THE
BOOK
OF
TRACES

edited by

V. Diekert
University of Stuttgart

G. Rozenberg
Leiden University

World Scientific
Singapore • New Jersey • London • Hong Kong

Published by

World Scientific Publishing Co. Pte. Ltd.

P O Box 128, Farrer Road, Singapore 9128

USA office: Suite 1B, 1060 Main Street, River Edge, NJ 07661

UK office: 57 Shelton Street, London WC2H 9HE

Library of Congress Cataloging-in-Publication Data

The book of traces / editors, V. Diekert, G. Rozenberg.
     p.   cm.
     Includes bibliographical references (p.   ).
     ISBN 9810220588
     1. Parallel processing (Electronic computers)   2. Combinatorial
analysis.   I. Diekert, Volker, 1955–   . II. Rozenberg, Grzegorz.
QA76.58.B66   1995
004'.35--dc20   94-39387
                                                     CIP

Printed in Singapore.

Preface

The theory of traces has two independent origins: combinatorial problems arising from the rearrangements of strings and the theory of concurrent systems. The book by P. Cartier and D. Foata (*Problèmes Combinatoires de Commutation et Rearrangements*, Lecture Notes in Mathematics 85, Springer Verlag, Berlin, 1969) was concerned with the former, and the paper by A. Mazurkiewicz (*Concurrent program schemes and their interpretations*, DAIMI Report PB-78, Department of Computer Science, Aarhus University, Aarhus, Denmark, 1977) was motivated by the latter area. One should also mention in this context the paper by R. Keller (*Parallel Program Schemata and Maximal Parallellism I. Fundamental Results*, Journal of the Association of Computing Machinery 20, pp. 514-537, 1973) where an approach similar to that of Mazurkiewicz is applied in the investigation of parallel program schemes.

It was the paper by Mazurkiewicz that made the theory of traces so popular. The research community quickly recognized it as a major contribution to the theory of concurrent systems and to the theory of formal languages. Since then the theory of traces has become a very active research area – the bibliography included in this book contains 278 entries. By today the main lines of research in trace theory employ techniques and tackle problems from quite diverse areas which include formal language theory, combinatorics, graph theory, algebra, logic, and the theory of concurrent systems. In all these areas the theory of traces has led to interesting problems and significant results. It is the combination of the broad scope and the considerable depth that makes the theory of traces so exciting.

All important research lines of the theory of traces are covered by this monograph – each chapter of the book is devoted to one research line and is written by leading experts. It is organized in such a way that each chapter can be read independently, and so it is very suitable for advanced courses/seminars in areas such as formal language theory, theory of concurrent systems, and combinatorics and algebra.

We are indebted to the authors of individual chapters for their contributions.

This book is a result of cooperation between two ESPRIT projects, ASMICS II, Basic Research Working Group No. 6317 and CALIBAN, Basic Research Working Group No. 6067, which again underlines the broad scope of trace theory: ASMICS II is concerned with algebraic and language theoretic techniques in computer science, while CALIBAN is concerned with concurrent systems.

Our special thanks go to W. Ebinger, whose technical expertise in TeX and devotion to all technical aspects of the production of this monograph were invaluable.

Finally we are indebted to Cartier, Foata and Mazurkiewicz for initiating the theory of traces, and to all the researchers in this area for making it so rich in interesting problems and beautiful results.

September 1994

V. Diekert, Stuttgart
G. Rozenberg, Leiden

Contents

IV   CONCURRENCY AND LOGIC   269

9   Trace Structures and other Models for Concurrency   271
(M. Nielsen, G. Winskel)

10 Traces and Logic   307
(W. Penczek, R. Kuiper)

V   GENERALIZATIONS   391

11 Infinite Traces   393
(P. Gastin, A. Petit)

I BASIC NOTIONS

Chapter 1

A. Mazurkiewicz
Introduction to Trace Theory

Chapter 2

H. J. Hoogeboom, G. Rozenberg
Dependence Graphs

Chapter 1

Introduction to Trace Theory

Antoni Mazurkiewicz

Institute of Computer Science, Polish Academy of Sciences
ul. Ordona 21, 01-237 Warszawa, and
Institute of Informatics, Jagiellonian University
ul. Nawojki 11, 31-072 Kraków, Poland
amaz@wars.ipipan.waw.pl

Contents

1.1 Introduction

The theory of traces has been motivated by the theory of *Petri Nets* and the theory of *formal languages and automata*.

Already in 1960's Carl Adam Petri has developed the foundations for the theory of concurrent systems. In his seminal work [226] he has presented a model which is based on the communication of interconnected sequential systems. He has also presented an entirely new set of notions and problems that arise when dealing with

3

concurrent systems. His model (or actually a family of "net-based" models) that has been since generically referred to as *Petri Nets*, has provided both an intuitive informal framework for representing basic situations of concurrent systems, and a formal framework for the mathematical analysis of concurrent systems. The intuitive informal framework has been based on a very convenient graphical representation of net-based systems, while the formal framework has been based on the token game resulting from this graphical representation.

The notion of a *finite automaton*, seen as a restricted type of Turing Machine, has by then become a classical model of a sequential system. The strength of automata theory is based on the "simple elegance" of the underlying model which admits powerful mathematical tools in the investigation of both the structural properties expressed by the underlying graph-like model, and the behavioural properties based on the notion of the *language* of a system. The notion of language has provided a valuable link with the theory of free monoids.

The original attempt of the theory of traces [189] was to use the well developed tools of formal language theory for the analysis of concurrent systems where the notion of concurrent system is understood in very much the same way as it is done in the theory of Petri Nets. The idea was that in this way one will get a framework for reasoning about concurrent systems which, for a number of important problems, would be mathematically more convenient that some approaches based on formalizations of the token game.

In 1970's when the basic theory of traces has been formulated, the most popular approach to deal with concurrency was *interleaving*. In this approach concurrency is replaced by *non-determinism* where concurrent execution of actions is treated as non-deterministic choice of the order of executions of those actions. Although the interleaving approach is quite adequate for many problems, it has a number of serious pitfalls. We will briefly discuss here some of them, because those were important drawbacks that we wanted to avoid in trace theory.

By reducing concurrency to non-determinism one assigns two different meanings to the term "non-deterministic choice": the choice between two (or more) possible actions that exclude each other, and the lack of information about the order of two (or more) actions that are executed independently of each other. Since in the theory of concurrent systems we are interested not only in the question "*what* is computed?" but also in the question "*how* it is computed?", this identification may be very misleading.

This disadvantage of the interleaving approach is well-visible in the treatment of *refinement*, see e.g. [49]. It is widely recognized that refinement is one of the basic transformations of any calculus of concurrent systems from theoretical, methodological, and practical point of view. This transformation must preserve the basic relationship between a system and its behaviour: the behaviour of the refined system is the refined behaviour of the original system. This requirement is not respected if the behaviour of the system is represented by interleaving.

Also in considerations concerning *inevitability*, see [192], the interleaving approach leads to serious problems. In non-deterministic systems where a choice between two partners may be repeated infinite number of times, a run discriminating against one of the partners is possible; an action of an a priori chosen partner is not inevitable. On the other hand, if the two partners repeat their actions *independently* of each other, an action of any of them is inevitable. However, in the interleaving approach one does not distinguish between these two situations: both are described in the same way. Then, as a remedy against this confusion, a special notion of fairness has to be introduced, where in fact this notion is outside of the usual algebraic means for the description of system behaviour.

Finally, the identification of non-deterministic choice and concurrency becomes a real drawback when considering *serializability of transactions* [104]. To keep consistency of a database to which a number of users have concurrent access, the database manager has to allow concurrent execution of those transactions that do not interfere with each other. To this end it is necessary to distinguish transactions that are in conflict from those which are independent of each other; the identification of the non-deterministic choice (in the case of conflicting transactions) with the choice of the execution order (in case of independent transactions) leads to serious difficulties in the design of database managing systems.

Above we have sketched some of the original motivations that led to the formulation of the theory of traces in 1977. Since then this theory has been developed both in breadth and in depth, and this volume presents the state of the art of the theory of traces. Some of the developments have followed the initial motivation coming from concurrent systems, while other fall within the areas such as formal language theory, theory of partially commutative monoids, graph grammars, combinatorics of words, etc.

In our paper we discuss a number of notions and results that have played a crucial role in the initial development of the theory of traces, and which in our opinion are still quite relevant.

1.2 Preliminary Notions

Let X be a set and R be a binary relation in X; R is an ordering relation in X, or X is ordered by R, if R is reflexive (xRx for all $x \in X$), transitive ($xRyRz$ implies xRz), and antisymmetric (xRy and yRx implies $x = y$); if, moreover, R is connected (for any $x, y \in X$ either xRy or yRx), then R is said to be a *linear*, or *total* ordering. A set, together with an ordering relation, is an *ordered set*. Let X be a set ordered by relation R. Any subset Y of X is then ordered by the restriction of R to Y, i.e. by $R \cap (Y \times Y)$.

The set $\{0, 1, 2, \ldots, n, \ldots\}$ will be denoted by ω. By an *alphabet* we shall understand a finite set of *symbols* (*letters*); alphabets will be denoted by Greek capital letters, e.g. $\Sigma, \Delta, \ldots$, etc. Let Σ be an alphabet; the set of all finite sequences of elements of Σ will be denoted by Σ^*; such sequences will be referred to as *strings* over Σ. Small initial letters $a, b, \ldots$, with possible sub- or superscripts will denote strings, small final Latin letters: $w, u, v, \ldots$, etc. will denote strings. If $u = (a_1, a_2, \ldots, a_n)$ is a string, n is called the *length* of u and is denoted by $|u|$. For any strings $(a_1, a_2, \ldots, a_n), (b_1, b_2, \ldots, b_m)$, the concatenation $(a_1, a_2, \ldots, a_n) \circ (b_1, b_2, \ldots, b_m)$

is the string $(a_1, a_2, \ldots, a_n, b_1, b_2, \ldots, b_m)$. Usually, sequences $(a_1, a_2, \ldots, a_n)$ are written as $a_1 a_2 \ldots a_n$. Consequently, a will denote symbol a as well as the string consisting of single symbol a; the proper meaning will be always understood by a context. String of length 0 (containing no symbols) is denoted by ϵ. The set of strings over an alphabet together with the concatenation operation and the empty string as the neutral element will be referred to as the *monoid* of strings over Σ, or the *free monoid* generated by Σ. Symbol Σ^* is used to denote the monoid of strings over Σ as well the set Σ^* itself.

We say that symbol a *occurs* in string w, if $w = w_1 a w_2$ for some strings w_1, w_2. For each string w define Alph (w) (the *alphabet* of w) as the set of all symbols occurring in w. By $w(a)$ we shall understand the number of occurrences of symbol a in string w.

Let Σ be an alphabet and w be a string (over an arbitrary alphabet); then $\pi_\Sigma(w)$ denotes the (string) *projection* of w onto Σ defined as follows:

$$\pi_\Sigma(w) = \begin{cases} \epsilon, & \text{if } w = \epsilon, \\ \pi_\Sigma(u), & \text{if } w = ua, a \notin \Sigma, \\ \pi_\Sigma(u)a, & \text{if } w = ua, a \in \Sigma. \end{cases}$$

Roughly speaking, projection onto Σ deletes from strings all symbols not in Σ. The subscript in π_Σ is omitted if Σ is understood by a context.

The *right cancellation* of symbol a in string w is the string $w \div a$ defined as follows:

$$\epsilon \div a = \epsilon, \tag{1.1}$$

$$(wb) \div a = \begin{cases} w, & \text{if } a = b, \\ (w \div a)b, & \text{otherwise.} \end{cases} \tag{1.2}$$

for all strings w and symbols a, b. It is easy to prove that projection and cancellation commute:

$$\pi_\Sigma(w) \div a = \pi_\Sigma(w \div a), \tag{1.3}$$

for all strings w and symbols a.

In our approach a *language* is defined by an alphabet Σ and a set of strings over Σ (i.e. a subset of Σ^*). Frequently, a language will be identified with its set of strings; however, in contrast to many other approaches, two languages with the same set of strings but with different alphabets will be considered as different; in particular, two singleton languages containing only empty strings, but over different alphabets, are considered as different. Languages will be denoted by initial Latin capital letters, e.g. $A, B, \ldots$, with possible subscripts and superscripts.

If A, B are languages over a common alphabet, then their concatenation AB is the language $\{uv \mid u \in A, v \in B\}$ over the same alphabet. If w is a string, A is a language, then (omitting braces around singletons)

$$wA = \{wu \mid u \in A\}, Aw = \{uw \mid u \in A\}.$$

The power of a language A is defined recursively:

$$A^0 = \{\epsilon\}, A^{n+1} = A^n A,$$

for each $n = 0, 1, \ldots$, and the iteration A^* of A is the union:

$$\bigcup_{n=0}^{\infty} A^n.$$

Extend the projection function from strings to languages defining for each language A and any alphabet Σ the projection of A onto Σ as the language $\pi_\Sigma(A)$ defined as

$$\pi_\Sigma(A) = \{\pi_\Sigma(u) \mid u \in A\}.$$

For each string w elements of the set

$$\mathrm{Pref}(w) = \{u \mid \exists v : uv = w\}$$

are called *prefixes* of w. Obviously, $\mathrm{Pref}(w)$ contains ϵ and w. For any language A over Σ define

$$\mathrm{Pref}(A) = \bigcup_{w \in A} \mathrm{Pref}(w).$$

Elements of $\mathrm{Pref}(A)$ are called prefixes of A. Obviously, $A \subseteq \mathrm{Pref}(A)$. Language A is *prefix closed*, if $A = \mathrm{Pref}(A)$. Clearly, for any language A the language $\mathrm{Pref}(A)$ is prefix closed. The *prefix relation* is a binary relation $\sqsubseteq$ in Σ^* such that $u \sqsubseteq w$ if and only $u \in \mathrm{Pref}(w)$. It is clear that the prefix relation is an ordering relation in any set of strings.

1.3 Dependency and Traces

By a *dependency* we shall mean any finite, reflexive and symmetric relation, i.e. a finite set of ordered pairs D such that if (a, b) is in D, then (b, a) and (a, a) are in D. Let D be a dependency; the the domain of D will be denoted by Σ_D and called the *alphabet* of D. Given dependency D, call the relation $I_D = (\Sigma_D \times \Sigma_D) - D$ *independency* induced by D. Clearly, independency is a symmetric and irreflexive relation. In particular, the empty relation, identity relation in Σ and the full relation in Σ (the relation $\Sigma \times \Sigma$) are dependencies; the first has empty alphabet, the second is the least dependency in Σ, the third is the greatest dependency in Σ. Clearly, the union and intersection of a finite number of dependencies is a dependency. It is also clear that each dependency is the union of a finite number of full dependencies (since any symmetric and reflexive relation is the union of its cliques).

Example 1.3.1 The relation $D = \{a, b\}^2 \cup \{a, c\}^2$ is a dependency; $\Sigma_D = \{a, b, c\}$, $I_D = \{(b, c), (c, b)\}$.

In this section we choose dependency as a primary notion of the trace theory; however, for other purposes it may be more convenient to take as a basic notion *concurrent alphabet*, i.e any pair (Σ, D) where Σ is an alphabet and D is a dependency, or any pair (Σ, I), where Σ is an alphabet and I is an independency, or *reliance alphabet*, i.e. any triple (Σ, D, I), where Σ is an alphabet, D is a dependency and I is independency induced by D.

Let D be a dependency; define the *trace equivalence* for D as the least congruence $\equiv_D$ in the monoid Σ_D^* such that for all a, b

$$(a, b) \in I_D \Rightarrow ab \equiv_D ba. \tag{1.4}$$

Equivalence classes of $\equiv_D$ are called *traces* over D; the trace represented by string w is denoted by $[w]_D$. By $[\Sigma^*]_D$ we shall denote the set $\{[w]_D \mid w \in \Sigma_D^*\}$, and by $[\Sigma]_D$ the set $\{[a]_D \mid a \in \Sigma_D\}$.

Example 1.3.2 For dependency $D = \{a, b\}^2 \cup \{a, c\}^2$ the trace over D represented by string $abbca$ is $[abbca]_D = \{abbca, abcba, acbba\}$.

By definition, a single trace arises by identifying all strings which differ only in the ordering of adjacent independent symbols. The quotient monoid $\mathbb{M}(D) = \Sigma_D^*/_{\equiv_D}$ is called the *trace monoid* over D and its elements the *traces* over D. Clearly, $\mathbb{M}(D)$ is generated by $[\Sigma]_D$. In the monoid $\mathbb{M}(D)$ some symbols from Σ commute (in contrast to the monoid of strings); for that reason $\mathbb{M}(D)$ is also called a *free partially commutative monoid* over D. As in the case of the monoid of strings, we use the symbol $\mathbb{M}(D)$ to denote the monoid itself as well as the set of all traces over D. It is clear that in case of full dependency, i.e. if D is a single clique, traces reduce to strings and $\mathbb{M}(D)$ is isomorphic with the free monoid of strings over Σ_D. We are going to develop the algebra of traces along the same lines as it has been done in case of of strings. Let us recall that the mapping $\varphi_D : \Sigma^* \longrightarrow [\Sigma^*]_D$ such that

$$\varphi_D(w) = [w]_D$$

is a homomorphism of Σ^* onto $\mathbb{M}(D)$, called the *natural homomorphism* generated by the equivalence $\equiv_D$.

Now, we shall give some simple facts about the trace equivalence and traces. Let D be fixed from now on; subscripts D will be omitted if it causes no ambiguity, I will be the independency induced by D, Σ will be the domain of D, all symbols will be symbols in Σ_D, all strings will be strings over Σ_D, and all traces will be traces over D, unless explicitly stated otherwise.

It is clear that $u \equiv v$ implies $\text{Alph}(u) = \text{Alph}(v)$; thus, for all strings w, we can define $\text{Alph}([w])$ as $\text{Alph}(w)$. Denote by $\sim$ a binary relation in Σ^* such that $u \sim v$ if and only if there are $x, y \in \Sigma^*$, and $(a, b) \in I$ such that $u = xaby, v = xbay$; it is not difficult to prove that $\equiv$ is the symmetric, reflexive, and transitive closure of $\sim$. In other words, $u \equiv v$ if and only if there exists a sequence $(w_0, w_1, \ldots, w_n), n \geq 0$, such that $w_0 = u, w_n = v$, and for each $i, 0 < i \leq n, w_{i-1} \sim w_i$.

Permutation is the least congruence $\simeq$ in Σ^* such that for all symbols a, b

$$ab \simeq ba. \tag{1.5}$$

If $u \simeq v$, we say that u is a permutation of v. Comparing (1.4) with (1.5) we see at once that $u \equiv v$ implies $u \simeq v$.

Define the *mirror image* w^R of string w as follows:

$$\epsilon^R = \epsilon, \quad (ua)^R = a(u^R),$$

for any string u and symbol a. It is clear that the following implication (the mirror rule) holds:

$$u \equiv v \Rightarrow u^R \equiv v^R; \tag{1.6}$$

thus, we can define $[w]^R$ as equal to $[w^R]$.

Since obviously $u \sim v$ implies $(u \div a) \sim (v \div a)$, and $\equiv$ is the transitive and reflexive closure of $\sim$, we have the following property (the cancellation property) of traces:

$$u \equiv v \Rightarrow (u \div a) \equiv (v \div a); \tag{1.7}$$

thus, we can define $[w] \div a$ as $[w \div a]$, for all strings w and symbols a.

We have also the following *projection rule*:

$$u \equiv_v \Rightarrow \pi_\Sigma(u) \equiv \pi_\Sigma(v) \tag{1.8}$$

for any alphabet Σ, being a consequence of the obvious implication $u \sim_v \Rightarrow \pi_\Sigma(u) \equiv \pi_\Sigma(v)$.

Let u, v be strings, a, b be symbols, $a \neq b$. If $ua \equiv vb$, then applying twice rule (1.7) we get $u \div b \equiv v \div a$; denoting $u \div b$ by w, by the cancellation rule again we get $u = (ua) \div a \equiv (vb) \div a = (v \div a)b \equiv wb$. Similarly, we get $v \equiv wa$. Since $ua \equiv vb$, $wba \equiv wab$ and by the definition of traces $ab \equiv ba$. Thus, we have the following implication for all strings u, v and symbols a, b:

$$ua \equiv vb \wedge a \neq b \Rightarrow (a, b) \in I \wedge \exists w : u \equiv wb \wedge v \equiv wa. \tag{1.9}$$

Obviously, $u \equiv v \Rightarrow xuy \equiv xvy$. If $xuy \equiv xvy$, by the cancellation rule $xu \equiv xv$; by the mirror rule $u^R x^R \equiv v^R x^R$; again by the cancellation rule $u^R \equiv v^R$, and again by the mirror rule $u \equiv v$. Hence, from the mirror property and the cancellation property it follows the following implication:

$$xuy \equiv xvy \Rightarrow u \equiv v. \tag{1.10}$$

Extend independency relation from symbols to strings, defining strings u, v to be independent, $(u, v) \in I$, if $\text{Alph}(u) \times \text{Alph}(v) \subseteq I$. Notice that the empty string is independent of any other: $(\epsilon, w) \in I$ trivially holds for any string w.

Proposition 1.3.3 *For all strings w, u, v and symbol $a \notin \text{Alph}(v)$: $uav \equiv wa \Rightarrow (a, v) \in I$.*

Proof: By induction. If $v = \epsilon$ the implication is clear. Otherwise, there is symbol $b \neq a$ and string x such that $v = xb$. By Proposition 1.9 $(a, b) \in I$ and $uaxb \equiv wa$. By cancellation rule, since $b \neq a$, we get $uax \equiv (w \div b)a$. By induction hypothesis $(a, x) \in I$. Since $(a, b) \in I$, $(a, xb) \in I$ which proves the proposition. $\qquad\square$

The next theorem is a trace generalization of the Levi Lemma for strings. which reads: for all strings u, v, x, y, if $uv = xy$, then there exists a string w such that either $uw = x, wy = v$, or $xw = u, wv = y$. In case of traces this useful lemma admits more symmetrical form:

Theorem 1.3.4 (Levi Lemma for traces) *For any strings u, v, x, y such that $uv \equiv xy$ there exist strings z_1, z_2, z_3, z_4 such that $(z_2, z_3) \in I$ and*

$$u \equiv z_1 z_2, v \equiv z_3 z_4, x \equiv z_1 z_3, y \equiv z_2 z_4. \tag{1.11}$$

Proof: Let u, v, x, y be strings such that $uv \equiv xy$. If $y = \epsilon$, the proposition is proved by setting $z_1 = u, z_2 = z_4 = \epsilon, z_3 = v$. Let w be a string and e be a symbol such that $y = we$. Then there can be two cases: either (1) there are strings v', v'' such that $v = v'ev''$ and $e \notin \text{Alph}(v'')$, or (2) there are strings u', u'' such that $u = u'eu''$, and $e \notin \text{Alph}(u''v)$.

In case (1) by the cancellation rule we have $uv'v'' \equiv xw$; by induction hypothesis there are z_1', z_2', z_3', z_4' such that

$$uv' \equiv z_1' z_2', v'' \equiv z_3' z_4', x \equiv z_1' z_3', w \equiv z_2' z_4',$$

and $(z_2', z_3') \in I$. Set $z_1 = z_1', z_2 = z_2'e, z_3 = z_3', z_4 = z_4'$. By Proposition 1.3.3 $(e, v'') \in I$, hence $(e, z_3') \in I$ and $(e, z_4') \in I$. Since $(e, z_4') \in I$, $ez_4' \equiv z_4'e$; and it is easy to check that equivalences (1.11) are satisfied. We have also $(z_2', z_3') \in I$ and $(e, z_3') \in I$; it yields $(z_2'e, z_3') \in I$ which proves $(z_2, z_3) \in I$.

In case(2) by cancellation rule we have $u'u''v \equiv xw$ and by induction hypothesis there are z_1', z_2', z_3', z_4' such that

$$u' \equiv z_1' z_2', u''v \equiv z_3' z_4', x \equiv z_1' z_3', w \equiv z_2' z_4'.$$

and $(z_2', z_3') \in I$. Set, as above, $z_1 = z_1', z_2 = z_2'e, z_3 = z_3', z_4 = z_4'$. By Proposition 1.3.3 $(e, u''v) \in I$, hence $(e, z_3') in I$ and $(e, z_4') \in I$. Since $ue \equiv z_2' z_4'e \equiv z_2'ez_4' = z_2 z_4)$, equivalences (1.11) are satisfied. By induction hypothesis $(z_2', z_3') \in I$; together with $(e, z_3') in I$ it implies $(z_2, z_3) \in I$. $\square$

Let $[u], [v]$ be traces over the same dependency. Trace $[u]$ is a *prefix* of trace $[v]$ (and $[v]$ is a *dominant* of $[u]$), if there exists trace $[x]$ such that $[ux] = [v]$. Similarly to the case of strings, the relation "to be a prefix" in the set of all traces over a fixed dependency is an ordering relation; however, in contrast to the prefix relation in the set of strings, the prefix relation for traces orders sets of traces (in general) only partially.

The structure of prefixes of the trace $[abbca]$ for dependency $\{a, b\}^2 \cup \{a, c\}^2$ is given in the Figure 1.2.

Proposition 1.3.5 *Let $[w]$ be a trace and $[u], [v]$ be prefixes of $[w]$. Then there exist the greatest common prefix and the least common dominant of $[u]$ and $[v]$.*

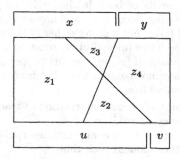

Figure 1.1: Graphical interpretation of Levi Lemma for traces.

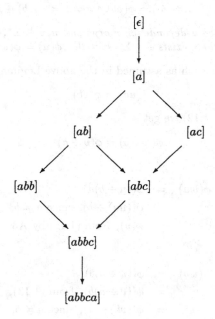

Figure 1.2: Structure of prefixes of $[abbca]_D$ for $D = \{a, b\}^2 \cup \{a, c\}^2$.

Proof: Since $[u], [v]$ are prefixes of $[w]$, there are traces $[x], [y]$ such that $ux \equiv vy$. Then, by Levi Lemma for traces, there are strings z_1, z_2, z_3, z_4 such that $u \equiv z_1 z_2, x \equiv z_3 z_4, v \equiv z_1 z_3, y \equiv z_2 z_4$, and z_2, z_3 are independent. Then $[z_1]$ is the greatest common prefix and $[z_1 z_2 z_3]$ is the least common dominant of $[u], [v]$. Indeed, $[z_1]$ is a common prefix of both $[u], [v]$; it is the greatest common prefix, since any symbol in z_2 does not occur in z_3 and any symbol in z_3 does not occur in z_2; hence any extension of $[z_1]$ is not a prefix either of $[z_1 z_2] = [u]$, or of $[z_1 z_3] = [v]$. Thus, any trace being a prefix of $[u]$ and of $[v]$ must be a prefix of $[z_1]$. Similarly, $[z_1 z_2 z_3]$ is a common dominant of $[u], [v]$; but any proper prefix of $[z_1 z_2 z_3]$ is either not dominating $[u]$, if it does not contain a symbol from z_2, or not dominating $[v]$, if it does not contain a symbol from z_3. $\square$

Let us close this section with a characterization of trace monoids by homomorphisms (so-called dependency morphisms).

A *dependency* morphism w.r.t. D is any homomorphism ϕ from the monoid of strings over Σ_D onto another monoid such that

$$A1: \quad \phi(w) = \phi(\epsilon) \Rightarrow w = \epsilon,$$
$$A2: \quad (a, b) \in I \Rightarrow \phi(ab) = \phi(ba),$$
$$A3: \quad \phi(ua) = \phi(v) \Rightarrow \phi(u) = \phi(v \div a),$$
$$A4: \quad \phi(ua) = \phi(vb) \wedge a \neq b \Rightarrow (a, b) \in I.$$

Lemma 1.3.6 *Let ϕ be a dependency morphism, $u, v \in \Sigma^*, a, b \in \Sigma$. If $\phi(ua) = \phi(vb)$ and $a \neq b$, then there exists $w \in \Sigma^*$ such that $\phi(u) = \phi(wb)$ and $\phi(v) = \phi(wa)$.*

Proof: Let u, v, a, b be such as assumed in the above Lemma and let

$$\phi(ua) = \phi(vb) \tag{1.12}$$

Applying twice A3 to (1.12) we get

$$\phi(u \div b) = \phi(v \div a) \tag{1.13}$$

Set $w = u \div b$. Then

$$
\begin{aligned}
\phi(wa) &= \phi((u \div b)a) \\
&= \phi((ua) \div b), \text{ since } a \neq b, \\
&= \phi(v), \text{ from (1.12) by A3,}
\end{aligned}
$$

and

$$
\begin{aligned}
\phi(wb) &= \phi((u \div b)b) \\
&= \phi((v \div a)b), \text{ from (1.13),} \\
&= \phi((vb) \div a), \text{ since } a \neq b, \\
&= \phi(u), \text{ from (1.12) by A3.}
\end{aligned}
$$

$\square$

Lemma 1.3.7 *Let* ϕ, ψ *be dependency morphisms w.r.t. the same dependency. Then* $\phi(x) = \phi(y) \Rightarrow \psi(x) = \psi(y)$ *for all* x, y.

Proof: Let D be a dependency and let ϕ, ψ be two concurrency mappings w.r.t. dependency D, $x, y \in \Sigma^*$, and $\phi(x) = \phi(y)$. If $x = \epsilon$, then by A1 $y = \epsilon$ and clearly $\psi(x) = \psi(y)$. If $x \neq \epsilon$, then $y \neq \epsilon$. Thus, $x = ua, y = vb$ for some $u, v \in \Sigma^*, a, b \in \Sigma$ and we have

$$\phi(ua) = \phi(vb). \tag{1.14}$$

There can be two cases. In the first case we have $a = b$, then by A3 $\phi(u) = \phi(v)$ and by induction hypothesis $\psi(u) = \psi(v)$; Thus $\psi(ua) = \psi(vb)$, which proves $\psi(x) = \psi(y)$. In the second case, $a \neq b$. By A4 $(a, b) \in I$. By Lemma 1.3.6 we get $\phi(u) = \phi(wb), \phi(v) = \phi(wa)$, for some $w \in \Sigma^*$. By induction hypothesis

$$\psi(u) = \psi(wb), \psi(v) = \psi(wa) \tag{1.15}$$

hence

$$\psi(ua) = \psi(wba), \psi(vb) = \psi(wab). \tag{1.16}$$

By A3, since $(a, b) \in I$,

$$\psi(ba) = \psi(ab), \tag{1.17}$$

hence $\psi(wba) = \psi(wab)$, which proves $\psi(x) = \psi(y)$. □

Theorem 1.3.8 *If* ϕ, ψ *are dependency morphisms w.r.t. the same dependency onto monoids* M, N, *then* M *is isomorphic with* N.

Proof: By Lemma 1.3.7 the mapping defined by the equality

$$\theta(\phi(w)) = \psi(w),$$

for all $w \in \Sigma^*$ is a homomorphism from M onto N. Since θ has its inverse, namely

$$\theta^{-1}(\psi(w)) = \phi(w),$$

which is a homomorphism also, θ is a homomorphism from N onto M, θ is an isomorphism. □

Theorem 1.3.9 *The natural homomorphism of the monoid of strings over* Σ_D *onto the monoid of traces over* D *is a dependency morphism.*

Proof: We have to check conditions A1 – A4 for $\phi(w) = [w]_D$. Condition A1 is obviously satisfied; condition A2 follows directly from the definition of trace monoids. Condition A3 follows from the cancellation property (1.7); condition A4 follows from (1.9). □

Corollary. If ϕ is a dependency morphism w.r.t. D onto M, then M is isomorphic with the monoid of traces over D and the isomorphism is induced by the mapping θ such that $\theta([a]_D) = \phi_D(a)$ for all $a \in \Sigma_D$.

Proof: It follows from Theorem 1.3.8 and Theorem 1.3.9. □

1.4   Dependence Graphs

Dependence graphs are thought as graphical representations of traces which make explicit the ordering of symbol occurrences within traces. It turns out that for a given dependency the algebra of traces is isomorphic with the algebra of dependency graphs, as defined below. Therefore, it is only a matter of taste which objects are chosen for representing concurrent processes: equivalence classes of strings or labelled graphs.

Let D be a dependency relation. Dependency graphs over D (or d-graphs for short) are finite, oriented, acyclic graphs with nodes labelled with symbols from Σ_D in such a way that two nodes of a d-graph are connected with an arc if and only if they are different and labelled with dependent symbols. Formally, a triple

$$\gamma = (V, R, \varphi)$$

is a dependence graph (d-graph) over D, if

$$V \text{ is a finite set (of nodes of } \gamma), \tag{1.18}$$
$$R \subseteq V \times V \text{ (the set of arcs of } \gamma), \tag{1.19}$$
$$\varphi : V \longrightarrow \Sigma_D \text{ (the labelling of } \gamma), \tag{1.20}$$

such that

$$R^+ \cap id_V = \emptyset, \quad \text{(acyclicity)} \tag{1.21}$$
$$(v_1, v_2) \in R \cup R^{-1} \cup id_V \Leftrightarrow (\varphi(v_1), \varphi(v_2)) \in D \quad \text{(D-connectivity)} \tag{1.22}$$

Two d-graphs γ', γ'' are isomorphic, $\gamma' \simeq \gamma''$, if there exists a bijection between their nodes preserving labelling and arc connections. As usual, two isomorphic graphs are identified; all subsequent properties of d-graphs are formulated up to isomorphism. The empty d-graph $(\emptyset, \emptyset, \emptyset)$ will be denoted by λ and the set of all isomorphism classes of d-graphs over D by Γ_D.

Example 1.4.1 Let $D = \{a, b\}^2 \cup \{a, c\}^2$. Then the node labelled graph (V, R, φ) with
$$V = \{1, 2, 3, 4, 5\},$$
$$R = \{(1, 2), (1, 3), (1, 4), (1, 5), (2, 4), (2, 5), (3, 5), (4, 5)\},$$
$$\varphi(1) = a, \varphi(2) = b, \varphi(3) = c, \varphi(4) = b, \varphi(5) = a,$$

is a d-graph. It is (isomorphic to) the graph in Fig.1.3

The following fact follows immediately from the definition:

Proposition 1.4.2 *Let D', D'' be dependencies, (V, R', φ) be a d-graph over D', (V, R'', φ) be a d-graph over D''. If $D' \subseteq D''$, then $R' \subseteq R''$.*

A vertex of a d-graph with no arcs leaving it (leading to it) is said to be a *maximum*(*minimum*, resp.) vertex. Clearly, a d-graph has at least one maximum

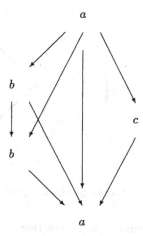

Figure 1.3: A dependence graph over $D = \{a, b\}^2 \cup \{a, c\}^2$.

and one minimum vertex. Since d-graphs are acyclic, the transitive and reflexive closure of d-graph arc relation is an ordering. Thus, each d-graph uniquely determines an ordering of symbol occurrences. This ordering will be discussed later on; for the time being we only mention that considering d-graphs as descriptions of non-sequential processes and dependency relation as a model of causal dependency, this ordering may be viewed as causal ordering of process events.

Observe that in case of full dependency D (i.e. if $D = S_D \times S_D$) the arc relation of any d-graph g over D is the linear order of vertices of g; in case of minimum dependency D (i.e. when D is an identity relation) any d-graph over D consists of a number of connected components, each of them being a linearly ordered set of vertices labelled with a common symbol.

Define the composition of d-graphs as follows: for all graphs γ_1, γ_2 in Γ_D the composition $(\gamma_1 \circ \gamma_2)$ with γ_1 with γ_2 is a graph arising from the disjoint union of γ_1 and γ_2 by adding to it new arcs leading from each node of γ_1 to each node of γ_2, provided they are labelled with dependent symbols. Formally, $(V, R, \varphi) \simeq (\gamma_1 \circ \gamma_2)$ iff there are instances $(V_1, R_1, \varphi_1), (V_2, R_2, \varphi_2)$ of γ_1, γ_2, respectively, such that

$$V = V_1 \cup V_2, V_1 \cap V_2 = \emptyset, \tag{1.23}$$
$$R = R_1 \cup R_2 \cup R_{12}, \tag{1.24}$$
$$\varphi = \varphi_1 \cup \varphi_2, \tag{1.25}$$

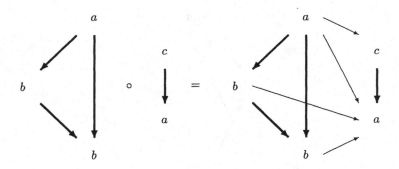

Figure 1.4: D-graphs composition

where R_{12} denotes a binary relation in V such that

$$(v_1, v_2) \in R_{12} \Leftrightarrow v_1 \in V_1 \wedge v_2 \in V_2 \wedge (\varphi(v_1), \varphi(v_2)) \in D. \qquad (1.26)$$

Example 1.4.3 In Fig. 1.4 the composition of two d-graphs is presented; thin arrows represent arcs added in the composition.

Proposition 1.4.4 *The composition of d-graphs is a d-graph.*

Proof: In view of (1.23) and (1.25) it is clear that the composition γ of two d-graphs γ_1, γ_2 is a finite graph, with nodes labelled with symbols from Σ_D. It is acyclic, since γ_1 and γ_2 are acyclic and by (1.26), in γ there is no arcs leading from nodes of γ_2 to nodes of γ_1. Let v_1, v_2 be nodes of γ with $(\varphi(v_1), \varphi(v_2)) \in D$. If both of them are nodes of γ_1 or of γ_2, then by D-connectivity of components and by (1.24) they are also joined in γ. If v_1 is a node of γ_1 and v_2 is a node of γ_2, then by (1.24) and (1.26) they are joined in γ, which proves D-connectivity of γ. $\qquad \square$

Composition of d-graphs can be viewed as "sequential" as well as "parallel": composing two independent d-graphs (i.e. d-graphs such that any node of one of them is independent of any node of the other) we get the result intuitively understood as "parallel" composition, while composing two dependent d-graphs, i.e. such that any node of one of them is dependent of any label of the other, the result can be viewed as the "sequential" or "serial" composition. In general, d-graph composition is a mixture of "parallel" and "sequential" compositions, where some (but not all) nodes of one d-graph are dependent on some nodes of the other, and some of them are not. The nature of composition of d-graphs depends on the nature of the underlying dependency relation.

Denote the empty graph (with no nodes) by e. The set of all d-graphs over a dependency D with composition ∘ defined as above and with the empty graph as a distinguished element forms an algebra denoted by $G(D)$.

Theorem 1.4.5 *The $G(D)$ is a monoid.*

Proof: Since the empty graph is obviously the neutral (left and right) element
w.r.t. to the composition, it suffices to show that the composition of d-graphs is
associative. Let, for $i = 1, 2, 3, (V_i, R_i, \varphi_i)$ be a representative of d-graph γ_i, such
that $V_i \cap V_j = \emptyset$ for $i \neq j$. By simple calculation we prove that $((\gamma_1 \circ \gamma_2) \circ \gamma_3)$ is
(isomorphic to) the d-graph (V, R, φ) with

$$V = V_1 \cup V_2 \cup V_3, \tag{1.27}$$
$$R = R_1 \cup R_2 \cup R_3 \cup R_{12} \cup R_{13} \cup R_{23} \tag{1.28}$$
$$\varphi = \varphi_1 \cup \varphi_2 \cup \varphi_3, \tag{1.29}$$

where R_{ij} denotes a binary relation in V such that

$$(v_1, v_2) \in R_{ij} \Leftrightarrow v_1 \in V_i \wedge v_2 \in V_j \wedge (\varphi(v_1), \varphi(v_2)) \in D,$$

and the same result we obtain for $(\gamma_1 \circ (\gamma_2 \circ \gamma_3))$. □

Let D be a dependency. For each string w over S_D denote by $\langle w \rangle_D$ the d-graph
defined recursively:

$$\langle \epsilon \rangle_D = e, \quad \langle wa \rangle_D = \langle w \rangle_D \circ (a, \emptyset, \{(a, a)\}) \tag{1.30}$$

for all strings w and symbols a. In other words, $\langle wa \rangle$ arises from the graph $\langle w \rangle$ by
adding to it a new node labelled with symbol a and new arcs leading to it from all
vertices of $\langle w \rangle$ labelled with symbols dependent of a.

D-graph $\langle abbca \rangle_D$ with dependency $D = \{a, b\}^2 \cup \{a, c\}^2$ is presented in Fig. 1.3.

Let dependency D be fixed from now on and let $\Sigma, I, \langle w \rangle$ denote $\Sigma_D, I_D, \langle w \rangle_D$,
respectively.

Proposition 1.4.6 *For each d-graph γ over D there is a string w such that $\langle w \rangle = \gamma$.*

Proof: It is clear for the empty d-graph. By induction, let γ be a non-empty
d-graph; remove from γ one of its maximum vertices. It is clear that the resulting
graph is a d-graph. By induction hypothesis there is a string w such that $\langle w \rangle$
is isomorphic with this restricted d-graph; then $\langle wa \rangle$, where a is the label of the
removed vertex, is isomorphic with the original graph. □

Therefore, the mapping $\langle \rangle$ is a surjection.

Proposition 1.4.7 *Mapping $\phi : \Sigma^* \longrightarrow G(D)$ defined by $\phi(w) = \langle w \rangle$ is a dependency morphism w.r.t. D.*

Proof: By Proposition 1.4.6 mapping ϕ is a surjection. By an easy induction we prove that for each strings u, v

$$\phi(uv) = \langle uv \rangle = \langle u \rangle \circ \langle v \rangle = \phi(u) \circ \phi(v),$$

and clearly $\phi(\epsilon) = \langle \epsilon \rangle = e$. Thus, ϕ is a homomorphism onto $G(D)$. Condition A1 is obviously satisfied. If $(a, b) \in I$, d-graph $\langle ab \rangle$ has no arcs, hence it is isomorphic with $\langle ba \rangle$. It proves A2. By definition, d-graph $\langle ua \rangle$, for string u and symbol a, has a maximum vertex labelled with a; if $\langle ua \rangle = \langle v \rangle$, then $\langle v \rangle$ has also a maximum vertex labelled with a; removing these vertices from both graphs results in isomorphic graphs; it is easy to see that removing such a vertex from $\langle v \rangle$ results in $\langle v \div a \rangle$. Hence, $\langle u \rangle = \langle v \div a \rangle$, which proves A3. If $\gamma = \langle ua \rangle = \langle vb \rangle$ and $a \neq b$, then γ has at least two maximum vertices, one of them labelled with a and the second labelled with b. Since both of them are maximum vertices, there is no arc joining them. It proves $(a, b) \in I$ and A4 is satisfied.   □

Theorem 1.4.8 *The trace monoid* $\mathbb{M}(D)$ *is isomorphic with the monoid* $G(D)$ *of d-graphs over dependency* D; *the isomorphism is induced by the bijection* θ *such that* $\theta([a]_D) = \langle a \rangle_D$ *for all* $a \in \Sigma_D$.

Proof: It follows from Corollary to Theorem 1.3.9.   □

The above theorem claims that traces and d-graphs over the same dependency can be viewed as two faces of the same coin; the same concepts can be expressed in two different ways: speaking about traces the algebraic character of the concept is stressed upon, while speaking about d-graphs its causality (or ordering) features are emphasized. We can consider some graph - theoretical features of traces (e.g. connectivity of traces) as well as some algebraic properties of dependence graphs (e.g. composition of d-graphs). Using this isomorphism, one can prove facts about traces using graphical methods and the other way around, prove some graph properties using algebraic methods. In fact, dual nature of traces, algebraic and graph-theoretical, was the principal motivation to introduce them for representing concurrent processes.

An illustration of graph-theoretical properties of traces consider the notion (useful in the other part of this book) of connected trace: a trace is connected, if the d-graph corresponding to it is connected. The algebraic definition of this notion could be the following: trace t is connected, if there is no non-empty traces t_1, t_2 with $t = t_1 t_2$ and such that $\mathrm{Alph}(t_1) \times \mathrm{Alph}(t_2) \subseteq I$. A *connected component* of trace t is the trace corresponding to a connected component of the d-graph corresponding to t; the algebraic definition of this notion is much more complex.

As the second illustration of graph representation of traces let us represent in graphical form projection π_1 of trace $[abcd]$ with dependency $\{a, b, c\}^2 \cup \{b, c, d\}^2$ onto dependency $\{a, c\}^2 \cup \{c, d\}^2$ and projection π_2 of the same trace onto dependency $\{a, b\}^2 \cup \{a, c\}^2 \cup \{c, d\}^2$ (Fig. 1.5). Projection π_1 is onto dependency with smaller alphabet than the original (symbol b is deleted under projection); projection π_2 preserves all symbols, but delete some dependencies, namely dependency (b, c) and (b, d).

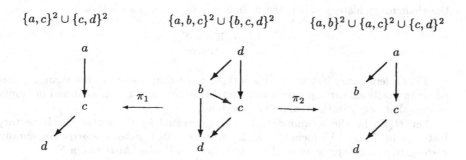

Figure 1.5: Trace projections

1.5 Histories

The concepts presented in this section originate in papers of M.W. Shields [253, 254, 255]. The main idea is to represent non-sequential processes by a collection of individual histories of concurrently running components; an individual history is a string of events concerning only one component, and the global history is a collection of individual ones. This approach, appealing directly to the intuitive meaning of parallel processing, is particularly well suited to CSP-like systems [138] where individual components run independently of each other, with one exception: an event concerning a number of (in CSP at most two) components can occur only coincidently in all these components ("handshaking" or "rendez-vous" synchronization principle). The presentation and the terminology used here have been adjusted to the present purposes and differ from those of the authors.

Let $\boldsymbol{\Sigma} = (\Sigma_1, \Sigma_2, \ldots, \Sigma_n)$ be a n-tuple of finite alphabets. Denote by $P(\boldsymbol{\Sigma})$ the product monoid

$$\Sigma_1^* \times \Sigma_2^* \times \ldots \times \Sigma_n^*. \tag{1.31}$$

The composition in $P(\boldsymbol{\Sigma})$ is component-wise: if $\mathbf{u} = (u_1, u_2, \ldots, u_n)$, $\mathbf{v} = (v_1, v_2, \ldots, v_n)$, then

$$\mathbf{uv} = (u_1 v_1, u_2 v_2, \ldots, u_n v_n), \tag{1.32}$$

for all $\mathbf{u}, \mathbf{v} \in \Sigma_1^* \times \Sigma_2^* \times \ldots \times \Sigma_n^*$.

Let $\Sigma = \Sigma_1 \cup \Sigma_2 \cup \cdots \cup \Sigma_n$ and let π_i be the projection from Σ onto Σ_i, for $i = 1, 2, \ldots, n$. By the *distribution* in $\boldsymbol{\Sigma}$ we understand here the mapping $\pi : \Sigma^* \longrightarrow \Sigma_1^* \times \Sigma_2^* \times \ldots \Sigma_n^*$ defined by the equality:

$$\pi(w) = (\pi_1(w), \pi_2(w), \ldots, \pi_n(w)). \tag{1.33}$$

For each $a \in \Sigma$ the tuple $\pi(a)$ will be called the *elementary history* of a. Thus, the elementary history of a is the n-tuple $(a_1, a_2, \ldots, a_n)$ such that

$$a_i = \begin{cases} a, & \text{if } a \in \Sigma_i, \\ \epsilon, & \text{otherwise.} \end{cases}$$

Thus, elementary history $\pi(a)$ is n-tuple consisting of one symbol strings a that occur in positions corresponding to components containing symbol a and of empty strings that occur in the remaining positions.

Let $H(\Sigma)$ be the submonoid of $P(\Sigma)$ generated by the set of all elementary histories in $P(\Sigma)$. Elements of $H(\Sigma)$ will be called *global histories* (or simply, *histories*), and components of global histories - *individual histories* in Σ.

Example 1.5.1 Let $\Sigma_1 = \{a, b\}, \Sigma_2 = \{a, c\}, \Sigma = (\Sigma_1, \Sigma_2)$. Then $\Sigma = \{a, b, c\}$ and the elementary histories of Σ are: $(a, a), (b, \epsilon), (\epsilon, c)$. The pair:

$$\pi(w) = (abba, aca)$$

is a global history in Σ, since

$$\begin{aligned} \pi(w) &= (a, a)(b, \epsilon)(b, \epsilon)(\epsilon, c)(a, a) \\ &= \pi(abbca). \end{aligned}$$

The pair $(abba, cca)$ is not a history, since it cannot be obtained by composition of elementary histories.

From the point of view of concurrent processes the subalgebra of histories can be interpreted as follows. There is n sequential components of a concurrent system, each of them is capable to execute (sequentially) some elementary actions, creating in this way a sequential history of the component run. All of components can act independently of each other, but an action common to a number of components can be executed by all of them coincidently. There is no other synchronization mechanisms provided in the system. Then the join action of all components is a n-tuple of individual histories of components; such individual histories are consistent with each other, i.e. – roughly speaking – they can be combined into one global history. The following theorem offers a formal criterion for such a consistency.

Proposition 1.5.2 *The distribution in Σ is a homomorphism from the monoid of strings over Σ onto the monoid of histories $H(\Sigma)$.*

Proof: It is clear that the distribution of any string over Σ is a history in $H(\Sigma)$. It is also clear that any history in $H(\Sigma)$ can be obtained as the distribution from a string over Σ, since any history is a composition of elementary histories: $\pi(a)_1\pi(a)_2\cdots\pi(a)_m = \pi(a_1a_2\cdots a_m)$. By properties of projection it follows the congruence of the distribution: $\pi(uv) = \pi(u)\pi(v)$.   □

Theorem 1.5.3 *Let* $\Sigma = (\Sigma_1, \Sigma_2, \ldots, \Sigma_n), D = \Sigma_1^2 \cup \Sigma_2^2 \cup \cdots \cup \Sigma_n^2$. *The distribution in* Σ *is a dependency morphism w.r.t.* D *onto the monoid of histories* $H(\Sigma)$.

Proof: Denote the assumed dependency by D and the induced independency by I. By Proposition 1.5.2 the distribution is a homomorphism onto the monoid of histories. By its definition we have at once $\pi(w) = \pi(\epsilon) \Rightarrow w = \epsilon$, which proves A1. By the definition of dependency, two symbols a, b are dependent iff there is index i such that a as well as b belongs to Σ_i, i.e. a, b are independent iff there is no index i such that Σ_i contains both of them. It proves that if $(a, b) \in I$, then $\pi(ab) = \pi(ba)$, since for all $i = 1, 2, \ldots, n$

$$\pi_i(ab) = \pi_i(ba) = \begin{cases} a, & \text{if } a \in \Sigma_i, \\ b, & \text{if } b \in \Sigma_i, \\ \epsilon, & \text{in the remaining cases.} \end{cases}$$

Thus, A2 holds. To prove A3, assume $\pi(ua) = \pi(v)$; then we have $\pi_i(ua) = \pi_i(v)$ for all $i = 1, 2, \ldots, n$; hence $\pi_i(ua) \div a = \pi_i(v) \div a$; since projection and cancellation commute, $\pi_i(ua \div a) = \pi_i(v \div a)$, i.e. $\pi_i(u) = \pi_i(v \div a)$ for all i, which implies $\pi(u) = \pi(v \div a)$. It proves A3. Suppose now $\pi(ua) = \pi(vb)$; if it were i with $a \in \Sigma_i, b \in \Sigma_i$, it would be $\pi_i(u)a = \pi_i(v)b$, which is impossible. Therefore, there is no such i, i.e. $(a, b) \in I$.   □

Theorem 1.5.4 *Monoid of histories* $H(\Sigma_1, \Sigma_2, \ldots, \Sigma_n)$ *is isomorphic with the monoid of traces over dependency* $\Sigma_1^2 \cup \Sigma_2^2 \cup \cdots \cup \Sigma_n^2$.

Proof: It follows from the Theorem 1.5.3 and Corollary to Theorem 1.3.9.   □

Therefore, similarly to the case of d-graphs, histories can be viewed as yet another, "third face" of traces; to represent a trace by a history, the underlying dependency should be converted to a suitable tuple of alphabets. One possibility, but not unique, is to take cliques of dependency as individual alphabets and then to make use of Theorem 1.5.4 for constructing histories. As an example consider trace $[abbca]$ over dependency $\{a, b\}^2 \cup \{a, c\}^2$ as in the previous sections; then the system components are $(\{a, b\}, \{a, c\})$ and the history corresponding to trace $[abbca]$ is the history $(abba, aca)$.

1.6 Ordering of Symbol Occurrences

Traces, dependence graphs and histories are the same objects from the algebraic point of view; since monoids of them are isomorphic, they behave in the same way under composition. However, actually they are different objects; their difference is visible when considering how symbols are ordered in corresponding objects: traces, graphs, and histories.

There are two kinds of ordering defined by strings: the ordering of symbols occurring in a string, called the occurrence ordering, and the ordering of prefixes of a strings, the prefix ordering. Looking at strings as at models of sequential processes, the first determines the order of event occurrences within a process. The second is the order of process states, since each prefix of a string can be interpreted as a partial execution of the process interpreting by this string, and such a partial execution determines uniquely an intermediate state of the process. Both orderings, although different, are closely related: given one of them, the second can be reconstructed.

Traces are intended to be generalizations of strings, hence the ordering given by traces should be a generalization of that given by strings. Actually, it is the case; as we could expect, the ordering resulting from a trace is partial. In this chapter we shall discuss in details the ordering resulting from trace approach.

We start from string ordering, since it gives us some tools and notions used next for defining the trace ordering. We shall consider both kinds of ordering: first the prefix ordering and next the occurrence ordering. Next, we consider ordering defined within dependence graphs; finally, ordering of symbols supplied by histories will be discussed.

In the whole section D will denote a fixed dependency relation, Σ be its alphabet, I the independency relation induced by D. All strings are assumed to be strings over Σ. The set of all traces over D will be denoted by the same symbol as the monoid of traces over D, i.e. by $\mathbf{M}(D)$.

Thus, in contrast to linearly ordered prefixes of a string, the set $Pref(t)$ is ordered by $[$ only partially. Interpreting a trace as a single run of a system, its prefix structure can be viewed as the (partially) ordered set of all intermediate (global) system states reached during this run. In this interpretation $[\epsilon]$ represents the initial state, incomparable prefixes represent states arising in effect of events occurring concurrently, and the ordering of prefix represents the temporal ordering of system states.

Occurrence ordering in strings. At the beginning of this section we give a couple of recursive definition of auxiliary notions. All of them define some functions on Σ_D^*; in these definitions w denotes always a string over Σ_D, and $e, e', e"$ symbols in Σ_D.

Let a be a symbol, w be a string; the number of occurrences of a in w is here denoted by $w(a)$. Thus, $\epsilon(a) = 0, wa(a) = w(a) + 1, wb(a) = w(a)$ for all strings w and symbols a, b. The *occurrence set* of w is a subset of $\Sigma \times \omega$:

$$\mathrm{Occ}\,(w) = \{(a, n) \mid a \in \Sigma \wedge 1 \leq n \leq w(a)\} \tag{1.34}$$

It is clear that a string and its permutation have the same occurrence set, since they have the same occurrence number of symbols; hence, all representatives of a trace over an arbitrary dependency have the same occurrence sets.

Example 1.6.1 -The occurrence set of string *abbca* is the set

$$\{(a, 1), (a, 2), (b, 1), (b, 2), (c, 1)\}.$$

Let $R \subseteq \Sigma \times \omega$ and A be an alphabet; define the projection $\pi_A(R)$ of R onto A as follows:

$$\pi_A(R) = \{(a, n) \in R \mid a \in A\}. \tag{1.35}$$

It is easy to show that

$$\pi_A(\text{Occ}\,(w)) = \text{Occ}\,(\pi_A(w)). \tag{1.36}$$

Thus, $\pi_A(\text{Occ}\,(w)) \subseteq \text{Occ}\,(w)$.

The *occurrence ordering* in a string w is an ordering $\text{Ord}\,(w)$ in the occurrence set of w defined recursively as follows:

$$\text{Ord}\,(\epsilon) = \emptyset, \quad \text{Ord}\,(wa) = \text{Ord}\,(w) \cup (\text{Occ}\,(wa) \times \{(a, w(a))\}). \tag{1.37}$$

Thus, $\text{Ord}\,(w) \subseteq \text{Occ}\,(w) \times \text{Occ}\,(w)$. It is obvious that $\text{Ord}\,(w)$ is a linear ordering for any string w.

Occurrence ordering in traces. In this section we generalize the notion of occurrence ordering from strings to traces. Let D be a dependency. As it has been already noticed, $u \equiv v$ implies $\text{Occ}\,(u) = \text{Occ}\,(v)$, for all strings u, v. Thus, the occurrence set for a trace can be set as the occurrence set of its arbitrary representative. Define now the occurrence ordering of a trace $[w]$ as the intersection of occurrence orderings of all representatives of $[w]$:

$$\text{Ord}\,([w]) = \bigcap_{u \equiv w} \text{Ord}\,(u). \tag{1.38}$$

This definition is correct, since all instances of a trace have the common occurrence set and the intersection of different linear ordering in a common set is a (partial) ordering of this set. Thus, according to this definition, ordering of all representatives of a single trace form all possible linearizations (extensions to the linear ordering) of the trace occurrence ordering. From this definition it follows that the occurrence ordering of a trace is the greatest ordering common for all its representatives. In the rest of this section we give some properties of this ordering and its alternative definitions.

We can interpret the ordering $\text{Ord}\,([w])$ from the point of view of concurrency as follows. Suppose there is a number of observers looking at the same concurrent process represented by a trace. Observation made by each of them is sequential; each of them sees only one representative of this trace. If two observers discover an opposite ordering of the same events in the observed process, it means that these events are actually not ordered in the process and that the difference noticed by observers results only because their specific points of view. Thus, such an ordering should not be taken into account, and consequently, two events can be considered as really ordered in the process if and only if they are ordered in the same way in all possible observations of the process (all observers agree on the same ordering).

D-graph ordering. Consider now d-graphs over D. Let $\gamma = (V, R, \varphi)$ be a dependence graph. Let, as in case of strings, $\gamma(a)$ denotes the number of vertices of γ labelled with a. Define the occurrence set of γ as the set

$$\text{Occ}\,(\gamma) = \{(a, n) \mid 1 \le n \le \gamma(a)\}. \tag{1.39}$$

We say that a vertex v *precedes* vertex u in γ, if there is an arc leading from v to u in γ. Let $v(a, n)$ denotes a vertex of γ labelled with a which is preceded in γ by

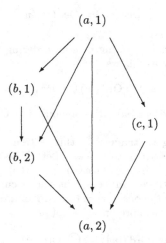

Figure 1.6. The occurrence relation for d-graph $\langle abbca \rangle_D$ over $D = \{a,b\}^2 \cup \{a,c\}^2$.

precisely $n-1$ vertices labelled with a. Observe that for each element (a,n) in the occurrence set of γ there exists precisely one vertex $v(a,n)$.

Occurrence relation for γ is the binary relation $Q(\gamma)$ in $\mathrm{Occ}(\gamma)$ such that

$$((a,n),(b,m)) \in Q(\gamma) \Leftrightarrow (v(a,n), v(b,m)) \in R). \tag{1.40}$$

Example 1.6.2 The diagram of the occurrence relation for the d-graph $\langle abbca \rangle$ over $\{a,b\}^2 \cup \{a,c\}^2$ is given in Fig.1.6

Since $Q(\gamma)$ is acyclic, its transitive and reflexive closure of $Q(\gamma)$ is an ordering relation in the set $\mathrm{Occ}(\gamma)$; this ordering will be called the *occurrence ordering* of γ and will be denoted by $\mathrm{Ord}(\gamma)$.

Proposition 1.6.3 *For each string w, the ordering $\mathrm{Ord}(w)$ is an extension of $\mathrm{Ord}(\langle w \rangle)$ to a linear ordering.*

Proof: It follows easily from the definition of arc connections in d-graphs by comparing it with the definition of $\mathrm{Ord}(w)$ given by (1.37)   □

Proposition 1.6.4 *Let γ be a d-graph, and let S be an extension of $\mathrm{Ord}(\gamma)$ to a linear ordering. Then there is a string u such that $S = \mathrm{Ord}(u)$ and $g = \langle u \rangle$.*

Proof: By induction. If γ is the empty graph, then set $u = \epsilon$. Let γ be not empty and let S be the extension of Ord (g) to a linear ordering. Let (a, n) be the maximum element of S. Then γ has a maximum vertex labelled with a. Delete from γ this vertex and denote the resulting graph by β; delete also the maximum element from S and denote the resulting ordering by R. Clearly, R is the linear extension of β; by induction hypothesis there is a string, say w, such that $R = \text{Ord}(w)$ and $\beta = \langle w \rangle$. But then $S = \text{Ord}(wa)$ and $\gamma = \langle wa \rangle$. Thus, $u = wa$ meets the requirement of the proposition.   □

Theorem 1.6.5 *For all strings w: $Ord([w]) = Ord(\langle w \rangle)$.*

Proof: Obvious in view of the definition of the trace ordering and propositions 1.6.3 and 1.6.4.   □

This theorem states that the intersection of linear orderings of representatives of a trace is the same ordering as the transitive and reflexive closure of the ordering of the d-graph corresponding to that trace.

History ordering. Now, let $(\Sigma_1, \Sigma_2, \ldots, \Sigma_n)$ be n-tuple of finite alphabets, $\Sigma = \Sigma_1 \cup \Sigma_2 \cup \cdots \cup \Sigma_n$, $D = \Sigma_1^2 \cup \Sigma_2^2 \cup \cdots \cup \Sigma_n^2$, π_i be the projection on Σ_i, and let π be the distribution function.

Fact 1.6.6 *For any string w over Σ and each $i \leq n$:*

$$\pi_i(Ord(w)) = Ord(\pi_i(w)). \tag{1.41}$$

Proof: Equality (1.41) holds for $w = \epsilon$. Let $w = ue$, for string u and symbol e. If $e \notin \Sigma_i$, equality (1.41) holds by induction hypothesis, since $\pi_i(w) = \pi_i(u)$. Let then $a \in \Sigma_i$. By definition, Ord $(ua) = $ Ord $(u) \cup (\text{Occ}(ua) \times \{(a, u(a)+1)\})$. By induction hypothesis $\pi_i(\text{Ord}(u)) = \text{Ord}(\pi_i(u))$; by (1.36) $\pi_i(\text{Occ}(ua)) = \text{Occ}(\pi_i(ua))$; $a \in \Sigma_i$ implies $\pi_i(u)(a) = u(a)$, hence $\pi(\text{Ord}(ua)) = \text{Occ}(\pi_i(ua)) \cup \{(a, \pi_i(u)(a) + 1\} = $ Ord $(\pi_i(ua))$. It ends the proof.   □

Fact 1.6.7 *For each string w over Σ:*

$$Occ(w) = \bigcup_{i=1}^{n} Occ(\pi_i(w)).$$

Proof: Since, by definition, $\pi_i(\text{Occ}(w)) \subseteq \text{Occ}(w)$, and $\pi_i(\text{Occ}(w)) = \text{Occ}(\pi_i(w))$ for each $i \leq n$, hence $\bigcup_{i=1}^{n} \text{Occ}(\pi_i(w)) \subseteq \text{Occ}(w)$. Let $(e, k) \in \text{Occ}(w)$; hence $(a, k) \in \pi_i(\text{Occ}(w))$ for i such that $a \in \Sigma_i$; thus, $(a, k) \in \text{Occ}(\pi_i(w))$ for this i; but it means that $(a, k) \in \bigcup_{i=1}^{n} \text{Occ}(\pi_i(w))$, which completes the proof.   □

Let $(w_1, w_2, \ldots, w_n)$ be a global history; define

$$\text{Ord}(w_1, w_2, \ldots, w_n) = (\bigcup_{i=1}^{n} \text{Ord}(w_i))^* \tag{1.42}$$

The following theorem close the comparison of different types of defining trace ordering.

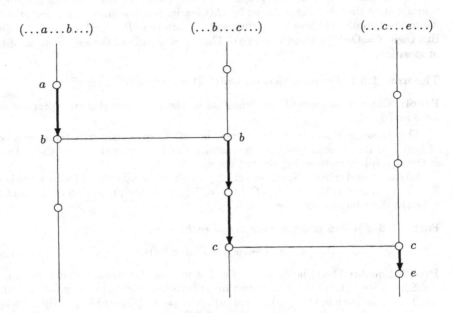

Figure 1.7: History ordering: e follows a.

Theorem 1.6.8 *Let $D = \bigcup \Sigma_i^2$, let $\pi(w)$ be distribution function in $(\Sigma_1, \Sigma_2, \ldots, \Sigma_n)$, and let $\langle w \rangle$ be the d-graph $\langle w \rangle_D$. Then for each string w $Ord(\pi(w)) = Ord(\langle w \rangle)$.*

Proof: Let D be such as assumed above, let $\langle w \rangle$ denotes $\langle w \rangle_D$, and let $\pi(w) = (w_1, w_2, \ldots, w_n)$. Thus, for each $i : w_i = \pi_i(w)$. Since $\mathrm{Occ}\,(w) = \mathrm{Occ}\,(\langle w \rangle)$, and $\mathrm{Occ}\,(w_i) \subseteq \mathrm{Occ}\,(w)$, we have $\mathrm{Occ}\,(w_i) \subseteq \mathrm{Occ}\,(\langle w \rangle)$. Any two symbols in Σ_i are dependent, hence $\mathrm{Ord}\,(w_i) \subseteq \mathrm{Ord}\,(\langle w \rangle)$. Therefore, $\bigcup_{i=1}^{n} \mathrm{Ord}\,(w_i) \subseteq \mathrm{Ord}\,(\langle w \rangle)$ and since $\mathrm{Ord}\,(\langle w \rangle)$ is an ordering, $(\bigcup_{i=1}^{n} \mathrm{Ord}\,(w_i))^* \subseteq \mathrm{Ord}\,(\langle w \rangle)$. To prove the inverse inclusion, observe that if there is an arc in an occurrence graph from (e', k') to (e'', k''), then $(e', e'') \in D$; it means that there is i such that $e', e'' \in \Sigma_i$ and that $((e', k'), (e'', k'')) \in \mathrm{Ord}\,(w_i)$, hence $((e', k'), (e'', k'')) \in \mathrm{Ord}\,(\pi(w))$. It ends the proof. □

The history ordering, defined by (1.42), is illustrated in Fig. 1.7.

It explains the principle of history ordering. Let us interpret ordering $\mathrm{Ord}\,(\pi w)$

in similar way as we have done it in case of traces. Each individual history of a component can be viewed as the result of a local observation of a process limited to events belonging to the repertoire of the component. From such a viewpoint, an observer can notice only events local to the component he is situated at; remaining actions are invisible for him. Thus, being localized at i-th component, he notices the ordering $\mathrm{Ord}\,(\pi_i(w))$ only. To discover the global ordering of events in the whole history, all such individual histories have to be put together; then events observed coincidently from different components form a sort of links between individual observations and make possible to discover an ordering between events local to separate and remote components. The rule is: an event occurrence (a'', n'') follows another event occurrence (a', n'), if there is a sequence of event occurrences beginning with (a', n') and ending with (a'', n'') in which every element follows its predecessor according to the individual history containing both of them. Such a principle is used by historians to establish a chronology of events concerning remote and separate historical objects.

Let us comment and compare all three ways of defining ordering within graphs, traces, and histories. They have been defined in the following way:

$\mathrm{Ord}\,(\langle w \rangle)$: as the transitive and reflexive closure of arc relation of $\langle w \rangle$;

$\mathrm{Ord}\,([w])$: as intersection of linear orderings of all representatives of $[w]$;

$\mathrm{Ord}\,(\pi(w))$: as the transitive closure of the union of linear orderings of all $\pi_i(w)$ components.

All of them describe processes as partially ordered sets of event occurrences. They have been defined in different way: in natural way for graphs, as the intersection of individually observed sequential orderings in case of traces, and as the union of individually observed sequential orderings in case of histories. In case of traces, observations were complete, containing every action, but sometimes discovering different orderings of some events; in case of histories, observations were incomplete, limited only to local events, but discovering always the proper ordering of noticed events. In the case of traces the way of obtaining the global ordering is by comparing all individual observations and rejecting a subjective and irrelevant information (by intersection of individual orderings); in case of histories, all individual observations are collected together to gain complementary and relevant information (by unifying individual observations). While the second method has been compared to the method of historians, the first one can be compared to that of physicists. In all three cases the results are the same; it gives an additional argument for the above mentioned definitions and indicates their soundness.

1.7 Trace Languages

Let D be a dependency; by a *trace language* over D we shall mean any set of traces over D. The set of all trace languages over D will be denoted by $\mathbf{T}_D$). For a given set L of strings over Σ_D denote by $[L]_D$ the set $\{[w]_D \mid w \in L\}$; and for a given set

T of traces over D denote by $\bigcup T$ the set $\{w \mid [w]_D \in T\}$. Clearly,

$$L \subseteq \bigcup[L]_D \text{ and } T = [\bigcup T]_D \tag{1.43}$$

for all (string) languages L and (trace) languages T over D. String language L such that $L = \bigcup[L]_D$ is called to be *(existentially) consistent* with dependency D [3]. The composition $T_1 T_2$ of trace languages T_1, T_2 over the same dependency D is the set $\{t_1 t_2 \mid t_1 \in T_2 \wedge t_2 \wedge T_2\}$. The iteration of trace language T over D is defined in the same way as the iteration of string language:

$$T^* = \bigcup_{n=0}^{\infty} T^n$$

where

$$T^0 = [\epsilon]_D \text{ and } T^{n+1} = T^n T.$$

The following proposition results directly from the definitions:

Proposition 1.7.1 *For any dependency D, any string languages L, L_1, L_2 over Σ_D, and for any family $\{L_i\}_{i \in I}$ of string languages over Σ_D:*

$$[\emptyset]_D = \emptyset, \tag{1.44}$$

$$[L_1]_D[L_2]_D = [L_1 L_2]_D, \tag{1.45}$$

$$L_1 \subseteq L_2 \Rightarrow [L_1]_D \subseteq [L_2]_D, \tag{1.46}$$

$$[L_1]_D \cup [L_2]_D = [L_1 \cup L_2]_D, \tag{1.47}$$

$$\bigcup_{i \in I}[L_i]_D = [\bigcup_{i \in I} L_i]_D, \tag{1.48}$$

$$[L]^*_D = [L^*]_D. \tag{1.49}$$

Before defining the synchronization of languages (which is the most important operation on languages for the present purpose) let us introduce the notion of projection adjusted for traces and dependencies.

Let C be a dependency, $C \subseteq D$, and let t be a trace over D; then the *trace projection* $\pi_C(t)$ of t onto C is a trace over C defined as follows:

$$\pi_C(t) = \begin{cases} [\epsilon]_C, & \text{if } t = [\epsilon]_D, \\ \pi_C(t_1), & \text{if } t = t_1[e]_D, e \notin \Sigma_C, \\ \pi_C(t_1)[e]_C, & \text{if } t = t_1[e]_D, e \in \Sigma_C. \end{cases}$$

Intuitively, trace projection onto C deletes from traces all symbols not in Σ_C and weakens the dependency within traces. Thus, the projection of a trace over dependency D onto a dependency C which is "smaller", but has the same alphabet as D, is a "weaker" trace, containing more representatives the the original one.

The following proposition is easy to prove:

Proposition 1.7.2 *Let C, D be dependencies, $D \subseteq C$. Then $u \equiv_C v \Rightarrow \pi_D(u) \equiv_D \pi_D(v)$.*

Define the *synchronization* of the string language L_1 over Σ_1 with the string language L_2 over Σ_2 as the string language $(L_1 \parallel L_2)$ over $(\Sigma_1 \cup \Sigma_2)$ such that

$$w \in (L_1 \parallel L_2) \Leftrightarrow \pi_{\Sigma_1}(w) \in L_1 \wedge \pi_{\Sigma_2}(w) \in L_2.$$

Proposition 1.7.3 *Let L, L_1, L_2, L_3 be string languages, Σ_1 be the alphabet of L_1, Σ_2 be the alphabet of L_2, let $\{L_i\}_{i \in I}$ be a family of string languages over a common alphabet, and let w be a string over $\Sigma_1 \cup \Sigma_2$. Then:*

$$L \parallel L = L,$$
$$L_1 \parallel L_2 = L_2 \parallel L_1,$$
$$L_1 \parallel (L_2 \parallel L_3) = (L_1 \parallel L_2) \parallel L_3,$$
$$\{[\epsilon]_{\Sigma_1}\} \parallel \{[\epsilon]_{\Sigma_2}\} = \{[\epsilon]_{\Sigma_1 \cup \Sigma_2}\},$$
$$\left(\bigcup_{i \in I} L_i\right) \parallel L = \bigcup_{i \in I}(L_i \parallel L)$$
$$(L_1 \parallel L_2)\{w\} = (L_1\{\pi_{\Sigma_1}(w)\}) \parallel (L_2\{\pi_{\Sigma_2}(w)\}),$$
$$\{w\}(L_1 \parallel L_2) = (\{\pi_{\Sigma_1}(w)\}L_1) \parallel (\{\pi_{\Sigma_2}(w)\}L_2).$$

Proof: Equalities (1.50) – (1.50) are obvious. Let $w \in (\bigcup_{i \in I} L_i) \parallel L$; it means that $\pi_{\Sigma'}(w) \in (\bigcup_{i \in I} L_i)$ and $\pi_{\Sigma}(w) \in (L)$; then $\exists i \in I : \pi_{\Sigma'}(w) \in L_i$ and $\pi_{\Sigma}(w) \in L$, i.e. $w \in (\bigcup_{i \in I}(L_i \parallel L))$, which proves (1.50). To prove (1.50), let $u \in (L_1 \parallel L_2)\{w\}$; it means that there exists v such that $v \in (L_1 \parallel L_2)$ and $u = vw$; by definition of synchronization, $\pi_{\Sigma_1}(v) \in L_1$ and $\pi_{\Sigma_2}(v) \in L_2$; because w is a string over $\Sigma_1 \cup \Sigma_2$, this is equivalent to $\pi_{\Sigma_1}(vw) \in L_1\{\pi_{\Sigma_1}(w)\}$ and $\pi_{\Sigma_2}(vw) \in L_2\{\pi_{\Sigma_2}(w)\}$; it means that $u \in (L_1\{\pi_{\Sigma_1}(w)\}) \parallel (L_2\{\pi_{\Sigma_2}(w)\})$. Proof of (1.50) is similar. $\square$

Define the *synchronization* of the trace language T_1 over D_1 with the trace language T_2 over D_2 as the trace language $(T_1 \parallel T_2)$ over $(D_1 \cup D_2)$ such that

$$t \in (T_1 \parallel T_2) \Leftrightarrow \pi_{D_1}(t) \in T_1 \wedge \pi_{D_2}(t) \in T_2.$$

Proposition 1.7.4 *For any dependencies D_1, D_2 and any string languages L_1 over Σ_{D_1}, L_2 over Σ_{D_2}:*

$$[L_1]_{D_1} \parallel [L_2]_{D_2} = [L_1 \parallel L_2]_{D_1 \cup D_2}$$

Proof:

$$
\begin{aligned}
[L_1]_{D_1} \parallel [L_2]_{D_2} &= \{t \mid \pi_{D_1}(t) \in [L_1]_{D_1} \wedge \pi_{D_2}(t) \in [L_2]_{D_2}\} \\
&= \{[w]_{D_1 \cup D_2} \mid \pi_{S_{D_1}}(w) \in L_1 \wedge \pi_{S_{D_2}}(w) \in L_2\} \\
&= \{[w]_{D_1 \cup D_2} \mid w \in L_1 \parallel L_2\} \\
&= [\{w \mid w \in (L_1 \parallel L_2)\}]_{D_1 \cup D_2} \\
&= [L_1 \parallel L_2]_{D_1 \cup D_2}.
\end{aligned}
$$

$\square$

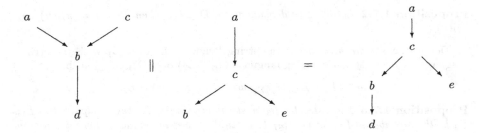

Figure 1.8: Synchronization of two singleton trace languages.

Proposition 1.7.5 *Let T, T_1, T_2, T_3 be trace languages, let D_1 be the dependency of T_1, D_2 be the dependency of T_2, let $\{T_i\}_{i \in I}$ be a family of trace languages over a common dependency, and let t be a trace over $D_1 \cup D_2$. Then:*

$$T \parallel T = T, \tag{1.50}$$

$$T_1 \parallel T_2 = T_2 \parallel T_1, \tag{1.51}$$

$$T_1 \parallel (T_2 \parallel T_3) = (T_1 \parallel T_2) \parallel T_3, \tag{1.52}$$

$$\{[\epsilon]_{D_1}\} \parallel \{[\epsilon]_{D_2}\} = \{[\epsilon]_{D_1 \cup D_2}\}, \tag{1.53}$$

$$(\bigcup_{i \in I} T_i) \parallel T = \bigcup_{i \in I} (T_i \parallel T) \tag{1.54}$$

$$(T_1 \parallel T_2)\{t\} = (T_1\{\pi_{D_1}(t)\}) \parallel (T_2\{\pi_{D_2}(t)\}), \tag{1.55}$$

$$\{t\}(T_1 \parallel T_2) = (\{\pi_{D_1}(t)\}T_1) \parallel (\{\pi_{D_2}(t)\}T_2). \tag{1.56}$$

Proof: It is similar to that of Proposition 1.7.3.   □

Example 1.7.6 Let $D_1 = \{a, b, d\}^2 \cup \{b, c, d\}^2, D_2 = \{a, b, c\}^2 \cup \{a, c, e\}^2, T_1 = \{[cabd]_{D_1}\}, T_2 = \{[acbe]_{D_2}\}$. The synchronization $T_1 \parallel T_2$ is the language $\{[acbde]_D\}$ over dependency $D = D_1 \cup D_2 = \{a, b, c, d\}^2 \cup \{a, c, e\}^2$. Synchronization of these two trace languages is illustrated in Fig. 1.8 where traces are represented by corresponding d-graphs (without arcs resulting by transitivity from others).

Observe that in a sense the synchronization operation is inverse w. r. to projection, namely we have for any trace t over $D_1 \cup D_2$ the equality:

$$\{t\} = \{\pi_{D_1}(t)\} \parallel \{\pi_{D_2}(t)\}.$$

Observe also that for any traces t_1 over D_1, t_2 over D_2, the synchronization $\{t_1\} \parallel \{t_2\}$ is either empty, or a singleton set. Thus the synchronization can be viewed as a partial operation on traces. In general, it is not so in case of strings: synchronization of two singleton string languages may not be a singleton. E.g., the synchronization of the string language $\{ab\}$ over $\{a, b\}$ with the string language $\{cd\}$ over $\{c, d\}$ is the string language $\{abcd, acbd, cabd, acdb, cadb, cdab\}$, while the synchronization of the trace language $\{[ab]\}$ over $\{a, b\}^2$ with the trace language $\{[cd]\}$ over $\{c, d\}^2$ is the singleton trace language $\{[abcd]\}$ over $\{a, b\}^2 \cup \{c, d\}^2$. It is yet another justification of using traces instead of strings for representing runs of concurrent systems.

Synchronization operation can be easily extended to an arbitrary number of arguments: for a family of trace languages $\{T_i\}_{i \in I}$, with T_i being a trace language over D_i, we define $\|_{i \in I} T_i$ as the trace language over $\bigcup_{i \in I} D_i$ such that

$$t \in \|_{i \in I} T_i \Leftrightarrow \forall_{i \in I} \pi_{D_i}(t) \in T_i.$$

Fact 1.7.7 *If T_1, T_2 are trace languages over a common dependency, then $T_1 \| T_2 = T_1 \cap T_2$.*

Proof: Let T_1, T_2 be trace languages over dependency D; then $t \in (T_1 \| T_2)$ if and only if $\pi_D(t) \in T_1$ and $\pi_D(t) \in T_2$; but since t is a trace over D, $\pi_D(t) = t$, hence $t \in T_1$ and $t \in T_2$. □

A trace language T is *prefix-closed*, if $s \sqsubseteq t \in T \Rightarrow s \in T$.

Proposition 1.7.8 *If T_1, T_2 are prefix-closed trace languages, then so is their synchronization $T_1 \| T_2$.*

Proof: Let T_1, T_2 be prefix-closed trace languages over dependencies D_1, D_2, respectively. Let $t \in (T_1 \| T_2)$ and let t' be a prefix of t; then there is t'' such that $t = t't''$. But then, by properties of projection, $\pi_{D_1}(t) = \pi_{D_1}(t't'') = \pi_{D_1}(t')\pi_{D_1}(t'') \in T_1$ and $\pi_{D_2}(t) = \pi_{D_2}(t't'') = \pi_{D_2}(t')\pi_{D_2}(t'') \in T_2$; since T_1, T_2 are prefix-closed, $\pi_{D_1}(t') \in T_1$ and $\pi_{D_2}(t') \in T_2$; hence, by definition, $t' \in (T_1 \| T_2)$. □

Fixed-point equations. Let $\mathbf{X}_1, \mathbf{X}_2, \ldots, \mathbf{X}_n, \mathbf{Y}$ be families of sets, $n > 0$, and let $f : \mathbf{X}_1 \times \mathbf{X}_2 \times \cdots \times \mathbf{X}_n \longrightarrow \mathbf{Y}$; f is *monotone*, if

$$(\forall i : X_i' \subseteq X_i'') \Rightarrow f(X_1', X_2', \ldots X_n') \subseteq f(X_1'', X_2'', \ldots, X_n'')$$

for each $X_i', X_i'' \in \mathbf{X}_i, i = 1, 2, \ldots, n$.

Fact 1.7.9 *Concatenation, union, iteration, and synchronization, operations on string (trace) languages are monotone.*

Proof: Obvious in view of corresponding definitions. □

Fact 1.7.10 *Superposition (composition) of any number of monotone operations is monotone.*

Proof: Clear. □

Let $D_1, D_2, \ldots, D_n, D$ be dependencies, $n > 0$, and let

$$f : 2^{\Sigma_{D_1}^*} \times 2^{\Sigma_{D_2}^*} \times \cdots \times 2^{\Sigma_{D_n}^*} \longrightarrow 2^{\Sigma_D^*};$$

f is *congruent*, if

$$(\forall i : [X_i']_{D_i} = [X_i'']_{D_i}) \Rightarrow [f(X_1', X_2', \ldots X_n')]_D = [f(X_1'', X_2'', \ldots, X_n'')]_D$$

for all $X_i', X_i'' \in 2^{\Sigma_{D_i}^*}, i = 1, 2, \ldots, n$.

Fact 1.7.11 *Concatenation, union, iteration, and synchronization operations on string languages are congruent.*

Proof: It follows from Proposition 1.7.1 and Proposition 1.7.4.   □

Fact 1.7.12 *Superposition (composition) of any number of congruent operations is congruent.*

Proof: Clear.   □

Let $D_1, D_2, \ldots, D_n, D$ be dependencies, $n > 0$, and let

$$f : 2^{\Sigma_{D_1}^*} \times 2^{\Sigma_{D_2}^*} \times \cdots \times 2^{\Sigma_{D_n}^*} \longrightarrow 2^{\Sigma_D^*}$$

be *congruent*. Denote by $[f]_D$ the function

$$[f]_D : 2^{\mathbf{T}_{D_1}} \times 2^{\mathbf{T}_{D_2}} \times \cdots \times 2^{\mathbf{T}_{D_n}} \longrightarrow 2^{\mathbf{T}_D}.$$

defined by the equality

$$[f]_D([L_1]_{D_1}, [L_2]_{D_2}, \ldots, [L_n]_{D_n}) = [f(L_1, L_2, \ldots, L_n)]_D$$

This definition is correct by congruence of f.

We say that the set x_0 is the least fixed point of function $f : 2^X \longrightarrow 2^X$, if $f(x_0) = x_0$ and for any set x with $f(x) = x$ the inclusion $x_0 \subseteq x$ holds.

Theorem 1.7.13 *Let D be a dependency and $f : 2^{\Sigma_D^*} \longrightarrow 2^{\Sigma_D^*}$ be monotone and congruent. If L_0 is the least fixed point of f, then $[L_0]_D$ is the least fixed point of $[f]_D$.*

Proof: Let D, f, and L_0 be such as defined in the formulation of Theorem. First observe that for any L with $f(L) \subseteq L$ we have $L_0 \subseteq L$. Indeed, let L' be the least set of strings such that $f(L') \subseteq L'$; then $L' \subseteq L$. Since f is monotone, $f(f(L') \subseteq f(L')$, hence $f(L')$ meets also the inclusion and consequently $L' \subseteq f(L')$; hence, $L' = f(L')$ and by the definition of L_0 we have $L_0 \subseteq L' \subseteq L$. Now,

$$[L_0]_D = [f(L_0)]_D = [f]_D([L_0]_D)$$

by congruence of f. Thus, $[L_0]_D$ is a fixed point of $[f]_D$. We show that $[L_0]_D$ is the least fixed point of $[f]_D$. Let T be a trace language over D such that $[f]_D(T) = T$ and set $L = \bigcup T$. Thus $[L]_D = T$ and $\bigcup T = \bigcup [L]_D = L$. By (1.43) we have $f(L) \subseteq \bigcup [f(L)]_D$; by congruence of f we have $\bigcup [f(L)]_D = \bigcup [f]_D([L]_D)$; by definition of L we have $\bigcup [f]_D([L]_D) = \bigcup [f]_D(T)$, and by definition of T we get $\bigcup [f]_D(T) = \bigcup T$ and again by definition of L: $\bigcup T = L$. Collecting all above relations together we get $f(L) \subseteq L$. Thus, as we have already proved, $L_0 \subseteq L$, hence $[L_0]_D \subseteq [L]_D = T$. It proves $[L_0]$ to be the least fixed point of $[f]_D$.   □

This theorem can be easily generalized for tuples of monotonic and congruent functions. As we have already mention, functions built up from variables and constants by means of union, concatenation and iteration operations can serve as examples of monotonic and congruent functions. Theorem 1.7.13 allows to lift the well-known and broadly applied method of defining string languages by fixed point equations to the case of trace languages. It offers also a useful and handy tool for analysis concurrent systems represented by elementary net systems, as shown in the next section.

It is worthwhile to note that, under the same assumptions as in Theorem 1.7.13, M_0 can be the greatest fixed point of a function f, while $[M_0]$ is not the greatest fixed point of $[f]$.

1.8 Elementary Net Systems

In this section we show how the trace theory is related to net models of concurrent systems. First, *elementary net systems*, introduced in [238] on the base of Petri nets and will be presented. The behaviour of such systems will be represented by string languages describing various sequences of system actions that can be executed while the system is running. Next, the trace behaviour will be defined and compared with the string behaviour. Finally, compositionality of behaviours will be shown: the behaviour of a net composed from other nets as components turns out to be the synchronization of the components behaviour.

Elementary net systems. By an *elementary net system*, called simply *net* from now on, we understand any ordered quadruple

$$N = (P_N, E_N, F_N, m_N^0)$$

where P_N, E_N are finite disjoint sets (of *places* and *transitions*, resp.), $F_N \subseteq P_N \times E_N \cup E_N \times P_N$ (the *flow* relation) and $m_N^0 \subseteq P_N$. It is assumed that $Dom(F_N) \cup Cod(F_N) = P_N \cup E_N$ (there is no "isolated" places and transitions) and $F \cap F^{-1} = \emptyset$. Any subset of P_N is called a *marking* of N; m_N^0 is called the (*initial marking*). A place in a marking is said to be *marked*, or *carrying a token*.

As all other types of nets, elementary net systems are represented graphically using boxes to represent transitions, circles to represent places, and arrows leading from circles to boxes or from boxes to circles to represent the flow relation; in such a representation circles corresponding to places in the initial marking are marked

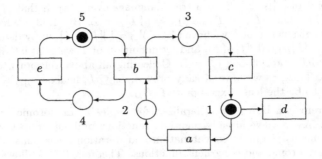

Figure 1.9: Example of an elementary net system.

with dots. In Fig. 1.9 the net (P, E, F, m) with

$$
\begin{aligned}
P &= \{1, 2, 3, 4, 5, 6\}, \\
E &= \{a, b, c, d, e\}, \\
F &= \{(1, a), (a, 2), (2, b), (b, 3), (3, c), (c, 1), \\
&\quad (1, d), (d, 4), (5, b), (b, 6), (6, e), (e, 5)\}), \\
m &= \{1, 5\}
\end{aligned}
$$

is represented graphically.

Define Pre, Post, Prox as functions from E to 2^P such that for all $a \in E$: as follows:

$$
\begin{aligned}
\text{Pre}_N(a) &= \{p \mid (p, a) \in F_N\}; & (1.57) \\
\text{Post}_N(a) &= \{p \mid (e, p) \in F_N\}; & (1.58) \\
\text{Prox}_N(a) &= \text{Pre}_N(a) \cup \text{Post}_N(a); & (1.59)
\end{aligned}
$$

places in $\text{Pre}_N(a)$ are called the *entry* places of a, those in $\text{Post}_N(a)$ are called the *exit* places of a, and those in $\text{Prox}_N(a)$ are *neighbours* of a; the set $\text{Prox}_N(a)$ is the neighbourhood of a in N. The assumption $F \cap F^{-1} = \emptyset$ means that no place can be an entry and an exit of the same transition. The subscript N is omitted if the net is understood.

Transition function of net N is a (partial) function $\delta_N : 2^P_N \times E_N \longrightarrow 2^{P_N}$ such that

$$
\delta_N(m_1, a) = m_2 \Leftrightarrow \left\{ \begin{array}{l} \text{Pre}(a) \subseteq m_1, \text{Post}(a) \cap m_1 = \emptyset, \\ m_2 = (m_1 - \text{Pre}(a)) \cup \text{Post}(a); \end{array} \right.
$$

As usual, subscript N is omitted, if the net is understood; this convention will hold for all subsequent notions and symbols related to them.

Clearly, this definition is correct, since for each marking m and transition a there exists at most one marking equal to $\delta(m, a)$. If $\delta(m, a)$ is defined for marking m and transition a, we say that a is *enabled* at marking m. We say that the transition function describes single steps of the system.

Reachability function of net N is the function $\delta_N^* : 2^P \times E^* \longrightarrow 2^P$ defined recursively by equalities:

$$\delta_N^*(m, \epsilon) = m, \tag{1.60}$$
$$\delta_N^*(m, wa) = \delta_N(\delta_N^*(m, w), a) \tag{1.61}$$

for all $m \in 2^P, w \in E^*, a \in E$.

Behavioural function of net N is the function $\beta_N : E^* \longrightarrow 2^P$ defined by $\beta_N(w) = \delta^*(m^0, w)$ for all $w \in E^*$.

As usual, the subscript N is omitted everywhere the net N is understood.

The set (of strings) $S_N = Dom(\beta)$ is the (sequential) behaviour of net N; the set (of markings) $R_N = Cod(\beta)$ is the set of *reachable* markings of N. Elements of S will be called *execution sequences* of N; execution sequence w such that $\beta(w) = m \subseteq P$ is said to *lead* to m.

The *sequential behaviour* of N is clearly a prefix closed language and as any prefix closed language it is ordered into a tree by the prefix relation. Maximal linearly ordered subsets of S can be viewed as sequential observations of the behaviour of N, i.e. observations made by observers capable to see only a single event occurrence at a time. The ordering of symbols in strings of S reflects not only the (objective) causal ordering of event occurrences but also a (subjective) observational ordering resulting from a specific view over concurrent actions. Therefore, the structure of S alone does not allow to decide whether the difference in ordering is caused by a conflict resolution (a decision made in the system), or by different observations of concurrency. In order to extract from S the causal ordering of event occurrences we must supply S with an additional information; as such information we take here the dependency of events.

Dependency relation for net N is defined as the relation $D_N \subseteq E \times E$ such that

$$(a, b) \in D_N \Leftrightarrow \mathrm{Prox}_N(a) \cap \mathrm{Prox}_N(b) \neq \emptyset.$$

Intuitively speaking, two transitions are dependent if either they share a common entry place (then they "compete" for taking a token away from this place), or they share a common exit place (and then they compete for putting a token into the place), or an entry place of one transition is the exit place of the other (and then one of them "waits" for the other). Transitions are independent, if their neighbourhoods are disjoint. If both such transitions are enabled at a marking, they can be executed concurrently (independently of each other).

Define the non-sequential behaviour of net N as the trace language $[S]_D$ and denote it by B_N. That is, the non-sequential behaviour of a net arises from its sequential behaviour by identifying some execution sequences; as it follows from the dependency definition, two such sequences are identified if they differ in the order of independent transitions execution.

Sequential and non-sequential behaviour consistency is guaranteed by the following proposition (where the equality of values of two partial functions means that either both of them are defined and then their values are equal, or both of them are undefined).

Proposition 1.8.1 *For any net N the behavioural function β is congruent w.r. to D, i.e. for any strings $u, v \in E^*, u \equiv_D v$ implies $\beta(u) = \beta(v)$.*

Proof: Let $u \equiv_D v$; it suffices to consider the case $u = xaby$ and $v = xbay$, for independent transitions a, b and arbitrary $x, y \in E^*$. Because of the behavioural function definition, we have to prove only

$$\delta(\delta(m, a), b) = \delta(\delta(m, b), a)$$

for an arbitrary marking m. By simple inspection we conclude that, because of independency of a and b, i.e. because of disjointness of neighbourhoods of a and b, both sides of the above condition are equal to a configuration

$$(m - (\mathrm{Pre}\,(a) \cup \mathrm{Pre}\,(b))) \cup (\mathrm{Post}\,(a) \cup \mathrm{Post}\,(b))$$

or both of them are undefined.   □

This is another motivation for introducing traces for describing concurrent systems behaviour: from the point of view of reachability possibilities, all equivalent execution sequences are the same. As we have shown earlier, firing traces can be viewed as partially ordered sets of symbol occurrences; two occurrences are not ordered, if they represent transitions that can be executed independently of each other. Thus, the ordering within firing traces is determined by mutual dependencies of events and then it reflects the causal relationship between event occurrences rather than the non - objective ordering following from the string representation of net activity.

Two traces are said to be *consistent*, if both of them are prefixes of a common trace. A trace language T is *complete*, if any two consistent traces in T are prefixes of a trace in T.

Proposition 1.8.2 *The trace behaviour of any net is a complete trace language.*

Proof: Let B be the trace behaviour of net N, I be the independence induced by D, and let $[w], [u] \in B$, and let $[wx] = [uy]$ for some strings x, y. Then by Levi Lemma for traces there are strings v_1, v_2, v_3, v_4 such that $v_1 v_2 \equiv w, v_3 v_4 \equiv x, v_1 v_3 \equiv u, v_2 v_4 = y$ and $(v_2, v_3) \in I$. Let $m = \beta(v_1)$. Since $w \in Dom(\beta), v_1 v_2 \in Dom(\beta)$; since $u \in \beta, (v_1 v_3) \in Dom(\beta)$; hence, $\delta^*(m, v_2)$ is defined and $\delta^*(m, v_3)$ is defined; since $(v_2, v_3) \in I, v_1 v_2 v_3 \equiv v_1 v_3 v_2$; moreover, $\delta^*(m, v_2 v_3)$ is defined, $\delta^*(m, v_3 v_2)$ is defined, and $\delta^*(m, v_2 v_3) = \delta^*(m, v_3 v_2)$. It means that $v_1 v_2 v_3 \equiv v_1 v_3 v_2 \in Dom(\beta)$, i.e. $wv_3 \equiv uv_2 \in Dom(\beta)$. It ends the proof.   □

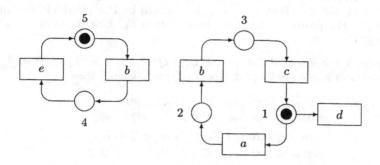

Figure 1.10: Decomposition of a net (into two sequential components).

Composition of nets and their behaviours. Here we are going to present a modular way of finding the behaviour of nets. It will be shown how to construct the behaviour of a net from behaviours of its parts: The first step is to decompose a given net into modules, next, to find their behaviours, and finally, to put them together finding in this way the behaviour of the original net.

Let $I = \{1, 2, \ldots, n\}$; we say that a net $N = (P, E, F, m)$ is composed of nets $N_i = (P_i, E_i, F_i, m_i), i \in I$, and write

$$N = N_1 + N_2 + \cdots + N_n,$$

if $i \neq j$ implies $P_i \cap P_j = \emptyset$ (N_i are pairwise place-disjoint), and

$$P = \bigcup_{i=1}^{n} P_i, E = \bigcup_{i=1}^{n} E_i, F = \bigcup_{i=1}^{n} F_i, m = \bigcup_{i=1}^{n} m_i.$$

The net in Fig. 1.9 is composed from two nets presented in Fig. 1.10.

Composition of nets could be defined without assuming the disjointness of sets of places; instead, we could use the disjoint union of sets of places rather than the set-theoretical union in the composition definition. However, it would require a new definition of nets, with two nets considered identical if there is an isomorphism identifying nets with different sets of places and preserving the flow relation and the initial marking. For sake of simplicity, we assume sets of places of the composition components to be disjoint, and we use the usual set-theoretical union in our definition.

Proposition 1.8.3 *Composition of nets is associative and commutative.*

Proof: Obvious. □

Let $I = \{1, 2, \ldots, n\}$ and let $N = N = N_1 + N_2 + \cdots + N_n$, $N_i = (P_i, E_i, F_i, m_i^0)$ for all $i \in I$. Let $\text{Pre}_{N_i}, \text{Post}_{N_i}, \text{Prox}_{N_i}$ be denoted by $\text{Pre}_i, \text{Post}_i, \text{Prox}_i$; moreover, let π_i be the projection functions from E onto E_i. Finally, let $m_i = m \cap P_i$ for any $m \subseteq P$.

Proposition 1.8.4 *Let $Q, R \subseteq P$ and set $Q_i = Q \cap P_I$, $R_i = R \cap P_I$. If $P = \bigcup_{i \in I} P_i$ and the members of the family $\{P_i\}_{i \in I}$ are pairwise disjoint, then*

$$Q \subseteq m \quad \Leftrightarrow \quad \forall i \in I : Q_i \subseteq m_i,$$
$$R = Q \cap m \quad \Leftrightarrow \quad \forall i \in I : R_i = Q_i \cap m_i,$$
$$m = Q \cup R \quad \Leftrightarrow \quad \forall i \in I : m_i = Q_i \cup R_i,$$
$$R = m - Q \quad \Leftrightarrow \quad \forall i \in I : R_i = m_i - Q_i.$$

and $Q = \bigcup_{i \in I} Q_i$, $R = \bigcup_{i \in I} R_i$.

Proof: Clear. □

Proposition 1.8.5 $D_N = \bigcup_{i=1}^{n} D_{N_i}.$

Proof: Let $(a, b) \in D(N)$; by definition, $\text{Prox}(a) \cap \text{Prox}(b) \neq \emptyset$; by (1.8.4) $\text{Prox}(a) \cap \text{Prox}(b) = Q \Leftrightarrow \forall_{i \in I} \text{Prox}_i(a) \cap \text{Prox}_i(b) = Q_i$; hence, by Proposition 1.8.4, $(a, b) \in D \Leftrightarrow \text{Prox}(a) \cap \text{Prox}(b) \neq \emptyset \Leftrightarrow Q \neq \emptyset \Leftrightarrow \bigcup_{i=1}^{n} Q_i \neq \emptyset \Leftrightarrow \bigcup_{i=1}^{n} \text{Prox}_i(a) \cap \text{Prox}_i(b) \neq \emptyset \Leftrightarrow (a, b) \in \bigcup_{i=1}^{n} D_{N_i}.$ □

Proposition 1.8.6 *Let δ_i denotes the transition function of N_i. Then*

$$\delta(m', a) = m'' \Leftrightarrow \forall i \in I : (a \in E_i \wedge \delta_i(m_i', a) = m_i'' \vee a \notin E_i \wedge m_i' = m_i'').$$

for all $m', m'' \in P$ and $a \in E$.

Proof: It is a direct consequence of Proposition 1.8.4. □

From the above proposition it follows by an easy induction:

$$\delta^*(m', w) = m'' \Leftrightarrow \forall i \in I : \delta_i^*(m_i', \pi_i(w)) = m_i''. \tag{1.62}$$

The main theorem of this section is the following:

Theorem 1.8.7

$$B_{N_1 + N_2 + \cdots + N_n} = B_{N_1} \parallel B_{N_2} \parallel \cdots \parallel B_{N_n}.$$

Proof: Set $\eta(m) = \{w \in E^* \mid \delta^*(m^0, w) = m\}$ for each $m \subseteq P$ and $\eta_i(m) = \{w \in E_i^* \mid \delta_i^*(m_i^0, w) = m\}$ for each $m_i \subseteq P_i$; by Proposition 1.62 $\delta^*(m^0, w) = m \Leftrightarrow \forall_{i \in I} \delta_i^*(m_i^0, \pi_i(w)) = m_i$; thus, $w \in \eta(m) \Leftrightarrow \forall_{i \in I} : \pi_i(w) \in \eta_i(m_i)$. It means that

$$\eta(m) = \eta_1(m_1) \parallel \eta_2(m_2) \parallel \cdots \parallel \eta_n(m_n).$$

Thus, by definition of the behaviour, the proof is completed. □

This theorem allows us to find the behaviour of a net knowing behaviours of its components. One can expect the behaviour of components to be easier to find than that of the whole net. As an example let us find the behaviour of the net in Fig. 1.9 using its decomposition into two components, as in Fig. 1.10. These components are sequential; from the theory of sequential systems it is known that their behaviour can be described by the least solutions of equations:

$$X_1 = X_1 be \cup b \cup \epsilon$$
$$X_2 = X_2 abc \cup ab \cup a \cup d \cup \epsilon$$

for languages X_1, X_2 over alphabets $\{b, e\}, \{a, b, c, d\}$, respectively. By definition of trace behaviour of nets, by Theorem 1.8.7, and Theorem 1.7.13 and we have

$$[X_1]_{D_1} = [X_1]_{D_1}[be]_{D_1} \cup [b]_{D_1} \cup [\epsilon]_{D_1}$$
$$[X_2]_{D_2} = [X_2]_{D_2}[abc]_{D_2} \cup [ab]_{D_2} \cup [a]_{D_2} \cup [d]_{D_2} \cup [\epsilon]_{D_2}$$

with $D_1 = \{b, e\}^2, D_2 = \{a, b, c, d\}^2$. The equation for the synchronization $X_1 \parallel X_2$, is, by properties of synchronization, as follows:

$$[X_1]_{D_1} \parallel [X_2]_{D_2} =$$
$$([X_1]_{D_1}[be]_{D_1} \cup [b]_{D_1} \cup [\epsilon]_{D_1}) \parallel ([X_2]_{D_2}[abc]_{D_2} \cup [ab]_{D_2} \cup [a]_{D_2} \cup [d]_{D_2} \cup [\epsilon]_{D_2})$$

and after some easy calculations (using Proposition 1.7.5 we get

$$[X_1 \parallel X_2]_D =$$
$$[X_1 \parallel X_2]_D \cup [abc \cup abe \cup ab \cup a \cup d \cup \epsilon]_D$$

with $D = D_1 \cup D_2 = \{b, e\}^2 \cup \{a, b, c, d\}^2$. Observe that composition of two components that are sequential results in a net with some independent transitions; in the considered case, the independent pairs of transitions are $(a, e), (c, e), (d, e)$ (and their symmetric images).

There exists a standard set of very simple nets, namely nets with a singleton set of places, the behaviours of which can be considered as known. Such nets are called *atomic* or *atoms*; an arbitrary net can be composed from such nets; hence, the behaviour of any net can be composed from the behaviours of atoms. Thus, giving the behaviours of atoms, we supply another definition of the elementary net system behaviour. More formally, let $N = (P, E, F, m^0)$ be a net; for each $p \in P$ the net

$$N_p = (\{p\}, \text{Prox}(p), F_p, (m^0)_p),$$

where

$$F_p = \{(e, p) \mid e \in \text{Pre}(p)\} \cup \{(p, e) \mid e \in \text{Post}(p)\}, (m^0)_p = m^0 \cap \{p\},$$

is called an *atom* of N (determined by p). Clearly, the following proposition holds:

Proposition 1.8.8 *Each net is the composition of all its atoms.*

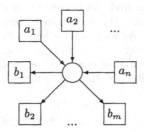

Figure 1.11: An example of atomic net

The behaviour of atoms can be easily found. Namely, let the atom N_0 be defined as $N_0 = (\{p\}, A \cup Z, F, m)$, where $A = \{e \mid (e, p) \in F\}, Z = \{e \mid (p, e) \in F\}$. Say that N_0 is marked, if $m = \{p\}$, and unmarked otherwise, i.e. if $m = \emptyset$. Then, by the definition of behavioural function, trace behaviour B_{N_0} is the trace language $[(ZA)^*(Z \cup \epsilon)]_D$, if it is marked, and $[(AZ)^*(A \cup \epsilon)]_D$, if it is unmarked, where $D = (A \cup Z)^2$.

1.9   Conclusions

Some basic notions of trace theory has been briefly presented. In the next chapters of this book this theory will be made broader and deeper; the intention of the present chapter was to show some initial ideas that motivated the whole enterprise. In the sequel the reader will be able to get acquainted with the development trace theory as a basis of non-standard logic as well as with the basic and involved results from the theory of monoids; with properties of graph representations of traces and with generalization of the notion of finite automaton that is consistent with the trace approach. All this work shows that the concurrency issue is still challenging and stimulating fruitful research.

Acknowledgements. The author is greatly indebted to Professor Grzegorz Rozenberg for his help and encouragement; without him this paper would not have appeared.

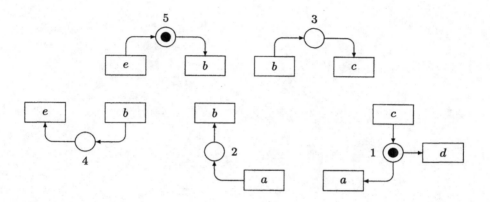

Figure 1.12: Atoms of net in Fig. 1.9

Chapter 2

Dependence Graphs

Hendrik Jan Hoogeboom   Grzegorz Rozenberg

Leiden University, Department of Computer Science,
P.O. Box 9512, 2300 RA Leiden, The Netherlands
hjh@rulwinw.leidenuniv.nl, rozenber@wi.leidenuniv.nl

Contents

2.1 Introduction

For a given dependence alphabet Γ, consisting of an alphabet Σ, and an independence relation I, every word x belonging to Σ^* determines a *trace*, viz., the set of all words that are Γ-equivalent with x; it will be denoted by $[x]_\Gamma$. Hence, in this way a trace is a set of words: it is an equivalence class of the equivalence relation generated by I. In this setting a trace may be given as a word x over an alphabet Σ, and an independence relation I over Σ.

There is another way of looking at traces. Rather than to see a trace as a *set* of objects (words) one can see a trace as a single object; this object is a *dependence graph*. A dependence graph is a node-labelled directed acyclic graph satisfying

43

certain conditions. It can be obtained from a word x belonging to Σ^* by "breaking up" the linear order of the occurrences of letters in x using the involved independence relation I (as a matter of fact, using the dependence relation D, which is the complement of I). Hence, e.g., if $x = abcd$ and $(b, c) \in I$, then the fact that b and c are linearly ordered in x is totally meaningless, it follows only from the fact that words are labelled linear orders and so in a word one cannot indicate that both bc and cb can be "inserted" between a and d. In order to indicate this, one has to break up the linear order of b and c and to represent what happens by a directed (acyclic) graph rather than by a linear order. Breaking up the linear relationships in x results in the partial order represented by the dependence graph.

It turns out that one obtains the same dependence graph by starting with any word y that is Γ-equivalent with x; hence this dependence graph g is an "invariant" for the whole trace of x. One can also obtain all words in $[x]_\Gamma$ by just taking all linear extensions of g. In this sense g is a very natural representation of $[x]_\Gamma$: it can be naturally obtained from any representative of $[x]_\Gamma$ and one can reconstruct from it all elements of $[x]_\Gamma$. Moreover, an advantage of working with g rather than with $[x]_\Gamma$ is that g is just *one* object, already well-understood in mathematics (viz., a directed acyclic graph).

Also, from the point of view of the theory of concurrent systems which underlies a big part of the research on traces, the notion of a dependence graph plays an important role. When traces are used to model concurrent systems (such as Elementary Net Systems) a trace represents all sequential observations of a run of the system, while the dependence graph of a trace represents the run itself (often called a process of the system).

In this chapter we present basic properties of dependence graphs. We discuss how to obtain dependence graphs from traces, how to obtain traces from dependence graphs, and we discuss a number of basic combinatorial properties of dependence graphs.

2.2   Preliminary Notions

In this section we recall some elementary notions concerning graphs, and establish the notation used in this chapter.

Let Σ be a finite alphabet. A *dependence relation* D over Σ is a reflexive and symmetric subset $D \subseteq \Sigma \times \Sigma$. The pair $\Gamma = (\Sigma, D)$ is called a *dependence alphabet*. If $(a, b) \in D$, then we say that a and b are *dependent* with respect to Γ. The *trace equivalence* $\equiv_\Gamma$ defined by Γ is the least congruence on Σ^* satisfying $ab \equiv_\Gamma ba$ for $a, b \in \Sigma$, $(a, b) \notin D$. Alternatively, two words x, y over Σ are trace equivalent with respect to Γ if y can be obtained from x by repeatedly interchanging adjacent independent letters. We will use $[x]_\Gamma$ to denote the equivalence class of x with respect to $\equiv_\Gamma$. In this chapter we will consider $[x]_\Gamma$ to be a set of equivalent words, rather than a single element in a quotient monoid.

A (directed, unlabelled) graph h is an ordered pair $h = (V, E)$, where V is the set of nodes, and $E \subseteq V \times V$ is the set of (directed) edges of h. We use V_h and E_h

to denote the sets of nodes and edges of a given graph h. In this chapter we will discuss *finite* graphs only.

The *symmetric and reflexive closure* of the graph h, denoted $\mathrm{symr}(h)$, is the graph (V, E_{symr}), where for all $u, v \in V$, $(u, v) \in E_{\mathrm{symr}}$ if and only if either $u = v$ or $(u, v) \in E$ or $(v, u) \in E$. We say that h is an *undirected* graph if $h = \mathrm{symr}(h)$. Note that $\mathrm{symr}(h)$ can be seen as the undirected version of the graph h, with a loop added for each node. These loops are convenient for a technical reason: their existence simplifies the definition of a homomorphism between undirected graphs. In order to keep figures readable, we will not draw these loops in pictorial representations of undirected graphs. Note that dependence alphabets are also undirected graphs !

Let h be an acyclic graph. The *Hasse graph* of h, denoted $\mathrm{hasse}(h)$, is the graph $g = (V, E_{\mathrm{hasse}})$, where $(u, v) \in E_{\mathrm{hasse}}$ if and only if $(u, v) \in E$ and there exists no path in h from u to v except for the path consisting of the edge (u, v). The (irreflexive and) *transitive closure* of h, denoted $\mathrm{tr}(h)$, is the graph $g = (V, E_{\mathrm{tr}})$, where $(u, v) \in E_{\mathrm{tr}}$ if and only if $u \neq v$ and there exists a path in h from u to v. If a graph is a transitive closure (of itself) then it is called a *transitive* graph.

It is well known that the Hasse graph of an acyclic graph represents the same (partial) order as the original graph, in our notation: $\mathrm{tr}(\mathrm{hasse}(g)) = \mathrm{tr}(g)$.

Let $h_1 = (V_1, E_1)$, $h_2 = (V_2, E_2)$ be graphs.
A function $\psi : V_1 \to V_2$ is a *homomorphism from h_1 into h_2* if, for all $u, v \in V_1$, $(u, v) \in E_1$ if and only if $(\psi(u), \psi(v)) \in E_2$; ψ is an *isomorphism* if ψ is also bijective. If h_1 and h_2 are *isomorphic*, then we write $h_1 \cong h_2$.

In this chapter we will only consider subgraphs induced by a set of nodes, i.e., h_2 is an (induced) *subgraph* of h_1 if $V_2 \subseteq V_1$ and $E_2 = E_1 \cap (V_2 \times V_2)$.

A (node) *labelling* of a graph h is a total function on V_h. A (directed) *node labelled graph* is a system (V, E, ℓ) where (V, E) is a graph and ℓ is a labelling of (V, E). For a node labelled graph $g = (V, E, \ell)$ we use V_g, E_g and ℓ_g to denote V, E, and ℓ respectively; we say that g is a graph *over* Σ if ℓ maps V into Σ.

A homomorphism of the labelled graph $g_1 = (V_1, E_1, \ell_1)$ into the labelled graph $g_2 = (V_2, E_2, \ell_2)$ is a (unlabelled graph) homomorphism ψ from (V_1, E_1) into (V_2, E_2) which additionally satisfies $\ell_1(u) = \ell_2(\psi(u))$ for each $u \in V_1$.

As for words, a set of graphs will be called a graph *language*.

2.3 Dependence Graphs via Words

In this section, after first defining the dependence graph for a given word over a dependence alphabet, we will formally prove its justification within trace theory: two words are trace-equivalent if and only if their dependence graphs are isomorphic (Theorem 2.3.7). We then illustrate the usefulness of dependence graphs in understanding some concepts from trace theory. These examples are taken from other chapters in this book.

In this chapter we consider finite traces only, and hence we deal with *finite* dependence graphs. Infinite traces and their dependence graphs are discussed in Chapter 11.

2.3.1 Definitions and Basic Properties

For a given dependence alphabet $\Gamma = (\Sigma, D)$ each word x over Σ corresponds to a dependence graph. This is a directed, acyclic node labelled graph which represents the "true structure" of x with respect to Γ. This structure results from the linear order on x by removing all the edges that do not comply with Γ.

Formally, one obtains the dependence graph for a given (finite) word as follows.

Definition 2.3.1 *Let $\Gamma = (\Sigma, D)$ be a dependence alphabet, and let $x = a_1 \cdots a_n$ be a word over Σ, where $n \geq 0$ and $a_i \in \Sigma$ for $1 \leq i \leq n$. The* concrete Γ-dependence graph *of x, denoted as $\langle x \rangle_\Gamma$, is the (directed, node labelled) graph $g = (V, E, \ell)$, where*

(i) $V = \{1, \ldots, n\}$,

(ii) *for all $i, j \in V$, $(i, j) \in E$ if and only if $i < j$ and $(a_i, a_j) \in D$, and*

(iii) *for all $i \in V$, $\ell(i) = a_i$.*

It is important to note that, in the definition of a dependence alphabet, D is assumed to be reflexive. Consequently, in the dependence graph nodes with equal labels will be connected.

Usually, one abstracts from the identities of the nodes in the concrete dependence graph, and considers *abstract graphs*, i.e., isomorphism classes of graphs. A graph g is called *a Γ-dependence graph* of x, if it is isomorphic with $\langle x \rangle_\Gamma$.

Example 2.3.2 Let $\Gamma_4 = (\Sigma_4, D_4)$ be the dependence alphabet with $\Sigma_4 = \{a, b, c, d\}$, and D_4 consisting of the pairs (a, b), (a, d), and (b, c) (together with the pairs needed to make D_4 reflexive and symmetric). Equivalently, $\Gamma_4 = (\Sigma_4, D_4)$ is the graph d—a—b—c.

The concrete Γ_4-dependence graphs $\langle w_i \rangle_{\Gamma_4}$ for $w_1 = acbdab$, $w_2 = cadbab$, and $w_3 = cadbba$ are given in Figure 2.1. Note that $\langle w_1 \rangle_{\Gamma_4}$ and $\langle w_2 \rangle_{\Gamma_4}$ are isomorphic graphs.

It turns out that dependence graphs are not really (non-linear) representations of words, but rather they represent traces. As a matter of fact, two words are elements of the same trace if and only if their dependence graphs are isomorphic (Theorem 2.3.7 below). As a first step in proving this fact, we demonstrate how the elements of a trace can be read from the dependence graph of one of the words representing the trace. We need the following notions.

A *topological ordering* of a graph $g = (V, E)$ is an total ordering $v_1, \ldots, v_n$ of the nodes of g such that $(v_i, v_j) \in E$ implies $i < j$. Hence a topological ordering of g is a linear ordering of the nodes (a linearization) of g compatible with the direction of the existing edges. A topological ordering exists if and only if the graph is acyclic. In that case it can be obtained by a (nondeterministic) process known as *topological sorting*: consecutively, for $i = 1, \ldots, n$ the node v_i is chosen to be one of the minimal nodes of the graph that results from g after removing the already

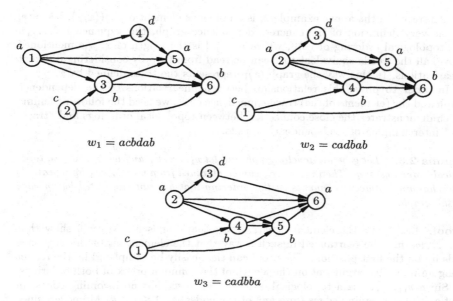

$$w_1 = acbdab \qquad w_2 = cadbab$$

$$w_3 = cadbba$$

Figure 2.1: some dependence graphs

chosen nodes $v_1, \ldots, v_{i-1}$ (together with their incident edges); a minimal node of a graph is a node without incoming edges.

The words that can be read from a labelled acyclic graph after performing a topological sort will be called the language of this graph. Note that the operation of topological sorting a graph and reading a word from it, is a kind of dual to the operation of constructing a dependence graph from a word: in the former one gets a word from an acyclic graph, in the latter one gets an acyclic graph from a word.

Definition 2.3.3 *Let $g = (V, E, \ell)$ be a node labelled acyclic graph. The* language *of g, denoted* $\mathrm{lan}(g)$*, is the set $\{\ell(v_1) \cdot \ldots \cdot \ell(v_n) : v_1, \ldots, v_n$ is a topological ordering of $g\}$.*

Example 2.3.4 Consider the dependence alphabet Γ_4 from Example 2.3.2, and let again $w_1 = acbdab$. The sequences $1, 2, 3, 4, 5, 6$ and $2, 1, 4, 3, 5, 6$ are topological orderings of the dependence graph $\langle w_1 \rangle_{\Gamma_4}$. Consequently, $w_1 = acbdab$ and $w_2 = cadbab$ are elements of $\mathrm{lan}(\langle w_1 \rangle_{\Gamma_4})$. As a matter of fact, since $\langle w_1 \rangle_{\Gamma_4}$ and $\langle w_2 \rangle_{\Gamma_4}$ are isomorphic, they have the same language. $w_3 = cadbba$ is not an element of the language of $\langle w_1 \rangle_{\Gamma_4}$, since in each linearization of this graph, node 5 (the second node with label a) precedes node 6 (the second node with label b).

Let $\Gamma = (\Sigma, D)$ be a dependence alphabet, and consider the (concrete) Γ-dependence graph $\langle x \rangle_\Gamma$ of a word x over Σ, constructed as in Definition 2.3.1.

As illustrated in the above example, x is an obvious element of $\mathrm{lan}(\langle x \rangle_\Gamma)$, because, by the very definition of the concrete dependence graph, the sequence $1, 2, \ldots, n$ is a topological ordering of $\langle x \rangle_\Gamma$, where $n = |x|$ is the length of x. As mentioned above, all the words equivalent to x can be read from $\langle x \rangle_\Gamma$ by considering different linearizations. In this way the graph $\langle x \rangle_\Gamma$ represents the trace defined by x.

In order to prove this relationship between linearizations of the dependence graph and the (elements of the) trace-equivalence class, we need the following lemma which demonstrates the close connection between topological orderings and "trace-like" interchanging of "independent" objects.

Lemma 2.3.5 *Let g be an acyclic graph and let $v_1, \ldots, v_n$ and $w_1, \ldots, w_n$ be topological orderings of g. Then $v_1, \ldots, v_n$ can be obtained from $w_1, \ldots, w_n$ by repeatedly interchanging adjacent elements in the ordering that are not connected by an edge in the graph.*

Proof: Let w_k be the element of $w_1, \ldots, w_n$ that equals v_1. We will show that $w_1, \ldots, w_n$ may be rearranged in such a way that the element w_k of this sequence ends up on the first position. The proof can then easily be completed by the reader using an inductive argument on the length of the common prefix of both orderings.

Since $v_1, \ldots, v_n$ is a topological ordering, $v_1 = w_k$ has no incoming edges, in particular no incoming edges from any of the nodes w_i, $1 \le i < k$. Moreover, since also $w_1, \ldots, w_n$ is a topological ordering, $v_1 = w_k$ has no outgoing edges to the nodes w_i, $1 \le i < k$. Consequently w_k is not connected to its predecessors in the ordering $w_1, \ldots, w_n$, and may be moved to the first position as described in the statement of the lemma.   □

We apply this lemma to dependence graphs.

Theorem 2.3.6 *Let $\Gamma = (\Sigma, D)$ be a dependence alphabet and let $x \in \Sigma^*$. Then $[x]_\Gamma = \mathrm{lan}(\langle x \rangle_\Gamma)$.*

Proof: We will show that, for $x, y \in \Sigma^*$, $y \in \mathrm{lan}(\langle x \rangle_\Gamma)$ if and only if $y \equiv_\Gamma x$.
Let ℓ be the labelling of the dependence graph $\langle x \rangle_\Gamma$. Obviously, according to the previous result $v_1, \ldots, v_n$ is a topological ordering of $\langle x \rangle_\Gamma$ if and only if it can be obtained from the sequence $1, \ldots, n$ by interchanging adjacent nodes that are unconnected in $\langle x \rangle_\Gamma$. Note however that node i and node j are not connected by an edge if and only if their labels $\ell(i)$ and $\ell(j)$ are independent according to Γ. Hence, $v_1, \ldots, v_n$ is a topological ordering of $\langle x \rangle_\Gamma$ if and only if $y = \ell(v_1) \cdot \ldots \cdot \ell(v_n) \equiv_\Gamma \ell(1) \cdot \ldots \cdot \ell(n) = x$.   □

It is now clear that words with isomorphic dependence graphs have to belong to the same trace. An elementary argument shows that the reverse is also true.

Theorem 2.3.7 *Let $\Gamma = (\Sigma, D)$ be a dependence alphabet and let x, y be words over Σ. Then $\langle x \rangle_\Gamma \cong \langle y \rangle_\Gamma$ if and only if $x \equiv_\Gamma y$.*

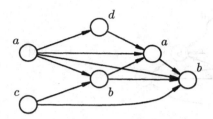

Figure 2.2: dependence graph of the trace $[acbdab]$

Proof: First assume that $\langle x \rangle_\Gamma \cong \langle y \rangle_\Gamma$. Obviously this implies $\mathrm{lan}(\langle x \rangle_\Gamma) = \mathrm{lan}(\langle y \rangle_\Gamma)$. Consequently, by Theorem 2.3.6, $[x]_\Gamma = [y]_\Gamma$, and so $x \equiv_\Gamma y$.

In order to prove the reverse implication, first assume that $x = x_1 ab x_2$ and $y = x_1 ba x_2$, where $x_1, x_2 \in \Sigma^*$ and a and b are independent. Clearly $\langle x \rangle_\Gamma$ and $\langle y \rangle_\Gamma$ are isomorphic, their only difference being the interchanged identity of two (unconnected) nodes labelled by independent letters. Then, for arbitrary x and y such that $x \equiv_\Gamma y$, the result follows by transitivity of the $\cong$ relation. □

Consequently, dependence graphs of equivalent words are isomorphic. Hence we may say that $\langle x \rangle_\Gamma$, regarded as an *abstract* graph, is the dependence graph of the *trace* $[x]_\Gamma$, rather than of the word x.

Example 2.3.8 The abstract graph corresponding to $\langle w_1 \rangle_{\Gamma_4}$ given in Figure 2.2 is the dependence graph of the trace $t = [acbdab]$.

2.3.2 Illustrations

There are several topics within trace theory that can be dealt with on the level of words (i.e., using words and studying the combinatorics of interchanging adjacent independent letters), but which become more elegant and intuitive on the level of dependence graphs. We will give three examples of such a situation: the study of normal forms for traces, the combinatorics of different compositions of the same trace, and Ochmański's concurrent trace iteration.

Foata normal form

Since traces are equivalence classes of words it is technically convenient to be able either to assign to a trace a unique (canonical) word which is the representative of the trace, or to find a unique decomposition into traces. In other words, one looks for a *normal form* of the trace. An important example of such a normal form is Foata normal form [34]. For infinite traces we refer to Proposition 11.2.15.

Let t be a trace over the dependence alphabet $\Gamma = (\Sigma, D)$. The *Foata normal form* of t is the unique decomposition of t of the form $t = t_1 \cdot \ldots \cdot t_n$ satisfying two requirements:

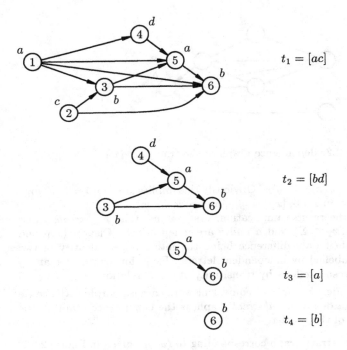

$$t_1 = [ac]$$

$$t_2 = [bd]$$

$$t_3 = [a]$$

$$t_4 = [b]$$

Figure 2.3: construction of Foata normal form

(i) the letters in each t_i are mutually independent, in particular, t_i does not have two occurrences of the same letter, and

(ii) for each letter in component t_{i+1} one can find a dependent letter in the preceding component t_i.

The Foata normal form of a trace $t = [x]_\Gamma$ is easily found performing a topological sort on the dependence graph $\langle x \rangle_\Gamma$: in each consecutive step of the linearization process one outputs the trace determined by *all* minimal (hence independent) nodes of the remaining part of the dependence graph.

Example 2.3.9 Consider again $t = [acbdab]$ from Example 2.3.2. The dependence graph $\langle acbdab \rangle_{\Gamma_4}$ has two minimal nodes, with labels a and c. Hence the first element t_1 in the Foata normal form of t is $t_1 = [ac]$. The remaining trace $[bdab]$ has again two minimal nodes, yielding $t_2 = [bd]$. Then in two more steps (see Figure 2.3) one obtains the complete decomposition $t = [ac] \cdot [bd] \cdot [a] \cdot [b]$.

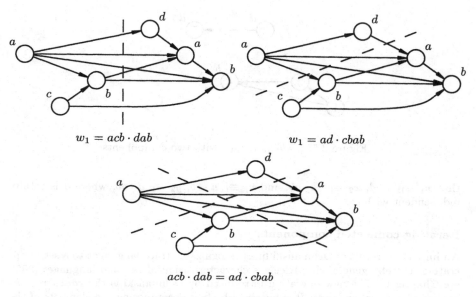

$$w_1 = acb \cdot dab \qquad\qquad w_1 = ad \cdot cbab$$

$$acb \cdot dab = ad \cdot cbab$$

Figure 2.4: Levi's Lemma

Levi's Lemma

Another example of a result that has an intuitively clear proof on the level of
dependence graphs is the celebrated Levi Lemma [177] (in its extension to traces
[47]) which relates different decompositions of the same trace. We will only illustrate
this lemma, for proofs we refer to Lemma 1.3.4 or Proposition **??** in other chapters
of this book. Observe that extensions to infinite traces and semi traces are presented
in Proposition 11.2.10 and Lemma 12.3.9.

The applicability of dependence graphs here stems from the fact that the different compositions of the traces in the lemma correspond to partitions of the nodes
in a dependence graph. By a *topological partition* of the graph $g = (V, E)$ we mean
a partition (V_1, V_2) of the nodes of g such that $E \cap (V_2 \times V_1) = \emptyset$ (i.e., no edge leads
from V_2 to V_1).

Theorem 2.3.10 (Levi's Lemma) *Let* $\Gamma = (\Sigma, D)$ *be a dependence alphabet,
and let* $x_1, x_2, y_1, y_2 \in \Sigma^*$. *Then* $x_1 x_2 \equiv_\Gamma y_1 y_2$ *if and only if there exist words*
$u, v_1, v_2, w \in \Sigma^*$ *such that* $x_1 \equiv_\Gamma uv_1$, $x_2 \equiv_\Gamma v_2 w$, $y_1 \equiv_\Gamma uv_2$, *and* $y_2 \equiv_\Gamma v_1 w$, *and,
every letter in* v_1 *is independent with every letter in* v_2.

Example 2.3.11 Once more consider $w_1 = acbdab$ from Example 2.3.2. As illustrated in Figure 2.4, $w_1 \equiv_\Gamma x_1 \cdot x_2$, where $x_1 = ad$, and $x_2 = cbab$, but also
$w_1 \equiv_\Gamma y_1 \cdot y_2$, where $y_1 = acb$, and $y_2 = dab$. The topological partitions corresponding to the decompositions are indicated in the figure by dashed lines. Note

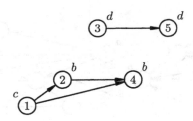

Figure 2.5: $[cbdbd]$, a trace with two components

that $x_1 \equiv_\Gamma a \cdot d$, $x_2 \equiv_\Gamma cb \cdot ab$, and $y_1 \equiv_\Gamma a \cdot cb$, $y_2 \equiv_\Gamma d \cdot ab$, where d is totally independent with cb.

Iterating connected components

An important result of Ochmański links recognizable trace languages to a set of operators, thereby generalizing Kleene's characterization of rational languages [205], see Chapter 6. The new operation introduced by Ochmański is the *concurrent iteration* of a trace language. It is obtained by first decomposing the elements of the language into their so-called connected components, and then using the ordinary Kleene iteration (star) on the decomposed language. Clearly, the definition of a connected component of a trace is elementary using the well known definition for graphs, whereas a reformulation of this notion on the word level (traces as equivalence classes of words) would be somewhat indirect, considering projections of the trace on connected components of the dependence alphabet.

Example 2.3.12 Consider the dependence alphabet Γ_4 from Example 2.3.2. The Γ_4-dependence graph of $w = cbdbd$ is depicted in Figure 2.5. It consists of two connected components, cbb and dd. The concurrent iteration of the singleton language $\{[w]\}$ equals the ordinary iteration of $\{[cbb], [dd]\}$, which is the language $\{[\varepsilon], [cbb], [dd], [cbbcbb], [cbbdd], [dddd], \ldots\}$.

2.4   The Structure of Dependence Graphs

A dependence graph g is a node labelled graph, i.e., a (unlabelled) graph h together with a node labelling ℓ. Moreover, g is a dependence graph over a specific dependence alphabet Γ; as a matter of fact ℓ maps h into Γ. Hence, in order to better understand the structure of g we will study the properties of the mapping ℓ, and the relationships between h and Γ induced by ℓ.

The structure of dependence graphs (in the above sense) will be discussed in subsection 2.4.1, and the relationship between a dependence graph and "its" dependence alphabet will be discussed in subsection 2.4.2

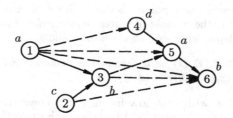

Figure 2.6: the composition of $\langle acb \rangle$ and $\langle dab \rangle$

2.4.1 Abstract View of Dependence Graphs

It follows directly from the definition that each dependence graph is acyclic and the presence of an edge between two nodes is determined by the labels of the nodes. Conversely, it is easily seen that, for a given acyclic graph g where the presence of edges is properly determined by the node labels, if x is a word from lan(g), then g is a dependence graph of x (cf. Definition 2.3.3).

These two observations yield an elegant characterization of those graphs that are dependence graphs of words over a given dependence alphabet.

Lemma 2.4.1 *Let* $\Gamma = (\Sigma, D)$ *be a dependence alphabet. A node labelled graph* $g = (V, E, \ell)$ *is a dependence graph over* Γ *if and only if it is acyclic, and, for every pair* $v_1, v_2 \in V$, $(\ell(v_1), \ell(v_2)) \in D$ *if and only if either* $v_1 = v_2$, *or* $(v_1, v_2) \in E$, *or* $(v_2, v_1) \in E$.

The above characterization is sometimes taken as the definition of the notion of dependence graph over a given dependence alphabet $\Gamma = (\Sigma, D)$. The set of all (abstract) graphs satisfying this property is then turned into a monoid (with the empty graph as unit) by introducing the following operation.

Definition 2.4.2 *Let* $\Gamma = (\Sigma, D)$ *be a dependence alphabet, and let* $g_1 = (V_1, E_1, \ell_1)$ *and* $g_2 = (V_2, E_2, \ell_2)$ *be two (abstract) dependence graphs over* Γ. *The* Γ-*composition of* g_1 *and* g_2, *denoted by* $g_1 \circ_\Gamma g_2$, *is the (abstract) graph that is obtained by taking the disjoint union of* g_1 *and* g_2 *and adding all edges* (v_1, v_2) *with* $v_1 \in V_1$, $v_2 \in V_2$, *satisfying* $(\ell_1(v_1), \ell_2(v_2)) \in D$.

Example 2.4.3 The dependence graph of $w_1 = acbdab$ from Figure 2.1 can be obtained by the Γ_4-composition of the dependence graphs of acb and dab. This is illustrated in Figure 2.6.

Note that we have already implicitly used graph compositions in Example 2.3.11 concerning Levi's Lemma: A topological partition of a graph corresponds to a (de)composition of this graph.

Concatenation of traces corresponds to composition of (dependence) graphs. Hence, by Theorem 2.3.7, the monoid of traces (equivalence classes of words) and the monoid of (finite) dependence graphs are isomorphic.

Theorem 2.4.4 *Let* $\Gamma = (\Sigma, D)$ *be a dependence alphabet and let* x, y *be words over* Σ. *Then we have* $\langle x \rangle_\Gamma \circ_\Gamma \langle y \rangle_\Gamma \cong \langle x \cdot y \rangle_\Gamma$.

In this chapter we deal with *finite* graphs only. It is however very well possible to take the characterization of Lemma 2.4.1 together with the notion of composition as defined above as the definition for a monoid of infinite dependence graphs (under a suitable restriction on the cardinality of the domains). The set of finite graphs is then a submonoid of this monoid. Another interesting submonoid is the set consisting of those graphs that have a countable number of nodes, each having a finite "past" (i.e., a finite number of predecessors in the partial ordering defined by the edge relation). These matters are discussed in Chapter 11.

2.4.2   Making Graphs into Dependence Graphs

Recall that by an *undirected* graph we mean a graph with a symmetric *and reflexive* edge relation.

Every acyclic (unlabelled) graph can be made into a dependence graph by labelling each node with a different symbol. More formally, by Lemma 2.4.1, for every acyclic graph $g = (V, E)$, (V, E, ℓ) is a Γ-dependence graph, where ℓ is the identity on V, and $\Gamma = \mathrm{symr}(g)$.

In this section we will investigate the less trivial problem of choosing a labelling for an unlabelled graph in order to make it a dependence graph over a *given* dependence alphabet Γ: given a graph $g = (V, E)$, does there exist a labelling ℓ such that (V, E, ℓ) is a Γ-dependence graph? In order to answer this question, we study the structural relationship between a dependence graph g and the dependence alphabet Γ over which it is defined.

The key observation in dealing with this problem, is the following. The labelling ℓ maps the nodes of one (directed) graph g to the nodes of another (undirected) graph Γ. Forgetting for a moment the directions of the edges of g, we have by Lemma 2.4.1 the following property: for every pair $v_1, v_2 \in V$, such that $v_1 \neq v_2$, $(v_1, v_2) \in E$ if and only if $(\ell(v_1), \ell(v_2)) \in D$. In other words: ℓ is a graph homomorphism from $\mathrm{symr}(g)$ to Γ.

Important structural information about an undirected graph is given by its resemblance relation.

Definition 2.4.5 *Let* $g = (V, E)$ *be an undirected graph. The resemblance relation of* g, *denoted* res_g, *is the binary relation on* V *defined by* $(v_1, v_2) \in res_g$ *if and only if*

(i) $(v_1, v_2) \in E$, *and*

(ii) *for all* $v \in V$, $(v, v_1) \in E$ *if and only if* $(v, v_2) \in E$.

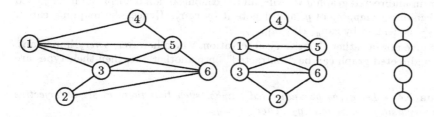

Figure 2.7: an undirected graph (twice) and its type

Actually, the first requirement in the above definition is somewhat superfluous: it follows from the second by taking $v = v_1$. We prefer to keep the requirement for clarity.

Example 2.4.6 Consider the undirected graph from Figure 2.7. Nodes 1 and 5 are in the resemblance relation: they are connected to each other, and they are each connected to the nodes 3, 4, and 6. Node 1 and 6 are not in the relation: although they are connected by an edge, they do not have the same neighbours in the graph.

It is easy to see that for a graph g, res_g is an equivalence relation. Moreover, edge connections in g are the same for equivalent nodes; res_g is a "congruence" with respect to the edge relation of g. More formally, if $v_1 \text{ res}_g v_2$ and $u_1 \text{ res}_g u_2$, then $(v_1, u_1) \in E_g$ if and only if $(v_2, u_2) \in E_g$. Hence it is possible to define the quotient structure of a graph g with respect to its equivalence res_g. We use $\mathbf{P}(\text{res}_g)$ to denote the set of equivalence classes of res_g.

Definition 2.4.7 *Let $g = (V_g, E_g)$ be an undirected graph. The type of g, denoted $\widehat{g}$, is the graph (V, E) such that $V = \mathbf{P}(\text{res}_g)$, and for all $u, v \in V_g$, $([u]_{\text{res}_g}, [v]_{\text{res}_g}) \in E$ if and only if $(u, v) \in E_g$.*

Example 2.4.8 The type of the graph from Example 2.4.6 is given in Figure 2.7.

Note that $\widehat{g}$ is isomorphic to any subgraph of g that is induced by a set of representatives of res_g.

Not surprisingly, there is a strong connection between the resemblance relation (an edge based congruence) we have defined above and the notion of graph homomorphism. A surjective homomorphism of one undirected graph onto another one can be seen as a "contraction" of the original graph: nodes that have the same connections to the other nodes in the graph (and are connected to each other) may be mapped by the homomorphism onto the same node in the image. Intuitively the type of an undirected graph formalizes the maximal contraction possible. Indeed, the next result implies that the type $\widehat{g}$ of an undirected graph g is the smallest (with respect to the number of nodes) undirected graph such that g can be "contracted" onto that graph.

For an undirected graph g we will call the canonical homomorphism from g onto $\widehat{g}$ the *canonical mapping* of g, and denote it by can_g. Hence, the mapping $\mathrm{can}_g : V_g \to V_{\widehat{g}}$, is defined by $\mathrm{can}_g(u) = [u]_{\mathrm{res}_g}$.

We give now a rather elementary observation, which however is very important. If one undirected graph can be "contracted" onto another one, then their types are equal.

Lemma 2.4.9 *Let g_1, g_2 be undirected graphs, such that there exists a surjective homomorphism from g_1 onto g_2. Then $\widehat{g_1} \cong \widehat{g_2}$.*

Proof: First we make an observation. Let φ be a surjective homomorphism from g_1 onto g_2. Then there exists a surjective homomorphism ψ from g_2 onto $\widehat{g_1}$ such that $\mathrm{can}_{g_1} = \psi \circ \varphi$.

This is seen as follows. It is straightforward to verify that, for $u_1, u_2 \in V_{g_1}$, $\varphi(u_1) = \varphi(u_2)$ implies $u_1 \, \mathrm{res}_{g_1} \, u_2$. This, together with the fact that φ is surjective, makes $\psi : V_h \to \mathbf{P}(\mathrm{res}_{g_1})$, defined by $\psi(v) = [u]_{\mathrm{res}_{g_1}}$ for $v = \varphi(u)$, a well-defined mapping from V_h onto $V_{\widehat{g_1}}$. Using the fact that both can_{g_1} and φ are homomorphisms, one easily shows that ψ is a homomorphism; it satisfies $\mathrm{can}_{g_1} = \psi \circ \varphi$ by definition. This proves our observation.

$$
\begin{array}{ccc}
 & \varphi & \\
g_1 & \longrightarrow & g_2 \\
{\scriptstyle \mathrm{can}_{g_1}}\Big\downarrow & {\scriptstyle \psi}\!\!\!\diagup & \Big\downarrow{\scriptstyle \mathrm{can}_{g_2}} \\
\widehat{g_1} & \longrightarrow & \widehat{g_2} \\
 & \varphi' &
\end{array}
$$

We return to the proof of the lemma. Observe that for $v_1 = \varphi(u_1)$ and $v_2 = \varphi(u_2)$ we have $v_1 \mathrm{res}_{g_2} v_2$ iff $u_1 \mathrm{res}_{g_1} u_2$ iff $\psi(v_1) = \psi(v_2)$. Hence, $\varphi' = \mathrm{can}_{g_2} \circ \psi^{-1}$ is an isomorphism between $\widehat{g_1}$ and $\widehat{g_2}$. $\qquad\square$

In the remainder of this section we return to dependence graphs. This means that the graphs that we will consider are directed rather than undirected graphs. The notion of *type* is extended to these graphs by defining the type of an arbitrary graph g to be the type of $\mathrm{symr}(g)$, i.e., the undirected version of g.

Theorem 2.4.10 ([93]) *Let $\Gamma = (\Sigma, D)$ be a dependence alphabet and let $g = (V, E)$ be an acyclic graph. Then there exists a labelling ℓ for g, such that (V, E, ℓ) is a Γ-dependence graph, if and only if $\widehat{g}$ is isomorphic to a (induced) subgraph of Γ.*

Proof: If there exists a homomorphism ℓ from $\mathrm{symr}(g)$ into Γ, then by Lemma 2.4.9, $\widehat{g}$ is isomorphic to the type of the range of ℓ. Hence $\widehat{g}$ is isomorphic to a subgraph of Γ, since the type of any subgraph of Γ is isomorphic to a subgraph of Γ.

The reverse implication is obvious. The canonical homomorphism from $\mathrm{symr}(g)$ onto its type $\widehat{g}$ combined with the isomorphism that maps this type to a subgraph of Γ yields a suitable labelling to make g a dependence graph. $\qquad\square$

Example 2.4.11 The graph in Figure 2.7 is the undirected version of the dependence graph of w_1 from Example 2.3.2. Indeed, a dependence alphabet with a structure as in Figure 2.7 is the smallest alphabet that can be used to label this dependence graph. Any other dependence alphabet that can be used to make this graph a dependence graph will have this structure as a subgraph.

As observed in the introduction to this section, every unlabelled acyclic graph can be labelled to make it a dependence graph if one is allowed to choose a dependence alphabet. For graph languages the situation is not that simple: if the language contains an infinite number of graphs, then the required dependence alphabet would need infinitely many symbols, which is not allowed in our setting.

As a corollary to the characterization above we obtain the following result. It characterizes the graph languages that can be turned into dependence graph languages as those that have a finite number of non-isomorphic types.

Corollary 2.4.12 *Let K be a graph language consisting of unlabelled acyclic graphs. The following conditions are equivalent.*
(1) There exists a dependence alphabet Γ such that for each $(V, E) \in K$ there exists a labelling ℓ such that (V, E, ℓ) is a dependence graph.
(2) There exists a constant n such that, for each $g \in K$, $\#(\mathbf{P}(\mathrm{res}_g)) \leq n$.

2.5 Transitive Closures

We now consider transitive closures of dependence graphs, i.e., we are dealing with partial orders induced by dependence graphs, rather than the dependence graphs themselves. In this sense we simply abstract from "unimportant" details of dependence graphs. As is usual with acyclic directed graphs, one can see a dependence graph as one "specific implementation" of the partial order it induces.

We investigate a problem similar to the last result presented in Section 2.4.2: to characterize those graph languages consisting of unlabelled graphs, for which a dependence alphabet Γ exists such that all graphs in the language can be labelled to become transitive closures of Γ-dependence graphs. Results in this section are taken from [92].

Assume we are given a dependence alphabet Γ and a labelled acyclic transitive graph g. If we want to check whether g is the transitive closure of a Γ-dependence graph, we have to verify at least the following two properties. First, every pair of nodes with dependent labels should be connected by an edge. Secondly, if two nodes are connected by an edge in hasse(g), i.e., this edge is not the shortcut of some path in g, then this edge should connect two nodes labelled by dependent letters.

This leads to the following notion.

Definition 2.5.1 *Let $\Gamma = (\Sigma, D)$ be a dependence alphabet, and let $g = (V, E)$ be an acyclic transitive graph. A mapping $\ell : V \to \Sigma$ is called a Γ-labelling of g, if*

(i) $(\ell(u), \ell(v)) \in D$, implies that either $u = v$, or $(u, v) \in E$ or $(v, u) \in E$, and

(ii) $(u, v) \in E_{\text{hasse}(g)}$ implies that $(\ell(u), \ell(v)) \in D$.

It is clear that labelling functions of the transitive closures of Γ-dependence graphs are examples of Γ-labellings. In fact, the two requirements in the definition above turn out to be sufficient to characterize transitive closures of dependence graphs in terms of their labellings. This result is strongly related to the characterization for dependence graphs in Lemma 2.4.1.

Lemma 2.5.2 *Let $\Gamma = (\Sigma, D)$ be a dependence alphabet, and let $g = (V, E)$ be an acyclic transitive graph. Then (V, E, ℓ) is the transitive closure of a Γ-dependence graph if and only if the mapping ℓ is a Γ-labelling of g.*

Proof: Assume that ℓ is a Γ-labelling of the acyclic transitive graph $g = (V, E)$. Consider the graph $h = (V, E_D, \ell)$ obtained from (V, E, ℓ) by removing all edges whose pair of labels is not in D. By Lemma 2.4.1 and (i) in the definition of Γ-labelling, h is a dependence graph.

Observe that, by (ii) in the definition of Γ-labelling, $E_{\text{hasse}(g)} \subseteq E_D \subseteq E$. Consequently, since $\text{tr}(\text{hasse}(g)) = \text{tr}(g) = g$, (V, E, ℓ) is the transitive closure of h. $\qquad\qquad\square$

Now assume that we are given an unlabelled acyclic transitive graph g and two specific nodes u and v of it. The question is whether there exists a dependence alphabet Γ and a Γ-labelling of g such that u and v are labelled by the same letter. First of all, the two nodes —having dependent labels— should be connected by an edge. Secondly, any node which is connected to one of the nodes by an edge in $\text{hasse}(g)$, must have a label that is dependent on the common label of the two nodes —consequently, it should also be connected to the other node (not necessarily in $\text{hasse}(g)$).

We formalize these two observations in the notion of the spine of a graph.

Definition 2.5.3 *Let $g = (V, E)$ be an acyclic transitive graph. The spine of g, denoted by $\text{sp}(g)$, is the graph (V, E_{sp}), where $(u, v) \in E_{\text{sp}}$ if and only if*

(i) $(u, v) \in E$,

(ii) *for each $z \in V$, $(u, z) \in E_{\text{hasse}(g)}$ implies $z = v$ or $(z, v) \in E$, and*

(iii) *for each $z \in V$, $(z, v) \in E_{\text{hasse}(g)}$ implies $u = z$ or $(u, z) \in E$.*

Note that in (ii) and (iii) of the definition of the spine of a graph only such nodes z are considered that are either direct successors of u, or direct predecessors of v. It is not necessary to consider the direct predecessors of u or the direct successors of v, since —by transitivity— these nodes are also connected to v and u, respectively.

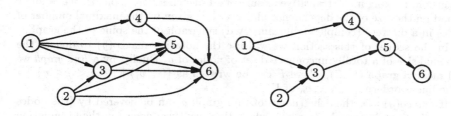

Figure 2.8: transitive closure and Hasse diagram

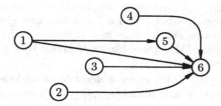

Figure 2.9: a spine

Example 2.5.4 Consider the graph g from Figure 2.8, which is the transitive closure of the (unlabelled version of the) dependence graph from Figure 2.1, Example 2.3.2. The Hasse graph and the spine of g are given in Figure 2.8 and Figure 2.9, respectively.

As an illustration of the construction of $\mathrm{sp}(g)$, note that (2,5) is not an edge in $\mathrm{sp}(g)$ because (4,5) is an edge in $\mathrm{hasse}(g)$, while (2,4) is not present in g (cf. (iii) from the above definition).

Observe that the spine of an acyclic transitive graph is again transitive. This observation simplifies both the construction and the representation of spines, since we can represent a spine by its Hasse graph.

As the following result shows, the spine fulfils its purpose: whenever two nodes of a transitive graph can be given the same label by some Γ-labelling, then they are connected in the spine of the graph. (This property has motivated the introduction of the notion of a spine; its proof is elementary.)

Lemma 2.5.5 *Let $g = (V, E)$ be an acyclic transitive graph, let Γ be a dependence alphabet, and let ℓ be a Γ-labelling of g. If $\ell(u) = \ell(v)$ for $u \neq v$, then u and v are connected by an edge in $\mathrm{sp}(g)$.*

Indeed, this lemma implies that if two nodes are unconnected in the spine of a graph, then they should get different labels if we want to construct a Γ-labelling for the graph, making it the transitive closure of a Γ-dependence graph. Hence, a lower bound on the size of the dependence alphabet Γ is given by the maximal number of nodes in a discrete (completely unconnected) subgraph of the spine of the graph.

In the sequel of this section we will use the notation $\text{maxco}(g)$ to denote the maximal size of a totally unconnected set of nodes of g. Dually, by a *line graph* we will mean a graph (V, E), where E can be written as $\{(v_i, v_j) \mid 1 \leq i < j \leq n\}$ for some linear ordering $v_1, \ldots, v_n$ of V.

If $\text{maxco}(g) = n$ then the (nodes of the) graph g can be covered by (the nodes of) n (disjoint) line graphs (see [66], where this result was shown in the formulation for partially ordered sets). Note that such a covering contains no edges other than those in g, but may very well leave some of the edges of g uncovered. Moreover, it may be clarifying to observe that a subgraph of a line graph is also a line graph.

As discussed above, the information present in the spine of a graph will help in constructing a dependence alphabet Γ and a Γ-labelling of a given graph. We will show that such a construction can be done in a uniform way for any set of graphs for which the maxco-values of the spines can be bounded by some constant.

Theorem 2.5.6 *Let $n \geq 1$. There exists a dependence alphabet Γ such that, for each acyclic transitive graph g with $\text{maxco}(\text{sp}(g)) \leq n$, there is a Γ-labelling of g.*

Proof: Fix an arbitrary alphabet Σ with cardinality n, and let Σ_1 be the alphabet $\{(a, A) \in \Sigma \times 2^{\Sigma} \mid a \in A\}$. Consider the dependence alphabet $\Gamma = (\Sigma_1, D)$, where (a, A) and (b, B) in Σ_1 are dependent (with respect to Γ) if and only if $a \in B$ or $b \in A$.

Let $g = (V, E)$ be an acyclic transitive graph with $\text{maxco}(\text{sp}(g)) \leq n$. Because of the bound on maxco, the nodes of $\text{sp}(g)$ can be covered by at most n disjoint line graphs. From this partition we construct a labelling $\psi : V \to \Sigma$ such that each pair of nodes with the same label is connected by an edge in $\text{sp}(g)$.

For each node u we add to the label $\psi(u)$ the labels of the immediate neighbours of u in $\text{hasse}(g)$, obtaining in this way the two component label: $\varphi(u) = (\psi(u), \{\psi(u)\} \cup \{\psi(v) \mid (v, u) \in E_{\text{hasse}(g)} \text{ or } (u, v) \in E_{\text{hasse}(g)}\}) \in \Sigma_1$.

We verify that φ is a Γ-labelling of g.

(1) First, we prove that every pair of dependent nodes is connected by an edge. Let u and v be nodes of g, and let $\varphi(u) = (a, A)$ and $\varphi(v) = (b, B)$ be such that $((a, A), (b, B)) \in D$. Without loss of generality we may assume that $a \in B$. Then, by the construction of φ there exists a node z with label (a, A_1) such that v and z are connected by an edge in $\text{hasse}(g)$. The nodes u and z (if $z \neq u$) are connected by an edge in $\text{sp}(g)$ since ψ labels both these nodes by the same label (u and z are on the same line).

If $z = u$, then it is clear that u and v are connected by an edge in g: the edges of $\text{hasse}(g)$ form a subset of those of g. Otherwise, one considers the different possibilities for the directions of the edge between u and z, and the edge between v and z. In all four cases it is easily verified that u and z are connected by an edge in g. This follows either by transitivity or by the definition of the spine.

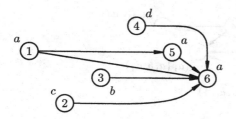

a. lines covering spine

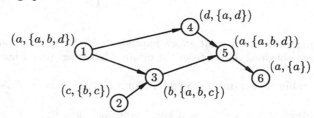

b. adding context information

Figure 2.10: construction of a dependence alphabet

(2) Conversely, if two nodes are connected by an edge in hasse(g), then their labels are dependent. This is an immediate consequence of the construction of the labelling φ. □

We give an example to illustrate the construction used in the proof.

Example 2.5.7 Let g be the transitive closure of the unlabelled version of the dependence graph from Example 2.3.2, as represented in Figure 2.8. The spine of g is given in Figure 2.9, Example 2.5.4. Clearly, maxco(sp(g)) = 4, so a dependence alphabet Γ which can be used to find a Γ-labelling for g, can be based on an alphabet with four letters, say $\Sigma = \{a, b, c, d\}$.

(1) sp(g) can be covered by the "lines" $\{1, 5, 6\}, \{3\}, \{2\}$, and $\{4\}$, inducing the labelling $\psi(1) = \psi(5) = \psi(6) = a, \psi(3) = b, \psi(2) = c$, and $\psi(4) = d$. Adding the context information, we get the labels $\varphi(1) = (a, \{a, b, d\}), \varphi(5) = (a, \{a, b, d\}), \varphi(6) = (a, \{a\}), \varphi(3) = (b, \{a, b, c\}), \varphi(2) = (c, \{b, c\})$, and $\varphi(4) = (d, \{a, d\})$. In this way we find a dependence alphabet with five distinct symbols. (See Figure 2.10.)

(2) As an alternative, consider the covering by $\{1, 5\}, \{3\}, \{2\}$, and $\{4, 6\}$. After naming these lines by a, b, c, and d, respectively, we get the labels $\varphi(1) = \varphi(5) = (a, \{a, b, d\}), \varphi(3) = (b, \{a, b, c\}), \varphi(2) = (c, \{b, c\})$, and $\varphi(4) = \varphi(6) = (d, \{a, d\})$. Note that this reduces to the labelling $\varphi_1(1) = \varphi_1(5) = a, \varphi_1(3) = b, \varphi_1(2) = c$, and $\varphi_1(4) = \varphi_1(6) = d$ over the dependence alphabet $\Gamma = (\{a, b, c, d\}, D)$, where D is the symmetric and reflexive relation containing the pairs $(a, b), (a, d)$ and (b, c).

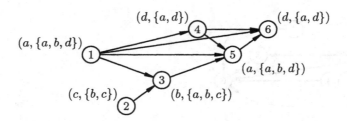

Figure 2.11:

Although this is the relation we have started with in Example 2.3.2, the labelling
we have obtained differs from the original labelling. (See Figure 2.11.)

Combining Lemma 2.5.5 and Theorem 2.5.6 yields the following result.

Corollary 2.5.8 *Let K be a graph language consisting of unlabelled acyclic transitive graphs. The following conditions are equivalent.*
*(1) There exists a dependence alphabet Γ such that for each $g \in K$ there exists a
Γ-labelling of g.*
(2) There exists a constant n such that, for each $g \in K$, $\mathrm{maxco}(\mathrm{sp}(g)) \leq n$.

The above result states that if the maxco-values of the set of spines of a language
of unlabelled acyclic transitive graphs can be bounded by some constant, then one
can find a dependence alphabet Γ such that all graphs in the language can be labelled
to become transitive closures of Γ-dependence graphs. This is a characterization in
terms of a graph-theoretical property of the spines of the graphs involved.

We will now present a more direct characterization in terms of the graphs themselves, rather than their spines. In order to adapt Corollary 2.5.8 in this sense,
we need to give a bound on the maxco-value of the spine of a graph in terms of
suitable properties of the graph itself. It is not possible to do this using only the
maxco-value of the graph, since, unfortunately, there exist classes of graphs for
which the maxco-values are bounded, while these values are not bounded for the
corresponding spines (see Example 2.5.10 below).

We will need the following notions.

Definition 2.5.9 *Let $g = (V, E)$ be an acyclic transitive graph.*
(1) The nodes $u_1, \ldots, u_n, v_1, \ldots, v_n$ of V induce a square graph (of size n) if
    - $(u_i, u_j) \in E$ for $1 \leq i < j \leq n$,
    - $(v_i, v_j) \in E$ for $1 \leq i < j \leq n$,
    - $(u_i, v_i) \in E_{\mathrm{hasse}(g)}$ for $1 \leq i \leq n$, and
    - $(v_i, u_j) \notin E$ for $1 \leq i, j \leq n$.
(2) $\mathrm{maxsq}(g) = \max\{n \mid g \text{ contains an induced square of size } n\}$.

Hence, when nodes $u_1, \ldots, u_n, v_1, \ldots, v_n$ induce a square graph, then we get a situation as in Figure 2.12, where edges required to be in the Hasse graph are given as dashed arcs and other edges as solid ones. Note that we have omitted arcs that follow by transitivity.

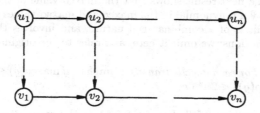

Figure 2.12: a square graph

Let $n > 1$, let $g = (V, E)$, and let the nodes $u_1, \ldots, u_n, v_1, \ldots, v_n$ of V induce a square graph. Then the nodes $u_1, \ldots, u_n$ form a totally unordered set in the spine of g. No edge $(u_i, u_j), i < j$, is present in $\mathrm{sp}(g)$ because $(u_i, v_i) \in E_{\mathbf{hasse}(g)}$, whereas $(v_i, u_j) \notin E$. This shows that if a graph contains an induced square of size n, then one can find at least n unconnected nodes in $\mathrm{sp}(g)$.

This implies that the maxsq-value of a given graph is bounded by the maxco-value of its spine. Moreover, it gives us an example of a class of graphs with unbounded maxco-values, while the maxco-values of their spines are bounded.

Example 2.5.10 Let K be the set of all square graphs, illustrated in Figure 2.13. Trivially these graphs contain induced squares of unbounded size, and consequently the spines of these graphs contain unbounded numbers of unconnected nodes. Note that the $\mathrm{maxco}(g) = 2$ for each graph g in K.

It is easily seen that, apart from the maxsq-value, also the maxco-value of a given graph is bounded by the maxco-value of its spine: nodes that are unconnected in g remain unconnected in $\mathrm{sp}(g)$.

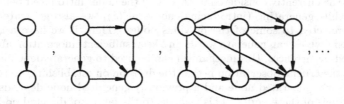

Figure 2.13: a language of squares

Lemma 2.5.11 *For each acyclic transitive graph g,* $\mathrm{maxco}(g) \leq \mathrm{maxco}(\mathrm{sp}(g))$, *and* $\mathrm{maxsq}(g) \leq \mathrm{maxco}(\mathrm{sp}(g))$.

Although we now have seen that the maxco-value of a spine cannot be bounded by the maxco-value of the original graph, some sort of converse of Lemma 2.5.11 can be shown. The next result shows that the maxco-value of the spine of a graph can be bounded by a polynomial in the maxco and maxsq-values of the graph. The proof of this result is of a combinatorial nature, and involves the introduction of some additional notions; we omit it here, and refer to the original paper [92].

Lemma 2.5.12 *For each acyclic transitive graph g, if* $\mathrm{maxco}(g) \leq n$ *and* $\mathrm{maxsq}(g) < m$, *then* $maxco(\mathrm{sp}(g)) < 2n^2 \cdot m$.

Combining Corollary 2.5.8, Lemma 2.5.11, and Lemma 2.5.12 we obtain the main result of this section.

Theorem 2.5.13 *Let K be a graph language consisting of unlabelled acyclic transitive graphs. The following three conditions are equivalent.*
(1) There exists a dependence alphabet Γ such that for each $g \in K$ there exists a Γ-labelling of g.
(2) There exists a constant n such that, for each $g \in K$, $\mathrm{maxco}(\mathrm{sp}(g)) \leq n$.
(3) There exists a constant n such that, for each $g \in K$, $\mathrm{maxco}(g) \leq n$ and $\mathrm{maxsq}(g) \leq n$.

Example 2.5.14 Consider again the graph language K illustrated in Figure 2.13. Since these graphs contain induced squares of unbounded size, by our last theorem, the graphs in K cannot be labelled using a common dependence alphabet Γ in such a way that they become transitive closures of Γ-dependence graphs.

2.6   Graph Grammars

Looking back at the definition of dependence graph that we have started with (Definition 2.3.1) one observes that it is of a grammatical nature in the following sense. While going through the word x from left to right we establish the edges between the currently considered node and all the nodes introduced before. In other words, while generating (introducing) nodes of $\langle x \rangle_\Gamma$ we also generate (introduce) edges connected to some of the previous nodes. Thus, if we have a grammatical mechanism which can generate words and keep sufficient information about already generated occurrences, this mechanism can be used to generate dependence graphs.

Now the crucial observation is that the decision on establishing an edge between the currently generated node and a previously generated node depends exclusively on the labels of these nodes. This leads us to the family of directed node-label controlled graph grammars (DNLC grammars) where the mechanism for establishing edges is based only on the labels of the nodes.

Definition 2.6.1 *A directed node-label controlled graph grammar, abbreviated a DNLC grammar, is a system* $G = (\Omega, \Xi, P, C_{in}, C_{out}, \xi)$, *where*

  (i) Ω *is an alphabet, called the* total alphabet *of G,*

  (ii) $\Xi \subseteq \Omega$ *is the* terminal alphabet *of G,*

  (iii) *P is a finite set of pairs* (X, h), *called* productions, *where* $X \in (\Omega - \Xi)$, *and h is a node labelled graph with labels from* Ω,

  (iv) $C_{in} \subseteq \Omega \times \Omega$. *and* $C_{out} \subseteq \Omega \times \Omega$ *are the* connection relations *of G, and*

  (v) ξ, *called the* axiom *of G, is a graph over* $\Omega - \Xi$ *consisting of one node only.*

Informally speaking, a DNLC grammar $G = (\Omega, \Xi, P, C_{in}, C_{out}, \xi)$ generates a set of graphs as follows.

Given a graph g to be rewritten and a production of the form (X, h), one chooses a node v of g labelled by X and replaces it by h (or, more precisely, by an isomorphic copy of h that is disjoint with g). Then one embeds h in the remainder of g (after removing v and its incident edges) by using the relations C_{in} and C_{out} in the following way. For *every* pair $(b, c) \in C_{in}$ one establishes an edge from *each* node u in the remainder of g labelled by c to each node of h labelled by b, provided that there was an edge from u to v in g. Analogously, for every pair $(b, c) \in C_{out}$ one establishes an edge from each node v of h labelled by b to each node u in the remainder of g labelled by c, provided that there was an edge from v to u in g. We say that the resulting graph is *directly derived* from g in G. Iterating these direct derivation steps, starting with the axiom ξ of G, and choosing only those derived graphs that are labelled by labels from the terminal alphabet Ξ, one gets the *(graph) language* $L(G)$ generated by G.

Example 2.6.2 Let $G = (\Omega, \Xi, P, C_{in}, C_{out}, \xi)$ be the DNLC grammar with $\Omega = \{S, a, b\}$, $\Xi = \{a, b\}$, $C_{in} = (\Omega \times \Omega) - \{(a, b), (b, a)\}$, $C_{out} = \emptyset$, ξ has a single node labelled by S, and P consists of the two productions depicted in Figure 2.14.

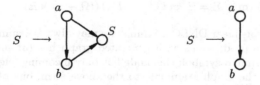

Figure 2.14: productions for a graph grammar

A sequence of derivation steps of G is given in Figure 2.15. Note that the node labelled by S remains connected to all other nodes in the graph. If this node is replaced by the right hand side of a production, the connections from nodes

labelled by b in the original graph to those labelled by a in the right-hand side will
be broken since (a, b) is not in the connection relation.

Note that none of the elements of the generated language is a dependence graph:
the graphs are acyclic, but the edges are not determined by node labels alone (cf.
Lemma 2.4.1).

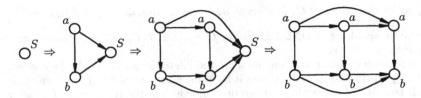

Figure 2.15: derivation in a graph grammar

The above notion of a DNLC grammar differs from the standard notion of a
DNLC grammar formally defined in [144] because we also allow erasing productions.

In accordance with the usual terminology, we say that a language K of dependence graphs over a dependence alphabet $\Gamma = (\Sigma, D)$ is *rational*, more precisely
that K is a *rational Γ-dependence graph language*, if it is constructed from a regular
word language R over Σ: $K = \{\langle x \rangle_\Gamma \mid x \in R\}$.

In order to properly generate rational dependence graph languages, we further
restrict the graph grammars we use. Not very surprisingly we will restrict ourselves
both to productions that have a right-linear form as well as to connection relations
that respect a given dependence relation.

Definition 2.6.3 *Let $\Gamma = (\Sigma, D)$ be a dependence alphabet and let $G = (\Omega, \Xi, P, C_{in},$
$C_{out}, \xi)$ be a DNLC grammar.*
(1) G is called right-linear *if every production of G is either of the form $(X, {}^\sigma \bullet \!\!\rightarrow\!\! \bullet {}^Y)$,
or of the form (X, ϕ), where $\sigma \in \Xi$, $X, Y \in \Omega - \Xi$, and ϕ denotes the empty graph.*
(2) G is called Γ-uniform *if $\Sigma = \Xi$ and $C_{in} = D \cup ((\Omega - \Xi) \times \Xi)$.*

Note that for a right-linear DNLC grammar we may always assume that $C_{out} =$
$\emptyset$: by the form of the productions each generated graph has (at most) one node
labelled with a nonterminal symbol; this node has only incoming edges.

Having restricted the graph grammars to the above form, one obtains the following correspondence between graph grammars and rational graph languages.

Theorem 2.6.4 ([5]) *Let $\Gamma = (\Sigma, D)$ be a dependence alphabet and let K be a set
of graphs with node labels in Σ. Then K is a rational Γ-dependence graph language
if and only if there exists a right-linear Γ-uniform DNLC grammar G such that
$K = L(G)$.*

Thus DNLC grammars provide yet another way of specifying (rational) trace languages.

In order to specify a trace language one has to specify an underlying word language and a dependence relation. To get dependence graphs from such a specification one uses an indirect way: for each word (which is a linear order) given by the specification of the language one "breaks it up" into the corresponding dependence graph using, e.g., the basic construction we gave in Definition 2.3.1. To specify an underlying language one can give, e.g., a regular expression or an automaton for it. One could also have a specification such as elementary net systems, which specify *both* the language (of firing sequences) and the dependence relation (obtained by considering two events independent if their neighbourhoods do not overlap).

Right-linear DNLC grammars specify a (possibly infinite) set of graphs using only a finite set of rules. Such a grammar *directly* specifies a set of dependence graphs. Moreover, the advantage is that from the grammar one can also "read off" an underlying word language (by considering the grammar as a right-linear word grammar) as well as the dependence relation (which is determined by the connection relation of the grammar).

II ALGEBRA AND COMBINATORICS

Chapter 3

C. Choffrut
Combinatorics in Trace Monoids I

Chapter 4

G. Duchamp, D. Krob
Combinatorics in Trace Monoids II

Chapter 5

A. Bertoni, M. Goldwurm, G. Mauri, N. Sabadini
Counting Techniques for Inclusion, Equivalence and
Membership Problems

Chapter 3

Combinatorics in Trace Monoids I

Christian Choffrut

Institut Blaise Pascal (LITP), Université Paris 7
2, place Jussieu, 75251 Paris Cedex 05, France
choffrut@litp.ibp.fr

Contents

3.1 Introduction

Let Ξ be an alphabet of *unknowns*. An *equation* is a pair $(e, e') \in \Xi^*$, also written $e = e'$. Given a dependence alphabet (Σ, D), a *solution* of the equation $e = e'$ in the trace monoid $\mathbb{M}(\Sigma, D)$, is a morphism $\theta : \Xi^* \to \mathbb{M}(\Sigma, D)$, such that $\theta(e) = \theta(e')$ holds.

The unknowns are denoted by the last letters of the Latin alphabet $x, y, \ldots$ or by $x_1, x_2, \ldots$, if they need to be ordered. The elements of Σ are denoted by the first letters of the Latin alphabet $a, b, \ldots$. We make the convention that all letters of Ξ appear in either e or e', i.e., $\Xi = \text{alpha}(e) \cup \text{alpha}(e')$.

Example 3.1.1 Consider $\Xi = \{x_1, x_2, x_3, x_4\}$, $\Sigma = \{a, b, c\}$ and $I = \{(a, b), (b, a), (a, c), (c, a)\}$. Then the morphism $\theta(x_1) = aa, \theta(x_2) = cbc, \theta(x_3) = c, \theta(x_4) = bcc$, is a solution of the equation $x_1 x_2 x_3 = x_3 x_4 x_1$.

An equation $e = e'$ is *trivial* if the two words e and e' are equal, e.g., $xyzx = xyzx$. Trivial equations have little mystery since all morphisms are solutions, so we assume thereafter that the equation is not trivial. Given a solution θ, an unknown $x \in \Xi$ *vanishes* if $\theta(x) = 1$ holds. The solution is *trivial* if all unknowns vanish. It is *cyclic* if there exists an element $t \in \mathbb{M}(\Sigma, D)$ such that $\theta(x) \in t^*$ for all $x \in \Xi$. As in elementary algebra, we will identify an unknown with its value assigned by some morphism, i.e., x with $\theta(x)$: if x is assigned the value u by θ then we write $x = u$ to mean $\theta(x) = u$.

Example 3.1.2 The equation $xyz = 1$ has a unique solution, the trivial one. In the free monoid $\{a, b\}^*$, the equation $x^2 y^2 = z^2$ has, e.g., the cyclic solution $x = ab, y = (ab)^3, z = (ab)^2$.

There is no formal definition of what it means to *solve* an equation. Indeed, it is clear that all equations have, at least, one solution, namely the trivial one. Also, given an equation and a dependence alphabet, determining whether or not the set of all the solutions in the corresponding trace monoid is finite, is decidable. Actually the finiteness does not depend on the specific trace monoid and it suffices to check this property for the solutions in the free monoid generated by a unique element. An attempt to formalize the intuitive idea of solving an equation makes use of the notion of parameterized words as exposed in [183], which are expressions involving word and integer variables. Here is an example that gives the intuition of what is meant by a parameterized word:

Example 3.1.3 Consider the equation $xy = yz$ in free monoids. An arbitrary cyclic solution is of the form $x = u^n, y = u^m, z = u^n$ for some word u and some integers n, m. Proposition 3.3.1 below shows that an arbitrary non cyclic solution is of the form $x = uv, y = (uv)^n u, z = vu$ for some words u, v and some integer n. Here, we have two types of parameters, word parameters u (resp. u, v) and integer parameters n, m (resp. n). Furthermore, $u^n, uv, (uv)^n u, vu$ are 4 examples of parameterized words.

It has been proven that the solutions in free monoids of equations with less than 4 unknowns are parameterizable, and that there exist equations with 4 unknowns that are not (cf. [137]). In practice however, this situation occurs for quite a few reasonable and natural equations. An apparently weaker question that is natural to ask, is whether or not an equation has a non cyclic solution. This is in fact usually difficult to determine, but, as shown by Pécuchet [213], using Makanin's deep result on equations [187], one can do more: one can effectively compute the maximal over all possible solutions, of the minimum number of word parameters used to express an arbitrary solution in free monoids of the given equation. In the previous example, this number is 1 for the cyclic solutions and 2 for the others. This number, called the *rank* of the equation, happens to always be less than the number of unknowns. Unfortunately, for trace monoids in general, no such result can hold.

There are two general approaches for solving equations in trace monoids both based on the experience in free monoids. The first one mimics the customary approach of free monoids. It compares the values of the two leftmost unknowns of the left- and right-hand sides of the equation. In free monoids one of these two unknowns is a prefix of the other: by cancellation one gets a new solution (of smaller size) of a new equation, which allows a proof by induction.

Example 3.1.4 Consider the equation $xyz = zyx$ and a solution $x = u, y = v, z = w$ in a free monoid. Then by comparing the prefixes u and w either $u = w$ or u is a prefix of w or w is a prefix of u. Assume, e.g., that u is a prefix of w and that it is different from the empty word. Then $w = uw'$ holds for some w'. Substituting in the original equation we get $uvuw' = uw'vu$, i.e., by cancellation to the left $vuw' = w'vu$. This shows that $x = u, y = v, z = w'$ is a solution of the new equation $yxz = zyx$. Observe that the sum of the lengths $|u| + |v| + |w'|$ is less than $|u| + |v| + |w|$.

For trace monoids, this simplicity is lost and this method leads us to equations whose solutions are submitted to extra conditions, see e.g., Proposition 3.2.2 below.

The second approach uses a process in two steps: one starts with studying the projections of the solutions over particular free submonoids yielding partial solutions, and then one tries to "reconstruct" these solutions into a global solution in the trace monoid.

Example 3.1.5 Consider the alphabet $\Sigma = \{a, b, c\}$, the equation $xy = yz$ and the independence relation $I = \{(a, c), (c, a)\}$. The submonoids generated by $\{a, b\}$ and $\{b, c\}$ respectively, are free. Projecting on $\{a, b\}^*$ for example gives a solution $\theta_1(x) = bba$, $\theta_1(y) = bb$, $\theta_1(z) = abb$. Projecting on $\{b, c\}^*$ gives a solution $\theta_2(x) = bc$, $\theta_2(y) = b$, $\theta_2(z) = cb$. Nonetheless, these partial solutions can not be combined into a solution in $\mathbb{M}(\Sigma, I)$ because the number of occurrences of the letter b in θ_1 and θ_2 do not match. Now, the solution $\theta_3(x) = bbc$, $\theta_3(y) = bb$, $\theta_3(z) = cbb$ can be combined with θ_1 yielding the solution: $\theta(x) = bbac$, $\theta(y) = bb$, $\theta(z) = acbb$.

One can wonder about the merit of these two techniques. In fact the first technique usually allows to verify the general form of the solutions relatively easily, once this form is known. However, this general form is usually worked out directly by applying the second technique.

3.2 Equations in Two Unknowns

The purpose of this section is to generalize to trace monoids the result stating that equations in two unknowns have only cyclic solutions in free monoids (cf. [176]):

Proposition 3.2.1 *Let $e = e'$ be a non trivial equation in two unknowns. Then all its solutions in a given trace monoid are cyclic.*

This statement has numerous consequences, since it implies in particular that two words in a free monoid commute if and only if they are powers of a common word. Another important consequence is that every non empty word is the power of a unique word of minimal length.

We will see that apart from the technical difficulty of having to deal with subalphabets, a similar proposition holds true in the more general case of trace monoids. The results are taken from [76] but our presentation differs in that it resorts to a more axiomatic approach, thereby avoiding the technicalities due to the method of reconstruction as mentioned in the previous section. This leads us to prove a general result stating that, under some mild assumption, equations having only cyclic solutions in free monoids have also only cyclic solutions in trace monoids. We first recall the "Levi type" equation which is the basis of this theory.

Proposition 3.2.2 Let $\mathbb{M}(\Sigma, I)$ be a trace monoid and let x, y, z, t be four of its elements satisfying the equality $xy = zt$. Then there exists u, v, α, β with $\mathrm{alpha}(\alpha) \times \mathrm{alpha}(\beta) \subseteq I$ such that

$$x = u\alpha, z = u\beta, y = \beta v, t = \alpha v$$

Proof: We first make a general observation concerning the prefixes of a trace. For each trace w, we denote by G_w, or simply by G when no confusion may arise, the dependence graph associated with it. Also, given a trace w and its dependence graph $G = (V, E)$, let $\prec$ be the order that is the transitive closure of the relation E, i.e., the relation defined for all nodes i and j by the condition: $i \prec j$ holds if and only if there exists a path in the graph leading from i to j. A subgraph $G' = (V', E')$ of G is a graph such that $V' \subseteq V$, $E' = E \cap V' \times V'$ and for all $(i, j) \in V'^2$ we have $(i, j) \in E'$ if and only if $(i, j) \in E$. Then the subgraph G' represents a prefix of w if and only if the set V' is an ideal, i.e., $i \in V'$ and $j \prec i$ implies $j \in V'$.

Now, consider the trace $w = xy = zt$ and its dependence graph G. The intersection of G_x and G_z represents a prefix, say u of w that is also a prefix of x and z, so we set: $x = u\alpha$ and $z = u\beta$. This entails $u\alpha y = u\beta t$, i.e., by cancellation to the left: $\alpha y = \beta t$. Now, each node of $G_x - G_z = G_\alpha$ is incomparable with each node of $G_z - G_x = G_\beta$, which shows that $\mathrm{alpha}(\alpha) \times \mathrm{alpha}(\beta) \subseteq I$ holds. Since G_α is disjoint from G_β, it is a subgraph of G_t: $t = \alpha v$ for some v and thus $y = \beta v$. $\qquad\square$

This result can be extended in the following way

Proposition 3.2.3 Let $x_1, \ldots, x_n, y_1, \ldots, y_m$ be elements satisfying the equality $x_1 \ldots x_n = y_1 \ldots y_m$. Then there exist nm elements $z_{ij}, 1 \leq i \leq n, 1 \leq j \leq m$ such that $\mathrm{alpha}(z_{ij})$ and $\mathrm{alpha}(z_{kl})$ are independent if (i, j) and (k, l) are incomparable (i.e., $i \leq k$ if and only if $l < j$)

$$x_i = \prod_{1 \leq j \leq m} z_{ij}, y_j = \prod_{1 \leq i \leq n} z_{ij}$$

Proof: We use an induction on the integer $n + m$. By Proposition 3.2.2 it suffices to consider the case $n \geq 2$, $m \geq 2$, $n + m \geq 5$. Applying the same result, we obtain for some $u, v, \alpha, \beta \in \mathbb{M}(\Sigma, D)$, alpha($\alpha$) $\times$ alpha(β) $\subseteq I$:

$$x_1 = u\alpha, y_1 = u\beta, x_2 \ldots x_n = \beta v, y_2 \ldots y_m = \alpha v$$

Applying Levi's property to equality $x_2 \ldots x_n = \beta v$, shows that for all $2 \leq i \leq n$ there exist $\beta_i, v_i \in \mathbb{M}(\Sigma, D)$ such that $\beta = \beta_2 \ldots \beta_n$ and $v = v'_2 \ldots v'_n$ and $x_i = \beta_i v'_i$. Equivalently, applying Levi's property to equality $y_2 \ldots y_m = \alpha v$, shows that for all $2 \leq j \leq m$ there exist $\alpha_j, v''_j \in \mathbb{M}(\Sigma, D)$ such that $\alpha = \alpha_2 \ldots \alpha_m$ and $v = v''_2 \ldots v''_m$ and $y_j = \beta_j v''_j$. Now, equality $v'_2 \ldots v'_n = v''_2 \ldots v''_m$ shows that there exist z_{ij} with $2 \leq i \leq n$, $2 \leq j \leq m$, such that $v'_i = \prod_{2 \leq j \leq m} z_{ij}, v''_j = \prod_{1 \leq i \leq n} z_{ij}$ and alpha(z_{ij}) $\times$ alpha(z_{kl}) $\subseteq I$ if (i, j) and (k, l) are incomparable. Set: $z_{11} = u$ and $z_{1j} = \alpha_j, z_{i1} = \beta_i$ for all $2 \leq i \leq n$ and $2 \leq j \leq m$. Then the condition alpha(z_{1j}) $\times$ alpha(z_{i1}) $\subseteq I$ for all $1 \leq i \leq n, 1 \leq j \leq m$ follows from alpha(α) $\times$ alpha(β) $\subseteq I$ and the verification is thus complete. $\square$

Under certain conditions all solutions split into partial solutions over independent subalphabets. In other words, it may happen that there exists a family of $p > 0$ pairwise independent subalphabets $\Sigma_1, \ldots, \Sigma_p$ such that solving the equation in $\mathbb{M}(\Sigma, D)$ reduces to independently solving the same equation in the trace monoids $\mathbb{M}(\Sigma_i, D_i)$ where $D_i = D \cap \Sigma_i \times \Sigma_i$ for $i = 1, \ldots, p$. Here is such a condition

Lemma 3.2.4 *Let $e = e'$ be an equation having only cyclic solutions in free monoids and let θ be a solution in the trace monoid $\mathbb{M}(\Sigma, D)$. Then for any two variables x, y, two arbitrary connected subalphabets of $\theta(x)$ and $\theta(y)$ are either disjoint or equal.*

Proof: Set $\theta(x) = u$ and $\theta(y) = v$ and let Σ_x (resp. Σ_y) be a connected subalphabet of u (resp. v). Assume their intersection is non empty: $a \in \Sigma_x \cap \Sigma_y$. For all $b \in \Sigma_x \cup \Sigma_y$, $(a, b) \in D$, consider the projection $\pi : \mathbb{M}(\Sigma, D) \rightarrow \{a, b\}^*$. Then, by composition of morphisms, $x = \pi(u)$, $y = \pi(v), \ldots$ is a solution of $e = e'$ in the free monoid $\{a, b\}^*$. Because all solutions are cyclic, this implies in particular that alpha($\pi(u)$) $=$ alpha($\pi(v)$), i.e., b belongs to the alphabet of u if and only if it belongs to the alphabet of v. The result follows by transitivity. $\square$

Proposition 3.2.5 *Let $e = e'$ be an equation having only cyclic solutions in free monoids and let θ be a solution in the trace monoid $\mathbb{M}(\Sigma, D)$. Assume that Σ is connected and that for all non vanishing unknowns alpha($\theta(x)$) $= \Sigma$ holds. Then θ is cyclic.*

Proof: Let us first make a general remark using the following notations inspired by the case of equations in free monoids. For all distinct $x, y \in \Xi$ consider the morphisms $\delta_x : \Xi^* \rightarrow (\Xi - \{x\})^*, \epsilon_{x,y} : \Xi^* \rightarrow (\Xi - \{x\})^*$ and $\phi_{x,y} : \Xi^* \rightarrow \Xi^*$ defined by the conditions

$$\delta_x(z) = z \text{ if } z \neq x \text{ and } \delta_x(z) = 1 \text{ otherwise}$$

$$\epsilon_{x,y}(z) = z \text{ if } z \neq x \text{ and } \epsilon_{x,y}(z) = y \text{ otherwise}$$

$$\phi_{x,y}(z) = z \text{ if } z \neq x \text{ and } \phi_{x,y}(z) = yx \text{ otherwise}$$

Then it is clear that for $\chi = \delta_x, \epsilon_{x,y}, \phi_{x,y}$ the equation $\chi(e) = \chi(e')$ has only cyclic solutions in the free monoids.

In order to prove the result we proceed by induction on the pair of integers $(\text{Card}(\Xi), \sum_{x \in \Xi} |\theta(x)|)$ where the first component is the number of unknowns and the second is the sum of the lengths of the images of the solution and where the pairs are lexicographically ordered (first compare the left components; if they agree, compare the right components). By cancelling out the maximal common prefix of e and e', either e and e' start with different unknowns x and y, or one of the two hand sides is the empty word. In this latter case, the result trivially holds. If $\theta(x) = 1$ or $\theta(y) = 1$ holds then we are done. Indeed, say $\theta(x) = 1$. The restriction θ' of θ to $(\Xi - \{x\})^*$ is a solution of the equation $\delta_x(e) = \delta_x(e')$. By the preliminary remark this latter equation has only cyclic solutions in free monoids and less unknowns than $e = e'$. It then suffices to apply the induction hypothesis.

We are thus left with an equation of the form

$$(2) \qquad\qquad xL(x, y, \ldots) = yR(x, y, \ldots)$$

where $L(x, y, \ldots)$ and $R(x, y, \ldots)$ are words over the free monoid Ξ^*. Because of Proposition 3.2.2, equality (2) implies that there exists $u, v, \alpha, \beta \in \mathbb{M}(\Sigma, D)$ such that $\text{alpha}(\alpha) \times \text{alpha}(\beta) \subseteq I$, $x = u\alpha$, $y = u\beta$, $L(x, y, \ldots) = \beta v$ and $R(x, y, \ldots) = \alpha v$. If $\alpha\beta = 1$ then we are done. Indeed, the restriction θ' of θ to $(\Xi - \{y\})^*$ is a solution of the equation $\epsilon_{y,x}(e) = \epsilon_{y,x}(e')$. This last equation has only cyclic solutions and fewer unknowns than $e = e'$. Therefore, the solution θ' is cyclic and so is the solution θ. Now if $\alpha = 1$ then we obtain $L(u, u\beta, \ldots) = \beta R(u, u\beta, \ldots)$ which shows that $\theta'(x) = u, \theta'(y) = \beta, \ldots$ is a solution of the equation $\phi_{y,x}(e) = \phi_{y,x}(e')$. Since the sum of the lengths of the images of the solution θ' is strictly smaller than that of θ, we may conclude by induction hypothesis.

We assume thereafter that α and β are different from the empty trace. Substituting the values of the variables x and y in (2) we get

$$(3) \qquad\qquad \alpha L(u\alpha, u\beta, \ldots) = \beta R(u\alpha, u\beta, \ldots)$$

Setting $\text{alpha}(\alpha) = \Sigma_\alpha$ and $\text{alpha}(\beta) = \Sigma_\beta$ and taking the projection π_α of the two hand sides on $(\Sigma - \Sigma_\beta)^*$, we obtain

$$(4) \qquad\qquad \alpha L(u'\alpha, u', \ldots) = R(u'\alpha, u', \ldots)$$

where $u' = \pi_\alpha(u)$. This shows that $x = \alpha, y = u', \ldots$ is a solution of the equation $\phi_{x,y}(e) = \phi_{x,y}(e')$. Because of $|u'| + |\alpha| < |u| + |v|$, we have $u', \alpha \in r^*$ for some $r \in \mathbb{M}(\Sigma, D)$ where $\text{alpha}(r) = \Sigma_\alpha$.

Equivalently, taking the projection π_β of the two hand sides on $(\Sigma - \Sigma_\alpha)^*$ yields

$$(5) \qquad\qquad L(u'', u''\beta, \ldots) = \beta R(u'', u''\beta, \ldots)$$

where $u'' = \pi_\beta(u)$. This shows that $x = u'', y = \beta, \ldots$ is a solution of the equation $\phi_{y,x}(e) = \phi_{y,x}(e')$. Because of $|u''| + |\beta| < |u| + |v|$, we have $u'', \beta \in t^*$ for some $t \in \mathbb{M}(\Sigma, D)$ where $alpha(t) = \Sigma_\beta$. We get $\Sigma = alpha(\theta(x)) = \Sigma = \Sigma_\alpha \cup \Sigma_\beta$ which together with $\Sigma_\alpha \cap \Sigma_\beta = \emptyset$ leads to a contradiction. We are thus left with $\alpha = 1$ or $\beta = 1$ which completes the proof. □

Before returning to the equations with two unknowns, we need a notion that is valid for all equations. An equation $e = e'$ is *balanced* if for all unknowns x, the right- and left-hand sides, as elements of Ξ^*, have the same number of occurrences of the letter x, i.e., $|e|_x = |e'|_x$. Otherwise, the equation is *unbalanced*.

Example 3.2.6 The equation $xyzx = zxxy$ is balanced but $xyzx = zxyz$ is not.

When the equation is unbalanced, the previous result can be made more precise, since it can be stated in analogous terms as for free monoids.

Proposition 3.2.7 *Let $e = e'$ be an unbalanced equation in two unknowns. Then every solution in the trace monoid is cyclic.*

Proof: Since the equation has only cyclic solutions in free monoids, via Lemma 3.2.4 and Proposition 3.2.5 there exist an integer $p > 0$, p pairwise independent subalphabets $\Sigma_1, \ldots, \Sigma_p$ and p elements $u_1 \in \mathbb{M}(\Sigma_1, D_1), \ldots, u_p \in \mathbb{M}(\Sigma_p, D_p)$, where $D_i = D \cap \Sigma_i \times \Sigma_i$ for $i = 1, \ldots, p$ such that $x = u_1^{i_1} \cdots u_p^{i_p}$ and $y = u_1^{j_1} \cdots u_p^{j_p}$ for some integers $i_1, \cdots, i_p$ and $j_1, \cdots, j_p$. Set $|e|_x - |e'|_x = \Delta_x$ and $|e|_y - |e'|_y = \Delta_y$. If, say, $\Delta_x = 0$, then $\Delta_y \neq 0$ and thus $\theta(y) = 1$ in all solutions, which is the result. Thus we may assume that $\Delta_x, \Delta_y \neq 0$. Consider the integers δ_x, δ_y satisfying $g.c.d(\delta_x, \delta_y) = 1$ and $\delta_y \Delta_x = \delta_x \Delta_y$. We get $i_k \Delta_x = j_k \Delta_y$ for all $k = 1, \ldots, p$, i.e., $i_k = r_k \delta_y$ and $j_k = r_k \delta_x$. Setting $t = u_1^{r_1} \cdots u_p^{r_p}$ we obtain $x = t^{\delta_y}$ and $y = t^{\delta_x}$. □

A trace $t \in \mathbb{M}(\Sigma, D) - \{1\}$ is called *primitive* if it is not a power of exponent greater than 1 of any other trace, i.e., $t = r^n$ implies $n = 1$.

Example 3.2.8 Consider $\Sigma = \{a, b, c\}$ and $I = \{(a, b), (b, a), (a, c), (c, a)\}$. Then $abacbc$ is not primitive since $abacbc = (abc)^2$ holds. However, $ababcbc$ is primitive.

Proposition 3.2.9 *For all traces $t \in \mathbb{M}(\Sigma, D) - \{1\}$ there exists a unique primitive trace r and a unique integer n such that $t = r^n$.*

Proof: Assume there exist two primitive traces $t = r_1^n = r_2^p$ for some integers $n, p > 0$. This means that the unbalanced equation $x^n = y^p$ with two unknowns has the solution $x = r_1$ and $y = r_2$. The previous Proposition violates the minimality of the lengths of r_1 and r_2. □

The trace r of the Proposition is called the *root* of t.

3.3   Conjugacy

Given an arbitrary monoid M, two elements $x, y \in M$ are *conjugate* if there exists
an element $z \in M$ such that $xz = zy$ holds. This equality can be viewed as an
equation in the three unknowns x, y, z. It is also one of the very few equations
whose set of solutions in free monoids can be entirely described. Indeed, we have
(cf.[176])

Proposition 3.3.1 *Let x, y be two nonempty words in a free monoid Σ^*. Then the
equality $xz = zy$ holds for some $z \in \Sigma^*$ if and only if there exist two words $u, v \in \Sigma^*$
and an integer $n \geq 0$ satisfying*

$$x = uv, y = vu \text{ and } z = (uv)^n u$$

The solutions in arbitrary trace monoids are more involved. They are described
in Theorem 3.3.3 taken from Duboc, [76]. Her approach uses the notion of recon-
structibility as briefly exposed in the preliminaries: this allows her to obtain more
information on the solutions (such as the uniqueness of the decomposition of x and
y in the case where x and y are primitive, a simple test for conjugacy etc ...) at the
cost of a more lengthy proof.

We first show how we can reduce the search to solutions of a more restricted
type.

Lemma 3.3.2 *Let $x, y, z \in \mathbb{M}(\Sigma, D)$ be three elements satisfying the equality $xz = zy$. Then there exist three subalphabets Σ_0, Σ' and Σ'', where $\Sigma' \subseteq \Sigma''$ and where Σ_0 and Σ'' are independent, satisfying $\text{alpha}(z) = \Sigma_0 \cup \Sigma'$ and $\text{alpha}(x) = \text{alpha}(y) = \Sigma''$.*

Proof: By simple counting arguments it is clear that x and y have the same
subalphabet. Set $\Sigma'' = \text{alpha}(x) = \text{alpha}(y)$ and $\Sigma_0 = \text{alpha}(z) - \Sigma''$. Assume
by contradiction there exist $a \in \Sigma_0$ and $b \in \Sigma''$ such that $(a, b) \in D$ holds. Denote
by $\pi_{a,b}$ the projection of $\mathbb{M}(\Sigma, D)$ on the free submonoids $\{a, b\}^*$. Then we get
$a \in \text{alpha}(\pi_{a,b}(z)) - \text{alpha}(\pi_{a,b}(x))$, contradicting Proposition 3.3.1.   □

As a consequence, without loss of generality we may assume that $\Sigma_0 = \emptyset$, i.e.,
$\text{alpha}(z) \subseteq \text{alpha}(x) = \text{alpha}(y)$. Let $\Sigma_1, \ldots, \Sigma_p$, be the decomposition of Σ' into
its $p > 0$ connected components. Set $D' = D \cap \Sigma' \times \Sigma'$, and $D_i = D \cap \Sigma_i \times \Sigma_i$ for
$i = 1, \ldots, p$. Denote by $\pi_i, i = 1, \ldots, p$ the projection of $\mathbb{M}(\Sigma', D')$ onto $\mathbb{M}(\Sigma_i, D_i)$.
Then we have

$$x = \pi_1(x) \cdots \pi_p(x), \quad y = \pi_1(y) \cdots \pi_p(y), \quad z = \pi_1(z) \cdots \pi_p(z)$$

and thus

$$\pi_i(x)\pi_i(z) = \pi_i(z)\pi_i(y) \text{ for } i = 1, \ldots, p$$

In other words, it suffices to be able to solve the conjugacy equality under the
hypothesis that the alphabet of x (or y) is connected. This is done in the next
result. We recall that the *diameter* of a connected undirected graph is the minimum

integer d for which two arbitrary vertices of the graph may be connected by a path of at most p edges. In the next result, the relation D is identified with the graph whose vertices are the letters of Σ and whose edges are the pairs $(a, b) \in D$.

Theorem 3.3.3 *Let $x, y \in \mathbb{M}(\Sigma, D) - \{1\}$ and $z \in \mathbb{M}(\Sigma, D)$ be three elements satisfying the equality $xz = zy$. Assume the graph D is connected and has diameter d. If $\mathrm{alpha}(x) = \Sigma$ holds then there exist $p \leq d$ elements $t_0, \ldots, t_p$ with $\mathrm{alpha}(t_i) \times \mathrm{alpha}(t_j) \subseteq I$ whenever $|i - j| > 1$ and an integer n such that*

$$x = t_0 \cdots t_p, y = t_p \cdots t_0, z = (t_0 \cdots t_p)^n t_0 \cdots t_{p-1} \cdots t_0 \cdots t_{p-2} \cdots t_0 t_1 t_0$$

Proof: We proceed by induction on the integer $|x| + |z|$. If $|x| + |z| = 1$ then $x = y = a$ for some letter $a \in \Sigma$ and $z = 1$. We may thus assume that $|x| + |z| > 1$. By Proposition 3.2.2, for some u, v, α, β, with $\mathrm{alpha}(\alpha) \times \mathrm{alpha}(\beta) \subseteq I$, we obtain

$$x = u\alpha, \quad z = u\beta = \beta v, \quad y = \alpha v$$

Since $|u| + |\beta| = (|x| + |z|) - |x|$ holds, by induction hypothesis applied to $u\beta = \beta v$ we obtain

$$u = t_0' \cdots t_p', \quad v = t_p' \cdots t_0', \quad \beta = (t_0' \cdots t_p')^n t_0' \cdots t_{p-1}' \cdots t_0' \cdots t_{p-2}' \cdots t_0' t_1' t_0'$$

If $\alpha = 1$ then we are done. Else if $n > 0$ then $\mathrm{alpha}(u) = \mathrm{alpha}(\beta)$ and thus $\mathrm{alpha}(\alpha)$ is independent of $\mathrm{alpha}(u)$ which contradicts the connectedness of x. It then suffices to set $t_i = t_i'$ for $i = 0, \ldots, p - 1$ and $t_p = t_p'\alpha (= \alpha t_p')$.

We are left with proving that $p \leq d$. First observe that if $d \leq 1$ then the monoid $\mathbb{M}(\Sigma, D)$ is free and the result follows from Proposition 3.3.1. We may thus assume $d > 1$ and therefore $p > 1$. For any two letters $a, b \in \Sigma$ denote by $d(a, b)$ the length of the shortest path in D between a and b. We verify by induction on p that if Σ is the union of $\Sigma_0, \ldots, \Sigma_p$ where Σ_i and Σ_j are independent whenever $|i - j| > 1$, then for any vertices $a \in \Sigma_0$ and $b \in \Sigma_p$ we have $d(a, b) \geq p$. This is clear for $p = 2$ since Σ_0 and Σ_p are independent. Now, consider a shortest path $c_0 = a, c_1, \ldots, c_r = b$ from $a \in \Sigma_0$ to $b \in \Sigma_p$. By the hypothesis on the subalphabets we have $c_{r-1} \in \Sigma_{p-1}$. Furthermore, $\bigcup_{0 \leq i \leq p-1} \Sigma_i$ is connected. Thus by the induction hypothesis we have $d(a, c_{r-1}) \geq p - 1$, i.e., $d(a, b) \geq p$ which completes the proof. $\qquad\square$

Our presentation is not well suited for investigating algorithmic aspects of conjugacy. Using the other approach (projection, solution in free monoids and reconstruction) it is possible to show that determining whether or not two given traces are conjugate, can be solved in time proportional to the length of the traces ([76], see also [180] and [212]).

A final remark on this subject. The notion of conjugacy is often given a different definition in the literature. In order to discuss it let us rename it and say that two elements x, y of a monoid are *transposed* if there exist u, v such that $x = uv, y = vu$ holds. Then y is obtained from x by one transposition. The previous Theorem ensures that whenever two traces are conjugate then it is possible to obtain one of them by applying a number of transpositions that is less than or equal to the diameter of the graph of the dependence relation (for finer results, see [76]). The reader is referred to [84] for the study of the structure of the centralizer of the free groups with partial commutations.

3.4   Related Topics

3.4.1   Equations with Constants

As discussed in a previous section, it is not clear what it should reasonably mean to solve an equation in trace monoids. We present a formalism that overcomes this difficulty and that is adapted from the case of free monoids and free groups. Here, the trace monoid in which the solution is sought, is part of the problem. Indeed, given an alphabet Ξ of unknowns and a dependence alphabet (Σ, D) of *constants*, an *equation with constants* Σ is a pair (e, e') of words over the alphabet $\Xi \cup \Sigma$: $(e, e') \in (\Xi \cup \Sigma)^* \times (\Xi \cup \Sigma)^*$. As for ordinary equations we write $e = e'$ instead of (e, e'). A solution of $e = e'$ is a morphism $\theta : (\Xi \cup \Sigma)^* \to \mathbb{M}(\Sigma, D)$ that leaves the constants invariant: $\theta(a) = a$ for all $a \in \Sigma$. What we gain by introducing constants is clear. The question whether or not, given an equation with constants, it has a solution, is no longer obvious. Actually, even in the case of free monoids the decidability of this question is a very profound result due to Makanin (cf.[187]).

Example 3.4.1 Consider $\Xi = \{x_1, x_2, x_3, x_4\}$, $\Sigma = \{a, b, c\}$ and $I = \{(a, b), (b, a), (a, c), (c, a)\}$. Then the equation $x_1 a x_2 x_1 = c x_3 b a x_4$ has the solution $\theta(x_1) = ac, \theta(x_2) = bba, \theta(x_3) = aab, \theta(x_4) = ac$.

An open question is to determine the dependence relations D for which Makanin's result still holds. For example, it certainly still holds in the case of direct products of free monoids since it amounts to deciding on each component separately whether or not the projection of the equation has a solution.

3.4.2   Trace Matching

Given a trace monoid $\mathbb{M}(\Sigma, D)$ and two traces x and y, the problem asks to determine whether or not x has an occurrence in y, i.e., whether or not $y = uxv$ holds for some traces u, v.

This is known as the string matching problem in the case of free monoids. Let us briefly recall one of its best known solutions due to Knuth, Morris and Pratt (cf. [156]), KMP for short. To fix the notations, x is the *string* and y is the *text*. The idea is to shift the string along the text from left to right. At each position in the text one compares the string against the text letter by letter by reading both from left to right. If the comparison fails before the string is entirely read, then another position of the string further to the right in the text must be tried. The authors observe that one can take advantage of the previous comparison so as to discard some positions that clearly lead to failure. Indeed, assume that x is the word *abaaabac*, that the prefix of x read so far is *abaaaba* and that the next letter in the text is different from *c*. Shifting x by one or two positions to the right would lead to a failure. Actually, the shortest shift to be tried is 4. In its simplified version, the algorithm proceeds by assigning to each prefix x' of the string x the value of the shortest shift that must be performed when a failure occurs after prefix x'. In the previous example, with $x' = abaa$ is associated the integer 3 and with $x' = abaaaba$ is associated the integer 4. This preprocessing reduces the number of letter comparisons to at most twice the length of the text.

In the case of trace matching some difficulties arise. However, as shown in [135] it is still possible to check in linear time whether or not a trace is a factor of another.

3.4.3 Free Trace Submonoids

Submonoids and equations are related in the theory of free monoids via the notion of Unique Decipherability and the Defect Theorem, cf. [12]. This connection no longer holds for trace monoids, however a notion of free trace submonoid can be defined as shown by the following.

In a free monoid Σ^*, each submonoid M admits a minimal set of generators, namely $X = M - \{1\} - (M - \{1\})^2$, i.e., $X^* = M$ holds and whenever $X'^* = M$ holds for some $X' \subseteq \Sigma^*$ then $X' = X$. It is also folklore that submonoids of Σ^* are not necessarily free. E.g., $X = \{a, ab, ba, \}$ is not free since *aba* admits two factorizations $(a)(ba) = (ab)(a)$. The minimal set of generators of free submonoids M is called a *code*. We also say that it is the *base* of M. The property for a finite subset to be a code is decidable as established by Sardinas and Paterson.

These questions have analogs for trace monoids. The first property holds for arbitrary free partially commutative monoids $\mathbb{M}(\Sigma, D)$, namely, there exists a unique minimum set that generates a given submonoid M of $\mathbb{M}(\Sigma, D)$ as can be readily seen. The second question on what it means to "freely generate a trace submonoid" remains to be defined formally. If one wants to extend this notion, one might be guided by what happens in the two particular cases of free commutative and free monoids. For free monoids one must end up with codes and for free commutative monoids one must end up with the notion of basis in linear algebra, since these monoids are embedded in a free $\mathbb{Z}$-module. Intuitively, we say that X freely generates the submonoid X^* if all elements in X^* have a unique expression as a product $x_1 \ldots x_n$ of elements of X up to commuting two consecutive factors whenever they commute in $\mathbb{M}(\Sigma, D)$. More formally, let $X \subseteq \mathbb{M}(\Sigma, D)$ be an arbitrary subset and consider a one to one mapping $\phi : \Delta \to X$ where X and Δ are disjoint. We define on the alphabet Δ, a relation of partial commutations J by setting for all $b_1, b_2 \in \Delta$

$$(b_1, b_2) \in J \text{ if and only if } \text{alpha}(\phi(b_1)) \times \text{alpha}(\phi(b_2)) \subseteq I$$

Then ϕ extends to a morphism $\phi : \mathbb{M}(\Delta, J) \to \mathbb{M}(\Sigma, I)$ and X is a *base* if this morphism is injective.

Example 3.4.2 Consider $\Sigma = \{a, b\}$, $D = \emptyset$ and $X = \{x_1, x_2\}$. Setting $\Delta = \{\delta_1, \delta_2\}$, $\phi(\delta_1) = ab^2$, $\phi(\delta_2) = a^2 b$, then X is a base if $x_1 = ab^2, x_2 = a^2 b$ but it is not if $x_1 = ab, x_2 = a^2b^2$ since $x_1x_1 = x_2$ holds.

Actually, it is undecidable to determine, given a trace monoid $\mathbb{M}(\Sigma, D)$ and a finite subset $X \subseteq \mathbb{M}(\Sigma, D)$, whether X has the unique decipherability property. This result is obtained by reducing the Post Correspondence Problem, PCP for short, to it. Indeed, an arbitrary instance of PCP is determined by a finite alphabet Σ and a set of $n \geq 1$ pairs of words $(u_1, v_1), \ldots, (u_n, v_n) \in \Sigma^* \times \Sigma^*$. Consider the alphabet $\Delta = \Sigma \cup N$ where $N = \{1, \ldots, n\}$ and define the independence relation $J = \Sigma \times N \cup N \times \Sigma$. Then assign to the previous instance of PCP the instance $X = \{(u_1, 1), \ldots, (u_n, n)\} \cup \{(v_1, 1), \ldots, (v_n, n)\}$ of Unique Decipherability in the trace monoid $\mathbb{M}(\Delta, J)$. It is clear that if the instance of PCP has a solution, i.e., if $u_{i_1} \ldots u_{i_k} = v_{i_1} \ldots v_{i_k}$ holds for some $k > 0$ and some $1 \leq i_1 \ldots i_k \leq n$ then the subset X of $\mathbb{M}(\Delta, J)$ does not have the unique decipherability property since

$$(u_{i_1}, i_1) \ldots (u_{i_k}, i_k) = (v_{i_1}, i_1) \ldots (v_{i_k}, i_k)$$

holds. The converse however only holds if the u's are forced to occur on the left hand side and the v's on the right-hand side. This can be achieved by using a standard technique of markers, cf. [141, 38]. Characterizing the trace monoids for which Unique Decipherability is decidable is still an open question.

Chapter 4

Combinatorics in Trace Monoids II

Gérard Duchamp   Daniel Krob

Institut Blaise Pascal (LITP) – Université Paris 7
2, place Jussieu, 75251 Paris Cedex 05, France
{ged,dk}@litp.ibp.fr

Contents

4.1 Introduction

This chapter is devoted to the presentation of three interesting combinatorial aspects of trace theory: elimination theory for trace monoids, Lyndon traces and shuffle product for traces. It should be noticed that one of our basic motivations through all this chapter was to be always able to make explicit computations with all the notions we introduced. This explains that an important part of our results are in fact effective formulas or relations on which algorithms can be based.

We begin this chapter with some preliminaries. Section 4.3, which is our first main section, deals with *elimination theory* for trace monoids. Very roughly speaking, elimination consists in looking how the study of $\mathbb{M}(\Sigma, I)$ can be related to the study of a trace monoid on a smaller alphabet, obtained by eliminating some letters from Σ. As we will see, a large part of our chapter is organized around this idea of elimination which is presented in Section 4.3.

Section 4.4 is devoted to the study of *Lyndon traces* that were initially introduced by Lalonde in the context of Viennot's theory of heaps of pieces. Lyndon traces are a natural generalization of Lyndon words in the framework of trace monoids. They are also highly connected with elimination theory. We present here how to obtain "good" generalizations of quite all the classical properties of Lyndon words.

In Section 4.5, we consider the notion of *shuffle product* for traces that we define using a notion of binomial coefficient for traces. This shuffle product is the nàtural generalization of the ordinary shuffle product for words. We give some properties of this shuffle product. We also present several methods for computing it.

We end finally this chapter by some exercises, by some remarks on other connected results and with some historical comments.

4.2 Preliminaries

In all this chapter, Σ denotes a *finite* alphabet.

4.2.1 Series over a Monoid

Let K be a semiring and let M be a monoid. A *series* S over M with multiplicities in K is a mapping from M into K. We represent the series S by

$$S = \sum_{m \in M} (S|m)\, m \ ,$$

where $(S|m) \in K$ denotes the image by S of $m \in M$. The set of all series over M with multiplicities in K is denoted by $K \ll M \gg$. A series of special interest is the *characteristic series* $\underline{M}$ of M which is defined by $(\underline{M}|m) = 1_K$ for every $m \in M$. A *polynomial* is a series S of $K \ll M \gg$ which has only finitely many coefficients $(S|m)$ that are not zero. The set of all polynomials is denoted by $K < M >$.

Observe that $K << M >>$ has a natural structure of K-module with addition and external product defined for $S, T \in K << M >>$ and $k \in K$ by setting

$$(S + T|m) = (S|m) + (T|m) \quad \text{and} \quad (k.S|m) = k(S|m)$$

for every $m \in M$. Let us now look whether it is possible to equip $K << M >>$ with a Cauchy product. The natural definition for such a product would be to define ST for $S, T \in K << M >>$ by setting

$$(ST|m) = \sum_{pq=m} (S|p)(T|q) \tag{4.1}$$

for every $m \in M$. Unfortunately this definition does not generally make sense since the set $\{(p, q) \in M \times M, \ pq = m\}$ may not be finite. However relation (4.1) can be used for defining ST in special cases even if the product of two series cannot be defined in general. For instance, we can always give sense to formula (4.1) when S or T is a polynomial. Hence $K < M >$ is always a K-algebra.

Thus, if we want to equip $K << M >>$ with the structure of K-algebra given by the previous definitions, we must suppose that M is a *finite decomposition* monoid, i.e. that the following property holds for every $m \in M$:

$$|\{(p, q) \in M \times M, \ p.q = m\}| < +\infty \ .$$

Observe that every trace monoid is clearly a finite decomposition monoid. Hence $K << \mathbb{M}(\Sigma, I) >>$ is always a K-algebra that we denote by $K << \Sigma, I >>$. The associated sub-K-algebra of polynomials is denoted by $K < \Sigma, I >$.

4.2.2 Factorization of a Monoid

Definition 4.2.1 *Let M be a monoid and let $\mathcal{F} = (M_i)_{i \in I}$ be a family of sub-monoids of M, indexed by some totally ordered set I. The family $\mathcal{F}$ is said to be a factorization of M iff every element m of M can be written in a unique way as*

$$m = m_{i_1} m_{i_2} \ldots m_{i_n}$$

where $m_{i_j} \in M_{i_j}$ for every $j \in [1, n]$ and where $i_1 < i_2 < \ldots < i_n$.

We express the fact that $\mathcal{F} = (M_k)_{k \in K}$ is a factorization of M by writing

$$\underline{M} = \prod_{k \in K} \underline{M_k} \ . \tag{4.2}$$

In fact the above expression is more than a simple notation. Indeed it is easily seen that the family $(M_k)_{k \in K}$ is a factorization of M iff relation (4.2) holds when interpreted as an equality between characteristic series in $\mathbb{Z}[[M]]$.

Example 4.2.2 Let Σ be an alphabet and let $T \subset \Sigma$. Then the free monoid Σ^* can be factorized into two free monoids as

$$\underline{\Sigma^* = \underline{T^*} \underline{((\Sigma - T)T^*)^*}} \ .$$

The previous identity expresses the very simple fact that every word over Σ can be uniquely decomposed as follows: a word over T, the first letter which is not in T, a word over T, the second letter which is not in T, a word over T, $\ldots$

Example 4.2.3 Let ρ_n be the cycle of order n of the symmetric group $\mathfrak{S}_n$ defined by $\rho_n = (1\,2\ldots n)$. Any permutation σ of $\mathfrak{S}_n$ can be written uniquely as

$$\sigma = \rho_n^i \tau \qquad \text{where } i \in [0, n-1] \text{ and } \tau(n) = n \ . \tag{4.3}$$

Indeed, it follows from relation (4.3) that $\sigma(n) = \rho_n^i\,(\tau(n)) = \rho_n^i(n) = \delta(i)$ where $\delta(i) = i$ when $i \in [1, n-1]$ and $\delta(0) = n$. Hence decomposition (4.3) is necessarily unique since we must have $i = \sigma(n)$ when $\sigma(n) \neq n$ and $i = 0$ when $\sigma(n) = n$. Conversely let us define i by these relations. It is then easy to check that the permutation τ defined by $\tau = \rho_n^{-i}\sigma$, satisfies to $\tau(n) = n$.

Relation (4.3) is exactly equivalent to the fact that $\mathfrak{S}_n$ can be factorized as

$$\underline{\mathfrak{S}_n} = \underline{< \rho_n >}\ \underline{\mathfrak{S}_{n-1}} \tag{4.4}$$

where $\mathfrak{S}_{n-1}$ is identified to the subgroup of $\mathfrak{S}_n$ composed of all permutations fixing n and where $< \rho_n >$ is the subgroup (isomorphic to $\mathbb{Z}/n\mathbb{Z}$) of $\mathfrak{S}_n$ generated by ρ_n. Factorization (4.4) can be iterated and leads to the factorization

$$\underline{\mathfrak{S}_n} = \underline{< \rho_n >}\ \underline{< \rho_{n-1} >}\ \cdots\ \underline{< \rho_2 >}$$

of $\mathfrak{S}_n$ into cyclic subgroups of order $n, n-1, \ldots, 2$.

Example 4.2.4 Let $Pla(a, b)$ denote the monoid defined by the presentation

$$Pla(a, b) = <a, b\,;\ aba \equiv baa,\ bba \equiv bab> \ .$$

Thus $Pla(a, b)$, which is called the plactic monoid of order 2, is the quotient monoid of $\{a, b\}^*$ by the congruence $\equiv$ generated by the two above relations. $Pla(a, b)$ can be factorized into the following product of three one-letter free monoids

$$\underline{Pla(a, b)} = \underline{\{ba\}^*}\ \underline{\{a\}^*}\ \underline{\{b\}^*} \ .$$

This property means that every $t \in Pla(a, b)$ can be uniquely written as

$$t = (ba)^i\, a^j\, b^k \ , \tag{4.5}$$

where $i, j, k \in \mathbf{N}$. Observe first that the defining relations of $Pla(a, b)$ exactly say that ba commutes with a and b. Hence ba commutes with every element of $Pla(a, b)$. This property shows that we can group all occurrences of ba in every $t \in Pla(a, b)$ at its beginning, decomposing therefore t as in (4.5).

To prove our factorization result, it remains to see that decomposition (4.5) is unique. Note first that the defining relations of $Pla(a, b)$ are compatible with relation $ba = 1$. Hence we can define a monoid morphism φ from $Pla(a, b)$ into the bicyclic monoid $Bi(a, b)$ which is the quotient monoid of $\{a, b\}^*$ by relation $ba \equiv 1$. If $t \in Pla(a, b)$ is written as in (4.5), we get $\varphi(t) = a^j b^k \in Bi(a, b)$. But it is a classical result (cf. [11] for instance) that every element of $Bi(a, b)$ can be uniquely written as a power of a followed by a power of b. Hence j and k are uniquely associated with t in relation (4.5). Observe finally that the number of a (or of b) is invariant under the defining relations of $Pla(a, b)$. This implies that $i + j$ (or $i + k$), and hence i, is also uniquely associated with t in relation (4.5).

4.2.3 Möbius Function

Let (Σ, I) be an independence alphabet. A trace $t = x_1 \ldots x_n$ is said to be a *clique* iff the letters x_i are different and commute altogether. The empty trace or any letter is always a clique. Note also that cliques are in one-to-one correspondence with the complete subgraphs [1] of the independence graph associated with (Σ, I) (which are also called cliques in the context of graph theory).

Definition 4.2.5 *Let* (Σ, I) *be an independence alphabet. Then the* Möbius *function associated with* (Σ, D) *is the mapping denoted* μ_I *from* $\mathbb{M}(\Sigma, I)$ *into* $\{-1, 0, 1\} \subset \mathbb{Z}$ *which is defined by*

$$\mu_I(t) = \begin{cases} (-1)^n & \text{if } t = x_1 \ldots x_n \text{ is a clique} \\ 0 & \text{otherwise .} \end{cases}$$

The Möbius function can also be identified with a series of $\mathbb{Z} << \Sigma, I >>$, which is here a polynomial of $\mathbb{Z} < \Sigma, I >$ since Σ is finite. In this case, we speak of the *Möbius polynomial* μ_I which is therefore defined by

$$\mu_I = \sum_{t \in \mathbb{M}(\Sigma, I)} \mu_I(t)\, t \; = \sum_{t \text{ clique of length } n} (-1)^n\, t \; .$$

Example 4.2.6 Let $I = \emptyset$. The associated trace monoid $\mathbb{M}(\Sigma, I)$ is exactly the free monoid over Σ. Using Definition 4.2.5, we easily get that

$$\mu_\emptyset = 1 - \sum_{x \in \Sigma} x \; .$$

Example 4.2.7 Let $|\Sigma| = n$ and let $I = \Sigma \times \Sigma$. The corresponding trace monoid $\mathbb{M}(\Sigma, I)$ is the free commutative monoid $\mathbb{N}^n$. Using Definition 4.2.5, we obtain

$$\mu_{\Sigma \times \Sigma} = \sum_{k=0}^{n} (-1)^n \sum_{x_i \neq x_j} x_1 \ldots x_k \; = \prod_{x \in \Sigma} (1 - x) \; .$$

Example 4.2.8 Let $\Sigma = \{a, b, c\}$ and let I be the independence relation defined by

$$a \text{——} b \qquad c$$

---

[1] A graph is said to be *complete* iff every pair of vertices is connected by an edge.

According to Definition 4.2.5, its Möbius polynomial is then equal to

$$\mu_I = 1 - a - b - c + ab .$$

The following result gives an important property of the Möbius polynomial.

Proposition 4.2.9 *Let (Σ, I) be an independence alphabet. The Möbius polynomial is then the inverse in $\mathbb{Z} \ll \Sigma, I \gg$ of the characteristic series of $\mathbb{M}(\Sigma, I)$. Thus*

$$\mu_I \; \underline{\mathbb{M}(\Sigma, I)} = \underline{\mathbb{M}(\Sigma, I)} \; \mu_I = 1$$

We refer to [34] for a proof of this classical result (see also Chapter 5 and Proposition 4.5.19 of Section 4.5.3).

4.2.4   Levi's Lemma for Traces

We present here a generalization for traces of Levi's classical lemma. It will be very useful for studying conjugacy.

Definition 4.2.10 *Let (Σ, I) be an independence alphabet. Two traces t and t' of $\mathbb{M}(\Sigma, I)$ are then said to be* independent *iff the two following conditions are satisfied*

     1. the alphabets of t and t' are disjoint,

     2. every letter of t is independent of every letter of t'.

Such a situation will be denoted by $t \, I \, t'$.

Remark 4.2.11 If t and t' are independent, we always have $t \, t' = t' \, t$.

Remark 4.2.12 The empty trace is independent from every other trace.

Example 4.2.13 Let us consider again the independence alphabet of Example 4.2.8. The independent non-empty traces are then necessarily of the form $t = a^n$ and $t' = b^m$ for some $n, m \geq 1$.

We can now give Levi's lemma for trace monoids.

Proposition 4.2.14 *Let (Σ, I) be an independence alphabet and let x, y, z, t be four traces of $\mathbb{M}(\Sigma, I)$. Then the two following assertions are equivalent*

     1. $xy = zt$

     2. There exists two traces u, v of $\mathbb{M}(\Sigma, I)$ and two independent *traces r, s of $\mathbb{M}(\Sigma, I)$ such that*

$$x = ur, \; y = sv \quad and \quad z = us, \; t = rv .$$

Proof: Observe first that assertion 2 implies clearly assertion 1. Thus we have only to show that $1 \implies 2$. We use an induction on $|x|$. Our result is true when $|x| = 0$ since assertion 2 holds then by taking $u = r = 1$, $s = z$ and $v = t$. Let now x, y, z, t be traces of $\mathbb{M}(\Sigma, I)$ with $|x| \geq 1$ such that $xy = zt$ and let us suppose that our result holds at order $|x| - 1$. Let us then write $x = ax'$ with $a \in \Sigma$. Hence $ax'y = zt$. Two opposite cases can now occur.

a) a is an initial letter of z. Thus $z = az'$ and by cancellability of $\mathbb{M}(\Sigma, I)$, we get $x'y = z't$. Using now the induction hypothesis, we can write $x' = u'r$, $y = sv$, $z' = u's$ and $t = rv$ where u', v, r, s are traces such that $r \; I \; s$. It follows that $x = (au')r$, $y = sv$, $z = (au')s$ and $z = rv$. Hence assertion 2 holds by setting $u = au'$.

b) a is not an initial letter of z. It follows then from relation $ax'y = zt$ that a is an initial letter of t which commutes with every letter of z. It follows in particular that a cannot belong to z. Hence we can write $t = at'$ where $a \; I \; z$. It follows that $ax'y = zat' = azt'$, thus that $x'y = zt'$ according to the cancellability of $\mathbb{M}(\Sigma, I)$. Using now the induction hypothesis, we get $x' = ur'$, $y = sv$, $z = us$ and $t' = r'v$ where u, v, r', s are traces such that $r' \; I \; s$. Note that $au = ua$ since $a \; I \; z$ and since u is a subword of z. It follows that $x = aur' = u(ar')$, $y = sv$, $z = us$ and $t = (ar')v$. From $a \; I \; z$ and from the fact that s is a subword of z, we get $a \; I \; s$. Thus $ar' \; I \; s$. Hence assertion 2 holds by setting $r = ar'$.

This ends our induction and our proof. $\square$

4.3 Elimination for Trace Monoids

4.3.1 Lazard's Factorization

This subsection is devoted to the study of the notion of Lazard's factorization of $\mathbb{M}(\Sigma, I)$. It is the natural generalization to the trace framework of the classical factorization of the free monoid that we presented in Example 4.2.2. This factorization is important since it can be seen as a combinatorial dictionary for similar results concerning other algebraic structures (cf. Section 4.7).

Let us first give some definitions. Let (Σ, I) be an independence alphabet. A subalphabet Z of Σ is said to be *non-commutative* iff $(x, y) \in D$ for every $x \neq y \in Z$. For every $T \subset \Sigma$, we denote by $< T >$ the submonoid of $\mathbb{M}(\Sigma, I)$ generated by T. Note that $< T >$ is isomorphic to the trace monoid $\mathbb{M}(T, I_T)$ where we set $I_T = I \cap T \times T$. Finally the *initial alphabet* of $t \in \mathbb{M}(\Sigma, I)$ is the set denoted $IA(t)$ that consists in the letters $a \in \Sigma$ such that $t = au$ for some $u \in \mathbb{M}(\Sigma, I)$.

We can now introduce one of the very keystone of this chapter.

Definition 4.3.1 *Let* (Σ, I) *be an independence alphabet, let* Z *be a* non-commutative *subalphabet of* Σ *and let* $T = \Sigma - Z$. *Then the* Z-code *is the subset of* $\mathbb{M}(\Sigma, I)$ *denoted* $C_Z(T)$ *which is defined by*

$$C_Z(T) = \{ z.t \mid t \in <T>, \; z \in Z, \; IA(z.t) = \{z\} \} \; .$$

Example 4.3.2 Let $I = \emptyset$ be the independence relation associated with the free monoid $\mathbb{M}(\Sigma, I) = \Sigma^*$. Every subset of Σ is then non-commutative and the condition on the initial alphabet involved in Definition 4.3.1 has no importance. Thus

$$C_Z(T) = Z\,T^*$$

for every $Z \subset \Sigma$ where we denoted $T = \Sigma - Z$ as in Definition 3.1.

Example 4.3.3 Let $I = \Sigma \times \Sigma$ be the independence relation associated with the free commutative monoid $\mathbb{M}(\Sigma, I) = \mathbb{N}^\Sigma$. In this case, the only non-commutative subalphabets of Σ are the one-element sets $T = \{x\}$ where x is a letter of Σ. Moreover the condition on the initial alphabet of the elements of a Z-code $C_Z(T)$ is also very restrictive and imply that we here have

$$C_Z(T) = \{x\}$$

for every $Z = \{x\}$ where $x \in \Sigma$.

Example 4.3.4 Let (Σ, I) be the independence alphabet defined by

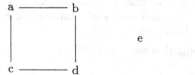

In this case, $Z = \{a, d\}$ is for instance a non-commutative subalphabet and the corresponding Z-code is equal to

$$C_Z(T) = ae(b + c + e)^* \cup de(b + c + e)^* \cup a \cup d$$

as the reader will easily check, using Definition 4.3.1.

We can now give our first main result that shows the role of Z-codes.

Theorem 4.3.5 Let (Σ, I) be an independence alphabet, let Z be a non-commutative subalphabet of Σ and let $T = \Sigma - Z$. Then every trace t of $\mathbb{M}(\Sigma, I)$ can be written in a unique way as

$$t = d\, c_n\, c_{n-1} \ldots c_1 \tag{4.6}$$

where every c_i belongs to $C_Z(T)$ and where d belongs to $<T>$.

Proof: We first prove the existence of decomposition (4.6) by induction on $|t|$. Our result is clear when $|t|$ is 0 or 1. Let $n \geq 2$ and let us suppose that any trace t with $|t| < n$ can be decomposed as in (4.6). Let now t be a trace of length n. We can write $t = at'$ with $a \in \Sigma$ and $|t'| = n - 1$. Using the induction hypothesis, we get

$$t' = d'\, c'_n\, c'_{n-1} \ldots c'_1 \tag{4.7}$$

where every c_i' belongs to $C_Z(T)$ and where $d' \in <T>$. If $a \in T$, it is clear using (4.7) that $t = at'$ still has a decomposition of type (4.6). Let us suppose now that $a \notin T$, i.e. that $a \in Z$. Two cases are to be considered.

a) $IA(ad') = \{a\}$: then $c_{n+1}' = ad' \in C_Z(T)$ according to Definition 4.3.1. Using (4.7), it immediately follows that $t = c_{n+1}' c_n' \ldots c_1'$ is a decomposition of type (4.6).

b) $IA(ad') \neq \{a\}$: we must then have $d' = bd''$ with some letter $b \in T$ such that $(a, b) \in I$. Thus $ad' = bad''$. It follows that t has an initial letter in T and our study showed that the conclusion was immediate in this case.

Let us now prove that decomposition (4.6) is unique. We again use an induction on the length of t. The unambiguity of decomposition (4.6) is clear when $|t|$ is 0 or 1. Let us then suppose that the unambiguity is proved for any t with $|t| < n$ for some $n \geq 2$. Let now t be a trace of length n which is decomposed in the two ways

$$t = d\, c_n\, c_{n-1} \ldots c_1 \quad \text{and} \quad t = d'\, c_m'\, c_{m-1}' \ldots c_1' \qquad (4.8)$$

with respect to (4.6). Let us suppose that $n = 0$. There are then no letters of Z in t : hence m must be equal to 0 and $d = d'$, proving therefore our unambiguity result. Thus we can suppose that $n, m \geq 1$. Let us now suppose that $d \neq 1$. We can then write $d = au$ with $a \in T$. Hence a belongs to the initial alphabet of t. But it follows from relations (4.8), from Definition 4.3.1 and from the non-commutativity of Z that an initial letter of t is either an initial letter of d' or the unique initial letter of c_m' which is in Z. Hence a is necessarily an initial letter of d' since $a \in T$. Thus $d' = au'$. By cancellability of $\mathbb{M}(\Sigma, I)$, we get

$$u\, c_n\, c_{n-1} \ldots c_1 = u'\, c_m'\, c_{m-1}' \ldots c_1' \; .$$

We can then apply our induction hypothesis to this last relation in order to conclude that $n = m$, $c_i = c_i'$ for every $i \in [1, n]$ and $d = d'$.

Let us finally suppose that d is empty. The previous argument shows that d' is also empty. Then we have

$$t = c_n\, c_{n-1} \ldots c_1 = c_m'\, c_{m-1}' \ldots c_1' \; .$$

Definition 4.3.1 and the non-commutativity of Z imply again that the initial alphabet of t is necessarily reduced to the unique initial letter of c_n. By symmetry, the unique initial letters of c_n and c_m' must coincide. Hence $c_n = zd$ and $c_m' = zd'$ with $d, d' \in <T>$ and $z \in Z$. By cancellability of $\mathbb{M}(\Sigma, I)$, we immediately get

$$d\, c_n\, c_{n-1} \ldots c_1 = d'\, c_m'\, c_{m-1}' \ldots c_1' \; .$$

We can apply our induction hypothesis to the above trace and thus obtain that $n = m$, $c_i = c_i'$ for every $i \leq n - 1$ and $d = d'$. It follows then from these relations that $c_i = c_i'$ for every $i \in [1, n]$. $\qquad \square$

Remark 4.3.6 The non-commutativity condition on Z of Definition 4.3.1 is clearly necessary for obtaining the unambiguity of decomposition (4.6).

Remark 4.3.7 The unambiguity of decomposition (4.6) immediately implies that every trace in $C_Z(T)^*$ can be uniquely decomposed as a product of elements of $C_Z(T)$. In other words, the submonoid $C_Z(T)^*$ of $\mathbb{M}(\Sigma, I)$ generated by $C_Z(T)$ is *free* with basis $C_Z(T)$. This explains our terminology of Z-code.

Theorem 4.3.5 equivalently claims that every trace $t \in \mathbb{M}(\Sigma, I)$ can be uniquely decomposed as a product of an element of $\mathbb{M}(T, I_T)$ with an element of $C_Z(T)^*$. Thus we can express Theorem 4.3.5 by writing that $\mathbb{M}(\Sigma, I)$ can be factorized as

$$\underline{\mathbb{M}(\Sigma, I)} \;=\; \underline{\mathbb{M}(T, I_T)}\; \underline{C_Z(T)^*} \tag{4.9}$$

which is called *Lazard factorization* of $\mathbb{M}(\Sigma, I)$.

Example 4.3.8 When $I = \emptyset$, it is easy to check that factorization (4.9) is exactly the factorization of Σ^* given in Example 4.2.2.

Example 4.3.9 Let us consider again the independence alphabet (Σ, I) of Example 4.3.4. The Lazard factorization of the associated trace monoid is then

$$\underline{\mathbb{M}(\Sigma, I)} = \underline{(b + c + e)^*}\; \underline{((a + d) + (a + d)e(b + c + e)^*)^*}\;.$$

$\mathbb{M}(\Sigma, I)$ is here factorized into two free monoids.

Observe that a trace monoid over a smaller alphabet appears at the left of relation (4.9). It is therefore natural to decompose it according to the same process and so on. But, before studying this construction, let us give the following definition.

Definition 4.3.10 *Let (Σ, I) be an independence alphabet. Then a chromatic partition of Σ is a partition $(\Sigma_i)_{i=1,N}$ of Σ into non-commutative subalphabets.*

Remark 4.3.11 The above terminology comes from the fact that a chromatic partition is equivalent to a colouring of the independence graph in such a way that two adjacent letters are coloured with different colours.

We can now give our next result which immediately follows by inductively iterating Lazard's factorization on the trace monoid of the left side of relation (4.9).

Corollary 4.3.12 *Let $(\Sigma_i)_{i=1,N}$ be a chromatic partition of some independence alphabet (Σ, I). Then $\mathbb{M}(\Sigma, I)$ can be factorized in the product of free monoids*

$$\underline{\mathbb{M}(\Sigma, I)} \;=\; \underline{C_{\Sigma_N}(T_N)^*}\; \cdots\; \underline{C_{\Sigma_1}(T_1)^*} \tag{4.10}$$

where we set $T_k = \bigcup_{j > k} \Sigma_j$ for every $k \in [1, N]$.

Corollary 4.3.12 allows us to associate with every chromatic partition a great variety of normal forms for representing traces inside Σ^*. Indeed it suffices to fix a normal form for all Z-codes involved in a factorization of type (4.10) in order to obtain normal forms for traces of $\mathbb{M}(\Sigma, I)$. Using this method, we can get normal forms that do not coincide nor with the Cartier-Foata, neither with the lexicographic normal forms as shown by the following example (see also Exercise 4.6.4).

Example 4.3.13 Let $\Sigma = \{a, b, c, d, e\}$ that we equip with the independence relation I defined by the independence graph

a ——————— b ——————— c ——————— d ——————— e

The family $(\Sigma_k)_{k=1,2,3}$ defined by $\Sigma_1 = \{a, c\}$, $\Sigma_2 = \{b, d\}$ and $\Sigma_3 = \{e\}$ is a chromatic partition of Σ. The factorization given by Corollary 4.3.12 is then

$$\underline{\mathbb{M}(\Sigma, I)} = \underline{e^*} \ (d + be^*)^* \ (a + a(d + e)e^*(d + be^*)^* + c(e + eb(b + d)^*)^*)^* \ . \quad (4.11)$$

We can interpret these expressions as rational expressions in Σ^*. Hence they give us normal forms for traces of $\mathbb{M}(\Sigma, I)$ that are different from the Cartier-Foata and from the lexicographic normal forms as we shall see. Let $t = edade \in \mathbb{M}(\Sigma, I)$. Its normal form given by (4.11) is $\tau = (e)(d)(ade) \in \Sigma^*$. τ cannot be in normal lexicographic form since $\tau \equiv_I (de)(ade) \equiv_I (e)(d)(a)(ed)$. Indeed if it were the case, the last computations show that we would both have $e < d$ and $d < e$. On the other hand, let $t' = adbc \in \mathbb{M}(\Sigma, I)$. Its normal form given by (4.11) is $\tau' = (adb)(c) \in \Sigma^*$. But the Cartier-Foata normal forms of t are exactly $(a)(dc)(b)$ and $(a)(cd)(b)$ according to the way Σ is ordered. This shows that τ' is not in Cartier-Foata normal form.

It is interesting to see that the chromatic number [2] of the independence graph of (Σ, I) can be interpreted in terms of factorizations into free monoids.

Proposition 4.3.14 *The chromatic number $\gamma(I)$ of the independence graph associated with an independence alphabet (Σ, I) is the minimal number of free monoids that can be involved in a factorization of $\mathbb{M}(\Sigma, I)$ into free monoids.*

Proof: Note first that $\mathbb{M}(\Sigma, I)$ can be factorized as a product of $\gamma(I)$ free monoids according to Corollary 4.3.12 and Theorem 4.3.5. Let us now consider a factorization

$$\underline{\mathbb{M}(\Sigma, I)} = \underline{M_1} \ \dots \ \underline{M_N} \ , \quad (4.12)$$

of $\mathbb{M}(\Sigma, I)$ into N free monoids $(M_k)_{k=1,N}$. It clearly suffices to prove that $N \geq \gamma(I)$ in order to conclude to our result. Note now that factorization (4.12) imply that every $x \in \Sigma$ belongs to a unique submonoid $M_{k(x)}$ of $\mathbb{M}(\Sigma, I)$ for some $k(x) \in [1, N]$. Let us denote by $k(\Sigma)$ the subset of $[1, N]$ consisting in the integers k such that $x \in M_k$ for some $x \in \Sigma$. Let us now define

---

[2] The *chromatic number* of a graph G is the minimal number of colours required for colouring the vertices of G in such a way that two adjacent vertices are coloured with distinct colours.

$$\Sigma_k = \{ x \in \Sigma, \ x \in M_k \}$$

for every $k \in k(\Sigma)$. Σ_k is in fact a non-commutative subalphabet of Σ for every $k \in k(\Sigma)$. Indeed, if it were not the case, we would have two distinct letters $x, y \in \Sigma$ that belong to the same free monoid M_k and such that $(x, y) \in I$. Hence $x = t^n$ and $y = t^m$ for some $t \in \mathbb{M}(\Sigma, I)$ since two elements of a free monoid commute iff they are power of a same element. By an immediate length argument, we get $|t| = n = m = 1$ and hence $x = y$. This contradiction shows that Σ_k is always non-commutative and that the family $(\Sigma_k)_{k \in k(\Sigma)}$ is a chromatic partition of Σ. Thus $N \geq |k(\Sigma)| \geq \gamma(I)$ according to Remark 4.3.11. $\square$

4.3.2   Some Properties of Z-Codes

In Section 4.3.1, we saw the importance of Z-codes for factorization properties of $\mathbb{M}(\Sigma, I)$. They also play an important role in the study of Lyndon traces. Therefore it is useful to know how to compute Z-codes. We now present two such methods.

Proposition 4.3.15 *Let (Σ, I) be an independence alphabet, let Z be a non-commutative subalphabet of Σ, let $T = \Sigma - Z$ and let μ_I and μ_{I_T} be the Möbius polynomials of $\mathbb{M}(\Sigma, I)$ and $\mathbb{M}(T, I_T)$. Then the characteristic series of $C_Z(T)$ is given by*

$$\underline{C_Z(T)} = 1 - \mu_I \ \mu_{I_T}^{-1} \ .$$

Proof: Relation (4.9) can be interpreted as an equality between characteristic series in $\mathbb{Z} \ll \Sigma, I \gg$. Taking the inverse in both sides of this equality, we get the relation

$$\underline{\mathbb{M}(\Sigma, I)}^{-1} = (\underline{C_Z(T)^*})^{-1} \ \underline{\mathbb{M}(T, I_T)}^{-1}$$

that holds in $\mathbb{Z} \ll \Sigma, I \gg$. But $(\underline{C_Z(T)^*})^{-1} = 1 - \underline{C_Z(T)}$ since $C_Z(T)^*$ is a free monoid of basis $C_Z(T)$. Using now this relation and Proposition 4.2.9, we get

$$\mu_I = (1 - \underline{C_Z(T)}) \ \mu_{I_T}$$

that holds in $\mathbb{Z} \ll \Sigma, I \gg$. It is now immediate to conclude. $\square$

Proposition 4.3.15 is useful when one wants to compute only the first traces (with respect to length) in the Taylor expansion of a Z-code. It suffices indeed to do a division of two polynomials of $\mathbb{Z} < \Sigma, I >$ in order to get the desired expansion.

Example 4.3.16 Let (Σ, I) be the independence alphabet defined by

$$a \ \text{———————} \ b \ \text{———————} \ c \qquad\qquad d$$

The subalphabet $Z = \{a, d\}$ is non-commutative. Proposition 4.3.15 gives us then

$$\underline{C_Z(T)} = 1 - (1 - a - b - c - d + ab + bc)(1 - b - c + bc)^{-1}$$

according to Definition 4.2.5. Computing now the quotient of the two polynomials of $\mathbb{Z} < \Sigma, I >$ involved in this last formula, we get

$$\underline{C_Z(T)} = a + d + db + dc + ac + dcb + dcc + dbb + acc + \ \ldots$$

where the reverse Euclidean division was made up to the order 3.

Let us now observe that we can write

$$C_Z(T) = \bigcup_{z \in Z} C_{\{z\}}(T) \tag{4.13}$$

for every Z-code $C_Z(T)$, where the denotation $C_{\{z\}}(T)$ is a slight extension of Definition 4.3.1 [3] and means

$$C_{\{z\}}(T) = \{\, z.t,\ t \in <T>,\ IA(z.t) = \{z\}\,\}\ .$$

We also call Z-code such a language since it is clearly a Z-code on a smaller alphabet. Relation (4.13) shows then that we can restrict us to the case where Z is a one-element set for obtaining exact expressions for Z-codes. This last problem is solved recursively by the following proposition.

Proposition 4.3.17 *Let (Σ, I) be an independence alphabet, let Z be a non-commutative subalphabet of Σ, let z be a letter of Z and let $T = \Sigma - Z$. Then only the two following opposite cases can occur*

- *every letter of T commute with z. We then have*

$$C_{\{z\}}(T) = \{z\}\ ;$$

- *there exists a non-commutative subalphabet U of T such that every letter of U is dependent of z. We then have*

$$C_{\{z\}}(T) = C_{\{z\}}(T - U)\ (C_U(T - U))^*\ .$$

Proof: The two above cases are clearly the only ones that can occur and they are obviously opposite. The first case follows from Definition 4.3.1. Thus let us suppose now that the second case holds. We can then consider Lazard's factorization

$$\underline{\mathbb{M}(T, I_T)} = \underline{\mathbb{M}(T - U, I_{T-U})}\ C_U(T - U)^* \tag{4.14}$$

of $\mathbb{M}(T, I_T)$. Let $t = z.u \in C_{\{z\}}(T)$ where $u \in <T>$ and where $IA(z.u) = \{z\}$. We can then decompose u according to relation (4.14). Thus we can write $t = zvc$ where $c \in C_U(T - U)^*$ and $v \in <T - U>$. Observe now that the condition on the initial alphabet of t immediately implies that $IA(zv)$ is also reduced to z. Hence zv belongs to $C_{\{z\}}(T - U)$. Thus we proved that

$$C_{\{z\}}(T) \subset C_{\{z\}}(T - U)\ C_U(T - U)^*\ . \tag{4.15}$$

To conclude, it suffices to show that the other inclusion also holds. Let therefore t be a trace in $C_{\{z\}}(T - U)\ C_U(T - U)^*$. We can then write

$$t = c\, c_n\, c_{n-1} \ldots c_1 \tag{4.16}$$

---

[3] As one can see, the only difference with Definition 4.3.1 is that one does not consider here all the letters of Z as possible initial letters of $C_{\{z\}}(T)$, but only one which is distinguished.

where every $c_i \in C_U(T - U)$ and where $c \in C_{\{z\}}(T - U)$. Relation (4.16) clearly shows that $t \in z\, \mathbb{M}(T, I_T)$. Hence to prove that $t \in C_{\{z\}}(T)$, it suffices to see that the initial alphabet of t is reduced to z. But relation (4.16) and the structure of Z-codes show that an initial letter of t is necessarily an initial letter of some c_i (that belongs to U) or the initial letter z of c. The non-commutativity of $U \cup \{z\}$ implies then that only the initial letter of c, i.e. z, can be the initial letter of t. Thus t belongs to $C_{\{z\}}(T)$. This proves the converse inclusion of (4.15). $\square$

Example 4.3.18 Let us consider the alphabet $\Sigma = \{\, a_{i,j},\ i, j \in \{-1, 0, 1\}\,\}$ equipped with the independence relation defined by the independence graph

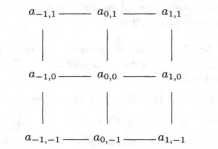

Let us compute the Z-code $C_{a_{0,0}}(T)$ where we set $Z = \{a_{0,0}\}$ and $T = \Sigma - Z$. Applying Proposition 4.3.17 with $U = \{a_{-1,-1}, a_{1,1}, a_{-1,1}, a_{1,-1}\}$, we obtain

$$C_{a_{0,0}} = C_{a_{0,0}}(V)\, C_U(V)^* = a_{0,0}\, C_U(V)^*$$

where $V = \{a_{0,1}, a_{1,0}, a_{0,-1}, a_{-1,0}\}$. Using relation (4.13) and the symmetry of the problem, the computation of $C_U(V)$ can be reduced for instance to the computation of $C_{a_{-1,1}}(V)$. Using again Proposition 4.3.17 with $W = \{a_{1,0}, a_{0,-1}\}$, we get

$$C_{a_{-1,1}}(V) = C_{a_{-1,1}}(V - W)\, C_W(V - W)^* = a_{-1,1}\, C_W(V - W)^* .$$

Going back to Definition 4.3.1, we easily get $C_W(V - W) = (a_{1,0} + a_{0,-1})\,(a_{0,1} + a_{-1,0})^*$. We can now use all the previous relations in order to obtain the expression

$$a_{0,0}\Big(a_{-1,1}\big((a_{1,0} + a_{0,-1})(a_{0,1} + a_{-1,0})^*\big)^* \cup a_{1,1}\big((a_{-1,0} + a_{0,-1})(a_{0,1} + a_{1,0})^*\big)^* \cup$$

$$a_{-1,-1}\big((a_{1,0} + a_{0,1})(a_{0,-1} + a_{-1,0})^*\big)^* \cup a_{1,-1}\big((a_{0,1} + a_{-1,0})(a_{1,0} + a_{0,-1})^*\big)^*\Big)^*$$

for the Z-code $C_{a_{0,0}}(T)$.

Proposition 4.3.17 and relation (4.13) clearly show that every Z-code is rational. They also give us a recursive way for computing a rational expression for any Z-code. However Z-codes are in fact recognizable and even star-free (cf. [129]) in a very low level of Straubing's hierarchy as shows the following proposition.

Proposition 4.3.19 *Let* (Σ, I) *be an independence alphabet, let* Z *be a non-commutative subalphabet of* Σ *and let* $T = \Sigma - Z$. *Then the* Z-*code* $C_Z(T)$ *belongs to the boolean closure of the trace languages*

$$x \, \mathbb{M}(\Sigma, I), \quad x \, \mathbb{M}(\Sigma, I) \, y \, \mathbb{M}(\Sigma, I)$$

where x *and* y *denote letters of* Σ.

Proof: According to relation (4.13), we can restrict us to prove our result when $Z = \{z\}$ is a one-element set. According to Definition 4.3.1, the Z-code $C_{\{z\}}(T)$ consists in this case in the traces that end with an element of $\mathbb{M}(T, I_T)$ and that begin by z, but not by another letter. In other terms, we have

$$C_{\{z\}}(T) = z \, \mathbb{M}(T, I_T) \; - \; \bigcup_{x \neq z} x \, \mathbb{M}(\Sigma, I) \ .$$

But the language $z \, \mathbb{M}(T, I_T)$ consists in the traces of $\mathbb{M}(\Sigma, I)$ that begin by z and whose other letters are not in Z. This shows that we have

$$z \, \mathbb{M}(T, I_T) = z \, \mathbb{M}(\Sigma, I) \; - \; \bigcup_{x \in Z} z \, \mathbb{M}(\Sigma, I) \, x \, \mathbb{M}(\Sigma, I) \ .$$

Our proposition now immediately follows from the two above relations. □

It clearly follows from Proposition 4.3.19 that every Z-code is star-free and recognizable (since recognizable trace languages are stable by all boolean operations and since all languages appearing in Proposition 4.3.19 are clearly recognizable).

4.4 Lyndon Traces

We deal in this section with Lyndon traces, which are a generalization of the classical notion of Lyndon word. Lyndon traces are also highly related with elimination results for $\mathbb{M}(\Sigma, I)$. However we first say some words on conjugacy and primitivity for traces that are two important notions used for defining Lyndon traces.

4.4.1 Transposition and Conjugacy

The classical notion of conjugacy splits here into the two following concepts (equivalent in the free case).

Definition 4.4.1 *Let* (Σ, I) *be an independence alphabet. Two traces* t, t' *are said to be* transposed *iff there exists two traces* $u, v \in \mathbb{M}(\Sigma, I)$ *such that*

$$t = uv \quad and \quad t' = vu \ . \tag{4.17}$$

A trace t *is said to be* conjugated *of* t' *iff there exists* $u \in \mathbb{M}(\Sigma, I)$ *such that*

$$tu = ut' \ . \tag{4.18}$$

Remark 4.4.2 Transposition is clearly a symmetric relation.

Remark 4.4.3 Conjugacy is transitive. Indeed if t is conjugated of t' and if t' is conjugated of $t"$, there exists then $u, v \in \mathbb{M}(\Sigma, I)$ such that $tu = ut'$ and $t'v = vt"$. It follows that t is conjugated of $t"$ since we can write $tuv = ut'v = uvt"$.

It clearly follows from the identities $(uv)u = u(vu)$ and $(vu)v = v(uv)$ that two transposed traces are always conjugated, one of the other. However the following example shows that the converse does not hold in general (contrary to the free case).

Example 4.4.4 Let $\Sigma = \{a, b, c\}$ equipped with the independence relation of Example 4.2.8. Then $t = aacbb$ is for instance conjugated of $t' = abcab$ since

$$t(aacab) = aacaabbcab = (aacab)t' .$$

But these two traces are not transposed since it is easy to check that $abbca$, $aabcb$, $aabbc$, $caabb$, $bcaab$, $acbba$ are the only traces obtained by transposition from t'.

The two notions of Definition 4.4.1 are connected. Indeed we shall see that conjugacy is the transitive closure of transposition. To this end, let us first give.

Proposition 4.4.5 Let (Σ, I) be an independence relation and let t, t' be two traces of $\mathbb{M}(\Sigma, I)$. Then the two following assertions are equivalent

> 1. t is conjugated of t'.
>
> 2. There exists a family $(z_i)_{i=1,n}$ of traces with $z_i I z_j$ for every $i < j - 1$ in $[1, n]$ such that
> $$t = z_1 z_2 \ldots z_n \quad and \quad t' = z_n z_{n-1} \ldots z_1 .$$

Proof: We first show that $2 \implies 1$. Thus let us suppose that assertion 2 holds. Let us then consider the trace $z(k)$ defined by

$$z(k) = (z_1 z_2 \ldots z_k)(z_1 z_2 \ldots z_{k-1}) \ldots (z_1 z_2) z_1$$

for every $k \in [0, n-1]$. Let us now prove by induction on k that we have

$$(z_1 z_2 \ldots z_{k+1}) z(k) = z(k)(z_{k+1} z_k \ldots z_1) \tag{4.19}$$

for every $k \in [0, n-1]$. This relation is obvious for $k = 0$ or $k = 1$. Let us now suppose that $k \geq 2$ and that relation (4.19) holds at order $k - 1$. Observe first that

$$(z_1 z_2 \ldots z_{k+1}) z(k) = (z_1 z_2 \ldots z_k) z_{k+1} (z_1 z_2 \ldots z_k) z(k-1) .$$

Using the induction hypothesis at order $k - 1$, it immediately follows that

$$(z_1 z_2 \ldots z_{k+1}) z(k) = (z_1 z_2 \ldots z_k) z_{k+1} z(k-1)(z_k z_{k-1} \ldots z_1) .$$

Note finally that $z_{k+1} I z(k-1)$ since $z_i I z_{k+1}$ for every $i < k$ by hypothesis. Hence it clearly follows from the last relation that

$$\begin{aligned} (z_1 z_2 \ldots z_{k+1}) z(k) &= (z_1 z_2 \ldots z_k) z(k-1) z_{k+1}(z_k z_{k-1} \ldots z_1) \\ &= z(k)(z_{k+1} z_k \ldots z_1) . \end{aligned}$$

Thus this ends our induction. It now immediately follows from relation (4.19) with $k = n - 1$ that t is conjugated of t'. Hence we proved that $2 \implies 1$.

Let us now prove $1 \implies 2$. In fact, we show the stronger following result.

Lemma 4.4.6 *Let (Σ, I) be an independence alphabet and let t, t' two traces of $\mathbb{M}(\Sigma, I)$ such that $tu = ut'$. Then there exists a trace z that commutes with t' and a family $(z_i)_{i=1,n}$ of traces with $z_i I z_j$ for every $i < j - 1$ in $[1, n]$ such that*

$$t = z_1 z_2 \ldots z_n, \ t' = z_n z_{n-1} \ldots z_1 \ \ and$$

$$u = (z_1 z_2 \ldots z_{n-1})(z_1 z_2 \ldots z_{n-2}) \ \ldots \ (z_1 z_2) z_1 z \ .$$

Proof: We prove this lemma by induction on $|t| + |u|$. Let then t, t' be two traces such that $tu = ut'$ with some $u \in \mathbb{M}(\Sigma, I)$. Our result is clearly true when $|t| + |u| = 0$ since $t = t' = u = 1$ in this case: thus we get our conclusion by setting $n = 0$ and $z = 1$. Let us suppose now that $|t| + |u| \geq 1$ and that our lemma is proved at any order strictly less than $|t| + |u|$. According to Proposition 4.2.14, there exists then four traces p, q, r, s with $r I s$ such that

$$t = pr \ u = sq = ps \ \ and \ \ t' = rq \ . \tag{4.20}$$

We have $ps = sq$ and $|p| + |s| < |u| + |t|$ since $|u| + |t| = |p| + |s| + |t'|$ by an easy computation and since $t' \neq 1$ by hypothesis. Hence we can apply our induction hypothesis to the relation $ps = sq$. Thus there exists a trace z commuting with q and a family of traces $(z_i)_{i=1,n}$ with $z_i I z_j$ when $i < j - 1$ in $[1, n]$, such that

$$p = z_1 z_2 \ldots z_n, \ q = z_n z_{n-1} \ldots z_1 \ , \tag{4.21}$$

$$\text{and} \ \ s = (z_1 z_2 \ldots z_{n-1})(z_1 z_2 \ldots z_{n-2}) \ \ldots \ (z_1 z_2) z_1 z \ . \tag{4.22}$$

Let us now set $z_{n+1} = r$. It follows then from relations (4.20) and (4.21) that

$$t = z_1 z_2 \ldots z_{n+1} \ \ and \ \ t' = z_{n+1} z_n \ldots z_1 \ . \tag{4.23}$$

Moreover we easily get that $z_i I z_{n+1}$ for every $i < n$ using relation (4.22) and the fact that $r I s$. Hence the traces z_i involved in relation (4.23) satisfy to $z_i I z_j$ for every $i < j - 1$ in $[1, n + 1]$. Relations (4.20), (4.21) and (4.22) also show that

$$u = (z_1 z_2 \ldots z_n)(z_1 z_2 \ldots z_{n-1}) \ \ldots \ (z_1 z_2) z_1 z \ .$$

We now immediately get that $r I z$ from the fact that $r I s$ and from relation (4.22). Hence, since z commutes with q by hypothesis, it easily follows from relation (4.20) that z commutes with t'. $\square$

Lemma 4.4.6 clearly implies that $1 \Longrightarrow 2$. This ends therefore our proof. $\square$

Remark 4.4.7 *Using relation (4.19), one can easily check that $tu = ut'$ when t, t', u are taken as in Lemma 4.4.6. Hence Lemma 4.4.6 gives the exact structure of all traces t, t', u such that $tu = ut'$.*

Corollary 4.4.8 *Let (Σ, I) be an independence alphabet and let t, t' be two traces of $\mathbb{M}(\Sigma, I)$. Then the two following assertions are equivalent*

   1. t is conjugated of t'.

2. There exists a finite sequence $(t_i)_{i=1,...,n}$ *of traces with* $t_1 = t$, $t_n = t'$ *and such that* t_i *and* t_{i+1} *are transposed for every* $i \in [1, n-1]$. [4]

Proof: Let us first show that $1 \implies 2$. Thus let us suppose that t is conjugated of t'. According to Proposition 4.4.5, there exists a family $(z_i)_{i=1,n}$ of traces with $z_i I z_j$ for every $i < j - 1$ in $[1, n]$ such that

$$t = z_1 z_2 \ldots z_n \quad \text{and} \quad t' = z_n z_{n-1} \ldots z_1 .$$

It follows that we can go from t to t' by the sequence of transpositions

$$t_1 = t, \ t_2 = z_n (z_1 \ldots z_{n-1}) = z_1 \ldots z_{n-2} (z_n z_{n-1}), \ \ldots ,$$
$$t_{n-1} = (z_n \ldots z_3) z_1 z_2 = z_1 (z_n \ldots z_2), \ t_n = t'$$

where one transposes at step i the trace $z_n \ldots z_{n-i+1}$. Hence property 2 holds.

On the other hand, $2 \implies 1$ easily follows from the fact that conjugacy is transitive and that transposed traces are always conjugated.   □

Remark 4.4.9 It follows from Corollary 4.4.8 that conjugacy is an equivalence relation, which is the transitive closure of transposition. Hence we now more simply say that two traces t, t' are conjugated when one is conjugated of the other.

Remark 4.4.10 One can always go from a trace to a transposed one by a sequence of *elementary transpositions*, i.e. of transpositions of the form ua and au where $a \in \Sigma$. Indeed if $v = a_1 \ldots a_n$ where every $a_i \in \Sigma$, one can go from $t = uv$ to $t' = vu$ by the sequence of elementary transpositions given by

$$t = t_1 = uv, \ t_2 = a_n(ua_1 \ldots a_{n-1}), \ldots, \ t_n = a_2 \ldots a_n(ua_1), \ t_{n+1} = t' = vu$$

where one only transposes at step i the letter a_{n-i+1}. It follows then from Corollary 4.4.8 that two traces are conjugated iff one can go from one to the other by a finite sequence of elementary transpositions.

4.4.2   Primitivity and Strong Primitivity

Another problem happens with the notion of primitivity. Indeed this classical concept also splits here into two distinct notions (equivalent in the free case).

Definition 4.4.11 *Let* (Σ, I) *be an independence alphabet and let* t *be a non-empty trace of* $\mathbb{M}(\Sigma, I)$. *Then* t *is said to be* primitive *iff we have*

$$t = u^n \quad \text{with } u \in \mathbb{M}(\Sigma, I) \text{ and } n \in \mathbb{N} \quad \implies \quad n = 1 \text{ and } t = u .$$

In the same way, t *is said to be* strongly primitive *iff we have*

$$t = uv = vu \quad \text{with some } u, v \in \mathbb{M}(\Sigma, I) \quad \implies \quad u = 1 \text{ or } v = 1 .$$

---

[4] In other words, this second condition means that one can go from t to t' by a finite sequence of transpositions.

Let us now recall a useful definition. Let (Σ, I) be an independence alphabet and let D be the associated dependence relation. A trace $t \in \mathbb{M}(\Sigma, I)$ is then said to be *connected* iff its alphabet is a connected subgraph of the dependence graph.

Proposition 4.4.12 *Let (Σ, I) be an independence alphabet and let t be a trace in $\mathbb{M}(\Sigma, I)$. Then the two following assertions are equivalent*

    1. t is strongly primitive.

    2. t is primitive and connected.

Proof: We first show that $1 \implies 2$. Thus let t be a strongly primitive trace. Let us suppose that t is not primitive. Hence $t = u^n$ with $n \geq 2$ and $u \neq 1$. Thus $t = uu^{n-1} = u^{n-1}u$. But since t is strongly primitive, u or u^{n-1} must be empty. Hence $u = 1$. This contradiction shows that t is primitive. On the other hand, let us suppose that t is not connected. This means that the alphabet of t can be divided into two disjoint non-empty subsets T and T' such that every letter of T commutes with every letter of T'. Taking the projections t_T and $t_{T'}$ of t on T and T' which are non-empty, we immediately get $t = t_T t_{T'} = t_{T'} t_T$, which is not possible since t is strongly primitive. Hence t must be connected.

Let us now prove that $2 \implies 1$. Let then t be a connected primitive trace and let us suppose that t is not strongly primitive. Hence we can write $t = uv = vu$ with some non-empty traces u and v. Proposition 4.2.14 shows then that there exists four traces p, q, r, s with $r \, I \, s$ such that $u = pr = rq$ and $v = ps = sq$. Before going further, let us show the lemma.

Lemma 4.4.13 *Let (Σ, I) be an independence alphabet and let t, t' and u be three traces of $\mathbb{M}(\Sigma, I)$ such that $tu = ut'$. Then every letter of u either is independent of t, or belongs to the alphabet of t.*

Proof: We prove this lemma by induction on the length of u. There is nothing to prove when $u = 1$. Let us now suppose that $|u| \geq 1$ and that our lemma holds at order $|u| - 1$. We can then write $u = av$ with $a \in \Sigma$. Since $tav = avt'$, a is an initial letter of tav. Two cases can now occur.

a) a does not belong to t. In this case, a must be independent of t and we clearly get $tv = vt'$. Hence we can apply our induction hypothesis to v and it is then easy to conclude that u satisfies the properties of our lemma.

b) a is an initial letter of t. Hence $t = at$" and the previous relation gives us here $(t"a)v = vt'$. Since the alphabets of t and of $t"a$ are the same, we can clearly conclude by applying our induction hypothesis to this last relation. $\qquad\square$

Let now R be the set consisting in the letters of r that do not belong to p. It easily follows from previous relations that $t = prps$. Thus the alphabet of t is the union of the alphabets of p, r and s, hence of P and R, where P denotes the union of the alphabets of s and p. However, according to Lemma 4.4.13 and to relation $pr = rq$, every letter of R is independent of p. Moreover every letter of R is independent of s since $r \, I \, s$. Hence the two subalphabets P and R are independent. Since t is connected, this implies that either P or R is empty.

If P was empty, we would have $p = s = 1$ and thus $v = 1$ which is not the case. Hence R is empty and every letter of r belong to the alphabet of p. By symmetry, we can also conclude that every letter of s belongs to the alphabet of p. Hence the alphabet of t is equal to the alphabet of p. Using now the relations $u = pr$, $v = ps$, we can conclude that the alphabets of u and v are equal to the alphabet of t which is connected for D. Since $uv = vu$, it follows from the results of Chapter 3 that there exists $w \in \mathbb{M}(\Sigma, I)$ such that $u = w^n$ and $v = w^m$ with $n, m \in \mathbb{N}$. Hence $t = w^{n+m}$. Since t is primitive, $n + m = 1$. Thus n or m is 0. Hence u or v is empty which is not the case. This contradiction ends our proof.   □

Thus a strongly primitive trace is also primitive. However the converse does not hold in general (conversely to the free case) as shows the following example.

Example 4.4.14 Let us consider again the independence alphabet of Example 4.2.8. Then $t = ab = ba$ is primitive, but is clearly not strongly primitive.

Let us finally give the following result that expresses some properties of primitivity and strong primitivity with respect to conjugacy.

Proposition 4.4.15 *Let (Σ, I) be an independence alphabet and let t be a primitive (resp. strongly primitive) trace. Then every trace of the conjugacy class of t is primitive (resp. strongly primitive).*

Proof: Connectedness is clearly preserved by transposition and hence by conjugacy according to Corollary 4.4.8. According to Proposition 4.4.12, it suffices to show that primitivity is preserved by conjugacy in order to get our proposition. But according to Remark 4.4.10, it suffices in fact to see that primitivity is preserved by elementary transpositions to obtain this result. Let then $t = ua$ be some primitive trace where $a \in \Sigma$. We must show that au is also primitive. Let us suppose that this is not the case. Hence $au = v^n$ with some $v \in \mathbb{M}(\Sigma, I)$ and some $n \geq 2$. The letter a must also be an initial letter of v. Hence we can write $v = av'$. It follows that

$$aua = (av')^n \, a = a \, (v'a)^n$$

and thus that $ua = (v'a)^n$ by cancellability of $\mathbb{M}(\Sigma, I)$. This contradicts the fact that $t = ua$ is primitive. Hence au is primitive.   □

4.4.3   Definition of Lyndon Traces

Let us recall that Lyndon words can be defined in the free case as the minimal words (for a fixed lexicographic order) in the conjugacy classes of primitive words of Σ^*. Lyndon words have several beautiful properties. Among them, there is the important property that every word of Σ^* can be uniquely written as a decreasing product of Lyndon words for the considered lexicographic order. This means that Σ^* can be factorized as

$$\underline{\Sigma^*} = \prod_{l \in Ly} \underline{l^*} \tag{4.24}$$

where Ly denotes the set of Lyndon words ordered by reverse lexicographic order.

The naive idea of taking the above definition in the general trace framework (with some suited order) does not work. Indeed one can not generalize with this definition several important classical properties of Lyndon words. For instance, let a and b be two independent letters such that $a < b$. Using the previous definition, we would be obliged to consider a, b and ab as Lyndon traces since they are primitive and the only elements in their conjugacy classes. It follows that $ab = (b)(a) = (ab)$ can be decomposed in two ways as an ordered product of Lyndon traces. This shows that the naive definition cannot be compatible with a factorization property of arbitrary Lyndon traces similar to the free case.

This example shows that the "good" definition of a Lyndon trace is to be carefully chosen. The first problem we now consider is the choice of a "good" order on $\mathbb{M}(\Sigma, I)$ (that corresponds to the lexicographic order in the free case).

From now to the end of Section 4.4, we fix a chromatic partition $(\Sigma_i)_{i=1,N}$ of the independence alphabet (Σ, I). We suppose that Σ is totally ordered by some fixed total order $<$ that respects the chromatic partition, i.e. such that

$$i < j \implies x_i < x_j$$

for every $i, j \in [1, N]$, every $x_i \in \Sigma_i$ and $x_j \in \Sigma_j$. We can now give the definition.

Definition 4.4.16 *Let t be a trace of $\mathbb{M}(\Sigma, I)$. Then the standard word associated with t is the word of Σ^*, that we denote by $std(t)$, which is the maximal word (for the lexicographic order on Σ^* induced by $<$) in the class $\varphi^{-1}(t) \subset \Sigma^*$ of t.*

We can now equip $\mathbb{M}(\Sigma, I)$ with the total order defined by

$$t < t' \quad \text{iff} \quad std(t) < std(t')$$

for every $t, t' \in \mathbb{M}(\Sigma, I)$. We always suppose in the sequel that $\mathbb{M}(\Sigma, I)$ is equipped with this order.

Example 4.4.17 In the free case, the standard word associated with a given word w is w itself. Hence the previous order is then just the usual lexicographic order on Σ^* induced by $<$.

Example 4.4.18 Let us consider the alphabet $\Sigma = \{a, b, c, d\}$ equipped with the independence relation defined by the independence graph

$$a \text{———} b \text{———} c \text{———} d$$

The family $(\Sigma_k)_{k=1,2,3}$ defined by $\Sigma_1 = \{a, d\}$, $\Sigma_2 = \{b\}$ and $\Sigma_3 = \{c\}$ is a chromatic partition of Σ. Let us order Σ by setting $a < d < b < c$. Let us now consider $t = abcd$ and $t' = dcba$ in $\mathbb{M}(\Sigma, I)$. The classes $\varphi^{-1}(t)$ and $\varphi^{-1}(t')$ are given by

$$\varphi^{-1}(t) = \{abcd, bacd, acbd, abdc, badc\} \subset \Sigma^*$$
$$\text{and} \quad \varphi^{-1}(t') = \{dcba, cdba, dbca, dcab, cdab\} \subset \Sigma^* \ .$$

We have $std(t) = bacd$ and $std(t') = cdba$. Hence $t < t'$ here.

The following proposition shows an easy but important property of our order.

Proposition 4.4.19 *Let t, t' be two traces of $\mathbb{M}(\Sigma, I)$. Then we have $t \leq tt'$.*

Proof: Observe that $\varphi(std(t)\,std(t')) = tt'$. Hence we necessarily have

$$std(t)\,std(t') \leq std(tt')$$

by definition of our order on $\mathbb{M}(\Sigma, I)$. It immediately follows that $std(t) \leq std(tt')$ which is equivalent to the fact that $t \leq tt'$.   □

It is now time to give the definition of Lyndon traces.

Definition 4.4.20 *Let (Σ, I) be an independence alphabet. A trace $t \in \mathbb{M}(\Sigma, I)$ is then said to be a* Lyndon trace *if and only if it is a minimal [5] strongly primitive trace in its conjugacy class.*

Example 4.4.21 In the free case, primitivity is equivalent to strong primitivity. Hence Lyndon traces are then exactly the usual Lyndon words.

Example 4.4.22 In the totally commutative case, the only strongly primitive traces are the letters of Σ. Hence Lyndon traces are here reduced to the letters of Σ.

Example 4.4.23 Let us again consider Example 4.4.18. It is then easy to check that $t = abcd$ is connected and primitive. Hence t is strongly primitive. Moreover the conjugacy class of t can easily be computed using Corollary 4.4.8 and is equal to

$$\{abcd, dabc, cabd, dcab, bdac, bdca, adcb, cadb\} \ .$$

The unique Lyndon trace conjugated to $abcd$ is then $acdb$.

Remark 4.4.24 By Proposition 4.4.15, a Lyndon trace is always strongly primitive.

4.4.4   Characterization Results

Let us first recall that Corollary 4.3.12 shows that $\mathbb{M}(\Sigma, I)$ can be factorized as

$$\underline{\mathbb{M}(\Sigma, I)} = \underline{C_{\Sigma_N}(T_N)^*} \ \ldots \ \underline{C_{\Sigma_2}(T_2)^*} \ \underline{C_{\Sigma_1}(T_1)^*} \tag{4.25}$$

---

[5] Minimality is here taken in the sense of the order on $\mathbb{M}(\Sigma, I)$ that we defined above.

where we set $T_j = \bigcup\limits_{k>j} \Sigma_k$ for every $j \in [1, N]$.

The total order $<$ put on $\mathbf{M}(\Sigma, I)$ orders also by restriction any Z-code $C_{\Sigma_i}(T_i)$. Hence the free monoid $C_{\Sigma_i}(T_i)^*$ is ordered by the usual lexicographic order extending the previous order on $C_{\Sigma_i}(T_i)$. On the other hand, $C_{\Sigma_i}(T_i)^*$ is also ordered by restriction of $<$. Thus we have two natural ways of ordering $C_{\Sigma_i}(T_i)^*$. In fact, it can be shown that they coincide. To this purpose, we need the following lemma.

Lemma 4.4.25 *Under the previous assumptions, let t be a trace of $\mathbf{M}(\Sigma, I)$ which is factorized with respect to (4.25) as*

$$t = (c_N^1 \ldots c_N^{k_N}) \ldots (c_1^1 \ldots c_1^{k_1})$$

where $c_i^j \in C_{\Sigma_i}(T_i)$ for every $i \in [1, N]$ and every $j \in [1, k_i]$. Then we have

$$std(t) = (std(c_N^1) \ldots std(c_N^{k_N})) \ldots (std(c_1^1) \ldots std(c_1^{k_1})) .$$

Proof: We prove this result by induction on the length of t. The lemma is clear when $|t| = 1$. Let now $t \in \mathbf{M}(\Sigma, I)$ decomposed with respect to (4.25) as

$$t = (c_i^1 \ldots c_i^{k_i}) \ldots (c_1^1 \ldots c_1^{k_1}) = c_i^1 t' \tag{4.26}$$

with some $i \in [1, N]$, where every $c_j^k \in C_{\Sigma_j}(T_j)$ and where we set

$$t' = (c_i^2 \ldots c_i^{k_i}) \ldots (c_1^1 \ldots c_1^{k_1}) .$$

Let us suppose our result proved at any order $< |t|$. We can write $c_i^1 = a_i u$ where $a_i \in \Sigma_i$ is the unique initial letter of c_i^1 and where $u \in <T_i>$. Hence the decomposition of u with respect to (4.25) has the form

$$u = (c_N^1 \ldots c_N^{k_N}) \ldots (c_{i+1}^1 \ldots c_{i+1}^{k_{i+1}}) \tag{4.27}$$

where $c_j^k \in C_{\Sigma_j}(T_j)$. Thus the decomposition of ut' with respect to (4.25) is just the concatenation of the decompositions of u and t' given by (4.26) and (4.27). Using now the induction hypothesis applied to ut', u and t, it is easy to prove that

$$std(ut') = std(u)\, std(t') . \tag{4.28}$$

On the other hand, Definitions 4.3.1 and 4.4.16 easily imply that $std(c_i^1) = a_i\, std(u)$ and $std(t) = a_i\, std(ut')$. Using now relation (4.28), we get

$$std(t) = a_i\, std(u)\, std(t') = std(c_i^1)\, std(t') . \tag{4.29}$$

It suffices now to apply the induction hypothesis to t' in order to conclude with relation (4.29) that our result holds for t. $\qquad\square$

Remark 4.4.26 As we saw in the proof of Lemma 4.4.25, we have $std(c) = a\, std(u)$ when $c = au$ belongs to a Z-code, a being the unique initial letter of c. This formula used together with Lemma 4.4.25 gives an inductive way of computing the standard word associated with any trace.

We can now prove that the two orders we defined on every submonoid $C_{\Sigma_i}(T_i)^*$ of $\mathbb{M}(\Sigma, I)$ are the same.

Proposition 4.4.27 *Let c and c' be two traces of $C_{\Sigma_i}(T_i)^*$ for some $i \in [1, N]$. Then $c < c'$ iff c is strictly less than c' for the lexicographic order on $C_{\Sigma_i}(T_i)^*$ induced by the ordering $<$ on the elements of $C_{\Sigma_i}(T_i)$.*

Proof: Let us denote by $<_{Lex}$ the lexicographic order on $C_{\Sigma_i}(T_i)^*$ induced by the ordering $<$ on $C_{\Sigma_i}(T_i)$. Let then $c, c' \in C_{\Sigma_i}(T_i)^*$ for some $i \in [1, N]$. Hence we have

$$c = c_1 \ldots c_n \quad \text{and} \quad c' = c'_1 \ldots c'_m \tag{4.30}$$

where every c_i and c'_i is in $C_{\Sigma_i}(T_i)$. It now follows from Lemma 4.4.25 that

$$std(c) = std(c_1) \ldots std(c_n) \quad \text{and} \quad std(c') = std(c'_1) \ldots std(c'_m). \tag{4.31}$$

Let us suppose that $c <_{Lex} c'$. Two cases can now occur. First c can be a strict prefix of c' in $C_{\Sigma_i}(T_i)^*$. Using relations (4.31), it is then easy to conclude that $c < c'$. On the other hand, if the previous situation does not hold, there exists $j \in \mathbb{N}$ such that the first $j - 1$ elements of $C_{\Sigma_i}(T_i)$ involved in relation (4.30) are equal and such that $c_j < c'_j$. In other words, we have

$$c = c_1 \ldots c_{j-1} c_j \ldots c_n \quad \text{and} \quad c' = c_1 \ldots c_{j-1} c'_j \ldots c'_m$$

with $std(c_j) < std(c'_j)$. Using now relations (4.31), we clearly get $std(c) < std(c')$. Hence we have $c < c'$.

Let us suppose conversely that $c < c'$. We must then have $c <_{Lex} c'$ since if it was not the case, we would have $c' \leq_{Lex} c$ and hence $c' \leq c$ according to our previous study, which is not possible. □

Remark 4.4.28 In the sequel, we always implicitly use the identification of the two orders on $C_{\Sigma_i}(T_i)^*$ given by Proposition 4.4.27, without explicitly referring to it.

Let us now give a useful lemma for the proof of the main result of this subsection.

Lemma 4.4.29 *Under the previous assumptions, let l be a trace of $\mathbb{M}(\Sigma, I)$ which is strictly less than all its proper transposed, i.e. such that*

$$l = uv \quad \text{with } u, v \neq 1 \quad \Longrightarrow \quad l < vu.$$

Then l is a usual Lyndon word over a Z-code $C_{\Sigma_i}(T_i)$ for some $i \in [1, N]$.

Proof: Let l be a trace of $\mathbb{M}(\Sigma, I)$ which is strictly less than all its proper transposed. Then l can be decomposed with respect to (4.25) as

$$l = c_i \, c_{i-1} \ldots c_j$$

where $i \geq j$, where $c_k \in C_{\Sigma_k}(T_k)^*$ for every $k \in [j, i]$ and where c_i and c_j are non-empty. Let us suppose that $i > j$. We can then consider the trace l' defined by

$$l' = c_{i-1} \ldots c_j \, c_i \tag{4.32}$$

which is a proper transposed of l. Hence $l < l'$. But the first letter of $std(l)$ is the unique initial letter a_i of $c_i = a_i \, v$. Thus it belongs to Σ_i. On the other hand, the initial letter of $std(l')$ belongs to the initial alphabet of l'. But, according to (4.32), to Definition 4.3.1 and to the non-commutativity of every Σ_k, an initial letter of l' must be an initial letter of some c_k with $k \in [j, i]$. Thus the first letter of $std(l')$ is necessarily the initial letter of some c_k with $k \in [j, i]$. Let us now suppose that the first letter a_k of $std(l')$ belongs to some Σ_k with $k < i$. Then we would have

$$std(l') = a_k \, u < a_i \, std(v \, c_{i+1} \ldots c_j) = std(l)$$

which is not the case. Hence the first letter of $std(l')$ must be the unique initial letter of c_i. Therefore l' and c_i have some common non-empty prefix. It follows by an immediate induction on length that the decomposition of the trace l' with respect to (4.25) is of the form

$$l' = c'_i \, c'_{i-1} \ldots c'_j$$

where c'_k belongs to $C_{\Sigma_k}(T_k)^*$ for every $k \in [j, i]$ and where c'_i is a non-empty prefix of c_i. Since $l \neq l'$, c_i and c'_i are also distinct. Hence $c'_i < c_i$ according to Proposition 4.4.19. By Lemma 4.4.25, we immediately get that $l' < l$ which is not the case.

Hence l belongs to a Z-code $C_{\Sigma_i}(T_i)$ for some $i \in [1, N]$. Using now Lemma 4.4.25, we easily get that l, considered as a word over the alphabet $C_{\Sigma_i}(T_i)$, is also strictly less than all its proper transposed. Hence it follows that l is a usual Lyndon word over $C_{\Sigma_i}(T_i)$ in the free monoid $C_{\Sigma_i}(T_i)^*$ according to a classical property of Lyndon words. $\qquad \square$

Corollary 4.4.30 *Let l be a trace of $\mathbb{M}(\Sigma, I)$ which is strictly less than all its proper transposed. Then the initial alphabet of l is reduced to a single letter.*

Proof: Lemma 4.4.29 shows that a trace l which is strictly less than all its proper transposed, belongs to $C_{\Sigma_i}(T_i)^*$ for some $i \in [1, N]$. It follows then from Definition 4.3.1 that the initial alphabet of l is reduced to a single letter in Σ_i. $\qquad \square$

We can now give our main characterization result.

Theorem 4.4.31 *Under the previous assumptions, let l be a trace of $\mathbb{M}(\Sigma, I)$. Then the following assertions are equivalent*

    1. l is a Lyndon trace.

2. l is a usual Lyndon word over the Z-code $C_{\Sigma_i}(T_i)$ for some $i \in [1, N]$.

3. l is strictly less than all its proper transposed, i.e.

$$l = uv \quad with \ u, v \neq 1 \quad \Longrightarrow \quad l < vu \ .$$

Proof: We first show that $2 \Longrightarrow 3$. Let then l be a usual Lyndon word over a Z-code $C_{\Sigma_i}(T_i)$ for some $i \in [1, N]$ that we can write

$$l = c_i^1 c_i^2 \ldots c_i^n \ . \tag{4.33}$$

Let now t be a proper transposed of l. If the transposition used for going from l to t respects decomposition (4.33), we can conclude that $l < t$ by using the corresponding classical property of usual Lyndon words. If it is not the case, there is an initial letter of t that belongs to T_i when the unique initial letter of l is in Σ_i. Since the order $<$ respects the chromatic partition, it follows from Definition 4.4.16 that we also have $l < t$ in this case. Hence we proved that l is strictly less than all its proper transposed. This shows that $2 \Longrightarrow 3$.

We can now prove that $2 \Longrightarrow 1$. Let then l again be a usual Lyndon word over a Z-code $C_{\Sigma_i}(T_i)$ for some $i \in [1, N]$. According to our previous study, assertion 3 holds. Hence l is in particular strongly primitive. By Proposition 4.4.15, every conjugated of t is also strongly primitive. Thus we can consider the unique Lyndon trace l' which is conjugated of l. l and l' can not be properly transposed since it would follow from assertion 3 that $l < l'$ which contradicts the fact that $l' \leq l$ according to Definition 4.4.20. Using now Proposition 4.4.5, we can write

$$l = z_1 z_2 \ldots z_M \quad and \quad l' = z_M z_{M-1} \ldots z_1$$

where $(z_k)_{k=1,M}$ is a family of traces such that $z_j \mathrm{I} z_k$ for every $j < k - 1$ in $[1, M]$. But, by Corollary 4.4.30, the initial alphabet of l and l' are reduced to a single letter, respectively denoted a and a', that belongs to Σ_i. Hence a and a' must respectively belong to the alphabet of z_1 and of z_M. But this is not possible if $M > 2$ since these two alphabets are independent in this case and since Σ_i is non-commutative. The case $M = 2$ is also not possible since l and l' would then be properly transposed and this is not the case. Hence $M = 1$ and $l = l'$. Thus l is a Lyndon trace. This shows that $2 \Longrightarrow 1$ holds.

We can now show that $1 \Longrightarrow 3$. Let then $l = uv$ be a Lyndon trace with $u, v \neq 1$. Since l is strongly primitive, we have $l \neq vu$. The minimality of l in its conjugacy class implies then that $l < vu$. This shows that $1 \Longrightarrow 3$ holds.

Let us finally observe that $3 \Longrightarrow 2$ was already proved in Lemma 4.4.29. $\quad\square$

Remark 4.4.32 It easily follows from Theorem 4.4.31 and Corollary 4.4.30 that every Lyndon trace has a unique initial letter which is its minimal letter.

Remark 4.4.33 In the free case, any partition $(\Sigma_i)_{i=1,N}$ of Σ is a chromatic partition. The associated factorization of Σ^* is then

$$\underline{\Sigma^*} = \underline{\Sigma_N^*} \ \underline{(\Sigma_{N-1} T_{N-1}^*)^*} \ \ldots \underline{(\Sigma_1 T_1^*)^*} \ .$$

Let now $<$ be any order that respects the previous chromatic partition of Σ. It follows then from Theorem 4.4.31 that the corresponding Lyndon words of Σ^* are exactly the Lyndon words over the alphabets $\Sigma_i(T_i)$ for $i \in [1, N]$.

Example 4.4.34 Let us again consider the independence alphabet of Example 4.4.18. We can equip it with the chromatic partition $(\Sigma_k)_{k=1,2,3}$ where $\Sigma_1 = \{a, d\}$, $\Sigma_2 = \{b\}$ and $\Sigma_3 = \{c\}$. We order Σ with the order $a < d < b < c$ which respects the above chromatic partition. Factorization (4.25) of $\mathbb{M}(\Sigma, I)$ is then

$$\underline{\mathbb{M}(\Sigma, I)} = \underline{c^*}\ \underline{b^*}\ \underline{(ac^* + db^*)^*}\ .$$

The order $<$ induces the following ordering on the Z-codes

$$a < ac < ac^2 < \ldots < d < db < db^2 < \ldots < b < c\ .$$

Going back to the classical free case with Theorem 4.4.31, it follows then that

$$b,\ c,\ aacdb,\ aadbdb,\ ac^2ac^2db^3,\ \ldots$$

are, for instance, Lyndon traces of $\mathbb{M}(\Sigma, I)$.

The following result shows that $\mathbb{M}(\Sigma, I)$ has – as in the free case – a factorization property with respect to Lyndon traces.

Corollary 4.4.35 *Every $t \in \mathbb{M}(\Sigma, I)$ can be uniquely decomposed as a decreasing product of Lyndon traces. In other words, $\mathbb{M}(\Sigma, I)$ can be factorized as*

$$\underline{\mathbb{M}(\Sigma, I)} = \prod_{l \in Ly(\Sigma, I)} \underline{l^*}$$

where $Ly(\Sigma, I)$ denotes the set of Lyndon traces totally ordered by the opposite order of $<$.

Proof: It suffices to apply the usual factorization property (4.24) of Lyndon words to every free monoid $C_{\Sigma_i}(T_i)^*$ for $i \in [1, N]$. Our corollary follows then from these factorizations, from (4.25) and from Theorem 4.4.31.   □

Usual Lyndon words can also be characterized by the fact that are strictly less than all their proper right factors. This property can also be generalized.

Proposition 4.4.36 *Under the previous assumptions, let l be a trace of $\mathbb{M}(\Sigma, I)$. Then the following assertions are equivalent*

1. *l is a Lyndon trace.*

2. *l is strictly less than all its proper right factors, i.e.*

$$l = uv \quad with\ u, v \neq 1 \quad \Longrightarrow \quad l < v\ .$$

Proof: We first show that $2 \Longrightarrow 1$. Let then $l \in \mathbb{M}(\Sigma, I)$ which is strictly less than all its proper right factors. Let $l = uv$ be a decomposition of l where u and v are non-empty. Using Proposition 4.4.19 and property 2, we get

$$l = uv < v < vu \ .$$

It now clearly follows from Theorem 4.4.31 that l is a Lyndon trace.

Conversely let l be a Lyndon trace. According to Theorem 4.4.31, there exists $i \in [1, N]$ such that l is a usual Lyndon word over $C_{\Sigma_i}(T_i)$. Hence we can write

$$l = c_i^1 c_i^2 \ldots c_i^{k_i} \tag{4.34}$$

where every $c_i^k \in C_{\Sigma_i}(T_i)$ and where l is a usual Lyndon word in the letters c_i. Let now v be a non-empty right factor of l. Two cases can occur.

a) $IA(v) \cap T_i \neq \emptyset$: in other words, v has a initial letter $a \in T_i$. Hence the first letter of $std(v)$ is greater or equal to a. On the other hand, according to Remark 4.4.26 and Lemma 4.4.25, the first letter of $std(l)$ belongs to Σ_i. Since every letter of Σ_i is strictly less than any letter of T_i, we immediately get $l < v$.

b) $IA(v) \cap T_i = \emptyset$: the initial letters of v are here in Σ_i. The non-commutativity of Σ_i and relation (4.34) imply then that the initial alphabet of v is reduced to a single letter and that $v = c_i^j c_i^{j+1} \ldots c_i^{k_i}$ for some $j \in [2, k_i]$. Using now the corresponding classical property of usual Lyndon words, we get that $l < v$. $\qquad\square$

Let us finally give the following interesting characterization of Lyndon traces.

Proposition 4.4.37 *Under the previous assumptions, let l be a trace of $\mathbb{M}(\Sigma, I)$. Then the following assertions are equivalent*

   1. l is a Lyndon trace.

   2. $std(l)$ is a usual Lyndon word in Σ^*.

Proof: We first prove that $1 \Longrightarrow 2$. Let l be a Lyndon trace. By Theorem 4.4.31, l is a usual word over the free monoid $C_{\Sigma_i}(T_i)^*$ for some $i \in [1, N]$. It follows that

$$l = c_i^1 c_i^2 \ldots c_i^{k_i} \tag{4.35}$$

where every $c_i^k \in C_{\Sigma_i}(T_i)$ and where l is a usual Lyndon word in the letters c_i^k. Using now Lemma 4.4.25, we get

$$std(l) = std(c_i^1) \, std(c_i^2) \ldots std(c_i^{k_i}) \ . \tag{4.36}$$

Let now u be a proper right factor of $std(l)$. Two cases are to be considered.

a) If u respects decomposition (4.36), $u = std(c_i^j) \ldots std(c_i^{k_i})$ for some $j > 1$. Hence, using Lemma 4.4.25, we get $u = std(c_i^j \ldots c_i^{k_i})$. It follows then from Proposition 4.4.36 that $std(l) < u$.

b) If u does not respect factorization (4.36), the first letter of u belongs necessarily to T_i and hence is strictly greater than the first letter of l which is in Σ_i. It immediately follows that $std(l) < u$.

Hence we showed that $std(l)$ is always strictly less than all its proper right factors. Thus this shows that $std(l)$ is a usual Lyndon word.

On the other hand, let us show that $2 \Longrightarrow 1$. Let then $l \in \mathbb{M}(\Sigma, I)$ such that $std(l)$ is a usual Lyndon word. We can decompose l with respect to (4.25) as

$$l = c_i\, c_{i-1}\, \dots\, c_j$$

where $i \geq j$, where every $c_k \in C_{\Sigma_k}(T_k)^*$ for $k \in [j, i]$ and where c_i and c_j are nonempty. Let us suppose that $i > j$. Since $std(l)$ is a usual Lyndon word, it follows from Lemma 4.4.25 that

$$std(l) = std(c_i)\, std(c_{i-1})\, \dots\, std(c_j) < std(c_j)\,.$$

But the first letter of $std(l)$ belongs to Σ_i when the first letter of $std(c_j)$ belongs to Σ_j and every letter of Σ_i is strictly greater than any letter of Σ_j. Hence the previous inequality is not possible. Thus $i = j$. Hence $l \in C_{\Sigma_i}(T_i)^*$ for some $i \in [1, N]$. Therefore l can be decomposed as in (4.35). Using relation (4.36) and Theorem 4.4.31, it now immediately follows from the fact that $std(l)$ is a Lyndon word that l is a Lyndon trace. This shows that $2 \Longrightarrow 1$. □

Remark 4.4.38 Proposition 4.4.37 gives an easy way for checking if a trace is a Lyndon trace, by going back to the free case with the help of standard words (that can be computed with the inductive method given at the beginning of this subsection).

4.4.5 Some Other Properties

We devote this last subsection to some other extensions to Lyndon traces of classical properties. Observe first that the following example shows that it is not true anymore – in opposition to the free case – that ll' is a Lyndon trace when l, l' are two Lyndon traces such that $l < l'$.

Example 4.4.39 Let us consider the free commutative monoid over $\Sigma = \{a, b\}$. Its independence relation is defined by the independence graph

$$a \underline{\hspace{5cm}} b$$

The family $(\Sigma_i)_{i=1,2}$ defined by $\Sigma_1 = \{a\}$ and $\Sigma_2 = \{b\}$ is a chromatic partition of Σ. We can order Σ by $a < b$. a and b are then two Lyndon traces such that $a < b$. But $ab = ba$ is not a Lyndon trace since it is even not strongly primitive.

Proposition 4.4.40 Let l, l' be two Lyndon traces and let a, a' be respectively the unique initial letters of l and l'. Then the following properties holds

1. If a and a' belong to the same Σ_i for some $i \in [1, N]$, then $l\,l'$ is a Lyndon trace when $l < l'$.

   2. *If $l\,l'$ is a Lyndon trace, then $l < l'$ and a' does not commute with l (excepted possibly if $l = a'$).*

Proof: We first show that assertion 1 holds. In this case, it easily follows from Theorem 4.4.31 that l and l' are both usual Lyndon words on the same alphabet $C_{\Sigma_i}(T_i)$. Hence $l\,l'$ is a Lyndon trace when $l < l'$ according to Lemma 4.4.25, Theorem 4.4.31 and the usual free property.

   Let us now show that assertion 2 holds. Indeed, if ll' is a Lyndon trace, we get $l \leq ll' < l'$ using Propositions 4.4.19 and 4.4.36. Hence $l < l'$. On the other hand, the unique initial letter a' of l' can not commute in general with l since if it was the case, a' would be an initial letter of ll'. The unambiguity of the initial letter of ll' implies that a' is equal to the initial letter a of l. Since a' commutes with l, it follows then from the strong primitivity of l that $l = a = a'$.   □

Remark 4.4.41 It can be showed by adapting the corresponding proof of Lalonde (cf. [168]) that $l\,l'$ is a Lyndon trace when l, l' are Lyndon traces such that $l < l'$ and such that the unique initial letter a' of l' does not commute with l (at the possible exception of the case $l = a'$).

   We now present the generalization of the notion of standard decomposition (see [182] for the usual free case).

Definition 4.4.42 *Let t be a trace of $\mathbb{M}(\Sigma, I)$ of length ≥ 2. Then t can be factorized in a unique way as a product $t = fn$ such that*

    1. $f \neq 1$,

    2. n is a Lyndon trace,

    3. n is minimal among all possible Lyndon traces such that $t = fn$.

The unique pair (f, n) defined by these conditions is then denoted $SD(t)$ and called the standard decomposition of t.

Example 4.4.43 Let us consider again the independence alphabet of Example 4.4.34 that we equip here with the chromatic partition $(\Sigma_i)_{i=1,4}$ defined by $\Sigma_1 = \{a\}$, $\Sigma_2 = \{b\}$, $\Sigma_3 = \{c\}$ and $\Sigma_4 = \{d\}$. The associated factorization of $\mathbb{M}(\Sigma, I)$ is then

$$\underline{\mathbb{M}(\Sigma, I)} = \underline{d^*}\ \underline{c^*}\ \underline{(bd^*)^*}\ \underline{(ac^*(db^*)^*)^*} .$$

Let us order Σ by setting $a < b < c < d$. Let us now consider $t = bdbdacd \in \mathbb{M}(\Sigma, I)$. We can find three factorizations of t

$$t = (bdbdac)(d) = (bdbdad)(c) = (bdbd)(acd) .$$

that satisfy conditions 1 and 2 of Definition 4.4.42. The last above decomposition gives the minimal right factor. Hence $SD(t) = (bdbd)(acd)$.

   Let us now see a method for computing standard decompositions.

Proposition 4.4.44 *Let t be a trace of $\mathbb{M}(\Sigma, I)$, let $t = l_1 l_2 \ldots l_k$ be its decreasing factorization in Lyndon traces given by Corollary 4.4.35 and let us suppose that $k \geq 2$. The standard decomposition of t is then equal to $SD(t) = (l_1 l_2 \ldots l_{k-1}, l_k)$.*

Proof: Let $t \in \mathbb{M}(\Sigma, I)$, let $SD(t) = (f, n)$ be its standard decomposition and let

$$t = (l_1^p \ldots l_{k_p}^p) \ldots (l_1^q \ldots l_{k_q}^q) \tag{4.37}$$

be its decreasing factorization in Lyndon traces, where $l_j^i \in C_{\Sigma_i}(T_i)^*$ for any $i \in [q, p]$. We suppose that at least two Lyndon words are involved in relation (4.37).

We have $n \leq l_{k_q}^q$ according to Definition 4.4.42. Hence the unique initial letter a of n is less or equal to the unique initial letter of $l_{k_q}^q$ which is in Σ_q. Relation (4.37) implies then that $a \in \Sigma_q$. It follows then from relation (4.37) – looking on the underlying decomposition over the Z-codes – that

$$n = v\, l_{i+1}^q \ldots l_{k_q}^q \tag{4.38}$$

for some $i \in [1, k_q]$ where v is a right factor of l_i^q. Using Propositions 4.4.19 and 4.4.36, our study shows that

$$l_i^q \leq v \leq n \leq l_{k_q}^q \leq l_{k_q-1}^q \leq \ldots \leq l_i^q \ .$$

Thus $v = l_i^q = l_{i+1}^q = \ldots = l_{k_q}^q$. Hence $n = (l_{k_q}^q)^{k_q-i+1}$. We get $k_q = i$ by primitivity of n. Relation (4.38) shows then that $n = l_{k_q}$. It is now immediate to conclude. $\square$

Remark 4.4.45 Example 4.4.43 can also be seen as a consequence of Proposition 4.4.44.

Proposition 4.4.46 *Let $t \in \mathbb{M}(\Sigma, I)$ be a Lyndon trace that belongs to $C_{\Sigma_i}(T_i)^*$ for some $i \in [1, N]$ and which has length ≥ 2 in the letters $C_{\Sigma_i}(T_i)$. Then the standard decomposition $SD(l) = (f, n)$ of l is equal to the usual standard decomposition of l considered in the free monoid $C_{\Sigma_i}(T_i)^*$.*

Proof: Let l be a Lyndon trace of $\mathbb{M}(\Sigma, I)$ that belongs to $C_{\Sigma_i}(T_i)^*$ for some $i \in [1, N]$ and which is of length ≥ 2 in the letters $C_{\Sigma_i}(T_i)$. Hence we can write

$$l = c_i^1 c_i^2 \ldots c_i^{k_i} \tag{4.39}$$

where $c_i^j \in C_{\Sigma_i}(T_i)$ for any $j \in [1, k_i]$ and where $k_i \geq 2$. We can consider the usual standard decomposition $l = FN$ of l considered as a word over $C_{\Sigma_i}(T_i)^*$ which is

$$F = c_i^1 c_i^2 \ldots c_i^k \quad \text{and} \quad N = c_i^{k+1} c_i^{k+2} \ldots c_i^{k_i}$$

for some $k \in [1, k_i - 1]$. F must be a Lyndon trace according to Theorem 4.4.31 and to the classical corresponding property in the free case.

Let now u be a proper right factor of l which is a Lyndon trace. If the initial letter of u is not in Σ_i, it must be in T_i. Comparing then the first letters of $std(u)$ and $std(N)$, we get $u > N$. On the other hand, let us suppose that the initial letter of u is in Σ_i. Hence $u = c_i^j \ldots c_i^{k_i}$ for some $j \in [2, k_i]$. Using now Lemma 4.4.25 and the definition of the standard decomposition in the free case, we get $N \leq u$. Hence it follows that (N, F) is the standard decomposition of l. $\square$

Proposition 4.4.47 *Let* $t = a_i u$ *be an element of some* Z-*code* $C_{\Sigma_i}(T_i)$ *where* $a_i \in \Sigma_i$ *is the unique initial letter of* t *and where* $u \in <T_i>$. *Then its standard decomposition* $SD(t) = (f, n)$ *is given by*

1. *If* u *is a Lyndon trace,* $f = a_i$ *and* $n = u$.

2. *If* u *is not a Lyndon trace, let* $SD(u) = (f', n')$ *be the standard decomposition of* u. *Then* $f = a_i f'$ *and* $n = n'$.

Proof: Let $t = a_i u \in C_{\Sigma_i}(T_i)$ as above and let $SD(t) = (f, n)$ be its standard decomposition. Let us first suppose that u is a Lyndon word. Then $n \leq u$ according to Definition 4.4.42. On the other hand, since a_i is the unique initial letter of t, a_i must also be the unique initial letter of f. It easily follows that n is in fact a right factor of u. Using now Proposition 4.4.19, we get $u \leq n$. Hence $u = n$ and thus $f = a_i$.

Let us now suppose that u is not a Lyndon trace and let $SD(u) = (f', n')$ be the standard decomposition of u. Since $t = a_i f' n'$, it follows from Definition 4.4.42 that $n \leq n'$. On the other hand, a_i must be the unique initial letter of f and we can write $f = a_i g$ with some trace g. g is non-empty, since if it was not the case, we would have $n = u$ and u would be a Lyndon trace which is not the case. Hence $u = g n$. Using again Definition 4.4.42, we get $n' \leq n$. Hence our study shows that $n = n'$. It follows that $f = a_i f'$. $\qquad\square$

Propositions 4.4.44, 4.4.46 and 4.4.47 give an inductive method, based on elimination, for computing the standard decomposition of a trace.

Example 4.4.48 Let us again consider the independence alphabet of Example 4.4.43. Let $t = accdbbd \in C_{\Sigma_1}(T_1)$. Proposition 4.4.47 says us then to study $u = ccdbbd$. The decomposition of u with respect to Lazard's factorization of $\mathbb{M}(\Sigma, I)$ is

$$u = (d)(c)(c)(b)(bd) = (d)(c)(c)(bbd) .$$

Since $b < bd$, the trace $bbd = (b)(bd)$ is a Lyndon trace according to Theorem 4.4.31. Hence the above relation gives the decreasing factorization of t in Lyndon traces. Hence using now Propositions 4.4.44 and 4.4.47, we easily get $SD(t) = (adcc, bbd)$.

The following result gives another interesting method for computing standard decompositions.

Proposition 4.4.49 *Let* t *be a trace of length* ≥ 2 *in* $\mathbb{M}(\Sigma, I)$, *let* $SD(t) = (f, n)$ *be its standard decomposition and let* $SD(std(t)) = (F, N)$ *be the usual standard decomposition of the word* $std(t) \in \Sigma^*$. *Then we have*

$$f = \varphi(F) \quad and \quad n = \varphi(N) .$$

Proof: Let us first show the following lemma of independent interest.

Lemma 4.4.50 *Let* t *be a trace of length* ≥ 2 *in* $\mathbb{M}(\Sigma, I)$ *and let* $SD(t) = (f, n)$ *be its standard decomposition. Then* $std(t) = std(f) \, std(n)$.

Proof: We prove this lemma by induction on $|t|$. When $|t| = 2$, $t = ab$ with $a, b \in \Sigma$. If $(a, b) \in I$, then $std(t) = ab$ and it is easy to check that the lemma holds. On the other hand, if a and b are dependent, let us suppose for instance that $a < b$. Then $std(t) = ba$ and our lemma is also easily checked.

Let us now suppose that $|t| > 2$ and that our lemma holds at any order strictly less than $|t|$. Several cases are to be considered.

a) t is not a Lyndon trace. Let then $t = l_1 l_2 \ldots l_k$ be the decreasing factorization of t in Lyndon traces given by Corollary 4.4.35. Since t is not a Lyndon trace, we have $k \geq 2$. It follows then from Lemma 4.4.25 and Theorem 4.4.31 that

$$std(t) = std(l_1 l_2 \ldots l_{k-1}) \, std(l_k) = std(l_1) \, std(l_2) \ldots std(l_{k-1}) \, std(l_k)$$

which, by unambiguity and by Proposition 4.4.37, is the usual decreasing factorization in Lyndon words of $std(t)$. The lemma follows then from Proposition 4.4.44.

b) t is a Lyndon trace. In this case, t is a usual Lyndon word over $C_{\Sigma_i}(T_i)^*$ for some $i \in [1, N]$. Hence we can write $t = c_i^1 \ldots c_i^k$ where $c_i^j \in C_{\Sigma_i}(T_i)$ for every $j \in [1, k]$. Two sub-cases are now to be considered.

α) $k \geq 2$. Then $std(t) = std(c_i^1) \ldots std(c_i^k)$ by Lemma 4.4.25. But Proposition 4.4.46 shows that the standard decomposition of t respects its factorization in Z-codes. Hence $f = c_i^1 \ldots c_i^j$ and $n = c_i^{j+1} \ldots c_i^k$ for some $j \in [1, k-1]$. Using Lemma 4.4.25 and the above expression of $std(t)$, it is now easy to conclude.

β) $k = 1$. In this case, $t = a_i u \in C_{\Sigma_i}(T_i)$ where $a_i \in \Sigma_i$ and $u \in < T_i >$. Then $std(t) = a_i \, std(u)$. If u is a Lyndon trace, our lemma immediately follows from Proposition 4.4.47. If u is not a Lyndon trace, let $SD(u) = (f', n')$ be the standard decomposition of u. Our induction hypothesis shows that $std(u) = std(f') \, std(n')$. But since $a_i f' \in C_{\Sigma_i}(T_i)$, we also have $std(a_i f') = a_i \, std(f')$. According to Proposition 4.4.47, we now get

$$std(f) \, std(n) = std(a_i f') \, std(n') = a_i \, std(f') \, td(n') = a_i \, std(u) = std(t) .$$

Hence our result also holds in this case.   □

Let us now go back to our proposition. We have $std(t) = std(f) \, std(n)$ according to Lemma 4.4.50. Using Definition 4.4.42 in the free case and Proposition 4.4.37, we get $N \leq std(n)$ or equivalently $\varphi(N) \leq n$. On the other hand, we have

$$t = \varphi(F) \, \varphi(N) . \tag{4.40}$$

But $std(\varphi(N)) = N$ according to Definition 4.4.16. Since N is a Lyndon word, $\varphi(N)$ is a Lyndon trace by Proposition 4.4.37. Hence relation (4.40) shows that $n \leq \varphi(N)$. Thus we showed that $n = \varphi(N)$. It is now easy to conclude.   □

Remark 4.4.51 Using the notations of Proposition 4.4.49, we can also say that

$$std(f) = F \quad \text{and} \quad std(n) = N .$$

In the free case, the two words occuring in the standard decomposition of a Lyndon word are still Lyndon words. The same property holds for Lyndon traces.

Corollary 4.4.52 *Let l be a Lyndon trace of $\mathbb{M}(\Sigma, I)$ of length ≥ 2 and let $SD(l) = (f, n)$ be its standard decomposition. Then f is also a Lyndon trace. Moreover we have $f < l < n$.*

Proof: Let $SD(std(l)) = (F, N)$ be the usual standard decomposition of $std(l)$. Since $std(l)$ is a Lyndon word by Proposition 4.4.37, it follows from the classical free case that F is a Lyndon word. But Proposition 4.4.49 shows that $F = std(f)$. Hence f is a Lyndon trace according to Proposition 4.4.37. It finally follows from Propositions 4.4.19 and 4.4.36 that $f < l = fn$ and $l < n$.   □

4.5 Shuffle Product

4.5.1 Definition and First Properties

Let us recall how the shuffle product is defined in the free case. Let u, v be two words of Σ^* of length n and m. Their shuffle product $u \sqcup\!\sqcup v$ is then the set of all words $w = x_1 x_2 \ldots x_{n+m}$ of length $n + m$ such that there exists two complementary subsequences $i_1 < i_2 < \ldots < i_n$ and $j_1 < j_2 < \ldots < j_m$ of $[1, n + m]$ with

$$u = x_{i_1} x_{i_2} \ldots x_{i_n} \quad \text{and} \quad v = x_{j_1} x_{j_2} \ldots x_{j_m} . \qquad (4.41)$$

In this definition, the shuffle of two words is considered as a language of Σ^*. However it is also convenient to consider it as a polynomial of $\mathbb{N} < \Sigma >$ defined by

$$u \sqcup\!\sqcup v = \sum_{w \in \Sigma^*} \binom{w}{u , v} \ w \ \in \mathbb{N} < \Sigma > \qquad (4.42)$$

where the coefficient of w denotes the number of complementary subsequences of $[1, n + m]$ such that (4.41) holds. The shuffle product in the first sense is then equal to the set of words that occur with a non-zero coefficient in relation (4.42). It is this last way of defining the shuffle product that we will use for traces.

Let $w = a_1 a_2 \ldots a_n$ be a word of length n of Σ^* and let $I = \{i_1, i_2, \ldots, i_k\}$ be some ordered subset of $[1, n]$. Then $w[I]$ denotes the subword $w[I] = a_{i_1} a_{i_2} \ldots a_{i_n}$ of w indexed by I. For every $I \subset [1, n]$, we write $w[-I]$ instead of $w[[1, n] - I]$. Let now (Σ, I) be an independence alphabet, let $u, v \in \mathbb{M}(\Sigma, I)$ and let $w \in \Sigma^*$ of length n. Then $NS(w, u, v)$ denotes the number of subsets I of $[1, n]$ such that

$$u = \varphi(w[I]) \quad \text{and} \quad v = \varphi(w[-I]) . \qquad (4.43)$$

The following result shows that $NS(w, u, v)$ depends only on $\varphi(w)$.

Lemma 4.5.1 *Let (Σ, I) be an independence alphabet and let u, v be two traces of $\mathbb{M}(\Sigma, I)$. Then, for every words w, w' of Σ^*, we have*

$$\varphi(w) = \varphi(w') \quad \Longrightarrow \quad NS(w, u, v) = NS(w', u, v) .$$

Proof: It clearly suffices to prove the lemma when w and w' are related by some elementary rewriting. Thus let us suppose that $w = a_1 \ldots a_{k-1} \, a_k \, a_{k+1} \, a_{k+2} \ldots a_n$ and $w' = a_1 \ldots a_{k-1} \, a_{k+1} \, a_k \, a_{k+2} \ldots a_n$ with $(a_k, a_{k+1}) \in I$. Let then $\mathcal{I}$ and $\mathcal{I}'$ be respectively the sets of subsets $I \subset [1, n]$ such that relation (4.43) holds for w and w'. Let us now define a mapping Φ from $\mathcal{I}$ into $\mathcal{I}'$ by setting

1. if $\{k, k+1\} \cap I = \{k, k+1\}$ or $\emptyset$, then $\Phi(I) = I$,
2. if $\{k, k+1\} \cap I = \{k\}$, then $\Phi(I) = I \cup \{k+1\} - \{k\}$,
3. if $\{k, k+1\} \cap I = \{k+1\}$, then $\Phi(I) = I \cup \{k\} - \{k+1\}$,

for every $I \in \mathcal{I}$. It is then easy to check that Φ is a one-to-one correspondence between $\mathcal{I}$ and $\mathcal{I}'$. The lemma immediately follows. $\square$

The previous lemma shows that the following definition makes sense.

Definition 4.5.2 *Let t be a trace of length n of $\mathbb{M}(\Sigma, I)$ and let u, v be two other traces in $\mathbb{M}(\Sigma, I)$. Then the binomial coefficient*

$$\begin{pmatrix} t \\ u \, , \, v \end{pmatrix}$$

is the number of subsets I of $[1, n]$ such that $\varphi(w[I]) = u$ and $\varphi(w[-I]) = v$ for any word $w \in \varphi^{-1}(t)$. The shuffle product $u \, \sqcup \, v$ of u and v is then the polynomial of $\mathbb{N}<\Sigma, I>$ defined by

$$u \, \sqcup \, v = \sum_{t \in \mathbb{M}(\Sigma, I)} \begin{pmatrix} t \\ u \, , \, v \end{pmatrix} t \ \in \mathbb{N}<\Sigma, I> .$$

Remark 4.5.3 Let K be a semiring. The definition of the shuffle product can then be easily extended by linearity to $K \ll \Sigma, I \gg$ by setting

$$S \, \sqcup \, T = \sum_{t \in \mathbb{M}(\Sigma, I)} \left(\sum_{u, v \in \mathbb{M}(\Sigma, I)} \begin{pmatrix} t \\ u \, , \, v \end{pmatrix} (P|u) \, (Q|v) \right) t$$

for every series $S, T \in K \ll \Sigma, I \gg$. The previous definition makes sense since the number of traces u, v such that the above binomial coefficient is not 0, is clearly always finite for every $t \in \mathbb{M}(\Sigma, I)$. Observe that the previous relation also defines the shuffle of two trace languages which is obtained by taking K equal to the boolean semiring $\mathcal{B} = \{0, 1\}$, where $1 + 1 = 1$.

Example 4.5.4 In the free case, Definition 4.5.2 is clearly equivalent to the usual definition given by relations (4.41) and (4.42).

Example 4.5.5 In the totally commutative case, it is easy to check that we have

$$t \, \sqcup \, t' = \left(\prod_{a \in \Sigma} \begin{pmatrix} |tt'|_a \\ |t|_a \, , \, |t'|_a \end{pmatrix} \right) tt'$$

for every traces t and t' of $\mathbb{M}(\Sigma, I) \simeq \mathbb{N}^\Sigma$. Thus it is easy to see that the shuffle product is then isomorphic to the usual Cauchy product.

Example 4.5.6 Let us consider the independence alphabet of Example 4.2.8. Then

$$ab \; \sqcup\!\sqcup \; c = abc + bca + acb + cab \; .$$

Let us now recall a definition. Let K be a semiring. Then, for every $u \in \mathbb{M}(\Sigma, I)$ and for every $S \in K \ll \Sigma, I \gg$, the series $u^{-1}S$ of $K \ll \Sigma, I \gg$ is defined by

$$u^{-1}S = \sum_{t \in \mathbb{M}(\Sigma, I)} (S|ut) \, t \; .$$

The following result shows that the shuffle product preserves recognizability.

Proposition 4.5.7 *Let P, Q be two recognizable trace languages of $\mathbb{M}(\Sigma, I)$. Then $P \sqcup\!\sqcup Q$ is also a recognizable trace language.*

Proof: Let us first prove the following lemma.

Lemma 4.5.8 *Let K be a semiring, let S, T be two series of $K \ll \Sigma, I \gg$, let t be a trace of length n in $\mathbb{M}(\Sigma, I)$ and let w be any word in $\varphi^{-1}(t)$. Then we have*

$$t^{-1}(S \; \sqcup\!\sqcup \; T) = \sum_{I \subset [1,n]} (\varphi(w[I])^{-1}S) \; \sqcup\!\sqcup \; (\varphi(w[-I])^{-1}T) \; . \qquad (4.44)$$

Proof: Let x be an arbitrary trace of $\mathbb{M}(\Sigma, I)$. It is then easy to see that the coefficient on x of the series involved at the right of relation (4.44) is

$$\sum_{I \subset [1,n]} \; \sum_{u,v \in \mathbb{M}(\Sigma, I)} \binom{x}{u \; , \; v} (S|\varphi(w[I])u) \, (T|\varphi(w[-I])v)$$

and thus is equal to

$$\sum_{u,v \in \mathbb{M}(\Sigma, I)} \; \sum_{I \subset [1,n]} \binom{x}{u \; , \; v} (S|\varphi(w[I])u) \, (T|\varphi(w[-I])v) \; ,$$

which can itself be rewritten as follows

$$\sum_{u,v \in \mathbb{M}(\Sigma, I)} \left(\sum_{I \subset [1,n]} \binom{x}{\varphi(w[I])^{-1}u \; , \; \varphi(w[-I])^{-1}v} \right) (S|u) \, (T|v) \; .$$

Let now w' be any word in $\varphi^{-1}(x)$. There clearly exists $J \subset [1, n + |x|]$ such that $\varphi(ww'[J]) = u$ and $\varphi(ww'[-J]) = v$ iff there exists $I \subset [1,n]$ and $K \subset [1, |x|]$ such that $\varphi(w[I]) \, \varphi(w'[K]) = u$ and $\varphi(w[-I]) \, \varphi(w'[-K]) = v$. Hence we get

$$\binom{tx}{u \; , \; v} = \sum_{I \subset [1,n]} \binom{x}{\varphi(w[I])^{-1}u \; , \; \varphi(w[-I])^{-1}v} \; .$$

It suffices now to report this last relation into the previous one in order to get

$$\left(\sum_{I \subset [1,n]} (\varphi(w[I])^{-1}S) \; \sqcup\!\sqcup \; (\varphi(w[-I])^{-1}T) | x \right) = \sum_{u,v \in \mathbb{M}(\Sigma, I)} \binom{tx}{u \; , \; v} (S|u) \, (T|v) \; .$$

Since this last term is equal to $(S \sqcup\!\sqcup T | x)$, it is now easy to conclude. $\qquad \square$

Let P, Q be two recognizable languages of $\mathbb{M}(\Sigma, I)$. This means that the sets $(t^{-1}P)_{t \in \mathbb{M}(\Sigma, I)}$ and $(t^{-1}Q)_{t \in \mathbb{M}(\Sigma, I)}$ are finite. Hence $R = (u^{-1}P \sqcup v^{-1}Q)_{u, v \in \mathbb{M}(\Sigma, I)}$ is also a finite set. But Lemma 4.5.8 shows that the trace languages $t^{-1}(P \sqcup Q)$ are always finite unions of the languages of R. Since R is finite, it follows that the set $(t^{-1}(P \sqcup Q))_{t \in \mathbb{M}(\Sigma, I)}$ is also finite. Hence $P \sqcup Q$ is a recognizable trace language of $\mathbb{M}(\Sigma, I)$.   □

Remark 4.5.9 Proposition 4.5.7 can be easily adapted in order to show that the shuffle product of two recognizable series (cf. [13, 244]) is also recognizable when K is a Noetherian ring or a finite semiring.

Remark 4.5.10 One may also ask if the shuffle product preserves rationality. This is true in the free case, since rationality is then equivalent to recognizability and in the totally commutative case, since the shuffle product of two trace languages is then equal to their product according to Example 4.5.5. However these are the two only cases for which such a result holds as shows the next example.

Example 4.5.11 Let us again consider the independence alphabet of Example 4.2.8 and let $L = (ab)^* \sqcup c^*$. It is a trace language which is the shuffle of two rational languages of $\mathbb{M}(\Sigma, I)$. Using the fact that $(a, b) \in I$, it is easy to check that

$$L = \{ t \in \mathbb{M}(\Sigma, I), \ |t|_a = |t|_b \} .$$

Suppose now that L is rational. Hence there would exist a rational subset R of Σ^* such that $L = \varphi(R)$. Applying the usual pumping lemma to R, we can conclude to the existence of $n \in \mathbb{N}$ such that every $w \in R$ of length $\geq n$ can be decomposed as $w = xyz$ with $|y| \geq 1$, $|xy| \leq n$ and $xy^m z \in R$ for every $m \geq 0$. But $w = a^n cb^n$ belongs necessarily to R since it is the only element in its commutation class. Decomposing w according to the pumping lemma, we can write $w = (a^p)(a^q)(a^r cb^n)$ with $x = a^p$, $y = a^q$, $z = a^r cb^n$, $p + q + r = n$ and $q \geq 1$. Thus $a^{p+mq+r} cb^n \in R$ for every $m \geq 0$ which is clearly not the case. Therefore L can not be a rational trace language.

4.5.2   Another Approach

We here denote by $\mathbb{M}(\Sigma, I) \otimes \mathbb{M}(\Sigma, I)$ the trace monoid $\mathbb{M}(\Sigma, I) \times \mathbb{M}(\Sigma, I)$ (which is also a trace monoid). We write then $u \otimes v$ instead of (u, v) for every $u, v \in \mathbb{M}(\Sigma, I)$. In particular, the product of two elements of $\mathbb{M}(\Sigma, I) \otimes \mathbb{M}(\Sigma, I)$ is defined by

$$(u \otimes v)(x \otimes y) = ux \otimes vy$$

for every u, v, x, y in $\mathbb{M}(\Sigma, I)$. Let us now introduce the mapping Δ from Σ into $\mathbb{N}[\mathbb{M}(\Sigma, I) \otimes \mathbb{M}(\Sigma, I)]$ defined by

$$\Delta(a) = 1 \otimes a + a \otimes 1$$

for every $a \in \Sigma$. It is then easy to check that

$$\Delta(a)\Delta(b) = (1 \otimes a + a \otimes 1)(1 \otimes b + b \otimes 1) = 1 \otimes ab + a \otimes b + b \otimes a + ab \otimes 1 .$$

It clearly follows from this last relation that $\Delta(a)\Delta(b) = \Delta(b)\Delta(a)$ when $(a, b) \in I$. Hence Δ can be extended to a monoid morphism, that we still call Δ, from $\mathbb{M}(\Sigma, I)$ into the multiplicative monoid $\mathbb{N}[\mathbb{M}(\Sigma, I) \otimes \mathbb{M}(\Sigma, I)]$ of polynomials over $\mathbb{M}(\Sigma, I) \otimes \mathbb{M}(\Sigma, I)$ with multiplicities in $\mathbb{N}$.

Proposition 4.5.12 *Let $\mathbb{M}(\Sigma, I)$ be a trace monoid, let t be a trace of length n in $\mathbb{M}(\Sigma, I)$ and let $w \in \Sigma^*$ be a word in $\varphi^{-1}(t)$. Then we have*

$$\Delta(t) = \sum_{I \subset [1,n]} \varphi(w[I]) \otimes \varphi(w[-I]) = \sum_{u,v \in \mathbb{M}(\Sigma, I)} \binom{t}{u \, , \, v} u \otimes v \ .$$

Proof: Let $u, v \in \mathbb{M}(\Sigma, I)$. The coefficient of $u \otimes v$ in the sum

$$\sum_{I \subset [1,n]} \varphi(w[I]) \otimes \varphi(w[-I]) \tag{4.45}$$

is equal to the number of $I \subset [1, |t|]$ such that $\varphi(w[I]) = u$ and $\varphi(w[-I]) = v$ where w denotes any word in $\varphi^{-1}(t)$, which is exactly a binomial coefficient. Hence the second equality of Proposition 4.5.12 is true. Moreover this also proves that the sum (4.45) does not depend of the representative w taken in $\varphi^{-1}(t)$.

We can now prove by induction on $|t|$ the first relation of Proposition 4.5.12 (which says that $\Delta(t)$ is equal to the sum (4.45)). Our result is true for $|t| = 0$ and for $|t| = 1$. Let now t be a trace of length $n \geq 2$ and let us suppose that our result holds at order $n - 1$. We can write $t = t' a$ with $a \in \Sigma$. Using the induction hypothesis and the definition of Δ, we get

$$\begin{aligned}
\Delta(t) &= \Big(\sum_{I \subset [1,n-1]} \varphi(w'[I]) \otimes \varphi(w'[-I]) \Big) \, (1 \otimes a + a \otimes 1) \\
&= \sum_{I \subset [1,n-1]} \varphi(w'[I]) \otimes \varphi(w'[-I])a \ + \sum_{I \subset [1,n-1]} \varphi(w'[I])a \otimes \varphi(w'[-I])
\end{aligned}$$

where $w' \in \varphi^{-1}(t')$. Let us now consider $w = w'a$ which is a word of Σ^* that belongs to $\varphi^{-1}(t)$. There is clearly a bijection between the set of pairs $(w[I], w[-I])$ for $I \subset [1, n]$ and the set of pairs $(w'[J]a, w'[-J])$ or $(w'[J], w'[-J]a)$ for $J \subset [1, n-1]$. It follows from this bijection and from the last above relation that $\Delta(t)$ is equal to the desired sum (4.45). $\qquad \square$

We can now give the following important result that gives the explicit connection between Δ and the shuffle product in $\mathbb{M}(\Sigma, I)$.

Corollary 4.5.13 *Let u, v, t be traces of $\mathbb{M}(\Sigma, I)$. Then we have*

$$\binom{t}{u \, , \, v} = (u \,\shuffle\, v | t) = (\Delta(t) | u \otimes v) \ .$$

Proof: The first above equality is clearly equivalent to Definition 4.5.2. The second one is an immediate reformulation of Proposition 4.5.12. $\qquad \square$

The following proposition shows that the operator $S \to a^{-1}S$ is a derivation for the shuffle product when $a \in \Sigma$.

Proposition 4.5.14 *Let* $\mathbb{M}(\Sigma, I)$ *be a trace monoid, let K be a semiring, let S, T be two series of $K \ll \Sigma, I \gg$ and let a be a letter of Σ. Then we have*

$$a^{-1}(S \amalg T) = (a^{-1}S) \amalg T + S \amalg (a^{-1}T) .$$

Proof: Let $t \in \mathbb{M}(\Sigma, I)$. By linearity, it suffices to prove our result when $S = u$ and $T = v$ where u, v are two traces of $\mathbb{M}(\Sigma, I)$. Then we can write

$$
\begin{aligned}
(a^{-1}(u \amalg v)|t) &= (u \amalg v|at) = (\Delta(at)|u \otimes v) = (\Delta(a)\Delta(t)|u \otimes v) \\
&= ((1 \otimes a)\Delta(t)|u \otimes v) + ((a \otimes 1)\Delta(t)|u \otimes v) \\
&= (\Delta(t)|u \otimes a^{-1}v) + (\Delta(t)|a^{-1}u \otimes v) \\
&= (u \amalg a^{-1}v + a^{-1}u \otimes v|t) ,
\end{aligned}
$$

using Corollary 4.5.13. Our proposition immediately follows.   □

Let us denote by ϵ the mapping from $\mathbb{M}(\Sigma, I)$ into $\mathbb{N}$ such that $\epsilon(1) = 1$ and $\epsilon(t) = 0$ for every non-empty trace t in $\mathbb{M}(\Sigma, I)$. Then we can give.

Proposition 4.5.15 *Let* $\mathbb{M}(\Sigma, I)$ *be a trace monoid. The binomial coefficient for traces is then entirely characterized by the fact that we have*

$$\binom{1}{u, \, v} = \epsilon(u)\,\epsilon(v) \quad and \quad \binom{at}{u, \, v} = \binom{t}{a^{-1}u, \, v} + \binom{t}{u, \, a^{-1}v}$$

for every traces u, v, t in $\mathbb{M}(\Sigma, I)$ and every letter a of Σ, where we set

$$\binom{t}{0, \, v} = \binom{t}{u, \, 0} = 0$$

for every u, v, t in $\mathbb{M}(\Sigma, I)$ by convention.

Proof: The first relation is a consequence from Definition 4.5.2. Let now $a \in \Sigma$ and $u, v, t \in \mathbb{M}(\Sigma, I)$. According to Proposition 4.5.14 and Corollary 4.5.13, we get

$$\binom{at}{u, \, v} = (u \amalg v|at) = (a^{-1}(u \amalg v)|t) = (a^{-1}u \amalg v|t) + (u \amalg a^{-1}v|t)$$

$$= \binom{t}{a^{-1}u, \, v} + \binom{t}{u, \, a^{-1}v} .$$

Thus the second formula also holds. Note now that the above formulas give an inductive way (based on an induction on the length of $|t|$) for computing the binomial coefficient, which is therefore characterized by them.   □

Example 4.5.16 When $\Sigma = \{a\}$, we easily get from Definition 4.5.2 that

$$\begin{pmatrix} a^n \\ a^p , \ a^q \end{pmatrix} = \delta_{n,p+q} \begin{pmatrix} n \\ p \end{pmatrix} .$$

Hence Proposition 4.5.15 is here equivalent to the usual Pascal triangle recursion.

Example 4.5.17 Let us consider the trace monoid of Example 4.2.8. Then we have

$$\begin{pmatrix} aabc \\ ab , \ ac \end{pmatrix} = \begin{pmatrix} aac \\ a , \ ac \end{pmatrix} = \begin{pmatrix} ac \\ 1 , \ ac \end{pmatrix} + \begin{pmatrix} ac \\ a , \ c \end{pmatrix}$$

$$= \begin{pmatrix} c \\ 1 , \ c \end{pmatrix} + \begin{pmatrix} c \\ 1 , \ c \end{pmatrix} = \begin{pmatrix} 1 \\ 1 , \ 1 \end{pmatrix} + \begin{pmatrix} 1 \\ 1 , \ 1 \end{pmatrix} = 2$$

according to Proposition 4.5.15.

Let $\tilde{w}$ denote the mirror image of w. Checking the property on elementary rewritings, it can be easily shown that $\varphi(\tilde{w}) = \varphi(\tilde{w'})$ when $\varphi(w) = \varphi(w')$ for every $w, w' \in \Sigma^*$. Hence the notion of *mirror image $\tilde{t}$* of a trace $t \in \mathbb{M}(\Sigma, I)$ is also well defined. We can then introduce the antipode which is the mapping S defined by

$$S(t) = (-1)^{|t|} \tilde{t} \in \mathbb{Z}<\Sigma, I>$$

for every $t \in \mathbb{M}(\Sigma, I)$. We can give antipodal formulas for the shuffle product.

Proposition 4.5.18 Let t be a trace of $\mathbb{M}(\Sigma, I)$. Then we have

$$\sum_{u,v \in \mathbb{M}(\Sigma,I)} \begin{pmatrix} t \\ u , \ v \end{pmatrix} S(u)v = \epsilon(t) \quad and \quad \sum_{uv=t} S(u) \ ⧢ \ v = \epsilon(t) .$$

Proof: The two above equalities are clear when $|t| = 0$. Let now t be a trace of length $n \geq 1$ of $\mathbb{M}(\Sigma, I)$. We can then write $t = at'$ with $a \in \Sigma$. Thus we have

$$\sum_{u,v \in \mathbb{M}(\Sigma,I)} \begin{pmatrix} at' \\ u , \ v \end{pmatrix} S(u)v = \sum_{u,v \in \mathbb{M}(\Sigma,I)} (\begin{pmatrix} t' \\ a^{-1}u , \ v \end{pmatrix} + \begin{pmatrix} t' \\ u , \ a^{-1}v \end{pmatrix})S(u)v$$

according to Proposition 4.5.15. It follows that the above sum is equal to

$$\sum_{u,v \in \mathbb{M}(\Sigma,I)} \begin{pmatrix} t' \\ u , \ v \end{pmatrix} (-1)^{|u|+1} \tilde{u}av + \sum_{u,v \in \mathbb{M}(\Sigma,I)} \begin{pmatrix} t' \\ u , \ v \end{pmatrix})S(u)av = 0 .$$

This shows the first relation of our proposition. Let now $x \in \mathbb{M}(\Sigma, I)$. Taking the coefficient of x of this first relation, we get

$$\sum_{\tilde{u}v=x} \begin{pmatrix} t \\ u , \ v \end{pmatrix} (-1)^{|u|} = (\epsilon(t)|x)$$

for every $t \in \mathbb{M}(\Sigma, I)$. Hence we have in particular

$$\sum_{uv=x} \begin{pmatrix} t \\ \tilde{u} \, , \, v \end{pmatrix} (-1)^{|u|} = (\epsilon(t)|x)$$

from which we deduce easily that

$$\begin{aligned}
\sum_{uv=x} S(u) \sqcup v &= \sum_{uv=x} \Big(\sum_{t\in\mathbb{M}(\Sigma,I)} \begin{pmatrix} t \\ \tilde{u} \, , \, v \end{pmatrix} (-1)^{|u|} t \Big) \\
&= \sum_{t\in\mathbb{M}(\Sigma,I)} \Big(\sum_{uv=x} \begin{pmatrix} t \\ \tilde{u} \, , \, v \end{pmatrix} (-1)^{|u|} \Big) \, t \\
&= \sum_{t\in\mathbb{M}(\Sigma,I)} (\epsilon(t)|x) = \epsilon(x) \, .
\end{aligned}$$

This shows the second relation. □

4.5.3 Recursive Formulas

In the free case, $u \sqcup v$ is classically inductively defined by the formulas

$$ua \sqcup vb = (u \sqcup vb)a + (ua \sqcup v)b$$
$$u \sqcup 1 = 1 \sqcup u = u$$

that give a recursive way of computing the shuffle product of two words. These formulas lead obviously to an exponential algorithm which seems to be unavoidable due to structure of the problem. We shall give here similar formulas for expressing the shuffle of two traces in terms of shuffles of some subwords.

The following result is essentially a reformulation of Proposition 4.2.9.

Proposition 4.5.19 (*Reconstruction lemma*) *Let* $\mathbb{M}(\Sigma, I)$ *be a trace monoid, let* K *be a ring and let* S *be a series of* $K \ll \Sigma, I \gg$. *Then we have*

$$S = (S|1) + \sum_{t \text{ is a clique}} (-1)^{|t|+1} \, t \, (t^{-1}S)$$

Proof: Observe that the relation to prove is equivalent to

$$(S|1) = \sum_{t \text{ is a clique}} (-1)^{|t|} \, t \, (t^{-1}S) \, . \tag{4.46}$$

Let now $x \in \mathbb{M}(\Sigma, I)$. Then the coefficient on x of the right member of (4.46) is

$$\sum_{t \text{ is a clique}} (-1)^{|t|} \sum_{tu=x} (S|tu) = (S|x) \Big(\sum_{tu=x} \mu_I(t) \Big) = (S|x) \, (\mu_I \, \underline{\mathbb{M}(\Sigma, I)}|x) \, .$$

It follows now from Proposition 4.2.9 that the last above expression is equal to 0 when $x \neq 1$ and to $(S|1)$ when $x = 1$. Our proposition immediately follows. □

We can then give a recursive formula for the shuffle product in $\mathbb{M}(\Sigma, I)$.

Proposition 4.5.20 *Let* $\mathbb{M}(\Sigma, I)$ *be a trace monoid. Then the relation*

$$u \sqcup\!\sqcup v = \sum_{t \text{ is a clique}} (-1)^{|t|+1} t \left(\sum_{xy=t} x^{-1}u \sqcup\!\sqcup y^{-1}v \right)$$

holds in $\mathbb{Z}\langle\Sigma, I\rangle$ *for every traces* u *and* v *of* $\mathbb{M}(\Sigma, I)$.

Proof: According to Proposition 4.5.19, we can write

$$u \sqcup\!\sqcup v = \sum_{t \text{ is a clique}} (-1)^{|t|+1} t \, t^{-1}(u \sqcup\!\sqcup v) . \tag{4.47}$$

Let us now show the following lemma.

Lemma 4.5.21 *Let* $\mathbb{M}(\Sigma, I)$ *be a trace monoid, let* u, v *be traces of* $\mathbb{M}(\Sigma, I)$ *and let* t *be a clique of* $\mathbb{M}(\Sigma, I)$. *Then we have*

$$t^{-1}(u \sqcup\!\sqcup v) = \sum_{xy=t} x^{-1}u \sqcup\!\sqcup y^{-1}v .$$

Proof: When $t = at'$ is a clique with $a \in \Sigma$, we have

$$xy = t \quad \text{iff} \quad (x = ax' \text{ and } y = y') \text{ or } (x = x' \text{ and } y = ay') \text{ with } x'y' = t' .$$

Using this property, it is now easy to deduce our lemma from Proposition 4.5.14 by induction on the length of t.   □

Relation (4.47) and Lemma 4.5.21 allows us immediately to conclude.   □

Remark 4.5.22 Even if the computations involved in the formula of Proposition 4.5.20 must be done in $\mathbb{Z}\langle\Sigma, I\rangle$, the result lies in fact in $\mathbb{N}\langle\Sigma, I\rangle$.

Remark 4.5.23 The shuffle product in $\mathbb{M}(\Sigma, I)$ is entirely characterized by the formula of Proposition 4.5.20 and by the fact that $u \sqcup\!\sqcup 1 = 1 \sqcup\!\sqcup u = u$ for every $u \in \mathbb{M}(\Sigma, I)$.

Example 4.5.24 Let us again consider the trace monoid of Example 4.2.8. Then Proposition 4.5.20 shows that the following relation

$$\begin{aligned}
u \sqcup\!\sqcup v = \ & a(a^{-1}u \sqcup\!\sqcup v) + a(u \sqcup\!\sqcup a^{-1}v) + b(b^{-1}u \sqcup\!\sqcup v) + b(u \sqcup\!\sqcup b^{-1}v) \\
& + c(c^{-1}u \sqcup\!\sqcup v) + c(u \sqcup\!\sqcup c^{-1}v) - ab((ab)^{-1}u \sqcup\!\sqcup v) \\
& - ab(a^{-1}u \sqcup\!\sqcup b^{-1}v) - ab(b^{-1}u \sqcup\!\sqcup a^{-1}u) - ab(u \sqcup\!\sqcup (ab)^{-1}v)
\end{aligned}$$

holds for every traces u, v in $\mathbb{M}(\Sigma, I)$. Using the previous formulas, we again get

$$\begin{aligned}
ab \sqcup\!\sqcup c &= a(b \sqcup\!\sqcup c) + b(a \sqcup\!\sqcup c) + c(ab \sqcup\!\sqcup 1) - ab(1 \sqcup\!\sqcup c) \\
&= abc + acb + bca + cab .
\end{aligned}$$

4.6 Exercises

Exercise 4.6.1 Let (Σ, I) be an independence alphabet, let Z be a non-commutative subalphabet of Σ and let $T = \Sigma - Z$. We define then inductively a *potential function* p from Σ^* into $\mathbf{N}$ by the conditions

$$p(1) = 0, \ p(wa) = p(w) \text{ if } a \in T \text{ and } p(wa) = p(w) + |w| + 1 \text{ if } a \in Z \ .$$

1) For every $S \subset \Sigma$ and for every $w \in \Sigma^*$, let us denote by $|w|_S$ the number of letters of w that belong to X. Let now $w \in \Sigma^*$. Show that one has

$$p(w) \leq \frac{1}{2}|w|_T \left(|w|_Z^2 + |w|_T\right)$$

and that this bound is reached once for some word commutatively equivalent to w.

2) Two words $x, y \in \Sigma^*$ are said to be *elementarily equivalent* iff there exists $u, v \in \Sigma^*$ and $(a, b) \in I$ such that $x = uabv$ and $y = ubav$. We also recall that a sequence $(k_i)_{i=0,n}$ of integers is said to be *unimodal* iff there exists some $k \in [0, n]$ such that $(k_i)_{i=0,k}$ is non-decreasing when $(k_i)_{i=k+1,n}$ is non-increasing.

Let now $u, v \in \Sigma^*$ such that $u \equiv_I v$. Show that there exists a chain of elementarily equivalent words $u_0 = u, u_1, \ldots, u_{n-1}, u_n = v$ going from u to v such that the sequence $(p(u_i))_{i=1,n}$ is unimodal.

3) Let $w \in \Sigma^*$ and let $w = w_0 z_1 w_1 \ldots z_n w_n$ be its decomposition with respect to the factorization of Example 4.2.2 where $z_i \in Z$ and $w_i \in <T>$ for any $i \in [1, n]$. Show that $p(w)$ is maximal in $\varphi^{-1}(w)$ iff $\varphi(z_i w_i) \in C_Z(T)$ for every $i \in [1, n]$.

4) We here denote by $\equiv_T$ the congruence on Σ^* induced by the independence graph $I \cap T \times T$. Let now $u \equiv_I v \in \Sigma^*$ such that $p(u)$ and $p(v)$ are maximal in their common equivalence class. Show that $u \equiv_T v$.

5) Deduce a new proof of Theorem 4.3.5 from the previous results.

Exercise 4.6.2 1) Analyze the complexity of the underlying algorithm given by the proof of Theorem 4.3.5 for computing the decomposition of a trace according to a given Lazard's factorization of the associated trace monoid.

2) Let (Σ, I) be an independence alphabet, let Z be a non-commutative subalphabet of Σ and let $T = \Sigma - Z$. Propose an efficient algorithm for computing Lazard's decomposition of a trace of type $z\, t$ where $z \in Z$ and $t \in <T>$.

3) Develop then a parallel algorithm for computing the decomposition of an arbitrary trace t according to Lazard's factorization and compare its complexity with the sequential algorithm given by Theorem 4.3.5. [6]

Exercise 4.6.3 Let K be a ring and let M be a monoid. We recall that M is said to be *locally finite* iff every $m \in M$ has only a finite number of decompositions of type $m = m_1 \ldots m_n$ where $m_i \in M - \{1_M\}$ for every $i \in [1, n]$.

---

[6] The idea is to factorize a representative of t in Σ^* with respect to the usual free Lazard's factorization (cf. Example 4.2.2) and then to apply in parallel the algorithm of the second question to each peace of the obtained factorization with an adapted synchronization methodology.

1) Let M be a locally finite monoid. Show that a series $S \in K \ll M \gg$ has an inverse in $K \ll M \gg$ iff $(S|1)$ has an inverse in K.

2) Show that any trace monoid $\mathbb{M}(\Sigma, I)$ is locally finite. Let $\mathfrak{Mg}_{\mathbb{Z}} \ll \Sigma, I \gg$ be the set of the series of $\mathbb{Z} < \Sigma, I >$ whose constant term is equal to 1. Show that $\mathfrak{Mg}_{\mathbb{Z}} \ll \Sigma, I \gg$ is a multiplicative group.

3) Show that one can define in a unique way a morphism μ from $\mathbb{M}(\Sigma, I)$ into $\mathfrak{Mg}_{\mathbb{Z}} \ll \Sigma, I \gg$ by setting $\mu(a) = 1 + a$ for every $a \in A$. Prove that μ is injective and hence that $\mathbb{M}(\Sigma, I)$ can be embedded in a group.

Exercise 4.6.4 Let $(\Sigma_i)_{i=1,N}$ be a chromatic partition of some independence alphabet (Σ, I) and let $<$ be a total order on Σ that respects the chromatic partition. Show that the normal forms for traces given by Corollary 4.3.12 are lexicographic.

Exercise 4.6.5 The *Lie bracket* on $\mathbb{Z} < \Sigma, I >$ is the operation defined by

$$[P, Q] = PQ - QP$$

for every $P, Q \in \mathbb{Z} < \Sigma, I >$. For every word $w = a_1 a_2 \ldots a_n \in \Sigma^*$, let us also define

$$[w] = [\ldots [[a_1, a_2], a_3], \ldots, a_n] \in \mathbb{Z} < \Sigma > .$$

1) Let $a \in \Sigma$ and let D_a denote the mapping defined by $D_a(P) = [a, P]$ for every polynomial $P \in \mathbb{Z} < \Sigma, I >$. Show that $D_a D_b = D_b D_a$ when $(a, b) \in I$. Deduce from this property that $[t] = [t'] \in \mathbb{Z} < \Sigma, I >$ when $t \equiv_I t' \in \Sigma^*$ and hence that one can define $[t] \in \mathbb{Z} < \Sigma, I >$ for every $t \in \mathbb{M}(\Sigma, I)$.

2) Let $a \in \Sigma$ and $t \in \mathbb{M}(\Sigma, I)$. Show then that one has

$$[at] = \sum_{x \in \mathbb{M}(\Sigma, I)} \left(\sum_{uav=x} (-1)^{|u|} \binom{t}{\tilde{u}, v} \right) x .$$

Exercise 4.6.6 Let M be a monoid. Then a total order $<$ on M *respects the monoid structure* iff $np < mq$ when $n < m$ and $p \le q$ for every $n, m, p, q \in M$.

1) Deduce from Exercise 4.6.3 that every trace monoid $\mathbb{M}(\Sigma, I)$ can be equipped with a total order that respects its monoid structure.

2) Let $u, v \in \mathbb{M}(\Sigma, I)$ such that $u^n = v^n$ with $n \in \mathbb{N} - \{0\}$. Show that $u = v$.

3) Let $u, v \in \mathbb{M}(\Sigma, I)$ such that $u^n v^m = v^m u^n$ with $n, m \in \mathbb{N} - \{0\}$. Show then that $uv = vu$.

4) A semiring K is said to be a *domain* iff either k or l is 0 when $kl = 0$ in K. Show that $K < \Sigma, I >$ is always a domain when K is a domain.

Exercise 4.6.7 Let M be a monoid defined by a presentation $< \Sigma; R >$ where $R = \{ (u, v), u, v \in \Sigma^* \}$ is some family of pairs of words over Σ. We denote by $M \otimes M$ the direct product $M \times M$ and use the same kinds of notations than in Section 4.5.2. Let then Δ be the mapping from Σ into $\mathbb{N}[M \otimes M]$ defined by

$$\Delta(a) = 1 \otimes a + a \otimes 1 .$$

We say that M can be equipped with a shuffle product iff one has $\Delta(u) = \Delta(v)$ for every pair $(u, v) \in R$. Show that the trace monoids are the only monoids that one can equip with a shuffle product.

4.7   Some Remarks on Other Related Structures

Let (Σ, I) be an independence alphabet. There are two interesting algebraic structures related to $\mathbb{M}(\Sigma, I)$. First we have the *free partially commutative group* $\mathbb{F}(\Sigma, I)$ which is the group presented by

$$\mathbb{F}(\Sigma, I) = \; < \Sigma \;; \; ab = ba \; \text{ for } (a, b) \in I >$$

(cf. [36, 186] for instance). Let K be a ring. We can then consider the *free partially commutative Lie K-algebra* $\mathbb{L}_K(\Sigma, I)$ which is the Lie K-algebra presented by

$$\mathbb{L}_K(\Sigma, I) = \; < \Sigma \;; \; [a, b] = 0 \; \text{ for } (a, b) \in I >$$

(cf. [28, 85] for instance). The results of Section 4.3 can be seen as a combinatorial dictionary for obtaining connected elimination results for $\mathbb{F}(\Sigma, I)$ and $\mathbb{L}_K(\Sigma, I)$. One can associate with every chromatic partition of (Σ, I) a decomposition of $\mathbb{L}_K(\Sigma, I)$ as a finite direct sum of free Lie algebras whose basic families can be computed with the associated Z-codes. This decomposition allows to effectively compute bases of $\mathbb{L}_K(\Sigma, I)$ (see [68, 78, 85, 87, 168, 169] for more details). More recently, Katsura and Kobayashi continued the study of the shuffle product in connection with $\mathbb{L}_K(\Sigma, I)$. They generalized Ree's theorem and Dynkin's formula (see [148, 147, 233]). The K-algebras $K < \Sigma, I >$ and $K \ll \Sigma, I \gg$ were also studied by several authors (see [51, 77, 87, 81, 80, 106, 152, 153, 260] for instance).

In the same way, one can associate with every chromatic partition of (Σ, I) a decomposition of $\mathbb{F}(\Sigma, I)$ as a finite semidirect product of free groups whose bases can be computed with the corresponding Z-codes (see [87]). Hence semidirect product seems to be the good tool for decomposing $\mathbb{F}(\Sigma, I)$ in a finite number of free groups. Note that there are free partially commutative groups that cannot be embedded in any finite limited direct product of free groups (cf. [55]). Using these elimination results, one can also construct a commutator calculus and a Magnus theory for $\mathbb{F}(\Sigma, I)$ connected as in the free case with $\mathbb{L}_K(\Sigma, I)$ (see [72, 84, 88]).

In fact $\mathbb{F}(\Sigma, I)$ has been intensively studied by several authors (see [36, 69, 70, 71, 72, 84, 87, 88, 250, 251, 252, 275, 276] for instance). It can be shown that $\mathbb{M}(\Sigma, I)$ embeds in a natural way into $\mathbb{F}(\Sigma, I)$ (see [36, 74]). One can prove that $\mathbb{F}(\Sigma, I)$ can be totally ordered (see [84, 89]). Complexities of several decision problems for $\mathbb{F}(\Sigma, I)$ have also been studied (see [53, 74, 275, 276]). Droms characterized the free partially commutative groups for which all subgroups are still free partially commutative groups by means of a property of their independence graph (see [55, 71]).

It is also interesting to know that one can solve the isomorphism problem for all these algebraic structures. Indeed two free partially commutative Lie algebras, groups, polynomial algebras or monoids are isomorphic iff their associated independence graphs are isomorphic (see [70, 152]).

Finally let us say that one can show that the trace framework is the maximal one in which one can both develop a Lie and a monoid theory. In particular $\mathbb{M}(\Sigma, I)$ is essentially the only monoid in which one can define good notions of subword and complement as in Section 4.5.1 and a good concept of shuffle product (see [82, 87] for more details).

4.8   Bibliographical Remarks

The material for Section 4.2 comes from different sources. Formal power series over monoids are considered by several authors (see [13, 94, 80, 106, 244] for instance). Factorization of monoids were introduced by Schützenberger in [248] (see also [182]) The plactic monoid considered in Example 4.2.4 was introduced by Lascoux and Schützenberger (see [171]). The Möbius function of $\mathbb{M}(\Sigma, I)$ was introduced by Cartier and Foata in a more general context (see [34]). It has been studied by several authors (see [52, 53, 56, 157, 159] for instance). Levi's lemma was proved in the free case in [177]. Its generalization to $\mathbb{M}(\Sigma, I)$ was done by several authors (see [47, 74, 223]). The proof given in Section 4.2.4 follows [47].

The idea of elimination goes back to Lazard who first used it in the context of free groups and free Lie algebras (see [28, 174, 175]). Schützenberger also used this idea in [247], strongly followed by Viennot who developed a combinatorial theory of bases of free Lie algebras (see [267, 268]). The idea of elimination in the trace context appears in [85], motivated by the construction of combinatorial bases for $\mathbb{L}_K(\Sigma, I)$. The material used in Section 4.3 comes essentially from [83].

Conjugacy $\mathbb{M}(\Sigma, I)$ was studied by Duboc (see [76, 74]). The material for Sections 4.4.1 and 4.4.2 comes from [76, 74, 168].

Lyndon words appear in a famous paper of Chen, Fox and Lyndon (cf. [35]) which was motivated by the basic commutator calculus in the free group (cf. [130, 185]). Lyndon words were then intensively studied in the context of combinatorics on words (see [182] for more details). The first definition of Lyndon traces was proposed by Lalonde (see [168, 169, 170]) using the framework of Viennot's theory of heaps of peaces (cf. [269]). Lalonde's definition corresponds to Definition 4.4.20 taken with a trivial chromatic partition (every Σ_i is reduced to a single letter). The presentation of Section 4.4.3 comes essentially from [160]. Another interpretation of Lyndon traces was proposed by Katsura and Kobayashi in [147]. The enumeration of Lyndon traces, generalizing the classical Witt's formulas (cf. [28, 182]), was also done independently by several authors (see [85, 168, 147] for instance).

Schmitt introduced the notions of binomial coefficient and of shuffle product of traces in [246]. The properties of the binomial coefficient given in Section 4.5.2 come from [148, 147]. It was also studied in [158]. The Hopf algebra presentation of the shuffle product (cf. [6]) given in Section 4.5.2 and the recursive formula of Section 4.5.3 come from [86].

Exercise 4.6.3 presents the Magnus transformation in the trace context (cf. [88]). Some answers to Exercise 4.6.2 are given in [83]. Exercise 4.6.4 comes from [148]. The results of Exercise 4.6.6 and Exercise 4.6.7 can be respectively found in [84, 88, 77, 260] and in [87].

Chapter 5

Counting Techniques for Inclusion, Equivalence and Membership Problems

Alberto Bertoni   Massimiliano Goldwurm
Giancarlo Mauri   Nicoletta Sabadini

Dip. Scienze dell'Informazione - Università di Milano, Italy
{bertoni,goldwurm,mauri,sabadini}@hermes.unimi.it

Contents

5.1   Introduction

Counting techniques based on properties of generating functions provide in several cases elegant and simple methods for solving problems on formal languages. Classical examples concern analytic techniques for proving the inherent ambiguity of context-free languages and for determining the solution of word enumeration problems: these techniques are related to the algebraicity of the generating functions of unambiguous context-free languages [37, 50, 103].

In this chapter we stress the role of counting techniques to study decidability and complexity of significant problems for rational trace languages: equivalence, inclusion and membership. These problems, defined for trace languages in the same way as for string languages, have been studied by several authors [19, 2, 4, 23] and are related to other classical problems in formal language and automata theory such as the equivalence problem for multi-tape automata [231, 101, 132].

The equivalence problem for rational trace languages has been proved to be decidable for transitive independence relations and undecidable in the general case [19]. The undecidability proof is obtained providing a reduction from the well-known equivalence problem for 2-tape nondeterministic finite state automata [101]. From this result the undecidability of the inclusion problem for rational trace languages follows immediately. A complete characterization has been given in [4] where both equivalence and inclusion problems for rational trace languages are proved to be decidable *if and only if* the independence relation is transitive. More recently a natural counting version of the equivalence problem has been studied in [266], where it is proved that the multiplicity equivalence for rational trace languages is decidable. The proof is based on the technique introduced in [132] to show the decidability of the multiplicity equivalence problem for deterministic multi-tape automata. This result also implies that the equivalence problem for unambiguous (rational) trace languages is decidable.

The membership problems for rational and context-free trace languages have been studied in [240, 41] and [23], where they are shown to be solvable in polynomial time. The combinatorial interest of the problem is related to the evaluation of the number of prefixes in traces of given length. Moreover, the corresponding algorithm can be seen as an instance of a general procedure scheme useful to solve several problems on trace languages as evaluating the multiplicity function of a rational trace language.

Our purpose is to present general methods to prove most results considered above. The main tools we consider are formal power series in partially commutative variables and generating functions associated with both string and trace languages. As a first example, using these tools, we prove that all the rational subsets of a trace monoid have rational generating function if and only if the independence relation is transitive. A first consequence of this result is that for non-transitive independence relations the class of unambiguous trace languages is properly included into the class of rational trace languages. The same result allows to prove the decidability of the inclusion problem in the case of transitive independence relations following a more general approach [17]: if a class of languages is closed under union and each one of its elements admits a rational generating function, then the inclusion problem is decidable.

Another example of application of counting techniques is related to the use of formal power series over division rings (non-commutative fields), which turns out to be a powerful decision tool. In particular, we show the decidability of the multiplicity equivalence problem for rational trace languages, following the proof given in [266], and we present a polynomial time decision algorithm in the case of a product of free monoids.

The last example of application of combinatorial techniques concerns the evaluation of the average number of prefixes in traces of given length. This combinatorial problem can be reduced to counting the strings of given length belonging to suitable regular languages whose generating functions are easily computable. The interest in counting the average number of prefixes is related to the average case analysis of a wide class of algorithms, described by a general procedure scheme, including algorithms for the membership problem.

This chapter is organized as follows. In the next section we present some basic definitions concerning free partially commutative monoids and the standard classification of trace languages. In particular we introduce the classes of rational, recognizable and unambiguous trace languages and study their inclusion properties.

In section 5.3 we introduce the formal power series in partially commutative variables and present the main properties of the Möbius function. Then we define the notion of generating function of trace languages, and characterize the family of trace monoids whose rational subset have rational generating function.

Section 5.4 is devoted to equivalence and inclusion problems both for rational and unambiguous trace languages. In this section we also study the decidability of the multiplicity equivalence for rational trace languages and consider its applications to other problems. Moreover, we give a sufficient condition on the independence relation for the inclusion problem of unambiguous trace languages to be undecidable.

Finally, Section 5.5 summarize the combinatorial results concerning the number of prefixes of traces of given length and shows the relationship with the worst case and average case analysis of algorithms for membership problems [16, 15, 123].

5.2 Rational Trace Languages

In this section we recall the main properties of rational, recognizable and unambiguous trace languages and state the relationships among these classes.

The class of rational trace languages was originally introduced as the set of trace languages obtained as closure of regular string languages under canonical morphism [189]. More precisely, given an independence alphabet (Σ, I) and a language $L \subseteq \Sigma^*$, the trace language *generated* by L is the set $T = \{\varphi(x) : x \in L\}$, where φ is the canonical morphism $\varphi : \Sigma^* \longrightarrow \mathbb{M}(\Sigma, I)$. In the following $\varphi(x)$ and $\varphi(L)$ are also denoted by $[x]$ and $[L]$ respectively. A trace language $T \subseteq \mathbb{M}(\Sigma, I)$ is *rational* if there exists a regular language $L \subseteq \Sigma^*$ that generates T. An algebraic characterization of the rational trace languages is based on the usual rational operations [189].

Theorem 5.2.1 *The class* $\mathrm{Rat}(\mathbb{M}(\Sigma, I))$ *of rational trace languages coincides with the smallest class of subsets of* $\mathbb{M}(\Sigma, I)$ *containing all finite sets and closed with respect to the operations of union* $(\cup)$*, product* $(\cdot)$ *and closure* $(^*)$*.*

Another natural class of languages is given by the set of all trace languages recognized by finite state automata over the trace monoid $\mathbb{M}(\Sigma, I)$.

Definition 5.2.2 *Given a monoid* M*, an* M*-automaton is a pair* $A = \langle Q, \delta \rangle$*, where* Q *is a finite set of states and* $\delta : M \times Q \to Q$ *is a transition function such that*

1. $\delta(1, q) = q$ *for every* $q \in Q$*;*

2. $\delta(mm', q) = \delta(m, \delta(m', q))$*, for every* $m, m' \in M$ *and* $q \in Q$*.*

Definition 5.2.3 *A language* $T \subseteq M$ *is said to be* recognizable *if and only if there exists an* M*-automaton with initial state* q_0 *and final states* $F \subseteq Q$ *such that* $T = \{t \in M : \delta(t, q_0) \in F\}$*.*

In the following we denote by $\mathrm{Rec}(\mathbb{M}(\Sigma, I))$ the class of recognizable languages over $\mathbb{M}(\Sigma, I)$. This class is particularly interesting since the recognizable languages represent in a natural way the behaviour of non-sequential models of computation. In fact, even if in $\mathbb{M}(\Sigma, I)$-automata independence of actions is represented by their commutation and parallelism is not explicitly described, it is possible to prove that they can be simulated by asynchronous devices. In particular, a deep result obtained by Zielonka gives a characterization of recognizable trace languages in terms of asynchronous automata [277]. Another interesting characterization of recognizable languages has been provided by Ochmański [205], using the operations of union, product and a restricted form of Kleene's closure, called coiteration. Further details on these topics can be found in the corresponding chapters of this book. Here we recall a simple characterization of the recognizable trace languages based on the set of all representatives. To this end, for any $T \subseteq \mathbb{M}(\Sigma, I)$, let us denote by $\mathrm{lin} T$ the language $\{x \in \Sigma^* : [x] \in T\}$.

Theorem 5.2.4 *For every independence alphabet* (Σ, I) *and every* $T \subseteq \mathbb{M}(\Sigma, I)$*,* T *is recognizable if and only if* $\mathrm{lin} T$ *is a regular language.*

It is easy to verify that every recognizable trace language is rational. Nevertheless it can be proved that the classes of rational and recognizable trace languages do not coincide unless the independence relation is empty; in other words a theorem analogous to Kleene's Theorem does not hold for rational trace languages. Here we prove these inclusion properties as a consequence of a stronger result concerning the hierarchy of subclasses of rational languages defined by bounding the number of representative strings of each trace.

Definition 5.2.5 *A trace language* T *is* k*-sequential if and only if* T *is generated by a regular language* L *such that every* $t \in T$ *contains at most* k *strings of* L*.*

In particular, a language T is 1-sequential or *deterministic* if and only if there exists a regular language L that generates T so that each trace in T contains exactly one word of L. This class is particularly interesting since it coincides with the class of *unambiguous* trace languages we introduce in the following.

Denoting by $\text{Rat}_k(\mathbb{M}(\Sigma, I))$ the class of k-sequential languages, as an immediate consequence of the definition, we get the following

Theorem 5.2.6 *For every independence alphabet* (Σ, I)*, it holds*

$$\text{Rat}_1(\mathbb{M}(\Sigma, I)) \subseteq \text{Rat}_2(\mathbb{M}(\Sigma, I)) \subseteq \ldots \subseteq \bigcup_{k=1}^{\infty} \text{Rat}_k(\mathbb{M}(\Sigma, I)) \subseteq \text{Rat}(\mathbb{M}(\Sigma, I)).$$

It is also possible to show that for some independence alphabet all these inclusions are proper [20]. For example, the language $T = [(ab)^* cd^* \cup a^* c(bd^*)]$, with independence relation $I = \{(a, b), (b, c), (b, d)\}$, is in $Rat_2(\mathbb{M}(\Sigma, I))$ but is not deterministic. In Section 5.3.3 we give alternative proofs of some of these inclusion results using properties of generating functions. Moreover, the class $\text{Rec}(\mathbb{M}(\Sigma, I))$ turns out to be properly included in the class of deterministic languages, provided the independence relation is non-empty. Here we briefly recall a simple proof of this fact.

Theorem 5.2.7 *Let* (Σ, I) *be an independence alphabet, with* $I \neq \emptyset$*. Then the class* $\text{Rec}(\mathbb{M}(\Sigma, I))$ *is properly contained into* $\text{Rat}_1(\mathbb{M}(\Sigma, I))$*.*

Proof: In order to prove that $\text{Rec}(\mathbb{M}(\Sigma, I)) \subseteq Rat_1(\mathbb{M}(\Sigma, I)))$, we recall that every trace can be represented by a suitable linearization of its Foata normal form. Such a correspondence defines a function $\gamma : \mathbb{M}(\Sigma, I) \longrightarrow \Sigma^*$ which maps every recognizable trace language T into a regular language [14]. Obviously $\gamma(T)$ generates T in a deterministic way, and hence the inclusion holds. To prove that the inclusion is proper, let us consider the language $T = [(ab)^*]$ on the independence alphabet (Σ, I) where $\Sigma = \{a, b\}$ and $I = \{(a, b), (b, a)\}$. This language is clearly in $\text{Rat}_1(\mathbb{M}(\Sigma, I))$ and its linearization $linT$ is not regular since it consists of all words containing the same number of a and b. Therefore, by Theorem 5.2.4, T is not recognizable. $\square$

As an immediate consequence of the previous result, we obtain the desired proper inclusion of $\text{Rec}(\mathbb{M}(\Sigma, I))$ into $\text{Rat}(\mathbb{M}(\Sigma, I))$.

Another interesting subclass of $\text{Rat}(\mathbb{M}(\Sigma, I))$ is the class of *unambiguous* rational trace languages [22]. The notion of unambiguous language over a monoid M was first introduced by Eilenberg and Schützenberger using the unambiguous restriction of rational operations [95]. Here, we give the definition concerning trace monoids:

Definition 5.2.8 *Given two trace languages* T_1 *and* T_2*, we define the* unambiguous sum $(\sqcup)$*, product* $(\circ)$ *and* closure $(^\circ)$ *as follows:*

1. $T_1 \sqcup T_2 = T_1 \cup T_2$ if $T_1 \cap T_2 = \emptyset$;

2. $T_1 \circ T_2 = T_1 \cdot T_2$ if $\forall x, z \in T_1, y, w \in T_2(xy = zw \Rightarrow x = z \wedge y = w)$;

3. $T_1^\diamond = T_1^*$ if T_1 is the basis of a free submonoid of $\mathbb{M}(\Sigma, I)$.

Definition 5.2.9 *The class* $UR(\mathbb{M}(\Sigma, I))$ *of unambiguous* trace languages is the *smallest class of subsets of* $\mathbb{M}(\Sigma, I)$ *containing the empty set, the singletons* $\{t\}$ *for all* $t \in \mathbb{M}(\Sigma, I)$, *and closed with respect to the unambiguous rational operations.*

It is well known that in free monoids every rational language is unambiguous and this property was extended to all commutative monoids by Eilenberg and Schützenberger:

Theorem 5.2.10 [95] *In every commutative monoid the class of the unambiguous rational sets coincides with the class of the rational sets.*

We are now interested in studying the general case of free partially commutative monoids. As a preliminary result, we state the equivalence between unambiguous and deterministic trace languages:

Theorem 5.2.11 [22] *For every independence alphabet* (Σ, I) *we have* $\mathrm{Rat}_1(\mathbb{M}(\Sigma, I)) = UR(\mathbb{M}(\Sigma, I))$ *and hence* $\mathrm{Rec}(\mathbb{M}(\Sigma, I)) \subseteq UR(\mathbb{M}(\Sigma, I)) \subseteq \mathrm{Rat}(\mathbb{M}(\Sigma, I))$.

At last we observe that the result of Eilenberg and Schützenberger cannot be extended to all partially commutative monoids.

Theorem 5.2.12 [22, 241] *For every independence alphabet* (Σ, I), $UR(\mathbb{M}(\Sigma, I)) = \mathrm{Rat}(\mathbb{M}(\Sigma, I))$ *if and only if* I *is transitive.*

5.3   Formal Series and Generating Functions

Algebraic techniques based on formal series and generating functions have widely been used in the literature to study properties of formal languages. A classical example is related to a well known result, due to Chomsky and Schützenberger, stating that every unambiguous context-free language admits an algebraic generating function [37]. This result allows to prove the inherent ambiguity of a context-free language by showing that its generating function is not algebraic. In [103] a variety of analytic methods are proposed to prove the inherent ambiguity of context-free languages which are based on this simple idea. Other applications concern problems of enumeration of strings in context-free languages which can be solved by studying the algebraic systems that define the corresponding generating functions (see for instance [50]).

In this section we present the basic notions and the main properties concerning formal power series and generating functions defined over partially commutative monoids. In particular we present a result that characterizes the trace monoid whose rational sets have rational generating functions. We use these concepts in the following sections to study the decidability of equivalence and inclusion problems for rational trace languages.

5.3.1 Preliminaries

We start by recalling standard properties of formal power series in non-commutative variables. Our presentation is not exhaustive and we only introduce the concepts actually used in the following sections. For a more general presentation see [13, 244].

Given an alphabet Σ and a field F, a formal power series (f.p.s.) in non-commutative variables Σ with coefficients in F is a function $r : \Sigma^* \to F$. The family of all formal series is denoted by $F\langle\langle\Sigma\rangle\rangle$. The support of an element $r \in F\langle\langle\Sigma\rangle\rangle$ is the set $\{x \in \Sigma^* : r(x) \neq 0\}$ and a polynomial is a f.p.s. that has finite support. The set of all polynomials is denotes by $F\langle\Sigma\rangle$. It is well-known that $F\langle\langle\Sigma\rangle\rangle$ forms a ring together with the operations of sum and Cauchy product of series. More precisely, considering the scalar product, $F\langle\langle\Sigma\rangle\rangle$ is a F-algebra.

Since F is a field, it can be proved that an element $r \in F\langle\langle\Sigma\rangle\rangle$ admits a multiplicative inverse $r^{-1} \in F\langle\langle\Sigma\rangle\rangle$ if and only if $r(\epsilon) \neq 0$. We say that a subring C of $F\langle\langle\Sigma\rangle\rangle$ is rationally closed if it contains the inverse r^{-1} for every $r \in C$ such that $r(\epsilon) \neq 0$.

The family of *rational* formal power series is defined as the smallest rationally closed subring of $F\langle\langle\Sigma\rangle\rangle$ containing the polynomials. It is known that a f.p.s. $r \in F\langle\langle\Sigma\rangle\rangle$ is rational if and only if there exists an integer $n \in \mathbf{N}$, two arrays $\pi, \eta \in F^n$ and a monoid morphism $A : \Sigma^* \to F^{n \times n}$ such that $r(x) = \pi A(x) \eta^T$ for every $x \in \Sigma^*$ [13]. We say that $\langle\pi, A, \eta\rangle$ is a *representation* of r and n is called *size* of the representation.

The Hadamard product of two f.p.s. $r, s \in F\langle\langle\Sigma\rangle\rangle$ is the f.p.s. $r \circ s$ defined by $(r \circ s)(x) = r(x) \cdot s(x)$, for every $x \in \Sigma^*$.

Proposition 5.3.1 *Let $r_1, r_2 \in F\langle\langle\Sigma\rangle\rangle$ be rational f.p.s.'s having representations of size n_1 and n_2 respectively. Then $r_1 - r_2$ and $r_1 \circ r_2$ are rational f.p.s. which admit a representation of size $n_1 + n_2$ and $n_1 n_2$ respectively.*

Proof: Let $\langle\pi_i, A_i, \eta_i\rangle$ be the representation of r_i for $i = 1, 2$. Then the f.p.s. $r_1 - r_2$ admits a representation $\langle\pi, A, \eta\rangle$ such that $\pi = (\pi_1, \pi_2)$, $\eta = (\eta_1, -\eta_2)$ and, for every $\sigma \in \Sigma$,

$$A(\sigma) = \begin{pmatrix} A_1(\sigma) & 0 \\ 0 & A_2(\sigma) \end{pmatrix}$$

Clearly such a representation has size $n_1 + n_2$. Analogously, the f.p.s. $r_1 \circ r_2$ can be represented by $\langle\pi_1 \otimes \pi_2, B, \eta_1 \otimes \eta_2\rangle$, where $\otimes$ is the Kronecker product and $B(\sigma) = A_1(\sigma) \otimes A_2(\sigma)$ for each $\sigma \in \Sigma$. It is easy to see that this representation has size $n_1 n_2$. $\square$

We now recall the traditional notion of generating function of a string language. These functions can be introduced as formal power series with coefficient in the field $\mathbb{Q}$ of rational numbers. Given an alphabet Σ and a formal variable z, let $\psi : \mathbb{Q}\langle\langle\Sigma\rangle\rangle \to \mathbb{Q}\langle\langle z\rangle\rangle$ be the morphism generated by the application which maps every $\sigma \in \Sigma$ into z. The *generating function* of a language $L \subseteq \Sigma^*$ is the formal power series f_L defined by

$$f_L = \psi(\chi_L) = \sum_{n=0}^{+\infty} \sharp\{x \in L : |x| = n\}z^n$$

where χ_L is the characteristic series of L.

Note that $\mathbb{Q}\langle\langle z \rangle\rangle$ is a commutative algebra since its elements are formal power series in only one variable. Moreover, it is useful to observe that in this case the definition of rational formal power series can be simplified: a f.p.s. $r \in \mathbb{Q}\langle\langle z \rangle\rangle$ is rational if and only if r is the quotient of two polynomials.

It is not difficult to prove that the generating function of every regular language is rational [37]. Moreover it is often possible to compute the generating function of a regular language L from the regular expression of L, without actually computing the number of words of given length in L. In order to see an example of this computation we observe that, for any pair of languages $L_1, L_2 \subseteq \Sigma^*$, $f_{L_1 L_2} = f_{L_1} + f_{L_2}$ whenever the product $L_1 L_2$ is unambiguous, i.e. every $x \in L_1 L_2$ admits a unique decomposition $x = x_1 x_2$ where $x_1 \in L_1$ and $x_2 \in L_2$. Analogously, $f_{L^*} = (1-f_L)^{-1}$ whenever the closure of L under the star operation is unambiguous, i.e. every $x \in L^+$ admits a unique decomposition $x = x_1 x_2 \cdots x_n$, where each $x_i \in L$ (note that, in this case, $\epsilon \notin L$).

Example 5.3.2 Consider the regular language $L = \{ab, c\}^* \cup \{cb, a\}^*$ and note that such a regular expression is unambiguous. Since the generating function of both $\{ab, c\}$ and $\{cb, a\}$ is $z + z^2$, we obtain

$$f_L = \frac{2}{(1 - z - z^2)}$$

Similar properties hold for unambiguous context-free languages. First we recall that a f.p.s. $r \in \mathbb{Q}\langle\langle z \rangle\rangle$ is said to be *algebraic* if, for a suitable $d \in \mathbb{N}$, there exist $d + 1$ polynomials $P_0, P_1, \ldots, P_d \in \mathbb{Q}\langle z \rangle$, such that $P_d \neq 0$ and $\sum_{k=0}^{d} P_k r^k = 0$. The minimum d for which such an equation holds is called *degree* of the function. A well-known result states that the generating function of every unambiguous context-free language is algebraic [37]. In this case the equation that implicitly defines the generating function can be obtained from an unambiguous grammar that generates the language. A classical example is given by the Dyck language $L \subseteq \{a, b\}^*$ generated by the grammar having productions $S \rightarrow aSbS, \epsilon$. The corresponding equation over $\mathbb{Q}\langle\langle z \rangle\rangle$ is $z^2 s^2 - s + 1 = 0$ which has one acceptable solution $s = \frac{1-(1-4z^2)^{1/2}}{2z^2}$, yielding the generating function $s = f_L(z) = \sum \binom{2n}{n}\frac{1}{n+1}z^{2n}$.

5.3.2 Formal Power Series over Free Partially Commutative Monoids

In this section we introduce basic definitions and results concerning formal power series in partially commutative variables. Here, our main goal is to describe some known properties of the Möbius function. For further details the reader is referred to [167].

Let $\mathbb{M}(\Sigma, I)$ be a free partially commutative monoid and let F be a field.

Definition 5.3.3 *A formal power series in partially commutative variables* (Σ, I) *is a function* $\phi : \mathbb{M}(\Sigma, I) \to F$. *The* support *of a formal power series* ϕ *is the language* $\text{supp}(\phi) = \{t : \phi(t) \neq 0\}$.

The formal power series ϕ is also represented by the sum $\sum_{t \in \mathbb{M}(\Sigma, I)} \phi(t)t$.

We denote by $F\langle\langle \Sigma, I \rangle\rangle$ the set of all formal power series in partially commutative variables (Σ, I). If $I = \emptyset$ we simply obtain $F\langle\langle \Sigma \rangle\rangle$. Also in this case the set $F\langle\langle \Sigma, I \rangle\rangle$ forms a F-algebra together with the operations of sum and Cauchy product defined by $(\phi + \psi)(t) = \phi(t) + \psi(t)$, $(\phi \cdot \psi)(t) = \sum_{uv=t} \phi(u)\psi(v)$. These operations are well defined, since every trace admits a finite number of decompositions of the form $t = t_1 t_2 \ldots t_n$, where $t_i \in \mathbb{M}(\Sigma, I)$ and $t_i \neq [\epsilon]$ for every i. We also recall that a polynomial over $\mathbb{M}(\Sigma, I)$ is a f.p.s. $\phi \in F\langle\langle \Sigma, I \rangle\rangle$ with finite support. The set of all polynomials over $\mathbb{M}(\Sigma, I)$ forms a subalgebra of $F\langle\langle \Sigma, I \rangle\rangle$ usually denoted by $F\langle \Sigma, I \rangle$.

The following examples are particularly important in our context. They describe formal power series in $\mathbb{Q}\langle\langle \Sigma, I \rangle\rangle$.

Example 5.3.4 Given a trace language T, the *characteristic function* of T is the f.p.s. $\chi_T = \sum_{t \in T} t$.

Example 5.3.5 Given the monoid $\mathbb{M}(\Sigma, I)$, let L be a language over Σ. We call *multiplicity* of L the f.p.s. $\natural_L$ such that $\natural_L(t)$ is the cardinality of the set $\{x \in L : [x] = t\}$. Clearly $[L] = supp(\natural_L)$. Moreover, if a trace language $T \subseteq \mathbb{M}(\Sigma, I)$ is unambiguous (i.e. deterministic) then there is a regular languages $L \subseteq \Sigma^*$ such that $\natural_L$ is the characteristic function of T.

Another interesting example is the f.p.s. representing the Möbius function; this function is used in the combinatorial proof of Mac Mahon's Master Theorem [34], that motivated the study of partially commutative monoids. In order to define this function, let us recall that a decomposition $t = t_1 t_2 \ldots t_n$, with $t_i \neq \epsilon$ for every i, is said to be odd (or even) if n is odd (even, respectively).

Example 5.3.6 Let $\text{dec}_0(t)$ $(\text{dec}_1(t))$ be the number of even (odd, respectively) decompositions of a trace t. If t is the empty trace, then $\text{dec}_0(t) = 1$ and $\text{dec}_1(t) = 0$. Then the *Möbius function* $\mu : \mathbb{M}(\Sigma, I) \longrightarrow \mathbb{Q}$ is defined by $\mu(t) = \text{dec}_0(t) - \text{dec}_1(t)$, for any $t \in \mathbb{M}(\Sigma, I)$.

The main property of the Möbius function is given by the following theorem:

Theorem 5.3.7 *Let* μ *and* ξ *be the formal power series representing respectively the Möbius function and the characteristic function of* $\mathbb{M}(\Sigma, I)$. *Then* $\mu \cdot \xi = \xi \cdot \mu = 1$.

The Möbius function can also be characterized in terms of cliques of (Σ, I). We recall that a clique of (Σ, I) is a set $c \subseteq \Sigma$ such that the relation I contains every pair of distinct symbols of c. In the following we denote by C the set of all cliques of (Σ, I). Each clique $c \in C$ can be interpreted in a natural way as a trace represented by a string of distinct independent elements.

Theorem 5.3.8 *Given a trace monoid* $\mathbb{M}(\Sigma, I)$, *the Möbius function* μ *is the formal power series*

$$\mu = \sum_{c \in C} (-1)^{|c|} c$$

where $|c|$ *denotes the length of* c.

5.3.3 Generating Functions of Trace Languages

We now introduce the generating functions of trace languages and present some properties used in the following section to study the decidability of the equivalence and inclusion problems. In particular we show that every rational trace language of a given trace monoid has rational generating function if and only if the independence relation is transitive.

Definition 5.3.9 *Given a trace language* $T \subseteq \mathbb{M}(\Sigma, I)$, *the* generating function *of* T *is the formal power series* $f_T(z) \in \mathbb{Q}\langle\langle z \rangle\rangle$ *defined by*

$$f_T(z) = \sum_{n=0}^{\infty} \sharp\{t \in T : |t| = n\} z^n$$

where $|t|$ *denotes the length of the trace* t.

We are now interested in studying the properties of the generating functions of rational trace languages. As a first immediate result we observe that every unambiguous rational trace language admits a rational generating function: to see this fact it is sufficient to recall that every regular language has rational generating function.

The question immediately arises whether *every* rational trace language admits a rational generating function. The answer to this question is negative; moreover it can be proved that every trace language in $\mathrm{Rat}(\mathbb{M}(\Sigma, I))$ has rational generating function if and only if I is transitive. Observe that in one direction this property is a consequence of Theorem 5.2.12 presented in Section 5.2: here we give an independent and direct proof of this result based on counting techniques.

Theorem 5.3.10 *Given an independence alphabet* (Σ, I), *the following statements are equivalent:*
  1) I *is transitive;*
  2) every rational trace language $T \subseteq \mathbb{M}(\Sigma, I)$ *has rational generating function.*

Proof: We first show that (2) implies (1). Given the independence alphabet $\langle\{a,b,c,\},\{(a,b),(b,a),(c,b),(b,c)\}\rangle$, we can consider the trace language T generated by the language $L = \{ab,c\}^* \cup \{cb,a\}^*$. It is easy to prove that every trace t of T admits at most two representatives in L and hence $T \in \text{Rat}_2(\mathbb{M}(\Sigma,I))$. Now, let us find the generating function of T. From Example 5.3.2 we know that the generating function of L is $2(1-z-z^2)^{-1}$. Moreover, we observe that a trace t admits two representatives in L if and only if $\#_a(t) = \#_b(t) = \#_c(t)$, where $\#_\beta(t)$ denotes the number of symbols β in t. Since there are $\binom{2k}{k}$ traces of this type having length $3k$, the generating function of T is

$$f_T(z) = \frac{2}{(1-z-z^2)} - \sum_{k=0}^{+\infty} \binom{2k}{k} z^{3k} = \frac{2}{(1-z-z^2)} - \frac{1}{(1-4z^3)^{1/2}}.$$

Hence $f_T(z)$ is algebraic but not rational.

Now, let us prove that (1) implies (2). We assume that I consists of two disjoint cliques C_1, C_2 since the proof in the general case is similar. Let $A = \langle Q, q_0, \delta, F \rangle$ be a finite state automaton over Σ recognizing the language $L \subseteq \Sigma^*$ such that $T = [L]$. For every set of states $S \subseteq Q$ and every $t \in \mathbb{M}(\Sigma,I)$ we define

$$\Delta(S,t) = \{q \in Q : \exists s \in S, \exists w \in \Sigma^* \ \delta(s,w) = q \wedge [w] = t\}$$

For $i = 1,2$ let $M^{(i)}$ be the monoid $\mathbb{M}(C_i, I_i)$, where I_i is the restriction of I to C_i. For every pair of sets of states $S, W \subseteq Q$ and every $i = 1,2$ let

$$U_{SW}^{(i)} = \{t \in M^{(i)} : \Delta(S,t) = W\},$$

$$T_W^{(i)} = \{t \in \mathbb{M}(\Sigma,I) : \Delta(q_0,t) = W, t = \hat{t}\alpha, \alpha \in M^{(i)}, \alpha \neq [\epsilon]\}.$$

Analogously, we can define the corresponding generating functions :

$$g_{SW}^{(i)}(z) = \sum_{n=1}^{+\infty} \#\{t \in U_{SW}^{(i)} : |t| = n\} z^n,$$

$$f_W^{(i)}(z) = \sum_{n=1}^{+\infty} \#\{t \in T_W^{(i)} : |t| = n\} z^n.$$

Observe that any trace language $U_{SW}^{(i)}$ is rational since

$$U_{SW}^{(i)} = \bigcup_{q \in S} \Big(\bigcap_{\tilde{q} \in W} [L_{q\tilde{q}}^{(i)}] \cap \big(\bigcup_{\tilde{q} \notin W} [L_{q\tilde{q}}^{(i)}]\big)^c \Big)$$

where $L_{q\tilde{q}}^{(i)} = \{x \in C_i^* : \delta(q,x) = \tilde{q}\}$, $i = 1,2$. Therefore, since $M^{(i)}$ is a commutative monoid, Eilenberg and Schützenberger's result mentioned in Theorem 5.2.10 implies that $U_{SW}^{(i)}$ is unambiguous and hence its generating function $g_{SW}^{(i)}(z)$ is rational.

Now we observe that every trace $t \in \mathbb{M}(\Sigma, I)$ admits a unique decomposition of the form $t = \alpha_1 \beta_1 \alpha_2 \beta_2 \cdots \alpha_n \beta_n$, where $\alpha_i \in M^{(1)}$ and $\beta_i \in M^{(2)}$ for all i, while $\alpha_i \neq [\epsilon]$ for $1 < i \leq n$, and $\beta_i \neq [\epsilon]$ for $1 \leq i < n$. This means that, for every $W \subseteq Q$ and every $n > 0$, we have

$$\sharp\{t \in T_W^{(1)} : |t| = n\} = \sharp\{t \in U_{\{q_0\}W}^{(1)} : |t| = n\}+$$
$$+ \sum_{S \subseteq Q} \sum_{k=0}^{n} \sharp\{t \in T_S^{(2)} : |t| = k\} \cdot \sharp\{t \in U_{SW}^{(1)} : |t| = n - k\},$$

$$\sharp\{t \in T_W^{(2)} : |t| = n\} = \sharp\{t \in U_{\{q_0\}W}^{(2)} : |t| = n\}+$$
$$+ \sum_{S \subseteq Q} \sum_{k=0}^{n} \sharp\{t \in T_S^{(1)} : |t| = k\} \cdot \sharp\{t \in U_{SW}^{(2)} : |t| = n - k\}$$

From these relations we can easily deduce a linear system of equations among the corresponding generating functions :

$$f_W^{(1)}(z) = g_{\{q_0\}W}^{(1)}(z) + \sum_{S \subseteq Q} f_S^{(2)}(z) \cdot g_{SW}^{(1)}(z)$$

$$f_W^{(2)}(z) = g_{\{q_0\}W}^{(2)}(z) + \sum_{S \subseteq Q} f_S^{(1)}(z) \cdot g_{SW}^{(2)}(z)$$

where $W \subseteq Q$. This implies that every function $f_W^{(i)}(z)$ is rational. At last, since $T_W^{(i)} \cap T_V^{(i)} = \emptyset$ whenever $W \neq V$, we have

$$T = \bigcup_{W \cap F \neq \emptyset} T_W^{(1)} \cup \bigcup_{W \cap F \neq \emptyset} T_W^{(2)},$$

and hence the generating function of T satisfies the equation

$$f_T(z) = \sum_{W \cap F \neq \emptyset} f_W^{(1)}(z) + f_W^{(2)}(z),$$

proving that also $f_T(z)$ is rational.   □

As a consequence of the first part of the proof we obtain the following stronger results

Proposition 5.3.11 *Let (Σ, I) be an independent alphabet such that I is not transitive. Then there are languages in $\mathrm{Rat}_2(\mathbb{M}(\Sigma, I))$ with nonrational generating functions.*

This remark gives an alternative direct proof of the proper inclusion $\mathrm{Rat}_1(\mathbb{M}(\Sigma, I)) \subsetneq \mathrm{Rat}_2(\mathbb{M}(\Sigma, I))$, and the question arises whether all languages in $\mathrm{Rat}_2(\mathbb{M}(\Sigma, I))$ have algebraic generating function. It is possible to show that this is not the case, and we can give a characterization of the class of the independence alphabets (Σ, I) such that every language in $\mathrm{Rat}_2(\mathbb{M}(\Sigma, I))$ has algebraic generating function [24].

5.4 Equivalence and Inclusion Problems

In this section we study the decidability of the equivalence and inclusion problems for rational trace languages. We illustrate the main results obtained in the literature and present some new proofs based on generating functions and counting techniques. In particular we apply a general method presented in [17] to show the decidability of inclusion problem for languages.

We first define our problems formally. Let (Σ, I) be an independence alphabet.

Definition 5.4.1 EQUIVALENCE(Σ, I) *problem:*
Instance: two finite state automata A_1 and A_2 over Σ, which recognize the languages L_1 and L_2 respectively.
Question: does $[L_1] = [L_2]$ hold?

Definition 5.4.2 INCLUSION(Σ, I) *problem:*
Instance: two finite state automata A_1 and A_2 over Σ which recognize the languages L_1 and L_2 respectively.
Question: does $[L_1] \subseteq [L_2]$ hold?

It is immediate to see that EQUIVALENCE(Σ, I) is reducible to INCLUSION(Σ, I) for every independence alphabet (Σ, I). Hence if INCLUSION(Σ, I) is decidable also EQUIVALENCE(Σ, I) is decidable. In [2] the following result has been proved:

Theorem 5.4.3 *If (Σ, I) is transitive then* INCLUSION(Σ, I) *is decidable.*

Here we give a new proof of this result based on Theorem 5.3.10 which follows a more general approach to decidability questions on languages [17]. To this end let us give some preliminary definitions.

Let $\mathcal{C}$ be a class of recursive trace languages over the independence alphabet (Σ, I). A *specification* of $\mathcal{C}$ is a pair $\langle S, \ell \rangle$, where S is a recursive subset of $\{0, 1\}^*$ and ℓ is a surjective function $\ell : S \to \mathcal{C}$ such that the set $\{(t, s) : t \in \mathbb{M}(\Sigma, I), s \in S, t \in \ell(s)\}$ is recursive. Given a specification $\langle S, \ell \rangle$ for a class $\mathcal{C}$ of trace languages, the inclusion problem for $\mathcal{C}$ can be defined as follows:
INCLUSION$(\mathcal{C})$ problem
    Instance: $s_1, s_2 \in S$;
    Question: does $\ell(s_1) \subseteq \ell(s_2)$ hold?
Now, let Rat_z be the field of rational functions in the variable z with coefficients in $\mathbb{Q}$. Clearly any function in Rat_z can be represented by two polynomials in $\mathbb{Q}\langle z \rangle$. We say that a class of trace languages is *functionally rational* if there exists a specification $\langle S, \ell \rangle$ of $\mathcal{C}$ and a total recursive function $f : S \to Rat_z$ such that, for every $s \in S$, $f(s)$ is the generating function of $\ell(s)$. We also say that $\mathcal{C}$ is *constructively* closed under union if there exists a total recursive function $g : S \times S \to S$ such that $\ell(g(s_1, s_2)) = \ell(s_1) \cup \ell(s_2)$ for every $s_1, s_2 \in S$. The following theorem gives a sufficient condition for INCLUSION$(\mathcal{C})$ problem to be decidable:

Theorem 5.4.4 *Let $\mathcal{C}$ be a class of recursive trace languages in $\mathbb{M}(\Sigma, I)$, with specification $\langle S, \ell \rangle$, which is functionally rational and constructively closed under union. Then* INCLUSION $(\mathcal{C})$ *problem is decidable.*

Proof: Observe that $\ell(s_1) \subseteq \ell(s_2)$ if and only if $f(g(s_1, s_2))$ and $f(s_2)$ are the same function. Since such a statement is clearly decidable the proposition is proved. □

By Theorem 5.3.10 we know that for every transitive independence relation (Σ, I) the class $\text{Rat}(\mathbb{M}(\Sigma, I))$ is functionally rational. Moreover, $\text{Rat}(\mathbb{M}(\Sigma, I))$ is constructively closed under union: hence Theorem 5.4.3 follows from the previous proposition.

As regards the nontransitive independence alphabets we have the following result due to Aalbersberg and Hogeboom:

Theorem 5.4.5 [4] *Let (Σ, I) be an independence alphabet such that $\Sigma = \{a, b, c\}$ and $I = \{(a, b), (b, a), (c, b), (b, c)\}$; then,* EQUIVALENCE$(\Sigma, I)$ *is undecidable.*

Proof: (outline). In this case, $\mathbb{M}(\Sigma, I)$ is a product of free monoids, i.e. $\mathbb{M}(\Sigma, I) = \{a, c\}^* \times \{b\}^*$. It can be proved that the morphism $\varphi : \{a, b, c\}^* \to \{a, c\}^* \times \{b\}^*$ induces a one-to-one correspondence between the rational trace languages in $\mathbb{M}(\Sigma, I)$ and the *regular transductions* from $\{a, c\}$ to $\{b\}$. Now, a result given by Ibarra [143] states that, for an arbitrary rational transduction R from $\{a, c\}$ to $\{b\}$, it is undecidable whether $R = \{a, c\}^* \times \{b\}^*$. Obviously, this implies the undecidability of the equivalence between a given trace language T and $\mathbb{M}(\Sigma, I)$. □

Therefore it is possible to prove the following characterization result for the equivalence and inclusion problems:

Theorem 5.4.6 *Both* EQUIVALENCE(Σ, I) *and* INCLUSION(Σ, I) *problems for rational trace languages are decidable if and only if the independence relation I is transitive.*

Proof: If (Σ, I) is transitive then INCLUSION(Σ, I) (and, a fortiori, EQUIVALENCE(Σ, I)) is decidable by Theorem 5.4.3. If (Σ, I) is not transitive then we can find three symbols $a, b, c \in \Sigma$ such that $(a, b), (b, c) \in I$ while $(a, c) \notin I$. Then, by the previous theorem, EQUIVALENCE(Σ, I) (and, a fortiori, INCLUSION(Σ, I)) is undecidable. □

5.4.1   The Multiplicity Equivalence Problem for Rational Trace Languages

In this section we study another version of the equivalence problem which takes into account the multiplicity of each trace. We recall that, given an independence alphabet (Σ, I) and a language $L \subseteq \Sigma^*$, $\natural_L$ denotes the multiplicity of L defined in Example 5.3.5.

Definition 5.4.7 $\natural$EQUIVALENCE(Σ, I) *problem:*
Instance: two finite state automata A_1 and A_2 over Σ which recognize the languages L_1 and L_2 respectively.
Question: does $\natural_{L_1} = \natural_{L_2}$ hold?

This problem is proved to be decidable in [266] using a technique introduced in [132] to show the decidability of the multiplicity equivalence problem for deterministic multitape automata. The proof is based on a deep algebraic result stating that the ring of polynomials $\mathbb{Q}\langle\Sigma, I\rangle$ is embeddable in a division ring [79]. Here we prove the decidability of $\sharp\mathrm{EQUIVALENCE}(\Sigma, I)$ problem following the proof given in [266], and present a different technique to obtain a polynomial time algorithm for solving the problem in the particular case $\Sigma = \{a, b, c\}$ and $I = \{(a, b), (b, a), (b, c), (c, b)\}$.

The main result requires two preliminary lemmas.

Lemma 5.4.8 *Let K be a division ring, π_i, η_i two vectors with m_i entries in K and A_i a $m_i \times m_i$ matrix with entries in K ($i = 1, 2$). Then the following sentences are equivalent:*
(1) $\pi_1 A_1^n \eta_1^T = \pi_2 A_2^n \eta_2^T$ for all $n \geq 0$;
(2) $\pi_1 A_1^n \eta_1^T = \pi_2 A_2^n \eta_2^T$ for $0 \leq n \leq m_1 + m_2$.

Proof: (outline) Let $\pi = (-\pi_1, \pi_2), \eta = (\eta_1, \eta_2)$, $A = \begin{pmatrix} A_1 & 0 \\ 0 & A_2 \end{pmatrix}$ with obvious notation, and let $m = m_1 + m_2$. We observe that

$$\pi A^n \eta^T = -\pi_1 A_1^n \eta_1^T + \pi_2 A_2^n \eta_2^T \tag{5.1}$$

Define $a_n = \pi A^n \eta^T$ and consider the vectors $\pi, \pi A, \ldots, \pi A^m$. Since every vector has m components in K and the number of vectors is $m + 1$, it is possible to find $m + 1$ coefficients $\lambda_0, \ldots, \lambda_m$ in K such that:
(i) there is an index i such that $\lambda_i \neq 0$,
(ii) $\sum_{k=0}^{m} \lambda_k \cdot \pi A^k = \underline{0}$.

Let $d \leq m$ be the maximum index such that $\lambda_d \neq 0$. Then $\sum_{k=0}^{d} \lambda_k \pi A^k = \underline{0}$ and, multiplying by $A^n \eta^T$, we obtain for every $n \geq 0$

$$\sum_{k=0}^{d} \lambda_k \cdot \pi A^{k+n} \eta^T = 0.$$

Therefore, for all $n \geq 0$

$$a_{d+n} = \sum_{k=0}^{d-1} \alpha_k a_{n+k}$$

where $\alpha_k = -\lambda_d^{-1} \lambda_k$.
Hence $a_n = 0$ for all n if and only if $a_n = 0$ for $0 \leq n \leq d - 1$ and this fact, together with equation 5.1, implies the thesis.   □

We state the second lemma without proof:

Lemma 5.4.9 [79, 266] *The ring $\mathbb{Q}\langle\Sigma, I\rangle$ of polynomials in partially commutative variables is embeddable in a division ring $K_{\Sigma, I}$.*

Now we are able to prove the main result of this section:

Theorem 5.4.10 $\sharp$EQUIVALENCE(Σ, I) *problem for rational trace languages is decidable for every independence alphabet* (Σ, I).

Proof: Let $\mathbb{M}(\Sigma, I)$ be a f.p.c.m. and let $K_{\Sigma, I}$ be the division ring that extends the ring of formal polynomials $\mathbb{Q}\langle\Sigma, I\rangle$. Let $A = \langle \Sigma, Q, q_0, \delta, F \rangle$ be a deterministic finite state automaton over the alphabet Σ, and consider the following objects:

1) the characteristic vector π of the initial state, i.e. a vector with components indexed by elements of Q such that $\pi_q = 1$ if $q = q_0$, and $\pi_q = 0$ otherwise;

2) the characteristic vector of the final states η, i.e. a vector with components indexed by elements of Q such that $\eta_q = 1$ if $q \in F$, and $\eta_q = 0$ otherwise;

3) a particular representation of the transition function δ, obtained as a $|Q| \times |Q|$ matrix A whose entries $A_{qq'}$ are polynomials in $\mathbb{Q}\langle\Sigma, I\rangle$, and hence in the division ring $K_{\Sigma, I}$, and are defined as follows :

$$A_{qq'} = \sum_{\delta(q,\sigma)=q'} [\sigma]$$

Let L be the language recognized by A. By a straightforward computation it can be verified that, for all n,

$$\sum_{|t|=n} \sharp_L(t) t = \pi A^n \eta^T$$

Let now consider two finite state automata A_1 and A_2 with m_1 and m_2 states, respectively, and let $\pi_1, \pi_2, A_1, A_2, \eta_1, \eta_2$ be the corresponding representations of the initial states, transition functions and final states.

If L_1 and L_2 are the languages recognized by A_1 and A_2, respectively, we obtain that $\sharp_{L_1} = \sharp_{L_2}$ if and only if $\pi_1 A_1{}^n \eta_1^T = \pi_2 A_2{}^n \eta_2^T$ for all n. By Lemma 5.4.8, $\pi_1 A_1{}^n \eta_1^T = \pi_2 A_2{}^n \eta_2^T$ for all n if and only if $\pi_1 A_1{}^n \eta_1^T = \pi_2 A_2{}^n \eta_2^T$, for $0 \leq n \leq m_1 + m_2$; therefore $\sharp_{L_1} = \sharp_{L_2}$ if and only if $\sharp_{L_1}(t) = \sharp_{L_2}(t)$ for all traces t such that $|t| \leq m_1 + m_2$. This means that EQUIVALENCE(Σ, I) is decidable since, as shown in Section 5.5.1, the values $\sharp_{L_1}(t)$ and $\sharp_{L_2}(t)$ are computable in polynomial time with respect to $|t|$. $\square$

We observe that, in the general case, the algorithm presented in the previous proof cannot be executed in polynomial time because the number of traces of length n grows exponentially with respect to n. In fact, given $\mathbb{M}(\Sigma, I)$, the number of traces of length n in $\mathbb{M}(\Sigma, I)$ is bounded by a polynomial in n if and only if $\mathbb{M}(\Sigma, I)$ is the free commutative monoid generated by Σ. In any other case, 2^n is a lower bound for the number of traces of length n in $\mathbb{M}(\Sigma, I)$, while $\sharp\Sigma^n$ is an upper bound. As a consequence of this discussion we obtain the following

Theorem 5.4.11 $\sharp$EQUIVALENCE(Σ, I) *belongs to EXPTIME; if the graph* $\langle \Sigma, I \rangle$ *is complete, then* $\sharp$EQUIVALENCE(Σ, I) *belongs to P.*

We conclude this section proving that $\sharp$EQUIVALENCE(Σ, I) is solvable in polynomial time if $\Sigma = \{a, b, c\}$ and $I = \{(a, b), (b, a), (b, c), (c, b)\}$; more precisely, we prove that in this case $\sharp$EQUIVALENCE(Σ, I) belongs to NC^2 (see [44] for a definition of NC^2 and related notions). However our technique is completely different from the previous one and cannot be simply extended to the general case.

Following the notation introduced in Section 5.3.2, let F be a field and, for every $\phi \in F\langle\langle \Sigma, I \rangle\rangle$ let $\hat{\phi}$ denote the function $\hat{\phi} : \{a, c\}^* \to F\langle\langle b \rangle\rangle$ such that

$$\hat{\phi}(w) = \sum_k \phi([wb^k]) \cdot b^k \qquad (w \in \{a, c\}^*).$$

Note that $\hat{\phi}$ is a formal power series in non-commutative variables $\{a, c\}$ with coefficients in $F\langle\langle b \rangle\rangle$. Let Rat_b^F be the field of rational functions in the variable b with coefficients in F. The main property is the following:

Proposition 5.4.12 *Consider the independence alphabet* (Σ, I) *such that* $\Sigma = \{a, b, c\}$ *and* $I = \{(a, b), (b, a), (b, c), (c, b)\}$. *Let* $L \subseteq \Sigma^*$ *be a regular language and let* $\sharp_L \in \mathbb{Q}\langle\langle \Sigma, I \rangle\rangle$ *be the multiplicity of* L. *Then* $\hat{\sharp}_L$ *is a rational f.p.s. in* $Rat_b^{\mathbb{Q}}\langle\langle a, c \rangle\rangle$.

Proof: Let $\langle \pi, A, \eta \rangle$ be a representation of the characteristic series of L. Setting $B(b) = \sum_0^\infty (A(b))^k \cdot b^k = (I - b \cdot A(b))^{-1}$, $\hat{\pi} = \pi B(b)$, $\hat{A}(\sigma) = A(\sigma)B(b)$ for $\sigma \in \{a, c\}$, the following equality can be verified:

$$\hat{\sharp}_L(x_1 \ldots x_m) = \hat{\pi}\hat{A}(x_1) \ldots \hat{A}(x_m)\eta^T, \qquad \text{for } x_1 \ldots x_m \in \{a, c\}^*.$$

Therefore $\langle \hat{\pi}, \hat{A}, \eta \rangle$ is a representation of $\hat{\sharp}_L$. $\qquad\square$

We observe that for any pair of regular languages L_1, $L_2 \subseteq \{a, b, c\}^*$ it holds that $\sharp_{L_1} = \sharp_{L_2}$ iff $\hat{\sharp}_{L_1} = \hat{\sharp}_{L_2}$ iff

$$(\hat{\sharp}_{L_1} - \hat{\sharp}_{L_2}) \circ (\hat{\sharp}_{L_1} - \hat{\sharp}_{L_2}) = 0.$$

By Propositions 5.3.1 and 5.4.12 the formal power series $\psi = (\hat{\sharp}_{L_1} - \hat{\sharp}_{L_2}) \circ (\hat{\sharp}_{L_1} - \hat{\sharp}_{L_2})$ is rational and hence it admits a representation $\langle \bar{\pi}, \bar{A}, \bar{\eta} \rangle$:

$$\psi(x_1 \cdots x_n) = \bar{\pi}\bar{A}(x_1) \cdots \bar{A}(x_m)\bar{\eta} \qquad \text{for } x_1 \ldots x_m \in \{a, c\}^*.$$

Now consider the generating function $R(b, z)$ defined by

$$R(b, z) = \sum_{w \in \{a, c\}^*} \psi(w) \cdot z^{|w|}.$$

By the previous discussion we have that $\sharp_{L_1} = \sharp_{L_2}$ if and only if $R(b, z)$ is identically null. Moreover a standard calculation proves that

$$R(b, z) = \bar{\pi}(\sum_0^{+\infty} (\bar{A}(a) + \bar{A}(c))^k z^k)\bar{\eta}^T = \bar{\pi}(I - \bar{A}(a)z - \bar{A}(c)z)^{-1}\bar{\eta}^T$$

The problem is thus NC^1-reducible to the problem of computing the inverse of a matrix whose entries are rational functions with coefficients in $\mathbb{Q}$: it can be proved that this computation is in NC^2 [44].

We conclude:

Theorem 5.4.13 *Let (Σ, I) be defined as in the Proposition 5.4.12. Then the problem* $\sharp\mathrm{EQUIVALENCE}(\Sigma, I)$ *is in NC^2.*

5.4.2   The Case of Unambiguous Trace Languages

Let us now consider the problems $\mathrm{EQUIVALENCE}(\Sigma, I)$ and $\mathrm{INCLUSION}(\Sigma, I)$ in the case of unambiguous trace languages. From the general result provided in Theorem 5.4.6, it follows that, when the independence relation is transitive, these problems are decidable.

Furthermore, from Theorem 5.4.10 since the multiplicity series of unambiguous languages have values in 0,1, we can conclude that $\mathrm{EQUIVALENCE}(\Sigma, I)$ problem for unambiguous languages is decidable *for every* independence alphabet (Σ, I). On the contrary, from a result due to Fisher and Rosenberg [101], it is easy to see that there are independence alphabets (Σ, I) such that $\mathrm{INCLUSION}(\Sigma, I)$ problem remains undecidable even for unambiguous languages.

Here we give a sufficient condition on (Σ, I) for $\mathrm{INCLUSION}(\Sigma, I)$ problem to be undecidable. In order to prove this result we need some preliminary definitions and results on a model of computation , the Multi-tape One Way Non-writing Automaton (MONA) introduced by Rabin and Scott [231].

This model has a finite-state control and m read-only one-way tapes. The state set of the machine is partitioned into m classes, and the class to which a particular state belongs determines which tape head is to be advanced. An initial state and a set of final states are given; the input string in each tape is delimited by two special symbols $\alpha, \beta \notin \Sigma$, with α on the left and β on the right. The machine starts in the initial state, with all the heads positioned on the symbol α. At each computation step, depending on the current state q, a single head is advanced of one position on the appropriate tape and the new symbol σ on this tape is read. In the nondeterministic model, the transition function δ of the machine yields a set of next states as a function of the current state q and symbol σ, while in the deterministic case δ yields a unique next state. The m-tuple of input strings is accepted if there is at least one computation for which the machine enters a final state, after reading all the input strings on the tapes.

In the following, we denote by D_m (N_m) the class of trace languages recognized by deterministic (nondeterministic, respectively) m-tape MONA's (obviously, the classes D_1 and N_1 coincide).

It is straightforward to verify the following properties:

Theorem 5.4.14 *If $T \in N_m$, then T is a rational trace language. If $T \in D_m$, then T is a unambiguous trace language.*

Furthermore, we recall the following result :

Theorem 5.4.15 [231] *For all m, D_m is closed under complementation.*

For sake of completeness, we summarize in Table 1 the closure properties under boolean operations of the classes $D_1 = N_1$, D_m and N_m $(m \geq 2)$ of languages recognized by m-tape MONA's, [231, 96]:

Operations	$D_1 = N_1$	$D_m (m \geq 2)$	$N_m (m \geq 2)$
Complementation	Yes	Yes	No
Intersection	Yes	No	No
Union	Yes	No	Yes

Now, we are ready to exhibit a sufficient condition on (Σ, I), for the problem INCLUSION(Σ, I) to be undecidable:

Theorem 5.4.16 *If the independence relation I contains the pattern $\{(a, d), (d, b), (b, c), (c, a)\}$, then* INCLUSION$(\Sigma, I)$ *problem for unambiguous trace language is undecidable.*

Proof: Since I contains the pattern $\{(a, d), (d, b), (b, c), (c, a)\}$, it is sufficient to prove the result for the free partially commutative monoid $\{a, b\}^* \times \{c, d\}^*$.
The proof is given by providing a reduction from the well known Post Correspondence Problem (PCP). Let us consider a Post Correspondence Set (PCS) over the alphabet $\{c, d\}$, that is a finite set of pairs of strings $\{(x_1, y_1), (x_2, y_2), \ldots, (x_m, y_m)\}$, where for each i $x_i, y_i \in \{c, d\}^*$. We say that such a PCS admits a solution if there is a sequence of indices $i_1, i_2, \ldots, i_t$, where each i_k belongs to $\{1, 2, \ldots, m\}$, such that $x_{i_1} x_{i_2} \cdots x_{i_t} = y_{i_1} y_{i_2} \cdots y_{i_t}$. We recall that the PCP is the problem of determining whether a given PCS admits a solution.

Now, given any PCS $\{(x_1, y_1), (x_2, y_2), \ldots, (x_m, y_m)\}$, we associate to it two trace languages $A, C \subseteq \{a, b\}^* \times \{c, d\}^*$ as follows. First of all, let us consider a code over the alphabet $\{a, b\}$, that is a finite set $\{z_1, z_2, \ldots, z_m\}$, $z_i \in \{a, b\}^*$, such that that every word $w \in \{z_1, z_2, \ldots, z_m\}^*$ admits a unique factorization in terms of $\{z_1, z_2, \ldots, z_m\}$. Let $A = \{[z_1 x_1], [z_2 x_2], \ldots, [z_m x_m]\}^*$ and $B = \{[z_1 y_1], [z_2 y_2], \ldots, [z_m y_m]\}^*$: it is easy to construct two deterministic MONA's recognizing A and B respectively. This implies that both A and B are deterministic. Since D_2 is closed under complementation, B^c is deterministic, too. This means that A, B, B^c are unambiguous trace languages. Now let $C = B^c$; it is straightforward to see that $A \subseteq C$ if and only if the PCS $\{(x_1, y_1), (x_2, y_2), \ldots, (x_m, y_m)\}$ does not have solution. Thus, a solution for INCLUSION(Σ, I) would yield a solution for the Post Correspondence Problem. $\square$

It remains open the problem of characterizing the independence alphabets (Σ, I) such that INCLUSION(Σ, I) for unambiguous trace languages is decidable.

5.5   On Counting the Prefixes of a Trace

In this section we summarize some results concerning the enumeration of the prefixes in free partially commutative monoids. Our main goal is to show that these enumeration problems can be reduced to computing the number of words of given length accepted by suitable finite state automata. Also in this case the generating functions of the corresponding languages are useful tools to obtain precise asymptotic evaluations. The results we obtain are also related to the analysis of algorithms for membership problems for rational and context-free trace languages.

Let us consider an independence alphabet (Σ, I) generating the free partially commutative monoid $\mathbb{M}(\Sigma, I)$. A prefix of an element $t \in \mathbb{M}(\Sigma, I)$ is a trace $t_1 \in \mathbb{M}(\Sigma, I)$ such that $t = t_1 t_2$ for a suitable $t_2 \in \mathbb{M}(\Sigma, I)$. We denote by $Pre(t)$ the set of all the prefixes of t and by $\Im(t)$ the number of prefixes of t. For the sake of simplicity, $\Im[x]$ will denote the number of prefixes of $[x]$ for any $x \in \Sigma^*$.

As an example consider the independence alphabet (Σ, I), where $\Sigma = \{a, b, c, d\}$, $I = \{(a, b), (b, a), (c, b), (b, c), (c, d), (d, c)\}$, and the trace $t \in \mathbb{M}(\Sigma, I)$, $t = [abcda]$.

In this case the set of the prefixes of t and its cardinality are given by

$$Pre(t) = \{[\epsilon], [a], [b], [ab], [ac], [abc], [abd], [abcd], [abcda]\}, \Im(t) = 9.$$

It is clear that the notion of prefix defines a natural partial order relation over $\mathbb{M}(\Sigma, I)$: for every $s, t \in \mathbb{M}(\Sigma, I)$, $s \leq_p t$ if and only if $s \in Pre(t)$. Such a partial order induces a structure of lattice on the set $Pre(t)$ that allows to characterize the prefixes of t as order ideals. To see this property, consider the partially ordered set $(P_t, \preceq_t)$ naturally defined by a trace $t \in \mathbb{M}(\Sigma, I)$, that is :

1. $P_t = \{(x_1, k_1), (x_2, k_2), \ldots, (x_n, k_n)\}$ where x_i belongs to Σ, $t = [x_1 x_2 \cdots x_n]$ and every k_i is the number of occurrences of x_i in $x_1 x_2 \cdots x_i$;

2. $\preceq_t$ is the transitive closure of the relation $\trianglelefteq$ defined by $(x_i, k_i) \trianglelefteq (x_j, k_j)$ iff $i \leq j$ and $(x_i, x_j) \notin I$.

We recall that an antichain A of P_t is a set $A \subseteq P_t$ such that $(x_i, k_i) \preceq_t (x_j, k_j)$ does not hold for any pair of distinct elements $(x_i, k_i), (x_j, k_j) \in A$. Moreover, a set $B \subseteq P_t$ is an order ideal generated by an antichain A of P_t if $B = \{(x_i, k_i) \in P_t : (x_i, k_i) \preceq_t (x_j, k_j), \text{for some } (x_j, k_j) \in A\}$. It is well-known that the set of order ideals of a partial order set is a lattice.

Proposition 5.5.1 *For any $t \in \mathbb{M}(\Sigma, I)$ the set $Pre(t)$ with the relation $\leq_p$ is isomorphic to the lattice of the order ideals of $(P_t, \preceq_t)$.*

Such an isomorphism clearly induces a one to one correspondence between $Pre(t)$ and the set of the antichains of $(P_t, \preceq_t)$ associating each prefix (order ideal) with the set of its maximal elements. We also observe that every antichain of P_t contains at most α elements, α being the size of the largest clique in the graph (Σ, I). Therefore we have $\Im(t) \leq \sum_{i=1}^{\alpha} \binom{|t|}{i}$, showing that $\Im(t) = O(|t|^{\alpha})$ as $|t|$ tends to $+\infty$ Actually it is not difficult to see that $\Im(t) \leq (1 + \frac{|t|}{\alpha})^{\alpha}$. Note that such a bound is tight since, if $\Sigma = \{a, b, c\}$, $I = \{(a, b), (b, a), (c, b), (b, c), (a, c), (c, a)\}$, and $t = [(abc)^n]$, where $n \in \mathbb{N}$, then $\Im(t) = (n + 1)^3$. Therefore the following proposition holds

Proposition 5.5.2 *Let (Σ, I) be an independence alphabet and let α be the size of the largest clique in (Σ, I). Then, denoting by $W(n)$ the maximum number of prefixes of a trace of length n in $\mathbb{M}(\Sigma, I)$, we have $W(n) = \Theta(n^{\alpha})$, as n tends to $+\infty$.*

5.5.1 Analysis of a General Procedure Scheme

The notion of prefix plays a relevant role in the design and analysis of certain algorithms for problems on trace languages. More precisely, by means of a general procedure scheme, we can define a class of algorithms for problems on f.p.c.m.'s which execute certain operations on each prefix of the input trace [16]. As a consequence the time and space complexity depends on the number of prefixes of the input. Examples of algorithms in such a class concern the Membership Problem for rational trace languages, the problem of computing the cardinality of a trace and the problem of computing $\sharp_L([x])$ for an input string x, where $\sharp_L$ is the formal series defined in Example 5.3.5 and L is a regular language [16].

The class of algorithms we consider is defined by the following procedure scheme which computes a function $f(x)$, for an input $x \in \Sigma^*$, depending on two symbols g and Op. Interpreting these symbols as suitable operations we obtain algorithms for particular problems.

```
Function f([x])
begin
     if |x| = 1 then f([x]) = g(x)
        else begin
                S = ∅
                for each t' ∈ Pre([x]) such that [x] = t'[a] and a ∈ Σ do
                        S = S ∪ {(f(t'), a)}
                return Op(S)
            end
end
```

As an example we describe an algorithm for the Membership Problem for rational trace languages. To this end let $T \subseteq \mathbb{M}(\Sigma, I)$ be the trace language generated by a regular language $L \subseteq \Sigma^*$. Consider a regular grammar $G = \langle V, \Sigma, S, P \rangle$ generating L, where V is the set of nonterminals, Σ is the set of terminals, S is the initial symbol and P the set of productions. The Membership Problem for T consists of verifying, for an input $x \in \Sigma^*$, whether S belongs to the set $U([x]) = \{A \in V : A \Rightarrow^* y, y \in \Sigma^*, [y] = [x]\}$, where $\Rightarrow^*$ denotes the usual relation of derivation induced by G. The problem is solved by the following procedure which computes the set $U([x])$ for every $x \in \Sigma^*$:

Function $U([x])$
begin
    if $|x| = 1$ then $U([x]) = \{A \in V/(A \to x) \in P\}$
      else begin
          $S = \emptyset$
          for each $t' \in Pre([x])$ such that $[x] = t'[a]$ and $a \in \Sigma$ do
               $S = S \cup \{(U(t'), a)\}$
$$U([x]) = \bigcup_{(W,a) \in S} \{A \in V/(A \to Ba) \in P, B \in W\}$$
        end
end

An iterative implementation of this procedure can be given which requires $O(\Im[x])$ time for an input x plus the time for computing a suitable representation of the prefixes of $[x]$. Such a representation can be computed by two different algorithms, described in [23] and [15, 121], which require respectively $O(|x|^\alpha)$ and $O(|x|\Im[x])$ time. Hence, recalling that $\Im[x] = O(|x|^\alpha)$, we obtain the following

Proposition 5.5.3 *The Membership Problem for rational trace languages can be solved in $O(|x|^\alpha)$ time for an input $x \in \Sigma^*$, where α is the size of the largest clique in (Σ, I). Moreover, the same problem can be solved in $O(|x|\Im[x])$ time and $O(\Im[x])$ space using a different procedure for computing a representation of the prefixes on the input trace.*

The same result holds for all problems solvable by suitable instances of the procedure scheme described above. In particular we have that $\sharp_L(t)$ is computable in polynomial time with respect to the length of t for any regular language L.

A similar analysis can also be developed for the Membership Problem of context-free trace languages. We recall that a trace language $T \subseteq \mathbb{M}(\Sigma, I)$ is context-free (algebraic) if the characteristic function of T is solution of an algebraic system of equations over the monoid $\mathbb{M}(\Sigma, I)$. It is known that T is algebraic if and only if $T = \{[x] : x \in L\}$ for a suitable context-free (string) language $L \subseteq \Sigma^*$ [18]. Membership to context-free trace languages can be tested using the same representation of prefixes and extending Valiant's algorithm for recognizing context-free (string) languages [23]. This analysis is summarized in the following

Proposition 5.5.4 *[23, 15] The Membership Problem for context-free trace languages can be solved in time $O(BM(\Im[x]))$ for an input $x \in \Sigma^*$, where $BM(m)$ is the time required to compute the product of two boolean matrices of size m.*

By the previous propositions it is clear that the average time and space complexity of the algorithms considered above depends on the average number of prefixes of a trace of given length. For this reason the following two subsections are devoted to the asymptotic analysis of the average number of prefixes of a trace of length n under different probability assumptions: in Section 5.5.2 we evaluate such a quantity assuming that all representative strings of given length are equiprobable; in Section 5.5.3 we suppose that all traces of fixed length are equiprobable, which is equivalent to assuming that each string $x \in \Sigma^n$ has probability $\sharp[x]/\sharp\Sigma^n$.

5.5.2 Probabilistic Analysis on Equiprobable Strings

Let (Σ, I) be an independence alphabet and, for every $n \in \mathbf{N}$, let $\Im_n$ be the cardinality of $Pre([z_n])$, where z_n is randomly chosen in $\Sigma^n = \{x \in \Sigma^* / |x| = n\}$ under the assumption that all words in Σ^n have the same probability. Clearly $\Im_n$ is an integer random variable whose values range from $n+1$ to $(n+1)^\alpha$. In this section we study the asymptotic behaviour of the average value of $\Im_n$, that is

$$E(\Im_n) = \sum_{|x|=n} \frac{\Im[x]}{\sharp \Sigma^n},$$

proving that there exists a constant η, only depending on the independence alphabet (Σ, I), such that

$$E(\Im_n) = \eta n^k + O(n^{k-1}),$$

where k is the number of connected components of the complementary graph (Σ, I^c) (i.e. the corresponding dependence alphabet). Similar expressions can be obtained for the variance and all moments of $\Im_n$. These results are obtained by showing that the sum $\sum_{|x|=n} \Im[x]$ equals the number of words of length n accepted by a finite state automaton of special kind, whose transition function induces a partial order on the set of states. To this end, we first introduce this kind of automaton and evaluate the number of accepted words of given length; then, we apply this result to compute the asymptotic expression of the first moment of $\Im_n$.

Partially Ordered Automata

Let $A = \langle Q, q_0, \delta \rangle$ be a finite state automaton over the alphabet Σ, where Q is the set of states, q_0 the initial state and δ the (partially defined) transition function $\delta : (Q \times \Sigma) \to Q \cup \{\perp\}$. Function δ is trivially extended to all words in Σ^* and a string $x \in \Sigma^*$ is accepted by A if and only if $\delta(q_0, x) \in Q$. Let us denote by $\leq_\delta$ the binary relation over Q such that, for every $q, q' \in Q$, $q \leq_\delta q'$ if and only if $\delta(q, a) = q'$ for some $a \in \Sigma$, and let $\leq_A$ be the reflexive and transitive closure of $\leq_\delta$. We also denote by $\ell(q)$ the number of loops occurring in the state q, i.e. $\ell(q) = \sharp\{a \in \Sigma : \delta(q, a) = q\}$. Another important coefficient in our context is H_A which denotes the largest number of loops in A, i.e. $H_A = \text{Max}\{\ell(q) : q \in Q\}$.

Definition 5.5.5 *The finite automaton $A = \langle Q, q_0, \delta \rangle$ is said to be partially ordered if the following conditions are satisfied :*

(i) $\leq_A$ is a partial order relation over Q such that q_0 is the smallest element and a suitable $\hat{q} \in Q$ is the largest element;

(ii) $H_A \geq 2$ and $\ell(q_0) = \ell(\hat{q}) = H_A$.

Given a partially ordered automaton $A = \langle Q, q_0, \delta \rangle$, let L_A and $f_A(n)$ be respectively the language recognized by A and the number of words of length n in L_A. It turns out that the asymptotic behaviour of $\{f_A(n)\}_{n>0}$ is related to the coefficients we define in the following list :

- For every $q \in Q$, q is called a *main state* if $\ell(q) = H_A$;

- A finite sequence of distinct states $\{q_i\}_{i=0,\dots,m}$ is called *complete chain* in A if q_0 is the initial state of A and, for every $j = 0,\dots,m-1$, $q_i \leq_\delta q_{i+1}$. Moreover, h_S denotes the number of main states in S, i.e. $h_S = \sharp\{q \in S : \ell(q) = H_A\}$;

- Similarly, let $h_A = \mathrm{Max}\{h_S : S \text{ is a complete chain in } A\}$;

- A complete chain S is called *main* if $h_S = h_A$. By Definition 5.5.5, we have $h_A \geq 2$ and $q_m = \hat{q}$ for every main complete chain $\{q_i\}_{i=0,\dots,m}$;

- We say that a string $x \in \Sigma^*$ is *recognized* by a complete chain $\{q_i\}_{i=0,\dots,m}$ if $\delta(q_0, x) = q_m$, $x = x_1 x_2 \cdots x_n$ and $q_1, q_2, \cdots, q_m$ is the ordered sequence of distinct states entered by A when the transition function δ is consecutively applied to $x_1, x_2, \cdots, x_n$;

- For every complete chain S we define $f_S(n) = \sharp\{x \in \Sigma^* : x \text{ is recognized by } S, |x| = n\}$, and denote by $f_S(z)$ the formal power series $\sum_{n=0}^{+\infty} f_S(n) z^n$;

- For every $q, q' \in Q$, $q \neq q'$, let $\omega(q, q') = \sharp\{a \in \Sigma : \delta(q, a) = q'\}$.

The following propositions give an asymptotic evaluation of $f_A(n)$. First of all we recall a well-known property of rational generating functions [136].

Proposition 5.5.6 *Let $f(z) = \sum_{n=0}^{+\infty} f_n z^n$ be the generating function of a sequence $\{f_n\}_{n>0} \subseteq \mathbb{C}$, and assume that $f(z) = \frac{a(z)}{b(z)(1-Hz)^{k+1}}$, where $k, H \in \mathbb{N}, k \neq 0, H \neq 0$, $a(z)$ and $b(z)$ are polynomials with complex coefficients, and $b(z)$ has no root of modulus smaller than or equal to H^{-1}. Then, if $a(H^{-1}) \neq 0$, as n tends to $+\infty$ we have*

$$f_n = \frac{a(H^{-1})H^n n^k}{b(H^{-1})k!} + O(H^n n^{k-1})$$

Proposition 5.5.7 *For every main complete chain $S = \{q_i\}_{i=0,\dots,m}$ of a partially ordered automaton $A = \langle Q, q_0, \delta \rangle$ we have*

$$f_S(z) = \left(\prod_{j=0}^{m-1} \omega(q_j, q_{j+1}) \right) z^m \prod_{j=0}^{m} \frac{1}{1 - \ell(q_j)z},$$

$$f_S(n) = \eta_S (H_A)^n \, n^{h_A - 1} + O((H_A)^n \, n^{h_A - 2}),$$

for a suitable rational constant $\eta_S > 0$ only depending on S.

Proof: Let L be the language of all strings recognized by S and, for every $j = 0,\dots,m$, define $\alpha_j = \{a \in \Sigma : \delta(q_j, a) = q_j\}$ and $\beta_j = \{a \in \Sigma : \delta(q_j, a) = q_{j+1}\}$. Then, the generating functions of the languages L, α_j^* and β_j are respectively $f_S(z)$, $(1 - \ell(q_j)z)^{-1}$ and $\omega(q_j, q_{j+1})z$. Since L is equal to the unambiguous product of the languages $\alpha_0^*, \beta_0, \alpha_1^*, \beta_1, \dots, \beta_{m-1}, \alpha_m^*$, arguing as in Example 5.3.2 it is easy to see that $f_S(z)$ is given by the product of the corresponding generating functions. This proves the first identity. Moreover, since S is a main chain, such an equality can be written in the form

$$f_S(z) = \left(\prod_{j=1}^{m-1} \omega(q_j, q_{j+1}) \right) \frac{z^m}{(1 - H_A z)^{h_A}} \left(\prod_{i=0}^{m-h_A} \frac{1}{1 - b_i z} \right)$$

where, for every $i = 0, \ldots, m - h_A$, $b_i < H_A$. Thus, applying Proposition 5.5.6, we obtain the result. □

Proposition 5.5.8 *Given a partially ordered automaton A, let S be a complete chain of A which is not main. Then $f_S(n) = O(H_A^n \, n^{h_A - 2})$.*

Proof: Let S be the complete chain $\{q_j\}_{j=0,\ldots,m}$. Arguing as in the previous proof, we obtain

$$f_S(z) = (\prod_{j=0}^{m-1} \omega(q_j, q_{j+1})) \frac{z^m}{(1 - H_A z)^T} (\prod_{i=0}^{m-T} \frac{1}{1 - b_i z})$$

where T is the number of main states in S and, for every $i = 0, \ldots, m - T$, $b_i < H_A$. Since S is not main, we have that $1 \leq T \leq h_A$. Then, applying Proposition 5.5.6, we obtain

$$f_S(n) = \Theta(H_A^n \, n^{T-1}) = O(H_A^n \, n^{h_A - 2}).$$

□

Proposition 5.5.9 *Let Γ be the set of all the main complete chains of a partially ordered automaton A. Then we have :*
  (i) $f_A(n) = \sum_{S \in \Gamma} f_S(n) + o(\sum_{S \in \Gamma} f_S(n))$, as n tends to $+\infty$;
  (ii) $f_A(n) = \eta_A H_A^n \, n^{h_A - 1} + O(H_A^n \, n^{h_A - 2})$, for a suitable rational constant $\eta_A > 0$ only depending on automaton A.

Proof: It is immediate to verify that, for every partially ordered automaton A, $f_A(n)$ equals the sum of all $f_S(n)$ where S ranges over the set of all complete chains of A. Then the result follows from Propositions 5.5.7 and 5.5.8. □

Analysis of the Mean Value

In this section we determine the asymptotic behaviour of the mean value of $\Im_n$, for any independence alphabet (Σ, I). Our main goal is to evaluate the sum $\sum_{|x|=n} \Im[x]$, where x ranges over the set Σ^n of all words in Σ^* having length n. To this purpose we first define a regular language $\mathcal{L}$, recognized by a suitable partially ordered automaton $\mathcal{A}$, such that the sum $\sum_{|x|=n} \Im[x]$ coincides with the number of words of length n in $\mathcal{L}$. Then, we use the results of the previous section to estimate the asymptotic behaviour of $f_{\mathcal{A}}(n)$.

Let Σ' be a disjoint isomorphic copy of the alphabet Σ. For each $a \in \Sigma$ let the symbol a' be the corresponding element in Σ'. Further, let the independence alphabet $(\tilde{\Sigma}, \tilde{I})$ be given by :
  - $\tilde{\Sigma} = \Sigma \cup \Sigma'$;
  - $\tilde{I} = \{(\alpha, \beta) \in (\tilde{\Sigma} \times \tilde{\Sigma}) : \exists (a, b) \in I$ s.t. $(\alpha = a \vee \alpha = a') \wedge (\beta = b \vee \beta = b')\}$.
Consider the trace language $T \subseteq \mathbb{M}(\tilde{\Sigma}, \tilde{I})$ given by

$$T = \{t \in \mathbb{M}(\tilde{\Sigma}, \tilde{I}) : t = t_1 \cdot t_2, t_1 \in \mathbb{M}(\Sigma, \tilde{I}), t_2 \in \mathbb{M}(\Sigma', \tilde{I})\}$$

and let $\mathcal{L}$ be the set $\{x \in \tilde{\Sigma}^* : [x] \in T\}$. It is easy to verify that a string $z \in \tilde{\Sigma}^*$ belongs to $\mathcal{L}$ if and only if, for every $a \in \Sigma$ occurring in z, we have $(a, b') \in \tilde{I}$ for every $b' \in \Sigma'$ which precedes a in z.

Proposition 5.5.10 *For every $n \in \mathbb{N}$ we have* $\sharp\{x \in \mathcal{L} : |x| = n\} = \sum_{|x|=n} \Im[x]$.

Proof: From the previous definition it is clear that there exists a bijective correspondence between the set $\{z \in \mathcal{L} : |z| = n\}$ and the set $D_n = \{(x, t) : x \in \Sigma^n, t \in \mathrm{Pre}([x])\}$. Therefore the result is a consequence of the following equality:

$$\sum_{|x|=n} \Im[x] = \sum_{t \in \mathbf{M}(\Sigma, I)} \sharp\{x \in \Sigma^* : |x| = n, t \in \mathrm{Pre}([x])\} = \sharp D_n.$$

$\square$

Let $\mathcal{A} = \langle Q, q_0, \delta \rangle$ be the finite automaton over $\tilde{\Sigma}$ such that $Q = \{B : B \subseteq \Sigma\}$, $q_0 = \Sigma$, and δ is defined as follows:

$$\forall B \subseteq \Sigma, \forall a \in \Sigma \quad \delta(B, a) = \begin{cases} B & \text{if } a \in B \\ \perp & \text{otherwise} \end{cases}$$

$$\forall B \subseteq \Sigma, \forall a' \in \Sigma' \quad \delta(B, a') = B \cap I(a)$$

where $I(a) = \{b \in \Sigma : (a, b) \in I\}$. Note that, for every $z \in \tilde{\Sigma}^*$, if $\delta(\Sigma, z) = B$ then, for each $a \in \Sigma$, za is accepted by $\mathcal{A}$ if and only if $a \in B$. In other words, za is accepted by $\mathcal{A}$ if and only if, for every $b' \in \Sigma'$ occurring in z, (a, b') belongs to $\tilde{I}$. By the definition of $\mathcal{L}$ this implies that $\mathcal{L}$ is the language recognized by $\mathcal{A}$. As a consequence we obtain the following statement

Proposition 5.5.11 *For every $n \in \mathbb{N}$ we have* $f_{\mathcal{A}}(n) = \sum_{|x|=n} \Im[x]$.

For any pair of states B, C in Q let $\ell(B)$ and $\omega(B, C)$ denote $\sharp\{\alpha \in \tilde{\Sigma} : \delta(B, \alpha) = B\}$ and $\sharp\{a' \in \Sigma' : \delta(B, a') = C\}$ respectively.

Proposition 5.5.12 *For every $B \in Q$, we have $\ell(B) \leq \sharp\Sigma$. Moreover $\ell(B) = \sharp\Sigma$ if and only if B is union of connected components of the dependency graph (Σ, I^c).*

Proof: Since I is irreflexive, we have that, for every $B \subseteq \Sigma$, $\{a \in \Sigma : B \subseteq I(a)\} \subseteq B^c$. Therefore, from the definition of δ, we obtain:

$$\begin{aligned} \ell(B) &= \sharp B + \sharp\{a' \in \Sigma' : \delta(B, a') = B\} = \\ &= \sharp B + \sharp\{a \in \Sigma : B \subseteq I(a)\} \leq \sharp B + \sharp B^c = \Sigma \end{aligned}$$

This becomes an identity if and only if

$$B^c \subseteq \{a \in \Sigma : B \subseteq I(a)\} \tag{5.2}$$

We claim that (5.2) is true if and only if B is a union of connected components of (Σ, I^c). It is clear that if B is such a union, then for every $a \in B^c$ and every $b \in B$

we have $(a, b) \in I$, and hence $b \in I(a)$. This implies $B \subseteq I(a)$ and hence inclusion (5.2) is proved. On the other hand (5.2) implies that, for every $b \in B$ and every $a \in B^c$, (a, b) belongs to I. This means that in the graph (Σ, I^c) there are no edges connecting a vertex in B with a vertex in B^c and hence B is union of connected components of (Σ, I^c). □

The previous proof also yields the following

Corollary 5.5.13 *For every $B \subseteq \Sigma$, $B^c = \{a \in \Sigma : B \subseteq I(a)\}$ if and only if B is a union of connected components of (Σ, I^c).*

Proposition 5.5.14 *Automaton $\mathcal{A}$ is a partially ordered automaton such that $H_{\mathcal{A}} = \sharp\Sigma$ and $h_{\mathcal{A}} = k + 1$, where k is the number of connected components of (Σ, I^c).*

Proof: It is straightforward to verify that the transition diagram of $\mathcal{A}$ is a partially ordered set with respect to the reflexive and transitive closure of $\leq_\delta$, where Σ and the empty set $\emptyset$ are respectively the smallest and the largest element. So, by Proposition 5.5.12, $\mathcal{A}$ is a partially ordered automaton such that $H_{\mathcal{A}} = \sharp\Sigma$ and a state B is a main state if and only if B is union of connected components of (Σ, I^c). A main complete chain in $\mathcal{A}$ is built in the following way. Let $X_1, X_2, \ldots, X_k$ be the connected components of the graph (Σ, I^c). Starting from state Σ, let us repeatedly apply the transition function δ to symbols $a' \in \Sigma'$ such that the corresponding element $a \in \Sigma$ belongs to X_1. Since $\bigcap_{a \in X_1} I(a) = \bigcup_{i=2}^k X_i$, Proposition 5.5.12 guarantees that, after some transitions, the automaton enters the state X_1^c. Then, we proceed from the state X_1^c by applying δ to symbols $a' \in \Sigma'$ such that $a \in X_2$. Again, after some transitions, the automaton enters the state $(X_1 \cup X_2)^c$ and, continuing this process, it eventually reaches the state $\emptyset$. Clearly such a complete chain contains $k + 1$ main states and it is easy to see that there is no complete chain in $\mathcal{A}$ having a greater number of main states. □

Propositions 5.5.9 and 5.5.14 yield the following

Proposition 5.5.15 *Let k be the number of connected components of (Σ, I^c); then, there exists a rational constant $\eta > 0$, only depending on (Σ, I), such that $E(\Im_n) = \eta n^k + O(n^{k-1})$.*

A natural problem arising from the last proposition is to evaluate the constant η. Clearly it is possible to give a general method to compute η for each independence alphabet. To this end let $S = \{q_j\}_{j=0,\ldots,m}$ be a main complete chain in $\mathcal{A}$. By Propositions 5.5.6 and 5.5.7, we have that $f_S(n) = \eta_S(\sharp\Sigma)^n n^k + O((\sharp\Sigma)^n n^{k-1})$, where η_S is given by

$$\eta_S = \frac{\prod_{j=0}^{m-1} \omega(q_j, q_{j+1})}{k!(\sharp\Sigma)^k \sum_{j=1}^{m-k} (\sharp\Sigma - b_j)} \tag{5.3}$$

and, for every $j = 1, 2, \ldots, m - k$, $b_j = \ell(p_j)$, p_j being the j-th non-main state of S. Hence by Proposition 5.5.9, point (i), we get the following

Proposition 5.5.16 *The constant η defined in the previous proposition equals the sum $\sum_{S \in \Gamma} \eta_S$, where Γ is the set of all main complete chains of $\mathcal{A}$ and each η_S is given by equation (5.3).*

Example 5.5.17 Let us consider the independence alphabet (Σ, I) defined by the following graph

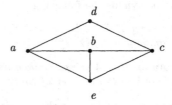

In this case the transition diagram of automaton $\mathcal{A}$ is represented in Figure 5.1. Such an automaton has 4 main states and 6 main complete chains; moreover $H_{\mathcal{A}} = 5$ and $h_{\mathcal{A}} = 3$. Using equation (5.3) to compute the coefficients η_S for any main complete chain S of $\mathcal{A}$, we get $\eta = 2/5$ and hence, in this case, we obtain $E(\Im_n) = \frac{2}{5}n^2 + O(n)$.

Variance, Moments and Limit Distributions

The method presented above can be used to obtain the asymptotic expressions of the variance and the moments of $\Im_n$. For every $i \in \mathbb{N}$ the i-th moment of $\Im_n$, that is $E(\Im_n^i) = \frac{\sum_{|x|=n}(\Im[x])^i}{\#\Sigma^n}$, can be computed defining a suitable partially ordered automaton $\mathcal{A}_i$ such that $\sum_{|x|=n}(\Im[x])^i$ is the number of words of length n in $\mathcal{A}_i$. Therefore, using the properties of partially ordered automata, it can be proved that $E(\Im_n^i) = \Theta(n^{ki})$ for every integer i [15].

Similarly an evaluation of the variance $\text{var}(\Im_n) = E(\Im_n^2) - (E(\Im_n))^2$ can be obtained comparing the partially ordered automaton $\mathcal{A}_2$ which yields $E(\Im_n^2)$ and the automaton of the same kind which allows to compute $(E(\Im_n))^2$. The analysis of the main states and the main complete chains of these two automata shows that $E(\Im_n^2)$ and $(E(\Im_n))^2$ have the same asymptotic behaviour. These results can also be extended to all central moments.

Proposition 5.5.18 [15, 123] *For every independence alphabet (Σ, I) we have :*
(i) $\text{var}(\Im_n) = O(n^{2k-1})$,
(ii) for every $i \in \mathbb{N}$, $E(\Im_n^i) = \eta^i n^{ki} + O(n^{ki-1})$,
where k is the number of connected components of the dependency graph (Σ, I^c) and η is the constant given in Proposition 5.5.15.

Using Chebyshev's inequality and equation (i) of the previous proposition it is easy to show that $\Im_n$ is asymptotic to ηn^k with probability tending to 1, that is

$$\lim_{n \to +\infty} \Pr\{|\frac{\Im_n}{\eta n^k} - 1| > \epsilon\} = 0$$

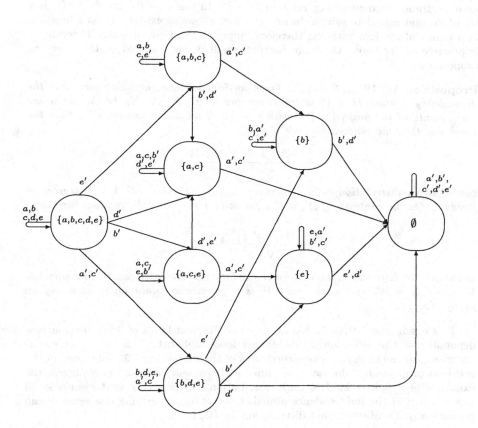

Figure 5.1:

for every $\epsilon > 0$ [123]. Roughly speaking this means that, for n large enough, $\Im_n$ is rather concentrated around its mean value.

Observe that all these results are based on the properties of the finite automata $\mathcal{A}_i$ which allow to calculate the exact value of the moments of $\Im_n$. This method is general and holds for any independence alphabet but it does not allow to determine the explicit expression of the probabilities $\Pr\{\Im_n = j\}$ for $j \in \mathbb{N}$. Actually we know a method to compute these values for those independence alphabets (Σ, I) that admit a transitive dependency relation $D = I^c$. In this case the graph (Σ, D) is a set of disjoint complete subgraphs and this fact allows to express $\Im_n$ as a function of a binomial random variable; therefore, applying the Central Limit Theorem, it is possible to determine the limit distribution of $\Im_n$ as specified by the following proposition.

Proposition 5.5.19 [122] *Let (Σ, I) be an independence alphabet such that the dependency relation $D = I^c$ is transitive and let $\Sigma_1, \Sigma_2, \ldots, \Sigma_k$ be the connected components of the graph (Σ, D), with $k \neq 1$. If all the components Σ_i have the same size then the random variable*

$$2\frac{k^{-k}n^k + k^{2-k}n^{k-1} - \Im_n}{k^{k-3}n^{k-1}}$$

converges in distribution to a chi-square random variable with $k - 1$ degrees of freedom. On the contrary, if $\sharp\Sigma_i \neq \sharp\Sigma_j$ for some $i \neq j$, then the random variable

$$\frac{\Im_n - n^k \prod_{i=1}^k p_i}{\sqrt{V} n^{k-\frac{1}{2}}}$$

converges in distribution to a normal random variable of mean 0 and variance 1, where $p_i = \frac{\sharp\Sigma_i}{\sharp\Sigma}$ for each i and V is a positive constant only depending on $p_1, p_2, \ldots, p_k$.

This result shows that $\Im_n$ has at least two different kinds of limit distributions depending on the definition of the independence alphabet. This fact is somewhat surprising since the asymptotic expressions of the moments of $\Im_n$, obtained in the previous propositions, do not show different behaviours and seem to suggest the existence of a unique kind of limit distribution. In fact note that even a small modification of the independence alphabet, as adding or erasing one symbol, can produce a quite different limit distribution for $\{\Im_n\}$.

5.5.3 Average Analysis on Equiprobable Traces

In this section we study the average number of prefixes of a trace of length n assuming that all traces of given size have the same probability. To this end let (Σ, I) be an independence alphabet and, for every $n \in \mathbb{N}$, let M_n be the set of all traces of length n in $\mathbb{M}(\Sigma, I)$. We define the random variable Δ_n as the number of prefixes of a trace t_n randomly chosen in M_n under the assumption that all traces in M_n have the same probability: $\Delta_n = \Im(t_n)$. We want to evaluate the average value

$$E(\Delta_n) = \frac{\sum_{|t|=n} \Im(t)}{T_n} = \frac{Y_n}{T_n},$$

where T_n is the cardinality of M_n and Y_n denotes the sum $\sum_{|t|=n} \Im(t)$.

Our analysis is based on some properties of formal power series in partially commutative variables and in particular on the Möbius function. Consider the characteristic series $\xi = \sum\limits_{t \in \mathbb{M}(\Sigma, I)} t$ and the Möbius function μ described in Section 5.4.2. We know that $\mu = \sum\limits_{t \in \mathcal{C}} (-1)^{|t|} t$, where $\mathcal{C} \subseteq \mathbb{M}(\Sigma, I)$ is the set of the cliques of the graph (Σ, I) and that $\xi \cdot \mu = [\epsilon]$.

Moreover, given a symbol z not in Σ let ψ be the morphism $\psi : \mathbb{Q}\langle\!\langle \Sigma, I \rangle\!\rangle \to \mathbb{Q}\langle\!\langle z \rangle\!\rangle$ induced by the function mapping each trace $t \in \mathbb{M}(\Sigma, I)$ into $z^{|t|}$. It is easy to verify that $\psi(\xi) = \sum_n T_n z^n$ and

$$\psi(\mu) = \sum_{j=0,\ldots,\alpha} (-1)^j \Gamma_j z^j,$$

where α is the size of the maximum clique of (Σ, I) and Γ_j is the number of cliques of size j in (Σ, I). Clearly, since $\xi^2 = \sum_t \Im(t) t$, we obtain

$$\psi(\xi^2) = \sum_{n=0}^{+\infty} \left(\sum_{|t|=n} \Im(t) \right) z^n = \sum_{n=0}^{+\infty} Y_n z^n$$

Denoting by $G(z)$ the polynomial $G(z) = \sum_{j=0,\ldots,\alpha} (-1)^j \Gamma_j z^j$ and recalling that ψ is a morphism, from the previous relations we get

$$\sum_{t \in \mathbb{M}(\Sigma, I)} T_n z^n = (\psi(\mu))^{-1} = (G(z))^{-1} \tag{5.4}$$

$$\sum_{n=0}^{+\infty} Y_n z^n = (\psi(\mu))^{-2} = (G(z))^{-2} \tag{5.5}$$

Also in this case we have to evaluate the asymptotic behaviour of two sequences from the corresponding generating functions.

Proposition 5.5.20 *Let Γ_j be the number of cliques of size j in (Σ, I) and let $G(z)$ be the polynomial $G(z) = \sum_{j=0,\ldots,\alpha} (-1)^j \Gamma_j z^j$. If $G(z)$ has only one root b of least modulus then $E(\Delta_n) = \Theta(n^h)$ where h is the multiplicity of b in $G(z)$.*

Proof: Applying Proposition 5.5.6 to equations (5.4) and (5.5) we have $T_n = \Theta(n^{h-1} b^{-n})$ and $Y_n = \Theta(n^{2h-1} b^{-n})$. Hence we conclude $E(\Delta_n) = \frac{Y_n}{T_n} = \Theta(n^h)$.
$\square$

5.5.4 Further Remarks

All results presented above can be applied to the analysis of the algorithms described in Section 5.5.1. In particular, assuming equiprobable all input strings of length n, the Membership Problem for rational trace languages can be solved in $O(n^{k+1})$ time and $O(n^k)$ space both in the average case and with probability tending to 1. The same holds for all algorithms represented by the procedure scheme described in [16] (see also [121]). Analogously the Membership Problem for context-free trace languages, on equiprobable input strings of length n, can be solved in $O(\mathrm{BM}(n^k))$ time both in the average case and with probability tending to 1, where $\mathrm{BM}(m)$ is the time required to multiply two boolean matrices of size m.

Note that, for a given free partially commutative monoid, the average time and space complexity of these algorithms depends on the values $E(\Im_n)$ and $E(\Delta_n)$, while the corresponding worst case complexity depends on $W(n)$ which represents the maximum number of prefixes of a trace of length n. Hence a comparison among these three values allows to evaluate the difference between average case and worst case behaviour of our algorithms.

In the following picture we compare the order of magnitude of $E(\Im_n)$, $E(\Delta_n)$ and $W(n)$ for some independence alphabets.

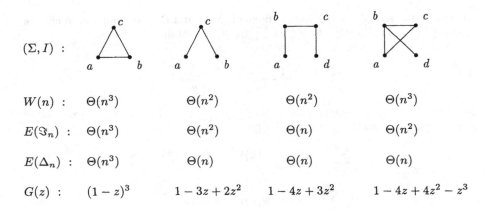

(Σ, I) :				
$W(n)$:	$\Theta(n^3)$	$\Theta(n^2)$	$\Theta(n^2)$	$\Theta(n^3)$
$E(\Im_n)$:	$\Theta(n^3)$	$\Theta(n^2)$	$\Theta(n)$	$\Theta(n^2)$
$E(\Delta_n)$:	$\Theta(n^3)$	$\Theta(n)$	$\Theta(n)$	$\Theta(n)$
$G(z)$:	$(1-z)^3$	$1 - 3z + 2z^2$	$1 - 4z + 3z^2$	$1 - 4z + 4z^2 - z^3$

Observe that for some independence alphabets the values of $E(\Im_n), E(\Delta_n)$ and $W(n)$ are equal up to a constant factor. On the contrary for other independence alphabets these values are completely different: in many cases we have $E(\Delta_n) = o(E(\Im_n))$ and $E(\Im_n) = o(W(n))$. While trivially $E(\Im_n) \le W(n)$ and $E(\Delta_n) \le W(n)$ we conjecture that $E(\Delta_n) \le E(\Im_n)$.

On the other hand, for most independence alphabets, it is clear that $W(n)$ is much larger than $E(\Im_n)$. In fact we have seen that $W(n) = \Theta(n^\alpha)$ and $E(\Im_n) = \Theta(n^k)$, where α is the size of the maximum clique of (Σ, I) and k is the number of connected components of (Σ, I^c). Clearly $k \le \alpha$ for every independence alphabet, but in most graphs the size of the maximum clique of a graph is greater than the number of connected components of its complement; therefore it is clear that $W(n)$ represents an overestimation of the number of prefixes of a trace of length n.

This fact is also confirmed by some properties of random graphs widely studied in the literature. It is known that, for m large enough, almost all graphs of size m have connected complement while the size of their largest clique is asymptotic to $2\log_2 m$ with probability 1 [146]. This means that, for most large independence alphabets (Σ, I), k equals 1 while α is close to $2\log_2(\sharp\Sigma)$ and hence, in these cases, the average number of prefixes is $O(n)$ while its largest value is a polynomial of high degree. By the previous observations this means that, for most free partially commutative monoids, there is a remarkable difference between the worst case and the average case behaviour of the algorithms for the Membership problems.

III LANGUAGES AND AUTOMATA

Chapter 6

E. Ochmański
Recognizable Trace Languages

Chapter 7

W. Zielonka
Asynchronous Automata

Chapter 8

V. Diekert, A. Muscholl
Construction of Asynchronous Automata

Chapter 6

Recognizable Trace Languages

Edward Ochmański

Polska Akademia Nauk, Instytut Podstaw Informatyki
Ordona 21, 01–237 Warszawa, Poland

Contents

The formal language theory over traces, limited to recognizable and rational trace languages, is the subject of this chapter. Section 6.1 presents basic concepts of monoid theory, related to the field of our interests. Section 6.2 introduces trace monoids. Algebraic characterizations of recognizable trace languages with rational expressions are given in Section 6.3. They disprove some informal conjectures (that rational expressions are useless for expressing recognizable trace languages) of early stage of development of trace theory. Perhaps the most famous open problem of trace theory is discussed in Section 6.4, with some partial solution. Section 6.5 contains a piece of information on trace morphisms. That area is still waiting for better exploration. So far, only partial results about trace codes (injective morphisms) are known, [32]. The last two sections 6.6 and 6.7 establish relations of recognizable trace languages to elementary Petri nets. Petri nets are regarded as devices generating trace languages. It is shown, using results of Section 6.3, that the class of recognizable subsets of any trace monoid is just equal to the class of languages generated by Petri nets (with possible labelling). The reader being familiar with asynchronous automata will certainly remark common points of both approaches.

6.1　Monoids and Their Subsets

In this preliminary section we study properties of monoids and their subsets, mostly those related to the common theme of the chapter. The studies are intensively illustrated with examples. The influence of [11] on this section is unhiddable.

A *monoid* $M = (M, \circ, 1)$ is a set M with a binary operation "$\circ$" on M, named *product*, and with a distinguished element $1 \in M$, named *unit*, satisfying the monoid axioms:

associativity $(x \circ y) \circ z = x \circ (y \circ z)$ for any $x, y, z \in M$

neutrality $1 \circ x = x \circ 1 = x$ for any $x \in M$

The sign of the product operation will be mostly omitted.

Given a monoid M, a *congruence* in M is an *equivalence relation* $\approx \subseteq M \times M$, i.e. a reflexive ($x \approx x$), symmetric ($x \approx y \Rightarrow y \approx x$), and transitive ($x \approx y \wedge y \approx z \Rightarrow x \approx z$) relation compatible with the product operation ($x \approx x' \wedge y \approx y' \Rightarrow xy \approx x'y'$). Any congruence $\approx$ in M induces the *quotient monoid* $(M_\approx, \circ, [1]_\approx)$, where $[m]_\approx = \{x \in M \mid x \approx m\}$, for $m \in M$, are equivalence classes of $\approx$, $M_\approx = \{[m]_\approx \mid m \in M\}$ and $[x]_\approx \circ [y]_\approx = [xy]_\approx$. For any $X \subseteq M_\approx$, the set $\bigcup X$ is the set-theoretical union of members of X, i.e. $\bigcup X = \{m \in M \mid [m]_\approx \in X\} \subseteq M$. Given a subset $L \subseteq M$, we denote by $[L]_\approx$ the set $[L]_\approx = \{[m]_\approx \mid m \in L\} \subseteq M_\approx$. The subsets containing just one member are named singletons; they are written without the set-braces, whenever it does not involve any confusion.

Let us denote by 2^M the set of all subsets (shortly, the *powerset*) of a monoid M. Clearly, the Boolean operations

union $X \cup Y = \{z \in M \mid z \in X \vee z \in Y\}$

intersection $X \cap Y = \{z \in M \mid z \in X \wedge z \in Y\}$

difference $X - Y = \{z \in M \mid z \in X \wedge z \notin Y\}$

work on 2^M. Let us extend the monoid product operation "$\circ$" on M to the set-product operation "$\bullet$" as follows:

set-product $X \bullet Y = \{x \circ y \mid x \in X \wedge y \in Y\}$

This way we have built a monoid $(2^M, \bullet, \{1\})$, the *power-monoid* over the monoid M.

Given two monoids M' and M''. The cartesian product $M' \times M''$, with the product operation $(x, u) \circ (z, v) = (xz, uv)$ and with the unit $1 = (1', 1'')$, is the *product-monoid* of M' and M''. The binary set-product operation induces the unary star operation in 2^M, defined as follows:

power $X^0 = \{1\}, X^{n+1} = X^n \bullet X$

star $X^* = \bigcup\{X^n \mid n \geq 0\}$

A subset X of a monoid M is said to be a *generator* of M iff $M = X^*$; we say M is *finitely generated* iff there exists a finite generator of M. A subset X of M is a *submonoid* of M iff $X = X^*$. For any $X \subseteq M$, the set $X^* \subseteq M$ is the least submonoid containing X.

Let Σ be a set, called an *alphabet*; members of alphabets are called *letters*; finite sequences of letters are called *words*. The set of all words over an alphabet Σ is denoted by Σ^*. The associative operation is the *concatenation*: $(a_1, \ldots, a_n) \circ (b_1, \ldots, b_m) = (a_1, \ldots, a_n, b_1, \ldots, b_m)$. We will write words omitting parenthesis and commas, i.e. $a_1 \ldots a_n$ instead of $(a_1, \ldots, a_n)$. The empty sequence $(\ )$ is called the empty word and is denoted by ε. For $w \in \Sigma^*$, we denote by $|w|$ the number of letter occurrences in w (formally: $|\varepsilon| = 0, (\forall a \in \Sigma) \, |a| = 1$ and $(\forall u, v \in \Sigma^*) \, |uv| = |u| + |v|$), named the *length* of w, and by $|w|_a$ (for $a \in \Sigma$) the number of occurrences of a in w (formally: $|\varepsilon|_a = 0, (\forall c \in \Sigma) \, |c|_a = $ if $c = a$ then 1 else 0 and $(\forall u, v \in \Sigma^*) \, |uv|_a = |u|_a + |v|_a$). The monoid $(\Sigma^*, \circ, \varepsilon)$ is the *free monoid* over the alphabet Σ; the alphabet Σ is the least generator of Σ^*. Subsets of free monoids are called *languages*.

Given two monoids M and M', a function $\Phi : M \to M'$ is a *morphism* iff $\Phi(xy) = \Phi(x)\Phi(y)$ for all $x, y \in M$ and $\Phi(1_M) = \Phi(1_{M'})$. Let us define some particular kinds of morphisms; we will utilize them in the course of the chapter.

substitution: any morphism $\Phi : M \to 2^{M'}$ from a monoid M into a power-monoid over a monoid M'.

canonical quotient morphism: a morphism $[\ ] : M \to M_\approx$ from a monoid M onto a quotient monoid $M_\approx$, where $\approx$ is a congruence in M, associating with each $x \in M$ its equivalence class $[x]_\approx$.

alphabetic morphism: any morphism $\varphi : \Sigma^* \to \Gamma^*$ from a free monoid Σ^* into a free monoid Γ^*, such that $\varphi(\Sigma) \subseteq \Gamma \cup \{\varepsilon\}$.

projection: an alphabetic morphism $\Pi_\Gamma : \Sigma^* \to \Gamma^*$, for $\Gamma \subseteq \Sigma$, such that (for any $a \in \Sigma$) $\Pi_\Gamma(a) = $ if $a \in \Gamma$ then a else ε.

6.1.1   Recognizable Subsets

Let M be a monoid. An M-*automaton* is a triple $\mathcal{A} = (Q, q_0, F)$. The set Q is identified with a subset $Q \subseteq Q^M$ of functions from M to Q; members of Q are named *states* of $\mathcal{A}$. States fulfil the composition rule: $(\forall q \in Q)(\forall x, y \in M)\ q(\varepsilon) = q$ and $q(xy) = q(x)(y)$. The state $q_0 \in Q$ is an *initial state* and the set $F \subseteq Q$ is the set of *final states*. An automaton is said to be a *finite automaton* iff its set Q of states is finite.

M-automata are regarded as devices recognizing subsets of the monoid M; the subset of M *recognized* by the automaton $\mathcal{A}$ is the set $L(\mathcal{A}) = \{m \in M \mid q_0(m) \in F\}$.

Definition 6.1.1 *A subset X of a monoid M is* recognizable *iff there exists a finite M-automaton recognizing X.*

A finite automaton $\mathcal{A}$ is said to be *minimal* iff its number of states is minimal among all automata recognizing $L(\mathcal{A})$. The family of all recognizable subsets of M will be denoted by $\mathrm{REC}(M)$. Recognizable subsets of free monoids will be mostly called *regular languages*, and the family of all regular languages in a free monoid Σ^* will be denoted by $\mathrm{REG}(\Sigma^*)$.

Now we are going to characterize recognizable subsets with the notions of the syntactic relations. These characterizations (Propositions 6.1.3, 6.1.6 and 6.1.7) will be frequently utilized in the investigations of this chapter, mostly in proofs.

Definition 6.1.2 *Let M be a monoid. The* left quotient *of a subset $X \subseteq M$ by an element $m \in M$ is the set $X/m = \{z \in M \mid mz \in X\}$. The* left syntactic relation *of X is the equivalence relation $\approx_X = \{(u, v) \in M \times M \mid X/u = X/v\}$. Clearly, $\approx_X$ is of finite index iff the family $\{X/m \mid m \in M\}$ is finite.*

Proposition 6.1.3 *Let M be a monoid and let X be a subset of M.*
   X is recognizable iff $\approx_X$ is of finite index.

Proof: $\Rightarrow$: if $q_0(m_1) = q_0(m_2)$ then $L(\mathcal{A})/m_1 = L(\mathcal{A})/m_2$.
   $\Leftarrow$: $Q = \{X/m \mid m \in M\}$; $(X/u)(v) = X/uv$; $q_0 = X/1 = X$; $F = \{X/m \mid m \in X\}$. □

The following example, being a corollary of the last proposition, presents two languages. They will be frequently used to show that a given language is not regular.

Example 6.1.4 Let Σ be a finite alphabet, let $a, b \in \Sigma$. The language $L = a^* b^*$ belongs to $\mathrm{REG}(\Sigma^*)$. Actually, $L/a = a^* b^*$, $L/b = b^*$ and $L/ba = \emptyset$ are the only left quotients of L. The language $K = \{a^n b^n \mid n \geq 0\}$ is perhaps the most popular non-regular language. Actually, $K/a^n \neq K/a^m$ whenever $n \neq m$.

Definition 6.1.5 *Let M be a monoid, let $X \subseteq M$ and let k be a nonnegative integer. Let $P = (p_1, \ldots, p_k)$ belong to M^k. The k-syntactic quotient of X by P, denoted by $X//P$, is a subset of M^{k+1} defined as follows: $(z_0, z_1, \ldots, z_k) \in X//(p_1, \ldots, p_k)$ iff $z_0 p_1 z_1 \ldots p_k z_k \in X$. The k-syntactic relation of X is the equivalence relation defined as follows: $(x_1, \ldots, x_k) \equiv_{X,k} (y_1, \ldots, y_k)$ iff $X//(x_1, \ldots, x_k) = X//(y_1, \ldots, y_k)$.*

Let us recall a well-known characterization of $\mathrm{REC}(M)$ with the 1-syntactic relation $\equiv_{X,1}$, denoted by $\equiv_X$ in the sequel.

Proposition 6.1.6 *Let M be a monoid and let X be a subset of M.*
X is recognizable iff $\equiv_X$ is of finite index.

Proof: $\Rightarrow$: Clearly, $X//(u) = \bigcup\{\{x\} \times X/xu \mid x \in X\}$. Observe that if $X/x = X/y$ then $X/xu = X/yu$. It allows us to write $X//(u) = \bigcup\{[x]_{\approx_X} \times X/xu \mid x \in X\}$. By Proposition 6.1.3, $\approx_X$ is of finite index, say equal to n. Then the index of $\equiv_X$ does not exceed n^n.

$\Leftarrow$: Remark that $(u) \equiv_X (v)$ implies $u \approx_X v$. Hence index of $\approx_X$ does not exceed the one of $\equiv_X$. Thus X is recognizable, by Proposition 6.1.3. $\quad\square$

The following generalization follows easily from Proposition 6.1.6:

Proposition 6.1.7 *Let M be a monoid, let X be a subset of M and let k be an integer. X is recognizable iff $\equiv_{X,k}$ is of finite index.*

Proof: If $k = 1$ then we have Proposition 6.1.6. One can easily show that if $(x_i) \equiv_X (y_i)$ for all $i = 1, \ldots, k$ then $(x_1, \ldots, x_k) \equiv_{X,k} (y_1, \ldots, y_k)$. Thus the index of $\equiv_{X,k}$ does not exceed n^k, where n is the index of $\equiv_X$. For the converse observe that if $(x, \varepsilon, \ldots, \varepsilon) \equiv_{X,k} (y, \varepsilon, \ldots, \varepsilon)$ then $(x) \equiv_X (y)$. $\quad\square$

Proposition 6.1.8 *Let M be a monoid.*
$\emptyset \in \mathrm{REC}(M)$.
$M \in \mathrm{REC}(M)$.
If X and Y are in $\mathrm{REC}(M)$, then $X \cup Y, X \cap Y$ and $X - Y$ are in $\mathrm{REC}(M)$.

Proof: $\emptyset/m = \emptyset$ for any $m \in M$. Thus the index of $\approx_\emptyset$ is equal to 1. $M/m = M$ for any $m \in M$. Thus the index of $\approx_M$ is equal to 1. By Proposition 6.1.3 the indices of $\approx_X$ and $\approx_Y$ are finite; say p and q, respectively. Observe that $(X \cup Y)/m = X/m \cup Y/m, (X \cap Y)/m = X/m \cap Y/m$ and $(X - Y)/m = X/m - Y/m$, for any $m \in M$. Thus the indices of $\approx_{X \cup Y}, \approx_{X \cap Y}$ and $\approx_{X-Y}$ do not exceed pq. Hence, all these sets are recognizable, by Proposition 6.1.3. $\quad\square$

Proposition 6.1.9 *Let M_0 and M be monoids; let $\Phi : M_0 \to M$ be a morphism. If $X \in \mathrm{REC}(M)$ then $\Phi^{-1}(X) \in \mathrm{REC}(M_0)$.*

Proof: We have $z \in \Phi^{-1}(X)/m$ iff $mz \in \Phi^{-1}(X)$ iff $\Phi(mz) \in X$ iff $\Phi(m)\Phi(z) \in X$ iff $\Phi(z) \in X/\Phi(m)$ iff $z \in \Phi^{-1}(X/\Phi(m))$. We have shown $\Phi^{-1}(X)/m = \Phi^{-1}(X/\Phi(m))$. Thus the index of $\approx_{\Phi^{-1}(X)}$ does not exceed the index of $\approx_X$. And Proposition 6.1.3 yields the result. $\quad\square$

It is well known that $\mathrm{REC}(\Sigma^*)$ is closed under product, star and morphisms. It does not hold for any monoid. The counter-examples (Example 6.1.11 – star and morphism, Example 6.1.12 – product) will be shown when we present some concrete monoids.

The following proposition allows to reason about (recognizable subsets of) quotient monoids from original monoids.

Proposition 6.1.10 *Let M be a monoid; let $\approx$ be a congruence in M. For any $X \subseteq M_\approx : X \in \mathrm{REC}(M_\approx)$ iff $\bigcup X \in \mathrm{REC}(M)$.*

Proof: Let $\alpha = [u]_\approx$ and $\beta = [v]_\approx$, for $\alpha, \beta \in M_\approx$ and $u, v \in M$. First remark that $X/\alpha = [(\bigcup X)/u]_\approx, X/\beta = [(\bigcup X)/v]_\approx$ and $[(\bigcup X)/u]_\approx = [(\bigcup X)/v]_\approx$ iff $(\bigcup X)/u = (\bigcup X)/v$. Hence $X/\alpha = X/\beta$ iff $(\bigcup X)/u = (\bigcup X)/v$, thus X and $\bigcup X$ have the same number of left quotients. $\qquad\square$

Let M be a monoid; let $\approx$ be a congruence in M. The operation $f_\approx : 2^M \to 2^M$ defined as $f_\approx(L) = \bigcup[L]_\approx$ is called the $\approx$-closure operation. A subset $L \subseteq M$ is said to be $\approx$-closed iff $L = f_\approx(L)$. Proposition 6.1.10 assures a one-to-one correspondence between $\mathrm{REC}(M_\approx)$ and $\approx$-closed members of $\mathrm{REC}(M)$. It is especially convenient when the original monoid M is free; then we can operate with the well known regular languages. Let us go into that field.

6.1.2 Equational Presentations

Let $M = \Sigma^*$ be a free monoid. Let $E \subseteq M \times M$ be a finite relation. The *congruence generated* by E is constructed as follows: $x \sim y$ iff $x = x'ux'', y = x'vx''$ and $(u, v) \in E \cup E^{-1}$. Let us denote the reflexive and transitive closure of $\sim$ by $\approx$; then $\approx$ is the congruence generated by E. Usually, the set E will be written as a set of equations $E = \{u_1 = v, \dots, u_n = v_n\}$, and the quotient monoid $M_\approx$ will be denoted by $M(\Sigma^*; u_1 = v_1, \dots, u_n = v_n)$. Clearly, $M(\Sigma^*; \emptyset)$ is (isomorphic to) the free monoid Σ^*.

Example 6.1.11 (star and morphism putting out of REC) Let $\Sigma = \{a, b\}$ and $M = M(\Sigma^*; ab = ba)$.

We show that $\mathrm{REC}(M)$ is not closed under star. Clearly, $[ab] \in \mathrm{REC}(M)$. For $[ab]^*$, however, we have $\bigcup[ab]^* \cap a^*b^* = \{a^n b^n \mid n \geq 0\} \notin \mathrm{REG}(\Sigma^*)$. So, by Proposition 6.1.10, $[ab]^* \notin \mathrm{REC}(M)$. Now we show a morphism that puts out of REC. Let $\varphi : \Sigma^* \to M$ be the morphism $\varphi(a) = [a]$ and $\varphi(b) = [b]$. We have $(ab)^* \in \mathrm{REC}(\Sigma^*)$ and $\varphi(ab)^* = [ab]^* \notin \mathrm{REC}(M)$.

We will see later that $\mathrm{REC}(M)$ of Example 6.1.11 is closed under product. So we have to exhibit another example:

Example 6.1.12 (product putting out of REC) Let $\Sigma = \{a, b\}$ and $M = M(\Sigma^*; ab = aabb)$.

Clearly, $[a]$ and $[b]$ are in $\mathrm{REC}(M)$. But $\bigcup\{[ab]\} = \{a^n b^n \mid n \geq 1\} \notin \mathrm{REG}(\Sigma^*)$. So, by Proposition 6.1.10, $[a][b] = [ab] \notin \mathrm{REC}(M)$.

Note that the above provides also an example of a monoid where finite sets are not recognizable, in general.

6.1.3 Rational Subsets

Definition 6.1.13 *Let M be a monoid.* $\mathrm{RAT}(M)$ *is the least family of subsets of M, such that:*
- *$\emptyset \in \mathrm{RAT}(M)$*
- *$\{m\} \in \mathrm{RAT}(M)$ for all $m \in M$*
- *if $X, Y \in \mathrm{RAT}(M)$ then $X \cup Y \in \mathrm{RAT}(M), X \bullet Y \in \mathrm{RAT}(M)$ and $X^* \in \mathrm{RAT}(M)$.*

Members of $\mathrm{RAT}(M)$ are called the rational subsets *of M.*

Given a monoid M, rational expressions *over M are members of the set $\mathrm{REX}(M)$ of finite strings over the alphabet $M \cup \{\emptyset, \cup, \bullet, *, (,)\}$, defined as the least set such that:*
- *$\emptyset \in \mathrm{REX}(M)$*
- *if $m \in M$ then $m \in \mathrm{REX}(M)$*
- *if $R, R' \in \mathrm{REX}(M)$ then $(R \cup R') \in \mathrm{REX}(M), (R \bullet R') \in \mathrm{REX}(M)$ and $R^* \in \mathrm{REX}(M)$.*

Setting the natural meaning on $R \in \mathrm{REX}(M)$, we obtain the subset $L(R) \subseteq M$ expressed by R. One can say that a subset is rational iff it is expressed by some rational expression. Remark that any rational subset is expressed by many different rational expressions.

It follows directly from the definition that $\mathrm{RAT}(M)$ is closed under union, product and star operations. The following two properties follow easily from the definition.

Proposition 6.1.14 *Let M be a monoid.* $M \in \mathrm{RAT}(M)$ *iff M is finitely generated.*

Proof: $\Leftarrow$: Obvious. $\Rightarrow$: Let $M = L(R)$ for some $R \in \mathrm{REX}(M)$. Let X be the set of members of M occurring in R. Clearly $M \subseteq X^* \subseteq M$, thus $M = X^*$. Since X is finite, M is finitely generated.   □

Proposition 6.1.15 *Let M and M' be monoids; let $\Phi : M \to M'$ be a morphism. If $X \in \mathrm{RAT}(M)$ then $\Phi(X) \in \mathrm{RAT}(M')$.*

Proof: Easily from the definition and the fact that for any morphism $\Phi(X \cup Y) = \Phi(X) \cup \Phi(Y), \Phi(XY) = \Phi(X)\Phi(Y), \Phi(X^*) = (\Phi(X))^*$.   □

Now we show the examples proving that RAT, unlike REC, is not closed under intersection, difference or inverse morphism.

Example 6.1.16 (intersection putting out of RAT) Let $\Sigma = \{a, b, c\}$, $M = M(\Sigma^*; ac = ca, bc = cb)$, $X = [(ac)^*b^*] \in \mathrm{RAT}(M)$, and $Y = [a^*(bc)^*] \in \mathrm{RAT}(M)$. For the projection $\Pi_{\{a,b\}}$ we have $\Pi_{\{a,b\}}(X \cap Y) = \{a^n b^n \mid n \geq 0\} \notin \mathrm{RAT}(M)$. Hence $X \cap Y \notin \mathrm{RAT}(M)$, by Proposition 6.1.15.

Example 6.1.17 (difference putting out of RAT) Let M and $X, Y \in \text{RAT}(M)$ be like in the last example. As M is finitely generated, it is rational (Proposition 6.1.14). As $X \cap Y = M - ((M - X) \cup (M - Y)) \notin \text{RAT}(M)$ and $\text{RAT}(M)$ is closed under union, difference of rational subsets is not rational, in general. Let us find an explicit example. $M - X = [(ac)^*(aa^* \cup cc^*)b^* \cup \Sigma^* ba\Sigma^*]$ and $M - Y = [a^*(bc)^*(bb^* \cup cc^*) \cup \Sigma^* ba\Sigma^*]$ as well as their union $Z = (M - X) \cup (M - Y)$ are in $\text{RAT}(M)$. Hence, $M - Z \notin \text{RAT}(M)$ whereas $M, Z \in \text{RAT}(M)$.

Example 6.1.18 (inverse morphism putting out of RAT) Let $\Sigma = \{a, b\}$ and $M = \Sigma^*, M' = M(\Sigma^*; ab = ba)$. Let $\Phi : M \to M'$ be defined as $\Phi(a) = [a]$ and $\Phi(b) = [b]$. Let $X = [(ab)^*] \in \text{RAT}(M')$. We have $\Phi^{-1}(X) \cap a^* b^* = \{a^n b^n \mid n \geq 0\} \notin \text{RAT}(M)$, thus $\Phi^{-1}(X) \notin \text{RAT}(M)$.

The commonly known Kleene's Theorem [155], identifying REC and RAT in finitely generated free monoids, is very fundamental for this chapter. For its proof see [243] or [94].

Theorem 6.1.19 (Kleene) *Let Σ be a finite alphabet.*
Then $\text{REC}(\Sigma^*) = \text{RAT}(\Sigma^*)$.

The following weaker version of Kleene's Theorem [193] holds for finitely generated monoids:

Proposition 6.1.20 (McKnight) $\text{REC}(M) \subseteq \text{RAT}(M)$ *iff M is finitely generated.*

Proof: $\Rightarrow$: As $M \in \text{REC}(M)$ for any monoid (Proposition 6.1.8), we have $M \in \text{RAT}(M)$. Since Proposition 6.1.14, M is finitely generated.

$\Leftarrow$: Let $\{g_1, \ldots, g_n\}$ be set of generators of M. Set $\Sigma = \{a_1, \ldots, a_n\}$. Let $\varphi : \Sigma^* \to M$ be the morphism defined by $\varphi(a_i) = g_i$, for $i = 1, \ldots, n$. Let $X \in \text{REC}(M)$. Then, by Proposition 6.1.9, $\varphi^{-1}(X) \in \text{REC}(\Sigma^*)$. By Kleene's Theorem, $\varphi^{-1}(X) \in \text{RAT}(\Sigma^*)$. Since Proposition 6.1.15, $\varphi(\varphi^{-1}(X)) = X \in \text{RAT}(M)$. $\square$

6.2   Trace Monoids and Trace Languages

Let Σ be a finite alphabet and let I be an irreflexive and symmetric relation on Σ, called *independence* relation. The couple (Σ, I) is then called a *concurrent alphabet*. The reflexive and symmetric relation $D = \Sigma \times \Sigma - I$ is called the *dependence* relation. The concurrent alphabet (Σ, I) induces the set of equations $E = \{ab = ba \mid (a, b) \in I\}$, and the monoid $M(\Sigma^*; E)$, called the *trace monoid*. Trace monoids will be mostly denoted by $M(\Sigma, I)$, and sometimes by $M(\Sigma, D)$. Clearly, a trace monoid is free iff $I = \emptyset$. Members of trace monoids are called *traces*; subsets of trace monoids are called *trace languages*. Traces will be represented graphically by so-called *dependence graphs*; see Chapter 2 of this book for their definition and properties. One can extend the notion of length to traces: $|\alpha| = n$ iff $\alpha = [w]$ and

$|w| = n$. Given a trace language $T \subseteq M = M(\Sigma, I)$, the language $\bigcup T = \{w \in \Sigma^* \mid [w] \in T\}$ is named the *flat* of T. The mapping $f_I : 2^{\Sigma^*} \to 2^{\Sigma^*}$ such that $f_I(L) = \bigcup[L]$ is the *closure* (with respect to I) function. The language $L \subseteq \Sigma^*$ is said to be *closed* (with respect to I) if $f_I(L) = L$. One can extend I and D to $\Sigma^* \times \Sigma^* : (u, v) \in I$ iff $\mathrm{alph}(u) \times \mathrm{alph}(v) \subseteq I$ and $(u, v) \in D$ iff $(\mathrm{alph}(u) \times \mathrm{alph}(v)) \cap D$ is nonempty, and even to $M(\Sigma, I) \times M(\Sigma, I) : (\alpha, \beta) \in I$ iff $\alpha = [u], \beta = [v]$ and $(u, v) \in I$. Given $x \in \Sigma^*$, we denote $I(x) = \{w \in \Sigma^* \mid (w, x) \in I\}$.

6.2.1 Some Combinatorial Properties

Let $M = M(\Sigma, I)$ be a trace monoid and let $x, y \in \Sigma^*$. A sequence $w_0, w_1, \ldots, w_n$ of words in Σ^* is called a *derivation* from x to y if and only if $w_0 = x, w_n = y$ and $(\forall i = 1, \ldots, n)(\exists a, b \in \Sigma \cup \{\varepsilon\}; u, v \in \Sigma^*)$ such that $(a, b) \in I, w_{i-1} = uabv, w_i = ubav$. Remark that empty derivation steps are allowed (for convenience only). Obviously, $[x] = [y]$ iff there is a derivation from x to y.

A monoid M is said to be *cancellative* iff $(\forall \alpha, \beta, \gamma, \delta \in M)$ $\gamma \alpha \delta = \gamma \beta \delta$ implies $\alpha = \beta$. Any trace monoid will be shown to be *cancellative*. Notice, however, that cancellation is not obliging in the class of all monoids.

Example 6.2.1 (non-cancellative monoid) Let $\Sigma = \{a, b\}$ and $M = M(\Sigma^*; ab = aabb)$. Clearly, $[a][b] = [a][abb]$ but $[b] \neq [abb]$.

Proposition 6.2.2 (cancellation) *Let* $M = M(\Sigma, I)$ *be a trace monoid.* $(\forall \alpha, \beta, \gamma, \delta \in M)$ $\gamma \alpha \delta = \gamma \beta \delta$ *implies* $\alpha = \beta$.

Proof: We shall show some auxiliary results.

Claim A Let $x, y, u \in \Sigma^*$ and $a \in \Sigma$. If $[xay] = [au]$ with $|x|_a = 0$, then $[xay] = [axy]$ and $[xy] = [u]$.

Proof: Clearly, $(b, a) \in I$ for any $b \in \mathrm{alph}(x)$; thus $[xay] = [axy]$. Let $xay = w_0, w_1, \ldots, w_n = au$ be a derivation from xay to au. It is easy to observe that the sequence $xy = v_0, v_1, \ldots, v_n = u$, obtaining by erasing the first occurrences of the letter a in the former derivation, is a derivation from xy to u. Hence $[xy] = [u]$. $\square$

Analogously, it holds

Claim B Let $x, y, u \in \Sigma^*$ and $a \in \Sigma$. If $[xay] = [ua]$ with $|y|_a = 0$, then $[xay] = [xya]$ and $[xy] = [u]$.

Now, inductively (with respect to $|x| + |y|$), we obtain from Claims A and B that $[u] = [v]$, whenever $[xuy] = [xvy]$. And the settlement $\alpha = [u], \beta = [v], \gamma = [x], \delta = [y]$ concludes the proof. $\square$

The following auxiliary lemma presents quite useful combinatorial property.

Lemma 6.2.3 *Let* $M = M(\Sigma, I)$ *be a trace monoid; let* $w, u, v \in \Sigma^*$. *Then* $[w] = [uv]$ *if and only if there is a factorization* $w = v_0 u_1 v_1 \ldots u_n v_n$, *such that* $[u_1 \ldots u_n] = [u], [v_0 v_1 \ldots v_n] = [v]$, *and* $(v_i, u_j) \in I$ *for* $i < j$.

Proof: Let us start with some auxiliary claim:

Claim 1 Let $x, y, u, v \in \Sigma^*$ and $a \in \Sigma$. If $[xay] = [uav]$ with $|x|_a = |u|_a$, then $[xy] = [uv]$.

Proof: Let $xay = w_0, w_1, \ldots, w_n = uav$ be a derivation from xay to uav. Clearly, for each w_i, there is a factorization $w_i = p_i a q_i$ with $|p_i|_a = |x|_a = |u|_a$. Let $v_i = p_i q_i$, for $i = 0, 1, \ldots, n$. The sequence $xy = v_0, v_1, \ldots, v_n = uv$ is a derivation (with possible repetitions) from xy to uv. Hence $[xy] = [uv]$. □

In order to define strictly the expected factorization, we have to define some kinds of subwords. Let $[w] = [uv]$. The *left subword of w with respect to u*, denoted by $\lambda(w, u)$, is the leftmost subword of w, containing all letter occurrences in u and only those; the *right subword of w with respect to v*, denoted by $\rho(w, v)$, is the rightmost subword of w, containing all letter occurrences in v and only those. Precisely:

Let $a \in \Sigma$, $u, v, w \in \Sigma^*$ and let $[w] = [uv]$.

$\lambda(aw, u) = $ if $u = \varepsilon$ then ε else if $(\exists u', u'')$ $u = u'au''$ then $a\lambda(w, u'u'')$ else $\lambda(w, u)$;

$\rho(wa, v) = $ if $v = \varepsilon$ then ε else if $(\exists v', v'')$ $v = v'av''$ then $\rho(w, v'v'')a$ else $\rho(w, v)$;

The following property holds:

Claim 2 Let $u, v, w \in \Sigma^*$ and let $[w] = [uv]$.
Then $[w] = [\lambda(w, u)\rho(w, v)]$, and $[\lambda(w, u)] = [u]$, $[\rho(w, v)] = [v]$.

Proof: Induction with respect to $n = |u| = |\lambda(w, u)|$. If $n = 0$, then it is trivial. Assume $|u| = n$ $(n > 0)$ and the statement holds for all lengths less than n. There are factorizations $w = w'aw''$ and $u = u'au''$ such that $\text{alph}(w') \cap \text{alph}(u) = \emptyset$ and $|u'_a| = 0$. Clearly, $(a, b) \in I$ for each $b \in \text{alph}(w')$; thus $[w'aw''] = [aw'w'']$. Moreover, $[w'w''] = [u'u''v]$, by Claim 1. By the induction hypothesis, we have $[w'w''] = [\lambda(w'w'', u'u'')\rho(w'w'', v)]$. Since $\lambda(w, u) = a\lambda(w'w'', u'u'')$ and $\rho(w, v) = \rho(w'w'', v)$, we have $[w] = [w'aw''] = [aw'w''] = [a\lambda(w'w'', u'u'')\rho(w'w'', v)] = [\lambda(w, u)\rho(w, v)]$. By the induction hypothesis we have also $[\lambda(w'w'', u'u'')] = [u'u'']$ and $[\rho(w'w'', v)] = [v]$. Therefore, we have $[\rho(w, v)] = [\rho(w'w'', v)] = [v]$ and $[\lambda(w, u)] = [a\lambda(w'w'', u'u'')] = [au'u''] = [u'au''] = [u]$ (where $[au'u''] = [u'au'']$, since $(a, b) \in I$ for all $b \in \text{alph}(u')$ (because $[w'aw''] = [u'au''v]$ and letters from u' do not occur in w')). This ends the proof of Claim 2. □

It is easily seen that the subwords $\lambda(w, u)$ and $\rho(w, v)$ define, thanks to Claim 2, the required factorization of w. Clearly, the if part of the lemma is trivial. □

The following corollary easily follows from Lemma 6.2.3. Its proof is left to the reader.

Corollary 6.2.4 (Levi's Lemma for traces) *Let $M = M(\Sigma, I)$ be a trace monoid; let $\alpha, \beta, \gamma, \delta \in M$.*
Then $\alpha\beta = \gamma\delta$ if and only if $(\exists \mu_1, \mu_2, \mu_3, \mu_4 \in M)$ such that $(\mu_2, \mu_3) \in I$ and $\alpha = \mu_1\mu_2$, $\beta = \mu_3\mu_4$, $\gamma = \mu_1\mu_3$, $\delta = \mu_2\mu_4$.

6.2.2 Rational Trace Languages

A family of sets is said to be a *Boolean algebra* iff it is closed under union, intersection and difference. Remind that $\mathrm{RAT}(M)$ is closed under union and, whenever M is a trace monoid, $M \in \mathrm{RAT}(M)$. As $X \cap Y = M - ((M - X) \cup (M - Y))$ and $X - Y = M - ((M - X) \cup Y)$, we have: $\mathrm{RAT}(M)$ is a Boolean algebra iff it is closed under complement.

The following characterization of trace monoids with rational sets forming a Boolean algebra was proved independently by Bertoni/Mauri/Sabadini [22], Aalbersberg/Welzl [2] and Sakarovitch [241]. We shorten "I is transitive" for "reflexive closure of I is transitive".

Theorem 6.2.5 *Let $M = M(\Sigma, I)$ be a trace monoid.*
  $\mathrm{RAT}(M)$ is a Boolean algebra if and only if I is transitive.

Note on the proof: The proof of the nontrivial "if" direction is omitted. The interested reader is encouraged to get to know one of the original proofs. Especially, Sakarovitch's paper is recommended, because of its relation to Theorem 6.2.7. For the "only if" direction see Example 6.1.16.

Let us repeat what we know about mutual relations between the classes REC and RAT in trace monoids:

Proposition 6.2.6 *Let $M = M(\Sigma, I)$ be a trace monoid. Then we have:*

 1. $\mathrm{REC}(M) \subseteq \mathrm{RAT}(M)$,

 2. $\mathrm{REC}(M) = \mathrm{RAT}(M)$ *iff* $I = \emptyset$.

Proof: (1): Directly from Proposition 6.1.20. (2): If $I = \emptyset$, we have Kleene's Theorem. If $I \neq \emptyset$, there are $a, b \in \Sigma$ such that $(a, b) \in I$. Then we have $[ab]^* \in \mathrm{RAT}(M) - \mathrm{REC}(M)$, as $\bigcup [ab]^* \cap a^* b^* = \{a^n b^n \mid n \geq 0\} \notin \mathrm{REG}(\Sigma^*)$. $\qquad\square$

In a natural way, the following decision problem arises.

RECOGNIZABILITY PROBLEM:
Instance: A trace monoid $M = M(\Sigma, I)$ and a trace language $T \in \mathrm{RAT}(M)$.
Question: Does T belong to $\mathrm{REC}(M)$?
The precise solution was given in [242]:

Theorem 6.2.7 (Sakarovitch) *The Recognizability Problem in $\mathrm{RAT}(M)$, $M = M(\Sigma, I)$, is decidable if and only if I is transitive.*

Note on the proof: The "only if" part is proved with the method of [143]. The proof of the "if" part exploits the method of [241].

Looking from outside, similarity of Theorems 6.2.5 and 6.2.7 seems to be unexpected. Both theorems are, however, closely related. And their proofs are based on the same idea. Look at the origins for details.

6.3   Recognizable Trace Languages

We present in this section three characterizations (Theorems 6.3.12, 6.3.13 and 6.3.16) of recognizable trace languages. All of them are of algebraic nature, and all of them are strongly based on the classical Kleene Theorem. Nevertheless, Theorems 6.3.13 and 6.3.16 are non-trivial trace generalizations of Kleene's Theorem, as well.

Let us start with some auxiliaries. The notions of rank (of distribution) as well as Proposition 6.3.2 are due to Hashiguchi [134]. They form quite powerful tool for proofs about recognizable trace languages.

Definition 6.3.1 *Let (Σ, I) be a concurrent alphabet; let L be a language in Σ^*; let $u, v \in \Sigma^*$ be words such that $[uv] \in [L]$. We say $rank_{L,I}(u, v) \leq n$ (for an integer n) iff there is $w \in L$ such that $w = v_0 u_1 v_1 \ldots u_n v_n$, $[u_1 \ldots u_n] = [u]$, $[v_0 v_1 \ldots v_n] = [v]$, and $(v_i, u_j) \in I$ for $i < j$. Thanks to Lemma 6.2.3, $rank_{L,I}$ is a total function from $\{(u, v) \mid [uv] \in [L]\}$ to the set N of integers, setting $rank_{L,I}(u, v) = \min\{n \in N \mid rank_{L,I}(u, v) \leq n\}$. Let us define $Rank_I(L) = \max\{rank_{L,I}(u, v) \mid [uv] \in [L]\}$, including ω as a possible value of $Rank_I(L)$.*

Proposition 6.3.2 (Hashiguchi) *Let (Σ, I) be a concurrent alphabet and $L \in REG(\Sigma^*)$.*

If $Rank_I(L)$ is finite, then $f_I(L)$ is regular.

Proof: We shall prove that the number of different left quotients of $f_I(L)$ is finite. Let n be an integer bounding $\{rank_{L,I}(u, v) \mid uv \in f_I(L)\}$. Taking into account Lemma 6.2.3, we get the following characterization of the set $f_I(L)/u$:

$v \in f_I(L)/u$ if $uv \in f_I(L)$ iff there is $w \in L$ such that

1. $w = v_0 u_1 v_1 \ldots u_n v_n$;

2. $[u_1 \ldots u_n] = [u]$ and $[v_0 v_1 \ldots v_n] = [v]$;

3. $(v_i, u_j) \in I$ whenever $i < j$.

Recall $I(x) = \{w \in \Sigma^* \mid (w, x) \in I\}$. Let us define $I_n(x_1, \ldots, x_n) = I(x_1 \ldots x_n) \times I(x_2 \ldots x_n) \times \cdots \times I(x_n) \times \Sigma^*$, for $(x_1, \ldots, x_n) \in (\Sigma^*)^n$.

Let us define, for $(x_1, \ldots, x_n) \in (\Sigma^*)^n$, the operation COMB : $2^{(\Sigma^*)^n} \to 2^{\Sigma^*}$ as follows: $\text{COMB}(X) = \{w \in \Sigma^* \mid w = x_1 \ldots x_n \text{ for some } (x_1, \ldots, x_n) \in X\}$. Now we can reformulate the (1)-(2)-(3) characterization of left quotients of $f_I(L)$, using the introduced notions. Namely, for any $u \in \Sigma^*$, the left quotient $f_I(L)/u$ is equal to the set $\bigcup\{f_I[\text{COMB}(L//(u_1, \ldots, u_n) \cap I_n(u_1, \ldots, u_n))] \mid [u_1 \ldots u_n] = [u]\}$. Clearly, the family $\{I(x) \mid x \in \Sigma^*\}$ is finite, so the family $\{I_n(x_1, \ldots, x_n) \mid x_i \in \Sigma^* \text{ for } 1 \leq i \leq n\}$ is finite, too. Since L is regular, the family $\{L//(x_1, \ldots, x_n) \mid x_i \in \Sigma^* \text{ for } 1 \leq i \leq n\}$ is finite, by Proposition 6.1.7. Therefore the family $\{f_I(L)/u \mid u \in \Sigma^*\}$ is finite, thus $f_I(L)$ is regular.   □

Remark that the converse of Proposition 6.3.2 is not true: $\Sigma = \{a, b\}, I = \{(a, b), (b, a)\}, L = (ab)^*(a^* \cup b^*)$. Then $f_I(L) = \Sigma^*$ is regular, although $\text{Rank}_I(L)$ is infinite (because $\text{rank}_{L,I}(a^n, b^n) = n$ for any integer n).

As we know (Example 6.1.12), there are monoids such that $\text{REC}(M)$ is not closed under product. We shall prove that trace monoids are not that case.

Proposition 6.3.3 *The class* $\text{REC}(M)$ *of recognizable subsets of any trace monoid* $M(\Sigma, I)$ *is closed under product:* $(\forall X, Y \in \text{REC}(M))\ XY \in \text{REC}(M)$.

Proof: Let $X, Y \in \text{REC}(M)$ and let $K = \bigcup X$ and $L = \bigcup Y$ be the flats of X and Y. As $K, L \in \text{REG}(\Sigma^*)$ (by Proposition 6.1.10), we have $KL \in \text{REG}(\Sigma^*)$. As K and L are closed with respect to I, we have $\text{Rank}_I(KL) \le 2$ by Levi's Lemma, 6.2.4. Therefore, by Proposition 6.3.2, $\bigcup(XY) = f_I(KL) \in \text{REG}(\Sigma^*)$. And Proposition 6.1.10 yields the assertion. $\square$

6.3.1 Lexicographic Order and Star-Connected Rational Expressions

Let $M = M(\Sigma, I)$ be a trace monoid. Any total order $<$ on Σ induces a *lexicographic order* on Σ^*, defined as follows:

- $(\forall u \in \Sigma^*)\, \varepsilon < u$;

- $(\forall u, v \in \Sigma^*)(\forall a, b \in \Sigma)\ au < bv$ iff $a < b$ or $(a = b\ \&\ u < v)$.

We assume from now on, that the lexicographic order is arbitrary, but fixed for the rest of the chapter. Thus all the following notions and results concerning lexicographic order concern any lexicographic order.

The *lexicographic representation* of the trace language $T \subseteq M(\Sigma, I)$ is the set $Lex(T) = \{u \in \bigcup T \mid (\forall v \in [u])\ u \le v\}$. Note that $Lex(T) = Lex(M) \cap \bigcup T$, for any $T \subseteq M(\Sigma, I)$. Members of $Lex(M)$ are said to be *minimal words* (with respect to I and the given alphabetic order). Clearly, any segment w of a minimal word uwv is minimal.

Proposition 6.3.4 *Let* $M = M(\Sigma, I)$ *be a trace monoid and* $T \subseteq M$.
If $T \in \text{REC}(M)$, *then* $Lex(T) \in \text{REG}(\Sigma^*)$.

Proof: As $Lex(T) = Lex(M) \cap \bigcup T$ and $\bigcup T \in \text{REG}(\Sigma^*)$, it is enough to show that $Lex(M) \in \text{REG}(\Sigma^*)$. Actually, $\Sigma^* - Lex(M) = \bigcup\{\Sigma^* b I(a) a \Sigma^* \mid (a, b) \notin I$ and $a < b\}$. As $I(a) = \{w \in \Sigma^* \mid (w, a) \in I\} = \{c \in \Sigma \mid (a, c) \in I\}^*$ is regular, $Lex(M)$ is regular, too. $\square$

Now, we introduce the notion of connectivity. This quite natural notion is crucial for the theory of recognizable trace languages.

Definition 6.3.5 (connectivity) *Let (Σ, D) be a concurrent alphabet. A word $w \in \Sigma^*$ is a* connected word *(with respect to D) iff the graph $\langle alph(w); D \cap alph(w) \times alph(w) \rangle$ is a connected graph; a trace $[w] \in M(\Sigma, D)$ is a* connected trace *iff w is a connected word. The trace language $T \subseteq M(\Sigma, D)$ is said to be a* connected trace language *iff any trace in T is connected.*

Example 6.3.6 $(\Sigma, D) = $ a — b ;   the trace $\alpha = [abc]$ is connected,
                                        | | the traces $\beta = [ad]$ and $\gamma = [bc]$ are
                                        c — d   non-connected.

Lemma 6.3.7 *Let $M = M(\Sigma, D)$ be a trace monoid.*
   If $w \in \Sigma^*$ is non-connected, then $ww \notin Lex(M)$.

Proof: Let $w \in \Sigma^*$ be a non-connected word. Then, there is a factorization $w = u_1 v_1 \ldots u_n v_n u_{n+1}$ such that :

   1. $n \geq 1$,

   2. $(u_1 \ldots u_n u_{n+1}, v_1 \ldots v_n) \in I$, and

   3. $u_i \neq \varepsilon \neq v_i$ for $i = 1, \ldots, n$.

Let us distinguish the initial letters: $u_i = a_i x_i, v_i = b_i z_i$ for $i = 1, \ldots, n$ and $u_{n+1} = a_{n+1} x_{n+1}$ if $u_{n+1} \neq \varepsilon$. Suppose $ww \in Lex(M)$. We have:
   if $u_{n+1} \neq \varepsilon$, then $a_1 < b_1 < \ldots < a_n < b_n < a_{n+1} < b_1$, but $(b_1 < b_1)$ is impossible; if $u_{n+1} = \varepsilon$, then $a_1 < b_1 < \ldots < a_n < b_n < a_1$, then $(a_1 < a_1)$ is also impossible. We have shown that the assumption $ww \in Lex(M)$ leads to a contradiction. $\Box$

Definition 6.3.8 (star-connected rational expression) *Let (Σ, D) be a concurrent alphabet. The rational expression $R \in \mathrm{REX}(\Sigma)$ is said to be* star-connected *(with respect to D) iff it operates with star over connected languages only. Formally: any R without star is star-connected; $R_1 \cup R_2$ and $R_1 \bullet R_2$ are star-connected iff R_1 and R_2 are star-connected; R^* is star-connected iff R is star-connected and $L(R)$ is connected.*

Example 6.3.9 Let $(\Sigma, D) = a—b—c$.
   All connected words: $a^* \cup c^* \cup \Sigma^* b \Sigma^*$.
   All non-connected words: $(a \cup c)^* - (a^* \cup c^*)$.
   $R = (abc)^* \cup ac$ is star-connected.
   $R' = ((abc)^* \cup ac)^*$ is not star-connected.
   $R_1 = (ac \cup a \cup c)^*$ is not star-connected.
   $R_2 = (a \cup c)^*$ is star-connected.
   Notice that $L(R_1) = L(R_2)$.

Proposition 6.3.10 *Let $M = M(\Sigma, I)$ be a trace monoid and let $R \in \mathrm{REX}(\Sigma)$ be a rational expression. If $L(R) \subseteq Lex(M)$, then R is star-connected.*

Proof: Assume R is not star-connected. Then there are $uwv, uwwv \in L(R)$ with a non-connected $w \in \Sigma^*$. But then, by Lemma 6.3.7, at least $uwwv \notin Lex(M)$. Contradiction. $\square$

Now we present a sufficient condition for recognizability of rational languages. The result is of quite big importance for the area of recognizable trace languages. Most of the following results of the present section, as well as the results of Sections 6.4, 6.5 and 6.7 will be derived with this proposition.

Proposition 6.3.11 *Let $M = M(\Sigma, I)$ be a trace monoid and let $R \in \mathrm{REX}(\Sigma)$ be a rational expression. If R is star-connected, then $[L(R^*)] \in \mathrm{REC}(M)$.*

Proof: Since $\mathrm{REC}(M)$ is closed under union and product (Proposition 6.3.3), it remains to show that $T^* \in \mathrm{REC}(M)$, whenever $T \in \mathrm{REC}(M)$ is connected. Let us prove an auxiliary claim.

Claim If L is closed and connected with respect to I, then $\mathrm{Rank}_I(L^*)$ is finite.

Proof: Let $uv \in f_I(L^*)$. Then there is $w \in L^*$ such that $[w] = [uv]$.

By Lemma 6.2.3, there is a factorization $w = v_0 u_1 v_1 \ldots u_n v_n$, such that

1. $[u_1 \ldots u_n] = [u], [v_0 v_1 \ldots v_n] = [v]$, and

2. $(v_i, u_j) \in I$ whenever $i < j$.

It is easily seen that, for any $uv \in f_I(L^*)$, there is $w \in (f_I(L))^*$ such that $[w] = [uv]$ and the factorization (1)-(2)-(3) fulfils additionally

3. $v_0 \in L^*$ and

4. $u_i v_i \in L^*$ for $i = 1, \ldots, n$.

As L is assumed to be closed (it means $L = f_I(L)$), we can assume such $w \in L^*$ is chosen that $[w] = [uv]$ and (1)-(2)-(3)-(4)-(5). Moreover, all u_i and v_i (possibly except v_0 and/or v_n) can be assumed to be nonempty. Observe now, that if $(u_i \notin L^*$ or $v_i \notin L^*)$ for some i, then (as L is connected) there are $a_i \in \mathrm{alph}(u_i)$ and $b_i \in \mathrm{alph}(v_i)$ such that $(a_i, b_i) \in D$. Hence, if $(u_i \notin L^*$ or $v_i \notin L^*)$ and $(u_j \notin L^*$ or $v_j \notin L^*)$ with $i < j$, then there are $a_i \in \mathrm{alph}(u_i), b_i \in \mathrm{alph}(v_i), a_j \in \mathrm{alph}(u_j)$ and $b_j \in \mathrm{alph}(v_j)$ such that $(a_i, b_i) \in D, (a_j, b_j) \in D$ and $(a_j, b_i) \notin D$; thus $a_i \neq a_j$. Therefore, $(u_i \notin L^*$ or $v_i \notin L^*)$ for at most $|\Sigma|$ cases, where $|\Sigma|$ is the cardinality of Σ. Let $(u_i \notin L^*$ or $v_i \notin L^*)$ and $(u_j \notin L^*$ or $v_j \notin L^*)$ for some $i < j$, let $(u_k \in L^*$ and $v_k \in L^*)$ for all $i < k < j$. Then, of course, $u_{i+1} \ldots u_{j-1} v_{i+1} \ldots v_{j-1} \in L^*$. We have proved $\mathrm{Rank}_I(L^*) \leq 2|\Sigma| + 1$. $\square$

Let $T \in \mathrm{REC}(M)$ be connected. As $L = \bigcup T$ is closed and connected, $\mathrm{Rank}_I(L^*)$ is finite by the Claim. As L^* is regular (Proposition 6.1.10), $f_I(L^*) = \bigcup T^*$ is regular (Proposition 6.3.2) and $T^* \in \mathrm{REC}(M)$, by Proposition 6.1.10. $\square$

And now we are completely prepared to characterize recognizable subsets of trace monoids. We present two characterizations: the first one is done with lexicographic representations, the second with star-connected rational expressions. The external forms of the characterizations seems to be quite distinct. Nevertheless, both characterizations are very common in their essence. And their proofs are very similar.

Theorem 6.3.12 *Let $M = M(\Sigma, I)$ be a trace monoid and let $T \subseteq M$ be a trace language.*

$T \in \mathrm{REC}(M)$ *if and only if* $Lex(T) \in \mathrm{REG}(\Sigma^*)$.

Proof: $\Rightarrow$ is exactly Proposition 6.3.4. $\Leftarrow$: If $Lex(T) \in \mathrm{REG}(\Sigma^*)$ then, by Kleene's Theorem, there is a rational expression R, such that $L(R) = Lex(T) \subseteq Lex(M)$. And R is star-connected, by Proposition 6.3.10. As $T = [Lex(T)] = [L(R)]$, Proposition 6.3.11 yields the result.   □

Theorem 6.3.13 *Let $M = M(\Sigma, I)$ be a trace monoid and let $T \subseteq M$ be a trace language.*

$T \in \mathrm{REC}(M)$ *iff* $T = [L(R)]$ *for a star-connected rational expression R.*

Proof: $\Rightarrow$: If $T \in \mathrm{REC}(M)$ then, by Proposition 6.3.4, $Lex(T) \in \mathrm{REG}(\Sigma^*)$. Hence, by Kleene's Theorem, there is a rational expression R, such that $L(R) = Lex(T) \subseteq Lex(M)$. And R is star-connected, by Proposition 6.3.10. As $T = [Lex(T)] = [L(R)]$, this direction is proved.

$\Leftarrow$ is exactly Proposition 6.3.11.   □

Let us mention a sufficient condition for recognizability. A word $w \in \Sigma^*$ is said to be an *iterating factor* of a language $L \subseteq \Sigma^*$ iff $(\exists u, v \in \Sigma^*)$ $uw^*v \subseteq L$. Obviously, if L is regular and all iterating factors of L are connected, then any R with $L(R) = L$ is star-connected. So, we have a trivial corollary of Theorem 6.3.13:

Corollary 6.3.14 *Let $M = M(\Sigma, I)$ be a trace monoid and let $L \in \mathrm{REG}(\Sigma^*)$.*

If any iterating factor of L is connected, then $[L] \in \mathrm{REC}(M)$.

6.3.2 Concurrent Star and Concurrent Meaning of Rational Expressions

Let $M = M(\Sigma, D)$ be a trace monoid and let α, γ be nonempty traces in M. The trace γ is a *component* of α iff γ is connected and $\alpha = \beta\gamma$ for some $\beta \in M$, such that $\mathrm{alph}(\beta) \times \mathrm{alph}(\gamma) \subseteq I$. The *decomposition of a trace* $\alpha \neq [\varepsilon]$ is the set $/\alpha/$ of all components of α; the decomposition of $[\varepsilon]$ is defined as $/[\varepsilon]/ = \{[\varepsilon]\}$. The *decomposition of a trace language* $T \subseteq M$ is the trace language $/T/ = \bigcup\{/\alpha/ \mid \alpha \in T\}$.

Lemma 6.3.15 *Let $M = M(\Sigma, D)$ be a trace monoid. If $T \in \mathrm{REC}(M)$, then $/T/ \in \mathrm{REC}(M)$.*

Proof: Let us denote $T_{X,Y} = \{\alpha \in M \mid \mathrm{alph}(\alpha) = X$ and $(\exists \beta \in M)\ \alpha\beta \in T$ and $\mathrm{alph}(\beta) \subseteq Y\}$, for $X, Y \subseteq \Sigma$. Clearly, $/T/ = \bigcup\{T_{X,Y} \mid X$ is connected and $X \times Y \subseteq I\}$. As $\{\alpha \in M \mid \mathrm{alph}(\alpha) = X\} = \bigcap\{[X^*aX^*] \mid a \in X\}$ is recognizable, it remains to show that $T_Y = \{\alpha \in M \mid (\exists \beta \in M)\ \alpha\beta \in T$ and $\mathrm{alph}(\beta) \subseteq Y\}$ is recognizable for any $Y \subseteq \Sigma$. Let $\mathcal{A} = (Q, q_0, F)$ be a finite M-automaton recognizing T. Changing the set of final states we obtain effectively a finite M-automaton $\mathcal{A}_Y = (Q, q_0, \{q \in Q \mid (\exists \beta \in M)\ q(\beta) \in F$ and $\mathrm{alph}(\beta) \subseteq Y\})$, recognizing T_Y. □

Let $M = M(\Sigma, I)$ be a trace monoid and let $T \subseteq M$ be a trace language. The *concurrent iteration* or *concurrent star* of T is the trace language $T^{c*} = /T/^*$. Let $R \in \mathrm{REX}(M)$ be a rational expression over M.

Let us recall the definition of the classical meaning of R : $L(\emptyset) = \emptyset, L(\alpha) = \alpha$ for $\alpha \in M, L(X \cup Y) = L(X) \cup L(Y), L(X \bullet Y) = L(X)L(Y), L(X^*) = (L(X))^*$.

The *concurrent meaning* of R is defined as follows: $T(\emptyset) = \emptyset, T(\alpha) = \alpha$ for $\alpha \in M, T(X \cup Y) = T(X) \cup T(Y), T(X \bullet Y) = T(X)T(Y), T(X^*) = /T(X)/^*$.

We see that the only difference is the meaning of star. Namely, star means the usual iteration for the classical meaning, and it means the concurrent iteration for the concurrent meaning of rational expressions. The following theorem yields a new characterization of the class of recognizable trace languages.

Theorem 6.3.16 *Let $M = M(\Sigma, I)$ be a trace monoid and let $T \subseteq M$ be a trace language.*

$T \in \mathrm{REC}(M)$ iff $T = T(R)$ for some rational expression $R \in \mathrm{REX}(M)$.

Proof: $\Rightarrow$: By Theorem 6.3.13, as $L(R) = T(R)$ for star-connected rational expressions.

$\Leftarrow$: Finite sets are recognizable in trace monoids, union is recognizable in any monoid, product is recognizable in trace monoids (Proposition 6.3.3), concurrent star is recognizable, by Lemma 6.3.15 and Theorem 6.3.13, as $/T/$ is connected. □

The last theorem, as well as the construction of Section 6.7, gives the reason for the notion and its name. Since now, the classical and concurrent meanings of rational expressions over trace monoids will be denoted by $\mathrm{Rat}(R)$ and $\mathrm{Rec}(R)$, respectively. Let $M(\Sigma, I)$ be a trace monoid and $R \in \mathrm{REX}(\Sigma)$ be a rational expression. Let $R_I \in \mathrm{REX}(M)$ denote the rational expression over M, obtained from R with the canonical substitution $a \leftarrow [a]_I$, for $a \in \Sigma \cup \{\varepsilon\}$. We will denote by $\mathrm{Rat}_I(R)$ and $\mathrm{Rec}_I(R)$ the meanings $\mathrm{Rat}(R_I)$ and $\mathrm{Rec}(R_I)$, respectively.

6.4 The Star Problem

The Star Problem is perhaps the most intriguing trace theoretical problem of the last years. Many attempts were done in order to solve it. Many subproblems were born during the investigations. Some of them are answered, most of them remain open. And even the recently obtained answers for a particular class of trace monoids approve the extraordinariness of this problem, contradicting possible intuitions.

STAR PROBLEM: *Instance:* Given a trace monoid $M = M(\Sigma, I)$ and a trace language $T \in \text{REC}(M)$.
Question: Does T^* belong to $\text{REC}(M)$?

As $\text{REC}(M) \subseteq \text{RAT}(M)$ and $T^* \in \text{RAT}(M)$, the Star Problem is decidable whenever the Recognizability Problem is decidable. The following proposition is a direct corollary of Theorem 6.2.7.

Proposition 6.4.1 *If I is transitive, then the Star Problem is decidable in $M(\Sigma, I)$.*

The following proposition, being a direct corollary of Theorem 6.3.13, is closely related to our problem.

Proposition 6.4.2 *Let $M = M(\Sigma, I)$ be a trace monoid.*
If $T \in \text{REC}(M)$ is connected, then $T^* \in \text{REC}(M)$.

Proof: By Theorem 6.3.13, $T = [L(R)]$ for a star-connected rational expression R. As T is connected, R^* is star-connected. And, by Theorem 6.3.13, $T^* = [L(R)] \in \text{REC}(M)$.   □

The converse is true for singletons and doubletons only, we prove it for singletons.

Proposition 6.4.3 *Let $M = M(\Sigma, I)$ be a trace monoid and $\alpha \in M$.*
$\alpha^* \in \text{REC}(M)$ if and only if α is connected.

Proof: Let α be non-connected. Then $\alpha = \beta\gamma = \gamma\beta$ for some non-empty traces β and γ with disjoint alphabets. Therefore, $\alpha^*/\beta^i \neq \alpha^*/\beta^j$ whenever $i \neq j$. So $\alpha^* \notin \text{REC}(M)$. The "if" part follows from Proposition 6.4.2.   □

Let us present now a collection of examples. Some of them seem to be quite unexpected.

Example 6.4.4 Let $M = \{a, c\}^* \times \{b\}^*$, $(\Sigma, D) = a\!-\!c \ b$.

1. $X = \{[ab], [aa], [b]\}$ and $\tau = [c]$.

    $X^* = [L(R)]$ for $R = (aa \cup b)^* \cup (aa \cup b)^* ab(aa \cup b)^*$. As R is star-connected, $X^* \in \text{REC}(M)$, by Theorem 6.3.13. This is a quite unexpected example. Adding the connected trace $\tau = [c]$ worsens the language. For $(X \cup \tau)^*$ we have $(\bigcup(X \cup [c])^*) \cap (ac)^* b^* = \{(ac)^m b^n \mid n \geq m\} \notin \text{REG}(\Sigma^*)$. Thus $(X \cup \tau)^* \notin \text{REC}(M)$, by Proposition 6.1.10.

2. $X = \{[acb], [ca], [c], [aa], [b]\}$ and $\tau = [ab]$.

    Now $X^* \notin \text{REC}(M)$, as $(\bigcup(X^*)) \cap (ac)^* b^* = \{(ac)^m b^n \mid n \geq m\} \notin \text{REG}(\Sigma^*)$. This is a completely surprising example. Adding the non-connected trace $\tau = [ab]$ betters the language. Since $[acb] = [ab][c]$, we have $(X \cup [ab])^* = \{[ab], [ca], [c], [aa], [b]\}^* = [L(R)]$ for $R = (ca \cup c \cup aa \cup b)^* \cup (ca \cup c \cup aa \cup b)^* ab(ca \cup c \cup aa \cup b)^*$. As R is star-connected, $(X \cup \tau)^* \in \text{REC}(M)$.

6.4.1 Star Problem in $M = A^* \times B^*$—Partial Results

Let us limit ourselves, for the rest of this section, to monoids being cartesian products $M = A^* \times B^*$ of finitely generated free monoids. Let us recall Mezei's characterization of $\mathrm{REC}(A^* \times B^*)$; for the proof, see [11].

Theorem 6.4.5 (Mezei) Let $M = A^* \times B^*$ and $T \subseteq M$. Then $T \in \mathrm{REC}(M)$ if and only if T is a finite union of sets of the form $X \times Y$, with $X \in \mathrm{REC}(A^*)$ and $Y \in \mathrm{REC}(B^*)$.

Observe that from the viewpoint of the Star Problem, only alphabets with at most two letters need to be considered.

Proposition 6.4.6 Let A, B be finite alphabets. Let $C = $ if $|A| > 2$ then $\{x, z\}$ else A, and $D = $ if $|B| > 2$ then $\{p, q\}$ else B.
  The Star Problem is decidable in $A^* \times B^*$ if and only if it is decidable in $C^* \times D^*$.

Proof: Order the alphabets $A = \{a_1, \ldots, a_n\}$ and $B = \{b_1, \ldots, b_m\}$. Let $f : A^* \to C^*$ and $g : B^* \to D^*$ be the classical codes: if $A = C$ then $f = $ identity else $(\forall i = 1, \ldots, n)$ $f(a_i) = xz^i$, if $B = D$ then $f = $ identity else $(\forall i = 1, \ldots, m)$ $f(b_i) = pq^i$. Let $\varphi : A^* \times B^* \to C^* \times D^*$ be the morphism $\varphi(u, v) = (f(u), g(v))$.

Claim $T \in \mathrm{REC}(A^* \times B^*)$ if and only if $\varphi(T) \in \mathrm{REC}(C^* \times D^*)$.

Proof: As φ is a connected morphism, the "only if" part follows from Theorem 6.5.6. As φ is injective, we have $T = \varphi^{-1}(\varphi(T))$ and the "if" part follows from Proposition 6.1.9. □

  Since $\varphi(T^*) = (\varphi(T))^*$, the proposition results from the claim. □

  Let T be a trace language in $M = A^* \times B^*$. We denote by C_T and N_T (or shortly by C and N, if T is clear) the sets of connected and non-connected traces of T. Throughout, we identify A^* and B^* to the submonoids $A^* \times \{\varepsilon\}$ and $\{\varepsilon\} \times B^*$ of M. We denote by $T_A, T_B, C_A, C_B, N_A, N_B$ the projections $\Pi_A(T), \Pi_B(T), \Pi_A(C)$, $\Pi_B(C), \Pi_A(N), \Pi_B(N)$, respectively.

Lemma 6.4.7 Let $M = A^* \times B^*$ and $T \in \mathrm{REC}(M)$.
  Then all sets $C_T, N_T, T_A, T_B, C_A, C_B, N_A, N_B$ are in $\mathrm{REC}(M)$.

Proof: As M is recognizable, $C_M = /M/$ is recognizable, by Lemma 6.3.15. Hence, $C_T = T \cap C_M$ and $N_T = T \setminus C_M$ are recognizable, by Proposition 6.1.8. As the projections Π_A and Π_B preserve connectivity, the sets $T_A, T_B, C_A, C_B, N_A, N_B$ are regular, by Theorem 6.5.6. □

  Given $T \subseteq M$, we use the abbreviations $T^{\leq n} = T^0 \cup T^1 \cup \ldots \cup T^n$ and $T^{\geq n} = T^n \cup T^{n+1} \cup \ldots$.

  We will use in a crucial way the *finite power property* (FPP for short): a set X has FPP iff there exists some integer n such that $X^* = X^{\leq n}$. Simon [256] and Hashiguchi [133] have shown independently:

Theorem 6.4.8 (Simon & Hashiguchi) *FPP is decidable for regular subsets of finitely generated free monoids.*

We will apply FPP to trace languages of the form $C^* \cup N$. Note that $(C^* \cup N)^{\leq n} \subseteq C^*(NC^*)^{\leq n} \subseteq (C^* \cup N)^{\leq 2n+1}$, for any integer n. Hence, the language $C^* \cup N$ has FPP iff there exists some integer n such that $(C^* \cup N)^* = C^*(NC^*)^{\leq n}$. We have:

Lemma 6.4.9 *If $C^* \cup N$ has FPP, then T^* is recognizable.*

Proof: $T^* = (C^* \cup N)^* = C^*(NC^*)^{\leq n}$, for some integer n. Since C is connected, C^* is recognizable, by Proposition 6.4.2. As $\mathrm{REC}(M)$ is closed under union (Proposition 6.1.8) and product (Proposition 6.3.3), the trace language T^* is recognizable. $\qquad\square$

Since any non-connected trace in $M = A^* \times B^*$ contains at least one letter of A and one letter of B, the following remark is obvious.

Remark 6.4.10 If $\alpha \in C^*(NC^*)^n$, then $n \leq \min(|\alpha|_A, |\alpha|_B)$.

We will use, thanks to Proposition 6.1.10, automata over the free monoid $(A \cup B)^*$ rather than automata over $A^* \times B^*$. The following property (Pumping Lemma) is obvious:

Fact 6.4.11 *Let $\mathcal{A}$ be a finite automaton (with n states) over a free monoid A^*. If $uwv \in L(\mathcal{A})$ with $|w| \geq n$, then*

1. *there is a factorization $w = prq$ such that $r \neq \varepsilon$ and $upr^*qv \subseteq L(\mathcal{A})$, and*

2. *there is a factorization $w = p_0 q_1 p_1 \ldots q_k p_k$ such that $|p_0 p_1 \ldots p_k| < n$ and $u p_0 p_1 \ldots p_k v \in L(\mathcal{A})$.*

The following proposition gives a necessary condition for the recognizability of T^*.

Proposition 6.4.12 *Let T be a trace language in $A^* \times B^*$.*
If T^* is recognizable, then $C_A^* \cup N_A$ and $C_B^* \cup N_B$ have FPP.

Proof: Let n be the number of states of the minimal automaton $\mathcal{A}$ recognizing $\bigcup T^*$. Let $u \in (C_A^* \cup N_A)^* = T_A^*$. There exists $v \in B^*$ such that $[uv] \in T^*$. By Fact 6.4.11, there is a subword v' of v such that $[uv'] \in T^*$ and $|v'| < n$. Therefore, $[uv'] \in C^*(NC^*)^{<n}$ (Remark 6.4.10) and $u = \Pi(uv') \in C_A^*(N_A C_A^*)^{<n}$. Analogously, $(C_B^* \cup N_B)^* = C_B^*(N_B C_B^*)^{<n}$. $\qquad\square$

Since Theorem 6.4.8, the condition of Proposition 6.4.12 is decidable whenever T is recognizable. Unfortunately, the condition is not sufficient, even if T is finite, as the following example shows.

Example 6.4.13 Let $A = \{a, c\}$, $B = \{b, d\}$ and $T = \{[ca], [c], [aa], [b], [d], [ab], [acd]\}$.

We have $C = C_A \cup C_B$, where $C_A = \{ca, c, aa\}$ and $C_B = \{b, d\}$; $N = \{[ab], [acd]\}$, so $N_A = \{a, ac\}$ and $N_B = \{b, d\}$. One can easily verify that $(C_A^* \cup N_A)^* = A^* = C_A^* \cup a C_A^* = C_A^* \cup N_A C_A^*$ and $(C_B^* \cup N_B)^* = C_B^*$. Therefore, the necessary condition is fulfilled. But T^* is not recognizable, since $(\bigcup T^*) \cap (ac)^* d^* = \{(ac)^n d^m \mid n \le m\}$ is not.

The following proposition gives a sufficient condition:

Proposition 6.4.14 Let T be a recognizable trace language in $A^* \times B^*$.
If $C_A^* \cup N_A$ and $C_B^* \cup N_B$ have FPP and $N = N_A \times N_B$, then T^* is recognizable.

Proof: Let n be an integer such that $(C_A^* \cup N_A)^* = C_A^* (N_A C_A^*)^{<n}$ and $(C_B^* \cup N_B)^* = C_B^* (N_B C_B^*)^{<n}$. Let $w \in C^* (NC^*)^{n^3}$. We can write $w = w_1 w_2 \ldots w_{n^2}$ with $w_i \in C^* (NC^*)^n$ for $i = 1, \ldots, n^2$. Set $w_{A,i} = \Pi_A(w_i)$ and $w_{B,i} = \Pi_B(w_i)$ for $i = 1, \ldots, n^2$.

As $C_A^* (N_A C_A^*)^{<n}$ and $(C_B^* \cup N_B)^* = C_B^* (N_B C_B^*)^{<n}$, there are integers $p_{A,i}$ and $p_{B,i}$ such that $1 \le p_{A,i} \le n$, $1 \le p_{B,i} \le n$, and $w_{A,i} \in C_A^* (N_A C_A^*)^{n-p_{A,i}}$ and $w_{B,i} \in C_B^* (N_B C_B^*)^{n-p_{B,i}}$. Since there are n^2 integers $p_{A,i}$ (resp. $p_{B,i}$), there exists some integer p_A (resp. p_B) such that $p_A = p_{A,i}$ (resp. $p_B = p_{B,i}$) for at least n different values of i.

Using $w_{A,i} \in C_A^* (N_A C_A^*)^{n-p_{A,i}}$ for p_B values of i, and $w_{A,i} \in C_A^* (N_A C_A^*)^n$ for other values of i, we obtain $\Pi(w) \in C_A^* (N_A C_A^*)^{n^3 - p_A p_B}$. In a similar way $\Pi(w) \in C_B^* (N_B C_B^*)^{n^3 - p_A p_B}$.

As $C^* = C_A^* C_B^*$ and $N = N_A \times N_B$, we deduce that $w = \Pi_A(w) \Pi_B(w) \in C^* (NC^*)^{n^3 - p_A p_B}$. Therefore $T^* = C^* (NC^*)^* = C^* (NC^*)^{<n^3}$, and the result follows from Lemma 6.4.9. $\square$

Again, this sufficient condition is not necessary, even for finite languages, as the following example shows.

Example 6.4.15 Let $A = \{a, c\}$, $B = \{b\}$ and $T = \{[aa], [c], [ca], [b], [abb], [acb]\}$.

Clearly, $C_A^* \cup N_A$ and $C_B^* \cup N_B$ have FPP, but $N \ne N_A \times N_B$. Nevertheless, using Proposition 6.4.17 we deduce easily that T^* is recognizable. Combining Propositions 6.4.12 and 6.4.14 we obtain a decidable (by Theorem 6.4.8) criterion for the recognizability of T^* for some special subclass of $\mathrm{REC}(A^* \times B^*)$.

Corollary 6.4.16 Let T be a recognizable trace language in $A^* \times B^*$ such that $N = N_A \times N_B$.
T^* is recognizable if and only if $C_A^* \cup N_A$ and $C_B^* \cup N_B$ have FPP.

6.4.2   Decidability of the Star Problem in $M = A^* \times \{b\}^*$

We deal in this subsection with trace monoids of the form $A^* \times \{b\}^*$. We shall prove that the Star Problem is decidable in this case. Note that it is not a case of Sakarovitch's characterization (Theorem 6.2.7) as long as A contains more than one letter.

First, we show a decidable sufficient condition:

Proposition 6.4.17 *Let T be a recognizable trace language in $A^* \times \{b\}^*$.*
If $C_A^* \cup N_A$ has FPP and $C_B \cap b^+ \neq \emptyset$, then T^* is recognizable.

Proof: By hypothesis, there exist two integers $n, m > 0$ with $T_A^* = C_A^* (N_A C_A^*)^{<n}$ and $b^m \in C_B$. Let k be the number of states of the minimal automaton $\mathcal{A}$ recognizing $\bigcup T$.

Claim $(\forall u \in T_A^*)(\exists p < nk)$ such that $[ub^p] \in C^* (NC^*)^{<n}$.

Proof: Let $u \in T_A^*$. Using FPP we write $u = v_0 u_1 v_1 \ldots u_j v_j$ with $v_i \in C_A^*, u_i \in N_A$ and $j < n$. For each $i = 1, \ldots, j$ there is $\lambda_i > 0$ such that $u_i b^{\lambda_i} \in N$. Using Fact 6.4.11, we may assume that $\lambda_i \leq k$. Set $p = \lambda_1 + \ldots + \lambda_j \leq jk < nk$. We have $ub^p = ub^{\lambda_1 + \ldots + \lambda_j} = v_0 u_1 b^{\lambda_1} v_1 \ldots u_j b^{\lambda_j} v_j$; thus $[ub^p] \in C_A^* (NC_A^*)^j \subseteq C^* (NC^*)^{<n}$.   □

Now we prove that $C^* \cup N$ has FPP. Let $[w] \in C^* (NC^*)^{(m+1)nk}$. We write $w = w_0 w_1 \ldots w_m$ with $[w_i] \in C^* (NC^*)^{nk}$ for $i = 0, \ldots, m$. For each $i = 0, 1, \ldots, m$, applying Claim to $u_i = \Pi_A(w_i)$, there exists some integer $p_i < nk$ such that $[u_i b^{p_i}] \in C^* (NC^*)^{<n}$. By Remark 6.4.10, we have $|w_i|_b \geq nk$, hence $q_i = |w_i|_b - p_i > 0$. Two of the $m + 1$ integers $q_0, q_0 + q_1, \ldots, q_0 + \cdots + q_m$ must be equal modulo m. Thus there are integers i, j $(0 \leq i < j \leq m)$ such that $q_{i+1} + \cdots + q_j = mq$, for some integer q. Therefore, $[w_{i+1} \ldots w_j] = [(u_{i+1} b^{p_{i+1}}) \ldots (u_j b^{p_j}) b^{mq}] \in C^* (NC^*)^{<(j-1)n} \subseteq C^* (NC^*)^{<(j-1)nk}$. Thus, we have $[w] \in C^* (NC^*)^{<(m+1)nk}$. This way, FPP for $C^* \cup N$ has been proved. And Lemma 6.4.9 concludes the proof.   □

As a first corollary we obtain the decidable criterion for finite languages:

Corollary 6.4.18 *Let T be a finite subset of $A^* \times \{b\}^*$.*
T^* is recognizable if and only if $C_A^* \cup N_A$ and $C_B^* \cup N_B$ have FPP.

Proof: The condition is necessary by Proposition 6.4.12. Conversely, if $C_B \cap b^+ \neq \emptyset$ the result follows from Proposition 6.4.17. If $C_B \cap b^+ = \emptyset$, then $C_B^* \cup N_B = \{\varepsilon\} \cup N_B$ has FPP iff $N_B \subseteq \{\varepsilon\}$. But then $N = \emptyset$, and $T^* = C^*$ is recognizable by Kleene's Theorem.   □

Unfortunately, as far as infinite languages are considered, FPP for $C_A^* \cup N_A$ and $C_B^* \cup N_B$ is not sufficient for recognizability:

Example 6.4.19 Let $A = \{a, c\}, B = \{b\}$ and $T = \{[a], [c], [ab]\} \cup [cb^+]$.
   FPP for $C_A^* \cup N_A$ and $C_B^* \cup N_B$ are obvious, but T^* is not recognizable, since $(\bigcup T^*) \cap a^* b^* = \{a^n b^m \mid n \geq m\}$.

Therefore, we need a more involved decidable criterion where $C_B \cap b^+ = \emptyset$. For this purpose, we split up N_A into two disjoint parts: $N_A = F_A + I_A$, when $F_A = \{u \in N_A \mid [ub^*] \cap N \text{ is finite}\}$ and $I_A = \{u \in N_A \mid [ub^*] \cap N \text{ is infinite}\}$. It follows easily from Mezei Theorem 6.4.5 that F_A and I_A are regular, whenever T is recognizable.

Proposition 6.4.20 *Let T be an infinite recognizable trace language in $A^* \times \{b\}^*$ with $C_B \cap b^+ = \emptyset$. T^* is recognizable if and only if (1) $C_A^* \cup N_A$ has FPP and (2) $(\exists s \geq 0) \ C_A^*(N_A C_A^*)^s \subseteq T_A^* I_A T_A^*$.*

Proof: $\Rightarrow$: Since Proposition 6.4.12, it remains to prove (2). Let s be the number of states of the minimal automaton $\mathcal{A}$ recognizing $\bigcup T^*$. Let $u \in C_A^*(N_A C_A^*)^s$. There exists $v \in b^*$ such that $[uv] \in C_A^*(N C_A^*)^s \subseteq T_A^*$. By Remark 6.4.10, $|v| \geq s$. By Fact 6.4.11, $[uv(b^q)^*] \subseteq T^*$ for some integer $q > 0$. Hence, $[ub^m] \in T^*$ for infinitely many integers m. Since $C_B \cap b^+ = \emptyset$, we have, by Remark 6.4.10, $[ub^m] \in C_A^*(N C_A^*) \leq |u|$ for infinitely many integers m. It follows that u admits a factorization in $T_A^* I_A T_A^*$. Therefore, $C_A^*(N_A C_A^*)^s \subseteq T_A^* I_A T_A^*$.

$\Leftarrow$: Let n and s be integers such that $T_A^* = C_A^*(N_A C_A^*) < n$ and $C_A^*(N_A C_A^*)^s \subseteq T_A^* I_A T_A^*$. Let $\mathcal{A}$ be the minimal automaton recognizing $\bigcup T$, let k be the number of states of $\mathcal{A}$ and let m be the least common multiple of the lengths of elementary (i.e. without internal loops) loops of $\mathcal{A}$. Note that, as T is infinite, $m > 0$.

Claim $(\forall u \in C_A^*(N_A C_A^*) \geq s)(\exists p < (2n+1)k)$ such that $[ub^p(b^m)^*] \subseteq C^*(NC^*)^{<2n}$.

Proof: We have $C_A^*(N_A C_A^*)^{\geq s} \subseteq T_A^* I_A T_A^* = CA^*(N_A C_A^*)^{<n} I_A C_A^*(N_A C_A^*)^{<n}$. Let $u \in C_A^*(N_A C_A^*)^{\geq s}$. We can write $u = u_1 u_2 u_3$ with $u_1, u_3 \in C_A^*(N_A C_A^*)^{<n}$ and $u_2 \in I_A$. Like in the Claim of the proof of Proposition 6.4.17, we find two integers $p_1, p_3 < nk$ such that $u_1 b^{p_1}, u_3 b^{p_3} \in C^*(NC^*)^{<n}$. Now, since $u_2 \in I_A$, we have $u_2 v_2 \in N$ for some $v_2 \in b^+$ with $|v_2| \geq k$. Applying Fact 6.4.11, we deduce that $u_2 b^{p_2}(b^m)^* \subseteq N$ for some $p_2 < k$. And the claim follows with $p = p_1 + p_2 + p_3$. $\square$

We shall show FPP for $C^* \cup N$. Let $h = \max(s, (2n+1)k)$ and let $w = w_0 \ldots w_m$ with $w_i \in C^*(NC^*)^h$ for $i = 1, \ldots, m$. For these i, let $u_i = \Pi_A(w_i)$ and let $p_i < (2n+1)k$ be such that $[u_i b^{p_i}(b^m)^*] \subseteq C^*(NC^*)^{<2n}$, as ensured by the Claim. Since $|w_i|_b \geq (2n+1)k$ (Remark 6.4.10), we have $q_i = |w_i|_b - p_i > 0$. Like in the proof of Proposition 6.4.17, we find two integers i, j such that $0 \leq i < j \leq m$ and $[w_{i+1} \ldots w_j] = [(u_{i+1} b^{p_{i+1}}) \ldots (u_j b^{p_j}) b^{mq}]$ for some integer q. Hence, $[w_{i+1} \ldots w_j] \in C^*(NC^*)^{<(j-1)2n} \subseteq C^*(NC^*)^{<(j-1)h}$ and we obtain $[w] \in C^*(NC^*)^{<(m+1)h}$. This way, FPP for $C^* \cup N$ has been proved. And Lemma 6.4.9 concludes the proof. $\square$

The following characterization follows directly from Propositions 6.4.17 and 4.15.

Corollary 6.4.21 *Let T be an infinite recognizable trace language in $A^* \times \{b\}^*$.*

T^* is recognizable if and only if $C_A^* \cup N_A$ has FPP and either $C_B \cap b^+ \neq \emptyset$ or $(\exists s \geq 0) \ C_A^*(N_A C_A^*)^s \subseteq T_A^* I_A T_A^*$.

It remains to show decidability.

Theorem 6.4.22 *The Star Problem is decidable in $A^* \times \{b\}^*$.*

Proof: Let T be a recognizable trace language in $A^* \times \{b\}^*$. Using the characterizations of Corollaries 6.4.18 and 6.4.21, it is sufficient to prove that FPP for $C_A^* \cup N_A$ and $C_B^* \cup N_B$ and the condition (2) of Proposition 6.4.20 are decidable.

As C_A, C_B, N_A and N_B are recognizable, FPP for $C_A^* \cup N_A$ and $C_B^* \cup N_B$ are ensured to be decidable by the Simon/Hashiguchi Theorem 6.4.8. We prove that the condition (2) $(\exists s \geq 0)\ C_A^*(N_A C_A^*)^s \subseteq T_A^* I_A T_A^*$ is decidable. Set $K = A^* \backslash (T_A^* I_A T_A^*)$; clearly, K is regular. Let n be the number of states of the minimal automaton $\mathcal{A}$ recognizing K.

Claim   The condition (2) holds if and only if $C_A^*(N_A C_A^*)^n \subseteq T_A^* I_A T_A^*$.

Proof: Suppose that $C_A^*(N_A C_A^*)^n \setminus T_A^* I_A T_A^* \neq \emptyset$. Then there exists a word $u \in K$ such that $u = u_0 v_1 u_1 \ldots v_n u_n$ with $u_i \in C_A^*$ and $v_i \in N_A$. Let q_0 be the initial state of $\mathcal{A}$ and let $q_i = q_0(u_0 v_1 \ldots u_{i-1} v_i)$ for $i = 1, \ldots, n$. We have $q_i = q_j$ for some $i < j$. Hence, $u_0 v_1 \ldots u_{i-1} v_i (u_i v_{i+1} \ldots u_{j-1} v_j)^* u_j v_{j+1} \ldots v_n u_n \subseteq K$ and there are arbitrary large integers s such that $C_A^*(N_A C_A^*)^s \cap K \neq \emptyset$. Therefore, the condition (2) does not hold. $\qquad\square$

As inclusion is decidable for regular subsets of free monoids, the proof is completed. $\qquad\square$

Note that the monoid $A^* \times \{b\}^*$ is not a case of Sakarovitch's characterization of the Recognizability Problem (Theorem 6.2.7). So, the monoid $A^* \times \{b\}^*$ is the first known example of a trace monoid with an undecidable Recognizability Problem and a decidable Star Problem. It proves that the both problems are of distinct nature. For recent progress concerning the Star Problem (and the FPP Problem) see [197, 236].

6.5   Morphisms on Trace Monoids

Let $M_1 = M(\Sigma_1, I_1)$ and $M_2 = M(\Sigma_2, I_2)$ be trace monoids. A mapping $F : M_1 \to M_2$ is a *trace morphism* iff $(\forall \alpha, \beta \in M_1)\ F(\alpha\beta) = F(\alpha)F(\beta)$. Let $f : \Sigma_1^* \to \Sigma_2^*$ be a morphism on free monoids (a word morphism). The trace morphism F is said to be induced by f iff $(\forall w \in \Sigma_1^*)\ F([w]_1) = [f(w)]_2$; then we write $F = [f]$. One can say: $F = [f]$ if and only if the following diagram commutes.

$$
\begin{array}{ccc}
\Sigma_1^* & \xrightarrow{\ f\ } & \Sigma_2^* \\
\Big\downarrow{\scriptstyle[\ ]} & & \Big\downarrow{\scriptstyle[\ ]} \\
M_1 & \xrightarrow{\ F\ } & M_2
\end{array}
$$

The natural question arises: when the following diagrams can be commutatively completed ?

$$
\begin{array}{ccc}
\Sigma_1^* & \xrightarrow{\ ?\ } & \Sigma_2^* \\
\Big\downarrow{\scriptstyle[\ ]} & & \Big\downarrow{\scriptstyle[\ ]} \\
M_1 & \xrightarrow{\ F\ } & M_2
\end{array}
\qquad\qquad
\begin{array}{ccc}
\Sigma_1^* & \xrightarrow{\ f\ } & \Sigma_2^* \\
\Big\downarrow{\scriptstyle[\ ]} & & \Big\downarrow{\scriptstyle[\ ]} \\
M_1 & \xrightarrow{\ ?\ } & M_2
\end{array}
$$

For the left diagram the answer is simple: always! Namely, any morphism defined on $a \in \Sigma_1$ as a member of $F([a])$ induces F. The following proposition is obvious.

Proposition 6.5.1 *Let $M_1 = M(\Sigma_1, I_1)$ and $M_2 = M(\Sigma_2, I_2)$ be trace monoids. Let $F : M_1 \to M_2$ and $f : \Sigma_1^* \to \Sigma_2^*$ be morphisms. $F = [f]$ iff $(\forall a \in \Sigma_1)\ f(a) \in F([a]_1)$.*

The inverse situation is different. Given trace monoids $M_1 = M(\Sigma_1, I_1)$ and $M_2 = M(\Sigma_2, I_2)$, a morphism $f : \Sigma_1^* \to \Sigma_2^*$ does not induce a trace morphism unconditionally.

Example 6.5.2 *Let $\Sigma_1 = \Sigma_2 = \{a, b\}$, $I_1 = \{(a, b), (b, a)\}$, $I_2 = \emptyset$, and $f = $ identity.*
Suppose $F = [f]$. We have $F([ab]_1) = [f(ab)]_2 = ab \neq ba = [f(ba)]_2 = F([ba]_1)$. But this is impossible, as $[ab]_1 = [ba]_1$.

Definition 6.5.3 (continuous morphism) *Let $M_1 = M(\Sigma_1, I_1)$ and $M_2 = M(\Sigma_2, I_2)$ be trace monoids. A word morphism $f : \Sigma_1^* \to \Sigma_2^*$ is said to be continuous (w.r.t. I_1 and I_2) iff $(\forall u, v \in \Sigma_1^*)\ [u]_1 = [v]_1$ implies $[f(u)]_2 = [f(v)]_2$. It is easily to observe that the word morphism is continuous if and only if $(\forall a, b \in \Sigma_1)\ (a, b) \in I_1$ implies $[f(ab)]_2 = [f(ba)]_2$.*

The following proposition characterizes word morphisms inducing trace morphisms. This way, it answers our question for the right hand side diagram.

Proposition 6.5.4 *Let $M_1 = M(\Sigma_1, I_1)$ and $M_2 = M(\Sigma_2, I_2)$ be trace monoids.*
A word morphism $f : \Sigma_1^* \to \Sigma_2^*$ induces a trace morphism $F : M_1 \to M_2$ iff it is continuous. Then F defined as $F([w]_1) = [f(w)]_2$ is the trace morphism.

Proof: $\Rightarrow$: Directly from Proposition 6.5.1. $\Leftarrow$: Since f is continuous, $[u]_1 = [v]_1$ implies $[f(u)]_2 = [f(v)]_2$. Thus F is well-defined. As f is a morphism, F is a morphism, too. $\square$

This way, the correspondence between trace morphisms and continuous word morphisms has been established.

6.5.1 Trace Morphisms and Recognizable Languages

We know that there are trace morphisms with non-recognizable images of recognizable languages. Let us recall an example:

Example 6.5.5 *Let $\Sigma_1 = \Sigma_2 = \{a, b\}$, $I_1 = \emptyset$, $I_2 = \{(a, b), (b, a)\}$, $M_1 = M(\Sigma_1, I_1)$, $M_2 = M(\Sigma_2, I_2)$, and $F(a) = [a], F(b) = [b]$. We have $(ab)^* \in \mathrm{REC}(\Sigma^*)$ and $F((ab)^*) = [ab]^* \notin \mathrm{REC}(M_2)$.*
Let $M_1 = M(\Sigma_1, I_1)$ and $M_2 = M(\Sigma_2, I_2)$ be trace monoids. A trace morphism $F : M_1 \to M_2$ is said to be *recognizable* iff $F(T) \in \mathrm{REC}(M_2)$ whenever $T \in \mathrm{REC}(M_1)$. A trace morphism $F : M_1 \to M_2$ is said to be *connected* iff $F(\alpha)$ is connected whenever $\alpha \in M_1$ is connected.

The following theorem, due to [75], characterizes recognizable trace morphisms with connected trace morphisms. As connectivity of trace morphisms is decidable (connected subalphabets of a finite alphabet have to be checked), this characterization proves the problem of recognizability of trace morphism to be decidable.

Theorem 6.5.6 (Duboc) *Let $M_1 = M(\Sigma_1, I_1)$ and $M_2 = M(\Sigma_2, I_2)$ be trace monoids.*
The trace morphism $F : M_1 \to M_2$ is recognizable iff it is connected.

Proof: $\Rightarrow$: If F is not connected then $F(\alpha)$ is non-connected for some connected α. As $F(\alpha^*) = (F(\alpha))^*$, we have, by Proposition 6.4.3, a non-recognizable image $F(\alpha^*)$ of a recognizable language α^*.

$\Leftarrow$: Let $T \in \mathrm{REC}(M_1)$. By Theorem 6.3.13, there is a star-connected rational expression $R \in \mathrm{REX}(\Sigma_1)$, such that $T = [L(R)]_1$. Let $f : \Sigma_1^* \to \Sigma_2^*$ be a word morphism inducing F. Let $f(R) \in \mathrm{REX}(\Sigma_2)$ means the rational expression obtained from R by the substitution $a \leftarrow f(a)$ for $a \in \Sigma_1$. Since, for any $X, Y \subseteq \Sigma_1, f(X \cup Y) = f(X) \cup f(Y), f(XY) = f(X)f(Y)$, and $f(X^*) = (f(X))^*$, we have $f(L(R)) = L(f(R))$. Thus, $F(T) = F([L(R)]_1) = [f(L(R))]_2 = [L(f(R))]_2$. As R is star-connected and $F = [f]$ is connected, $f(R)$ is star-connected, too. Therefore, $F(T) \in \mathrm{REC}(M_2)$, by Theorem 6.3.13. $\qquad\Box$

Let us mention an interesting result of Chrobak/Rytter [38], lying out of scope of the chapter. Namely, unlike the free case, the decision problem "is a given trace morphism injective?" is undecidable. This result can also be found in [141][Satz 14, page 102].

6.6   Petri Nets and Their Behaviour

Petri nets form a well-known model for concurrent systems. In this chapter we deal with the simplest Petri nets, which are named elementary Petri nets. Recall that Mazurkiewicz's paper [189], initiating trace theory within computer science, concerned just the relations of trace languages to elementary Petri nets. The reader interested in more involved Petri nets (place/transition systems) is referred to Chapter 8 of the present book (see also Diekert's book [53] and [58]).

A *net* is a triple $N = (\Sigma, C, \varphi)$, where: Σ is a finite set of *actions*; C is a finite set of *conditions*, $\Sigma \cap C = \emptyset; \varphi = (^\bullet\varphi, \varphi^\bullet) : \Sigma \to 2^C \times 2^C$

$^\bullet\varphi(a)$ and $\varphi^\bullet(a)$ are mostly denoted by $^\bullet a$ and $a^\bullet$, respectively; $^\bullet a$ is the set of *preconditions* of $a, a^\bullet$ is the set of *postconditions* of $a, {}^\bullet a^\bullet$ is the shortened denotation for $^\bullet a \cup a^\bullet$.

Any net N induces the independence relation $I_N \subseteq \Sigma \times \Sigma$ and the dependence relation $D_N = \Sigma \times \Sigma \setminus I_N$, so the trace monoid $M(N) = M(\Sigma, D_N)$, as follows: $(a, b) \in I_N$ iff $a \neq b$ and $^\bullet a^\bullet \cap {}^\bullet b^\bullet = \emptyset, (a, b) \in D_N$ iff $a = b$ or $^\bullet a^\bullet \cap {}^\bullet b^\bullet \neq \emptyset$.

The following convention is used in this chapter, for graphical representations of nets: actions are denoted by letters, conditions are denoted by digits, $1 \to a$ means $1 \in {}^\bullet a, a \to 1$ means $1 \in a^\bullet$.

Example 6.6.1 (1) $N:$
$$1 \;\to\; a \;\to\; 2 \qquad (\Sigma, D_N): \quad a \;-\; b$$
$$\uparrow \qquad\qquad \uparrow \qquad\qquad\qquad\qquad | \qquad\quad |$$
$$d \qquad\qquad b \qquad\qquad\qquad\qquad d \;-\; c$$
$$\uparrow \qquad\qquad \uparrow$$
$$4 \;\leftarrow\; c \;\leftarrow\; 3$$

(2) $N: \quad a \;\to\; 1 \;\to\; b \;\to\; 2 \;\to\; c \qquad (\Sigma, D_N): \quad a \;-\; b \;-\; c$

A *net system* is a triple $S = (N, s, W)$, where:
$N = (\Sigma, C, \varphi)$ is a net, called the *underlying net* of S;
$s \subseteq C$ is an initial state;
$W \subseteq 2^C$ is a set of *final states*. (if $W = \{Z\}$ is a singleton, we will write Z instead of $\{Z\}$).

We will also denote the net system by the quintuple $S = (\Sigma, C, \varphi, s, W)$; the independence I_N, the dependence D_N and the trace monoid $M(N)$ will be also denoted by I_S, D_S and $M(S)$, if N is the underlying net of S.

Let $u, v \in \Sigma^*$ and let $X, Z \subseteq C$ be subsets of conditions. We write $(u, X) \Rightarrow (v, Z)$ iff $(\exists a \in \Sigma)\; v = ua$ and $^\bullet a \subseteq X, a^\bullet \setminus {}^\bullet a \subseteq C \setminus X, Z = (X \setminus {}^\bullet a) \cup a^\bullet$. The *flat transition relation* of S is the reflexive and transitive closure $\Rightarrow^*$ of the relation $\Rightarrow$. The *flat language generated* by S is the language $L(S) = \{w \in \Sigma^* \mid (\varepsilon, s) \Rightarrow^* (w, Z)$ for some $Z \in W\}$.

Proposition 6.6.2 *For any net system $S = (\Sigma, C, \varphi, s, W)$, the flat language $L(S)$ is regular.*

Proof: Let $G = (\Sigma, 2^C, P, s, W)$ be the regular grammar with the set of productions $P = \{X \to aY \mid (\varepsilon, X) \Rightarrow (a, Y)\}$ (see Section 6.7 for the definition of regular grammars). Clearly, $L(G) = L(S)$. $\square$

Proposition 6.6.3 *Let $S = (\Sigma, C, \varphi, s, W)$ be a net system, let $I = I_S$ be the independence induced by S, let $L = L(S)$ be the flat language generated by S. Then $L = f_I(L)$; it means L is closed with respect to I.*

Proof: Let $uabv \in L$ with $(a, b) \in I$. Then $(\varepsilon, s) \Rightarrow^* (u, X) \Rightarrow (ua, Y') \Rightarrow (uab, Y) \Rightarrow^* (uabv, Z)$ for some $X, Y, Y' \subseteq C$ and some $Z \in W$. As $(a, b) \in I$, we have $^\bullet a \cap {}^\bullet b = \emptyset$ and $(u, X) \Rightarrow^* (uba, Y)$. So $ubav \in L$. Let $w \in L$ and $w' \in f_I(w)$. As w' is derivable from w with a finite number of such commutations, we conclude inductively that $w' \in L$. $\square$

The last proposition allows us to consider net systems as devices generating trace languages. As Petri nets are concurrent devices, the following version of the definition of the transition relation is more adequate to them: Let $S = (\Sigma, C, \varphi, s, W)$ be a net system. Let $\alpha, \beta \in M(S)$ and let $X, Z \subseteq C$. We write $(\alpha, X) \Rightarrow (\beta, Z)$ iff $(\exists a \in \Sigma)\; \beta = \alpha \circ [a]$ and $^\bullet a \subseteq X, a^\bullet \setminus {}^\bullet a \subseteq C \setminus X, Z = (X \setminus {}^\bullet a) \cup a^\bullet$. The *transition relation* of S is the reflexive and transitive closure $\Rightarrow^*$ of the relation $\Rightarrow$. The *trace language generated* by S is the trace language $T(S) = \{\alpha \in M(S) \mid ([\varepsilon], s) \Rightarrow^* (\alpha, Z)$ for some $Z \in W\}$. Since Proposition 6.6.3, one can say now: The *flat language generated* by S is the language $L(S) = \bigcup T(S) = \{w \in \Sigma^* \mid [w] \in T(S)\}$.

Example 6.6.4 **(1)** N: $1 \rightarrow a \rightarrow 2$ (Σ, D_N): $a \, - \, b$

$$
\begin{array}{ccc}
1 & \rightarrow \; a \; \rightarrow & 2 \\
\uparrow & & \uparrow \\
d & & b \\
\uparrow & & \uparrow \\
4 & \leftarrow \; c \; \leftarrow & 3
\end{array}
\qquad
\begin{array}{ccc}
a & - & b \\
| & & | \\
d & - & c
\end{array}
$$

For $S_1 = (N, \{1\}, \{1\})$ we have: $T(S_1) = [abcd]^*, L(S_1) = (abcd)^*$

For $S_2 = (N, \{1,3\}, \{1,3\})$ we have: $T(S_2) = [acbd]^*, L(S_2) = ((ac \cup ca)(bd \cup db))^*$

(2) N: $a \rightarrow 1 \rightarrow b \rightarrow 2 \rightarrow c$ (Σ, D_N): $a \, - \, b \, - \, c$

For $S = (N, \emptyset, \emptyset)$ we have: $L(S) = \varepsilon \cup a(b(ac \cup ca))^*bc$;

$T(S) = [abc]^*$ and its first elements have the following dependence graphs:

$$[\varepsilon], \qquad [abc] = a \rightarrow b \rightarrow c, \qquad [abc]^2 = a \rightarrow b \; \overset{a}{\underset{c}{\diagdown\!\!\diagup}} \; b \rightarrow c,$$

$$[abc]^3 = a \rightarrow b \; \overset{a}{\underset{c}{\diagdown\!\!\diagup}} \; b \; \overset{a}{\underset{c}{\diagdown\!\!\diagup}} \; b \rightarrow c, \quad \cdots \quad \cdots$$

Proposition 6.6.5 *For any net system S, the trace language $T(S)$ is recognizable.*

Proof: As $L(S) = \bigcup T(S)$, the proposition results from Propositions 6.6.2 and 6.1.10. $\square$

As far as we are interested in occurrences of actions only, the approach "$T(S)$ is the behaviour of S" is enough. However, we have to be aware that such approach keeps out quite essential aspects of the net behaviour, namely, the occurrences of conditions. The following example illustrates this remark.

Example 6.6.6 Let us consider the following net systems (members of initial states are marked with parenthesis):

$$
S_1: \quad
\begin{array}{ccc}
(1) & \rightarrow \; a \; \rightarrow & 2 \\
\uparrow & & \downarrow \\
c & \leftarrow \; 3 \; \leftarrow & b
\end{array}
\qquad\qquad
S_2: \quad
\begin{array}{ccc}
(1) & \rightarrow \; a \; \rightarrow & 3 \\
\uparrow & & \downarrow \\
b & \leftarrow \; (2) \; \leftarrow & c
\end{array}
$$

Both the nets define the same concurrent alphabet $\begin{array}{c} a - b \\ \diagdown \; \diagup \\ c \end{array}$.

Assuming the sets of final states $W_1 = \{\{1\}\}$ for S_1 and $W_2 = \{\{1,2\}\}$ for S_2, both the systems generate the same trace languages $T(S_1) = T(S_2) = (abc)^*$. But, obviously, they behave in distinct ways. We intend to express the distinction.

6.6.1 Occurrence Traces

We are going to define a tool, allowing to capture all aspects of elementary net systems. Let $N = (\Sigma, C, \varphi)$ be a net. The *occurrence alphabet* induced by N is the couple $(\Sigma \cup C, D)$, where:

$(\forall a, b \in \Sigma) \ (a, b) \in D$ iff $\bullet a \bullet \cap \bullet b \bullet \neq \emptyset$;

$(\forall x, y \in C) \ (x, y) \in D$ iff $x = y$;

$(\forall a \in \Sigma)(\forall x \in C) \ (a, x) \in D$ iff $x \in \bullet a \bullet$.

Example 6.6.7 The underlying nets of our net systems S_1 and S_2 are the following:

$$N_1: \quad \begin{array}{ccccc} 1 & \to & a & \to & 2 \\ \uparrow & & & & \downarrow \\ c & \leftarrow & 3 & \leftarrow & b \end{array} \qquad\qquad N_2: \quad \begin{array}{ccccc} 1 & \to & a & \to & 3 \\ \uparrow & & & & \downarrow \\ b & \leftarrow & 2 & \leftarrow & c \end{array}$$

They induce the following occurrence alphabets:

$(\Sigma \cup C, D_1):$

$$\begin{array}{c} 2 \\ \diagup \ | \ \diagdown \\ a - b \\ \diagup \diagdown \diagup \diagdown \\ 1 - c - 3 \end{array}$$

$(\Sigma \cup C, D_2):$

$$\begin{array}{c} 1 \\ \diagup \ | \ \diagdown \\ a - b \\ \diagup \diagdown \diagup \diagdown \\ 3 - c - 2 \end{array}$$

Let $N = (\Sigma, C, \varphi)$ be a net. Let D be the above defined dependence relation on $\Sigma \cup C$ and let D_Σ mean $D \cap \Sigma \times \Sigma$; let I and I_Σ mean the complements of D and D_Σ, respectively. Let $F[a] = [aa\bullet]$ for $a \in \Sigma$. As $[a(a\bullet)b(b\bullet)]_I = [b(b\bullet)a(a\bullet)]_I$ whenever $(a, b) \in I_\Sigma$, one can extend F to the morphism $F : M(\Sigma, D_\Sigma) \to M(\Sigma \cup C, D)$.

Let $S = (\Sigma, C, \varphi, s, W)$ be a net system. The *full behaviour* of S is the trace language $OT(S) = [s] \circ F(T(S))$. Members of $OT(S)$ are called *occurrence traces* of S.

Example 6.6.8 Let us come back once again to our net systems

$$S_1: \quad \begin{array}{ccccc} (1) & \to & a & \to & 2 \\ \uparrow & & & & \downarrow \\ c & \leftarrow & 3 & \leftarrow & b \end{array} \qquad\qquad S_2: \quad \begin{array}{ccccc} (1) & \to & a & \to & 3 \\ \uparrow & & & & \downarrow \\ b & \leftarrow & (2) & \leftarrow & c \end{array}$$

with the sets of final states $W_1 = \{\{1\}\}$ for S_1 and $W_2 = \{\{1, 2\}\}$ for S_2. Their full behaviours are the following:

$$OT(S_1) = \{1 \to a \to 2 \to b \to 3 \to c\}^*$$

$$OT(S_2) = \left\{ \begin{array}{ccccccccccc} 1 & \to & a & \to & 3 & \to & c & \to & 2 & \to & b \\ & & & \searrow & & \nearrow & & \searrow & & \nearrow & & \searrow \\ & & 2 & \to & b & \to & 1 & \to & a & \to & 3 & \to & c \end{array} \right\}^*$$

Proposition 6.6.9 *For any net system S, the full behaviour $OT(S)$ is recognizable.*

Proof: Observe that F is a connected morphism. Hence, $OT(S)$ is recognizable by Propositions 6.6.5 and Theorem 6.5.6. □

6.7 Labelled Petri Nets

We have seen in Section 6.6 that elementary Petri nets generate recognizable trace languages (Proposition 6.6.5). Remark, however, that there are even very simple languages which cannot be generated by them. The language $\{a, aa\}$, for instance. Such situations result from the individuality of actions. In order to put into work the full power of Petri nets, we have to allow labelling of actions. Then distinct actions having the same label deliver the same production. The labelling must be done carefully, respecting independences induced by net structures. We present an algorithm producing, for any recognizable trace language, a labelled Petri net generating it. The reader being familiar with Zielonka's [277] asynchronous automata (see the Chapter 7 of the book) will certainly remark common points of both approaches. First, we have to do some preparatory work.

6.7.1 Interpretation of Trace Languages

Let $M_1 = M(\Sigma_1, I_1)$ and $M_2 = M(\Sigma_2, I_2)$ be trace monoids, let $T \subseteq M_1$ be a trace language and let $\lambda : \Sigma_1 \to \Sigma_2 \cup \{\varepsilon\}$ define the morphism $\lambda : \Sigma_1^* \to \Sigma_2^*$. Then λ is said to be an *interpretation* of T in M_2 iff $(\forall \alpha \in T)\ \lambda(\alpha) \in M_2$. The trace language $\lambda(T) = \{\lambda(\alpha) \mid \alpha \in T\} \subseteq M_2$ is then called the λ-*interpretation* of T.

Remark 6.7.1 Recall that traces were defined as congruency classes, so they can be regarded as (finite) subsets of Σ^*. In the course of this section we mean $\lambda(\alpha)$, for a trace α, as the image $\lambda(\alpha) \subseteq \Sigma_2^*$ of $\alpha \subseteq \Sigma_1^*$. In the framework of this convention, the formula "$\lambda(\alpha) \in M_2$" is equivalent to the conjunction "$\lambda(\alpha)$ is closed with respect to I_2 and $(\forall u, v \in \alpha)\ [\lambda(u)]_2 = [\lambda(v)]_2$".

Lemma 6.7.2 *Let $M_1 = M(\Sigma_1, I_1)$ and $M_2 = M(\Sigma_2, I_2)$ be trace monoids, let $T \subseteq M_1$ be a trace language and let $\lambda : \Sigma_1 \to \Sigma_2 \cup \{\varepsilon\}$ define the morphism $\lambda : \Sigma_1^* \to \Sigma_2^*$. If (i) and (ii) are satisfied, where*

(i) *If $\lambda(a) = \varepsilon$ and $[uav] \in T$, then $\lambda(v) = \varepsilon$.*

(ii) *If $\lambda(a) \neq \varepsilon \neq \lambda(b)$ and $[uabv] \in T$, then $(a, b) \in I_1$ iff $(\lambda(a), \lambda(b)) \in I_2$.*

then λ is an interpretation of T in M_2.

Proof: Let f_1 and f_2 be the closures with respect to I_1 and I_2, respectively.

(1) We prove that $(\forall \alpha \in T)$ $f_2(\lambda(\alpha)) = \lambda(\alpha)$. Clearly, $\lambda(\alpha) \subseteq f_2(\lambda(\alpha))$. Let $uabv \in \lambda(\alpha)$ and $(a, b) \in I_2$. As λ is alphabetic, there is $xpyqz \in \alpha$ such that $\lambda(x) = u, \lambda(p) = a, \lambda(y) = \varepsilon, \lambda(q) = b, \lambda(z) = v$. We have $y = \varepsilon$, from (i), and $(p, q) \in I_1$, from (ii). Hence $xqpz \in \alpha$, thus $ubav \in \lambda(\alpha)$. Inductively, $f_2(\lambda(\alpha)) \subseteq \lambda(\alpha)$.

(2) We prove that $(\forall \alpha \in T)(\forall u, v \in \alpha)$ $[\lambda(u)]_2 = [\lambda(v)]_2$. Let $u, v \in \alpha$ and let $u = xpqz, v = xqpz$ with $(p, q) \in I_1$. If $\lambda(p) = \varepsilon$ or $\lambda(q) = \varepsilon$ then, by (i), $\lambda(p) = \lambda(q) = \varepsilon$ and $\lambda(z) = \varepsilon$. Thus then $\lambda(u) = \lambda(v) = \lambda(x)$. Assume now $\lambda(p) = a \neq \varepsilon$ and $\lambda(q) = b \neq \varepsilon$. By (ii), $(a, b) \in I_2$. Hence $[\lambda(u)]_2 = [\lambda(x)ab\lambda(z)]_2 = [\lambda(x)ba\lambda(z)]_2 = [\lambda(v)]_2$. Inductively, $[\lambda(u)]_2 = [\lambda(v)]_2$ for all $u, v \in \alpha$. Therefore, by (1) + (2), we have $\lambda(\alpha) \in M_2$ for any $\alpha \in T$. $\qquad\square$

Example 6.7.3 1. Let $\Sigma = \Sigma_1 = \Sigma_2 = \{a, b\}$, $D_1 = id$, $D_2 = \Sigma \times \Sigma$, $\lambda = id$.

With $\alpha = [ab] = \{ab, ba\}$, $\lambda(\alpha) = \{ab, ba\} \notin M_2$, (ii) is not satisfied.

2. Let $\Sigma = \Sigma_1 = \Sigma_2 = \{a, b\}$, $D_1 = \Sigma \times \Sigma$, $D_2 = id$, $\lambda = id$.

With $\alpha = [ab] = \{ab\}$, $\lambda(\alpha) = \{ab\} \notin M_2$, (ii) is not satisfied.

3. Let $(\Sigma_1, D_1) = (\Sigma_2, D_2) = a\text{ ---}b\text{ ---}c$; $\lambda = \Pi_{\{a,c\}}$.

With $\alpha = [abc] = \{abc\}$, $\lambda(\alpha) = \{ac\} \notin M_2$, (i) is not satisfied.

4. If λ is strictly alphabetic ($\lambda : \Sigma_1 \to \Sigma_2$) and $(a, b) \in D_1$ iff $(\lambda(a), \lambda(b)) \in D_2$, then λ is an interpretation in M_2 of any $T \subseteq M_1$.

Definition 6.7.4 *A (properly) labelled net system is a triple $\mathcal{S} = (S, M, \lambda)$, where $S = (\Sigma, C, \varphi, s, W)$ is a net system, $M = M(\Gamma, D)$ is a trace monoid, and $\lambda : \Sigma^* \to \Gamma^*$ is an interpretation of $T(S) \subseteq M(\Sigma, D_S)$ in M. Then the trace language $T(\mathcal{S}) = \lambda(T(S))$ is the* trace language *of $\mathcal{S}$ and the language $L(\mathcal{S}) = \lambda(L(S)) = \bigcup T(\mathcal{S})$ is the* flat language *of $\mathcal{S}$.*

Proposition 6.7.5 *Let $\mathcal{S}$ be a labelled net system. The flat $L(\mathcal{S})$ and the trace $T(\mathcal{S})$ languages of $\mathcal{S}$ are both recognizable.*

Proof: Since $L(S)$ is regular, by Proposition 6.6.2, its morphic image $L(\mathcal{S}) = \lambda(L(S))$ is regular. As $\bigcup T(\mathcal{S}) = L(\mathcal{S})$, $T(\mathcal{S})$ is recognizable by Proposition 6.1.10. $\square$

6.7.2 Cliques of (Σ, D)

A subalphabet $C \subseteq \Sigma$ is a *clique* in (Σ, D) iff $C \times C \subseteq D$. A family $\{C_1, \ldots, C_n\}$ of cliques in (Σ, D) *covers* (Σ, D) iff $\bigcup \{C_i \times C_i \mid i = 1, \ldots, n\} = D$. Conversely, any set $\{C_1, \ldots, C_n\}$ of subsets of Σ covering Σ (i.e. such that $C_1 \cup \ldots \cup C_n = \Sigma$) can be regarded as a family of cliques for Σ, defining the dependence relation $D = \bigcup \{C_i \times C_i \mid i = 1, \ldots, n\}$.

Example 6.7.6 (1) $(\Sigma, D) = a$—b—c

$C_1 = \{a, b\}, C_2 = \{b, c\}; \{C_1, C_2\}$ covers (Σ, D).

(2) $(\Sigma, D) =$

$$a - c - d - e$$
$$\searrow \nearrow$$
$$b$$

The family $C_1 = \{a, b, c\}, C_2 = \{c, d\}, C_3 = \{d, e\}$ covers (Σ, D).

Also the family $C_1 = \{a, b\}, C_2 = \{a, c\}, C_3 = \{b, c\}, C_4 = \{c, d\}, C_5 = \{d, e\}$ covers (Σ, D).

6.7.3 Regular Grammars

A *regular grammar* is a quintuple $G = (\Sigma, N, P, \sigma, F)$, where: Σ is a finite set of *terminals*; N is a finite set of *non-terminals*, $\Sigma \cap N = \emptyset$; $P \subseteq \{X \to aY \mid X, Y \in N, a \in \Sigma \cup \{\varepsilon\}\}$ is a set of *productions*; $\sigma \in N$ is an *initial symbol*; $F \subseteq N$ is a set of *final symbols* (if $F = \{Z\}$ is a singleton, we will write Z instead of $\{Z\}$, for simplicity).

Let $u, v \in \Sigma^*$ and $X, Y \in N$. We write $uX \Rightarrow vY$ iff $(\exists p \in P)$ $p = X \to aY$ and $v = ua$. The *transition relation* $\Rightarrow^*$ is the reflexive and transitive closure of $\Rightarrow$. Grammars are regarded as devices generating languages over their terminal alphabets. The *language generated* by G is defined as $L(G) = \{w \in \Sigma^* \mid \sigma \Rightarrow^* wZ$ with $Z \in F\}$. Remark that regular grammars are labelled net systems of special type. Namely, with $^\bullet a, a^\bullet$, initial state s and final states (members of W) restricted to singletons.

It is easily seen how to transform regular grammar to finite automaton and vice versa. So, the following fact is obvious.

Proposition 6.7.7 *A language L is regular iff there is a regular grammar generating L.*

The following construction (grammar corresponding to rational expression) and transformations of grammars (deleting empty productions and putting the unique exit) form a preparing part of the further algorithm. It is assumed that the respective steps of the algorithm (Steps 2, 3, 4 and 7) are done precisely as described below.

6.7.4 Grammars Corresponding to Rational Expressions

Let R be a rational expression over a finite alphabet Σ. The *grammar G_R corresponding to R* is defined inductively as follows.

$R = \emptyset$: $G_R = (\Sigma, \{\sigma\}, \emptyset, \sigma, \emptyset)$

$R = \varepsilon$: $G_R = (\Sigma, \{\sigma\}, \emptyset, \sigma, \{\sigma\})$

$R = a$: $G_R = (\Sigma, \{\sigma, Z\}, \{\sigma \to aZ\}, \sigma, Z)$

Let R_1 and R_2 be rational expressions, let $G_1 = (\Sigma, N_1, P_1, \sigma_1, F_1)$ and $G_2 = (\Sigma, N_2, P_2, \sigma_2, F_2)$ be grammars corresponding to R_1 and R_2, respectively. We may assume $N_1 \cap N_2 = \emptyset$.

$R = R_1 \cup R_2$: $G_R = (\Sigma, N, P, \sigma, F)$, where $N = N_1 \cup N_2 \cup \{\sigma\}, P = \{\sigma \to \sigma_1, \sigma \to \sigma_2\} \cup P_1 \cup P_2, \sigma \notin N_1 \cup N_2, F = F_1 \cup F_2$.

$R = R_1 \bullet R_2$: $G_R = (\Sigma, N, P, \sigma, F)$, where $N = N_1 \cup N_2, P = P_1 \cup \{X \to \sigma_2 \mid X \in F_1\} \cup P_2, \sigma = \sigma_1, F = F_2$.

$R = R_1^*$: $G_R = (\Sigma, N, P, \sigma, F)$, where $N = N_1, P = P_1 \cup \{X \to \sigma_1 \mid X \in F_1\}, \sigma = \sigma_1, F = \sigma_1$.

Obviously, $L(G_R) = L(R)$. Be aware that the above construction is exactly what we need for the following algorithm. An attempt to take (in the second step of the algorithm) any grammar G such that $L(G) = L(R)$ fails.

DELETING EMPTY PRODUCTIONS

Let $G = (\Sigma, N, P, \sigma, F)$ be a regular grammar. A production $X \to aY$ is said to be empty production iff $a = \varepsilon$. Let $P' = \{X \to aZ \mid a \in \Sigma, X, Z \in N$ and $(\exists Y \in N)\ X \Rightarrow^* Y \Rightarrow aZ\}$ and let $F' = \{X \in N \mid X \Rightarrow^* Z$ and $Z \in F\}$. Let $G' = (\Sigma, N, P', \sigma, F')$. Clearly, G' has no empty production and $L(G') = L(G)$.

PUTTING THE UNIQUE EXIT

Let $G = (\Sigma, N, P, \sigma, F)$ be a regular grammar. Let $G'' = (\Sigma, N \cup \{\#\}, P'', \sigma, \#)$, where $\# \notin N$ is a new nonterminal and $P'' = P \cup \{X \to \# \mid X \in F\}$. Clearly, G'' has the unique exit $\#$ and $L(G'') = L(G)$.

ALGORITHM

ENTRY: Concurrent alphabet (Σ, I) and Rational Expression $R \in$ REX(Σ)

EXIT: Labelled Net System $\mathcal{S}$, such that $T(\mathcal{S}) = \text{Rec}_I(R)$

Step 1: Set $D = \Sigma \times \Sigma \setminus I$. Find any family $C = \{C_1, \ldots, C_n\}$ of cliques covering (Σ, D).

Step 2: Build the grammar $G = G_R$ corresponding to R.

Step 3: Delete empty productions from $G; G \leftarrow G'$.

Step 4: Put the unique exit $\#$ into $G; G \leftarrow G''$.

Let $G = (\Sigma, N, P, \sigma, \#)$ be the current grammar.

This must be necessarily done, even if G has already a single exit. Let $G, G_1 \cup G_2, G_1 \bullet G_2$ and G^* denote resulting grammars of this step for expressions $R, R_1 \cup R_2, R_1 \bullet R_2$ and R^*, respectively. It follows directly from the construction that $L(G) = L(R), L(G_1 \cup G_2) = L(R_1 \cup R_2), L(G_1 \bullet G_2) = L(R_1 \bullet R_2)$ and $L(G^*) = L(R^*)$.

Step 5: Build the grammar of programs (possible sequences of productions) for G:

Set $T = \{X \to pY \mid p \in P$ and $p = X \to aY\}$. Set $H = (P, N, T, \sigma, \#)$. Let $\lambda_0 : P \to \Sigma \cup \{\varepsilon\}$ be the function $\lambda_0(p) = a$ iff $p = X \to aY$. It follows directly from the construction that $L(G) = \lambda_0(L(H))$. Let $H, H_1 \cup H_2, H_1 \bullet H_2$ and H^* denote resulting grammars of this step for expressions $R, R_1 \cup R_2, R_1 \bullet R_2$ and R^*, respectively. It follows directly from the construction that $L(H) =$

$L(R)$, $L(H_1 \cup H_2) = L(H_1) \cup L(H_2)$, $L(H_1 \bullet H_2) = L(H_1) \circ L(H_2)$ and $L(H^*) = (L(H))^*$.

Set $B_i = \lambda_0^{-1}(C_i \cup \{\varepsilon\})$ for $i = 1, \ldots, n$. Since $B_1 \cup \ldots \cup B_n = P$, we can regard the set $\{B_1, \ldots, B_n\}$ as the family of cliques for P. It induces the dependence $D_P \subseteq P \times P = \bigcup \{B_i \times B_i \mid i = 1, \ldots, n\}$ and the independence $I_P = P \times P \setminus D_P$.

Step 6: Decompose H with respect to cliques: For $i = 1, \ldots, n$: $H_i = (B_i, N, T_i, \sigma, \#)$, where $T_i = \{X \to pY \mid X \to pY \in T \text{ and } p \in B_i\} \cup \{X \to Y \mid X \to pY \in T \text{ and } p \notin B_i\}$.

Step 7: Delete empty productions from all H_i. $H_i \leftarrow H_i''$ for $i = 1, \ldots, n$. Remark that, after putting the unique exit $\#$ (Step 4), only empty productions ended with $\#$. Any clique of the new family $\{B_1, \ldots, B_n\}$ of cliques (Step 5) contains all empty productions. Since that and definition of T_i (Step 6), there is no empty production ended with $\#$ in T_i. Therefore, the current step does not change final symbols $\#$ in grammars H_i.

Step 8: Disjoint nonterminals in H_i ($i = 1, \ldots, n$):
$N_i = N \times \{i\}$ for $i = 1, \ldots, n$; we write X_i for $(X, i) \in N_i$.
$T_i \leftarrow \{X_i \to pY_i \mid X \to pY \in T_i\}$ for $i = 1, \ldots, n$. $H_i \leftarrow (B_i, N_i, T_i, \sigma_i, \#_i)$ for $i = 1, \ldots, n$.

Step 9: Build the net system $S = (Q, C, \varphi, s, W)$:
Let \$ be a special symbol out of $T_1 \cup \ldots \cup T_n$; set $T_i \leftarrow T_i \cup \{\$\}$ for $i = 1, \ldots, n$.
Set $Q_p = \{(q_1, \ldots, q_n) \in T_1 \times \ldots \times T_n \mid (\forall i = 1, \ldots, n) \text{ if } p \in B_i \text{ then } q_i = X \to pY \text{ (for some } X, Y \in N_i) \text{ else } q_i = \$\}$, for any $p \in P$.
Actions of S : $Q = \bigcup \{Q_p \mid p \in P\}$.
Conditions of S : $C = N_1 \cup \ldots \cup N_n$
$^\bullet(q_1, \ldots, q_n) = \{X \mid (\exists i)\, q_i = X \to pY\}$ $(q_1, \ldots, q_n)^\bullet = \{Y \mid (\exists i)\, q_i = X \to pY\}$
$\varphi = (^\bullet\varphi, \varphi^\bullet)$, where $^\bullet\varphi(q_1, \ldots, q_n) = {}^\bullet(q_1, \ldots, q_n)$ and $\varphi^\bullet(q_1, \ldots, q_n) = (q_1, \ldots, q_n)^\bullet$.
Initial state: $s = \{\sigma_1, \ldots, \sigma_n\}$ One final state: $W = \{\{\#_1, \ldots, \#_n\}\}$

Step 10: Define the labelling $\lambda : Q \to \Sigma \cup \{\varepsilon\}$:
Set $\lambda'(q_1, \ldots, q_n) = p$ iff $(q_1, \ldots, q_n) \in Q_p$; it is a function, as sets Q_p are pairwise disjoint.
Let $\lambda_0 : P \to \Sigma \cup \{\varepsilon\}$ be that one of Step 5.
Labelling function: $\lambda(q_1, \ldots, q_n) = \lambda_0(\lambda'(q_1, \ldots, q_n))$
END OF ALGORITHM

The correctness of the algorithm will be proved in two steps. First, we shall prove that $\lambda : M(S) \twoheadrightarrow M(\Sigma, I)$ is an interpretation of $T(S)$ in $M = M(\Sigma, I)$, so $\mathcal{S} = (S, M, \lambda)$ is really a properly labelled net system. Next, we shall prove that the trace language $T(\mathcal{S}) = \lambda(T(S))$ is really equal to $\text{Rec}_I(R)$.

Lemma 6.7.8 *Let $M = M(\Sigma, I)$ be a trace monoid and let R be a rational expression over Σ.*

The triple $\mathcal{S} = (S, M, \lambda)$ produced by the algorithm, is a properly labelled net system.

Proof: We have to prove that the labelling function $\lambda : Q \to \Sigma \cup \{\varepsilon\}$, defined in Steps 5 and 10 of the algorithm and extended to the morphism $\lambda : Q^* \to \Sigma^*$, is the interpretation of $T(S)$ in $M = M(\Sigma, I)$. We shall prove that the conditions (i) and (ii) of Lemma 6.7.2 are satisfied:

(i) if $\lambda(q) = \varepsilon$ and $[uqv] \in T$, then $\lambda(v) = \varepsilon$ and

(ii) if $\lambda(q) \neq \varepsilon \neq \lambda(q')$ and $[uqq'v] \in T$, then $(q,q') \in I_S$ iff $(\lambda(q), \lambda(q')) \in I$

(i) Let $q \in Q$ and $\lambda(q) = \varepsilon$; Let $\lambda'(q) = p$. Then $\lambda(q) = \lambda_0(p) = \varepsilon$; it means p is an empty production. After Steps 3 and 4, the only empty productions are of the form $Y \to \#$. Thus $p = Y \to \#$ and $(\forall i)$ $p \in B_i$ (Step 5). Since there is no production from $\#$, we have $\varphi^\bullet(q) = \{\#_1, \ldots, \#_n\}$ and q cannot be followed.

(ii) Let I_P be the independence relation on P induced by the set $\{B_1, \ldots, B_n\}$ of cliques (Step 5), i.e. $(p,q) \in D_P$ iff $(\exists i)$ $\{p,q\} \subseteq B_i, I_P = P \times P \setminus D_P$. Let $q, q' \in Q$ and $\lambda(q) \neq \varepsilon, \lambda(q') \neq \varepsilon$. Let $\lambda'(q) = p$ and $\lambda'(q') = p'$. The implication $(p,p') \in I_P \Rightarrow (q,q') \in I_S$ follows from:

— construction of grammars H_i (Step 6) with respect to cliques,
— disjoining of nonterminals in grammars H_i (Step 8),
— definition of $\varphi = (^\bullet\varphi, \varphi^\bullet)$ (Step 9).

Now, assume that $(q,q') \in I_S$ and $uqq'v \in L(S)$. Suppose $(p,p') \in D_P$. Then $(\exists i)$ $\{p,p'\} \subseteq B_i$ and there are $X_i \to pY_i$ and $Y_i \to p'Z_i$ in T_i. As then $Y_i \in q^\bullet \cap {}^\bullet q' \neq \emptyset$, we have $(q,q') \in D_S$, contradiction. Thus $(p,p') \in I_P$. We have shown that if $q, q' \in Q, \lambda(q) \neq \varepsilon, \lambda(q') \neq \varepsilon$ and $uqq'v \in L(S)$, then $(q,q') \in I_S$ iff $(p,p') \in I_P$ (where $p = \lambda'(q)$ and $p' = \lambda'(q')$). Let $\lambda_0(p) = a$ and $\lambda_0(p') = b$, for some $a, b \in \Sigma$. Equivalence $(p,p') \in I_P$ iff $(a,b) \in I$ follows directly from construction of $\{B_1, \ldots, B_n\}$ (Step 5). Thus we have $(q,q') \in I_S$ iff $(p,p') \in I_P$ iff $(a,b) \in I$. But $\lambda(q) = \lambda_0(p) = a$ and $\lambda(q') = \lambda_0(p') = b$. So (ii) is proved.

Hence λ is an interpretation of $T(S)$ in $M = M(\Sigma, I)$, by Lemma 6.7.2. So $\mathcal{S} = (S, M, \lambda)$ is a properly labelled net system. $\square$

It remains to prove that $\mathcal{S} = (S, M, \lambda)$ generates exactly $\mathrm{Rec}_I(R)$. First, we shall prove it for R being star-connected (Proposition 6.7.9). It will be enough to characterize recognizable trace languages with Petri nets (Theorem 6.7.10).

Proposition 6.7.9 *Let $M = M(\Sigma, I)$ be a trace monoid and let R be a star-connected rational expression over Σ. Let $\mathcal{S} = (S, M, \lambda)$ be the labelled net system produced by the algorithm. Then $T(\mathcal{S}) = \lambda(T(S))$ is equal to $\mathrm{Rec}_I(R)$ $(= \mathrm{Rat}_I(R))$ in this case.*

Proof: Clearly, $L(G) = L(R)$ for the grammar G of Step 4. Next, observe that $\lambda_0(L(H)) = L(G) = L(R)$ for the grammar H, built in Step 5. Remark, that the construction of Step 9 gives nothing else than a rule of executions of actions of grammars of Step 8. And the rule is the following: any action p can be executed in S if and only if it can be executed in all grammars H_i such that $p \in B_i$. Let I_P be the independence on P defined in Step 5. We shall prove that $\lambda'(L(S)) = f_I(L(H))$. First, observe that $L(H) \subseteq \lambda'(L(S))$, thanks to Step 7. Next, observe that if $xpqz \in \lambda'(L(S))$ (for some $x, z \in P^*, p, q \in P$) and $(p,q) \in I_P$, then $xqpz \in \lambda'(L(S))$; it results from Steps 6–9. Concluding, $f_I(L(H)) \subseteq \lambda'(L(S))$. The inverse inclusion will be shown inductively. It is clear, if the algorithm starts with $R = \emptyset$, $R = \varepsilon$ or $R = a$ ($a \in \Sigma$). Induction: Let H, H_1, H_2 denote the results of Step 5 of the algorithm and S, S_1, S_2 denote the results of Step 9 of the algorithm, for the expressions R, R_1 and R_2, respectively. Induction hypothesis: $\lambda'(L(S_1)) = f_I(L(H_1))$ and $\lambda'(L(S_2)) = f_I(L(H_2))$.

Let $R = R_1 \cup R_2$. As nonterminals in the grammars H_1 and H_2 are disjoint, any jump from H_1 to H_2 or from H_2 to H_1 is impossible. Thus $\lambda'(L(S)) = \lambda'(L(S_1)) \cup \lambda'(L(S_2))$. Now, using remark of Step 5 and induction hypothesis we obtain $\lambda'(L(S)) = \lambda'(L(S_1)) \cup \lambda'(L(S_2)) = f_I(L(H_1) \cup f_I(L(H_2)) = f_I(L(H_1) \cup (L(H_2)) = f_I(L(H_1 \cup H_2)) = f_I(L(H))$.

Let $R = R_1 \bullet R_2$. The situation is quite similar, as nonterminals in H_1 and H_2 are disjoint, except exits from H_1 are entries to H_2. Hence, a withdrawal from H_2 is impossible. Only some "delayed" independent actions can be executed. Thus $\lambda'(L(S)) = f_I(\lambda'(L(S_1)) \circ \lambda'(L(S_2)))$. Again, by remark of Step 5 and induction hypothesis we obtain $\lambda'(L(S)) = f_I(\lambda'(L(S_1)) \circ \lambda'(L(S_2))) = f_I(f_I(\lambda'(L(S_1))) \circ f_I(\lambda'(L(S_2)))) = f_I(f_I(L(H_1)) \circ f_I(L(H_2))) = f_I(L(H_1) \circ (L(H_2)) = f_I(L(H_1 \bullet H_2)) = f_I(L(H))$.

Let $R = R_1^*$. This case is slightly different, as this time H_1 may be visited arbitrary often. We have to use the assumption R is star-connected. Then $L(H_1)$ is connected. Suppose the net system reaches the final state having produced only a proper subword u of a member w of $L(S_1)$. Then $\lambda'(\text{alph}(u)) \times \lambda'(\text{alph}(w) \setminus \text{alph}(u)) \subseteq I_P$, so $\lambda'(w) \in f_I(L(H_1))$ is non-connected. Contradiction, as $L(H_1)$ is connected. Hence, the equality $\lambda'(L(S)) = f_I((\lambda'(L(S_1)))^*)$ has been proved. By remark of Step 5 and induction hypothesis we have $\lambda'(L(S)) = f_I((\lambda'(L(S_1)))^*) = f_I((f_I(L(H_1)))^*) = f_I((L(H_1))^*) = f_I(L(H_1^*)) = f_I(L(H))$.

We have proved $\lambda'(L(S)) = f_I(L(H))$, what is equivalent to $[\lambda'(L(S))] = [L(H)]$. As $\lambda_0(L(H)) = L(G) = L(R)$ and $\lambda = \lambda_0(\lambda')$ is the interpretation of $T(S)$ in $M = M(\Sigma, I)$ (Lemma 6.7.8), we have $T(S) = \lambda(T(S)) = \lambda_0(\lambda'(T(S))) = \lambda_0[\lambda'(L(S))] = \lambda_0[L(H)] = [L(G)] = [L(R)] = T(R) = \text{Rat}_I(R) = \text{Rec}_I(R)$. $\square$

Be aware that the assumption R is star-connected was substantially utilized during the last proof. And the equality $[\lambda'(L(S))]_{I_S} = [L(H)]_{I_P}$, as well as the final sequence of equalities do not hold for arbitrary R. Nevertheless, the algorithm works properly for any R, producing always a labelled net system S with $T(S) = \text{Rec}_I(R)$. It will be better supported soon (Proposition 6.7.11). But we are already prepared, since Theorem 6.3.13, to formulate a general characterization of recognizable trace languages with Petri nets:

Theorem 6.7.10 *Let $M = M(\Sigma, I)$ be a trace monoid and let $T \subseteq M$ be a trace language.*

$T \in \text{REC}(M)$ iff $T = T(S)$ for some labelled net system S.

Proof: $\Rightarrow$: From Theorem 6.3.13 and Proposition 6.7.9.

$\Leftarrow$: Proposition 6.7.5. $\square$

As it was mentioned, the algorithm works for arbitrary $R \in \text{REX}(\Sigma)$ (not necessarily star-connected), producing a labelled net system S with $T(S) = \text{Rec}_I(R)$. Since Theorem 6.7.10, the following proposition is of practical rather than theoretical meaning. As the precise proof involves complications (of technical nature only), it is sketched with some hints.

Proposition 6.7.11 *Let $M = M(\Sigma, I)$ be a trace monoid and let $R \in \text{REX}(\Sigma)$ be a rational expression. Let $S = (S, M, \lambda)$ be the labelled net system produced by the algorithm.*

Then $T(S) = \lambda(T(S))$ is equal to $\text{Rec}_I(R)$.

Proof: (sketch with hints at 7.5) First of all, the equality $[\lambda'(L(S))] = [L(H)]$ does not hold, in general. Therefore, we have to do induction on the equality $\lambda_0[\lambda'(L(S))] = \text{Rec}_I(R)$. The inductive steps for $R = R_1 \cup R_2$ and $R = R_1 \bullet R_2$ are, in their essence, the same. And we obtain directly $\lambda_0[\lambda'(L(S))] = \text{Rec}_I(R_1) \cup \text{Rec}_I(R_2) = \text{Rec}_I(R)$ and $\lambda_0[\lambda'(L(S))] = \text{Rec}_I(R_1) \circ \text{Rec}_I(R_2) = \text{Rec}_I(R)$, respectively. The case $R = R_1^*$ is different. This time $(\text{Rec}_I(R_1))^* \subseteq \lambda_0[\lambda'(L(S))]$, but the inverse inclusion does not hold, in general. One can prove, however, that $\lambda_0[\lambda'(L(S))] = /\text{Rec}_I(R_1)/^* = \text{Rec}_I(R)$. It finishes the induction. The rest is easy: $T(S) = \lambda(T(S)) = \lambda_0(\lambda'(T(S))) = \lambda_0[\lambda'(L(S))] = \text{Rec}_I(R)$. $\square$

6.8 Bibliographical Remarks

The preliminaries of Section 6.1 belong to the classical theories of formal languages and monoids. Their historical attribution can be found in [11], [94] or [243]. The importance of Kleene's Theorem cannot be underestimated.

Trace monoids were introduced by Cartier/Foata [34], where some combinatorial properties (among others, cancellation in trace monoids (Proposition 6.2.2)) were proved. Levi's Lemma for traces (Corollary of Lemma 6.2.3) was proved by Cori/Perrin [47]. The characterization of trace monoids with a decidable Recognizability Problem is due to Sakarovitch [242].

The results of Section 6.3 form the main part of the author's Ph.D. Thesis [204] (extended abstract [205]). The powerful Proposition 6.3.2 of Hashiguchi [134] allowed to shorten some proofs. Proposition 6.3.3 was obtained by Fliess [107] in a quite involved way. The present proof is probably the best illustration of the power of Proposition 6.3.2. The concept of lexicographic representatives of traces was introduced by Anisimov/Knuth [7], where the trivial "only if" direction of Theorem 6.3.12 was remarked. The Corollary of Theorem 6.3.13 (on iterating factors) was independently obtained by Métivier [194].

Section 6.4, about the Star Problem, is based on [209] and mostly on [112]. Proposition 6.4.2 is from [204, 205]; it was independently proved by Clerbout and Latteux [42] (in the more general framework of semi-commutations) and by Métivier [195]. Theorem 6.4.8 (on finite power property in free monoids) was proved independently by Simon [256] and Hashiguchi [133].

Section 6.5, on morphisms, is based on [207]. Theorem 6.5.6 (on recognizable morphisms) is due to Duboc [75].

Trace theory, in the framework of computer science, has begun with Mazurkiewicz's paper [189] dealing with Petri nets. Just that paper and [206] are the origins of Section 6.6.

The algorithm of Section 6.7 and the proof of its correctness are applications of results of Section 6.3 (mainly, of the characterizing Theorems 6.3.13 and 6.3.16). The contents of that section were described in the author's unpublished papers [202] and [203].

Chapter 7

Asynchronous Automata

Wiesław Zielonka

Université Bordeaux I, LaBRI, URA CNRS 1304
351, cours de la Libération, 33405 Talence Cedex, France
zielonka@geocub.greco-prog.fr

Contents

7.1 Introduction

The problem of inventing a suitable machine-like model for traces was implicitly
present since the advent of trace theory. Such devices should exhibit two properties

- they should have an adequate computational power, i.e. they should accept
  exactly recognizable[2] sets of traces and

- the independency of actions should be reflected by the "true" concurrency of
  their executions and not just by the interleaving.

---

[2] "Recognizable" means here recognizable in the abstract way — by means of morphisms from
the free partially commutative monoids into finite monoids

The condition-event nets used in Mazurkiewicz's seminal paper [189], which introduced traces in the domain of concurrency, satisfy the second condition, but their computational power is clearly insufficient — as it is well-known there are recognizable subsets of the free monoid that cannot be recognized by unlabelled Petri nets. The direct possibility of enhancing the power of condition-event nets passes by endowing them with a labelling of transitions. Unfortunately some labellings give rise to behaviours that are expressed by labelled acyclic graphs that are not interpretable in the framework of trace theory. Thus actually in this case we should specify a class of admissible labellings but such objects become too complex and difficult to handle.

Asynchronous automata introduced in this chapter overcome these difficulties, they have the desired computational power, allow the "real" concurrency of actions and have a nice regular structure. Moreover they place trace theory in the framework of the well-established theory of finite automata.

The chapter is organized as follows.

In Section 7.2 asynchronous transition systems are introduced.

Two natural non-interleaving semantics for these systems are proposed in Section 7.3.

The first of these semantics has been patterned on the process semantics of Petri nets. However we can note that while processes in Petri nets are always represented by directed acyclic graphs, to represent faithfully the behaviour of finite asynchronous transition systems we are obliged to admit in general some cycles (still if an asynchronous transition system can be directly represented as a Petri net then both process semantics are identical, in particular all processes are acyclic.)

The second semantics examined in this section is directly related to traces, actually it yields a trace representation adapted for asynchronous transition systems.

In Section 7.4 a special class of asynchronous transition systems, finite asynchronous cellular transition systems, is presented. In the next Section 7.5 we show that not only asynchronous cellular transition systems have particularly simple and appealing internal structure but in fact they can simulate without any loss of potential concurrency between actions a much larger class of asynchronous transition systems.

In Section 7.6 asynchronous (cellular) transition systems are equipped with the sets of initial and final states and the recognizability power of the automata obtained in this way is examined.

7.2   Asynchronous Transition Systems

The following notation will be used throughout the chapter. By $id_X = \{(x, x) \mid x \in X\}$ we shall denote the identity relation over a set X, if the domain of this relation is clear from the context then the subscript X will often be skipped. Let E be a binary relation. For any element x and a set B: $xE = \{y \mid (x, y) \in E\}$ is the image of x under E, $Ex = \{y \mid (y, x) \in E\}$ is the inverse image of x under E, $BE = \bigcup_{x \in B} xE$, $EB = \bigcup_{x \in B} Ex$ are respectively the image and the inverse image of B under E, finally $E^{-1} = \{(x, y) \mid (y, x) \in E\}$ is the inverse of E. The composition of two binary relations E and F is defined as $E \circ F = \{(x, y) \mid \exists z, (x, z) \in E \text{ and } (z, y) \in F\}$.

The transitive closure of a relation $E \subseteq X \times X$ is defined as $E^+ = \bigcup_{i=0}^{\infty} E^i$, where $E^1 = E$ and $E^{i+1} = E^i \circ E$, while $E^* = id_X \cup E^+$ denotes the transitive and reflexive closure of E.

The relation E is said to be acyclic if its graph is acyclic, i.e. if $id_X \cap E^+ = \emptyset$.

For any two sets X and Y, $\mathbf{F}(X; Y)$ denotes the family of all mappings from X into Y and $\mathcal{P}(X)$ stands for the family of all subsets of X.

For any word $x \in \Sigma^*$ by $|x|$ we denote the length of x, while $|x|_a$ is the number of occurrences of $a \in \Sigma$ in x. The empty word is denoted by $\mathbf{1}$, Rec_Σ stands for the family of recognizable subsets of Σ^*.

After these preliminaries we can pass to the main subject of this chapter. A *signature* is a triple $\sigma = (\Sigma, R, E)$, where

— Σ is the set actions,

— R is the set of registers,

— $E \subseteq \Sigma \times R \cup R \times \Sigma$ is the connection relation.

We assume that R and Σ are disjoint.

Intuitively, a signature represents a static structure of a distributed system, for each action $a \in \Sigma$, $Ea = \{r \in R \mid (r, a) \in E\}$ is the set of registers that a reads when it is executed and $aE = \{r \in R \mid (a, r) \in E\}$ is the set of registers that a modifies (i.e. where it writes a new value).

A *finite asynchronous transition system* (or a fat-system for short) is a tuple $\tau = (\Sigma, R, E, X, \Delta)$, where

— (Σ, R, E) is a signature of τ,

— X is a finite set of values (local states),

— Δ is a family of local transition relations.

The set $\Delta = \{\delta_a \mid a \in \Sigma\}$ consists of local transition relations, for each action $a \in \Sigma$, Δ contains a transition relation δ_a

$$\delta_a \subseteq \mathbf{F}(Ea; X) \times \mathbf{F}(aE; X)$$

To describe precisely how fat-systems work and how local transition relations are used by the actions we need some additional notation.

We assume that at each moment every register contains some value from the set X of values, thus the global state of the system is described by a mapping $s : R \longrightarrow X$ assigning to each register $r \in R$ its values $s(r) \in X$. By S we shall denote the set $\mathbf{F}(R; X)$ of all global states of τ.

For every $s \in S$ and $\alpha \subseteq R$ by $s_{|\alpha}$ we denote the restriction of s to α. Note that $s_{|\alpha} \in \mathbf{F}(\alpha; X)$. In general the mappings from a subset α of R into X will be called partial states.

Elements of the local transition relation δ_a are called *local transitions*. A local transition $(s_1, s_2) \in \delta_a$ is said to be *enabled* at a global state $s' \in S$ if $s_1 = s'_{|Ea}$. The action a is enabled at $s' \in S$ if some of its local transition is enabled. If transition $(s_1, s_2) \in \delta_a$ is enabled at $s' \in S$ then it can be executed by a yielding a new global state $s'' \in S$ such that

$$\forall r \in R, \quad s''(r) = \begin{cases} s'(r) & \text{if } r \notin aE \\ s_2(r) & \text{otherwise} \end{cases}$$

Intuitively, the execution of an action a can be interpreted in the following way. First a reads the values of all registers from its reading domain Ea obtaining a partial state $s' \in \mathbf{F}(Ea; X)$. Next it chooses a partial state $s'' \in \mathbf{F}(aE; X)$ such that $(s', s'') \in \delta_a$ and modifies the values of registers of its writing domain aE writing to each register $r \in aE$ the value $s''(r)$. The execution of a described above is atomic.

Formally, the modifications of global states by execution of actions are specified by means of the global transition relation Δ:

$$\Delta \subseteq S \times \Sigma \times S$$

(Let us note that the symbol Δ is slightly overloaded since it is used also to denote the family of local transition relations of τ, however the context will always indicate unambiguously the actual meaning of Δ.)

Let $s', s'' \in S$ and $a \in \Sigma$. Then $(s', a, s'') \in \Delta$ if

$$(s'_{|Ea}, s''_{|aE}) \in \delta_a$$

and

$$s''_{|R \setminus (aE)} = s'_{|R \setminus (aE)}$$

Sometimes it is convenient to interpret Δ as a mapping from $S \times \Sigma$ into $\mathcal{P}(S)$, where $\Delta(s, a) = \{s' \in S \mid (s, a, s') \in \Delta\}$ for $s \in S$ and $a \in \Sigma$.

A fat-system τ is *deterministic* if for each $a \in \Sigma$ and each global state $s \in S$ there is at most one global state s' such that $(s, a, s') \in \Delta$. In this case Δ can be interpreted as a partial mapping from $S \times \Sigma$ into S, where $s' = \Delta(s, a)$ iff $(s, a, s') \in \Delta$. Note that τ is deterministic if all relations δ_a are (partial) functions — $\forall a \in \Sigma, \forall s \in \mathbf{F}(Ea; X), \text{card}\{s' \in \mathbf{F}(aE; X) \mid (s, s') \in \delta_a\} \leq 1$, i.e. for each action a and each global state there is at most one local transition of a enabled at this state.

The global transition relation can be extended in the standard way to finite sequences of actions:

$$\Delta \subseteq S \times \Sigma^* \times S$$

by setting $(s, \mathbf{1}, s) \in \Delta$ for each $s \in S$ and $(s', ua, s'') \in \Delta$ iff there exists $s \in S$ such that $(s', u, s) \in \Delta$ and $(s, a, s'') \in \Delta$ for any word $u \in \Sigma^*$ and $a \in \Sigma$.

Example 7.2.1 Let $R = \{r_1, r_2\}$, $\Sigma = \{a, b, c\}$, $X = \{0, 1, 2\}$ and let σ be as on Figure 7.1

Here and in the sequel the elements of R are represented by circles while the elements of Σ by boxes.

The local transition relations of τ are given by the following tables

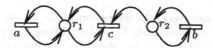

Figure 7.1: A signature σ.

δ_a	r_1 $\parallel$ r_1
	0 $\parallel$ 1
	1 $\parallel$ 2

δ_b	r_2 $\parallel$ r_2
	2 $\parallel$ 1
	1 $\parallel$ 2

δ_c	r_1 r_2 $\parallel$ r_1
	2 1 $\parallel$ 0
	1 2 $\parallel$ 0

In general, for every $a \in \Sigma$, a row of a transition table of δ_a corresponds to a local transition $(s', s'') \in \delta_a$, s' is given by the first part of the row, while s'' is coded by the part after the double vertical line. For example the second row of the transition table for c shows that $(s', s'') \in \delta_c$, where $s' \in \mathbf{F}(\{r_1, r_2\}; X)$, $s'' \in \mathbf{F}(\{r_1\}; X)$ are such that $s'(r_1) = 1$, $s'(r_2) = 2$, $s''(r_1) = 0$. In other words, this transition describes the fact that if r_1 contains 1 and r_2 contains 2 then c is enabled and if this transition is executed then 0 is written to r_1.

Figure 7.2 presents the graph of the global transition relation Δ. (In the graphical representation of Δ global states are given by tuples of values from X, where the i-th element of the tuple gives the value of the register r_i. A directed edge from s' to s'' labelled by $a \in \Sigma$ denotes the fact that $(s', a, s'') \in \Delta$.) This fat-system is deterministic.

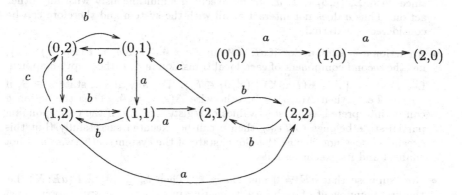

Figure 7.2: Global transition relation

The main interest in the fat-systems results from their ability to execute some actions in parallel. Intuitively, the execution of an action $a \in \Sigma$, consisting of reading the contents of registers from Ea and modifying the values of registers from aE is atomic. This implies that the execution of another action $b \in \Sigma$ cannot overlap the execution of a if b writes to one of the registers $r \in aE \cup Ea$ used by a. Dependence and potential parallelism between actions are captured by means of binary relations over Σ that are defined below.

With each signature $\sigma = (\Sigma, R, E)$ we associate four binary relations over Σ:

— $C = \{(a, b) \in \Sigma^2 \mid aE \cap Eb \neq \emptyset\}$ — *direct causality* relation,

— $W = \{(a, b) \in \Sigma^2 \mid aE \cap bE \neq \emptyset\}$ — *writing conflict* relation,

— $D = C \cup C^{-1} \cup W$ — *conflict* relation,

— $I = \Sigma^2 \backslash D$ — *independence* relation.

Note that two actions $a, b \in \Sigma$ are independent, $(a, b) \in I$, if $aE \cap bE = aE \cap Eb = Ea \cap bE = \emptyset$. In fact these are well-known Bernstein's conditions [10] specifying the pairs of non-interfering actions that can be executed in any order without altering the result of the computation, actually any pair of independent actions can be executed even simultaneously. This point is discussed in detail in Section 7.3.

Given a fat-system τ we can classify all actions as belonging to one of the following four classes: external, test, reset and internal actions:

- An action $a \in \Sigma$ is *external* if $aE \cup Ea = \emptyset$, i.e. a neither reads nor writes to any register. Note that in this case either δ_a is empty or $\delta_a = \{(\emptyset, \emptyset)\}$, i.e. only one local transition consisting of the pair of the empty mappings is possible for a. In the first case a is never enabled, while in the second case it is always enabled but its execution does not change the global state and, since $\forall b \in \Sigma$, $(a, b) \in I$, a can be executed simultaneously with any other action. Thus a does not interact at all with the system and therefore can be considered as external.

- An action a is a *test* action if $aE = \emptyset$ but $Ea \neq \emptyset$. Then $\delta_a \subseteq \mathbf{F}(Ea; X) \times \{\emptyset\}$, i.e. the second component of each local transition in δ_a is the empty mapping. Let $Test_a = \{s' \in \mathbf{F}(Ea; X) \mid (s', \emptyset) \in \delta_a\}$. For any global state $s \in S$, if $s_{|Ea} \in Test_a$ then $\Delta(s, a) = s$, otherwise $\Delta(s, a) = \emptyset$. Thus the action a can be interpreted as a test of values of registers in Ea, if the corresponding partial state belongs to $Test_a$ then a can be executed successfully (but this execution does not change the global state of the system), otherwise a is not enabled and its execution fails.

- Now suppose that $aE \neq \emptyset$ and $Ea = \emptyset$. Then $\delta_a \subseteq \{\emptyset\} \times \mathbf{F}(aE; X)$, i.e. the first component of each local transition in δ_a is the empty mapping. Let $Reset_a = \{s \in \mathbf{F}(aE; X) \mid (\emptyset, s) \in \delta_a\}$. Now for all global states $s_1, s_2 \in S$, $(s_1, a, s_2) \in \Delta$ if and only if $s_{2|aE} \in Reset_a$ and $s_{2|R \backslash aE} = s_{1|R \backslash aE}$. In other words, since a does not read anything, it is always enabled and upon its execution a partial state is chosen from $Reset_a$ and the registers from the set aE are modified according to this partial state. Thus intuitively, a can be interpreted as a *reset* action that can always be executed and whenever activated it resets the values of registers from aE.

- Finally, by *internal* action we mean any action $a \in \Sigma$ such that both aE and Ea are non-empty.

Example 7.2.2 Let $\Sigma = \{a, b, c\}$, $R = \{r_1, r_2\}$, $X = \{0, 1\}$. The signature is presented on Figure 7.3.

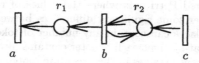

Figure 7.3: A signature σ.

Note that a is a test action, c is a reset action and b is an internal action. The following tables give the transition relations of a, b and c.

δ_a

r_1
0

δ_b

	r_2	r_1	r_2
	0	0	1
	1	1	1

δ_c

r_2
0

Figure 7.4 presents the global transition graph of this system.

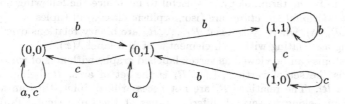

Figure 7.4: Global transition graph

In the rest of the paper we restrict our attention to asynchronous transition systems that have only internal and reset actions. (Since the executions of the other actions does not have any influence on the system state they can be ignored, if necessary it is always possible to include them in the system by the addition of supplementary registers.)

Thus from now on we assume that each signature $\sigma = (\Sigma, R, E)$ satisfies the following condition

$$\forall a \in \Sigma, \ aE \neq \emptyset$$

i.e. each action writes to some register. Let us note that this condition implies that the writing conflict relation W is reflexive, $id_\Sigma \subseteq W$.

The graphical representation of the signatures that is used here is the same as the graphical representation of unmarked Petri nets. This resemblance is in fact intended — actions and registers of fat-systems play the same role as transitions and places in Petri nets and in some cases a direct translation of the fat-systems into (labelled) Petri nets is possible [277]. To some extent fat-systems can be considered as special coloured Petri nets where the values of registers are viewed as coloured tokens. However some significant differences between these models exist. In coloured Petri nets places can contain any number of tokens, in particular they can be empty, while in fat-systems each register contains always exactly one token. Even more notable difference resides in the execution mode. A firing of a transition in a Petri net results in removing some tokens from the input places and adding new tokens to the output places. The execution semantics of fat-systems is quite different — the input registers are only read, their contents is not modified if they are not in the writing domain of the executed action. Implicitly this implies that different actions sharing only their reading registers can be executed simultaneously. Also the contents of the output registers changes in a different way, rather than adding a new token to the existing one a fat-system replaces the old token by a new one.

7.3   Non-Interleaving Semantics of Asynchronous Transition Systems

In order to unify the terminology it is useful to introduce the following notion.

Labelled relational structures are (isomorphism classes) of tuples $(X, R_1, \ldots, R_n, \lambda)$, where X is a set, $R_1, \ldots, R_n$ are binary relations over X and λ is a labelling associating with each element x of X a label $\lambda(x)$.

Such systems can be viewed as vertex labelled graphs with arcs of various types: the set X is the set of vertices, $\bigcup_{i=1}^{n} R_i$ is the set of arcs, R_i being the set of arcs of type R_i. The relations R_i are not necessarily disjoint, thus an arc (x, y), $x, y \in X$ can belong to several different types at the same time. Two labelled relational structures $(X, R_1, \ldots, R_n, \lambda)$ and $(X', R'_1, \ldots, R'_n, \lambda')$ are isomorphic if they represent the same graph up to a renaming of vertices, i.e. if there exists a bijection $f : X \longrightarrow X'$ such that

$$\forall x \in X, \ \lambda(x) = \lambda'(f(x))$$

and

$$\forall i, 1 \leq i \leq n, \ \forall x_1, x_2 \in X, \ (x_1, x_2) \in R_i \Longleftrightarrow (f(x_1), f(x_2)) \in R'_i$$

In the sequel we identify isomorphic labelled relational structures.

To describe precisely how the asynchronous transition systems work we should present semantics that is capable to reflect the asynchronous and parallel aspects of computations of such systems.

Let us recall that with each signature $\sigma = (\Sigma, R, E)$ we have associated the following conflict relation

$$D = \{(a, b) \in \Sigma^2 \mid aE \cap bE \neq \emptyset \text{ or } aE \cap Eb \neq \emptyset \text{ or } Ea \cap bE \neq \emptyset\}$$

and the independence relation $I = \Sigma^2 \setminus D$. The conflict relation D is obviously symmetric and, since we have assumed that $\forall a \in \Sigma$, $aE \neq \emptyset$, it is also reflexive.

Let $\sim_I$ be the least congruence over the free monoid Σ^* such that $ab \sim_I ba$ for all $(a, b) \in I$. Let $\mathbf{M}(\Sigma, I)$ be the corresponding free partially commutative monoid, i.e. the quotient of the free monoid Σ^* by $\sim_I$. As always the elements of $\mathbf{M}(\Sigma, I)$ are called traces, $[u]_I$ will denote the trace generated by a word $u \in \Sigma^*$.

Intuitively, the relation $\sim_I$ identifies the strings in Σ^* that generate the same computation. In fact a suitable representation of traces shows explicitly which actions can be executed in parallel — this is the main subject of the present section.

Immediately we can note the following remark:

Remark 7.3.1 For all $x, y \in \Sigma^*$ and for all global states $s \in S$ of a fat-system over the signature σ, if $x \sim_I y$ then $\Delta(s, x) = \Delta(s, y)$.

Proof: Direct verification shows that for each pair of independent actions, $(a, b) \in I$, we have $\Delta(s, ab) = \Delta(s, ba)$.

Now note that $x \sim_I y$ iff there exists a sequence $z_0, z_1, \ldots, z_k$ of words of Σ^* such that $x = z_0$, $y = z_k$ and $z_i = w_i a_i b_i v_i$, $z_{i+1} = w_i b_i a_i v_i$ for some $w_i, v_i \in \Sigma^*$ and $(a_i, b_i) \in I$, $i = 0, \ldots, k-1$, therefore $\Delta(s, z_i) = \Delta(s, z_{i+1})$ results immediately from the preceding remark. $\square$

Remark 7.3.1 shows that the global transition relation can be extended to traces:

$$\Delta \subseteq S \times \mathbf{M}(\Sigma, I) \times S$$

by setting for $s, s' \in S$, $t \in \mathbf{M}(\Sigma, I)$, $(s, t, s') \in \Delta$ if $(s, x, s') \in \Delta$ for some (or equivalently for all) $x \in \Sigma^*$ such that $[x]_I = t$. As in the case of words we shall sometimes view Δ as a mapping $\Delta : S \times \mathbf{M}(\Sigma, I) \longrightarrow \mathcal{P}(S)$ or as a partial mapping from $S \times \mathbf{M}(\Sigma, I)$ into S if the fat-system is deterministic.

7.3.1 Processes

Let $\tau = (\Sigma, R, E, X, \Delta)$ be a fat-system. In this section we shall note local transitions $(s', s'') \in \delta_a$, $a \in \Sigma$, of τ as triples (s', a, s''). We begin with the definition of sequential processes.

A *sequential process* in τ is a sequence

$$p = (s_1, a_1, s_1'), (s_2, a_2, s_2'), \ldots, (s_n, a_n, s_n')$$

of transitions such that

Seq1: for all i, j $(1 \leq i < j \leq n)$ and for all $r \in R$, if $r \in Ea_i \cap Ea_j$ and $\forall k$, $(i \leq k < j)$, $r \notin a_k E$ then $s_i(r) = s_j(r)$.

Seq2: for all i, j $(1 \leq i < j \leq n)$ and for all $r \in R$, if $r \in a_i E \cap E a_j$ and $\forall k, i < k < j, r \notin a_k E$ then $s_i'(r) = s_j(r)$,

Intuitively, **Seq1** states that if two actions a_i and a_j read the value of a register r and this register was not modified by any action following a_i and preceding a_j then they should read the same value. Condition **Seq 2** specifies which value a_j reads from a register r, this is the value written by the last action preceding a_j and writing into r. Note that **Seq1** is redundant for actions preceded by some writing action, since in this case **Seq2** implies **Seq1**. However, **Seq1** is necessary if a_i and a_j are not preceded by any action writing into r in order to specify that in this case both actions read the same "initial" value of r.

Example 7.3.2 Let us consider the fat-system of Example 7.2.1. Then $p = u_1 u_2 u_3 u_4 u_5 u_6 u_7$ is a sequential process in τ, where
$u_1 = (\{(r_1, 0)\}, a, \{(r_1, 1)\})$, $u_2 = (\{(r_2, 1)\}, b, \{(r_2, 2)\})$,
$u_3 = (\{(r_1, 1), (r_2, 2)\}, c, \{(r_1, 0)\})$, $u_4 = (\{(r_2, 2)\}, b, \{(r_2, 1)\})$,
$u_5 = (\{(r_1, 0)\}, a, \{(r_1, 1)\})$, $u_6 = (\{(r_1, 1)\}, a, \{(r_1, 2)\})$,
$u_7 = (\{(r_1, 2), (r_2, 1)\}, c, \{(r_1, 0)\})$.

Intuitively, to obtain a concurrent process from a sequential process p we transform each local transition (s_i, a_i, s_i') of p into the labelled graph presented on Figure 7.5, where $Ea = \{r_{i_1}, \ldots, r_{i_k}\}$, $aE = \{r_{j_1}', \ldots, r_{j_n}'\}$, $\forall l \ (1 \leq l \leq k) \ s_i(r_{i_l}) = x_{i_l}$; $\forall l \ (1 \leq l \leq n) \ s_i'(r_{j_l}') = x_{j_l}'$.

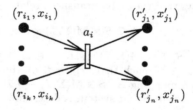

Figure 7.5: Causal dependence relation for a single local transition

The vertices labelled by (r_{i_l}, x_{i_l}) represent the events consisting of reading the value x_{i_l} from register r_{i_l}, the vertices labelled by (r_{j_l}', x_{j_l}') represent the events of writing x_{j_l}' into r_{j_l}', finally the vertex labelled by a_i represents the execution of a_i. Next we simply identify the reading events with the corresponding writing events produced by preceding local transitions. In this way we obtain the causal precedence relation *Caus* over the set of events. As it turns out there are temporal precedence relations between the events that do not result from the causality relation, e.g. when we have two actions writing into the same register that mutually do not communicate directly. This temporal precedence is captured by the relation *Pred* over the events. The description of *Pred* being a bit tricky, is postponed for a moment.

Now we pass to the formal definition.

A concurrent process is a labelled relational structure $cp = (Events, Caus, Pred, \lambda)$, where

— *Events* is a set of events,

— *Caus* and *Pred* are two relations over *Events*, they are called respectively *direct causality* and *direct precedence* relations,

— $\lambda : Events \longrightarrow \Sigma \cup (R \times X)$ is a labelling of events.

Intuitively, if an event $e \in Events$ is labelled by $a \in \Sigma$, i.e., $\lambda(e) = a$, then e represents an execution of the action a in cp, otherwise, if $\lambda(e) = (r, x) \in R \times X$ then e represents a state of r, where r contains the value x.

The relation *Caus* describes the causal dependence between events, if $z_1 Caus^* z_2$, $z_1 \neq z_2$, then z_1 is, possibly indirect, cause of z_2. The relation *Pred* describes the necessary temporal relations between events, if $z_1 Pred^* z_2$, $z_1 \neq z_2$, then the event z_1 precedes z_2. We always have the inclusion $Caus \subseteq Pred$, i.e. causality implies temporal precedence.

Instead of giving a list of condition characterizing concurrent processes we describe how a sequential process can be transformed into a concurrent one. This transformation will be denoted by Ψ.

Let

$$p = (s_1, a_1, s_1'), \ldots, (s_n, a_n, s_n') \tag{7.1}$$

be a sequential process. The corresponding concurrent process is the labelled relational structure

$$cp = \Psi(p) = (Events, Caus, Pred, \lambda)$$

The set *Events* is the union of two disjoint sets $Events_\Sigma$ and $Events_R$. The set $Events_\Sigma$ consists of exactly n elements:

$$Events_\Sigma = \{e_1, \ldots, e_n\}$$

where $n = |p|$ is the number of transition occurrences in p. An event $e_i \in Events_\Sigma$ represents the action occurrence a_i, hence

$$\lambda(e_i) = a_i, \quad 1 \leq i \leq n$$

The set $Events_R$ is the union

$$Events_R = \bigcup_{r \in R} Events_r$$

where

$$Events_r = \lambda^{-1}(\{r\} \times X), \quad r \in R$$

is the set of events representing consecutive states of the register r. This set is obtained in the following way.

Let $\Pi_r : \Sigma^* \longrightarrow \Sigma^*$ be the erasing morphism preserving only actions writing into r:

$$\Pi_r(a) = \left\{ \begin{array}{ll} a & \text{if } (a, r) \in E \\ 1 & \text{otherwise} \end{array} \right.$$

Let $m_r = |\Pi_r(a_1 \dots a_n)|$, i.e. there are exactly m_r action occurrences in p writing into r. Then

$$Events_r = \left\{ \begin{array}{ll} \{w_{r0}, w_{r1}, \dots, w_{rm_r}\} & \text{if } \exists k \ (1 \leq k \leq n) \ (r, a_k) \in E \text{ and} \\ & \Pi_r(a_1 \dots a_{k-1}) = 1 \\ \{w_{r1}, \dots, w_{rm_r}\} & \text{otherwise} \end{array} \right.$$

Intuitively, w_{rk}, $1 \leq k \leq m_r$, represents the state of r after k-th writing into r. If there is k, $1 \leq k \leq n$, such that the k-th transition of p reads r but no preceding transition writes into r then $Events_r$ contains also the event w_{r0} corresponding to the "initial" state of r.

For each k, $1 \leq k \leq m_r$, we set

$$i_k = \min\{j \mid 1 \leq j \leq n \text{ and } |\Pi_r(a_1 \dots a_j)| = k\} \qquad (7.2)$$

From the definition of Π_r it follows that $(a_{i_k}, r) \in E$ and, in fact, a_{i_k} is the k-th action occurrence writing into r in p. The label of w_{rk} is defined by

$$\lambda(w_{rk}) = (r, s'_{i_k}(r))$$

i.e. w_{rk} is labelled by a pair (r, x), where $x \in X$ is the k-th value written into r. If $w_{r0} \in Events_r$ then we set additionally

$$\lambda(w_{r0}) = (r, s_k(r))$$

for any k such that $(r, a_k) \in E$ and $\Pi_r(a_1 \dots a_{k-1}) = 1$. (Note that if there are several actions reading the value of r before this value is overwritten by other actions of p then **Seq1** assures that all of them read the same value, i.e. this definition is consistent.)

The relation $Caus$ is the union of two relations

$$Caus = Read_R \cup Write_R$$

where

$$Read_R = \bigcup_{r \in R} Read_r \text{ and } Write_R = \bigcup_{r \in R} Write_r$$

The relation $Write_r$ codes the direct causality relation between action occurrences writing into r and events representing the state of r immediately after this writing:

$$Write_r = \{(e_{i_k}, w_{rk}) \in Events_\Sigma \times Events_r \mid 1 \leq k \leq m\}$$

where i_k is given by Eq. 7.2.

The relation $Read_r$, $r \in R$, consists of pairs of events (w_{rj}, e_l) such that a_l is the action occurrence reading the state of r represented by w_{rj}:

$$Read_r = \{(w_{rj}, e_l) \in Events_r \times Events_\Sigma \mid (r, a_l) \in E \text{ and } j = |\Pi_r(a_1 \ldots a_{l-1})|\}$$

Note that in particular if $\Pi_r(a_1 \ldots a_{l-1}) = 1$ and $r \in Ea_l$ then $(w_{r0}, e_l) \in Read_r$, i.e. a_l reads the initial value of r.

As an example we show on Figure 7.6 the concurrent process $\Psi(p) = (Events, Caus, Pred, \lambda)$ obtained for the sequential process p from Example 7.3.2.

From now on we assume that the following rule is adopted in the graphical representation of concurrent processes: continuous arcs represent the elements of the direct causality relation $Caus$, while dashed arcs represent the elements of $Pred \setminus Caus$, i.e. the pairs of events that should be added to $Caus$ to obtain the direct precedence relation $Pred$; since always $Caus \subseteq Pred$ this representation is unambiguous. (The relation $Pred$ is defined below.)

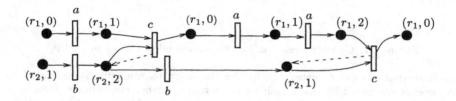

Figure 7.6: The concurrent process $\Psi(p)$.

The direct precedence relation $Pred$ is the union

$$Pred = Caus \cup Before_R \cup While_R$$

where
$$Before_R = \bigcup_{r \in R} Before_r \text{ and } While_R = \bigcup_{r \in R} While_r$$

To introduce the relation $Before_R$ let us consider the following example:

Example 7.3.3 Let

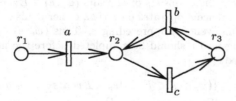

be a signature of a fat-system with the following local transitions relations

δ_a

r_1	r_2
1	1

δ_b

r_3	r_2
2	2

δ_c

r_2	r_3
1	2
2	0

Let $u_a = (\{(r_1,1)\}, a, \{(r_2,1)\})$, $u_b = (\{(r_3,2)\}, b, \{(r_2,2)\})$, $u_1 = (\{(r_2,1)\}, c, \{(r_3,2)\})$, $u_2 = (\{(r_2,2)\}, c, \{(r_3,0)\})$ and let $p_1 = u_a u_b$, $p_2 = u_b u_a$ be two sequential processes in this system. Both processes yield the same causality relation $(Events, Caus, \lambda)$ that is presented on Figure 7.7.

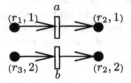

Figure 7.7: Causality relation for the sequential processes p_1 and p_2.

Note that the events generated by the transition u_a are causally unrelated to the events generated by the transition u_b, actually neither the value written by a is used by b nor the result of execution of b is used by a. Although, the transitions u_a and u_b are completely causally unrelated, their order is important for the final state of the system — in p_1 the final value of r_2 is 2, in p_2 it is 1. The difference between p_1 and p_2 is even more evident if we remark that $u_a u_b u_2$ and $u_b u_a u_1$ are valid sequential processes while $u_a u_b u_1$ and $u_b u_a u_2$ are not valid. The causality relations for $u_a u_b u_2$ and $u_b u_a u_1$ are presented on Figure 7.8.

From this example we see that the information provided by the relation $Caus$ is somehow incomplete. For these reason we add information about the temporal precedence of events which is captured by the relation $Pred$. In fact in the processes p_1 and p_2 in Example 7.3.3 actions a and b cannot be executed in parallel since u_a and u_b modify r_2, in p_1 we cannot start the execution of b before the modification of r_2 by a is completed, which yields the situation presented on Figure 7.9.

The temporal precedence just described is captured by the relations $Before_r$, $r \in R$. Intuitively, $Before_r$ consists of all pairs $(w_r, e) \in Events_r \times Events_\Sigma$ such that the action occurrence e operates on r (i.e., either reads r or writes into r) and w_r is the last writing event for r preceding e. Thus $(w_r, e) \in Before_r$ represents the fact that writing into r should be completed before the next action operating on r can be executed

$$Before_r = \{(w_{rj}, e_l) \in Events_r \times Events_\Sigma \mid r \in a_l E \cup E a_l \text{ and } |\Pi_r(a_1 \ldots a_{l-1})| = j\}$$

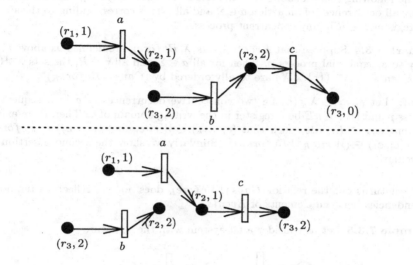

Figure 7.8: Causality relations for $u_a u_b u_2$ and $u_b u_a u_1$.

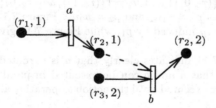

Figure 7.9: *Caus* and *Before$_R$* relations for p_1

Note that always $Read_r \subseteq Before_r$. To complete the definition we set $Before_R = \bigcup_{r \in R} Before_r$.

The following remark shows that the relation $Caus \cup Before_R$ enables to order totally all occurrences of an action $a \in \Sigma$ and all events corresponding to the states of a register $r \in R$ in any concurrent process.

Remark 7.3.4 Suppose that $Events, Caus, \lambda, Before_R$ are defined as above relatively to a sequential process p. Then for all $a \in \Sigma$ and all $r \in R$, the sets $\lambda^{-1}(a)$ and $Events_r = \lambda^{-1}(\{r\} \times X)$ are totally ordered by $(Caus \cup Before_R)^*$.

Proof: Let $e_i, e_j \in \lambda^{-1}(a)$ be two consecutive occurrences of a in a sequential process p and let $r \in aE$ be a register in the writing domain of a. Then there exists an event $w_{rk} \in Events_r$ such that $(e_i, w_{rk}) \in Write_r$ and $(w_{rk}, e_j) \in Before_r$. Thus $(e_i, e_j) \in (Write_R \cup Before_R)^2$. Similarly we show the second assertion of the remark.

$\square$

As it turns out the relation $Caus \cup Before_R$ does not yet reflect all temporal dependencies between elements of $Events$.

Example 7.3.5 Let us consider a fat-system with the signature

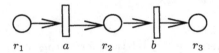

$$r_1 \qquad a \qquad r_2 \qquad b \qquad r_3$$

and the following transition relations

δ_a	r_1	r_2
	0	1
	1	0

δ_b	r_2	r_3
	0	0
	1	1

Let $u_1 = (\{(r_2, 0)\}, b, \{(r_3, 0)\})$ and $u_2 = (\{(r_1, 1)\}, a, \{(r_2, 0)\})$ and let us consider the sequential processes $p_1 = u_1 u_2$ and $p_2 = u_2 u_1$. Figure 7.10 represents the relations $Caus$ and $Before_R$ induced by p_1, while Figure 7.11 gives the same relations for p_2.

Note that Figure 7.11 indicates clearly that a is executed before b, while Figure 7.10 may suggest that a and b can be executed in parallel. However, since a modifies r_2 it cannot be executed until the action b operating also on r_2 is completed.

To complete the definition of the direct precedence relation $Pred$ we should closely analyse the situation. First let us note that the events of $Events_\Sigma$ and of $Events_R$ are of quite different nature. Each element e of $Events_\Sigma$ represents an action occurrence, i.e. an event that is instantaneous (or at least that can be considered as such by the assumption of atomicity of the action execution). On the other hand, the elements of $Events_R$ represent states of registers, i.e. by their very nature

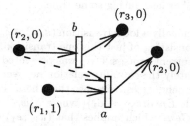

Figure 7.10. Relations $Caus$ and $Before_R$ for p_1 (dashed arrow represents an element of $Before_R \setminus Caus$).

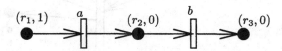

Figure 7.11. $Caus$ and $Before_R$ relations for p_2 (here $Before_R \subseteq Caus$, therefore $Before_R$ is not visible on the picture).

they are not instantaneous but rather span over some period of time. This point of view can also be justified by the following consideration. As it was mentioned previously, intuitively, elements of $Events_R$ are obtained by an identification of events consisting in writing into registers with subsequent matching reading events. While both writing and reading regarded separately can be considered as instantaneous (atomic), we cannot pretend by any means that the resulting composed events are instantaneous, they rather last during some time.

Let us consider specifically a local transition $(s, s') \in \delta_a$ of $a \in \Sigma$ and a sequential process $p' = (s, a, s')$ consisting of just this one transition. The causality relation of the corresponding concurrent process $\Psi(p')$ was presented on Figure 7.5. While this graph represents accurately the causality relation between events, it may not reflect all possible temporal dependencies. Suppose that there is a register $r \in (Ea) \setminus (aE)$. Then $Events_r = \{w_{r0}\}$, $Events_\Sigma = \{e_1\}$, where $\lambda(w_{r0}) = (r, s(r))$ and $\lambda(e_1) = a$. Moreover, $(w_{r0}, e_1) \in Caus$ which implies that $(w_{r0}, e_1) \in Pred$, i.e. w_{r0} precedes e_1 in the temporal order. However in some sense w_{r0} also coexists with e_1 and immediately follows e_1 in the temporal order. In fact, during the execution of a no other action can write into r, therefore during this execution and immediately after it the value of r remains unchanged and we can assume that also $(e_1, w_{r0}) \in Pred$. Thus the parallel process $\Psi((s, a, s'))$ should be represented by the labelled relational structure given on Figure 7.12.

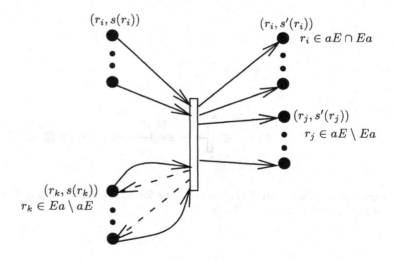

Figure 7.12: Concurrent process generated by one transition (s, a, s').

In general for a sequential process p of the form (7.1) the precedence relation discussed above is captured by the relations $While_r$:

$$While_r = U_r \cup U_r^{-1}, \text{ where}$$
$$U_r = \{(w_{rj}, e_k) \in Events_r \times Events_\Sigma \mid \ r \in (Ea_k) \setminus (a_k E) \text{ and}$$
$$j = |\Pi_r(a_1 \ldots a_{k-1})|\}$$

Now we set

$$While_R = \bigcup_{r \in R} While_r$$

and we can complete the definition of concurrent processes by defining

$$Pred = Caus \cup Before_R \cup While_R$$

Note that $U_r \subseteq Write_r$ and if $U_r \neq \emptyset$ for some $r \in R$ then the relation $Pred$ is not acyclic.

We shall illustrate the complete definition of processes with a few examples. First, to terminate Example 7.3.5 we give on Figure 7.13 the representation of the concurrent processes $\Psi(p_1)$ and $\Psi(p_2)$.

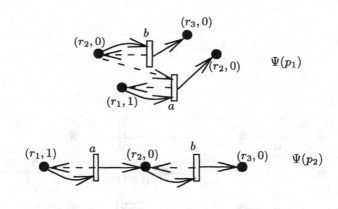

Figure 7.13: Concurrent processes $\Psi(p_1)$ and $\Psi(p_2)$.

Example 7.3.6 Let τ be a fat-system with the signature σ presented on Figure 7.14.

The transition relations of τ are presented below:

δ_a	r_1	r_3	r_1
	0	0	1
	1	1	0

δ_b	r_3	r_2
	0	1
	1	0

δ_c	r_1	r_2	r_3
	1	1	1
	0	0	0

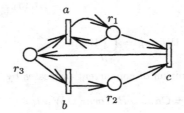

Figure 7.14: A signature σ.

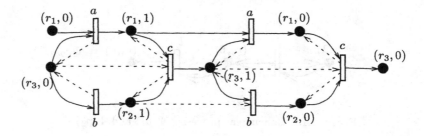

Figure 7.15: A concurrent process.

Figure 7.15 represents a concurrent process in τ.

At the end let us note that there is also an alternative possibility of defining the concurrent processes as equivalence classes of sequential processes.

Let Tr be the set of local transitions of a fat-system τ and let I be the independence relation over Σ induced by the signature of τ. This relation extends naturally to Tr: two transitions $u_1 = (s_1, a, s_1')$ and $u_2 = (s_2, b, s_2')$ are said to be independent, $(u_1, u_2) \in I$, if the underlying actions are independent, $(a, b) \in I$. Analogously we can define the relation $\sim_I$ over the set Tr^* of sequences of transitions as the smallest congruence such that $\forall (u_1, u_2) \in I,\ u_1 u_2 \sim_I u_2 u_1$. Let $\Pi : Tr^* \longrightarrow \Sigma^*$ be the morphism mapping each transition (s, a, s') to the underlying action a. Then for all sequences $p_1, p_2 \in Tr^*$ of transitions, $p_1 \sim_I p_2$ iff $\Pi(p_1) \sim_I \Pi(p_2)$. As it turns out for each sequential process p in τ we can identify the corresponding concurrent process $\Psi(p)$ with the equivalence class of p under $\sim_I$:

Proposition 7.3.7 *(i) Let p be a sequential process in τ and let $p' \in Tr^*$ be any sequence of transitions such that $p \sim_I p'$. Then p' is a sequential process.*
(ii) Let p, p' be two sequential processes in τ. Then $p \sim_I p'$ if and only if $\Psi(p) = \Psi(p')$.

Proof: Straightforward but tedious induction on the length of p. □

Proposition 7.3.7 implies that we can identify concurrent processes with the equivalence classes $[p]_I$ of $\sim_I$ for p ranging over sequential processes. This definition would have had the advantage of being technically simpler than the definition of the labelled relational structures $\Psi(p)$, which is rather complicate. Nevertheless, we have preferred to introduce the concurrent processes by means of $\Psi(p)$ since this representation reflects better the intuitive ideas lying behind this concept — it provides explicitly the causality and temporal precedence relations between events giving direct insight into the behaviour of the fat-systems.

7.3.2 Semantics Based on Partial Order of Action Occurrences

In this subsection we introduce non-interleaving semantics of the fat-systems that takes into account only the action occurrences. As we shall see below cp-graphs representing the behaviour of the fat-systems in this semantics are directly related to traces, actually they constitute a representation of traces suitable for the fat-systems.

Let $\sigma = (\Sigma, R, E)$ be a fixed signature and let x be a word of Σ^*, $x = a_1 a_2 \ldots a_n$. A *causal and precedence graph* (cp-graph for short) for x is the labelled relational structure $\Psi_\sigma(x) = (Ev_x, Ca_x, Pr_x, \lambda_x)$, where

— $Ev_x = \{e_1, \ldots, e_n\}$ is the set of events, $\mathrm{card}(Ev_x) = |x|$,

— $\lambda_x : Ev_x \longrightarrow \Sigma$ is a labelling such that $\forall i,\ (1 \leq i \leq n),\ \lambda(e_i) = a_i$,

— Ca_x and Pr_x are acyclic relations over Ev_x called respectively *direct causality relation* and *direct precedence relation*.

The direct causality relation is defined in the following way:

$$Ca_x = \{(e_i, e_j) \in Ev_x \times Ev_x \mid \ 1 \leq i < j \leq n \text{ and}$$
$$\exists r \in a_i E \cap Ea_j, \ \forall l \ (i < l < j) \ r \notin a_l E\}$$

The direct precedence relation is defined in the following way:
$(e_i, e_j) \in Pr_x$ if $1 \leq i < j \leq n$ and at least one of the following conditions holds:

- $\exists r \in a_i E \cap Ea_j, \ \forall l \ (i < l < j) \ r \notin a_l E$

- $\exists r \in a_i E \cap a_j E, \ \forall l \ (i < l < j) \ r \notin a_l E$

- $\exists r \in Ea_i \cap a_j E, \ \forall l \ (i \leq l < j) \ r \notin a_l E$

The elements of Ev_x correspond to the occurrences of actions in the word x, e_i being the occurrence of a_i. A pair of events (e_i, e_j) is in Ca_x if for some register r the action occurrence $a_i = \lambda_x(e_i)$ writes into r a value that is subsequently read by the action occurrence $a_j = \lambda_x(e_j)$, i.e. no other action between a_i and a_j overwrites the value written into r by a_i (intuitively, there is a direct communication from a_i to a_j by means of the register r).

The direct precedence relations Pr_x consists of pairs of events (e_i, e_j) that are in conflict for some register r. Three cases are distinguishable:

- the action occurrence a_i writes into r a value that is subsequently read by the action occurrence a_j,

- the action occurrences a_i and a_j write to the same register and a_j overwrites the value written by a_i (there is no action occurrence between a_i and a_j writing into r),

- the action occurrence a_i reads the value of r and a_j is the first subsequent action occurrence modifying r.

Note that the first of these conditions corresponds to the definition of Ca_x, i.e. $Ca_x \subseteq Pr_x$.

Intuitively, Ca_x illustrates how the information passes from one action occurrence to another during the execution of x by any fat-system with the signature σ while $Prec_x$ represents the the pairs of action occurrences that are in conflict over some register and for this reason their order is significant for the final outcome of the execution and cannot be altered. Taking the reflexive and transitive closures of Ca_x and Pr_x we obtain partial orders over the set Ev_x: $(e_i, e_j) \in Ca_x^*$ if e_i is (possibly indirect) cause of e_j and $(e_i, e_j) \in Pr_x^*$ if e_i necessarily precedes e_j. If neither $(e_i, e_j) \in Pr_x^*$ nor $(e_j, e_i) \in Pr_x^*$ then the events e_i and e_j can occur simultaneously or in any order.

cp-graphs are closely related to concurrent processes. Let τ be a fat-system over a signature σ. Let $p = u_1 \ldots u_n$ be a sequential process in τ, where $u_i = (s_i, a_i, s_i')$ and let $\Psi(p) = (Events, Caus, Pred, \lambda)$ be the corresponding concurrent process. It is easy to see that $\Psi(p)$ determines (up to isomorphism) the cp-graph $\Psi_\sigma(y)$ of the sequence $y = a_1 \ldots a_n$ of actions of p.

Example 7.3.8 Let σ be the signature of Example 7.2.1 and let $x = abcbabac$. The cp-graph $\Psi_\sigma(x)$ is presented on Figure 7.16. As in the case of parallel processes, continuous arcs show elements of Ca_x while dashed arcs indicate the elements of Pr_x that are not in Ca_x.

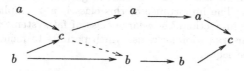

Figure 7.16: cp-graph $\Psi_\sigma(abcbaac)$

As it turns out the cp-graphs constitute in fact a representation of traces:

Proposition 7.3.9 *Let σ be a signature, $x, y \in \Sigma^*$, $\Psi_\sigma(x) = (Ev_x, Ca_x, Pr_x, \lambda_x)$, $\Psi_\sigma(y) = (Ev_y, Ca_y, Pr_y, \lambda_y)$ and finally let I be the independence relation induced by σ. Then the following facts are equivalent*

- $x \sim_I y$,

- $\Psi_\sigma(x) = \Psi_\sigma(y)$ *(i.e. the cp-graphs of x and y are isomorphic)*,

- (Ev_x, Pr_x, λ_x) *and* (Ev_y, Pr_y, λ_y) *are isomorphic labelled graphs,*

Proof: Straightforward induction on the length of words.   □

One may wonder why we use the cp-graph $\Psi_\sigma(x)$ to characterize the trace $[x]_I$, as Proposition 7.3.9 shows that the trace is characterized unambiguously by the triple (Ev_x, Pr_x, λ_x) and therefore the relation Ca_x seems to be useless. However, the relation Ca_x that is essential for the characterization of the runs of the asynchronous automata over traces and therefore determines the recognizability power of asynchronous automata (cf. Section 7.6). On the other hand the relation Pr_x is also necessary since Ca_x cannot in general characterize traces as the following example shows.

Example 7.3.10 Let σ be the following signature:

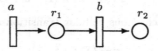

Then the traces $[y]_I$ and $[z]_I$, where $y = aba$, $z = aab$, are different but (Ev_y, Ca_y, λ_y) and (Ev_z, Ca_z, λ_z) are isomorphic labelled relational structures.

7.4 Asynchronous Cellular Transition Systems

In this section we introduce a special subclass of fat-systems — asynchronous cellular transition systems. This class is characterized by a particularly simple form of signatures. The simplicity of asynchronous cellular transition systems often facilitates formal reasoning and enables better insight into constructions carried out in the next sections. The importance of this class is also emphasizes by the fact that, as we shall see in Section 7.5, a large class of fat-systems is equivalent with asynchronous cellular transition systems, which permits to focus our attention on the latter class in the sequel.

Definition 7.4.1 *A signature $\sigma = (\Sigma, R, E)$ is simple if $\forall a \in \Sigma, \mathrm{card}(aE) = 1$ and the mapping associating with each action $a \in \Sigma$ the unique register of aE is a bijection between Σ and R.*

Formally, *finite asynchronous cellular transition systems* (or fact-systems in short) are asynchronous transition systems with simple signatures.

Up to now we have assumed that the sets Σ and R are disjoint, however in the case of fact-systems it is convenient to identify every action a with the unique register r_a that a can modify, $aE = \{r_a\}$.

Let $\tau = (\Sigma, R, E, X, \Delta)$ be a finite asynchronous cellular transition system. Let $C = \{(a, b) \in \Sigma \mid aE \cap Eb \neq \emptyset\}$ be the direct causality relation induced by σ. Let us note that $E \cap (R \times \Sigma) = \{(r_a, b) \in R \times \Sigma \mid (a, b) \in C\}$, while $E \cap (\Sigma \times R) = \{(a, r_a) \mid a \in \Sigma\}$. Thus we see that if we identify every register r_a with a then $E \cap (\Sigma \times R)$ becomes the identity relation while $E \cap (R \times \Sigma)$ collapses to C.

Let $s \in \mathbf{F}(\alpha; X)$, $\alpha \subseteq R$, be a partial state and let $\alpha' = E\alpha = \{a \in \Sigma \mid r_a \in \alpha\}$. Then s will be identified with the mapping $s' \in \mathbf{F}(\alpha'; X)$ such that $s'(a) = s(r_a)$, in particular, for each $a \in \Sigma$, $\mathbf{F}(Ea; X)$ is replaced by $\mathbf{F}(Ca; X)$. Therefore, instead of speaking of the state of register r_a we can speak about the state of the cell $a \in \Sigma$. (In the case of fact-systems we use double terminology when speaking about elements of Σ— we call them cells if we have in mind the registers associated with $a \in \Sigma$, or actions if we consider them rather as actions in the system).

Let us consider the set $\mathbf{F}(aE; X) = \mathbf{F}(\{r_a\}; X)$. Now this set is replaced by $\mathbf{F}(\{a\}; X)$. However, the set of mappings from a one element domain is naturally isomorphic with the co-domain X, under this isomorphism each $s \in \mathbf{F}(\{a\}; X)$ is identified with the value $x = s(a)$. Therefore we replace the local transition relations $\delta_a \subseteq \mathbf{F}(Ea; X) \times \mathbf{F}(aE; X)$, $a \in \Sigma$ by the relations

$$\delta_a \subseteq \mathbf{F}(Ca; X) \times X, \quad a \in \Sigma \tag{7.3}$$

In conclusion, an asynchronous cellular transition system can be viewed as a quadruple

$$\tau = (\Sigma, C, X, \Delta)$$

where

— Σ is the set of cells (actions),

— C is a binary relation over Σ,

— X is the set of values (local states),

— $\Delta = \{\delta_a \mid a \in \Sigma\}$ is the set of transition relations that have the form defined by (7.3).

As previously the global states of τ are mappings from Σ into X and $S = \mathbf{F}(\Sigma; X)$ will stand for the set of global states.

The global transition relation

$$\Delta \subseteq S \times \Sigma \times S$$

is defined in the following way:

for all $s', s'' \in S$ and $a \in \Sigma$, $(s', a, s'') \in \Delta$ if

$$(s'_{|Ca}, s''(a)) \in \delta_a \text{ and} \tag{7.4}$$

$$\forall b \in \Sigma \setminus \{a\}, \ s''(b) = s'(b) \tag{7.5}$$

To maintain the analogy with fat-systems the pair $\sigma = (\Sigma, C)$ will be called the signature of the fact-system τ.

We can imagine an asynchronous cellular transition system in the following way. Let $\mathcal{G} = (\Sigma, C)$ be the (directed) graph of the relation C. A global state $s \in \mathbf{F}(\Sigma; X)$ associates with each vertex $a \in \Sigma$ of $\mathcal{G}$ its state $s(a) \in X$. How an action a is executed in this automaton? Intuitively, a reads the states of all vertices b such that there is an arc from b to a in $\mathcal{G}$ ($(b, a) \in C$), which yields a mapping $s \in \mathbf{F}(Ca; X)$ — the partial state of the system induced by the neighbourhood of a. Next a chooses a value $x \in X$ such that $(s, x) \in \delta_a$ and takes this value as its new state. (If for all $x \in X$, $(s, x) \notin \delta_a$ then a is not enabled and cannot be executed.) Thus the execution of a does not change the states of the other cells (cf. 7.5), and the new state of a depends only on the states of its neighbours from Ca (cf. 7.4).

Let us note that in fact-systems the writing conflict relation W is the identity thus the conflict relation has the form

$$D = C \cup C^{-1} \cup id_\Sigma$$

i.e. two different actions cannot be executed simultaneously iff their cells are adjacent in the graph $\mathcal{G}$.

From now on we shall always note fact-systems as quadruples $\tau = (\Sigma, C, X, \Delta)$ defined above. Thus formally fact-systems have different form than fat-systems, nevertheless we continue to view them as a special kind of fat-systems since we can always recover the underlying fat-system by reintroducing a register r_a for each action $a \in \Sigma$.

Example 7.4.2 Let C be the binary relation over $\Sigma = \{a, b, c, d\}$ presented below and let $X = \{0, 1\}$.

We shall consider an fact-system with the following local transition relations

δ_a	d	a
	0	1
	1	0

δ_b	a	b	b
	1	0	1
	0	1	0

δ_c	b	d	c
	0	0	1
	1	1	0

δ_d	c	d	d
	1	0	1
	0	1	0

The graph of the global transition relation for this system is presented on Figure 7.17.

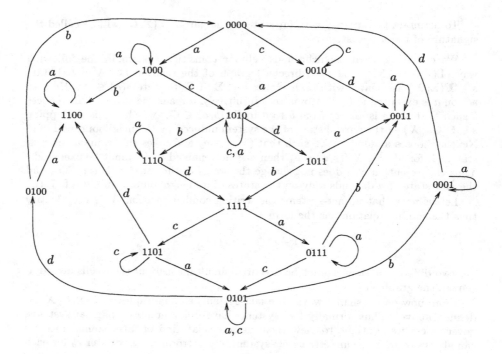

Figure 7.17. Global transition relation. Each global state s is represented by the vector $(s(a), s(b), s(c), s(d))$ of four values of cells a, b, c, d.

At the end let us note that cp-graph semantics for fact-systems has particularly simple form. Let $\sigma = (\Sigma, C)$ be a signature of a fact-system and let $y = a_1 \ldots a_n$. Then the cp-graph $\Psi_\sigma(y)$ for y is the labelled relational structure

$$\Psi_\sigma(y) = (Ev_y, Ca_y, Pr_y, \lambda_y)$$

where
— $Ev_y = \{e_1, \ldots, e_n\}$, $\text{card}(Ev_y) = n$,
— $\lambda_y(e_i) = a_i$ for $1 \leq i \leq n$,
— $Ca_y = \{(e_i, e_j) \in Ev_y \times Ev_y \mid i < j \text{ and } (a_i, a_j) \in C \text{ and } \forall k \ (i < k < j) \ a_i \neq a_k \neq a_j\}$
— $Pr_y = \{(e_i, e_j) \in Ev_y \times Ev_y \mid i < j \text{ and } (a_i, a_j) \in D \text{ and } \forall k \ (i < k < j) \ a_i \neq a_k \neq a_j\}$, where $D = C \cup C^{-1} \cup id_\Sigma$ is the conflict relation induced by σ.

As in the general case of fat-systems, $Ca_y \subseteq Pr_y$ and both these relations are acyclic.

7.5 Simulations Between Asynchronous Transition Systems

In this section we examine the question of how to simulate one fat-system by another. First we fix the terminology.

A subset U of the set S of global states of a fat-system τ is *closed under transitions* if $\forall s \in U, \forall a \in \Sigma, \Delta(s, a) \subseteq U$.

Let τ_i, $i = 1, 2$, be fat-systems over the same alphabet Σ and let S_i, Δ_i be respectively the sets of global states and the global transition relations of τ_i.

Definition 7.5.1 *The fat-system τ_2 covers τ_1 if there exists a subset U of S_2 closed under transitions and a surjective mapping (called* covering *of τ_2) $c : U \longrightarrow S_1$ such that $\forall s \in U, \forall a \in \Sigma$, c maps bijectively the set $\Delta(s, a)$ onto $\Delta(c(s), a)$.*

Intuitively the covering relation describes the simulation of τ_2 by τ_1.

Proposition 7.5.2 *Let τ_i, $i = 1, 2$, be two fat-systems and let $c : U \longrightarrow S_1$ be a covering of τ_1 by τ_2, $U \subseteq S_2$. Then*
(i) for all $s' \in U$, for all $x \in \Sigma$, if $s'' \in \Delta_2(s', x)$ then $s'' \in U$ and $c(s'') \in \Delta_1(c(s'), x)$
(ii) for all $s'_1, s''_1 \in S_1$, for all $x \in \Sigma^*$, if $s''_1 \in \Delta_1(s'_1, x)$ then $\forall s'_2 \in c^{-1}(s'_1)$, $\exists s''_2 \in c^{-1}(s''_1)$, $s''_2 \in \Delta_2(s'_2, x)$

Proof: Straightforward.   □

The covering relation is transitive, if τ_1 is covered by τ_2 and τ_2 is covered by τ_3 then τ_3 covers τ_1. It is also reflexive, τ covers itself by the identity mapping. Not all covering mappings are of interest, for example each fat-system τ_1 is covered by a sequential fat-system τ_2 with the signature $(\Sigma, \{r\}, \Sigma \times \{r\} \cup \{r\} \times \Sigma)$, τ_2 stores in r the global state of τ_1. This trivial covering replacing a distributed system by its sequential simulation is not very useful. The coverings that are of interest should not diminish the degree of parallelism of the distributed system — we shall call them faithful.

The rest of this section is devoted to simulations between fat-systems and fact-systems.

One of the main structural properties of fact-systems is the absence of writing conflicts between distinct actions. As it turns out this property is essential since a fat-system τ_1 can be simulated faithfully by an fact-system τ_2 if in τ_1 all writing conflicts between different actions are in some sense redundant.

Let $\sigma = (\Sigma, R, E)$ be a fixed signature. Let us recall that two distinct actions $a, b \in \Sigma$ are in writing conflict if $aE \cap bE \neq \emptyset$. We say that this writing conflict is *redundant* if $(a, b) \in C \cap C^{-1}$, where $C = (E \circ E) \cap \Sigma^2$ is the direct causality relation induced by σ.

In the sequel we shall study signatures σ where all writing conflicts between distinct actions are redundant, i.e. we assume that the condition

$$W \setminus id_\Sigma \subseteq C \cap C^{-1} \tag{7.6}$$

holds, where W and C are respectively the writing conflict and the direct causality relation induced by σ. A signature satisfying (7.6) will be called *w-redundant*.

Example 7.5.3 Let us consider the signature presented on Figure 7.18.

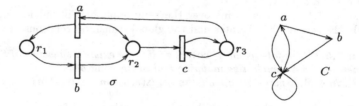

Figure 7.18. A signature with a non-redundant writing conflict relation and its direct causality relation.

The actions a and b are in writing conflict since they write into the same register r_2. The action a can send informations directly to b by means of the register r_1, $(a, b) \in C$, however $(b, a) \notin C$, i.e. this writing conflict is not redundant.

Proposition 7.5.4 *Let $\sigma = (\Sigma, R, E)$ be a w-redundant signature and let $\tau = (\Sigma, R, E, X, \Delta)$ be an asynchronous transition system over σ. Let $C = (E \circ E) \cap \Sigma^2$ be the direct causality relation induced by σ. Then there exists an asynchronous cellular transition system $\tau' = (\Sigma, C, X', \Delta')$ covering τ.*

Proof: In our simulation each local state of a cell $a \in \Sigma$ of the constructed fact-system τ' will consist of two components f and st.

The first component f is a mapping from the set aE of registers that are modified by a in τ into the set X of local states of τ. Intuitively, $f(r)$, for $r \in aE$, gives the last value written into r by a. If a was not yet performed then $f(r)$ contains any initial value of r. However to simulate the behaviour of τ the information provided by f is insufficient.

Suppose for example that for some $r \in R$, $Er = \{a_{i_0}, \ldots, a_{i_{k-1}}\}$ and $b \in rE$ (cf. Figure 7.19).

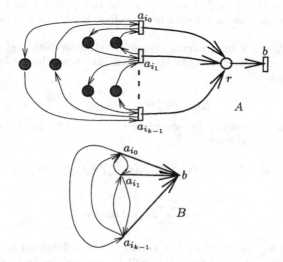

Figure 7.19. (A) In τ, $Er = \{a_{i_0}, \ldots, a_{i_{k-1}}\}$ and $b \in rE$. If σ is w-redundant then $\forall a_{i_m}, a_{i_l} \in Er$, $m \neq l \implies a_{i_m} E \cap E a_{i_l} \neq \emptyset$. (B) In τ', $\{a_{i_0}, \ldots, a_{i_{k-1}}\} \times \{b\} \subseteq C$. If σ is w-redundant then $\forall a_{i_m}, a_{i_l} \in Er$, $(m \neq l)$ $(a_{i_m}, a_{i_l}) \in C$.

Thus $(a_{i_m}, b) \in C$ for all $a_{i_m} \in Er$ and, since the writing conflicts are redundant in τ, we have $(a_{i_m}, a_{i_l}) \in C$ for all $a_{i_m}, a_{i_l} \in Er$, $a_{i_m} \neq a_{i_l}$, i.e. Er is a clique of C. Now suppose that b is executed in τ. Then b reads the contents of r and this value, together with the values of the other registers read by b, is used to determine the transition performed by b.

Let us consider the execution of b in τ': b reads the states of the cells $a_{i_0}, \ldots a_{i_{k-1}}$ obtaining mappings $f_{i_0}, \ldots f_{i_{k-1}}$ respectively and $f_{i_l}(r)$, $0 \leq l < k$, give the last value written into r by a_{i_l}. However to simulate τ, b should know the actual value of r in τ, i.e. it should be able to determine the action of Er that was performed as the last.

To this end the second component of each state of τ' is used — it is called time-stamp. Intuitively, looking solely at the time-stamps of the cells $a_{i_0}, \ldots, a_{i_{k-1}}$ the agent b will be able to determine which of them was performed as the last.

For each register $r \in R$, $TS_r = \{0, \ldots, k-1\}$, where $k = \mathrm{card}(Er)$, will stand for the set of time-stamps associated with r. For each action $a \in \Sigma$ we need a time-stamp for every register $r \in aE$, thus the time-stamps for a are elements of the direct product $T_a = \prod_{r \in aE} TS_r$. Now we can specify formally the set X_a' of local states of $a \in \Sigma$ in τ':

$$X_a' = \mathbf{F}(aE; X) \times T_a$$

Thus $X' = \cup_{a \in \Sigma} X_a'$ is the set of all local states of τ'.

A partial state $u \in \mathbf{F}(\alpha; X')$, $\alpha \subseteq \Sigma$, is said to be valid if $\forall a \in \alpha$, $u(a) \in X_a'$. To explain how time-stamps are used in τ' we fix a linear order $\prec$ over the set Σ of actions.

If $u \in \mathbf{F}(\alpha; X')$ is a valid partial state of τ' then for each register $r \in R$ such that $Er \subseteq \alpha$ we can determine the last action that wrote into r by means of the following algorithm.

Let

$$Er = \{a_{i_0} \prec \ldots \prec a_{i_{k-1}}\} \tag{7.7}$$

i.e. we order the elements of Er according to $\prec$. To determine the value of r we use the local states of the cells of Er.

Let

$$u(a_{i_0}) = (f_{i_0}, ts_{i_0}), \ldots, u(a_{i_{k-1}}) = (f_{i_{k-1}}, ts_{i_{k-1}})$$

and

$$p = \sum_{l=0}^{k-1} ts_{i_l}(r) \bmod k$$

Then the action a_{i_p}, i.e. the $(p+1)$st action on the ordered list (7.7) is considered as the last writing into r. This action will be denoted by $last_u(r)$. Accordingly, $f_{i_p}(r) \in X$ will be taken as the state of r determined by u, this value will be denoted by $value_u(r)$.

Let us note that formally the algorithm given above defines for each valid state $u \in \mathbf{F}(\alpha; X')$ of τ' two mappings

$$last_u : R_u \longrightarrow \Sigma$$

and

$$value_u : R_u \longrightarrow X$$

where $R_u = \{r \in R \mid Er \subseteq \alpha\}$ and such that $\forall r \in R_u$, $last_u(r) \in Er$.

Moreover to compute $last_u(r)$ and $value_u(r)$ we use in fact only the local states $u(a_{i_0}), \ldots, u(a_{i_{k-1}})$, i.e. the partial state $u_{|Er}$.

Now we can define the covering mapping c, its domain is the set

$$U_{valid} = \{u \in \mathbf{F}(\Sigma; X') \mid \forall a \in \Sigma, u(a) \in X_a'\}$$

of valid global states and for $u \in U_{valid}$ we set

$$c(u) = value_u.$$

Now we are able to describe in detail how an execution of an action $a \in \Sigma$ in τ is simulated in τ'.

Let $s_1, s_2 \in S$ be two global states of τ such that $(s_1, a, s_2) \in \Delta$. Let us suppose that s_2 is obtained from s_1 by means of a transition $(s', s'') \in \delta_a$, i.e.

$$s_{1|Ea} = s', \quad s_{2|aE} = s'' \quad \text{and} \quad s_{1|R\setminus(aE)} = s_{2|R\setminus(aE)}.$$

Let $u_1 \in U_{valid}$ be a valid global state of τ' such that

$$c(u_1) = value_{u_1} = s_1, \tag{7.8}$$

i.e. u_1 covers s_1.

Simulating the transition (s_1, a, s_2) of τ in τ' we should obtain a valid global state $u_2 \in U_{valid}$ of τ' such that

(A) $c(u_2) = value_{u_2} = s_2$ (u_2 covers s_2),

(B) $\forall b \in \Sigma \setminus \{a\}$, $u_1(b) = u_2(b)$ (execution of a changes only the local state of a in τ'),

(C) the new local state $u_2(a)$ of a in τ' depends only on the partial state $u_{1|Ca}$ (a cannot access cells that are outside of Ca).

Let $u' = u_{1|Ca}$. First of all let us note that for each $r \in Ea$, $Er \subseteq Ca$, i.e. r is in the domain of $value_{u'}$ and since u_1 covers s_1 we have

$$\forall r \in Ea, \ value_{u'}(r) = value_{u_1}(r) = s_1(r) = s'(r)$$

Thus, intuitively, a can reconstruct s' by means of the partial state u'. Now note that s'' gives the new values of all registers in aE that are written during the execution of a, which implies that s'' is the first component of the new state $u_2(a)$ of a in τ'.

The new time-stamp ts'' of a should be chosen in such a way that immediately after the execution of a this action is indicated as the last action writing into each register $r \in aE$. We shall show how to calculate $ts''(r)$ for $r \in aE$ by means of u'. First note that the signature σ is w-redundant, i.e.

$$(Er \times Er) \setminus id_\Sigma \subseteq C \cap C^{-1}$$

which implies that in particular

$$Er \setminus \{a\} \subseteq Ca \tag{7.9}$$

(see Figure 7.19). Let $Er = \{a_{i_0}, \ldots, a_{i_{k-1}}\}$, where $a_{i_0} \prec \ldots \prec a_{i_{k-1}}$. Since $a \in Er$, there exists m, $0 \leq m < k$, such that $a = a_{i_m}$. From 7.9 it follows that $Er \setminus \{a\}$ is included in the domain of u'. Let

$$(f_{i_l}, ts_{i_l}) = u'(a_{i_l}) \quad \text{for} \quad l \neq m, \ 0 \leq l < k$$

and

$$p_r = \sum_{l=0, l \neq m}^{k-1} ts_{i_l}(r)$$

There exists a unique integer w_r, $0 \leq w_r < k$, such that

$$(p_r + w_r) \bmod k = m$$

and we set

$$ts''(r) = w_r$$

to obtain the time-stamp with required property. In this way we have translated a transition $(s', s'') \in \delta_a$ of τ into a transition $(u', u'') \in \delta'_a$ of τ', where $u'' = (s'', ts'')$. $\square$

Note that the covering constructed in Proposition 7.5.4 is faithful, the conflict relation in the simulated fat-system τ is equal $D = C \cup C^{-1} \cup W$, where W is the writing conflict relation induced by σ, while the conflict relation in the constructed fact-system τ' is equal $D' = C \cup C^{-1} \cup id_\Sigma$. Since $id_\Sigma \subseteq W$ we see that the actions independent in τ remain independent in τ'. The time-stamp system used in the proof of Proposition 7.5.4 is adapted from [178].

Proposition 7.5.5 *Let $\tau = (\Sigma, C, X, \Delta)$ be an fact-system and let $\sigma = (\Sigma, R, E)$ be a w-redundant signature inducing the same causality relation C. Then there exists a fat-system $\tau' = (\Sigma, R, E, X', \Delta')$ over σ covering τ.*

Proof: The main idea of the simulation is the following: at each moment every register $r \in R$ of the constructed fat-system τ' will contain a partial state of the simulated fact-system τ, more precisely it will contain the values of the cells from the set Er in τ.

For each register $r \in R$ of τ' the local states of r are mappings from Er into X, by $X'_r = \mathbf{F}(Er; X)$ we denote the set of all such mappings and $X' = \bigcup_{r \in R} X'_r$ is the set of local states of τ'.

Let $\alpha \subseteq R$ and let $u \in \mathbf{F}(\alpha; X')$ be a partial state of τ'. The state u is said to be consistent if

1. $\forall r \in \alpha, \ u(r) \in X'_r$ and

2. $\bigcup_{r \in \alpha} u(r)$ is a mapping from $\bigcup_{r \in \alpha} Er \subseteq \Sigma$ into X.

To explain the last condition let us note that for $r \in \alpha$, $u(r) \in \mathbf{F}(Er; X)$ and the union of these mappings is again a mapping if they all agree on common parts of their domains, i.e. if $u(r')(a) = u(r'')(a)$ for all $r', r'' \in \alpha$ and $a \in Er' \cap Er''$. This mapping will be denoted by $\overline{u}$, i.e. $\overline{u}(a) = u(r)(a)$, where $r \in \alpha$ and $a \in Er$. Note that if u is a consistent global state of τ' then $\overline{u}$ is a mapping from $\bigcup_{r \in R} Er = \Sigma$ into X, i.e. $\overline{u}$ is a global state of τ.

On the other hand, if $s \in \mathbf{F}(\Sigma; X)$ is a global state of τ then it determines in a natural way the corresponding global state $u \in \mathbf{F}(R; X')$:

$$\text{for all } r \in R, \ u(r) = s_{|Er}.$$

This global state u is consistent and moreover $\overline{u} = \bigcup_{r \in R} u(r) = s$.

Let U be the set of consistent global states of τ'. As we have seen the mapping $c : u \longmapsto \overline{u}$, $u \in U$, is a bijection between the set U of global consistent states of τ' and the set S of global states of τ. The transition relations of τ' will be constructed in such a way that this bijection will constitute the required covering of τ by τ'.

First we shall prove the following facts.

Let $u_1 \in \mathbf{F}(Ea; X')$ be a consistent partial state of τ'. Then

$$\begin{aligned} & \overline{u_1} \in \mathbf{F}(Ca; X) \text{ and} \\ & \forall r \in aE, \ Er \setminus \{a\} \subseteq Ca \end{aligned} \qquad (7.10)$$

To prove the first assertion let us note that by the definition of the direct causality relation

$$\bigcup_{r \in Ea} \mathrm{dom}(u_1(r)) = \bigcup_{r \in Ea} Er = (E \circ E)a = Ca$$

($\mathrm{dom}(f)$ denotes here the domain of a partial function f).

Now suppose that $r \in aE$ and $b \in Er \setminus \{a\}$. Thus a and b are in writing conflict and, since σ is w-redundant, $(a, b) \in C \cap C^{-1}$, in particular $b \in Ca$. This proves second assertion.

Now we define transition relations of τ'.

Let δ'_a, $a \in \Sigma$, be a transition relation of τ' and let $u_1 \in \mathbf{F}(Ea; X')$, $u_2 \in \mathbf{F}(aE; X')$. Then $(u_1, u_2) \in \delta'_a$ if

1. u_1 is a consistent partial state of τ' and

2. there exists $x \in X$ such that $(\overline{u_1}, x) \in \delta_a$ and
   $\forall r \in aE, \ \forall b \in Er$,

$$u_2(r)(b) = \begin{cases} x & \text{if } b = a \\ \overline{u_1}(b) & \text{if } b \neq a \end{cases}$$

By 7.10 this definition is sound and the state u_2 is obviously consistent.

Now it suffices to observe two facts (their easy verification is left to the reader)

1. if $s_1, s_2 \in S$ are global states of τ and $(s_1, a, s_2) \in \Delta$ then $(u_1, a, u_2) \in \Delta'$, where $u_1, u_2 \in U$ are such that $\overline{u_i} = s_i$, $i = 1, 2$,

2. if $u_1 \in U$ and $(u_1, a, u_2) \in \Delta'$ then $u_2 \in U$ and $(\overline{u_1}, a, \overline{u_2}) \in \Delta$.

Since $U \ni u \longmapsto \overline{u}$ is a bijection, these condition imply that this mapping is a covering of τ.

$\square$

7.6 Language Recognizability by Asynchronous Automata

In this section we enrich the structure of asynchronous transition systems by adding to them initial and final states and we examine the recognizability power of the automata obtained in this way.

A *finite asynchronous automaton* (faa in short) is a tuple $\mathcal{A} = (\Sigma, R, E, X, \Delta, I, F)$, where $\tau = (\Sigma, R, E, X, \Delta)$ is a fat-system and $I, F \subset \mathbf{F}(R; X)$ are respectively the sets of initial and final states. The language $L(\mathcal{A})$ recognized by $\mathcal{A}$ is defined in the standard way:

$$L(\mathcal{A}) = \{x \in \Sigma^* \mid \exists s_0 \in I, \Delta(s_0, x) \cap F \neq \emptyset\}$$

Finite asynchronous cellular automata (faca) are defined in the analogous way.

A finite asynchronous (cellular) automaton is *deterministic* if it has at most one initial state, $\mathrm{card}(I) \leq 1$, and its global transition relation is a partial mapping, i.e. for each global state s and $a \in \Sigma$, $\mathrm{card}(\Delta(s, a)) \leq 1$.

The main problem considered here is which classes of languages are recognized by finite asynchronous (cellular) automata over a fixed signature.

Let σ be a signature ($\sigma = (\Sigma, R, E)$ for faa or $\sigma = (\Sigma, C)$ for faca). By $\mathcal{L}_\sigma^d$ ($\mathcal{L}_\sigma^n$) we denote the class of languages recognized by deterministic (respectively non-deterministic) finite asynchronous (cellular) automata over signature σ.

Lemma 7.6.1 *Let τ_1 and τ_2 be two fat-systems. Let $\mathcal{A}_1 = (\tau_1, I_1, F_1)$ be a finite asynchronous automaton, $I_1, F_1 \subseteq S_1$. If τ_2 covers τ_1 then there exist sets $I_2, F_2 \subseteq S_2$ such that $\mathrm{card}(I_2) = \mathrm{card}(I_1)$ and $L(\mathcal{A}_1) = L(\mathcal{A}_2)$, where $\mathcal{A}_2 = (\tau_2, I_2, F_2)$ and S_i is the set of global states of τ_i.*

Proof: Let $c : U \longrightarrow S_1$ be a covering of τ_1 by τ_2. First we set $F_2 = c^{-1}(F_1)$. To obtain the set I_2 of initial states of $\mathcal{A}_2$ we choose exactly one global state from each set $c^{-1}(s)$, $s \in I_1$. (Thus I_2 is any subset of S_2 such that $I_2 \subseteq c^{-1}(I_1)$ and $\forall s \in I_1, \mathrm{card}(I_2 \cap c^{-1}(s)) = 1$.)

From the definition of covering and from the fact that $\mathrm{card}(I_1) = \mathrm{card}(I_2)$ it results that if $\mathcal{A}_1$ is deterministic then $\mathcal{A}_2$ is also. Directly from Proposition 7.5.2 we deduce that $L(\mathcal{A}_1) = L(\mathcal{A}_2)$.   □

Proposition 7.6.2 *Let $\sigma_1 = (\Sigma, R, E)$ be a w-redundant signature and let $\sigma_2 = (\Sigma, C)$ be a signature of a fat-system such that $C = (E \circ E) \cap \Sigma^2$ is the direct causality relation induced by σ_1. Then*

$$\mathcal{L}_{\sigma_1}^d = \mathcal{L}_{\sigma_2}^d \text{ and } \mathcal{L}_{\sigma_1}^n = \mathcal{L}_{\sigma_1}^n$$

Proof: Directly from Proposition 7.5.4, Proposition 7.5.5 and Lemma 7.6.1.   □

Note that if σ_1 and σ_2 are as in Proposition 7.6.2 then the conflict relation induced by σ_2 is included in the conflict relation for σ_1. Thus any language recognized by a w-redundant faa can be recognized by a faca without any loss of concurrency. For this reason in the sequel we restrain our attention to languages recognized by finite asynchronous cellular automata.

First we shall prove that without loss of generality we can assume in the sequel that there is always only one initial state.

Lemma 7.6.3 *For each faca $\mathcal{A} = (\Sigma, C, X, \Delta, I, F)$ there exists a faca $\mathcal{A}'$ over the same signature $\sigma = (\Sigma, C)$ and with only one initial state recognizing the same language.*

Proof: Let $I = \{s_o^1, \ldots, s_0^k\}$. The local states of the constructed automaton $\mathcal{A}'$ are k-tuples of the local states of $\mathcal{A}$, $X' = X^k$. For each i, $1 \le i \le k$, using the i-th component of the local states of $\mathcal{A}'$ we can easily simulate the behaviour of $\mathcal{A}$ with the initial state s_0^i. The details are left to the reader.

$\square$

Lemma 7.6.4 *Let $\sigma_1 = (\Sigma_1, C_1)$ and $\sigma_2 = (\Sigma_2, C_2)$ be two signatures such that $\Sigma_1 \subseteq \Sigma_2$ and $C_1 = C_2 \cap (\Sigma_1 \times \Sigma_1)$. Then for each language $L \subseteq \Sigma_1^*$*

$$L \in \mathcal{L}_{\sigma_1}^u \text{ iff } L \in \mathcal{L}_{\sigma_2}^u$$

where u means either d or n.

Proof: Let us note that for each $a \in \Sigma_1$, $C_2a = C_1a \cup (C_2a \setminus C_1a)$, i.e. the reading domain of a in σ_2 is the disjoint union of the reading domain C_1a of a in σ_1 and the subset $C_2a \setminus C_1a$ of $\Sigma_2 \setminus \Sigma_1$. This property is crucial in the construction.

Let $\mathcal{A}_1 = (\Sigma_1, C_1, X_1, \Delta_1, s_0^1, F_1)$ be a fca recognizing L. The idea is to build a faca $\mathcal{A}_2 = (\Sigma_2, C_2, X_2, \Delta_2, s_0^2, F_2)$ that works exactly as $\mathcal{A}_1$ for the words of Σ_1^* by ignoring the local states of the cells of $\Sigma_2 \setminus \Sigma_1$. As the set of local states of $\mathcal{A}_2$ we take $X_2 = X_1 \cup \{y_1, y_2\}$, where y_1, y_2 are new values not belonging to X_1. The initial state s_0^2 is such that $s_{0|\Sigma_1}^2 = s_0^1$ and $s_0^2(a) = y_1$ for all $a \in \Sigma_2 \setminus \Sigma_1$. The execution of any action $a \in \Sigma_2 \setminus \Sigma_1$ writes the value y_2 into the cell a. For $a \in \Sigma_1$ and $s \in \mathbf{F}(C_2a; X_2)$, $(s, x) \in \delta_a^2 \in \Delta_2$ if $(s_{|C_1a}, x) \in \delta_a^1$, i.e. a ignores the local states of $C_2a \setminus C_1a$ and is executed exactly as in $\mathcal{A}_1$. Now it suffices to take as final states of $\mathcal{A}_2$ the states $s \in \mathbf{F}(\Sigma_2; X_2)$ such that $s_{|\Sigma_1} \in F_1$ and $s(a) = y_1$ for all $a \in \Sigma_2$.

Suppose now that $\mathcal{A}_2 = (\Sigma_2, C_2, X_2, \Delta_2, s_0^2, F_2)$ is a faca recognizing $L \subseteq \Sigma_1^*$. We construct a faca $\mathcal{A}_1 = (\Sigma_1, C_1, X_1, \Delta_1, s_0^1, F_1)$ that simulates $\mathcal{A}_2$ for all computations generated by the words of Σ_1^* and starting at s_0^2. Note that since $L(\mathcal{A}_2) \subseteq \Sigma_1^*$, $s \in \Delta(s_0^2, u) \cap F_2$ implies that $s_{|\Sigma_2 \setminus \Sigma_1} = s_{0|\Sigma_2 \setminus \Sigma_1}^2$ (otherwise some action of $\Sigma_2 \setminus \Sigma_1$ should have been executed in u.)

Thus it suffices to take: $X_1 = X_2$, $s_0^1 = s_{0|\Sigma_1}^2$, $F_1 = \{s \in \mathbf{F}(\Sigma_1; X_1) \mid \exists s' \in F_2, s'_{|\Sigma_1} = s \text{ and } s'_{|\Sigma_2 \setminus \Sigma_1} = s_{0|\Sigma_2 \setminus \Sigma_1}^2\}$ and finally, for $a \in \Sigma_1$, $s \in \mathbf{F}(C_1a; X_1)$, $x \in X_1$, $(s, x) \in \delta_a^1 \in \Delta_1$ if there exists $(s', x) \in \delta_a^2 \in \Delta_2$ such that $s'_{|C_1a} = s$ and

$s'_{|C_2a\backslash C_1a} = s^2_{0|C_2a\backslash C_1a}$. It is clear that $\forall u \in \Sigma_1^*$, $(s_0^1, u, s) \in \Delta_1$ iff $(s_0^2, u, s') \in \Delta_2$, where $s'_{|\Sigma_1} = s$ and $s'_{|\Sigma_2\backslash\Sigma_1} = s^2_{0|\Sigma_2\backslash\Sigma_1}$.

□

Lemma 7.6.5 *Let $C_1, C_2 \subseteq \Sigma^2$ and $C_1 \subseteq C_2$, $\sigma_i = (\Sigma, C_i)$, $i = 1, 2$. Then $\mathcal{L}_{\sigma_1}^d \subseteq \mathcal{L}_{\sigma_2}^d$ and $\mathcal{L}_{\sigma_1}^n \subseteq \mathcal{L}_{\sigma_2}^n$.*

Proof: Let $\mathcal{A}_1$ be a faca over σ_1. To obtain a faca $\mathcal{A}_2$ over σ_2 recognizing the same language it suffices to modify slightly the transition relations. Intuitively, although the automaton $\mathcal{A}_2$ executing an action a reads the states of all cells of C_2a it will use effectively only the states of the cells of C_1a. Formally, for $a \in \Sigma$, $s \in \mathbf{F}(C_2a; X)$, $x \in X$, $(s, x) \in \delta_a^2 \in \Delta_2$ iff $(s_{|C_1a}, x) \in \delta_a^1 \in \Delta_1$. Note that if $\mathcal{A}_1$ is deterministic then $\mathcal{A}_2$ is deterministic as well. □

In the sequel we shall use the notion of computation paths in a faca $\mathcal{A} = (\Sigma, C, X, \Delta, s_0, F)$. Such a path is a sequence

$$s_{i_0} \overset{a_1}{\Longrightarrow} s_{i_1} \overset{a_2}{\Longrightarrow} \ldots \overset{a_n}{\Longrightarrow} s_{i_n}$$

where s_{i_k} are global states, a_k actions and $\forall k$, $(1 \leq k \leq n)$ $s_{i_k} \in \Delta(s_{i_{k-1}}, a_k)$. This computation path is *initial* if $s_{i_0} = s_0$, and is *accepting* if it is initial and s_{i_n} is a final state.

Lemma 7.6.6 *Let $\Sigma = \{a\}$, $C = \emptyset$, $\sigma = (\Sigma, C)$. Then $\mathcal{L}_\sigma^d = \mathcal{L}_\sigma^n = \{\emptyset, 1, a^+, a^*\}$.*

Proof: First we show that all four languages $\emptyset, 1, a^+, a^*$ belong to $\mathcal{L}_\sigma^d$. Taking $\delta_a = \{(\emptyset, (a, 1))\}$, $s_0 = \{(a, 0)\}$, $x = \{0, 1\}$ we get a faca recognizing either 1 if $F = \{\{(a, 0)\}\}$ or a^+ if $F = \{\{(a, 1)\}\}$. The trivial automata recognizing a^* and $\emptyset$ are left to the reader.

Let $L \in \mathcal{L}_\sigma^d$. To prove that L is one of the four languages given in the thesis it suffices to show that $a^i \in L$, $i > 0$, implies $a^+ \subseteq L$.

Let $\mathcal{A}$ be a faca over σ recognizing a word a^i. We consider an accepting computation path for a^i:

$$s_0 \overset{a}{\Longrightarrow} s_1 \overset{a}{\Longrightarrow} \ldots \overset{a}{\Longrightarrow} s_{i-1} \overset{a}{\Longrightarrow} s_i$$

where s_0 is the initial and s_i a final state. Since $C = \emptyset$ the last transition used in this computation is always enabled and leads directly to the final state. Thus for each $n > 0$, using n times this transition we obtain the computation path

$$s_0 \underbrace{\overset{a}{\Longrightarrow} s_i \overset{a}{\Longrightarrow} s_i \overset{a}{\Longrightarrow} \ldots \overset{a}{\Longrightarrow} s_i}_{n \text{ times}}$$

accepting a^n. Thus $\mathcal{L}_\sigma^n \subseteq \{\emptyset, 1, a^+, a^*\} \subseteq \mathcal{L}_\sigma^d$, and since $\mathcal{L}_\sigma^d \subseteq \mathcal{L}_\sigma^n$ trivially we get the thesis. □

Lemma 7.6.7 *Let* $\Sigma = \{a\}$, $C = \{(a,a)\}$, $\sigma = (\Sigma, C)$. *Then* $\mathcal{L}_\sigma^d = \mathcal{L}_\sigma^n = \mathrm{Rec}_\Sigma$.

Proof: Let us note that this is just a special case of the general Theorem 7.6.11. Intuitively, if $\mathcal{A}$ is a faca over σ then we get immediately an equivalent finite automaton $\mathcal{B}$ by identifying the state of the unique cell of $\mathcal{A}$ with the state of $\mathcal{B}$. This yields the thesis since the deterministic and non-deterministic finite automata recognize the class Rec_Σ of languages. $\quad\square$

Lemma 7.6.8 *Let* $\Sigma = \{a,b\}$ $(a \neq b)$, $C_1 = \{(b,a)\}$, $C_2 = \{(a,a),(a,b),(b,b)\}$, $\sigma_i = (\Sigma, C_i)$ $(i = 1, 2)$.
Let $L = a^+ b^+$, $L' = b^+ a(a \cup b)^* b$.
Then $L \in \mathcal{L}_{\sigma_1}^d$, $L \notin \mathcal{L}_{\sigma_2}^d$, $L \in \mathcal{L}_{\sigma_2}^n$, $L' \in \mathcal{L}_{\sigma_1}^n$, $L' \notin \mathcal{L}_{\sigma_1}^d$.

Proof: To simplify the notation we shall present the global states $s \in \mathbf{F}(\{a,b\}; X)$ as pairs $(s(a), s(b))$ of values of X.

To show that $L \in \mathcal{L}_{\sigma_1}^d$ we set $X = \{0,1\}$, $s_0 = (0,0)$, $F = \{(1,1)\}$ and

δ_a	b	a
	0	1

δ_b	b
	1

Figure 7.20 presents the transition diagram of the faca defined above.

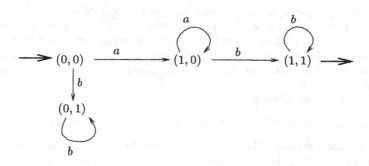

Figure 7.20: A deterministic finite asynchronous cellular automaton recognizing L

To show that $L \in \mathcal{L}_{\sigma_2}^n$ we take the following faca: $X = \{0,1\}$, $s_0 = (0,0)$, $F = \{(1,1)\}$,

δ_a	a	a
	0	0
	0	1

δ_b	a	b	b
	1	0	1
	1	1	1

The transition diagram of this automaton is given on Figure 7.21.
Finally we shall prove that $L \notin \mathcal{L}_{\sigma_2}^d$.

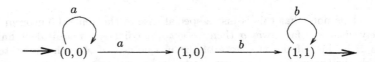

Figure 7.21. A non-deterministic finite asynchronous cellular automaton recognizing L. Note that only the global states reachable from the initial state are presented on faca diagrams.

Suppose that $\mathcal{A}_2 = (\Sigma, C_2, X, \Delta, s_0, F)$ is a deterministic faca recognizing L and let $n = \mathrm{card}(X)$. Let us examine the accepting computation path for the word $a^n b \in L$:

$$s_0 \overset{a}{\Longrightarrow} s_1 \overset{a}{\Longrightarrow} \ldots \overset{a}{\Longrightarrow} s_n \overset{b}{\Longrightarrow} s_{n+1} \in F \qquad (7.11)$$

Let $s_0 = (x_0, y_0)$. Since a can change only its local state we have $s_i = (x_i, y_0)$, $0 \le i \le n$, for some $x_i \in X$. Similarly as b can modify only its local state we have $s_{n+1} = (x_n, y_1)$ for some $y_1 \in X$. Since $n = \mathrm{card}(X)$, some elements should occur more then once in the sequence

$$x_0, \ldots, x_n \qquad (7.12)$$

i.e. $\exists i, j,\ 0 \le i < j \le n,\ x_i = x_j$ (which implies $s_i = s_j$.) Now we can deduce that for some $l,\ 0 \le l < n,\ x_l = x_n$, i.e. the last element in (7.12) occurs at least twice. (Otherwise suppose that x_k is the last element occuring more than once in (7.12) and let $x_i = x_k$ for $0 \le i < k \le n$. If $k \ne n$ then $s_k = s_i \overset{a}{\Longrightarrow} s_{i+1}$ and $s_k \overset{a}{\Longrightarrow} s_{k+1}$ and as $\mathcal{A}_2$ is deterministic, we get $s_{i+1} = s_{k+1}$ and $x_{i+1} = x_{k+1}$, in contradiction with our choice of k.)

Now we take the subpath

$$s_n = s_l = (x_l, y_0) \overset{a}{\Longrightarrow} s_{l+1} = (x_{l+1}, y_0) \overset{a}{\Longrightarrow} \ldots \overset{a}{\Longrightarrow} s_n = (x_n, y_0) \qquad (7.13)$$

of the computation path (7.11). Since $C_2 a = \{a\}$ the executions of a do not depend of the local state of b, therefore replacing y_0 by y_1 in each global state of (7.13) we obtain again a valid computation path:

$$s_{n+1} = (x_n, y_1) = (x_l, y_1) \overset{a}{\Longrightarrow} (x_{l+1}, y_1) \overset{a}{\Longrightarrow} \ldots \overset{a}{\Longrightarrow} (x_n, y_1) = s_{n+1}$$

which shows that $s_{n+1} = \Delta(s_{n+1}, a^{n-l})$. Therefore $s_{n+1} = \Delta(\Delta(s_0, a^n b), a^{n-l}) = \Delta(s_0, a^n b a^{n-l}) \cap F$, i.e. $a^n b a^{n-l} \in L(\mathcal{A}_2)$ and $\mathcal{A}_2$ recognizes a word not belonging to L.

To show that $L' \in \mathcal{L}_{\sigma_1}^n$ we set:
$X = \{0, 1, 2\}$, $s_0 = (0, 0)$, $F = \{(1, 2)\}$ and

δ_a	b	a
	1	1

δ_b	b
	1
	2

Figure 7.22 presents the transition graph for this faca.

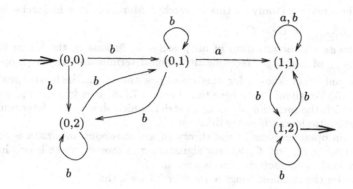

Figure 7.22. A non-deterministic finite asynchronous cellular automaton recognizing L'

To prove that $L' \notin \mathcal{L}_{\sigma_1}^d$ let us take a deterministic faca $\mathcal{A}_1 = (\Sigma, C_1, X, \Delta, s_0, F)$ over σ_1. Since $\mathcal{A}_1$ is deterministic and the reading domain of b is empty, δ_b is either empty or consists of just one transition: $\delta_b = \{(\emptyset, \{(b, y_1)\})\}$ for some $y_1 \in X$. In the first case $\mathcal{A}_1$ can never execute b and $L(\mathcal{A}_1) \neq L'$. In the second case b is always enabled and the first execution of b writes y_1 into the cell b and all subsequent executions of b do not change the local state of b. Thus executing ba or bab^n, $n > 0$, at the initial state we arrive at the same global state, i.e. $ba \in L(\mathcal{A}_1)$ iff $bab \in L(\mathcal{A}_1)$ and $L' \neq L(\mathcal{A}_1)$.

$\square$

Theorem 7.6.9 (Hierarchy Theorem) *Let* $C_1, C_2 \subseteq \Sigma^2$, $\sigma_i = (\Sigma, C_i)$, $i = 1, 2$. *Then* $\mathcal{L}_{\sigma_1}^d \subseteq \mathcal{L}_{\sigma_2}^d$ *iff* $C_1 \subseteq C_2$.

Proof: The right to left implication is given by Lemma 7.6.5.

Now suppose that C_1 is not included in C_2. There are two cases to examine.

CASE 1: There exists $a \in \Sigma$ such that $(a, a) \in C_1 \setminus C_2$.

Then by Lemma 7.6.6, Lemma 7.6.7 and Lemma 7.6.4 any recognizable subset of a^* different from $\emptyset, 1, a^+, a^*$ belongs to $\mathcal{L}_{\sigma_1}^d$ but not to $\mathcal{L}_{\sigma_2}^d$, for example $(aa)^* \in \mathcal{L}_{\sigma_1}^d \setminus \mathcal{L}_{\sigma_2}^d$.

CASE 2: There exist $a, b \in \Sigma$, $a \neq b$, such that $(b, a) \in C_1 \setminus C_2$.

Let $\Sigma_r = \{a, b\}$ and $C' = C_1 \cap (\Sigma_r \times \Sigma_r)$, $C'' = C_2 \cap (\Sigma_r \times \Sigma_r)$, $\sigma' = (\Sigma_r, C')$, $\sigma'' = (\Sigma_r, C'')$. Then $\{(b, a)\} \subseteq C'$ and $C'' \subseteq \{(a, a), (a, b), (b, b)\}$. By Lemma 7.6.5 and Lemma 7.6.8, $a^+b^+ \in \mathcal{L}_{\sigma'}^d \setminus \mathcal{L}_{\sigma''}^d$ and applying Lemma 7.6.4 we see that $a^+b^+ \in \mathcal{L}_{\sigma_1}^d \setminus \mathcal{L}_{\sigma_2}^d$.

$\square$

Theorem 7.6.9 describes all possible inclusions between families $\mathcal{L}^d_{(\Sigma,C)}$ with C ranging over all binary relations over Σ. We see that $\mathcal{L}^d_{(\Sigma,\emptyset)}$ is the least while $\mathcal{L}^d_{(\Sigma,\Sigma^2)}$ the greatest family in this hierarchy. Moreover this hierarchy is proper: $\mathcal{L}^d_{(\Sigma,C_1)} = \mathcal{L}^d_{(\Sigma,C_2)}$ iff $C_1 = C_2$.

The precise characterization of all possible inclusions in the hierarchy of the classes $\mathcal{L}^n_{(\Sigma,C)}$ of languages recognized by non-deterministic faca is an open problem. The only fact known for this classes is the trivial inclusion provided by Lemma 7.6.5. We should note here that Lemma 7.6.8 gives two examples of signatures for which the inclusion $\mathcal{L}^d_\sigma \subset \mathcal{L}^n_\sigma$ is strict, which shows that deterministic and non-deterministic hierarchies are different.

The main open problem in the theory of asynchronous automata is to characterize the classes $\mathcal{L}^d_\sigma$ and $\mathcal{L}^n_\sigma$ for any signature σ. However, there is one important case where such a characterization is known.

Let $\simeq_C$ be the smallest congruence over Σ^* such that

- $ab \simeq_C ba$ if $(a,b) \notin C \cup C^{-1}$

- $aa \simeq_C a$ if $(a,a) \notin C$

Let

$$\mathrm{Rec}(\Sigma^*, C) = \{L \subseteq \Sigma^* \mid L \in \mathrm{Rec}_\Sigma \text{ and } \forall x, y \in \Sigma^*,\ x \simeq_C y \implies (x \in L \Leftrightarrow y \in L)\}$$

Thus $\mathrm{Rec}(\Sigma^*, C)$ consists of all recognizable languages that are closed under $\simeq_C$.

The following inclusions are obvious.

Fact 7.6.10 *If* $C \subseteq \Sigma^2$ *and* $\Sigma = (\Sigma, C)$ *then*

$$\mathcal{L}^d_\sigma \subseteq \mathcal{L}^n_\sigma \subseteq \mathrm{Rec}(\Sigma^*, C)$$

Proof: It suffices to note that if $\mathcal{A}$ is a faca over σ then $ab \simeq_C ba$ and $aa \simeq_C a$ imply $\Delta(s, ab) = \Delta(s, ba)$ and $\Delta(s, aa) = \Delta(s, a)$ respectively. □

The main result of the theory of asynchronous automata (cf. [46, 277]) indicates that under some condition imposed on C the inclusions in Fact 7.6.10 can be replaced by equalities.

Theorem 7.6.11 (Main Theorem) *Let* $\sigma = (\Sigma, C)$. *If the relation* $C \subseteq \Sigma^2$ *is symmetric and reflexive* $(C = C \cup C^{-1} \cup id_\Sigma)$ *then*

$$\mathcal{L}^n_\sigma = \mathcal{L}^d_\sigma = \mathrm{Rec}(\Sigma^*, C)$$

Let us note that if the relation C is symmetric and reflexive then C is equal with the conflict relation D and the family $\mathrm{Rec}(\Sigma^*, C)$ can be identified with the family of recognizable subsets of the free partially commutative monoid $\mathbf{M}(\Sigma, I)$, where $I = \Sigma^2 \setminus D$ is the independency relation induced by σ. Thus Theorem 7.6.11 states that if C is symmetric and reflexive then finite asynchronous cellular automata can recognize exactly all recognizable subsets of the corresponding free partially commutative monoid.

On the other hand if C is not symmetric or not reflexive, i.e. if C is strictly included in D then by the Hierarchy Theorem (Theorem 7.6.9) $\mathcal{L}_\sigma^d$ is also strictly included in the family of recognizable subsets of $\mathbf{M}(\Sigma, I)$.

We end this section with a discussion of the adequacy of cp-graph semantics for finite asynchronous automata, for the sake of simplicity of presentation we restrain our considerations to cellular automata. As we noted in Subsection 7.3.2 (Proposition 7.3.9) cp-graphs constitute actually a representation of traces. However there are other trace representations, for example by equivalence classes of words under $\sim_I$ relation or by dependence graphs (cf. Chapter 2, [1]) and the question can be raised why we still need this new trace model. Let $\sigma = (\Sigma, C)$ and $u \in \Sigma^*$. First note that each event of the cp-graph $\Psi_\sigma(u) = (Ev_u, Ca_u, Pr_u, \lambda_u)$ has uniformly bounded in-degree for Ca_u and Pr_u:

if $e \in Ev_u$ and $\lambda_u(e) = a$ then $\mathrm{card}(\{e' \in Ev_u \mid (e', e) \in Ca_u\}) \leq \mathrm{card}(Ca)$ and $\mathrm{card}(\{e' \in Ev_u \mid (e', e) \in Pr_u\}) \leq \mathrm{card}(Da)$, where D is the conflict relation induced by σ (cf. the end of Section 7.4 for the definition of cp-graphs adapted for cellular automata). This boundedness property enables to introduce directly finite automata over cp-graphs. For such an automaton $\mathcal{B}$ we should specify

- a finite set X of states,

- initial states that are associated with each initial event $e \in Ev_u$ (e is initial if $\{e' \in Ev_u \mid (e', e) \in Ca_u\} = \emptyset$, we can have several initial events with the same label, cf. Example 7.3.10, in this case they all have the same initial state); these states depend on the label of e but not of e itself,

- a transition mapping enabling to calculate the state of each non-initial event $e \in Ev_u$ if the following information is provided

  - the label $\lambda_u(e)$ of e and
  - the labels and the states of all the events e' such that $(e', e) \in Ca_u$,

- the set of final states, these states are partial mappings from Σ into X.

A run of the automaton $\mathcal{B}$ over cp-graph $\Psi_\sigma(u) = (Ev_u, Ca_u, Pr_u, \lambda_u)$ is a mapping r from Ev_u into X associating with each initial event its initial state and with the other events the state calculated by means of the transition mapping of $\mathcal{B}$. The run r is accepting if

$$\{(\lambda_u(e), r(e)) \mid e \in Ev_u \text{ is a final event}\} \tag{7.14}$$

is a final state (an event e is final if $\forall e' \in Ev_u, \lambda_u(e') = \lambda_u(e) \implies (e', e) \in Pr_u^*$).

Note that Pr_u^* totally orders all events with the same label, i.e. (7.14) defines a partial mapping from Σ into X, the domain of this mapping is the set of letters that occur in u.

Given a faca $\mathcal{A} = (\Sigma, C, X, \Delta, s_0, F)$ it is trivial to construct a corresponding cp-graph automaton $\mathcal{B}$. The set of states of $\mathcal{B}$ is simply equal X. For $\alpha \subseteq \Sigma$,

$s : \alpha \longrightarrow X$ is a final state of $\mathcal{B}$ iff the mapping $s' : \Sigma \longrightarrow X$ such that $\forall a \in \alpha$, $s'(a) = s(a)$ and $\forall a \in \Sigma \setminus \alpha$, $s'(a) = s_0(a)$ is a final state of $\mathcal{A}$.

Let $u \in \Sigma^*$ and $\Psi_\sigma(u) = (Ev_u, Ca_u, Pr_u, \lambda_u)$. We shall describe how a run r of $\mathcal{B}$ over $\Psi_\sigma(u)$ simulates the execution of $\mathcal{A}$ on u (this will implicitly explain how the transition of $\mathcal{B}$ is constructed from the transition relations of $\mathcal{A}$).

The initial state $r(e)$ of each initial event $e \in Ev_u$ is set to be equal $s_0(\lambda_u(e))$. Let e be a non-initial event such that r is already defined for all events e' such that $(e', e) \in Ca_u$. Suppose that $\lambda_u(e) = a$. Then we set $r(e) = x \in X$ if there exists a transition $(s, x) \in \delta_a$ of $\mathcal{A}$ such that

- $\forall e'$ such that $(e', e) \in Ca_u$, $s(\lambda_u(e')) = r(e')$,

- $\forall b \in Ca \setminus \{\lambda_u(e') \mid (e', e) \in Ca_u\}$, $s(b) = s_0(b)$ (note that always $\{\lambda_u(e') \mid (e', e) \in Ca_u\} \subseteq Ca$).

In a similar way we can easily transform a cp-graph automata to finite asynchronous cellular automata.

Thus we see that asynchronous cellular automata can be interpreted, after some minor modifications, as automata over cp-graphs.

It should be noted that, actually only the direct causality relation Ca_u is really essential for cp-graph automata, the role of the direct precedence relation Pr_u is limited to indicate the last occurrence of each action — this information is needed in order to find the final state of a run. If the relation C is reflexive then we can get rid of Pr_u at all since in this case Ca_u^* orders totally all occurrences of the same action in Ev_u in the same way as Pr_u.

The fact that asynchronous automata can be viewed as finite automata over labelled acyclic graphs associated to traces was noted explicitly by Thomas[263]. However Thomas originally used reduced dependence graphs, which makes the transformations between asynchronous automata and graph automata a bit more complex. Let us note also that for non-reduced dependence graphs there is no natural way to define finite automata since the in-degree of vertices of these graphs is not bounded.

7.7   Bibliographical Remarks

The Main Theorem (Theorem 7.6.11) was proved in Zielonka[277]. Subsequently the proof was simplified and improved in Cori et al.[46]. The reader can find one of the direct general constructions of deterministic asynchronous (cellular) automata in Chapter 8. Unfortunately all known such constructions are quite involved and give rise to a considerable explosion of the number of states. We should note however that in some interesting cases it is possible to present simpler and more transparent constructions.

The first case is when we allow nondeterminism. Nondeterministic asynchronous automata for a given trace language were built by Pighizzini[228, 227]. Recently methods for converting nondeterministic asynchronous automata to deterministic ones were devised by Muscholl[198] and Klarlund et al.[154].

The construction of deterministic asynchronous automata becomes also simpler if we add some constraints on their topology, for example if the signature can be represented by an undirected tree Métivier[196], Perrin[223], Bertoni et al.[21]. Let us note that the last paper [21] can be considered as a precursor of the theory, although written in the context of labelled Petri nets, it actually provides a nontrivial special case of Theorem 7.6.11. Unfortunately, this paper had little impact on the further development of the theory since it did not appear in the proceedings and its circulation was very limited. An elegant extension of these methods to the case of triangulated dependency graphs was proposed by Diekert and Muscholl and is presented in Chapter 8.

Reductions between various types of asynchronous automata were studied by Cori et al.[48], Pighizzini[229, 227]. Section 7.5 generalizes these results.

The minimalization problem for asynchronous automata was considered by Bruschi et al.[31], and Pighizzini[229, 227]. The main result is that in general the category of deterministic asynchronous (cellular) automata recognizing a given trace language does not admit the unique minimal automaton.

Probabilistic asynchronous automata were examined by Jesi et al. [145] and Pighizzini [227].

Recently asynchronous automata were successfully used to recognize sets of infinite traces (Gastin et al.[113], Diekert et al.[62].)

Asynchronous cellular automata were introduced by Zielonka[278]. In this paper also a "safety" property of asynchronous automata is considered. (A safe automaton is an automaton such that each initial computation path can be extended to an accepting path.)

Theorem 7.6.9 (Hierarchy Theorem) is new. Also the general definitions of asynchronous (cellular) automata given in this chapter are new; previously only automata inducing symmetric and reflexive conflict relations were considered in the literature.

Let us note finally that although asynchronous automata were introduced explicitly in [277], actually similar models have much longer history and were used to solve problems in distributed computing. In this domain especially some topologies, for example with circular connection relation, give rise to appealing and non-trivial problems. For example the computational model used by Dijkstra [65] in his famous self-stabilization problem has immediate representation as an asynchronous automaton (intuitively the system considered in [65] consists of a ring of finite state automata each of them able to read the state of its two neighbours). As another interesting algorithmic problem solved by Mazurkiewicz in a similar model we can mention the ranking problem [191]. We should indicate that the problems such as the two ones mentioned above have quite different flavour than the problems considered in this chapter — the possible sequences of actions executed in the system are of no interest for self-stabilization or ranking problems, in both of them we want to construct automata such that ultimately all reachable global states verify some special property.

Chapter 8

Construction of Asynchronous Automata

Volker Diekert   Anca Muscholl

Universität Stuttgart, Institut für Informatik
Breitwiesenstr. 20–22, 70565 Stuttgart, Germany
{diekert,muscholl}@informatik.uni-stuttgart.de

Contents

8.1 Introduction

In this chapter we consider recognizable trace languages from the viewpoint of automata-theoretical characterizations. We use the asynchronous (cellular) automaton, which is characterized by a distributed control structure. A detailed investigation about these automata and their control structures is given in Chapter 7.

By Zielonka's theorem [277, 278], both, deterministic asynchronous automata (an *exclusive-read-exclusive-write* model) and deterministic cellular asynchronous automata (a *concurrent-read-owner-write* model) characterize recognizability of trace languages precisely. This characterization is in fact one of the major contributions in the theory of Mazurkiewicz traces, due to the non-interleaving semantics of asynchronous (cellular) automata.

Zielonka's construction starts with a trace language recognized by a homomorphism to a finite monoid, and it yields a deterministic asynchronous cellular automaton. Its basic component is a bounded time-stamping which allows to determine the actuality of information received in a distributed way.

A crucial aspect of Zielonka's construction is given however by the notion of asynchronous mapping, which will be presented in Section 8.3.2. Asynchronous mappings, originally introduced by R. Cori and Y. Métivier [45] (see also [53]), are mappings which can be computed in a distributed manner. This property makes them directly translatable into deterministic asynchronous cellular automata. In Zielonka's original construction asynchronous mappings appear implicitly, only. Once one has constructed a deterministic asynchronous cellular automaton, the translation to an asynchronous automaton (as originally defined by Zielonka) is straightforward. The difference between both models is of minor importance here. The polynomial-time transformations from asynchronous cellular automata into equivalent asynchronous automata and vice-versa have been already discussed in Chapter 7, see also e.g. [227, 229].

The question whether a substantially simpler construction for Zielonka's theorem exists, is still open. Recently, two determinization constructions for asynchronous (cellular) automata have been presented [154, 198], both still relying on Zielonka's time-stamping function. So far, only in the special case of acyclic dependence graphs a simpler solution is known: in [196] Y. Métivier exhibited a surprisingly elegant construction which provides in a natural way deterministic asynchronous automata. The drawback of this construction is the fact that the hypothesis of an acyclic dependence relation is a strong restriction, which is often violated. In fact, even the special case of complete dependence, i.e. the free monoid, is not included. Following the presentation of [63] we generalize in the next section Métivier's construction to the larger class of *triangulated* graphs. From a practical point of view, this means that by adding sufficient dependence, i.e. triangulating in a dependence alphabet, we can obtain simple deterministic asynchronous automata for every recognizable trace languages, by loosing some concurrency, only.

We conclude this section by fixing the notations used in this chapter, which are in fact the standard ones.

By (Σ, D) we denote a finite *dependence alphabet*, with Σ being a finite alphabet and $D \subseteq \Sigma \times \Sigma$ a reflexive and symmetric relation called *dependence relation*. The complementary relation $I = (\Sigma \times \Sigma) \setminus D$ is called *independence relation*. The monoid of *finite traces*, $\mathbb{M}(\Sigma, D)$, is defined as a quotient monoid with respect to the congruence relation induced by I, i.e., $\mathbb{M}(\Sigma, D) = \Sigma^* / \{ ab = ba \mid (a, b) \in I \}$.

Recognizability for trace languages can be defined by recognizing homomorphisms: a trace language $L \subseteq \mathbb{M}(\Sigma, D)$ is *recognizable* if there exists a finite monoid S and a homomorphism $\eta : \mathbb{M}(\Sigma, D) \to S$ recognizing L, i.e. satisfying $L = \eta^{-1}\eta(L)$. Alternatively, by Zielonka's characterization theorem, recognizability can be defined by means of asynchronous (cellular) automata. (We shall work here with deterministic automata, only.) We denote the family of recognizable trace languages by $\mathrm{Rec}(\mathbb{M}(\Sigma, D))$ (or $\mathrm{Rec}(\mathbb{M})$ for short).

Definition 8.1.1 *An asynchronous automaton* $\mathcal{A}$ *is a tuple*

$$\mathcal{A} = (\prod_{i=1}^{m} Q_i, (\delta_a)_{a \in \Sigma}, q_0, F)$$

satisfying the following conditions:

- *The global state set* $Q = \prod_{i=1}^{m} Q_i$ *is a direct product of local states sets* Q_i, $1 \leq i \leq m$.

- *Each letter* $a \in \Sigma$ *has an associated domain* $\mathrm{dom}(a) \subseteq \{1, \ldots, m\}$ *such that for all* $(a, b) \in I$ *we have* $\mathrm{dom}(a) \cap \mathrm{dom}(b) = \emptyset$.

- *Each letter* $a \in \Sigma$ *has a (partially defined) local transition function* $\delta_a : \prod_{i \in \mathrm{dom}(a)} Q_i \to \prod_{i \in \mathrm{dom}(a)} Q_i$. *A global transition step* $q' = \delta(q, a)$, $q = (q_i)_{1 \leq i \leq m}$, $q' = (q'_i)_{1 \leq i \leq m} \in Q$, *is defined if and only if* $\delta_a((q_i)_{i \in \mathrm{dom}(a)})$ *is defined. In this case only the components of the domain of a change, i.e. we have*

  1. $q'_j = q_j$ *if* $j \notin \mathrm{dom}(a)$
  2. $(q'_i)_{i \in \mathrm{dom}(a)} = \delta_a((q_i)_{i \in \mathrm{dom}(a)})$

  The language accepted by $\mathcal{A}$ *is* $L(\mathcal{A}) = \{t \in \mathbb{M}(\Sigma, D) \mid \delta(q_0, t) \in F\}$.

Note that asynchronous automata enable concurrent transitions, since write- and read-domains of independent letters do not overlap. They can be seen as EREW (*exclusive-read-exclusive-write*) devices, whereas asynchronous cellular automata, which are defined in the following, correspond to the CROW (*concurrent-read-owner-write*) type.

Definition 8.1.2 *An asynchronous cellular automaton* $\mathcal{A}$ *is a tuple*

$$\mathcal{A} = ((Q_a)_{a \in \Sigma}, (\delta_a)_{a \in \Sigma}, q_0, F)$$

For each letter $a \in \Sigma$ *a set of local states* Q_a *and a (partially defined) local transition function* $\delta_a : (\prod_{b \in D(a)} Q_b) \to Q_a$ *are given. Further,* $q_0 \in \prod_{a \in \Sigma} Q_a$ *denotes the global initial state and* $F \subseteq \prod_{a \in \Sigma} Q_a$ *denotes the set of final global states. The (partially defined) global transition function* $\delta : \prod_{a \in \Sigma} Q_a \times \Sigma \to \prod_{a \in \Sigma} Q_a$ *is defined by*

$$q' = \delta(q, a) \quad \Leftrightarrow \quad q'_a = \delta_a((q_b)_{b \in D(a)}) \quad and$$
$$q'_c = q_c, \qquad\qquad for\ all\ c \neq a$$

Thus, an a-transition $q' = \delta(q, a)$ is defined if and only if $\delta_a((q_b)_{b \in D(a)})$ is defined; and in this case, the change affects only the local a-state. The accepted language is defined as above.

8.2 Métivier's Construction for Triangulated Dependence Graphs

Before giving the proof of Zielonka's theorem, which turns out to be rather technical, we consider here the much easier case of triangulated dependence graphs. We show that Métivier's construction can be extended from acyclic graphs to this case and that triangulated graphs represent the maximal graph class where this construction may be applied to.

The aim of this section is to give a flavour of the behaviour of asynchronous automata and of the problems the general solution has to deal with, without the necessity of using the bounded time-stamping.

We also think that this section may serve as the basis for a course on distributed automata, where the important aspect of asynchronous automata can be presented without having the time to present the general solution.

Let us start with the paradigm behind Métivier's construction. The idea is that each component of the state set is associated with a single letter of the alphabet. Thus, we consider $Q = \prod_{a \in \Sigma} Q_a$ as set of global states. The communication between different components is realized as usual by defining for each $a \in \Sigma$ a set $dom(a) \subseteq \Sigma$ such that $(a, b) \in I$ implies $dom(a) \cap dom(b) = \emptyset$. The main idea is to use a suitable linear ordering on the alphabet, i.e. we have $\Sigma = \{a_1, \ldots, a_n\}$ and $a_1 < \ldots < a_n$. We now transmit the information between components in a fixed, directed way, by letting $dom(a) = \{b \in D(a) \mid a \leq b\}$. The natural question is to determine the class of dependence graphs where this approach yields an asynchronous automaton.

8.2.1 Triangulated Graphs

An undirected graph $G = (V, E)$ with vertex set V and edge set E is *triangulated* if all its chord-less cycles are of length three. Trivial examples are complete graphs (i.e. graphs where $E = \binom{V}{2}$), or acyclic graphs.

For $u \in V$ let $E(u)$ denote the set of vertices adjacent to u, i.e. $E(u) = \{v \in V \mid uv \in E\}$. A *perfect vertex elimination scheme* is a linear ordering $\leq$ of the vertices such that for all $u \in V$ the set $\{v \in E(u) \mid u \leq v\}$ forms a clique (i.e. a complete subgraph). We may represent a perfect vertex elimination scheme by a list $[v_1, \ldots, v_n]$ such that $v_i \leq v_j$ if and only if $i \leq j$.

By induction on n it is easy to see that a graph having a perfect vertex elimination scheme is triangulated. The converse is also true. This characterization of triangulated graphs is due to G. A. Dirac [67]. The result can be found e.g. in the textbook of M. C. Golumbic [125][Thm. 4.1]. For convenience we sketch the proof:

let $G = (V, E)$ be a triangulated graph. If G is a complete graph, then any ordering of the vertex set is a perfect vertex elimination scheme. Otherwise, let us prove by induction that there are at least two vertices $c, d \in V$ such that $cd \notin E$ and $E(c)$ as well as $E(d)$ are cliques.

Start with two vertices $a, b \in V$ with $ab \notin E$. Let S be some minimal separator of a, b. This is any subset $S \subseteq V$ of minimal cardinality with the property that removing S from G puts a and b in two different connected components C_a and C_b respectively. Since G is triangulated, an easy reflection shows that S is a (possibly empty) clique.

Let G_a (G_b respectively) be the induced subgraph of G by $C_a \cup S$ ($C_b \cup S$ respectively). Either G_a (G_b respectively) is a complete graph or we apply the induction hypothesis in order to obtain a vertex c of G_a (d of G_b respectively), which does not belong to S and such that the set of vertices adjacent to c (d respectively) is a clique in G_a (G_b respectively). Note that all neighbors of c (d respectively) are contained in G_a (G_b respectively). Hence, $E(c)$ and $E(d)$ are both cliques of G. Since $c, d \notin S$ we also have $cd \notin E$ and the induction step follows. This completes the proof of Dirac's result.

If $G = (V, E)$ is acyclic, then any ordering which represents a topological sorting yields a perfect vertex elimination scheme. For a complete graph every order is a perfect vertex elimination scheme. Hence, the construction given below will apply to acyclic graphs and complete graphs as well.

8.2.2 Métivier's Construction

In [196] Y. Métivier gave an elegant and amazingly simple construction for asynchronous automata in the case of acyclic dependence alphabets (Σ, D) (see also the survey of D. Perrin [223]). The basic idea is to choose a tree (forest) structure and to move the distributed information to the top of the tree(s) as soon as available. We will show here that the construction applies to triangulated graphs, too. All we need is a perfect vertex elimination scheme, as defined in the previous subsection.

Let (Σ, D) be any triangulated dependence alphabet and let $\leq$ be a linear ordering of Σ such that for all $a, b, c \in \Sigma$, $a \leq b \leq c$, $(a, c) \in D$ and $(b, c) \in D$, we have $(a, b) \in D$, too. Thus, if $\Sigma = \{a_1, \ldots, a_n\}$ ($n = |\Sigma|$) is written in increasing order $a_1 < \cdots < a_n$, then $[a_n, \ldots, a_1]$ is a perfect vertex elimination scheme of (Σ, D).

Let $\eta : \mathbb{M}(\Sigma, D) \to S$ be a homomorphism to a finite monoid S and $L = \eta^{-1}(R)$ for some subset $R \subseteq S$. We are going to construct an asynchronous automaton $\mathcal{A}$ recognizing L.

The state set of $\mathcal{A}$ will be an n-fold direct product of S, $n = |\Sigma|$. First we define ordered products in S. Let $\Gamma \subseteq \Sigma$ and $s_c \in S$, for all $c \in \Gamma$. Define the ordered product $\prod_{c \in \Gamma} s_c$ by $\prod_{c \in \Gamma} s_c = s_{c_1} \cdots s_{c_m}$, if $\Gamma = \{c_1, \ldots, c_m\}$, $m \geq 0$, with $c_1 < \cdots < c_m$. All products of elements of S used in the following will be ordered ones.

Let now $\mathcal{A} = (\prod_{a \in \Sigma} Q_a, \delta, q_0, F)$ be defined by

$$\delta : \prod_{a \in \Sigma} Q_a \times \Sigma \to \prod_{a \in \Sigma} Q_a,$$

where for every $a \in \Sigma$:

$$Q_a = S$$

$$\delta(q, a) = q \cdot a = q' \quad \text{with} \quad q_b' = \begin{cases} (\prod_{\substack{a \leq c, \\ (a,c) \in D}} q_c) \cdot \eta(a) & \text{if } b = a \\ 1 & \text{if } a < b, \ (a, b) \in D \\ q_b & \text{otherwise} \end{cases}$$

Furthermore, let $q_0 = (1)_{a \in \Sigma}$ and $F = \{(q_a)_{a \in \Sigma} \in \prod_{a \in \Sigma} Q_a \mid \prod_{a \in \Sigma} q_a \in \eta(L)\}$.

Proposition 8.2.1 *Let $L \in \mathrm{Rec}(\mathbb{M})$ be recognized by the homomorphism $\eta :$ $\mathbb{M}(\Sigma, D) \to S$ to the finite monoid S. Let $\mathcal{A}$ be the automaton defined above. Then $\mathcal{A}$ is asynchronous and we have $L(\mathcal{A}) = L$.*

Proof: First we show that $\mathcal{A}$ is asynchronous. The write- and read-domain of a letter $a \in \Sigma$ is given by the index set $\{c \in \Sigma \mid a \leq c$ and $(a, c) \in D\}$. Assume that for some $a, b, c \in \Sigma$, $a \leq b \leq c$ we have $(a, c) \in D$ and $(b, c) \in D$. Then $(a, b) \in D$ follows, due to the ordering. Hence, if $(a, b) \in I$, then a and b have disjoint write- and read-domains. Thus, $\mathcal{A}$ is asynchronous. In particular, for any trace $w \in \mathbb{M}(\Sigma, D)$, the global state $q_0 \cdot w = \delta((1)_{a \in \Sigma}, w)$ is well-defined.

For $(q_a)_{a \in \Sigma} = q_0 \cdot w$ we show the following two invariants:

1. $a \leq b$ and $(a, b) \in I$ imply $q_b \, \eta(a) = \eta(a) \, q_b$.

2. $a \leq b \leq c$, $(a, b) \in I$, and $(a, c) \in D$ imply $q_b \, q_c = q_c \, q_b$.

In order to verify these invariants we need some alphabetic information. We observe that for each local state q_a, $a \in \Sigma$, there exists some subset $\Gamma_a \subseteq \Sigma$ with the following properties: q_a is an element of the submonoid generated by $\eta(c)$, with $c \in \Gamma_a$, and for each $c \in \Gamma_a$ there exists a chain $a = a_0 < \cdots < a_k = c$, $k \geq 0$, such that $(a_{i-1}, a_i) \in D$ for $1 \leq i \leq k$. This crucial observation can be easily derived from the inductive definition of the transition function δ.

Consider now $a \leq b \leq c$ with $(a, b) \in I$ and $\Gamma_b, \Gamma_c \subseteq \Sigma$ as introduced above. Invariant (1) follows by showing that $\{a\} \times \Gamma_b \subseteq I$. Invariant (2) follows by showing that $\Gamma_b \times \Gamma_c \subseteq I$, whenever $(a, c) \in D$.

For invariant (1) let $b_k \in \Gamma_b$ and $b = b_0 < \cdots < b_k$, $k \geq 0$, such that $(b_{i-1}, b_i) \in D$ for $1 \leq i \leq k$. Assume that we would have $(a, b_k) \in D$. Then $k \geq 1$ and $(b_{k-1}, b_k) \in D$ implies $(a, b_{k-1}) \in D$. We can continue this way and we arrive to $(a, b_0) \in D$ (see also Figure 8.1). This is a contradiction to $(a, b) \in I$. Thus, $(a, b_i) \in I$ for all $1 \leq i \leq k$; this fact will be used below, too.

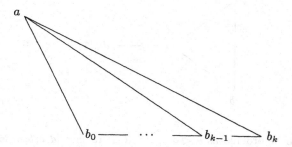

Figure 8.1: Consequence of $(a, b_k) \in D$.

For invariant (2) let $(a, c) \in D$, $b_k \in \Gamma_b$, $c_m \in \Gamma_c$ with $b = b_0 < \cdots < b_k$ and $c = c_0 < \cdots < c_m$, $k, m \geq 0$, such that $(b_{i-1}, b_i) \in D$ and $(c_{j-1}, c_j) \in D$ for $1 \leq i \leq k$, $1 \leq j \leq m$. We show by induction that $(b_i, c_j) \in I$ for all i, j. Assume first that $c_m \leq b_k$. Then we have $k \geq 1$ (since $b < c$) and $(c_m, b_k) \in D$, $(b_{k-1}, b_k) \in D$ imply $(c_m, b_{k-1}) \in D$. Hence we may assume $b_k < c_m$. Suppose next that $m \geq 1$. Then $(b_k, c_m) \in D$, $(c_{m-1}, c_m) \in D$ imply $(b_k, c_{m-1}) \in D$. Hence, we may assume $m = 0$ and we obtain the following situation:

$$a < b = b_0 < \cdots < b_k < c, \quad k \geq 0.$$

Finally, suppose that we would have $(b_i, c) \in D$ for some $1 \leq i \leq k$. Since $(a, c) \in D$ this implies $(a, b_i) \in D$, contradicting the fact mentioned in the proof of (1) above. Thus, both invariants (1) and (2) are valid.

The proposition follows from the following claim:

$$\text{For } (q_a)_{a \in \Sigma} = q_0 \cdot w \quad \text{we have} \quad \prod_{a \in \Sigma} q_a = \eta(w).$$

The claim is satisfied for $|w| = 0$ since $q_0 = (1)_{a \in \Sigma}$. By induction assume that the claim holds for $q = q_0 \cdot w$ and let $q' = q \cdot a$ for some letter $a \in \Sigma$. It is enough to show:

$$\left(\prod_{a \leq c} q_c \right) \eta(a) = \left(\prod_{\substack{a \leq c, \\ (a,c) \in D}} q_c \right) \eta(a) \left(\prod_{\substack{a < b, \\ (a,b) \in I}} q_b \right).$$

However, this last formula is immediate from the two invariants shown above. This completes the proof of the proposition. $\qquad\square$

The example below illustrates the construction for a dependence alphabet on four letters $\Sigma = \{a, b, c, d\}$ with the following dependence relation D:

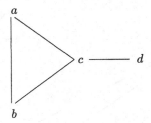

The alphabet Σ can be ordered as $a < b < c < d$ (note that $[d, c, b, a]$ is a perfect vertex elimination scheme). Let $\eta : \mathbb{M}(\Sigma, D) \to \mathbb{Z}/n\mathbb{Z}$ be a homomorphism computing the length of a trace modulo n, $n \geq 1$. Then the construction for asynchronous automata given above yields e.g. the following transition mappings, together with some concrete computations in $\mathbb{Z}/n\mathbb{Z}$:

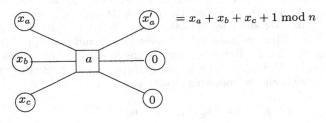

$$x'_a = x_a + x_b + x_c + 1 \bmod n$$

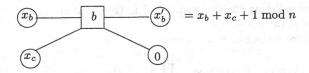

$$x'_b = x_b + x_c + 1 \bmod n$$

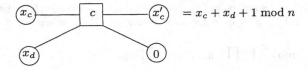

$$x'_c = x_c + x_d + 1 \bmod n$$

$$x'_d = x_d + 1 \bmod n$$

$$\delta(q_0, c \overset{a\text{---}b}{\underset{d}{\diagup}} \,) = \begin{pmatrix} 2 \\ 1 \\ 0 \\ 1 \end{pmatrix}$$

$$\delta(q_0, a\text{---}b\text{---}c\text{---}d) = \begin{pmatrix} 1 \\ 1 \\ 1 \\ 1 \end{pmatrix} \qquad \delta(q_0, d\text{---}c\text{---}b\text{---}a) = \begin{pmatrix} 4 \\ 0 \\ 0 \\ 0 \end{pmatrix}$$

Remark 8.2.2 Note that as soon as the dependence graph contains a chordless cycle of length greater than three, the automaton constructed above is not asynchronous anymore. More precisely, for any ordering $\leq$ of the alphabet Σ there exist letters $a < b < c$ (on the cycle) satisfying $(a, c) \in D$, $(b, c) \in D$, but $(a, b) \in I$. In this case however, c belongs to both write- and read-domains of a and b.

8.3 Asynchronous Cellular Automata for Recognizable Trace Languages

In this section we give the general solution of constructing asynchronous automata for arbitrary (symmetric and reflexive) dependence alphabets. The presentation follows ideas from [277, 278, 45, 53, 46]. The main piece of work is to construct a suitable asynchronous mapping, as proposed in [45] (see also [53] for a corrected version). From an asynchronous mapping one can easily obtain a deterministic asynchronous cellular automaton, which furthermore can be easily transformed in a deterministic asynchronous equivalent automaton. This last step is not done here, since it has been already discussed in Chapter 7.

8.3.1 Prefix Order for Traces

Let us recall in this section some basic notions concerning prefixes of traces and ordering between them. We denote by $\leq$ the partial (prefix) order given by $u \leq v$ if $v = ut$ for some $t \in \mathbb{M}(\Sigma, D)$. As usual, for $u, v \in \mathbb{M}(\Sigma, D)$, $u < v$ if both $u \leq v$ and $v \neq u$; we denote by $u \sqcap v$ the greatest lower bound of u, v with respect to the prefix order. Whenever it exists, the least upper bound of u, v is denoted by $u \sqcup v$. Clearly, $u \sqcup v$ exists if and only if $u \leq w$ and $v \leq w$ for some $w \in \mathbb{M}(\Sigma, D)$.

Another notation used frequently is $\max(t)$ for $t \in \mathbb{M}(\Sigma, D)$, denoting the labellings of the maximal elements of the partial order represented by t, i.e. $\max(t) = \{a \in \Sigma \mid \exists x \in \Sigma^* : xa \in \varphi^{-1}(t)\}$, for the canonical surjective homomorphism $\varphi : \Sigma^* \to \mathbb{M}(\Sigma, D)$. Since the elements of $\max(t)$ are pairwise independent and therefore commute, $\max(t)$ can also be viewed as a trace.

The following definition introduces a basic notation for studying properties of the prefix order.

Definition 8.3.1 *Let $t \in \mathbb{M}(\Sigma, D)$, $A \subseteq \Sigma$. We define the least prefix of t which contains all letters from A by*

$$\partial_A(t) = \sqcap\{u \leq t \mid \forall a \in A : |u|_a = |t|_a\}$$

For $A, B \subseteq \Sigma$ we write $\partial_{A,B}(t)$ instead of $\partial_A(\partial_B(t))$. Additionally, whenever $A = \{a\}$ we write directly $\partial_a(t)$ (resp. $\partial_{a,B}(t)$ etc.).

The following lemma gives an equivalent characterization of $\partial_A(t)$.

Lemma 8.3.2 *Let $t \in \mathbb{M}(\Sigma, D)$ and $A \subseteq \Sigma$. Then*

$$\partial_A(t) = \sqcup\{u \leq t \mid \max(u) \subseteq A\}.$$

Proof: Clearly $\max(\partial_A(t)) \subseteq A$, hence $\partial_A(t) \leq \sqcup\{u \leq t \mid \max(u) \subseteq A\}$. For the other direction, consider $u, v \leq t$ such that $\max(u) \subseteq A$ and $|v|_a = |t|_a$, for every $a \in A$. Let $x, y \in \mathbb{M}(\Sigma, D)$ be such that $t = ux = vy$ and let us apply Levi's lemma to this equation. We obtain traces $p, r, s \in \mathbb{M}(\Sigma, D)$ with $\text{alph}(r) \times \text{alph}(s) \subseteq I$ and $u = pr$, $v = ps$.

Finally, $\max(u) \subseteq A$ implies $\max(r) \subseteq A$, hence $r \neq 1$ would contradict the definition of v. $\square$

Remark 8.3.3 Note that for every $A \subseteq \Sigma$, the prefix $\partial_A(t)$ is equal to $\sqcup_{a \in A} \partial_a(t)$. Furthermore, for every $t \in \mathbb{M}(\Sigma, D)$ we have $t = \partial_\Sigma(t) = \partial_{\max(t)}(t)$.

The following proposition summarizes some basic properties of $\partial_A(t)$ prefixes. The easy proof is omitted and left to the reader.

Proposition 8.3.4 *Let $t, u, v \in \mathbb{M}(\Sigma, D)$, $A, B \subseteq \Sigma$ and $a \in \Sigma$. We have*

1. $t \leq u$ *implies* $\partial_A(t) \leq \partial_A(u)$.

2. $\partial_{A,A}(t) = \partial_A(t)$.

3. $A \subseteq B$ *implies both* $\partial_A(t) \leq \partial_B(t)$ *and* $\partial_A(t) = \partial_{A,B}(t) = \partial_{B,A}(t)$.

4. $\partial_A(tu) = \partial_{A \cup D(B)}(t)\partial_A(u)$, *where* $B = \text{alph}(\partial_A(u))$. *Especially we have* $\partial_a(ta) = \partial_{D(a)}(t)a$.

5. *If* $u \sqcup v$ *exists, then* $\partial_A(u) \sqcup \partial_A(v)$ *exists, too, and* $\partial_A(u) \sqcup \partial_A(v) = \partial_A(u \sqcup v)$.

6. $\partial_{a,A}(t) = \sqcup_{b \in A} \partial_{a,b}(t)$. *Hence, for* $A \neq \emptyset$ *we have* $\partial_{a,A}(t) = \partial_{a,b}(t)$ *for some* $b \in A$.

7. *For* $A \neq \emptyset$, $\partial_a(t) \leq \partial_A(t)$ *implies* $\partial_a(t) = \partial_{a,b}(t)$ *for some* $b \in A$.

In the remaining part of this section we consider a typical situation which will be encountered in the context of asynchronous mappings. Briefly speaking, we are interested in the interconnection between two prefixes $\partial_A(t), \partial_B(t)$ of a trace $t = \partial_{A \cup B}(t)$.

Proposition 8.3.5 *Let* $A, B \subseteq \Sigma$ *and* $t \in \mathbb{M}(\Sigma, D)$ *such that* $t = \partial_{A \cup B}(t)$. *We denote in the following* $t_A = \partial_A(t)$, $t_B = \partial_B(t)$. *Consider traces* r, u, v *as given by Levi's lemma such that* $r = t_A \sqcap t_B$, $t_A = ru$, $t_B = rv$ *with* $\mathrm{alph}(u) \times \mathrm{alph}(v) \subseteq I$. *Then with* $C = \{c \in \Sigma \mid \partial_c(t_A) = \partial_c(t_B)\}$ *the following assertions hold:*

1. *For every* $a \in \Sigma$ *we have* $\partial_a(t_A) < \partial_a(t_B)$ *if and only if* $a \in \mathrm{alph}(v)$. *Moreover,* $a \in \mathrm{alph}(v)$ *implies* $\partial_a(t_A) = \partial_a(r)$.

2. $r = \partial_C(t) = \partial_C(t_A) = \partial_C(t_B)$. *In particular,* $\max(r) \subseteq C$.

3. $\Sigma \setminus C = \mathrm{alph}(uv)$.

Proof:

1. Use Proposition 8.3.4(4) and $\mathrm{alph}(u) \times \mathrm{alph}(v) \subseteq I$.

2. With the definition of C and Proposition 8.3.4(5) it is easily seen that we have both $\partial_C(t) = \partial_C(t_A) = \partial_C(t_B)$ and $\partial_C(t) < r$.

   If $r \neq 1$ consider $a \in \max(r)$ and let us assume $\partial_a(t_A) < \partial_a(t_B)$. With (1) we obtain $a \in \mathrm{alph}(v)$. Furthermore, $D(a) \cap \mathrm{alph}(u) \neq \emptyset$, since with Proposition 8.3.4(4)

   $$ru = \partial_A(ru) = \partial_{A \cup D(B)}(r)\partial_A(u), \text{ where } B = \mathrm{alph}(\partial_A(u)).$$

   hence $r = \partial_{A \cup D(B)}(r)$ and $u = \partial_A(u)$, and thus $\max(r) \subseteq A \cup D(\mathrm{alph}(u))$. Now, with $a \in A$ one obtains by Proposition 8.3.4(3) $\partial_a(t_A) = \partial_a(t)$, thus contradicting the assumption $\partial_a(t_A) < \partial_a(t_B)$.

   Hence, we obtained a contradiction to $\mathrm{alph}(u) \times \mathrm{alph}(v) \subseteq I$. By symmetry, $\partial_a(t_A) = \partial_a(t_B)$, which yields $a \in C$ and finally $r = \partial_{\max(r)}(r) \leq \partial_C(r) \leq \partial_C(t)$.

3. Follows directly with the definition of C together with (1).

$\square$

Corollary 8.3.6 *Let* $t \in \mathbb{M}(\Sigma, D)$ *and* $\emptyset \neq A, B \subseteq \Sigma$, *and suppose that the sets* $C_{a,b} = \{c \in \Sigma \mid \partial_{c,a}(t) = \partial_{c,b}(t)\}$ *are known for all* $a, b \in A \cup B$. *Then we are able to determine for every* $c \in \Sigma$ *which of the following situations occurs:*

- $\partial_{c,A}(t) = \partial_{c,B}(t)$

- $\partial_{c,A}(t) < \partial_{c,B}(t)$

- $\partial_{c,B}(t) < \partial_{c,A}(t)$

Proof: Assume $a, b \in A \cup B$ and let $r, u, v \in \mathbb{M}(\Sigma, D)$ such that $\partial_a(t) = ru$, $\partial_b(t) = rv$ with $\text{alph}(u) \times \text{alph}(v) \subseteq I$. Applying Proposition 8.3.5(1) we obtain $\partial_{c,a}(t) < \partial_{c,b}(t)$ if and only if $c \in \text{alph}(v)$. By Proposition 8.3.5(3) we obtain that $c \in \text{alph}(v)$ implies that c, b belong to the same connected component of $\Sigma \setminus C_{a,b}$. Furthermore, c and a can not be connected by a path in $\Sigma \setminus C_{a,b}$, since $\text{alph}(u) \times \text{alph}(v) \subseteq I$.

Applying this argument to all pairs $(a, a') \in A \times A$ we determine $a \in A$ such that $\partial_{c,A}(t) = \partial_{c,a}(t)$. An analogous calculation yields b with $\partial_{c,B}(t) = \partial_{c,b}(t)$ and finally we have to compare $\partial_{c,a}(t)$ and $\partial_{c,b}(t)$. $\qquad\square$

8.3.2 Asynchronous Mappings

The aim of this section is to introduce the notion of asynchronous mapping due to Cori and Métivier and to show the close connection to asynchronous cellular automata. Briefly speaking, asynchronous mappings are mappings which can be computed stepwise in a distributed way, thus being easily transformed into an equivalent asynchronous cellular automaton (with respect to recognition).

Definition 8.3.7 *A mapping* $\mu : \mathbb{M}(\Sigma, D) \to S$ *is called* asynchronous *if for any* $t \in \mathbb{M}(\Sigma, D)$, $a \in \Sigma$ *and* $A, B \subseteq \Sigma$ *the following conditions are satisfied.*

- $\mu(\partial_{D(a)}(t))$ *and the letter* a *uniquely determine the value* $\mu(\partial_a(ta))$.

- $\mu(\partial_A(t))$ *and* $\mu(\partial_B(t))$ *uniquely determine the value* $\mu(\partial_{A \cup B}(t))$.

The relevance of asynchronous mappings is given by the following proposition, which establishes the connection to asynchronous cellular automata. Note that in general, an asynchronous mapping $\mu : \mathbb{M}(\Sigma, D) \to S$ does not give any natural monoid automaton structure. This is due to the fact that for $t \neq \partial_{D(a)}(t)$ the value of $\mu(t)$ does not suffice for computing $\mu(ta)$, where $a \in \Sigma$.

However, given $(\mu(\partial_b(t)))_{b \in \max(t)}$, one can compute $\mu(ta)$, since for $A = \max(t) \cap I(a)$ we have $ta = \partial_A(t) \sqcup \partial_a(ta)$. Furthermore, $\mu(\partial_A(t))$ is computable from $(\mu(\partial_b(t)))_{b \in A}$ (by the 2nd condition in Definition 8.3.7), whereas $\mu(\partial_a(ta))$ is determined analogously using both conditions by a and $(\mu(\partial_b(t)))_{b \in D(a)}$. Finally, $\mu(ta)$ can be computed using again the 2nd condition (note that $\partial_A(t) = \partial_A(ta)$).

Proposition 8.3.8 *Let* $\mu : \mathbb{M}(\Sigma, D) \to S$ *be an asynchronous mapping and* $R \subseteq S$ *a subset of* S. *Then there exists an asynchronous cellular automaton* $\mathcal{A}_\mu$ *such that* $L(\mathcal{A}_\mu) = \mu^{-1}(R)$.

Proof: Let us define $\mathcal{A}_\mu = ((Q_a)_{a \in \Sigma}, (\delta_a)_{a \in \Sigma}, q_0, F)$ by

$$Q_a = \{\mu(\partial_a(t)) \mid t \in \mathbb{M}(\Sigma, D)\}, \qquad a \in \Sigma$$

$$\delta((\mu(\partial_a(t)))_{a \in \Sigma}, b) = (\mu(\partial_a(tb)))_{a \in \Sigma}$$

With $\partial_a(tb) = \partial_a(t)$ for $a \neq b$ it is easily seen that a b-transition merely changes the local b-state. Moreover, with $\partial_b(tb) = \partial_{D(b)}(t)b$ and due to the ability of computing $\mu(\partial_b(tb))$ from $(\mu(\partial_a(t)))_{a \in D(b)}$ and b we obtain that the change of the local b-state depends only on the local states corresponding to the subset $D(b)$. Hence, δ is well-defined and the automaton is asynchronous cellular. We accomplish the construction by letting $q_0 = (\mu(1))_{a \in \Sigma}$ and $F = \{(\mu(\partial_a(t)))_{a \in \Sigma} \mid t \in \mu^{-1}(R)\}$.

In order to show $L(\mathcal{A}_\mu) = \mu^{-1}(R)$ note that $t \in L(\mathcal{A}_\mu)$ if and only if for some $u \in \mu^{-1}(R)$,

$$\mu(\partial_a(t)) = \mu(\partial_a(u)), \qquad \text{for all } a \in \Sigma.$$

Finally, with $t = \partial_\Sigma(t)$ we note that $\mu(t)$ (and $\mu(u)$ as well) is determined by $(\mu(\partial_a(t)))_{a \in \Sigma}$, hence it follows that $\mu(t) = \mu(u)$. $\qquad\square$

8.3.3 Asynchronous Mappings for Recognizable Trace Languages

The first aim in this section is to exhibit an asynchronous mapping ν independent from the given recognizable trace language, which corresponds to a bounded time-stamping. This mapping contains crucial information about the prefix order between prefixes $\partial_a(t)$, $a \in \Sigma$, needed in order to be able to establish actuality of information. Concretely, the value $\nu(t)$ contains enough information in order to compute the set $C = \{c \in \Sigma \mid \partial_{c,A}(t) = \partial_{c,B}(t)\}$ for any $t \in \mathbb{M}(\Sigma, D)$, $A, B \subseteq \Sigma$.

The main idea for the construction consists in labelling trace prefixes of the form $\partial_x(t)$, $x \in \Sigma$, in such a way that for $a, b, c \in \Sigma$ the equality $\partial_{c,a}(t) = \partial_{c,b}(t)$ holds if and only if the labellings of these two traces coincide.

Definition 8.3.9 *Let $\nu : \mathbb{M}(\Sigma, D) \to \mathbb{N}^{\Sigma \times \Sigma}$ be defined inductively as follows:*

- $\nu(1)(a, b) = 0$.

- *If $t \neq \partial_{a,b}(t)$ then $\nu(t)(a, b) = \nu(\partial_{a,b}(t))(a, a)$.*

- *If $t = \partial_a(t)$ and $t \neq 1$ then*

$$\nu(t)(a, a) = \min\{n > 0 \mid n \neq \nu(t)(a, c) \text{ for all } c \neq a\}$$

Lemma 8.3.10 *The mapping $\nu : \mathbb{M}(\Sigma, D) \to \mathbb{N}^{\Sigma \times \Sigma}$ is well-defined and satisfies for every $t \in \mathbb{M}(\Sigma, D)$, $a, b, c \in \Sigma$, and $A, B \subseteq \Sigma$ the following properties:*

1. $0 \leq \nu(t)(a, b) \leq |\Sigma|$.

2. $\nu(t)(a, b) = \nu(\partial_b(t))(a, a) = \nu(\partial_{a,b}(t))(a, a)$.

3. $\nu(t)(a, b) = 0$ is equivalent to $\partial_{a,b}(t) = 1$.

4. $\partial_{c,a}(t) = \partial_{c,b}(t)$ is equivalent to $\nu(t)(c, a) = \nu(t)(c, b)$.

5. $\partial_{c,A}(t) = \partial_{c,B}(t)$ is equivalent to $\nu(\partial_A(t))(c, c) = \nu(\partial_B(t))(c, c)$.

Proof:

1. Follows directly from $|\{n > 0 \mid n \neq \nu(t)(a,c) \text{ for every } c \neq a\}| \leq |\Sigma| - 1$.

2. Obvious.

3. Follows directly from $\nu(t)(a,b) = \nu(\partial_{a,b}(t))(a,a)$ using the definition of ν.

4. The implication from left to right is clear due to (2). Conversely, assume w.l.o.g. that $\partial_{c,a}(t) < \partial_{c,b}(t)$. By Proposition 8.3.5 we have with $r = \partial_a(t) \sqcap \partial_{c,b}(t)$ the equality $\partial_{c,a}(t) = \partial_c(r)$. Hence, for some $d \in \max(r)$ (for $r \neq 1$) we obtain $\partial_{c,a}(t) = \partial_{c,d}(r) = \partial_{c,d}(\partial_{c,b}(t))$ $(= \partial_{c,d}(\partial_a(t)))$. Note also that $d \neq c$, since otherwise $\partial_{c,a}(t) = \partial_{c,b}(t)$.

   Finally, the definition of ν yields:

   $$\nu(t)(c,b) = \nu(\partial_{c,b}(t))(c,c) \overset{c \neq d}{\neq} \nu(\partial_{c,b}(t))(c,d) = \nu(\partial_{c,d}(\partial_{c,b}(t)))(c,c),$$

   thus contradicting the hypothesis $\nu(t)(c,a) = \nu(t)(c,b)$.

5. Assume that $A, B \neq \emptyset$ (otherwise we use (3) and the definition of ν). For suitable $a \in A$, $b \in B$ we have $\partial_{c,A}(t) = \partial_{c,a}(t)$ and $\partial_{c,B}(t) = \partial_{c,b}(t)$. Together with

   $$\nu(\partial_A(t))(c,c) \overset{(2)}{=} \nu(\partial_{c,A}(t))(c,c) = \nu(\partial_{c,a}(t))(c,c) \overset{(2)}{=} \nu(t)(c,a),$$

   $(\nu(t)(c,b) = \nu(\partial_B(t))(c,c)$ analogously) and (4) the result follows immediately.

$\square$

Remark 8.3.11 Note that the value of $\nu(t)$ allows to determine whether $\partial_a(t) \leq \partial_b(t)$ holds, with $a, b \in \Sigma$. To see this note that $\partial_a(t) \leq \partial_b(t)$ is equivalent to $\partial_a(t) = \partial_{a,b}(t)$, hence to $\nu(t)(a,a) = \nu(t)(a,b)$ by Lemma 8.3.10.

For the asynchronous cellular automaton A_ν defined at the beginning of the section this implies the following: given a trace t and the local states $q_x := \delta(q_0, t)_x$, $x \in \{a, b\}$, one can determine if $\partial_a(t) \leq \partial_b(t)$ or $\partial_b(t) \leq \partial_a(t)$ holds, or $\partial_a(t)$ and $\partial_b(t)$ are incomparable, since:

$$\partial_a(t) \leq \partial_b(t) \Longleftrightarrow$$
$$\nu(\partial_a(t))(a,a) \overset{8.3.10(2)}{=} \nu(t)(a,a) = \nu(t)(a,b) \overset{8.3.10(2)}{=} \nu(\partial_b(t))(a,a) \Longleftrightarrow$$
$$q_a(a,a) = q_b(a,a)$$

Proposition 8.3.12 *The mapping ν is asynchronous.*

Proof: Let us first show that for any $t \in \mathbb{M}(\Sigma, D)$, $a \in \Sigma$ the value $\nu(\partial_{D(a)}(t))$ and the letter a suffice for determining $\nu(\partial_a(ta))$. With Lemma 8.3.10(2) we directly obtain for $b, c \in \Sigma$ with $c \neq a$ resp. $c = a \neq b$,

$$\nu(\partial_a(ta))(b, c) = \nu(\partial_{D(a)}(t))(b, c),$$

since $\partial_{b,c,a}(ta) = \partial_{b,c}(\partial_{D(a)}(t)a) = \partial_{b,c}(\partial_{D(a)}(t))$, resp. $\partial_{b,a,a}(ta) = \partial_b(\partial_{D(a)}(t)a) = \partial_{b,D(a)}(t) = \partial_{b,a}(\partial_{D(a)}(t))$.

Finally, $\nu(\partial_a(ta))(a, a) = \min\{n > 0 \mid n \neq \nu(\partial_a(ta))(a, d), d \neq a\}$, which is computable using $\nu(\partial_a(ta))(a, d) = \nu(\partial_{D(a)}(t))(a, d)$ (note that $a \neq d$ implies $\partial_{a,d,D(a)}(t) = \partial_{a,d,a}(ta)$).

Now assume that $\nu(\partial_A(t))$ and $\nu(\partial_B(t))$ are given, with $A, B \subseteq \Sigma$. Due to Lemma 8.3.10(2) it suffices to show that using $\nu(\partial_A(t))$, $\nu(\partial_B(t))$ we are able to determine whether for a given $c \in \Sigma$,

$$\partial_{c,B}(t) \leq \partial_{c,A}(t) (= \partial_{c,A \cup B}(t)) \quad \text{or} \quad \partial_{c,A}(t) < \partial_{c,B}(t) (= \partial_{c,A \cup B}(t))$$

holds. By Corollary 8.3.6 it suffices to know the sets $C_{a,b} = \{c \in \Sigma \mid \partial_{c,a}(t) = \partial_{c,b}(t)\}$ for $a, b \in A \cup B$. This can be achieved using the information provided by $\nu(\partial_A(t))$ and $\nu(\partial_B(t))$, since $\nu(t)(c, a) \stackrel{8.3.10(2)}{=} \nu(\partial_A(t))(c, a)$ for $a \in A$ (analogously for B) and

$$\partial_{c,a}(t) = \partial_{c,b}(t) \stackrel{8.3.10(4)}{\Longleftrightarrow} \nu(t)(c, a) = \nu(t)(c, b)$$

$\square$

The information provided by Zielonka's time-stamping is sufficient in order to obtain a more complex structural information about a trace. More precisely, with the knowledge of $\nu(t)$ we are able to compute the second approximation introduced by Cori and Métivier in [45] and used in the construction of asynchronous cellular automata. The second approximation $\Delta_2(t)$ of a trace t is the directed graph with vertex set $\Sigma \times \Sigma$ and edge set $\{((a, c), (b, d)) \mid \partial_{a,c}(t) \leq \partial_{b,d}(t)\}$. However, Cori, Métivier and Zielonka showed that the computation of the mapping ν provides sufficient information about trace prefixes in order to obtain an asynchronous mapping [46]. Since the second approximation is an interesting information for itself, we show in the following how to compute it.

First, let us show the following property for $\Delta_2(t)$, which is a stronger variant of the first property required for asynchronous mappings.

Lemma 8.3.13 Let $t \in \mathbb{M}(\Sigma, D)$ and $a \in \Sigma$. Then the second approximation $\Delta_2(ta)$ is computable using $\Delta_2(t)$ and the letter a.

Proof: Let $b, c \in \Sigma$. Then we have

$$\partial_{b,c}(ta) = \begin{cases} \partial_{b,c}(t) & \text{if } c \neq a \\ \partial_{b,D(a)}(t) & \text{if } b \neq c = a \\ \partial_{D(a)}(t)a = \partial_a(ta) & \text{if } b = c = a \end{cases}$$

Note that if $b \neq c = a$ holds, then we can use $\Delta_2(t)$ for computing a letter $c' \in D(a)$ with $\partial_{b,D(a)}(t) = \partial_{b,c'}(t)$.

Finally, we note that $\partial_{D(a)}(t)a$ is not a prefix of t; conversely, a prefix of t is a prefix of $\partial_{D(a)}(t)a$ if and only if it is a prefix of $\partial_{D(a)}(t)$. To conclude, we have $\partial_{D(x)}(t)x \leq \partial_{D(y)}(t)y$ if and only if $x = y$. □

Proposition 8.3.14 *Let $t \in \mathbb{M}(\Sigma, D)$ and $A, B \subseteq \Sigma$ be given and denote $t_1 = \partial_A(t)$, $t_2 = \partial_B(t)$, $r = t_1 \sqcap t_2$, $t_1 = ru$ and $t_2 = rv$ with $u, v \in \mathbb{M}(\Sigma, D)$, $\mathrm{alph}(u) \times \mathrm{alph}(v) \subseteq I$.*

Let $\mu(t_i) = (\nu(t_i), \Delta_2(t_i))$, $i = 1, 2$. Then we can compute the second approximation $\Delta_2(t)$ from $\mu(t_1), \mu(t_2)$.

Proof: Let $C = \{c \in \Sigma \mid \partial_c(t_1) = \partial_c(t_2)\} \overset{8.3.10}{=} \{c \in \Sigma \mid \nu(t_1)(c,c) = \nu(t_2)(c,c)\}$. For convenience we use the following notations: for $x, y \in \Sigma$ we denote (x,y) a u-point if $\partial_{x,C}(t_1)$ is a strict prefix of $\partial_{x,y}(t_1)$, i.e. $\partial_{x,C}(t_1) < \partial_{x,y}(t_1)$; (x,y) is a v-point if $\partial_{x,C}(t_2) < \partial_{x,y}(t_2)$. Otherwise, (x,y) is r-point. The above notations illustrate the graphical meaning, i.e. the position of the maximal vertex of $\partial_{x,y}(t)$ in the subgraph of the dependence graph which corresponds to u, v, or r respectively.

Note that if $C = \emptyset$ then (x,y) is a u-point if and only if $\partial_{x,y}(t_1) \neq 1$, hence if $\nu(t_1)(x,y) \neq 0$; analogously, (x,y) is a v-point if and only if $\nu(t_2)(x,y) \neq 0$ and finally, (x,y) is a r-point if and only if $\nu(t_1)(x,y) = \nu(t_2)(x,y) = 0$.

If $C \neq \emptyset$, then with Corollary 8.3.6 we may use $\nu(t_1)$ in order to determine whether (x,y) is a u-point (resp. $\nu(t_2)$ for a v-point). We assume in the following $C \neq \emptyset$. Observe that for $a, c \in \Sigma$,

$$\partial_{a,c}(t) = \begin{cases} \partial_{a,c}(t_1) & \text{if } (a,c) \text{ is a } u\text{-point} \\ \partial_{a,c}(t_2) & \text{if } (a,c) \text{ is a } v\text{-point} \\ \bigsqcup_{i=1,2} \partial_{a,c}(t_i) \leq \partial_a(r) & \text{if } (a,c) \text{ is a } r\text{-point} \end{cases}$$

Furthermore, if (a,c) is a r-point, then we have to distinguish if (c,c) is a u-, v- or r-point. Note that we have $\partial_{a,c}(t) = \partial_{a,c}(t_1)$, if (c,c) is a u-point, respectively $\partial_{a,c}(t) = \partial_{a,c}(t_2)$, if (c,c) is a v-point and finally, $\partial_{a,c}(t) = \partial_{a,c}(t_i)$ $(i = 1,2)$, if (c,c) is a r-point (hence, $c \in C$).

Consider now for $a, b, c, d \in \Sigma$ the question, whether or not $\partial_{a,c}(t) \leq \partial_{b,d}(t)$ holds and suppose (a,c) is a α-point and (b,d) is a β-point, where $\alpha, \beta \in \{u, v, r\}$.

First, observe that if $\{\alpha, \beta\} = \{u, v\}$ or $(\beta = r$ and $\alpha \neq r)$, then the answer is negative. Else, if $\alpha = \beta$, then we can provide an answer using either $\Delta_2(t_1)$ or $\Delta_2(t_2)$.

We now consider the situation $\alpha = r$, $\beta = u$ (the case $\beta = v$ can be handled analogously). Now, if (c,c) is either a u- or a r-point, then we can use again $\Delta_2(t_1)$ (see remark above) and check $\partial_{a,c}(t_1) \leq \partial_{b,d}(t_1)$.

Finally, we consider the case where $\alpha = r$, $\beta = u$ and (c,c) is a v-point, hence $\partial_{a,c}(t) = \partial_{a,c}(t_2)$. It suffices to show that a letter $f \in \Sigma$ exists effectively such that $\partial_{a,c}(t_2) = \partial_{a,f}(t_1)$ holds.

Assume $\partial_{a,c}(t_2) \neq 1$ (otherwise, $\partial_{a,c}(t_1) = 1$, too, and we choose $f = c$). Recall $r = \partial_C(t) = \partial_C(t_1) = \partial_C(t_2)$ and consider the trace $r' = r \sqcap \partial_c(t_2)$, with $r = r'x$, $\partial_c(t_2) = r'y$ and $\mathrm{alph}(x) \times \mathrm{alph}(y) \subseteq I$ (see also Figure 8.2).

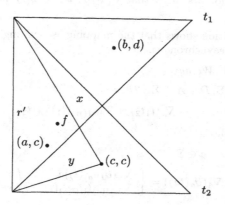

Figure 8.2: $\alpha = r$, $\beta = u$ and (c, c) is a v-point.

With $\partial_{a,c}(t_2) = \partial_{a,c}(t) \leq \partial_a(r)$ we immediately obtain $\partial_{a,c}(t_2) = \partial_a(r')$, in particular $r' \neq 1$. Let $C' = \{e \in \Sigma \mid \partial_e(\partial_c(t_2)) = \partial_e(r)\}$, hence with Proposition 8.3.5 we obtain $C' \supseteq \max(r') \neq \emptyset$. Furthermore, with Proposition 8.3.4 we have $\partial_{a,c}(t_2) = \partial_a(r') = \partial_{a,f}(r') = \partial_{a,f}(r)$ for some $f \in \max(r')$, hence $f \in C'$. We show $\partial_f(r) = \partial_f(t_1)$. For this, note that by definition of r', we have $f \notin \mathrm{alph}(x)$. Moreover, due to $y \neq 1$ (otherwise we contradict (c, c) being a v-point), together with $f \in \max(r')$, we obtain $f \in D(\mathrm{alph}(y))$, hence $f \in D(\mathrm{alph}(v))$. Thus, since $\mathrm{alph}(u) \times \mathrm{alph}(v) \subseteq I$, we deduce $f \notin \mathrm{alph}(u)$. Finally, since $t_1 = r'xu$ we immediately conclude $\partial_f(t_1) = \partial_f(r') = \partial_f(r)$.

A letter f with $\partial_{a,c}(t_2) = \partial_{a,f}(t_1)$ can now be computed effectively as follows: using $\nu(t_1)$, $\nu(t_2)$ we first determine the sets C and $\mathrm{alph}(v)$ (see Corollary 8.3.6). Using again $\nu(t_2)$ we compute C'. Finally, using $\nu(t_1)$ we choose $f \in C' \cap D(\mathrm{alph}(v))$ such that $\partial_{a,C}(t_1) \leq \partial_{a,f}(t_1)$. We obtain finally

$$\partial_{a,f}(t_1) \overset{f \in D(\mathrm{alph}(v))}{=\!=\!=} \partial_{a,f}(r) \overset{f \in C'}{=\!=} \partial_{a,f,c}(t_2) \leq \partial_{a,c}(t_2) \leq \partial_{a,C}(t_2) = \partial_{a,C}(t_1) \leq \partial_{a,f}(t_1)$$

$\square$

In the remaining of this section we accomplish the construction of an asynchronous mapping $\mu : \mathbb{M}(\Sigma, D) \to S$ for a given trace language $L \in \mathrm{Rec}(\mathbb{M})$, such that $L = \mu^{-1}\mu(L)$. The mapping μ is obtained by augmenting the basic mapping ν by a component depending on a homomorphism to a finite monoid recognizing L. For this new component we use Zielonka's ∇ notation.

Definition 8.3.15 *Let $t \in M(\Sigma, D)$, $A \subseteq \Sigma$. By $\nabla_A(t)$ we denote the maximal suffix of t containing letters from A, only, i.e. the unique suffix s of t with $t = \partial_{\bar{A}}(t)s$, where $\bar{A} = \Sigma \setminus A$.*

Remark 8.3.16 It follows easily that $\nabla_A \nabla_B(t) = \nabla_{A \cap B}(t)$, for every $t \in M(\Sigma, D)$, $A, B \subseteq \Sigma$.

The next proposition shows that the mapping associating with each trace t the tuple $(\nabla_A(t))_{A \subseteq \Sigma}$ is asynchronous.

Proposition 8.3.17 *We have*

1. *Let $t_1, t_2 \in M(\Sigma, D)$, $A \subseteq \Sigma$. Then*

$$\nabla_A(t_1 t_2) = \nabla_{A \cap I(B)}(t_1) \nabla_A(t_2),$$

   where $B = \mathrm{alph}(\partial_{\bar{A}}(t_2))$.

2. *Let $t \in M(\Sigma, D)$, $a \in \Sigma$. Then*

$$\nabla_A(\partial_a(ta)) = \begin{cases} \nabla_A(\partial_{D(a)}(t))a & \text{for } a \in A \\ \nabla_{A \cap I(a)}(\partial_{D(a)}(t)) & \text{else} \end{cases}$$

3. *Let $t \in M(\Sigma, D)$, $A, B \subseteq \Sigma$ such that $t = \partial_{A \cup B}(t)$. With the notations of Proposition 8.3.5 we have for every $E \subseteq \Sigma$*

$$\nabla_E(t) = \nabla_{E \cap I(F)}(t_A) \nabla_{E \cap \bar{C}}(t_B), \quad \text{where } F = \mathrm{alph}(\partial_E(v)).$$

Proof:

1. By Proposition 8.3.4(4) we obtain $\partial_{\bar{A}}(t_1 t_2) = \partial_{\bar{A} \cup D(B)}(t_1) \partial_{\bar{A}}(t_2)$. With Remark 8.3.16 and the cancellative property of $M(\Sigma, D)$ the result immediately follows.

2. Is a direct consequence of (1) for $t_1 = \partial_{D(a)}(t)$, $t_2 = a$.

3. First note that for $E \subseteq \Sigma$ and $G := \mathrm{alph}(\partial_E(uv)) \supseteq F$,

$$\nabla_E(t) \overset{(1)}{=} \nabla_{E \cap I(G)}(r) \nabla_E(uv) = \nabla_{E \cap I(G)}(r) \nabla_E(u) \nabla_E(v),$$

   where the last equality is due to $\mathrm{alph}(u) \times \mathrm{alph}(v) \subseteq I$. Let us now consider the right side of the claimed identity, noting that $\partial_{E \cup D(F)}(u) = \partial_E(u)$ (since $F \subseteq \mathrm{alph}(v)$):

   - $\nabla_{E \cap I(F)}(t_A) \overset{(1)}{=} \nabla_{E \cap I(G)}(r) \nabla_E(u)$
   - Let $H = \mathrm{alph}(\partial_{E \cup C}(v))$. Then,

$$\nabla_{E \cap \bar{C}}(t_B) \overset{(1)}{=} \nabla_{E \cap \bar{C} \cap I(H)}(r) \nabla_{E \cap \bar{C}}(v) = \nabla_E(v),$$

   due to $\max(r) \subseteq C$ and $\nabla_{\bar{C}}(v) = v$ by Proposition 8.3.5, together with Remark 8.3.16.

$\square$

Corollary 8.3.18 *Let N be a finite monoid and $\eta : \mathbb{M}(\Sigma, D) \to N$ a homomorphism. Let S be the finite set*

$$S = \{(\nu(t), (\eta(\nabla_A(t)))_{A \subseteq \Sigma}) \mid t \in \mathbb{M}(\Sigma, D)\}$$

Then the mapping $\mu : \mathbb{M}(\Sigma, D) \to S$, $\mu(t) = (\nu(t), (\eta(\nabla_A(t)))_{A \subseteq \Sigma})$ is asynchronous and the homomorphism η factorizes through μ.

Proof: The mapping μ is asynchronous by Propositions 8.3.12, 8.3.17. Since $t = \nabla_\Sigma(t)$ for any $t \in \mathbb{M}(\Sigma, D)$, $\mu(t) = \mu(t')$ implies $\eta(t) = \eta(t')$, hence the assertion. $\quad\square$

Main Theorem 8.3.19 *Let $D \subseteq \Sigma \times \Sigma$ be a symmetric and reflexive dependence relation and $L \subseteq \mathbb{M}(\Sigma, D)$ a recognizable trace language. Then there exists a deterministic finite asynchronous cellular automaton recognizing L.*

Proof: Corollary 8.3.18 provides an asynchronous mapping with finite image such that $L = \mu^{-1}\mu(L)$. The asynchronous cellular automaton $\mathcal{A}_\mu$ constructed in Proposition 8.3.8 accepts exactly L. $\quad\square$

8.4 Concluding Remarks

Relating the algebraic recognizability of trace languages to recognizability by devices with distributed control has been a subject of considerable efforts during the eighties. Very interesting constructions providing partial solutions have been given, like C. Duboc's mixed products of automata [75] or Y. Métivier's solution for acyclic dependence graphs [196], presented in a generalized form in Section 8.2. Of course, the most important contribution is W. Zielonka's solution for the general case [277, 278] (see also [45, 46, 53]). The construction given by Zielonka is involved and the question, whether a simpler construction exists, is still of actuality.

The importance of constructing asynchronous automata is also underlined by applications, where automata of small size are highly required. Considerations concerning efficient (and simpler) constructions are also the topic of two kinds of current contributions. The first one concerns modular constructions of asynchronous automata, based on concurrent rational representations of recognizable trace languages, and yields non-deterministic asynchronous automata [228]. The second one deals also with a classical approach and can be regarded as a completion of the first one: determinization of asynchronous automata. The inherent difficulty of the problem of constructing deterministic asynchronous automata is also suggested by both determinization procedures given recently by Klarlund et. al. [154] and by the second author [198].

IV   CONCURRENCY AND LOGIC

Chapter 9

Trace Structures and other Models for Concurrency

Mogens Nielsen   Glynn Winskel

Computer Science Department, Aarhus University, Denmark
{mnielsen,gwinskel}@daimi.aau.dk

Contents

9.1   Introduction

Trace structures were introduced originally by Mazurkiewicz in 1977 [189] as a model for concurrency. The simple but yet powerful new idea was to equip the alphabet of formal languages with an extra structure of independence, interpreted as computational independence between atomic actions while the strings of the language represent the potential evolution of a system. In this chapter we survey a number of results which highlight the power of this idea with respect to other prominent models for concurrency.

More specifically, we shall relate trace structures to the following models: Hoare structures, event structures, prime algebraic domains, Petri nets and asynchronous transition systems. Of course, this is but a small subset of the models for concurrency which have been introduced and studied in recent years. We have chosen to present a few results in some detail, at the expense of the range of models covered.

And how do we relate traces to the other models? Any model for concurrency is meant to model the behaviour of distributed systems at a certain level of abstraction, focussing on certain aspects of the behaviour, deliberately abstracting from others. Here, we shall attempt to classify models according to their "level of abstraction". In stating and proving such relationships we shall use the language of category theory—in particular the notion of an adjunction. In many contexts this has proven to be a convenient language succinctly expressing such relationships, abstracting away from the details of the often very different mathematical formalisms of the individual models. As the reader will see, trace structures relate nicely to most of our chosen models, in the sense that one of the models "embed" into the other; "embedding" is formalized here by special adjunctions called coreflections.

Since the notion of coreflection is quite central to our presentation, let us briefly comment on their formal definition and the intuitive way to understand them.

All our models are introduced as a class of objects, which are equipped with a notion of (behaviour preserving) morphisms, making each model into a category. An adjunction between two such categories, M_0 and M_1, consists of ways of translating from one model to the other, satisfying certain properties. Formally, (see [184] for alternatives) we shall express an adjunction in terms of two functors $L : M_0 \to M_1$ and $R : M_1 \to M_0$ (the left/right adjoint of the adjunction) satisfying:

> for any object m_0 of M_0, there is a morphism $u : m_0 \to R \circ L(m_0)$ (the unit at m_0) such that for any object m_1 of M_1, if there is a morphism $f_0 : m_0 \to R(m_1)$, then there is a unique morphism $f_1 : L(m_0) \to m_1$, such that $f_0 = R(f_1) \circ u$.

If all units of an adjunction are isomorphisms then the adjunction is called a coreflection. It follows that the left adjoint L of a coreflection is always a full and faithful functor.

So much for the formal definition. Notice, how we may interpret a coreflection directly as a way of saying that M_0 embeds into M_1—with L telling us how to embed M_0 into M_1, and R telling us how to project M_1 onto M_0. This will be our formal way of saying that "M_0 is an abstract version of M_1".

The structure of this chapter is straightforward. Categorical relationships between trace structures and the other models are presented in sequence: Hoare traces (section 2), event structures (section 3), domains (section 4), Petri nets (section 5) and asynchronous transition systems (section 6).

Most of the results presented here are based on work by the authors. However, section 5 is based on joint work with G. Rozenberg and P.S. Thiagarajan.

9.2 Trace Structures and Hoare Structures

In this section we shall introduce trace structures as a simple, but yet powerful generalization of classical formal languages. As a model for concurrency, formal languages have been advocated and studied primarily by C.A.R. Hoare and his coworkers [139].

9.2.1 Hoare Structures

The use of formal languages as a model for concurrency is based on the view that the behaviour of a distributed system may be thought of and modeled by its set of possible sequences of occurrences of atomic actions. Let us illustrate the idea by an example.

Example 9.2.1 We consider a simple version of a 'mutual exclusion' system with two processes, P_0 and P_1, and one scheduler, S. The processes work independently, except that every now and then they may request access to a critical region, e.g. accessing common data. The task of the scheduler is to ensure mutually exclusive access to critical regions by appropriately synchronizing with the two processes.

P_i is intended to repeatedly perform the following sequence of four atomic actions:

w_i, representing 'working outside critical region',

e_i, representing 'entering critical region',

c_i, representing 'working inside critical region',

ℓ_i, representing 'leaving critical region'.

S is intended to repeatedly synchronize with either P_0 or P_1 on their respective enter/leave actions:

e_i/ℓ_i representing 'permitting P_i to enter/leave the critical region'.

In process algebra the system may be described as follows, with the convention that parallel components must synchronize on common action-names, as in TCSP [139],

where $\|$ represents parallel composition, $+$ represents nondeterministic choice, and
" . " denotes action prefixing:

$$
\begin{aligned}
\text{SYS} &= P_0 \parallel S \parallel P_1 \\
P_0 &= w_0 \, . \, e_0 \, . \, c_0 \, . \, \ell_0 \, . \, P_0 \\
P_1 &= w_1 \, . \, e_1 \, . \, c_1 \, . \, \ell_1 \, . \, P_1 \\
S &= (e_0 \, . \, \ell_0 \, . \, S) + (e_1 \, . \, \ell_1 \, . \, S)
\end{aligned}
$$

Modelling the behaviour of SYS in terms of sets of sequences of action occurrences,
as suggested in [139], the behaviour of P_i and S will be the sets (ϵ representing the
empty string):

P_i: $\{\epsilon, \, w_i, \, w_i e_i, \, w_i e_i c_i, \, \ldots\}$
S: $\{\epsilon, \, e_0, \, e_1, \, e_0 \ell_0, \, e_1 \ell_1, \ldots\}$

Following [139], the behaviour of SYS will consist of all those strings over the
joint alphabet of actions, which 'project' down to strings in the sets associated with
P_0, P_1, and S (where 'projecting' a string down to a component erases all occurrences of symbols not in the alphabet of the component). I.e. you get a prefix
closed set of strings over the alphabet of actions, where the initial elements (and
their prefix ordering) will be as shown in Figure 9.1.

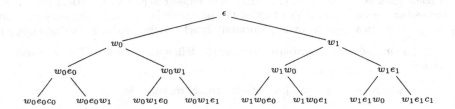

Figure 9.1:

Following our intuition, correctness of the system could be expressed by the fact
that no element in this set will have two consecutive occurrences of c-actions.

Formally, we have

Definition 9.2.2 *A Hoare Structure is a pair (H, Σ) where Σ is an alphabet (of
atomic actions), and H is a nonempty, prefix closed subset of the monoid Σ^*.*

Actually, such structures are called traces in [139], but we prefer to reserve the word
traces to the kind of structures introduced next—the topic of this book.

9.2.2 Trace Structures

Note that in the example above, the Hoare structure does not capture the intention that either of the processes may work outside its critical region completely independently of (in parallel with) other activities of SYS—one of the main points of the 'mutual exclusion' exercise! To be more precise, the very same Hoare structure will be associated with a completely sequential, 'interleaved' TCSP version of SYS.

The idea suggested by Mazurkiewicz [189] is to allow the modelling of such independent activities of components of system by introducing the extra structure of an independence relation, I, on the action alphabet. For process algebras like TCSP, following our intuition we would relate two actions as independent iff they involve disjoint sets of components (from parallel components like P_0, P_1 and S), i.e. they occur at physically different sites of the system. So, in our example we would get the symmetric closure of

$$I = \quad \{w_0, c_0\} \times \{e_1, \ell_1, w_1, c_1\}$$
$$\cup \{w_1, c_1\} \times \{e_0, \ell_0, w_0, c_0\}$$

Based on an independence alphabet, the behaviour of our system will be modeled in terms of traces, i.e. on equivalence classes of

$\simeq_I$ — the smallest congruence of Σ^* satisfying $a \ I \ b \Rightarrow ab \simeq_I ba$.

In our example $w_0 w_1 e_0 \simeq_I w_0 e_0 w_1$, and the equivalence class of $w_0 w_1 e_0$ is $[w_0 w_1 e_0] = \{w_0 w_1 e_0, w_0 e_0 w_1, w_1 w_0 e_0\}$.

Now, Hoare structures generalize from subsets of Σ^* to subsets of the monoid of traces, denoted $M(\Sigma, I)$. The prefix ordering of Hoare structures generalize to a prefix ordering of traces, defined in terms of the following preorder on strings:

$$s \ _I \ t \ \text{iff} \ \exists \ u. \ su \approx_I t$$

which induces the following partial order (prefix order) on traces:

$$\sqsubseteq_I \ = \ _I \ / \approx_I$$

i.e.

$$[s] \sqsubseteq_I [t] \ \text{iff} \ \exists \ u, v. \ s \approx_I u \ _I \ v \approx_I t.$$

In our example $[\epsilon] \sqsubseteq_I [w_0] \sqsubseteq_I [w_0 w_1] \sqsubseteq_I [w_0 \ e_0 \ w_1]$, and the initial traces and their prefix ordering are as shown in Figure 9.2.

So, the extra modelling power boils down to the presence of traces like $[w_0 w_1]$ in our example, representing actions w_0 and w_1 in any (unspecified) order, and interpreted as their concurrent or independent occurrences. To be more precise, consider the following two TCSP terms:

$$T_0 \ = \ w_0 \parallel w_1$$
$$T_1 \ = \ (w_0 \ . \ w_1) + (w_1 \ . \ w_0)$$

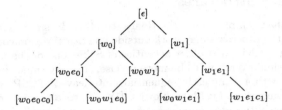

Figure 9.2:

Figure 9.3: Hoare structure of T_0 and T_1

The Hoare structures associated with these two terms will be identical:
whereas the independence alphabet over $\{w_0, w_1\}$ will be different for the two systems, following our interpretation of independence as 'activity of different components'. Hence the trace structures of the two systems will be different:

Figure 9.4: Trace structure of T_0 , trace structure of T_1

We are now ready for our formal definition of trace structures. Conceptually, we follow [190] where a trace structure is defined to be a prefix closed, proper subset of the monoid $M(\Sigma, I)$. However, for technical reasons (only!) we prefer in our formal definition to work with such structures in terms of consistent subsets of Σ^*—with the traces a derived notion, as in Proposition 9.2.4 below

Definition 9.2.3 *A trace structure is a triple* $T = (M, \Sigma, I)$ *where* (Σ, I) *is an independence alphabet, i.e.* I *an irreflexive, symmetric relation* $\subseteq \Sigma \times \Sigma$, *and* M *a*

consistent, prefix closed, proper subset of Σ^*, i.e. a subset satisfying for all $t, t' \in \Sigma^*$ and $a, b \in \Sigma$:

$$consistency \quad : \quad - t \approx_I t' \in M \Rightarrow t \in M$$
$$prefix\ closure \quad : \quad - ta \in M \Rightarrow t \in M$$
$$properness \quad : \quad - ta, tb \in M \ \& \ aIb \Rightarrow tab \in M$$

We use the notation $M / \approx_I$ for the traces of T, i.e.

$$M / \approx_I = \{[w] \mid w \in M\}$$

We may (as we shall often do) think of a trace structure as a prefix closed set of traces, in the sense that from the axioms of consistency and prefix closure above, we get:

Proposition 9.2.4 *Given a trace structure* $T = (M, \Sigma, I)$ *as in Definition 9.2.3, then* $(M / \approx_I, \sqsubseteq_I)$ *satisfies*

$$w \in M \Leftrightarrow [w] \in M / \approx_I$$

and

$$[w] \sqsubseteq_I [w'] \in M / \approx_I \Rightarrow [w] \in M / \approx_I$$

We also assume here properness as part of the definition of a trace structure (as in [190]). Our main reason is that this is most often done when considering trace languages as a model for concurrency. Based on our view above as independence being activity of different components of a distributed system, it certainly seems very natural to assume properness. However, from the point of view of this chapter, most of what we are going to say about relationships to other models could have been said without assuming properness and, correspondingly, slightly changing the definition of the other models. We have mainly included properness for convenience, and leave these modifications for the interested reader.

9.2.3 Their Relationship

We have introduced trace structures as a generalization of Hoare structures, and argued based on examples that we get more expressive power, viewed as a model for concurrency. Is there a more formal way of saying this? As indicated in the introduction, we shall state the 'embedding' of Hoare structures into trace structures as a categorical coreflection. First we equip our models with notions of behaviour preserving morphisms.

Morphisms of languages are partial functions on their alphabets which send strings in one language to strings in another:

Definition 9.2.5 *A partial function* $\lambda : \Sigma \rightarrow_* \Sigma'$ *extends to strings by defining*

$$\widehat{\lambda}(sa) = \begin{cases} \widehat{\lambda}(s)\lambda(a) & \text{if } \lambda(a) \text{ defined} \\ \widehat{\lambda}(s) & \text{if } \lambda(a) \text{ undefined} \end{cases}$$

A morphism *of Hoare structures* $(H, \Sigma) \to (H', \Sigma')$ *consists of a partial function* $\lambda : \Sigma \to_* \Sigma'$ *such that* $\forall s \in H.\ \widehat{\lambda}(s) \in H'$.
We write **H** *for the category of Hoare structures with the above understanding of morphisms, where composition is our usual composition of partial functions.*

Behaviour preserving morphisms such as these may be thought of as specifying correctness properties. E.g. we may specify the 'correctness' of the mutual exclusion example by the fact that the function λ from the alphabet of actions, which is undefined for $\{w_0, w_1\}$ and the identity function for all other action symbols, *is* a morphism from the Hoare structure of the mutual exclusion example to the Hoare structure consisting of all prefixes of the regular language $(e_0 c_0 l_0 \cup e_1 c_1 l_1)^*$.

Morphisms between trace structures are morphisms between the underlying languages which preserve independence:

Definition 9.2.6 *A morphism of trace structures* $(M, \Sigma, I) \to (M', \Sigma', I')$ *consists of a partial function* $\lambda : \Sigma \to_* \Sigma'$ *which*

- *preserves independence:* aIb & $\lambda(a)$ *defined* & $\lambda(b)$ *defined* $\Rightarrow \lambda(a)I'\lambda(b)$ *for all* $a, b \in \Sigma$,

- *preserves strings:* $s \in M \Rightarrow \widehat{\lambda}(s) \in M'$ *for all strings s.*

It is easy to see that morphisms of trace structures preserve traces and the ordering between them.

Proposition 9.2.7 *Let* $\lambda : (M, \Sigma, I) \to (M', \Sigma', I')$ *be a morphism of trace structures. If $s \sqsubseteq t$ in the trace structure (M, Σ, I) then $\widehat{\lambda}(s) \sqsubseteq \widehat{\lambda}(t)$ in the trace language* (M', Σ', I').

We write **T** for the category of trace structures with composition that of partial functions. Note that for both **H** and **T** the derived notions of isomorphisms become 'identity up to names of elements of Σ'.

The promised coreflection between **H** and **T** is formed by the functors $ht : \mathbf{H} \to \mathbf{T}$ and $th : \mathbf{T} \to \mathbf{H}$.

$$
\begin{aligned}
\text{on objects} \quad &: ht(H, \Sigma) = (H, \Sigma, \emptyset) \\
&\quad th(M, \Sigma, I) = (M, \Sigma) \\
\text{on morphisms} &: ht(\lambda) = \lambda \\
&\quad th(\lambda) = \lambda
\end{aligned}
$$

So, ht views a Hoare structure as a trace structure with no independence, and th simply forgets about the independence relation.

Theorem 9.2.8 *ht, th form a coreflection between **H** and **T** with ht as left adjoint.*

Proof: It is easy to see that for every Hoare Structure (H, Σ) : $th \circ ht(H, \Sigma) = (H, \Sigma)$. Furthermore, for every trace structure (M, Σ, I), the identity function Id : $\Sigma \to \Sigma$ is a morphism $ht \circ th(M, \Sigma, I) \to (M, \Sigma, I)$, which is seen to be the counit of the coreflection, in the sense that for every Hoare structure (H, Σ') with morphism λ : $ht(H, \Sigma') \to (M, \Sigma, I)$ there is a unique λ' : $ht(H, \Sigma') \to ht \circ th(M, \Sigma, I)$ such that $\lambda = Id \circ \lambda'$ (obviously $\lambda' = \lambda$). $\qquad\square$

Before we continue our survey of relationships between trace structures and other models for concurrency, let us briefly mention that there is more to categorical view of models such as **T**. As it turns out, all our models, including **T**, have certain universal constructs, which first of all are essential building blocks in understanding and modelling of many of the standard combinators from process algebra, and secondly for general reasons, many of these universal constructs translate via our adjunctions from one model to another. Let us illustrate the first of these points by two examples: the product and coproduct in **T**.

We start by commenting on these universal constructions in the category of sets with partial functions. Assume that X and Y are sets not containing the distinguished symbol $*$. Write $f : X \to_* Y$ for a function $f : X \cup \{*\} \to Y \cup \{*\}$ such that $f(*) = *$. When $f(x) = *$, for $x \in X$, we say $f(x)$ is *undefined* and otherwise *defined*. We say $f : X \to_* Y$ is *total* when $f(x)$ is defined for all $x \in X$. Of course, such total morphisms $X \to_* Y$ correspond to the usual total functions $X \to Y$, with which they shall be identified. For the category **Set**$_*$, we take as objects sets which do not contain $*$, and as morphisms functions $f : X \to_* Y$, with the composition of two such functions being the usual composition of total functions (but on sets extended by $*$). Of course, **Set**$_*$ is isomorphic to the category of sets with partial functions, as usually presented.

We remark on some categorical constructions in **Set**$_*$. A coproduct of X and Y in **Set**$_*$ is the disjoint union $X \uplus Y$ with the obvious injections. A product of X and Y in **Set**$_*$ has the form $X \times_* Y =$

$$\{(x, *)|x \in X\} \cup \{(*, y)|y \in Y\} \cup \{(x, y)|x \in X, y \in Y\}$$

with projections those partial functions to the left and right coordinates.

Proposition 9.2.9 *Let* (M_0, Σ_0, I_0) *and* (M_1, Σ_1, I_1) *be trace structures. Their product is* (M, Σ, I) *where* $\Sigma = \Sigma_0 \times_* \Sigma_1 = \Sigma_0 \times \{*\} \cup \{*\} \times \Sigma_1 \cup \Sigma_0 \times \Sigma_1)$, *the product in* **Set**$_*$, *with projections* $\pi_0 : \Sigma \to_* \Sigma_0$ *and* $\pi_1 : \Sigma \to_* \Sigma_1$, *with*

$$aIb \Leftrightarrow (\pi_0(a), \pi_0(b) \ \textit{defined} \ \Rightarrow \pi_0(a)I_0\pi_0(b)) \ \&$$
$$(\pi_1(a), \pi_1(b) \ \textit{defined} \ \Rightarrow \pi_1(a)I_1\pi_1(b)),$$

and

$$M = \widehat{\pi}_0^{-1}M_0 \cap \widehat{\pi}_1^{-1}M_1.$$

Their coproduct *is* (M, Σ, I) *where* $\Sigma = \Sigma_0 \uplus \Sigma_1$, *the disjoint union, with injections* $j_0 : \Sigma_0 \to \Sigma, j_1 : \Sigma_0 \to \Sigma$, *the relation* I *satisfies*

$$aIb \Leftrightarrow \exists a_0, b_0. \ a_0 I_0 b_0 \ \& \ a = j_0(a_0) \ \& \ b = j_0(a_0) \ \textit{or}$$
$$\exists a_1, b_1. \ a_1 I_1 b_1 \ \& \ a = j_1(a_1) \ \& \ b = j_1(a_1)$$

and

$$M = \widehat{j_0} M_0 \cup \widehat{j_1} M_1.$$

Example 9.2.10 Let $T_i = (\{\epsilon, a_i\}, \{a_i\}, \emptyset)$, $i = 0, 1$, be two trace structures, $a_0 \neq a_1$. Then the product of T_0 and T_1 is the trace structure:

$$[\epsilon] \longrightarrow [(a_0, a_1)]$$

$$[(a_0, *)] \qquad [(*, a_1)]$$

$$[(a_0, *)(*, a_1),$$
$$(*, a_1)(a_0, *)]$$

The coproduct of T_0 and T_1 is the trace structure

$$[\epsilon]$$

$$[a_0] \qquad [a_1]$$

Note that the product of two trace structures may be thought of as a trace structure over an alphabet of actions belonging to $\Sigma_0((a_0, *))$, $\Sigma_1((*, a_1))$ or a combined (synchronizing) action $((a_0, a_1))$. The strings in the product structure represent exactly those which project down to strings in M_0 and M_1. Notice the close relationship to the interpretation of the parallel combinator of process algebra like TCSP. This is no coincidence! Notice also that there is a similar close relationship between the coproduct of trace structures and the operational understanding of the sum (nondeterministic choice) combinator of process algebra. This is not a coincidence either! The close connection between products/coproducts in models like trace structures and parallel/sum combinators in process algebra have been studied in detail by Winskel, and may be found in [273].

9.3   Trace Structures and Event Structures

Consider again the prefix ordering of strings. It is easy to see that the orderings associated with Hoare structures will be standard tree structures. An interesting question is, what happens when we generalize to trace structures, i.e. what can be said about the orderings associated with trace structures? In the next section we shall provide a characterization of these orderings in terms of a well-known class of Scott-like domains. But in the process of providing this result, we shall show here, that these orderings are exactly the orderings associated with another well-known model for concurrency, the event structures originally introduced in [199]. And as a corollary of this we provide an independent strong relationship between trace structures and event structures.

9.3.1 Event Structures

The tree ordering of the elements of a Hoare structure may be viewed as a structure over action occurrences, where individual occurrences may be either ordered or not ordered (belonging to the same or different computations). Event structures may be seen as a generalization of such structures, allowing a third relationship between occurrences, that of concurrency (belonging to the same computation, but with no causal/temporal ordering).

Definition 9.3.1 *Define an* event structure *to be a structure* $(E, \leq, \#)$ *consisting of a set E, of* events *which are partially ordered by $\leq$, the* causal dependency relation, *and a binary, symmetric, irreflexive relation $\# \subseteq E \times E$, the* conflict relation, *which satisfy*

$$\{e' \mid e' \leq e\} \text{ is finite,}$$
$$e \# e' \leq e'' \Rightarrow e \# e''$$

for all $e, e', e'' \in E$.

Say two events $e, e' \in E$ are concurrent, *and write e co e', iff $\neg(e \leq e'$ or $e' \leq e$ or $e \# e')$. Write W for $\# \cup 1_E$, i.e. the reflexive closure of the conflict relation.*

The finiteness assumption restricts attention to discrete processes where an event occurrence depends only on finitely many previous occurrences. The axiom on the conflict relation expresses that if two events causally depend on events in conflict then they too are in conflict.

Guided by our interpretation we can formulate a notion of computation state of an event structure $(E, \leq, \#)$. Taking a computation state of a process to be represented by the set x of events which have occurred in the computation, we expect that

$$e' \in x \ \& \ e \leq e' \Rightarrow e \in x$$

—if an event has occurred then all events on which it causally depends have occurred too—and also that

$$\forall e, e' \in x. \neg(e \# e')$$

—no two conflicting events can occur together in the same computation.

Definition 9.3.2 *Let $(E, \leq, \#)$ be an event structure. Define its* configurations, *$\mathcal{D}(E, \leq, \#)$, to consist of those subsets $x \subseteq E$ which are*

- conflict-free: $\forall e, e' \in x. \ \neg(e \# e')$ *and*

- downwards-closed: $\forall e, e'. \ e' \leq e \in x \Rightarrow e' \in x$.

In particular, define $\lceil e \rceil = \{e' \in E \mid e' \leq e\}$. (Note that $\lceil e \rceil$ is a configuration as it is conflict-free.)

Write $\mathcal{D}^0(E, \leq, \#)$ for the set of finite configurations.

The important relations associated with an event structure can be recovered from its finite configurations (or indeed similarly from its configurations):

Proposition 9.3.3 *Let $(E, \leq, \#)$ be an event structure. Then*

- $e \leq e' \Leftrightarrow \forall x \in \mathcal{D}^0(E, \leq, \#).\ e' \in x \Rightarrow e \in x.$

- $e \# e' \Leftrightarrow \forall x \in \mathcal{D}^0(E, \leq, \#).\ e \in x \Rightarrow e' \notin x.$

- $e \text{ co } e' \Leftrightarrow \exists x, x' \in \mathcal{D}^0(E, \leq, \#).\ e \in x \ \& \ e' \notin x \ \& \ e' \in x' \ \& \ e \notin x' \ \& \ x \cup x \in \mathcal{D}^0(E, \#, \leq).$

Events manifest themselves as atomic jumps from one configuration to another, and later it will follow that we can regard such jumps as transitions in an asynchronous transition system.

Definition 9.3.4 *Let $(E, \leq, \#)$ be an event structure. Let x, x' be configurations. Write*

$$x \xrightarrow{\ e\ } x' \Leftrightarrow e \notin x \ \& \ x' = x \cup \{e\}.$$

Proposition 9.3.5 *Two events e_0, e_1 of an event structure are in the concurrency relation co iff there exist configurations x, x_0, x_1, x' such that*

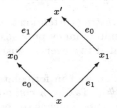

Morphisms on event structures are defined as follows [271]:

Definition 9.3.6 *Let $ES = (E, \leq, \#)$ and $ES' = (E', \leq', \#')$ be event structures. A morphism from ES to ES' consists of a partial function $\eta : E \to_* E'$ on events which satisfies*

$$x \in \mathcal{D}(ES) \Rightarrow \eta x \in \mathcal{D}(ES') \ \& $$
$$\forall e_0, e_1 \in x.\ \eta(e_0), \eta(e_1) \text{ both defined } \ \& \ \eta(e_0) = \eta(e_1) \Rightarrow e_0 = e_1.$$

A morphism $\eta : ES \to ES'$ between event structures expresses how behaviour in ES determines behaviour in ES'. The partial function η expresses how the occurrence of events in ES implies the simultaneous occurrence of events in ES'; the fact that $et(e) = e'$ can be understood as expressing that the event e' is a 'component' of the event e and, in this sense, that the occurrence of e implies the simultaneous occurrence of e'. If two distinct events in ES have the same image in ES' under η then they cannot belong to the same configuration.

Morphisms of event structures preserve the concurrency relation. This is a simple consequence of Proposition 9.3.5, showing how the concurrency relation holding between events appears as a 'little square' of configurations.

Proposition 9.3.7 *Let E be an event structure with concurrency relation co and E' an event structure with concurrency relation co'. Let $\eta : E \to E'$ be a morphism of event structures. Then, for any events e_0, e_1 of E,*

$$e_0 \ co \ e_1 \ \& \ \eta(e_0), \eta(e_1) \ both \ defined \Rightarrow \eta(e_0) \ co' \ \eta(e_1).$$

Morphisms between event structures can be described more directly in terms of the causality and conflict relations of the event structure:

Proposition 9.3.8 *A morphism of event structures from $(E, \leq, \#)$ to $(E', \leq', \#')$ is a partial function $\eta : E \to_* E'$ such that*

(i) $\eta(e)$ defined $\Rightarrow \lceil \eta(e) \rceil \subseteq \eta\lceil e \rceil$ and
(ii) $\eta(e_0), \eta(e_1)$ both defined $\& \ \eta(e_0)\mathsf{w}'\eta(e_1) \Rightarrow e_0\mathsf{w}e_1$.

Let **E** Denote the category of event structures with morphism as in Def. 9.3.6, and composition named composition of partial functions.

The category of event structures also possesses products and coproducts useful in modelling parallel compositions and nondeterministic sums.

Proposition 9.3.9 *Let $(E_0, \leq_0, \#_0)$ and $(E_1, \leq_1, \#_1)$ be event structures. Their coproduct in the category **E** is the event structure $(E_0 \uplus E_1, \leq, \#)$ where*

$$e \leq e' \Leftrightarrow (\exists e_0, e_0'. \ e_0 \leq_0 e_0' \ \& \ j_0(e_0) = e \ \& \ j_0(e_0') = e') \ or$$
$$(\exists e_1, e_1'. \ e_1 \leq_1 e_1' \ \& \ j_1(e_1) = e \ \& \ j_1(e_1') = e')$$

and

$$\# = \#_0 \cup \#_1 \cup (j_0 E_0) \times (j_1 E_1),$$

with injections $j_0 : E_0 \to E_0 \uplus E_1, j_1 : E_1 \to E_0 \uplus E_1$ the injections of E_0 and E_1 into their disjoint union.

It is tricky to give a direct construction of product on event structures. However, a construction of the product will follow from the coreflection from event structures to trace languages (see later in this section), and we postpone the construction till then.

9.3.2 A Representation Theorem

Throughout this section assume (M, Σ, I) is a trace structure, and we shall study its associated preorder

$$s \ t \Leftrightarrow \exists u. \ su \approx t$$

and show that its quotient $/\approx$ can be represented by the finite configurations of an event structure. We limit ourselves here to a sketch of the main steps in this representation, and refer to [273] for a complete proof of the representation theorem. Alternative proofs may be found in [9] and [239].

Events of (M, Σ, I), to be thought of as event occurrences, are taken to be equivalence classes of nonempty strings with respect to the equivalence relation $\sim$ now defined.

Definition 9.3.10 *The relation $\sim$ is the smallest equivalence relation on nonempty strings such that*

$$sa \;\sim\; sba \quad if \;\; bIa, \;\; and$$
$$sa \;\sim\; ta \quad if \;\; s \approx t$$

for $sa, sba, ta \in M$.

Definition 9.3.11 *Let $s \in M$. Define the events of s, to be*

$$ev(s) = \{\{u\}_\sim \mid u \text{ is a nonempty prefix of } s\},$$

and the events of M to be

$$ev(M) = \cup\{ev(s) \mid s \in M\}$$

Example 9.3.12 From the prefixes shown in Figure 9.2, there are the following events:

$$\{w_0\}_\sim, \; \{w_1\}_\sim, \; \{w_0 e_0\}, \; \{w_1, e_1\}_\sim, \; \{w_0 e_0 c_0\}_\sim, \{w_1 e_1 c_1\}_\sim$$

where e.g.

$$\{w_0 e_0 c_0\}_\sim = \{w_0 e_0 c_0, w_0 e_0 w_1 c_0, w_0 w_1 e_0 c_0, w_1 w_0 e_0 c_0\}$$

Before giving the complete definition of an event structure, we list some important properties of the events of a trace structure:

Lemma 9.3.13 *Let $s, t \in M$.*

$$s \; t \Leftrightarrow ev(s) \subseteq ev(t).$$

The next lemma shows that incompatibility between traces stems from a lack of independence between events.

Lemma 9.3.14 *Let $s, t \in M$.*

$$\exists u \in M. \; ev(u) = ev(s) \cup ev(t)$$

iff

$$\forall v \in M, a, b \in \Sigma. \; \{va\}_\sim \in ev(s) \; \& \; \{vb\}_\sim \in ev(t) \Rightarrow a(I \cup 1_\Sigma)b.$$

The following lemma says that each event has a -minimum representative.

Lemma 9.3.15 *For all events e there is $sa \in e$ such that*

$$\forall ta \in e. \; sa \; ta.$$

With these properties of the events of a trace structure, we are ready for the main construction in our representation theorem:

Definition 9.3.16 *Let $T = (M, \Sigma, I)$ be a trace structure. Define a corresponding event structure*

$$te(M, \Sigma, I) = (E, \leq, \#)$$

where

- *E is the set of events of (M, Σ, I),*

- *$\leq$ is a relation between events e, e' given by $e \leq e'$ iff $e \in ev(s)$ where sa is a minimum representative of e', and*

- *the relation $e \# e'$ holds between events iff*

$$\exists e_0, e_0'. \; e_0 \# _0 e_0' \; \& \; e_0 \leq e \; \& \; e_0' \leq e'$$

where, by definition,

$$e_0 \# _0 e_0' \text{ iff } \exists v, a, b. \; va \in e_0 \; \& \; vb \in e_0' \; \& \; \neg(a(I \cup 1_\Sigma)b).$$

Furthermore, define $\lambda_T : E \to \Sigma$ by taking $\lambda_T(\{sa\}_\sim) = a$. (From the definition of $\sim$, it follows that λ_T is well-defined as a function.)

Proposition 9.3.17 *Let $T = (M, \Sigma, I)$ be a trace structure. Then the structure $te(T) = (E, \leq, \#)$ given by Definition 9.3.16 is an event structure for which*

$$e \leq e' \quad \text{iff} \quad \forall s \in M. \; e' \in ev(s) \Rightarrow e \in ev(s)$$

$$e \# e' \quad \text{iff} \quad \forall s \in M. \; e \in ev(s) \Rightarrow e' \notin ev(s).$$

We now present the representation theorem for trace structures.

Theorem 9.3.18 *Let $T = (M, \Sigma, I)$ be a trace structure. Let $te(T) = (E, \leq, \#)$. There is an order isomorphism*

$$Ev : (M/ \approx, \; /\approx) \to (\mathcal{D}^0(E, \leq, \#), \subseteq)$$

where $Ev(\{s\}_\approx) = ev(s)$.
Moreover, for $s \in M$, $x \in \mathcal{D}^0(E, \leq, \#)$ and $a \in \Sigma$,

$$(\exists e. \; ev(s) \xrightarrow{\;e\;} x \text{ in } \mathcal{D}^0(E, \leq, \#) \; \& \; \lambda_T(e) = a) \Leftrightarrow (sa \in M \; \& \; ev(sa) = x). \quad (\dagger)$$

Proof: Let $s \in M$. By the 'only if' direction of Lemma 9.3.14 it follows that $ev(s)$ is a conflict-free subset of events. By Lemma 9.3.15, $ev(s)$ is downwards-closed with respect to $\leq$. The fact that Ev is well-defined, 1-1, order preserving and reflecting follows from Lemma 9.3.13. To establish that Ev is an isomorphism it suffices to check Ev is onto. To this end we first prove ($\dagger$).

The '⇐' direction of the equivalence (†) follows directly, as follows. Assume $sa \in M$, and $ev(sa) = x$. Then taking $e = \{sa\}_{\approx}$ yields an event for which $ev(s) \xrightarrow{e} x$ and $\lambda_T(e) = a$. To show '⇒', assume $ev(s) \xrightarrow{e} x$ and $\lambda_T(e) = a$. Let ta be a minimum representative of the event e. As x is downwards-closed

$$ev(t) \subseteq ev(s).$$

Because x is conflict-free we meet the conditions of lemma 9.3.14 ('if' direction, with s for s and ta for t) and obtain the existence of $u \in M$ such that

$$ev(u) = ev(s) \cup ev(ta) = x.$$

Hence $s \sqsubseteq u$, i.e. $sw \approx u$ for some string w. But $ev(s) \xrightarrow{e} ev(sw)$, so w must be a with $sa \in e$.

Now a simple induction on the size of $x \in \mathcal{D}^0(E, \leq, \#)$ shows that there exists $s \in M$ for which $ev(s) = x$. From this it follows that Ev is onto, and consequently that Ev is an order isomorphism.   □

Via the representation theorem we can see how to read the concurrency relation of an event structure in trace-language terms:

Proposition 9.3.19 *For a trace structure $T = (M, \Sigma, I)$ the construction $te(M, \Sigma, I)$ is an event structure in which the concurrency relation satisfies*

$$e \text{ co } e' \text{ iff } \exists va, vb \in M.\ va \in e\ \&\ vb \in e'\ \&\ aIb. \tag{†}$$

9.3.3   Some Relationships

The representation theorem extends to a coreflection between the categories of event structures and trace structures. This may be interpreted as the perhaps surprising result, that trace structures are more expressive than event structures, despite the fact that event structures seem to have more structure in terms of the explicit conflict relation.

Definition 9.3.20 *Let E be an event structure. Define $et(E)$ to be (M, E, co), where $s = e_1 \ldots e_n \in M$ iff there is a chain*

$$\emptyset \xrightarrow{e_1} x_1 \xrightarrow{e_2} x_2 \ldots \xrightarrow{e_n} x_n$$

of configurations of E.
Let η be a morphism of event structures $\eta : E \to E'$. Define $et(\eta) = \eta$.

Proposition 9.3.21 *et is a functor $\mathbf{E} \to \mathbf{T}$.*

Proof: The only nontrivial part of the proof is that showing that η is a morphism from $et(E)$ to $et(E')$ provided η is a morphism $E \to E'$. However, this follows from the Proposition 9.3.7 and the observation that if a sequence of events s is associated with a chain of configurations in E then $\hat{\eta}(s)$ is associated with a chain of configurations in E'.   □

The function λ_T, for T a trace structure, will be the counit of the adjunction.

Proposition 9.3.22 *Let $T = (M, \Sigma, I)$ be a trace structure. Then,*

$$\lambda_T : et \circ te(T) \rightarrow T$$

is a morphism of trace structures.

Proof: Let $e_1 e_2 \cdots e_n$ be a string in the trace structure $et \circ te(T)$. Then there is a chain of configurations of the event structure $te(T)$

$$\emptyset \xrightarrow{e_1} \{e_1\} \xrightarrow{e_2} \{e_1, e_2\} \cdots \xrightarrow{e_n} \{e_1, e_2, \cdots, e_n\}.$$

By repeated use of ($\dagger$) in the representation theorem 9.3.18, we obtain that $\widehat{\lambda_T}(e_1 e_2 \cdots e_n) \in M$. If e co e', for events e, e', then by Proposition 9.3.19, it follows directly that $\lambda_T(e) I \lambda_T(e')$. Thus $\lambda_T : et \circ te(T) \rightarrow T$ is a morphism of trace structures. $\square$

Lemma 9.3.23 *Let $ES = (E, \leq, \#)$ be an event structure, such that $et(ES) = (M, E, co)$. Let $\lambda : et(ES) \rightarrow T'$ be a morphism in **T**. If $\lambda(e)$ is defined then for all $se, s'e \in M$*

$$\hat{\lambda}(se) \sim \hat{\lambda}(s'e)$$

in $T' = (M', \Sigma', I')$.

Proof: It suffices to consider the following two cases.

The first case is where we assume $s = ue_0 e_1 v$ and $s' = ue_1 e_0 v$ where $u, v \in E^*$, $e_0, e_1 \in E$, e_0 co e_1 in ES: In this case e_0 and e_1 are independent in $et(ES)$. But then $\lambda(e_0) I' \lambda(e_1)$ in T' if both defined (from properties of morphisms in **T**), and hence $\hat{\lambda}(ue_0 e_1 v) \sim \hat{\lambda}(ue_1 e_0 v)$ in T'.

The second case arises when $s = s'e'$ for some $e' \in E$ such that e co e' in ES: In this case e and e' are independent in $et(ES)$. But then $\lambda(e) I' \lambda(e')$ in T' if $\lambda(e')$ is defined and hence $\hat{\lambda}(se) = \hat{\lambda}(s'e)$. $\square$

Theorem 9.3.24 *Let $T' = (M', \Sigma', I')$ be a trace structure. Then the pair $et \circ te(T')$, $\lambda_{T'}$, is cofree over T' with respect to the functor et. That is, for any event structure ES and morphism $\lambda : et(ES) \rightarrow T'$ there is a unique morphism $\eta : ES \rightarrow te(T')$ such that $\lambda = \lambda_{T'} \circ et(\eta)$.*

Proof: Let $ES = (E, \leq, \#)$, $te(T') = (E', \leq', \#')$ and $et(ES) = (M, E, co)$. Define $\eta : E \rightarrow^* E'$ by

$$\eta(e) = \begin{cases} * & \text{if } \lambda(e) = * \\ \{\hat{\lambda}(se)\}_\sim, & \text{where } se \in M, \text{ if } \lambda(e) \neq * \end{cases}$$

It follows from Lemma 9.3.23 that η is a well-defined partial function from E to E'. We need to prove that

(a) η is a morphism $ES \to te(T')$

(b) $\lambda = \lambda_{T'} \circ \eta$

(c) η is unique satisfying (a) and (b).

For a proof of these, see [273]. $\square$

Corollary 9.3.25 *The operation te on trace structures extends to a functor, right adjoint to et, forming a coreflection between* **E** *and* **T**; *the functor te sends the morphism* $\lambda : T \to T'$ *to* $\eta : te(T) \to te(T')$ *acting on events* $\{sa\}_\sim$ *of* $te(T)$ *so that*

$$\eta(\{sa\}_\sim) = \begin{cases} * & \text{if } \lambda(a) \text{ undefined }, \\ \{\widehat{\lambda}(sa)\}_\sim & \text{if } \lambda(a) \text{ defined} . \end{cases}$$

The existence of a coreflection from event structures to trace languages has the important consequence of yielding an explicit product construction on event structures, which is not so easy to define directly. The product of event structures E_0 and E_1 can be obtained as

$$te(et(E_0) \times et(E_1)),$$

that is by first regarding the event structures as trace languages, forming their product as trace languages, and then finally regarding the result as an event structure again. That this result is indeed a product of E_0 and E_1 follows because the right adjoint *te* preserves limits and the unit of the adjunction is a natural isomorphism (i.e. from the coreflection).

The coreflection expresses the sense in which the model of event structures 'embeds' in the model of trace languages. Because of the coreflection we can restrict trace languages to those which are isomorphic to images of event structures under *et* and obtain a full subcategory of trace languages equivalent to that of event structures. Let the subcategory consist of all trace languages T at which the counit

$$\lambda_T : et \circ te(T) \to T$$

is an isomorphism. By a general argument, this subcategory, call it $\mathbf{T}_E$, whose objects have a simple characterization, will be equivalent to the category of event structures. The following proposition characterizes exactly those trace structures in the image of event structures, i.e. we may interpret the following as 'a trace structure version of event structures'. The characterization is phrased in terms of three axioms, two of which ((i) and (ii)) are 'innocent', abandoning redundant elements of Σ and I (which could have been a sensible convention for general trace structures. Axiom (iii) is the 'serious' axiom cutting down $\mathbf{T}$ to $\mathbf{T}_E$.

Proposition 9.3.26 *The trace structures in* $\mathbf{T}_E$ *are those* (M, Σ, I) *for which*

(i) $\forall e \in \Sigma \exists s.\ se \in M$,

(ii) $\forall e_1, e_2.\ e_1 I e_2 \Rightarrow \exists s.\ se_1 \in M\ \&\ se_2 \in M$,

(iii) $\forall e \in E \forall s_1, s_2.\ s_1 e, s_2 e \in M \Rightarrow s_1 e \sim s_2 e.$

The functors $et : \mathbf{E} \to \mathbf{T},\ te : \mathbf{T} \to \mathbf{E}$ *restrict to functors* $\mathbf{E} \to \mathbf{T}_E$ *and* $\mathbf{T}_E \to \mathbf{E}$ *forming an equivalence of categories.*

Proof: The properties 1, 2, 3 are precisely those required of a trace structure T for $\lambda_T : \{se\}_\sim \mapsto e$ to be a bijection preserving and reflecting independence and strings between $et \circ te(T)$ and T, and hence for the counit at T to be an isomorphism. The equivalence of categories now follows by a standard argument from category theory as indicated above, see e.g. [184]. $\qquad\square$

As seen from Proposition above, the extra expressive power in $\mathbf{T}$ compared to $\mathbf{E}$ lies in the possibility of repeatedly occurring action symbols, where the events of event structures from definition represent unique occurrences. We shall now show that the extra power of trace structures has only got to do with this aspect, in the sense that if we equip event structures with a labelling structure, the relationship between the two models turn around, and trace structures embed (reflectively) into labelled event structures.

First we extend event structures with a labelling function into alphabets with independence, resulting in the following category $\mathcal{L}_I(\mathbf{E})$.

Definition 9.3.27 *Define the category* $\mathbf{Set}_I$ *of sets with independence to consist of objects* (L, I) *where* L *is a set and* I, *the independence relation, is a binary, irreflexive relation on* L, *and morphisms* $(L, I) \to (L', I')$ *to be partial functions* $\lambda : L \to_* L'$ *which preserve independence in the sense that*

$$aIb\ \&\ \lambda(a)\ defined\ \&\ \lambda(b)\ defined\ \Rightarrow \lambda(a)I'\lambda(b);$$

composition is that of partial functions.

Definition 9.3.28 *The category* $\mathcal{L}_I(\mathbf{E})$ *has objects* $(ES, l : (E, co) \to (L, I))$ *where* ES *is an event structure with events* E, *and concurrency relation* co, *and the labelling function* $l : (E, co) \to (L, I)$ *is a total function in* $\mathbf{Set}_I$ *(which therefore sends concurrent events to independent labels). We remark that one way an ordinary set* L *can be regarded as a set with independence is as* $(L, L \times L \setminus 1_L)$. *The restriction on labelling functions to such sets with independence amounts to the commonly used restriction of banning* autoconcurrency. *A morphism in* $\mathcal{L}_I(\mathbf{E})$ *has the form*

$$(\eta, \lambda) : (ES, l : (E, co) \to (L, I)) \to (ES', l' : (E', co') \to (L', I'))$$

and consists of a morphism of event structures

$$\eta : ES \to ES'$$

and a morphism

$$\lambda : (L, I) \to (L', I')$$

in $\mathbf{Set}_I$ *such that*

$$l' \circ \eta = \lambda \circ l.$$

The right adjoint of the reflection is $\mathcal{E} : \mathbf{T} \to \mathcal{L}_I(\mathbf{E})$ defined as follows:

Definition 9.3.29 *Let $T = (M, \Sigma, I)$ be a trace language. Define $\mathcal{E}(M, \Sigma, I)$ to be $(E, \leq, \#, \lambda_T)$ where $(E, \leq, \#)$ is the event structure $te(T)$ and $\lambda_T : (E, co) \to (\Sigma, I)$ in $\mathbf{Set}_I$ is given by the counit at T of the coreflection between (unlabelled) event structures and trace languages.*

Let $\lambda : T \to T'$ be a morphism of trace languages. Define $\mathcal{E}(\lambda)$ to be $(te(\lambda), \lambda)$.

In constructing a left adjoint we make use of the following property.

Proposition 9.3.30 *Let $\lambda : (L', I') \to (L, I)$ be a morphism in $\mathbf{Set}_I$. Let (M', L', I') be a trace language. Define $\lambda_!(M', L', I')$ to be (M, L, I) where M is the smallest consistent, prefix-closed, and proper subset containing $\widehat{\lambda} M'$. Then $\lambda : (M', L', I') \to \lambda_!(M', L', I')$ is a morphism of trace languages.*

The left adjoint of the reflection is now given by:

Definition 9.3.31 *Let $(ES, l) \in \mathcal{L}_I(\mathbf{E})$, where $ES = (E, \leq, \#)$ and $l : (E, co) \to (L, I)$ in $\mathbf{Set}_I$. Define*

$$\mathcal{T}(ES, l) = l_! \circ et(ES)$$

For $(\eta, \lambda) : (ES, l) \to (ES', l')$ a morphism of $\mathcal{L}_I(\mathbf{E})$, define

$$\mathcal{T}(\eta, \lambda) = \lambda$$

Theorem 9.3.32 *$\mathcal{E} : \mathbf{T} \to \mathcal{L}_I(\mathbf{E})$ and $\mathcal{T} : \mathcal{L}_I(\mathbf{E}) \to \mathbf{T}$ are functors with $\mathcal{T}$ left adjoint to $\mathcal{E}$. In fact, if $T = (M, L, I)$ is a trace structure then*

$$1_L : \mathcal{T}\mathcal{E}(T) \to T$$

is the counit at T making the adjunction a reflection.

Proof: It is easy to check $\mathcal{E}, \mathcal{T}$ are functors. The fact that $\mathcal{T}\mathcal{E}(T) = T$ follows from the representation theorem (theorem 9.3.18), and ensures that $1_L : \mathcal{T}\mathcal{E}(T) \to T$ is a morphism in $\mathbf{T}$, for any $T \in \mathbf{T}$ with labelling set L.

Let $(ES, l) \in \mathcal{L}_I(\mathbf{E})$, with $l : (E, co) \to (L', I')$, and $T = (M, L, I) \in \mathbf{T}$. We show the cofreeness property, that for any $\lambda : \mathcal{T}(ES, l) \to T$ there is a unique morphism $(\eta, \lambda) : (ES, l) \to \mathcal{E}(T)$ such that

$$
\begin{array}{ccc}
T & \xleftarrow{\ 1_L\ } & \mathcal{T}\mathcal{E}(T) \\
 & \lambda \nwarrow & \uparrow {\scriptstyle \mathcal{T}(\eta, \lambda) = \lambda} \\
 & & \mathcal{T}(ES, l)
\end{array}
$$

commutes. This follows from a corresponding cofreeness property associated with the coreflection from $\mathbf{E} \to \mathbf{T}$.

Note, that the morphism

$$l : et(ES) \to l_! \circ et(ES) = \mathcal{T}(ES)$$

from Proposition 9.3.30, composes with

$$\lambda : \mathcal{T}(ES) \to T$$

to yield a morphism

$$\lambda \circ l : et(ES) \to T.$$

By definition, $(\eta, \lambda) : (ES, l) \to \mathcal{E}(T) = (te(T), \lambda_T)$ is a morphism in $\mathcal{L}_I(\mathbf{E})$ iff $\eta : ES \to te(T)$ is a morphism in $\mathbf{E}$ and $\lambda_T \circ \eta = \lambda \circ l$. This is equivalent to

$\eta : ES \to te(T)$ is a morphism in $\mathbf{E}$ such that the following diagram commutes:

$$T \xleftarrow{\lambda_T} et \circ te(T)$$
$$\lambda \circ l \nwarrow \qquad \uparrow \eta = et(\eta)$$
$$et(ES)$$

The coreflection between $\mathbf{E}$ and $\mathbf{T}$ ensures the existence of a unique such $\eta : ES \to te(T)$. □

We finish this section by mentioning that this last result is paralleled by a similar result embedding Hoare traces reflectively into synchronization trees. So, in this formal way labeled event structures generalize synchronization trees in the same way that trace structures generalize Hoare traces (from an interleaving to a noninterleaving model).

9.4 Trace Structures and Domains

We return to the question of characterizing the class of partial orders associated with trace structures. Following the last section, we know that these orderings are exactly the orderings of configurations of event structures. In one direction this is stated in the representation theorem for trace structures. In the other direction, it follows as an immediate corollary to this and the coreflection between event structures and trace structures, which implies that for any event structure ES, $et(ES)$ is a trace structure such that $te(et(ES))$ is is isomorphic to ES and hence from the representation theorem:

Corollary 9.4.1 *Let $ES = (E, \leq, \#)$ be an event structure. Let $et(T) = (M, E, co)$. Then there is an order isomorphism between $(\mathcal{D}^0(E, \leq, \#), \subseteq)$ and $(M/\approx_{co}, /\approx_{co})$.*

Our characterization of the partial orders of trace structures in terms of special Scott domains below, has been formulated and proved in the literature as a similar characterization of the orderings of domains of configurations of event structures, see e.g. [199]. Our formulation below is simply a translation of the results from there using our equivalence between orders of trace structures and event structures.

In the formulation of the characterization result, we need a few standard definitions from domain theory.

Definition 9.4.2 *Let* $(D, \sqsubseteq)$ *be a partial order with least upper bounds of subsets* X *written as* $\bigsqcup X$ *when they exist.*

Say D *is* bounded complete *iff all subsets* $X \subseteq D$ *which have an upper bound in* D *have a least upper bound* $\bigsqcup X$ *in* D.

Say D *is* coherent *iff all subsets* $X \subseteq D$ *which are pairwise bounded (i.e. such that all pairs of elements* $d_0, d_1 \in X$ *have upper bounds in* D) *have least upper bounds* $\bigsqcup X$ *in* D. *(Note that coherence implies bounded completeness.)*

A complete prime *of* D *is an element* $p \in D$ *such that*

$$p \sqsubseteq \bigsqcup X \Rightarrow \exists x \in X. \, p \sqsubseteq x$$

for any set X *for which* $\bigsqcup X$ *exists.*

D *is* prime algebraic *iff*

$$x = \bigsqcup \{ p \sqsubseteq x \mid p \text{ is a complete prime} \},$$

for all $x \in D$. *If furthermore the sets*

$$\{ p \sqsubseteq q \mid p \text{ is a complete prime} \}$$

are always finite when q *is a complete prime, then* D *is said to be* finitary.

If D *is bounded complete and prime algebraic it is a* prime algebraic domain.

For $d_0, d_1 \in D$ *say that* d_1 covers d_0, $d_0 \leq d_1$ *iff* $d_0 \sqsubseteq d_1$, *and for every* d, $d_0 \sqsubseteq d \sqsubseteq d_1$ *implies* $d = d_0$ *or* $d = d_1$.

Theorem 9.4.3 *Let* $T = (M, \Sigma, I)$ *be a trace structure. The partial order* $(M/\approx_I, I)$ *is a coherent, finitary, prime algebraic domain; the complete primes are the set* $\{ [s] \mid s \text{ is a minimal representative of an event of } T \}$.

Proof: Follows from representation theorem and [199, 272]. □

Conversely, any coherent, finitary, prime algebraic domain is associated with a trace structure:

Theorem 9.4.4 *Let* $(D, \sqsubseteq)$ *be a coherent, finitary, prime algebraic domain. Define* (M, Σ, I) *as the trace structure*

$$
\begin{aligned}
\Sigma \quad &= \quad \text{the complete primes of } (D, \sqsubseteq) \\
p I p' \quad &\quad \text{iff } p' \not\sqsubseteq p, \, p \not\sqsubseteq p' \text{ and } p \text{ and } p' \text{ have an upper bound} \\
M \quad &= \quad \{ p_0 p_1 \ldots p_n \mid \text{for every } i, \, 0 \leq i \leq n, \, \bigsqcup \{ p_0, \ldots, p_i \} \text{ exists and} \\
&\qquad \text{for every complete prime} \\
&\qquad p \sqsubseteq \bigsqcup \{ p_0, \ldots, p_i \} \Rightarrow p \in \{ p_0, \ldots, p_i \} \}
\end{aligned}
$$

Then $(D, \sqsubseteq)$ *and* $(M/\approx_I, I)$ *are isomorphic partial orders.*

Proof: Follows from Theorem above and [199], the representation theorem and a few simple observations. □

Actually, the relationship between event structures and coherent, finitary prime algebraic domains is very strong, in that they are equivalent; one can be used to represent the other. This may be formalized also in terms of a categorical equivalence between $\mathbf{T}_E$ and a category of coherent, finitary prime algebraic domains equiped with stable functions as morphisms.

Theorem 9.4.5 *Let $\mathbf{P}$ denote the category of coherent, finitary prime algebraic domains with morphism functions $f : (D_0, \sqsubseteq_0) \to (D_1, \sqsubseteq_1)$ satisfying:*

(i) additivity:
   for all $x, y \in D_0$ such that $x \sqcup y$ exists,
   $$f(x \sqcup y) = f(x) \sqcup f(y)$$

(ii) stability:
   for all $x, y \in D_0$ such that $x \sqcup y$ exists,
   $$f(x \sqcap y) = f(x) \sqcap f(y)$$

(iii) covering preserving:
   for all $x, y \in D_0$:
   $$x \leq_0 y \text{ implies } f(x) \leq_1 f(y).$$

Then $\mathbf{P}$ and $\mathbf{T}_E$ are equivalent categories.

Proof: See [272]. □

Also, the characterizing domains are familiar in another guise. (Recall that the dI-domains of Berry are distributive algebraic cpos in which every finite element only dominates finitely many elements [11].)

Theorem 9.4.6 *The finitary, prime algebraic domains are precisely the dI-domains of Berry.*

Proof: See [272]. □

9.5 Trace Structures and Petri Nets

The theory of Petri Nets was originally a strong source of inspiration behind the introduction of traces by Mazurkiewicz in [189]. Also, the relationship between traces and nets have been extensively studied, see in particular the survey papers by Rozenberg and Thiagarajan in [238, 258]. The presentation here is based on joint work with Rozenberg and Thiagarajan, [200], in which proofs and details may be found.

9.5.1 Elementary Net Systems

Elementary net systems were introduced by Thiagarajan, [258], as a fundamental class of net systems. His definitions were as follows.

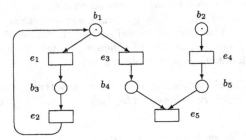

Figure 9.5:

Definition 9.5.1 *A* net *is a triple* $N = (B, E, F)$ *where B and E are sets and* $F \subseteq (B \times E) \cup (E \times B)$ *are such that*

(i) $B \cap E = \emptyset$

(ii) $domain(F) \cup range(F) = B \cup E$ *where*

$domain(F) = \{x \mid \exists y.(x, y) \in F\}$ *and*
$range(F) = \{y \mid \exists x.(x, y) \in F\}.$

Thus a net may be viewed as a directed bipartite graph with no isolated elements.

Definition 9.5.2 *An* elementary net system *is a quadruple* $\mathcal{N} = (B, E, F, c_{in})$ *where*

(i) $N_{\mathcal{N}} = (B, E, F)$ *is a net called the* underlying net *of $\mathcal{N}$.*

(ii) $c_{in} \subseteq B$ *is the* initial case *of $\mathcal{N}$.*

An elementary net system may be viewed as a directed bipartite graph with a specified subset of B-elements.

Presenting an elementary net system as a graph, following standard practise, the B-elements will be drawn as circles, the E-elements as boxes, the elements of the flow relation, F, as directed arcs, and the initial case will be indicated by dots (tokens) on its members. Figure 9.5 is an example of a net.

As a model for concurrency, B-elements are used to denote the (local) atomic states (or resources) called *conditions* and the E-elements are used to denote (local) atomic changes-of-states called *events*. The flow relation models the effect on conditions by an occurrence of an event, in the form of a *fixed* neighbourhood relation between the conditions and events of a system. Following this intuition, we see that our critical region example may be described as the elementary net system in Figure 9.6, where the center condition represents a kind of semaphore controlling the access to critical regions by the two processes.

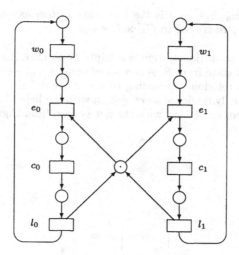

Figure 9.6:

The dynamics of an elementary net system are simple. A state (usually called a *case*) of the system consists of a set of conditions holding concurrently. An event can occur at a case iff all its pre-conditions and none of its post-conditions hold at the case. When an event occurs each of its pre-conditions ceases to hold and each of its post-conditions begins to hold. Let us formalize this dynamics of net systems. In doing so, it will be convenient to use the following standard notation: Let $N = (B, E, F)$ be a net. Then $X_N = B \cup E$ is the set of *elements* of N. Let $x \in X_N$. Then

$$^\bullet x = \{y \mid (y, x) \in F\} \quad \text{(the set of } \textit{pre-elements} \text{ of } x\text{)}$$
$$x^\bullet = \{y \mid (x, y) \in F\} \quad \text{(the set of } \textit{post-elements} \text{ of } x\text{)}$$

This 'dot' notation is extended to subsets of X_N in the obvious way. For $e \in E$ we shall call $^\bullet e$ the set of *pre-conditions* of e and we shall call $e^\bullet$ the set of *post-conditions* of e.

Definition 9.5.3 Let $N = (B, E, F)$ be a net. Then $\longrightarrow_N \subseteq 2^B \times E \times 2^B$ is the (elementary) transition relation generated by N and is given by

$$\longrightarrow_N = \{(k, e, k') \mid k - k' = {}^\bullet e \, \& \, k' - k = e^\bullet\}$$

Definition 9.5.4 Let $\mathcal{N} = (B, E, F, c_{in})$ be a net system.

(i) $C_\mathcal{N}$, *the state space of* $\mathcal{N}$ (also denoted as $[c_{in} >)$ is the least subset of 2^B containing c_{in} such that if $c \in C_\mathcal{N}$ and $(c, e, c') \in \longrightarrow_{N_\mathcal{N}}$ then $c' \in C_\mathcal{N}$.

(ii) $TS_\mathcal{N} = (C_\mathcal{N}, c_{in}, E, \longrightarrow_\mathcal{N})$ is *the transition system associated with* $\mathcal{N}$ *where* $\longrightarrow_\mathcal{N}$ *is* $\longrightarrow_{N_\mathcal{N}}$ *restricted to* $C_\mathcal{N} \times E \times C_\mathcal{N}$.

We recall that a transition system is a triple $TS = (S, i, A, \rightarrow)$ where S is a set of states, i an initial state from S, A is a set of actions and $\longrightarrow \subseteq S \times A \times S$ is the (labelled) transition relation. According to the above definition there is a natural way of explaining the dynamics of a net system with the help of a transition system. The transition system associated with the net system from Figure 9.5 is presented in Figure 9.7.

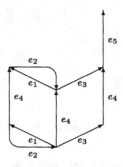

Figure 9.7:

Basic concepts concerning the behaviour of distributed systems such as causality, choice, concurrency, and confusion ('glitch') can now be cleanly defined—and separated from each other—with the help of net systems. The interested reader is referred to Thiagarajan [258] for details. Here we just bring out a few important behavioural concepts: We illustrate by means of a few small examples how nets can be used to model nondeterminism and concurrency.

Example 9.5.5

(1) Concurrency:

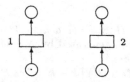

The events 1 and 2 can occur concurrently, in the sense that they both have concession and are independent in not having any pre or post conditions in common.

(2) Conflict:

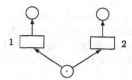

Either one of events 1 and 2 can occur, but not both. This shows how nondeterminism can be represented in a net.

(3) Contact:

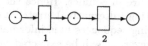

The event 2 has concession. The event 1 does not—its post condition holds—and it can only occur after 2.

Example (3) above illustrates contact. In general, there is *contact* at a marking M when for some event e

$$^\bullet e \subseteq M \ \& \ e^\bullet \cap (M \setminus {}^\bullet e) \neq \emptyset.$$

9.5.2 Trace Semantics

Following the definition of the transition relation we may associate the following (standard) Hoare structure with an elementary net system.

The set of *firing sequences* of $\mathcal{N}$—denoted $FS_\mathcal{N}$—is the least subset of E^* (recall that $\mathcal{N} = (B, E, F, c_{in})$) given by

(i) $\epsilon \in FS_\mathcal{N}$ and $c_{in} [\![\epsilon > c_{in}$

(ii) Suppose $\rho \in FS_\mathcal{N}$, $c_{in} [\![\rho > c$ and $c \xrightarrow{e} c'$ then $\rho e \in FS_\mathcal{N}$ and $c_{in} [\![\rho e > c'$.

Thus $[\![\ >$ is the natural 'extension' of $\longrightarrow_\mathcal{N}$ to $\{c_{in}\} \times E^* \times C_\mathcal{N}$.

One of the essential aspects of nets is that they allow an explicit representation of the distributed nature of computations. As an example, in the net for our mutual exclusive example in Figure 9.6, the independence between actions w_0 and w_1 is represented, following our intuitive understanding of the net, by the disjointness of their local effects. However, as with Hoare structures in general, firing sequences 'hide' aspects of the behaviour of a net system to do with parallel or independent activities.

To bring out this deficiency more clearly, we follow the original way of introducing independence between events of elementary net systems. In net theory this relation is most often referred to as the concurrency relation:

Let $e_1 \neq e_2$ and $e_1, e_2 \in E$. Let $c \in C_\mathcal{N}$. We say that e_1 and e_2 can occur *concurrently* at c—denoted $c [\![\{e_1, e_2\} >$—iff $c[e_1 >$ and $c[e_2 >$ and $({}^\bullet e_1 \cup e_1^\bullet) \cap ({}^\bullet e_2 \cup e_2^\bullet) = \emptyset$.

Thus e_1 and e_2 can occur concurrently at c iff they can occur individually and their neighbourhoods are disjoint. For the system $\mathcal{N}$ from Figure 9.5, at the initial case e_1 and e_4 can occur concurrently. Consequently, the firing sequences $e_1e_2e_4$ and $e_4e_1e_2$ and $e_1e_4e_2$ all represent the *same* (non-sequential) stretch of behaviour of $\mathcal{N}$.

The 'dual' of the notion of concurrency is conflict. Then we say that e_1 and e_2 are in *conflict* at c iff $c[e_1 >$ and $c[e_2 >$ *but not* $c[\{e_1, e_2\} >$. Thus at c either e_1 may occur or e_2 may occur but not both. The choice as to whether e_1 or e_2 will occur is assumed to be resolved by the 'environment' of the system. In $\mathcal{N}$ from Figure 9.5, at the initial case e_1 and e_3 are in conflict. Hence the firing sequences $e_1e_2e_4$ and $e_3e_4e_5$ represent two conflicting (alternative) stretches of behaviour of $\mathcal{N}$.

It is in this sense that firing sequences hide information concerning concurrency and conflict-resolution. However, as will be expected by now, this information may be retrieved by associating a trace structure with a net, with concurrency as the appropriate independence relation.

Theorem 9.5.6 *Let* $\mathcal{N} = (B, E, F, c_{in})$ *be an elementary net system. Then* $nt(\mathcal{N})$ *= ($FS_\mathcal{N}$, E, I) is a trace structure, where I denotes the independence relation associated with* $\mathcal{N} = (B, E, F, c_{in})$:

$$I = \{(e_1, e_2) \mid e_1, e_2 \in E \wedge (\,^\bullet e_1 \cup e_1\,^\bullet) \cap (\,^\bullet e_2 \cup e_2^\bullet) = \emptyset\}$$

Proof: The required properties follow from definition. Note in particular that $nt(\mathcal{N})$ is consistent and proper from definition of the (elementary) transition relation. □

For the net system $\mathcal{N}$ from Figure 9.5, Figure ?? shows an initial portion of the associated poset of traces:

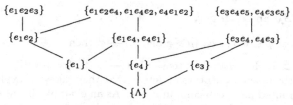

The beauty of the trace semantics is its simplicity. One of the classical results from concurrency theory is that the trace semantics is 'consistent' with an alternative way of defining the behaviour of net systems in terms of unfoldings into processes (or occurrence nets). Several results of this type have been shown, [26]. The presentation in the following is adapted from [200]. For the sake of convenience we shall assume here that $\mathcal{N}$ is *contact-free*. In other words, we shall assume,

$$\forall c \in C_\mathcal{N}.\forall e \in E.[\,^\bullet e \in c \Rightarrow e^\bullet \cap (c \backslash\,^\bullet e) = \emptyset].$$

As is well-known (see for instance [238]), this does not—at least for the study of behavioural issues—involve any loss of generality.

A process of N will be a *labelled net* of the form $\tilde{N} = (\tilde{B}, \tilde{E}, \tilde{F}, \tilde{\varphi})$ where $(\tilde{B}, \tilde{E}, \tilde{F})$ is a restricted kind of a net called a *causal net* and $\tilde{\varphi} : \tilde{B} \cup \tilde{E} \rightarrow B \cup E$ (recall that $\mathcal{N} = (B, E, F, c_{in}))$ is the labelling function required to satisfy certain constraints. For a definition of a process along these lines, see [238].

Here we shall define processes with the help of firing sequences. This will enable us to build up the finite processes of $\mathcal{N}$ inductively. Moreover, our method of construction will enable us to obtain the unfolding of a net system in a smooth fashion. As we will see, this method of constructing processes will be very helpful for proving the desired results. For a similar development of the process notion, see [26].

For each firing sequence ρ, we will define a process $N_\rho = (B_\rho, E_\rho, F_\rho, \varphi_\rho)$. In doing so it will be convenient to keep track of the conditions that hold in $\mathcal{N}$ after the run represented by the firing sequence ρ. This set of conditions will be encoded as c_ρ.

Definition 9.5.7 *Let $\rho \in FS$. Then $N_\rho = (B_\rho, E_\rho, F_\rho, \varphi_\rho)$ is given by:*

    (i) $\rho = \epsilon$. *Then*

$$N_\epsilon = (\phi, \phi, \phi, \phi) \text{ and}$$
$$c_\epsilon = \{(b, \phi) \mid b \in c_{in}\}$$
$$\text{recall that } \mathcal{N} = (B, E, F, c_{in})$$

    (ii) $\rho \neq \epsilon$. *Let $\rho = \rho'e$ and assume that $N_{\rho'} = (B_{\rho'}, E_{\rho'}, F_{\rho'}, \varphi_{\rho'})$ and $c_{\rho'}$ are defined. Then*
$$N_\rho = (B_\rho, E_\rho, F_\rho, \varphi_\rho) \text{ with}$$
$$E_\rho = E_{\rho'} \cup \{(e, X)\}$$
$$\quad \text{where } X = \{(b, D) \mid b \in {}^\bullet e \text{ and } (b, D) \in c_{\rho'}\},$$
$$B_\rho = B_{\rho'} \cup X \cup Y \text{ where } Y = \{(b, \{(e, X)\}) \mid b \in e^\bullet\},$$
$$F_\rho = F_{\rho'} \cup (X \times \{(e, X)\}) \cup (\{(e, X)\} \times Y), \text{ and}$$
$$\varphi_\rho \text{ is defined by: } \forall (z, Z) \in B_\rho \cup E_\rho. \ \varphi_\rho((z, Z)) = z.$$
$$\text{Finally, } c_\rho = (c_{\rho'} - X) \cup Y.$$

It will turn out that N_ρ as defined above is a labelled net. For $\rho = e_1 e_2 e_4 e_3$ in the system $\mathcal{N}$ of Figure 9.5 we show N_ρ in Figure 9.8. For convenience we have displayed φ_ρ by writing the value of $\varphi_\rho(x)$ inside the graphical representation of x for each $x \in B\rho \cup E_\rho$.

In order to establish a relationship between the traces of $\mathcal{N}$ and its processes it is necessary to define an ordering relation over the processes of $\mathcal{N}$.

Definition 9.5.8

    (i) *The set of finite processes of N is denoted as $P_\mathcal{N}$ and is given by: $P_\mathcal{N} = \{N_\rho \mid \rho \in FS\}$ where N_ρ is as given by Definition 9.5.7.*

    (ii) *$\subseteq' \subseteq P_\mathcal{N} \times P_\mathcal{N}$ is defined as:*

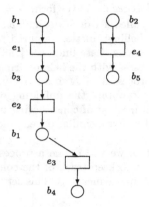

Figure 9.8:

$$N_\rho = (B_\rho, E_\rho, F_\rho, \varphi_\rho) \ \subseteq' \ N_{\rho'} = (B_{\rho'}, E_{\rho'}, F_{\rho'}, \varphi_{\rho'}) \quad iff$$
$$B_\rho \subseteq B_{\rho'} \ and \ E_\rho \subseteq E_{\rho'} \ and \ F_\rho \subseteq F_{\rho'}.$$

Clearly $\subseteq'$ is a partial ordering relation. The main result relating trace semantics to processes is the following:

Theorem 9.5.9 *For any elementary net system $\mathcal{N}$, $(P_\mathcal{N}, \subseteq')$ and the ordering of the traces from $nt(\mathcal{N})$, $(FS_\mathcal{N}/ \approx_{I}, I)$, are isomorphic posets. In fact, $f : FS_\mathcal{N}/ \approx_I \to P$ given by $f([\rho]) = N_\rho$ is an isomorphism.*

Proof: see [200]. □

9.5.3 Some Relationships

As usual we start by turning elementary net systems into a category. As morphisms we take:

Definition 9.5.10 *Let $N = (B, M_0, E, pre, post)$ and $N' = (B', M_0', pre', post')$ be nets. A morphism $(\beta, \eta) : N \to N'$ consists of a relation $\beta \subseteq B \times B'$, such that β^{op} is a partial function $B' \to B$, and a partial function $\eta : E \to E'$ such that*

$$\beta M_0 = M_0',$$
$$\beta^\bullet e = {}^\bullet \eta(e) \ and$$
$$\beta e^\bullet = \eta(e)^\bullet$$

Thus morphisms on nets preserve initial markings and events when defined. A morphism $(\beta, \eta) : N \to N'$ expresses how occurrences of events and conditions in N induce occurrences in N'. Morphisms on nets preserve behaviour:

Proposition 9.5.11 *Let* $N = (B, M_0, E, pre, post)$, $N' = (B', M'_0, E', pre', post')$ *be nets. Suppose* $(b, \eta) : N \to N'$ *is a morphism of net.*

- *If* $M \xrightarrow{e} M'$ *in* N *then* $\beta M \xrightarrow{\eta(e)} \beta M'$ *in* N'.

- *If* $^\bullet e_1^\bullet \cap {}^\bullet e_2^\bullet = \emptyset$ *in* N *then* $^\bullet \eta(e_1)^\bullet \cap {}^\bullet \eta(e_2)^\bullet = \emptyset$ *in* N'.

Proof: It is easily seen that

$$^\bullet\eta(e) = \beta^\bullet e \text{ and } \eta(e)^\bullet = \beta e^\bullet$$

for e an event of N. Observe too that because β^{op} is a partial function, β in addition preserves intersections and set differences. These observations mean that $\beta M \xrightarrow{\eta(e)} \beta M'$ in N' follows from the assumption that $M \xrightarrow{e} M'$ in N, and that independence is preserved. $\square$

Proposition 9.5.12 *Nets and their morphisms form a category in which the composition of two morphisms* $(\beta_0, \eta_0) : N_0 \to N_1$ *and* $(\beta_1, \eta_1) : N_1 \to N_2$ *is* $(\beta_1 \circ \beta_0, \eta_1 \circ \eta_0) : N_0 \to N_2$ *(composition in the left component being that of relations and in the right that of partial functions).*

Definition 9.5.13 *Let* **N** *be the category of nets described above.*

The choice of morphisms here may not be as obvious and intuitively understandable as the other notions of morphisms, we have been considering. And indeed other notions of categories of net systems have been studied—see e.g. [273]. Let us just mention that from the results above, we do get what might be called a behaviour (and concurrency) preserving notion of morphisms, a fact which has been explored by e.g. [29] using such morphism as expressing correctness properties between nets. Also, we note that the derived notion of isomorphism becomes identity up to names of conditions and events.

Furthermore, this notion of net morphisms does relate to the notion of trace structure morphisms in the sense that as proved in [273]:

Theorem 9.5.14 *The trace semantics given above extends to a functor nt: from* **N** *to* **T**.

However, this functor is not part of any adjunction. One 'solution' to this is to modify nt to nt' by composing with $te \circ te$ to get a functor from **N** to $\mathbf{T}_E$, yielding a more abstract trace semantics, forgetting about the names of individual event occurrences. It is known ([200]) that this is part of a coreflection embedding $\mathbf{T}_E$ into **N**, a result which may be interpreted that elementary net systems 'unfold' nicely (read 'universally') via nt into the trace structures equivalent to event structures.

Theorem 9.5.15 *nt' is the right adjoint of a coreflection between* **N** *and* $\mathbf{T}_E$.

Proof: The proof of this is rather involved, but may be found in [201], and for more general forms of net systems in [273] and [140]. $\square$

But the remaining question is if there a system model 'corresponding' to **T**, in the sense that it unfolds naturally (coreflectively) into **T**? This question will be addressed and answered positively in the next section.

9.6　Trace Structures and Asynchronous Transition Systems

Asynchronous transition systems deserve to be better known as a model of parallel computation. They were introduced independently by Bednarczyk in [9] and Shields in [255], heavily inspired by trace theory. The idea on which they are based is simple enough: extend transition systems by, in addition, specifying which transitions are independent of which. More accurately, transitions are to be thought of as occurrences of events which bear a relation of independence. This interpretation is supported by axioms which essentially generalize those from trace structures.

9.6.1　Asynchronous Transition Systems

Definition 9.6.1 *An* asynchronous transition system *consists of* $(S, i, E, I, Tran)$ *where* $(S, i, E, Tran)$ *is a transition system,* $I \subseteq E^2$, *the* independence relation *is an irreflexive, symmetric relation on the set* E *of events such that*

(1) $e \in E \Rightarrow \exists s, s' \in S.\ (s, e, s') \in Tran$

(2) $(s, e, s') \in Tran\ \&\ (s, e, s'') \in Tran \Rightarrow s' = s''$

(3) $e_1 I e_2\ \&\ (s, e_1, s_1) \in Tran\ \&\ (s, e_2, s_2) \in Tran$
　　$\Rightarrow \exists u.\ (s_1, e_2, u) \in Tran\ \&\ (s_2, e_1, u) \in Tran$

(4) $e_1 I e_2\ \&\ (s, e_1, s_1) \in Tran\ \&\ (s_1, e_2, u) \in Tran$
　　$\Rightarrow \exists s_2.\ (s, e_2, s_2) \in Tran\ \&\ (s_2, e_1, u) \in Tran$

Axiom (1) says every event appears as a transition, and axiom (2) that the occurrence of an event at a state leads to a unique state. Axioms (3) and (4) express properties of independence: if two events can occur independently from a common state then they should be able to occur together and in so doing reach a common state (3); if two independent events can occur one immediately after the other then they should be able to occur with their order interchanged (4). Axiom (3) corresponds to the properness axiom on trace structures and, as there, a great deal of the theory have been be developed without it.

As an example of an asynchronous transition system, consider the transition system from Figure 9.7, with I the independence relation inherited from the net of Figure 9.5, i.e. the symmetric closure of

$$(\{e_1, e_2\} \times \{e_4, e_5\}) \cup (\{e_2, e_4\} \times \{e_3\})$$

It is easy to see that the axioms of Definition 9.6.1 are satisfied. Similarly, the transition system associated with the mutual exclusion net from Figure 9.6, and with the inherited independence relation over its events (equal to the independence relation over the actions of the mutual exclusion example from Section 2), will be an asynchronous transition system. As a matter of fact, these observations follow from a general relationship between nets and asynchronous transition systems, see [201] and [273]. But here we focus instead on a formal relationship to traces, viewing asynchronous transition systems as *the* system model for trace structures.

First, we turn asynchronous transition systems into a category, by equipping them with behaviour preserving morphisms:

Definition 9.6.2 *Let $T = (S, i, E, I, Tran)$ and $T' = (S', i', E', I', Tran')$ be asynchronous transition systems. A morphism*

$$(\sigma, \eta) : (S, i, E, Tran) \to (S', i', E', Tran')$$

consists of

$$\rho : S \to S' \text{ and } \eta : E \to_* E'$$

such that

$$
\begin{array}{ll}
(s_0, e_1, s_1) \in Tran \text{ and } \eta(e) \text{ defined} & \Rightarrow \quad (\sigma(s_0), \eta(e), \sigma(s_1)) \in Tran' \\
(s_0, e_1, s_1) \in Tran \text{ and } \eta(e) \text{ undefined} & \Rightarrow \quad \sigma(s_0) = \sigma(s_1) \\
e_1 I e_2 \ \& \ \eta(e_1), \eta(e_2) \text{ both defined} & \Rightarrow \quad \eta(e_1) I' \eta(e_2).
\end{array}
$$

Morphisms of asynchronous transition systems compose as morphisms between their underlying transition systems, and are readily seen to form a category. Write $\mathbf{A}$ for the category of asynchronous transition systems.

The category $\mathbf{A}$ has categorical constructions which essentially generalize those of transition systems and Mazurkiewicz traces. To illustrate this point, here are the product and coproduct constructions for the category $\mathbf{A}$:

Definition 9.6.3 *Assume asynchronous transition systems $T_0 = (S_0, i_0, E_0, I_0, Tran_0)$ and $T_1 = (S_1, i_1, E_1, I_1, Tran_1)$. Their product $T_0 \times T_1$ is $(S, i, E, I, Tran)$ where $(S, i, E, Tran)$ is the product of transition systems $(S_0, i_0, E_0, Tran_0)$ and $(S_1, i_1, E_1, Tran_1)$ with projections (ρ_0, π_0) and (ρ_1, π_1), and the independence relation I is given by*

$$
\begin{array}{l}
aIb \Leftrightarrow (\pi_0(a), \pi_0(b) \text{ defined } \Rightarrow \pi_0(a)I_0\pi_0(b)) \ \& \\
\qquad (\pi_1(a), \pi_1(b) \text{ defined } \Rightarrow \pi_1(a)I_1\pi_1(b)).
\end{array}
$$

Definition 9.6.4 *Assume asynchronous transition systems $T_0 = (S_0, i_0, E_0, I_0, Tran_0)$ and $T_1 = (S_1, i_1, E_1, I_1, Tran_1)$. Their coproduct $T_0 + T_1$ is $(S, i, E, I, Tran)$ where $(S, i, E, Tran)$ is the coproduct of transition systems $(S_0, i_0, E_0, Tran_0)$ and $(S_1, i_1, E_1, Tran_1)$ with injections (in_0, j_0) and (in_1, j_1), and the independence relation I is given by*

$$
\begin{array}{l}
aIb \Leftrightarrow (\exists a_0, b_0. \ a = j_0(a_0) \ \& \ b = j_0(b_0) \ \& \ a_0 I_0 b_0) \text{ or} \\
\qquad (\exists a_1, b_1. \ a = j_1(a_1) \ \& \ b = j_1(b_1) \ \& \ a_1 I_1 b_1).
\end{array}
$$

9.6.2   The Relationship

That asynchronous transition systems generalize trace structures is backed up by a straightforward coreflection between categories of trace structures and asynchronous transition systems. To obtain the adjunction we need to restrict trace structures slightly to those where every element of the alphabet occurs in some trace (this matches property (1) required by the definition of asynchronous transition systems).

Definition 9.6.5 *Define* $\mathbf{T}_0$ *to be the full subcategory of trace structures* (M, Σ, I) *satisfying*

$$\forall e \in \Sigma \; \exists s. \; se \in M.$$

A trace structure forms an asynchronous transition system in which the states are traces.

Definition 9.6.6 *Let* (M, Σ, I) *be a trace structure in* $\mathbf{T}_0$, *with trace equivalence* $\approx$. *Define* $ta(M, \Sigma, I) = (S, i, \Sigma, I, Tran)$ *where*

$$S \;=\; M/\approx$$
$$(t, e, t') \in Tran \quad \Leftrightarrow \quad \exists s, se \in M. \; t = \{s\}_\approx \; \& \; t' = \{se\}_\approx$$

Let $\eta : (M, \Sigma, I) \to (M', \Sigma', I')$ *be a morphism of trace structures. Define* $ta(\eta) = (\sigma, \eta)$ *where*

$$\sigma(\{s\}_\approx) = \{\hat{\eta}(s)\}_\approx.$$

(Note this is well-defined because morphisms between trace structures respect $\approx$.*)*

Proposition 9.6.7 *The operation* ta *is a functor* $\mathbf{T}_0 \to \mathbf{A}$.

An asynchronous transition system determines a trace structure:

Definition 9.6.8 *Let* $T = (S, i, E, I, Tran)$ *be an asynchronous transition system. Define* $at(T) = (Seq, E, I)$ *where* Seq *consists of all sequences of events, possibly empty,* $e_1 e_2 \ldots e_n$ *for which there are transitions*

$$(s, e_1, s_1), (s_1, e_2, s_2), \ldots, (s_{n-1}, e_n, s_n) \in Tran$$

Let $(\sigma, \eta) : T \to T'$ *be a morphism of asynchronous transition systems. Define* $at(\sigma, \eta) = \eta$.

Proposition 9.6.9 *The operation* at *is a functor* $\mathbf{A} \to \mathbf{T}_0$.

In fact, the functors ta, at form a coreflection:

Theorem 9.6.10 *The functor* $ta : \mathbf{T}_0 \to \mathbf{A}$ *is left adjoint to* $at : \mathbf{A} \to \mathbf{T}_0$.
    Let $L = (M, \Sigma, I)$ *be a trace structure. Then* $at \circ ta \, (M, \Sigma, I) = (M, \Sigma, I)$ *and the unit of the adjunction at* (M, Σ, I) *is the identity* $1_E : (M, \Sigma, I) \to at \circ ta(M, \Sigma, I)$.
    Let T *be an asynchronous transition system, with events* E. *Then* $(\sigma, 1_E) : ta \circ at(T) \to T$ *is the counit of the adjunction at* T, *where* $\sigma(t)$, *for a trace* $t = \{e_1 e_2 \ldots e_n\}_\approx$, *equals the unique state* s *for which* $i \xrightarrow{e_1 e_2 \ldots e_n} s$.

Proof: Let $L = (M, \Sigma, I)$ be a Trace Structure in $\mathbf{T}_0$ and $T = (S, i, E', I', \mathit{Tran'})$ be an asynchronous system. Given a morphism of trace languages

$$\eta : L \to at(T)$$

there is a unique morphism of asynchronous transition systems

$$(\sigma, \eta) : ta(L) \to T$$

—the function σ must act so $\sigma(t)$, on a trace $t = \{e_1 e_2 \ldots e_n\}_{\approx}$, equals the unique state s_n for which there are transitions, possibly idle,

$$(i, \eta(e_1), s_1), (s_1, \eta(e_2), s_2), \ldots, (s_{n-1}, \eta(e_n), s_n)$$

in T. That this is well-defined follows from T satisfying axiom 4 in the definition of asynchronous transition systems. The stated coreflection, and the form of the counit, follow. $\square$

We note that a coreflection between event structures and asynchronous transition systems follows by composing the coreflections between event structures and trace languages and that between trace languages and asynchronous transition systems. It is easy to see that the coreflection from event structures $\mathbf{E}$ to trace languages $\mathbf{T}$ restricts to a coreflection to $\mathbf{T}_0$. The left adjoint of the resulting coreflection, is the composition

$$\mathbf{E} \xrightarrow{et} \mathbf{T}_0 \xrightarrow{ta} \mathbf{A}.$$

9.7 Conclusion

We have presented a few formal relationships between trace structures and other models for concurrency. Many important and related models have been left out. Some of the closely related models include the pomsets of Pratt [230] and the partial words of Grabowsky [127]. For some recent results on trace relationships to these models, see [245].

Also, it should be noted that we have not gone into any comparisons between the theories developed around our individual models. Some of our models have been further developed in this respect than others, but we leave any such comparison for the reader to judge himself.

Also, there is more to the categorical view of models than we have presented here. For instance, the universal constructs like product and coproduct serve as basis for giving semantics to process algebras, see [273] for more detail. And since our morphisms are "behaviour preserving", the existence of a morphism may be seen as a demonstration that one object (implementation) satisfies another (specification). This has been pursued in a nontrivial setting by [29].

Finally, we would like to acknowledge many colleagues who have been part of developing the material behind this chapter. In particular, we acknowledge our close collaboration with P.S. Thiagarajan on many parts of this work.

Chapter 10

Traces and Logic

Wojciech Penczek

Institute of Computer Science
Polish Academy of Sciences
Ordona 21, 01-237 Warsaw, Poland
penczek@wars.ipipan.waw.pl

Ruurd Kuiper

Eindhoven University of Technology
Department of Mathematics and Computing Science
P.O. Box 513, 5600 MB Eindhoven, The Netherlands
wsinruur@info.win.tue.nl

Contents

10.1   Introduction

Trace systems were introduced by Mazurkiewicz [189, 190] as semantics for concurrent systems (think, for example, about Petri Nets). The reader is briefly reminded about some of the characteristics that are relevant to appreciate the logics developed in connection with them.

The most characteristic feature of trace systems is that they model the distinction between concurrency and non-deterministic choice explicitly, while at the same time abstracting from interleaving. The former is achieved through an independence relation on actions, the latter through defining traces as equivalence classes of finite sequences modulo interleaving.

One evident limitation is the restriction of the independence relation to a context-independent one. As a consequence, for example Place Transition Nets [235] can not be expressed; this can, retaining the concept of traces, be remedied by going to semi-commutations (see chapter 12). Another limitation is the exclusion of non-determinism between actions with the same label. To overcome this restriction, instances of actions have to be distinguished explicitly. This means going to, e.g., event structures, which amounts to leaving the realm of trace systems. The choice to allow only finite traces has the advantage of simplicity but the drawback that an additional notion, run, is required to capture infinitary properties. Intuitively, this notion incorporates the view that executions should be fair with respect to concurrently enabled actions. Analogous approaches based on infinite traces exist; see chapter 11.

The first area in which logics for trace systems make their appearance is formal verification using program proof systems, i.e., verification by hand.

Interleaving Set Temporal Logic, ISTL, developed by Katz and Peled [149, 150] can be viewed as the starting point of logics for trace systems. Historically, their aim was to make the verification of Linear Time Temporal Logic (LTL) properties of concurrent programs easier by exploiting the idea that sequences that differ only in their interleaving are in some sense equivalent. For certain properties only one, arbitrary, representative from each equivalence class of execution sequences then needs to be considered. This clearly resembles the idea of abstraction in the concept of trace. However, at that stage the relation to traces was not made explicit.

In [218], Peled and Pnueli, as a side issue, discuss the connection between trace systems and ISTL. This paper also considers the other side of the trace system view, namely the ability to distinguish concurrency explicitly, and the possibilities of ISTL to reason about these matters. ISTL can thus be seen as a logic that is, maybe somewhat retrospectively, directly geared to trace systems and enables to exploit both features of that approach.

The second area in which logics and trace systems appear is verification by means of model checking, i.e., fully automated verification. Programs here are essentially finite state and the logics are propositional.

The ability to abstract away from interleaving of concurrent actions was again investigated first, now with the intention to avoid the state explosion problem. Godefroid [119] presents constructions of reduced finite trace automata that generate representatives for finite executions of a program. Godefroid and Wolper [120] consider model checking of safety properties using reduced trace automata.

The further aim to likewise simplify model checking of an LTL formula against a program, possibly involving liveness properties and hence infinite sequences, is present in the approach of Peled [215]. Note that again the temporal logic itself is not a trace system logic, but that the idea of representatives is used to enhance efficiency.

As regards expressiveness, model checking for propositional ISTL could be considered. As yet, this has not been investigated.

Apart from the linear logics mentioned so far, various others exist, for instance ones that deal with branching. They will make their appearance in the rest of the chapter. A state-of-the-art overview of logics and results about them like the ones just discussed is presented in the conclusions.

Further topics as well as the organization of the rest of the chapter are as follows. Didactic rather than historical considerations dictated the organization of the material.

Section 10.2.1 contains preliminaries: trace systems together with the associated models and acceptors. Furthermore, Elementary Petri Nets are chosen as the representation of finite state concurrent systems. Also the two running examples, taken from [218], are introduced. In Section 10.3 various temporal logics for trace systems are compared as to their ability to distinguish between models. Section 10.4 deals with model checking from the efficiency point of view: LTL without the next step operator. Section 10.5 adapts the efficient model checking to branching time logics without the next step operator. Section 10.6 again concerns model checking, but now from the expressiveness point of view: CTL_P. In Section 10.7 program proof systems for ISTL with past operators are presented, considering both expressiveness and efficiency. Section 10.8 contains an axiomatization of an essential subset of ISTL with past operators. Section 10.9 contains some conclusions. Then in the Appendix by W. Ebinger logical definability of trace languages is discussed. In particular the equivalence of recognizability and monadic second order logic, and the equivalence of star-freeness and first order logic are demonstrated.

10.2 Trace Systems

This section provides notions used in the rest of the chapter. For a comparison of trace structures with other models for concurrency see chapter 9.

10.2.1 Traces

The starting point is an *independence alphabet*: an ordered pair (Σ, I), where Σ is a finite set of symbols (*actions*) and $I \subseteq \Sigma \times \Sigma$ is a symmetric and irreflexive binary relation on Σ (the *independence* relation). Actions not related are said to be *dependent*.

Let $\equiv$ be an equivalence relation defined on Σ^* by $u \equiv u'$, if there is a finite sequence of action sequences $u_1, \ldots, u_n$ such that $u_1 = u$, $u_n = u'$, and for each $i < n$, $u_i = sabt$, $u_{i+1} = sbat$, for some $(a, b) \in I$ and $s, t \in \Sigma^*$. The *traces* over (Σ, I) are the equivalence classes of $\equiv$. The trace of which a string u is a representative is denoted by $[u]$. The following notations are used.

- $[\Sigma^*] = \{[u] \mid u \in \Sigma^*\}$ - the set of all traces over (Σ, I),

- $[\Sigma] = \{[a] \mid a \in \Sigma\}$ - the set of all traces corresponding to actions.

10.2.2 Operations on Traces

Concatenation of traces $[u]$, $[t]$, denoted $[u][t]$, is defined as $[ut]$.

The *successor* relation $\rightarrow$ in $[\Sigma^*]$ is defined by: $\tau_1 \rightarrow \tau_2$ iff there is $a \in \Sigma$ such that $\tau_1[a] = \tau_2$. The *prefix* relation $\leq$ in $[\Sigma^*]$ is defined as the reflexive and transitive closure of the successor relation, i.e., $\leq = (\rightarrow)^*$. The relation $<$ denotes the transitive closure of $\rightarrow$, i.e., $(\rightarrow)^+$. Let $\tau \in [\Sigma^*]$ and $Q \subseteq [\Sigma^*]$. The following notations are used.

- $\downarrow \tau = \{\tau' \in [\Sigma^*] \mid \tau' \leq \tau\}$, $\uparrow \tau = \{\tau' \in [\Sigma^*] \mid \tau \leq \tau'\}$, $\downarrow Q = \bigcup_{\tau \in Q} \downarrow \tau$, $\uparrow Q = \bigcup_{\tau \in Q} \uparrow \tau$.

A set of traces R is *prefix-closed*, if $R = \downarrow R$. A set R of traces has the *I-diamond* property, if for all $\tau \in R$, $a, b \in \Sigma$ with $(a, b) \in I$, $(\tau[a] \in R$ and $\tau[b] \in R)$ implies $\tau[ab] \in R$. Notice that $(a, b) \in I$ implies $[ab] = [ba]$ and therefore $\tau[ba] \in R$.

10.2.3 Connection to Computing

In this section the notions of trace system and interpreted trace system are defined. They may be viewed as representations, corresponding to two levels of abstraction, of the behaviour of concurrent systems. The concurrent systems themselves are mostly left implicit. Therefore, intuitive notions like executions are only identified in the representation.

Definition 10.2.1 *A trace system $\mathcal{T}$ over (Σ, I) is a prefix-closed subset of $[\Sigma^*]$ with the I-diamond property.*

Where no confusion is likely, (Σ, I) is omitted. This may be viewed as representing the behaviour of a concurrent system in terms of the executed actions.

To interpret the effect of actions, a set of variables $\mathcal{Y}$ and a domain of interpretation $\mathcal{D}$ can be added.

Definition 10.2.2 *An* interpreted trace system $(\mathcal{T}, \mathcal{I})$, *interpreted over* $(\mathcal{Y}, \mathcal{D})$, *is a trace system $\mathcal{T}$ together with an interpretation function $\mathcal{I} : \mathcal{T} \longrightarrow (\mathcal{Y} \longrightarrow \mathcal{D})$.*

This may be viewed as representing the behaviour of a concurrent system in a less abstract way, where also values of variables after executing the actions in a trace are specified. Throughout the chapter, where the interpretation is not relevant and extension straightforward the exposition just considers trace systems.

A trace represents a partial execution of a concurrent system. Executions with different ordering of dependent actions yield different traces; executions that differ only in the ordering of independent actions yield the same trace.

Omitting from the definition of I-diamond the requirement that the actions involved are from I yields the following notion. A set R of traces has the *diamond* property, if for all $\tau \in R$, $a, b \in \Sigma$, $(\tau[a] \in R$ and $\tau[b] \in R)$ implies $(a, b) \in I$ and $\tau[ab] \in R$. Considering the fact that in trace systems closed diamonds only occur for actions from I, this notion is used to indicate that for some subset of traces diamonds only open with actions from I and that the trace closing the diamond is present in the subset. A *run* R of T is a maximal (with respect to the inclusion ordering) subset of T with the diamond property. A run represents a complete execution of T, providing all the traces that occur in the different interleavings for that execution.

A sequence $x = \tau_0 a_0 \tau_1 a_1 \dots$ in $S \subseteq T$ such that $\tau_i[a_i] = \tau_{i+1}$ for all $i \geq 0$ is a *path* in S. A path in S is *maximal* if is either infinite or its last trace does not have a successor in S. $x/\Sigma \overset{def}{=} a_0 a_1 \dots$ is the *restriction of x to actions*. $x/T \overset{def}{=} \tau_0 \tau_1 \dots$ is the *restriction of x to traces*. Where no confusion is likely, restrictions are referred to by just x as well. $\downarrow x = \{\tau \in T \mid \tau \leq \tau_i$, for $i \geq 0\}$ denotes the set of traces dominated by a path x. An *observation* of a run R of T is any maximal path x in R such that $R = \downarrow x$. Note that an observation is a path which is cofinal with some run. Thus, it carries information about all actions executed in the run. A maximal path is called an observation (of T) if it is an observation of some run in T. A suffix $\tau_i \tau_{i+1} \dots$ of an observation x is said to be an observation starting at τ_i. An observation, like a run, represents a complete execution of T, now by providing all traces that occur in just one interleaving for that execution. An arbitrary path in a run might not enable to recover the run, as not even all actions occurring in the run need to be present.

The following Lemma provides an alternative characterization for observations, independent of the notion of run.

Lemma 10.2.3 *A maximal path* $x = \tau_0 a_0 \tau_1 a_1 \dots$ *in* T *is an observation iff*

$$(\forall a \in \Sigma)(\forall i \in I\!N)(\exists j \geq i)(\tau_j[a] \notin T \text{ or } (a, a_j) \notin I).$$

Proof: See [218] and [161].   □

Obviously, the above lemma also holds for suffixes of observations. Intuitively, if an action is independent with all actions present in a suffix of a path and could be have be added at any point, it is concurrently enabled without being taken. The lemma states, that such situation does not occur in observations. The reader familiar with fair computations may notice that observations are paths that are *concurrency fair* in the sense that for each continuously concurrently enabled action either that action itself or a dependent one is eventually taken.

Note that all notions concerning trace systems are defined in terms of traces and the successor relation only. Once a trace system is given as a set of equivalence classes, i.e., subsets of action sequences, the successor relation between traces can also be obtained without recourse to (Σ, I). Namely, by defining $\tau_1 \rightarrow \tau_2$ iff there are representatives $u_1 \in \tau_1$, $u_2 \in \tau_2$ and $a \in \Sigma$ such that $u_1 a = u_2$. Thus, the set of traces contains all information about a trace system, except for the independence alphabet that defines its superset. A (Σ, I) that could serve this purpose can be obtained by taking as Σ all actions that occur in the traces, and as I the pairs of actions that extend two different traces to one and the same trace. Two trace systems are considered to be identical if their sets of traces are, irrespective of (Σ, I).

Trace systems and the associated notions are illustrated by the following two examples, respectively concerning abstraction and expressiveness; an example of an interpreted trace system is given in Section 10.2.7.

Example 10.2.4 [inevitability] The following property is one for which abstraction of interleaving is useful.

- A subset $Q \subseteq T$ is *inevitable*, if each observation of T contains a trace in Q.

It is not always the case that to check whether a property is inevitable, abstraction of interleaving can be applied. Only one observation of each run can be considered for stable properties (i.e., properties Q such that with each trace $\tau \in Q$, $\uparrow \tau \cap T \subseteq Q$), and properties of sets of actions.

A concrete example of the latter property is as follows. Consider the independence alphabet (Σ, I).

- $\Sigma = \{a, b, c, d\}$,

- $I = \{(a, c), (c, a), (a, d), (d, a)\}$.

Figure 10.1 shows the trace system T_1 over (Σ, I), together with the successor relation. T_1 contains infinitely many finite runs R_i and one infinite run R.

- $R_i = \downarrow [(cd)^i b]$, for $i \geq 0$,

- $R = \bigcup_{i=1}^{\infty} \downarrow [(cd)^i a]$.

Every path in T_1 except for $x = [\epsilon][c][cd][cdc]...$, which ignores a, is an observation of T_1.

- Let $Q = \{\tau \mid a \in \Sigma(\tau) \text{ or } b \in \Sigma(\tau)\}$,
  where $\Sigma(\tau)$ is the set of actions occurring in τ.

  Inevitability of Q means that either a or b will be executed eventually.

Since the observations of the same run differ only in the ordering of independent actions, it suffices to check whether one, arbitrary, observation of each run contains a trace in Q.

It might seem surprising that Q is inevitable, as there is an infinite path $x = [\epsilon][c][cd][cdc] ...$ which does not contain any trace from Q. However, this path is not an observation, as the action a is continuously concurrently enabled and never executed, and a property is inevitable if it holds for each observation.

Example 10.2.5 [serializability] Serializability is a property for which expression of independence is useful. This notion in terms of trace semantics was introduced in [218].

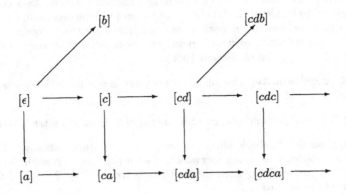

Figure 10.1: Trace system T_1 with successor relation

- Two subsets $T_1 \subseteq \Sigma$ and $T_2 \subseteq \Sigma$ are *serializable* for T, if in every run of T, there exists an observation containing traces τ and τ' such that

  1. $T_1 \subseteq \Sigma(\tau)$, $T_2 \cap \Sigma(\tau) = \emptyset$, and $T_2 \subseteq \Sigma(\tau')$ or
  2. $T_2 \subseteq \Sigma(\tau)$, $T_1 \cap \Sigma(\tau) = \emptyset$, and $T_1 \subseteq \Sigma(\tau')$,

  i.e., all the operations of T_1 appear before those of T_2, or the other way round.

A concrete example is as follows. Consider the independence alphabet (Σ, I).

- $\Sigma = \{a_1, a_2, a_3, b_1, b_2, b_3\}$,

- $I = \{(a_1, b_1), (b_1, a_1), (a_3, b_1), (b_1, a_3), (a_1, b_3), (b_3, a_1), (a_2, b_1), (b_1, a_2),$

  $(a_1, b_2), (b_2, a_1)\}$. Note that the action a_1 commutes with all b_i actions, but that a_2 and a_3 commute with b_1 only.

Figure 10.2 shows the trace system T_2 together with the successor relation. T_2 contains two runs, marked by the thin and the thick lines, respectively.

T_2 can be thought of as implementing a database with two transactions.

- Let $T_1 = \{a_1, a_2, a_3\}$ and $T_2 = \{b_1, b_2, b_3\}$.

Each transition represents a database read or write operation. For a correct implementation, transactions should be serializable. One can check that, indeed, in each run there is an observation satisfying the requirement of serializability, namely:

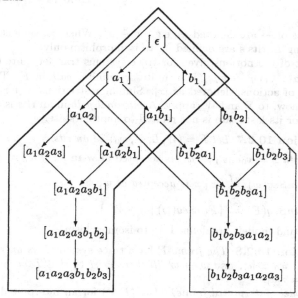

Figure 10.2: Trace system $\mathcal{T}_2$ with successor relation

- $[\epsilon][a_1][a_1a_2][a_1a_2a_3][a_1a_2a_3b_1][a_1a_2a_3b_1b_2][a_1a_2a_3b_1b_2b_3]$ in the run marked by the thick line, and

- $[\epsilon][b_1][b_1b_2][b_1b_2b_3][b_1b_2b_3a_1][b_1b_2b_3a_1a_2][b_1b_2b_3a_1a_2a_3]$ in the run marked by the thin line.

The rest of this section mainly deals with various representations of trace systems, used in the sequel. At the end of it, a choice for a syntax for finite state concurrent systems is shown.

10.2.4 Frames and Models for Trace Systems

The notions of frame and model for trace systems respectively interpreted trace systems are introduced to interpret temporal logics. To start with labelled transition systems are defined.

Definition 10.2.6 *A rooted labeled transition system (rlts) is a four-tuple $F = (W, L, \rightarrow, w_0)$, where W is a set of states, L a set of actions, $\rightarrow \subseteq W \times L \times W$ a labelled relation and w_0 the root.*
An interpreted rooted labeled transition system (F, V), interpreted over $(\mathcal{Y}, \mathcal{D})$, is an rlts F together with an interpretation function $V : W \longrightarrow (\mathcal{Y} \longrightarrow \mathcal{D})$.

Elements of $\rightarrow$ are denoted as, e.g., $w \xrightarrow{a} w'$. When convenient, labels are omitted. Excepting L, rlts's are defined up to isomorphism only.

Most of the notions given for trace systems transfer quite directly to rlts. $x = w_0 a_0 w_1 a_1 \dots, w_i \xrightarrow{a_i} w_{i+1}$ is a, finite or infinite, *path* in F. The *length* of x is its number of actions, denoted as $|x|$. Similar restrictions as for trace systems, to Σ and T, now, to Σ and W, apply. A *maximal path* in an rlts is a path that is either infinite or its last state is not related to another state.

Definition 10.2.7 *Let* $F = (W, L, \rightarrow, w_0)$ *be an rlts.*

- *Path* $x = w_0 a_0 w_1 \dots w_n$ *is accepted at* w *in* F, *if* $w_n = w$.

- $FinSeq(w) \overset{def}{=} \{x \mid x \ is \ accepted \ at \ w\}$.

- $FinSeq(F) \overset{def}{=} \{FinSeq(w) \mid w \in W \}$.

Frames and models are defined up to isomorphism.

Definition 10.2.8 *The frame* F *for a trace system* T *is an rlts for which* $L = \Sigma$, $W \simeq T$, $w_0 \simeq [\epsilon]$, *and* $w \xrightarrow{a} w'$ *iff there exist* $\tau, \tau' \in T$ *such that* $w \simeq \tau$, $w' \simeq \tau'$ *and* $\tau' = \tau[a]$.
The model (interpreted frame) $M = (F, V)$ *for an interpreted trace system* $(T, \mathcal{I})$ *is an interpreted rlts for which* F *is the frame for* T *and for all* $w \in W$, $\tau \in T$, $w \simeq \tau$ *implies* $V(w) = \mathcal{I}(\tau)$.

When convenient traces of T will be used as the names of the states of the model for $(T, \mathcal{I})$.

Note that (Σ, I) is not part of the above definition. This is in line with the observation made in connection with Definition 10.2.1 of trace system, that no essential information is present therein.

Example 10.2.9 The frame for the trace system in Example 10.2.4 is as follows. $F = (W, L, \rightarrow, w_0)$, where

- $W = \{w_0, w_{11}, w_{13}, \dots, w_{21}, w_{22}, \dots, w_{31}, w_{32}, \dots\}$,

- $L = \{a, b, c, d\}$.

Figure 10.3 shows the frame.

The main difference between trace systems and frames is that an equivalence class of action sequences, a trace, is now presented more indirectly as the set of action sequences that is accepted at one and the same state. This can be viewed as transferring the information about independence of actions from the states, i.e., the traces, to the structure, i.e., the labelled relation.

Lemma 10.2.10 *Let* F *be the frame for trace system* T.

- *If* $w \simeq \tau$, *then* $\{x/\Sigma \mid x \in FinSeq(w)\} = \tau$.

- $\{\{x/\Sigma \mid x \in FinSeq(w)\} \mid w \in W\} = T$.

Proof: Directly from Definition 10.2.8 $\square$

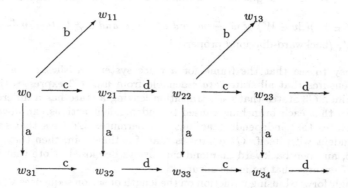

Figure 10.3: The frame for trace system T_1

(Interpreted) trace systems and (interpreted) frames can be viewed as different ways of representing the same information. To clarify the connection it is now shown which properties need to be satisfied by rlts in order to be frame for some trace system.

For an rlts F the relation $I_F \subseteq \Sigma \times \Sigma$ is defined as follows: $I_F = \{(a,b) \mid (\exists w, w', w'' \in W) : w' \xrightarrow{a} w, w'' \xrightarrow{b} w$ and $a \neq b\}$. Note that this relation is well-defined, irrespectively of whether or not the rlts corresponds to a trace system. Condition $C4$ in the Lemma below ensures that if for two actions a diamond is closed once, it is closed wherever it occurs, i.e., that I_F is context independent.

Lemma 10.2.11 *An rlts F is the frame for a trace system iff it satisfies the following conditions:*

C1. $W = \{w \mid w_0 \rightarrow^* w\}$ *(reachability),*

C2. $\{w \mid w \rightarrow w_0\} = \emptyset$ *(beginning),*

C3. $(\forall w, w', w'' \in W)\ w \xrightarrow{a} w'$ *and* $w \xrightarrow{a} w''$ *implies* $w' = w''$ *(forward determinism),*

C4. $(\forall w, w', w'' \in W)(\exists v \in W)$ *if* $w \xrightarrow{a} w'$ *and* $w \xrightarrow{b} w''$ *and* $(a,b) \in I_F$, *then* $w' \xrightarrow{b} v$ *and* $w'' \xrightarrow{a} v$ *(forward I_F-diamond property),*

C5. $(\forall w, w', w'' \in W)(\exists v \in W)$ *if* $w \xrightarrow{a} w' \xrightarrow{b} w''$ *and* $(a,b) \in I_F$, *then* $w \xrightarrow{b} v \xrightarrow{a} w''$ *(concurrency closure property).*

C6. $(\forall w, w', w'' \in W)$ $w' \xrightarrow{a} w$ and $w'' \xrightarrow{a} w$ implies $w' = w''$ (no auto-concurrency),

C7. $(\forall w, w', w'' \in W)(\exists v \in W)$ if $w' \xrightarrow{a} w$ and $w'' \xrightarrow{b} w$ and $a \neq b$, then $v \xrightarrow{a} w''$ and $v \xrightarrow{b} w'$, (backward-diamond property),

Proof: It is easy to see that the frame for a trace system satisfies the above conditions. $C1$ ensures that all states are reachable from w_0. $C2$ expresses that w_0 is the beginning. $C3$ states that each transition leaving a state has a different label. $C4$ ensures that each branching caused by independent actions can always be closed. $C5$ states that independent actions can permute. $C6$ says that each action a is dependent with itself. $C7$ expresses that if actions join, then they are independent. So, an open backward diamond can always be closed. Note that $C2$ together with $C7$ ensures that no loops occur.

It is equally straightforward, using induction on the length of action sequences where necessary, to show that each rlts satisfying the conditions $C1 - C7$ is a frame for a trace system, namely for $\{\{x/\Sigma \mid x \in FinSeq(w)\} \mid w \in W\}$ over (Σ, I_F). The full proof can be found in [221]. □

Some notions given for trace systems transfer to frames for trace systems.

Definition 10.2.12 Let $F = (W, \Sigma, \rightarrow, w_0)$ be the frame for a trace system.

a) $F' = (W', \Sigma, \rightarrow', w_0)$ is a subframe of F if
$$W' \subseteq W \quad and \quad \rightarrow' = \rightarrow \cap (W' \times \Sigma \times W').$$

b) A subframe F' has the forward-diamond property, if for all $w, w', w'' \in W'$, $a, b \in \Sigma$, $w \xrightarrow{a} w'$ and $w \xrightarrow{b} w''$ implies that there is $v \in W'$ such that $w' \xrightarrow{b} v$ and $w'' \xrightarrow{a} v$.

c) A subframe F' is a run of F if W' is a maximal subset of W such that F' has the diamond property.

Let $x = w_0 a_1 w_1 a_1 \ldots$ be a maximal path in F. $\downarrow x$ denotes the subframe of F obtained by restricting the set of states to $\{w \in W \mid w \rightarrow^* w_i, \text{ for } i \geq 0\}$. An *observation* of a run F' of F is any maximal path x in F' such that $F' = \downarrow x$. A suffix $w_i a_i w_{i+1} \ldots$ of an observation x is said to be an observation starting at w_i.

The isomorphism $\simeq$ could be used to identify corresponding structures in the realms of trace systems respectively frames; the above notions are defined so as to give the same names to corresponding notions.

10.2.5 Acceptors

The rlts defined in the previous section accept sets of sequences at each state. Special rlts, frames, were shown to be equivalent to trace systems in the ability to characterize sets of sets of action sequences, i.e., sets of traces. In this section, a less restricted subclass of rlts is considered that enables, for instance, to accept trace systems that are infinite but which correspond to finite state programs, in a finite way. The idea is to enable acceptors to be more concise by allowing loops, but still requiring that the representatives of a trace are accepted at the same state. The reason for this requirement is that acceptors are to represent concurrent programs for which different interleavings of the same partial run lead to the same state. The consequences of doing so are that closure of diamonds may occur also if actions are not independent and that sequences of different length can be accepted at a state. The first consequence means in fact that the independence information can no longer be retrieved from the structure in the rlts; this is remedied by putting the independence relation back in explicitly. This enables to partition the sets of action sequences accepted at a state into traces again.

Definition 10.2.13 *An* acceptor *for a trace system* T *is a five-tuple* $F = (W, \Sigma, \rightarrow, I, w_0)$, *where* $(W, \Sigma, \rightarrow, w_0)$ *is an rlts and* I *is an independency relation in* Σ, *satisfying the following conditions:*

1) $\{[FinSeq(w)/\Sigma] \mid w \in W\} = T$,

2) *if* $x \in FinSeq(w)$, *then for each* $y \in [x]$, $y \in FinSeq(w)$, *for all* $w \in W$.

As in case of frames it is now shown which properties need to be satisfied by rlts with I in order to be an acceptor for some trace system. Notice that $C1 - C2$ and $C6 - C7$ are dropped from the characterization of a frame.

Lemma 10.2.14 $F = (W, \Sigma, \rightarrow, I, w_0)$ *is an acceptor of a trace system iff it satisfies the following conditions:*

$C3$. $(\forall w, w', w'' \in W)$ $w \xrightarrow{a} w'$ *and* $w \xrightarrow{a} w''$ *implies* $w' = w''$ *(forward determinism)*,

$C4$. $(\forall w, w', w'' \in W)(\exists v \in W)$ *if* $w \xrightarrow{a} w'$ *and* $w \xrightarrow{b} w''$ *and* $(a, b) \in I$, *then* $w' \xrightarrow{b} v$ *and* $w'' \xrightarrow{a} v$ *(forward I-diamond property)*,

$C5$. $(\forall w, w', w'' \in W)(\exists v \in W)$ *if* $w \xrightarrow{a} w' \xrightarrow{b} w''$ *and* $(a, b) \in I$, *then* $w \xrightarrow{b} v \xrightarrow{a} w''$ *(concurrency closure property)*.

Proof: See chapter 9. □

In the literature rlts equipped with I satisfying the above conditions $C3 - C5$ are called *rooted concurrent transition systems* [257, 73] or *rooted asynchronous transition systems (rats)* [9]. The latter name will be used in this chapter.

Rats are used as acceptors for both trace systems as well as frames. As before, the connection to the former is made by defining which traces are accepted at each state of the rats. As to the latter, the frame can be viewed as being represented by the sequences accepted at each state, but now together with the relation I rather than just the structure of the frame.

Definition 10.2.15 *Let* F *be an rats.*

- $Tr(w) \overset{def}{=} \{[x/\Sigma] \mid x \in FinSeq(w)\}.$

- $Tr(F) \overset{def}{=} \{Tr(w) \mid w \in W\}.$

Note that just one trace system is accepted by an rats. This allows the following somewhat indirect definition of acceptor for a frame. The indirectness is caused by the fact that in a frame the relation I is encoded in the structure.

Definition 10.2.16 *An rats F' is an* acceptor *for a frame F if F is the frame for the trace system accepted by F'.*

To enable identifying at which state of an rats F which traces are accepted, an *acceptance function* $AC : Tr(F) \longrightarrow W$ is defined, assigning to each trace accepted by F the state of F which accepts a representative of this trace, i.e., $AC(\tau) = w$ iff for some $x \in FinSeq(w)$, $[x/\Sigma] = \tau$. Thanks to conditions $C4$ and $C5$ in Lemma 10.2.14, AC is well defined. AC is extended in the standard way on subsets of $Tr(F)$: $AC(P) = \{AC(\tau) \mid \tau \in P\}$, for $P \subseteq Tr(F)$.

Interpreted trace systems are accepted by rats's equipped with interpretation functions.

Definition 10.2.17 *An interpreted rats (F, V) is an* acceptor *for an interpreted trace system $(T, \mathcal{I})$ if $Tr(F) = T$ and $V(w) = \mathcal{I}(\tau)$, for each τ such that $AC(\tau) = w$.*

Note that just one interpreted trace system is accepted by an interpreted rats. This allows the following definition of acceptor for a model.

Definition 10.2.18 *An interpreted rats (F, V) is an* acceptor *for a model M if M is the model for the interpreted trace system accepted by (F, V).*

10.2.6   Finite State Trace Systems

Since one of the aims of this chapter is to show methods of proving properties of interpreted trace systems by model checking, trace systems that are finite state are of interest. These trace systems are a subclass of the recognizable trace systems (see chapter 6).

Definition 10.2.19 *A trace system T is* finite state, *if there is an equivalence relation $EQ \subseteq T \times T$ satisfying the following conditions.*

   1 EQ has a finite index,

   2 $(\forall \tau, \tau' \in T)(\forall \alpha \in [\Sigma])$ $((\tau \, EQ \, \tau'$ and $\tau\alpha \in T)$ implies $(\tau\alpha \, EQ \, \tau'\alpha))$.

An interpreted trace system $(T, \mathcal{I})$ is finite state, *if in addition to the above two conditions the following condition is satisfied.*

   3 $(\forall \tau, \tau' \in T)(\tau \, EQ \, \tau'$ implies $\mathcal{I}(\tau) = \mathcal{I}(\tau'))$.

The above definition states that the number of traces that are distinguishable with respect to their continuations (clause 2) and with respect to their interpretation (clause 3) is finite. However, $\mathcal{T}$ may well have infinitely many traces with different prefixes i.e., $\downarrow \tau \neq \downarrow \tau'$ for infinitely many $\tau, \tau' \in \mathcal{T}$.

Example 10.2.20 The trace system $\mathcal{T}_1$ of Example 10.2.4 is finite state. The equivalence classes of the relation $EQ \subseteq \mathcal{T}_1 \times \mathcal{T}_1$ are the following.

- $[[\epsilon]]_{EQ} = [(cd)^*]$,

- $[[a]]_{EQ} = [(cd)^*a]$,

- $[[b]]_{EQ} = [(cd)^*b]$,

- $[[c]]_{EQ} = [(cd)^*c]$,

- $[[ac]]_{EQ} = [(dc)^*ac]$.

One can build a quotient structure of $\mathcal{T}$ by EQ.

Definition 10.2.21 *The* quotient structure *of $\mathcal{T}$ by an equivalence relation EQ is a five-tuple $F = (W, \Sigma, \rightarrow, I, w_0)$, where:*

- $W = \{[\tau]_{EQ} \mid \tau \in \mathcal{T}\}$ *is the set of states,*

- (Σ, I) *is the given independence alphabet,*

- $\rightarrow \subseteq W \times \Sigma \times W$ *is the transition relation such that $[\tau]_{EQ} \xrightarrow{a} [\tau']_{EQ}$, if there are traces $\tau_1 \in [\tau]_{EQ}, \tau_1' \in [\tau']_{EQ}$, and $a \in \Sigma$ such that $\tau_1[a] = \tau_1'$,*

- $w_0 = [\epsilon]_{EQ}$.

Lemma 10.2.22 *The* quotient structure *of $\mathcal{T}$ by an equivalence relation EQ is an* rats.

Proof: By straightforward verification of the conditions from Lemma 10.2.14. □

Lemma 10.2.23 *A trace system has a finite acceptor iff it is finite state.*

Proof: ($\Rightarrow$) If a trace system has a finite acceptor, then a relation EQ is defined as follows: $\tau \, EQ \, \tau'$ iff $AC(\tau) = AC(\tau')$.
($\Leftarrow$) If a trace system is finite state, then from Lemma 10.2.22 its quotient structure with respect to EQ is a finite rats. □

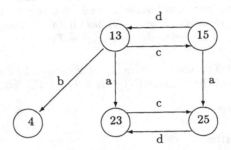

Figure 10.4: The rats F_1 accepting the trace system T_1

Corollary 10.2.24 *A frame has a finite acceptor iff it is the frame for a finite state trace system.*

The above notions are straightforwardly extended to the interpreted case.

Example 10.2.25 [acceptors of trace systems] Below, the definition of a finite acceptor of the trace system T_1 of the Example 10.2.4 is given. The acceptor is shown in Figure 10.4.

The rats $F_1 = (W_1, \Sigma_1, \rightarrow_1, I_1, w_0^1)$ accepting the trace system T_1 is defined as follows:

- $W_1 = \{13, 15, 4, 23, 25\}$,

- $\Sigma_1 = \{a, b, c, d\}$,

- $\rightarrow_1 = \{(13, b, 4), (13, a, 23), (13, c, 15), (15, d, 13), (15, a, 25), (25, d, 23),$
  $(23, c, 25)\}$,

- $I_1 = \{(a, c), (c, a), (d, a), (a, d)\}$,

- $w_0^1 = 13$.

10.2.7   A Syntax for Finite State Concurrent Systems: Elementary Net-Systems

Elementary Net systems are a subclass of Petri Nets, namely those corresponding to finite state programming languages. They may be viewed as programs for which trace systems provide semantics; they serve as an easy representation of finite state concurrent programs. Extensions covering the infinite state case are available and extensively studied. As such extensions are not used in the present exposition, they are not considered here. For further information see, e.g., [235].

Definition 10.2.26 *An* Elementary Net system, *EN-system for short, is an or-dered quadruple* $N = (B, E, F, c_0)$, *where* B *and* E *are finite, disjoint, nonempty sets of places and transitions, respectively,* $F \subseteq B \times E \cup E \times B$ *is the* flow *relation, with* $dom(F) = B \cup E$, *and* c_0 *is a subset of* B, *called the* initial case.

Any subset c of B is called a *case*. A case can be viewed as a state the EN-system is in; c_0 is then the starting state. Nets are represented graphically using lines for transitions, circles for places, and arrows for the flow relation. The initial case is represented by dots in circles (see Figure 10.5).

Definition 10.2.27 *Let* N *be an EN-system. For each* $x \in B \cup E$, *the following sets are defined:*

- $Pre(x) = \{y \mid (y, x) \in F\}$ *(preconditions)*,

- $Post(x) = \{y \mid (x, y) \in F\}$ *(postconditions)*,

- $Prox(x) = Pre(x) \cup Post(x)$ *(proxconditions)*.

Definition 10.2.28 (firing sequence) *A transition* t *is* fire-able *at a case* c *and leads to the case* c' *(written* $c[t > c')$, *if* $Pre(t) \subseteq c$, $Post(t) \subseteq c'$, *and* $c - Pre(t) = c' - Post(t)$.
    A finite sequence of transitions $u = t_0 t_1 \ldots t_n$ *is a firing sequence of* N, *if there is a sequence of cases* $c_1, \ldots, c_{n+1}$ *such that* $c_i[t_i > c_{i+1}$, *for* $i \leq n$. *This is denoted by* $c_0[u > c_{i+1}$. *A case* c *is* reachable, *if there is a firing sequence that leads to it.*

The last clause of the fire-ability condition prohibits firings that would fill an already occupied place, unless that place first gets emptied by the firing.

Definition 10.2.29 *An EN-system* N *is said to be* contact-free *if for each reachable case* c *and for all* $t \in E$, *the following condition holds:*

- $Pre(t) \subseteq c$ *implies* $Post(t) \cap (c - Pre(t)) = \emptyset$.

So, if a reachable case contains the preconditions of a transition, then it does not contain its postconditions, unless they coincide. Therefore, for contact-free nets a transition t is fire-able at c, just when $Pre(t) \subseteq c$.
    All EN-systems used in this chapter as examples are contact-free.

Example 10.2.30 In Figure 10.5, the EN-system N_1 is represented graphically.

The EN-system $N_1 = (B_1, E_1, F_1, c_0^1)$, where

- $B_1 = \{1, 2, 3, 4, 5\}$,

- $E_1 = \{a, b, c, d\}$,

- $F_1 = \{(1, a), (a, 2), (1, b), (b, 4), (3, b), (3, c), (c, 5), (5, d), (d, 3)\}$,

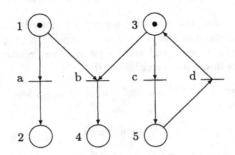

Figure 10.5: EN-system N_1

- $c_0^1 = \{1, 3\}$.

Next, it is shown how interpreted trace systems provide a semantics for EN-systems.

Definition 10.2.31 [trace semantics] *The* semantics *of an EN-system $N = (B, E, F, c_0)$, is the interpreted trace system $(\mathcal{T}, \mathcal{I})$ over (Σ, I) and $(\mathcal{Y}, \mathcal{D})$ such that the following conditions hold.*

- $\Sigma = E$,

- $(a, b) \in I$ *iff* $Prox(a) \cap Prox(b) = \emptyset$, *and*

- $\mathcal{T} = \{[u] \in [\Sigma^*] \mid u$ *is a firing sequence of transitions in $N\}$,*

- $\mathcal{Y} = \{p_b \mid b \in B\}$,

- $\mathcal{D} = \{true, false\}$,

- $\mathcal{I}([u])(p_b) = true$ *iff* $b \in c$, *for* $c_0[u > c$.

One can easily see that the semantics of the EN-system N_1 of Example 10.2.30 is the trace system $\mathcal{T}_1$ of Example 10.2.4, extended with the obvious interpretation function.

Example 10.2.32 In Figure 10.6, the EN-system N_2 is represented graphically.

The EN-system $N_2 = (B_2, E_2, F_2, c_0^2)$ is defined as follows:

- $B_2 = \{1, 2, 3, 4, 5, 6, 7, 8, 9\}$,

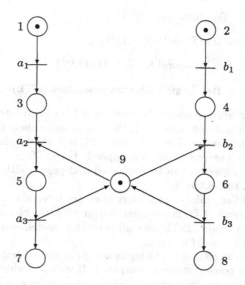

Figure 10.6: EN-system N_2

- $E_2 = \{a_1, a_2, a_2, b_1, b_2, b_3\}$,

- $F_2 = \{(1, a_1), (a_1, 3), (3, a_2), (a_2, 5), (5, a_3), (a_3, 7), (a_3, 9), (9, a_2), (9, b_2),$

    $(2, b_1), (b_1, 4), (4, b_2), (b_2, 6), (6, b_3), (b_3, 9), (b_3, 8)\}$,

- $c_0^2 = \{1, 2, 9\}$.

One can easily see that the semantics of the EN-system N_2 of Example 10.2.32 is the trace system T_2 of Example 10.2.5, extended with the obvious interpretation function.

Example 10.2.33 Notice that the interpreted trace systems which are semantics of EN-systems are finite state. Let $N = (B, E, F, c_0)$ be an EN-system and let (T, I) be its semantics. Then, EQ can then be defined as follows:

$(\forall [u], [u'] \in T)(\forall c \subseteq B) \; [u] \; EQ \; [u']$ iff $(c_0[u > c \Leftrightarrow c_0[u' > c)$.

10.3 Comparison of Temporal Logics on Trace Systems

In this section temporal logics are introduced. These are propositional versions of:

- Linear Time Temporal Logic (LTL),

- Computation Tree Logic$^{(*)}$ (CTL$^{(*)}$),

- Interleaving Set Temporal Logic$^{(*)}$ (ISTL$^{(*)}$),

- Computation Tree Logic with Past Operators (CTL$_P$).

These four logics are considered because they have been interpreted on models for interpreted trace systems. Moreover, they allow us to show the main advantages of using the trace semantics. For LTL and CTL it is shown that model checking can be more effective if trace semantics is applied. For ISTL and CTL$_P$ it is shown that new important properties can be expressed and proved either by proof rules or by model checking, respectively.

The logics differ mainly in the way they are interpreted over models for interpreted trace systems. LTL is interpreted over all paths of a model, CTL$^{(*)}$ over the tree defined by a model, ISTL over all runs of a model, and CTL$_P$ over the whole partial order structure of a model.

Next, formal definitions of the logics are given and their distinguishing power between models for trace systems is compared. It is shown which logics can distinguish branching points and which can distinguish concurrency from non-determinism.

10.3.1   Collection of Logics

In this section the syntax and semantics are defined for LTL, CTL*, ISTL*, and CTL$_P$. Propositional versions of these logics are defined on models for interpreted trace systems over $(\mathcal{Y}, \mathcal{D})$, where $\mathcal{Y}$ is equal to the set of propositional variables PV and $\mathcal{D}$ is equal to the set of Boolean variables $\{true, false\}$. It is convenient to start with the definition of CTL*.

Computation Tree Logic* (CTL*)

The language of CTL* [98, 39] is composed of state and path formulas. As the names indicate, state formulas are interpreted over states and path formulas are interpreted over paths.

Syntax of CTL*

Syntactically, the languages of all other logics considered in this paper are extensions or restrictions of this well-known language.

The set of state formulas and the set of path formulas is defined inductively:

S1. Each $q \in PV$ is a state formula,

S2. if φ and ψ are state formulas, then so are $\neg\varphi$ and $\varphi \wedge \psi$,

S3. if φ is a path formula, then $E\varphi$ is a state formula,

P1. any state formula φ is also a path formula,

P2. if φ, ψ are path formulas, then so are $\varphi \wedge \psi$ and $\neg \varphi$,

P3. if φ, ψ are path formulas, then so are $X\varphi$ and $(\varphi U \psi)$.

E is a path quantifier with the intuitive meaning: there is a path. X is the next step operator and U denotes Until.

The following abbreviations will be used for all the discussed logics:

- $\varphi \vee \psi \stackrel{def}{=} \neg(\neg\varphi \wedge \neg\psi)$; $true \stackrel{def}{=} \varphi \vee \neg\varphi$, for any φ; $\varphi \rightarrow \psi \stackrel{def}{=} \neg\varphi \vee \psi$,

- $\varphi \oplus \psi \stackrel{def}{=} (\varphi \wedge \neg\psi) \vee (\neg\varphi \wedge \psi)$; $\varphi \equiv \psi \stackrel{def}{=} (\varphi \rightarrow \psi) \wedge (\psi \rightarrow \varphi)$,

- $F\varphi \stackrel{def}{=} true U \varphi$; $A(\varphi U \psi) \stackrel{def}{=} \neg(E(\neg\psi U(\neg\varphi \wedge \neg\psi)) \vee EG(\neg\psi))$,

- $AG\varphi \stackrel{def}{=} \neg EF\neg\varphi$, $AH\varphi \stackrel{def}{=} \neg EP\neg\varphi$.

Semantics of CTL*

Let $M = ((W, \Sigma, \rightarrow, w_0), V)$ be a model and $p = x_0 x_1 \ldots$ be a maximal path starting at $x_0 \in W$. Let p_i denote the suffix $x_i x_{i+1} \ldots$ of p.

S1. $x \models q$ iff $V(x)(q) = true$, for $q \in PV$,

S2. $x \models \neg\varphi$ iff not $x \models \varphi$,

$\quad x \models \varphi \wedge \psi$ iff $x \models \varphi$ and $x \models \psi$,

S3. $x \models E\varphi$ iff $p \models \varphi$ for some path p starting at x,

P1. $p \models \varphi$ iff $x_0 \models \varphi$ for any state formula φ,

P2. $p \models \varphi \wedge \psi$ iff $p \models \varphi$ and $p \models \psi$,

$\quad p \models \neg\varphi$ iff not $p \models \varphi$,

P3. $p \models X\varphi$ iff $p_1 \models \varphi$,

$\quad p \models (\varphi U \psi)$ iff $(\exists i \geq 0)\, p_i \models \psi$ and $(\forall j : 0 \leq j < i)\, p_j \models \varphi$.

A CTL* formula φ is said to be valid in a model M (written $M \models_{CTL^*} \varphi$) iff $M, w_0 \models \varphi$.

Example 10.3.1 Let $M = (F, V)$ be the model for an interpreted trace system $(\mathcal{T}, \mathcal{I})$. For instance, the following properties can be expressed in CTL*:

- $M \models_{CTL^*} AG\varphi$ – φ is an invariant in $(\mathcal{T}, \mathcal{I})$,

- $M \models_{CTL^*} AF\varphi$ – φ will eventually hold in $(\mathcal{T}, \mathcal{I})$,

- $M \models_{CTL^*} EF\varphi$ – φ is possible in $(\mathcal{T}, \mathcal{I})$.

Computation Tree Logic (CTL)

The language of the logic CTL is the restriction of the language of CTL* such that only one single linear time operator (F,G,X, or U) can follow a path quantifier (A or E).

Syntax of CTL

The set of CTL formulas is the maximal one generated by the rules:

S1. Each $q \in PV$ is a formula,

S2. if α and ψ are formulas, then so are $\neg\varphi$ and $\varphi \wedge \psi$,

S3'. if φ, ψ are formulas, then so are $EX\varphi$, $EG\varphi$, and $E(\varphi U \psi)$.

The semantics is the subset of the semantics of CTL* concerning CTL formulas.

Example 10.3.2 The following are CTL* formulas, which are not expressible in CTL:

- $AFG\varphi$,

- $AGF\varphi$.

Linear Time Temporal Logic (LTL)

The language of the logic LTL [188] is the restriction of the language of CTL* such that it does not contain path quantifiers.

Syntax of LTL

The set of LTL formulas is the maximal one generated by the rules $S1 - S2$ and $P1 - P3$.

Semantics of LTL

LTL formulas are interpreted over models corresponding to executions of concurrent systems. These correspond to maximal paths through interpreted trace systems in the present framework.

The semantics is the subset of the semantics of CTL* concerning LTL formulas.

An LTL formula φ is said to be valid in a model M (written $M \models_{LTL} \varphi$) iff $p \models \varphi$, for all maximal paths p starting at w_0 in M.

Example 10.3.3 Let $M = (F, V)$ be the model for an interpreted trace system $(\mathcal{T}, \mathcal{I})$. For instance, the following properties can be expressed in LTL:

- $M \models_{LTL} G\varphi - \varphi$ is an invariant in $(\mathcal{T}, \mathcal{I})$,

- $M \models_{LTL} F\varphi - \varphi$ is inevitable in $(\mathcal{T}, \mathcal{I})$.

Interleaving Set Temporal Logic* (ISTL*)

ISTL* was introduced in Peled's thesis [214] and then extensively studied in [149, 150]. The logic enables explicit reasoning about the observations and the runs they belong to.

Syntax of ISTL*

The syntax of ISTL* is the same as that of CTL*.

Semantics of ISTL*

Although the syntax of ISTL* is the same as that of CTL*, the semantics is different. ISTL* formulas are interpreted over models for runs of interpreted trace systems.

Let $M = (F, V)$ be the model for an interpreted trace system $(\mathcal{T}, \mathcal{I})$. $M' = (F', V')$ is an *ISTL* model* for M if F' is a run of F and $V' = V|W'$.

One can easily notice that for each ISTL* model M' there is the run R of $\mathcal{T}$ such that M' is the model for the interpreted run $(R, \mathcal{I}|R)$.

Let O_{x_0} be the set of all observations of M' starting at $x_0 \in W'$ and let $o = x_0 x_1 \ldots \in O_{x_0}$. Let o_i denote the suffix $x_i x_{i+1} \ldots$ of o.

S1, S2, P1 - P3 like for CTL*,

S3. $x_0 \models E\varphi$ iff $o \models \varphi$ for some observation $o \in O_{x_0}$ starting at x_0.

An ISTL* formula φ is said to be valid in a model M (written $M \models_{ISTL^*} \varphi$) iff $M', w_0 \models \varphi$, for all ISTL* models M' for M.

Example 10.3.4 In addition to properties expressible in LTL (but quantified now over observations) formulas of ISTL* can express partial order properties.

- $M \models_{ISTL^*} AG\varphi - \varphi$ is an invariant in $(\mathcal{T}, \mathcal{I})$,

- $M \models_{ISTL^*} AF\varphi - \varphi$ is inevitable in $(\mathcal{T}, \mathcal{I})$ (under the concurrency fairness assumption),

- $M \models_{ISTL^*} EF\varphi - \varphi$ holds at some state of each run in $(\mathcal{T}, \mathcal{I})$.

It will be show in the next section that serializability can be expressed in ISTL*.

Interleaving Set Temporal Logic (ISTL)

The language of ISTL is the same as that of CTL. Therefore, the logic ISTL is a restriction of ISTL* in the same manner as the logic CTL was a restriction of CTL*. Again, only a single linear time operator (F,G,X, or U) can follow a path quantifier (A or E).

Computation Tree Logic with Past Operators (CTL$_P$)

CTL$_P$ was introduced in [222, 220] in order to reason about partial order properties. The language of CTL$_P$ is an extension of the language of CTL by past operators. The original definition of CTL$_P$ included next step modalities labelled with actions. It is further shown that if a valuation function encodes names of action executed between successive states, then the labelled modalities are expressible using the unlabelled versions.

Syntax of CTL$_P$

Now, the set of CTL$_P$ formulas is defined.

S1. Each $p \in PV$ is a formula,

S2. if φ and ψ are formulas, then so are $\varphi \wedge \psi$, $\neg\varphi$,

S3. if φ is a formula, then so are $EX\varphi$, $EG\varphi$, and $E(\varphi U \psi)$,

S4. if φ is a formula, then so are $EY\varphi$ and $EP\varphi$,

The symbols E and A can be called observation quantifiers (they correspond to path quantifiers in CTL). The other symbols have the following intuitive meaning: X - next step, U - Until, Y - backward step, P - somewhere in the past. Formulas of the form $EY\varphi$ and $EP\varphi$ are called past formulas. Notice that the past formulas are not symmetric to the future formulas. This is motivated by the requirement of defining the simplest logic enabling to express partial order properties. Extensions with $EH\varphi$ and $E(\varphi S \psi)$ are possible, but will not be discussed in this chapter.

Semantics of CTL$_P$

Let $M = ((W, \Sigma, \rightarrow, w_0), V)$ be a model and $x \in W$. The notion of *truth* in M is defined by the relation $\models$ as follows:

S1. $M, x \models q$ iff $V(x)(q) = true$, for $q \in PV$,

S2. if φ, ψ are state formulas,

$M, x \models \neg\varphi$ iff not $M, x \models \varphi$,

$M, x \models \varphi \wedge \psi$ iff $M, x \models \varphi$ and $M, x \models \psi$,

S3. $M, x \models EX\varphi$ iff $M, x' \models \varphi$ for some $x' \in W$ with $x \rightarrow x'$,

$M, x_0 \models EG\varphi$ iff there is an observation $o = x_0 x_1 \ldots$ such that for all $i \geq 0$ $M, x_i \models \varphi$,

$M, x_0 \models E(\varphi U \psi)$ iff there is an observation $o = x_0 x_1 \ldots$ and $k \geq 0$ such that $M, x_k \models \psi$, and for all $0 \leq i < k$: $M, x_i \models \varphi$,

S4. $M, x \models EY\varphi$ iff $M, x' \models \varphi$, for some $x' \in W$ with $x' \to x$,

$M, x \models EP\varphi$ iff $M, x' \models \varphi$, for some $x' \in W$ with $x' \to^* x$.

A formula φ is *valid in a model* M (written $M \models_{CTL_P} \varphi$), if $M, w_0 \models \varphi$. A formula φ is said to be *valid*, if $M \models \varphi$, for all models M.

The language of CTL_P contains all the CTL formulas (with slightly different semantics, tuned to observations) and moreover the formulas with the past modalities EP and EY.

Example 10.3.5 In addition to the properties expressible in CTL (but quantified now over observations), CTL_P formulas can express partial order properties, i.e., requiring the distinction between concurrency and non-determinism.

- $M \models_{CTL_P} AG\varphi$ – φ is an invariant in $(\mathcal{T}, \mathcal{I})$,

- $M \models_{CTL_P} AF\varphi$ – φ is inevitable in $(\mathcal{T}, \mathcal{I})$, (under a concurrency fairness assumption),

- $M \models_{CTL_P} EF\varphi$ – φ is possible in $(\mathcal{T}, \mathcal{I})$,

- $M \models_{CTL_P} EF(AH\varphi)$ – there is a partial execution in $(\mathcal{T}, \mathcal{I})$ such that φ holds at all its states,

- $M \models_{CTL_P} EG(AH\varphi)$ – there is a run in $(\mathcal{T}, \mathcal{I})$ such that φ holds at all its states,

- $M \models_{CTL_P} AF(EP\varphi)$ – φ holds at some state of each run in $(\mathcal{T}, \mathcal{I})$,

- $M \models_{CTL_P} AG(\varphi \to EP\psi)$ – always if φ holds, ψ held in the past; this formula allows for specifying snapshots of concurrent programs (φ and ψ do not contain temporal formulas).

Examples of snapshots of concurrent systems are shown in [151, 217]. It is further shown that serializability can be expressed in the language of CTL_P.

10.3.2 Encoding Labelled Next Step Operators

The label of the transition between two adjacent states of a model can be encoded by the valuation of these states. This encoding allows to derive labelled next step operators EX_a and EY_a.

Let M be the model for an interpreted trace system, $PV_\Sigma = \{p_a \mid a \in \Sigma\}$ and $PV_\Sigma \subseteq PV$.

Definition 10.3.6 *The valuation function V encodes actions if for all $p_a \in PV_\Sigma$, $V(w)(p_a) = true$ iff the number of occurrences of $\xrightarrow{a}$-transitions in a path accepted at w is odd.*

The definition is correct since the paths accepted at w in M have the same numbers of $\xrightarrow{a}$- transitions. The condition in this definition enables to find the label of the transition between two adjacent states only by looking at its valuations, i.e., the label is a iff p_a holds at exactly one of the two states.

Therefore, the following abbreviations can be defined for all the logics using EX and/or EY:

- $EX_a\varphi \stackrel{def}{=} (p_a \to EX(\varphi \wedge \neg p_a)) \wedge (\neg p_a \to EX(\varphi \wedge p_a))$,

- $EY_a\varphi \stackrel{def}{=} (p_a \to EY(\varphi \wedge \neg p_a)) \wedge (\neg p_a \to EY(\varphi \wedge p_a))$.

$EX_a\varphi$ ($EY_a\varphi$) expresses that there is the a-successor (a-predecessor, resp.) state satisfying φ.

Example 10.3.7 It follows from the definition of the model M for a trace system $\mathcal{T}$ that $M \models EF(EY_a(true) \wedge EY_b(true))$ for $a \neq b$ expresses that actions a and b are independent, i.e., $(a, b) \in I$.

10.3.3 Examples of Inevitability and Serializability

Example 10.3.8 The partial order properties discussed in the former examples can be formally expressed in the logics ISTL and CTL$_P$. Let $PV_i = \{p_b \mid b \in B_i\}$, where B_i is the set of places of EN-system N_i, and $M_i = (F_i, V_i)$ be the model for trace semantics $(\mathcal{T}_i, \mathcal{I}_i)$ of N_i, for $i \in \{1, 2\}$ (see Examples 10.2.30 and 10.2.32).

In the following way, the property discussed in Example 10.2.4 can be expressed by ISTL and CTL$_P$ formulas:

INEVITABILITY (in ISTL) $M_1 \models_{ISTL} AF(p_2 \vee p_4)$,

INEVITABILITY (in CTL$_P$) $M_1 \models_{CTL_P} AF(p_2 \vee p_4)$.

In the following way, the property discussed in Example 10.2.5 can be expressed by ISTL and CTL$_P$ formulas:

SERIALIZABILITY (in ISTL):

1. $M_2 \models_{ISTL} (p_1 \wedge p_2 \wedge p_9) \to EF((p_7 \wedge p_2 \wedge p_9) \vee (p_1 \wedge p_8 \wedge p_9))$,
2. $M_2 \models_{ISTL} AG[((p_7 \wedge p_2 \wedge p_9) \vee (p_1 \wedge p_8 \wedge p_9)) \to EF(p_7 \wedge p_8 \wedge p_9)]$.

SERIALIZABILITY (in CTL$_P$):

1. $M_2 \models_{CTL_P} (p_1 \wedge p_2 \wedge p_9) \to AFEP((p_7 \wedge p_2 \wedge p_9) \vee (p_1 \wedge p_8 \wedge p_9))$,
2. $M_2 \models_{CTL_P} AG[((p_7 \wedge p_2 \wedge p_9) \vee (p_1 \wedge p_8 \wedge p_9)) \to AF(EP(p_7 \wedge p_8 \wedge p_9))]$.

The first formula expresses that each run contains a state at which either control is before the execution of T_1 and after the execution of T_2, or the other way round. The second formula says that each run contains a state at which control is after the execution of T_1 and T_2.

10.3.4 Equivalence Notions for Frames for Trace Systems

In order to investigate equivalences imposed on models by temporal logics it is assumed that the valuation functions do not encode any structural information, but only actions executed between successive states. This is ensured by taking $PV = PV_{\Sigma}$ and requiring that V encodes actions (see Definition 10.3.6).

As before, it is possible to find the label of the transition between two adjacent states only by looking at its valuations. Let $M = (F, V)$ be a model. Notice that V satisfies the following conditions:

- $V(w_0)(p_a) = false$, for each $p_a \in PV$, and

- $V(w)(p_a) \neq V(w')(p_a)$ iff $w \xrightarrow{a} w'$.

Now, equivalence notions for frames for trace systems are formally defined.

The following definitions contain four notions of equivalences. The notion of maximal interleaving path equivalence is defined first. Let F and F' be frames for trace systems.

Definition 10.3.9 F and F' are said to be maximal interleaving path equivalent $(F \sim_{mip-e} F')$ iff $\{x/\Sigma \mid x \text{ is a maximal path in } F\} = \{x'/\Sigma \mid x' \text{ is a maximal path in } F'\}$.

Now, Park's and Milner's notion of forward bisimulation for F and F' are given, denoted here as $F \sim_{f-b} F'$, and referred to as f-bisimulation.

Definition 10.3.10 A relation $Z \subseteq W \times W'$ is an f-bisimulation between F and F' iff $(w_0, w_0') \in Z$ and if $(w, w') \in Z$,

- if $w \xrightarrow{a} v$, then there exists $v' \in W'$ such that $w' \xrightarrow{a}' v'$ and $(v, v') \in Z$, and

- the symmetric condition.

F and F' are f-bisimilar $(F \sim_{f-b} F')$, if there exists an f-bisimulation between F and F'.

Then, definitions of a run trace equivalence and backward-forward bisimulation are given.

Definition 10.3.11 F and F' are run trace equivalent $(F \sim_{r-t} F')$ iff

- for each run F_1 in F, there is a run F_1' in F' such that F_1 and F_1' are isomorphic, and

- the symmetric condition

Definition 10.3.12 A relation $Z \subseteq F \times F'$ is a bf-bisimulation for F and F' iff Z is an f-bisimulation and if $(w, w') \in Z$,

- *if $v \xrightarrow{a} w$, then there exists $v' \in W'$ such that $v' \xrightarrow{a}' w'$ and $(v, v') \in Z$, and*

- *the symmetric condition.*

F and F' are bf-bisimilar ($F \sim_{bf-b} F'$), if there exists a bf-bisimulation for F and F'.

10.3.5   Equivalences Imposed by Temporal Logics

In this section it is investigated which equivalences are imposed on models corresponding to interpreted trace systems by the different logics considered in this chapter. Each induced equivalence will be shown to coincide with one equivalence defined in the former section.

Let $M = (F, V)$ and $M' = (F', V')$ be the propositional models for interpreted trace systems $(\mathcal{T}, \mathcal{I})$ and $(\mathcal{T}', \mathcal{I}')$ over $(PV_\Sigma, \{true, false\})$, respectively. The interpretations $\mathcal{I}$ and $\mathcal{I}'$ are defined like the valuation functions in Definition 10.3.6.

Modal equivalences of M and M' are defined in the following way:

Definition 10.3.13 (modal equivalence) *The* modal equivalence $\equiv_L$ *imposed by the logic $L \in \{LTL, CTL, CTL^*, ISTL, ISTL^*, CTL_P\}$ is defined as follows:*
$$M \equiv_L M' \text{ iff } (M \models_L \varphi \Leftrightarrow M' \models_L \varphi) \text{ for each formula } \varphi \text{ of the logic } L.$$

The next four theorems match equivalences of frames for trace systems with those induced by the considered temporal logics.

The equivalence induced by LTL coincides with maximal interleaving path equivalence.

Theorem 10.3.14 *F and F' are maximal interleaving path equivalent iff $M \equiv_{LTL} M'$, where ($\Leftarrow$) holds, provided the sets of maximal paths in F and F' are finite in size.*

The equivalence induced by CTL$^{(*)}$ coincides with forward bisimulation.

Theorem 10.3.15 *F and F' are f-bisimilar iff $M \equiv_{CTL^{(*)}} M'$,*

The equivalence induced by ISTL$^{(*)}$ coincides with run trace equivalence.

Theorem 10.3.16 *F and F' are run trace equivalent iff $M \equiv_{ISTL^{(*)}} M'$, where ($\Leftarrow$) holds, provided F and F' have finitely many runs.*

The equivalence induced by CTL$_P$ coincides with backward-forward bisimulation.

Theorem 10.3.17 *F and F' are bf-bisimilar iff $M \equiv_{CTL_P} M'$.*

The proofs of the above theorems can be found in [124, 257].

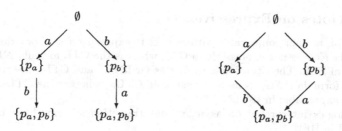

Figure 10.7: Models M and M'

10.3.6   Comparing Equivalences

The aim of this section is to compare equivalences.

The following theorem shows that backward-forward bisimulation and run trace equivalence coincide with isomorphism, whereas maximal interleaving path equivalence is equal to forward bisimulation for trace systems.

Theorem 10.3.18 *The following equalities hold:*

- $\sim_{bf-b} = \sim_{r-e} = iso$

- $\sim_{f-b} = \sim_{mip-e} \neq iso$

The proof can be found in [124]. The reason for both above equalities is forward determinism of frames. The relaxation of this condition, as in case of occurrence transition systems [124], makes $\sim_{bf-b}$ stronger than $\sim_{r-e}$ and $\sim_{f-b}$ stronger than $\sim_{mip-e}$.

Example 10.3.19 The models M and M' (see Figure 10.7, where the displayed propositions hold at the states) for the following two interpreted trace systems $(\mathcal{T}, \mathcal{I})$ and $(\mathcal{T}', \mathcal{I}')$ (over $(PV_\Sigma, \{true, false\})$) cannot be distinguished by any LTL and CTL* formulas.

- $\mathcal{T} = \{[\epsilon], [a], [b], [ab], [ba]\}$, $\Sigma = \{a, b\}$, $I = \emptyset$, with the obvious $\mathcal{I}$,

- $\mathcal{T}' = \{[\epsilon], [a], [b], [ab]\}$, $\Sigma' = \{a, b\}$, $I' = \{(a, b), (b, a)\}$, with the obvious $\mathcal{I}'$.

But, these models can be distinguished by ISTL and CTL$_P$ formulas.

- $M \not\models_{ISTL} EXp_a \wedge EXp_b$, $M' \models_{ISTL} EXp_a \wedge EXp_b$,

- $M \not\models_{CTL_P} EF(EYp_a \wedge EYp_b)$, $M' \models_{CTL_P} EF(EYp_a \wedge EYp_b)$.

10.3.7 Notes on Expressiveness

LTL and CTL are not comparable with respect to expressiveness. For example, the LTL formula FGp is not expressible in CTL whereas the CTL formula EFp is not expressible in LTL. The situation is similar as far ISTL* and CTL$_P$ are concerned. The ISTL* formula $AFGp$ is not expressible in CTL$_P$, whereas the CTL$_P$ formula EFp is not expressible in ISTL*.

Modal logics interpreted on asynchronous transition systems have been also investigated in [181].

10.4 Efficient Model Checking for a Subset of LTL

Model checking for linear time temporal logic is linear in the size of the model acceptor and $PSPACE - complete$ in the length of the tested formula. In the context of automatic verification, a finite state concurrent system could, in principle, be given as an interpreted trace system, but, in practice, is usually given in a program-like form; for this chapter one could think of EN-systems.

Starting from a suitable description of a concurrent system, a finite interpreted rats can be obtained algorithmically that accepts all executions. However, the number of states is frequently exponential in the number of actions. Thus, the rats is often so large as to transgress the boundaries of available computing power. Therefore, methods for reducing rats's are of interest as they can improve the feasibility of model checking. Unfortunately, since checking whether an LTL formula holds for an EN-system (i.e., it is true in its model) was proved to be $NP - hard$ in the number of the transitions of the EN-system, it is unlikely that a polynomial algorithm can be found.

In this section it is shown that if trace semantics is used, a different, smaller, structure than the rats, called a *trace automaton* suffices; various algorithms that check a formula against an rats can be applied on the trace automaton as well. The idea is that a much smaller transition graph suffices to generate for each equivalence class of sequences a representative with respect to the independence relation. Of course, this puts a constraint on the formulas to be checked: Formulas should evaluate to the same result on each representative of a class. This is called *equivalence robustness*. A, rather mild, constraint is needed to ensure equivalence robustness: Formulas should not contain next step operators. The subset of LTL formulas satisfying this property is called LTL-x.

To start with, a standard method of model checking is given, after which it is shown how the model acceptors it employs can be reduced using trace automata.

10.4.1 Standard Approach

Let P be an EN-system and $(\mathcal{T}, \mathcal{I})$ be its trace semantics. Then, let $M_P = (F, V_P)$ be a model acceptor for the model for $(\mathcal{T}, \mathcal{I})$.

The standard method of model checking of LTL [274, 265] using automata-theoretic constructions is then as follows. Since this method ignores the independence relation I, the substructure of F equal to $(W, \Sigma, \rightarrow, w_0)$ and denoted by F_P is used. To start with, F_P is turned into a generalized Büchi automaton (gba, for short) $A_P = (W, \Sigma, \rightarrow, w_0, \mathcal{F})$, where $\mathcal{F} = \{F_1, ..., F_k\} \subseteq 2^W$, by adding a set of accepting conditions. Accepting conditions are needed to accommodate fairness; they enable defining certain subsets of maximal paths (computations), called sets of *accepting computations* of F_P. A computation of A_P is accepting if for each F_j, there is some state in F_j that repeats infinitely often in the computation. $L(A_P)$ denotes the set of all accepting computations of A_P. For instance, $L(A_P)$ is equal to the set of all maximal paths of A_P, if $\mathcal{F} = \emptyset$.

Now, let $M_P = (A_P, V_P)$ be a gba with valuation function V_P and let $L(M_P)$ denote the accepting computations of M_P.

Example 10.4.1 The new notions are explained on the EN-system N_1 of Example 10.2.30. The model acceptor is defined as follows. Let $PV_1 = \{p_1, p_2, p_3, p_4, p_5\}$. $M_{N_1} = (F_1, V_1)$, where the rats F_1 is shown in Figure 10.4 (Example 10.2.25) and $V_1(w)(p_i) = true$ iff w corresponds to a case with the place i marked.

Assume that formulas are to be checked over observations of F_1. Since the method deals with infinite paths only, all observations need to be extended to be infinite. This can be easily achieved by adding one more transition looping at the state 4 and labelling the transition with an action name, say, b. This extension can obviously change some properties satisfied by N_1. Since the property under consideration remains unchanged, it is not discussed here how properties of extended rats's can be related to properties of original ones.

Next, $\mathcal{F}_1 = \{\{4, 23\}\}$ is defined. Now, the set of accepting computations is equal to the set of observations.

Now, let φ be an LTL formula. To verify that each accepting computation of $L(M_P)$ satisfies the formula φ (written $M_P \models \varphi$), a gba with a valuation function $M_{\neg\varphi}$ should be built with $L(M_{\neg\varphi})$ equal exactly to all accepting computations satisfying $\neg\varphi$. Then $L(M_P) \cap L(M_{\neg\varphi}) = \emptyset$ should be verified.

Since M_P has got only one beginning state w_0, the above intersection may be non-empty only if $M_{\neg\varphi}$ contains a computation starting at a state with the same valuation as w_0. Therefore, first a gba with a valuation function accepting all computations satisfying $\neg\varphi$ is found and then it is restricted to its reachable part starting at the state with the same valuation as w_0. The construction used in the proof of Theorem 10.4.2 guarantees that there are no two states with the same valuation function.

Theorem 10.4.2 ([265]) *One can build a generalized Büchi automaton with a valuation function $M_\varphi = (F_\varphi, V_\varphi)$, where $F_\varphi = (W, \Sigma, \rightarrow, W_0, \mathcal{F})$, $|W| \leq 2^{O(|\varphi|)}$ such that $L(M_\varphi)$ is exactly the set of computations satisfying an LTL formula φ.*

The above theorem is a slightly modified version of the original theorem as states rather than transitions are labelled with sets of propositions. The transitions are labelled with actions of Σ.

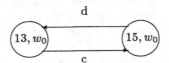

Figure 10.8: The product automaton $F_{N_1, \neg\varphi_1}$

Example 10.4.3 Let $\varphi_1 = F(p_2 \vee p_4)$ be a given formula to be checked over M_{N_1} of Example 10.4.1. Then, $\neg\varphi_1 = G(\neg p_2 \wedge \neg p_4)$. A gba with a valuation function for $\neg\varphi_1$ is then $M_{\neg\varphi_1} = ((\{w_0\}, \Sigma_1, \{(w_0, a, w_0) \mid a \in \Sigma_1\}, \{w_0\}, \{\{w_0\}\}), V_{\neg\varphi_1})$, where $V_{\neg\varphi_1}(w_0)(p_i) = false$, for $i = 2, 4$.

Next, it is checked whether $L(M_P) \cap L(M_{\neg\varphi}) = \emptyset$. This is done by taking the product of M_P and the appropriate reachable part of $M_{\neg\varphi}$ (see the definition below), and establishing whether it contains any accepting computation. If so, then M_P satisfies φ. The time complexity of the algorithm is $O(size(M_P) \times 2^{O(|\varphi|)})$.

Definition 10.4.4 (product) *The* product *of two generalized Büchi automata* $A_1 = (W_1, \Sigma, \rightarrow_1, w_1, \mathcal{F}_1)$ *and* $A_2 = (W_2, \Sigma, \rightarrow_2, w_2, \mathcal{F}_2)$ *is the automaton* $A = (W, \Sigma, \rightarrow, w_0, \mathcal{F})$ *defined by*

- $W = W_1 \times W_2$, $w_0 = (w_1, w_2)$,
- $\mathcal{F} = \bigcup_{F_j \in \mathcal{F}_1} \{F_j \times W_2\} \cup \bigcup_{F_j \in \mathcal{F}_2} \{W_1 \times F_j\}$,
- $((v_1, v_2), a, (u_1, u_2)) \in \rightarrow$ *when* $(v_1, a, u_1) \in \rightarrow_1$ *and* $(v_2, a, u_2) \in \rightarrow_2$.

A further simplification is obtained by considering only the states for which both M_P and $M_{\neg\varphi}$ have consistent valuations. This leads to the following definition for $M_{P, \neg\varphi} = (F_{P, \neg\varphi}, V_{P, \neg\varphi})$.

$F_{P, \neg\varphi}$ is equal to the product of $F_P \times F_{\neg\varphi}$ restricted to the states W', for which both components have consistent valuations, i.e., $W' = \{(v, v') \in W \times W_{\neg\varphi} \mid V_P(v) \cap Subformulas(\varphi) = V_{\neg\varphi}(v')\}$, $V_{P, \neg\varphi}((v, v')) = V_P(v)$.

Example 10.4.5 The product of the structures M_{N_1} and $M_{\neg\varphi_1}$ is the following structure $M_{N_1, \neg\varphi_1} = (F_{N_1, \neg\varphi_1}, V_{N_1, \neg\varphi_1})$, where $F_{N_1, \neg\varphi_1} = (\{(13, w_0), (15, w_0)\}, \Sigma_1, \{((13, w_0), c, (15, w_0)), ((15, w_0), d, (13, w_0))\}, \{(13, w_0)\}, \{\emptyset, \{(13, w_0), (15, w_0)\}\})$, (see Figure 10.8), and $V_{N_1, \neg\varphi_1}((xy, w_0))(p_i) = true$, for $i = x, y$.

Note that $L(M_{N_1, \neg\varphi_1}) = \emptyset$. Therefore, $M_{N_1} \models \varphi_1$.

10.4.2 Trace Approach

In order to use the power of traces in model checking the notion of trace automaton is introduced. Following that, several ways of obtaining such automata are discussed.

Trace Automata

Trace systems are also accepted by certain rooted labelled transition systems, called *trace automata*, which do not need to be rats's and can often be smaller than these. Trace automata accept the same traces as some rats, but using a different definition of acceptance.

Definition 10.4.6 *A trace automaton is a five-tuple* $TA = (W, \Sigma, \rightarrow, I, w_0)$ *such that* $(W, \Sigma, \rightarrow, w_0)$ *is a rooted labelled transition system and* I *is an independence relation.* TA *accepts a trace* τ*, if there is a finite path* x *in* TA *such that* $\tau \in \downarrow [x/\Sigma]$. *The set of traces accepted by* TA *is denoted by* $Tr(TA)$.

Notice, that a trace τ is accepted by TA if TA accepts a path corresponding to a representative of a trace extending τ. This means that a trace automaton does not need to contain paths corresponding to all representatives of all accepted traces.

Lemma 10.4.7 *Let* $F = (W, \Sigma, \rightarrow, I, w_0)$ *be an rats and* $TA = (W', \Sigma, \rightarrow', I, w_0)$ *be a trace automaton such that*

- $W' \subseteq W$, $\rightarrow' \subseteq \rightarrow$, *and*

- *for each trace* $\tau \in Tr(F)$, *there is a finite path* x *in* TA *such that* $\tau \in \downarrow [x/\Sigma]$.

Then, $Tr(F) = Tr(TA)$.

Trace automata are used for model checking of certain safety properties, where they can just replace rats's. The method of model checking, to be explained shortly, uses the fact that a trace automaton contains a path corresponding to a representative of each trace or its extension. For example, for checking termination it is sufficient to analyse only one representative of each maximal trace.

Example 10.4.8 Figure 10.9 shows the trace automaton accepting the trace system T_1 (see Example 10.2.4) of EN-system N_1 of Figure 10.5.

However, a trace automaton does not necessarily contain an infinite path corresponding to some observation of each run of the accepted trace system. Even worse, a trace automaton may not contain any infinite path corresponding to an observation (see Example 10.4.9). This disallows to model check liveness properties, i.e., these requiring analysis of observations (as inevitability, for example) as the standard method of model checking relies on testing whether the product of gba's with valuation functions contains an accepting computation, i.e., an infinite path satisfying some conditions. This method does not use any information given by I. So, the lack of an observation in a trace automaton might make the standard method incorrect when the rats is replaced by the trace automaton.

Example 10.4.9 Consider rats F_1 as given in Figure 10.10, with $I = \{(a, b), (b, a)\}$. Definition 10.4.6 allows two non-trivial reductions: TA_1^1 and TA_1^2. TA_1^1 correctly represents the infinite observation ba^ω, whereas TA_1^2 represents only the infinite path a^ω, which is not an observation

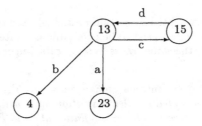

Figure 10.9: Trace automaton accepting the trace system $\mathcal{T}_1$

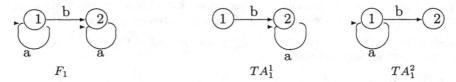

Figure 10.10: Rcts F_1 and two trace automata TA_1^1 and TA_1^2

In order to also allow one checking liveness properties, trace automata have to correctly represent runs of trace systems. The way they need to represent them is similar to the way they represent traces. This means that for each run of the accepted trace system, a trace automaton should contain a path corresponding to one of its observations.

Definition 10.4.10 *A* trace automaton on runs *is a trace automaton TA for which $Tr(TA)$ is a trace system and which satisfies the following auxiliary property:*

- *for each run R of $Tr(TA)$, there is a path $x = w_0 a_0 w_1 a_1 \ldots$ in TA such that $[\epsilon][a_0][a_0 a_1] \ldots$ is an observation of R.*

It follows from the definition that for each observation in rats F there is at least one path in TA that is an observation of the same run, if $Tr(F) = Tr(TA)$.

10.4.3 Algorithmically Generating Trace Automata on Runs

The main task is to obtain, in an algorithmic manner, a trace automaton on runs from some suitable description of P, say from an EN-system, without first building the whole rats. So, let N be an EN-system and $(\mathcal{T}, \mathcal{I})$ be its trace semantics. Obviously, first having to construct the rats in order to obtain the trace automaton would not make the new model checking approach more efficient. Below it is described how trace theoretical ideas are used to obtain the trace automaton. The main idea is to construct the graph of a trace automaton from the EN-system by recursively expanding cases, starting from the initial case. During this construction, extra information is preserved at each case that enables to expand the graph by only some rather that all transitions that are, according to the EN-system, enabled at a case. During the construction, the graph therefore has as nodes cases plus some extra information - what kind of information and how it is represented is explained below.

There are essentially two approaches. One approach acquires the information used to determine these subsets dynamically, i.e., choices made when building the reduced automaton influence what needs to be added in subsequent construction steps. This is the *sleep set* method, developed by Godefroid (see [119]). The other approach first determines all information statically; this approach was pursued by Peled as the *ample set* method. Peled later combined the two methods (see [215]).

To simplify the exposition, in the sequel, unless stated otherwise, only concurrently fair executions are considered. This ties in with considering observations.

Definition 10.4.11 (concurrency fairness assumption) *For every infinite execution, for every action a that is enabled from some state on, either that action or an action dependent with it is taken in the execution at some later state.*

The sleep set method

In this approach, historically, rather than supplying sets of enabled actions that need to be added, sets that need not be added are used. Obviously, this is no essential difference, as complementation with respect to enabled actions immediately shows.

The idea is, that at some stage in the construction of the automaton an action can be ignored at a state if the extensions of paths through that state by that action can also be obtained as extensions of another, equivalent, path through the automaton. Note that at that stage of the expansion such extensions need not yet be available - it is enough to know that they will be available at some stage. As this information depends on what has been put into the graph in previous expansion steps, it can only be obtained during the construction of the graph, i.e., dynamically. For each node, it is represented as a set of enabled actions that need not be considered for addition; this set is called a *sleep set*.

Let N be an EN-system and $(\mathcal{T}, \mathcal{I})$ be its trace semantics.

Definition 10.4.12 (Sleep set) *At some stage in the construction of a trace automaton $(W, \Sigma, \rightarrow, I, w_0)$ to accept the trace system $\mathcal{T}$, a set $Sleep(w) \subseteq en(w)$ is a sleep set for a case $w \in W$ if for each firing sequence u of N such that $w_0[u> w$, with $w \xrightarrow{a} w'$ and $a \in Sleep(w)$, there is a case $v \in W$ and a finite path y accepted at v such that $[u][a]$ is a prefix of $[y/\Sigma]$.*

An abstract algorithm for the construction of the graph that generates and uses the sleep sets is presented in Figure 10.11. The algorithm is abstract in the sense that it is highly nondeterministic: neither the order in which nodes are expanded nor the order in which actions are selected for expansion is fixed. Several different choices for this order have been investigated and various heuristics exist that improve the efficiency of the algorithm or the extend of the reduction. We shall not enter into this as the present aim is just to show how the trace theoretical ideas are used, not to present particular algorithms.

The ample set method

The idea now is that enough actions need to be added at each state to ensure that every path reaching that node extends into every run. This information does not depend on previous expansion steps and is therefore obtained through a static analysis of the system. At each node, it is presented as a set of actions, indicating that only these need to be considered for addition to the graph.

Let N be an EN-system and $(\mathcal{T}, \mathcal{I})$ be its trace semantics.

Definition 10.4.13 (Ample set) *A set $Ample(w) \subseteq en(w)$ is* ample *for a case $w \in W$ in a trace automaton $(W, \Sigma, \to, I, w_0)$ accepting $\mathcal{T}$ if for each firing sequence u of N such that $w_0[u> w$, for each run R of $\mathcal{T}$ such that $[u] \in R$, $\{a \in \Sigma \mid [u][a] \in R\} \cap Ample(w) \neq \emptyset$.*

Thus, for each run which contains the trace $[u]$, there is an action from the ample set extending that trace within the run.

The first task is to obtain ample sets. Various approaches exist. In [215] an approach is presented where as ample sets faithful ones are taken.

Definition 10.4.14 *A set $F(w) \subseteq en(w)$ is* faithful *at a case w if at w until an action from $F(w)$ is executed, only actions outside $F(w)$ that are independent of all actions in $F(w)$ are enabled.*

The second task is to generate the reduced graph using a given ample set assignment. An abstract algorithm for the construction of the graph that uses the ample sets is presented in Figure 10.12. Again, the aim is just to show how trace theoretical ideas are used - again various heuristics exist that yield improvements.

Trace automata generated by the algorithms are not necessarily minimal, but time complexity of the algorithms is $O(|\Sigma|^2 \times n)$, where n is the number of transitions investigated when generating the trace automaton. Since it was proved that obtaining minimal trace automata is $NP - hard$, one should not aim at that.

Remarks

The different ways in which sleep sets respectively ample sets are used, the former expressing which actions need not, and the latter expressing which actions need to be added are just historically determined. Interpreting the sleep set as expressing that from the enabled actions, say en(w), those not in the sleep set need to be added makes comparison more straightforward: $en(w) \setminus Sleep(w)$ can than be compared to $Ample(w)$ and $en(w) \setminus Ample(w)$ to $Sleep(w)$. The two approaches differ in an essential way: The above correspondences do not always yield ample from sleep sets

1 Build the starting node $(w_0, \emptyset)$, where $w_0 = c_0$ - (the initial case).

Nodes $(w, Sleep(w))$ are expanded as follows. One by one, in some order that is left implicit here, all enabled transitions that are not in the $Sleep(w)$ are added.

Firstly, the case is considered where a new transition, say $w \xrightarrow{a} v$, $a \notin Sleep(w)$, is added for which the target node v was not yet present.

2 If transition $w \xrightarrow{b} v'$ with $(a, b) \in I$ is already present, then b is added to $Sleep(v)$.

Motivation: A representative for each $\sigma[ab]\sigma'$ will be generated as $\sigma[ab] = \sigma[ba]$ (as $(a, b) \in I$).

3 If $c \in Sleep(w)$ with $(a, c) \in I$, then c is added to $Sleep(v)$.

Motivation: A representative for each $\sigma[ac]\sigma''$ will be generated as $\sigma[ac] = \sigma[ca]$ (as $(a, c) \in I$) and $c \in Sleep(w)$.

Secondly, the case is considered where the expansion reuses a node that was already present.

4 If the transition does not close a loop in the expansion, i.e. it does not connect to a state which expansion has been started but not yet finished, a new sleep set is constructed as before, then the intersection of the old one and the new sleep set is taken and then the node is expanded again with this set as its sleep set.

Motivation: Reaching a node via different routes may allow to ignore different sets of transitions; only a transitions that can be ignored in both cases can safely be part of the sleep set. As this set determines which transitions need to be added, a new expansion is necessary.

5 If the transition closes a loop, then it is not added to the sleep set.

Motivation: A loop generates an infinite sequence of actions. If an action independent with all the actions in the sequence were added to the sleep set, it might be the case that some infinite sequence including infinite number of occurrences of that independent action would not be accepted by the automaton and therefore no observations of some run would be represented.

Example: Consider the trace system over $\Sigma = \{a, b\}$ and $I = \{(a, b), (b, a)\}$ accepted by the rats with two states 1 and 2, where a is continuously enabled, looping in states 1 and 2 and b is enabled only at state 1 until it is executed once, making the transition to state 2 (see Figure 10.10). Clause 5 disallows the erroneous trace automaton where the reduction consists in the removal of the loop on state 2. The sequence containing b and infinitely many $a's$ would not be then accepted.

Note that 5 can still not be omitted if only concurrency fair executions are considered: The above mentioned sequence is concurrency fair.

Figure 10.11: Algorithm building a trace automaton on runs using sleep sets

1 Build the starting node $(w_0, Ample(w_0))$, where $w_0 = c_0$ - (the initial case),

2 If no transition from $Ample(w)$ does close a loop in the expansion, i.e. no transition does connect to a state which expansion has been started but not yet finished, then

   nodes $(w, Ample(w))$ are expanded as follows. One by one, in some order left implicit here, all enabled transitions that are in the $Ample(w)$ are added. If the corresponding target node is already present in the graph it is used, otherwise it is added.

3 If a transition from $Ample(w)$ closes a loop, then all transitions enabled at w are added. If the corresponding target node is already present in the graph it is used, otherwise it is added.

Figure 10.12: Algorithm building a trace automaton on runs using ample sets

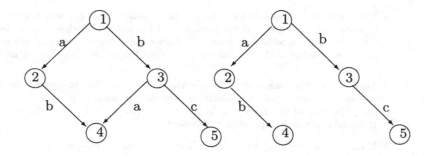

Figure 10.13: Sleep set reduction that is not an ample set reduction

or vice versa. The difference is even stronger: not every reduction obtained by the sleep set approach can be obtained by the ample set approach or vice versa.

Figure 10.13 shows an example of this fact starting with a sleep set reduction. For sleep set $Sleep(3) = \{a\}$, the corresponding set is $en(3) \setminus Sleep(3) = \{c\}$. As from state 3 extensions in both runs are possible, only $Ample(3) = \{a, c\}$ is allowed. This also implies, that no ample set reduction can remove a at 3.

Figure 10.14 takes ample sets as a starting point. For ample set $Ample(1) = \{b\}$, the corresponding set is $en(1) \setminus Ample(1) = \{a\}$. As at that state only $Sleep(1) = \emptyset$ is allowed. This also implies, that no sleep set reduction can remove a at 1.

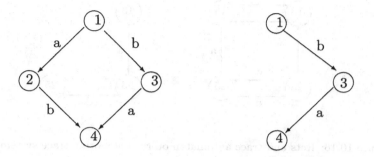

Figure 10.14: Ample set reduction that is not a sleep set reduction

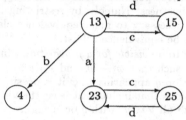

Figure 10.15: Trace automaton on runs accepting the trace system T_1

Examples

Next, two examples of trace automata on runs that are generated by the ample set algorithm are given.

Example 10.4.15 Figure 10.15 shows the trace automaton on runs accepting the trace system T_1 (see Example 10.2.4) of EN-system N_1 of Figure 10.5.

Example 10.4.16 Consider EN-system N_1 from which the transition b is removed. Figure 10.16 shows an rats and trace automaton on runs accepting the trace semantics (without interpretation) T_1' of N_1. Remember that this trace automaton is built under the assumption that only concurrency fair executions need to be represented.

As mentioned in the introduction, only equivalence robust formulas are amenable to this approach. This is due to the fact that some formulas of LTL-x can hold in some, but not in all the equivalent maximal paths of models. Therefore, a model checking algorithm using a reduced structure would give another answer that the algorithm applied to the full structure.

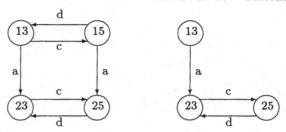

Figure 10.16: Rcts and trace automaton on runs accepting trace system T_1'

Given a formula φ, it is possible to choose the independence relation such as to ensure equivalence robustness. Namely, by restricting the independence relation I in F_P whenever it is necessary to make equivalence classes of maximal sequences small enough for φ to be equivalence robust.

An action a is said to be *visible for a proposition q* in a structure M_P if there are two states $w, w' \in W$ such that $w \overset{a}{\to} w'$ and $V_P(w)(q) \neq V_P(w')(q)$. It is assumed that for each proposition q appearing in φ it is possible to calculate efficiently the set $Vis(q) \subseteq \Sigma$ of actions that includes at least the visible actions for q. $Vis(\varphi)$ is defined as the union of all $Vis(q)$ with q occuring in φ.

Firstly, a sufficient condition for φ to be equivalent robust is given.

Lemma 10.4.17 *If $(Vis(\varphi) \times Vis(\varphi)) \cap I = \emptyset$, then φ is equivalent robust.*

The proof relies on showing that each two equivalent maximal paths with valuation function restricted to propositions appearing in φ are equivalent up to stuttering, i.e, repeating the same state finitely many times. This implies that they cannot be distinguished by any LTL-x formula.

Next, I' can be defined as $I - I_\varphi$, where $I_\varphi = Vis(\varphi) \times Vis(\varphi)$, which ensures that φ can be checked over a gba with valuation function built over a trace automaton accepting $Tr(F_P')$ with $F_P' = (W, \Sigma, \to, I', w_0)$.

However, it turns out that I_φ can be even smaller than the one defined above. This follows from the fact that equivalence robustness is preserved by Boolean operators. (Notice that it is not preserved by temporal operators.)

Therefore, if $\varphi = \varphi_1 \vee \varphi_2$ (or $\varphi_1 \wedge \varphi_2$), then I_φ can be defined as $(\Sigma(\varphi_1) \times \Sigma(\varphi_1)) \cup (\Sigma(\varphi_2) \times \Sigma(\varphi_2))$, which is usually smaller than $Vis(\varphi) \times Vis(\varphi)$.

A strategy to define I_φ as small as possible is to rewrite the formula φ in an equivalent form in which as many as possible boolean operators are not in the scope of a temporal modality. This procedure can also be automated efficiently. It is worth mentioning here that one should avoid striving for optimal rewriting as the complexity of achieving such is $NP - hard$ in the size of the formula.

Example 10.4.18 Notice that $\varphi_1 = F(p_2 \vee p_4)$ is equivalence robust for $M_{N_1} = (F_1, V_1)$ of Example 10.4.1. Therefore, a trace automaton can be used instead of F_1 in the standard way for model checking. Such a trace automaton is shown in Example 10.4.15.

The above presented method has been shown to be much better than the standard method when there is no very tight coupling between the concurrent components of the system. As examples indicate model checking of LTL-x using trace automata can be efficiently used in practical applications.

Remarks

An independent approach that achieves reductions has been developed by Valmari [264]. It is comparable to the ample set approach in that reductions are achieved by assigning *stubborn* sets to states, again based on static analysis that fulfil a similar role as ample sets. It fundamentally differs from the ample set approach in that these assignments are not based on trace theoretical ideas nor seem to be reducible to such ideas.

10.5 Efficient Model Checking for a Subset of CTL

Model checking for CTL is linear in the size of the model acceptor and linear in the length of the tested formula [39]. However, as in the case of LTL, the number of states of the model acceptor is frequently exponential in the number of program actions. Moreover, also like for LTL, checking whether a CTL formula holds for an EN-system (i.e., it is true in its model) was proved to be $NP - hard$ in the number of transitions of the EN-system. It is therefore unlikely that a polynomial algorithm can be found.

In this section it is shown that the approach used to make model checking more efficient for LTL can be adapted to CTL. Equivalence robustness is redefined for CTL and reductions (trace automata) are redefined accordingly to respect this equivalence.

Again, formulas should not contain next step operators. The subset of CTL formulas satisfying this property is called CTL-x.

To start with, a standard method of CTL-x model checking is given, after which it is shown how the model acceptors it employs can be reduced using trace automata.

10.5.1 Standard Approach

Let P be an EN-system and $(\mathcal{T}, \mathcal{I})$ be its trace semantics. Then, let $M_P = (F, V)$ be a model acceptor for the model M for $(\mathcal{T}, \mathcal{I})$ and φ be a given formula to be checked.

The method of CTL-x model checking is inductive, i.e., given a formula ψ, starting from its shortest and most deeply nested subformula φ the algorithm labels with φ these states of M_P, which accept traces, at which φ holds in M. Therefore, in case of checking a one level less deeply nested subformula, it can be assumed that the states have just been labelled with all its subformulas. This process ends when ψ is attached to states; $M_P \models \psi$ iff ψ is attached to the root. Notice that the information about independent actions is not used.

Below, algorithms for labelling states of M_P are given.

Labelling p, $\neg\varphi$, $\varphi \wedge \gamma$

Notice, that:

1. $M_P, w \models q$ iff $V(w)(q) = true$, for $q \in PV$,

2. $M_P, w \models \neg\varphi$ iff not $M_P, w \models \varphi$,

   $M_P, w \models \varphi \wedge \gamma$ iff $M_P, w \models \varphi$ and $M_P, w \models \gamma$.

Therefore, in the first case it is checked whether $V(w)$ gives q the value $true$, in the second case it is checked whether w has been labelled φ and in the third case it is checked whether w has been labelled φ and γ.

Labelling $E(\varphi U \gamma)$

Observe that $M_P, w \models E(\varphi U \gamma)$ iff there is a state $v \in W$ and a sequence of states $w_0, \ldots, w_n \in W$ such that $w = w_0 \to \ldots \to w_n = v$ and $M_P, v \models \gamma$, $M_P, w_i \models \varphi$ for $0 \leq i < n$.

Firstly, all the states at which γ holds are labelled with $E(\varphi U \gamma)$. Secondly, the algorithm goes backward using the relation $\to^{-1}$ and labels all states at which φ holds with $E(\varphi U \gamma)$.

Labelling $EG\varphi$

Observe that $M_P, w \models EG\varphi$ iff there is a maximal path x starting at w such that $M_P, v \models \varphi$, for each v on x.

Let $W_\varphi = \{v \in W \mid M_P, v \models \varphi\}$ be the subset of W, labelled φ. A *strongly connected component* in W_φ is any subset $U \subseteq W_\varphi$ satisfying one of the following conditions:

- $(\forall v, v' \in U)$: $v \to^* v'$ and $v' \to^* v$, or

- U contains only one state that does not have any successor in W.

Secondly, all the maximal strongly connected components in W_φ are selected. Notice that they are disjoint. Then, w is labelled $EG\varphi$ iff w is labelled φ and there is a maximal strongly connected component U in W_φ reachable from w by a path contained in W_φ.

10.5.2 Trace Approach

The idea is to use special kind of reduced model acceptors such they preserve all CTL-x formulas. First, it is shown which conditions should be satisfied by two model acceptors ensuring that the accepted models are CTL-x equivalent.

Let M and M' be two finite model acceptors.

Definition 10.5.1 ([30]) *A relation $\sim \subseteq W \times W'$ is a* stuttering equivalence *between M and M' if the following conditions hold:*

1. *$w_0 \sim w'_0$,*

2. *if $w \sim w'$, then $V(w) = V'(w')$ and for every maximal path π of M that starts at w, there is a maximal path π' in M' that starts at w', a partition $B_1, B_2 \ldots$ of π, and a partition $B'_1, B'_2 \ldots$ of π' such that for all $j \geq 0$, B_j and B'_j are nonempty and finite, and every state in B_j is related by '$\sim$' to every state in B'_j and*

3. *the same condition as (2) interchanging π and M with π' and M'.*

M and M' are said to be stuttering equivalent, *if there is a stuttering equivalence relation between them.*

In [30] stuttering equivalence is defined using approximants $\sim^n$. Because model acceptors are finite, it is easy to see that the two definitions are equivalent.

In order to avoid frequent referring to the model accepted by a model acceptor, the following convention is assumed : a formula φ is said to hold in a model acceptor M' (denoted $M' \models \varphi$) if φ holds in the model accepted by M'.

Theorem 10.5.2 ([30]) *Let φ be a CTL*-x formula. Let M and M' be two stuttering equivalent model acceptors. Then, $M \models \varphi$ iff $M' \models \varphi$.*

The next task is to generate a smaller model acceptor which is stuttering equivalent to the model acceptor M_P without first building M_P.

10.5.3 The Ample Set Algorithm

In the Section 10.4 two algorithms are given that generate trace automata preserving LTL-x formulas interpreted over observations. Presently, it is only known how to modify the ample set algorithm (see Figure 10.12) to generate automata preserving CTL-x formulas. The following exposition is based on the paper [118].

The idea is to sharpen the requirements on generated subsets of successor states without changing the original ample set algorithm. Let Vis denote the set of *visible actions* in Σ, i.e., $Vis = \bigcup_{q \in PV} Vis(q)$. Note that if the formulas that need to be checked are known, then in order to get better reductions one should take PV to be the propositions occuring in these formulas only. The actions of $\Sigma \setminus Vis$ are called *invisible*.

The following are the restrictions put on $Ample(w)$ in the ample set algorithm. If $Ample(w) \neq en(w)$, then:

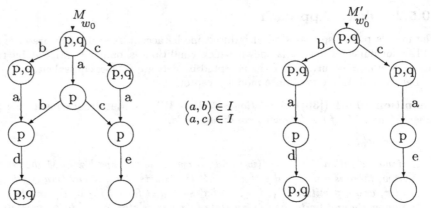

Let $\varphi = AG((p \wedge \neg q) \rightarrow (AFq \vee AF\neg p))$. Notice that $M', w_0' \models \varphi$, but $M, w_0 \not\models \varphi$.

Figure 10.17: A reduction under **C1** and **C2** that does not preserve CTL-x

C1 - $Ample(w)$ is a faithful set (see Definition 10.4.14),

C2 - $Ample(w) \cap Vis = \emptyset$,

C3 - $Ample(w)$ is a singleton set.

C1 ensures that $Ample(w)$ is indeed an ample set. **C2** and **C3** say that $Ample(w)$ contains exactly one invisible action. The conditions are strongly influenced by the definition of stuttering equivalence. They ensure that in case some action enabled at w is removed, for each maximal path beginning with $wa\ldots$, the reduced structure contains a stuttering equivalent path beginning with $wb\ldots$, where $Ample(w) = \{b\}$.

In the former section about efficient LTL model checking, as ample sets faithful ones were taken. However, this guaranteed only correct reductions for concurrency fair version of LTL-x. If unfair version of LTL is considered, then it was shown in [216] that **C1**, **C2** are sufficient to guarantee the correct reductions. But, branching temporal properties can be more sensitive to the removal of branching points and therefore **C3** is added.

In Figure 10.17, the branching point after the execution of the visible operation a is omitted in the reduction, which causes a distinction between the truth value of a CTL-x property in the full model acceptor (left) in which it does not hold and the reduced model acceptor (right) in which it holds.

An example of a reduction obtained by the algorithm using $Ample(w)$ satisfying the conditions **C1**–**C3** is shown in Figure 10.18. Another example of a reduction for formulas for which d is invisible is shown in Figure 10.15

Let $M' = (F', V')$ be the model acceptor such that F' is a trace automaton on runs generated by the ample set algorithm under the assumption that $Ample(w)$ satisfies **C1** $-$ **C3**, and $V' = V|W'$.

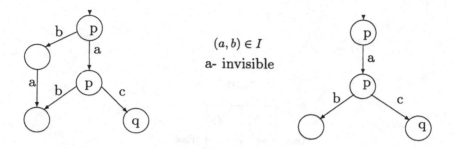

Figure 10.18: A correct CTL-x reduction

Theorem 10.5.3 *M_P and M' are stuttering equivalent.*

Proof: See [118]   □

The above theorem together with Theorem 10.5.2 guarantees that the result of checking any CTL-x formula φ over M_P is the same as checking φ over M'.

Several experimental results showing how substantial reductions can be obtained by the ample set algorithm for LTL-x and CTL-x are shown in [118].

10.6   Model Checking for CTL$_P$

The logic CTL$_P$ has been introduced in order to express and prove partial order properties by model checking. Let's start the presentation with giving definitions of decidability and model checking for a logic.

Decidability of a logic concerns the existence of an algorithm to determine satisfiability of formulas. Such algorithm should decide the question: given a formula φ, is there a model M such that φ holds in M ? Model checking concerns the existence of an algorithm to determine satisfaction of formulas in given models. Such algorithm should decide the question: given a formula φ and a finite model acceptor M', does φ hold in the model M accepted by M' ? In Section 10.4, it has been shown that if a logic has a decision procedure of a certain form, namely using a finite structure representing all models, a model checking algorithm can be obtained in a standard manner.

Unfortunately, CTL$_P$ turns out to be not decidable, so this route could not be followed here. However, CTL$_P$ nevertheless does admit of a model checking algorithm. In this section undecidability of CTL$_P$ is shown and a model checking algorithm is presented.

The present exposition is based on the paper of Penczek [222].

North

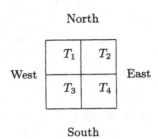

South

Figure 10.19: A compound tile c

10.6.1   Undecidability of CTL$_P$

Undecidability of CTL$_P$ is proved using the fact that the *recurring tiling problem* is known to be undecidable (see [131]). This problem concerns the existence of a certain covering with patterned tiles of the grid $\omega \times \omega$.

It will be shown that the grid can be encoded as a CTL$_P$ frame and that the covering can be encoded as a CTL$_P$ formula. The recurring tiling problem then reduces to deciding the satisfiability of that formula.

To start with, the *recurring tiling problem* is stated. Let Γ be a finite set of types of tiles such that for each $T \in \Gamma$ each side - North, East, South and West - is assigned a number (N(T), E(T), S(T), and W(T), resp.). Let $Co \subseteq \Gamma^4$ be a set of *compound tiles*, i.e., big tiles, consisting of four tiles being put together as follows: $c = (T_1, T_2, T_3, T_4) \in Co$ iff $S(T_1) = N(T_3)$, $E(T_1) = W(T_2)$, $N(T_4) = S(T_2)$, and $W(T_4) = E(T_3)$ (see Figure 10.19).

The idea is now to try to cover each lattice point with a compound tile in such a manner that a certain pattern ensues.

For each $c = (T_1, T_2, T_3, T_4) \in Co$, let $U(c), R(c) \subseteq Co$, where U stands for *Up* and R stands for *Right*, with $U(c) = \{c' \in Co \mid c' = (T, T', T_1, T_2),$ for some $T, T'\}$, $R(c) = \{c' \in Co \mid c' = (T_2, T, T_4, T'),$ for some $T, T'\}$. Let $T_0, T_f \in \Gamma$ be two special types. The problem is to find a compound tile assignment $c : \omega \times \omega \longrightarrow Co$ such that for all $i, j \in \omega$, $c(i, j) \in Co$, $c(0, 0) \in \{c' \in Co \mid c' = (T, T', T_0, T''),$ for some $T, T', T''\}$, $c(i, j+1) \in U(c(i, j))$, and $c(i+1, j) \in R(c(i, j))$, and there are infinitely many compound tiles in the leftmost column, which contain the tile type T_f. The above formulation means that one has to find a compound tile assignment of the lattice points in the plane such that if a point is assigned a compound tile c, then the point just above is assigned a compound tile from the set $U(c)$ and the point to the right is assigned a compound tile from the set $R(c)$, the beginning is assigned a

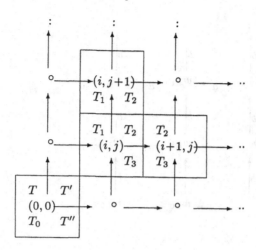

Figure 10.20: The patterning requirements of a covering with compound tiles

compound tile of a given subset of Co and the given tile type T_f occurs infinitely often in the leftmost column (see Figure 10.20).

Next, it is shown how to reduce the recurrent tiling problem to the satisfiability of a CTL$_P$ formula. This is possible since CTL$_P$ formulas can characterize frames (and models) of trace systems up to isomorphism (see Section 10.3.6).

To enable the encoding of the tiling problem into CTL$_P$, a frame for CTL$_P$ that is isomorphic with the grid $\omega \times \omega$ is defined.

Let $\Sigma = \{a, b\}$ and $I = \{(a, b), (b, a)\}$. Consider the trace system $\mathcal{T} = [\Sigma^*]$. The frame for $\mathcal{T}$ is defined as $F = (\{w_{i,j} \mid (i, j) \in \omega \times \omega\}, \Sigma, \rightarrow, w_{0,0})$, where $w_{i,j} \xrightarrow{a} w_{i',j'}$ iff $i' = i + 1$ and $j' = j$ and $w_{i,j} \xrightarrow{b} w_{i',j'}$ iff $i' = i$ and $j' = j + 1$

F is obviously isomorphic (up to the labels of transitions) with the grid $\omega \times \omega$ (see Figure 10.21).

Let $PV = \{C_i \mid c_i \in Co\} \cup \{p_a, p_b\}$, i.e., each compound tile c_i is assigned the atomic proposition C_i. The atomic propositions p_a and p_b are defined to encode the labels of transitions, which allows to define the labelled next step operators (see Section 10.3.2).

Now it is possible to give a set of formulas of CTL$_P$ such that its conjunction is satisfiable iff the recurring tiling problem has a solution.

The following CTL$_P$ formulas characterize F up to isomorphism.

(A):

1. $AG(EX_a true \wedge EX_b true)$

2. $EF(EY_a true \wedge EY_b true)$

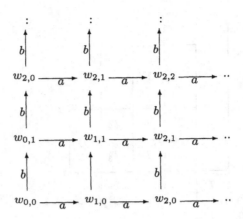

Figure 10.21: The frame F isomorphic with the grid $\omega \times \omega$

1) expresses that two actions a and b are executed at each state. 2) says that a and b are independent at some state. Thus, by the definition of independence relation, a and b are independent at each state.

The following formulas describe the tiling.

(B):

1. $\bigvee\{C_i \mid c_i = (T, T', T_0, T''),$ for some $T, T', T''\}$,

2. $AG(\bigvee(\{C_i \mid c_i \in Co\}) \wedge (\bigwedge\{C_i \rightarrow \neg C_j \mid i \neq j\}))$,

3. $AG(\bigwedge(\{C_i \rightarrow EX_a(\bigvee\{C_j \mid c_j \in R(c_i)\}) \mid c_i \in Co\}))$,

4. $AG(\bigwedge(\{C_i \rightarrow EX_b(\bigvee\{C_j \mid c_j \in U(c_i)\}) \mid c_i \in Co\}))$,

5. $AG(\neg EY_a true \rightarrow EF(\neg EY_a true \wedge \bigvee\{C_i \mid$ type T_f occurs in compound tile $c_i\}))$.

1) expresses that the tile type T at the beginning is T_0. 2) enforces exactly one compound tile at each point of the grid. 3) and 4) ensure that successors have the right compound tile. 5) requires that the tile type T_f occurs infinitely often in the leftmost column.

The recurring tiling problem has a solution iff the conjunction of the formulas A) and B) is satisfiable. Therefore, the validity problem for CTL_P is undecidable.

In fact, using the same method, one can show that if labelled next step operators can be encoded in the language of ISTL, then ISTL is not decidable as well.

10.6.2   NP-hardness of CTL$_P$ Model Checking

The model checking problem for CTL$_P$ is formulated as: given a formula φ and given a finite model acceptor M', does φ hold in the model M accepted by M' ?

NP-hardness of CTL$_P$ model checking problem follows intuitively from the fact that the logic allows to express properties about selected states of a path (by using past operators over models which look like tree). Model checking problem for CTL is of polynomial complexity, but CTL allows only for saying something about all states or some state of a path.

Then, NP-hardness of CTL$_P$ model checking is proved using the fact that the *3-SAT problem* is NP-hard. This problem concerns the decidability of certain propositional formulas, i.e., whether or not a model exists for which such formula holds.

It will be shown that this problem can be encoded as checking whether or not some CTL$_P$ formula holds in some model and that the encoding is polynomial (in fact, even linear).

Note that here a decidability problem in one framework is reduced to a model checking problem in another framework.

It is proved that 3-SAT problem is polynomially reducible to determining whether $M \models \varphi$, for some CTL$_P$ formula φ and some model acceptor M' of M.

To start with, the 3-SAT problem is stated. Let $\psi = b_1 \wedge \ldots \wedge b_m$ be a boolean formula in 3-CNF, i.e., $b_i = l_{i_1} \vee l_{i_2} \vee l_{i_3}$, for $1 \leq i \leq m$, $l_{i_j} = x_k$ or $\neg x_k$ for some k such that $1 \leq k \leq n$, where $x_1, \ldots, x_n$ are the propositional variables appearing in ψ.

Next, it is shown how to polynomially reduce the 3-SAT problem to a CTL$_P$ model checking problem.

Let $M' = (F', V')$ be a model acceptor (see Figure 10.22), defined as follows:

- Let $X = \{x_i \mid 1 \leq i \leq n\} \cup \{x_i' \mid 1 \leq i \leq n\}$, $Y = \{y_i \mid 0 \leq i \leq n\}$, where $X \cap Y = \emptyset$,

- $F' = (W', \Sigma, \rightarrow', I, w_0')$, where

- $W' = X \cup Y$, $\Sigma = X \times Y \cup Y \times X$, $I = \emptyset$,

- $\rightarrow' = \{(y_{i-1}, (y_{i-1}, x_i), x_i), (y_{i-1}, (y_{i-1}, x_i'), x_i'), (x_i, (x_i, y_i), y_i),$
  $(x_i', (x_i', y_i), y_i) \mid 1 \leq i \leq n\}$,

- $w_0' = y_0$,

- $PV = \{b_i \mid 1 \leq i \leq m\}$,

- $V'(x_i)(b_j) = true$ iff x_i appears as a literal in b_j,

- $V'(x_i')(b_j) = true$ iff $\neg x_i$ appears as a literal in b_j,

- $V'(y_i)(b_j) = false$, for $0 \leq i \leq n$ and $0 \leq j \leq m$.

The following equivalence holds:

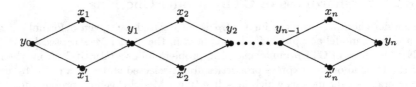

Figure 10.22: The rats F' of the model acceptor M'

*) ψ is satisfiable iff $M \models EF(EPb_1 \wedge \ldots \wedge EPb_m)$,

where M is the model accepted by M'.

Each path represents one of the possible valuations of the propositional variables x_i. Since the independence relation $I = \emptyset$, the model accepted by M' is a tree. Therefore, to satisfy ψ, there must be one such path on which each b_i is true somewhere. As the number of states in the model acceptor is linear in the number of propositions in the formula, this reduction is linear. Hence, model checking for CTL_P is NP-hard.

10.6.3 Model Checking for CTL_{P-}

To ease the exposition, initially a restricted version of the logic, called CTL_{P-}, is considered which contains only CTL_P formulas without nested past modalities.

Although CTL_{P-} seems to be a small extension of CTL, it turns out that all the partial order properties discussed so far are expressible in CTL_{P-}. Therefore it is easy to see that the proofs of undecidability and of NP-hardness of model checking also hold for CTL_{P-}.

Because of NP-hardness, only a one exponential model checking algorithm is presented for the restricted logic. It is shown at the end of the section that the algorithm can be extended for CTL_P model checking.

Unfortunately, neither of the two known methods for model checking applied to CTL* (LTL) or CTL, can be used directly in the case of CTL_{P-}.

The first known method, for CTL* model checking [99] or as encountered in Section 10.4 for LTL model checking [179, 265], requires building a model structure for a formula. It follows from the undecidability of CTL_P that this is not possible now.

The second known method, as encountered in Section 10.5, is for CTL [39]. The idea there is to iteratively label with progressively more complicated subformulas of the formula (which is checked) the states of M' where these subformulas hold. Showing where this methods fails in the present setting is used as an introduction to the method presented here.

The problem is caused by the combination of past operators and partial order semantics. As stated in Section 10.2.6, the requirements on an equivalence relation used to construct a model acceptor are just that traces from one equivalence class can neither be distinguished by their interpretation nor by their continuations. As CTL formulas are only concerned with the future, a CTL formula then has the same value on each trace of such class - which enables to decide whether or not the formula should be added as a label.

The equivalence relation provides no such property for the prefixes of the traces from one equivalence class. Indeed, as will be shown, CTL$_{P-}$ formulas with past time operators turn out to potentially evaluate differently on different traces from one class - which makes it no longer possible to decide about adding such formulas as labels. The solution is of course to sharpen the equivalence relation accordingly.

Contrary to what naively might be expected, this is not a simple extension of the ideas from CTL. Herein lies the novelty of the approach presented as well as the connection with trace theory.

To ease the understanding, it is first shown how the requirements on the equivalence relation defined on the model need to be strengthened to accommodate CTL$_{P-}$ and next how a model acceptor that satisfies these requirements can be constructed directly from a given model acceptor, i.e., without referring to the model.

Let $M' = (F', V')$ be the model acceptor of a model M built using an equivalence relation as defined in Definition 10.2.19. There are two cases to be investigated, corresponding to the past time operators EP and EY.

> Consider two traces $[abc]$ and $[def]$ such that they belong to the same equivalence class and $M, [abc] \models p$ (then also $M, [def] \models p$). All actions are interdependent.
>
> 1. Let $M, [\epsilon] \models p$, $M, [a] \models p$, $M, [ab] \models p$, and $M, [d] \models \neg p$, $M, [de] \models p$.
>
>   Then, EPp evaluates differently on $M, [abc]$ than on $M, [def]$, but EYp evaluates to the same value on both.
>
> 2. Now, let $M, [\epsilon] \models p$, $M, [a] \models p$, $M, [ab] \models \neg p$, and $M, [d] \models \neg p$, $M, [de] \models p$.
>
>   Then, EYp evaluates differently on $M, [abc]$ than on $M, [def]$, but EPp evaluates to the same value on both.

To achieve that such formulas do not evaluate differently on one equivalence class, the original equivalence relation is strengthened, by the following extra requirements.

Let M'' be a new model acceptor, defined using an equivalence relation satisfying the conditions as before plus the requirement that its acceptance function AC'' satisfies the following properties concerning the prefixes of traces, defined in terms of AC': $AC''(\tau) = AC''(\tau')$ implies

P1) $AC'(\downarrow \tau) = AC'(\downarrow \tau')$, and

P2) for each $a \in \Sigma$, if $\tau = \tau_1[a]$, then $\tau' = \tau'_1[a]$ and $AC'(\tau_1) = AC'(\tau'_1)$, for $\tau_1, \tau'_1 \in [\Sigma^*]$.

P1) ensures that traces accepted by the same state in M'' satisfy the same EP formulas, whereas P2) ensures the same for EY formulas. In fact, AC'' ensures that each CTL_{P-} formula receives just one value on all traces accepted at the same state.

The next task is to construct M'' directly from M' rather than define M'' via the model M. To see how this can be done, an equivalence relation EQ that provides an AC'' with the above properties is defined, again, firstly on the states $Tr(F')$ of the model M.

Let $P(\Sigma)$ be the family of all subsets of Σ and one be the following function $one : Tr(F') \longrightarrow \{tt, ff\}$ such that $one(\tau) = tt$, if $|\tau| = 1$, and $one(\tau) = ff$, if $|\tau| \neq 1$, where (tt stands for $true$ and ff stands for $false$).

Now a function $Rep : Tr(F') \longrightarrow 2^{W' \times P(\Sigma) \times \{tt, ff\}}$ is defined such that $Rep(\tau) = \{(AC'(\tau_1), \Sigma(\tau_2), one(\tau_2)) \mid \tau_1 \tau_2 = \tau\}$. The intuitive meaning is as follows. $AC'(\tau_1)$ records states of W' accepting the prefixes of τ. $\Sigma(\tau_2)$ records names of actions which occur in the trace leading from the prefix to τ. $one(\tau_2)$ says whether that trace contained one or more actions.

Then, using Rep, the equivalence relation EQ and its equivalence classes are defined.

- $\tau\ EQ\ \tau'$ iff $Rep(\tau) = Rep(\tau')$, for $\tau, \tau' \in Tr(F')$

- $[\tau]_{EQ} = \{\tau' \in Tr(F') \mid \tau\ EQ\ \tau'\}$,

Let $F'' = (W'', \Sigma, \rightarrow'', I, w_0'')$ be the quotient structure of $Tr(F')$ by the equivalence relation EQ such that the elements of W'' are of the form $Rep(\tau)$ for $\tau \in Tr(F')$ rather than $[\tau]_{EQ}$. It is shown in [222] that the acceptance function AC'' for F'' satisfies the properties P1) and P2).

It is now shown that F'' can be defined directly from F'. The following notions simplify the rest of the construction.

- a function $last : W'' \longrightarrow W'$, such that $last(w'') = w'$, if $(w', \emptyset, ff) \in w''$,

  $last(w'')$ gives the state of M' accepting the traces accepted by w'' in M'',

- a function $emp : P(\Sigma) \longrightarrow \{tt, ff\}$ such that $emp(\Delta) = tt$, if $\Delta = \emptyset$, and $emp(\Delta) = ff$, if $\Delta \neq \emptyset$.

The following partial function $Next : W'' \times \Sigma \longrightarrow W''$ allows to construct for a given $w'' \in W''$ and $a \in en(w'')$ the state reached in W'' after executing a at w'', i.e., $w'' \xrightarrow{a}'' Next(w'', a)$ holds.

- $Next$ is defined as: $Next(w'', a) = \{(w', \Delta \cup \{a\}, emp(\Delta)) \mid (w', \Delta, q) \in w''\} \cup \{(w_a', \Delta, q) \mid (w', \Delta, q) \in w'' \text{ and } \{a\} \times \Delta \subseteq I\}$, for any $w'' \in W''$ and $a \in en(last(w''))$, where w_a' denotes the state in W' reached after executing a at w'.

The correctness of the definition of $Next$ follows from the following special case of Levi's Lemma for traces [190].

Lemma 10.6.1 *For each* $\tau, \tau_1, \tau_2 \in [\Sigma^*]$ *and* $\alpha \in [\Sigma]$ *the following condition holds:*

$$\tau\alpha = \tau_1\tau_2 \text{ iff}$$

1) $\tau_2 = \tau''\alpha$ *and* $\tau_1\tau'' = \tau$, *for some* $\tau'' \in [\Sigma^*]$ *or*

2) $\tau_1 = \tau'\alpha$, $\{a\} \times \Sigma(\tau_2) \subseteq I$, *and* $\tau'\tau_2 = \tau$, *for some* $\tau' \in [\Sigma^*]$ *and* $[a] = \alpha$.

This lemma allows to represent $Next(w'', a)$ as the union of two sets corresponding to the conditions 1) and 2).

Construction of F''

The construction of F'' is performed now inductively, in stages.

Let $F_1'' = (W_1'', \Sigma, \emptyset, I, w_0'')$, where $W_1'' = \{w_0''\}$ and $w_0'' = \{(w_0', \emptyset, ff)\}$. Now, for each node w'' of $W_i'' - W_{i-1}''$ (with $W_0'' = \emptyset$) the algorithm adds all its successors in W'' and extends $\rightarrow_i''$, respectively. Let $F_i'' = (W_i'', \Sigma, \rightarrow_i'', I, w_0'')$ and $W_i^\emptyset = W_i'' - W_{i-1}''$. Then, $F_{i+1}'' = (W_{i+1}'', \Sigma, \rightarrow_{i+1}'', I, w_0'')$, where

- $W_{i+1}'' = W_i'' \cup \{Next(w'', a) \mid w'' \in W_i^\emptyset, a \in en(last(w''))\}$,

- $\rightarrow_{i+1}'' = \rightarrow_i'' \cup \{(w'', a, Next(w'', a)) \mid w'' \in W_i^\emptyset, a \in en(last(w''))\}$.

The construction stops at the least integer m with $F_m'' = F_{m+1}''$. It is easy to see that F_m'' is isomorphic to F''.
Then, the new model acceptor $M'' = (F'', V'')$ is defined as follows:

- $F'' = (W'', \Sigma, \rightarrow'', I, w_0'')$,

- $V''(w'')(q) = V'(last(w''))(q)$, for $q \in PV$.

The complexity of building M'' is: $O(|\rightarrow'| \times |P(\Sigma)| \times 2^{2 \times |W'| \times |P(\Sigma)|})$.
Notice that for each subformula φ of CTL$_{P-}$ formula ψ and for each $\tau, \tau' \in Tr(F'')$, if $AC''(\tau) = AC''(\tau')$, then $M, \tau \models \varphi$ iff $M, \tau' \models \varphi$. Therefore, $w'' \in W''$ is labelled φ (written $M'', w'' \models \varphi$), if $M, \tau \models \varphi$, for some τ with $AC''(\tau) = w''$.

Obviously, for each subformula φ without past operators, for each $\tau, \tau' \in Tr(F')$, if $AC'(\tau) = AC'(\tau')$, then $M, \tau \models \varphi$ iff $M, \tau' \models \varphi$. Therefore, $w' \in W'$ is labelled φ (written $M', w' \models \varphi$), if $M, \tau \models \varphi$, for some τ with $AC'(\tau) = w'$.

Next, algorithms labelling the states of M'' are shown. The method is inductive, i.e., given a formula ψ, starting from its shortest and most deeply nested subformula φ the algorithm labels with φ these states of M'', which accept traces, at which φ holds in M. Therefore, in case of checking a less nested subformula, it can be assumed that the states have just been labelled with all its subformulas.

Firstly, the states of M' are labelled with all the subformulas of ψ which do not contain past subformulas. Then, the states of M'' are labelled with all the subformulas of ψ. Below, algorithms for labelling states of M'' are given.

Labelling p, $\neg\varphi$, $\varphi \wedge \gamma$, $E(\varphi U \gamma)$

The algorithms have been shown in Section 10.5.

Labelling $EY\varphi$

Observe that $M'', w'' \models EY\varphi$ iff there is $(w', \Delta, tt) \in w''$ such that $M', w' \models \varphi$.

Labelling $EP\varphi$

Observe that $M'', w'' \models EP\varphi$ iff there is $(w', \Delta, q) \in w''$, such that $M', w' \models \varphi$.

Labelling $EX\varphi$

Observe that $M'', w'' \models EX\varphi$ iff there is $v'' \in W''$ such that $w'' \rightarrow'' v''$ and $M'', v'' \models \varphi$. Therefore, the algorithm finds all the states at which φ holds and labels all its predecessors with $EX\varphi$.

Labelling $EG\varphi$

Observe that $M'', w'' \models EG\varphi$ iff there is an observation x starting at w'' such that $M'', v'' \models \varphi$, for each v'' on x.

Let $W''_\varphi = \{v'' \in W'' \mid M'', v'' \models \varphi\}$ be the subset of W'', labelled φ. A *strongly connected component* in W''_φ is any subset $U \subseteq W''_\varphi$ satisfying one of the following conditions:

- $(\forall v, v' \in U)$: $v \rightarrow''^* v'$ and $v' \rightarrow''^* v$, or

- U contains only one state that does not have any successor in W''.

Secondly, all the maximal strongly connected components in W''_φ are selected. Notice that they are disjoint. Then, w'' is labelled $EG\varphi$ iff w'' is labelled φ and there is a maximal strongly connected component U in W''_φ reachable from w'' by a path contained in W''_φ and for all $a \in \Sigma$ there is v in U such that a is not enabled at v or a is dependent with at least one action enabled at v and leading to a state from U (i.e., U "contains" an observation).

Complexity of CTL$_{P-}$ Model Checking

In order to handle an arbitrary CTL$_{P-}$ formula ψ, the state-labelling algorithm is applied to the subformulas of ψ starting with the shortest and most deeply nested one. Since ψ contains at most $length(\psi)$ different subformulas, the algorithm requires time

$$O(length(\psi) \times | \rightarrow' | \times |P(\Sigma)| \times 2^{2 \times |W'| \times |P(\Sigma)|}).$$

In [222], several improvements are defined to the algorithm that decrease its complexity.

Example 10.6.2 [proving serializability] Below, it is shown how to prove serializability of the trace system T_2 of Example 10.2.5.

It is to be verified:

1. $M_2 \models p_1 \wedge p_2 \wedge p_9 \rightarrow AFEP((p_7 \wedge p_2 \wedge p_9) \vee (p_1 \wedge p_8 \wedge p_9))$,

2. $M_2 \models AG[((p_7 \wedge p_2 \wedge p_9) \vee (p_1 \wedge p_8 \wedge p_9)) \rightarrow AF(EP(p_7 \wedge p_8 \wedge p_9)]$.

Since M_2 is finite, it is taken as its model acceptor M_2'. Moreover, observe that in this case M_2'' is equal to M_2'. Therefore, the states of M_2 are labelled. The only difficult task is to label the states of M_2 with the formulas:

F1= $AFEP((p_7 \wedge p_2 \wedge p_9) \vee (p_1 \wedge p_8 \wedge p_9))$,

F2= $AFEP(p_7 \wedge p_8 \wedge p_9)$.

It is shown how to do that for the formula F1. First notice that:
$AFEP((p_7 \wedge p_2 \wedge p_9) \vee (p_1 \wedge p_8 \wedge p_9)) \equiv \neg EG \neg EP\varphi$, where $\varphi = ((p_7 \wedge p_2 \wedge p_9) \vee (p_1 \wedge p_8 \wedge p_9)$. Next, the states of M_2 are labelled with $EG \neg EP\varphi$.

- $M_2, w \models \varphi$, if $w \simeq [a_1 a_2 a_3]$ or $w \simeq [b_1 b_2 b_3]$.

- $M_2, w \models EP\varphi$ for all w such that $w \simeq \tau$ for $\tau \in \uparrow [a_1 a_2 a_3] \cup \uparrow [b_1 b_2 b_3]$.

- M_2, w_0 is not labelled $EG \neg EP\varphi$.

Thus, $M_2, w_0 \models AFEP((p_7 \wedge p_2 \wedge p_9) \vee (p_1 \wedge p_8 \wedge p_9))$. Consequently, $M_2, w_0 \models p_1 \wedge p_2 \wedge p_9 \rightarrow AFEP((p_7 \wedge p_2 \wedge p_9) \vee (p_1 \wedge p_8 \wedge p_9))$.

Extending Model Checking to CTL_P

The presented method of model checking can be extended such that past formulas can be nested.

Define a sequence of unfoldings $M_1, \ldots, M_n$, where $M_1 = M''$, n is the maximal depth of nested past formulas in ψ, M_{i+1} is obtained from M_i in the same way as M'' was obtained from M'. Then, the states of M_i are labelled inductively with subformulas of ψ containing the nested past formulas of depth at most i. Then, $M, w_0 \models \psi$ iff the beginning state of M_n has been labelled with ψ. In the worst case the complexity is $exp_n(2 \times |W'| \times |P(\Sigma)|)$.

10.7   Proving Program Properties using ISTL_P

As discussed in the introduction to this chapter, trace systems are special in that they both enable very detailed modelling and also offer opportunities for abstraction. Interleaving Set Temporal Logic* (ISTL*), the propositional version of which was introduced in Section 10.3, enables to exploit both features. This leads to two separate approaches; an example of both will be given. The part concerning expressiveness is based on Peled and Pnueli's [218], the part concerning abstraction is based on Katz and Peled's [151].

The need for verification by hand is most obvious where automated verification is intrinsically impossible. This is foremost the case when properties of systems are considered that concern potentially unbounded data. Finite state descriptions no longer suffice there. Consequently, propositional logics, representing data values as propositions, do not apply. The ensuing extension to first order logic precludes automated verification.

To allow giving a trace semantics to programs with variables, trace systems are used that support state variables. Propositional ISTL is then extended accordingly to first order ISTL. Furthermore, past time modalities are added. The resulting logic is called ISTL$_P$. These extra modalities are, as will be seen, crucial for the proof system. Following that, programs are introduced and the connection between behaviour of programs and ISTL$_P$ formulas is made. Finally, a proof system, or, in fact, two proof systems, for the program part are presented, corresponding to the two different strengths of trace systems.

As the interesting features of the approach can already be demonstrated on simple finite state examples, only such are presented.

10.7.1 Programs

Like before, interpreted trace systems are used as the basis for program behaviour; interpretation is used in this case to accommodate state variables.

Because ISTL$_P$ is interpreted on models rather than on interpreted trace systems, the corresponding models will be taken as the semantics of programs.

Programs themselves are taken as quadruples consisting of an independence alphabet, an ordered set of variables and the initial condition. Programs are defined in a first order language $\mathcal{L}$ interpreted over a first order structure $\mathcal{A}$ for which the standard interpretation of the relation and function symbols is assumed.

An *interpretation* $\mathcal{J}$ of a vector of variables $\vec{y}$ is a mapping associating with each variable y from $\vec{y}$ a value $\mathcal{J}(y)$ from its domain. Let $\mid \vec{y} \mid$ denote the number of variables in $\vec{y}$.

Definition 10.7.1 *A program $\mathcal{P}$ is a quadruple $< \Sigma, I, \vec{y}, \Theta >$, where (Σ, I) is an independence alphabet, $\vec{y}$ a finite vector of program variables and Θ a first order formula with free variables from $\vec{y}$ (the initial condition). Furthermore, with each action a is associated a first order formula en_a (the enabling condition) and a $\mid \vec{y} \mid$-tuple of terms f_a (transformation function), satisfying the following consistency requirements for each $(a, b) \in I$:*

- $(en_a(\vec{y}) \wedge en_b(\vec{y})) \rightarrow f_a(f_b(\vec{y})) = f_b(f_a(\vec{y}))$

  (commutativity of independent operations),

- $en_a(\vec{y}) \rightarrow (en_b(\vec{y}) \leftrightarrow en_b(f_a(\vec{y})))$

  (independent operations do not influence each others enabledness).

The enabling condition en_a holds if the action a is enabled, whereas the transformation function f_a gives the new values to the variables of $\vec{y}$ after executing a.

The consistency requirements ensure that the effect of the actions on the variables is compatible with inverting the order of execution between adjacent independent actions.

To simplify the exposition, the programs are restricted such that Θ uniquely determines the value of $\vec{y}$. The extension to the unrestricted case is straightforward.

It is easy to see, especially considering their semantics, that EN-systems (see Definition 10.2.26) can be regarded as a special case of the programs defined above. Therefore the running examples can again be used, as these have been shown, in Section 10.2.3 to be expressible as EN-systems.

Semantics

The semantics of programs is defined in two steps: the interpreted trace system corresponding to a program is defined and then the program semantics is given as the model corresponding to that.

Definition 10.7.2 *The* interpreted trace system corresponding to a program $\mathcal{P} =< \Sigma, I, \vec{y}, \Theta >$, *is* $(\mathcal{T}, \mathcal{I})$ *where:*

- $\mathcal{T}$ *is the minimal set of traces over* (Σ, I) *containing* $[\varepsilon]$ *such that if* $\tau \in \mathcal{T}$ *and* $\mathcal{I}(\tau)$ *validates* en_a *(a is enabled at* τ*), then* $\tau[a] \in \mathcal{T}$,

- $\mathcal{I}[\varepsilon]$ *validates* Θ *and if* $\tau[a] \in \mathcal{T}$*, then* $\mathcal{I}(\tau[a]) = f_a(\mathcal{I}(\tau))$.

Note that the consistency conditions in the definition of program ensures that $\mathcal{I}$ is well defined.

Also note that the use of variables is quite different than in Section 10.3.4. The concern there was to code into the state precisely the information needed to capture transition labellings. The aim here is to capture for each action the effect on the state variables - this may or may not capture the transition labellings.

Definition 10.7.3 *The* semantics *of a program* $\mathcal{P} =< \Sigma, I, \vec{y}, \Theta >$ *is the model for the interpreted trace system* $(\mathcal{T}, \mathcal{I})$ *representing the behaviour of* $\mathcal{P}$.

This model is called the model for P.

10.7.2   First Order ISTL_P

The definition of ISTL is extended to its first order version with past operators.

Syntax of first order ISTL$_P$

Only two entries in the definition of ISTL, given in Section 10.3, change, as follows.

S1. if φ is a first order formula, then φ is a formula,

S3. if φ, ψ are formulas, then so are $EX\varphi$, $EG\varphi$, $E(\varphi U\psi)$, $EY\varphi$ and $EP\varphi$.

EY is the backward step modality and EP denotes sometime in the past. As in case of CTL$_P$, only two past modalities are added to the language of ISTL. Extensions with $EH\varphi$ and $E(\varphi S\psi)$ are possible, but will not be discussed in this chapter.

Semantics of first order ISTL$_P$

Because a first order version of ISTL$_P$ is considered, models are extended by the first order structure $\mathcal{A}$. Let (F, V) be the model for an interpreted trace system $(\mathcal{T}, \mathcal{I})$, as defined in Section 10.3.1. Then $M = (\mathcal{A}, F, V)$ is the extension to first order, i.e., for every world $x \in W$, $(\mathcal{A}, V(x))$ is a first order model on which formulas without temporal operators can be interpreted.

Clause $S1$ below just states that then evaluation of non-temporal formulas is as usual. Let $F' = (W', \Sigma, \rightarrow', w_0)$ be a run of F. Clause $S3$ gives the semantics of the two new entries in the syntax, where $x \in W'$ and o is an observation of F'.

S1. $x \models \varphi$ iff $(\mathcal{A}, V(x)) \models \varphi$, for non-temporal φ,

S3. $M, x \models EY\varphi$ iff $M, x' \models \varphi$, for some $x' \in W$ with $x' \rightarrow x$,

   $M, x \models EP\varphi$ iff $M, x' \models \varphi$, for some $x' \in W$ with $x' \rightarrow^* x$.

As before, a first order ISTL$_P$ formula φ is *valid* in a model M (written $M \models_{ISTL_P} \varphi$) iff $(\mathcal{A}, F', V'), w_0 \models \varphi$, for all runs F' of F, where $V' = V|W'$.

Definition 10.7.4 *A formula φ is* valid for a program $\mathcal{P}$ *if it is valid in the model* $(\mathcal{A}, F, V)$ *for P.*

10.7.3   Proof Systems for Programs

When a *logic* is used to describe properties of *programs* that manipulate *data*, three different parts can be distinguished accordingly in the proof system:

- the logic part - to deal with logical truth,

- the (data) domain part - to deal with domain properties, and

- the program part - to deal with program properties.

The program part is used to remove the references to the program from formulas. The logic and domain part are then used to derive the truth of the resulting formulas.

Because of the incompleteness incurred generally for first order logics over interpreted domains, only relative completeness can be achieved. This means that applying the program part enables to reduce the proof obligation about the program to proving validity of formula, without further reference to the program. The validity of some of the resulting formulas then has to be given by an oracle. These formulas could be temporal formulas, expressing a complicated mixture of properties of the data domain and the trace structure. As the incompleteness is really due to the interpretation of the data domain in first order logic and the modal logic is introduced primarily to express properties of the interdependency of actions, the oracle should preferably be limited to first-order non-temporal formulas only. This result is achieved for ISTL$_P$, both in case of exploiting expressiveness as when exploiting abstraction.

Rather than giving full proof systems, the present exposition is limited to the relevant and novel aspects of the programming part of the two systems considered.

10.7.4 Proof System to Exploit Expressiveness

Linear Time Temporal Logic, as discussed in Section 10.3, uses sequences, i.e., paths, of states as models. ISTL* uses observations of runs. The small discrepancy between the set of paths and the set of observations generated by a program can be taken care of by requiring the appropriate condition explicitly by means of the LTL formula

$$Fair \;=\; \bigwedge_{a \in \Sigma} (FGinden_a \rightarrow GFex_a),$$

where $inden_a$ means that a is enabled and independent with the action which is executed, ex_a means that a is executed.

ISTL* can be viewed as extending Linear Time Temporal Logic in the sense that an LTL formula $Fair \rightarrow \varphi$ is equivalent to ISTL* formula $A\varphi$.

Considering proof systems, this means that ISTL formulas corresponding to LTL-ones can be handled as these. Program proof rules for LTL can be found in [188]. ISTL$_P$ formulas that exploit the extra expressiveness of ISTL$_P$, i.e., do not quantify over all observations but rather assert the existence of one, have no LTL analogon. At present, complete proof rules are only known for certain, important, classes of such formulas, namely, those of form

$$AG(\varphi \rightarrow EX\psi)$$

and

$$AG(\varphi \rightarrow E(\phi U \psi))$$

as well as their past time counterparts.

A general strategy to prove eventuality properties is firstly to prove properties that hold after one step and then, secondly, to combine these results. The crucial proof principles for this approach, considering future time only, are discussed. The most relevant rules of the approach are presented.

To focus thought, the exposition is exemplified on one of the running examples, serializability. A trace is also, slightly abusing notation, used as a formula characterizing the state after the execution of its actions. It is shown how to establish the following formula:

$$AG([\varepsilon] \rightarrow EF([a_1 a_2 a_3] \vee [b_1 b_2 b_3])).$$

To do so, one has to first show how to establish formulas of the form $AG(\varphi \rightarrow EX\psi)$.

Proof Rule for $AG(\varphi \rightarrow EX\psi)$

The semantical meaning of $AG(\varphi \rightarrow EX\psi)$ is: for every run, for every trace τ in that run satisfying φ, there is an action a such that $\tau[a]$ is in that run and satisfies ψ.

To establish this formula, it suffices to provide a set F of actions with the following properties.

> For each trace τ satisfying φ,

> - for each run which contains τ, there is an action from F extending τ within the run;

> - extended traces satisfy ψ.

> Such a set is called a *forward intercepting* set.

For the serializability example

- The formula to be established is $AG([\varepsilon] \rightarrow EX([a_1]))$.

- The required set is $\{a_1\}$.

Runs are difficult to handle in a finitary way. Therefore, the first idea is to describe the set of actions without having to consider runs. In order to do so, notice that the observations of a run are equivalent modulo permuting independent actions. The requirement about the set F can thus be expressed as follows.

> For each trace τ satisfying φ, for each extension, i.e., action sequence u such that $\tau[u]$ is a trace of the program (thus extending into all runs), one of the following two options should hold.

(OK -Now). The extension contains some action a from F that can be permuted to occur immediately after the original trace, i.e., for all b in u that precede a, $(a, b) \in I$.

(OK -Later). The extension is not yet long enough to contain an action of F but there is some action from F that is concurrently enabled in the extension, i.e., $\tau \models en_a$ and for all b in v, $(a, b) \in I$. (Note that this option may hold for all finite prefixes of an infinite sequence of traces without a ever be taken: in that case the sequence is not an observation and nothing needs to be shown. Also note that because of the consistency requirements a remains enabled throughout v.)

For the serializability example:

- The first option covers the sequences a_1, $b_1 a_1$ and their extensions.

- The second one covers b_1, $b_1 b_2$ and $b_1 b_2 b_3$.

An extension is called *violating*, if it contains no actions from F that can be permuted back to its beginning and has no concurrently enabled action from F. This requirement can be formulated negatively as: there are no violating extensions.

Now, there are still infinitely many extensions to consider. The second idea is to show that no violating extensions exist by providing a finite graph that generates all potentially harmful candidates.

The nodes of the graph are of form $G_i = < \varphi_i, F_i >$. The intuitive meaning is the following. φ_i is a first order formula that denotes which traces could have been generated when arriving at this node. F_i indicates which actions from F are still enabled at this node.

The edges of the graph carry the transitions that build potentially violating extensions.

The structure of the graph is, intuitively, as follows.

1. The starting node allows all traces τ such that $\tau \models \varphi$ and also enables all actions from F.

2. For each node G_i, every enabled transition $a \notin F_i$ contributes to a potentially violating sequence and therefore is present on the edge to some G_j. To comply with the above intuition, the corresponding φ_j then allows at least all traces that are obtained by extending already generated ones by a. Also, just those actions from F_i that can not be permuted back over a are removed from F_i to yield F_j.

3. To keep the graph finite, it is required that different nodes have different sets of enabled actions.

4. Extensions generated by such a graph are violating ones just if a node G_i is reached where $F_i = \emptyset$. Therefore, in that case $\varphi_i = false$ should hold.

5. At each state satisfying φ every action a in F satisfies the weakest precondition of ψ, $wp_a(\psi)$, i.e., is enabled and, if executed, yields ψ.

The corresponding proof rule is NEXT.

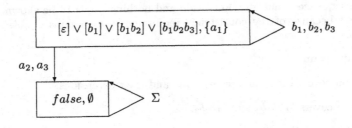

Figure 10.23: Graph for the serializability example

N1. $G_0 = (\varphi_0, F_0)$, such that $AG(\varphi \rightarrow \varphi_0)$

N2. If $G_i \xrightarrow{a} G_j$ then $(\varphi_i \wedge en_a) \rightarrow wp_a(\varphi_j)$ and $F_j = F_i - \{b \mid (a, b) \in D\}$

N3. If $G_i \neq G_j$, then $F_i \neq F_j$

N4. If $F_i = \emptyset$, then $\varphi_i = false$

N5. $AG(\varphi \rightarrow wp_a(\psi))$, for each $a \in F$

$$\overline{\qquad\qquad\qquad\qquad\qquad\qquad\qquad\qquad\qquad\qquad\qquad}$$

$AG(\varphi \rightarrow EX\psi)$

For the serializability example, to establish $AG([\varepsilon] \rightarrow EX([a_1]))$, the graph is shown in Figure 10.23.

A proof rule for $AG(\varphi \rightarrow EF\psi)$

The difference with the NEXT situation is that now ψ should be satisfied in the present in any subsequent state rather than after the execution of a single action.

The idea is to establish in a novel inductive manner that some property ψ holds for every run for some observation in some future state. It turns out that just applying induction forward in time, i.e., providing intermediate assertions $EX\psi_i$ that hold along observations serving as an induction path to the desired state and together achieve ψ fails.

The reason is the implicit universal quantification over runs. Because of this, where runs overlap, intermediate assertions that hold along the observation serving as the induction path to the desired state for one run, may be required to also hold for some second run (for which that observation was never destined to be the induction path). There are situations that this requirement can not be met, i.e., in which the straightforward approach fails. There are cases in which in some state along the induction path of the first run no intermediate assertion can be found at all, because the desired state in the second run can no more be reached. There are situations that this is the case for all induction paths, i.e., situations where the straightforward inductive approach fails.

Serializability again provides an example. To prove is:

$$AG([\varepsilon] \rightarrow EF([a_1 a_2 a_3] \vee [b_1 b_2 b_3])).$$

The first intermediate assertion, suitable for the thick-lined run in the Figure 10.2, would be $AG([\varepsilon] \rightarrow EX[a_1])$ (or, equivalently, $AG([\varepsilon] \rightarrow EX[b_1])$) - choosing $[a_1] \vee [b_1]$ would only worsen the situation.

The next step would then require $AG([a_1] \rightarrow EX[a_1 b_1])$. Now the assertion for the subsequent step, $AG([a_1 b_1] \rightarrow EF([a_1 a_2 a_3] \vee [b_1 b_2 b_3]))$, does not hold anymore.

Already at state $[a_1]$ in fact only $[a_1 a_2 a_3]$ is reachable anymore, satisfying the requirement for only the thick-lined run. However, at this state the runs still overlap, thus requiring extensions into both. It is evident, that no other choice of inductive paths and corresponding intermediate assertions would escape this situation.

A closer analysis indicates how to overcome the problem.

As runs are directed, there must be some turning state further on in the second run that

1. still can be reached and

2. from which, going backward, the desired state can be reached.

Now if only backward paths are used that subsume the origin where one started, this implies that there is also a path from the origin along which the desired state can be reached by just going forward. That the origin is subsumed is necessary, as otherwise this approach might not be sound; only a forward/backward but no forward path leading to the desired state might exist. The idea is to find an assertion characterizing the turning state and then to show that the desired state can be reached by standard induction applied forward as well as backward.

For the serializability example, from $[a_1]$, and also even from $[a_1 b_1]$, $[a_1 a_2 a_3 b_1]$ and $[b_1 b_2 b_3 a_1]$ can both be reached. From these states, there are backwards paths to the desired $[a_1 a_2 a_3]$ and $[b_1 b_2 b_3]$. As $[\varepsilon]$ was the origin state, no subsystems need be considered for the backwards paths.

That backward paths subsume the origin is achieved by changing for the backward part to the subsystem rooted in the state where φ held. In [218] this is formalized, here just the notation to indicate this subsystem, P_φ, is borrowed.

The corresponding proof rule is FRBK.

F1 $AG(\varphi \rightarrow EF\hat{\psi})$

F2 $P_\varphi \vdash AG(\hat\psi \to EP\psi)$

─────────────────────────────

$AG(\varphi \to EF\psi)$

For the example, by repeated application of the rule NEXT and the use of, essentially, variants of familiar future time temporal logic rules, $F1$ can be established: $AG([\varepsilon] \to EF([a_1a_2a_3b_1] \vee [b_1b_2b_3a_1]))$. Using similar backward rules, $F2$ is established: $AG([a_1a_2a_3b_1] \vee [b_1b_2b_3a_1] \to EP([a_1a_2a_3] \vee [b_1b_2b_3]))$. The desired result then follows directly by FRBK.

The need to go to a subsystem for the backward part can also be seen from the example. Consider, for instance, starting from $[a_1]$ rather than $[\varepsilon]$. Again a forward path to $[b_1b_2b_3a_1]$ exists, as well as a backward one to $[b_1b_2b_3]$. However, a path from $[a_1]$ to $[b_1b_2b_3]$ does not exist.

10.7.5   Proof System to Exploit Abstraction

The first idea is that in certain cases to establish $AG(\varphi \to AF\psi)$ for a program it is sufficient to prove the weaker property $AG(\varphi \to EF\psi)$. Namely, for certain combinations of programs and properties. This might especially simplify proofs, when for some convenient observations the desired property is easier to establish than for others.

Unfortunately, the rules for proving EF-properties as discussed in the previous section are still very complicated. The second idea is therefore, to simplify the rules as well. Rules are simplified in the sense that they remain sound for all programs and properties, but generally not complete. Of course again a, maybe different, subclass of programs and properties could be provided for which such rules are complete.

The question of simplifying the rules is addressed first. Secondly, a class of programs and properties is defined for which OF properties imply OF-ones. It turns out that for this class the simplified rules are in fact complete.

The inevitability property of the second example program is used to illustrate the approach.

A simplified rule for $AG(\varphi \to EF\psi)$

To limit the number of actions to be considered when iteratively assessing representative sequences, for each state τ a subset H_τ of helpful actions is defined.

The idea is to find a set of actions that are helpful in that in any state satisfying φ, each of them yields ψ. The set should also be such that in each run there is an observation where such an action is executed at the right moment, i.e., in a state where φ holds.

The former requirement will be seen to be incorporated in the premises of a proof rule. The latter requirement is achieved by the following definition, provided that an action from the set is continuously enabled.

Definition 10.7.5 *A faithful decomposition of a program in a state τ is a subset of actions $\mathcal{H}_\tau \subseteq \Sigma$ such that each action in its complement, $\overline{\mathcal{H}_\tau}$, is either independent of each action in $\mathcal{H}_\tau$ or disabled in τ and its successors as long as no action from $\mathcal{H}_\tau$ is executed.*

Let faithful$(\varphi, \mathcal{H})$ *denote that $\mathcal{H}$ is a faithful decomposition in each state satisfying φ.*

The idea is then to establish $AG(\varphi \to EF\psi)$ as follows. Find a set $\mathcal{H}$ with the following properties.

1. To ensure availability of helpful actions, $\mathcal{H}$ should be faithful for φ.

2. To ensure enabledness of a helpful action, there should be an action a in $\mathcal{H}$ that is enabled if φ holds.

   Furthermore, the following should hold about this action.

3. Actions from the faithful set that are independent from a need not be helpful themselves, as they leave a enabled - they should leave φ true though, as otherwise a might not yield ψ anymore. Of course, if "perchance" they yield the desired ψ, this is allowed too.

4. Actions from $\mathcal{H}$ that are not independent from a, for instance a itself, should yield ψ. This is required, because such actions might disable actions from $\mathcal{H}$.

This leads to the following rule.

EVENTUAL

E1. $faithful(\varphi, \mathcal{H})$,

   For some $a \in \mathcal{H}$,

E2. $AG(\varphi \to en_a)$;

E3. for each $b \in \mathcal{H}$ such that $(b, a) \in I$, $AG((\varphi \wedge en_b) \to wp_b(\varphi \vee \psi))$;

E4. for each $b \in \mathcal{H}$ such that $(b, a) \notin I$, $AG((\varphi \wedge en_b) \to wp_b(\psi))$

$AG(\varphi \to EF\psi)$

Using this rule to prove $AG(\neg(a \in \Sigma(\tau) \vee b \in \Sigma(\tau)) \to EF(a \in \Sigma(\tau) \vee b \in \Sigma(\tau)))$ for the inevitability example, $faithful(\neg(a \in \Sigma(\tau) \vee b \in \Sigma(\tau)), \{a, b, c, d\})$ is chosen. The premises of the EVENTUAL rule are then fulfilled:

E1. $\{a,b,c,d\}$ is trivially faithful, as $\overline{\{a, b, c, d\}} = \emptyset$

Choose a as the special action in $\{a, b, c, d\}$,

E2. indeed a is enabled if it and b have not occurred yet;

E3. the actions from $\{a, b, c, d\}$ that are independent of a, i.e., c and d, preserve
$\neg(a \in \Sigma(\tau) \vee b \in \Sigma(\tau))$;

E4. the only action from $\{a, b, c, d\}$ that is not independent of a, b,
yields $(a \in \Sigma(\tau) \vee b \in \Sigma(\tau))$

$$AG(\neg(a \in \Sigma(\tau) \vee b \in \Sigma(\tau)) \rightarrow EF(a \in \Sigma(\tau) \vee b \in \Sigma(\tau)))$$

A condition under which replacement of E by A is allowed

To allow E in $EF\psi$ to be replaced by A, the following should hold for the combination of program P and properties φ and ψ. For each run, there cannot be observations o_1 and o_2 starting from a state τ_0 where φ holds such that ψ holds eventually in some state τ_1 on o_1, but $\neg\psi$ continually holds on o_2. From this, a sufficient, more manageable, condition is now argued.

Assume such an offending pair of observations exists. Because o_1 and o_2 are observations of the same run, there is a state τ_2 on o_2 that is reachable from τ_1. The resulting path p_1 from τ_0 to τ_2, shown in Figure 10.24, and the path p_2 from τ_0 to τ_2 on o_2 form a large diamond, and hence are equivalent. Therefore, p_2 can be transformed into p_1 by repeatedly exchanging the order between adjacent independent actions - "flipping". Always flipping the lowest of such pairs, one of these flippings will cause, on a prefix of p_2, the first occurrence of a state where ψ holds. Hence there exists a diamond on o_2, defined as follows.

Definition 10.7.6 *An offending diamond for ψ is a state in which $\neg\psi$ holds, with two immediate successors τ' and τ'', generated by two independent actions a and b. The state τ' satisfies ψ and the state τ'' satisfies $\neg\psi$. Furthermore, the b-successor of τ', which is also the a-successor of τ'', satisfies $\neg\psi$.*

This leads to the following theorem (see Figure 10.24).

Theorem 10.7.7 *The non-existence of offending diamonds is sufficient to ensure that $AG(\varphi \rightarrow EF\psi)$ implies $AG(\varphi \rightarrow AF\psi)$.*

For the inevitability example: There exists no offending diamond, as once the program establishes $a \in \Sigma(\tau) \vee b \in \Sigma(\tau)$, this can not be made undone.

Therefore, $AG(\neg(a \in \Sigma(\tau) \vee b \in \Sigma(\tau)) \rightarrow AF(a \in \Sigma(\tau) \vee b \in \Sigma(\tau)))$ has now been shown.

For the class of programs and properties defined by the requirement that no offending diamond exists, the EVENTUAL rule (together with the other rules) is complete in the following sense. If $\mathcal{H} = \Sigma$ is chosen, the rule reduces to the LTL rule to prove $AG(\varphi \rightarrow AF\psi)$. For the restricted class of programs and properties, this is exactly what the EVENTUAL rule achieves.

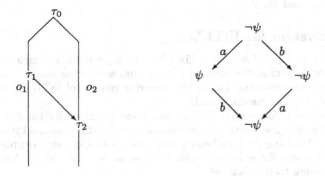

Figure 10.24: An offending pair and an offending diamond

10.8 Axiomatization of a Subset of Propositional ISTL$_P$

In this section, a complete infinitary proof system for a subset of propositional ISTL with past operators is presented.

In Section 10.6, it has been shown how to reduce the validity problem for CTL$_P$ to the recurring tiling problem. This proof also goes through for ISTL$_P$, because the grid encoded has the forward-diamond property and ISTL with past operators is at least as expressive as CTL$_P$ over such models. The complexity of the recurring tiling problem, and thus also of the validity problem, is known to be Π_1^1-hard. Hence, a complete finitary axiomatization of ISTL$_P$ does not exist. This motivates the presence of infinitary rules.

In what follows, only trace systems with infinite runs are dealt with. This inessential restriction allows to consider only infinite models for ISTL$_P$ and admits of a simpler axiomatization.

The part of the proof system concerned with characterizing the logical operators is standard, as for CTL with past and labelled operators.

The part of the axiom system concerned with characterizing models is obtained as follows. A frame for ISTL$_P$ corresponds to a run of a trace system. Properties of ISTL$_P$ frames given in Lemma 10.2.11, where the forward I_F-diamond property $C4$ is strengthen to the forward-diamond property b) of Definition 10.2.12, are axiomatized. The only property which cannot be expressed in the logic and therefore axiomatized is $C1$.

The present exposition is based on the paper of Penczek [221], where the complete proof system has been given for a subset of ISTL$_P$ extended with the past formulas of form $EH\varphi$ and $E\varphi S\psi$.

10.8.1   Proof System for ISTL'$_P$

As an intermediate step, a proof system is given for the logic ISTL'$_P$ which is like ISTL$_P$ except for the fact that the forward path quantifiers range over maximal paths rather than over observations, i.e., in the semantic rule $S3$ of ISTL the word "observation" is replaced by "maximal path".

The current literature is followed in that a proof system is given for the floating version of the logic, i.e., the logic with validity (denoted $\models_f$) defined over all models and all states. Both (floating and anchored) versions are of the same expressive power, and a proof system for either one can be used as a proof system for the other, using the following translation rules.

1. $\models \psi$ iff $\models_f AYfalse \rightarrow \psi$,

2. $\models_f \psi$ iff $\models AG\psi$.

1) says that ψ holds in all models at the beginning states iff $AYfalse \rightarrow \psi$ holds in all models at all states. Note that the formula trivializes at all but the beginning state. 2) expresses that ψ holds in all models at all states iff $AG\psi$ holds in all models at the beginning states.

Denote by:

- $EX^i(\varphi) \stackrel{def}{=} \varphi \wedge EX(\varphi \wedge EX(\varphi \wedge ...EX(\varphi)...)$
  (the operator EX occurs i times, for $i \geq 0$),

- $EX^0(\varphi, \psi) \stackrel{def}{=} \psi$, $EX^i(\varphi, \psi) \stackrel{def}{=} \varphi \wedge EX(\varphi \wedge EX(\varphi \wedge ...EX(\psi)...)$
  (the operator EX occurs i times, for $i \geq 1$),

- $EX_\epsilon\varphi \stackrel{def}{=} \varphi$, $EX_u\varphi \stackrel{def}{=} EX_{a_1}EX_{a_2}...EX_{a_n}\varphi$, for $u = a_1a_2...a_n$.

- $I(a,b) \stackrel{def}{=} EPEF(EY_a true \wedge EY_b true)$, for $a \neq b$, $a, b \in \Sigma$.

$I(a, b)$ expresses that the actions a and b are executed independently in the model.

Axioms

A1. all formulas of the form of tautologies of the classical prop. calculus

A2. $EG\varphi \equiv \varphi \wedge EX(EG\varphi)$ (fixed-point characterization of EG)

A3. $E(\varphi U\psi) \equiv \psi \vee (\varphi \wedge EX(E(\varphi U\psi)))$ (fixed-point characterization of EU)

A4. $EP\psi \equiv \psi \vee EYEP\psi$ (fixed-point characterization of EP)

A5. $\varphi \rightarrow AX_a EY_a \varphi$ (relating past and future)

A6. $\varphi \to AY_a EX_a \varphi$ (relating past and future)

A7. $EX\,true$ (infiniteness)

A8. $EP(AY\,false)$ (beginning)

A9. $EX_a(\varphi \wedge \psi) \equiv EX_a(\varphi) \wedge EX_a(\psi)$ (forward determinism)

A10. $EX_a AX_b \varphi \to AX_b EX_a \varphi$, for $a \neq b$ (forward-diamond property)

A11. $(I(a,b) \wedge EX_a EX_b \varphi) \to EX_b EX_a \varphi$ (concurrency closure property)

A12. $EY_a(\varphi \wedge \psi) \equiv EY_a(\varphi) \wedge EY_a(\psi)$ (no auto-concurrency)

A13. $EY_a AY_b \varphi \to AY_b EY_a \varphi$, for $a \neq b$ (backward-diamond property)

Proof Rules

MP. $\varphi, \varphi \to \psi \vdash \psi$ (modus ponens)

R1. $\varphi \to \psi \vdash EX_a \varphi \to EX_a \psi$

R2. $\varphi \to \psi \vdash EY_a \varphi \to EY_a \psi$

R3. $\{\phi \to EX_u EX^i(\varphi)\}_{i \in \omega} \vdash \phi \to EX_u EG\varphi$, for $u \in \Sigma^*$

R4. $\{EX_u EX^i(\varphi, \psi) \to \phi\}_{i \in \omega} \vdash EX_u E(\varphi U \psi) \to \phi$, for $u \in \Sigma^*$

R5. $AY\,false \to AG\varphi \vdash \varphi$.

MP is the standard modus ponens rule. $R1$ and $R2$ are rules expressing deductive closures. $R3$ and $R4$ are infinitary rules characterizing EG and EU. $R5$ characterizes the beginning state.

The "only if" part of the following lemma is used to prove that $R3$ and $R4$ preserve validity.

Lemma 10.8.1 *For every model M and each state w,*

(a) $M, w \models EG\varphi$ iff $M, w \models EX^i(\varphi)$, for each $i \in \omega$,

(b) $M, w \models E(\varphi U \psi)$ iff $M, w \models EX^i(\varphi, \psi)$, for some $i \in \omega$.

Proof: a) $(\Rightarrow)$ follows directly from the definition of the temporal operator EG.

Since Σ is finite, each state in M has only finitely many successors. Therefore, a) $(\Leftarrow)$ follows from König's lemma.

b) similarly follows directly from the definitions of the operators EU and $EX^i(.,.)$.

$\square$

Note that the use of maximal paths rather than observations is crucial here; the right hand sides of the two clauses guarantee the existence of a maximal path, but not necessarily of an observation.

Theorem 10.8.2 *The proof system is sound (i.e., $\vdash \varphi$ implies $\models_f \varphi$).*

Proof: It is easy to check that the axioms are valid and the proof rules preserve validity. For the rules $R3$ and $R4$, this follows from Lemma 10.8.1 and the forward determinism of frames.   □

Completeness of the Proof System for ISTL'$_P$

The construction in this section builds a model for a consistent formula. An outline of the construction is as follows:

- The Lindenbaum-Tarski algebra for the logic is built.

- The infinite operations, say Q, corresponding to the infinitary rules are defined in the algebra.

- Q-filters in the algebra are defined. These are then used as worlds of the model.

- The model is built. The axioms are used to prove that the model is isomorphic with a run.

Let $\sim \subseteq Form \times Form$ be the following relation: $\varphi \sim \psi \; iff \; \vdash \varphi \equiv \psi$.

Note that $\sim$ is a congruence with respect to all the logical and modal operators. Let $Form/\sim$ denote the set of all equivalence classes of $\sim$. Elements of $Form/\sim$ are denoted as follows $[\varphi], [\psi], ...$

Definition 10.8.3 *The* Lindenbaum-Tarski algebra *for ISTL'$_P$ is a 6-tuple $LTA = (Form/\sim, \cup, \cap, -, [true], [false])$, where*

- $[\varphi] \cup [\psi] = [\varphi \vee \psi]$,

- $[\varphi] \cap [\psi] = [\varphi \wedge \psi]$,

- $-[\varphi] = [\neg\varphi]$.

Theorem 10.8.4 *The Lindenbaum-Tarski algebra LTA satisfies the following conditions:*

1. *LTA is a non-degenerate Boolean algebra,*

2. *$\vdash \varphi$ iff $[\varphi] = [true]$,*

3. *$\nvdash \varphi$ iff $[\neg\varphi] \neq [false]$.*

The proof of the above theorem is standard and can be found in [232] (p. 257). Let $\leq$ be a partial ordering in $Form/\sim \times Form/\sim$, defined as follows:

$$[\varphi] \leq [\psi] \;\; iff \;\; \vdash \varphi \to \psi.$$

Lemma 10.8.5 *In the algebra LTA the following conditions hold:*

(a) $[EX_u EG\varphi] = inf_{i\in\omega}\{[EX_u EX^i\varphi]\}$, *for* $u \in \Sigma^*$,

(b) $[EX_u E(\varphi U\psi)] = sup_{i\in\omega}\{[EX_u EX^i(\varphi,\psi)]\}$, *for* $u \in \Sigma^*$.

Proof: Follows from axioms $A2$, $A3$, and rules $R3$ and $R4$.   □

Let Q denote the following infinite operations in the algebra LTA: $inf_{i\in\omega}\{EX_u EX^i(.)\}$, and $sup_{i\in\omega}\{EX_u EX^i(.,.)\}$, for $u \in \Sigma^*$.

Definition 10.8.6 *A Q-filter in LTA is a maximal proper filter A which satisfies the following conditions:*

- *if $[EX_u E(\varphi U\psi)] \in A$, then there is $i \in \omega$ such that $[EX_u EX^i(\varphi,\psi)] \in A$,*

- *if $[EX_u EG\varphi] \notin A$, then there is $i \in \omega$ such that $[EX_u EX^i\varphi] \notin A$.*

Notice that the number of infinite operations is enumerable. The following standard result is assumed (see [232]).

Lemma 10.8.7 *If a set Q of infinite operations in a Boolean algebra is at most enumerable, then every non-zero element of the Boolean algebra belongs to a Q-filter.*

Completeness can now be argued.

Theorem 10.8.8 *The proof system is complete (i.e., $\models_f \phi$ implies $\vdash \phi$).*

Proof. (sketch)
It is shown that if $\not\vdash \phi$, then there is a model for $\neg\phi$, which by contraposition implies that the theorem holds. Let UF be the family of all ultrafilters in the algebra LTA and $QF \subseteq UF$ be the family of all Q-filters in LTA. Define the following relation in $UF \times \Sigma \times UF$:

- $D \xrightarrow{a}_F D'$ iff $\{[EX_a\varphi] \mid [\varphi] \in D'\} \subseteq D$.

The following lemma is needed in order to build a required model for $\neg\phi$.

Lemma 10.8.9 *If D is a Q-filter and $[EX_a\varphi] \in D$, then there is the Q-filter D' s.t. $D \xrightarrow{a}_F D'$ and $[\varphi] \in D'$.*

Proof: Using the standard construction method (cf. [232]), an ultrafilter D' can be built s.t. $D \xrightarrow{a}_F D'$ and $[\varphi] \in D'$. To show that D' is a Q-filter, assume that $[EX_u E(\psi U\phi)] \in D'$. Then, by definition of $\xrightarrow{a}_F$, $[EX_a EX_u E(\psi U\phi)] \in D$. Since D is a Q-filter, there is $i \in \omega$ such that $[EX_a EX_u EX^i(\psi,\phi)] \in D$. Therefore, $[EX_u EX^i(\psi,\phi)] \in D'$. To complete the proof that D' is a Q-filter, assume that $[EX_u EG\psi] \notin D'$. Then, by definition of $\xrightarrow{a}_F$, $[EX_a EX_u EG\psi] \notin D$. Since D is a Q-filter, there is $i \in \omega$ such that $[EX_a EX_u EX^i\psi] \notin D$. Therefore, $[EX_u EX^i\psi] \notin D'$, which proves that D' is a Q-filter.

It follows from $A10$ that D' is the only ultrafilter s.t. $D \xrightarrow{a}_F D'$.   □

Then, if $\not\vdash \phi$, then, by $R5$, $\not\vdash AYfalse \rightarrow AG\phi$. Then, by Theorem 10.8.4, $[AYfalse \wedge \neg AG\phi] \neq [false]$. Therefore, by Lemma 10.8.7, there is a Q-filter $C \in QF$ such that $[AYfalse] \in C$ and $[EF(\neg\phi)] \in C$. Next, the structure $F = (W, \Sigma, \rightarrow, C)$ and the structure $M = (F, V)$ is defined as follows:

- $W = \{D \in QF \mid \exists D_1, ..., D_n \in QF, \ D_1 \rightarrow_F ... \rightarrow_F D_n, \ D_1 = C, \ D_n = D\}$,

- $\rightarrow \ = \ \rightarrow_F \cap (W \times \Sigma \times W)$,

- $q \in V(D)$ iff $[q] \in D$, where $q \in PV$ and $D \in W$.

Now, the proof can be completed.

Lemma 10.8.10 *The following conditions hold:*

   a) F is a frame for $ISTL_P$,

   b) For each $\varphi \in Form$, $D \in W$: $M, D \models \varphi$ iff $[\varphi] \in D$.

Proof: a) All the conditions stated in Lemma 10.2.11, where the forward I_F-diamond property $C4$ is strengthen to the forward-diamond property b) of Definition 10.2.12, hold for F.

- $C1$ holds by the definition of W,

- F is infinite by $A7$,

- For $2 \leq i \leq 7$, Ci holds by the axiom Ak, where $k = i + 6$.

b) The proof is by induction on a formula φ using a well-founded relation in the set of formulas. $\square$

10.8.2   Proof System for a Subset of $ISTL_P$

In the original semantics of $ISTL_P$, the quantifiers E and A range over observations rather than over forward paths. It is now shown that a small modification of the proof system for $ISTL'_P$ leads to a complete proof system for the subset of $ISTL_P$ without formulas of the form $EG\varphi$, but with the formulas of the form $E(\varphi U\phi)$ and $A(\varphi U\phi)$.

Let A_o and E_o denote the quantifiers ranging over observations. $E_o(\varphi U\psi)$ and $A_o(\varphi U\psi)$ can be expressed in the defined language and therefore derived using the proof system.

Firstly, observe that $M, w \models E_o(\varphi U\psi)$ iff $M, w \models E(\varphi U\psi)$. Unfortunately, the analogous property does not hold for $A_o(\varphi U\psi)$. This problem can be solved as follows. Select a proposition $\sigma \in PV$ and add the following three new axioms characterizing its values in the models:

$A\sigma1.\ AYfalse \rightarrow \sigma$,

$A\sigma2.$ $\sigma \to EX_!\sigma \wedge (AY\,false \vee EY_!\sigma),$

     where $EX_!\sigma \overset{def}{=} \bigoplus_{a\in\Sigma} EX_a\sigma,$ $EY_!\sigma \overset{def}{=} \bigoplus_{a\in\Sigma} EY_a\sigma.$

$A\sigma3.$ $EF\sigma.$

The axioms $A\sigma1\text{-}2$ express that σ holds in exactly one path in the model. $A\sigma3$ ensures that the path at which σ holds is an observation, namely, by stating that it is cofinal with the run.

Now, the formulas of the form $A_o(\varphi U\psi)$ are shown to be expressible in the defined language:

Theorem 10.8.11 *The following equivalence holds:*

$$\models_f A_o(\varphi U\psi) \ \ iff \ \ \models_f \sigma \to E((\varphi \wedge \sigma)U(\psi \wedge \sigma)),$$

where ψ, φ and ψ do not contain σ.

The proof of ($\Leftarrow$) follows from the fact that the formula $(\varphi U\psi)$ must hold in each model at the observation marked σ. Since for each run and each its observation there is a model in which this observation is marked σ, $(\varphi U\phi)$ holds in all models at all observations.

In order to express formulas containing several subformulas of the form $A_o(\varphi_i U\phi_i)$, for each of them a special proposition σ_i has to be selected and three new axioms for σ_i, are added, as above.

Therefore, the extended proof system contains a complete axiomatization of ISTL_P without formulas of the form $E_o G\varphi$.

Moreover, it follows from the completeness theorem that the set of theorems of the axiomatized fragment of ISTL is at most Π_1^1. Therefore, the validity problem for this subset is Π_1^1-complete.

The given proof system for ISTL_P can be adapted to a proof system for CTL_P [221] by strengthening $A10$ to the axiom

    $(I(a,b) \wedge EX_a AX_b\varphi) \to AX_b EX_a\varphi,$ for $a \neq b$ (I-diamond property).

10.9 Conclusions

Except for the introductory material and the rather independent topic considered in the appendix, the table below follows from the organization of the material in this chapter. The possible entries generated by the tabular presentation provide some guidance to assess the state-of-the-art. In the following table ?? indicates current absence of a result; - indicates that a slot can not be filled in a meaningful way.

logic	model checking		decidable	axiomatization	proof rules	
	standard	efficient			standard	efficient
LTL	YES	YES	YES	YES	YES	YES
CTL	YES	YES	YES	YES	YES	??
CTL*	YES	YES	YES	??	??	??
ISTL	??	-	??	??	??	-
ISTL*	??	-	NO	??	??	-
ISTL$_P$	??	-	NO	YES	YES	-
ISTL*$_P$	??	-	NO	??	??	-
CTL$_P$	YES	-	NO	YES	??	-
CTL*$_P$	??	-	NO	??	??	-

The linear temporal logic LTL and its extension CTL* that enables to identify forward branching points are conventional temporal logics in the sense that they do not address partial order properties. The restriction CTL of CTL* is included because in that case the complexity of standard model checking is linear. The information about the existence of standard model checking procedures, axiomatizations, decision procedures and program proof rules for these logics is included in the table not so much because of direct relevance to partial order considerations, but to provide a somewhat wider context. Most of the results are discussed in [97].

As shown in Sections 10.4 and 10.5, partial order techniques can make model checking more efficient for these logics without next step operators. Note that efficient model checking is based on the idea that logics can only distinguish up to permutations of independent actions, plus that in case of CTL also branching points are relevant. Formulas can therefore be checked over any acceptor that respects the corresponding equivalence. The independence of actions is thus only used for reducing the acceptors; the logics considered are not partial order logics themselves. Because of the very fact that the logics ISTL and CTL$_P$ and their extensions do enable to distinguish between permutations, efficient model checking is not an option, as indicated in the table. Methods based on ample sets as well as on sleep sets are presented for LTL. The adaptation of the ample set approach for CTL (and, as only reducing acceptors is involved, also for CTL*) is quite recent; the sleep set direction has not yet been explored.

The same remark about enhancing efficiency as made in the case of model checking applies in principle to program proof rules: It is the efficiency of proving LTL formulas about programs that is enhanced, again the approach does not apply for ISTL* and CTL$_P$. There is a difference though, in that model checking is a semantic activity but proving formulas occurs at the syntactic level. Therefore, independence of actions cannot be hidden in the model but needs to be present in the proof system. So in fact proving an LTL formula efficiently amounts to proving a formula from a subset of ISTL* formulas. The table indicates what is in fact achieved: efficient proving of LTL formulas about programs.

Program proof systems for branching time logics were slow to develop. The proof system Fix and Grumberg provide for fair CTL [102] is the first result in this area. Whether or not simplifying proof rules for CTL and extensions to CTL* are feasible remains yet to be seen.

ISTL* extends the expressive power of LTL by enabling to explicitly mention representatives of runs, i.e., exploit independence of actions. ISTL*$_P$ [218] is an extension of ISTL* with CTL*-like nested past operators. As discussed in Section 10.7, on the one hand syntactically restricted and on the other hand extended, namely with past operators, version ISTL$_P$, admits of an axiomatization and program proof system. In the absence of the past operators, i.e., for ISTL, no results are available. The program proof rules and axiomatization for ISTL$_P$ is still incomplete in that it does not cover formulas of form $EG\varphi$. The relevance of such formulas for expressing properties of programs is still a matter of debate, though. CTL$_P$ extends the expressive power of CTL by enabling to identify backward branching. This enables to express independence of actions; together with the capability to identify forward branching already present in CTL, properties of runs can be described, be it in a less direct manner than in the case of ISTL*. Note that in the case of both ISTL$_P$ and CTL$_P$ the axiomatizations are infinitary.

The results in Section 10.6 about CTL$_P$ are that this logic, exploiting the expressiveness of the trace approach, is undecidable but that NP-hard model checking applies; a one-exponential algorithm is presented for a restricted version without nested past operators.

Some other options are the following. LTL extended with past operators is not discussed, as the interpretation over sequences causes the expressiveness to remain the same as for LTL. QISTL [150] and CCTL [219] can be viewed as ISTL-like extensions of branching rather than linear time logics. As both logics are quite involved and their practical relevance is yet to be assessed more fully, these are not included in the table. A perhaps somewhat less obvious but interesting new direction is proposed by Thiagarajan in [259]. The main idea there is to interpret a multi-agent linear temporal logic over independence graphs of infinite traces. This approach is motivated by the aim to connect decidability and model checking problem for the logic to testing for non-emptiness of asynchronous Büchi automata.

10.10   Appendix:
Logical Definability of Trace Languages

Werner Ebinger

Universität Stuttgart, Institut für Informatik
Breitwiesenstr. 20–22, 70565 Stuttgart, Germany
ebinger@informatik.uni-stuttgart.de

In this appendix we show the equivalence between recognizability and monadic second order logic definability, and the equivalence of star-freeness and first order logic for trace languages. This connects logic on traces to the theory of recognizable trace languages (Chapters 6, 7, 8, and 11) and extends classical results of Büchi, McNaughton, Ladner and Thomas on word languages to traces. Monadic second order logic on traces has been first considered by Thomas. This section is based on a joint work with Muscholl [91] and on the dissertation of the author [90].

10.10.1   First Order Logic and Monadic Second Order Logic on Traces

The underlying structures for the logical setting considered in the following are single (finite or infinite) traces. A finite trace $t \in \mathbb{M}(\Sigma, D)$, respectively an infinite (real) trace $t \in \mathbb{R}(\Sigma, D)$ (Chapter 11), can be represented as a labelled partial order $(V, <, \ell)$, corresponding to the dependence graph of t (see Chapter 1 and 2). A logical formula is interpreted over a *structure* with signature $(V, <, (P_a)_{a \in \Sigma})$, where P_a is the set of vertices labelled by a. We allow the empty structure $V = \emptyset$ in order to include the empty trace.

First order formulae and monadic second order formulae are based on first order variables $x, y, z, \ldots$ ranging over V and monadic second order variables $X, Y, Z, \ldots$ ranging over the power set $\mathcal{P}(V)$. First order predicates of the form $x < y$, $P_a(x)$ $(a \in \Sigma)$ and monadic second order predicates of the form $X(y)$ are the atomic formulae. Formulae are built inductively using the logical operators $\wedge$ (and), $\vee$ (or), and $\neg$ (not), as well as quantification $\exists$, $\forall$ of first order and second order variables. Formulae ψ defined in this way are called *monadic second order formulae* (denoted by $\psi \in \mathcal{L}_2(\Sigma, D)$). A formula ψ is called *first order formula* (denoted by $\psi \in \mathcal{L}_1(\Sigma, D)$) if it contains no second order variable.

A real trace t is a model for a sentence (i. e. a formula without free variables) ψ, if ψ is satisfied by t under the canonical interpretation (denoted by $t \models \psi$). This means that variables are mapped to (sets of) vertices of the dependence graph of t. The predicate $P_a(x)$ is "x is labelled with $a \in \Sigma$", the relation $<$ is interpreted as the partial order of the dependence graph and $X(y)$ is "y belongs to X".

We also write $y \in X$ instead of $X(y)$ and freely use abbreviations like $\rightarrow$, $\leftrightarrow$, $X \subseteq Y$ for $\forall x \ (x \in X \rightarrow x \in Y)$ and $x = y$ for $\bigvee_{a \in \Sigma} (P_a(x) \wedge P_a(y) \wedge \neg (x < y) \wedge \neg (y < x))$.

For the special case of complete dependency $D = \Sigma \times \Sigma$, we obtain the monadic second order logic $\mathcal{L}_2(\Sigma)$ and the first order logic $\mathcal{L}_1(\Sigma)$ on (finite and infinite) words.

Example 10.10.1 We can express the property "t contains the trace factor ab" by

$$t \models \exists x \, \exists y \, (P_a(x) \wedge P_b(y) \wedge \neg y < x \wedge \neg \exists z \, (x < z \wedge z < y)) \ .$$

The power of monadic second order logic on traces does not depend on whether the $<$-relation or the edge relation E of the Hasse diagram of $(V, <, \ell)$ are chosen to be incorporated in the logic, since they can be expressed one into another. The edge relation E constitutes some kind of successor relation and is expressible by the partial order relation $<$ (even in first order logic):

$$x \, E \, y \quad \text{iff} \quad x < y \wedge \neg \exists z \, (x < z \wedge z < y) \ ,$$

and vice versa (in monadic second order logic):

$$x < y \quad \text{iff} \quad \exists x' \Big(x \, E \, x' \, \wedge$$
$$\forall X (x' \in X \wedge \forall z \forall z' (z \in X \wedge z \, E \, z' \rightarrow z' \in X)$$
$$\rightarrow y \in X) \Big) \ .$$

Therefore we are free to use both, the $<$-relation and the edge relation E in monadic second order formulae.

10.10.2 Characterizations for Finite Traces

The truth value of a formula depends on whether it is interpreted on words or on traces. For example the formula $\forall x \, \forall y \, (x \leq y \ \vee \ y \leq x)$ is not satisfied by any dependence graph which contains an anti-chain (i. e. a set of pairwise incomparable vertices), but it is always true in the word case, i. e. when $<$ is interpreted as a linear order. Our first result connects the logical definability of finitary word languages to the logical definability of finitary trace languages. By $\varphi : \Sigma^* \rightarrow \mathbb{M}(\Sigma, D)$ we denote the canonical homomorphism associating to a word the corresponding trace.

Theorem 10.10.2 *Let $A \subseteq \mathbb{M}(\Sigma, D)$ be a language of finite traces. Then the following holds:*

1. *The language A is definable in first order logic $\mathcal{L}_1(\Sigma, D)$ if and only if $\varphi^{-1}(A)$ is definable in first order logic $\mathcal{L}_1(\Sigma)$.*
2. *The language A is definable in second order logic $\mathcal{L}_2(\Sigma, D)$ if and only if $\varphi^{-1}(A)$ is definable in second order logic $\mathcal{L}_2(\Sigma)$.*

Proof: In both cases, it suffices to express the partial order on traces by the linear order on words and vice versa (in first-order logic).

"$\Rightarrow$": In the following we denote the linear order on words by $<_{lin}$. For the formula below note that if there is a path in the dependence graph from a vertex x to a vertex y, then there is also a path with distinct labellings (up to the fact that x and y may have the same labelling). $x < y$ if and only if

$$\bigvee_{\substack{1 \leq l \leq |\Sigma| \\ \text{with } (a_i, a_{i+1}) \in D \\ \text{for } 1 \leq i \leq l}} \bigvee_{a_1,\ldots,a_l,a_{l+1} \in \Sigma} \exists x_2 \ldots \exists x_l \Big(P_{a_1}(x) \wedge P_{a_2}(x_2) \wedge \ldots \wedge P_{a_l}(x_l) \wedge P_{a_{l+1}}(y) \wedge \\ x <_{lin} x_2 <_{lin} \ldots <_{lin} x_l <_{lin} y \Big) .$$

"$\Leftarrow$": In order to interpret a formula for words on traces, we view the trace t as one of its representing words, since the formula from $\mathcal{L}_1(\Sigma)$ or $\mathcal{L}_2(\Sigma)$ is satisfied either by all words w with $\varphi(w) = t$ or by none. As representing word we consider the lexicographic normal form of t. Given a linear ordering $<_\Sigma$ of Σ, the lexicographically first representing word $w \in \varphi^{-1}(t)$ is called the *lexicographic normal form* of t. A word $w \in \Sigma^*$ is the lexicographic normal form of $\varphi(w)$ if and only if for each factor aub of w with $a, b \in \Sigma$, $u \in \Sigma^*$, satisfying $(au, b) \in I$, it holds $a <_\Sigma b$ [7, 53].

Let x, y be vertices in the dependence graph of t and let $lex(x, y)$ denote the predicate which means that x is before y in the lexicographic normal form. Assume that $lex(x, y)$ holds and let $x_0 \cdots x_n$ correspond to the factor in the lexicographic normal form with $x_0 = x$ and $x_n = y$. Let i be minimal, $0 \leq i \leq n$, such that $x_i \leq y$ in the partial order. Then we have $(x_0 \cdots x_{i-1}, x_i) \in I$ and hence $\ell(x_0) \leq_\Sigma \ell(x_i)$. Therefore $lex(x, y)$ is equivalent with $\exists z \, (\ell(x) \leq_\Sigma \ell(z) \wedge z \leq y \wedge lex(x, z))$. This observation leads to a definition of $lex(x, y) = \bigvee_{a,b \in \Sigma} \big(P_a(x) \wedge P_b(y) \wedge lex_{a,b}(x, y) \big)$ where $lex_{a,b}(x, y)$ is defined recursively as

$$lex_{a,b}(x, y) = \begin{cases} x < y & \text{for } a = b , \\ \neg \, lex_{b,a}(y, x) & \text{for } a <_\Sigma b , \\ \exists z \Big(\bigvee_{c \geq_\Sigma a} \big(P_c(z) \wedge z \leq y \wedge lex_{a,c}(x, z) \big) \Big) & \text{for } a >_\Sigma b . \end{cases}$$

The recursion ends after at most $2 \cdot |\Sigma|$ rounds and and yields a first-order formula (of exponential size in $|\Sigma|$). The quantifier depth is bounded by $|\Sigma| - 1$. $\square$

Note that for words, monadic second-order definability is equivalent to recognizability [33, 262], and first-order definability is equivalent to star-freeness [166], which is equivalent to aperiodicity [249]. The family of *star-free* finitary trace languages $SF(M(\Sigma, D))$ is the closure of the sets $\{a\}$ ($a \in \Sigma$) by Boolean operations and concatenation and is equal to the set of aperiodic trace languages [129].

Corollary 10.10.3 *A trace language $A \subseteq M(\Sigma, D)$ is definable in monadic second-order logic $\mathcal{L}_2(\Sigma, D)$ if and only if it is recognizable.*

Corollary 10.10.4 *A trace language $A \subseteq M(\Sigma, D)$ is definable in first-order logic $\mathcal{L}_1(\Sigma, D)$ if and only if it is star-free.*

10.10.3   Equivalence of Recognizability and Monadic Second Order Logic for Finite and Infinite Traces

In the proof of the theorem above, the step from traces to words holds for any language of real traces. Since the lexicographic normal form is in general undefined for real traces, the step from words to traces can not be generalized directly to real traces. A different approach is needed to show the equivalence of recognizability and monadic second order logic definability for the family of real trace languages. We will use *c-rational trace languages* [205, 115]. The family of c-rational trace languages (Definition 11.7.31) is the closure of $\emptyset$ and the sets $\{a\}$ $(a \in \Sigma)$ by concatenation, union, $*$-iteration and ω-iteration, where iterations are restricted to connected c-rational trace languages (Corollary 11.7.24; for connectivity see Definition 6.3.5).

Theorem 10.10.5 *Let $A \subseteq \mathbb{R}(\Sigma, D)$ be a real trace language. Then A is recognizable if and only if it is definable in monadic second order logic $\mathcal{L}_2(\Sigma, D)$.*

Proof: The figure below sketches what we intend to show.

$$
\begin{array}{ccc}
 & \varphi^{-1}(A) \text{ is} & \overset{(Büchi)}{\Longleftrightarrow} & \varphi^{-1}(A) \text{ is} \\
 & \text{definable} & & \text{recog-} \\
A \text{ is} & \overset{(1)}{\Longrightarrow} \text{ in } \mathcal{L}_2(\Sigma) & & \text{nizable} \overset{Th. 11.7.4}{\Longleftrightarrow} \\
\text{definable} & & & & A \text{ is} \\
\text{in } \mathcal{L}_2(\Sigma, D) & & & & \text{recog-} \\
 & & & & \text{nizable} \\
 & \overset{(2)}{\Longleftarrow} & A \text{ is} & \overset{Th. 11.7.32}{\Longleftrightarrow} \\
 & & \text{c-rational}
\end{array}
$$

(1): See the the first part of the proof of Theorem 10.10.2.
(2): This implication is shown by induction over c-rational expressions. Since we deal simultaneously with finite and infinite traces, every formula states whether the satisfying traces are finite or not.

- Languages $\{a\}$ for $a \in \Sigma$: A formula stating that there is exactly one vertex, labelled by a.

- $A \cup B$ for c-rational sets A and B: Combine the formulae ψ_A and ψ_B for A and B to $\psi_{A \cup B} = \psi_A \vee \psi_B$.

- $A \cdot B$ for c-rational sets $A \subseteq \mathbb{M}(\Sigma, D)$ and $B \subseteq \mathbb{R}(\Sigma, D)$: For $\psi_{A \cdot B}$ we need formulae with restricted quantification. Let $\psi|_X$ for some set variable X be the formula ψ where we replace every subformula $\exists x \psi'$ by $\exists x \, (x \in X \wedge \psi')$, $\forall x \psi'$ by $\forall x \, (x \in X \rightarrow \psi')$, $\exists Y \psi'$ by $\exists Y \, (Y \subseteq X \wedge \psi')$, and $\forall Y \psi'$ by $\forall Y \, (Y \subseteq X \rightarrow \psi')$. The formula $\psi_{A \cdot B}$ is now given by

$$
\bigvee_{0 \leq k \leq |\Sigma|} \exists x_1 \dots \exists x_k \left(\psi_A|_{\{x| \underset{1 \leq i \leq k}{\wedge} \neg x_i \leq x\}} \wedge \psi_B|_{\{x| \underset{1 \leq i \leq k}{\vee} x_i \leq x\}} \right) ,
$$

where the variables $x_1, \dots, x_k$ cover the minimal elements of the suffix claimed to be in B.

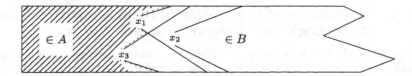

- A^*, A^ω for a connected c-rational set $A \subseteq \mathbb{M}(\Sigma, D)$: Let ψ_A denote the formula defining A and assume for convenience $1 \notin A$.

The formula below is based on a colouring of the vertices of the dependence graph of a factorization $t_1 \, t_2 \ldots$, such that every factor $t_i \in \mathbb{M}(\Sigma, D)$ is one-coloured and, if two different factors have the same colour, then there is no edge between them in the Hasse diagram. Two factors t_i, t_j will have the same colour only if they have the same alphabet, $\mathrm{alph}(t_i) = \mathrm{alph}(t_j)$. Hence, for every $\Sigma' \subseteq \Sigma$ we take two colours and colour alternatingly the factors t_i with the colours of $\Sigma' = \mathrm{alph}(t_i)$. (Note that factors with the same alphabet are totally ordered.)

We define ψ_{A^*} and ψ_{A^ω} as

$$\exists X_1 \ldots \exists X_k \, (\psi_1 \wedge \psi_2 \wedge \psi_3 \wedge \psi_4) \ ,$$

where $X_1, \ldots, X_k$ express the colouring mentioned above, with $k = 2 \cdot 2^{|\Sigma|}$.

Let ψ_1 be a formula stating that V is the disjoint union of all X_i. For the next two subformulae we define some abbreviations. By $mocs(X)$ we express that X is a "maximal one-coloured connected subgraph" of the Hasse diagram; formally, we define $mocs(X)$ as

$$\bigvee_{1 \leq i \leq k} \left(X \subseteq X_i \ \wedge \ \text{``}X \text{ is connected''} \right.$$
$$\left. \wedge \ \forall y \forall z \, \big((y \in X \wedge z \in X_i \wedge (z \, E \, y \vee y \, E \, z)) \to z \in X \big) \right),$$

where E is the edge relation of the Hasse diagram. The subformula "X is connected" simply states that for every $x, y \in X$ there is an undirected path between x and y, lying in X.

The formula ψ_2 ensures that every $mocs$-component is an element of A and is defined as

$$\forall X \, (mocs(X) \to \psi_A|_X) \ .$$

Note that since A is a finitary language, the $mocs$-components satisfying ψ_2 will be finite.

The underlying interpretation of the *mocs*-components is being factors of the given trace which belong to A. In order to ensure that the *mocs*-components can be ordered, thus corresponding to a factorization, we first define $X \prec Y$ as

$$\exists x \exists y \ (x \in X \land y \in Y \land x < y) \ .$$

The formula ψ_3 ensures that there are no cycles in the relation $\prec$ restricted to *mocs*-components. Note that cycles longer than $|\Sigma|$ can be shortened. Therefore we define ψ_3 as follows:

$$\neg \bigvee_{2 \leq l \leq |\Sigma|} \exists Y_1 \ldots \exists Y_l \Big(\bigwedge_{1 \leq i \leq l} mocs(Y_i) \ \land$$
$$Y_1 \prec Y_2 \land \ldots \land Y_{l-1} \prec Y_l \land Y_l \prec Y_1 \Big) \ .$$

Finally ψ_4 expresses whether the trace is finite or not, depending on the type of iteration (* or ω).

$\square$

Remark 10.10.6 In Theorem 10.10.2 we directly transform formulae on finite words to formulae on finite traces and vice versa. Note that this provides, together with Theorem 10.10.5, a new proof for Métivier's [195, Theorem 2.3] and Ochmański's [205, Lemma 8.2] result on the recognizability of the iteration of connected recognizable languages of finite traces (Prop. 6.3.11).

Remark 10.10.7 Theorem 10.10.5 can also be proved [90] using Büchi asynchronous (cellular) automata, first investigated by P. Gastin and A. Petit [113].

10.10.4 Equivalence of First Order Logic and Star-Free Expressions for Finite and Infinite Traces

We already introduced the family of *star-free* finitary trace languages $SF(\mathbb{M}(\Sigma, D))$ as the closure of singleton sets $\{a\}$ ($a \in \Sigma$) by Boolean operations and concatenation. The family $SF(\mathbb{R}(\Sigma, D))$ of *star-free real trace languages* is the closure of $SF(\mathbb{M}(\Sigma, D))$ by concatenation from the left with languages of $SF(\mathbb{M}(\Sigma, D))$ and by Boolean operations, where the complement is taken with respect to $\mathbb{R}(\Sigma, D)$.

We will consider formulae and languages with *free variables*. For a finite set W of variables we add to the structure $(V, <, \ell)$ a mapping $\sigma : W \to V$, associating every variable to a vertex in the dependence graph of the trace. Thus we obtain a new structure $(V, <, \ell, \sigma)$ of a trace with variables. If a trace has no variables, then the new structure $(V, <, \ell, \emptyset)$ can be identified with $(V, <, \ell)$. The sets $\mathbb{M}(\Sigma, D)$, $\mathbb{R}(\Sigma, D)$, A, B, ... with variables W are denoted by $\mathbb{M}_W$, $\mathbb{R}_W$, A_W, B_W, ...; a trace t with variable set W is denoted by t_W. Often we omit the subscript of a set A_W; we write W_t for the set of variables of $t \in \mathbb{R}_W$. Concatenation of traces with variables is defined only on traces with disjoint sets of variables. If $u = (V_u, <_u, \ell_u, \sigma_u)$ and $v = (V_v, <_v, \ell_v, \sigma_v)$ are traces with sets W_u, W_v of variables and $W_u \cap W_v = \emptyset$, then the dependence graph of the concatenation $t = uv = (V_t, <_t, \ell_t, \sigma_t)$ is defined as the usual concatenation of the two traces together with the mapping $\sigma_t = \sigma_u \cup \sigma_v$. The complement of a language $A_W \subseteq \mathbb{R}_W$ is taken with respect to $\mathbb{R}_W$.

The following lemma states some useful properties of star-free trace languages over the extended structures defined above. We define the left and right quotients $t^{-1}A$ and At^{-1} for $t \in \mathbb{R}_U$, $A \subseteq \mathbb{R}_W$ as $t^{-1}A = \{v \mid tv \in A\}$ and $At^{-1} = \{v \mid vt \in A\}$. Note that the partial monoid of real traces $\mathbb{R}$ is not cancellative: If uv, uv', vu, and $v'u$ are defined, we have $uv = uv' \Rightarrow v = v'$, but $vu = v'u$ does not imply $v = v'$. In particular it does not hold that $\{t\}t^{-1} = \{1\}$, for example $\{a^\omega\}(a^\omega)^{-1} = a^* \neq \{1\}$.

Lemma 10.10.8   *1. For any subalphabet $\Sigma' \subseteq \Sigma$ and finite variable set W, the languages $\{t \in \mathbb{M}_W \mid \mathrm{alph}(t) \subseteq \Sigma'\}$ and $\{t \in \mathbb{R}_W \mid \mathrm{alph}(t) \subseteq \Sigma'\}$ are star-free.*
  2. The left and right quotients $t^{-1}A$ and At^{-1} commute with $\cup$ and $\cap$. Moreover, for $t \in \mathbb{R}_U$ and $A \subseteq \mathbb{R}_W$ with $U \subseteq W$, we have $\overline{t^{-1}A} = t^{-1}\overline{A} \cup \{u \in \mathbb{R}_{W \setminus U} \mid tu \notin \mathbb{R}_W\}$ and $\overline{At^{-1}} = \overline{A}t^{-1} \cup \{u \in \mathbb{R}_{W \setminus U} \mid ut \notin \mathbb{R}_W\}$.
  3. Let $A \in \mathrm{SF}(\mathbb{R}_W)$ and $U \subseteq W$. Then the set of left (right) quotients $\{t^{-1}A \mid t \in \mathbb{R}_U\}$ $(\{At^{-1} \mid t \in \mathbb{R}_U\})$ is a finite subset of $\mathrm{SF}(\mathbb{R}_{W \setminus U})$.

Proof: 1: Obvious.

2: Note that for $u \in \mathbb{R}_{W \setminus U}$ we have $u \notin t^{-1}A$ if and only if either $tu \in \overline{A}$ or tu is not a real trace.

3: Let $A \in \mathrm{SF}(\mathbb{R}_W)$. The proof is given by induction on the star-free expression for A. We denote the number of different languages $t^{-1}A$ by n_A.

If $A = \{a\}$ for some $a \in \Sigma_W$, then $t^{-1}A = \{t^{-1}a\}$ and $n_A \leq 2$.

If $A = B \cup C$, then $\{t^{-1}(B \cup C) \mid t \in \mathbb{R}_U\} = \{t^{-1}B \cup t^{-1}C \mid t \in \mathbb{R}_U\} \subseteq \{t^{-1}B \cup t'^{-1}C \mid t, t' \in \mathbb{R}_U\}$ and $n_A \leq n_B \cdot n_C$ ($A = B \cap C$ analogously).

If $A = \overline{B}$, then with $t^{-1}\overline{B} = \overline{t^{-1}B} \setminus \{v \in \mathbb{R}_{W \setminus U} \mid D \cap \mathrm{alph}(v) \times \mathrm{alphinf}(t) \neq \emptyset\}$ we obtain $n_A \leq n_B \cdot 2^{|\Sigma|}$. (By $\mathrm{alphinf}(t)$ we denote the set of letters occurring infinitely often in t.)

If $A = BC$, then $t^{-1}(BC) = \bigcup_{rs=t}(r^{-1}B \cap F_s)(s^{-1}C)$, where $F_s = \{p \in \mathbb{R}_{W'} \mid (p, s) \in I, W' \subseteq W\}$, thus

$$\{t^{-1}(BC) \mid t \in \mathbb{R}_U\} = \{\bigcup_{rs=t}\underbrace{(\underbrace{r^{-1}B}_{\leq n_B} \cap \underbrace{F_s}_{\leq 2^{|\Sigma|}})}_{\leq n_B \cdot 2^{|\Sigma|}}\underbrace{(s^{-1}C)}_{\leq n_C} \mid t \in \mathbb{R}_U\},$$

and $n_A \leq 2^{n_B}\, 2^{|\Sigma|}\, n_C$.

Right quotients are treated symmetrically.

$\square$

Theorem 10.10.9 *A trace language $A \subseteq \mathbb{R}(\Sigma, D)$ is definable in first order logic $\mathcal{L}_1(\Sigma, D)$ if and only if it is star-free.*

Proof: "$\Leftarrow$": In order to construct logical formulae from star-free expressions, we replace the set operations by the corresponding logical operations. For concatenation we use the first order formula given in Theorem 10.10.5.

"$\Rightarrow$": We give a proof by induction on formulae.

Predicates: The set of infinite traces with a finite set of variables W satisfying $x < y$ for some variables $x, y \in W$, is the star-free trace language (we omit the subscripts for $\mathbb{M}, \mathbb{R}$)

$$\bigcup_{\text{finite}} \quad \bigcup_{\substack{a_1 \in \Sigma_X, a_l \in \Sigma_Y,\ x \in X,\ y \in Y \\ \text{with } (a_i, a_{i+1}) \in D \text{ for } 1 \leq i \leq l-1}} \mathbb{M}a_1\mathbb{M}\dots\mathbb{M}a_l\mathbb{R}\ .$$

Note that the variable sets omitted above form a partition of W and $l \leq |\Sigma|$.

The language with set of variables W satisfying $P_a(x)$ is $\bigcup_{\text{finite}} \mathbb{M}a\mathbb{R}$ with $x \in W_a$. For $x = y$ we have $\bigcup_{\text{finite}} \bigcup_{\substack{a \in \Sigma_w \\ x,y \in W}} \mathbb{M}a\mathbb{R}$.

Induction step: For $\wedge, \vee, \neg$ we use the corresponding set theoretical operations. Finally, for quantified formulae, if $A \in \mathrm{SF}(\mathbb{R})$ is a language defined by ψ and $x \in W_A$, then we can represent A as [224]

$$A = \bigcup_{\substack{a \in \Sigma,\ ua \in \mathbb{R} \\ x \in W_a}} B(u)\, a\, C(u)$$

with

$$C(u) = (ua)^{-1}A, \quad B(u) = \bigcap_{v \in C(u)} A(av)^{-1}\ .$$

By Lemma 10.10.8 the union in the expression for A is finite. Finally, the language defined by the formula $\exists x \psi$ is

$$A' = \bigcup_{ua \in \mathbb{R}} B(u)\, a\, C(u)$$

with $W_{A'} = W_A \setminus \{x\}$.

$\square$

Similar to the result of Thomas [261] and of Perrin and Pin [224], this can be generalized to embed a hierarchy of first order formulae, where the alternations of negation and existential quantification are counted, between two hierarchies of star-free languages, where the alternations of complementation and concatenation are counted [90].

10.10.5 Notes

Monadic second order logic on traces has been first investigated by Thomas [263] using an automata-theoretic approach [262, for example]. These results have been generalized to infinite traces and extended to the first order case [90, 91]. Independently, the first order case has also been considered by Thomas and Zielonka (personal communication).

In the present appendix we have used single traces as underlying structures instead of trace structures as in the other parts of this chapter. This yields the decidability of the logic as an immediate consequence of decidability in the word case, shown by Büchi [33, 262]. This appendix does not deal with temporal logic. A temporal logic based on single traces as underlying structures has been proposed in [90]. As a main result about this logic it is shown there that for finite traces definability in this new logic is equivalent with definability in first order logic.

V GENERALIZATIONS

Chapter 11

P. Gastin, A. Petit
Infinite Traces

Chapter 12

M. Clerbout, M. Latteux, Y. Roos
Semi-Commutations

Chapter 11

Infinite Traces

Paul Gastin

Institut Blaise Pascal, LITP
4, place Jussieu
75252 Paris Cédex 05, France
gastin@litp.ibp.fr

Antoine Petit

ENS Cachan, LIFAC
61 av. President Wilson
94235 Cachan Cedex, France
petit@lifac.ens-cachan.fr

Contents

11.1   Introduction

Finite traces were introduced by A. Mazurkiewicz as a semantic model for non-sequential processes. The motivation for an infinitary extension of traces is twofold.

First, some non-sequential systems are not designed to terminate, e.g. distributed operating systems. In order to abstract their behaviors, the notion of infinite traces is clearly needed. Since an infinite behavior may be seen as the *limit* of a sequence of finite behaviors, the set of infinite traces has to be the *completion* of the set of finite traces. In other words, each infinite trace must be the limit of a sequence of finite traces and, conversely, each "good" sequence of finite traces must converge to an infinite trace.

Second, some programming structures do not admit convenient semantics within the monoid of finite traces. For instance, behaviors of recursive programs are frequently described by solutions of fix-point equations of the form $x = f(x)$. Depending on the mapping f, different techniques may be used to obtain these fix-points.

- Assume first that the mapping f is non decreasing with respect to some partial order on the semantic domain. Iterating the mapping f starting from the least element $\perp$ of the semantic domain, we obtain a non decreasing sequence $(f^n(\perp))_{n \geq 0}$. If the mapping f is continuous and if the semantic domain is complete with respect to this partial order, this non decreasing sequence admits a least upper bound which is the least fix-point of f.

- Assume now that the mapping f is contracting with respect to some metric on the semantic domain. The sequence $(f^n(x))_{n \geq 0}$ is Cauchy for any starting point x. If the semantic domain is complete as a metric space, this sequence converges to the unique fix-point of f.

For both techniques, complete semantic domains are needed. Unfortunately, the set of finite traces is not complete, neither with respect to the prefix order nor with respect to any semantically satisfactory metric (see Section 11.5.3). Therefore, both an order and a metric completion of the set of finite traces must be introduced. This gives rise to different notions of infinite traces.

The order completion of the set of finite traces defines the set of infinite *real* traces where a real trace may be identified with an ideal (a prefix-closed and directed set) of finite traces (see Sections 11.2 and 11.3). Note that, when a semantic domain is not complete, fix-point equations are frequently solved in the power set of the domain. Solutions are then directed sets which may be identified with elements of the order completion of the domain. Hence, the two approaches (solving fix-point equations in the power set of a semantic domain on one hand, and in the order completion of the domain on the other hand) are closely related. From this point of view, infinite real traces may simply be seen as convenient abstractions of directed sets of finite traces.

Unfortunately, no metric on the set of real traces is fully satisfactory. In order to obtain a *good* metric completion of the set of finite traces, a slight generalization of real traces, namely complex traces, was introduced by V. Diekert (see Sections 11.4 and 11.5).

In this chapter, we also introduce transfinite traces as transfinite generalizations of dependence graphs (see Chapter 2). The semantic motivation for transfinite traces may seem more difficult. This is due to the implicit assumption that there is a positive lower bound to the execution time of all actions. If this restriction is removed, an infinite process may be executed within a finite amount of time. For instance, being inspired by oscillating mechanisms, one may consider an infinite process where each step takes half the time taken by the previous step. Such a process terminates within a finite amount of time and may be followed by another activity. The set of transfinite traces is the natural semantic domain for such situations. Apart from this semantic motivation, transfinite traces are also useful because they allow a uniform framework for the definition of both real and complex traces. Indeed, the set of real traces is embedded in the set of transfinite traces while the set of complex traces is a quotient of the set of transfinite traces.

Real and transfinite traces are defined in Section 11.2. Their basic properties are also investigated in this section. The set of transfinite traces equipped with a natural concatenation forms a left-cancellative monoid. On the other hand, the set of real traces is only a partial monoid since the concatenation of two real traces may give a transfinite (non-real) trace. As a basic tool, products of infinite (and even transfinite) sequences of traces are defined. In particular, these products allow us to relate infinite words and infinite traces and to state a Foata normal form theorem for infinite traces.

In Section 11.3, we study the properties of the sets of real traces and of transfinite traces with respect to the prefix order. We are mainly interested in the *completeness* and the *algebraicity* of these posets (partially ordered sets). More precisely, we prove that the set of real traces is coherently complete (every coherent set of real traces admits a least upper bound) whereas the set of transfinite traces is only bounded complete (every bounded set of transfinite traces admits a least upper bound). Moreover, we show that the set of real traces and the set of transfinite traces are both algebraic: every real trace (transfinite trace resp.) is the least upper bound of a set of compact real traces (compact transfinite traces resp.). Finally, we prove that a real trace is compact if and only if it is a finite trace. Altogether, this shows that the set of real traces is a Scott domain which is precisely the prefix order completion of the set of finite traces.

As it turns out, however, the set of real traces is not fully satisfactory with respect to the concatenation which is only partially defined. Moreover, although the set of real traces may be provided with metrics which make it a complete metric space, the concatenation (even restricted to finite traces) is not continuous for these metrics. Complex traces are introduced in order to obtain a metric completion of the set of finite traces equipped with a uniformly continuous concatenation.

In Section 11.4, the monoid of complex traces is defined as a quotient of the monoid of transfinite traces by a suitable congruence. Basic properties of the concatenation and of infinite products on complex traces are investigated. In fact, complex traces are simply a slight generalization of real traces: the set of real traces is embedded in the set of complex traces and a complex trace may be identified with a real trace together with an alphabetic information.

The topological properties of complex traces are studied in Section 11.5. The set of complex traces equipped with a natural ultrametric is a complete and compact metric space. For the topology induced by this metric, the set of finite traces is an open, discrete and dense subset of the set of complex traces. Moreover, the concatenation on complex traces is uniformly continuous. In other words, the set of complex traces is the metric completion of the set of finite traces and the concatenation on complex traces is the unique continuous extension of the concatenation on finite traces.

Among all the infinite trace languages describing the behaviors of non-sequential systems, rational and recognizable languages play a central role. Indeed, as in any monoid used as a semantic domain, rational languages describe the behaviors of systems which can be built in a modular way from a finite set of very simple systems. On the other hand, recognizable languages represent the behaviors of finite state systems. Recall that in the case of word languages (i.e. in the case of sequential systems), Kleene's and Büchi's theorems state that the two families coincide: a word language is rational if and only if it is recognizable. Concerning finite traces (i.e. in the case of finite non-sequential systems), the family of recognizable languages is included in the family of rational languages. Moreover, the inclusion is strict as soon as the independence relation is not empty. Nevertheless, Ochmański's theorem (Chapter 6) asserts that a language of finite traces is recognizable if and only if it is concurrent rational. The remainder of this Chapter is devoted to the study of the families of rational and recognizable infinite trace languages and in particular to a generalization of Kleene's, Büchi's and Ochmański's theorems to infinite trace languages.

In Section 11.6, we introduce and study the rational languages of infinite traces. Formally, the family of rational languages is defined as the smallest family which contains the finite sets of finite traces and which is closed under union, concatenation, $*$-iteration and ω-iteration. Depending on the concatenation and the ω-product used, either the family of rational real trace languages or the family of rational complex trace languages is obtained. The main results of this section are normal forms for rational sets of real traces and of complex traces. We also give the links between rational real trace languages and rational word languages on one hand and between rational complex trace languages and rational real trace languages on the other hand. Apart from these characterizations, we prove that the intersection, the left quotient and the right quotient of a rational set by a recognizable set are rational too.

We introduce and study in Section 11.7 the family of recognizable languages of real traces. These languages are defined by extending in a natural way the definition of recognizable word languages using recognizing morphisms. We prove that the family of recognizable real trace languages is closed under union, intersection, complement and (real) concatenation. These results together with the closure by iterations restricted to connected languages yield a normal form theorem for recognizable real trace languages. Next, finite and infinite concurrent iterations on real trace languages are defined. It turns out that the family of recognizable real trace languages is closed under these new operations. Then the main result of this section states that the family of recognizable real trace languages coincides with the family of concurrent rational real trace languages. This last family is defined as the family of rational real trace languages by simply replacing the classical iterations by their concurrent versions. Besides, we prove that the family of recognizable real trace languages is closed under left and right quotients by arbitrary real trace languages.

Finally, we deal with recognizable complex trace languages in Section 11.8. First we give the links between recognizable real trace languages and recognizable complex trace languages. We then prove that the family of recognizable complex trace languages is closed under union, intersection, complement, concatenation, quotients by arbitrary languages and iterations restricted to connected languages. Next, we obtain a normal form theorem for recognizable complex trace languages which generalizes the corresponding result on recognizable real trace languages. Finally, we extend Kleene's and Büchi's theorems on words and Ochmański's theorem on finite traces by proving that the family of recognizable complex trace languages coincides with the family of concurrent rational complex trace languages, i.e. the smallest family of complex trace languages which contains the finite sets of finite traces and which is closed under union, concatenation, finite and infinite concurrent iterations.

11.2 Real and Transfinite Traces

In this section, we introduce *real* and *transfinite* traces which are infinitary generalizations of finite traces. Although it would be possible to introduce directly an equivalence relation on ω-words (transfinite words resp.) in order to define real traces (transfinite traces resp.), we prefer to use the framework of dependence graphs (see Chapter 2). This approach provides a much more natural extension of finite traces and allows to define uniformly real traces, transfinite traces and complex traces (defined in Section 11.4).

The notion of ordinal will be extensively used throughout. We refer to [237] for a complete course on ordinals. In fact, we will use very few results from ordinal theory. Mainly, we will use ordinals to number sequences. In order to fix notations, we recall that the finite ordinals are the natural numbers, the first non-finite ordinal is denoted by ω and the first non-countable ordinal is denoted by $\aleph_1$.

11.2.1   Definition

Let Σ be a finite alphabet and let $D \subseteq \Sigma \times \Sigma$ be a reflexive and symmetric relation over Σ, called the dependence relation. Its complement $I = \Sigma \times \Sigma \setminus D$ is the independence relation. The pair (Σ, D) is called the dependence alphabet. Throughout this chapter, we will depict a dependence alphabet by its graph (without reflexive edges). For instance, the dependence alphabet (Σ, D) defined by $\Sigma = \{a, b, c, d, e\}$ and $D = \{(a, a), (b, b), (c, c), (d, d), (e, e), (a, b), (b, a), (b, c), (c, b), (d, e), (e, d)\}$ will be represented by the following graph:

$$(\Sigma, D) = a \text{\textemdash\textemdash} b \text{\textemdash\textemdash} c \qquad d \text{\textemdash\textemdash} e$$

Throughout this section, all examples will be given with respect to this dependence alphabet.

A dependence graph will be defined as an isomorphism class of labelled directed graphs. Recall that two labelled graphs $[V_1, E_1, \lambda_1]$ and $[V_2, E_2, \lambda_2]$ are said to be isomorphic if there exists a bijection $\xi : V_1 \longrightarrow V_2$ between their sets of vertices which preserves the edges $((p, q) \in E_1 \iff (\xi(p), \xi(q)) \in E_2)$ and the labelling $(\lambda_1(p) = \lambda_2(\xi(p)))$. For the sake of simplicity, we will often identify a concrete labelled graph and its isomorphism class.

Definition 11.2.1 *A dependence graph over the dependence alphabet (Σ, D) is an isomorphism class of labelled directed acyclic graphs $[V, E, \lambda]$, where the set V of vertices is countable, $E \subseteq V \times V$ is the set of edges, $\lambda : V \to \Sigma$ is the labelling function and it holds*

- *edges are between dependent vertices: for all $p, q \in V$,*

$$(\lambda(p), \lambda(q)) \in D \iff p = q \text{ or } (p, q) \in E \text{ or } (q, p) \in E$$

- *the induced partial order $\preceq = E^*$ (the reflexive and transitive closure of the edge relation E) is well-founded: there is no infinite strictly decreasing sequence of vertices $p_0 \succ p_1 \succ p_2 \succ \cdots$*

The set of dependence graphs is denoted by $\mathbb{G}(\Sigma, D)$, or simply by $\mathbb{G}$. A dependence graph is also called a (transfinite) trace. The set of finite dependence graphs (finite traces) is denoted by $\mathbb{M}(\Sigma, D)$, or simply by $\mathbb{M}$.

This is a very natural generalization of the definition of finite dependence graphs presented in Chapter 2. We simply allow the set of vertices to be countable and we require in addition that the reflexive and transitive closure of the edge relation is

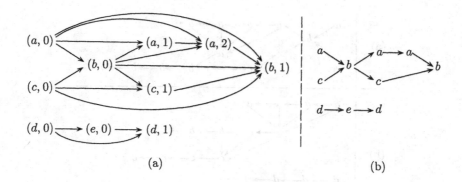

(a)   (b)

Figure 11.1: A *finite* dependence graph

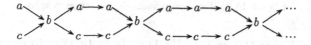

Figure 11.2: A *real* dependence graph

well-founded. This restriction ensures that every dependence graph admits a finite set of initial actions.

Moreover, for each dependence graph $g = [V, E, \lambda]$ and each letter $a \in \Sigma$, this last restriction implies that the set $V_a = \lambda^{-1}(a) = \{p \in V \mid \lambda(p) = a\}$ of vertices with label a is a *well-ordered* subset of V, i.e., the restriction of the induced partial order $\preceq$ to V_a is a well-founded *total* order. We denote by $|g|_a$ the number of occurrences of a in g, i.e., $|g|_a$ is the countable ordinal associated with the well-ordered set V_a. Hence, every dependence graph g admits a standard representation where its set of vertices is $V = \{(a, i) \mid a \in \Sigma \text{ and } i < |g|_a\}$ and the labelling is trivially defined by $\lambda((a, i)) = a$ for all $(a, i) \in V$.

For instance, the standard representation of a finite dependence graph is presented in Figure 11.1 (a). Since a dependence graph is an isomorphism class of graphs, we will only write the labels of the vertices. Still in order to simplify the pictures, we will not necessarily draw the edges which can be obtained by composition of other edges. Using these remarks, the dependence graph of Figure 11.1 (a) can be simply presented by its *Hasse diagram* as in Figure 11.1 (b). Finally, three infinite dependence graphs are presented in Figures 11.2 and 11.3.

Let $g = [V, E, \lambda]$ be a dependence graph and $p \in V$ be a vertex of g. The *past* of p for the induced partial order $\preceq = E^*$ is the set $\downarrow_g p = \{q \in V \mid q \preceq p\}$. When no confusion may arise, the past of p will be simply denoted by $\downarrow p$. For instance,

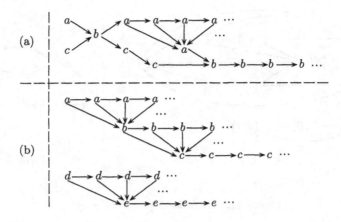

Figure 11.3: Two *transfinite* dependence graphs

in the graph of Figure 11.1 we have $\downarrow(a,1) = \{(a,0),(a,1),(b,0),(c,0)\}$. Note that the infinite graph of Figure 11.2 satisfies a stronger property than merely the well-foundedness of its induced partial order: all its vertices have a finite past. On the other hand, in the graph of Figure 11.3 (b), the vertices labelled by b, c or e have an infinite past. This important remark leads to the following definition.

Definition 11.2.2 *Let* $g = [V,E,\lambda] \in \mathbb{G}(\Sigma,D)$ *be a dependence graph.*

The real part $\mathrm{Re}(g)$ *and the* transfinite part $\mathrm{Tr}(g)$ *of* g *are the restrictions of the graph* g *to the sets of vertices* $\{p \in V \mid \downarrow p \text{ is finite}\}$ *and* $\{p \in V \mid \downarrow p \text{ is infinite}\}$ *respectively.*

A real trace *(or* real *dependence graph) is a dependence graph with an empty transfinite part. The set of real traces will be denoted by* $\mathbb{R}(\Sigma,D)$, *or simply by* $\mathbb{R}$.

The alphabet *of* g, $\mathrm{alph}(g) = \lambda(V)$, *is the set of letters which occur in* g. *The* alphabet at infinity *of* g *is* $\mathrm{alphinf}(g) = \{a \in \Sigma \mid \lambda^{-1}(a) \text{ is infinite}\} \cup \mathrm{alph}(\mathrm{Tr}(g))$.

Note that $\mathrm{Re}(g)$ and $\mathrm{Tr}(g)$ are dependence graphs. Moreover, $\mathrm{Re}(g)$ is clearly a real trace. This is a direct consequence of the following easy fact.

Remark 11.2.3 The restriction of a dependence graph $g = [V,E,\lambda]$ to any subset of V is a dependence graph too.

For instance, the graphs of Figures 11.1 and 11.2 are real whereas the graphs of Figure 11.3 are not real. Their real parts and transfinite parts are presented in Figure 11.4. The alphabets of the graphs of Figures 11.1–11.3 are respectively Σ, $\{a,b,c\}$, $\{a,b,c\}$ and Σ. Their alphabets at infinity are respectively $\emptyset$, $\{a,b,c\}$, $\{a,b\}$ and Σ.

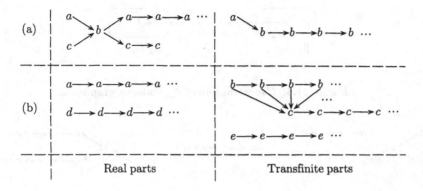

Figure 11.4: *Real* and *transfinite* parts

We end this subsection with some semantic considerations concerning real and non-real dependence graphs. A very natural point of view in computer science is to assume that there exist a uniform lower bound and a uniform upper bound on the execution time of all actions. Then real graphs are exactly those graphs in which each action may be executed within a finite amount of time. This is probably the main reason for which real traces may be considered as the most semantically significant infinite traces. Moreover, we will see throughout the chapter that real traces possess very good properties.

Therefore, one may wonder why we do not restrict ourselves to the study of real traces. There are in fact three main reasons for this. First, we will see in the next subsection that only a partial concatenation is defined on real traces. Hence, the algebraic structure of transfinite traces or complex traces (defined in Section 11.4) is more satisfactory. Second, as shown in Section 11.5, the monoid of complex traces is the topological completion of the monoid of finite traces for a very natural ultrametric. Note that there is no metric for which a similar result holds for real traces. Third, if we do not assume the existence of the uniform lower bound, transfinite traces admit a good semantic interpretation too. Namely, in such a case, infinitely many actions may be performed within a finite amount of time. Therefore, actions with an infinite past may be executed and it is then natural to consider the non-real dependence graphs as transfinite traces.

11.2.2 Concatenation

In this subsection, we first define the concatenation of transfinite traces (or dependence graphs). Then we derive the partial concatenation of real traces and study properties of these products. Informally, the concatenation of two graphs g_1 and g_2 is their disjoint union together with new arcs from g_1 to g_2 (see Figure 11.5).

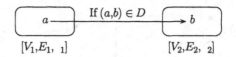

$$[V_1, E_1, \ _1] \qquad\qquad\qquad [V_2, E_2, \ _2]$$

Figure 11.5: *Concatenation* of dependence graphs

$$
\begin{array}{l}
a\searrow \\
\quad\searrow b \nearrow \quad a\longrightarrow a\longrightarrow a \cdots \\
c\nearrow \quad\searrow c
\end{array}
\qquad
\begin{array}{l}
c\longrightarrow c\longrightarrow c \cdots
\end{array}
\quad = \quad
\begin{array}{l}
a\searrow \\
\quad\searrow b \nearrow \quad a\longrightarrow a\longrightarrow a \cdots \\
c\nearrow \quad\searrow c\longrightarrow c\longrightarrow c \cdots
\end{array}
$$

Figure 11.6: *Concatenation* of two real traces

Definition 11.2.4 *Let $g_1 = [V_1, E_1, \lambda_1]$ and $g_2 = [V_2, E_2, \lambda_2]$ be two dependence graphs with $V_1 \cap V_2 = \emptyset$. The concatenation $g_1 \cdot g_2 = [V, E, \lambda]$ is defined by*

$$
\begin{aligned}
V &= V_1 \cup V_2 \\
E &= E_1 \cup E_2 \cup \{(p_1, p_2) \in V_1 \times V_2 \mid (\lambda_1(p_1), \lambda_2(p_2)) \in D\} \\
\lambda &= \lambda_1 \cup \lambda_2
\end{aligned}
$$

For instance, the concatenation of two real traces is presented in Figure 11.6.

It is easy to verify that the concatenation is an associative operation in $\mathbb{G}$ and that the empty graph $\mathbf{1} = [\emptyset, \emptyset, \emptyset]$ is the unity. Hence $(\mathbb{G}, \cdot)$ is a monoid.

As usual, a prefix relation, denoted by $\leq$, is associated with the concatenation:

$$f \leq h \text{ if and only if } h = f \cdot g \text{ for some } g \in \mathbb{G}.$$

This prefix relation admits the following useful characterization.

Proposition 11.2.5 *A trace $f \in \mathbb{G}(\Sigma, D)$ is a prefix of a trace $h \in \mathbb{G}(\Sigma, D)$ if and only if f is a downward closed subgraph of h.*

Proof: The 'only if' part is clear. Conversely, for each dependence graph $g \in \mathbb{G}$, we denote by V_g, E_g and λ_g the set of vertices, the set of edges and the labelling function of g respectively. Let $f \in \mathbb{G}$ be a downward closed subgraph of $h \in \mathbb{G}$, i.e., $V_f = \downarrow_h V_f$, $E_f = E_h \cap (V_f \times V_f)$ and $\lambda_f = \lambda_{h|V_f}$. Let $g \in \mathbb{G}$ be the restriction of h to $V_g = V_h \setminus V_f$. Since V_f is downward closed, there is no edge in h from V_g to V_f. Hence, for $(p, q) \in V_f \times V_g$ we have

$$(p, q) \in E_h \quad \Longleftrightarrow \quad (\lambda(p), \lambda(q)) \in D \quad \Longleftrightarrow \quad (p, q) \in E_{f \cdot g}$$

which proves that $h = f \cdot g$. $\qquad\qquad\qquad\qquad\qquad\qquad\qquad\qquad\qquad\qquad\qquad\square$

Using Proposition 11.2.5 we deduce that, for every dependence graph g, the real part $\mathrm{Re}(g)$ is a prefix of g. Clearly the corresponding suffix is the transfinite part of g. Therefore, every dependence graph g is the concatenation of its real part by its transfinite part (see for instance Figures 11.3 and 11.4):

$$g = \mathrm{Re}(g) \cdot \mathrm{Tr}(g)$$

Note that the concatenation is an internal operation in the set $\mathbf{M}$ of finite traces (finite dependence graphs) which is therefore a submonoid of $\mathbb{G}$. This is not true for real traces. For instance, the two graphs of Figure 11.4 (a) are real but their concatenation is the non real graph of Figure 11.3 (a). Hence the set $\mathbb{R}$ of real traces is not a submonoid of $\mathbb{G}$. Nevertheless, the concatenation of two real traces may also be real (Figure 11.6). The following easy characterization will be useful.

Remark 11.2.6 The concatenation of two real traces g_1 and g_2 is real if and only if $\mathrm{alphinf}(g_1) \times \mathrm{alph}(g_2) \subseteq I$.

The fact that the set $\mathbb{R}$ of real traces is not a monoid for the very natural concatenation of Definition 11.2.4 explains why we consider transfinite dependence graphs and not simply real ones. Nevertheless, the concatenation on $\mathbb{G}$ induces a partial concatenation on $\mathbb{R}$. Whenever ambiguous, we denote the concatenation on $\mathbb{G}$ by $\cdot_{\mathbb{G}}$ and the concatenation on $\mathbb{R}$ by $\cdot_{\mathbb{R}}$.

Definition 11.2.7 *The partial concatenation $\cdot_{\mathbb{R}}$ on $\mathbb{R}$ is defined for two real traces r and s by*

$$r \cdot_{\mathbb{R}} s = \begin{cases} r \cdot_{\mathbb{G}} s & \text{if } r \cdot_{\mathbb{G}} s \in \mathbb{R} \\ \text{undefined} & \text{otherwise} \end{cases}$$

It is also possible to define this concatenation on $\mathbb{R}$ using a *Rees-quotient* of the monoid $(\mathbb{G}, \cdot_{\mathbb{G}})$ of transfinite traces. Clearly, the set $\mathcal{I} = \mathbb{G} \setminus \mathbb{R}$ of non-real traces is an *ideal* for the concatenation $\cdot_{\mathbb{G}}$ in $\mathbb{G}$: the left- or right-concatenation of a non-real trace by any dependence graph is a non-real trace too. Hence the *Rees-quotient* of the monoid $\mathbb{G}$ of dependence graphs by the ideal $\mathcal{I}$ of non-real traces, $\mathbb{G}/\mathcal{I} = \mathbb{R} \cup \{\mathbf{0}\}$, is a monoid. Since $\mathbf{0}$ stands for all non-real traces, this yields precisely the concatenation of Definition 11.2.7, apart from the fact that *undefined* is denoted by $\mathbf{0}$.

We turn now to the study of some properties of the monoid $(\mathbb{G}, \cdot_{\mathbb{G}})$ of transfinite traces and of the partial monoid $(\mathbb{R}, \cdot_{\mathbb{R}})$ of real traces. We first prove that $(\mathbb{G}, \cdot_{\mathbb{G}})$ is left-cancellative and right-cancellative by finite traces. Note that, as a direct corollary, the same results hold for the partial monoid $(\mathbb{R}, \cdot_{\mathbb{R}})$ of real traces if we assume that all products are well-defined.

Proposition 11.2.8 *Let $r, s, t \in \mathbb{G}(\Sigma, D)$ be traces.*

- If $r \cdot s = r \cdot t$, then $s = t$.

- If $s \cdot r = t \cdot r$ and r is finite, then $s = t$.

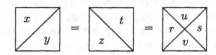

Figure 11.7: *Levi's Lemma* for real traces

Proof: We only prove the left-cancellativity. The proof of the right-cancellativity
is similar. For each dependence graph $g \in \mathbb{G}$, we denote by V_g, E_g, λ_g and $\preceq_g$ the
set of vertices, the set of edges, the labelling function and the induced partial order
of g respectively. We may assume that $V_r \cap V_s = V_r \cap V_t = \emptyset$. Since $r \cdot s = r \cdot t$,
there exists an isomorphism ξ between $[V_{r \cdot s}, E_{r \cdot s}, \lambda_{r \cdot s}]$ and $[V_{r \cdot t}, E_{r \cdot t}, \lambda_{r \cdot t}]$, that is,
a bijection ξ from $V_{r \cdot s} = V_r \cup V_s$ to $V_{r \cdot t} = V_r \cup V_t$ which preserves the edges
$((p, q) \in E_{r \cdot s} \iff (\xi(p), \xi(q)) \in E_{r \cdot t})$ and the labelling $(\lambda_{r \cdot s}(p) = \lambda_{r \cdot t}(\xi(p)))$. In
order to prove that $s = t$ we will show that the restriction of ξ to V_s induces an
isomorphism between $[V_s, E_s, \lambda_s]$ and $[V_t, E_t, \lambda_t]$.

First, we claim that the restriction of ξ to V_r is the identity. We proceed by
induction on the well-founded set $(V_r, \preceq_r)$. Let $p \in V_r$ and assume that $\forall q \prec_r$
$p, \xi(q) = q$. Since ξ preserves the labelling, p and $\xi(p)$ in $r \cdot t$ on one hand and p and
$\xi^{-1}(p)$ in $r \cdot s$ on the other hand must be ordered. Using the induction hypothesis
and the injectivity of ξ, we deduce that $p \preceq_{r \cdot t} \xi(p)$ and $p \preceq_{r \cdot s} \xi^{-1}(p)$. Since ξ
preserves the edges, the last inequality implies that $\xi(p) \preceq_{r \cdot t} p$. Hence, we obtain
$\xi(p) = p$ and the claim is proved.

Let ζ be the restriction of ξ to V_s. Using the claim above, we deduce that ζ is
a bijection from V_s onto V_t. Then, for all $p, q \in V_s$, we have

$$\lambda_s(p) = \lambda_{r \cdot s}(p) = \lambda_{r \cdot t}(\xi(p)) = \lambda_t(\zeta(p))$$

$$(p, q) \in E_s \iff (p, q) \in E_{r \cdot s} \iff (\xi(p), \xi(q)) \in E_{r \cdot t} \iff (\zeta(p), \zeta(q)) \in E_t$$

That is, ζ preserves the edges and the labelling.   □

Remark 11.2.9 From this proposition, we deduce that if a trace $r \in \mathbb{G}$ is a prefix
of a trace $t \in \mathbb{G}$, that is, if there exists a trace $s \in \mathbb{G}$ such that $t = r \cdot s$, then this
suffix s is unique and will be denoted by $r^{-1} \cdot t$ throughout the chapter.

We end this subsection with a characterization of the solutions of the equation
$x \cdot y = z \cdot t$ in the monoid $(\mathbb{G}, \cdot_\mathbb{G})$ of transfinite traces. Again the same result
holds in the monoid $(\mathbb{R}, \cdot_\mathbb{R})$ of real traces if we assume that both products are well-
defined. This important result generalizes to traces Levi's classical Lemma on the
free monoid Σ^* (see also Example 2.3.11, Theorem 2.3.10, and Proposition 4.2.14).

Proposition 11.2.10 Let $x, y, z, t \in \mathbb{G}(\Sigma, D)$ be such that $x \cdot y = z \cdot t$. Then, there
exist four traces $r, u, v, s \in \mathbb{G}(\Sigma, D)$ such that

$$x = r \cdot u, \quad y = v \cdot s, \quad z = r \cdot v, \quad t = u \cdot s$$

and

$$\text{alph}(u) \times \text{alph}(v) \subseteq I$$

Proof: As in the proof above, for each dependence graph $g \in \mathbb{G}$, we denote by V_g, E_g and λ_g the set of vertices, the set of edges and the labelling function of g respectively. Let $[V, E, \lambda]$ be the graph $x \cdot y = z \cdot t$. By definition, the graphs x, y, z and t are subgraphs of $[V, E, \lambda]$. Hence the set V admits two partitions $V = V_x \cup V_y = V_z \cup V_t$. Let r, u, v, s be the restrictions of $[V, E, \lambda]$ to $V_r = V_x \cap V_z$, $V_u = V_x \cap V_t$, $V_v = V_y \cap V_z$ and $V_s = V_y \cap V_t$ respectively (see Figure 11.7). By Remark 11.2.3, we have $r, u, v, s \in \mathbb{G}$. We claim that

$$x = r \cdot u, \quad y = v \cdot s, \quad z = r \cdot v, \quad t = u \cdot s$$

We only prove that $x = r \cdot u$. The other cases are similar. Considering the definitions of r and u, it is enough to verify that the edges between V_r and V_u are the same in the graphs $r \cdot u$ and x. Let $p \in V_r$ and $q \in V_u$. Since $p \in V_z$, $q \in V_t$ and $z \cdot t = x \cdot y$, there is no edge from q to p in the graph of x. Hence,

$$(p, q) \in E_{r \cdot u} \iff (\lambda(p), \lambda(q)) \in D \iff (p, q) \in E \iff (p, q) \in E_x$$

Finally, since $x \cdot y = z \cdot t$, there is no edge from V_y to V_x nor from V_t to V_z. Hence, there is no edge between V_u and V_v, which implies that $\text{alph}(u) \times \text{alph}(v) \subseteq I$. $\square$

Note that, in the proposition above, the traces r, u, v, s are uniquely determined. The proof of this fact is left to the reader.

11.2.3 Infinite Products

We generalize the definitions and results of the previous subsection to infinite products. When we deal with an infinitary extension of a monoid of finite objects, infinite products arise very naturally. They allow to describe the infinite objects by means of infinite products of finite objects. In the case of ω-words, we use the classical ω-product. When we consider infinite traces, the ω-product of a sequence of finite traces always results in a real trace (Remark 11.2.13). In order to generate all transfinite traces of $\mathbb{G}$ as infinite products of finite traces, we need to consider α-products where α is any countable ordinal. Readers who are interested in real traces only may restrict α to be at most ω throughout the end of this section.

Definition 11.2.11 *Let α be a countable ordinal and let $g_i = [V_i, E_i, \lambda_i] \in \mathbb{G}(\Sigma, D)$ be a dependence graph for each $i < \alpha$. We may assume that $V_i \cap V_j = \emptyset$ for all $i < j < \alpha$. The α-product of the α-sequence $(g_i)_{i<\alpha}$ is the dependence graph $\prod_{i<\alpha} g_i = [V, E, \lambda]$ where*

$$
\begin{aligned}
V &= \bigcup_{i<\alpha} V_i \\
E &= \left(\bigcup_{i<\alpha} E_i\right) \cup \{(p, q) \in V_i \times V_j \mid i < j < \alpha \text{ and } (\lambda_i(p), \lambda_j(q)) \in D\} \\
\lambda &= \bigcup_{i<\alpha} \lambda_i
\end{aligned}
$$

The α-power of the trace $g \in \mathbb{G}(\Sigma, D)$ is $g^\alpha = \prod_{i<\alpha} g$.

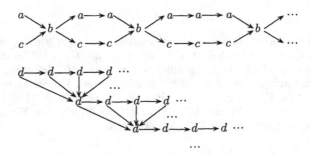

Figure 11.8: An $(\omega \cdot 3)$-product of dependence graphs

This definition allows a simple denotation of traces. For all $a \in \Sigma$, the trace $[\{p\}, \emptyset, p \mapsto a]$ which consists of a single vertex labelled by a will be simply denoted by a. Then, an α-sequence of letters $u = (u_i)_{i<\alpha}$ will denote the trace $\prod_{i<\alpha} u_i$.

For instance, the traces of Figures 11.1–11.3 may be denoted by $acbadeacbd$, $acbaaccbaaaccb\ldots$, $acbccaaa\ldots abbb\ldots$ and $adadad\ldots bebebe\ldots ccc\ldots$ respectively. Note that a trace is well-defined by its denotation but the denotation is not unique: $dcaebdcaab$ is another denotation of the trace of Figure 11.1. Subsection 11.2.4 investigates the relationship between traces and sequences of letters.

Let us give another example of an infinite product. For $i < \omega$, let $g_i = (ac)^i b$, let $g_{\omega+i} = d$ and let $g_{\omega \cdot 2 + i} = d^\omega = ddd\ldots$. Then, the ω-product $\prod_{i<\omega} g_i$ is the graph of Figure 11.2 and the $(\omega \cdot 3)$-product $\prod_{i<\omega \cdot 3} g_i$ is the graph of Figure 11.8.

Remark 11.2.12 The infinite product is associative. More precisely, let α be a countable ordinal and let $(\alpha_j)_{j<\alpha}$ be an α-sequence of countable ordinals. For all $j \leq \alpha$, let $\beta_j = \sum_{i<j} \alpha_i$ and let $(g_i)_{i<\beta_\alpha}$ be a β_α-sequence of dependence graphs. Then

$$\prod_{i<\beta_\alpha} g_i = \prod_{j<\alpha} \left(\prod_{i<\alpha_j} g_{\beta_j+i} \right)$$

Let us illustrate the associativity on the previous example. Let $\alpha = \omega$, $\alpha_0 = \alpha_1 = \omega$ and $\alpha_i = 1$ for all $1 < i < \alpha$. We have $\beta_\alpha = \omega \cdot 3$ and this associativity may be written as

$$\prod_{i<\omega \cdot 3} g_i = (acbaaccbaaaccb \cdots) \cdot (d^\omega) \cdot (d^\omega) \cdot (d^\omega) \cdots$$

Indeed, the infinite product is not an internal operation in the set of real traces. For instance, the $(\omega \cdot 3)$-product of real traces presented in Figure 11.8 is a non-real trace. Hence, as for the concatenation, the infinite product on $\mathbb{G}$ induces a partial infinite product on $\mathbb{R}$. With the same example as above, the *real* infinite product $\prod_{i<\omega\cdot 3} g_i$ is undefined, the *real* infinite product $\prod_{i<\omega} g_i$ is the real trace of Figure 11.2 and the *real* infinite product $\prod_{i<\omega\cdot 2} g_i$ is the real part of the graph of Figure 11.8.

In fact, we only need ω-products when dealing with real traces. Indeed, it is easy to verify that a $(\omega \cdot |\Sigma| + 1)$-product of non-empty real traces is always a non-real trace. Hence, all *real* infinite products may be obtained using ω-products and concatenations only.

The following remark gives a useful characterization of well-defined real ω-products. In particular, it ensures that an ω-product of finite traces is a real trace. Moreover, a product which contains at least $|\Sigma| + 1$ infinite traces is necessarily a non-real trace. Hence, the well-defined real ω-products are ultimately products of finite traces.

Remark 11.2.13 The ω-product of a sequence $(g_i)_{i<\omega}$ of real traces is a real trace if and only if $\mathrm{alphinf}(g_i) \times \mathrm{alph}(g_j) \subseteq I$ for all $i < j < \omega$.

Note that, Proposition 11.2.10 generalizes easily to infinite products as stated in the next remark. The proof of this remark is left as an exercise to the reader.

Remark 11.2.14 Let $x, y, (z_i)_{i<\alpha}$ be dependence graphs such that $x \cdot y = \prod_{i<\alpha} z_i$. Then, there exist two sequences (uniquely determined) $(x_i)_{i<\alpha}$ and $(y_i)_{i<\alpha}$ of dependence graphs such that

$$x = \prod_{i<\alpha} x_i, \quad y = \prod_{i<\alpha} y_i \quad \text{and} \quad z_i = x_i \cdot y_i \text{ for all } i < \alpha$$

and

$$\mathrm{alph}(y_i) \times \mathrm{alph}(x_j) \subseteq I \text{ for all } i < j < \alpha$$

We now turn to the generalization to infinite traces of the *Foata Normal Form* (FNF) of finite traces (see Chapter 2). Intuitively, this normal form gives the fastest execution of the trace on a synchronous parallel machine. The trace is decomposed in *steps*. Since a step is a set of pairwise independent actions (a *clique* of (Σ, I)), it may be executed in one unit of time on a parallel machine. Formally, let the set of steps be

$$\mathcal{S} = \{S \subseteq \Sigma \mid S \neq \emptyset \text{ and } (a, b) \in I \text{ for all } a, b \in S \text{ such that } a \neq b\}.$$

Each step S will be identified with the trace $\prod_{a \in S} a$. Note that, it is not necessary to precise the order in this product since the actions of a step are pairwise independent.

Let $g = [V, E, \lambda] \in \mathbb{G}$ be a trace, we define its set of *minimal actions* by $\min(g) = \{\lambda(p) \mid p$ is a minimal vertex of $g\}$. Since there is no edge between two minimal vertices of a graph, the letters of $\min(g)$ are pairwise independent, that is, $\min(g) \in \mathcal{S}$. Clearly, $\min(g)$ is a prefix of g.

We give now the *Foata Normal Form* theorem for infinite traces. Note that the third condition below is useless if we consider real traces only.

Theorem 11.2.15 *Let $g \in \mathbb{G}(\Sigma, D)$ be a trace. There exist a unique countable ordinal α and a unique α-sequence of steps $(S_i)_{i<\alpha} \subseteq S$ such that*

1. $g = \prod_{i<\alpha} S_i$,

2. *for all successor ordinal i with $0 < i < \alpha$, for all $b \in S_i$ there exists $a \in S_{i-1}$ such that $(a,b) \in D$,*

3. *for all limit ordinal $i < \alpha$, for all $b \in S_i$, $i = \sup\{j < i \mid \exists a \in S_j, (a,b) \in D\}$.*

Moreover, if g is a real trace (a finite trace resp.) then $\alpha \leq \omega$ (α is finite resp.).

Proof: We define the sequence $(S_i)_{i<\alpha}$ by induction. Let i be an ordinal and assume that for all $j < i$, S_j is already defined in such a way that $\prod_{k \leq j} S_k$ is a prefix of g. An easy verification shows that $\prod_{j<i} S_j$ is a prefix of g. Then, either $g = \prod_{j<i} S_j$ and the construction is over by setting $\alpha = i$. Or $\prod_{j<i} S_j$ is a strict prefix of g and we set $S_i = \min((\prod_{j<i} S_j)^{-1} \cdot g)$. Note that, since S_i is a prefix of $(\prod_{j<i} S_j)^{-1} \cdot g$, $\prod_{k \leq i} S_k$ is a prefix of g.

Since each step is non-empty and a dependence graph is countable, this construction must stop with a countable ordinal α and, by construction, we obtain $g = \prod_{i<\alpha} S_i$. For the same reason, we must have α finite if $g \in \mathbb{M}$ is a finite trace.

Now assume that $\alpha \geq \omega$, then

$$\mathrm{Re}(g) = \prod_{i<\omega} S_i \qquad\qquad (11.1)$$

Indeed, by Remark 11.2.13 it is clear that $\prod_{i<\omega} S_i$ is a real prefix of g. Conversely, let p be a vertex of g which is not in $\prod_{i<\omega} S_i$. For all $i < \omega$, p is not a minimal vertex of $(\prod_{j<i} S_j)^{-1} \cdot g$. Hence, there is at least a vertex in S_i which is in the past of p. Therefore, the past of p is infinite and p is not in the real part of g, which proves Equation 11.1. We deduce immediately that $\alpha \leq \omega$ if g is a real trace.

To complete the existence part of this proof, it remains to show that the sequence $(S_i)_{i<\alpha}$ satisfies conditions 2 and 3. Let $i < \alpha$ and let $b \in S_i$. We claim that for all $j < i$ there exists an ordinal k such that $j \leq k < i$ and a letter $a \in S_k$ with $(a,b) \in D$.

Let p be the vertex labelled by b in S_i. Since p is not a minimal vertex of $(\prod_{m<j} S_m)^{-1} \cdot g$, the past of p with respect to this graph contains a vertex q labelled by some a with $(a,b) \in D$. Since p is a minimal vertex of $(\prod_{m<i} S_m)^{-1} \cdot g$, q must be a vertex of some S_k with $j \leq k < i$ and the claim is proved.

Condition 2 is a direct consequence of this claim (just take $j = i-1$). Since the alphabet Σ is finite, the third condition follows easily from the claim, too.

Finally, from conditions 2 and 3, we deduce that

$$\min\left(\prod_{i<\alpha} S_i\right) = S_0$$

Using the left-cancellativity in $\mathbb{G}$, the unambiguity follows easily by induction. $\square$

For instance, the *Foata Normal Forms* of the graphs of Figures 11.1 and 11.3 (b) are the following sequences of length 5 and $\omega \cdot 3$ respectively:

$$S_0 = \{a, c, d\}, S_1 = \{b, e\}, S_2 = \{a, c, d\}, S_3 = \{a\}, S_4 = \{b\}$$

and

$$S_i = \{a, d\}, S_{\omega+i} = \{b, e\}, S_{\omega \cdot 2+i} = \{c\}, \text{ for all } i < \omega.$$

11.2.4 Words and Infinite Traces

We will now study the relationship between words and infinite traces. For this purpose, we first recall some notations and definitions concerning words. For a countable ordinal α, we denote by Σ^α the set of all α-sequences over Σ, that is, sequences of letters indexed by α. In particular, Σ^ω is the classical set of all ω-words. The length of a word $u \in \Sigma^\alpha$ is α and we write $|u| = \alpha$.

The free monoid over Σ is the set $\Sigma^* = \cup_{i<\omega}\Sigma^i$ of all finite words with the usual concatenation. We denote by $\Sigma^\infty = \cup_{i\leq\omega}\Sigma^i = \Sigma^* \cup \Sigma^\omega$ the set of all finite and ω-words. Finally, the monoid of (countably) transfinite words is the set $\Sigma^{<\aleph_1} = \cup_{i<\aleph_1}\Sigma^i$ of all countable words equipped with the natural concatenation: the concatenation of two words $u = (u_i)_{i<|u|}$ and $v = (v_i)_{i<|v|}$ is $u \cdot v = (w_i)_{i<|u|+|v|}$ where $w_i = u_i$ for $i < |u|$ and $w_{|u|+i} = v_i$ for $i < |v|$.

Since the concatenation on $\Sigma^{<\aleph_1}$ is left-cancellative, the prefix relation $\leq$, defined for $x, z \in \Sigma^{<\aleph_1}$ by $x \leq z$ if $z = x \cdot y$ for some $y \in \Sigma^{<\aleph_1}$, is a partial order on $\Sigma^{<\aleph_1}$.

As for infinite traces, the concatenation is extended to general α-products and α-powers: let $(u_i)_{i<\alpha} \subseteq \Sigma^{<\aleph_1}$ be a sequence of words indexed by a countable ordinal α, its α-product $\prod_{i<\alpha} u_i \in \Sigma^{<\aleph_1}$ is the concatenation of the words u_i for $i < \alpha$.

Let $u \in \Sigma^\alpha$ be a word and let $(V, \sqsubseteq)$ be a well-ordered set representing the ordinal α. The word u defines a labelling function $\lambda : V \longrightarrow \Sigma$. Hence u may be identified with the labelled well-ordered set $[V, \sqsubseteq, \lambda]$. This remark allows an easy definition of the canonical mapping φ from the set $\Sigma^{<\aleph_1}$ of (transfinite) words to the set $\mathbb{G}(\Sigma, D)$ of (transfinite) traces.

Definition 11.2.16 *The mapping* $\varphi : \Sigma^{<\aleph_1} \longrightarrow \mathbb{G}(\Sigma, D)$ *is defined as follows. Let* $u = [V, \sqsubseteq, \lambda] \in \Sigma^{<\aleph_1}$ *be a word. Then* $\varphi(u)$ *is the dependence graph* $[V, E, \lambda]$ *where* $E = \{(p, q) \in V \times V \mid (\lambda(p), \lambda(q)) \in D \text{ and } p \sqsubset q\}$.

For instance, this canonical mapping φ maps the words $u = acbadeacbd$, $v = acbaaccbaaaccccb\ldots$ and $w = aaa\ldots bbb\ldots ccc\ldots ddd\ldots eee\ldots$ to the traces of Figures 11.1, 11.2 and 11.3 (b) respectively.

In other words, the mapping φ weakens the total order $\sqsubseteq$ to an edge relation E which satisfies the conditions of Definition 11.2.1.

Conversely, a linearization of a trace $g = [V, E, \lambda] \in \mathbb{G}$ is a labelled totally ordered set $[V, \sqsubseteq, \lambda]$ where $\sqsubseteq$ is a linear extension of the induced partial order $\preceq = E^*$, that is, for all $p, q \in V$, $p \preceq q \implies p \sqsubseteq q$. Then, the inverse image by φ of a graph $g = [V, E, \lambda] \in \mathbb{G}$ is the set of linearizations of g. Indeed, every word of

$\varphi^{-1}(g)$ is, by definition, a linearization of g. Now, let $[V, \sqsubseteq, \lambda]$ be any linearization of g. We just have to prove that $[V, \sqsubseteq, \lambda]$ is a word, i.e., that $(V, \sqsubseteq)$ is well-ordered. Assume that there exists a decreasing ω-sequence $p_0 \; p_1 \; p_2 \; \ldots$ in $[V, \sqsubseteq, \lambda]$. Since Σ is finite, we may assume that all $(p_i)_{i<\omega}$ are labelled by the same letter of Σ. Hence, the sequence $(p_i)_{i<\omega}$ must be totally ordered in g. Since $[V, \sqsubseteq, \lambda]$ is a linearization of g it follows that $(p_i)_{i<\omega}$ is a decreasing ω-sequence in g which is a contradiction with the well-foundedness of g.

Proposition 11.2.17 *The mapping $\varphi : \Sigma^{<\aleph_1} \longrightarrow \mathbb{G}(\Sigma, D)$ is a morphism with respect to every α-product where α is a countable ordinal.*

Proof: Let α be a countable ordinal and for all $i < \alpha$, let $u_i = [V_i, \sqsubseteq_i, \lambda_i] \in \Sigma^{<\aleph_1}$ be a word. By definition of the α-product, we have $u = \prod_{i<\alpha} u_i = [V, \sqsubseteq, \lambda]$ where

$$V = \bigcup_{i<\alpha} V_i, \quad \sqsubseteq = \left(\bigcup_{i<\alpha} \sqsubseteq_i \right) \cup \left(\bigcup_{i<j<\alpha} V_i \times V_j \right) \quad \text{and} \quad \lambda = \bigcup_{i<\alpha} \lambda_i.$$

For all $i < \alpha$, let $g_i = \varphi(u_i) = [V_i, E_i, \lambda_i]$ and let $g = \varphi(u) = [V, E, \lambda]$. An easy verification shows that

$$E = \left(\bigcup_{i<\alpha} E_i \right) \cup \{(p, q) \in V_i \times V_j \mid i < j < \alpha \text{ and } (\lambda_i(p), \lambda_j(q)) \in D\}.$$

Therefore, $g = \prod_{i<\alpha} g_i$. $\square$

Note that, for a word $u = (u_i)_{i<\alpha} \in \Sigma^\alpha$, we may write $u = \prod_{i<\alpha} u_i$ as well as $\varphi(u) = \prod_{i<\alpha} \varphi(u_i) = \prod_{i<\alpha} u_i$ (since we identify u_i and $\varphi(u_i)$ as in Section 11.2.3). According to the context, the α-product $\prod_{i<\alpha} u_i$ is understood to be a word-product in the first case and a trace-product in the second case.

Proposition 11.2.18 *The mapping $\varphi : \Sigma^{<\aleph_1} \longrightarrow \mathbb{G}(\Sigma, D)$ is surjective. Moreover, $\varphi(\Sigma^\infty) = \mathbb{R}(\Sigma, D)$ and $\varphi(\Sigma^*) = \mathbb{M}(\Sigma, D)$.*

Proof: Let $g \in \mathbb{G}$ be a trace and let $(S_i)_{i<\alpha}$ be its Foata Normal Form. For all $i < \alpha$, let $u_i \in \Sigma^*$ be any linearization of S_i. Then, $g = \prod_{i<\alpha} S_i = \prod_{i<\alpha} \varphi(u_i) = \varphi(\prod_{i<\alpha} u_i)$. Moreover, if g is a real trace (a finite trace resp.) then the number of steps in its FNF is at most ω (finite resp.). Hence, $\prod_{i<\alpha} u_i \in \Sigma^\infty$ ($\prod_{i<\alpha} u_i \in \Sigma^*$ resp.). $\square$

As a direct consequence of Remark 11.2.13 and Proposition 11.2.18 we obtain:

Corollary 11.2.19 *A trace is real if and only if it may be written as an ω-product of finite traces:*

$$\mathbb{R}(\Sigma, D) = \mathbb{M}(\Sigma, D)^\omega$$

If the independence relation I is empty, then φ is clearly injective. Hence, φ is an isomorphism between $\Sigma^{<\aleph_1}$ and $\mathbb{G}(\Sigma, \Sigma \times \Sigma)$. But, as soon as the independence relation is non-empty, φ is not injective. For instance, for $a, b \in \Sigma$ we have $\varphi(ab) = \varphi(ba)$ if and only if $(a, b) \in I$. This leads to the definition of the *trace congruence* on $\Sigma^{<\aleph_1}$.

Definition 11.2.20 *The trace congruence $\sim_I$, or simply $\sim$, on $\Sigma^{<\aleph_1}$ is the congruence associated with the morphism φ: for all $u, v \in \Sigma^{<\aleph_1}$,*

$$u \sim v \iff \varphi(u) = \varphi(v)$$

For instance, $baacb \sim bacab \sim bcaab$. Note that, for a finite trace g, all words of $\varphi^{-1}(g)$ have the same length. Hence the length $|g|$ of a finite trace g is well defined. But the words which represent the same infinite trace may have different lengths. For instance, $acacac \cdots \sim aaa \cdots ccc \cdots$. Hence, the length of an infinite trace is not well-defined.

Remark 11.2.21 From Proposition 11.2.18 and Definition 11.2.20 we deduce immediately that

$$\mathbb{M}(\Sigma, D) = \Sigma^*/\sim, \quad \mathbb{R}(\Sigma, D) = \Sigma^\infty/\sim \quad \text{and} \quad \mathbb{G}(\Sigma, D) = \Sigma^{<\aleph_1}/\sim$$

Note that the trace equivalence on $\Sigma^{<\aleph_1}$ is the equivalence relation associated with the I-prefix quasi-order relation defined for $x, z \in \Sigma^{<\aleph_1}$ by $x \leq_I z$ if $\varphi(x) \leq \varphi(z)$, or equivalently if $z \sim x \cdot y$ for some $y \in \Sigma^{<\aleph_1}$.

Since many words represent the same trace, it may be useful to have canonical words which represent traces. Besides the Foata Normal Form, the *Lexicographic Normal Form* defines such canonical representatives. Let us first introduce the lexicographic order $\leq_{\text{lex}}$ on $\Sigma^{<\aleph_1}$. We assume that the alphabet Σ is provided with a total order which is also denoted by $\leq_{\text{lex}}$. Let $u = (u_i)_{i < |u|}$ and $v = (v_i)_{i < |v|}$ be two words of $\Sigma^{<\aleph_1}$. Then, $u <_{\text{lex}} v$ if

- either $|u| < |v|$ and $u_i = v_i$ for all $i < |u|$, i.e., u is a strict prefix of v,

- or there exists $i < \min(|u|, |v|)$ such that $u_i <_{\text{lex}} v_i$ and $u_j = v_j$ for all $j < i$.

Clearly, $\leq_{\text{lex}}$ is a total order on $\Sigma^{<\aleph_1}$. Since, for a finite trace $g \in \mathbb{M}$, the set $\varphi^{-1}(g)$ of representatives of g is finite, it admits a least element for the lexicographic order. This trivial result may be extended to transfinite traces.

Proposition 11.2.22 *Let $g \in \mathbb{G}(\Sigma, D)$ be a dependence graph. The set $\varphi^{-1}(g)$ of words which represent g admits a least element for the lexicographic order. This least representative is the* Lexicographic Normal Form *of g.*

Proof: We first define by induction a representative u of g. Then, we prove that this word u is the least representative of g for the lexicographic order.

Let i be a countable ordinal. Assume that for all $j < i$, $u_j \in \Sigma$ is defined and that $f = \varphi(\prod_{j<i} u_j)$ is a prefix of g. Then, either $f = g$ and the construction is over: we let $u = (u_j)_{j<i}$. Or, f is a strict prefix of g and thus $f^{-1} \cdot g$ is well defined by Remark 11.2.9. We define u_i as the least letter for the lexicographic order in the set $\min(f^{-1} \cdot g)$ of minimal letters of $f^{-1} \cdot g$. Since g is countable, this construction must stop and defines a word $u \in \Sigma^{<\aleph_1}$.

By definition, u is a representative of g, that is, $\varphi(u) = g$. Now, let $v \in \varphi^{-1}(g)$ be another representative of g. First, assume that there exists $i < \min(|u|, |v|)$ such that $u_i \neq v_i$ and $u_j = v_j$ for all $j < i$. Let $f = \varphi(\prod_{j<i} u_j) = \varphi(\prod_{j<i} v_j)$. Then, both u_i and v_i are in the set $\min(f^{-1} \cdot g)$. Hence, by construction, $u_i <_{\text{lex}} v_i$ and we deduce $u <_{\text{lex}} v$. Second, assume that v is a prefix of u (or vice versa). Then,

$$g = \varphi(u) = \varphi(v) \cdot \varphi(v^{-1} \cdot u) = g \cdot \varphi(v^{-1} \cdot u)$$

By Proposition 11.2.8, we deduce that $v^{-1} \cdot u = 1$, that is, $u = v$ which concludes the proof. $\square$

For instance, if we assume that $a <_{\text{lex}} b <_{\text{lex}} c <_{\text{lex}} d <_{\text{lex}} e$, the Lexicographic Normal Forms of the traces of Figures 11.1– 11.3 are respectively $acbaacbded$, $acbaaccbaaaacccb \cdots$, $acba^\omega accb^\omega$ and $a^\omega b^\omega c^\omega d^\omega e^\omega$. Note that the Lexicographic Normal Form of a real trace may be of length strictly greater than ω. For instance, the Lexicographic Normal Form of the real trace $\varphi((ac)^\omega)$ is $a^\omega c^\omega$.

We will now characterize the trace congruence $\sim$ using projections on cliques of the dependence alphabet (Σ, D). Recall that a clique of (Σ, D) is a complete subgraph of (Σ, D). For instance, the cliques of the dependence alphabet used for the examples of this section are $\{a\}, \{b\}, \{c\}, \{d\}, \{e\}, \{a, b\}, \{b, c\}$ and $\{d, e\}$.

For each subalphabet $C \subseteq \Sigma$ and for each trace $g \in \mathbb{G}$, let $\pi_C(g) \in \mathbb{G}$ be the restriction of g to the set $\lambda^{-1}(C)$. Clearly, π_C is a surjective morphism from $\mathbb{G}(\Sigma, D)$ onto $\mathbb{G}(C, D \cap C \times C)$ which preserves α-products for all countable ordinals α. Moreover, if C is a clique of (Σ, D) then the projection $\pi_C(g)$ is a word of $C^{<\aleph_1}$. The next proposition shows that $\mathbb{G}(\Sigma, D)$ may be identified with a submonoid of a direct product of word-monoids. This result generalizes the classical embedding theorem for finite traces (see for instance[53]).

Proposition 11.2.23 *Let $((C_1, C_1 \times C_1), \ldots, (C_k, C_k \times C_k))$ be a covering of (Σ, D) by cliques. Then, the mapping $\pi : \mathbb{G}(\Sigma, D) \longrightarrow C_1^{<\aleph_1} \times \cdots \times C_k^{<\aleph_1}$ defined for a trace $g \in \mathbb{G}(\Sigma, D)$ by $\pi(g) = (\pi_{C_1}(g), \ldots, \pi_{C_k}(g))$ is an injective morphism (which preserves α-products for all countable ordinals α). Hence,*

$$\mathbb{G}(\Sigma, D) \hookrightarrow C_1^{<\aleph_1} \times \cdots \times C_k^{<\aleph_1}$$

Proof: Let $g \in \mathbb{G}$ and let $\pi(g) = (g_1, \ldots, g_k)$. Clearly, we have

$$\min(g) = \{a \in \Sigma \mid \text{ for all } 1 \leq n \leq k, a \in C_n \implies g_n \in aC_n^{<\aleph_1}\} \tag{11.2}$$

Let $g, h \in \mathbb{G}$ be two traces such that $\pi(g) = \pi(h)$. We prove by induction that g and h have the same Foata Normal Form. Let $(S_i)_{i<\alpha}$ and $(T_i)_{i<\beta}$ be the FNF of g and h respectively. Let $i \leq \min(\alpha, \beta)$ and assume that for all $j < i$ we have $S_j = T_j$. Since π is a morphism and the monoids $C_1^{<\aleph_1}, \ldots, C_k^{<\aleph_1}$ are left-cancellative, we deduce that

$$\pi\left(\left(\textstyle\prod_{j<i} S_j\right)^{-1} \cdot g\right) = \pi\left(\left(\textstyle\prod_{j<i} T_j\right)^{-1} \cdot h\right)$$

Hence, either $\left(\prod_{j<i} S_j\right)^{-1} \cdot g = 1 = \left(\prod_{j<i} T_j\right)^{-1} \cdot h$ and $\alpha = \beta = i$, or $S_i = T_i$ by Equation 11.2. □

Note that the projections on subalphabets are also well-defined for words. Hence, we deduce the following characterizations of the trace congruence and of the I-prefix quasi-order on $\Sigma^{<\aleph_1}$.

Corollary 11.2.24 *Let* $((C_1, C_1 \times C_1), \ldots, (C_k, C_k \times C_k))$ *be a covering of* (Σ, D) *by cliques. Then, for all* $u, v \in \Sigma^{<\aleph_1}$ *we have*

$$u \leq_I v \iff \text{for all } 1 \leq n \leq k, \quad \pi_{C_n}(u) \leq_I \pi_{C_n}(v)$$

$$u \sim v \iff \text{for all } 1 \leq n \leq k, \quad \pi_{C_n}(u) = \pi_{C_n}(v)$$

Note that, the characterization of Proposition 11.2.23 may be used to define directly (without using dependence graphs) the trace equivalence $\sim$ on words, and thence the monoid of transfinite traces $\Sigma^{<\aleph_1}/\sim$ and the (partial) monoid of real traces $\Sigma^\infty/\sim$. But such a definition would make it necessary to verify that it does not depend on the covering of (Σ, D) by cliques.

In fact, the trace equivalence on Σ^∞ was originally defined by several authors using the following characterization. Note that this characterization only uses the classical trace equivalence on finite words which may be defined as the least congruence generated by $\{(ab, ba) \mid (a, b) \in I\}$.

Remark 11.2.25 Let $u, v \in \Sigma^\infty$. Then, $u \sim v$ if and only if for all finite prefix x of u, there exists a finite prefix y of v such that $x \leq_I y$, i.e., $y \sim x \cdot z$ for some finite word $z \in \Sigma^*$; and vice versa.

The proof of this remark is left as an exercise to the reader.

11.2.5 Notes

Infinite traces were introduced independently, implicitly or explicitly, by several authors. The various motivations which led to these works clearly indicate that infinite traces form a natural model in semantics of parallelism.

In order to deal with the serializability of concurrent access to data bases, Flé and Roucairol [105] have introduced an equivalence relation on Σ^∞ based on the projections on pairs of dependent letters. The definition of this equivalence is related to the characterization of the trace equivalence stated in Proposition 11.2.23.

The first explicit definition of infinite (real) traces seems to be in a survey on trace theory by Mazurkiewicz [190]. He introduced the set of infinite traces as the classical ideal completion of the set of finite traces partially ordered by the prefix relation. He then showed that infinite traces may be represented by real dependence graphs. We will prove in Section 11.3 that the poset of real traces is the ideal completion of the poset of finite traces.

In order to define infinite behaviors of Petri nets, Best and Devillers [25] introduced an equivalence relation on Σ^∞ which, in this context, turns out to be precisely the trace equivalence. Their definition is in the same vein as the characterization of Remark 11.2.25.

In order to define a semantics for infinite behaviors of CSP programs, Fauconnier [100] was led to introduce an equivalence relation on Σ^∞ whose definition corresponds to the characterization of Remark 11.2.25, as well.

An infinitary vector semantic model for distributed systems was introduced by Gastin [108, 110]. The finitary part of this model was proved to be equivalent to the finitary trace monoid. Hence, this model may be seen as an infinitary extension of the monoid of finite traces. Again, this led to the definition of the trace equivalence on Σ^∞.

Finally, Kwiatkowska [161, 163] introduced real traces in order to obtain a semantic model suitable to the study of fairness, liveness and safety properties in distributed systems.

The concatenation on real traces was defined both in [108, 109] and in [161, 163]. Gastin defines a total operation which uses 0 to denote the ideal of non-real traces, whereas Kwiatkowska uses a partial operation.

The monoid of dependence graphs (or transfinite traces) was introduced by Diekert [Die91] in order to define complex traces (see Section 11.4). The major contribution to the theory of transfinite trace can be found in that paper.

These definitions led naturally to the investigation of the properties of trace monoids. The cancellativity for infinite trace monoids (Proposition 11.2.8) was proved by Gastin [108, 109] for real traces and by Diekert [54, 57] for transfinite traces. The generalization of Levi's Lemma to trace monoids (Proposition 11.2.10) was given by Cori and Perrin [47] for finite traces, by Gastin [108, 109] for real traces and by Diekert [54, 57] for transfinite traces. The Foata Normal Form for finite traces was introduced by Foata [34] and generalized to real traces independently by Gastin [109] and by Bonizzoni, Mauri and Pighizzini [27]. This result was then extended to transfinite traces by Kwiatkowska and Stannett [165]. Finally, the characterization using projections on cliques of the trace equivalence was proved by Cori and Perrin [47] for finite traces and generalized to real traces by Gastin [109].

11.3   Poset Properties of Infinite Traces

There are several possible ways to obtain an infinitary generalization of the monoid $\mathbb{M}$ of finite traces. In Section 11.2 we have introduced "directly" the set $\mathbb{R}$ of real traces and the set $\mathbb{G}$ of transfinite traces. In Section 11.4, we will define "directly" another extension of the monoid of finite traces, namely, the monoid $\mathbb{C}$ of complex traces. Other methods come up naturally, as well. One may consider first the ideal completion of the set $\mathbb{M}$ partially ordered by the prefix relation and second the topological completion of the metric space $(\mathbb{M}, d)$ for a suitable metric which will be studied in Section 11.5. We will see that the set $\mathbb{R}$ of real traces is the best infinitary extension with respect to the prefix relation, whereas the monoid $\mathbb{C}$ of complex traces has the best topological properties.

The aim of this section is thus to study the properties of the sets $\mathbb{R}$ and $\mathbb{G}$ of real and transfinite traces with respect to the prefix relation. In every (partial) monoid M, this relation, defined by $x \leq y$ if $y = x \cdot z$ for some $z \in M$, is reflexive and transitive. Using the left-cancellativity in $\mathbb{G}$ (Proposition 11.2.8), we deduce easily that the prefix relation on $\mathbb{G}$ is anti-symmetric, and hence it is a partial order on both $\mathbb{G}$ and $\mathbb{R}$.

We will be interested in the *completeness* and in the *algebraicity* of the *posets* (partially ordered sets) $\mathbb{R}$ and $\mathbb{G}$ of real and transfinite traces. More precisely, we will study, on one hand, sufficient conditions for the existence of least upper bounds and, on the other hand, the possibility to reconstruct all traces by means of least upper bounds of "simple" traces, namely, compact and prime traces.

These two questions are fundamental from a semantic point of view. Indeed, the semantics of recursive terms often uses least upper bounds, and this motivates the study of the completeness of the considered poset. On the other hand, infinite traces are abstractions of limit behaviors which are naturally least upper bounds of partial (finite) behaviors. Thus, in some sense, algebraicity means that every infinite trace is the limit behavior of "simple" traces.

Throughout this section, we will use the standard representation of a dependence graph (see Section 11.2.1) where its set of vertices is $V = \{(a, i) \mid a \in \Sigma$ and $i < |g|_a\}$ and the labelling function is trivially defined by $\lambda((a, i)) = a$ for all $(a, i) \in V$. Moreover, for each dependence graph $g \in \mathbb{G}$, we denote by V_g, E_g, λ_g and $\preceq_g$ the set of vertices, the set of edges, the labelling function and the induced partial order of g respectively.

11.3.1 Completeness

First, we recall some classical definitions. Let $(Z, \leq)$ be a poset, i.e., a partially ordered set. A subset $Y \subseteq Z$ is *coherent* if for all $x, y \in Y$, there exists $z \in Z$ such that $x \leq z$ and $y \leq z$. A subset $Y \subseteq Z$ is *directed* if it is non empty and for all $x, y \in Y$, there exists $z \in Y$ such that $x \leq z$ and $y \leq z$. A subset $Y \subseteq Z$ is *bounded above* if there exists $z \in Z$ such that $x \leq z$ for all $x \in Y$. The poset $(Z, \leq)$ is a *directed complete partial order* (a *dcpo* for short) if every directed subset of Z has a least upper bound. Similarly, the poset $(Z, \leq)$ is a *coherently complete partial order* (a *ccpo* for short) if every coherent subset of Z has a least upper bound in Z. Finally, the poset $(Z, \leq)$ is a *bounded complete partial order* (a *bcpo* for short) if every bounded subset of Z has a least upper bound in Z. Whenever they exist, the least upper bound and the greatest lower bound of a subset $Y \subseteq Z$ will be denoted by $\sqcup Y$ and $\sqcap Y$ respectively.

We will see that only a countable set of traces may have a least upper bound. Hence, we first give some useful sufficient conditions for a set of traces to be countable.

Lemma 11.3.1 *Every coherent set of real traces is countable. Every bounded above set of transfinite traces is countable.*

Proof: For each transfinite trace $g \in \mathbb{G}$, we denote by $\Lambda(g) = (|g|_a)_{a \in \Sigma}$ the tuple of partial lengths of g (see Section 11.2.1). We claim that this mapping Λ restricted to any coherent subset $G \subseteq \mathbb{G}$ is injective. Indeed, let $f, g \in G$ be such that $\Lambda(f) = \Lambda(g)$. Since G is coherent, we have $f \leq h$ and $g \leq h$ for some $h \in \mathbb{G}$. Using Proposition 11.2.5, we deduce easily that the graph f is the restriction of the graph h to the subset $\{(a, i) \mid a \in \Sigma$ and $i < |f|_a\}$ of V_h. Since the same fact holds for g, we deduce that $f = g$ which proves the claim.

Now, for $G \subseteq \mathbb{R}$, we have $\Lambda(G) \subseteq \{(i_a)_{a \in \Sigma} \mid i_a \leq \omega, \forall a \in \Sigma\}$ which is countable. By the above claim, every coherent set of real traces is countable.

Similarly, let $h \in \mathbb{G}$ be an upper bound of the subset $G \subseteq \mathbb{G}$. We have $\Lambda(G) \subseteq \{(i_a)_{a \in \Sigma} \mid i_a \leq |h|_a, \forall a \in \Sigma\}$ which is countable. By the above claim, every bounded above set of transfinite traces is countable.   □

Using this lemma, we will prove the main theorem of this subsection. It gives a necessary and sufficient condition for a set of transfinite traces to admit a least upper bound. Moreover, whenever it exists, the least upper bound of a set of traces is simply the union of the (standard representations) of its members.

Theorem 11.3.2 *Let $G \subseteq \mathbb{G}(\Sigma, D)$ be a set of transfinite traces. Then, G has a least upper bound if and only if G is coherent and countable.*

In this case, $\sqcup G = [V, E, \lambda]$, where $V = \bigcup_{g \in G} V_g$, $E = \bigcup_{g \in G} E_g$ and $\lambda((a, i)) = a$ for all $(a, i) \in V$.

Proof: The "only if" part is clear: a subset which has a least upper bound is in particular bounded above. Therefore, it is coherent and by Lemma 11.3.1, it is countable.

Conversely, let $G \subseteq \mathbb{G}$ be a coherent and countable set of transfinite traces. We will first prove that the graph $[V, E, \lambda]$ defined in Theorem 11.3.2 is a dependence graph and then we will check that it is the least upper bound of G. We start with two easy claims.

Claim 1 Let $(p, q) \in E$ and let $g \in G$ be such that $q \in V_g$. Then, $p \in V_g$ and $(p, q) \in E_g$.

Let $f \in G$ be such that $(p, q) \in E_f$. Since G is coherent, we have $f \leq h$ and $g \leq h$ for some $h \in \mathbb{G}$. This implies clearly that $(p, q) \in E_h$. Since $g \leq h$ and $q \in V_g$, it follows from Proposition 11.2.5 that $p \in V_g$ and $(p, q) \in E_g$.

Let $\preceq = E^*$ be the reflexive and transitive closure of the edge relation E. From Claim 1, it follows directly by induction that

Claim 2 Let $p, q \in V$ be such that $p \preceq q$ and let $g \in G$ be such that $q \in V_g$. Then, $p \in V_g$ and $p \preceq_g q$.

We now prove that $[V, E, \lambda]$ is a dependence graph. Since G is countable, so is the set of vertices $V = \bigcup_{g \in G} V_g$.

Let us check that edges are between dependent vertices. Let $(p, q) \in E$, we have $(p, q) \in E_g$ for some $g \in G$. Hence, $(\lambda(p), \lambda(q)) \in D$. Conversely, let $p, q \in V$ be such that $p \neq q$ and $(\lambda(p), \lambda(q)) \in D$. We have $p \in V_f$ and $q \in V_g$ for some $f, g \in G$. Since G is coherent, there exists $h \in \mathbb{G}$ such that $f \leq h$ and $g \leq h$. Since h is a dependence graph, we have either $(p, q) \in E_h$ or $(q, p) \in E_h$. Using Proposition 11.2.5 we deduce that either $p \in V_g$ and $(p, q) \in E_g$ or $q \in V_f$ and $(q, p) \in E_f$. Therefore, either $(p, q) \in E$ or $(q, p) \in E$.

Now, we prove that $[V, E, \lambda]$ is acyclic. Assume that $p \preceq q$ and $q \preceq p$ for some $p, q \in V$. We have $q \in V_g$ for some $g \in G$. From Claim 2, it follows $p \in V_g$, $p \preceq_g q$ and $q \preceq_g p$. Since g is acyclic, we obtain $p = q$.

Finally, assume that there exists in $[V, E, \lambda]$ an infinite strictly decreasing sequence of vertices $p_0 \succ p_1 \succ p_2 \succ \ldots$. Let $g \in G$ be such that $p_0 \in V_g$. Using Claim 2, we deduce that $p_n \in V_g$ for all $n \geq 0$ and that $p_0 \succ_g p_1 \succ_g p_2 \succ_g \ldots$ which is in contradiction with the well-foundedness of $\preceq_g$.

It remains to prove that $[V, E, \lambda]$ is the least upper bound of G. Let $g \in G$, using Claim 1, we deduce easily that g is a downward closed subgraph of $[V, E, \lambda]$. Hence, by Proposition 11.2.5, g is a prefix of $[V, E, \lambda]$. Conversely, let $h \in \mathbb{G}$ be an upper bound of G. Clearly, $V \subseteq V_h$ and $E \subseteq E_h$. Now, let $(p, q) \in E_h$ with $q \in V$. We have $q \in V_g$ for some $g \in G$. Since $g \leq h$, we deduce that $p \in V_g$ and $(p, q) \in E_g$. Therefore, $p \in V$ and $(p, q) \in E$ which proves that $[V, E, \lambda]$ is a downward closed subgraph of h. Hence, by Proposition 11.2.5, $[V, E, \lambda]$ is a prefix of h. $\square$

Note that, for each letter a, the set $G_a = \{a^i \mid i \text{ is a countable ordinal}\}$ of transfinite traces is directed but non-countable. Hence $\mathbb{G}$ is neither a dcpo nor a ccpo. Nevertheless, from Theorem 11.3.2 we obtain directly.

Corollary 11.3.3 *The poset $(\mathbb{G}(\Sigma, D), \leq)$ of transfinite traces is a bcpo. Moreover, let α be a countable ordinal and let $(g_i)_{i < \alpha}$ be an increasing α-sequence of transfinite traces, that is, $g_j \leq g_i$ for all $j < i < \alpha$. Then, $(g_i)_{i < \alpha}$ has a least upper bound in $\mathbb{G}(\Sigma, D)$.*

Note that α-products are closely related to least upper bounds of increasing sequences. More precisely, let α be a countable limit ordinal and let $(g_i)_{i < \alpha}$ be an α-sequence of transfinite traces. For all $i < \alpha$, let $h_i = \prod_{j < i} g_j$. Then, the α-sequence $(h_i)_{i < \alpha}$ is increasing since $h_i = h_j \cdot \prod_{j \leq k < i} g_k$ for all $j < i < \alpha$. Moreover, it holds

$$\prod_{i < \alpha} g_i = \bigsqcup_{i < \alpha} h_i \tag{11.3}$$

Indeed, the α-sequence $(h_i)_{i < \alpha}$ is bounded above by $g = \prod_{i < \alpha} g_i$. Therefore, $h =$

$\bigsqcup_{i<\alpha} h_i \leq g$. Conversely, since α is a limit ordinal, it holds

$$V_g = \bigcup_{i<\alpha} V_{g_i} = \bigcup_{i<\alpha} \left(\bigcup_{j<i} V_{g_j}\right) = \bigcup_{i<\alpha} V_{h_i} = V_h.$$

Therefore, $g = h$ and Formula 11.3 is proved. Note also that if $(h_i)_{i<\alpha}$ is an increasing α-sequence of transfinite traces with $h_0 = 1$ then Formula 11.3 holds with $g_i = h_i^{-1} \cdot h_{i+1}$ for all $i < \alpha$.

The situation for real traces is much better than for transfinite traces and we will obtain a stronger completeness property. Note that this is not a direct consequence of the above results. Indeed, let $(X, \leq)$ be a subposet of $(Z, \leq)$, a subset $Y \subseteq X$ may have a least upper bound in $(X, \leq)$ but not in $(Z, \leq)$ and vice versa. However, this situation does not arise for the subposet of real traces.

Lemma 11.3.4 *Let $G \subseteq \mathbb{R}(\Sigma, D)$. Then, G has a least upper bound $\bigsqcup_\mathbb{R} G$ in $(\mathbb{R}(\Sigma, D), \leq)$ if and only if G has a least upper bound $\bigsqcup_\mathbb{G} G$ in $(\mathbb{G}(\Sigma, D), \leq)$. Moreover, in this case, $\bigsqcup_\mathbb{R} G = \bigsqcup_\mathbb{G} G$.*

Proof: First, assume that $\bigsqcup_\mathbb{R} G$ exists. Then, G is bounded above in $\mathbb{R}$, whence in $\mathbb{G}$ and $\bigsqcup_\mathbb{G} G$ exists (Corollary 11.3.3).

Conversely, assume that $h = \bigsqcup_\mathbb{G} G$ exists. We claim that h is in fact a real trace. Let $q \in V_h$ and let $g \in G$ be such that $q \in V_g$. Using Claim 2 of the proof of Theorem 11.3.2, we deduce that $\downarrow_h q = \downarrow_g q$. Hence, the past of q in h is finite and h is a real trace which proves the claim. It follows directly that h is the least upper bound of G in $\mathbb{R}$. This proves both that $\bigsqcup_\mathbb{R} G$ exists and that $\bigsqcup_\mathbb{R} G = \bigsqcup_\mathbb{G} G$.   □

Using Lemma 11.3.1 and Theorem 11.3.2, we deduce that every coherent set of real traces has a least upper bound *in* $\mathbb{G}$. By Lemma 11.3.4, this least upper bound is *in* $\mathbb{R}$. Therefore,

Theorem 11.3.5 *The poset $(\mathbb{R}(\Sigma, D), \leq)$ of real traces is a ccpo.*

Since every directed set (bounded set resp.) is coherent, we deduce immediately:

Corollary 11.3.6

1. *The poset $(\mathbb{R}(\Sigma, D), \leq)$ of real traces is a bcpo.*

2. *The poset $(\mathbb{R}(\Sigma, D), \leq)$ of real traces is a dcpo with the empty trace as least element.*

3. *Let α be a countable ordinal. Every increasing α-sequence of real traces has a least upper bound in $\mathbb{R}(\Sigma, D)$.*

From classical results on posets, we also get that every non-empty subset of $\mathbb{R}$ (of $\mathbb{G}$ resp.) has a greatest lower bound in $\mathbb{R}$ (in $\mathbb{G}$ resp.). Indeed, let $F \subseteq \mathbb{G}$ ($F \subseteq \mathbb{R}$ resp.) be a non-empty set of traces and let $G = \{g \in \mathbb{G} \mid g \leq f \text{ for all } f \in F\}$ be the set of lower bounds of F. Since F is non-empty, G is bounded above, and hence it admits a least upper bound $\sqcup G \in \mathbb{G}$ ($\sqcup G \in \mathbb{R}$ resp.). It is easy to verify that $\sqcup G$ is the greatest lower bound of F. Note that this existence result does not provide us with any characterization of the greatest lower bound. The following exercise gives such a characterization when the non-empty set F is also coherent.

Exercise 11.3.1 Show that the greatest lower bound of a non-empty and coherent set $F \subseteq \mathbb{G}(\Sigma, D)$ is $\sqcap F = [V, E, \lambda]$ where $V = \cap_{f \in F} V_f$, $E = \cap_{f \in F} E_f$ and $\lambda((a, i)) = a$ for all $(a, i) \in V$.

Finally, the following exercise may be used to prove the generalization of Levi's Lemma to traces (see Proposition 11.2.10).

Exercise 11.3.2 Let $g, h \in \mathbb{G}(\Sigma, D)$ be two coherent traces. Show that there exist $g', h' \in \mathbb{G}(\Sigma, D)$ such that $\text{alph}(g') \times \text{alph}(h') \subseteq I$ and

$$g = (g \sqcap h)g', \quad h = (g \sqcap h)h' \quad \text{and} \quad g \sqcup h = (g \sqcap h)g'h' = (g \sqcap h)h'g'$$

11.3.2 Algebraicity

Again, we recall some classical definitions. Let $(Z, \leq)$ be a poset. An element $x \in Z$ is *prime* if for all subset $Y \subseteq Z$ admitting a least upper bound, $x \leq \sqcup Y$ implies $x \leq y$ for some $y \in Y$. For $z \in Z$, let $P(z) = \{x \in Z \mid x \leq z \text{ and } x \text{ is prime}\}$ be the set of prime elements less than or equal to z.

Similarly, an element $x \in Z$ is *compact* if for all *directed* subset $Y \subseteq Z$ admitting a least upper bound, $x \leq \sqcup Y$ implies $x \leq y$ for some $y \in Y$. For $z \in Z$, let $C(z) = \{x \in Z \mid x \leq z \text{ and } x \text{ is compact}\}$ be the set of compact elements less than or equal to z.

A poset $(Z, \leq)$ is *prime algebraic* (*algebraic* resp.) if $z = \sqcup P(z)$ ($C(z)$ is directed and $z = \sqcup C(z)$ resp.) for all $z \in Z$. Finally, an algebraic dcpo is called a Domain. Frequently, one restricts oneself to domains with a countable set of compact elements.

We start with the characterization of prime and of compact transfinite traces. To this purpose, we introduce the following definition: let $g \in \mathbb{G}$ be a dependence graph, a subset of vertices $P \subseteq V_g$ dominates g if

$$V_g = \downarrow P = \{q \in V_g \mid q \preceq_g p \text{ for some } p \in P\}.$$

Proposition 11.3.7 *Let $f \in \mathbb{G}(\Sigma, D)$ be a transfinite trace.*

1. *f is prime if and only if f is dominated by one vertex.*

2. *f is compact if and only if f is dominated by a finite set of vertices.*

Proof: 1. We first assume that f is dominated by the vertex $p \in V_f$. Let $G \subseteq \mathbb{G}$ be such that $h = \sqcup G$ exists and $f \leq h$. From Proposition 11.2.5, f is the restriction of h to V_f. Hence, $p \in V_h$ and by Theorem 11.3.2, there exists $g \in G$ such that $p \in V_g$. From Proposition 11.2.5, g is the restriction of h to V_g. Moreover, $V_f = \downarrow_f p = \downarrow_h p = \downarrow_g p$. Therefore, f is the restriction of g to $\downarrow_g p$. That is, $f \leq g$ and we have proved that f is prime.

Conversely, let us assume that f is prime. For each $p \in V_f$, we denote by f_p the restriction of f to $\downarrow_f p$. Let $G = \{f_p \mid p \in V_f\}$. The trace f is an upper bound of the set G. Hence, $\sqcup G$ exists (Corollary 11.3.3) and we have $\sqcup G = \bigcup_{p \in V_f} f_p = f$ (Theorem 11.3.2). Since f is prime, we obtain $f \leq f_p$ for some $p \in V_f$, that is, f is dominated by the vertex p.

2. The proof is similar. Let us assume that f is dominated by a finite set of vertices $P \subseteq V_f$ and let G be a directed subset of $\mathbb{G}$ such that $h = \sqcup G$ exists and $f \leq h$. As above, we deduce that $P \subseteq V_h$. Since G is directed, we deduce from Theorem 11.3.2 that $P \subseteq V_g$ for some $g \in G$. Hence, $V_f = \downarrow_f P = \downarrow_h P = \downarrow_g P$ and we obtain $f \leq g$ which proves that f is compact.

Conversely, let us assume that f is compact. For each $P \subseteq V_f$, we denote by f_P the restriction of f to $\downarrow_f P$. Let $G = \{f_P \mid P \subseteq V_f \text{ and } P \text{ is finite}\}$. Observe that $\sqcup\{f_P, f_Q\} = f_{(P \cup Q)}$ for all $P, Q \subseteq V_f$. Therefore, the set G is directed. As above, we deduce that $\sqcup G = f$. Since f is compact, we obtain $f \leq f_P$ for some $P \subseteq V_f$, that is, f is dominated by the finite set of vertices P.   □

Using this characterization of prime traces, we derive the algebraicity and the prime algebraicity of the poset of transfinite traces. Unfortunately, $\mathbb{G}$ is not a Domain since we have seen in Section 11.3.1 that $\mathbb{G}$ is not a dcpo.

Theorem 11.3.8 *The poset* $(\mathbb{G}(\Sigma, D), \leq)$ *of transfinite traces is algebraic and prime algebraic.*

Proof: We first show that $\mathbb{G}$ is prime algebraic. Let $f \in \mathbb{G}$ be a transfinite trace. As in the proof of Proposition 11.3.7, for each $p \in V_f$, we denote by f_p the restriction of f to $\downarrow_f p$. Using Proposition 11.3.7, we deduce that the set of prime traces less than or equal to f is $P(f) = \{f_p \mid p \in V_f\}$. Finally, $\sqcup P(f) = \bigcup_{p \in V_f} f_p = f$.

Since every prime element is also compact, we deduce that $\sqcup C(f) = \sqcup P(f) = f$ for all $f \in \mathbb{G}$. To obtain the algebraicity of $\mathbb{G}$, it remains to prove that $C(f)$ is directed for all $f \in \mathbb{G}$. This follows from the bounded completeness of $\mathbb{G}$. Indeed, it is easy to verify that, if each coherent pair of a poset $(Z, \leq)$ has a least upper bound then $C(z)$ is directed for all $z \in Z$.   □

We now turn to the study of the algebraicity of the poset of real traces. As for completeness, the results do not follow directly from the previous ones. Indeed, let $(X, \leq)$ be a subposet of $(Z, \leq)$, an element $x \in X$ may be prime in $(X, \leq)$ but not in $(Z, \leq)$ and vice versa. However, such a situation does not arise for the subposet of real traces.

Lemma 11.3.9

1. Let $G \subseteq \mathbb{G}(\Sigma, D)$ be a coherent and countable set. Then

$$\mathrm{Re}(\sqcup G) = \sqcup \mathrm{Re}(G)$$

2. Let $f \in \mathbb{R}(\Sigma, D)$ be a real trace. Then, f is prime (compact resp.) in the poset $(\mathbb{R}(\Sigma, D), \leq)$ if and only if f is prime (compact resp.) in the poset $(\mathbb{G}(\Sigma, D), \leq)$.

Proof: 1. Let $h = \sqcup G$ (Theorem 11.3.2). For all $g \in G$, we have $\mathrm{Re}(g) \leq g \leq h$, whence $\mathrm{Re}(g) \leq \mathrm{Re}(h)$. Hence, the set $\mathrm{Re}(G)$ is bounded by $\mathrm{Re}(h)$ and has a least upper bound $\sqcup \mathrm{Re}(G) \in \mathbb{R}$ (Theorem 11.3.5). Moreover, $\sqcup \mathrm{Re}(G) \leq \mathrm{Re}(h)$. Now,

$$
\begin{aligned}
p \in V_{\mathrm{Re}(h)} \quad &\Longleftrightarrow \quad p \in V_h \text{ and } \downarrow_h p \text{ is finite} \\
&\Longleftrightarrow \quad p \in V_g \text{ and } \downarrow_g p \text{ is finite, for some } g \in G \\
&\Longleftrightarrow \quad p \in V_{\mathrm{Re}(g)} \text{ for some } g \in G
\end{aligned}
$$

Therefore, $V_{\mathrm{Re}(h)} = \bigcup_{g \in G} V_{\mathrm{Re}(g)}$ and we obtain $\mathrm{Re}(h) = \sqcup \mathrm{Re}(G)$.

2. The "if" part is clear. Conversely, let $f \in \mathbb{R}$ be prime (compact resp.) in $(\mathbb{R}, \leq)$. Assume that $f \leq \sqcup G$ for some set $G \subseteq \mathbb{G}$ (some coherent set $G \subseteq \mathbb{G}$ resp.) which admits a least upper bound. Then, $f \leq \mathrm{Re}(\sqcup G) = \sqcup \mathrm{Re}(G)$. Since f is prime (compact resp.) in $(\mathbb{R}, \leq)$, we have $f \leq \mathrm{Re}(g) \leq g$ for some $g \in G$. Therefore, f is prime (compact resp.) in the poset $(\mathbb{G}, \leq)$. $\qquad \square$

Note that a real trace which is dominated by a finite set of vertices is necessarily finite. Hence the characterization of prime real traces and of compact real traces follows directly from Proposition 11.3.7 and Lemma 11.3.9.

Proposition 11.3.10 Let $f \in \mathbb{R}(\Sigma, D)$ be a real trace.

1. f is prime if and only if f is finite and has only one maximal vertex.

2. f is compact if and only if f is finite.

Finally, we obtain the main theorem which states roughly that the poset of real traces has all the good properties one can wish for.

Theorem 11.3.11

1. The poset $(\mathbb{R}(\Sigma, D), \leq)$ of real traces is prime algebraic.

2. The poset $(\mathbb{R}(\Sigma, D), \leq)$ of real traces is a domain with a countable basis of compact elements which is the set $\mathbb{M}(\Sigma, D)$ of finite traces.

3. Every real trace is the least upper bound of an increasing sequence of finite traces.

Proof: 1. Let $g \in \mathbb{R}$ be a real trace. By Lemma 11.3.9, we have

$$\begin{aligned} P(g) &= \{f \in \mathbb{R} \mid f \le g \text{ and } f \text{ is prime in } (\mathbb{R}, \le)\} \\ &= \{f \in \mathbb{G} \mid f \le g \text{ and } f \text{ is prime in } (\mathbb{G}, \le)\} \end{aligned}$$

Using Theorem 11.3.8, we obtain $g = \sqcup_{\mathbb{G}} P(g)$. Finally, $g = \sqcup_{\mathbb{R}} P(g)$ by Lemma 11.3.4. This proves that $(\mathbb{R}, \le)$ is prime algebraic.

2. A similar proof shows the algebraicity of $(\mathbb{R}, \le)$. Using Corollary 11.3.6 we deduce that $(\mathbb{R}, \le)$ is a domain. Finally, the set of compact real traces is the set $\mathbb{M}$ of finite traces (Proposition 11.3.10) which is indeed countable.

3. This is an easy result from poset theory which only uses the fact that the poset $(\mathbb{R}, \le)$ is algebraic with a countable basis of compact elements. More precisely, let $g \in \mathbb{R}$ be a real trace. Since $C(g)$ is countable, we may enumerate the compact traces less than or equal to g in a sequence $(f_n)_{n<\omega}$. Using the fact that $C(g)$ is directed, we define inductively an increasing sequence $(g_n)_{n<\omega} \subseteq C(g)$ as follows. Let $g_0 = f_0$ and if $g_n \in C(g)$ is already defined then let g_{n+1} be any upper bound in $C(g)$ of g_n and f_{n+1}. Clearly, we obtain $g = \sqcup C(g) = \sqcup_{n<\omega} f_n = \sqcup_{n<\omega} g_n$. □

In order to state the last result of this section, we need some new definitions and general results from poset theory (see for instance [173]). Let $(Z, \le)$ be a poset. An ideal of Z is a subset $Y \subseteq Z$ which is directed and downward closed, i.e., $Y = \downarrow Y = \{x \in Z \mid x \le y \text{ for some } y \in Y\}$. Let $(Id(Z), \subseteq)$ be the poset of ideals of Z ordered by inclusion. Then the poset $(Id(Z), \subseteq)$ is a domain and the mapping $i : Z \longrightarrow Id(Z)$ defined by $i(z) = \downarrow z$ is an order embedding. The poset $(Id(Z), \subseteq)$ is called the ideal completion of the poset $(Z, \le)$. Moreover, if the poset $(Z, \le)$ is a domain, then the ideal completion of the subposet $(C(Z), \le)$ of compact elements of Z is order isomorphic to the poset $(Z, \le)$. Hence, we obtain directly from Theorem 11.3.11 the following result.

Corollary 11.3.12 *The poset* $(\mathbb{R}(\Sigma, D), \le)$ *of real traces is the ideal completion of the poset* $(\mathbb{M}(\Sigma, D), \le)$ *of finite traces.*

11.3.3 Notes

The poset properties of real traces were studied independently by Kwiatkowska [162, 164] and by Gastin and Rozoy [117]. More precisely, Kwiatkowska proved that the poset of real traces is a bounded complete domain which is the ideal completion of the poset of finite traces. In addition, Gastin and Rozoy proved that the poset of real traces is coherently complete and prime algebraic.

Later, the poset properties of transfinite traces were investigated by Gastin and Petit [114]. This last paper contains most of the results presented in this section. In addition, it deals with the poset properties of complex traces (see Section 11.4).

11.4 Complex Traces

Infinite words can be obtained from finite words in several ways. For instance, the poset of finite and infinite words is the ideal completion of the poset of finite words.

The set of finite words can also be provided with a metric based on prefixes such that concatenation on finite words is uniformly continuous. The metric completion of the metric space of finite words is once again the set of infinite words. In particular, the concatenation can be extended in a unique continuous way to infinite words and is still uniformly continuous.

For traces, we have seen in Section 11.3 that the set of real traces is the ideal completion of the poset of finite traces. Concerning metrics, the situation is much less satisfactory. Namely, as we will see more precisely in Section 11.5, there does not exist a natural metric on the set of finite traces such that, simultaneously, the concatenation is uniformly continuous and the metric completion of the set of finite traces is the set of real traces.

Complex traces were introduced in order to obtain a metric completion with a uniformly continuous concatenation. However, we first present these traces without any metric consideration. The reader interested in topology is referred to Section 11.5 for the study of a natural metric which makes the set of complex traces complete and compact.

11.4.1 Definition using Indistinguishability

Let (Σ, D) be a dependence alphabet. In general, the equivalence relation associated with the mapping $\mathrm{Re} : \mathbb{G} \to \mathbb{R}$ (which associates with each dependence graph its real part) is not a congruence. For instance, if $(\Sigma, D) = a \relbar\joinrel\relbar b \relbar\joinrel\relbar c$, $\mathrm{Re}(a^\omega) = \mathrm{Re}(a^\omega b) = a^\omega$ whereas $\mathrm{Re}(a^\omega c) = ca^\omega \neq a^\omega = \mathrm{Re}(a^\omega bc)$. We say that an equivalence relation on $\mathbb{G}$ respects real parts if two equivalent dependence graphs have the same real part. The identity on $\mathbb{G}$ clearly defines the finest congruence which respects real parts. It is easy to verify that the coarsest congruence which respects real parts is the transitive closure of the union of all the congruences which respect real parts.

Definition 11.4.1 *Let $\equiv$ be the coarsest congruence on $\mathbb{G}(\Sigma, D)$ which respects real parts. The monoid $\mathbb{C}(\Sigma, D)$, or simply $\mathbb{C}$, of complex traces is the quotient $\mathbb{G}(\Sigma, D)/\equiv$.*

The canonical surjection from $\mathbb{G}$ onto $\mathbb{C}$ is denoted by χ. The concatenation in the set $\mathbb{C}$ of complex traces, induced by the congruence $\equiv$, will be denoted $\cdot_{\mathbb{C}}$ or simply $\cdot$ if there is no risk of confusion.

Two dependence graphs g, h such that $\chi(g) = \chi(h)$ are said *indistinguishable*. Note that distinct real traces are always distinguishable, that is, χ is an embedding of the set of real traces $\mathbb{R}(\Sigma, D)$ into the set of complex traces $\mathbb{C}(\Sigma, D)$. In the sequel, a real trace r will be identified with its image $\chi(r)$ and we will simply write $r \in \mathbb{C}$.

11.4.2 A More Concrete View

Two dependence graphs with distinct real parts are of course distinguishable. But the previous definition does not give any direct way to decide whether two graphs with same real parts are congruent or not. To this purpose, we need a more explicit definition of complex traces. We first introduce some more notations and definitions on dependence graphs.

Let $A \subseteq \Sigma$, we define the set $D(A)$ of letters which depend on A by

$$D(A) = \{b \in \Sigma \mid (a,b) \in D \text{ for some } a \in A\}$$

and we define the set $I(A)$ of letters independent from A by

$$I(A) = \Sigma \setminus D(A) = \{b \in \Sigma \mid (a,b) \in I \text{ for all } a \in A\}.$$

In Definition 11.2.2, the real part, the transfinite part and the alphabet at infinity of a dependence graph g were introduced. In addition, we define $D(g) = D(\text{alph}(g))$ and we define the imaginary part of g by $\text{Im}(g) = D(\text{alphinf}(g))$.

For instance, let $(\Sigma, D) = a \text{ --- } b \text{ --- } c \text{ --- } d \text{ --- } e$. Let f_1, f_2, f_3, f_4, f_5, and f_6 be the dependence graphs represented in Figure 11.9. The real parts, transfinite parts, alphabets at infinity and imaginary parts of these dependence graphs are given below. Note that f_1 and f_2 have not the same real parts, and hence are distinguishable. On the contrary, f_3, f_4, f_5, and f_6 have the same real part, but we do not know whether they are distinguishable.

	$\text{Re}(\cdot)$	$\text{Tr}(\cdot)$	$\text{alphinf}(\cdot)$	$\text{Im}(\cdot)$	$D(\cdot)$
f_1	ae^ω	d	$\{d,e\}$	$\{c,d,e\}$	$\{a,b,c,d,e\}$
f_2	$b^2c^2da^\omega$	1	$\{a\}$	$\{a,b\}$	$\{a,b,c,d,e\}$
f_3	$ab(ac)^\omega$	1	$\{a,c\}$	$\{a,b,c,d\}$	$\{a,b,c,d\}$
f_4	$ab(ac)^\omega$	b^ω	$\{a,b,c\}$	$\{a,b,c,d\}$	$\{a,b,c,d\}$
f_5	$ab(ac)^\omega$	bd	$\{a,b,c,d\}$	$\{a,b,c,d,e\}$	$\{a,b,c,d,e\}$
f_6	$ab(ac)^\omega$	de	$\{a,c,d,e\}$	$\{a,b,c,d,e\}$	$\{a,b,c,d,e\}$

Since we are looking for a congruence which respects real parts, we will need to compute the real part of the concatenation of two dependence graphs. To this purpose, for any dependence graph g and any subset A of Σ, we extract the maximal real prefix of g containing letters from $I(A)$ only. Formally, if $g = [V, E, \lambda]$, $\mu_A(g)$ is the restriction of g to $\{p \in V \mid \downarrow p \text{ is finite and } \text{alph}(\downarrow p) \subseteq I(A)\}$. From Remark 11.2.3 and Proposition 11.2.5, we deduce that $\mu_A(g)$ is a prefix of g. The corresponding suffix $\mu_A(g)^{-1}g$ (see Remark 11.2.9) will be denoted by $\text{suff}_A(g)$.

Remark 11.4.2 If g is a dependence graph and A a subset of Σ, it holds, from the very definition,

$$\mu_A(g) = \mu_A(\text{Re}(g))$$

and hence, by left-cancellativity of $\mathbb{G}$ (Proposition 11.2.8),

$$\text{suff}_A(g) = \text{suff}_A(\text{Re}(g)) \cdot \text{Tr}(g)$$

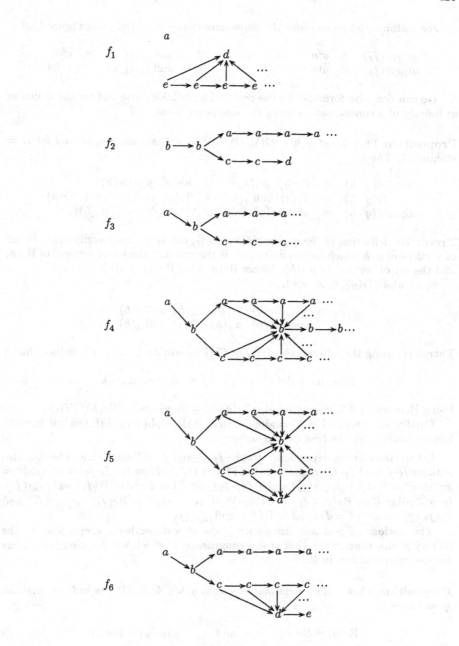

Figure 11.9: Some dependence graphs

For instance, let us consider the dependence graphs f_2 and f_5 of Figure 11.9.

$$\mu_{\{d,e\}}(f_2) = b^2 a^\omega \qquad\qquad \mathrm{suff}_{\{d,e\}}(f_2) = c^2 d$$
$$\mu_{\{d,e\}}(f_5) = aba^\omega \qquad\qquad \mathrm{suff}_{\{d,e\}}(f_5) = c^\omega bd$$

We can now give formulas for the real and transfinite parts and for the alphabet at infinity of a concatenation using the mappings μ and suff.

Proposition 11.4.3 *Let* $g, h \in \mathbb{G}(\Sigma, D)$ *be two dependence graphs and let* $A = \mathrm{alphinf}(g)$. *Then.*

$$\mathrm{Re}(g \cdot h) = \mathrm{Re}(g) \cdot \mu_A(h) = \mathrm{Re}(g) \cdot \mu_A(\mathrm{Re}(h))$$
$$\mathrm{Tr}(g \cdot h) = \mathrm{Tr}(g) \cdot \mathrm{suff}_A(h) = \mathrm{Tr}(g) \cdot \mathrm{suff}_A(\mathrm{Re}(h)) \cdot \mathrm{Tr}(h)$$
$$\mathrm{alphinf}(g \cdot h) = \mathrm{alphinf}(g) \cup \mathrm{alphinf}(h) \cup \mathrm{alph}(\mathrm{suff}_A(\mathrm{Re}(h)))$$

Proof: By definition of the concatenation in $\mathbb{G}$, one may easily verify that the set of vertices of $g \cdot h$ which have a finite past is the union of the set of vertices of $\mathrm{Re}(g)$ and the set of vertices of $\mu_A(h)$. Hence $\mathrm{Re}(g \cdot h) = \mathrm{Re}(g) \cdot \mu_A(h)$.

Since $\mathrm{alph}(\mathrm{Tr}(g)) \subseteq A$, we have

$$g \cdot h = \mathrm{Re}(g) \cdot \mathrm{Tr}(g) \cdot \mu_A(h) \cdot \mathrm{suff}_A(h)$$
$$= \mathrm{Re}(g) \cdot \mu_A(h) \cdot \mathrm{Tr}(g) \cdot \mathrm{suff}_A(h)$$

Therefore, using the left-cancellativity of $\mathbb{G}$ (Proposition 11.2.8), we deduce that

$$\mathrm{Tr}(g \cdot h) = \mathrm{Re}(g \cdot h)^{-1}(g \cdot h) = \mathrm{Tr}(g) \cdot \mathrm{suff}_A(h).$$

Using Remark 11.4.2, we obtain also $\mathrm{Tr}(g \cdot h) = \mathrm{Tr}(g) \cdot \mathrm{suff}_A(\mathrm{Re}(h)) \cdot \mathrm{Tr}(h)$.

Finally, since $\mathrm{alphinf}(g \cdot h) = \mathrm{alphinf}(\mathrm{Re}(g \cdot h)) \cup \mathrm{alph}(\mathrm{Tr}(g \cdot h))$, the last formula follows easily from the first two formulas. □

Let us consider the dependence graphs f_1, f_2 and f_5 of Figure 11.9. The concatenations $f_1 \cdot f_2$ and $f_1 \cdot f_5$ are presented in Figure 11.10. Then $\mathrm{Re}(f_1 \cdot f_2) = ab^2(ae)^\omega = ae^\omega \cdot b^2 a^\omega = \mathrm{Re}(f_1) \cdot \mu_{\{d,e\}}(f_2)$ and $\mathrm{Tr}(f_1 \cdot f_2) = dc^2 d = d \cdot c^2 d = \mathrm{Tr}(f_1) \cdot \mathrm{suff}_{\{d,e\}}(f_2)$. In a similar way, $\mathrm{Re}(f_1 \cdot f_5) = a^2 b(ae)^\omega = ae^\omega \cdot aba^\omega = \mathrm{Re}(f_1) \cdot \mu_{\{d,e\}}(f_5)$ and $\mathrm{Tr}(f_1 \cdot f_5) = dc^\omega bd = d \cdot c^\omega bd = \mathrm{Tr}(f_1) \cdot \mathrm{suff}_{\{d,e\}}(f_5)$.

The notions of real and imaginary parts of a dependence graph lead to the following nice characterization of the congruence $\equiv$ which will be used intensively for the computations in $\mathbb{C}$.

Proposition 11.4.4 *Two dependence graphs* $g, h \in \mathbb{G}(\Sigma, D)$ *are indistinguishable if and only if*

$$\mathrm{Re}(g) = \mathrm{Re}(h) \qquad \text{and} \qquad \mathrm{Im}(g) = \mathrm{Im}(h)$$

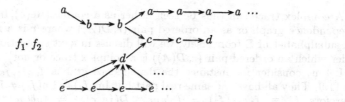

$f_1 \cdot f_2$

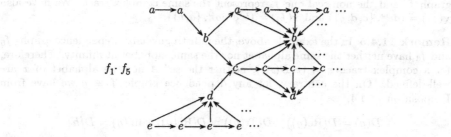

$f_1 \cdot f_5$

Figure 11.10: Concatenations

Proof: In $\mathbb{G}$, the relation "to have the same real and imaginary parts" is clearly an equivalence relation. Let $f, g \in \mathbb{G}$ be such that $\mathrm{Re}(f) = \mathrm{Re}(g)$ and $\mathrm{Im}(f) = \mathrm{Im}(g)$. We may have $\mathrm{alphinf}(f) \neq \mathrm{alphinf}(g)$ but $I(\mathrm{alphinf}(f)) = I(\mathrm{alphinf}(g))$, hence $\mu_{\mathrm{alphinf}(f)} = \mu_{\mathrm{alphinf}(g)}$ and $\mathrm{suff}_{\mathrm{alphinf}(f)} = \mathrm{suff}_{\mathrm{alphinf}(g)}$. Therefore, using Proposition 11.4.3, it may be easily verified that, for any $h \in \mathbb{G}$, $\mathrm{Re}(f \cdot h) = \mathrm{Re}(g \cdot h)$, $\mathrm{Im}(f \cdot h) = \mathrm{Im}(g \cdot h)$ and $\mathrm{Re}(h \cdot f) = \mathrm{Re}(h \cdot g)$, $\mathrm{Im}(h \cdot f) = \mathrm{Im}(h \cdot g)$. Thus "to have the same real and imaginary parts" is a congruence which respects real parts.

Conversely, suppose that $f, g \in \mathbb{G}$ are indistinguishable. By definition, $\mathrm{Re}(f) = \mathrm{Re}(g)$. Assume for instance that $a \in \mathrm{Im}(f) \setminus \mathrm{Im}(g)$. From Proposition 11.4.3, $\mathrm{Re}(fa) = \mathrm{Re}(f)$ whereas $\mathrm{Re}(ga) = \mathrm{Re}(g) \cdot a \neq \mathrm{Re}(g)$. Hence we get $\mathrm{Re}(fa) \neq \mathrm{Re}(ga)$ which is in contradiction with the facts that $f \equiv g$ and $\equiv$ is a congruence. $\square$

A complex trace can thus be seen either as a couple $(\mathrm{Re}(g), \mathrm{Im}(g))$ where g is a dependence graph or as an ordered pair $(r, D(A))$ where r is a real trace and A is a subalphabet of Σ (conversely, we will discuss in next subsection the conditions under which an ordered pair $(r, D(A))$ is a complex trace or not).

Let us consider for instance the dependence graphs f_3, f_4, f_5 and f_6 of Figure 11.9. They all have the same real part but $\mathrm{Im}(f_3) = \mathrm{Im}(f_4) \neq \mathrm{Im}(f_5) = \mathrm{Im}(f_6)$. Therefore $f_3 \equiv f_4$, $\chi(f_3) = (ab(ac)^\omega, D(\{a,c\})) = (ab(ac)^\omega, D(\{a,b,c\})) = (ab(ac)^\omega, \{a,b,c,d\})$ and $f_5 \equiv f_6$, $\chi(f_5) = (ab(ac)^\omega, D(\{a,b,c,d\})) = (ab(ac)^\omega, D(\{a,c,d,e\})) = (ab(ac)^\omega, \{a,b,c,d,e\})$. Note that the real dependence graph f_3 and the non-real one f_4 represent the same complex trace. We have also $\chi(f_1) = (ae^\omega, \{c,d,e\})$ and $\chi(f_2) = (b^2c^2da^\omega, \{a,b\})$.

Remark 11.4.5 In the example above, the indistinguishable dependence graphs f_5 and f_6 have neither the same alphabet nor the same alphabet at infinity. Therefore, for a complex trace $x = (r, D(A))$, neither the set A nor the alphabet of x are well-defined. On the contrary, for any dependence graphs $f \equiv g$ we have from Proposition 11.4.4,

$$D(g) = D(\mathrm{Re}(g)) \cup D(\mathrm{Tr}(g)) = D(\mathrm{Re}(g)) \cup \mathrm{Im}(g) = D(h)$$

Thus, the notation $D(.)$ factorizes to complex traces and for $x = (r, D(A)) \in \mathbb{C}$, we have $D(x) = D(\mathrm{alph}(r)) \cup D(A)$. Finally, note that $D(\mathrm{alphinf}(r)) \subseteq D(A)$.

From Proposition 11.4.3, we deduce easily a direct formula for the concatenation of two complex traces.

Proposition 11.4.6 *Let $(r, D(A))$ and $(s, D(B))$ be two complex traces in $\mathbb{C}(\Sigma, D)$.*

$$(r, D(A)) \cdot_{\mathbb{C}} (s, D(B)) = (r\mu_A(s), D(A) \cup D(B) \cup D(\mathrm{suff}_A(s)))$$

Let f_1, f_2 and f_5 be the dependence graphs of Figure 11.9. Using the previous examples and the formula of Proposition 11.4.6, we get:

$$\begin{aligned}
\chi(f_1) \cdot \chi(f_2) &= (ae^\omega \cdot b^2 a^\omega, D(\{d,e\}) \cup D(\{a\}) \cup D(c^2 d)) \\
&= (ab^2(ae)^\omega, D(\{a,c,d,e\}))
\end{aligned}$$

and

$$\chi(f_1) \cdot \chi(f_5) = (ae^\omega \cdot aba^\omega, D(\{d, e\}) \cup D(\{a, b, c, d\}) \cup D(c^\omega))$$
$$= (a^2 b(ae)^\omega, D(\{a, b, c, d, e\}))$$

With the representations of Figure 11.10, it can be checked that, of course,

$$\chi(f_1) \cdot_{\mathbb{C}} \chi(f_2) = \chi(f_1 \cdot_{\mathbb{G}} f_2) \quad \text{and} \quad \chi(f_1) \cdot_{\mathbb{C}} \chi(f_5) = \chi(f_1 \cdot_{\mathbb{G}} f_5).$$

Recall that the monoid $\mathbb{G}$ and the partial monoid $\mathbb{R}$ are left-cancellative. In contrast, the set of complex traces is not cancellative since, for instance, $a^\omega \cdot a^\omega = a^\omega$ for any letter $a \in \Sigma$. But, from Proposition 11.4.6, a finite trace $p \in \mathbb{M}$ is a prefix of a complex trace $x = (r, D(A))$ if and only if p is a prefix of the real part r of x. Hence,

Remark 11.4.7 The monoid $\mathbb{C}$ is left-cancellative by finite traces.

As we have seen in Section 11.2 infinite products are naturally defined in the set $\mathbb{G}$ of dependence graphs. In order to define these products for complex traces, we first explicit the real part and the alphabet at infinity of an infinite product of dependence graphs.

Lemma 11.4.8 *Let α be a countable ordinal and let $(g_i)_{i<\alpha}$ be an α-sequence of dependence graphs. For all $0 \le i \le \alpha$, let $A_i = \text{alphinf}(\prod_{j<i} g_j)$ (note that $A_0 = \emptyset$) and for all $0 \le i < \alpha$, let $r_i = \mu_{A_i}(g_i) = \mu_{A_i}(\text{Re}(g_i))$. Then, for all $0 \le i \le \alpha$,*

$$\text{Re}\left(\prod_{j<i} g_j\right) = \prod_{j<i} r_j$$

and

$$A_i = \begin{cases} (\bigcup_{j<i} A_j) \cup \text{alphinf}(\prod_{j<i} r_j) & \text{if } i \text{ is a limit ordinal} \\ A_{i-1} \cup \text{alphinf}(g_{i-1}) \cup \text{alph}(\text{suff}_{A_{i-1}}(\text{Re}(g_{i-1}))) & \text{otherwise} \end{cases}$$

Proof: We prove by induction the first formula of the lemma. Let $i \le \alpha$ and assume that $\text{Re}(\prod_{k<j} g_k) = \prod_{k<j} r_k$ for all $j < i$.

If i is a successor ordinal then $\prod_{j<i} g_j = (\prod_{j<i-1} g_j) \cdot g_{i-1}$. By Proposition 11.4.3 and the induction hypothesis we deduce $\text{Re}(\prod_{j<i} g_j) = (\prod_{j<i-1} r_j) \cdot \mu_{A_{i-1}}(g_{i-1}) = \prod_{j<i} r_j$.

If i is a limit ordinal then, using Formula 11.3 of Section 11.3.1, Lemma 11.3.9 and the induction hypothesis we deduce

$$\text{Re}\left(\prod_{j<i} g_j\right) = \text{Re}\left(\bigsqcup_{j<i}\left(\prod_{k<j} g_k\right)\right) = \bigsqcup_{j<i} \text{Re}\left(\prod_{k<j} g_k\right) = \bigsqcup_{j<i}\left(\prod_{k<j} r_k\right) = \prod_{j<i} r_j$$

We do not need an induction to prove the second formula of the lemma. If i is a successor ordinal, the formula follows directly from Proposition 11.4.3. Now, let us assume that i is a limit ordinal. Clearly, $(\bigcup_{j<i} A_j) \cup \text{alphinf}(\prod_{j<i} r_j) \subseteq A_i$. Conversely, it is enough to show that $\text{alph}(\text{Tr}(\prod_{j<i} g_j)) \subseteq \bigcup_{j<i} A_j$. Let $a \in \text{alph}(\text{Tr}(\prod_{j<i} g_j))$, there exists $k < i$ such that $a \in \text{alph}(\text{Tr}(\prod_{j\le k} g_j))$. Hence, $a \in A_{k+1} \subseteq \bigcup_{j<i} A_j$. $\square$

Let $(g_i)_{i<\alpha}$ be an α-sequence of dependence graphs. Using Lemma 11.4.8, it follows directly by induction that the α-sequences $(r_i)_{i<\alpha}$ and $(D(A_i))_{i\le\alpha}$ depend only on the α-sequences $(\text{Re}(g_i))_{i<\alpha}$ and $(\text{Im}(g_i))_{i<\alpha}$. Therefore, indistinguishability is also preserved by α-products, that is, $\prod_{i<\alpha} g_i$ and $\prod_{i<\alpha} h_i$ are indistinguishable if $(g_i)_{i<\alpha}$ and $(h_i)_{i<\alpha}$ are two α-sequences of dependence graphs such that g_i and h_i are indistinguishable for all ordinal $i < \alpha$. Moreover, from Lemma 11.4.8 we obtain formulas for α-products of complex traces which generalize Proposition 11.4.6.

Corollary 11.4.9 *For all countable ordinal α, the α-product is well-defined in the set $\mathbb{C}(\Sigma, D)$ of complex traces. Moreover, let $(x_i)_{i<\alpha}$ be an α-sequence of complex traces and let $(A_i)_{i\le\alpha}$ be an (increasing) sequence of subalphabets such that $A_0 = \emptyset$ and for all $1 \le i \le \alpha$,*

$$D(A_i) = \begin{cases} (\bigcup_{j<i} D(A_j)) \cup D(\text{alphinf}(\prod_{j<i} \mu_{A_j}(x_j))) & \text{if } i \text{ is a limit ordinal} \\ D(A_{i-1}) \cup \text{Im}(x_{i-1}) \cup D(\text{suff}_{A_{i-1}}(\text{Re}(x_{i-1}))) & \text{otherwise} \end{cases}$$

Then, for all $0 \le i \le \alpha$,

$$\text{Re}\left(\prod_{j<i} x_j\right) = \prod_{j<i} \mu_{A_j}(x_j) \quad and \quad \text{Im}\left(\prod_{j<i} x_j\right) = D(A_i)$$

For instance, let $(\Sigma, D) = a \textemdash b \textemdash c \textemdash d$ and let g be the real dependence graph $abcd^\omega$. We have $\chi(g) = (abcd^\omega, D(\{d\}))$ and hence $\chi(g)^2 = (abcabd^\omega, D(\{c,d\}))$ and $\chi(g)^3 = (abcabad^\omega, D(\{b,c,d\}))$. Therefore, for any countable ordinal $\alpha \ge 3$, $\chi(g)^\alpha = \chi(g)^3$.

Let h be the non real dependence graph $ac^\omega d$. For any countable ordinal α, we have $h^\alpha = a^\alpha(c^\omega d)^\alpha$ and therefore for any integer $n < \omega$, $\chi(h)^n = \chi(h^n) = (a^n c^\omega, D(\{c,d\}))$ whereas for any countable ordinal $\alpha \ge \omega$, $\chi(h)^\alpha = ((ac)^\omega, D(\{a,c,d\}))$.

11.4.3 Links with Real Traces

Let $(\Sigma, D) = \Sigma \times \Sigma$ be a full dependence alphabet. In this particular case, $\mathbb{M} = \Sigma^*$ is the free monoid and a real trace is nothing else but a finite or ω-word. Moreover, if $(r, D(A)) \in \mathbb{C}$, then either r is finite and $A = D(A) = \emptyset$ or r is infinite and $D(A) = \Sigma$. Therefore the second component is redundant and we can identify the sets Σ^∞, $\mathbb{R}(\Sigma, \Sigma \times \Sigma)$ and $\mathbb{C}(\Sigma, \Sigma \times \Sigma)$. More generally, if the dependence relation D is transitive, (Σ, D) is a disjoint union $\bigcup_{i=1}^{k}(\Sigma_i, \Sigma_i \times \Sigma_i)$ and the sets $\prod_{i=1}^{k} \Sigma_i^\infty$, $\mathbb{R}(\Sigma, D)$ and $\mathbb{C}(\Sigma, D)$ can be identified.

When the dependence relation D is not transitive, $\mathbb{R}(\Sigma, D)$ and $\mathbb{C}(\Sigma, D)$ are distinct. However, we have seen in the previous subsection that the set of real traces $\mathbb{R}(\Sigma, D)$ is always embedded in the set of complex traces $\mathbb{C}(\Sigma, D)$. More precisely, a real trace r is identified with the complex trace $(r, D(\text{alphinf}(r)))$.

Let r, s be two real traces, we have seen (Remark 11.2.6) that $r \cdot_{\mathbb{R}} s$ is well-defined if and only if $\text{alphinf}(r) \times \text{alph}(s) \subseteq I$. In this case, it holds $\mu_{\text{alphinf}(r)}(s) = s$ and thus (Proposition 11.4.6),

$$
\begin{aligned}
r \cdot_{\mathbb{C}} s &= (r, D(\text{alphinf}(r))) \cdot_{\mathbb{C}} (s, D(\text{alphinf}(s))) \\
&= (r \cdot_{\mathbb{R}} s, D(\text{alphinf}(r)) \cup D(\text{alphinf}(s))) \\
&= r \cdot_{\mathbb{R}} s
\end{aligned}
$$

On the contrary, note that the concatenation $r \cdot_{\mathbb{C}} s$ may be a real trace even when $r \cdot_{\mathbb{R}} s$ is undefined. For instance, if $a \in \Sigma$, $a^\omega \cdot_{\mathbb{C}} a^\omega = a^\omega$ whereas $a^\omega \cdot_{\mathbb{R}} a^\omega$ is undefined.

Besides, each complex trace is an ordered pair $(r, D(A))$ where r is a real trace and A is a subalphabet of Σ. To summarize, it holds thus $\mathbb{R} \subseteq \mathbb{C} \subseteq \mathbb{R} \times \mathcal{P}(\Sigma)$ where $\mathcal{P}(\Sigma)$ denotes the set of subalphabets of Σ. Conversely, in order to study under which conditions an element of $\mathbb{R} \times \mathcal{P}(\Sigma)$ is a complex trace, we need some more notations and definitions on dependence graphs.

For a dependence graph $g = [V, E, \lambda] \in \mathbb{G}$, we recall that $\min(g)$ is the set of labels of the minimal vertices in g (see Section 11.2.3). Since these labels are pairwise independent, $\min(g)$ can also be seen as a finite trace of $\mathbf{M}$. The reduction of g, denoted by $\text{red}(g)$, is the restriction of g to the set $\{p \in V \mid \forall q \in V, \lambda(p) = \lambda(q) \implies (p, q) \in E^*\}$. From Remark 11.2.3, $\text{red}(g)$ is also a finite trace.

For instance, the minimal vertices and the reductions of the dependence graphs of Figure 11.9 are presented in Figure 11.4.3.

The following formulas, obvious from the definitions, will be used throughout.

Lemma 11.4.10 Let $g \in \mathbb{G}(\Sigma, D)$ be a dependence graph.

$$
\begin{aligned}
\min(\min(g)) &= \min(g) \\
\min(\text{red}(g)) &= \min(g) \\
\text{alph}(\text{red}(g)) &= \text{alph}(g) \\
\text{red}(\text{red}(g)) &= \text{red}(g)
\end{aligned}
$$

We can now characterize the elements of $\mathbb{R} \times \mathcal{P}(\Sigma)$ which are complex traces.

Proposition 11.4.11 Let $(r, D(B)) \in \mathbb{R}(\Sigma, D) \times \mathcal{P}(\Sigma)$ and let $A \subseteq \Sigma$ be such that $D(\text{alphinf}(r)) = D(A)$. The following assertions are equivalent:

1. $(r, D(B)) \in \mathbb{C}(\Sigma, D)$

2. $\exists f \in \mathbf{M}(\Sigma, D)$ such that $r \cdot_{\mathbb{C}} f = (r, D(B))$

3. $\exists f \in \mathbf{M}(\Sigma, D)$ such that $|f| \leq |\Sigma|$, $\min(f) \subseteq D(A)$ and $D(A) \cup D(f) = D(B)$

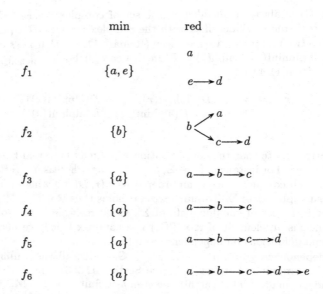

Figure 11.11: Minimal vertices and reductions

Proof: 3) ⇒ 2) Since $\min(f) \subseteq D(A)$, we have $\mu_A(f) = 1$. Hence, by Proposition 11.4.6, it holds $r \cdot_{\mathbb{C}} f = (r, D(B)) \cdot_{\mathbb{C}} (f, \emptyset) = (r, D(A) \cup D(f)) = (r, D(B))$.

2) ⇒ 1) follows directly from the containment $\mathbb{M} \subseteq \mathbb{C}$.

1) ⇒ 3) Let g be a dependence graph such that $\chi(g) = (r, D(B))$. Let us define $f = \text{red}(\text{Tr}(g))$. By definition of the reduction of a dependence graph, f is a finite trace which verifies $|f| \leq |\Sigma|, \min(f) = \min(\text{Tr}(g))$ and $\text{alph}(f) = \text{alph}(\text{Tr}(g))$ (Lemma 11.4.10). By definition of the transfinite part of a dependence graph, it holds $\min(\text{Tr}(g)) \subseteq D(\text{alphinf}(\text{Re}(g))) = D(\text{alphinf}(r)) = D(A)$. Moreover, $D(A) \cup D(f) = D(\text{alphinf}(\text{Re}(g))) \cup D(\text{alph}(\text{Tr}(g))) = D(\text{alphinf}(g)) = D(B)$. □

Note that if $A = \emptyset$, only the empty trace satisfies $\min(f) \subseteq D(A)$. Hence an ordered pair $(r, D(B))$ of $\mathbb{R} \times \mathcal{P}(\Sigma)$ with r finite is a complex trace if and only if $B = \emptyset$.

For instance, with the dependence graphs of Figure 11.9, we have:

$$\chi(f_1) = (ae^\omega, D(\{d, e\})) = (ae^\omega, D(\{e\})) \cdot (d, \emptyset) = ae^\omega \cdot_{\mathbb{C}} d$$
$$\chi(f_2) = (b^2 c^2 da^\omega, D(\{a\})) = (b^2 c^2 da^\omega, D(\{a\})) \cdot (1, \emptyset) = b^2 c^2 da^\omega$$
$$\chi(f_4) = (ab(ac)^\omega, D(\{a, b, c\})) = (ab(ac)^\omega, D(\{a, c\})) \cdot (b, \emptyset) = ab(ac)^\omega \cdot_{\mathbb{C}} b$$
$$\chi(f_5) = (ab(ac)^\omega, D(\{a, b, c, d\})) = (ab(ac)^\omega, D(\{a, c\})) \cdot (bd, \emptyset) = ab(ac)^\omega \cdot_{\mathbb{C}} bd$$

Since each real trace is a product of at most ω finite traces (Corollary 11.2.19), we get the following corollary from Proposition 11.4.11.

Corollary 11.4.12 *A complex trace may be written as the product of at most* $\omega + 1$ *finite traces.*

$$\mathbb{C}(\Sigma, D) = \mathbb{M}(\Sigma, D)^{\omega+1}$$

From Proposition 11.4.11 3), the fact that an ordered pair $(r, D(B))$ of $\mathbb{R} \times \mathcal{P}(\Sigma)$ belongs to $\mathbb{C}$ does not depend on r and B but on $D(\mathrm{alphinf}(r))$ and $D(B)$ only. More precisely, if f is a finite trace such that $r \cdot f = (r, D(B))$ then $s \cdot f = (s, D(B))$ for any real trace s with $D(\mathrm{alphinf}(s)) = D(\mathrm{alphinf}(r))$. An ordered pair (A, B) of subsets of Σ is said *consistent* if $(r, D(B)) \in \mathbb{C}$ for some real trace r such that $D(\mathrm{alphinf}(r)) = D(A)$.

For all complex trace language L and for all subset B of Σ, we define

$$L_B = \{x \in L \mid \mathrm{Im}(x) = D(B)\}.$$

In particular, $\mathbb{R}_B = \{r \in \mathbb{R} \mid D(\mathrm{alphinf}(r)) = D(B)\}$. For all subsets A, B of Σ, it holds

$$\mathrm{Re}(L_B) \cap \mathbb{R}_A = \{r \in \mathbb{R} \mid D(\mathrm{alphinf}(r)) = D(A) \text{ and } (r, D(B)) \in L\}.$$

Note that either (A, B) is not consistent and $\mathrm{Re}(L_B) \cap \mathbb{R}_A = \emptyset$ or (A, B) is consistent and there exists a finite trace $s_{A,B} \in \mathbb{M}$ such that

$$(\mathrm{Re}(L_B) \cap \mathbb{R}_A) \cdot s_{A,B} = \{(r, D(B)) \in L \mid D(\mathrm{alphinf}(r)) = D(A)\}$$

This proves the following proposition which makes the link between real and complex trace languages.

Proposition 11.4.13 *Let L be a language of $\mathbb{C}(\Sigma, D)$.*

$$L = \bigcup_{(A,B) \text{ consistent}} (\mathrm{Re}(L_B) \cap \mathbb{R}(\Sigma, D)_A) \cdot s_{A,B}$$

where, for each consistent pair (A, B), $s_{A,B}$ is a finite trace such that $r \cdot s_{A,B} = (r, D(B))$ for any real trace r with $D(\mathrm{alphinf}(r)) = D(A)$.

11.4.4 Notes

The notion of complex traces has been introduced by Diekert in [54]. In the original paper, the concept of α-complex traces was also defined and studied as an intermediary tool. Roughly speaking, the α-complex trace associated with a dependence graph g is $(\mathrm{Re}(g), \mathrm{alphinf}(g))$. Hence, in an α-complex trace, the information given by the second component is more precise than in a complex trace. Nevertheless, the theory of complex traces proves that the perfect knowledge of the alphabet at infinity is not necessary. Only the letters which depend on this alphabet, that is, the imaginary part of a representing dependence graph, have to be known.

At least two natural orders can be studied on the set of complex traces. First, using the inclusion $\mathbb{C} \subseteq \mathbb{R} \times \mathcal{P}(\Sigma)$, a product order $\sqsubseteq$ can be defined from the prefix order in $\mathbb{R}$ and the inclusion order in $\mathcal{P}(\Sigma)$. More precisely, $(r, D(A)) \sqsubseteq (s, D(B))$ if $r \leq s$ and $D(A) \subseteq D(B)$. Second, the concatenation in $\mathbb{C}$ defines also a prefix order $\leq$ in $\mathbb{C}$. Note that, from Proposition 11.4.6, it is clear that, if x, y are two complex traces, $x \leq y$ implies $x \sqsubseteq y$. For these two orders, the poset properties of complex traces have been investigated by Gastin and Petit [114]. Both posets $(\mathbb{C}, \sqsubseteq)$ and $(\mathbb{C}, \leq)$ are shown to be coherently complete. But, in general, they are neither algebraic nor prime algebraic. In fact, the situation slightly differs for the two orders.

First, for the product order, a complex trace is compact if and only if it is finite. This result is satisfactory from a semantic point of view. But, since whenever it exists, the least upper bound of a set of finite traces is a real trace it follows that the poset $(\mathbb{C}, \sqsubseteq)$ is algebraic if and only if $\mathbb{C} = \mathbb{R}$, i.e., when the dependence relation D is transitive.

Second, for the prefix order, there may exist prime complex traces which are not real traces. When the dependence relation D is transitive, the poset $(\mathbb{C}, \leq)$ of complex traces is order isomorphic to the poset $(\mathbb{R}, \leq)$ of real traces, and hence it is a domain. In the other cases, depending on the dependence relation D, there may exist complex traces which are not the least upper bound of their compact (prime resp.) lower bounds.

11.5   Topology on Complex Traces

This section is devoted to the study of the topological properties of complex traces. These traces were presented in Section 11.4 without any metric consideration. However, the original motivation for their introduction lies in the results of this section. Note that, these results are not required for the sequel of the chapter.

11.5.1   Basic Properties

We begin with some reminders on the topology on finite and ω-words which will guide us through the approach to the topology on traces. We refer to [225] for a detailed study of the topology on words.

The set Σ^∞ of finite and ω-words over the alphabet Σ can be provided with a metric $d_{\mathrm{pref}} : \Sigma^\infty \times \Sigma^\infty \longrightarrow \mathbb{R}$ defined by

$$d_{\mathrm{pref}}(u, v) = 2^{-l_{\mathrm{pref}}(u,v)}$$

where the function $l_{\mathrm{pref}} : \Sigma^\infty \times \Sigma^\infty \longrightarrow \mathbb{N} \cup \{\infty\}$ is defined by

$$l_{\mathrm{pref}}(u, v) = sup\{n \in \mathbb{N} \mid \forall p \in \Sigma^*, |p| \leq n \Longrightarrow (p \leq u \Longleftrightarrow p \leq v)\}$$

and $2^{-\infty} = 0$ by convention. In other words, if $u \neq v$, $l_{\mathrm{pref}}(u, v)$ is the first integer n such that the $(n+1)st$ letter of u differs from the $(n+1)st$ letter of v.

The concatenation is uniformly continuous in the metric space $(\Sigma^*, d_{\mathrm{pref}})$. The metric completion of $(\Sigma^*, d_{\mathrm{pref}})$ is precisely $(\Sigma^\infty, d_{\mathrm{pref}})$. Furthermore, the set Σ^∞ is compact for the topology induced by d_{pref}.

It can be shown (see Section 11.5.3) that there does not exist a natural metric based on prefixes only, such that the concatenation in $\mathbb{M}$ is uniformly continuous. Therefore, suffixes also must be taken into account. The basic idea is that the alphabet of the suffixes, or rather the letters dependent on this alphabet , must be considered. Rather than proposing a metric on $\mathbb{M}$ and then extending it to $\mathbb{C}$, we will introduce a metric directly on complex traces. From Remark 11.4.7, if a finite trace p is a prefix of a complex trace $x = (r, D(A))$, there exists a unique complex trace y such that $p \cdot y = x$. This complex trace is $y = (p^{-1}r, D(A))$ and will be denoted by $p^{-1}x$.

The following convention for partially defined functions will be used: if p is a finite trace and x, y are two complex traces, an equation such as $D(p^{-1}x) = D(p^{-1}y)$ means that either both $p^{-1}x$ and $p^{-1}y$ are undefined or both are defined and the values of $D(p^{-1}x)$ and $D(p^{-1}y)$ are equal.

Definition 11.5.1 *The function* $l_{\mathbb{C}} : \mathbb{C}(\Sigma, D) \times \mathbb{C}(\Sigma, D) \longrightarrow \mathbb{N} \cup \{\infty\}$ *is defined by:*

$$l_{\mathbb{C}}(x, y) = sup\{n \in \mathbb{N} \mid \forall p \in \mathbb{M}(\Sigma, D), \mid p \mid < n \Longrightarrow D(p^{-1}x) = D(p^{-1}y)\}$$

and the function $d_{\mathbb{C}} : \mathbb{C}(\Sigma, D) \times \mathbb{C}(\Sigma, D) \longrightarrow \mathbb{R}$ *is defined by:*

$$d_{\mathbb{C}}(x, y) = 2^{-l_{\mathbb{C}}(x,y)}$$

Proposition 11.5.2 *The function* $d_{\mathbb{C}}$ *is an ultrametric distance on* $\mathbb{C}(\Sigma, D)$.

Proof: Assume first that $x = (r, D(A))$ and $y = (s, D(B))$ are two distinct complex traces. If $r \neq s$, there exists some finite trace p which is, for instance, a prefix of r but not of s. In this case, we have $l_{\mathbb{C}}(x, y) \leq |p|$ and hence $d_{\mathbb{C}}(x, y) \geq 2^{-|p|} > 0$. If r and s are equal, then $D(A) \neq D(B)$. Let p be a finite prefix of r such that $\text{alph}(p^{-1}r) = \text{alphinf}(r)$. Then we have $D(p^{-1}x) = D(p^{-1}r) \cup D(A) = D(\text{alphinf}(r)) \cup D(A) = D(A) \neq D(B) = D(p^{-1}y)$. Therefore, once again, $d_{\mathbb{C}}(x, y) \geq 2^{-|p|} > 0$.

It is clear that $d_{\mathbb{C}}(x, y) = d_{\mathbb{C}}(y, x)$ for any complex traces x, y.

It remains to verify that $d_{\mathbb{C}}(x, y) \leq max\{d_{\mathbb{C}}(x, z), d_{\mathbb{C}}(y, z)\}$ for any complex traces x, y and z. If $d_{\mathbb{C}}(x, y) = 0$, the result is trivial. Otherwise, let $p \in \mathbb{M}$ be such that $|p| = l_{\mathbb{C}}(x, y)$ and $D(p^{-1}x) \neq D(p^{-1}y)$. Then we cannot have simultaneously $D(p^{-1}x) = D(p^{-1}z)$ and $D(p^{-1}y) = D(p^{-1}z)$. Therefore, either $l_{\mathbb{C}}(x, z) \leq |p|$ or $l_{\mathbb{C}}(y, z) \leq |p|$ that is, $max\{d_{\mathbb{C}}(x, z), d_{\mathbb{C}}(y, z)\} \geq 2^{-|p|} = d_{\mathbb{C}}(x, y)$.   □

For instance, let $(\Sigma, D) = a \text{ ——— } b \text{ ——— } c \text{ ——— } d$. Let $x = (abcb^\omega, D(\{b\}))$ and $y = (abcb^\omega, D(\{b, c\}))$. The real trace $r = abcb^\omega$ admits a (ab, abc resp.) as unique prefix of length 1 (2, 3 resp.). Moreover $D(a^{-1}r) = D((ab)^{-1}r) = D(\{b, c\})$ whereas $D((abc)^{-1}r) = D(\{b\})$, hence $D(a^{-1}x) = D((ab)^{-1}x) = D((ab)^{-1}y) = D(a^{-1}y)$ but $D((abc)^{-1}x) \neq D((abc)^{-1}y)$. Therefore we have $d_{\mathbb{C}}(f, g) = 2^{-3}$.

Let $x = abc$, $y = ac$ and $z = a$, $d_{\mathbb{C}}(x, z) = d_{\mathbb{C}}(y, z) = 2^0$, moreover c is a prefix of y but is not a prefix of x, hence $d_{\mathbb{C}}(x, y) = 2^{-1}$.

For $n \geq 1$, let $f_n = c^n bd^\omega$ and $g_n = c^n ba^\omega$. Although the real traces f_n and g_n have neither the same alphabet nor the same imaginary parts, it holds $d_{\mathbb{C}}(f_n, g_n) =$

2^{-n}. Namely, for $k \leq n$, f_n and g_n both admit c^k as unique prefix of length k. Furthermore, if $k < n$, $D((c^k)^{-1}f_n) = D(c^{n-k}bd^{\omega}) = D(\{b,c,d\}) = D((c^k)^{-1}g_n)$ but $D((c^n)^{-1}f_n) = D(bd^{\omega}) = D(\{b,d\}) \neq D(\{a,b\}) = D((c^n)^{-1}g_n)$.

Theorem 11.5.3 *The concatenation is uniformly continuous in the metric space* $(\mathbb{C}(\Sigma, D), d_{\mathbb{C}})$: $\forall x, y, z, t \in \mathbb{C}(\Sigma, D)$,

$$d_{\mathbb{C}}(xy, zt) \leq \inf(d_{\mathbb{C}}(x, z), d_{\mathbb{C}}(y, t))$$

Proof: Let $n < \omega$ and let $x = (r, D(A))$, $y = (s, D(B))$, $z = (u, D(C))$ and $t = (v, D(E))$ be four complex traces such that $d_{\mathbb{C}}(x, z) \leq 2^{-n}$ and $d_{\mathbb{C}}(y, t) \leq 2^{-n}$. We will show that $d_{\mathbb{C}}(xy, zt) \leq 2^{-n}$. By symmetry, it is enough to show that for all $p \in \mathbb{M}$ such that $|p| < n$, we have $D(p^{-1}xy) = D(p^{-1}zt)$.

By Proposition 11.4.6 it holds

$$x \cdot_{\mathbb{C}} y = (r\mu_A(s), D(A) \cup D(B) \cup D(\text{suff}_A(s)))$$
$$z \cdot_{\mathbb{C}} t = (u\mu_C(v), D(C) \cup D(E) \cup D(\text{suff}_C(v)))$$

Let $p \in \mathbb{M}$ be such that $|p| < n$ and $p \leq xy$. Hence, there exists some real trace q such that $r\mu_A(s) = pq$. By Proposition 11.2.10, there exist four real traces $\alpha, \beta, \gamma, \delta$ such that $\text{alph}(\beta) \times \text{alph}(\gamma) \subseteq I$ and

$$
\begin{array}{llll}
r & = & \alpha\beta & \qquad\qquad p & = & \alpha\gamma \\
\mu_A(s) & = & \gamma\delta & \qquad\qquad q & = & \beta\delta
\end{array}
$$

From $|p| < n$, it holds $|\alpha| < n$ and $|\gamma| < n$. Since $d_{\mathbb{C}}(x, z) \leq 2^{-n}$ and $\alpha \leq r$, we deduce $\alpha \leq u$. Hence $u = \alpha\beta'$ for some real trace β' and

$$D(\alpha^{-1}x) = D(\beta) \cup D(A) = D(\beta') \cup D(C) = D(\alpha^{-1}z) \qquad (11.4)$$

In a similar way, $s = \mu_A(s)\,\text{suff}_A(s) = \gamma\delta\,\text{suff}_A(s)$ therefore $\gamma \leq v$ and

$$D(\gamma^{-1}y) = D(\delta\,\text{suff}_A(s)) \cup D(B) = D(\gamma^{-1}v) \cup D(E) = D(\gamma^{-1}t) \qquad (11.5)$$

Besides, we claim that $\gamma \leq \mu_C(v)$. Indeed, $\gamma \leq \mu_A(s)$ and thus $\text{alph}(\gamma) \cap D(A) = \emptyset$, moreover $\text{alph}(\beta) \times \text{alph}(\gamma) \subseteq I$ and then $\text{alph}(\gamma) \cap D(\beta) = \emptyset$. These two equalities together with (11.4), imply

$$\text{alph}(\gamma) \cap D(C) = \emptyset \text{ and } \text{alph}(\gamma) \cap D(\beta') = \emptyset \qquad (11.6)$$

Then we have $\gamma \leq v$ and $\text{alph}(\gamma) \cap D(C) = \emptyset$, hence by definition of the operator μ_C, the claim is proved. More precisely, $\mu_C(v) = \gamma\delta'$. Thus $u\mu_C(v) = \alpha\beta'\gamma\delta' = \alpha\gamma\beta'\delta'$ since, from (11.6), $\text{alph}(\beta') \times \text{alph}(\gamma) \subseteq I$. Hence $u\mu_C(v) = p\beta'\delta'$, therefore p is a prefix of $u\mu_C(v)$ and thus of zt. It remains to verify that $D(p^{-1}xy) = D(p^{-1}zt)$.

$$
\begin{array}{rll}
D(p^{-1}xy) & = & D(p^{-1}r\mu_A(s)) \cup D(A) \cup D(B) \cup D(\text{suff}_A(s)) \\
& = & D(q) \cup D(A) \cup D(B) \cup D(\text{suff}_A(s)) \\
& = & D(\beta) \cup D(\delta) \cup D(A) \cup D(B) \cup D(\text{suff}_A(s)) \\
& = & D(\beta') \cup D(C) \cup D(\gamma^{-1}v) \cup D(E) \qquad\qquad \text{by (11.4) and (11.5)} \\
& = & D(\beta') \cup D(C) \cup D(\delta'\,\text{suff}_C(v)) \cup D(E) \\
& = & D(\beta'\delta') \cup D(C) \cup D(E) \cup D(\text{suff}_C(v)) \\
& = & D(p^{-1}u\mu_C(v)) \cup D(C) \cup D(E) \cup D(\text{suff}_C(v)) \\
& = & D(p^{-1}zt)
\end{array}
$$

□

We have seen in Corollary 11.3.6 that every increasing sequence of real traces admits a least upper bound. In fact, this least upper bound is also the limit of the sequence for the metric $d_{\mathbb{C}}$.

Lemma 11.5.4 *Let* $(r_n)_{n<\omega}$ *be an increasing sequence of real traces. Then* $\bigsqcup_{n<\omega} r_n$ *is the limit of the sequence* $(r_n)_{n<\omega}$ *in the metric space* $((\mathbb{C}(\Sigma, D), d_{\mathbb{C}})$.

Proof: Let $r = \bigsqcup_{n<\omega} r_n = [V, E, \lambda]$. Let p be a finite prefix of r such that $\text{alph}(p^{-1}r) = \text{alphinf}(r)$. For each integer $n < \omega$, we consider the least prefix s_n of r containing all the vertices of p and the n first vertices of $p^{-1}r$ with label a, for all $a \in \text{alphinf}(r)$.

Let now $n < \omega$, there exists some $N < \omega$ such that $s_n \leq r_N$ and $\text{alph}(s_n^{-1}r_N) = \text{alphinf}(r)$. Let $m \geq N$ and let p be a finite trace such that $|p| < n$. If $p \leq r_m$ then clearly $p \leq r$. Conversely, if $p \leq r$, we have by construction $p \leq s_n \leq r_N$ and since the sequence $(r_i)_{i<\omega}$ is increasing, we deduce $p \leq r_m$. Moreover

$$
\begin{aligned}
D(p^{-1}r) &= D(p^{-1}s_n) \cup D(s_n^{-1}r) \\
&= D(p^{-1}s_n) \cup D(\text{alphinf}(r)) \\
&= D(p^{-1}s_n) \cup D(s_n^{-1}r_m) \\
&= D(p^{-1}r_m)
\end{aligned}
$$

Hence, $d_{\mathbb{C}}(r_m, r) \leq 2^{-n}$ for all $m \geq N$ and the lemma is proved.   □

In order to prove that $(\mathbb{C}, d_{\mathbb{C}})$ is the metric completion of $(\mathbb{M}, d_{\mathbb{C}})$, we will need the following result.

Theorem 11.5.5 *For the topology induced by the metric* $d_{\mathbb{C}}$, $\mathbb{M}(\Sigma, D)$ *is an open, discrete and dense subspace of* $\mathbb{C}(\Sigma, D)$.

Proof: Let $f \in \mathbb{M}$ be a finite trace. In order to prove that $\mathbb{M}$ is open and discrete, we will show that $B(f) = \{x \in \mathbb{C} \mid d_{\mathbb{C}}(f, x) < 2^{-|f|}\} = \{f\}$. Namely, assume that $x \in B(f)$, it holds $l_{\mathbb{C}}(f, x) \geq |f| + 1$. Since $|f| < |f| + 1$, we have thus $D(f^{-1}x) = D(f^{-1}f) = \emptyset$. Hence $x = f$. Therefore $\mathbb{M}$ is an open and discrete subspace of $\mathbb{C}$.

To prove the density, let $x = (r, D(A))$ be a complex trace and let f be a finite trace such that $x = r \cdot f$. Let $(r_n)_{n<\omega}$ be an increasing sequence of finite traces such that $r = \bigsqcup_{n<\omega} r_n$ (see Theorem 11.3.11). From Lemma 11.5.4, we obtain that $\lim_{n \longrightarrow \omega} d_{\mathbb{C}}(r_n, r) = 0$. Since the concatenation is continuous, we deduce that $x = r \cdot f$ is the limit in $(\mathbb{C}, d_{\mathbb{C}})$ of the sequence $(r_n \cdot f)_{n<\omega}$ of finite traces.   □

11.5.2 Completeness and Compactness

We are now ready to prove the main theorem of this section.

Theorem 11.5.6 *The metric space* $(\mathbb{C}(\Sigma, D), d_{\mathbb{C}})$ *is complete.*

Proof: Let $(x_n = (r_n, D(B_n)))_{n < \omega}$ be a Cauchy sequence in $\mathbb{C}$.

Since a Cauchy sequence admits a limit if and only if any of its infinite subsequences admits a limit and since Σ is finite, we may assume without restriction that there exist two subalphabets $A, B \subseteq \Sigma$ such that, for all $n < \omega$, $\mathrm{alphinf}(r_n) = A$ and $D(B_n) = D(B)$. Moreover we assume also that, for all $n < \omega$ and for all $m \geq n$,

$$d_{\mathbb{C}}(x_n, x_m) \leq 2^{-n} \tag{11.7}$$

Let $m \geq n$ be two integers and let p be any finite trace such that $|p| < n$. It holds

$$p \leq r_n \Longleftrightarrow p \leq r_m \text{ and } D(p^{-1}r_m) \cup D(B) = D(p^{-1}r_n) \cup D(B) \tag{11.8}$$

Let $p_n = \bigsqcup \{p \in \mathbb{M} \mid p \leq r_n \text{ and } |p| < n\}$ (such a least upper bound exists from Corollary 11.3.6). From (11.8), we get, for all $m \geq n$,

$$p_n = \bigsqcup \{p \in \mathbb{M} \mid p \leq r_m \text{ and } |p| < n\} \tag{11.9}$$

In particular, $p_n \leq p_m$. The sequence of finite traces $(p_n)_{n < \omega}$ is thus increasing and admits then a least upper bound (Corollary 11.3.6) $r = \bigsqcup_{n < \omega} p_n$.

Since, for any $n < \omega$, $\mathrm{red}(p_n^{-1}r_n)$ is a finite trace of length at most $|\Sigma|$, we may assume that there exists some finite trace f_1 such that $\mathrm{red}(p_n^{-1}r_n) = f_1$ for all $n < \omega$.

For any $n < \omega$, $x_n = (r_n, D(B))$ is a complex trace with $\mathrm{alphinf}(r_n) = A$, hence there exists (see Proposition 11.4.11) a finite trace f_2 with $\min(f_2) \subseteq D(A)$ and $D(A) \cup D(f_2) = D(B)$ such that $x_n = r_n \cdot f_2$ for all $n < \omega$.

Let $f = f_1 \cdot f_2$. Using two intermediary claims, we will prove that the limit of the Cauchy sequence $(x_n)_{n < \omega}$ is $r \cdot f$.

Using Lemma 11.4.10, we have $\min(f_2) \subseteq D(\mathrm{alphinf}(r_n)) \subseteq D(p_n^{-1}r_n) = D(f_1)$. Therefore $\min(f) = \min(f_1)$.

Claim 1 $\forall p \in \mathbb{M} \mid |p| < n, (p \leq p_n \cdot f \Longrightarrow p \leq p_n)$

Indeed, let p be a finite trace of minimal length such that $p \leq p_n \cdot f$ and $p \not\leq p_n$. Thus, from Proposition 11.2.10, $p = p' \cdot p''$ for some traces p', p'' such that $p' \leq p_n$, $p'' \leq f$ and $\mathrm{alph}(p'^{-1}p_n) \times \mathrm{alph}(p'') \subseteq I$. Since p is of minimal length, we deduce that $p'' = a \in \min(f) = \min(f_1)$. Hence we obtain, from Lemma 11.4.10, $a \in \min(p_n^{-1}r_n)$ and thus $p' \cdot a \leq r_n$. Since $p' \cdot a \not\leq p_n$, this implies, from the definition of p_n, that $|p' \cdot a| \geq n$ and this first claim is proved.

Claim 2 $d_{\mathbb{C}}(x_n, p_n \cdot f) \leq 2^{-n}$ for all $n < \omega$

Namely, let $p \in \mathbb{M}$ be such that $|p| < n$. From Claim 1, we have

$$p \leq x_n \Longleftrightarrow p \leq r_n \Longleftrightarrow p \leq p_n \Longleftrightarrow p \leq p_n \cdot f$$

Moreover

$$\begin{aligned}
D(p^{-1}x_n) &= D(p^{-1}r_n) \cup D(B) \\
&= D(p^{-1}p_n) \cup D(p_n^{-1}r_n) \cup D(B) \\
&= D(p^{-1}p_n) \cup D(f_1) \cup D(f_2) \\
&= D(p^{-1}(p_n \cdot f))
\end{aligned}$$

and the second claim is thus proved.

At last, we have from Lemma 11.5.4, $\lim_{n \longrightarrow \omega} d_{\mathbb{C}}(p_n, r) = 0$. Since the concatenation is continuous, we deduce that $\lim_{n \longrightarrow \omega} d_{\mathbb{C}}(p_n \cdot f, r \cdot f) = 0$. Therefore, from Claim 2, it follows $\lim_{n \longrightarrow \omega} d_{\mathbb{C}}(x_n, r \cdot f) = 0$. Hence the Cauchy sequence $(x_n)_{n < \omega}$ admits $r \cdot f$ as limit in $(\mathbb{C}, d_{\mathbb{C}})$ which is thus a complete metric space. □

Let $(\Sigma, D) = a \text{ —— } b \text{ —— } c \text{ —— } d$ and, for any integer $n < \omega$, let $x_n = (c^n b d^\omega, D(\{d\}))$. The limit of the Cauchy sequence $(x_n)_{n < \omega}$ is $(c^\omega, D(\{b, c, d\}))$.

Note that a sequence of complex traces may converge whereas the sequence of its real parts diverges. For instance, let $(\Sigma, D) = a \text{ —— } b \text{ —— } c \text{ —— } d \text{ —— } e$ and, for any integer $n < \omega$, let $x_{2n} = (a^{2n} e^\omega, \Sigma)$ and $x_{2n+1} = (a^{2n+1} b e^\omega, \Sigma)$. The limit of the Cauchy sequence $(x_n)_{n < \omega}$ is $((ae)^\omega, \Sigma)$. Note however that the limit of the sequence $\text{Re}(x_{2n})_{n < \omega}$ is $(ae)^\omega = ((ae)^\omega, \{a, b, d, e\})$ and the limit of the sequence $\text{Re}(x_{2n+1})_{n < \omega}$ is $((ae)^\omega, \Sigma)$.

The concatenation is continuous (and even uniformly continuous) on $\mathbb{C}$ (Theorem 11.5.3) and $\mathbb{M}$ is dense in $\mathbb{C}$ (Theorem 11.5.5). Therefore, we deduce the following corollary by unicity of the completion of a metric space.

Corollary 11.5.7 *The completion of the metric space* $(\mathbb{M}(\Sigma, D), d_{\mathbb{C}})$ *is the metric space* $(\mathbb{C}(\Sigma, D), d_{\mathbb{C}})$. *Moreover, the concatenation* $\cdot_{\mathbb{C}}$ *on* $(\mathbb{C}(\Sigma, D), d_{\mathbb{C}})$ *is the unique continuous extension of the concatenation* $\cdot_{\mathbb{M}}$ *on* $(\mathbb{M}(\Sigma, D), d_{\mathbb{C}})$.

To conclude this section on topology, we will show that the metric space $(\mathbb{C}, d_{\mathbb{C}})$ is in fact compact. Note that to prove this result, we use the completeness of $(\mathbb{C}, d_{\mathbb{C}})$.

Theorem 11.5.8 *The metric space* $(\mathbb{C}(\Sigma, D), d_{\mathbb{C}})$ *is compact.*

Proof: Let $\bigcup_{i=1}^{k} (\Sigma_i, \Sigma_i \times \Sigma_i)$ be a covering by cliques of the dependence alphabet (Σ, D) such that, for any $a \in \Sigma$, there exists some $i \in \{1, \cdots, k\}$ such that $\Sigma_i = \{a\}$. For $t \in \mathbb{M}$, let t_i be the projection of t on Σ_i^*. The embedding theorem states that $\zeta : \mathbb{M}(\Sigma, D) \longrightarrow \prod_{i=1}^{k} \Sigma_i^*, \zeta(t) = (t_i)_{i=1,\cdots,k}$ is injective (see Proposition 11.2.23).

On each free monoid Σ_i^*, we consider, as we recalled in the preliminaries of this section, the metric d_{pref} based on prefixes. As usual, these metrics give on the direct product $\prod_{i=1}^{k} \Sigma_i^*$, a metric, still denoted by d_{pref}, defined by $d_{\text{pref}}((s_i)_{i=1,\cdots,k}, (t_i)_{i=1,\cdots,k}) = \max\{d_{\text{pref}}(s_i, t_i)/1 \leq i \leq k\}$. Even if it should be noticed that $\zeta : (\mathbb{M}(\Sigma, D), d_{\mathbb{C}}) \longrightarrow (\prod_{i=1}^{k} \Sigma_i^*, d_{\text{pref}})$ is not continuous, we are interested in the inverse image of ζ restricted to the image of $\mathbb{M}$. So, let $\xi : \zeta(\mathbb{M}) \longrightarrow \mathbb{M}$ be the inverse image of ζ. We will prove that $\xi : (\zeta(\mathbb{M}), d_{\text{pref}}) \longrightarrow (\mathbb{M}, d_{\mathbb{C}})$ is uniformly continuous.

Let $s, t \in \mathbb{M}$ and $n \in \mathbb{N}$ be such that $\max\{d_{\text{pref}}(s_i, t_i)/1 \leq i \leq k\} \leq 2^{-(n+1)}$. We claim that $d_{\mathbb{C}}(s, t) \leq 2^{-n}$. Let $p \in \mathbb{M}$ such that $|p| < n$. Suppose that $p \leq s$, by Proposition 11.2.23, we get $p_i \leq s_i$ for all $1 \leq i \leq k$. Therefore, $p_i \leq t_i$ for all $1 \leq i \leq k$ and $p \leq t$, too. It remains to show that $D(p^{-1}s) \subseteq D(p^{-1}t)$. By symmetry, it is enough to prove that $a \in \text{alph}(p^{-1}s)$ implies $a \in \text{alph}(p^{-1}t)$. Consider the index i such that $\Sigma_i = \{a\}$. Then $p_i = a^m$ for some $m < n$. From

$a \in \mathrm{alph}(p^{-1}s)$, we get $a^{m+1} \leq s_i$. Then, since $d_{\mathrm{pref}}(s_i, t_i) \leq 2^{-(n+1)}$, we obtain $a^{m+1} \leq t_i$. Therefore $a \in \mathrm{alph}(p^{-1}t)$ which proves the claim.

The uniformly continuous mapping $\xi : (\zeta(\mathrm{M}), d_{\mathrm{pref}}) \longrightarrow (\mathrm{M}, d_{\mathbb{C}})$ extends uniquely in a continuous way to the completions of $(\zeta(\mathrm{M}), d_{\mathrm{pref}})$ and of $(\mathrm{M}, d_{\mathbb{C}})$. By Corollary 11.5.7, the completion of $(\mathrm{M}, d_{\mathbb{C}})$ is exactly $(\mathbb{C}, d_{\mathbb{C}})$.

Besides, we know that the metric space $(\prod_{i=1}^{k} \Sigma_i^{\infty}, d_{\mathrm{pref}})$ is compact and the metric completion of $(\prod_{i=1}^{k} \Sigma_i^*, d_{\mathrm{pref}})$. Therefore the metric completion of $(\zeta(\mathrm{M}), d_{\mathrm{pref}})$ is exactly the closure $\overline{\zeta(\mathrm{M})}$ of $\zeta(\mathrm{M})$ in $\prod_{i=1}^{k} \Sigma_i^{\infty}$. Furthermore, this closure is compact too.

In conclusion $\mathbb{C}$ is compact being the continuous image by ξ of the compact space $\overline{\zeta(\mathrm{M})}$. □

11.5.3 Notes

The topological properties of the set of complex traces have been studied by Diekert [54, 57]. In these papers, the compactness and the completeness of the set of complex traces was inferred from the compactness and the completeness of the set of α-complex traces (see Section 11.4.4). Nevertheless, the proof of Theorem 11.5.8 is very close to the original proofs for α-complex traces.

A natural attempt to define a metric on the set $\mathbb{R}$ of real traces is to extend on traces the function l_{pref} and the metric d_{pref} on words. This leads naturally Kwiatkowska [163] to define the function $l_{\mathrm{pref}} : \mathbb{R}(\Sigma, D) \times \mathbb{R}(\Sigma, D) \longrightarrow \mathbb{N} \cup \{\infty\}$ by

$$l_{\mathrm{pref}}(r, s) = sup\{n \in \mathbb{N} \mid \forall p \in \mathrm{M}(\Sigma, D), \mid p \mid \leq n \implies (p \leq r \iff p \leq s)\}$$

and the metric associated with l_{pref} by

$$d_{\mathrm{pref}}(r, s) = 2^{-l_{\mathrm{pref}}(r,s)}$$

Note that it is straightforward to verify that the function d_{pref}, defined above, is an ultra-metric on the set of real traces.

Unfortunately, the behavior of the concatenation in the metric space $(\mathbb{R}, d_{\mathrm{pref}})$ is far from being satisfactory. For instance, assume that $(\Sigma, D) = a \text{——} b \text{——} c$. Although $a^{\omega} \cdot_{\mathbb{R}} c^{\omega} = (ac)^{\omega}$ is well-defined, the concatenation is not continuous at (a^{ω}, c^{ω}). Namely, the sequences $(c^n)_{n \in \mathbb{N}}$ and $(c^n b)_{n \in \mathbb{N}}$ both admit c^{ω} as limit. But while the limit of the sequence $(a^{\omega} c^n)_{n \in \mathbb{N}}$ is $a^{\omega} \cdot c^{\omega}$, all the terms of the sequence $(a^{\omega} c^n b)_{n \in \mathbb{N}}$ are undefined in $\mathbb{R}$ and hence the sequence does not converge. Since the concatenation is (uniformly) continuous for $d_{\mathbb{C}}$, it follows in particular that the metrics d_{pref} and $d_{\mathbb{C}}$ are not uniformly equivalent.

Nevertheless, Kwiatkowska proved that the metric space $(\mathbb{R}(\Sigma, D), d_{\mathrm{pref}})$ is complete and compact. In fact, it is the metric completion of $(\mathrm{M}(\Sigma, D), d_{\mathrm{pref}})$. These results can also be obtained as corollaries of results of Section 11.5.2. Namely, the mapping from $(\mathbb{C}(\Sigma, D), d_{\mathbb{C}})$ to $(\mathbb{R}(\Sigma, D), d_{\mathrm{pref}})$ which maps each complex trace to its real part is continuous and surjective. Therefore, the metric space $(\mathbb{R}(\Sigma, D), d_{\mathrm{pref}})$ is compact as the continuous image of a compact. Hence, the compact metric space

$(\mathbb{R}(\Sigma, D), d_{\text{pref}})$ is complete, and it is the metric completion of $(\mathbb{M}(\Sigma, D), d_{\text{pref}})$ since $\mathbb{M}(\Sigma, D)$ is dense in $\mathbb{R}(\Sigma, D)$.

Bonizzoni, Mauri and Pighizzini [27] defined a different metric on real traces. The distance between two traces is the distance of their Foata normal forms (see Section 11.2) in the free monoid S^∞ where S is the set of cliques of the graph $(\Sigma \times \Sigma, I)$ (see Section 11.2.3). This distance is uniformly equivalent to the distance d_{pref} and therefore has the same properties.

To remedy the deficiencies of the distance d_{pref} on traces, we could try to define a metric d on finite traces such that the concatenation $\cdot_M$ is uniformly continuous. Moreover, such a metric should be compatible with the PoSet structure of $(\mathbb{M}, \leq)$. More precisely, the following conditions should at least be fulfilled:

1. Let $(x_n)_{n \geq 0}$ be an increasing sequence of finite traces and let $x = \bigsqcup_{n \geq 0} x_n$ then $(x_n)_{n \geq 0}$ converges to x.

2. Let $(x_n)_{n \geq 0}$ be a sequence of finite traces which converges to x. Then any finite prefix p of x is ultimately a prefix of the x_n.

From the first condition, we deduce that the set of real traces is contained in such a completion of the monoid of finite traces. In fact, this inclusion is strict if the dependence relation D on Σ is not transitive (the proof of this fact is left as an exercise to the reader). On the other hand, we know that the monoid of complex traces is such a completion of the monoid of finite traces. Moreover, if the dependence relation is transitive, the set of complex traces coincides with the set of real traces.

Finally, Gastin proposed in [109] a third metric on real traces. Even if the concatenation is not uniformly continuous on finite traces for this distance, it seems to be the most satisfactory for what concerns real traces and concatenation. Namely, the concatenation on real traces is continuous at each point $(r, s) \in \mathbb{R} \times \mathbb{R}$ such that $r \cdot_{\mathbb{R}} s$ is well-defined. In particular, this metric is not uniformly equivalent to d_{pref}. Nevertheless, the set of real traces is still the metric completion of the set of finite traces.

11.6 Rational Languages of Infinite Traces

In this section, we introduce and study the rational languages of infinite traces. As usual, the family of rational languages will be defined as the smallest family which contains the finite sets of finite traces and which is closed under union, concatenation, $*$-iteration and ω-iteration. Depending on the concatenation and the ω-product used, different families of rational languages will be obtained. Using the partial concatenation $\cdot_{\mathbb{R}}$ on real traces (see Section 11.2.2) and the partial ω-product on real traces (see Section 11.2.3), this yields the family Rat $\mathbb{R}$ of rational real trace languages. On the contrary, using the concatenation and the ω-product on complex traces (see Section 11.4) the family Rat $\mathbb{C}$ of rational complex trace languages is defined.

We will prove similar results for the two families Rat $\mathbb{R}$ and Rat $\mathbb{C}$ but since the proofs are radically different, we divide this section in two subsections, each of them devoted to the study of one family.

The main results of this section are normal forms for rational sets of real traces and of complex traces (Theorems 11.6.2 and 11.6.12). In these theorems, we also give the links between rational real trace languages and rational word languages on one hand and between rational complex trace languages and rational real trace languages on the other hand. Apart from these characterizations, we prove that the intersection, the left and right quotients of a rational set by a recognizable set are rational too. To this purpose, we use a characterization of recognizable languages which will be proved in Sections 11.7 and 11.8.

11.6.1   Rational Real Trace Languages

In any monoid M, the concatenation is extended to languages $K, L \subseteq M$ by

$$K \cdot L = \{x \cdot y \mid x \in K \text{ and } y \in L\}.$$

The $*$-iteration of a language $L \subseteq M$ is the submonoid of M generated by L:

$$L^* = \bigcup_{n \geq 0} L^n$$

where $L^0 = \{1\}$ and $L^{n+1} = L \cdot L^n$ for all $n \geq 0$.

In a monoid M, the family of rational languages is defined as the least family which contains some elementary languages: the empty set and the singletons $\{m\}$ for all $m \in M$, and which is closed under the rational operations: union, concatenation and $*$-iteration [11]. When the monoid $M = \Sigma^*$ is the free monoid over Σ, we obtain the family Rat Σ^* of rational word languages and when the monoid $M = \mathbb{M}(\Sigma, D)$ is the trace monoid over (Σ, D), we obtain the family Rat $\mathbb{M}(\Sigma, D)$ of rational languages of finite traces.

This definition does not apply for rational ω-word languages. In fact, even singletons may be not rational. For instance, the singleton $\{aba^2ba^3b\ldots\}$ is not a rational language. Actually, only singletons which consists of a single letter are allowed as elementary languages. In order to generate infinite words in rational languages a new rational operation is introduced, the ω-iteration of a language $L \subseteq \Sigma^\infty$:

$$L^\omega = \{\prod_{i < \omega} u_i \mid (u_i)_{i < \omega} \subseteq L\}.$$

Then, the family Rat Σ^∞ is the least family which contains the empty set and the singletons $\{a\}$ for all $a \in \Sigma$ and which is closed under union, concatenation, $*$-iteration and ω-iteration. Note that, the concatenation and the ω-product defined in Section 11.2.4 are not internal operations in Σ^∞. In the definition above of Rat Σ^∞, the concatenation, $*$-iteration and ω-iteration should be understood as the restrictions to Σ^∞ of the corresponding operations on transfinite words defined in Section 11.2.4.

We will use a similar definition for rational infinite trace languages. To this purpose, we first define the concatenation, $*$-iteration and ω-iteration on real trace languages. Using the partial concatenation on real traces (Section 11.2.2), we define the total *real* concatenation of real trace languages $R, S \subseteq \mathbb{R}$ by:

$$R \cdot_{\mathbb{R}} S = \{r \cdot_{\mathbb{R}} s \mid r \in R \text{ and } s \in S\}$$
$$= \{r \cdot s \mid r \in R, s \in S \text{ and } \mathrm{alphinf}(r) \times \mathrm{alph}(s) \subseteq I\}$$

For instance, let $(\Sigma, D) = a \relbar\joinrel\relbar b \relbar\joinrel\relbar c \qquad d \relbar\joinrel\relbar e$ be the dependence alphabet and let $R = \{a^\omega, b^2, c^\omega, d\}$ and $S = \{c^\omega, c^2 be, c^2\}$ be two real trace languages. Then,

$$R \cdot S = \{(ac)^\omega, c^2 a^\omega, b^2 c^\omega, b^2 c^2 be, b^2 c^2, dc^\omega, dc^2 be, dc^2\}$$

The $*$-iteration of a real trace language $R \subseteq \mathbb{R}$ is

$$R^* = \bigcup_{n \geq 0} R^n$$

where $R^0 = \{1\}$ and $R^{n+1} = R \cdot R^n$ for all $n \geq 0$ and its ω-iteration is defined by:

$$R^\omega = \{\prod_{i < \omega} r_i \mid (r_i)_{i<\omega} \subseteq R \text{ and } \mathrm{alphinf}(r_i) \times \mathrm{alph}(r_j) \subseteq I \text{ for all } i < j\}.$$

Since a well-defined product of real traces contains at most $|\Sigma|$ infinite traces (see Section 11.2.3), we obtain easily the following formulæ:

$$R^* = \bigcup_{k \leq |\Sigma|} (R_{\mathrm{fin}}^* \cdot R_{\mathrm{inf}})^k \cdot R_{\mathrm{fin}}^* \tag{11.10}$$

and

$$R^\omega = \bigcup_{k \leq |\Sigma|} (R_{\mathrm{fin}}^* \cdot R_{\mathrm{inf}})^k \cdot R_{\mathrm{fin}}^\omega \tag{11.11}$$

where $R_{\mathrm{fin}} = R \cap \mathbb{M}$ and $R_{\mathrm{inf}} = R \setminus R_{\mathrm{fin}}$.

For instance, with the dependence alphabet and the language R defined above, it holds $R_{\mathrm{fin}} = \{b^2, d\}, R_{\mathrm{inf}} = \{a^\omega, c^\omega\}$ and we obtain:

$$R^* = \{b^2, d\}^* \cdot \{1, a^\omega, c^\omega, (ac)^\omega\}$$

and

$$R^\omega = \{b^2, d\}^* \cdot \{b^\omega, d^\omega, (bd)^\omega, (ad)^\omega, (cd)^\omega, (acd)^\omega\}$$
$$= \{d\}^* \cdot \{b^\omega\} \cup \{(bd)^\omega\} \cup \{b^2\}^* \cdot \{d^\omega, (ad)^\omega, (cd)^\omega, (acd)^\omega\}$$

Definition 11.6.1 *The family* Rat $\mathbb{R}(\Sigma, D)$ *of rational real trace languages is the smallest family*

- *which contains the empty set and all singletons $\{a\}$ for $a \in \Sigma$,*

- *which is closed under union and under concatenation, $*$-iteration and ω-iteration on* real *traces.*

A real trace language $R \subseteq \mathbb{R}$ is monoalphabetic if $\mathrm{alph}(r) = \mathrm{alph}(s)$ for all $r, s \in R$. When a monoalphabetic language R is non empty, we denote by $\mathrm{alph}(R)$ the common alphabet of its elements.

The following theorem characterizes rational real trace languages by means of rational languages of finite traces and of rational word languages.

Theorem 11.6.2 *Let $T \subseteq \mathbb{R}(\Sigma, D)$ be a language of real traces. The following assertions are equivalent:*

1. *T is rational.*

2. *T is a finite union of sets of the form $R \cdot S^\omega$ where $R, S \in \mathrm{Rat}\ \mathbb{M}(\Sigma, D)$ are rational monoalphabetic languages of finite traces.*

3. *$T = \varphi(L)$ for some rational word language $L \in \mathrm{Rat}\ \Sigma^\infty$.*

Proof: $1 \Longrightarrow 2$: Let $\mathcal{R}$ be the family of languages which are finite union of sets of the form $R \cdot S^\omega$ where $R, S \in \mathrm{Rat}\ \mathbb{M}(\Sigma, D)$ are rational monoalphabetic languages of finite traces. We will prove that $\mathcal{R}$ contains the elementary languages and is closed under the rational operators. Therefore, we will obtain $\mathrm{Rat}\ \mathbb{R} \subseteq \mathcal{R}$.

We have $\emptyset = \emptyset \cdot \emptyset^\omega$, hence $\emptyset \in \mathcal{R}$. Similarly, for all $a \in \Sigma$, we have $\{a\} = \{a\} \cdot \{1\}^\omega \in \mathcal{R}$ (note that $\{1\} = \emptyset^* \in \mathrm{Rat}\ \mathbb{M}$).

Clearly, the family $\mathcal{R}$ is closed under union.

Now let $R, S, R', S' \in \mathrm{Rat}\ \mathbb{M}$ be four non empty monoalphabetic rational languages of finite traces. Either $\mathrm{alph}(S) \times \mathrm{alph}(R'S') \subseteq I$ and we have $(R \cdot S^\omega) \cdot (R' \cdot S'^\omega) = (RR') \cdot (SS')^\omega$. Or $\mathrm{alph}(S) \times \mathrm{alph}(R'S') \cap D \neq \emptyset$ and we have $(R \cdot S^\omega) \cdot (R' \cdot S'^\omega) = \emptyset$. Therefore, the family $\mathcal{R}$ is closed under concatenation.

In order to prove that the family $\mathcal{R}$ is closed under $*$-iteration and ω-iteration, we first show the following claim.

Claim Let $R \in \mathrm{Rat}\ \mathbb{M}$ be a rational language of finite traces. Then, $R, R^\omega \in \mathcal{R}$.

Indeed, for all $A \subseteq \Sigma$, the language $\mathbb{M}_A = \{t \in \mathbb{M} \mid \mathrm{alph}(t) = A\}$ is a recognizable language of finite traces. Since the intersection of a rational language of finite traces with a recognizable language of finite traces is rational, we deduce that the monoalphabetic language $R_A = R \cap \mathbb{M}_A$ is rational for all $A \subseteq \Sigma$. Therefore, $R = \bigcup_{A \subseteq \Sigma} R_A \cdot \{1\}^\omega \in \mathcal{R}$. Now, it is easy to verify that

$$R^\omega = \bigcup_{B \subseteq A \subseteq \Sigma} (R^+)_A \cdot ((R^+)_B)^\omega.$$

For all $A \subseteq \Sigma$, the language $(R^+)_A$ is a monoalphabetic rational language of finite traces. Therefore, $R^\omega \in \mathcal{R}$ and the claim is proved.

Note that $T_{\text{fin}} \in \text{Rat } \mathbb{M}$ and $T_{\text{inf}} \in \mathcal{R}$ for all language $T \in \mathcal{R}$. Therefore, the closure of the family $\mathcal{R}$ under the $*$-iteration and the ω-iteration follows from the claim, from the formulæ 11.10 and 11.11 and from the closure of the family $\mathcal{R}$ under union and concatenation.

$2 \Longrightarrow 3$: Let $T = \bigcup_{1 \leq i \leq n} R_i \cdot S_i^\omega$ be a language of $\mathcal{R}$. Since $\varphi : \Sigma^* \longrightarrow \mathbb{M}$ is a surjective morphism, there exist rational word languages $X_i, Y_i \in \text{Rat } \Sigma^*$ such that $\varphi(X_i) = R_i$ and $\varphi(Y_i) = S_i$ for all $1 \leq i \leq n$. Then, $L = \bigcup_{1 \leq i \leq n} X_i \cdot Y_i^\omega \in \text{Rat } \Sigma^\infty$ is a rational word language and $\varphi(L) = T$.

$3 \Longrightarrow 1$: Let $L = \bigcup_{1 \leq i \leq n} X_i \cdot Y_i^\omega \in \text{Rat } \Sigma^\infty$ be a rational word language. For all $1 \leq i \leq n$, the languages $\varphi(X_i)$ and $\varphi(Y_i)$ are rational languages of finite traces. Therefore, $\varphi(L) = \bigcup_{1 \leq i \leq n} \varphi(X_i) \cdot \varphi(Y_i)^\omega \in \text{Rat } \mathbb{R}$. $\square$

The last results of this subsection state that the intersection and the left and right quotients of a rational real trace language by a *recognizable* real trace language are rational too. The recognizable real trace languages will be defined in Section 11.7. To prove the following results, we will only use the characterization of Theorem 11.7.4 which states that a real trace language R is recognizable if and only if the word language $\varphi^{-1}(R)$ is recognizable.

Corollary 11.6.3 *Let $R \subseteq \mathbb{R}(\Sigma, D)$ be a recognizable real trace language and let $T \subseteq \mathbb{R}(\Sigma, D)$ be a rational real trace language. Then, the language $R \cap T$ is rational too.*

Proof: Let $L \in \text{Rat } \Sigma^\infty$ be a rational word language such that $\varphi(L) = T$ (Theorem 11.6.2). By Theorem 11.7.4, $\varphi^{-1}(R) \in \text{Rec } \Sigma^\infty$ is a recognizable word language. Since the family $\text{Rat } \Sigma^\infty = \text{Rec } \Sigma^\infty$ is closed under intersection, we deduce from Theorem 11.6.2 that $R \cap T = \varphi(\varphi^{-1}(R) \cap L)$ is a rational real trace language. $\square$

In order to prove the results concerning the left and right quotients, we introduce the I-shuffle and the I-shuffle quotients which are the word counterparts of the concatenation and the quotients on real traces. The I-shuffle of two words $u, v \in \Sigma^\infty$ is defined by:

$$u \sqcup\!\sqcup_I v = \{u_0 v_0 u_1 v_1 \ldots \in \Sigma^\infty \quad | \quad u_i, v_i \in \Sigma^* \text{ for all } i \geq 0,$$
$$u = u_0 u_1 \ldots, v = v_0 v_1 \ldots \text{ and}$$
$$(v_i, u_j) \in I \text{ for all } 0 \leq i < j\}$$

Classically, this operation is extended to word languages $U, V \subseteq \Sigma^\infty$ by:

$$U \sqcup\!\sqcup_I V = \bigcup_{u \in U, v \in V} u \sqcup\!\sqcup_I v$$

Finally, the left and right I-shuffle quotients are defined by:

$$U^{-1} \sqcup\!\sqcup_I V = \{v \in \Sigma^\infty \mid (U \sqcup\!\sqcup_I v) \cap V \neq \emptyset\}$$
$$U \sqcup\!\sqcup_I V^{-1} = \{u \in \Sigma^\infty \mid (u \sqcup\!\sqcup_I V) \cap U \neq \emptyset\}$$

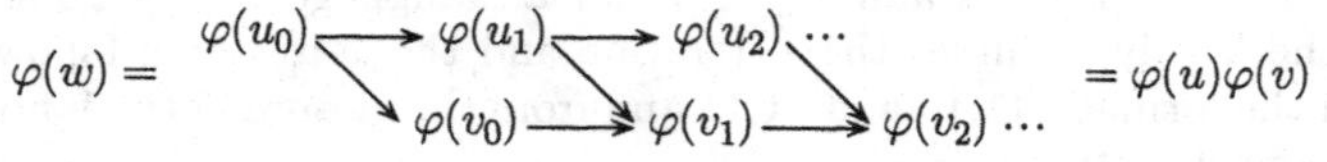

$$\varphi(w) = \begin{array}{ccc} \varphi(u_0) \to \varphi(u_1) \to \varphi(u_2) \cdots \\ \searrow \quad \searrow \quad \searrow \\ \varphi(v_0) \to \varphi(v_1) \to \varphi(v_2) \cdots \end{array} = \varphi(u)\varphi(v)$$

Figure 11.12: I-shuffle and concatenation

For instance, let $(\Sigma, D) = a \,\text{---}\, b \,\text{---}\, c \qquad d \,\text{---}\, e$ be the dependence alphabet. Then,

$$aeba^\omega \sqcup\!\sqcup_I dc^\omega = ae(db + ba^*d)a^*(c^+a^+)^\omega$$

$$a^*ba^\omega \sqcup\!\sqcup_I c^*dc^\omega = (a^*da^*b + a^*b(a^*c^*)^*d)a^*(c^+a^+)^\omega$$

$$(a^* + c^\omega + ba^* + bc^\omega)^{-1} \sqcup\!\sqcup_I a^*ba^*(c^+a^+)^\omega = a^*ba^*(c^+a^+)^\omega + a^*(c^+a^+)^\omega + a^\omega$$

$$a^*ba^*(c^+a^+)^\omega \sqcup\!\sqcup_I (c^* + a^\omega + bc^\omega + b(ac)^\omega)^{-1} = a^*ba^*(c^+a^+)^\omega + a^*ba^*(c^+a^+)^*c^\omega + a^*$$

The following lemma establishes the relationship between these I-shuffle operations and the concatenation and the left and right quotients on real trace languages. A word language $U \subseteq \Sigma^\infty$ is closed with respect to the trace congruence $\sim$ if U is a union of $\sim$-classes, i.e. $u \sim v$ and $u \in U$ imply $v \in U$ for all $u, v \in \Sigma^\infty$.

Lemma 11.6.4 *Let $U, V \subseteq \Sigma^\infty$ be two word languages. Then,*

1. $\varphi(U \sqcup\!\sqcup_I V) = \varphi(U) \cdot \varphi(V)$,

2. if in addition U is closed, then $\varphi(U^{-1} \sqcup\!\sqcup_I V) = \varphi(U)^{-1} \cdot \varphi(V)$,

3. if in addition V is closed, then $\varphi(U \sqcup\!\sqcup_I V^{-1}) = \varphi(U) \cdot \varphi(V)^{-1}$.

Proof: The proof of this lemma is based on the following two claims.

Claim 1 Let $u, v, w \in \Sigma^\infty$ be such that $w \in u \sqcup\!\sqcup_I v$ then $\varphi(w) = \varphi(u) \cdot \varphi(v)$.

For $i \geq 0$, let $u_i, v_i \in \Sigma^*$ be such that $w = u_0 v_0 u_1 v_1 \ldots$, $u = u_0 u_1 \ldots$, $v = v_0 v_1 \ldots$ and $(v_i, u_j) \in I$ for all $0 \leq i < j$. The equation $\varphi(w) = \varphi(u) \cdot \varphi(v)$ is illustrated in Figure 11.12. Its easy verification is left to the reader.

Claim 2 Let $r, s \in \mathbb{R}$ be such that $\text{alphinf}(r) \times \text{alph}(s) \subseteq I$ and let $w \in \varphi^{-1}(r \cdot s)$. There exist $u \in \varphi^{-1}(r)$ and $v \in \varphi^{-1}(s)$ such that $w \in u \sqcup\!\sqcup_I v$.

We may write $w = w_0 w_1 \ldots$ with $w_i \in \Sigma \cup \{1\}$ for all $i \geq 0$. We construct inductively two sequences $u_0, u_1, \ldots, v_0, v_1, \ldots$ of $\Sigma \cup \{1\}$ as follows. Assume that $u_0, v_0, \ldots, u_{i-1}, v_{i-1}$ are already defined for some $i \geq 0$. Then we set

$$u_i = \begin{cases} w_i & \text{if } w_i \neq 1 \text{ and } |w_0 \ldots w_i|_{w_i} \leq |r|_{w_i} \\ 1 & \text{otherwise} \end{cases}$$

and
$$v_i = \begin{cases} w_i & \text{if } w_i \neq 1 \text{ and } |w_0 \dots w_i|_{w_i} > |r|_{w_i} \\ 1 & \text{otherwise} \end{cases}$$

Note that $w_i = u_i v_i$ for all $i \geq 0$ and $(v_i, u_j) \in I$ for all $0 \leq i < j$. Therefore, if we set $u = u_0 u_1 \dots$ and $v = v_0 v_1 \dots$, we obtain $w \in u \sqcup\!\sqcup_I v$. Moreover, it is easy to verify that $\varphi(u) = r$ and $\varphi(v) = s$.

1. $\varphi(U \sqcup\!\sqcup_I V) \subseteq \varphi(U) \cdot \varphi(V)$ follows directly from Claim 1. Conversely, let $t \in \varphi(U) \cdot \varphi(V)$, there exist $u \in U$ and $v \in V$ such that alphinf$(u) \times$ alph$(v) \subseteq I$ and $t = \varphi(u) \cdot \varphi(v)$. Let $u = u_0 u_1 \dots$ be a factorization of u on Σ^* with alph$(u_i) = $ alphinf(u) for all $i > 0$. Let $v = v_0 v_1 \dots$ be any factorization of v on Σ^*. Clearly, we have $w = u_0 v_0 u_1 v_1 \dots \in u \sqcup\!\sqcup_I v$. Hence, from Claim 1, we deduce $t = \varphi(u) \cdot \varphi(v) = \varphi(w) \in \varphi(U \sqcup\!\sqcup_I V)$.

2. Let $v \in U^{-1} \sqcup\!\sqcup_I V$. There exists $w \in (u \sqcup\!\sqcup_I v) \cap V$ for some $u \in U$. Hence, $\varphi(u) \cdot \varphi(v) = \varphi(w) \in \varphi(V)$ and $\varphi(v) \in \varphi(U)^{-1} \cdot \varphi(V)$. Conversely, let $s \in \varphi(U)^{-1} \cdot \varphi(V)$. There exists $r \in \varphi(U)$ such that $r \cdot s = \varphi(w)$ for some $w \in V$. By Claim 2, there exist $u \in \varphi^{-1}(r)$ and $v \in \varphi^{-1}(s)$ such that $w \in u \sqcup\!\sqcup_I v$. Since U is a closed language, we have $u \in U$. Hence, $v \in U^{-1} \sqcup\!\sqcup_I V$ and $s = \varphi(v) \in \varphi(U^{-1} \sqcup\!\sqcup_I V)$.

3. The proof for the right quotient is similar and left to the reader. □

The second lemma states that the family Rec Σ^∞ of recognizable word languages is closed under I-shuffle and I-shuffle quotients. To this purpose, it uses an easy fact: the closure of the family Rec Σ^∞ under morphism and inverse morphism (see [225]).

Lemma 11.6.5 *Let $U, V \in$ Rec Σ^∞ be two recognizable word languages. Then, $U \sqcup\!\sqcup_I V$, $U^{-1} \sqcup\!\sqcup_I V$ and $U \sqcup\!\sqcup_I V^{-1}$ are recognizable too.*

Proof: Let Σ_1 and Σ_2 be two disjoint copies of Σ and let $\widehat{\Sigma} = \Sigma_1 \cup \Sigma_2$. For $i = 1, 2$, we denote by a_i the copy in Σ_i of the letter $a \in \Sigma$. We define three morphisms h, p_1, p_2 from $\widehat{\Sigma}^\infty$ onto Σ^∞ by

- $h(a_1) = h(a_2) = a$ for all $a \in \Sigma$,

- $p_1(a_1) = a$ and $p_1(a_2) = 1$ for all $a \in \Sigma$,

- $p_2(a_1) = 1$ and $p_2(a_2) = a$ for all $a \in \Sigma$.

Finally, we define the recognizable language $K \in$ Rec Σ^∞ by its complement
$$\overline{K} = \bigcup_{(a,b)\in D} \widehat{\Sigma}^* b_2 \widehat{\Sigma}^* a_1 \widehat{\Sigma}^\infty.$$

The I-shuffle and the I-shuffle quotients may be expressed using these morphisms by the following formulæ which are easy to verify:
$$\begin{aligned} U \sqcup\!\sqcup_I V &= h(p_1^{-1}(U) \cap p_2^{-1}(V) \cap K) \\ U^{-1} \sqcup\!\sqcup_I V &= p_2(p_1^{-1}(U) \cap h^{-1}(V) \cap K) \\ U \sqcup\!\sqcup_I V^{-1} &= p_1(h^{-1}(U) \cap p_2^{-1}(V) \cap K) \end{aligned}$$

This concludes the proof of the lemma since the family Rec Σ^∞ is closed under morphism, inverse morphism and intersection. □

Using the previous results, we easily deduce the following proposition.

Proposition 11.6.6 *Let $R \subseteq \mathbb{R}(\Sigma, D)$ be a recognizable real trace language and let $S \subseteq \mathbb{R}(\Sigma, D)$ be a rational real trace language. Then, the left and right quotients $R^{-1} \cdot S$ and $S \cdot R^{-1}$ are rational too.*

Proof: Let $L \in \text{Rat } \Sigma^\infty$ be a rational word language such that $\varphi(L) = S$ (Theorem 11.6.2). By Theorem 11.7.4, $\varphi^{-1}(R) \in \text{Rec } \Sigma^\infty$ is a recognizable word language. Hence, the word languages $\varphi^{-1}(R)^{-1} \sqcup_I L$ and $L \sqcup_I \varphi^{-1}(R)^{-1}$ are recognizable too (Lemma 11.6.5). Since $\varphi^{-1}(R)$ is a closed language, we deduce from Lemma 11.6.4 that $R^{-1} \cdot S = \varphi(\varphi^{-1}(R)^{-1} \sqcup_I L)$ and $S \cdot R^{-1} = \varphi(L \sqcup_I \varphi^{-1}(R)^{-1})$. Therefore, $R^{-1} \cdot S$ and $S \cdot R^{-1}$ are rational (Theorem 11.6.2). □

Note that the same techniques may be used to establish that the family of recognizable real trace languages is closed under concatenation, left quotient and right quotient. The proof is left as an exercice to the reader with the following hint: prove first that for $R, S \subseteq \mathbb{R}$ the following formulæ hold

$$\varphi^{-1}(R) \sqcup_I \varphi^{-1}(S) = \varphi^{-1}(R \cdot S)$$
$$\varphi^{-1}(R)^{-1} \sqcup_I \varphi^{-1}(S) = \varphi^{-1}(R^{-1} \cdot S)$$
$$\varphi^{-1}(R) \sqcup_I \varphi^{-1}(S)^{-1} = \varphi^{-1}(R \cdot S^{-1})$$

In Section 11.7, the proof of these closure results will be done using recognizing morphisms. In fact, a stronger result will be obtained for the quotients (Proposition 11.7.11): the left and right quotients of a recognizable real trace language by *any* real trace language are recognizable too.

11.6.2 Rational Complex Trace Languages

As mentioned in the introduction of this section, the difference between rational real trace languages and rational complex trace languages lies in the concatenation and the ω-product used. In case of ambiguity, we will add a subscript to distinguish between the concatenation $\cdot_\mathbb{R}$ on real traces and the concatenation $\cdot_\mathbb{C}$ on complex traces, but in most cases, the concatenation used should be clear from the context.

As in any monoid, the concatenation on complex traces is extended to complex trace languages and is used to define the $*$-iteration, while the ω-product on complex traces yields the ω-iteration (see Section 11.6.1).

For instance, if there exists two independent letters $(a, c) \in I$ then $ca^\omega \cdot_\mathbb{C} ca^\omega = c^2 a^\omega$ whereas $ca^\omega \cdot_\mathbb{R} ca^\omega$ is undefined. For a more elaborate example, let $(\Sigma, D) = a \relbar b \relbar c \qquad d \relbar e$ be the dependence alphabet and let $R = \{a^\omega, b^2, c^\omega, d\}$ and $S = \{c^\omega, c^2 be, c^2\}$ be the real trace languages defined in the first example of Section 11.6.1. Then, their concatenation $R \cdot_\mathbb{R} S$ as real trace languages given in this example is different from their concatenation $R \cdot_\mathbb{C} S$ as complex trace languages:

$$R \cdot_\mathbb{C} S = \{(ac)^\omega, c^2 e a^\omega b, c^2 a^\omega, b^2 c^\omega, b^2 c^2 be, b^2 c^2, c^\omega, ec^\omega b, dc^\omega, dc^2 be, dc^2\}.$$

Note however that there is an important case where the *real* concatenation and the *complex* concatenation of two real trace languages $R, S \subseteq \mathbb{R}$ coincide. Namely, $R \cdot_{\mathbb{R}} S = R \cdot_{\mathbb{C}} S$ when $\mathrm{alphinf}(r) \times \mathrm{alph}(s) \subseteq I$ for all $r \in R$, $s \in S$. Similarly, the *real* $*$-iteration (ω-iteration resp.) of a language of finite traces is equal to its *complex* $*$-iteration (ω-iteration resp.).

As another example, consider the complex trace language $T = \{a^\omega, ba^\omega b, cdb^\omega\}$. Then

$$T \cdot_{\mathbb{C}} \{c^\omega, d^\omega\} = \{(ac)^\omega, (ad)^\omega, ba^\omega b, b(ad)^\omega b, cdb^\omega, c(bd)^\omega\}$$

Moreover, $T^0 = \{1\}$, $T^1 = T$ and it is easy to verify by induction that for all $n \geq 2$,

$$T^n = T^{n-1} \cup \{d^{n-2}a^\omega b, d^{n-1}ca^\omega b, d^{n-1}ba^\omega b, d^n cb^\omega\}$$

Hence, $T^* = 1 + a^\omega + d^*(a^\omega b + ba^\omega b) + d^+(ca^\omega b + cb^\omega)$. Similarly, we obtain

$$T^\omega = a^\omega + d^* a^\omega b + (ad)^\omega b + cd^+ a^\omega b + c(ad)^\omega b + d^* ba^\omega b + b(ad)^\omega b + cd^+ b^\omega + c(bd)^\omega.$$

Definition 11.6.7 *The family* Rat $\mathbb{C}(\Sigma, D)$ *of rational complex trace languages is the smallest family*

- *which contains the empty set and all singletons $\{a\}$ for $a \in \Sigma$,*

- *which is closed under union and under concatenation, $*$-iteration and ω-iteration on* complex *traces.*

In order to prove the results on rational complex trace languages, we will extensively use some operators introduced in Section 11.4.

Let $A \subseteq \Sigma$ be a subset of the alphabet. Recall that, for a dependence graph g, $\mu_A(g)$ denotes the maximal real prefix of g independent from A. Since the mapping μ_A depends only on the real part of a dependence graph, we can generalize it to complex traces by setting $\mu_A(x) = \mu_A(r)$ for all $x = (r, D(B)) \in \mathbb{C}$. We extend this mapping to complex trace languages by setting $\mu_A(T) = \{\mu_A(x) \mid x \in T\}$ for all $T \subseteq \mathbb{C}$.

Let $A, B \subseteq \Sigma$ be subsets of the alphabet and let $T \subseteq \mathbb{C}$ be a complex trace language. The language $T_A = \{x \in T \mid \mathrm{Im}(x) = D(A)\}$ was already defined in Section 11.4. In fact, we will need a finer decomposition of the complex trace language T. We introduce the mapping $\mathrm{shift}_{A,B}$ from complex trace languages to complex trace languages which gives the subset of traces which shift the imaginary part from $D(A)$ to $D(B)$:

$$\mathrm{shift}_{A,B}(T) = \{y \in T \mid \mathrm{Im}(xy) = D(B) \text{ for some } x \in \mathbb{C}_A\}.$$

Due to the properties of concatenation on complex traces (see Proposition 11.4.6), the existential quantifier *for some* may be replaced by the universal quantifier *for all* in the definition of $\mathrm{shift}_{A,B}$. Note that $\mathrm{shift}_{A,B}(T) = \emptyset$ if $D(A) \not\subseteq D(B)$. More generally, from Proposition 11.4.11, it follows that $\mathrm{shift}_{A,B}(\mathbb{M}) \neq \emptyset$ if and only if the ordered pair (A, B) is consistent (cf. Section 11.4.3).

Finally, we define a new mapping $\mu_{A,B}$ from complex trace languages to real trace languages by

$$\mu_{A,B}(T) = \mu_A(\text{shift}_{A,B}(T)).$$

Remark 11.6.8 The mappings $\text{shift}_{A,B}$ and $\mu_{A,B}$ may be considered as basic since they allow an easy expression of the other operations:

$$
\begin{aligned}
T_A &= \text{shift}_{\emptyset,A}(T) & \mu_A(T) &= \bigcup_{B \subseteq \Sigma} \mu_{A,B}(T) \\
\text{Re}(T) &= \mu_\emptyset(T) & \text{Re}(T_A) &= \mu_{\emptyset,A}(T)
\end{aligned}
$$

For instance, let $(\Sigma, D) = a \,\text{---}\, b \,\text{---}\, c \qquad d \,\text{---}\, e$ be the dependence alphabet and let $T = c^*a^\omega + cd^*b + b^*d^\omega + d(ac)^\omega + ba^\omega b$ be a complex trace language. Then,

$$
\begin{aligned}
\text{shift}_{\emptyset,\emptyset}(T) = T_\emptyset &= cd^*b & \text{shift}_{\{a\},\{b\}}(T) &= cd^*b + d(ac)^\omega + ba^\omega b \\
\text{shift}_{\emptyset,\{a\}}(T) = T_{\{a\}} &= c^*a^\omega & \text{shift}_{\{a\},\{a,e\}}(T) &= d^\omega \\
\text{shift}_{\emptyset,\{b\}}(T) = T_{\{b\}} &= d(ac)^\omega + ba^\omega b & \text{shift}_{\{a\},\Sigma}(T) &= b^+d^\omega \\
\text{shift}_{\emptyset,\Sigma}(T) = T_\Sigma &= \emptyset & \text{shift}_{\{b\},\{a\}}(T) &= \emptyset
\end{aligned}
$$

and

$$
\begin{aligned}
\text{Re}(T) = \mu_\emptyset(T) &= c^*a^\omega + cd^*b + b^*d^\omega + d(ac)^\omega + ba^\omega & \mu_{\{a\},\{b\}}(T) &= cd^* + dc^\omega \\
\mu_{\{a\}}(T) &= c^* + cd^* + d^\omega + dc^\omega & \mu_{\{a\},\{a,e\}}(T) &= d^\omega \\
\mu_{\{b\}}(T) &= d^* + d^\omega & \mu_{\{a\},\Sigma}(T) &= d^\omega \\
\mu_\Sigma(T) &= 1 & \mu_{\{b\},\{a\}}(T) &= \emptyset
\end{aligned}
$$

We will prove that rational trace languages are preserved by all these operations. To this purpose, we will use the following technical lemma which relates the rational operations with the basic mappings $\text{shift}_{A,B}$ and $\mu_{A,B}$.

Lemma 11.6.9 *Let* $R, S \in \text{Rat } \mathbb{C}(\Sigma, D)$ *be two complex trace languages, let* $A, B \subseteq \Sigma$ *be two subalphabets and let* $\mathcal{C} = \{C \subseteq \Sigma \mid D(A) \subseteq D(C) \subseteq D(B)\}$. *It holds*

$$
\begin{aligned}
\text{shift}_{A,B}(R \cup S) &= \text{shift}_{A,B}(R) \cup \text{shift}_{A,B}(S) & (11.12) \\
\mu_{A,B}(R \cup S) &= \mu_{A,B}(R) \cup \mu_{A,B}(S) & (11.13) \\
\text{shift}_{A,B}(R \cdot S) &= \bigcup_{C \in \mathcal{C}} \text{shift}_{A,C}(R) \cdot \text{shift}_{C,B}(S) & (11.14) \\
\mu_{A,B}(R \cdot S) &= \bigcup_{C \in \mathcal{C}} \mu_{A,C}(R) \cdot_{\mathbb{R}} \mu_{C,B}(S) & (11.15)
\end{aligned}
$$

Moreover, let

$$
\begin{aligned}
\mathcal{A} &= \{(A_0, \ldots, A_k) \mid k \geq 0 \text{ and } D(A) = D(A_0) \subsetneq \cdots \subsetneq D(A_k) = D(B)\} \\
\mathcal{B} &= \{(A_0, \ldots, A_k) \mid k \geq 0 \text{ and } D(A) = D(A_0) \subsetneq \cdots \subsetneq D(A_k) \subseteq D(B)\} \\
T_{A,C,B} &= \{x \in \mathbb{C} \mid D(C \cup \text{alphinf}(\mu_A(x))) = D(B)\} \\
S_{A,C,B} &= \{r \in \mathbb{R} \mid \text{alph}(r) \subseteq I(A) \text{ and } D(C \cup \text{alphinf}(r)) = D(B)\}
\end{aligned}
$$

Then

$$\text{shift}_{A,B}(R^*) = \bigcup_{(A_0,\ldots,A_k)\in\mathcal{A}} (\text{shift}_{A_0,A_0}(R))^* \cdot \text{shift}_{A_0,A_1}(R) \cdots \tag{11.16}$$
$$(\text{shift}_{A_{k-1},A_{k-1}}(R))^* \cdot \text{shift}_{A_{k-1},A_k}(R) \cdot (\text{shift}_{A_k,A_k}(R))^*$$

$$\mu_{A,B}(R^*) = \bigcup_{(A_0,\ldots,A_k)\in\mathcal{A}} (\mu_{A_0,A_0}(R))^* \cdot_\mathbb{R} \mu_{A_0,A_1}(R) \cdots \tag{11.17}$$
$$(\mu_{A_{k-1},A_{k-1}}(R))^* \cdot_\mathbb{R} \mu_{A_{k-1},A_k}(R) \cdot_\mathbb{R} (\mu_{A_k,A_k}(R))^*$$

$$\text{shift}_{A,B}(R^\omega) = \bigcup_{(A_0,\ldots,A_k)\in\mathcal{B}} T_{A,A_k,B} \cap (\text{shift}_{A_0,A_0}(R))^* \cdot \text{shift}_{A_0,A_1}(R) \cdots \tag{11.18}$$
$$(\text{shift}_{A_{k-1},A_{k-1}}(R))^* \cdot \text{shift}_{A_{k-1},A_k}(R) \cdot (\text{shift}_{A_k,A_k}(R))^\omega$$

$$\mu_{A,B}(R^\omega) = \bigcup_{(A_0,\ldots,A_k)\in\mathcal{B}} S_{A,A_k,B} \cap (\mu_{A_0,A_0}(R))^* \cdot_\mathbb{R} \mu_{A_0,A_1}(R) \cdots \tag{11.19}$$
$$(\mu_{A_{k-1},A_{k-1}}(R))^* \cdot_\mathbb{R} \mu_{A_{k-1},A_k}(R) \cdot_\mathbb{R} (\mu_{A_k,A_k}(R))^\omega$$

Proof: The first two formulæ are trivial and the third one is easy to verify. Formula 11.15 is a direct consequence of Formula 11.14 and the following claim with $\alpha = 3$. We give a more general claim since it will also be used for the iterations. In fact, we will only use this claim for $\alpha \leq \omega$.

Claim Let $A \subseteq \Sigma$ and let α be a countable ordinal. Let $(x_i)_{1\leq i<\alpha}$ be a sequence of complex traces and let $(A_i)_{1\leq i\leq\alpha}$ be a sequence of subalphabets such that $A_1 = A$ and $\prod_{1\leq j<i} x_j \in \text{shift}_{A,A_i}(\mathbb{C})$ for all $1 \leq i \leq \alpha$. Then

$$\mu_A\left(\prod_{1\leq i<\alpha} x_i\right) = \prod_{1\leq i<\alpha} \mu_{A_i}(x_i)$$

Indeed, let $x_0 \in \mathbb{C}_A$ and let $A_0 = \emptyset$. From Corollary 11.4.9 we deduce $\text{Re}(\prod_{0\leq i<\alpha} x_i) = \prod_{0\leq i<\alpha} \mu_{A_i}(x_i)$. Now, by Proposition 11.4.6, $\text{Re}(\prod_{0\leq i<\alpha} x_i) = \text{Re}(x_0) \cdot \mu_A(\prod_{1\leq i<\alpha} x_i)$. Since $\text{Re}(x_0) = \mu_\emptyset(x_0) = \mu_{A_0}(x_0)$, the claim follows from the left cancellativity of $\mathbb{R}$ (Proposition 11.2.8).

The formulæ for the iterations are more intricate. In order to deal with both iterations simultaneously, let $\dagger$ stand for either iteration ($*$ or ω). Let $x \in \text{shift}_{A,B}(R^\dagger)$. There exists a sequence of complex traces $(x_i)_{1\leq i<\alpha} \subseteq R$ for some $1 \leq \alpha \leq \omega$ such that $x = \prod_{1\leq i<\alpha} x_i$. Let $y \in \mathbb{C}_A$. Since the increasing sequence of subalphabets $(\text{Im}(y \prod_{1\leq i<j} x_i))_{1\leq j\leq\alpha}$ takes only finitely many values, there exist an integer $k \geq 0$, a finite sequence $A_0,\ldots,A_k$ of subalphabets and a finite sequence of integers $0 = i_0 < i_1 < \cdots < i_k < i_{k+1} = \alpha$ such that $D(A) = D(A_0) \subsetneq \cdots \subsetneq D(A_k)$, $x_{i_j} \in \text{shift}_{A_{j-1},A_j}(R)$ for all $1 \leq j \leq k$ and $x_p \in \text{shift}_{A_j,A_j}(R)$ for all $0 \leq j \leq k$ and $i_j < p < i_{j+1}$. Therefore,

$$x \in (\text{shift}_{A_0,A_0}(R))^* \cdot \text{shift}_{A_0,A_1}(R) \cdots \tag{11.20}$$
$$(\text{shift}_{A_{k-1},A_{k-1}}(R))^* \cdot \text{shift}_{A_{k-1},A_k}(R) \cdot (\text{shift}_{A_k,A_k}(R))^\dagger$$

- If α is finite, we deduce from Formula 11.20 that $x \in \text{shift}_{A_0, A_k}(R^*)$. Hence $(A_0, \ldots, A_k) \in \mathcal{A}$ and the first inclusion of Formula 11.16 is proved. The converse inclusion is clear.

- If $\alpha = \omega$, by Corollary 11.4.9 we obtain $\text{Im}(yx) = D(A_k) \cup D(\text{alphinf}(\text{Re}(yx)))$. Since $\text{Re}(yx) = \text{Re}(y)\mu_A(x)$ and $D(\text{alphinf}(\text{Re}(y))) \subseteq D(A) \subseteq D(A_k)$, we obtain $D(B) = \text{Im}(yx) = D(A_k) \cup D(\text{alphinf}(\mu_A(x)))$. Therefore, $x \in T_{A, A_k, B}$ and $D(A_k) \subseteq D(B)$, whence $(A_0, \ldots, A_k) \in \mathcal{B}$. The first inclusion of Formula 11.18 is proved and, again, the converse inclusion is an easy consequence of Corollary 11.4.9.

Let $(A_0, \ldots, A_k) \in \mathcal{B}$, it follows from the claim that

$$\mu_A((\text{shift}_{A_0, A_0}(R))^* \cdot \text{shift}_{A_0, A_1}(R) \cdots \text{shift}_{A_{k-1}, A_k}(R) \cdot (\text{shift}_{A_k, A_k}(R))^\dagger) =$$
$$(\mu_{A_0, A_0}(R))^* \cdot_\mathbb{R} \mu_{A_0, A_1}(R) \cdots \mu_{A_{k-1}, A_k}(R) \cdot_\mathbb{R} (\mu_{A_k, A_k}(R))^\dagger$$

Moreover, it is easy to verify that $\mu_A(T_{A, C, B}) = S_{A, C, B}$. Therefore, Formulæ 11.17 and 11.19 follows from Formulæ 11.16 and 11.18. $\qquad\square$

Using Lemma 11.6.9, we will prove that the rationality of trace languages is preserved by the mappings μ_A, $\mu_{A, B}$ and Re. This is also true for the mapping $\text{shift}_{A, B}$ but this result will be obtained as a corollary of Theorem 11.6.12 which characterizes rational complex trace languages.

Proposition 11.6.10 *Let $T \subseteq \mathbb{C}(\Sigma, D)$ be a rational complex trace language. Then for all $A, B \subseteq \Sigma$, the languages $\mu_{A, B}(T), \mu_A(T), \text{Re}(T_A), \text{Re}(T) \subseteq \mathbb{R}(\Sigma, D)$ are rational real trace languages.*

Proof: We first prove the result for $\mu_{A, B}$ by induction. The other cases will follow from Remark 11.6.8.

First, $\mu_{A, B}(\emptyset) = \emptyset$ and for all $a \in \Sigma$,

$$\mu_{A, B}(\{a\}) = \begin{cases} \{a\} & \text{if } D(A) = D(B) \text{ and } a \in I(A) \\ \emptyset & \text{otherwise} \end{cases}$$

Now, let $R, S \in \text{Rat } \mathbb{C}$ be rational complex trace languages and assume that for all $A, B \subseteq \Sigma$, $\mu_{A, B}(R), \mu_{A, B}(S) \in \text{Rat } \mathbb{R}$ are rational real trace languages. Using Formulæ 11.13, 11.15 and 11.17 of Lemma 11.6.9, we deduce directly that for all $A, B \subseteq \Sigma$, $\mu_{A, B}(R \cup S), \mu_{A, B}(R \cdot S), \mu_{A, B}(R^*) \in \text{Rat } \mathbb{R}$ are rational real trace languages. Finally, the rationality of $\mu_{A, B}(R^\omega)$ follows from Formula 11.19 and Corollary 11.6.3 since for all $A, B, C \subseteq \Sigma$, the language $S_{A, C, B}$ defined in Lemma 11.6.9 is clearly a recognizable real trace language. Indeed, this language is recognized by the alphabetic morphism alph : $\mathbb{M} \longrightarrow \mathcal{P}(\Sigma)$ (see Section 11.7.1). $\qquad\square$

Corollary 11.6.11 *Let $T \subseteq \mathbb{R}(\Sigma, D)$ be a real trace language. Then T is rational as a real trace language if and only if T is rational as a complex trace language:*

$$\text{Rat } \mathbb{R}(\Sigma, D) = \text{Rat } \mathbb{C}(\Sigma, D) \cap \mathcal{P}(\mathbb{R}(\Sigma, D))$$

Proof: Let $T \in \mathrm{Rat}\ \mathbb{R}$ be a rational real trace language. From Theorem 11.6.2, T is a finite union of sets of the form $R \cdot_{\mathbb{R}} S^{\omega_{\mathbb{R}}}$ where $R, S \in \mathrm{Rat}\ \mathbb{M}$ are rational languages of finite traces. In this case, the concatenation and the ω-product in $\mathbb{R}$ and $\mathbb{C}$ coincide: $R \cdot_{\mathbb{R}} S^{\omega_{\mathbb{R}}} = R \cdot_{\mathbb{C}} S^{\omega_{\mathbb{C}}}$. Hence, $T \in \mathrm{Rat}\ \mathbb{C}$. Conversely, let $T \in \mathrm{Rat}\ \mathbb{C}$ be a rational complex trace language such that $T \subseteq \mathbb{R}$. From Proposition 11.6.10 we deduce that $T = \mathrm{Re}(T) \in \mathrm{Rat}\ \mathbb{R}$ is a rational real trace language. $\qquad\square$

The following theorem gives a charaterization of rational complex trace languages by means of rational real trace languages and by means of rational languages of finite traces. This last characterization is a (non unique) normal form for rational complex trace languages.

Theorem 11.6.12 *Let* $T \subseteq \mathbb{C}(\Sigma, D)$ *be a language of complex traces. The following assertions are equivalent:*

1. *T is rational.*

2. *$\mathrm{Re}(T_A) \in \mathrm{Rat}\ \mathbb{R}(\Sigma, D)$ is a rational real trace language for all $A \subseteq \Sigma$.*

3. *T is a finite union of sets of the form $R \cdot S^{\omega} \cdot t$ where $R, S \in \mathrm{Rat}\ \mathbb{M}(\Sigma, D)$ are rational monoalphabetic languages of finite traces and $t \in \mathbb{M}(\Sigma, D)$ is a finite (shift) trace.*

Proof: $1 \Longrightarrow 2$ is already proved in Proposition 11.6.10.

$2 \Longrightarrow 3$: Let $A \subseteq \Sigma$, by Theorem 11.6.2 we have $\mathrm{Re}(T_A) = \bigcup_{1 \leq i \leq n} R_i S_i^{\omega}$ where $R_i, S_i \in \mathrm{Rat}\ \mathbb{M}$ are rational monoalphabetic languages of finite traces for all $1 \leq i \leq n$. By Proposition 11.4.11, there exist finite traces $(t_i)_{1 \leq i \leq n}$ such that $T_A = \bigcup_{1 \leq i \leq n} R_i S_i^{\omega} t_i$. The result follows since $T = \bigcup_{A \subseteq \Sigma} T_A$.

Note that this implication is also a direct consequence of Proposition 11.4.13, Corollary 11.6.3 and Theorem 11.6.2 since the language $\mathbb{R}_A$ is clearly recognizable for all $A \subseteq \Sigma$.

$3 \Longrightarrow 1$ is trivial. $\qquad\square$

Extending the corresponding results for real trace languages, we will prove now that the intersection, the left quotient and the right quotient of a rational complex trace language by a *recognizable* complex trace language are rational too. Recognizable complex trace languages will be defined in Section 11.8 but in order to prove these results we only need the characterization of Proposition 11.8.7 which states that a complex trace language $R \subseteq \mathbb{C}$ is recognizable if and only if the real trace languages $(\mathrm{Re}(R_A))_{A \subseteq \Sigma}$ are recognizable.

Corollary 11.6.13 *Let* $R \subseteq \mathbb{C}(\Sigma, D)$ *be a recognizable complex trace language and let* $T \subseteq \mathbb{C}(\Sigma, D)$ *be a rational complex trace language. Then, the language $R \cap T$ is rational too.*

Proof: We have $\mathrm{Re}((R \cap T)_A) = \mathrm{Re}(R_A \cap T_A) = \mathrm{Re}(R_A) \cap \mathrm{Re}(T_A)$ for all $A \subseteq \Sigma$. Hence, the result follows from Proposition 11.8.7 and Theorem 11.6.12 and Corollary 11.6.3. $\qquad\square$

For all $A, B \subseteq \Sigma$ and $T \subseteq \mathbb{C}$, we have $\text{shift}_{A,B}(T) = T \cap \text{shift}_{A,B}(\mathbb{C})$. Since the complex trace language $\text{shift}_{A,B}(\mathbb{C})$ is recognizable (Lemma 11.8.12), we deduce that $\text{shift}_{A,B}(T)$ and T_A are rational whenever T is rational.

Proposition 11.6.14 *Let $R \subseteq \mathbb{C}(\Sigma, D)$ be a recognizable complex trace language and let $T \subseteq \mathbb{C}(\Sigma, D)$ be a rational complex trace language. Then, the left and right quotients $R^{-1} \cdot T$ and $T \cdot R^{-1}$ are rational too.*

Proof: First, note that by Proposition 11.8.7 and Theorem 11.6.12, the real trace languages $\text{Re}(R_A)$ and $\text{Re}(T_A)$ are recognizable and rational respectively, for all $A \subseteq \Sigma$.

We start with the right quotient. Let $A \subseteq \Sigma$, we have

$$(T \cdot R^{-1})_A = \bigcup_{B \subseteq \Sigma} (T_B \cdot R^{-1})_A = \bigcup_{B \subseteq \Sigma} (T_B \cdot \text{shift}_{A,B}(R)^{-1})_A$$

It is easy to verify that

$$
\begin{aligned}
\text{Re}((T_B \cdot \text{shift}_{A,B}(R)^{-1})_A) &= \{s \in \text{Re}(\mathbb{C}_A) \mid s \cdot \mu_A(y) \in \text{Re}(T_B) \\
&\qquad\qquad \text{for some } y \in \text{shift}_{A,B}(R)\} \\
&= \text{Re}(\mathbb{C}_A) \cap \text{Re}(T_B) \cdot \mu_{A,B}(R)^{-1}
\end{aligned}
$$

By Lemma 11.8.12, $\mu_{A,B}(R)$ is a recognizable real trace language. Hence, it follows from Proposition 11.6.6 and Corollary 11.6.3 that $\text{Re}((T_B \cdot \text{shift}_{A,B}(R)^{-1})_A)$ is a rational real trace language. Therefore, by Theorem 11.6.12, $T \cdot R^{-1}$ is a rational complex trace language.

The computation for the left quotient is slightly different. First, note that

$$R^{-1} \cdot T = \bigcup_{A,C \subseteq \Sigma} R_A^{-1} \cdot T_C$$

Next, let $B \subseteq \Sigma$, we have

$$
\begin{aligned}
(R_A^{-1} \cdot T_C)_B &= \{y \in \mathbb{C}_B \mid xy \in T_C \text{ for some } x \in R_A\} \\
&= \{y \in \mathbb{C}_B \cap \text{shift}_{A,C}(\mathbb{C}) \mid \mu_A(y) \in \text{Re}(R_A)^{-1} \cdot \text{Re}(T_C)\}
\end{aligned}
$$

Therefore,

$$
\begin{aligned}
\text{Re}((R_A^{-1} \cdot T_C)_B) &= \text{Re}(\mathbb{C}_B) \cap \text{Re}(\text{shift}_{A,C}(\mathbb{C})) \\
&\qquad \cap \{s \in \mathbb{R} \mid \mu_A(s) \in \text{Re}(R_A)^{-1} \cdot \text{Re}(T_C)\}
\end{aligned}
$$

Clearly, $\mathbb{C}$ is a recognizable complex trace language and by Lemma 11.8.12, the language $\text{shift}_{A,C}(\mathbb{C})$ is recognizable too. Moreover, by Proposition 11.6.6, the language $\text{Re}(R_A)^{-1} \cdot \text{Re}(T_C)$ is rational. Hence the result follows from Corollary 11.6.13 and the claim:

Claim Let $L \subseteq \mathbb{R}$ be a rational real trace language then $K = \{s \in \mathbb{R} \mid \mu_A(s) \in L\}$ is rational too.

Indeed, it is easy to verify that $K = (L \cap \{s \in \mathbb{R} \mid \mathrm{alph}(s) \subseteq I(A)\}) \cdot \mathrm{suff}_A(\mathbb{R})$ The real trace language $\{s \in \mathbb{R} \mid \mathrm{alph}(s) \subseteq I(A)\}$ is clearly recognizable. Moreover, $\mathrm{suff}_A(\mathbb{R}) = \mathbb{R} \setminus \bigcup_{a \in I(A)} a \cdot \mathbb{R}$ is recognizable, whence is rational (Corollary 11.7.5). Therefore, K is rational.   □

Note that the same proof may be used to prove Theorem 11.8.10 which states that the left and right quotients of a recognizable complex trace language by any complex trace language are recognizable too.

11.6.3   Notes

Rational real trace languages were introduced and first studied in [111]. In this paper, it was only proved that a real trace language T is recognizable if and only if T is a finite union of sets of the form $R_1 S_1^\omega R_2 S_2^\omega \cdots R_k S_k^\omega$, where $k \leq |\Sigma|$ and $R_i, S_i \in \mathrm{Rat}\ \mathbb{M}$ are rational languages of finite traces. Next, the study of rational real trace languages was pursued in [116] where the main characterizations of these languages (Theorem 11.6.2) were established.

The family of rational complex trace languages was introduced in [59]. In this paper, rational languages were defined by characterization 2 of Theorem 11.6.12 whereas Definition 11.6.7 was obtained as a characterization. All the results presented in Section 11.6.2 and Proposition 11.6.6 were proved in [59].

11.7   Recognizable Real Trace Languages

We introduce and study in this section the family Rec $\mathbb{R}$ of recognizable languages of real traces. These languages are defined by extending in a natural way the definition of recognizable word languages using recognizing morphisms.

We prove that the family of recognizable real trace languages is closed under union, intersection, complement and (real) concatenation. These results together with the closure of Rec $\mathbb{R}$ by iterations restricted to connected languages yield a normal form theorem for recognizable real trace languages (Theorem 11.7.23).

Next, finite and infinite concurrent iterations on real trace languages are defined. It turns out that the family Rec $\mathbb{R}$ is closed under these new operations. This leads to the main result of this section which states that the family of recognizable real trace languages coincides with the family of c—rational real trace languages (Theorem 11.7.32). This last family is defined similarly to the family of rational real trace languages introduced in Section 11.6 by simply replacing the classical iterations by their concurrent versions.

On the other hand, we prove that the family Rec $\mathbb{R}$ is closed under left and right quotients by arbitrary real trace languages (Proposition 11.7.11).

11.7.1 Definition and Closure Properties

The family Rec Σ^∞ of recognizable languages of finite and infinite words can be defined in the following way. A language of finite and infinite words $L \subseteq \Sigma^\infty$ is recognizable if there exists some morphism η from Σ^* to a finite monoid S such that, for any sequence $(u_i)_{i<\omega}$ of finite words, if $\prod_{i<\omega} u_i \in L$ then $\prod_{i<\omega} \eta^{-1}(\eta(u_i)) \subseteq L$ (see e.g. [225]). We extend this definition in a natural way in order to introduce the recognizable languages of real traces.

Definition 11.7.1 *A morphism η from $\mathbb{M}(\Sigma, D)$ to a finite monoid S recognizes a real trace language $T \subseteq \mathbb{R}(\Sigma, D)$ if for all sequences of finite traces $(r_i)_{i<\omega}, (s_i)_{i<\omega} \subseteq \mathbb{M}(\Sigma, D)$ such that $\eta(r_i) = \eta(s_i)$ for all $i < \omega$, it holds*

$$\prod_{i<\omega} r_i \in T \Longleftrightarrow \prod_{i<\omega} s_i \in T$$

A real trace language $T \subseteq \mathbb{R}(\Sigma, D)$ is recognizable if it is recognized by some morphism from $\mathbb{M}(\Sigma, D)$ to a finite monoid.

The family of recognizable real trace languages over a dependence alphabet (Σ, D) is denoted by Rec $\mathbb{R}(\Sigma, D)$ or simply by Rec $\mathbb{R}$.

The family Rec $\mathbb{M}(\Sigma, D)$ of recognizable languages of finite traces has been defined and studied in Chapter 6. As in any monoid (see e.g. [11]), this family can be characterized using morphisms into finite monoids. A language of finite traces $T \subseteq \mathbb{M}(\Sigma, D)$ is recognizable if $T = \eta^{-1}(\eta(T))$ for some morphism η from $\mathbb{M}(\Sigma, D)$ to a finite monoid S. The following result asserts that this definition and Definition 11.7.1 (restricted to languages of finite traces) yield the same family of languages.

Proposition 11.7.2 Rec $\mathbb{M}(\Sigma, D) = $ Rec $\mathbb{R}(\Sigma, D) \cap \mathcal{P}(\mathbb{M}(\Sigma, D))$

Proof: Let $T \subseteq \mathbb{M}$ be a language of finite traces recognized, in the sense of Definition 11.7.1, by a morphism η from $\mathbb{M}$ to a finite monoid S. Let $r, s \in \mathbb{M}$ be such that $\eta(r) = \eta(s)$. It holds $r \in T \Longleftrightarrow r1^\omega \in T \Longleftrightarrow s1^\omega \in T \Longleftrightarrow s \in T$. Hence $T \in $ Rec $\mathbb{M}$.

Conversely, suppose that there exists some morphism η from $\mathbb{M}$ to a finite monoid S with identity 1 such that $T = \eta^{-1}(\eta(T))$. Without loss of generality we can assume that $\eta^{-1}(1) = \{1\}$. (If η does not satisfy this assumption then we take the morphism $\eta' : \mathbb{M} \longrightarrow S^u$, where $S^u = S \cup \{u\}$ and $u \notin S$ is a new unit element, i.e. multiplication in S is completed by $s \cdot u = u \cdot s = s$ for all $s \in S^u$, and $\eta'(t) = \eta(t)$ if $t \neq 1$, $\eta'(1) = u$. Note also that all alphabetic morphism (Definition 11.7.8) satisfy the assumption). Then the fact that η recognizes T in the sense of Definition 11.7.1 follows immediately from the formula $\eta^{-1}(\eta(t_0)) \ldots \eta^{-1}(\eta(t_k)) \subseteq \eta^{-1}(\eta(t_0 \ldots t_k))$ which is valid for all $t_0, \ldots, t_k \in \mathbb{M}$. □

For instance, any morphism η from $\mathbf{M}(\Sigma, D)$ to a finite monoid S recognizes $\mathbb{R}$. Let 1 be the identity of S. If, in addition, $\eta^{-1}(1) = \{1\}$ then the languages $\mathbb{M}$ and $\mathbb{R} \setminus \mathbb{M}$ are also recognized by η. Now, let alph : $\mathbf{M}(\Sigma, D) \longrightarrow \mathcal{P}(\Sigma)$ be the morphism which associates with each finite trace its alphabet. Let $(u_i)_{i < \omega}$ and $(v_i)_{i < \omega}$ be two sequences of finite traces such that $\mathrm{alph}(u_i) = \mathrm{alph}(v_i)$ for all $i < \omega$. We have thus $\mathrm{alph}(\prod_{i < \omega} u_i) = \mathrm{alph}(\prod_{i < \omega} v_i)$ and $\mathrm{alphinf}(\prod_{i < \omega} u_i) = \mathrm{alphinf}(\prod_{i < \omega} v_i)$. Therefore, the morphism alph recognizes the real trace languages $\{u \in \mathbb{R}(\Sigma, D) \mid \mathrm{alph}(u) = A\}$ and $\mathbb{R}_A = \{u \in \mathbb{R}(\Sigma, D) \mid D(\mathrm{alphinf}(u)) = D(A)\}$ for any $A \subseteq \Sigma$. Finally, for all $A, B, C \subseteq \Sigma$, the morphism alph recognizes also the language $S_{A,C,B} = \{r \in \mathbb{R} \mid \mathrm{alph}(r) \subseteq I(A) \text{ and } D(C \cup \mathrm{alphinf}(r)) = D(B)\}$ used in Lemma 11.6.9.

In order to provide a link between the recognizability of a real trace language T and the recognizability of the word language $\varphi^{-1}(T)$, we first define the syntactic congruence of T.

Definition 11.7.3 *Let $T \subseteq \mathbb{R}(\Sigma, D)$ be a real trace language. The syntactic congruence $\sim_T$ of T is the equivalence relation over $\mathbf{M}(\Sigma, D)$ defined for $r, s \in \mathbf{M}(\Sigma, D)$ by*

$$r \sim_T s \text{ if } \quad \forall u, v, w \in \mathbf{M}(\Sigma, D), \quad urvw^\omega \in T \Longleftrightarrow usvw^\omega \in T \text{ and}$$
$$u(vrw)^\omega \in T \Longleftrightarrow u(vsw)^\omega \in T$$

It is straightforward to verify that $\sim_T$ is indeed a congruence over the monoid $\mathbf{M}(\Sigma, D)$. When the dependence relation is full (i.e. $D = \Sigma \times \Sigma$), we obtain exactly the syntactic congruence for word languages defined by Arnold [8].

With each congruence $\sim$ over $\mathbf{M}(\Sigma, D)$, a morphism from $\mathbf{M}(\Sigma, D)$ into $\mathbf{M}(\Sigma, D)/ \sim$ is canonically associated which maps any trace t to its equivalence class $[t]_\sim$. A congruence *recognizes* a language $T \subseteq \mathbb{R}$ if the associated morphism recognizes T. On the other hand, if a morphism η from $\mathbf{M}(\Sigma, D)$ to a finite monoid S recognizes a real trace language $T \subseteq \mathbb{R}$ then the relation $\sim$ defined for $r, s \in \mathbf{M}(\Sigma, D)$ by: $r \sim s$ if $\eta(r) = \eta(s)$ is a congruence recognizing T.

Thus a real trace language $T \subseteq \mathbb{R}$ is recognizable iff there exists a congruence $\sim$ of finite index (i.e. with a finite number of equivalence classes) over $\mathbf{M}(\Sigma, D)$ recognizing T.

Arnold [8] has proved that a word language $L \subseteq \Sigma^\infty$ is recognizable if and only if its syntactic congruence $\sim_L$ has finite index and recognizes L. We will use this result to characterize the recognizability of a real trace language T by its syntactic congruence or by the recognizability of $\varphi^{-1}(T)$.

Theorem 11.7.4 *Let $T \subseteq \mathbb{R}(\Sigma, D)$ be a real trace language. Then the following conditions are equivalent:*

1. *T is recognizable*

2. *$\varphi^{-1}(T) \subseteq \Sigma^\infty$ is a recognizable word language*

3. *the syntactic congruence $\sim_T$ of T has finite index and recognizes T.*

Proof: $1 \implies 2$. Let η be a morphism from $\mathbb{M}$ to a finite monoid S recognizing T. Using Proposition 11.2.17, it is straightforward to verify that the morphism $\eta \circ \varphi$ from Σ^* to S recognizes the word language $\varphi^{-1}(T)$.

$2 \implies 3$. Assume that $L = \varphi^{-1}(T)$ is a recognizable word language. From Arnold's result, the syntactic congruence $\sim_L$ of L has finite index and recognizes L. From the very definition of $\sim_L$ and $\sim_T$ and Proposition 11.2.17, it holds

$$\forall x, y \in \Sigma^*, x \sim_L y \text{ iff } \varphi(x) \sim_T \varphi(y).$$

Hence the syntactic congruences $\sim_L$ and $\sim_T$ have the same finite index. Moreover, $\sim_L$ recognizes L if and only if $\sim_T$ recognizes T.

$3 \implies 1$. Trivial   □

Büchi's theorem states that the families Rec Σ^∞ of recognizable word languages and Rat Σ^∞ of rational word languages coincide. Hence, from Theorems 11.6.2 and 11.7.4, we deduce

Corollary 11.7.5 Rec $\mathbb{R}(\Sigma, D) \subseteq$ Rat $\mathbb{R}(\Sigma, D)$

However, the converse is false as soon as there exists a pair $(a, b) \in I$ of independent letters. Indeed, the rational language $L = \varphi(ab)^* \subseteq \mathbb{M}(\Sigma, D)$ is not recognizable (since $\varphi^{-1}(L) = \{w \in \{a, b\}^* \mid |w|_a = |w|_b\}$ is not a recognizable word language).

An example of an ω-language $L \subseteq \mathbb{R}(\Sigma, D) \setminus \mathbb{M}(\Sigma, D)$ which is rational but not recognizable, can be constructed on three letters, say a, b, c, where there is at least one pair of independent letters, say $(a, b) \in I$. Then the rational language $L = \varphi(ab)^* \cdot \varphi(c)^\omega$ is not recognizable since the projection of $\varphi^{-1}(L)$ to $\{a, b\}^\infty$ is $\{w \in \{a, b\}^* \mid |w|_a = |w|_b\}$. We leave it as an exercise to the reader to show that no such example exists on a two-letter alphabet.

From Definition 11.7.1, we deduce easily the first closure properties of the family Rec $\mathbb{R}$.

Proposition 11.7.6 *The family Rec $\mathbb{R}(\Sigma, D)$ is closed under the operations of union, intersection and complement.*

Proof: If a morphism η from $\mathbb{M}$ to a finite monoid S recognizes the languages $T_1, T_2 \subseteq \mathbb{R}$, it follows directly from Definition 11.7.1 that η recognizes the languages $T_1 \cup T_2$, $T_1 \cap T_2$ and $\overline{T_1}$ too. Using these results, the proposition is an easy consequence of the following claim.

Claim For $j = 1, 2$, let η_j from $\mathbb{M}$ to a finite monoid S_j be a morphism recognizing a language $T_j \subseteq \mathbb{R}$. Let γ from $\mathbb{M}(\Sigma, D)$ to $S_1 \times S_2$ be the morphism defined by $\gamma(t) = (\eta_1(t), \eta_2(t))$ for any trace $t \in \mathbb{M}$. Then γ recognizes T_1 and T_2.

Indeed, for any finite trace t we have

$$\gamma^{-1}(\gamma(t)) = \{u \in \mathbb{M} \mid \eta_1(u) = \eta_1(t) \text{ and } \eta_2(u) = \eta_2(t)\} = \eta_1^{-1}(\eta_1(t)) \cap \eta_2^{-1}(\eta_2(t))$$

Hence, if $(t_i)_{i<\omega} \subseteq \mathbf{M}$ verifies $\prod_{i<\omega} t_i \in T_j$ for some $j = 1, 2$, it holds

$$\prod_{i<\omega} \gamma^{-1}(\gamma(t_i)) \subseteq \prod_{i<\omega} \eta_i^{-1}(\eta_i(t_i)) \subseteq T_j$$

and the claim is proved. $\qquad\qquad\qquad\qquad\qquad\qquad\qquad\qquad\qquad\qquad\qquad\quad$ $\square$

Let $T \subseteq \mathbb{R}$ be a real trace language. Assume that T is recognizable. As we noticed previously the languages $\mathbf{M}$ and $\mathbb{R} \setminus \mathbf{M}$ are recognizable and thus, by Proposition 11.7.6, the languages $T_{\mathrm{fin}} = T \cap \mathbf{M}$ and $T_{\mathrm{inf}} = T \cap (\mathbb{R} \setminus \mathbf{M}) = T \setminus T_{\mathrm{fin}}$ are recognizable too. Conversely, if T_{fin} and T_{inf} are recognizable, then so is $T = T_{\mathrm{fin}} \cup T_{\mathrm{inf}}$. Hence we have proved:

Remark 11.7.7 Let $T \subseteq \mathbb{R}(\Sigma, D)$ be a real trace language. Then T is recognizable if and only if $T_{\mathrm{fin}} = T \cap \mathbf{M}(\Sigma, D)$ and $T_{\mathrm{inf}} = T \setminus T_{\mathrm{fin}}$ are recognizable.

In order to deal with independent traces, it will be useful in the sequel to consider morphisms such that two finite traces with the same image have the same alphabet.

Definition 11.7.8 *A morphism η from $\mathbf{M}(\Sigma, D)$ to a monoid S is* alphabetic *if η is surjective and*

$$\forall u, v \in \mathbf{M}(\Sigma, D), \eta(u) = \eta(v) \implies \mathrm{alph}(u) = \mathrm{alph}(v)$$

Then, for all $s \in S$, the alphabet of s, denoted by $\mathrm{alph}(s)$, is the common alphabet of the traces of $\eta^{-1}(s)$.

Let η be a morphism from $\mathbf{M}(\Sigma, D)$ to a finite monoid S. Let also $\bar{\eta}$ be the direct product of the morphisms η and alph, that is, $\bar{\eta}$ is the morphism from $\mathbf{M}(\Sigma, D)$ to $\eta(S) \times \mathcal{P}(\Sigma)$ defined by $\bar{\eta}(t) = (\eta(t), \mathrm{alph}(t))$ for all $t \in \mathbf{M}$. By the claim of the proof of Proposition 11.7.6, if η recognizes a real trace language then $\bar{\eta}$ recognizes this language as well. Moreover, $\bar{\eta}$ is alphabetic. Thus we obtain:

Proposition 11.7.9 *A real trace language is recognizable if and only if it is recognized by some alphabetic morphism into a finite monoid.*

This result will allow us to assume in the sequel, whenever necessary, that a recognizable real trace language is recognized by an alphabetic morphism into some finite monoid.

In order to prove that the family Rec $\mathbb{R}$ is closed under (real) concatenation, we will introduce a new operator on morphisms. Let S_1, S_2 be two finite monoids. Let $\eta_1 : \mathbf{M}(\Sigma, D) \longrightarrow S_1$ and $\eta_2 : \mathbf{M}(\Sigma, D) \longrightarrow S_2$ be two alphabetic morphisms. We first define the diamond product $\diamond_I(S_1, S_2)$ as the set $\mathcal{P}(S_1 \times S_2)$ provided with the multiplication specified for all $R, R' \subseteq S_1 \times S_2$, by:

$$R \circ R' = \{(s_1 s_1', s_2 s_2') \mid (s_1, s_2) \in R, (s_1', s_2') \in R' \text{ and } (s_2, s_1') \in I\}.$$

Here, $(s_2, s_1') \in I$ is an abbreviation for $\mathrm{alph}(s_2) \times \mathrm{alph}(s_1') \subseteq I$.

Note that the definition of the law ∘ depends in fact on the morphisms η_1 and η_2 since, by definition, $(s_2, s_1') \in I$ means $\text{alph}(\eta_1^{-1}(s_1')) \times \text{alph}(\eta_2^{-1}(s_2)) \subseteq I$. Hence the diamond product should be denoted by $\Diamond_{I,\eta_1,\eta_2}(S_1, S_2)$. Nevertheless, we use the notation $\Diamond_I(S_1, S_2)$ to lighten the formulas.

To see that $\Diamond_I(S_1, S_2)$ has a monoid structure, it suffices to verify that the multiplication is associative. To this purpose, one can easily verify that

$$
\begin{aligned}
(R \circ R') \circ R'' &= \{(s_1 s_1' s_1'', s_2 s_2' s_2'') \mid (s_1, s_2) \in R, (s_1', s_2') \in R', (s_1'', s_2'') \in R'' \\
&\qquad \text{and } (s_1', s_2) \in I, (s_1'', s_2) \in I, (s_1'', s_2') \in I\} \\
&= R \circ (R' \circ R'')
\end{aligned}
$$

Now, the diamond product $\Diamond_I(\eta_1, \eta_2)$ of two alphabetic morphisms $\eta_1 : \mathbb{M}(\Sigma, D) \longrightarrow S_1$ and $\eta_2 : \mathbb{M}(\Sigma, D) \longrightarrow S_2$ is the mapping

$$
\begin{aligned}
\Diamond_I(\eta_1, \eta_2): \quad \mathbb{M}(\Sigma, D) &\longrightarrow \Diamond_I(S_1, S_2) \\
t &\longmapsto \{(\eta_1(u), \eta_2(v)) \mid t = uv\}
\end{aligned}
$$

We shall show that $\Diamond_I(\eta_1, \eta_2)$ is a morphism from $\mathbb{M}(\Sigma, D)$ into $\Diamond_I(S_1, S_2)$. Let $t = t_1 t_2 \in \mathbb{M}$. Then $\Diamond_I(\eta_1, \eta_2)(t) = \{(\eta_1(u), \eta_2(v)) \mid t_1 t_2 = uv\}$. Recall that two real traces x and y are independent, denoted by $(x, y) \in I$, if $\text{alph}(x) \times \text{alph}(y) \subseteq I$. By Theorem 2.3.10 (see also Proposition 4.2.14), $t_1 t_2 = uv$ if and only if there exist traces z_0, z_1, z_2, z_3 of $\mathbb{M}$ such that

$$
t_1 = z_0 z_1, \ t_2 = z_2 z_3, u = z_0 z_2, v = z_1 z_3 \text{ and } (z_1, z_2) \in I
$$

Hence, we obtain

$$
\begin{aligned}
\Diamond_I(\eta_1, \eta_2)(t) &= \{(\eta_1(z_0 z_2), \eta_2(z_1 z_3)) \mid t_1 = z_0 z_1, t_2 = z_2 z_3 \text{ and } (z_1, z_2) \in I\} \\
&= \{(\eta_1(z_0)\eta_1(z_2), \eta_2(z_1)\eta_2(z_3)) \mid t_1 = z_0 z_1, t_2 = z_2 z_3 \text{ and } (z_1, z_2) \in I\} \\
&= \{(\eta_1(z_0), \eta_2(z_1)) \mid t_1 = z_0 z_1\} \circ \{(\eta_1(z_2), \eta_2(z_3)) \mid t_2 = z_2 z_3\} \\
&= \Diamond_I(\eta_1, \eta_2)(t_1) \circ \Diamond_I(\eta_1, \eta_2)(t_2)
\end{aligned}
$$

We are now ready to prove the closure of Rec $\mathbb{R}$ under (real) concatenation.

Proposition 11.7.10 *Let* $T', T'' \subseteq \mathbb{R}(\Sigma, D)$ *be two recognizable real trace languages then the language* $T' \cdot_\mathbb{R} T''$ *is recognizable too.*

Proof: Let $\eta' : \mathbb{M}(\Sigma, D) \longrightarrow S'$ and $\eta'' : \mathbb{M}(\Sigma, D) \longrightarrow S''$ be two alphabetic morphisms into finite monoids recognizing T' and T'' respectively. We claim that $\Diamond_I(\eta', \eta'')$ recognizes $T' \cdot_\mathbb{R} T''$.

Let $t \in T'T''$. We have $t = t't''$ for some $t' \in T'$ and $t'' \in T''$. Let $(u_i)_{i<\omega}$ be a sequence of finite traces such that $t = \prod_{i<\omega} u_i$. By Remark 11.2.14, there exist sequences $(u_i')_{i<\omega}$ and $(u_i'')_{i<\omega}$ of finite traces such that

$$
t' = \prod_{i<\omega} u_i', \quad t'' = \prod_{i<\omega} u_i'', \quad u_i = u_i' u_i'' \text{ for all } i < \omega
$$
$$
\text{and } (u_i'', u_j') \in I \text{ for all } i < j.
$$

Let $(v_i)_{i<\omega}$ be a sequence of finite traces such that

$$\Diamond_I(\eta',\eta'')(v_i) = \Diamond_I(\eta',\eta'')(u_i) \text{ for all } i < \omega. \tag{11.21}$$

For all $i < \omega$, by definition of $\Diamond_I(\eta',\eta'')$, there exist two finite traces v_i', v_i'' such that

$$v_i = v_i'v_i'', \quad \eta_1(v_i') = \eta_1(u_i') \quad \text{and} \quad \eta_2(v_i'') = \eta_2(u_i'') \tag{11.22}$$

Since the morphisms η' and η'' are alphabetic, we obtain $\text{alph}(v_i') = \text{alph}(u_i')$ and $\text{alph}(v_i'') = \text{alph}(u_i'')$ for all $i < \omega$. Hence,

$$(v_i'', v_j') \in I \text{ for all } i < j. \tag{11.23}$$

To prove our claim we have to show that $\prod_{i<\omega} v_i \in T'T''$. Let $r' = \prod_{i<\omega} v_i'$ and $r'' = \prod_{i<\omega} v_i''$. Since η' recognizes T' and $t' \in T'$, Formula 11.22 implies that $r' \in T'$. Similarly, we obtain $r'' \in T''$. But from Formula 11.23 we get then

$$\prod_{i<\omega} v_i = \prod_{i<\omega}(v_i'v_i'') = \left(\prod_{i<\omega} v_i'\right)\left(\prod_{i<\omega} v_i''\right) = r'r'' \in T'T''$$

$\square$

We end this section by the proof of the closure of recognizable real trace languages under quotients by arbitrary real trace languages.

Proposition 11.7.11 *Let $K \subseteq \mathbb{R}(\Sigma, D)$ be an arbitrary real trace language and let $L \subseteq \mathbb{R}(\Sigma, D)$ be a recognizable real trace language. Then the following left and right quotients are recognizable too:*

$$K^{-1} \cdot_{\mathbb{R}} L = \{y \in \mathbb{R} \mid x \cdot y \in L \text{ for some } x \in K$$
$$\text{such that } \text{alphinf}(x) \times \text{alph}(y) \subseteq I\}$$
$$L \cdot_{\mathbb{R}} K^{-1} = \{x \in \mathbb{R} \mid x \cdot y \in L \text{ for some } y \in K$$
$$\text{such that } \text{alphinf}(x) \times \text{alph}(y) \subseteq I\}$$

Proof: We prove this proposition for $K^{-1} \cdot_{\mathbb{R}} L$ only, the case of $L \cdot_{\mathbb{R}} K^{-1}$ being similar.

Let η be an alphabetic morphism from $\mathbb{M}$ into a finite monoid S recognizing L. Let $(y_i)_{i<\omega}$ be a sequence of finite traces such that $y = \prod_{i<\omega} y_i \in K^{-1} \cdot_{\mathbb{R}} L$. By definition, there exists a real trace $x \in K$ such that $x \cdot y \in L$ and $\text{alphinf}(x) \times \text{alph}(y) \subseteq I$. Let $(x_i)_{i<\omega}$ be a sequence of finite traces such that $x = \prod_{i<\omega} x_i$ and $\text{alph}(x_i) = \text{alphinf}(x)$ for all $i \geq 1$. We have

$$x \cdot_{\mathbb{R}} y = (x_0 y_0)(x_1 y_1)\ldots \in L$$

Now, let $(z_i)_{i<\omega}$ be a sequence of finite traces such that $\eta(z_i) = \eta(y_i)$ for all $i < \omega$. Since η recognizes L, we get $(x_0 z_0)(x_1 z_1)\ldots \in L$. But η is alphabetic, so it holds

$$(x_0 z_0)(x_1 z_1)\ldots = x \cdot z \in L \quad \text{and} \quad \text{alphinf}(x) \times \text{alph}(z) \subseteq I$$

Therefore $z \in K^{-1} \cdot_{\mathbb{R}} L$ and the proposition is proved. $\square$

11.7.2   Normal Form

The notion of weakly recognizable word languages has been proposed in [225] where it is proved that the families of recognizable word languages and weakly recognizable word languages coincide. We will now extend this result to real trace languages which will then help us to prove the closure of Rec $\mathbb{R}$ under iterations restricted to connected languages.

For a finite monoid S, the set $P(S)$ of linked pairs of S is defined by $P(S) = \{(s, e) \in S \times S \mid s \cdot e = s \text{ and } e \cdot e = e\}$.

Definition 11.7.12 *Let η be a morphism from $\mathbb{M}(\Sigma, D)$ into a finite monoid S and let $T \subseteq \mathbb{R}(\Sigma, D)$ be a real trace language. Then η weakly recognizes T if*

$$T = \bigcup_{(s,e) \in P_T(S)} \eta^{-1}(s)(\eta^{-1}(e))^{\omega}$$

where $P_T(S) = \{(s, e) \in P(S) \mid \eta^{-1}(s)(\eta^{-1}(e))^{\omega} \subseteq T\}$.

A language T of real traces is weakly recognizable if it is weakly recognized by some morphism into a finite monoid.

Let η be a morphism from $\mathbb{M}(\Sigma, D)$ into a finite monoid S and let $\overline{\eta} = \eta \times \text{alph} :$ $\mathbb{M} \longrightarrow S \times \mathcal{P}(\Sigma)$ be defined by $\overline{\eta}(t) = (\eta(t), \text{alph}(t))$ for all $t \in \mathbb{M}$. Assume that η weakly recognizes a real trace language T. Let $t \in T$ and let $(s, e) \in P_T(S)$ be such that $t \in \eta^{-1}(s)(\eta^{-1}(e))^{\omega}$. Let $(t_i)_{i<\omega} \subseteq \mathbb{M}$ be a sequence of finite traces verifying $t = \prod_{i<\omega} t_i$, $\eta(t_0) = s$ and $\eta(t_i) = e$ for all $i \geq 1$. Since (s, e) is a linked pair, we may assume without loss of generality that $\text{alph}(t_0) = \text{alph}(t)$ and $\text{alph}(t_i) = \text{alphinf}(t)$ for all $i \geq 1$. Hence $t \in \overline{\eta}^{-1}(s, \text{alph}(t))\overline{\eta}^{-1}(e, \text{alphinf}(t))^{\omega}$ and since $(\text{alph}(t), \text{alphinf}(t))$ is a linked pair of $\mathcal{P}(\Sigma)$, we deduce that $\overline{\eta}$ weakly recognizes T. Therefore, we get the following remark which can be seen as a counterpart of Proposition 11.7.9 for weakly recognizable real trace languages.

Remark 11.7.13 *Any weakly recognizable real trace language is weakly recognized by an alphabetic morphism into some finite monoid.*

The existence of Ramsey factorizations will be essential in the study the relationship between the families of recognizable and weakly recognizable real trace languages. Therefore, we include a simple and direct proof of this result inspired from [225]. It is also a trivial application of Ramsey's Theorem [128].

Lemma 11.7.14 *Let η be a morphism from an arbitrary monoid M into a finite monoid S and let $(u_i)_{i<\omega}$ be a sequence of elements of M. There exist a strictly increasing sequence of integers $(i_j)_{j<\omega}$ and a linked pair $(s, e) \in P(S)$ such that*

$$s = \eta(u_0 \ldots u_{i_0-1}) \text{ and } e = \eta(u_{i_j} \ldots u_{i_k-1}) \text{ for all } 0 \leq j < k$$

This is called a Ramsey factorization of the infinite sequence $(u_i)_{i<\omega}$.

Proof: Let $V = \{(i,j) \in \mathbb{N}^2 \mid i < j\}$. We consider the mapping $c : V \longrightarrow S$ defined by $c(i,j) = \eta(u_i \ldots u_{j-1})$.

We define inductively a sequence of infinite sets of integers $N_0 \supset N_1 \supset N_2 \ldots$ and a sequence of integers $(n_i)_{i<\omega}$ as follows. First, we set $N_0 = \mathbb{N}$. Assume that N_p is already defined. Let $n_p = \min(N_p)$. Since S is finite and N_p is infinite, there exist $s_p \in S$ and an infinite subset $N_{p+1} \subset N_p$ such that $c(n_p, m) = s_p$ for all $m \in N_{p+1}$.

Finally, since S is finite, there exist $e \in S$ and an infinite sequence $(p_i)_{i<\omega}$ such that $s_{p_j} = e$ for all $j < \omega$. Then, for all $j \geq 0$, we set $i_j = n_{p_j}$. For all $0 \leq j < k$ we have $\eta(u_{i_j} \ldots u_{i_k-1}) = c(i_j, i_k) = s_{p_j} = e$. Note that $e^2 = s_{p_0} s_{p_1} = c(n_{p_0}, n_{p_1}) c(n_{p_1}, n_{p_2}) = c(n_{p_0}, n_{p_2}) = s_{p_0} = e$. Moreover, if we set $s = s_0$, we obtain $s = c(0, n_{p_1}) = c(0, n_{p_0}) c(n_{p_0}, n_{p_1}) = se$ and the result is proved. □

Now we are able to prove that each recognizable real trace language is weakly recognizable.

Proposition 11.7.15 *Let η be a morphism from $\mathbb{M}(\Sigma, D)$ into a finite monoid S recognizing a language T of real traces. Then η weakly recognizes T.*

Proof: To get the thesis it suffices to show that if η recognizes T then for any $t \in T$ there exists a linked pair $(s,e) \in P_T(S)$ such that $t \in \eta^{-1}(s)(\eta^{-1}(e))^\omega$. Let $(t_i)_{i<\omega}$ be a sequence of finite traces such that $t = \prod_{i<\omega} t_i$. By Lemma 11.7.14, there exists a linked pair $(s,e) \in P(S)$ and a strictly increasing sequence of integers $(i_j)_{j<\omega}$ such that $s = \eta(t_0 \ldots t_{i_0-1})$ and $e = \eta(t_{i_j} \ldots t_{i_k-1})$ for all $0 \leq j < k$. Therefore

$$t = (t_0 \ldots t_{i_0-1})(t_{i_0} \ldots t_{i_1-1})(t_{i_1} \ldots t_{i_2-1}) \ldots \in \eta^{-1}(s)(\eta^{-1}(e))^\omega$$

Moreover, since η recognizes T, we deduce

$$\eta^{-1}(s)(\eta^{-1}(e))^\omega = \eta^{-1}(\eta(t_0 \cdots t_{i_0-1})) \prod_{k<\omega} \eta^{-1}(\eta(t_{i_k} \cdots t_{i_{k+1}-1})) \subseteq T$$

which concludes the proof. □

The converse of Proposition 11.7.15 does not hold even in the case of infinite words; a morphism η may weakly recognize a language L of Σ^∞ without recognizing it. Nevertheless, using Schützenberger's product, it can be proved that the families of recognizable word languages and of weakly recognizable word languages coincide [225]. We will extend this result to real trace languages using the diamond product of morphisms (defined in Section 11.7.1) which can be seen as a trace generalization of Schützenberger's product. First we need a technical lemma on equivalent sequences of finite traces.

Lemma 11.7.16 *Let $(t_i)_{i<\omega}, (z_i)_{i<\omega} \subseteq \mathbb{M}(\Sigma, D)$ be two sequences of finite traces. Then $\prod_{i<\omega} t_i = \prod_{i<\omega} z_i$ if and only if there exist strictly increasing sequences of integers $(m_i)_{i<\omega}$ and $(n_i)_{i<\omega}$ with $m_0 = n_0 = 0$ and sequences of finite traces $(x_i)_{i<\omega}$ and $(y_i)_{i<\omega}$ with $y_0 = 1$ such that, for all $i < \omega$:*

$$\begin{aligned} t_{m_i} \ldots t_{m_{i+1}-1} &= y_i x_i \\ z_{n_i} \ldots z_{n_{i+1}-1} &= x_i y_{i+1} \end{aligned}$$

A rough picture of the situation described in the lemma above is given in the following picture.

$$
\begin{aligned}
\prod_{i<\omega} t_i &= \underbrace{t_0 \ldots t_{m_1-1}}_{x_0} \quad \underbrace{t_{m_1} \ldots t_{m_2-1}}_{y_1 x_1} \quad \underbrace{t_{m_2} \ldots t_{m_3-1}}_{y_2 x_2} \quad \cdots \\
&= \quad\quad x_0 \quad\quad\quad\quad y_1 x_1 \quad\quad\quad\quad y_2 x_2 \quad\quad \cdots \\
&= \quad\quad\quad x_0 y_1 \quad\quad\quad\quad x_1 y_2 \quad\quad\quad\quad x_2 y_3 \quad\quad \cdots \\
&= \quad \underbrace{z_0 \ldots z_{n_1-1}}_{} \quad \underbrace{z_{n_1} \ldots z_{n_2-1}}_{} \quad \underbrace{z_{n_2} \ldots z_{n_3-1}}_{} \quad \cdots \\
&= \prod_{i<\omega} z_i
\end{aligned}
$$

Proof: It is clear that the conditions imply $\prod_{i<\omega} t_i = \prod_{i<\omega} z_i$. Conversely, assume that $\prod_{i<\omega} t_i = \prod_{i<\omega} z_i$. We construct the appropriate sequences by induction. Let $y_0 = 1$, $x_0 = t_0$, $m_0 = n_0 = 0$ and $m_1 = 1$. Then, assume that for some $k < \omega$ we have defined indices $0 = m_0 < \ldots < m_{k+1}$, $0 = n_0 < \ldots < n_k$ and finite traces $y_0 = 1, x_0, \ldots, y_k, x_k$ such that

$$
\begin{aligned}
t_{m_i} \ldots t_{m_{i+1}-1} &= y_i x_i \quad \text{for } 0 \leq i \leq k \\
z_{n_i} \ldots z_{n_{i+1}-1} &= x_i y_{i+1} \quad \text{for } 1 \leq i \leq k-1
\end{aligned}
$$

Since $y_0 x_0 \ldots y_k x_k$ is a finite prefix of $\prod_{i<\omega} t_i = \prod_{i<\omega} z_i$ and $y_0 x_1 \ldots x_{k-1} y_k = z_{n_0} \ldots z_{n_k-1}$ it follows from the left-cancellativity of $\mathbb{R}$ (Proposition 11.2.8) that x_k is a finite prefix of $\prod_{n_k \leq i < \omega} z_i$. Hence we find some $n_{k+1} > n_k$ such that x_k is a prefix of $z_{n_k} \ldots z_{n_{k+1}-1}$, i.e., $x_k y_{k+1} = z_{n_k} \ldots z_{n_{k+1}-1}$ for some $y_{k+1} \in \mathbb{M}$. A symmetric argument yields that for some $m_{k+2} > m_{k+1}$, there exists $x_{k+1} \in \mathbb{M}$ such that $y_{k+1} x_{k+1} = t_{m_{k+1}} \ldots t_{m_{k+2}-1}$. This concludes the proof of the lemma. $\square$

We can now prove the following result which claims that each weakly recognizable real trace language is recognizable.

Proposition 11.7.17 *Let $T \subseteq \mathbb{R}(\Sigma, D)$ be a language of real traces weakly recognized by an alphabetic morphism η from $\mathbb{M}(\Sigma, D)$ into a finite monoid S. Then the morphism $\diamond_I(\eta, \eta)$ recognizes T.*

Proof: Let $\gamma = \diamond_I(\eta, \eta)$ and let $(u_i)_{i<\omega}$ be a sequence of finite traces such that $u = \prod_{i<\omega} u_i \in T$. Since η weakly recognizes T, there exists a linked pair $(s, e) \in P_T(S)$ such that

$$
u \in \eta^{-1}(s)(\eta^{-1}(e))^\omega \subseteq T
$$

We claim that

$$
\prod_{i<\omega} \gamma^{-1}(\gamma(u_i)) \subseteq \eta^{-1}(s)(\eta^{-1}(e))^\omega
$$

Indeed, let $(v_i)_{i<\omega}$ be a sequence of finite traces such that

$$
\gamma(v_i) = \gamma(u_i) \text{ for all } i < \omega
$$

Since $u \in \eta^{-1}(s)(\eta^{-1}(e))^\omega$ there exists a sequence of finite traces $(w_i)_{i<\omega} \subseteq \mathbf{M}$ such that $w_0 \in \eta^{-1}(s)$ and $w_i \in \eta^{-1}(e)$ for all $i \geq 1$ with

$$\prod_{i<\omega} u_i = u = \prod_{i<\omega} w_i$$

From Lemma 11.7.16, there exist strictly increasing sequences of integers $(m_i)_{i<\omega}$ and $(n_i)_{i<\omega}$ with $m_0 = n_0 = 0$ and sequences of finite traces $(x_i)_{i<\omega}$ and $(y_i)_{i<\omega}$ with $y_0 = 1$ such that for all $i < \omega$:

$$
\begin{aligned}
w_{m_i} \ldots w_{m_{i+1}-1} &= y_i x_i \\
u_{n_i} \ldots u_{n_{i+1}-1} &= x_i y_{i+1}
\end{aligned}
$$

Since (s, e) is a linked pair we get in particular

$$\eta(x_0) = s \text{ and } \eta(y_i x_i) = e \text{ for all } 1 \leq i < \omega$$

Since $\Diamond_I(\eta, \eta)$ is a morphism, $\Diamond_I(\eta, \eta)(v_{n_i} \ldots v_{n_{i+1}-1}) = \Diamond_I(\eta, \eta)(u_{n_i} \ldots u_{n_{i+1}-1})$ for all $i < \omega$. Hence, by definition of the diamond product $\Diamond_I(\eta, \eta)$, there exist two sequences $(x_i')_{i<\omega}$ and $(y_i')_{i<\omega}$ of finite traces with $y_0' = 1$ such that:

$$v_{n_i} \ldots v_{n_{i+1}-1} = x_i' y_{i+1}', \eta(x_i') = \eta(x_i) \text{ and } \eta(y_i') = \eta(y_i), \text{ for all } i < \omega$$

Now we have $\prod_{i<\omega} v_i = (x_0' y_1')(x_1' y_2') \ldots = (y_0' x_0')(y_1' x_1') \ldots$ and $\eta(y_0' x_0') = \eta(x_0') = \eta(x_0) = s$, and $\eta(y_i' x_i') = \eta(y_i x_i) = e$ for all $1 \leq i < \omega$. Therefore $\prod_{i<\omega} v_i \in \eta^{-1}(s)(\eta^{-1}(e))^\omega$ and the claim is proved. Hence we get $\prod_{i<\omega} \gamma^{-1}(\gamma(u_i)) \subseteq T$ and γ recognizes the real trace language T. $\qquad\square$

As a corollary of Propositions 11.7.15 and 11.7.17 we obtain the following result.

Theorem 11.7.18 *A real trace language is weakly recognizable if and only if it is recognizable.*

As in the case of the finite iteration, the infinite iteration of a recognizable real trace language is not necessarily recognizable as shown in the following example.

Let $(\Sigma, D) = a \text{ —— } b \text{ —— } c$ and let $T = \{ac, b\}$. T is obviously recognizable whereas T^ω is not. Indeed, $\varphi^{-1}(T^\omega) \cap \{a, c\}^* b^\omega = \{u \in \{a, c\}^* \mid |u|_a = |u|_c\} b^\omega$ which is not a recognizable word language and the result follows from Theorem 11.7.4.

Nevertheless, the following result provides an interesting sufficient condition ensuring the recognizability of the infinite iteration T^ω of a language of finite traces.

Proposition 11.7.19 *Let $T \subseteq \mathbf{M}(\Sigma, D)$ be a recognizable language of finite traces such that $T \cdot T \subseteq T$. Then T^ω is recognizable.*

Note that the condition $T \cdot T \subseteq T$ is equivalent to $T = T^+$.

Proof: Let η be a morphism from $\mathbb{M}$ into a finite monoid S recognizing T. We shall show that η weakly recognizes T^ω.

Let $t \in T^\omega$ and let $(t_i)_{i<\omega}$ be a sequence of traces of T such that $t = \prod_{i<\omega} t_i$. Applying Lemma 11.7.14, we obtain a strictly increasing sequence $(i_j)_{j<\omega}$ of integers and a linked pair $(s, e) \in P(S)$ such that

$$\eta(t_0 \cdots t_{i_0-1}) = s \quad \text{and} \quad \eta(t_{i_k} \cdots t_{i_{k+1}-1}) = e \text{ for all } k < \omega \qquad (11.24)$$

Now note that since $T \cdot T \subseteq T$, all traces $(t_0 \cdots t_{i_0-1})$ and $(t_{i_k} \cdots t_{i_{k+1}-1})$, $k < \omega$, belong to T, thus $s, e \in \eta(T)$. But η recognizes T, hence $\eta^{-1}(\eta(T)) = T$, in particular $\eta^{-1}(s) \subseteq T$ and $\eta^{-1}(e) \subseteq T$, which together with (11.24) implies that

$$t = \prod_{i<\omega} t_i \quad \in \quad \eta^{-1}(s)(\eta^{-1}(e))^\omega \quad \subseteq \quad T^\omega$$

The proposition follows then from Theorem 11.7.18. $\qquad\qquad\qquad\qquad\qquad$ $\square$

A language T of finite traces verifies $T^+ \cdot T^+ \subseteq T^+$ and $T^\omega = (T^+)^\omega$. Since T^+ is recognizable if and only if T^* is, we obtain immediately the following consequence of the previous proposition.

Corollary 11.7.20 Let $T \subseteq \mathbb{M}(\Sigma, D)$ be a language of finite traces. If T^* is recognizable then T^ω is a recognizable real trace language.

Note that the inverse of Corollary 11.7.20 does not hold: the recognizability of T and T^ω does not imply that T^* is recognizable. Indeed, assume that there exists two independent letters $(a, b) \in I$. Let $T = \{ab\}$, T is of course recognizable. Note also that T^ω is recognized by any alphabetic morphism. On the contrary, T^* is not recognizable since $\varphi^{-1}(T^*) = \{u \in \{a, b\}^* \mid |u|_a = |u|_b\}$ is not a recognizable word language.

Exercise 11.7.1 Using Formulas 11.10 and 11.11, prove that Proposition 11.7.19 (and thus Corollary 11.7.20) can be generalized to real trace languages: if $T \subseteq \mathbb{R}(\Sigma, D)$ is a recognizable real trace language such that $T \cdot T \subseteq T$ then T^ω is recognizable.

The relevance of Corollary 11.7.20 stems from the fact that numerous sufficient conditions ensuring the recognizability of the finite iteration T^* of a language $T \subseteq \mathbb{M}$ are known (see Chapter 6) and each of them applies now directly to the infinite iteration as well.

Recall that a finite trace t is connected if the dependence graph t is connected. Equivalently, a finite trace t is connected if and only if the restriction of the dependence relation D to $\text{alph}(t) \times \text{alph}(t)$ is a connected graph. We will use intensively in this section and in the next one the following result which is proved in Chapter 6.

Theorem 11.7.21 Let $T \subseteq \mathbb{M}(\Sigma, D)$ be a recognizable language of connected finite traces, then T^* is recognizable.

From this theorem and Corollary 11.7.20, we get the following condition that will be used several times in the sequel.

Corollary 11.7.22 *Let* $T \subseteq \mathbb{M}(\Sigma, D)$ *be a recognizable language of finite traces such that all traces of T are connected. Then T^ω is a recognizable real trace language.*

In the next subsection, we will define a notion of connected real traces and extend this result to recognizable languages of connected real traces (Proposition 11.7.28).

A non-empty subset A of Σ is said to be connected if $D \cap (A \times A)$ is a connected graph. For each $\emptyset \neq A \subseteq \Sigma$ there exists a unique family $\{A_1, \ldots, A_k\}$ of non-empty connected sets such that $\bigcup_{i=1}^{k} A_i = A$ and $A_i \times A_j \subseteq I$ for $i \neq j$. The sets $A_1, \ldots, A_k$ are the connected components of A.

We can now state the main result of this subsection.

Theorem 11.7.23 *A real trace language $T \subseteq \mathbb{R}(\Sigma, D)$ is recognizable if and only if it can be written as a finite union of languages of the form*

$$M \cdot N_1^\omega \cdots N_k^\omega = M \cdot (N_1 \cdots N_k)^\omega$$

where $M, N_1, \ldots, N_k \subseteq \mathbb{M}(\Sigma, D)$ are monoalphabetic recognizable languages such that $\mathrm{alph}(N_i)$ *is connected for all $1 \leq i \leq k$ and* $\mathrm{alph}(N_i) \times \mathrm{alph}(N_j) \subseteq I$ *for all $i \neq j$.*

Proof: First, it is clear by Propositions 11.7.6 and 11.7.10, Corollary 11.7.22 that every such finite union is recognizable. Also, given the alphabetic conditions, we have $M \cdot N_1^\omega \cdots N_k^\omega = M \cdot (N_1 \cdots N_k)^\omega$.

Conversely, let η be an alphabetic morphism which recognizes T. By Proposition 11.7.15, η weakly recognizes T and thus

$$T = \bigcup_{(s,e) \in P_T(S)} \eta^{-1}(s)(\eta^{-1}(e))^\omega$$

For each $e \in S$, we consider the connected components $A_1, \ldots, A_k$ of $\mathrm{alph}(e)$ and we define the finite set

$$E = \{(e_1, \ldots, e_k) \mid e = e_1 \cdots e_k \text{ and } \mathrm{alph}(e_i) = A_i, \text{ for all } 1 \leq i \leq k\}$$

By definition of alphabetic morphisms, η is surjective. Let $f, g \in S$ be such that $\mathrm{alph}(f) = A_i$ and $\mathrm{alph}(g) = A_j$ for some $1 \leq i \neq j \leq k$. Let $u \in \eta^{-1}(f)$ and let $v \in \eta^{-1}(g)$. Since η is alphabetic, it holds $fg = \eta(u)\eta(v) = \eta(uv) = \eta(vu) = \eta(v)\eta(u) = gf$. Hence, it is easy to verify that E is a submonoid of S^k.

We claim that

$$\eta^{-1}(s)(\eta^{-1}(e))^\omega = \bigcup_{(e_1, \ldots, e_k) \in E} \eta^{-1}(s)(\eta^{-1}(e_1) \cdots \eta^{-1}(e_k))^\omega$$

Indeed, $\eta^{-1}(e_1) \cdots \eta^{-1}(e_k) \subseteq \eta^{-1}(e)$ and one inclusion is clear.

Conversely, we define a morphism $\psi : \eta^{-1}(e) \rightarrow E$ as follows. Let x be in $\eta^{-1}(e)$. Since $\mathrm{alph}(x) = \mathrm{alph}(e)$, x admits a unique decomposition in connected components $x = x_1 \cdots x_k$ such that $\mathrm{alph}(x_i) = A_i$ for all $1 \leq i \leq k$. Then we set $\psi(x) = (\eta(x_1), \ldots, \eta(x_k))$.

Now, let $\prod_{i<\omega} y_i \in \eta^{-1}(s)(\eta^{-1}(e))^\omega$ with $y_0 \in \eta^{-1}(s)$ and $y_i \in \eta^{-1}(e)$ for all $i \geq 1$. Using Ramsey factorization (Lemma 11.7.14), we obtain an infinite sequence of integers $(i_j)_{j<\omega}$ and a tuple $(e_1, \ldots, e_k) \in E$ such that $\psi(y_{i_j} \cdots y_{i_k-1}) = (e_1, \ldots, e_k)$ for all $0 \leq j < k$. Hence, $y_{i_j} \cdots y_{i_{j+1}-1} \in \eta^{-1}(e_1) \cdots \eta^{-1}(e_k)$ for all $j < \omega$ and we obtain $y_{i_0} y_{1+i_0} y_{2+i_0} \cdots \in (\eta^{-1}(e_1) \cdots \eta^{-1}(e_k))^\omega$. This proves the claim since $\eta(y_0 y_1 \cdots y_{i_0-1}) = se \cdots e = se = s$.

This claim provides a normal form for the language $\eta^{-1}(s)(\eta^{-1}(e))^\omega$ which concludes the proof.   □

As a direct consequence of the previous theorem and of Propositions 11.7.6 and 11.7.10 and Corollary 11.7.22, we obtain the following characterization of recognizable real trace languages.

Corollary 11.7.24 *The family of recognizable real trace languages is the smallest family which contains the finite languages of finite traces and which is closed under union, concatenation and $*$-iteration and ω-iteration both restricted to languages of connected finite traces.*

11.7.3 C-Rational Real Trace Languages

We introduce in this subsection the new family of concurrent rational real trace languages and prove that this family coincides with the family of recognizable real trace languages.

First we need to define the notion of connected real traces.

Definition 11.7.25 *A real trace $t \in \mathbb{R}(\Sigma, D)$ is connected if the dependence graph t is connected.*

For instance, the real trace of Figure 11.2 and the real traces f_2 and f_3 of Figure 11.9 are connected. On the contrary, let $(\Sigma, D) = a \text{——} b \text{——} c \text{——} d \text{——} e$, then the real traces presented in Figure 11.13 are not connected.

It is easy to verify that a real trace t is connected if and only if the graph $D \cap (\mathrm{alph}(t) \times \mathrm{alph}(t))$ is connected. Moreover, if t is a non-connected real trace then there exists a unique family $\{t_1, \ldots, t_k\}$ of pairwise independent connected non-empty traces such that $t = t_1 \cdots t_k$. The traces $t_1, \ldots, t_k$ are called the connected components of t. Note that, in this case, $\{alph(t_1), \ldots, alph(t_k)\}$ is the family of connected components of $alph(t)$.

In the sequel, for any real trace $t \in \mathbb{R}$, we denote by $\mathrm{C}(t)$ the set of *connected components* of t. Moreover, for a language $T \subseteq \mathbb{R}$, we set $\mathrm{C}(T) = \bigcup_{t \in T} \mathrm{C}(t)$. For instance, let f_1 and f_2 be the real traces of Figure 11.13, then $\mathrm{C}(f_1) = \{ab(ac)^\omega, e^\omega\}$ and $\mathrm{C}(f_2) = \{aa, c^\omega, e^\omega\}$.

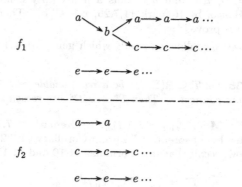

Figure 11.13: Two *non connected* dependence graphs

Remark 11.7.26 Let $r, t \in \mathbb{R}(\Sigma, D)$ be two real traces. Then

$$r \in C(t) \iff r \text{ is a connected non empty trace}$$
$$\text{and } t = rs \text{ for some } s \in \mathbb{R}(\Sigma, D) \text{ such that } (r, s) \in I$$

We first prove that the operator C preserves the recognizable real trace languages. A language is said to be connected if all its elements are connected.

Proposition 11.7.27 *If $T \subseteq \mathbb{R}(\Sigma, D)$ is a recognizable real trace language then $C(T)$ is recognizable as well.*

Proof: Suppose that T is recognized by an alphabetic morphism η from $\mathbb{M}$ into a finite monoid S. We shall show that η recognizes $C(T)$. Let $(u_i)_{i<\omega}$ be a sequence of finite traces such that $u = \prod_{i<\omega} u_i \in C(T)$. Then there exists a trace $r \in \mathbb{R}$ such that $(u, r) \in I$ and $ur \in T$. Let $(r_i)_{i<\omega}$ be any sequence of finite traces such that $r = \prod_{i<\omega} r_i$. Since $(u, r) \in I$, we have

$$(u_i, r_j) \in I \text{ for all } i, j < \omega$$

Therefore $ur = (\prod_{i<\omega} u_i)(\prod_{i<\omega} r_i) = \prod_{i<\omega} u_i r_i$.

Now let $(v_i)_{i<\omega}$ be a sequence of finite traces such that $\eta(u_i) = \eta(v_i)$ for all $i < \omega$. Since η is a morphism, we get for all $i < \omega$, $\eta(u_i r_i) = \eta(v_i r_i)$. Hence, as $ur \in T$ and η recognizes T, we obtain

$$\prod_{i<\omega} v_i r_i \in T$$

Since η is alphabetic, it holds $(v_i, r_j) \in I$ for all $i, j < \omega$. Thus, we have

$$vr = \left(\prod_{i<\omega} v_i \right) \left(\prod_{i<\omega} r_i \right) = \prod_{i<\omega} v_i r_i \in T$$

Moreover $alph(u) = alph(v)$ and v is thus a non empty connected trace which verifies $(v, r) \in I$. Hence, by Remark 11.7.26, $v \in C(T)$. Therefore η recognizes $C(T)$ and the lemma is proved. □

We can now prove the following result which generalizes Theorem 11.7.21 on finite traces.

Proposition 11.7.28 *Let $T \subseteq \mathbb{R}(\Sigma, D)$ be a recognizable real trace language such that all traces of T are connected. Then T^* and T^ω are recognizable.*

Proof: Let $T_{\text{fin}} = T \cap \mathbb{M}$ and $T_{\text{inf}} = T \setminus T_{\text{fin}}$. By Remark 11.7.7, T_{fin} and T_{inf} are recognizable and thus, by Theorem 11.7.21 and Corollary 11.7.22, T_{fin}^* and T_{fin}^ω are recognizable too. Now, recall that (see Formulas 11.10 and 11.11):

$$T^* = \bigcup_{k \leq |\Sigma|} (T_{\text{fin}}^* \cdot T_{\text{inf}})^k \cdot T_{\text{fin}}^*$$

and

$$T^\omega = \bigcup_{k \leq |\Sigma|} (T_{\text{fin}}^* \cdot T_{\text{inf}})^k \cdot T_{\text{fin}}^\omega$$

Hence the result follows directly from the closure of the family of recognizable real trace languages under union and concatenation (Propositions 11.7.6 and 11.7.10). □

We are now ready to introduce and examine two new operations on real trace languages, namely, the finite and infinite concurrent iterations. These operations generalize the concurrent iteration of languages of finite traces introduced in Chapter 6.

Definition 11.7.29 *Let $T \subseteq \mathbb{R}(\Sigma, D)$ be a real trace language. Then the finite and infinite concurrent iterations of T are defined by*

$$T^{c-*} = (C(T))^* \ \text{and} \ T^{c-\omega} = (C(T))^\omega.$$

As a direct consequence of Propositions 11.7.27 and 11.7.28 we obtain the following result.

Theorem 11.7.30 *If $T \subseteq \mathbb{R}(\Sigma, D)$ is a recognizable real trace language then T^{c-*} and $T^{c-\omega}$ are recognizable too.*

The family of c-rational trace languages is then defined like the family of rational real trace languages (see Definition 11.6.1) by simply replacing the classical iterations by their concurrent versions.

Definition 11.7.31 *The family $c - \text{Rat} \, \mathbb{R}(\Sigma, D)$ of c-rational real trace languages is the smallest family*

- *which contains the empty set and all singletons $\{a\}$ for $a \in \Sigma$,*

- *which is closed under union, concatenation and under finite and infinite concurrent iterations on real traces.*

If we do not allow in this definition the infinite concurrent iteration, we obtain the family $c - \text{Rat } \mathbb{M}(\Sigma, D)$ of c-rational languages of finite traces introduced by Ochmański. It turns out that this family coincide with the family $\text{Rec } \mathbb{M}(\Sigma, D)$ of recognizable languages of finite traces (see Chapter 6). We will now show that this result generalizes to real trace languages.

Theorem 11.7.32 $c - \text{Rat } \mathbb{R}(\Sigma, D) = \text{Rec } \mathbb{R}(\Sigma, D)$

Proof: First, from the closure properties of the family $\text{Rec } \mathbb{R}$ (Propositions 11.7.6 and 11.7.10 and Theorem 11.7.30), it follows directly that $c - \text{Rat } \mathbb{R}(\Sigma, D) \subseteq \text{Rec } \mathbb{R}$.

Conversely, let $T \in \text{Rec } \mathbb{R}$. By Theorem 11.7.23, T is a finite union of sets of the form $M \cdot N_1^\omega \cdots N_k^\omega$, where $M, N_1, \ldots, N_k$ belong to $\text{Rec } \mathbb{M} = c - \text{Rat } \mathbb{M}$ and all traces of the sets N_i are connected. Hence $N_i^\omega = N_i^{c-\omega}$ for all $1 \leq i \leq n$ and thus $T \in c - \text{Rat } \mathbb{R}$ and the theorem is proved. $\square$

The classical Kleene's theorem states the equality of recognizable and rational languages of the free monoid Σ^*. By Büchi's theorem, a similar fact holds also for languages of Σ^∞: recognizable and ω-rational subsets of Σ^∞ coincide [225]. Ochmański's theorem, stating that $c - \text{Rat } \mathbb{M}(\Sigma, D) = \text{Rec } \mathbb{M}(\Sigma, D)$, and Theorem 11.7.32 can be interpreted as trace counterparts of Kleene's and Büchi's theorems with finite and infinite iterations replaced by concurrent iterations.

11.7.4   Notes

Recognizable real trace languages were introduced and first studied in [111]. In this paper, the syntactic congruence of a real trace language was proposed and the equivalence between the recognizability of a real trace language T and the recognizability of the word language $\varphi^{-1}(T)$ was established. Using this equivalence, it was also proved that the family $\text{Rec } \mathbb{R}$ is closed under union, intersection, complement and concatenation.

The main results of this section (Theorems 11.7.20, 11.7.23 and 11.7.32) have been first proved in [115]. The proofs presented in this section are inspired from [116] where the notion of diamond product and weakly recognizable real trace languages were proposed. The closure of recognizable real trace languages under quotients by arbitrary real trace languages was first shown, with a different proof, in [59].

At last, note that characterizations of recognizable real trace languages in terms of Büchi non-deterministic asynchronous cellular automata [113], Muller deterministic asynchronous cellular automata [61, 62] and logic formulas [91] have been recently established.

11.8   Recognizable Complex Trace Languages

This section is devoted to the study of recognizable complex trace languages. We first prove that the family of recognizable complex trace languages is closed under union, intersection, complement and quotients by an arbitrary language.

Next, using the links between real and complex trace languages explained in Section 11.4 and some results of Section 11.7, we show that the family of recognizable complex trace languages is closed under concatenation.

Then, we define the notion of connected complex traces and we prove that the family of recognizable complex trace languages is closed under finite and infinite iterations restricted to connected languages. Finally, we extend Kleene's and Büchi's theorems on words and Ochmański's theorem on finite traces by proving that the families of recognizable complex trace languages and of c-rational complex trace languages coincide (Theorem 11.8.24). To this purpose, we prove, as an intermediary result, that the iteration of a recognizable language of connected complex traces is recognizable (Theorem 11.8.21).

11.8.1   Definition

Since a product of at most ω finite traces is always a real trace (see Corollary 11.2.19), Definition 11.7.1 cannot be used to define recognizable complex trace languages. But the equality $\mathbb{C}(\Sigma, D) = \mathbb{M}(\Sigma, D)^{\omega+1}$ (Corollary 11.4.12) suggests to modify this definition by substituting $(\omega + 1)-$ sequences for $\omega-$sequences. Following this approach, we obtain the definition of recognizable complex trace languages.

Definition 11.8.1 *A morphism η from $\mathbb{M}(\Sigma, D)$ into a finite monoid S recognizes a complex trace language $L \subseteq \mathbb{C}(\Sigma, D)$ if for all $(\omega + 1)-$sequences of finite traces $(r_i)_{i<\omega+1}, (s_i)_{i<\omega+1} \subseteq \mathbb{M}(\Sigma, D)$ such that $\eta(r_i) = \eta(s_i)$ for all $i < \omega + 1$, it holds*

$$\prod_{i<\omega+1} r_i \in T \Longleftrightarrow \prod_{i<\omega+1} s_i \in T$$

A complex trace language $L \subseteq \mathbb{C}(\Sigma, D)$ is recognizable if it is recognized by some morphism into a finite monoid.

The family of recognizable complex trace languages over a dependence alphabet (Σ, D) is denoted by Rec $\mathbb{C}(\Sigma, D)$ or simply by Rec $\mathbb{C}$.

For instance, any morphism η from $\mathbb{M}$ into a finite monoid S recognizes $\mathbb{C}$. The trivial morphism η from $\mathbb{M}(\Sigma, D)$ onto $\{1\}$ recognizes the complex trace language $\mathbb{C}$ but does not recognize the language $\mathbb{M}$. In a similar way, this morphism does not recognize the complex trace language $\mathbb{R}$ as soon as $\mathbb{C} \neq \mathbb{R}$ i.e. when D is not transitive.

Let alph be the morphism from $\mathbb{M}(\Sigma, D)$ into $\mathcal{P}(\Sigma)$ which maps each finite trace to its alphabet. This morphism clearly recognizes the complex trace languages $\mathbb{M}$ and $\mathbb{C}$. But, in general, this morphism does not recognize the languages $\mathbb{C}_A = \{x \in$

$\mathbb{C} \mid \text{Im}(x) = D(A)\}$ for $A \subseteq \Sigma$. For instance, let $(\Sigma, D) = a \text{---} b \text{---} c \text{---} d$. Let $(u_i)_{i<\omega+1}$ $((v_i)_{i<\omega+1}$ respectively) be the sequence of finite traces defined by $u_i = a$ for all $i < \omega$ and $u_\omega = bc$ $(v_i = a$ for all $i < \omega$ and $v_\omega = cb$ respectively). Clearly, $\text{alph}(u_i) = \text{alph}(v_i)$ for all $i < \omega + 1$. But $\prod_{i<\omega+1} u_i = (a^\omega, D(\{a, b, c\})) \in \mathbb{C}_\Sigma$ whereas $\prod_{i<\omega+1} v_i = (ca^\omega, D(\{a, b\})) \notin \mathbb{C}_\Sigma$.

Remark 11.8.2 As in the case of real traces (Proposition 11.7.9), it is easy to show that a complex trace language is recognizable if and only if it is recognized by some alphabetic morphism (see Definition 11.7.8) from $\mathbf{M}(\Sigma, D)$ into a finite monoid S.

Since a real trace language can be viewed as a complex trace language, Definition 11.8.1 can also be used for real trace languages. In case of ambiguity, if a morphism η recognizes a real trace language T in the sense of Definition 11.8.1, we will say that η $(\omega + 1)$–recognizes T. On the contrary, if a morphism η recognizes T in the sense of Definition 11.7.1, we will say that η ω–recognizes T. Obviously, if a morphism η $(\omega + 1)$–recognizes a real trace language T, then it ω–recognizes it, as well. But the converse is clearly false since, for instance, as soon as D is not transitive, the trivial morphism defined by $\eta(t) = 1$ for all $t \in \mathbf{M}$ ω–recognizes the language $\mathbb{R}$ without $(\omega + 1)$–recognizing it. Nevertheless, we will show that the recognizability of a real trace language does not depend on the definition chosen. To this purpose, we first emphasize some results on $(\omega + 1)$–sequences of finite traces which follow directly from Corollary 11.2.19 and Proposition 11.4.6.

Remark 11.8.3 Let $(u_i)_{i<\omega+1}$ be a sequence of finite traces, let $u = \prod_{i<\omega+1} u_i$ and let $A = \text{alphinf}(\prod_{i<\omega} u_i)$. Then

1. $\text{Re}(u) = (\prod_{i<\omega} u_i) \cdot_\mathbb{R} \mu_A(u_\omega)$

2. $\text{Im}(u) = D(A) \cup D(\text{suff}_A(u_\omega))$

3. $\text{alphinf}(\text{Re}(u)) = A$

Let alph from $\mathbf{M}(\Sigma, D)$ to $\mathcal{P}(\Sigma)$ be the morphism defined above. We will prove that alph $(\omega + 1)$–recognizes the trace language $\mathbb{R}$ and more generally the trace languages $\text{Inf}_A(\mathbb{R}) = \{r \in \mathbb{R}(\Sigma, D) \mid \text{alphinf}(r) = A\}$ for all $A \subseteq \Sigma$. Indeed, let $(u_i)_{i<\omega+1}$ be a sequence of finite traces such that $u = \prod_{i<\omega+1} u_i \in \mathbb{R}$. Let $A = \text{alphinf}(\prod_{i<\omega} u_i)$. From Remark 11.8.3, $\text{Im}(u) = D(A) \cup D(\text{suff}_A(u_\omega))$. Since $u \in \mathbb{R}$ it holds $\text{Im}(u) = D(A)$ and thus $D(\text{suff}_A(u_\omega)) \subseteq D(A)$. Therefore the sets $B = \text{alph}(\mu_A(u_\omega))$ and $C = \text{alph}(\text{suff}_A(u_\omega))$ verify $B \times C \subseteq I$. Let now $(v_i)_{i<\omega+1}$ be a sequence of finite traces such that $\text{alph}(u_i) = \text{alph}(v_i)$ for all $i < \omega + 1$. In particular $\text{alph}(u_\omega) = \text{alph}(v_\omega) = B \cup C$. Since $B \times C \subseteq I$, this yields $v_\omega = v'_\omega v''_\omega$ for some traces v'_ω and v''_ω such that $\text{alph}(v'_\omega) = B$ and $\text{alph}(v''_\omega) = C$. From $\text{alphinf}((u_i)_{i<\omega}) = \text{alphinf}((v_i)_{i<\omega}) = A$, we get $\text{Re}(\prod_{i<\omega+1} v_i) = (\prod_{i<\omega} v_i)v'_\omega$ and $\text{Im}(\prod_{i<\omega+1} v_i) = D(A) \cup D(v''_\omega) = D(A) \cup D(C) = D(A)$. Therefore $\prod_{i<\omega+1} v_i \in \text{Inf}_A(\mathbb{R})$ and the morphism alph $(\omega + 1)$–recognizes the trace language $\text{Inf}_A(\mathbb{R})$.

Let η be a morphism from $\mathbf{M}(\Sigma, D)$ into a finite monoid S which ω–recognizes a real trace language T. We will construct a new morphism $\Box\eta$ which $(\omega +$

1)–recognizes T. First, let us consider the mapping from $\mathbb{M}(\Sigma, D)$ into $\prod_{A \subseteq \Sigma} S \times \mathcal{P}(\Sigma)$ specified by:

$$\forall t \in \mathbb{M}, \, \Box\eta(t) = (\eta(\mu_A(t)), \text{alph}(\text{suff}_A(t)))_{A \subseteq \Sigma}$$

From the definition of the operators μ_A and suff_A (see Section 11.4), it is easy to verify that, if t, t' are two finite traces and A is a subset of Σ, it holds $\mu_A(tt') = \mu_A(t)\mu_{A \cup B}(t')$ and $\text{suff}_A(tt') = \text{suff}_A(t)\text{suff}_{A \cup B}(t')$ where $B = \text{alph}(\text{suff}_A(t))$. Therefore, in order to transform the mapping above into a morphism, we provide the set $\prod_{A \subseteq \Sigma} S \times \mathcal{P}(\Sigma)$ with the internal operation $\odot$ defined by:

$$(s_A, X_A)_{A \subseteq \Sigma} \odot (s'_A, X'_A)_{A \subseteq \Sigma} = (s_A s'_{A \cup X_A}, X_A \cup X'_{A \cup X_A})_{A \subseteq \Sigma}$$

It is easy to verify that $(\prod_{A \subseteq \Sigma} S \times \mathcal{P}(\Sigma), \odot)$ has a structure of monoid with identity $(1, \emptyset)_{A \subseteq \Sigma}$. This monoid will be denoted by $\Box S$ in the sequel. Finally, it is straightforward to verify that the mapping $\Box\eta$ is a morphism from $\mathbb{M}$ into $\Box S$.

This morphism $\Box\eta$ will help us to prove several interesting results in the sequel. We collect in the following lemma all the properties of this morphism that will be used throughout this section.

Lemma 11.8.4 *Let η be a morphism from $\mathbb{M}(\Sigma, D)$ into a finite monoid S. Let $(u_i)_{i < \omega+1}$ and $(v_i)_{i < \omega+1}$ be two sequences of finite traces such that $\Box\eta(u_i) = \Box\eta(v_i)$ for all $i < \omega + 1$. Let $u = \prod_{i < \omega+1} u_i$ and let $v = \prod_{i < \omega+1} v_i$. Then*

   1. $\eta(u_i) = \eta(v_i)$ and $\text{alph}(u_i) = \text{alph}(v_i)$ for all $i < \omega + 1$

   2. $\text{alphinf}(\text{Re}(u)) = \text{alphinf}(\text{Re}(v))$ and $\text{Im}(u) = \text{Im}(v)$

Proof: Let $i < \omega + 1$. By definition of $\Box\eta$, it holds

$$(\eta(\mu_A(u_i)), \text{alph}(\text{suff}_A(u_i)))_{A \subseteq \Sigma} = (\eta(\mu_A(v_i)), \text{alph}(\text{suff}_A(v_i)))_{A \subseteq \Sigma}$$

In particular, for $A = \emptyset$, it holds $\eta(\mu_\emptyset(u_i)) = \eta(\mu_\emptyset(v_i))$, i.e. $\eta(u_i) = \eta(v_i)$, and for $A = \Sigma$, we have $\text{alph}(\text{suff}_\Sigma(u_i)) = \text{alph}(\text{suff}_\Sigma(u_i))$, i.e. $\text{alph}(u_i) = \text{alph}(v_i)$. Thus 1 is proved.

Let $A = \text{alphinf}(\prod_{i < \omega} u_i)$. From 1 and Remark 11.8.3, we deduce that $A = \text{alphinf}(\text{Re}(u)) = \text{alphinf}(\text{Re}(v))$. Once again, by Remark 11.8.3, $\text{Im}(u) = D(A) \cup D(\text{suff}_A(u_\omega)) = \text{Im}(v)$ since $\text{alph}(\text{suff}_A(u_\omega)) = \text{alph}(\text{suff}_A(v_\omega))$. This concludes the proof. $\Box$

Let η be the trivial morphism from $\mathbb{M}(\Sigma, D)$ onto $\{1\}$. Let $(u_i)_{i < \omega+1}$ and $(v_i)_{i < \omega+1}$ be two sequences of finite traces such that $\Box\eta(u_i) = \Box\eta(v_i)$ for all $i < \omega + 1$. By Lemma 11.8.4, it holds $\text{Im}(\prod_{i < \omega+1} u_i) = \text{Im}(\prod_{i < \omega+1} v_i)$. Therefore the morphism $\Box\eta$ $(\omega + 1)$–recognizes the complex trace languages $\mathbb{C}_A = \{x \in \mathbb{C} \mid \text{Im}(x) = D(A)\}$ for all $A \subseteq \Sigma$.

Exercise 11.8.1 Prove that the morphism $\Box(\text{alph})$ recognizes the languages $\text{shift}_{A,B}(\mathbb{C})$, introduced in Section 11.6, for all $A, B \subseteq \Sigma$.

We can now relate ω−recognition and $(\omega+1)$−recognition of real trace languages.

Proposition 11.8.5 *Let η be a morphism from $\mathbb{M}(\Sigma, D)$ into a finite monoid S ω−recognizing a real trace language $T \subseteq \mathbb{R}(\Sigma, D)$. Then the morphism $\square\eta$ from $\mathbb{M}(\Sigma, D)$ to $\square S$ $(\omega+1)$−recognizes T.*

Proof: Let $(u_i)_{i<\omega+1}$ and $(v_i)_{i<\omega+1}$ be two sequences of finite traces such that $u = \prod_{i<\omega+1} u_i \in T$ and $\square\eta(u_i) = \square\eta(v_i)$ for all $i < \omega+1$. Let $A = \mathrm{alphinf}(\prod_{i<\omega} u_i)$ and let $v = \prod_{i<\omega+1} v_i$. By Remark 11.8.3 and Lemma 11.8.4, $\mathrm{Re}(u) = (\prod_{i<\omega} u_i) \cdot_{\mathbb{R}} \mu_A(u_\omega)$ and $\mathrm{Re}(v) = (\prod_{i<\omega} v_i) \cdot \mu_A(v_\omega)$. By definition of A, there exists an integer n such that

$$\left(\prod_{i<\omega} u_i\right) \cdot \mu_A(u_\omega) = \left(\prod_{i<n} u_i\right) \mu_A(u_\omega) \left(\prod_{n\leq i<\omega} u_i\right)$$

and

$$\left(\prod_{i<\omega} v_i\right) \cdot \mu_A(v_\omega) = \left(\prod_{i<n} v_i\right) \mu_A(v_\omega) \left(\prod_{n\leq i<\omega} v_i\right)$$

By Lemma 11.8.4, $\eta(u_i) = \eta(v_i)$ for all $i < \omega$. Moreover $\eta(\mu_A(u_\omega)) = \eta(\mu_A(v_\omega))$ by definition of $\square\eta$. Since $\mathrm{Re}(u) = u \in T$, it follows from Definition 11.7.1 that $\mathrm{Re}(v) \in T$. Finally, by Lemma 11.8.4 and by the fact that u is a real trace, we obtain $\mathrm{Im}(v) = \mathrm{Im}(u) = D(\mathrm{alphinf}(\mathrm{Re}(u))) = D(\mathrm{alphinf}(\mathrm{Re}(v)))$. Therefore v is a real trace and $v = \mathrm{Re}(v) \in T$. $\square$

As a direct consequence, we obtain the following corollary which asserts that the recognizability of a real trace language does not depend on the chosen definition.

Corollary 11.8.6 Rec $\mathbb{R}(\Sigma, D) = \mathcal{P}(\mathbb{R}(\Sigma, D)) \cap$ Rec $\mathbb{C}(\Sigma, D)$

Using the morphism $\square\eta$ we get the first characterization of the recognizability of a complex trace languages in terms of the recognizability of some of its real parts.

Proposition 11.8.7 *A complex trace language $L \subseteq \mathbb{C}(\Sigma, D)$ is recognizable if and only if, for all subset A of Σ, $\mathrm{Re}(L_A)$ is a recognizable real trace language.*

Proof: Let η be an alphabetic morphism from $\mathbb{M}$ into a finite monoid S $(\omega+1)$−recognizing the language L. We claim that η ω−recognizes the languages $\mathrm{Re}(L_A)$ for all $A \subseteq \Sigma$. Let $(u_i)_{i<\omega}$ and $(v_i)_{i<\omega}$ be two sequences of finite traces such that $u = \prod_{i<\omega} u_i \in \mathrm{Re}(L_A)$ for some $A \subseteq \Sigma$ and $\eta(u_i) = \eta(v_i)$ for all $i < \omega$. By Proposition 11.4.11, there exists some finite trace f such that $(\prod_{i<\omega} u_i) \cdot f \in L_A \subseteq L$ and $\min(f) \subseteq D(\mathrm{alphinf}(\prod_{i<\omega} u_i))$. Since η $(\omega+1)$−recognizes L, we get $(\prod_{i<\omega} v_i) \cdot f \in L$. Moreover since η is alphabetic, $\mathrm{Re}((\prod_{i<\omega} v_i) \cdot f) = \prod_{i<\omega} v_i$ and $\mathrm{Im}((\prod_{i<\omega} v_i) \cdot f) = \mathrm{Im}((\prod_{i<\omega} u_i) \cdot f) = D(A)$. Therefore $\prod_{i<\omega} v_i \in \mathrm{Re}(L_A)$ and the claim is proved.

Conversely we may assume from the claim of Proposition 11.7.6 that there exists a morphism $\eta : \mathbb{M} \longrightarrow S$ which ω−recognizes the languages L_A for all $A \subseteq \Sigma$. We claim that the language L is $(\omega+1)$−recognized by the morphism $\Box\eta$. Let $(u_i)_{i<\omega+1}$ and $(v_i)_{i<\omega+1}$ be two sequences of finite traces such that $u = \prod_{i<\omega+1} u_i \in L$ and $\Box\eta(u_i) = \Box\eta(v_i)$ for all $i < \omega + 1$. Let $A \subseteq \Sigma$ be such that $u \in L_A$. If $B = \text{alphinf}(\prod_{i<\omega} u_i)$, we get $\text{Re}(u) = (\prod_{i<\omega} u_i) \cdot \mu_B(u_\omega) \in \text{Re}(L_A)$ by Remark 11.8.3. Therefore, by Lemma 11.8.4, we deduce $\text{Im}(v) = \text{Im}(u) = D(A)$ and $\text{Re}(v) = (\prod_{i<\omega} v_i) \cdot \mu_B(u_\omega)$. Moreover, once again by Lemma 11.8.4, $\eta(u_i) = \eta(v_i)$ for all $i < \omega$. Besides, $\eta(\mu_B(u_\omega)) = \eta(\mu_B(v_\omega))$ by definition of $\Box\eta$. Thus since η ω-recognizes $\text{Re}(L_A)$ we obtain (as in the proof of Proposition 11.8.5) that $\text{Re}(v) \in \text{Re}(L_A)$. Finally, $v \in L_A$ which concludes the proof. $\Box$

Using the characterizations of rational and recognizable complex trace languages in terms of real parts (Theorem 11.6.2 and Proposition 11.8.7), it follows directly by Corollary 11.7.5:

Corollary 11.8.8 Rec $\mathbb{C}(\Sigma, D) \subseteq$ Rat $\mathbb{C}(\Sigma, D)$

Once again, the converse is false as soon as there exists a pair $(a, b) \in I$ of independent letters.

11.8.2   Closure Properties

By a proof very similar to that of Proposition 11.7.6, we easily deduce from Definition 11.8.1 the following closure properties of the family Rec $\mathbb{C}$.

Proposition 11.8.9 *The family* Rec $\mathbb{C}(\Sigma, D)$ *is closed under the operations of union, intersection and complement.*

Before proving the closure of Rec $\mathbb{C}$ under concatenation, we first extend Theorem 11.7.11 to complex trace languages. Then we will use this result to deal with the concatenation problem.

Theorem 11.8.10 *Let* $K \subseteq \mathbb{C}(\Sigma, D)$ *be a complex trace language and let* $L \subseteq \mathbb{C}(\Sigma, D)$ *be a recognizable complex trace language. Then the following left and right quotients are recognizable too:*

$$
\begin{aligned}
L \cdot K^{-1} &= \{x \in \mathbb{C} \mid xy \in L \text{ for some } y \in K\} \\
K^{-1} \cdot L &= \{y \in \mathbb{C} \mid xy \in L \text{ for some } x \in K\}
\end{aligned}
$$

Proof: Let η be an alphabetic morphism from $\mathbb{M}$ into a finite monoid S which $(\omega + 1)$-recognizes the complex trace language L. We will prove that the morphism $\Box\eta$ $(\omega + 1)$-recognizes both $L \cdot K^{-1}$ and $K^{-1} \cdot L$.

Let $(r_i)_{i<\omega+1} \subseteq \mathbb{M}$ be a sequence of finite traces such that $r = \prod_{i<\omega+1} r_i \in L \cdot K^{-1}$. Let $t \in K$ be such that $rt \in L$. Let $A, B \subseteq \Sigma$ be such that $D(A) = D(\text{alphinf}(\text{Re}(r)))$ and $D(B) = \text{Im}(r)$. By definition of the concatenation in $\mathbb{C}$, it holds

$$
\text{Re}(rt) = \text{Re}(r)\mu_B(t)
$$

By Remark 11.8.3, $\text{Re}(r) = (\prod_{i<\omega} r_i)\mu_A(r_\omega)$. By Proposition 11.4.11, there exists a finite trace f such that $rt = \text{Re}(rt)f$. In particular, $\min(f) \subseteq D(\text{alphinf}(\text{Re}(rt)))$. Therefore

$$rt = \left(\prod_{i<\omega} r_i\right)\mu_A(r_\omega)\mu_B(t)f.$$

Let n be an integer such that $\text{alph}(r_i) \subseteq A$ for all $i \geq n$. Then $(r_i, \mu_A(r_\omega)) \in I$ for all $i \geq n$. Moreover, since $D(A) \subseteq D(B)$, it holds $I(B) \subseteq I(A)$ and hence the traces r_i are independent from $\mu_B(t)$ for all $i \geq n$. Let now $(t_i)_{i<\omega}$ be a sequence of finite traces such that $\mu_B(t) = \prod_{i<\omega} t_i$. From the independences above, we deduce:

$$rt = \left(\prod_{i<n} r_i\right)\mu_A(r_\omega)\left(\prod_{n\leq i<\omega} r_i t_{i-n}\right)f \in L \qquad (11.25)$$

Let now $(s_i)_{i<\omega+1}$ be a sequence of finite traces such that $\Box\eta(r_i) = \Box\eta(s_i)$ for all $i < \omega+1$. By definition of $\Box\eta$ and by Lemma 11.8.4, we have $\eta(\mu_A(r_\omega)) = \eta(\mu_A(s_\omega))$ and $\eta(r_i) = \eta(s_i)$ for all $i < \omega$. Since η $(\omega+1)$-recognizes the language L, we deduce from Formula 11.25 that

$$\alpha = \left(\prod_{i<n} s_i\right)\mu_A(s_\omega)\left(\prod_{n\leq i<\omega} s_i t_{i-n}\right)f \in L$$

Since η is alphabetic, we have $(s_i, \mu_A(s_\omega)) \in I$ and $(s_i, \mu_B(t)) \in I$ for all $i \geq n$. Therefore

$$\alpha = \left(\prod_{i<\omega} s_i\right)\mu_A(s_\omega)\mu_B(t)f \in L$$

Let $s = \prod_{i<\omega+1} s_i$. By Lemma 11.8.4, we have $\text{Re}(s) = (\prod_{i<\omega} s_i)\mu_A(s_\omega)$ and $\text{Im}(s) = \text{Im}(r) = D(B)$. Hence $(\prod_{i<\omega} s_i)\mu_A(s_\omega)\mu_B(t) = \text{Re}(st)$. Moreover,

$$\text{Im}(st) = D(B) \cup \text{Im}(t) \cup D(\text{alph}(\text{suff}_B(\text{Re}(t)))) = \text{Im}(rt)$$

and

$$\text{alphinf}(\text{Re}(st)) = \text{alphinf}(\text{Re}(s)) \cup \text{alphinf}(\mu_B(t)) = \text{alphinf}(\text{Re}(rt)).$$

Therefore $st = \text{Re}(st)f$. Finally $\alpha = st \in L$ which proves that η $(\omega+1)$-recognizes the complex trace language $L \cdot K^{-1}$.

We now turn to $K^{-1} \cdot L$. Let $(r_i)_{i<\omega+1} \subseteq \mathbf{M}$ be a sequence of finite traces such that $r = \prod_{i<\omega+1} r_i \in K^{-1} \cdot L$. Let $t \in K$ be such that $tr \in L$. Let $A, B \subseteq \Sigma$ be such that $D(A) = \text{Im}(t)$ and $D(B) = \text{Im}(tr)$. By definition of the concatenation in $\mathbb{C}$, it holds

$$\text{Re}(tr) = \text{Re}(t)\mu_A(r)$$

Let $(A_i)_{i\leq\omega+1}$ be a sequence of subalphabets of Σ such that $D(A_i) = \mathrm{Im}(t\cdot\prod_{j<i}r_j)$ for all $i \leq \omega + 1$. By the claim of the proof of Lemma 11.6.9, it holds

$$\mu_A(r) = \prod_{i<\omega+1}\mu_{A_i}(r_i)$$

Let $(t_i)_{i<\omega}$ be a sequence of finite traces such that $\mathrm{Re}(t) = \prod_{i<\omega}t_i$ and $\mathrm{alph}(t_i) = \mathrm{alphinf}(\mathrm{Re}(t))$ for all $1 \leq i < \omega$. We get

$$\mathrm{Re}(tr) = \left(\prod_{i<\omega}t_i\mu_{A_i}(r_i)\right)\mu_{A_\omega}(r_\omega)$$

By Proposition 11.4.11, there exists a finite trace f such that $tr = \mathrm{Re}(tr)f$. In particular, $\min(f) \subseteq D(\mathrm{alphinf}(\mathrm{Re}(tr)))$. Therefore

$$tr = \left(\prod_{i<\omega}t_i\mu_{A_i}(r_i)\right)\mu_{A_\omega}(r_\omega)f \in L$$

Let now $(s_i)_{i<\omega+1}$ be a sequence of finite traces such that $\Box\eta(r_i) = \Box\eta(s_i)$ for all $i < \omega + 1$ and let $s = \prod_{i<\omega+1}s_i$. By definition of $\Box\eta$ we have $\eta(\mu_{A_i}(r_i)) = \eta(\mu_{A_i}(s_i))$ for all $i < \omega + 1$. Since η $(\omega + 1)$-recognizes the language L, we obtain

$$\left(\prod_{i<\omega}t_i\mu_{A_i}(s_i)\right)\mu_{A_\omega}(s_\omega)f \in L$$

Since η is alphabetic, we deduce

$$\left(\prod_{i<\omega}t_i\right)\left(\prod_{i<\omega+1}\mu_{A_i}(s_i)\right)f \in L$$

By definition of $\Box\eta$, $\mathrm{alph}(\mathrm{suff}_{A_i}(s_i)) = \mathrm{alph}(\mathrm{suff}_{A_i}(r_i))$ for all $i < \omega + 1$. Hence we obtain $\mathrm{Im}(t\prod_{j<i}s_j) = D(A_i)$ for all $i \leq \omega+1$ by an immediate induction and thus $\prod_{i<\omega+1}\mu_{A_i}(s_i) = \mu_A(s)$. Therefore

$$\mathrm{Re}(ts)f = \mathrm{Re}(t)\mu_A(s)f = \left(\prod_{i<\omega}t_i\right)\mu_A(s)f \in L$$

Moreover $\mathrm{Im}(ts) = D(A_{\omega+1}) = \mathrm{Im}(tr)$ and $\mathrm{alphinf}(\mathrm{Re}(ts)) = \mathrm{alphinf}(\mathrm{Re}(t))\cup \mathrm{alphinf}(\mu_A(s)) = \mathrm{alphinf}(\mathrm{Re}(tr))$. Hence $ts = \mathrm{Re}(ts)f$. Therefore, $ts \in L$ which proves that η $(\omega + 1)$-recognizes the complex trace language $K^{-1} \cdot L$.

$\square$

In order to study the closure of Rec $\mathbb{C}$ under concatenation, the formulæ given in the next lemma will be useful. Recall that, for $A, B \subseteq \Sigma$, the operators $\text{shift}_{A,B}$ and $\mu_{A,B}$ have been defined in Section 11.6 by

$$\text{shift}_{A,B}(L) = \{y \in L \mid \text{Im}(xy) = D(B) \text{ for some } x \in \mathbb{C}_A\}$$
$$\mu_{A,B}(L) = \mu_A(\text{shift}_{A,B}(L))$$

for any complex trace language L.

Remark 11.8.11 Let $K, L \subseteq \mathbb{C}(\Sigma, D)$ be complex trace languages and let $B \subseteq X$. Remark 11.6.8 and Formulæ (11.14) and (11.15) applied to $A = \emptyset$ yield

1. $(KL)_B = \bigcup_{C \subseteq X} K_C \, \text{shift}_{C,B}(L)$

2. $\text{Re}((KL)_B) = \bigcup_{C \subseteq X} \text{Re}(K_C) \mu_{C,B}(L)$

From Proposition 11.4.13 and Lemma 11.8.11, we deduce that for any complex trace languages K and L,

$$KL = \bigcup_{(A,B) \text{ consistent}} \left(\bigcup_{C \subseteq X} \text{Re}(K_C) \mu_{C,B}(L) \cap \mathbb{R}(\Sigma, D)_A \right) \cdot s_{A,B} \qquad (11.26)$$

where, for (A, B) consistent, $s_{A,B}$ is a finite trace of $\text{shift}_{A,B}(\mathbb{M}(\Sigma, D))$ such that $\mu_A(s_{A,B}) = 1$.

We will use this formula to prove that Rec $\mathbb{C}$ is closed under concatenation. First we need a lemma which shows that the operators $\text{shift}_{A,B}$ and $\mu_{A,B}$ preserve recognizability.

Lemma 11.8.12 *Let $L \subseteq \mathbb{C}(\Sigma, D)$ be a recognizable complex trace language and let $A, B \subseteq X$. Then the languages $\mu_A(L) \subseteq \mathbb{R}(\Sigma, D)$ and $\text{shift}_{A,B}(L) \subseteq \mathbb{C}(\Sigma, D)$ are recognizable.*

Proof: By definition of the operator μ_A, it holds $\mu_A(L) = \mu_A(\text{Re}(L))$. Moreover since $\text{Re}(L)$ is a recognizable real trace language (Propositions 11.8.7 and 11.7.6), it is enough to prove that $\mu_A(T)$ is recognizable for any recognizable real trace language T. By the very definition of the operator μ_A (see Section 11.4), it is straightforward to verify that

$$\mu_A(T) = T \cdot \{u \in \mathbb{R} \mid \min(u) \subseteq D(A)\}^{-1} \cap \{u \in \mathbb{R} \mid \text{alph}(u) \subseteq I(A)\}$$

By Proposition 11.7.11, the language $T \cdot \{u \in \mathbb{R} \mid \min(u) \subseteq D(A)\}^{-1}$ is recognizable. We have seen in Section 11.7 that the language $\{u \in \mathbb{R} \mid \text{alph}(u) \subseteq I(A)\}$ is recognizable too. Since Rec $\mathbb{R}$ is closed under intersection (Proposition 11.7.6), we conclude that $\mu_A(T)$ is a recognizable real trace language.

By definition of the operator $\text{shift}_{A,B}$ it is immediate to see that $\text{shift}_{A,B}(L) = \text{shift}_{A,B}(\mathbb{C}) \cap L$ and $\text{shift}_{A,B}(\mathbb{C}) = \mathbb{C}_A^{-1} \mathbb{C}_B$. As we have seen previously, $\mathbb{C}_B$ is a recognizable language and hence $\text{shift}_{A,B}(\mathbb{C})$ is also recognizable by Theorem 11.8.10. We conclude that $\text{shift}_{A,B}(L)$ is recognizable by Proposition 11.8.9. $\qquad \square$

We can now conclude on the closure of Rec $\mathbb{C}$ under concatenation.

Proposition 11.8.13 Rec $\mathbb{C}(\Sigma, D)$ *is closed under concatenation.*

Proof: First, let $A, B \subseteq \Sigma$. Let $R \subseteq \mathbb{R}(\Sigma, D)$ be a recognizable real trace language such that $R = R_A$ and let s be a finite trace in $\text{shift}_{A,B}(\mathbb{M}(\Sigma, D))$ such that $\mu_A(s) = 1$. We claim that $R \cdot_{\mathbb{C}} s$ is a recognizable complex trace language. Indeed, by definitions of concatenation in $\mathbb{C}$ and of shift traces, it holds $R \cdot_{\mathbb{C}} s = (R \cdot_{\mathbb{C}} s)_B$ and $\text{Re}((R \cdot_{\mathbb{C}} s)_B) = R_A = R$. Hence the recognizability of $R \cdot_{\mathbb{C}} s$ follows directly from the recognizability of R and Proposition 11.8.7.

The proposition follows easily from this claim, Lemma 11.8.12 and Formula 11.26.   □

We can now give a normal form theorem for recognizable complex trace languages which generalizes the corresponding result for recognizable real trace languages (Theorem 11.7.23).

Theorem 11.8.14 *A complex trace language $L \subseteq \mathbb{R}(\Sigma, D)$ is recognizable if and only if it can be written as a finite union of languages of the form*

$$M \cdot N_1^\omega \cdots N_k^\omega \cdot s = M \cdot (N_1 \cdots N_k)^\omega \cdot s$$

where $M, N_1, \ldots, N_k \subseteq \mathbb{M}(\Sigma, D)$ are monoalphabetic recognizable languages such that $\text{alph}(N_i)$ is connected and $\text{alph}(N_i) \times \text{alph}(N_j) \subseteq I$ for all $i \neq j$, and where $s \in \mathbb{M}(\Sigma, D)$ is a finite trace.

Proof: Note that the alphabetic conditions yield $N_1^\omega \cdots N_k^\omega \cdot s = (N_1 \cdots N_k)^\omega \cdot s$. Let L be a recognizable complex trace language. Using Proposition 11.4.13, L is a finite union of languages $(\text{Re}(L_B) \cap \mathbb{R}_A)s_{A,B}$. By Proposition 11.8.7, $\text{Re}(L_B)$ is a recognizable real trace language for any $B \subseteq \Sigma$. Moreover we have seen in Section 11.7 that the languages $\mathbb{R}_A$ are recognizable for all $A \subseteq \Sigma$. Thus from the closure of Rec $\mathbb{R}$ under intersection (Proposition 11.7.6) we deduce that $\text{Re}(L_B) \cap \mathbb{R}_A$ is a recognizable real trace language for all $A, B \subseteq \Sigma$. Hence the normal form for L follows directly from Theorem 11.7.23.

Conversely, assume that a complex trace language L can be written as a finite union of languages of the form $M \cdot (N_1 \cdots N_k)^\omega \cdot s$. Again, the alphabetic conditions yield $N_1^\omega \cdots N_k^\omega = (N_1 \cdots N_k)^\omega$. Any language of the form $M \cdot (N_1 \cdots N_k)^\omega$ is a recognizable real trace language by Theorem 11.7.23. Therefore, L is recognizable by Corollary 11.8.6 and since Rec $\mathbb{C}$ is closed under union (Proposition 11.8.9) and concatenation (Proposition 11.8.13).   □

Contrary to the real case (see Formulæ 11.10 and 11.11), an arbitrary large number of non-finite traces may be relevant in a product of complex traces. For instance, if $a, b \in \Sigma$ are two independent letters, it holds $(ab^\omega)^n = a^n b^\omega$ for any integer n and $(ab^\omega)^\omega = (ab)^\omega$. Nevertheless, we will see that such a product can be written in a nice way using some particular traces. The basic idea is that if $(x_i)_{i<\omega}$ is a sequence of complex traces, the sequence of imaginary parts $(\text{Im}(\prod_{j<i} x_j))_{i<\omega}$

is an increasing sequence which takes therefore a finite number of distinct values. Thus, for a complex trace language L, we define $\nu_A(L) = \mu_{A,A}(L) = \{\mu_A(y) \mid y \in L$ and $\text{Im}(xy) = D(A)$ for some $x \in \mathbb{C}_A\}$. Note that, by Proposition 11.4.6, an element $y \in \nu_A(L)$ verifies $\text{alphinf}(y) \subseteq \text{alph}(y) \subseteq I(A)$ and $D(\text{alphinf}(y)) \subseteq \text{Im}(y) \subseteq D(A)$. Hence $\text{alphinf}(y) = \emptyset$ and $\nu_A(L) \subseteq \mathbb{M}$ is a language of finite traces.

Lemma 11.8.15 *Let $L \subseteq \mathbb{C}(\Sigma, D)$ be a complex trace language and $\dagger \in \{*, \omega\}$. Let C be the finite set of sequences $C = \{(A_0, \ldots, A_k) \mid \emptyset = D(A_0) \subsetneq \cdots \subsetneq D(A_k) \subseteq \Sigma\}$. Then the language $L^\dagger$ is the finite union*

$$L^\dagger = \bigcup_{(A_0, \ldots, A_k) \in C} \nu_{A_0}(L)^* \, \text{shift}_{A_0, A_1}(L) \ldots \nu_{A_{k-1}}(L)^* \, \text{shift}_{A_{k-1}, A_k}(L) \nu_{A_k}(L)^\dagger$$

Proof: By Remark 11.6.8, $L^\dagger = \cup_{B \subseteq \Sigma} \text{shift}_{\emptyset, B}(L^\dagger)$. Then, from Formulæ 11.16 and 11.18, it is easy to verify that

$$L^\dagger = \bigcup_{(A_0, \ldots, A_k) \in C} (\text{shift}_{A_0, A_0}(L))^* \cdot \text{shift}_{A_0, A_1}(L) \cdots$$
$$(\text{shift}_{A_{k-1}, A_{k-1}}(L))^* \cdot \text{shift}_{A_{k-1}, A_k}(L) \cdot (\text{shift}_{A_k, A_k}(L))^\dagger$$

Moreover, for all $A \subseteq \Sigma$ and for all complex trace languages $K \subseteq \mathbb{C}_A$ and $K' \subseteq \mathbb{C}$, it holds $K\nu_A(K') = K \, \text{shift}_{A,A}(K')$. Thus

$$L^\dagger = \bigcup_{(A_0, \ldots, A_k) \in C} \nu_{A_0}(L)^* \, \text{shift}_{A_0, A_1}(L) \cdots \nu_{A_{k-1}}(L)^* \, \text{shift}_{A_{k-1}, A_k}(L) \nu_{A_k}(L)^\dagger$$

and the lemma is proved. □

Using Lemma 11.8.12 and the closure of Rec $\mathbb{C}$ under union (Proposition 11.8.9) and concatenation (Proposition 11.8.13), we deduce from the previous lemma the weakest known condition ensuring the recognizability of the finite and infinite iterations of a recognizable complex trace language.

Corollary 11.8.16 *Let $L \subseteq \mathbb{C}(\Sigma, D)$ be a recognizable complex trace language such that $\nu_A(L)^* \subseteq \mathbb{M}(\Sigma, D)$ is recognizable for all $A \subseteq \Sigma$. Then L^* and L^ω are recognizable complex trace languages too.*

11.8.3 C-Rational Complex Trace Languages

Recall that a real trace t is connected if the dependence graph t is connected (see Section 11.7). This definition can of course be extended to arbitrary dependence graphs of $\mathbb{G}(\Sigma, D)$. Unfortunately, this notion does not factorize to complex traces. The same complex trace may have connected as well as non connected representing dependence graphs. For instance, let $(\Sigma, D) = a \text{----} b \text{----} c$. Then the complex trace $((ac)^\omega, \Sigma)$ is represented by the connected dependence graph $(ac)^\omega b$ as well as by the non connected graph $a^\omega c^\omega$. Intuitively, a trace is connected if it cannot be split in two non-empty independent traces. Therefore, we will bypass the problem of defining connected complex traces by first introducing the notion of independent traces. This notion is clear in $\mathbb{G}(\Sigma, D)$: two graphs f and g are independent if $\mathrm{alph}(f) \times \mathrm{alph}(g) \subseteq I$. In this case, we simply write $(f, g) \in I$. Unfortunately, we cannot use this definition in $\mathbb{C}(\Sigma, D)$ since the alphabet of a complex trace is not well-defined. Nevertheless, the independence relation in $\mathbb{G}(\Sigma, D)$ factorizes to complex traces:

Lemma 11.8.17 *Let $x, y \in \mathbb{C}(\Sigma, D)$ be two complex traces. Let $f, f', g, g' \in \mathbb{G}(\Sigma, D)$ be dependence graphs such that $\chi(f) = \chi(f') = x$ and $\chi(g) = \chi(g') = y$. Then*

$$(f, g) \in I \iff (f', g') \in I$$

Proof: By symmetry, it is enough to prove that $(f, g) \in I \implies (f', g) \in I$. By definition, $(f, g) \in I \iff \mathrm{alph}(f) \times \mathrm{alph}(g) \subseteq I \iff D(\mathrm{alph}(f)) \cap \mathrm{alph}(g) = \emptyset$. But f and f' represent the same complex trace x, so it holds $D(\mathrm{alph}(f)) = D(\mathrm{alph}(\mathrm{Re}(f)) \cup D(\mathrm{alphinf}(f)) = D(\mathrm{alph}(\mathrm{Re}(x)) \cup Im(x) = D(\mathrm{alph}(f'))$ and the lemma is proved.   □

Therefore, we can define without ambiguity the notion of *independent* complex traces. Two complex traces $x = (u, D(A))$, $y = (v, D(B)) \in \mathbb{C}(\Sigma, D)$ are independent if so are any two dependence graphs representing x and y respectively. Moreover, by the proof of Lemma 11.8.17, we obtain immediately the following useful characterization: x and y are independent if and only if $(\mathrm{alph}(u) \cup A) \times (\mathrm{alph}(v) \cup B) \subseteq I$. In this case we will simply write $(x, y) \in I$.

For instance, let $(\Sigma, D) = a\!-\!b\overset{\displaystyle e}{\overset{\textstyle \diagup\diagdown}{}}c\!-\!d\!-\!f\!-\!g$ be the dependence alphabet. The complex traces $(d^\omega, D(\{c, d\}))$ and $(gga^\omega, D(\{a\}))$ are independent whereas the complex traces $(gga^\omega, D(\{a, b\}))$ and $(d^\omega, D(\{c, d\}))$ are not.

Using the above characterization of independent complex traces, we obtain easily:

Remark 11.8.18 *Let $(u_i)_{i<\omega+1}$ and $(v_i)_{i<\omega+1}$ be two sequences of finite traces. Then the complex traces $u = \prod_{i<\omega+1} u_i$ and $v = \prod_{i<\omega+1} v_i$ are independent if and only if $(\bigcup_{i<\omega+1} \mathrm{alph}(u_i)) \times (\bigcup_{i<\omega+1} \mathrm{alph}(v_i)) \subseteq I$.*

We can now define the notions of connected and finitarily connected complex traces.

Definition 11.8.19 *A complex trace z is called* connected *if for all factorization $z = xy$ where x, y are independent, either $x = 1$ or $y = 1$. A trace x is called a* connected component *of $z \in \mathbb{C}(\Sigma, D)$ if either $x = z = 1$ or x is a non-empty connected trace such that $z = xy$ for some y independent of x. The trace z is said to be* finitarily connected *if it admits at most one finite connected component.*

For any non-empty trace z, we denote by $\mathrm{C}(z)$ ($\mathrm{FC}(z) = \mathrm{C}(z) \cap \mathbb{M}(\Sigma, D)$ respectively) the set of connected components (finite connected components respectively) of z. These notations are extended as usual to languages. A language is said to be connected (finitarily connected respectively) if all its elements are connected (finitarily connected respectively).

With the dependence alphabet above, the trace $x = (gg(ad)^\omega, D(\{a,c,d\}))$ is not connected since $x = (gga^\omega, D(\{a\})) \cdot (d^\omega, D(\{c,d\}))$ is the product of two independent traces. The connected components of x are $(gg,\emptyset)$, $(a^\omega, D(\{a\}))$, $(d^\omega, D(\{c,d\}))$, $(a^\omega, D(\{a,b\}))$ and $(d^\omega, D(\{d\}))$. Note that x admits several decompositions in connected components: $x = (gg,\emptyset)(a^\omega, D(\{a\}))(d^\omega, D(\{c,d\}))$ $= (gg,\emptyset)(a^\omega, D(\{a,b\}))(d^\omega, D(\{d\})) = (gg,\emptyset)(a^\omega, D(\{a,b\}))(d^\omega, D(\{c,d\}))$ but $(gg,\emptyset)(a^\omega, D(\{a\}))(d^\omega, D(\{d\})) = (gg(ad)^\omega, D(\{a,d\})) \neq x$.

Exercise 11.8.2 This exercice investigates the relationship between the two notions of connectedness in $\mathbb{G}(\Sigma, D)$ and $\mathbb{C}(\Sigma, D)$. Let $x \in \mathbb{C}(\Sigma, D)$ be a complex trace. Prove that x is connected if and only if all its representatives in $\mathbb{G}(\Sigma, D)$ are connected. Now, let $f \in \mathbb{G}(\Sigma, D)$ be any representative of x and let $\{f_1, \ldots, f_k\}$ be the set of finite connected components of f. Prove that $FC(x) = \{f_1, \ldots, f_k\}$.

The operators C and FC preserve the recognizability of complex trace languages.

Lemma 11.8.20 Let $L \subseteq \mathbb{C}(\Sigma, D)$ be a recognizable complex trace language. Then $FC(L)$ and $C(L)$ are recognizable too.

Proof: Let NC be the set of non-connected complex traces. By definition of a connected complex trace it holds

$$NC = \bigcup_{(A \cup B) \times (E \cup F) \subseteq I} K(A, B) \cdot K(E, F)$$

where, for all $A, B \subseteq \Sigma$, $K(A, B) = \{x \in \mathbb{C}_B \setminus \{1\} \mid \mathrm{alph}(\mathrm{Re}(x)) = A\}$.

Let alph be the morphism which maps each finite traces to its alphabet. We claim that $\square(\mathrm{alph})$ recognizes the languages $K(A, B)$ for all $A, B \subseteq \Sigma$. Indeed, let $(u_i)_{i < \omega+1}, (v_i)_{i < \omega+1} \subseteq \mathbb{M}$ be sequences of finite traces such that $\square(\mathrm{alph})(u_i) = \square(\mathrm{alph})(v_i)$ for all $i < \omega + 1$. Let $u = \prod_{i < \omega+1} u_i$ and let $v = \prod_{i < \omega+1} v_i$. By Lemma 11.8.4, it holds $\mathrm{Im}(u) = \mathrm{Im}(v)$. Let $C = \mathrm{alphinf}(\mathrm{Re}(u))$. By Remark 11.8.3 and the definition of $\square(\mathrm{alph})$, it holds $\mathrm{alph}(\mathrm{Re}(u)) = \bigcup_{i < \omega} \mathrm{alph}(u_i) \cup \mathrm{alph}(\mu_C(u_\omega)) = \mathrm{alph}(\mathrm{Re}(v))$. Therefore, $u \in K(A, B)$ if and only if $v \in K(A, B)$ and the claim is proved.

Hence, by Propositions 11.8.9 and 11.8.13, the set $\overline{NC} = \mathbb{C} \setminus NC$ of connected complex traces is recognizable.

Now, it turns out that

$$C(L) \setminus \{1\} = \left(\bigcup_{(A \cup B) \times (E \cup F) \subseteq I} K(A, B)^{-1} \cdot K(E, F) \right) \cap \overline{NC}$$

From Proposition 11.8.9 and Theorem 11.8.10, we deduce that $C(L)$ is recognizable. Finally, the language $FC(L)$ is equal to $C(L) \cap \mathbb{M}$ and hence is recognizable as well. $\square$

Extending the corresponding results on (finite) real traces, we can now prove that the iteration of a recognizable connected complex trace language remains recognizable.

Theorem 11.8.21 *Let $L \subseteq \mathbb{C}(\Sigma, D)$ be a recognizable complex trace language. If L is finitarily connected (in particular if L is connected) then L^* and L^ω are recognizable too.*

Proof: Let us first define, for any complex trace language K, $\mathrm{FinComp}(K) = \{t \in \mathbb{M} \mid \exists u \in \mathbb{C}$ such that $(t, u) \in I$ and $tu \in K\}$. The following claim will be crucial for the proof.

Claim $\mathrm{FinComp}(L) = \bigcup_{A \subseteq X} \nu_A(L)$

Let $t \in \nu_A(L)$. We already observed that t is finite. By definition, there exists a complex trace $x \in \mathrm{shift}_{A,A}(L)$ such that $t = \mu_A(x)$. Hence $x = t \cdot (\mathrm{suff}_A(\mathrm{Re}(x)), \mathrm{Im}(x))$. Moreover, since $x \in \mathrm{shift}_{A,A}(L)$, we have $D(\mathrm{suff}_A(\mathrm{Re}(x))) \cup \mathrm{Im}(x) \subseteq D(A)$. Thus, t and $(\mathrm{suff}_A(\mathrm{Re}(x)), \mathrm{Im}(x))$ are independent since $\mathrm{alph}(t) \subseteq I(A)$. Therefore $t \in \mathrm{FinComp}(L)$.

Conversely, let $t \in \mathrm{FinComp}(L)$, there exist $v \in L$ and $u \in \mathbb{C}$ such that $v = tu$ with $(t, u) \in I$. Let $B = \mathrm{alph}(t)$ and $A = I(B)$. Note that $B \subseteq I(A)$. Let $u = (r, D(C))$. Since $(t, u) \in I$, we have $(\mathrm{alph}(r) \cup C) \subseteq I(B) = A$. Hence $\mathrm{alph}(r) \subseteq A$ and then $\mu_A(v) = t$. We also get $D(\mathrm{alph}(r)) \cup D(C) \subseteq D(A)$, and hence $v \in \mathrm{shift}_{A,A}(L)$, so that the claim is proved.

Assume now that L is finitarily connected. Then $\mathrm{FinComp}(L)$ is connected, and by the claim above, $\nu_A(L)$ is a connected language of finite traces for all $A \subseteq X$. Since $\nu_A(L)$ is also recognizable by Lemma 11.8.12, the iteration $\nu_A(L)^*$ is recognizable (Theorem 11.7.21). Hence L^* and L^ω are recognizable by Corollary 11.8.16. $\square$

Exercise 11.8.3 **1)** Let $L \subseteq \mathbb{C}(\Sigma, D)$ be a recognizable complex trace language such that $\mathrm{FC}(L) \subseteq L^*$. Prove that L^* and L^ω are recognizable too.

2) Prove that if x is a complex trace such that $\{x\} \in \mathrm{Rec}(\mathbb{C}(\Sigma, D))$, then x^ω is recognizable too. Hint: show first that $\{x^\omega\} = ((\mathrm{FC}(\{x\}) \cup \{x\})^\omega)_A$ where $D(A) = \mathrm{Im}(x^\omega)$. A solution to these exercises can be found in [59].

Now, we generalize the definition of concurrent iterations and c-rational languages introduced in the previous section to complex trace languages.

Definition 11.8.22 *Let $L \subseteq \mathbb{C}(\Sigma, D)$ be a complex trace language. Then the concurrent iterations of L are defined by $L^{c-*} = (\mathrm{C}(L))^*$ and $L^{c-\omega} = (\mathrm{C}(L))^\omega$.*

The family $c - \mathrm{Rat}\,\mathbb{C}(\Sigma, D)$ of c-rational complex trace languages is the smallest family

- *which contains the empty set and all singletons $\{a\}$ for $a \in \Sigma$,*

- *which is closed under union and under concatenation, finite and infinite concurrent iterations.*

By definition, $C(L)$ is connected for all complex trace language L, hence we obtain directly from Lemma 11.8.20 and Theorem 11.8.21:

Corollary 11.8.23 *Let $L \subseteq \mathbb{C}(\Sigma, D)$ be a recognizable complex trace language. Then L^{c-*} and $L^{c-\omega}$ are recognizable.*

We conclude this section with the main result concerning recognizable complex trace languages, which can be seen as a generalization to complex traces of Kleene's and Büchi's theorems on finite and infinite words.

Theorem 11.8.24 $\text{Rec } \mathbb{C}(\Sigma, D) = c - \text{Rat } \mathbb{C}(\Sigma, D)$

Proof: We have seen that $\text{Rec } \mathbb{C}$ is a boolean algebra closed under concatenation (Proposition 11.8.13) and finite and infinite concurrent iterations (Corollary 11.8.23). Hence $c - \text{Rat } \mathbb{C} \subseteq \text{Rec } \mathbb{C}$.

Conversely, every recognizable complex trace language can be written as a finite union over languages of type $MN_1^\omega \ldots N_k^\omega s$ where $M, N_1, \ldots, N_k \subseteq \mathbb{M}$ belong to $\text{Rec } \mathbb{M} = c - \text{Rat } \mathbb{M}$ and $s \in \mathbb{M}$ is a finite trace (Theorem 11.8.14). Moreover all traces in each language N_i are connected and hence $N_i^\omega = N_i^{c-\omega}$. Thus $MN_1^\omega \ldots N_k^\omega s$ is in $c - \text{Rat } \mathbb{C}$ and the theorem is proved. $\square$

11.8.4 Notes

Recognizable complex trace languages were introduced and studied in [60, 59]. In these papers, recognizable languages were defined by the characterization of Proposition 11.8.7, whereas Definition 11.8.1 was obtained as a characterization in [59]. All the results presented in this section were proved in [59] but, due to the choice of the basic definition of recognizable complex trace languages, the proofs are, in general, quite different.

We end these notes by a brief discussion on recognizability by morphisms and ordinals. Let α be a countable ordinal. Generalizing Definitions 11.7.1 and 11.8.1, we say that a morphism η from $\mathbb{M}$ to a finite monoid S α-recognizes a complex trace language L if for any α-sequences $(r_i)_{i<\alpha}, (s_i)_{i<\alpha} \subseteq \mathbb{M}$ such that $\eta(r_i) = \eta(s_i)$ for all $i < \alpha$, it holds

$$\prod_{i<\alpha} r_i \in L \iff \prod_{i<\alpha} s_i \in L$$

A complex trace language $L \subseteq \mathbb{C}$ is α-recognizable if it is α-recognized by some morphism from $\mathbb{M}$ into a finite monoid. The family of α-recognizable complex trace languages is denoted by α-$\text{Rec } \mathbb{C}$.

A very natural question is to compare these notions of α-recognizability for all countable ordinals α. First, it is clear that if $\alpha < \beta$ are two countable ordinals, a morphism β-recognizing a trace language L, α-recognizes it too.

Assume now that we restrict ourselves to languages of finite traces. Proposition 11.7.2 can be simply reformulated by:

$$1 - \text{Rec } \mathbb{C} \cap \mathcal{P}(\mathbb{M}) = \omega - \text{Rec } \mathbb{C} \cap \mathcal{P}(\mathbb{M})$$

In fact, a proof very similar to that of Proposition 11.7.2 establishes that, for all countable ordinal $\alpha \geq 1$:

$$1 - \text{Rec } \mathbb{C} \cap \mathcal{P}(\mathbb{M}) = \alpha - \text{Rec } \mathbb{C} \cap \mathcal{P}(\mathbb{M})$$

If we consider languages of real traces, Proposition 11.8.5 asserts that:

$$\omega - \text{Rec } \mathbb{C} \cap \mathcal{P}(\mathbb{R}) = (\omega + 1) - \text{Rec } \mathbb{C} \cap \mathcal{P}(\mathbb{R})$$

Once again, using Corollary 11.4.9, the proof of Proposition 11.8.5 can be generalized to prove that, for all countable ordinal $\alpha \geq \omega$,

$$\omega - \text{Rec } \mathbb{C} \cap \mathcal{P}(\mathbb{R}) = \alpha - \text{Rec } \mathbb{C} \cap \mathcal{P}(\mathbb{R})$$

Note that, on the contrary, any language $L \subseteq \mathbb{R} \backslash \mathbb{M}$ is n-recognized by any morphism for any ordinal $n < \omega$. Therefore, for all ordinal $n < \omega$, the family $n - \text{Rec } \mathbb{C} \cap \mathcal{P}(\mathbb{R})$ is uncountable and hence cannot be defined by rational expressions. Therefore, the notion of n-recognizability, for $n < \omega$, is not suitable for real trace languages.

Concerning complex trace languages, it can be shown (see [59] for some hints) that for all countable ordinal $\alpha \geq \omega + 1$,

$$(\omega + 1) - \text{Rec } \mathbb{C} = \alpha - \text{Rec } \mathbb{C}$$

whereas for any ordinal $\beta < \omega + 1$, any language $L \subseteq \mathbb{C} \setminus \mathbb{R}$ is β-recognized by any morphism. In particular, for all ordinal $\beta < \omega + 1$, the family $\beta - \text{Rec } \mathbb{C}$ is uncountable and hence cannot be defined by rational expressions. Hence, the notion of β-recognizability for $\beta < \omega + 1$ is not suitable for complex trace languages.

In conclusion, all these results prove that Definition 11.7.1 (Definition 11.8.1 respectively) is "minimal" when dealing with recognizing morphisms and real trace languages (complex trace languages respectively). On the contrary, we could have adopted the following "maximal" definition, valid in all cases: a language L is recognized by a morphism η from $\mathbb{M}$ into a finite monoid S if, for all countable ordinal α and for all α-sequences $(r_i)_{i<\alpha}, (s_i)_{i<\alpha} \subseteq \mathbb{M}$ such that $\eta(r_i) = \eta(s_i)$ for all $i < \alpha$, it holds $\prod_{i<\alpha} r_i \in L \iff \prod_{i<\alpha} s_i \in L$.

Acknowledgement: We thank Pascal Weil for many helpful comments and suggestions.

Chapter 12

Semi-Commutations

Mireille Clerbout   Michel Latteux   Yves Roos

CNRS URA 369, L.I.F.L., Université des Sciences et Technologies de Lille
U.F.R. I.E.E.A. Informatique, 59655 Villeneuve d'Ascq Cédex, France
{clerbout,latteux,yroos}@lifl.lifl.fr

Contents

12.1   Introduction

Semi-commutations introduced in [40] are natural extensions of partial commutations. The only change is that the dependence relation is not anymore symmetric. So, we can have two letters, let say p (as *Producer*) and c (as *Consumer*) such that c depends on p, but p does not depend on c. In that case, we allow to rewrite cp in pc but the converse is forbidden.

Some recent papers (see [142],[209]) show that semi-commutations are suitable tools for the study of Petri nets. As a matter of fact, they are convenient for expressing process synchronization. Let us point out this fact with the *Readers and Writers problem*. In computer systems, it is common to have some processes (called *readers*) that read data and others (called *writers*) that write it. Because readers do not change the contents of the database, many readers may access the database at once. But a writer can modify the data, so it must have exclusive access. When a writer is active, no other readers or writers may be active.

Let us take the alphabet $\Sigma = \{r, \bar{r}, w, \bar{w}\}$ where r (resp. w) stands for the beginning of a reading (resp. writing) and $\bar{r}$ (resp. $\bar{w}$) for an ending. Now let us consider L, the set of words representing loops on the initial state that are allowed by the above protocol. Since many readers may access the database at once, a reader does not need to wait for the end of a reading to begin its reading, that is r does not depend on $\bar{r}$ then L is closed for the semi-commutation $\theta = \{(\bar{r}, r)\}$. More precisely, L is the θ-closure of the regular language $(r\bar{r} + w\bar{w})^*$ that represents the purely sequential behaviour of readers and writers.

A variant of this protocol gives the priority to the writers, that is the beginning of a reading is not allowed if a writer is waiting. Then we enlarge the alphabet Σ with the letter q representing the request of a writer. Now the language expressing this protocol is nothing else that the closure of the language $(r\bar{r} + qw\bar{w})^*$ under the semi-commutation $\{(\bar{r}, r), (\bar{r}, q), (w, q), (\bar{w}, q)\}$.

Thus in some cases, the parallel behaviour is the closure of a regular language representing the sequential behaviour under a semi-commutation expressing the rules of the protocol. This shows that the closure of regular languages under a semi-commutation is of interest. So, in section 12.7, a characterization of semi-commutations converting regular languages into context-free ones is given. A similar characterization is stated without any proof in the last section for the semi-commutations preserving the family of multi-counter languages.

Concerning the family $\operatorname{Reg}_\theta(\Sigma^*)$, a sufficient condition ensuring that the θ-closure of a given regular language remains regular is proved in section 12.6. This yields naturally to the study of the family $\operatorname{R}_\theta(\Sigma^*)$, that is the least family containing elementary languages and closed under union, θ-concatenation and θ-iteration. Unfortunately, the equality $\operatorname{Reg}_\theta(\Sigma^*) = \operatorname{R}_\theta(\Sigma^*)$ holds only if θ is symmetric. In others words, the nice Ochmański's theorem on partial commutation (Theorem 12.6.15, Theorem 6.3.16) cannot be extended to semi-commutations in this way.

Other important results on semi-commutations seen as language operations are proved in sections 12.4 and 12.5. The decomposition theorem (Theorem 12.4.14) says that each semi-commutation function can be effectively factorized into atomic semi-commutations functions which are in some sense the simplest semi-commutations. The composition criterion (Theorem 12.5.9) allows to decide whether the composition of two given semi-commutation functions remains a semi-commutation function. This criterion is revealed lately very useful (see [270]). In particular, it gives directly an effective criterion to decide confluence of semi-commutations.

Some connections between semi-commutations and Petri nets are presented in section 12.8. For instance, it is shown that a Petri language can be obtained from a regular language by using a semi-commutation and an inverse morphism.

In the last section, two recent but interesting results are stated without any proof. Next we present some important problems not yet solved which are missing inside the theory of semi-commutations.

12.2 Preliminaries

12.2.1 Some Notations

In the following text Σ is the used alphabet ; u, v and w are words in Σ^*. We shall denote by $|w|$ the length of the word w and by $|w|_a$ the number of occurrences of the letter a that appear in the word w.

We shall say that v is a *subword* of u if there exist words $w_0, w_1', w_1, \ldots, w_n', w_n$ in Σ^* such that $u = w_0 w_1' w_1 \ldots w_i' w_i \ldots w_n' w_n$ and $v = w_1' w_2' \ldots w_n'$.

We denote by $F(w)$ (respectively $LF(w)$) the set of *factors* (respectively *left factors*) of the word w, that is:

$$F(w) = \{u \in \Sigma^* \mid \exists v, v' \in \Sigma^* with\ w = vuv'\}$$

$$LF(w) = \{u \in \Sigma^* \mid \exists v \in \Sigma^* with\ w = uv\}$$

and if $L \subseteq \Sigma^*$, we extend these definitions by:

$$F(L) = \bigcup_{w \in L} F(w)$$

$$LF(L) = \bigcup_{w \in L} LF(w)$$

We denote by $\Pi_Y(w)$ the *projection* of the word w over the *subalphabet* Y, i.e. the image of w by the homomorphism Π_Y which is defined by:

$$\forall x \in \Sigma,\ if\ x \in Y\ then\ \Pi_Y(x) = x\ ,\ else\ \Pi_Y(x) = \varepsilon$$

We shall often write $\Pi_u(w)$ instead of $\Pi_{\mathbf{alph}(u)}(w)$.

We denote by $\preceq$ the order defined over the set of mappings from 2^{Σ^*} to 2^{Σ^*} by:

$$(f \preceq g) \Longleftrightarrow (\forall L \subseteq \Sigma^*, f(L) \subseteq g(L))$$

$\tilde{u}$ is the reverse of the word u i.e. if $u = x_1 x_2 \ldots x_n$ then $\tilde{u} = x_n \ldots x_2 x_1$.

$u \sqcup\!\sqcup v$ is the *shuffle* of the two words u and v that is

$$u \sqcup\!\sqcup v = \{u_1 v_1 u_2 v_2 ... u_n v_n \mid u_i \in \Sigma^*, v_i \in \Sigma^*, u = u_1 u_2 ... u_n, v = v_1 v_2 ... v_n\}$$

$u \sqcap v$ is the *synchronized shuffle* of the two words u and v that is

$$u \sqcap v = \{w \in (\mathrm{alph}(u) \cup \mathrm{alph}(v))^* \mid \Pi_{\mathrm{alph}(u)}(w) = u, \Pi_{\mathrm{alph}(v)}(w) = v\}$$

$\mathrm{com}(w) = \{u \in \Sigma^* \mid \forall a \in \Sigma, |w|_a = |u|_a\}$ is the *commutative closure* of the word w and if $L \subseteq \Sigma^*$, we extend this definition by:

$$\mathrm{com}(L) = \bigcup_{w \in L} \mathrm{com}(w)$$

$D_1^*(x, y)$ is the *Dyck language* on the alphabet $\{x, y\}$, that is

$$D_1^*(x, y) = \{w \in \{x, y\}^* \mid |w|_x = |w|_y\} = \mathrm{com}((xy)^*)$$

$D_1'^*(x, y)$ is the *semi-Dyck language* on $\{x, y\}$, that is

$$D_1'^*(x, y) = \{w \in D_1^*(x, y) \mid \forall u \in LF(w), |u|_x \geq |u|_y\}$$

Rat will denote the family of *rational languages*, Reg the family of *regular languages*, Alg the family of *algebraic languages* and Ocl the one counter languages family which is the smallest set of languages which contains $D_1'^*(x, y)$ and which is closed under rational transductions, product, union and star.

12.2.2 Semi-Commutations.

Definition 12.2.1 *A* semi-commutation relation *defined over an alphabet Σ is an irreflexive relation: it is a subset of $\Sigma \times \Sigma \setminus \{(a, a) \mid a \in \Sigma\}$.*

Definition 12.2.2 *To each semi-commutation relation θ, we associate a rewriting system $S = < \Sigma, P >$ which is named* semi-commutation system *in which P is the set $\{xy \longrightarrow yx \mid (x, y) \in \theta\}$.*

We shall write $u \xrightarrow[\theta]{} v$ if there is a rule $ab \longrightarrow ba$ in P and two words w and w' such that $u = wabw'$ and $v = wbaw'$.

We shall write $u \xrightarrow[\theta]{*} v$ if there are words $w_1, w_2, ..., w_n (n \geq 1)$ such that $w_1 = u, w_n = v$, and for each $i < n, w_i \xrightarrow[\theta]{} w_{i+1}$. Then we shall write that there is a *derivation* from u to v, and the integer $n - 1$ is named the *derivation length*.

When we have $u \xrightarrow[\theta]{*} v$ with a known derivation length n, we shall also write:

$u \xrightarrow[\theta]{n} v$.

Definition 12.2.3 *To each semi-commutation θ we associate its* commutation graph *which is the directed graph defined by $< \Sigma, \theta >$ where Σ is the node-set and θ the edge-set.*

The *non commutation relation* associated with the semi-commutation relation θ is denoted by $\bar{\theta}$. Hence:

$$\bar{\theta} = \{(a, b) \mid (a, b) \notin \theta\}$$

The *converse semi-commutation* relation associated with the semi-commutation relation θ is denoted by θ^{-1}. Hence:

$$\theta^{-1} = \{(b, a) \mid (a, b) \in \theta\}$$

Definition 12.2.4 *To each semi-commutation θ we associate its* non commutation graph *which is the directed graph defined by* $< \Sigma, \{(a, b) \mid a \neq b \text{ and } (a, b) \notin \theta\} >$ *where Σ is the node-set and $\{(a, b) \mid a \neq b \text{ and } (a, b) \notin \theta\}$ the edge-set.*

A lot of properties concerning regularity of languages which are closed under a semi-commutation relation depend on properties of connectivity of the associated non commutation graph. Let us recall some classical connectivity notions in graph theory:

Definition 12.2.5 *A directed graph $G = < V, E >$ is said to be* strongly connected *(resp.* connected*) if for every two nodes v_1, v_2 in V, there exists a directed path (resp. a path) of edges from E joining v_1 and v_2.*

Definition 12.2.6 *Any maximal strongly connected subgraph (resp. connected subgraph) of a graph G is named a* strongly connected component *(resp.* connected component*) of the graph G.*

In the light of semi-commutations, we shall extend these definitions to words:

Definition 12.2.7 *Let Σ be an alphabet, and θ be a semi-commutation relation defined over Σ. A word w of Σ^* is said to be* strongly connected *(for the semi-commutation relation θ) if the non commutation graph of the restriction of θ to* alph(w) *is strongly connected.*

Example 12.2.8 Let $\Sigma = \{a, b, c, d\}$ and

$$\theta = \{(a, c), (a, d), (b, a), (b, c), (c, a), (c, d), (d, a), (d, b)\}.$$

Then θ is a semi-commutation relation and its non commutation graph is given in Fig.12.1. This non commutation graph is not strongly connected (but it is connected). Its strongly connected components are $\{a\}$ and $\{b, c, d\}$. The word $bcbbcbdcb$ is strongly connected but the words $bcbbcbcb$ and $bcbabcbdcb$ are not.

Definition 12.2.9 *To each semi-commutation relation θ defined over the alphabet Σ, we associate a* semi-commutation function $f_\theta : 2^{\Sigma^*} \longrightarrow 2^{\Sigma^*}$ *which is defined by:*

$$\forall L \subseteq \Sigma^*, f_\theta(L) = \bigcup_{w \in L} \{u \in \Sigma^* \mid w \xrightarrow{*}_{\theta} u\}$$

If $f_{\theta_1}, f_{\theta_2}, \ldots, f_{\theta_n}$ are semi-commutation functions defined over Σ, we shall write $f_{\theta_n} \circ f_{\theta_{n-1}} \circ \ldots \circ f_{\theta_1}$ for the composition of these functions. Hence:

$$\forall w \in \Sigma^* f_{\theta_n} \circ f_{\theta_{n-1}} \circ \ldots \circ f_{\theta_1}(w) = f_{\theta_n}(f_{\theta_{n-1}}(\ldots (f_{\theta_1}(w))\ldots))$$

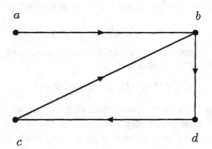

Figure 12.1: The non commutation graph of θ

12.3   Basic Lemmas

When working with semi commutations, it is often very convenient to deal with permutation words, that is with words not containing several occurrences of the same letter.

Definition 12.3.1 *The set of* permutation words *over an alphabet Σ, denoted by $P(\Sigma^*)$, is equal to $\{u \in \Sigma^* \mid \forall\, a \in \text{alph}(u), |u|_a = 1\}$.*

Definition 12.3.2 *Let $u \in P(\Sigma^*)$ be a permutation word over an alphabet Σ. We set: $E_u = \{(b, a) \in \Sigma \times \Sigma \mid u = xbyaz$ for some $x, y, z \in \Sigma^*\}$.*

Remark 12.3.3 For $u \in P(\Sigma^*)$ and $a, b \in \text{alph}(u)$, exactly one of the three following assertions does hold:

1. $a = b$

2. $(b, a) \in E_u$

3. $(a, b) \in E_u$

Lemma 12.3.4 (Permutation Lemma) *Let θ be a semi-commutation over an alphabet Σ, $u \in P(\Sigma^*)$, $v \in com(u)$ and $k = \text{Card}(E_u \setminus E_v)$. Then:*

  $-$ $v \in f_\theta(u)$ *if and only if $E_u \setminus E_v \subseteq \theta$.*

  $-$ *If $v \in f_\theta(u)$, k is the length of a shortest derivation $u \xrightarrow{\;*\;}_{\theta} v$.*

Proof: Clearly, the proof results directly from the two following assertions:

1. If $u \xrightarrow{\;n\;}_{\theta} v$ then $E_u \setminus E_v \subseteq \theta$ with $n \geq k$

2. If $E_u \setminus E_v \subseteq \theta$ then $u \xrightarrow[\theta]{k} v$

The proof of 1 is by induction on n.

If $n = 0$, we are done since $u = v$, hence $E_u \setminus E_v = \emptyset$ and $k = 0$.

If $n > 0$, then $u \xrightarrow[(b,a)]{} u' \xrightarrow[\theta]{n-1} v$.

By induction, we get $E_{u'} \setminus E_v \subseteq \theta$ with $n - 1 \geq \mathrm{Card}(E_{u'} \setminus E_v)$. Since $(b, a) \in \theta$ and $E_u \setminus E_v \subseteq (E_{u'} \setminus E_v) \cup \{(b, a)\}$, we get the result.

For the proof of 2, we shall reason by induction on k.

If $k = 0, E_u = E_v$, hence $u = v$ and $u \xrightarrow[\theta]{0} v$.

If $k > 0, u \neq v$. Then there exist $a, b \in \Sigma, x, y \in \Sigma^*$ such that $u = xbay$ with $(a, b) \in E_v$. Thus $u \xrightarrow[(b,a)]{} u' = xaby$. Since $E_{u'} \setminus E_v = (E_{u'} \setminus E_v) \setminus \{(b, a)\}, E_{u'} \setminus E_v \subseteq \theta$

with $\mathrm{Card}(E_{u'} \setminus E_v) = k - 1$. Then, by induction hypothesis, we get $u' \xrightarrow[\theta]{k-1} v$. Hence

$u \xrightarrow[(b,a)]{} u' \xrightarrow[\theta]{k-1} v$.

$\square$

For words having several occurrences of the same letter, we number these occurrences in order to get a permutation word.

Definition 12.3.5 *For a semi-commutation θ over an alphabet Σ, we set:*

- $\Sigma_{num} = \Sigma \times \mathbb{N}_+$

- $\theta_{num} = \{((b, i), (a, j)) \mid i, j \in \mathbb{N}_+, (b, a) \in \theta\}$

We define inductively the mapping $\mathrm{num} : \Sigma^* \to P(\Sigma^*_{num})$ *by:*

- $\mathrm{num}(\epsilon) = \epsilon$

- $\forall u \in \Sigma^*, \forall a \in \Sigma, \mathrm{num}(ua) = \mathrm{num}(u)(a, |ua|_a)$

The morphism $\mathrm{denum} : \Sigma^*_{num} \to \Sigma^*$ *is defined by:*

- $\forall x = (a, i) \in \Sigma_{num}, \mathrm{denum}(x) = a$

Remark 12.3.6 *For $\Sigma' \subseteq \Sigma$, we have:*
$\mathrm{num} \circ \Pi_{\Sigma'} = \Pi_{\Sigma'_{num}} \circ \mathrm{num}$ and $\mathrm{denum} \circ \Pi_{\Sigma'_{num}} = \Pi_{\Sigma'} \circ \mathrm{denum}$

By definition of θ_{num}, for $u, v \in \Sigma^*$, we have $u \xrightarrow[\theta]{} v$ if and only if $\mathrm{num}(u) \xrightarrow[\theta_{num}]{}$ $\mathrm{num}(v)$. Conversely, for $u', v' \in \Sigma^*_{num}, u' \xrightarrow[\theta_{num}]{} v'$ implies $\mathrm{denum}(u') \xrightarrow[\theta]{} \mathrm{denum}(v')$. Thus, we deduce immediately the following result which permits to reduce many problems on words to problems on permutation words.

Lemma 12.3.7 (Enumeration Lemma) *Let θ be a semi-commutation over an alphabet Σ.*

- *For $u, v \in \Sigma^*, u \xrightarrow[\theta]{n} v$ if and only if* $\mathrm{num}(u) \xrightarrow[\theta_{num}]{n} \mathrm{num}(v)$.

- *For $u', v' \in \Sigma^*_{num}, u' \xrightarrow[\theta_{num}]{n} v'$ implies* $\mathrm{denum}(u') \xrightarrow[\theta]{n} \mathrm{denum}(v')$.

If Σ' is a subalphabet of Σ and θ a semi-commutation over Σ, it is easy to verify that $u \xrightarrow[\theta]{} v$ implies $\Pi_{\Sigma'}(u) \xrightarrow[\theta]{*} \Pi_{\Sigma'}(v)$. Hence, if $v \in f_\theta(u)$, then $\Pi_{\Sigma'}(v) \in f_\theta(\Pi_{\Sigma'}(u))$. The following basic lemma telling that it suffices to look at the projections on the two letter subalphabets of Σ is a kind of converse of this fact.

Lemma 12.3.8 (Projection Lemma) *Let θ be a semi-commutation over an alphabet Σ and $u, v \in \Sigma^*$. The following assertions are equivalent:*

1. *$v \in f_\theta(u)$*

2. *$\forall\ a, b \in \Sigma, \Pi_{ab}(v) \in f_\theta(\Pi_{ab}(u))$*

Proof:
   Clearly it suffices to prove 2) $\Rightarrow$ 1). Let us set $u' = \mathrm{num}(u)$ and $v' = \mathrm{num}(v)$. From the two previous lemmas, it is enough to establish the inclusion $E_{u'} \setminus E_{v'} \subseteq \theta_{num}$. Let us take $(y, x) = ((b, i), (a, j)) \in E_{u'} \setminus E_{v'}$. Then $\Pi_{xy}(u') = yx$ and $\Pi_{xy}(v') = xy$. But $\Pi_{xy}(u') = \Pi_{xy} \circ \mathrm{num} \circ \Pi_{ab}(u)$ and $\Pi_{xy}(v') = \Pi_{xy} \circ \mathrm{num} \circ \Pi_{ab}(v)$. By hypothesis $\Pi_{ab}(u) \xrightarrow[\theta]{*} \Pi_{ab}(v)$. Hence, $\Pi_{xy}(u') \xrightarrow[\theta_{num}]{*} \Pi_{xy}(v')$ which implies $(y, x) \in \theta_{num}$.

$\square$

   The two first lemmas are also useful to prove another basic result on semi-commutation

Lemma 12.3.9 (Levi's lemma for semi-traces) *Let θ be a semi-commutation relation over an alphabet $\Sigma, u, v \in \Sigma^*$ and $zt \in f_\theta(uv)$. There exist u', u'', v', v'' such that:*

1. *$z \in f_\theta(u'v')$ and $t \in f_\theta(u''v'')$*

2. *$u'u'' \in f_\theta(u)$ and $v'v'' \in f_\theta(v)$*

3. *$\mathrm{alph}(u'') \times \mathrm{alph}(v') \subseteq \theta$.*

Proof:
   According to the Enumeration Lemma, one can assume that uv and zt are permutation words. We shall show that by choosing $u' = \Pi_z(u), u'' = \Pi_t(u), v' = \Pi_z(v)$ and $v'' = \Pi_t(v)$, properties 1), 2) and 3) are satisfied.

1. Since $uv \xrightarrow[\theta]{*} zt, u'v' = \Pi_z(uv) \xrightarrow[\theta]{*} \Pi_z(zt) = z$. Hence, $z \in f_\theta(u'v')$. Similarly, $t \in f_\theta(u''v'')$.

2. Let us take $(y, x) \in E_u \setminus E_{u'u''}$. Then $y \in \text{alph}(u'') \subseteq \text{alph}(z)$ and $x \in \text{alph}(u') \subseteq \text{alph}(z)$. Thus, $(y, x) \in E_{uv} \setminus E_{zt}$. According to the Permutation Lemma, $E_{uv} \setminus E_{zt} \subseteq \theta$, hence $(y, x) \in \theta$ and $u \xrightarrow[\theta]{*} u'u''$. Similarly, $v \xrightarrow[\theta]{*} v'v''$.

3. Let us take $(y, x) \in \text{alph}(u'') \times \text{alph}(v')$. Then $y \in \text{alph}(t)$ and $x \in \text{alph}(z)$. Thus, $(y, x) \in E_{uv} \setminus E_{zt} \subseteq \theta$.

$\square$

This lemma can be easily generalized in the following way:

Lemma 12.3.10 (Generalized Levi's lemma for semi-traces) *Let θ be a semi-commutation relation over an alphabet Σ, $z, t, x_1, x_2, \ldots, x_n \in \Sigma^*$ such that $zt \in f_\theta(x_1 x_2 \ldots x_n)$. There exist $x'_i, x''_i \in \Sigma^*, 1 \le i \le n$ such that:*

1. for $1 \le i \le n$, $x'_i x''_i \in f_\theta(x_i)$

2. $z \in f_\theta(x'_1 x'_2 \ldots x'_n)$ and $t \in f_\theta(x''_1 x''_2 \ldots x''_n)$

3. $\forall i, \forall j > i$, $\text{alph}(x''_i) \times \text{alph}(x'_j) \subseteq \theta$

Proof:

We make an induction on n. If $n \ge 2$, when applying Levi's lemma for semi-traces, we can find x'_1, x''_1, v', v'' such that $z \in f_\theta(x'_1 v')$, $t \in f_\theta(x''_1 v'')$, $x'_1 x''_1 \in f_\theta(x_1)$, $v'v'' \in f_\theta(x_2 \ldots x_n)$ and $\text{alph}(x''_1) \times \text{alph}(v') \subseteq \theta$.

As $v'v'' \in f_\theta(x_2 \ldots x_n)$, we apply induction hypothesis and we get the result.

$\square$

Definition 12.3.11 *For $u \in \Sigma^*$ and $v \in \text{com}(u)$, the distance between u and v, denoted by $d(u, v)$, is equal to $\text{Card}(E_{\text{num}(u)} \setminus E_{\text{num}(v)})$.*

Remark 12.3.12 *It is clear that $d(u, v) = d(\text{num}(u), \text{num}(v))$. Thus, if $v \in f_\theta(u)$ for some semi-commutation θ, then $d(u, v)$ is the length of a shortest derivation $u \xrightarrow[\theta]{*} v$.*

The following lemma states that for $v \in f_\theta(u)$, each step decreasing the distance is a "good" step.

Lemma 12.3.13 (Distance Lemma) *Let θ be a semi-commutation over an alphabet Σ, $u, v \in \Sigma^*$ and $v \in f_\theta(u)$. If $u \xrightarrow[(b,a)]{} w$ with $d(w, v) < d(u, v)$ then $v \in f_\theta(w)$*

Proof:

Let us set $u' = \text{num}(u)$, $w' = \text{num}(w)$, $v' = \text{num}(v)$. Then $u' \xrightarrow[(y,x)]{} w'$ with $y = (b, i)$ and $x = (a, j)$. Then $\text{Card}(E_{w'} \setminus E_{v'}) = d(w, v) < d(u, v) = \text{Card}(E_{u'} \setminus E_{v'})$. Since $E_{w'} = E_{u'} \setminus \{(y, x)\} \cup \{(x, y)\}$ we get $(x, y) \in E_{v'}$ then $E_{w'} \setminus E_{v'} \subseteq E_{u'} \setminus E_{v'}$. Since $u' \xrightarrow[\theta_{num}]{*} v'$, the Permutation Lemma implies $E_{u'} \setminus E_{v'} \subseteq \theta_{num}$, hence, $E_{w'} \setminus E_{v'} \subseteq \theta_{num}$ and $w' \xrightarrow[\theta_{num}]{*} v'$, which implies $w \xrightarrow[\theta]{*} v$.

$\square$

In a semi-commutation system $< \Sigma, P >$, associated with a semi-commutation θ, each rule in P is of the form $u \longrightarrow \tilde{u}$. Thus, for words w, w' such that $w \xrightarrow[\theta]{} w'$, we have not only $w' \xrightarrow[\theta^{-1}]{} w$ but also $\tilde{w}' \xrightarrow[\theta]{} \tilde{w}$. A simple induction yields to the obvious but useful property:

Lemma 12.3.14 (Reversal Lemma) *Let θ be a semi-commutation over an alphabet Σ and $u, v \in \Sigma^*$. The following assertions are equivalent:*

1. $u \xrightarrow[\theta]{n} v$

2. $v \xrightarrow[\theta^{-1}]{n} u$

3. $\tilde{v} \xrightarrow[\theta]{n} \tilde{u}$

12.4   The Decomposition Theorem

Definition 12.4.1 *θ is an atomic semi-commutation over an alphabet Σ if $\theta = \Sigma_1 \times \Sigma_2$ where Σ_1 and Σ_2 are disjoint subalphabets of Σ.*

Definition 12.4.2 *A semi-commutation relation θ is said to be decomposable if there are semi-commutations $\theta_1 \subsetneq \theta, \dots, \theta_n \subsetneq \theta$ such that $f_\theta = f_{\theta_n} \circ \dots \circ f_{\theta_1}$.*

The aim of this section is to prove that a semi-commutation is decomposable if and only if it is not atomic. Moreover, we shall give an algorithm to decompose any semi-commutation in terms of atomic semi-commutations.

Definition 12.4.3 *For a semi-commutation θ over an alphabet Σ and $(b, a) \in \theta$, we set:*
$$\theta_{ba} = \{(y, x) \in \theta \mid (y, a) \in \theta \ \& \ (b, x) \in \theta\} \ and \ \theta_{-ba} = \theta \setminus \{(b, a)\}.$$

Lemma 12.4.4 *Let θ be a semi-commutation over an alphabet Σ. Then the following assertions are equivalent:*

1. θ is an atomic semi-commutation

2. $\forall (b, a) \in \theta, \theta_{ba} = \theta$.

Proof:
 i) 1.$\Rightarrow$ 2.
 Let us take $(b, a) \in \theta = \Sigma_1 \times \Sigma_2$. It suffices to prove the inclusion $\theta \subseteq \theta_{ba}$. For $(y, x) \in \theta, y, b \in \Sigma_1$ and $x, a \in \Sigma_2$. Hence, $(y, a) \in \Sigma_1 \times \Sigma_2 = \theta$ and $(b, x) \in \Sigma_1 \times \Sigma_2 = \theta$. Thus $(y, x) \in \theta_{ba}$.
 ii) 2.$\Rightarrow$ 1.
 Let us set $\Sigma_1 = \{b \in \Sigma \mid (b, x) \in \theta \ for \ some \ x \in \Sigma\}$ and $\Sigma_2 = \{a \in \Sigma \mid (y, a) \in \theta \ for \ some \ y \in \Sigma\}$. Since $\theta \subseteq \Sigma_1 \times \Sigma_2$, it suffices to prove the reverse inclusion. Let us take $(b, a) \in \Sigma_1 \times \Sigma_2$. Then $(b, x), (y, a) \in \theta$ for some $x, y \in \Sigma$. As $(y, a) \in \theta_{ya} = \theta = \theta_{bx}$, it follows from definition of θ_{bx} that $(b, a) \in \theta$.

$\square$

Lemma 12.4.5 *Let θ be a semi-commutation over an alphabet Σ and $u, v \in \Sigma^*$. If $v \in f_\theta(u)$, then there exists $u \xrightarrow[\theta_{ba}]{n} w \xrightarrow[\theta_{-ba}]{k} v$ with $n + k = d(u, v)$.*

Proof:

We shall reason by induction on $d(u, v)$.

1. If $d(u, v) = 0$, we take $w = u = v$ and $n = k = 0$.

2. For $d(u, v) > 0$, we shall distinguish two cases:

   - If $v \in f_{\theta_{-ba}}(u)$, we take $w = u, n = 0$ and $k = d(u, v)$.
   - If $v \notin f_{\theta_{-ba}}(u)$, then there exist (b, i) and (a, j) in Σ_{num} such that $((b, i), (a, j)) \in E_{u'} \setminus E_{v'}$ where $u' = \text{num}(u)$ and $v' = \text{num}(v)$. Let us set $u' = \alpha(b, i)\beta(a, j)\gamma = \alpha z_0 \ldots z_p \gamma$ where $z_i's$ are letters in Σ_{num}. Let s be the least index such that $(z_s, z_0) \in E_{v'}$. Note that s exists since $(z_p, z_0) = ((a, j), (b, i)) \in E_{v'}$. From this choice, we get $(z_s, z_{s-1}) \in E_{v'}$ and $(z_p, z_{s-1}) \in E_{v'}$. Thus $(z_{s-1}, z_s), (z_{s-1}, z_p), (z_0, z_s) \in E_{u'} \setminus E_{v'}$. Set $y = \text{denum}(z_{s-1})$ and $x = \text{denum}(z_s)$. Then $(y, x), (b, x), (y, a) \in \theta$, which implies $(y, x) \in \theta_{ba}$. Let w' such that $u' \xrightarrow[(z_{s-1}, z_s)]{} w'$ and $w = \text{denum}(w')$. Then $u \xrightarrow[\theta_{ba}]{} w$ and $d(w, v) = d(w', v') = d(u', v') - 1 = d(u, v) - 1$. The Distance Lemma implies that $v \in f_\theta(w)$ and the induction hypothesis permits to conclude the proof.

$\square$

For any $(b, a) \in \theta, \theta_{-ba}$ is strictly included in θ. Thanks to Lemma 12.4.4, if θ is not atomic, there is some $(y, x) \in \theta$ such that θ_{yx} is strictly included in θ. From Lemma 12.4.5, it follows that any non atomic semi-commutation is decomposable in two semi-commutations.

Example 12.4.6 Consider the semi-commutation $\theta = \{(c, b), (c, a), (a, b)\}$. Then $\theta_{cb} = \theta$, but $f_\theta = f_\nu \circ f_\mu$ where $\mu = \theta_{ca} = \{(c, b), (c, a)\} = \{c\} \times \{a, b\}$ is atomic and $\nu = \theta_{-ca} = \{(c, b), (a, b)\} = \{a, c\} \times \{b\}$ is atomic. This decomposition is not unique since we have also $f_\theta = f_\mu \circ f_\nu$. Indeed, one can check that $\nu = \theta_{ab}$ and $\mu = \theta_{-ab}$.

Example 12.4.7 Consider the semi-commutation $\theta' = \theta \cup \{(b, a)\}$. Since $\theta'_{-ba} = \theta$, we get, from the above example, $f_{\theta'} = f_\mu \circ f_\nu \circ f_\lambda$ where $\lambda = \theta'_{ba} = \{c, b\} \times \{a\}$ is atomic.

Remark 12.4.8 For the semi-commutation θ' of example 12.4.7 and for $v \in f_{\theta'}(u)$, there exist words u', u'' such that $u \xrightarrow[\lambda]{n} u' \xrightarrow[\nu]{p} u'' \xrightarrow[\mu]{q} v$ with $n + p + q = d(u, v)$. As a matter of fact, using Theorem 12.5.9, one get $f_{\theta'} = f_\mu \circ f_\lambda$. So, for $bac \in f_{\theta'}(cba)$, the only word $u' \in f_\lambda(cba)$ with $bac \in f_\mu(u')$ is $u' = acb$. Then we have $cba \xrightarrow[\lambda]{2} acb \xrightarrow[\mu]{2} bac$ with $2 + 2 > d(cba, bac) = 2$.

Now, from the two above lemmas, it is easy to get, by induction on the number of elements of the semi-commutations, the following result:

Theorem 12.4.9 *Let θ be a semi-commutation over an alphabet Σ. Then one can find atomic semi-commutations $\theta_1, \ldots, \theta_n$ such that $f_\theta = f_{\theta_n} \circ \ldots \circ f_{\theta_1}$.*

Now, we shall prove that none atomic semi-commutation is decomposable. For that we need two auxiliary results:

Lemma 12.4.10 *Let θ be a semi-commutation over an alphabet Σ and $u, v \in \Sigma^*$. Then $f_\theta(u \sqcup\!\sqcup v) \subseteq f_\theta(u) \sqcup\!\sqcup f_\theta(v)$.*

Proof:

Clearly, by using the Enumeration Lemma, one can reduce the proof to the case where uv is a permutation word. Thus, we shall assume that $\Sigma_1 = \text{alph}(u)$ and $\Sigma_2 = \text{alph}(v)$ are disjoint subsets of Σ. Let us take $w \in u \sqcup\!\sqcup v$ and $w' \in f_\theta(w)$. Then $u = \Pi_{\Sigma_1}(w) \xrightarrow{*} \Pi_{\Sigma_1}(w')$ and $v = \Pi_{\Sigma_2}(w) \xrightarrow{*} \Pi_{\Sigma_2}(w')$. Thus $w' \in \Pi_{\Sigma_1}(w') \sqcup\!\sqcup \Pi_{\Sigma_2}(w') \subseteq f_\theta(u) \sqcup\!\sqcup f_\theta(v)$.

$\square$

Lemma 12.4.11 *Let Σ_1, Σ_2 be two disjoint subsets of the alphabet Σ and $\theta_1, \ldots, \theta_n$ be semi-commutations included in $\Sigma_1 \times \Sigma_2 \cup \Sigma_2 \times \Sigma_1$. One considers the words $u = b_n \ldots b_1 a_1 \ldots a_n$ and $v = a_1 \ldots a_n b_n \ldots b_1$ with $\forall i \in [1, n], (b_i, a_i) \in \Sigma_1 \times \Sigma_2 \setminus \theta_i$. Then $v \notin f_{\theta_n} \circ \ldots \circ f_{\theta_1}(u)$.*

Proof:

By construction, $f_{\theta_1}(u) = u$. Similarly, $\forall i \in [1, n], f_{\theta_i}(b_n \ldots b_i a_i \ldots a_n) = b_n \ldots b_i a_i \ldots a_n$. According to Lemma 12.4.10,

$$f_{\theta_{i+1}}(b_n \ldots b_{i+1} a_{i+1} \ldots a_n \sqcup\!\sqcup \Sigma^*) \subseteq f_{\theta_{i+1}}(b_n \ldots b_{i+1} a_{i+1} \ldots a_n) \sqcup\!\sqcup f_{\theta_{i+1}}(\Sigma^*)$$
$$= b_n \ldots b_{i+1} a_{i+1} \ldots a_n \sqcup\!\sqcup \Sigma^*$$

Since it is clear that

$$b_n \ldots b_i a_i \ldots a_n \sqcup\!\sqcup \Sigma^* \subseteq b_n \ldots b_{i+1} a_{i+1} \ldots a_n \sqcup\!\sqcup \Sigma^*$$

we get

$$f_{\theta_{i+1}}(b_n \ldots b_i a_i \ldots a_n \sqcup\!\sqcup \Sigma^*) \subseteq b_n \ldots b_{i+1} a_{i+1} \ldots a_n \sqcup\!\sqcup \Sigma^*$$

Now, a simple induction yields to $f_{\theta_n} \circ \ldots \circ f_{\theta_1}(u) \subseteq b_n a_n \sqcup\!\sqcup \Sigma^*$, which implies $v \notin f_{\theta_n} \circ \ldots \circ f_{\theta_1}(u)$.

$\square$

Theorem 12.4.12 *Let θ be a semi-commutation over an alphabet Σ. Then θ is decomposable if and only if it is not atomic.*

Proof:

It has been seen that any non atomic semi-commutation is decomposable. Thus, it remains to prove that an atomic semi-commutation is not decomposable. Let us consider an atomic semi-commutation $\theta = \Sigma_1 \times \Sigma_2$ and assume that θ is decomposable, that is $f_\theta = f_{\theta_n} \circ \ldots \circ f_{\theta_1}$ with $\theta_1 \subsetneqq \theta, \ldots, \theta_n \subsetneqq \theta$. Let us consider now the words $u = b_n \ldots b_1 a_1 \ldots a_n$ and $v = a_1 \ldots a_n b_n \ldots b_1$ with $\forall i \in [1, n], (b_i, a_i) \in \theta \setminus \theta_i$. According to Lemma 12.4.11, $v \notin f_{\theta_n} \circ \ldots \circ f_{\theta_1}(u)$. Hence, we get a contradiction since, clearly, $v \in f_\theta(u)$.

$\square$

We shall conclude this section by showing that the same kind of results does hold for partial commutations. Clearly, a non empty atomic semi-commutation is not symmetric, hence, is not a partial commutation. Atomic partial commutations will be simply defined as symmetric closures of atomic semi-commutations:

Definition 12.4.13 *A partial commutation θ over the alphabet Σ is an atomic partial commutation if $\theta = \Sigma_1 \times \Sigma_2 \cup \Sigma_2 \times \Sigma_1$ for some disjoint subsets of Σ.*

From Theorem 12.4.12, it follows directly that any partial commutation can be expressed as a composition of atomic partial commutations:

Theorem 12.4.14 *Let θ be a partial commutation over an alphabet Σ. Then one can find atomic partial commutations $\theta_1, \ldots, \theta_n$ such that $f_\theta = f_{\theta_n} \circ \ldots \circ f_{\theta_1}$.*

Proof:

From Theorem 12.4.12, one can find atomic semi-commutations $\theta_1', \ldots, \theta_n'$ such that $f_\theta = f_{\theta_n'} \circ \ldots \circ f_{\theta_1'}$. It is easy to check that we have also $f_\theta = f_{\theta_n} \circ \ldots \circ f_{\theta_1}$ where $\forall i \in [1, n], \theta_i$, the symmetric closure of θ_i' is an atomic partial commutation.

$\square$

As a matter of fact, it has been shown in [43] that, like for semi-commutations, a non atomic partial commutation can always be decomposed in two partial commutations. Now a non empty atomic partial commutation is a decomposable semi-commutation since it is not an atomic semi-commutation. More precisely, for $\theta = \Sigma_1 \times \Sigma_2 \cup \Sigma_2 \times \Sigma_1$, one can easily check that $f_\theta = f_\nu \circ f_\mu$ with $\mu = \Sigma_1 \times \Sigma_2$ and $\nu = \Sigma_2 \times \Sigma_1$. However, one can define:

Definition 12.4.15 *A partial commutation θ is a decomposable partial commutation if there are partial commutations $\theta_1 \subsetneqq \theta, \ldots, \theta_n \subsetneqq \theta$ such that $f_\theta = f_{\theta_n} \circ \ldots \circ f_{\theta_1}$.*

Theorem 12.4.16 *Let θ be a partial commutation over an alphabet Σ. Then θ is a decomposable partial commutation if and only if θ is not an atomic partial commutation.*

Proof:

Theorem 12.4.14 shows that that every non atomic partial commutation is a decomposable partial commutation. Indeed, if $f_\theta = f_{\theta_n} \circ \ldots \circ f_{\theta_1}$ where θ_i's are atomic partial commutations, then it is obvious that $\forall i \in [1,n], \theta_i \subseteq \theta$. These inclusions are necessarily strict since θ is not atomic.

Now, let us consider an atomic partial commutation $\theta = \Sigma_1 \times \Sigma_2 \cup \Sigma_2 \times \Sigma_1$ and assume that θ is a decomposable partial commutation, that is $f_\theta = f_{\theta_n} \circ \ldots \circ f_{\theta_1}$ with $\theta_1 \subsetneq \theta, \ldots, \theta_n \subsetneq \theta$. Since θ_i's are symmetric, it follows that $\forall i \in [1,n]$, there exists $(b_i, a_i) \in (\Sigma_1 \times \Sigma_2) \setminus \theta_i$. Let us consider now the words $u = b_n \ldots b_1 a_1 \ldots a_n$ and $v = a_1 \ldots a_n b_n \ldots b_1$ with $\forall i \in [1,n], (b_i, a_i) \in (\Sigma_1 \times \Sigma_2) \setminus \theta_i$. According to Lemma 12.4.11, $v \notin f_{\theta_n} \circ \ldots \circ f_{\theta_1}(u)$. Hence, we get a contradiction since, clearly, $v \in f_\theta(u)$.

$\square$

12.5 A Composition Criterion

When new operators, as semi-commutation functions, are defined a natural question is *what about their composition?* In section 12.4, it has been seen that semi-commutation functions can be decomposed into weaker semi-commutation functions if and only if they are not atomic.

Unfortunately the composition of two semi-commutation functions, even atomic, is not always a semi-commutation function:

Example 12.5.1 Let $\Sigma = \{a,b,c\}$ and $\mu = \{(a,c)\}, \nu = \{(b,c)\}$ be two semi-commutations over Σ. Let us suppose that there exists a semi-commutation θ over Σ which satisfies: $f_\nu \circ f_\mu = f_\theta$. As $f_\mu \preceq f_\nu \circ f_\mu = f_\theta$, (a,c) must belongs to θ. Similarly, (b,c) must belongs to θ. Let us consider the two words abc and cab. Clearly, $cab \in f_\theta(abc)$ but $f_\nu \circ f_\mu(abc) = \{abc, acb\}$. This contradiction implies that $f_\nu \circ f_\mu$ is not a semi-commutation function.

Our purpose, in this section, is to give a decidable characterization of semi-commutations μ, ν such that the composition $f_\nu \circ f_\mu$ is a semi-commutation function. The characterization is based on the commutation graphs of μ and ν, and the non commutation graphs of μ and ν^{-1}.

12.5.1 Preliminary Results

Lemma 12.5.2 Let $\theta_1, \theta_2, \ldots, \theta_n$ be semi-commutations over an alphabet Σ. If $f_{\theta_n} \circ f_{\theta_{n-1}} \circ \ldots \circ f_{\theta_1}$ is equal to a semi-commutation function f_θ then $f_{\theta_n} \circ f_{\theta_{n-1}} \circ \ldots \circ f_{\theta_1} = f_{\theta_1} \circ f_{\theta_2} \circ \ldots \circ f_{\theta_n}$

Proof:

Let u and v be two words of Σ^* such that $u \xrightarrow[\theta]{*} v$. From Lemma 12.3.14 we have $u \xrightarrow[\theta]{*} v \Longleftrightarrow \tilde{u} \xrightarrow[\theta^{-1}]{*} \tilde{v}$. As

$$f_{\theta^{-1}} = f_{\theta_1^{-1}} \circ f_{\theta_2^{-1}} \circ \ldots \circ f_{\theta_n^{-1}}$$

we have:

$$\tilde{u} = w_n \xrightarrow[\theta_n^{-1}]{*} w_{n-1} \xrightarrow[\theta_{n-1}^{-1}]{*} \ldots \xrightarrow[\theta_1^{-1}]{*} w_0 = \tilde{v}$$

So for each i in $[1, n]$ we have $w_i \xrightarrow[\theta_i^{-1}]{*} w_{i-1}$. From Lemma 12.3.14, we have, for each i in $[1, n]$, $\tilde{w_i} \xrightarrow[\theta_i]{*} \tilde{w}_{i-1}$. So we have:

$$u = \tilde{w}_n \xrightarrow[\theta_n]{*} \tilde{w}_{n-1} \xrightarrow[\theta_{n-1}]{*} \ldots \xrightarrow[\theta_1]{*} \tilde{w}_0 = v$$

$\square$

Generally the converse of Lemma 12.5.2 is false:

Example 12.5.3 Let $\Sigma = \{a, b, c\}$, $\theta_1 = \{(a, c)\}$, $\theta_2 = \{(a, b)\}$ and $\theta_3 = \theta_1$. We have $f_{\theta_3} \circ f_{\theta_2} \circ f_{\theta_1} = f_{\theta_1} \circ f_{\theta_2} \circ f_{\theta_3}$ but $f_{\theta_3} \circ f_{\theta_2} \circ f_{\theta_1}$ is not a semi-commutation function: $f_{\theta_3} \circ f_{\theta_2} \circ f_{\theta_1}(abcb) = \{abcb, bacb, bcab\}$ and $(f_{\theta_3} \circ f_{\theta_2} \circ f_{\theta_1}) \circ (f_{\theta_3} \circ f_{\theta_2} \circ f_{\theta_1})(abcb) = \{abcb, bacb, bcab, bcba\}$

Nevertheless when we work with only two semi-commutations we have:

Proposition 12.5.4 Let μ and ν be two semi-commutations over an alphabet Σ. These following assertions are equivalent:

1. $f_\nu \circ f_\mu$ is a semi-commutation function

2. $f_\nu \circ f_\mu = f_\mu \circ f_\nu$

3. $f_\mu \circ f_\nu \preceq f_\nu \circ f_\mu$

4. $f_\nu \circ f_\mu = f_{\mu \cup \nu}$

Proof:

It is obvious that $(2) \Longrightarrow (3)$ and $(4) \Longrightarrow (1)$. From Lemma 12.5.2 we have $(1) \Longrightarrow (2)$. We have only to prove: $(3) \Longrightarrow (4)$ that is

$$(f_\nu \circ f_\mu \preceq f_\mu \circ f_\nu) \Longrightarrow (f_\nu \circ f_\mu = f_{\mu \cup \nu})$$

It is easily seen that $f_\nu \circ f_\mu \preceq f_{\mu \cup \nu}$ (see example 12.5.1). It remains to prove that $f_{\mu \cup \nu} \subseteq f_\nu \circ f_\mu$: Let u and v be two words of Σ^* such that $v \in f_{\mu \cup \nu}(u)$. We shall reason by induction on the distance between u and v: $d(u, v)$. If $d(u, v) = 0$, then $u = v$ and $v \in f_\nu \circ f_\mu(u)$. If $d(u, v) > 0$ then there exists a word w such that $u \xrightarrow[\mu \cup \nu]{} w$ with $v \in f_{\mu \cup \nu}(w)$ and $d(w, v) = d(u, v) - 1$. With the induction hypothesis, we get: $v \in f_\nu \circ f_\mu(w)$ and, as $u \xrightarrow[\mu \cup \nu]{} w$, we have too: $w \in f_\mu(u)$ or $w \in f_\nu(u)$.

1. If $w \in f_\mu(u)$ then $w \in f_\nu \circ f_\mu \circ f_\mu(u) = f_\nu \circ f_\mu(u)$.

2. If $w \in f_\nu(u)$ then $w \in f_\nu \circ f_\mu \circ f_\nu(u)$. As $f_\mu \circ f_\nu \preceq f_\nu \circ f_\mu$, we have: $f_\nu \circ f_\mu \circ f_\nu(u) \subseteq f_\nu \circ f_\mu(u)$, hence $w \in f_\nu \circ f_\mu(u)$.

$\square$

12.5.2   A Decidable Characterization

In this part, Σ is the used alphabet, μ and ν are two semi-commutations defined over Σ.

Thanks to proposition 12.5.4 we know that the composition of the two semi-commutation functions $f_\nu \circ f_\mu$ is a semi-commutation function if and only if there do not exist two words u and v such that $v \notin f_\nu \circ f_\mu(u)$ and $v \in f_{\mu \cup \nu}(u)$. We shall say that if such words u and v exist, the couple (u, v) satisfies *property P*.

We shall see that there exist two words satisfying property P if and only if there exist two permutation words satisfying property P. The following notion will be useful to represent the image of a permutation word by a semi-commutation function.

Definition 12.5.5 *Let θ be a semi-commutation over an alphabet Σ and u a permutation word of Σ^*. The ocurrency graph of $f_\theta(u)$, denoted by $\gamma(u, \theta)$ is the directed graph $< V, E >$, where the vertices set V is equal to Σ and the edges set E is equal to $E_u \cap \bar{\theta}$, that is the set of couples of letters (a, b) such that ab is a subword of u and (a, b) does not belong to θ.*

The aim of the next lemma is to propose a necessary and sufficient condition for a permutation word to belong to the image of another word by the composition $f_\nu \circ f_\mu$.

Lemma 12.5.6 *Let u and v be two permutation words of Σ^*. Then v belongs to $f_\nu \circ f_\mu(u)$ if and only if $\gamma(u, \mu) \cup \gamma(v, \nu^{-1})$ does not contain any directed cycle.*

Proof:

Let $\Gamma = \gamma(u, \mu) \cup \gamma(v, \nu^{-1})$.

$\Longrightarrow$

We know that v belongs to $f_\nu \circ f_\mu(u)$ so there exists a word w of Σ^* such that w belongs to $f_\mu(u) \cap f_{\nu^{-1}}(v)$. Set $w = x_0 x_1 \dots x_n$.

Suppose Γ contains a directed cycle. Let x_i be the first letter of w belonging to a directed cycle of Γ. There exists x_j belonging to the same directed cycle as x_i in Γ such that (x_j, x_i) belongs to Γ. Either (x_j, x_i) belongs to $\gamma(u, \mu)$ or (x_j, x_i)

belongs to $\gamma(v, \nu^{-1})$. Then from the Projection Lemma (Lemma 12.3.8), we have $\Pi_{\{x_i, x_j\}}(w) = x_j x_i$. This leads us to a contradiction: x_i is not the first letter of w belonging to a directed cycle.

$\Longleftarrow$

Hypothesis: there exists no directed cycle in Γ. Let *is_before* be the relation on $\Sigma \times \Sigma$ defined by:

$$x \ is\_before \ y \Longleftrightarrow (x, y) \in \Gamma$$

The relation *is_before* is an order on Σ whence there exists a word w of Σ^* such that $w = x_0 x_1 \ldots x_n$ with $w \in \text{com}(u)$ and for each $i, j \in [0, n]$ $(x_i \ is\_before \ x_j)$ implies $(i < j)$. Now for each $i, j \in [0, n]$ $(x_i \ is\_before \ x_j)$ implies $(\Pi_{\{x_i, x_j\}}(w) = x_i x_j)$ and so, from the Projection Lemma, we get $w \in f_\mu(u) \cap f_{\nu^{-1}}(v)$.

$\square$

In this light, we can state:

Lemma 12.5.7 *There exist a couple of words of Σ^* satisfying property P if and only if there exist a couple of permutation words of Σ^* satisfying property P.*

Proof:
Clearly, we have only to show the only if part. We shall use the Enumeration Lemma (Lemma 12.3.7).

We denote P_{num} the property: a couple of words (w_1, w_2) of $\Sigma_{num}^* \times \Sigma_{num}^*$ satisfies the property P_{num} if and only if $w_2 \in f_{\mu_{num} \cup \nu_{num}}(w_1)$ and $w_2 \notin f_{\nu_{num}} \circ f_{\mu_{num}}(w_1)$.

Let (u, v) be a couple of words of $\Sigma^* \times \Sigma^*$ satisfying property P and $\Gamma_{num} = \gamma(u, \mu_{num}) \cup \gamma(v, \nu_{num}^{-1})$.

From the Enumeration Lemma we know that $(\text{num}(u), \text{num}(v))$ satisfies the property P_{num}, so, from Lemma 12.5.6, we know that Γ_{num} contains a directed cycle. Let C be a smaller directed cycle in Γ_{num}.

It is easily seen that $C = \{(y_0, y_1), (y_1, y_2), \ldots, (y_n, y_0)\}$ where all y_i are different from each other because C is a smaller directed cycle. Moreover, if (y_i, y_j) belongs to Γ_{num} then (y_i, y_j) belongs to C.

Let us suppose that there exist a letter y_i and a letter y_j such that $\text{denum}(y_i) = \text{denum}(y_j) = a$. Let $y_i = (a, q)$ and $y_j = (a, p)$ with $p > q$. We know that there exists $x \in \Sigma_{num}$ such that $((a, p), x) \in C$:

- either $((a, p), x) \in \gamma(\text{num}(u), \mu_{num})$ and $p > q$ therefore, from the definition of Γ_{num}, $((a, q), x) \in \Gamma_{num}$

- or $((a, p), x) \in \gamma(\text{num}(v), \nu_{num}^{-1})$ and $p > q$ therefore, from the definition of Γ_{num}, $((a, q), x) \in \Gamma_{num}$

whence $((a, q), x) \in \Gamma_{num}$. As (a, q) and x belong to the smallest directed cycle C we have $((a, q), x) \in C$. But we know that $((a, q), (a, p))$ belongs to $\gamma(\text{num}(u), \mu_{num})$ so $((a, q), (a, p))$ belongs to C hence $x = (a, p)$, this leads us to a contradiction:

$((a, p), (a, p))$ belongs to C and num(u) does not contain two occurrences of the same letter. So denum$(\Pi_Y(\text{num}(u)))$ does not contain two occurrences of the same letter, where $Y = \{x \in \Sigma_{num} \mid \exists y \in \Sigma_{num} : (x, y) \in C \text{ or } (y, x) \in C\}$.

Let $u' = \text{denum}(\Pi_Y(\text{num}(u)))$ and $v' = \text{denum}(\Pi_Y(\text{num}(v)))$

The couple $(\Pi_Y(\text{num}(u)), \Pi_Y(\text{num}(v)))$ satisfies the property P$_{num}$ therefore, from the Enumeration lemma, the couple of words (u', v') satisfies the property P. Then there exists a couple of permutations words on Σ which satisfies the property P.

$\square$

The next lemma proves that if there exists a couple of words satisfying the property P then there exists a couple of words (u, v) satisfying the property P such that the derivation of u in v uses at least one rule of μ and only one rule of $\bar{\mu} \cap \nu$.

Lemma 12.5.8 *If there exists a couple of permutation words (u, v) satisfying the property P then there exists a couple of words (u', v') such that:*

- *the couple (u', v') satisfies the property P*

- $u' \xrightarrow[\bar{\mu} \cap \nu]{} w_1 \xrightarrow[\mu]{*} w_2 \xrightarrow[\mu \cap \bar{\nu}]{} v'$ *with $d(u', v') = d(w_1, v') + 1$*

- u' *belongs to* com(u)

Proof:

The couple (u, v) satisfies the property P, let us write a derivation:

$$u = u_0 \xrightarrow[\mu \cup \nu]{} u_1 \xrightarrow[\mu \cup \nu]{} \ldots \xrightarrow[\mu \cup \nu]{} u_i \xrightarrow[\mu \cup \nu]{} \ldots \xrightarrow[\mu \cup \nu]{} u_{n-1} \xrightarrow[\mu \cup \nu]{} u_n = v$$

Let j be the greatest positive such that (u_j, u_n) satisfies the property P. Clearly $j \neq n$.

Suppose that $u_j \xrightarrow[\mu]{} u_{j+1}$. We know that the couple (u_{j+1}, u_n) does not satisfy the property P, therefore $u_{j+1} \xrightarrow[\mu]{*} m \xrightarrow[\nu]{*} u_n$. This leads us to a contradiction:

$u_j \xrightarrow[\mu]{*} u_{j+1} \xrightarrow[\mu]{*} m \xrightarrow[\nu]{*} u_n$ hence (u_j, u_n) does not satisfy the property P.

So we have:

$$u_j = w_0 \xrightarrow[\bar{\mu} \cap \nu]{} w_1 \xrightarrow[\mu]{} \ldots \xrightarrow[\mu]{} w_l \xrightarrow[\nu]{} \ldots \xrightarrow[\nu]{} w_{k-1} \xrightarrow[\nu]{} w_k = u_n$$

Now let h be the smallest integer such that the couple (w_0, w_h) satisfies the property P. Clearly $h \neq 0$.

Suppose that $w_{h-1} \xrightarrow[\nu]{*} w_h$. we know that the couple (w_0, w_{h-1}) does not satisfy the property P, hence we have $w_0 \xrightarrow[\mu]{*} m' \xrightarrow[\nu]{*} w_{h-1}$. This leads us to a contradiction: $w_0 \xrightarrow[\mu]{*} m' \xrightarrow[\nu]{*} w_{h-1} \xrightarrow[\nu]{*} w_h$ but the couple (w_0, w_h) satisfies the property P.

It is easily seen that:

$$w_0 \xrightarrow[\bar{\mu} \cap \nu]{} w_1 \xrightarrow[\mu]{*} w_{h-1} \xrightarrow[\mu \cap \bar{\nu}]{} w_h$$

As $w_0 = u_j$ and u_j belongs to $com(u)$, w_0 belongs to $com(u)$.

It remains to verify that $d(w_0, w_h) = d(w_1, w_h) + 1$. As $w_0 \xrightarrow[\bar{\mu} \cap \nu]{} w_1$, there exits two letters a, b such that $\Pi_{ab}(w_0) = ab$, $\Pi_{ab}(w_1) = ba$ and $(a, b) \in \bar{\mu} \cap \nu$. Let us suppose that $\Pi_{ab}(w_h) = ab$. As $w_1 \xrightarrow[\mu]{*} w_h$ and thanks to the Projection Lemma, we have $w_0 \xrightarrow[\mu]{*} w_h$. This leads us to a contradiction since the couple (w_0, w_h) satisfies the property P. Then $\Pi_{ab}(w_h) = ba$ and $d(w_0, w_h) = d(w_1, w_h) + 1$.

$\square$

Due to Lemma 12.5.7, we can decide if the composition of two semi-commutation functions is a semi-commutation function: it is sufficient to compare the image by the composition and by the union of the two semi-commutation functions for each permutation word on Σ.

The next proposition proposes another characterization using the commutation graphs of μ and of ν and the non commutation graphs of μ and of ν^{-1}.

Theorem 12.5.9 *Let μ and ν be two semi-commutations over an alphabet Σ. The composition of two semi-commutation functions $f_\nu \circ f_\mu$ is a semi-commutation function if and only if for each set $\{(x_0, x_1), (x_1, x_2), \ldots, (x_i, x_{i+1}), \ldots, (x_n, x_0)\}$ included in $\bar{\mu} \cup \bar{\nu}^{-1}$ such that:*

- *$x_p = x_q \Longleftrightarrow p = q$*

- *$(x_0, x_n) \in \mu \cap \bar{\nu}$*

- *$(x_i, x_{i+1}) \in \nu \cap \bar{\mu}$*

there exist two positives $h \in [0, i]$ and $j \in [i+1, n]$ such that (x_h, x_j) belongs to $\bar{\mu} \cap \bar{\nu}$.

Proof:

$\Longrightarrow$

Let us suppose that there exists a directed cycle

$$\{(x_0, x_1), (x_1, x_2), \ldots, (x_i, x_{i+1}), \ldots, (x_n, x_0)\} \subseteq \bar{\mu} \cup \bar{\nu}^{-1}$$

such that

- $x_p = x_q \Longleftrightarrow p = q$

- $(x_0, x_n) \in \mu \cap \bar{\nu}$

- $(x_i, x_{i+1}) \in \nu \cap \bar{\mu}$

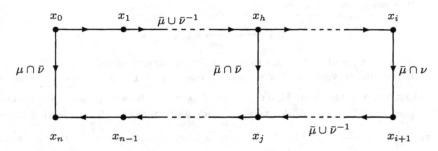

Figure 12.2: The graph criterion to decide composition

and there are no positives $h \in [0, i]$ and $j \in [i+1, n]$ such that $(x_h, x_j) \in \bar{\mu} \cap \bar{\nu}$.
Let $w_1 = x_0 x_1 \ldots x_i$ and $w_2 = x_{i+1} x_{i+2} \ldots x_n$.
It is easily seen that $w_1 w_2 \xrightarrow[\mu \cup \nu]{*} w_2 w_1$.
Let us consider $\Gamma = \gamma(w_1 w_2, \mu) \cup \gamma(w_2 w_1, \nu^{-1})$:
For each couple (x_k, x_{k+1}) with $k \neq i$ we have:

- either $(x_k, x_{k+1}) \in \gamma(w_1 w_2, \mu)$ if $(x_k, x_{k+1}) \in \bar{\mu}$

- or $(x_k, x_{k+1}) \in \gamma(w_2 w_1, \nu^{-1})$ if $(x_k, x_{k+1}) \in \bar{\nu}^{-1}$

therefore each couple (x_k, x_{k+1}), with $k \neq i$, belongs to Γ. Moreover we have:

- $(x_0, x_n) \in \mu \cap \bar{\nu}$ and $\Pi_{\{x_0, x_n\}}(w_2 w_1) = x_n x_0$ hence $(x_n, x_0) \in \Gamma$

- $(x_i, x_{i+1}) \in \nu \cap \bar{\mu}$ and $\Pi_{\{x_i x_{i+1}\}}(w_1 w_2) = x_i x_{i+1}$ hence $(x_i, x_{i+1}) \in \Gamma$

Γ contains a directed cycle so, from Lemma 12.5.6, $w_2 w_1 \notin f_\nu \circ f_\mu(w_1 w_2)$.
$\Longleftarrow$
Let us suppose that the composition $f_\nu \circ f_\mu$ is not a semi-commutation function.
Thanks to Lemma 12.5.7 we know that there exists a couple of words of minimum
length (u', v') satisfying the property P. From lemma 12.5.8 we know that there
exists a couple of words (u, v) such that:

- the couple (u, v) satisfies the property P

- $u \xrightarrow[\bar{\mu} \cap \nu]{} u_1 \xrightarrow[\mu]{*} v_1 \xrightarrow[\mu \cap \bar{\nu}]{} v$

- u belongs to com(u')

The couple (u, v) satisfies the property P hence, from Lemma 12.5.6, there exists
a directed cycle in $\gamma(u, \mu) \cup \gamma(v, \nu^{-1})$. Let Γ be $\gamma(u, \mu) \cup \gamma(v, \nu^{-1})$. As (u, v) satisfies

the property P and u belongs to com(u'), (u, v) is a couple of words of minimum length satisfying the property P, therefore it is easily seen that u does not contain two occurrences of the same letter. Suppose there exist two different directed cycles in Γ or there exists a letter which does not belong to a directed cycle then, from Lemma 12.5.6 , the projection of the couple of words (u, v) over the smaller directed cycle gives a couple of words of minimum length satisfying the property P hence a contradiction. So all the letters used in u belong to the unique directed cycle of Γ . Therefore $\Gamma = \{(x_0, x_1), \ldots, (x_i, x_{i+1}), \ldots, (x_n, x_0)\}$ with all the x_i different from each other and u belongs to com($x_0 x_1 \ldots x_n$).

v is given from v_1 by using one rule of $\mu \cap \bar{\nu}$, let a and b be the two letters which commute such that $\Pi_{\{a,b\}}(v) = ba$. Hence (b, a) belongs to $\bar{\nu}^{-1}$ therefore (b, a) belongs to $\gamma(v, \nu^{-1})$. Then we can write $x_0 = a$ and $x_n = b$.

u_1 is given from u by using one rule of $\nu \cap \bar{\mu}$, let x_i and x_j be the two letters which commute such that $\Pi_{\{x_i, x_j\}}(u) = x_i x_j$. Hence (x_i, x_j) belongs to $\bar{\mu}$ therefore (x_i, x_j) belongs to $\gamma(u, \mu)$ which is included in Γ. We cannot have $i = n$ and $j = 0$ because (x_0, x_n) belongs to $\bar{\nu}$, hence we have $j = i + 1$.

So we have $\Gamma = \{(x_0, x_1), \ldots, (x_i, x_{i+1}), \ldots, (x_n, x_0)\}$ included in $\bar{\mu} \cup \bar{\nu}^{-1}$ and we know that (x_0, x_n) belongs to $\mu \cap \bar{\nu}$ and (x_i, x_{i+1}) belongs to $\nu \cap \bar{\mu}$. Now we shall prove that there do not exist two positives h in $[0, i]$ and j in $[i + 1, n]$ such that (x_h, x_j) belongs to $\bar{\mu} \cap \bar{\nu}$.

We have $u_1 \xrightarrow{*}_{\mu} v$, therefore for each couple of letters (x, y) of $\gamma(u_1, \mu)$ we have $\Pi_{\{x,y\}}(v) = xy$. From the definition of $\gamma(v, \nu^{-1})$, we know that for each couple (x, y) of $\gamma(v, \nu^{-1})$ we have $\Pi_{\{x,y\}}(v) = xy$. Hence for each couple (x, y) of $\gamma(v, \nu^{-1}) \cup \gamma(u_1, \mu)$, we have $\Pi_{\{x,y\}}(v) = xy$. It is easily seen that $\Gamma \setminus \{(x_i, x_{i+1})\}$ is included in $\gamma(v, \nu^{-1}) \cup \gamma(u_1, \mu)$. Hence we have $v = x_{i+1} \ldots x_n x_0 \ldots x_i$.

Let us suppose now that there exist h in $[0, i]$ and j in $[i + 1, n]$ such that $(h, j) \neq (0, n)$ and (x_h, x_j) belongs to $\bar{\nu}$: this leads us to a contradiction: (x_j, x_h) belongs to $\bar{\nu}^{-1}$ and $\Pi_{\{x_h, x_j\}}(v) = x_j x_h$ so (x_j, x_h) belongs to $\gamma(v, \nu^{-1})$ and $(h, j) \neq (0, n)$ so Γ contains two directed cycles.

$\square$

12.5.3 Applications

The two following results are direct consequences of Theorem 12.5.9

Partial Commutations

As a partial commutation is a symmetric semi-commutation we can use the theorem 12.5.9 to decide if the composition of two partial commutation functions is a partial commutation function. In this case, Theorem 12.5.9 becomes:

Corollary 12.5.10 *The composition of two partial commutation functions $f_\nu \circ f_\mu$ is a partial commutation function if and only if there exists no subalphabet A of Σ such that the graph $(A, \overline{\mu \cap \nu})$ is a cycle which is neither in $(A, \bar{\mu})$, nor in $(A, \bar{\nu})$*

Confluent Semi-Commutations

Definition 12.5.11 *A semi-commutation θ defined over an alphabet Σ is said to be confluent if and only if its associated semi-commutation system is confluent: for all words u, v, w in Σ^* such that $w \xrightarrow[\theta]{*} u$ and $w \xrightarrow[\theta]{*} v$ there exist a word w' of Σ^* such that $u \xrightarrow[\theta]{*} w'$ and $v \xrightarrow[\theta]{*} w'$.*

As a consequence of proposition 12.5.4, we obtain a characterization of confluent semi-commutations

Corollary 12.5.12 *A semi-commutation θ is confluent if and only if $f_{\theta^{-1}} \circ f_\theta$ is a semi-commutation function.*

Proof:
Shown in Fig. 12.3

□

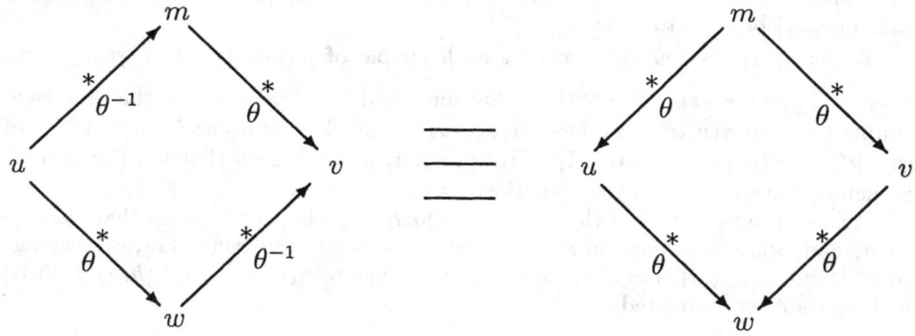

Figure 12.3: $f_\theta \circ f_{\theta^{-1}} \preceq f_{\theta^{-1}} \circ f_\theta \Longleftrightarrow < \Sigma, \theta >$ *is confluent*

Theorem 12.5.9 gives us a decidable graphic criterion of such confluent semi-commutations systems. As a matter of fact, we obtain another proof of the following result of V. Diekert, E. Ochmański and K. Reinhardt [64].

Theorem 12.5.13 *A semi-commutation θ is not confluent if and only if the graph $< \Sigma, \bar{\theta} >$ contains a directed cycle going through at least two directed edges but without any undirected chord.*

Atomic Semi-Commutations and Composition

We have seen in section 12.4 that atomic semi-commutations can not be decomposed into weaker semi-commutations. It is natural to find a characterization of composable semi-commutations using atomic semi-commutations. The following corollary is clearly another formulation of Theorem 12.5.9.

Corollary 12.5.14 *Let μ, ν be two semi-commutation relations defined over an alphabet Σ. Then $f_\nu \circ f_\mu$ is a semi-commutation function if and only if there do not exist two permutation words w_1 and w_2 in Σ^* such that:*

- $\text{alph}(w_1) \times \text{alph}(w_2) \subseteq (\mu \cup \nu)$

- $w_2 w_1 \notin f_\nu \circ f_\mu(w_1 w_2)$

Then it follows:

Proposition 12.5.15 *Let μ, ν be two semi-commutation relations defined over an alphabet Σ. Then $f_\nu \circ f_\mu$ is a semi-commutation function if and only if every (maximal) atomic semi-commutation θ included in $\mu \cup \nu$ satisfies: $f_\theta \preceq f_\nu \circ f_\mu$.*

Proof: Clearly, the *only if* part follows directly from proposition 12.5.4. Conversely, let us suppose that $f_\nu \circ f_\mu$ is not a semi-commutation function. From corollary 12.5.14, we know that there exist two permutation words w_1 and w_2 in Σ^* such that:

- $\text{alph}(w_1) \times \text{alph}(w_2) \subseteq (\mu \cup \nu)$

- $w_2 w_1 \notin f_\nu \circ f_\mu(w_1 w_2)$

As $\text{alph}(w_1) \times \text{alph}(w_2) \subseteq (\mu \cup \nu)$, there exists an atomic semi-commutation θ included in $\mu \cup \nu$ which contains $\text{alph}(w_1) \times \text{alph}(w_2)$, hence $w_2 w_1 \in f_\theta(w_1 w_2)$, then $f_\theta \npreceq f_\nu \circ f_\mu$.
□

12.6 Recognizability and Rationality

In this section we investigate closure properties of regular semi-commutation closed languages under rational operators and we intend to generalize to semi-commutation case the characterization of regular languages closed under a partial commutation relation in terms of co-rational expressions due to E. Ochmański.

What means recognizability?

Let θ be a semi-commutation relation over an alphabet Σ, and f_θ the semi-commutation function associated with θ. It is rather easy to generalize the definitions and notations of trace theory: the *semi-trace monoid* over (Σ, θ) is the triple $\mathbf{M}(\Sigma, \theta) = (M, ., 1)$ where $M = \{f_\theta(u) \mid u \in \Sigma^*\}$, the concatenation is defined by $f_\theta(u).f_\theta(v) = f_\theta(uv)$ and $1 = f_\theta(\varepsilon) = \{\varepsilon\}$.

An element $f_\theta(u)$ of $\mathbb{M}(\Sigma, \theta)$ is so called a semi-trace. The big difference between a trace monoid and a semi-trace monoid is that a semi-trace monoid is not a quotient monoid.

We may define recognizable part of a semi-trace monoid as usual: a subset L of a semi-trace monoid $\mathbb{M}(\Sigma, \theta)$ is recognizable if and only if the set of its left quotients $\{u^{-1}L \mid u \in M\}$ is finite; recall that $u^{-1}L = \{v \in M \mid uv \in L\}$.

E. Ochmański characterizes in [208] recognizable languages of $\mathbb{M}(\Sigma, \theta)$ and so proved that the family of recognizable languages of $\mathbb{M}(\Sigma, \theta)$ does not coincide with the family of recognizable θ-closed languages of Σ^*. We present now this result, and next we will study recognizability in the family of θ-closed languages.

12.6.1   Recognizability in the Semi-Trace Monoid

Let θ be a semi-commutation relation over the alphabet Σ and $\mathbb{M}(\Sigma, \theta)$ the semi-trace monoid defined over (Σ, θ).

We denote by θ_s the symmetric part of θ that is

$$\theta_s = \{(a, b) \in \Sigma \times \Sigma \mid (a, b) \in \theta, (b, a) \in \theta\} = \theta \cap \theta^{-1}$$

For a language $L \in \mathbb{M}(\Sigma, \theta)$, we denote by

$$\cup L = \bigcup_{f_\theta(u) \in L} f_\theta(u)$$

and

$$\cup_s L = \bigcup_{f_\theta(u) \in L} f_{\theta_s}(u)$$

E. Ochmański proved that a language L of $\mathbb{M}(\Sigma, \theta)$ is recognizable if and only if $\cup_s L$ is a regular part of Σ^*.

Lemma 12.6.1 $f_\theta(u) = f_\theta(v)$ *if and only if* $f_{\theta_s}(u) = f_{\theta_s}(v)$

Proof: The sufficient condition is obvious since $\theta_s \subseteq \theta$. For the necessary condition, we have $u \xrightarrow{*}_{\theta} v$ since $u \in f_\theta(v)$ and $v \in f_\theta(u)$ and it is clear that only symmetric rules are used in these derivations so $u \xrightarrow{*}_{\theta_s} v$ and $f_{\theta_s}(u) = f_{\theta_s}(v)$.   □

Lemma 12.6.2 $f_\theta(u) \in L$ *if and only if* $u \in \cup_s L$

Proof: The necessary condition is trivial. For the sufficient condition, we get

$$
\begin{aligned}
u \in \cup_s L \;&\Longrightarrow\; \exists w \in \Sigma^*, \; u \in f_{\theta_s}(w) \text{ and } f_\theta(w) \in L \\
&\Longrightarrow\; \exists w \in \Sigma^*, \; f_{\theta_s}(u) = f_{\theta_s}(w) \text{ and } f_\theta(w) \in L \\
&\Longrightarrow\; f_\theta(u) = f_\theta(w) \text{ and } f_\theta(w) \in L \text{ (Lemma 12.6.1)} \\
&\Longrightarrow\; f_\theta(u) \in L
\end{aligned}
$$

□

Lemma 12.6.3 $f_\theta(u)^{-1}L = f_\theta(u^{-1} \cup_s L)$

Proof:

$$
\begin{aligned}
f_\theta(u)^{-1}L &= \{f_\theta(v) \mid f_\theta(uv) \in L\} \\
&= \{f_\theta(v) \mid uv \in \cup_s L\} \text{ (Lemma 12.6.2)} \\
&= f_\theta(u^{-1} \cup_s L)
\end{aligned}
$$

$\square$

Lemma 12.6.4 $f_\theta(u^{-1} \cup_s L) = f_\theta(v^{-1} \cup_s L)$ *if and only if* $u^{-1} \cup_s L = v^{-1} \cup_s L$

Proof: The sufficient condition is trivial. For the necessary one, we get

$$
\begin{aligned}
x \in u^{-1} \cup_s L &\implies f_\theta(x) \in f_\theta(u^{-1} \cup_s L) \\
&\implies f_\theta(x) \in f_\theta(v^{-1} \cup_s L) \\
&\implies \exists w \in v^{-1} \cup_s L,\ vw \in \cup_s L \text{ and } f_\theta(x) = f_\theta(w)
\end{aligned}
$$

From Lemma 12.6.1, it follows

$$
\begin{aligned}
&\implies \exists w \in v^{-1} \cup_s L,\ vw \in \cup_s L \text{ and } f_{\theta_s}(x) = f_{\theta_s}(w) \\
&\implies \exists w \in v^{-1} \cup_s L,\ vw \in \cup_s L \text{ and } f_{\theta_s}(vx) = f_{\theta_s}(vw) \\
&\implies vx \in \cup_s L \\
&\implies x \in v^{-1} \cup_s L
\end{aligned}
$$

$\square$

Proposition 12.6.5 *A language* $L \subseteq \mathbf{M}(\Sigma, \theta)$ *is recognizable if and only if* $\cup_s L$ *is a regular subset of* Σ^*.

Proof: $f_\theta(u)^{-1}L = f_\theta(v)^{-1}L$ if and only if $f_\theta(u^{-1} \cup_s L) = f_\theta(v^{-1} \cup_s L)$ (Lemma 12.6.3) and this is true if and only if $u^{-1} \cup_s L = v^{-1} \cup_s L$ (Lemma 12.6.4). So, L and $\cup_s L$ have the same number of left quotients.

$\square$

So it appears that such a language as $L = \{f_\theta((ab)^n) \mid n \geq 0\}$ where $\theta = \{(b, a)\}$ is recognizable in $\mathbf{M}(\{a, b\}, \theta)$ since $\theta_s = \emptyset$ and $\cup_s L = f_{\theta_s}((ab)^*) = (ab)^*$ is regular.

On the other hand, let $\Sigma = \{a, b, c\}$ and $\theta = \{(a, b), (b, a), (a, c), (b, c)\}$. Let $R = c(ab)^* + (a + b)^*c$. The language $f_\theta(R)$ is a regular θ-closed language since $f_\theta(R) = (a + b)^*c(a + b)^*$. But $f_{\theta_s}(R) \cap ca^*b^* = \{ca^n b^n \mid n \geq 0\}$ is not regular, so $\{f_\theta(u) \mid u \in R\}$ is not recognizable in $\mathbf{M}(\Sigma, \theta)$.

The family of regular θ-closed languages seems to be of greatest interest for learning about semi-commutation and we are now going to study some of its properties. Before, let us name it:

Definition 12.6.6 *We denote by* $\mathrm{Reg}_\theta(\Sigma^*)$ *the set of regular languages of* Σ^* *which are closed under the semi-commutation* θ.

12.6.2   Regular Closed Languages and Automata

Up to now there does not exist something like asynchronous automata for regular semi-commutation closed languages. But a deterministic automaton that recognizes such a language satisfies a decidable property. With this property, we are able to find what is the biggest semi-commutation relation under which a regular language defined with a deterministic automaton is closed. So it is possible to decide if, for some regular language R, and for some semi-commutation relation θ, $R = f_\theta(R)$.

Let $A = (\Sigma, Q, q_0, \delta, F)$ be a deterministic automaton. If $q \in Q$, we set

$$R_q = \{u \in \Sigma^* \mid \delta(q, u) \in F\}$$

Let us define the following order relation on the set Q of states:

$$q \leq q' \iff R_q \subseteq R_{q'}$$

If $q \leq q'$, we say that q' is better than q: q' allows to recognize at least all words recognized from q.

And it is easy to see that

Lemma 12.6.7 *Let $A = (\Sigma, Q, q_0, \delta, F)$ be a deterministic automaton and $q, q' \in Q$ such that $q \not\leq q'$. If $\delta(q_1, a) = q$ and $\delta(q_1', a) = q'$ then $q_1 \not\leq q_1'$.*

It is very easy to decide, for two given states q and q' of Q, if q is better than q': for that we construct the complementary of the graph of the relation with the following algorithm (that looks like the minimalization algorithm of a deterministic automaton):

Let the sequence $\{H_i\}_{i \in \mathbb{N}}$ be defined by

1. $H_0 = F \times (Q \setminus M)$

2. for every i, $H_{i+1} = H_i \cup \{(q, q') \mid \exists a \in \Sigma, \ (\delta(q, a), \delta(q', a)) \in H_i\}$

It is clear that there exists a value $N \in \mathbb{N}$ such that $\forall i \geq N$, $H_i = H_N$: the sequence $\{H_i\}_{i \in \mathbb{N}}$ is ascending (for inclusion) and $Q \times Q$ is a finite set.

Let us set

$$H = \bigcup_{i \in \mathbb{N}} H_i$$

We prove now that H is the complementary of the relation $\leq$.

Lemma 12.6.8 $H = \{(q, q') \mid q \not\leq q'\}$

Proof: To prove that $H \subseteq \{(q, q') \mid q \not\leq q'\}$, we make an induction:
   $(q, q') \in H_0$ means that $q \in F$ and $q' \notin F$, so $\varepsilon \in R_q$ and $\varepsilon \notin R_{q'}$, so $R_q \not\subseteq R_{q'}$.
   Let us assume now that $\forall i < n$, $(q, q') \in H_i \Rightarrow q \not\leq q'$ and let $(q, q') \in H_n \setminus H_{n-1}$.
   There exist a letter $a \in \Sigma$ and two states $q_1, q_1' \in Q$ such that $\delta(q, a) = q_1$, $\delta(q', a) = q_1'$ and $(q_1, q_1') \in H_{n-1}$. So by induction, $q_1 \not\leq q_1'$ and with Lemma 12.6.7 we get $q \not\leq q'$.

For the reverse inclusion, let q, q' be two states of Q such that $q \not\leq q'$. There exist a word $u \in \Sigma^*$ such that $\delta(q, u) \in F$ and $\delta(q', u) \notin F$. We prove that $(q, q') \in H$ by induction on $|u|$, the length of u.

If $|u| = 0$, it is clear that $q \in F$, $q' \notin F$ and so $(q, q') \in H_0$. If $u = av$ with $a \in \Sigma$, we have $\delta(\delta(q, a), v) \in F$ and $\delta(\delta(q', a), v) \notin F$. We deduce that $\delta(q, a) \not\leq \delta(q', a)$ and by induction hypothesis, $(\delta(q, a), \delta(q', a)) \in H_n$ for some $n \in \mathbb{N}$. Then $(q, q') \in H_{n+1} \subseteq H$.

$\square$

Proposition 12.6.9 *Let R be a regular language recognized by the deterministic automaton $A = (\Sigma, Q, q_0, \delta, F)$, and let θ be a semi-commutation relation.*

$$R = f_\theta(R) \Longleftrightarrow \forall q \in Q, \ \forall (a, b) \in \theta, \ \delta(q, ab) \leq \delta(q, ba)$$

Proof: If we assume that $R = f_\theta(R)$, let $q \in Q$ and $(a, b) \in \theta$. Let $u \in \Sigma^*$ be such that $\delta(q_0, u) = q$. For each word $v \in R_{\delta(q,ab)}$, $uabv \in R = f_\theta(R)$, then $ubav \in R$ and $v \in R_{\delta(q,ba)}$.

On the other side, let $uabv$ be a word of R, with $(a, b) \in \theta$. Let us set $q = \delta(q_0, u)$. We have $v \in R_{\delta(q,ab)}$ and $\delta(q, ab) \leq \delta(q, ba)$ so $v \in R_{\delta(q,ba)}$ and $ubav \in R$. We conclude that $R = f_\theta(R)$.

$\square$

Corollary 12.6.10 *Let $R \subseteq \Sigma^*$ a regular language recognized by the deterministic automaton $A = (\Sigma, Q, q_0, \delta, F)$. The biggest semi-commutation relation under which R is closed is $\theta_R = \{(a, b) \in \Sigma \times \Sigma \mid \forall q \in Q, \delta(q, ab) \leq \delta(q, ba)\}$.*

Proof: With the previous proposition, it is clear that $R = f_{\theta_R}(R)$ and that θ_R is the biggest semi-commutation under which R is closed. We just have to notice that the definition of θ_R does not depend on the chosen deterministic automaton:

Let $A' = (\Sigma, Q', q_0', \delta', F')$ be the minimal deterministic automaton which recognizes R and let $\theta_R' = \{(a, b) \in \Sigma \times \Sigma \mid \forall q \in Q', \delta'(q, ab) \leq \delta'(q, ba)\}$. We have to prove that $\theta_R = \theta_R'$.

If $(a, b) \in \theta_R$, let $q' \in Q'$. There exists a state $q \in Q$ such that $R_q = R_{q'}$. Then $R_{\delta'(q',ab)} = R_{\delta(q,ab)}$ and $R_{\delta'(q',ba)} = R_{\delta(q,ba)}$. So $R_{\delta'(q',ab)} \subseteq R_{\delta'(q',ba)}$ and $(a, b) \in \theta_R'$. Conversely, if $(a, b) \in \theta_R'$, let $q \in Q$. There exists a state $q' \in Q'$ such that $R_q = R_{q'}$. Then $R_{\delta(q,ab)} = R_{\delta'(q',ab)} \subseteq R_{\delta'(q',ba)} = R_{\delta(q,ba)}$ and we get $(a, b) \in \theta_R$.

$\square$

Corollary 12.6.11 *Let $R \subseteq \Sigma^*$ be a regular language and θ be a semi-commutation relation defined on Σ.*

$$R = f_\theta(R) \Longleftrightarrow \theta \subseteq \theta_R$$

12.6.3   Closure Properties of $\text{Reg}_\theta(\Sigma^*)$

The results we present in this part are quite generalizations of those obtained in the case of trace theory and the proofs are similar. So there will be not detailed.

It is obvious that $\text{Reg}_\theta(\Sigma^*)$ is closed under union. The first interesting result states that if two languages are in $\text{Reg}_\theta(\Sigma^*)$, the θ-closure of their concatenation is also in $\text{Reg}_\theta(\Sigma^*)$.

Proposition 12.6.12 *If L_1 and L_2 are in $\text{Reg}_\theta(\Sigma^*)$ then the language $f_\theta(L_1 L_2)$ is also in $\text{Reg}_\theta(\Sigma^*)$.*

Proof: For a word $u \in \Sigma^*$, let us define the set

$$V(u) = \{(x^{-1}L_1, y^{-1}L_2, \text{alph}(y)) \mid u \in f_\theta(xy)\}$$

Since L_1 and L_2 are recognizable, the set $\{V(u) \mid u \in \Sigma^*\}$ is finite. We prove that $V(u) = V(v) \implies u^{-1}f_\theta(L_1 L_2) = v^{-1}f_\theta(L_1 L_2)$ in just the same way that in the case of partial commutation, when using the Levi's Lemma for semi-traces.   □

It is clear that this result cannot be extended to the star operation. The following condition which ensures that $f_\theta(R^*) \in \text{Reg}_\theta(\Sigma^*)$ if each word of R is strongly connected has been established simultaneously for partial commutation in [195] and [205] and in [42] for semi-commutation. The proof in the semi-commutative case can also be easily obtained from the commutative one using the generalized Levi lemma for semi-traces (Lemma 12.3.10):

Proposition 12.6.13 *If each word of a language L of $\text{Reg}_\theta(\Sigma^*)$ is strongly connected, then $f_\theta(L^*)$ is recognizable and so $f_\theta(L^*) \in \text{Reg}_\theta(\Sigma^*)$.*

Proof: For a word $u \in \Sigma^*$, let us define the set

$$\begin{aligned}
V(u) = \{ \quad & (\quad x_1^{-1}L, \ldots, x_n^{-1}L, \text{alph}(x_1), \ldots, \text{alph}(x_n), \\
& \text{alph}(y_0), \text{alph}(y_1), \ldots, \text{alph}(y_n)) \mid \\
& n \geq 0, x_i, y_i \in \Sigma^*, x_i \neq \varepsilon, y_i \in L^*, \\
& \text{alph}(x_i) \neq \text{alph}(x_j) \text{ if } i \neq j \text{ and} \\
& u \in f_\theta(y_0 x_1 y_1 \ldots x_n y_n)\}
\end{aligned}$$

Since L is recognizable and $\text{alph}(x_i) \neq \text{alph}(x_j)$ for $i \neq j$, the set $V(u)$ is finite and the set $\{V(u) \mid u \in \Sigma^*\}$ to. So in order to get the result, it is enough to prove that for each word $u \in \Sigma^*$, $V(u) = V(u')$ implies $u^{-1}f_\theta(L^*) = u'^{-1}f_\theta(L^*)$.

Let $u, u', v \in \Sigma^*$ be such that $V(u) = V(u')$ and $v \in u^{-1}f_\theta(L^*)$. Since $uv \in f_\theta(L^*)$, we can find words $p_1, p_2, \ldots p_m$ of L such that $uv \in f_\theta(p_1 p_2 \ldots p_m)$ and by Lemma 12.3.10 there are $x_i, z_i \in \Sigma^*$, $1 \leq i \leq m$ such that $u \in f_\theta(x_1 \ldots x_m)$, $v \in f_\theta(z_1 \ldots z_m)$, $x_i z_i \in f_\theta(p_i)$ and $\text{alph}(z_i) \times \text{alph}(x_j) \subseteq \theta$ for all $j > i$.

If for $i < j$ we rename in y_{ij} words as $x_i \ldots x_j$ where $z_i \ldots z_j = \varepsilon$ and in t_{ij} words as $z_i \ldots z_j$ where $x_i \ldots x_j = \varepsilon$, by a conversion of indices we get

$$u \in f_\theta(y_0 x_1 y_1 \ldots x_n y_n), \quad y_i \in L^*, \ x_i \neq \varepsilon$$
$$v \in f_\theta(t_0 z_1 t_1 \ldots z_n t_n), \quad t_i \in L^*, \ z_i \neq \varepsilon$$
$$x_i z_i \in L,$$
$$\mathrm{alph}(z_i) \times \mathrm{alph}(y_i x_{i+1} \ldots y_n) \subseteq \theta \text{ for } 1 \leq i \leq n$$
$$\mathrm{alph}(t_i) \times \mathrm{alph}(x_{i+1} \ldots y_n) \subseteq \theta \text{ for } 0 \leq i \leq n$$

Since $x_i z_i \in L$, $x_i z_i$ is strongly connected and since $\mathrm{alph}(z_i) \times \mathrm{alph}(x_j) \subseteq \theta$ for $i < j$ and $x_j, z_i \neq \varepsilon$, we get $\mathrm{alph}(x_i) \neq \mathrm{alph}(x_j)$ whenever $i < j$. So

$$(x_1^{-1} L, \ldots, x_n^{-1} L, \mathrm{alph}(x_1), \ldots, \mathrm{alph}(x_n), \mathrm{alph}(y_0), \ldots, \mathrm{alph}(y_n)) \in V(u)$$

Since $V(u) = V(u')$, there exist $x_1', \ldots x_n' \in \Sigma^+, y_0', \ldots, y_n' \in L^*$ such that $u' \in f_\theta(y_0' x_1' y_1' \ldots x_n' y_n')$, $x_i^{-1} L = x_i'^{-1} L$, $\mathrm{alph}(x_i) = \mathrm{alph}(x_i')$ and $\mathrm{alph}(y_i) = \mathrm{alph}(y_i')$. Then

$$\begin{aligned} u'v \ &\in \ f_\theta(y_0' x_1' y_1' \ldots x_n' y_n' t_0 z_1 t_1 \ldots z_n t_n) \\ &\subseteq \ f_\theta(y_0' t_0 x_1' z_1 y_1' t_1 \ldots x_n' z_n y_n' t_n) \\ &\subseteq \ L^* \end{aligned}$$

Similarly, if $v \in u'^{-1} L$ then $v \in u^{-1} L$ and we get the result.

$\square$

This condition is not necessary, just as in partial commutation. And we only obtain a complete characterization in the following particular case:

Corollary 12.6.14 *Let $u \in \Sigma^*$. $f_\theta(u^*) \in \mathrm{Reg}_\theta(\Sigma^*)$ if and only if u is strongly connected.*

Proof: The sufficient condition is an immediate consequence of Proposition 12.6.13. For the necessary condition, if u is not strongly connected, we can find a partition of the alphabet: $\Sigma = B \cup C$ where $B \cap C = \emptyset$ and $C \times B \subseteq \theta$. Then $\Pi_B(u) \Pi_C(u) \in f_\theta(u)$ and $\Pi_C(u) \Pi_B(u) \in f_\theta(\Pi_B(u) \Pi_C(u))$.

So $f_\theta(u^*) \cap \Pi_B(u)^* \Pi_C(u)^* = \{ \Pi_B(u)^n \Pi_C(u)^n \mid n \geq 0 \}$ is not recognizable. $\square$

12.6.4   What about Rational Expressions?

When looking at the previous results, it seems quite natural to introduce and study a family of θ-closed languages which could be obtained from elementary sets using union, product and iteration with respect to the semi-commutation relation θ. The purpose is to compare the family of recognizable θ-closed languages and this new family and the hope is to get equality. Let us define more formally this new family:

In the sequel Σ denotes a totally ordered alphabet and θ a semi-commutation relation over Σ. Let us defined the following operations on θ-closed languages of Σ^*:

1. θ-union: $R_1 \cup_\theta R_2 = f_\theta(R_1 \cup R_2) = R_1 \cup R_2$

2. θ-concatenation: $R_1._\theta R_2 = f_\theta(R_1.R_2)$

3. θ-iteration: if $\forall u \in R$, $(\mathrm{alph}(u), \bar{\theta})$ is strongly connected, then $R^{*\theta} = f_\theta(R^*)$

Note that θ-iteration as defined here is a partial operator.

So we define $\mathrm{R}_\theta(\Sigma^*)$ as the smallest family of languages containing elementary languages that are $\emptyset$, $\{\varepsilon\}$ and $\{x\}$ where $x \in \Sigma$ and closed under θ-union, θ-concatenation and θ-iteration.

In the case of partial commutations, the equality of these two families is an important result due to E. Ochmański (Theorem 6.3.16):

Theorem 12.6.15 *[205] If θ is a partial commutation relation defined over Σ then* $\mathrm{Reg}_\theta(\Sigma^*) = \mathrm{R}_\theta(\Sigma^*)$.

In the case of semi-commutation, we have at least an inclusion:

Proposition 12.6.16 *If θ is a semi-commutation relation defined over Σ,*

$$\mathrm{R}_\theta(\Sigma^*) \subseteq \mathrm{Reg}_\theta(\Sigma^*)$$

Proof: $\mathrm{Reg}_\theta(\Sigma^*)$ is closed under union and we saw in Propositions 12.6.12 and 12.6.13 that it is also closed under θ-product and θ-iteration. $\qquad\square$

The following result is a direct consequence of the definition of $\mathrm{R}_\theta(\Sigma^*)$:

Proposition 12.6.17 *Let θ be a semi-commutation relation defined over Σ. If $L \subseteq \Sigma^*$ is recognizable and if each iterating factor of L is strongly connected then $f_\theta(L) \in \mathrm{R}_\theta(\Sigma^*)$*

Proof: The proof is carried on by structural induction of L.

If L is an elementary subset of Σ^*, the result is obvious.

If $L = L_1 \cup L_2$ or $L = L_1 L_2$ where L_1 and L_2 are recognizable parts of Σ^*, since each iterating factor of L_1 or of L_2 is an iterating factor of L, by induction hypothesis, $f_\theta(L_1)$, $f_\theta(L_2) \in \mathrm{R}_\theta(\Sigma^*)$. Hence $f_\theta(L_1 \cup L_2) = f_\theta(L_1) \cup f_\theta(L_2) \in \mathrm{R}_\theta(\Sigma^*)$ and $f_\theta(L_1 L_2) = f_\theta(f_\theta(L_1) f_\theta(L_2)) = f_\theta(L_1)._\theta f_\theta(L_2) \in \mathrm{R}_\theta(\Sigma^*)$.

If $L = L_1^*$ where $L_1 \subseteq \Sigma^*$ is recognizable, then each iterating factor of L_1 is one of L and then $f_\theta(L_1) \in \mathrm{R}_\theta(\Sigma^*)$ by induction hypothesis. Moreover, each word of L_1 is an iterating factor of L and so is strongly connected. Thus $f_\theta(L_1^*) = f_\theta((f_\theta(L_1))^*) = (f_\theta(L_1))^{*\theta} \in \mathrm{R}_\theta(\Sigma^*)$. $\qquad\square$

We introduce now some subsets of a semi-commutation closed set, which are representatives of the semi-traces included in this set.

Recall that θ_s denotes the symmetric part of θ.

For $u \in \Sigma^*$, $Lex(u)$ denotes the smallest element of $f_{\theta_s}(u)$ for the lexicographic ordering of Σ^*. For $L \subseteq \Sigma^*$, $Lex(L) = \cup_{u \in L} Lex(u)$ and LEX is the set $\{Lex(u) \mid u \in \Sigma^*\}$.

For $R \subseteq \Sigma^*$, $MAX_\theta(R) = \{u \in R \mid \forall v \in R, \ u \in f_\theta(v) \Rightarrow v \in f_\theta(u)\}$.

The following properties of these sets are well known or are easy to prove.

Lemma 12.6.18 *[205] Let θ be a semi-commutation relation defined over Σ. LEX is a recognizable set of Σ^* and each factor of a word of LEX is also a word of LEX.*

Lemma 12.6.19 *[205] If θ is a partial commutation relation over Σ, and if R is a θ-closed language, then $Lex(R) = R \cap LEX$ and $R = f_\theta(Lex(R))$.*

Moreover, $R \in \mathrm{Reg}_\theta(\Sigma^*) \Longleftrightarrow Lex(R) \in \mathrm{Reg}(\Sigma^*)$.

Lemma 12.6.20 *Let θ be a semi-commutation relation defined over Σ.*

If $L = MAX_\theta(L)$ then $\forall L' \subseteq L$, $L' = MAX_\theta(L')$.

If $L = Lex(L)$ then $\forall L' \subseteq L$, $L' = Lex(L')$.

Lemma 12.6.21 *Let θ be a semi-commutation relation defined over Σ.*

If $L = L_1.L_2$ then

$$L = MAX_\theta(L) \Rightarrow L_1 = MAX_\theta(L_1) \quad and \quad L_2 = MAX_\theta(L_2)$$

$$L = Lex(L) \Rightarrow L_1 = Lex(L_1) \quad and \quad L_2 = Lex(L_2)$$

Lemma 12.6.22 *[205] Let θ be a partial commutation relation defined on Σ and $u \in \Sigma^*$. If $u^* \subseteq LEX$ then u is connected.*

It is easy to see that if R is a θ-closed language,

$$MAX_\theta(R) = f_{\theta_s}(MAX_\theta(R)) \quad and \quad R = f_\theta(MAX_\theta(R))$$

It means that $MAX_\theta(R)$ is a good string representation of the semi-traces included in R. Moreover, if R is recognizable, $MAX_\theta(R)$ is also recognizable as states the following lemma:

Lemma 12.6.23 *Let θ be a semi-commutation relation defined over Σ.*

If $R \in \mathrm{Reg}_\theta(\Sigma^*)$, then $MAX_\theta(R) \in \mathrm{Reg}(\Sigma^*)$.

Proof: In order to construct $MAX_\theta(R)$ from R, we have to take out of R words which are obtained from a word of R by a first step of a derivation using a commutation in $\theta \setminus \theta_s$ and following derivations in θ_s (that cannot be done before the first step of derivation).

As R is a recognizable θ-closed language, so it is θ_s-closed and the minimal deterministic automaton which recognizes R, $M = (X, Q, q_0, \delta, F)$, satisfies

$$if \ (x, y) \in \theta_s \ and \ \delta(q, xy) = q', then \ \delta(q, yx) = q'$$

For a letter $b \in \Sigma$ let us denote by I_b the set $\{a \in X \mid (a, b) \in \theta_s\}$ and if q and q' are in Q, let us denote by $R_{q,q'}$ the recognizable θ_s-closed set of words w such that $\delta(q, w) = q'$ (The fact that $R_{q,q'}$ is θ_s-closed is due to the above property of the minimal automaton). So, in order to obtain $MAX_\theta(R)$ from R, we have to take out of R the sets of words

$$R_{q_0,q_1} b f_{\theta_s}((R_{q_1,q_2} \cap I_b^*)(R_{q_3,q_4} \cap I_a^*)) a R_{q_4,q_5}$$

where q_1, q_2, q_3, q_4, q_5 and a, b are such that $(a, b) \in \theta \setminus \theta_s$, $\delta(q_2, ab) = q_3$ and $q_5 \in F$

Since $R_{q_1,q_2} \cap I_b^*$ and $R_{q_3,q_4} \cap I_a^*$ are θ_s-closed languages, we deduced from Proposition 12.6.12 that $f_{\theta_s}((R_{q_1,q_2} \cap I_b^*)(R_{q_3,q_4} \cap I_a^*))$ is recognizable so each set that has to be taken out of R is recognizable and $MAX_\theta(R)$ is recognizable. □

A necessary and sufficient condition to be in $\mathrm{R}_\theta(\Sigma^*)$

Let θ be a semi-commutation relation and let $R \subseteq \Sigma^*$ be a θ-closed language

If θ is symmetric, i.e in the case of partial commutation, then Ochmański has proved that $R \in \mathrm{Reg}_\theta(\Sigma^*)$ if and only if $Lex(R) \in \mathrm{Reg}(\Sigma^*)$.

Similarly, in the case of semi-commutation we should like to find a language $L \subseteq R$ such that $R \in \mathrm{Reg}_\theta(\Sigma^*)$ if and only if $L \in \mathrm{Reg}(\Sigma^*)$. Since $f_\theta(MAX_\theta(R)) = R$, the language $Lex(MAX_\theta(R))$ seems to be a good candidate.

Unfortunately, $Lex(MAX_\theta(R)) \in \mathrm{Reg}(\Sigma^*)$ is not a sufficient condition to conclude that $R \in \mathrm{R}_\theta(\Sigma^*)$: if $\Sigma = \{a, b\}$, $\theta = \{(b, a)\}$ and $R = \{w \in \{a, b\}^* \mid |w|_a = |w|_b$ and $w = uv \Rightarrow |u|_a \geq |u|_b\}$, we get $MAX_\theta(R) = (ab)^* \in \mathrm{Reg}(\Sigma^*)$ but $R \notin \mathrm{R}_\theta(\Sigma^*)$ since $R \notin \mathrm{Reg}_\theta(\Sigma^*)$. As we shall see, the reason of it is that ab is an iterating factor of $MAX_\theta(R)$ which is not strongly connected.

So, we can give the following condition for a θ-closed language R to be in $\mathrm{R}_\theta(\Sigma^*)$, and we shall see that it is a necessary and sufficient condition:

Condition 1

1. The language $K = Lex(MAX_\theta(R))$ is in $\mathrm{Reg}(\Sigma^*)$.

2. Each iterating factor of K is strongly connected.

The following result state that Condition 1 is sufficient:

Proposition 12.6.24 *Let θ be a semi-commutation relation over Σ. Let R be a θ-closed language such that $K = Lex(MAX_\theta(R))$ is in $\mathrm{Reg}(\Sigma^*)$ and such that each iterating factor of K is strongly connected, then R is in $\mathrm{R}_\theta(\Sigma^*)$.*

Proof: Since K is a recognizable language whose each iterating factor is strongly connected, we get with Proposition 12.6.17 $f_\theta(K) \in \mathrm{R}_\theta(\Sigma^*)$. On the other hand, we have $f_\theta(K) = f_\theta(f_{\theta_s}(Lex(MAX_\theta(R)))) = f_\theta(MAX_\theta(R))$ (Lemma 12.6.19) $= R$, so $R \in \mathrm{R}_\theta(\Sigma^*)$. □

We are now going to prove that each language R of $R_\theta(\Sigma^*)$ satisfies a Condition which is in fact equivalent with Condition 1:

Condition 2

1. The language $K = MAX_\theta(R)$ is in $Reg(\Sigma^*)$.

2. Each iterating factor u of K such that $u^* \subseteq LEX$ is strongly connected.

We immediately show that **Condition 2** is at least stronger that **Condition 1**:

Lemma 12.6.25 *If a θ-closed language R satisfies Condition 2 then it satisfies Condition 1.*

Proof: It is clear that if we set $K' = Lex(K)$, then K' is in $Reg(\Sigma^*)$ (We know that $K = MAX_\theta(R)$ is a θ_s-closed language and we use Lemma 12.6.19).

Moreover, if u is an iterating factor of K', then u is also an iterating factor of K since $K' \subseteq K$. And we can find two words x and y such that $xu^*y \subseteq K' \subseteq LEX$. As LEX is closed under factor (Lemma 12.6.18), we get $u^* \subseteq LEX$ so u is strongly connected. □

We know that if a language R is in $R_\theta(\Sigma^*)$, then it is in $Reg_\theta(\Sigma^*)$ (Proposition 12.6.16) and so $MAX_\theta(R)$ is in $Reg(\Sigma^*)$ (Lemma 12.6.23). It is rather more difficult to establish the second part of Condition 2, and we need some results about iterating factors.

Lemma 12.6.26 *Let K_1 and K_2 be two recognizable languages of Σ^* and u be an iterating factor of $K_1 \cup K_2$. Then we can find a positive integer k and $i \in \{1,2\}$ such that u^k is an iterating factor of K_i.*

Proof: There exist two words x,y of Σ^* such that $xu^*y \subseteq K_1 \cup K_2$. So, at least one of the sets $xu^*y \cap K_i$, $i = 1,2$, is infinite. Let $M = (X, Q, q_0, \delta, F)$ be a deterministic automaton which recognizes K_i. Since $xu^*y \cap K_i$ is infinite, we can find two different non negative integers n and m such that $\delta(q_0, xu^n) = \delta(q_0, xu^m)$, $\delta(q_0, xu^n y) \in F$ and $\delta(q_0, xu^m y) \in F$

If $n < m$, then $xu^n(u^{m-n})^*y \subseteq K_i$ and so u^{m-n} is an iterating factor of K_i. □

Lemma 12.6.27 *Let θ be a partial commutation defined on Σ, K_1, K_2 be two θ-closed recognizable languages and $u \in \Sigma^*$ a connected word (for θ) which is an iterating factor of $K_{1.\theta}K_2$. Then there exists $k \geq 1$ such that u^k is an iterating factor of K_1 or K_2.*

Proof: Let $(X, Q_1, q_1, \delta_1, F_1)$ (resp. $(X, Q_2, q_2, \delta_2, F_2)$) a deterministic automaton which recognizes K_1 (resp. K_2).

Let N_1 (resp N_2) be the cardinality of Q_1 (resp. Q_2).

As u is an iterating factor of $K_{1.\theta}K_2$, we can find two words x,y such that $\forall n \in \mathbb{N}, xu^n y \in K_{1.\theta}K_2$.

Let us choose an integer n such that $n \geq N_1 + N_2 + |u| + 2$.

There exist two words $w_1 \in K_1$ and $w_2 \in K_2$ such that $f_\theta(xu^n y) = f_\theta(w_1 w_2)$.

By Lemma 12.3.10 we can find words $x', x'', y', y'', u_i', u_i''$ for $i \in \{1, 2, ..., n\}$ such that

$$f_\theta(w_1) = f_\theta(x' u_1' u_2' ... u_n' y')$$
$$f_\theta(w_2) = f_\theta(x'' u_1'' u_2'' ... u_n'' y'')$$
$$f_\theta(x' x'') = f_\theta(x), \ f_\theta(y' y'') = f_\theta(y)$$
$$f_\theta(u_i' u_i'') = f_\theta(u), \ \forall 1 \le i \le n$$
$$\forall 1 \le i \le n, \ \text{alph}(u_i'') \times \text{alph}(u_{i+1}' ... u_n') \subseteq \theta$$

If we set $w_1' = x' u_1' u_2' ... u_n' y'$ and $w_2 = x'' u_1'' u_2'' ... u_n'' y''$, it is clear that $w_1' \in K_1$ and $w_2 \in K_2$ since these languages are θ-closed.

Let p_1 be the first value such that $u_{p_1}'' \ne \varepsilon$.

Note that $\forall i < p_1, \ f_\theta(u_1') = f_\theta(u)$ and if $p_1 > N_1 + 1$, then $x' u_1' ... u_{N_1+1}'$ is a left factor of $w_1' \in K_1$ and since K_1 is θ-closed also $x' u^{N_1+1}$ is a left factor of a word of K_1. So, as N_1 is the number of states of the automaton which recognizes K_1, we can find two integers $0 < n < m \le N_1$ such that $\delta_1(q_1, xu^n) = \delta_1(q_1, xu^m)$, therefore u^{m-n} is an iterating factor of K_1.

If $p_1 \le N_1 + 1$, then $\forall q \ge p_1, \ \forall y \in \text{alph}(u_{q+1}')$, we have $y \notin \text{alph}(u_1'' u_2'' ... u_q'')$ as y and each letter of this set are independent. Since $\forall 1 \le j \le n, \ \text{alph}(u) = \text{alph}(u_j') \cup \text{alph}(u_j'')$ we get $\forall 1 \le j \le q, \ y \in \text{alph}(u_j')$. So

$$\forall q \ge p_1, \quad \text{alph}(u_{q+1}') \subseteq \text{alph}(u_q')$$

We are now going to prove that $\forall q \ge p_1$, if $u_q' \ne \varepsilon$, then $\text{alph}(u_{q+1}') \subsetneq \text{alph}(u_q')$.

As u is connected we can find a letter a in $\text{alph}(u_q')$, and a letter b in $\text{alph}(u_q'')$ such that $(a, b) \notin \theta$. So $a \notin \text{alph}(u_{q+1}' ... u_n')$ since b and each letter of this set are independent, then $a \in \text{alph}(u_q')$, $a \notin \text{alph}(u_{q+1}')$ and $\text{alph}(u_{q+1}') \subsetneq \text{alph}(u_q')$.

It means that we shall find a value $p_2 \le p_1 + |u|$ (in fact, $p_1 + |\text{alph}(u)|$ is a best bound) such that $u_{p_2}' = \varepsilon$, that is $\forall j \ge p_2, \ \text{alph}(u) = \text{alph}(u_{p_2}'') = \text{alph}(u_j'')$ and $\forall j \ge p_2, \ f_\theta(u_j'') \in f_\theta(u)$.

We know that $w_2' = x'' u_1'' u_2'' ... u_n'' y''$ is in K_2 which is θ-closed, so $u^{N_2+1} y''$ is a right factor of a word of K_2 ($p_1 \le N_1 + 1$ and $n > |u| + N_1 + N_2 + 1$). With the same proof as above, we conclude that u^k is an iterating factor of K_2, for some positive integer k. □

The following lemma is a generalization of the previous one, in the case of concatenation of more than two languages:

Lemma 12.6.28 *Let θ be a partial commutation defined over Σ, $K_1, K_2, ..., K_n$ be n recognizable θ-closed languages and $u \in \Sigma^*$ be a connected word (for θ) which is an iterating factor of $K_1._\theta K_2 ... ._\theta K_n$. Then there exist a positive integer k and $i \in \{1, 2, ..., n\}$ such that u^k is an iterating factor of K_i.*

Proof: It is an induction on n.

If $n = 1$, the result is obvious.

If $n > 1$, we can write: u is an iterating factor of $(K_{1 \cdot \theta} K_2 \ldots {}_{\cdot \theta} K_{n-1}){}_{\cdot \theta} K_n$.

Thanks to Lemma 12.6.27, there exists $k \geq 1$ such that u^k is an iterating factor of K_n or of $K_{1 \cdot \theta} K_2 \ldots {}_{\cdot \theta} K_{n-1}$, and we conclude with the induction hypothesis. $\square$

The next lemma characterizes $f_\theta(u^*)$ for any strongly connected word u.

Lemma 12.6.29 *Let θ be a semi-commutation relation defined over Σ and u be a strongly connected word of Σ^*.*

Then for each factor w of $f_\theta(u^*)$ such that there exists a letter y which satisfies $|w|_y > 2|u|_y \, Card(alph(u))$, we have $\forall x \in alph(u)$, $|w|_x \geq 1$.

Proof: Let x, y two different letters of $alph(u)$.

Since u is strongly connected, we can find letters of $alph(u)$:

$$a_0, a_1, \ldots, a_q, a_{q+1}, \ldots, a_p$$

such that

$$a_0 = a_p = y \text{ and } a_q = x,$$
$$\forall 0 \leq i, j \leq q, \text{ if } i \neq j, \ a_i \neq a_j,$$
$$\forall q \leq i, j \leq p, \text{ if } i \neq j, \ a_i \neq a_j,$$
$$\forall 1 \leq i \leq p, \ (a_{i-1}, a_i) \notin \theta$$

Let us set $v = a_0 a_1 \ldots a_q a_{q+1} \ldots a_p$. By construction, v satisfies the two following properties:

$$f_\theta(v) = \{v\} \text{ and } |v| < 2Card(alph(u))$$

On the other hand, let w be a factor of a word of $f_\theta(u^*)$ which satisfies: $|w|_y > 2|u|_y Card(alph(u))$. Let us set $N = 2Card(alph(u))$.

We have $w = w_1 y_j w_2 y_{j+N|u|_y} w_3$ where y_j denotes the jth occurrence of y in w and there exist $w_0, w_4 \in \Sigma^*$ and $i \in \mathbb{N}$ such that $w_0 w_1 y_j w_2 y_{j+N|u|_y} w_3 w_4 \in f_\theta(u^i)$. So $u^i = v_0 y_j v_1 u^{N-2} v_2 y_{j+N|u|_y} v_3$ and we conclude that v is a subword of $y_j v_1 u^{N-2} v_2 y_{j+N|u|_y}$ with $a_0 = y_j$ and $a_p = y_{j+N|u|_y}$.

Since $f_\theta(v) = \{v\}$, v is also a factor of $y_j w_2 y_{j+N|u|_y}$ and we get that x occurs in w. $\square$

We are now ready to prove the necessary condition (Condition 2) for a θ-closed language to be in $R_\theta(\Sigma^*)$.

Proposition 12.6.30 *Let θ be a semi-commutation relation defined over Σ. Let R be a θ-closed language of Σ^*. If $R \in R_\theta(\Sigma^*)$ then R satisfies the two following assertions:*

1. *The language $K = MAX_\theta(R)$ is in $Reg(\Sigma^*)$*

2. *Each iterating factor u of K such that $u^* \subseteq LEX$ is strongly connected.*

Proof: Proposition 12.6.16 enables us to state that if R is in $R_\theta(\Sigma^*)$, then it is in $Reg_\theta(\Sigma^*)$ and then we conclude with Lemma 12.6.23 that $MAX_\theta(R) \in Reg(\Sigma^*)$. So the first assertion is true.

We prove the second one by structural induction.

1. If $R = \emptyset$ or $R = \{\varepsilon\}$ or $R = \{a\}$ for some letter $a \in \Sigma$, the result is obvious.

2. If $R = R_1 \cup_\theta R_2$, where R_1, R_2 are two languages of $R_\theta(\Sigma^*)$, then for an iterating factor u of $MAX_\theta(R)$ with $u^* \subseteq LEX$, we can find two words $x, y \in \Sigma^*$ such that

$$xu^*y \subseteq MAX_\theta(R) \subseteq MAX_\theta(R_1) \cup MAX_\theta(R_2)$$

and these two languages are in $Reg(\Sigma^*)$.

So with Lemma 12.6.26, we can find a positive integer k such that u^k is an iterating factor of one of the two languages $MAX_\theta(R_1)$ or $MAX_\theta(R_2)$.

And $(u^k)^* \subseteq u^* \subseteq LEX$, so by induction hypothesis, we conclude that u^k and u are strongly connected.

3. If $R = R_1._\theta R_2$ where R_1, R_2 are two languages of $R_\theta(\Sigma^*)$, and if u is an iterating factor of $MAX_\theta(R)$ with $u^* \subseteq LEX$, we can find two words $x, y \in \Sigma^*$ such that
$$xu^*y \subseteq MAX_\theta(R) \subseteq MAX_\theta(R_1)._{\theta_s} MAX_\theta(R_2)$$

and these two θ_s-closed languages are in $Reg(\Sigma^*)$.

By Lemma 12.6.22 u is connected for θ_s and with Lemma 12.6.27, we get that u^k is an iterating factor of one of these languages, and just as above, we conclude that u is strongly connected.

4. If $R = R_1^{*_\theta}$, where R_1 is a language of $R_\theta(\Sigma^*)$ such that each of its words is strongly connected, then

$$K = MAX_\theta(R) \subseteq (MAX_\theta(R_1))^{*_{\theta_s}}$$

Let us set $K_1 = MAX_\theta(R_1)$. K_1 is a θ_s-closed language.

Let u be an iterating factor of K such that $u^* \subseteq LEX$. So we can find two words $x, y \in \Sigma^*$ such that $xu^*y \subseteq K$, and we know (Lemmas 12.6.18 and 12.6.22) that u is θ_s-connected.

We have to distinguish two cases:

(a) There exists a value N such that

$$xu^*y \subseteq f_{\theta_s}((K_1 \cup \{\varepsilon\})^N)$$

Then due to Lemma 12.6.28, we conclude that u^k is an iterating factor of K_1 and that, by induction hypothesis, u is strongly connected.

(b) If we cannot find such a value, it means that

$$\forall n \in \mathbb{N}, \exists p, q > n, \ xu^p y \in f_{\theta_s}((K_1 \setminus \{\varepsilon\})^q)$$

so we can find q words $u_1, u_2, ..., u_q$ of $K_1 \setminus \{\varepsilon\}$ such that

$$f_{\theta_s}(xu^p y) = f_{\theta_s}(u_1 u_2 ... u_q)$$

Since u is connected for θ_s, when choosing a sufficiently great value for n we obtain the following fact by applying Lemma 12.6.29:

(1) $\exists i, j, k \in \{1, 2, ..., q\}, \ \mathrm{alph}(u) = \mathrm{alph}(u_i ... u_j) = \mathrm{alph}(u_{j+1} ... u_k)$

Suppose that u is not strongly connected. Then there exist two subsets B, C of $\mathrm{alph}(u)$ such that $B \cup C = \mathrm{alph}(u)$, $B \times C \subseteq \theta$ but $C \times B \cap \theta = \emptyset$. As each word of K_1 is strongly connected ($K_1 \subseteq R_1$),

$$\forall i \in \{1, 2, ..., q\}, \ \mathrm{alph}(u_i) \subseteq B \ or \ \mathrm{alph}(u_i) \subseteq C$$

Let $u_{i_1}, u_{i_2}, ..., u_{i_l}$ be the words of $\{u_i, u_{i+1}, ..., u_k\}$ whose letters are in B ($i_1 < i_2 < ... < i_l$) and $u_{j_1}, u_{j_2}, ..., u_{j_m}$ the other ones ($\mathrm{alph}(u_{j_\alpha}) \subseteq C$). From (1), we are sure that $\{i_1, i_2, ..., i_l\} \cap \{i, ..., j\}$, $\{i_1, i_2, ..., i_l\} \cap \{j + 1, ..., k\}$, $\{j_1, j_2, ..., j_m\} \cap \{i, ..., j\}$ and $\{j_1, j_2, ..., j_m\} \cap \{j + 1, ..., k\}$ are all non-empty.
Then

$$u_i ... u_j ... u_k \ \neq \ u_{i_1} u_{i_2} ... u_{i_l} u_{j_1} u_{j_2} ... u_{j_m} \ and$$
$$u_i ... u_j ... u_k \ \in \ f_\theta(u_{i_1} u_{i_2} ... u_{i_l} u_{j_1} u_{j_2} ... u_{j_m})$$

but the converse is not true:

$$u_{i_1} u_{i_2} ... u_{i_l} u_{j_1} u_{j_2} ... u_{j_m} \notin f_\theta(u_i ... u_j ... u_k)$$

So $u_1 ... u_q$ is not in $MAX_\theta(R)$ since it has a factor which is not maximal, hence $xu^* y$ is not in $MAX_\theta(R)$ since $f_{\theta_s}(xu^* y) = f_{\theta_s}(u_1 u_2 ... u_q)$.
The hypothesis was impossible: u is strongly connected.

$\square$

When putting Proposition 12.6.24 , Proposition 12.6.30 and Lemma 12.6.25 together, we obtain

Proposition 12.6.31 *Let θ be a semi-commutation relation over Σ and $R \in \Sigma^*$ be a θ-closed language. Then the following three assertions are equivalent:*

1. $R \in R_\theta(\Sigma^*)$

2. (a) The language $K = Lex(MAX_\theta(R))$ is in $\mathrm{Reg}(\Sigma^*)$ and

(b) *Each iterating factor of K is strongly connected*

3.   (a) *The language* $K = MAX_\theta(R)$ *is in* $\text{Reg}(\Sigma^*)$ *and*

   (b) *Each iterating factor u of K such that* $u^* \subseteq LEX$ *is strongly connected.*

We are now able to state that

Theorem 12.6.32 *Let θ be a semi-commutation relation over Σ. We have $R_\theta(\Sigma^*) = \text{Reg}_\theta(\Sigma^*)$ if and only if θ is a symmetric relation.*

Proof: When θ is a partial commutation, the result is due to E. Ochmański [205].

In the other cases, it suffices to find a language of $\text{Reg}_\theta(\Sigma^*)$ which does not satisfy the properties announced in Proposition 12.6.31.

Since θ is not symmetric, there exist two letters a, b such that $(b, a) \in \theta$ and $(a, b) \notin \theta$. Let $R = (ba)^*a(a + b)^*$.

It is clear that $R = f_\theta(R)$. Note that $(a + b)^* \subseteq LEX$ and $MAX_\theta(R) = R \setminus R'$ where $R' = \{xaby|\ xbay \in R\}$. We get $MAX_\theta(R) = (ba)^*a(a^* + b + bb + bba + bbb^+a^*)$.

Now note that although ba is an iterating factor of $MAX_\theta(R)$, it is not strongly connected. $\square$

An other definition of $R_\theta(\Sigma^*)$

In the case of trace languages, E. Ochmański introduced a new kind of iteration: the concurrent iteration which is defined for each language (unlike the partially defined iteration which was previously introduced).

We are going to see that this operator can be extended in a quite natural way to θ-closed languages, and we will be able to defined a new sub family of recognizable θ-closed languages associated with quasi-rational expressions. Then we prove that this new family is equal to $R_\theta(\Sigma^*)$.

Definition 12.6.33 *Let Σ be an alphabet and θ be a semi-commutation relation defined over Σ.*

For $u \in \Sigma^*$, let $(\Sigma_1, \Sigma_2, ..., \Sigma_n)$ be the partition of the graph $(\text{alph}(u), \bar\theta)$ into strongly connected components. Then the strongly connected components of u is the set defined as

$$AS(\varepsilon) = \{\varepsilon\}$$

$AS(u) = \{\Pi_{\Sigma_i}(u)|\ \Sigma_i$ *is a strongly connected component of* $(\text{alph}(u), \bar\theta)\}$ *if* $u \neq \varepsilon$

and, for any language $R \subseteq \Sigma^*$,

$$AS(R) = \bigcup_{u \in R} AS(u)$$

Then the "concurrent iteration" (co$_\theta$-iteration in the sequel) of a language R: R^{co_θ} is defined by

$$R^{co_\theta} = f_\theta((AS(R))^*)$$

Definition 12.6.34 $R'_\theta(\Sigma^*)$ *denotes the least family containing elementary subsets of Σ^* and closed under union, θ-concatenation and co_θ-iteration.*

E. Ochmański proved that in the symmetric case $R_\theta(\Sigma^*) = R'_\theta(\Sigma^*)$.

This result remains true in the non-symmetric case, but it is not immediate. It is clear that $R_\theta(\Sigma^*) \subseteq R'_\theta(\Sigma^*)$. For the converse, the difficulty is to prove that if a language R is in $R_\theta(\Sigma^*)$ then $AS(R)$ is also in $R_\theta(\Sigma^*)$, and the characterization of $R_\theta(\Sigma^*)$ obtained previously will be useful.

First of all we give some properties of the operator AS.

Lemma 12.6.35 *Let θ be a semi-commutation relation over Σ, u be a word of Σ^* and $(\Sigma_1, \Sigma_2, ..., \Sigma_n)$ be the strongly connected components of $(\mathrm{alph}(u), \bar\theta)$.*
There exist permutations $(i_1, i_2, ..., i_n)$ and $(k_1, k_2, ..., k_n)$ of $\{1, 2, ..., n\}$ such that

1. $\Pi_{\Sigma_{i_1}}(u)\Pi_{\Sigma_{i_2}}(u)...\Pi_{\Sigma_{i_n}}(u) \in f_\theta(u)$

2. $u \in f_\theta(\Pi_{\Sigma_{k_1}}(u)\Pi_{\Sigma_{k_2}}(u)...\Pi_{\Sigma_{k_n}}(u))$

Proof: We make inductions on n, the number of strongly connected components of $(\mathrm{alph}(u), \bar\theta)$.

1. If $n = 1$, the result is obvious.

   If $n > 1$, then we can find an i such that $\Sigma_i \times \bar\Sigma_i \subseteq \theta$. It means that $\Pi_{\bar\Sigma_i}(u)\Pi_{\Sigma_i}(u) \in f_\theta(u)$.

   The restriction of the non-commutation graph to $\mathrm{alph}(\Pi_{\bar\Sigma_i}(u))$ has $n - 1$ strongly connected components $(\Sigma_1, \Sigma_2, .., \Sigma_{i-1}, \Sigma_{i+1}, ..., \Sigma_n)$, so by induction hypothesis, we can find a permutation $(j_1, j_2, ..., j_{n-1})$ of $\{1, 2, ..., n\} \setminus \{i\}$ such that

$$\Pi_{\Sigma_{j_1}}(u)\Pi_{\Sigma_{j_2}}(u)...\Pi_{\Sigma_{j_{n-1}}}(u) \in f_\theta(\Pi_{\bar\Sigma_i}(u))$$

   and we get the result.

2. As previously the case $n = 1$ is obvious.

   If $n > 1$, there exists k such that $\bar\Sigma_k \times \Sigma_k \subseteq \theta$, this implies that $u \in f_\theta(\Pi_{\Sigma_k}(u)\Pi_{\bar\Sigma_k}(u))$. Now it suffices to apply the induction hypothesis to $\Pi_{\bar\Sigma_k}(u)$ in the same way that in the proof of -1-.

$\square$

We deduce the two following corollaries:

Corollary 12.6.36 *Let θ be a semi-commutation defined on Σ and u be a word of Σ^*. Let P be the number of strongly connected components of $(\mathrm{alph}(u), \bar\theta)$. Then $u \in f_\theta((AS(u))^P)$*

Corollary 12.6.37 *Let θ be a semi-commutation defined over Σ. There exists a constant N bounded by the cardinality of Σ such that*

$$\forall u \in \Sigma^*, \ u \in f_\theta((AS(u) \cup \{\varepsilon\})^N)$$

Lemma 12.6.38 *Let θ be a semi-commutation relation on Σ and $u \in \Sigma^*$, then*

$$f_\theta(AS(u)) = AS(f_\theta(u))$$

Proof:

Since $\forall Y \subseteq \Sigma$, $\Pi_Y(f_\theta(u)) \subseteq f_\theta(\Pi_Y(u))$, it is clear that $AS(f_\theta(u)) \subseteq f_\theta(AS(u))$. For the converse inclusion, let w be a word of $f_\theta(AS(u))$. Then we can find a strongly connected component Y of $(\text{alph}(u), \bar\theta)$ such that $w \in f_\theta(\Pi_Y(u))$, and thanks to the previous lemma, we can write $\Pi_{\Sigma_{i_1}}(u)\Pi_{\Sigma_{i_2}}(u)...\Pi_{\Sigma_{i_n}}(u) \in f_\theta(u)$ where $(\Sigma_{i_1}, \Sigma_{i_2}, ...\Sigma_{i_n})$ are the ordered strongly connected components of $(\text{alph}(u), \bar\theta)$. If $Y = \Sigma_{i_k}$, then $u' = \Pi_{\Sigma_{i_1}}(u)...\Pi_{\Sigma_{i_{k-1}}}(u)\ w\ \Pi_{\Sigma_{i_{k+1}}}(u)...\Pi_{\Sigma_{i_n}}(u)$ belongs to $f_\theta(\Pi_{\Sigma_{i_1}}(u)\Pi_{\Sigma_{i_2}}(u)...\Pi_{\Sigma_{i_n}}(u))$ which is included in $f_\theta(u)$. So $w = \Pi_Y(u')$ with $u' \in f_\theta(u)$ and $w \in AS(f_\theta(u))$. □

We prove now that the function AS defined on Σ^* is a rational transduction.

Lemma 12.6.39 *Let θ be a semi-commutation relation defined over Σ.*
The function AS defined on Σ^* by:

$$AS(\varepsilon) = \{\varepsilon\} \text{ and for } u \neq \varepsilon,$$
$$AS(u) = \{\Pi_{\Sigma_i}(u)|\ \Sigma_i \text{ is a strongly connected component of } (\text{alph}(u), \bar\theta)\}$$

is a rational transduction.

Proof: If Y is a non-empty subset of Σ and if Σ_i is a strongly connected component of $(Y, \bar\theta)$, let us define the rational transduction $\tau_{Y,\Sigma_i} = (Id_Y, \cap R_Y, \Pi_{\Sigma_i})$, where Id_Y is the identity on Y, Π_{Σ_i} is the projection over the subalphabet Σ_i of Y and R_Y is the rational language of words $u \in \Sigma^*$ such that $\text{alph}(u) = Y$:

$$R_Y = \bigcap_{x \in Y} Y^*xY^*$$

If $Y = \emptyset$, let us set $\tau_{\emptyset, \emptyset}(u) = \{\varepsilon\}$ if and only if $u = \varepsilon$.

It may be seen that for any word $u \in \Sigma^*$, $\tau_{Y,\Sigma_i}(u) = \Pi_{\Sigma_i}(u)$ if $\text{alph}(u) = Y$, and $\tau_{Y,\Sigma_i}(u) = \emptyset$ if not. So let us define the rational transduction τ as the finite union of τ_{Y,Σ_i} where $Y \subseteq \Sigma$ and Σ_i is a strongly connected component of $(Y, \bar\theta)$. It is clear that $AS(u) = \tau(u)$ □

Lemma 12.6.40 *Let θ be a semi-commutation relation defined over Σ.*
If $R \subseteq \Sigma^*$ is in $\text{Reg}_\theta(\Sigma^*)$, $AS(R)$ is also in $\text{Reg}_\theta(\Sigma^*)$.

Proof: From Lemma 12.6.38, $f_\theta(AS(R)) = AS(f_\theta(R)) = AS(R)$ so $AS(R)$ is a θ-closed language, and directly from Lemma 12.6.39, we get $AS(R)$ is a recognizable set. □

Now we prove the same kind of result for the family $R_\theta(\Sigma^*)$.

Lemma 12.6.41 *Let θ be a semi-commutation relation over Σ.*

$$R \in R_\theta(\Sigma^*) \Longrightarrow AS(R) \in R_\theta(\Sigma^*)$$

Proof: We use the second necessary and sufficient condition for a θ-closed language to be in $R_\theta(\Sigma^*)$ obtained in Proposition 12.6.31.

From the previous lemma, we know that $AS(R) \in \text{Reg}_\theta(\Sigma^*)$, so $MAX_\theta(AS(R))$ is in $\text{Reg}(\Sigma^*)$ (Lemma 12.6.23).

We prove now that each iterating factor u of $MAX_\theta(AS(R))$ such that $u^* \subseteq LEX$ is strongly connected, with a structural induction on R.

1. If R is an elementary subset of Σ^*, the result is obvious.

2. If $R = R_1 \cup R_2$ with $R_1, R_2 \in R_\theta(\Sigma^*)$, then

$$MAX_\theta(AS(R)) = MAX_\theta(AS(R_1) \cup AS(R_2))$$

which is included in $MAX_\theta(AS(R_1)) \cup MAX_\theta(AS(R_2))$. From Lemma 12.6.26, we can find $k > 0$ and $i \in \{1, 2\}$ such that u^k is an iterating factor of $MAX_\theta(AS(R_i))$. So, when using the induction hypothesis, we deduce that u is strongly connected.

3. If $R = R_1._\theta R_2$ with $R_1, R_2 \in R_\theta(\Sigma^*)$:

For any word w of $AS(R)$ we can find two words $u_1 \in R_1$, $u_2 \in R_2$ and a strongly connected component B of $(\text{alph}(u_1 u_2), \bar{\theta})$ such that

$$\begin{aligned} w \quad &\in \quad \Pi_B(f_\theta(u_1 u_2)) \\ &\subseteq \quad f_\theta(\Pi_B(u_1)\Pi_B(u_2)) \end{aligned}$$

It is clear that for $i \in \{1, 2\}$, $B \cap \text{alph}(u_i)$ is an union of strongly connected components of $(\text{alph}(u_i), \bar{\theta})$ and $AS(\Pi_B(u_i)) \subseteq AS(u_i) \cup \{\varepsilon\}$, so we have

$$\begin{aligned} w \quad &\in \quad f_\theta(\Pi_B(u_1)\Pi_B(u_2)) \\ &\subseteq \quad f_\theta(f_\theta((AS(u_1) \cup \{\varepsilon\})^N)f_\theta((AS(u_2) \cup \{\varepsilon\})^N)) \text{ (Corollary 12.6.37)} \\ &\subseteq \quad f_\theta(f_\theta((AS(R_1) \cup \{\varepsilon\})^N)f_\theta((AS(R_2) \cup \{\varepsilon\})^N)) \\ &= \quad f_\theta((AS(R_1) \cup \{\varepsilon\})^N)._\theta f_\theta((AS(R_2) \cup \{\varepsilon\})^N) \end{aligned}$$

Let us set for $i = 1, 2$, $R_i' = R_i \cup \{\varepsilon\}$. Then $AS(R_1._\theta R_2)$ is a subset of $f_\theta((AS(R_1'))^N)._\theta f_\theta(AS(R_2'))^N)$ and $MAX_\theta(AS(R_1._\theta R_2))$ is a subset of $MAX_\theta(f_\theta((AS(R_1'))^N)._\theta f_\theta((AS(R_2'))^N))$ which is included in

$$MAX_\theta(f_\theta((AS(R_1'))^N))._{\theta_s} MAX_\theta(f_\theta((AS(R_2'))^N))$$

Hence, if u is an iterating factor of $MAX_\theta(AS(R_1._\theta R_2))$ such that $u^* \subseteq LEX$ (which implies that u is connected for θ_s), using Lemma 12.6.27, we get: for some k, u^k is an iterating factor of $MAX_\theta(f_\theta((AS(R_1'))^N))$ or of $MAX_\theta(f_\theta((AS(R_2'))^N))$. Thanks to Lemma 12.6.38 we have for $i \in \{1,2\}$

$$MAX_\theta(f_\theta((AS(R_i'))^N)) \subseteq MAX_\theta(AS(R_i')._\theta AS(R_i')...._\theta AS(R_i'))$$

which is included in $MAX_\theta(AS(R_i'))._{\theta_s} MAX_\theta(AS(R_i'))...._{\theta_s} MAX_\theta(AS(R_i'))$. Then from Lemma 12.6.28, we deduce that there exists $i \in \{1,2\}$ such that u^k is an iterating factor of $MAX_\theta(AS(R_i))$. And by induction hypothesis, we conclude that u is strongly connected.

4. If $R = R_1^{*\theta}$ with $R_1 \in R_\theta(\Sigma^*)$ where each word of R_1 is strongly connected, then $AS(R_1) = R_1$ and $AS(R) \subseteq R$. So u is an iterating factor of $MAX_\theta(R)$ with $u^* \subseteq LEX$ and since $R \in R_\theta(\Sigma^*)$, u is strongly connected (necessary condition of Proposition 12.6.31). Then we deduce from Proposition 12.6.31 that $AS(R)$ is in $R_\theta(\Sigma^*)$.

$\square$

And we finish with the following result:

Proposition 12.6.42 *If θ is a semi-commutation relation defined over the alphabet Σ,*

$$R_\theta(\Sigma^*) = R_\theta'(\Sigma^*)$$

Proof:

The inclusion $R_\theta(\Sigma^*) \subseteq R_\theta'(\Sigma^*)$ is clear.

We prove the reverse inclusion with an induction.

Let R be a language of $R_\theta'(\Sigma^*)$.

1. If R is an elementary subset of Σ^*, it is also in $R_\theta(\Sigma^*)$.

2. If R is the union or the θ-concatenation of two languages R_1, R_2 of $R_\theta'(\Sigma^*)$, then by induction hypothesis R_1 and R_2 are in $R_\theta(\Sigma^*)$ and so is R.

3. If $R = R_1^{co_\theta}$ for some language R_1 of $R_\theta'(\Sigma^*)$, then by induction hypothesis, $R_1 \in R_\theta(\Sigma^*)$.

   And by definition $R = f_\theta((AS(R_1))^*)$.

   It is clear that all words of $AS(R_1)$ are strongly connected, so it remains to prove that $AS(R_1)$ is in $R_\theta(\Sigma^*)$, and it is true with Lemma 12.6.41.

$\square$

12.7   Algebraic Rational Functions

In section 12.6, we have tried to see when our new operators on languages, the semi-commutation functions, preserve regularity. Clearly, for any semi-commutation function f_θ such that θ is not empty, there exist regular languages such that their image by f_θ is not regular. A natural extension is to examine the case where the condition is to stay in the context free languages family. More precisely, in this section, we answer to the following question: *If f_θ is a semi-commutation function, is it decidable to know whether the image of any regular language by f_θ is algebraic?* We name such functions *algebraic rational functions* and we give a decidable characterization of semi-commutation functions which are algebraic rational .

Definition 12.7.1 *A semi-commutation function f defined on an alphabet Σ is algebraic rational if and only if for any regular language R included in Σ^*, the language $f(R)$ is algebraic.*

The main result is the following characterization of algebraic rational functions: A semi-commutation function f defined on an alphabet Σ is algebraic rational if and only if the semi-commutation graph of f has no subgraph isomorphic to •→•→•←•→•→• or •→•→•→• The proof of this result is based on an induction on the cardinality of the alphabet Σ. Clearly, when Σ contains only one letter, the only possible semi-commutation θ on Σ is the empty relation. Then, its commutation graph cannot contain a subgraph isomorphic to •→•→•←•→•→• or •→•→•→• . The corresponding semi-commutation function is the identity which is algebraic rational. To give an idea of what happens in the general case, we will also examine the case of a two-letter alphabet.

12.7.1 Over a Two-Letter Alphabet

Let $\Sigma = \{a, b\}$. As in the case of a one-letter alphabet, we have to verify that each semi-commutation function defined on Σ is algebraic rational . There are four semi-commutation functions on a two-letter alphabet: the identity (no commutation at all), com (the total commutation), $f_{ab\to ba}$ associated to the rule $ab \to ba$, and symmetrically $f_{ba\to ab}$.

At first, we give a necessary and sufficient condition for a word w' to be in the image of a word w of Σ^* by $f_{ab\to ba}$ (the proof of this result is in [40]):

Lemma 12.7.2 *Let w and w' be two words of Σ^*. $w' \in f_{ab\to ba}(w)$ if and only if $w' \in \text{com}(w)$ and $\forall(u,v) \in LF(w) \times LF(w'), |u| = |v| \implies |u|_b \le |v|_b$.*

Then we can state:

Proposition 12.7.3 *Any semi-commutation function defined on $\Sigma = \{a, b\}$ is algebraic rational .*

Proof:

If f is the identity, the result is obvious: $f(R) = R \in \text{Rat} \subseteq \text{Alg}$. If $f = \text{com}$, M.Latteux proved that: $\forall R \in \text{Rat}, \text{com}(R) \in \text{Ocl}$ (see [172]). So we have to establish that $f_{ab\to ba}(R)$ is context-free, for each regular language R. The proof is symmetric for $f_{ba\to ab}$. Let h be the morphism defined on $\{a, b, \bar{b}\}$ by $h(a) = a, h(b) = b, h(\bar{b}) = \varepsilon$ and let g be the morphism defined on the same alphabet by $g(a) = a, g(b) =$

$\varepsilon, g(\bar{b}) = b$. We have: $\forall u \in \Sigma^*, f(u) = g(h^{-1}(u) \cap (D_1'^*(\bar{b}, b) \sqcup a^*))$. Indeed, set $u' \in f(u)$ and let us denote by $\bar{u}'$ the word u' where each occurrence of the letter b has been marked. ($\bar{u}' = m(u')$ with $m : \{a, b\} \longmapsto \{a, \bar{b}\}, m(a) = a, m(b) = \bar{b}$). Set $v = u \sqcap \bar{u}' \cap (\bar{b}^* b^* a)^*$. Thanks to Lemma 12.7.2, it is clear that $\Pi_{\{b, \bar{b}\}}(v) \in D_1'^*(\bar{b}, b)$ so $v \in h^{-1}(u) \cap D_1'^*(\bar{b}, b) \sqcup a^*$ and $u' = g(v)$. On the other hand, if $u' \in h^{-1}(u) \cap (D_1'^*(\bar{b}, b) \sqcup a^*)$ then each left factor α of $LF(u')$ satisfies: $|\alpha|_{\bar{b}} \geq |\alpha|_b$. So $g(u') \in f(\Pi_{\{a, b\}}(u')) = f(u)$. As $D_1'^*(\bar{b}, b) \in$ Ocl which is a family closed under regular transduction, each regular language has its image by f in Ocl, so f is algebraic rational .

$\square$

Remark 12.7.4 We have seen in section 12.6 (more precisely in subsection 12.6.3) the differences between semi-commutations and partial commutations concerning regularity. The two following counter-examples show the same kind of difference.

1. $f_{ab \to ba}(\text{Alg}) \not\subseteq \text{Alg}$

   If L is an algebraic language, there is a regular language R such that $\text{com}(L) = \text{com}(R)$ (see [172]) so $\text{com}(L)$ is an algebraic language . However, $f_{ab \to ba}(L)$ is not always context-free: Set $L = \{(ba)^n b^n \mid n \geq 0\}$. $L \in \text{Alg}$, but $f_{ab \to ba}(L) \cap b^* a^* b^* = \{b^{n+k} a^n b^{n-k} \mid n \geq k \geq 0\} = L_1$. And $LF(b^* L_1) = \{b^n a^p b^q \mid n \geq p \geq q \geq 0\} \notin \text{Alg}$.

2. $f_{ab \to ba}(\text{Rat})$ is not closed under intersection

   Let $L_1 = (aab)^*$ and $L_2 = (ab)^* a^*$. Let us consider $L = f_{ab \to ba}(L_1) \cap f_{ab \to ba}(L_2)$. Clearly, $L = f_{ab \to ba}(\{(ab)^n a^n, n \geq 0\})$, and $L \cap b^* a^* ba^* = \{b^{n-1} a^{n-k} b a^{n+k} \mid n \geq k \geq 0\}$. Then $L \notin \text{Alg}$ and, as $f_{ab \to ba}$ is algebraic rational, it is not possible to find a regular language R in $(a + b)^*$ such that $L = f_{ab \to ba}(R)$.

12.7.2   A Decidable Criterion

Let us now suppose that the cardinality of the alphabet Σ is greater than 2.

Definition 12.7.5 *Let f be a semi-commutation function defined on the alphabet Σ. We say that f satisfies the (C) condition if the semi-commutation graph of f has no subgraph isomorphic to* •──•◄──•─•──•► *or* •─•─•─•►

Proposition 12.7.6 *If a semi-commutation function is algebraic rational then it satisfies the (C) condition .*

Proof:

Let f be the semi-commutation function defined on $\Sigma = \{a, b, c\}$ by the commutation graph shown in Fig. 12.4

Set $R = (abc)^*$. Then

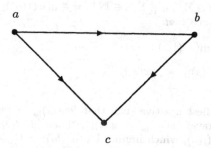

Figure 12.4:

$$f(R) \cap c^*b^*a^* = \{c^n b^n a^n \mid n \in \mathbb{N}\} \notin \text{Alg}$$

Let g be the function defined on $\{a, b, c, d\}$ by the commutation graph shown in Fig. 12.5

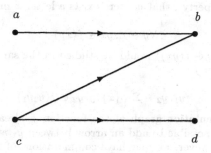

Figure 12.5:

Set $R' = (cd)^*(ab)^*$. Then

$$g(R') \cap d^*b^*c^*a^* = \{d^n b^p c^n a^p, \ n, p \in \mathbb{N}\} \notin \text{Alg}$$

A function which does not satisfy the (C) condition would never be algebraic rational .

□

We shall now prove the converse of this proposition by induction on the cardinality of the alphabet Σ. The following lemma will be useful.

Notation: For $w \in \Sigma^*$, and $t \in \mathbb{N}^+$, $w(t)$ denotes the left factor of length t of the word w.

Lemma 12.7.7 *Let $u \in \Sigma^+$, $a \notin \Sigma$, $i \in \mathbb{N}^+$, $w \in a(u \sqcup\!\sqcup a^i)$, $w' \in u \sqcup\!\sqcup a^i a^+$. Then we can find $t_0 \in \mathbb{N}^+$ such that:*

1. $\mathrm{com}(w(t_0)) = \mathrm{com}(w'(t_0))$

2. $\forall\, 0 < s < t_0, \; |w'(s)|_a \; < \; |w(s)|_a$

Proof:

Let t_0 be the smallest positive such that $|w'(t_0)|_a \geq |w(t_0)|_a$. This t_0 exists since, if $t = |w|$, we have: $|w'(t)|_a \geq |w(t)|_a$. Then $|w'(t_0)|_a = |w(t_0)|_a$ and thus $|\Pi_\Sigma(w'(t_0))| = |\Pi_\Sigma(w(t_0))|$ which implies $\Pi_\Sigma(w'(t_0)) = \Pi_\Sigma(w(t_0))$ since these two words are left factors of u. Therefore $\mathrm{com}(w(t_0)) = \mathrm{com}(w'(t_0))$. And $\forall 0 < s < t_0, |w'(s)|_a < |w(s)|_a$ is satisfied because of the definition of t_0.

$\square$

In order to prove the converse of proposition 12.7.6, we will consider two cases:

Definition 12.7.8 *We say that a semi-commutation function f defined on Σ satisfies (P) property if and only if there exists a letter x in Σ such that for each letter y in Σ, $yx \in f(xy)$ or such that for each letter y in Σ, $xy \in f(yx)$.*

So, let f be a semi-commutation function defined on Σ which satisfies both (C) condition and (P) property , that is there exists a letter x in Σ such that:

$$\forall y \in \Sigma, yx \in f(xy)$$

The other case ($xy \in f(yx)$) would be studied in the same way. Let us explain what does the function f:

$$\forall y_1, y_2 \in \Sigma \setminus \{x\}, y_1 y_2 \notin f(y_2 y_1)$$

Because the commutation graph of the function f already contains $y_1 \longleftarrow x$ and $x \longrightarrow y_2$, it is impossible to add an arrow between y_1 and y_2, since f satisfies the (C) condition. However, we may have commutations of the kind $yx \longrightarrow xy$ for some letters y of $\Sigma \setminus \{x\}$. Thus the alphabet Σ may be partition-ned into three disjoint subsets: $\Sigma = \Sigma_1 \cup \Sigma_2 \cup \{x\}$, with $\Sigma_1 = \{y \in \Sigma \setminus \{x\}, \; xy \in f(yx)\}$, $\Sigma_2 = \{y \in \Sigma, \; xy \notin f(yx)\}$. It means that, in a word $w \in \Sigma^*$, the occurrences of the letter x are going to move on left or right, in each factor of w which is in Σ_1^*, but an occurrence of x may move over a letter of Σ_2 only from left to right. When adding in w the new positions of marked occurrences of the letter x ($\bar{x}$ instead of x), we get factors in this new word which are members of $D_1^*(x, \bar{x}) \sqcup\!\sqcup \Sigma_1^*$ and factors which are members of $D_1'^*(x, \bar{x}) \sqcup\!\sqcup (\Sigma_1 \cup \Sigma_2)^*$. It is what is formalized in the following lemma

Notation: If w is a word of Σ^*, $\bar{w}$ denotes the image of w by the morphism which marks the letter x: $m : \Sigma \longmapsto \Sigma \cup \{\bar{x}\}$, $m(x) = \bar{x}$, and $\forall y \in \Sigma \setminus \{x\}, m(y) = y$.

Lemma 12.7.9 *Let f be a semi-commutation function defined on Σ, which satisfies the (C) condition and for which there exists a letter x such that $\forall y \in \Sigma, yx \in f(xy)$. Let $u \in \Sigma^*$, and $u' \in f(u)$. Then we can find a word v in $u \sqcap \bar{u}'$ such that*

$$v \in ((D_1^*(x,\bar{x}) \sqcup \Sigma_1^*)(D_1'^*(x,\bar{x}) \sqcup (\Sigma_1 \cup \Sigma_2)^*))^*$$

where $\Sigma_1 = \{y \in \setminus\{x\}, xy \in f(yx)\}$ *and* $\Sigma_2 = \{y \in \Sigma, xy \notin f(yx)\}$.

Proof: We proceed by induction on the length of the word u.

1. If $|u| = 0$, the property is clearly true.

2. If $|u| > 0$, $\Pi_{\Sigma_1 \cup \Sigma_2}(u) = \Pi_{\Sigma_1 \cup \Sigma_2}(u')$ is always true because no letter of $\Sigma_1 \cup \Sigma_2$ can commute one with the other.

   On the other hand, we may assume that the first letters of u and u' are different:

   - If u and u' begin with a same letter of $\Sigma_1 \cup \Sigma_2$, we apply the induction hypothesis to the words u and u' where the first letter has been erased.
   - If u and u' begin with the letter x, we have $u = xw$, $u' = xw'$, and, with the induction hypothesis, we can find a word $v_1 \in w \sqcap w'$ in $((D_1^*(x,\bar{x}) \sqcup \Sigma_1^*)(D_1'^*(x,\bar{x}) \sqcup (\Sigma_1 \cup \Sigma_2)^*))^*$ and then, the word $x\bar{x}v_1$ is in $u \sqcap \bar{u}' \cap ((D_1^*(x,\bar{x}) \sqcup \Sigma_1^*)(D_1'^*(x,\bar{x}) \sqcup (\Sigma_1 \cup \Sigma_2)^*))^*$.

   We may also assume that $|u|_{\Sigma_2} \neq 0$: If $|u|_{\Sigma_2} = 0$, $f(u) = \Pi_{\Sigma_1}(u) \sqcup x^i$, with $i = |u|_x$ and thus $u \sqcap \bar{u}' \subseteq D_1^*(x,\bar{x}) \sqcup \Sigma_1^*$.

   So u or u' begins with x.

   - The first letter of u' is x.

     Then the first letter of u belongs to Σ_1: if u begins with a letter of Σ_2, so does u'. It follows that: $u = u_1 c u_2$, $u' = u_1' c u_2'$, $|u_1|_{\Sigma_2} = |u_1'|_{\Sigma_2} = 0$, $c \in \Sigma_2$, and we have $\Pi_{\Sigma_1}(u_1) = \Pi_{\Sigma_1}(u_1')$ and $|u_1|_x \geq |u_1'|_x$ because $xc \notin f(cx)$. Then, $u_1 \in \Pi_{\Sigma_1}(u_1) \sqcup x^j$, $u_1' \in x\Pi_{\Sigma_1}(u_1) \sqcup x^i$, with $j = |u_1|_x$, $i + 1 = |u_1'|_x$, $j \geq i + 1$. From Lemma 12.7.7 there exist decompositions: $u_1 = v_1 w_1$, $u_1' = v_1' w_1'$, with $v_1 \neq \varepsilon$ and $\text{com}(v_1) = \text{com}(v_1')$, thus $v_1 \sqcap \bar{v}_1' \cap D_1^*(x,\bar{x}) \sqcup \Sigma_1^* \neq \emptyset$. Then

     $$(v_1 \sqcap \bar{v}_1')(w_1 c u_2 \sqcap \bar{w}_1' c \bar{u}_2') \subseteq u \sqcap \bar{u}'$$

     Moreover, $v_1' w_1' c u_2' \in f(v_1 w_1 c u_2)$ and $\text{com}(v_1) = \text{com}(v_1')$ imply $w_1' c u_2' \in f(w_1 c u_2)$ (see [40]). Then we may apply the induction hypothesis to $w_1 c u_2$, which gives the result.

   - The first letter of u is x.

     We may then write: $u \in x(\Pi_{\Sigma_1 \cup \Sigma_2}(u) \sqcup x^i)$, $u' \in \Pi_{\Sigma_1 \cup \Sigma_2}(u') \sqcup x^j$, with $j = i + 1 = |u|_x$. From Lemma 12.7.7, it follows: $u = w_1 w_2$, $u' = w_1' w_2'$, with $w_1 \neq \varepsilon$, $\text{com}(w_1) = \text{com}(w_1')$ and thus $w_2' \in f(w_2)$. Let $\{v\} = w_1 \sqcap \bar{w}_1' \cap (x^*\bar{x}^*(\Sigma_1 \cup \Sigma_2))^*$. Then, clearly, $v \in D_1'^*(x,\bar{x}) \sqcup (\Sigma_1 \cup \Sigma_2)^*$, because of property 2 of Lemma 12.7.7, and $v(w_2 \sqcap \bar{w}_2') \subseteq u \sqcap \bar{u}'$. Then from the induction hypothesis on w_2, we get the result. $\square$

Then we can state:

Proposition 12.7.10 *Let f be a semi-commutation function defined on the alphabet Σ, which satisfies the (C) condition and for which there exists a letter x such that $\forall y \in \Sigma, yx \in f(xy)$. Then, we can find morphisms h and g and two subsets of Σ, Σ_1 and Σ_2 such that*

$$\forall u \in \Sigma^*, f(u) = g(h^{-1}(u) \cap ((D_1^*(x, \bar{x}) \sqcup \Sigma_1^*)(D_1'^*(x, \bar{x}) \sqcup (\Sigma_1 \cup \Sigma_2)^*))^*)$$

So f is algebraic rational .

Proof:

Set $\Sigma_1 = \{y \in \Sigma \setminus \{x\}, xy \in f(yx)\}$ and $\Sigma_2 = \Sigma \setminus (\Sigma_1 \cup \{x\})$. Let h and g be the morphisms defined on $\Sigma \cup \{\bar{x}\}$ by $\forall y \in \Sigma_1 \cup \Sigma_2$, $h(y) = y$, $g(y) = y$; $h(x) = x$, $g(x) = \varepsilon$; $h(\bar{x}) = \varepsilon$, $g(\bar{x}) = x$. Set $L = (D_1^*(x, \bar{x}) \sqcup \Sigma_1^*)(D_1'^*(x, \bar{x}) \sqcup (\Sigma_1 \cup \Sigma_2)^*)$. We prove that:

$$\forall u \in \Sigma^*, f(u) = g(h^{-1}(u) \cap L^*).$$

Let $u' \in f(u)$. It is clear that $u \sqcap \bar{u}' \subseteq h^{-1}(u)$ and according to Lemma 12.7.9, we can find a word $v \in u \sqcap \bar{u}' \cap L^*$; on the other hand, $g(v) = u'$. Consequently

$$u' \in g(h^{-1}(u) \cap ((D_1^*(x, \bar{x}) \sqcup \Sigma_1^*)(D_1'^*(x, \bar{x}) \sqcup (\Sigma_1 \cup \Sigma_2)^*))^*).$$

Conversely, let $u' \in h^{-1}(u) \cap L^*$. We can find a number p such that $u' \in h^{-1}(u) \cap L^p$. We proceed by induction on p: If $p = 0$, $u' = \varepsilon$ so $u = \varepsilon$ and $g(u') \in f(u)$. If $p \geq 1$, $u' \in h^{-1}(u) \cap LL^{p-1}$. Thus $u' = u_1'u_2'v'$ where $u_1' \in D_1^*(x, \bar{x}) \sqcup \Sigma_1^*$, $u_2' \in D_1'^*(x, \bar{x}) \sqcup (\Sigma_1 \cup \Sigma_2)^*$ and $v' \in L^{p-1}$.

So we can write $u = u_1u_2v$ where $u_1 = \Pi_\Sigma(u_1')$, $u_2 = \Pi_\Sigma(u_2')$, and $v = \Pi_\Sigma(v')$. Moreover, $g(u_1') \in f(u_1)$ (only with commutations $xy \leftrightarrow yx, y \in \Sigma_1$) since $\Pi_{\Sigma_1}(u_1') = \Pi_{\Sigma_1}(u_1)$ and $|u_1'|_x = |u_1|_x = |u_1'|_{\bar{x}}$. In the same way, $g(u_2') \in f(u_2)$: it's clear that $\text{com}(g(u_2')) = \text{com}(f(u_2))$ and $\forall 0 < t < |g(u_2')|, |g(u_2')(t)|_x \geq |g(u_2)(t)|_x$. And by induction hypothesis, $g(v') \in f(v)$ $(v' \in h^{-1}(u) \cap L^{p-1})$. Thus

$$g(u') = g(u_1')g(u_2')g(v') \in f(u_1)f(u_2)f(v) \subseteq f(u_1u_2v) = f(u).$$

$\square$

For a given semi-commutation function f, if no letter may commute with each of the others, shuffles will be local. So, to get the image of a word by f, it is sufficient to make shuffles on factors which are defined on a smaller alphabet. This motivates the following lemma:

Lemma 12.7.11 *Let f be a semi-commutation function defined on Σ, which satisfies (C) condition but not (P) property. Then, for any word u of Σ^*, for any word v of $f(u)$, we can find decompositions $u = u_1u_2$ and $v = v_1v_2$ with $u_1 \neq \varepsilon$, $\text{alph}(u_1) \subsetneq \Sigma$ and $v_1 \in f(u_1)$.*

Proof: If $alph(u) \subsetneq \Sigma$, the result is obvious. If not, set $u = au', v = dv', a \in \Sigma, d \in \Sigma$. If $a = d$, we can choose $u_1 = v_1 = a$, else we set $D = \{z \in \Sigma \setminus \{a\} \mid za \in f(az)\}$, and $\Sigma' = \Sigma \setminus (D \cup \{a\})$. Then $d \in D$, so $D \neq \emptyset$; $\Sigma' \neq \emptyset$ because f does not satisfy (P) property; if z_1 and z_2 are in D, the commutation graph of f contains a subgraph $z_1 \longleftarrow a \longrightarrow z_2$, thus there is no commutation between z_1 and z_2 because f satisfies (C) condition. We shall distinguish two cases:

1. $\forall y \in \Sigma', \forall z \in D, zy \notin f(yz)$

   Then, let us set $u = awyu'', v = dw'y'v''$ with $w, w' \in (D \cup \{a\})^*$ and $y, y' \in \Sigma'$. No occurrence of the letter a in the word aw can over-step the occurrence of the letter y, because for any letter x in Σ', $xa \notin f(ax)$. So we have $|aw|_a \leq |w'|_a$ then $|w'|_a > |w|_a$. On the other hand, for two letters $(d_1, y_1) \in D \times \Sigma'$, it is possible to have $y_1 d_1 \in f(d_1 y_1)$, but since $d_1 y_1 \notin f(y_1 d_1)$, we get $\Pi_D(dw') \in LF(\Pi_D(w))$. Then $u = u'yu''$ with $u' \in a(\Pi_D(dw') \sqcup a^i)(w'' \sqcup a^{i'})$ and $v = v'y'v''$ with $v' \in \Pi_D(dw') \sqcup a^j$, where $j = |w'|_a, i + i' = |w|_a$, so $j > i$. From Lemma 12.7.7, it follows: $u' = u_1 u'_2$ and $v' = v_1 v'_2$ where $u_1 \neq \varepsilon$ and $com(u_1) = com(v_1)$, so $v_1 \in f(u_1)$. Moreover, $alph(u_1) \subseteq D \cup \{a\} \subsetneq \Sigma$. So, the couple (u_1, v_1) answers the problem.

2. $\exists y \in \Sigma', \exists d_1 \in D \mid d_1 y \in f(yd_1)$

   Then, $D = \{d\}$: if two different letters d_1 and d_2 belong to D, we will find in the commutation graph of f the subgraph $y \longrightarrow d_1 \longleftarrow a \longrightarrow d_2$, which contradicts the hypothesis: f satisfies (C) condition. Then we set: $E = \{z \in \Sigma \setminus \{d\} \mid dz \in f(zd)\}$ and $Z = \Sigma \setminus (E \cup \{d\})$. We have $E \neq \emptyset$ because $y \in E$; $Z \neq \emptyset$ because f does not satisfy (P) property; if z_1 and z_2 are two different letters of E, there is no commutation between z_1 and z_2 because the commutation graph of f already contains the subgraph $z_1 \longrightarrow d \longleftarrow z_2$ and f satisfies (C) condition.

   Let us set $u = awzu'', v = dw'z'v''$ with $w, w' \in (E \cup \{d\})^*$, $z, z' \in Z$.

   No occurrence of the letter d in the word u'' can over-step z or z', but it is possible to have rules such as $dt \longrightarrow td$ for a letter t in Z. So we get $|dw'|_d \leq |aw|_d$ then $|w|_d > |w'|_d$.

   On the other hand, for every letter x in $E \setminus \{a\}$, for every letter z in Z, the commutation graph of f contains the subgraph $a \longrightarrow d \longleftarrow x$. No arrow like $x \longrightarrow z$ can be added and $za \notin f(az)$ because $D = \{d\}$ and $d \notin Z$. Then for every letter x in E and for every letter z in Z, $zx \notin f(xz)$. But we can find a rule as $z_1 x_1 \longrightarrow x_1 z_1$ for (x_1, z_1) in $E \times Z$. So we have $\Pi_E(aw) \in LF(\Pi_E(dw')) = LF(\Pi_E(w'))$. Then: $u = u'zu''v = v'z'v''$ with $u' \in \Pi_E(aw) \sqcup d^j$ and $v' \in d(\Pi_E(aw) \sqcup d^i)(w'' \sqcup d^{i'})$, where $j = |aw|_d$, $i + i' = |w'|_d$ which implies $j > i$.

   Thanks to Lemma 12.7.7, we get $u' = u_1 u''_2$ and $v' = v_1 v''_2$ with $u_1 \neq \varepsilon$ and $com(u_1) = com(v_1)$ (so $v_1 \in f(u_1)$), and $alph(u_1) \subseteq E \cup \{d\} \subsetneq \Sigma$. The couple (u_1, v_1) answers the problem. $\qquad\square$

We are now able to state:

Theorem 12.7.12 *A semi-commutation function f is algebraic rational if and only if the semi-commutation graph of f does not contain any subgraph of the kind* •→•→• •←•→• *or* •↔•→•↔•

Proof: Thanks to proposition 12.7.6, we have only to prove the if part. We proceed by induction on the cardinality of the alphabet Σ.

1. If $\mathrm{Card}(\Sigma) = 2$, the result is true (Proposition 12.7.3).

2. If $\mathrm{Card}(\Sigma) > 2$:

   - If f satisfies (P) property, the result is true because of Proposition 12.7.10.

   - If not, we are going to show that for each rational language R, $f(R) \in Alg$. Let $R \in RAT$. We can define a deterministic automaton $M = (\Sigma, Q, q_0, \delta, F)$ which accepts R. If $q, q' \in Q$, we set $R_{q,q'} = \{w \in \Sigma^* \mid \delta(q, w) = q'\}$. Let s be the substitution defined on $Q \times Q$ by

$$\forall (q, q') \in Q \times Q, \; s((q, q')) = \bigcup_{x \in \Sigma} f(R_{q,q'} \cap (\Sigma \setminus \{x\})^*)$$

By induction hypothesis, s is an algebraic substitution. Let K be the rational language defined on $Q \times Q$ by

$$K = \{(q_0, q_1)(q_1, q_2)....(q_{p-1}, q_p), \; p \geq 1, \; \forall i \in \{1, ..., p\}, \; q_i \in Q, \; q_p \in F\}$$

It remains to verify if $f(R) = s(K)$, the proof will be done since the image of a rational language by an algebraic substitution is an algebraic language:

- $s(K) \subseteq f(R)$?
  Let $w = (q_0, q_1)(q_1, q_2) \ldots (q_{p-1}, q_p) \in K$. Then

$$\forall w' \in s(w), w' = u_0 u_1 \ldots u_{p-1} \mid \forall i \in \{0, \ldots, p-1\}, u_i \in s((q_i, q_{i+1}))$$

So

$$\forall i \in \{0, \ldots, p-1\}, \exists x_i \in \Sigma, \exists v_i \in R_{q_i, q_{i+1}} \cap (\Sigma \setminus \{x_i\})^* \mid u_i \in f(v_i)$$

and

$$w' \in f(v_0)f(v_1) \ldots f(v_{p-1}) \subseteq f(v_0 v_1 \ldots v_{p-1})$$

As $\delta(q_0, v_0 v_1 \ldots v_{p-1}) = q_p \in F$, we obtain $v_0 v_1 \ldots v_p \in R$.

- $f(R) \subseteq s(K)$?
  If q and q' are two states of Q, we set:

$$K_{q,q'} = \{(q_1, q_2)(q_2, q_3) \ldots (q_p, q_{p+1}) \mid p \geq 1, q_1 = q, q_{p+1} = q'\}$$

We shall prove by induction on the length of a word w in $R_{q,q'}$ that for each word w in $f(w)$, we have w' in $s(K_{q,q'})$.

  - $\text{alph}(w) \subsetneq \Sigma$
    Then $f(w) \subseteq s((q, q'))$
  - $\text{alph}(w) = \Sigma$
    Thanks to Lemma 12.7.11, we can find two decompositions $w = w_1 w_2$ and $w' = w_1' w_2'$, where $w_1 \neq \varepsilon, \text{alph}(w_1) \subsetneq \Sigma$ and $w_1' \in f(w_1)$. If $\delta(q, w_1) = q_1$, we get $f(w_1) \subseteq s(q, q_1)$ and, by induction hypothesis, $f(w_2) \subseteq s(K_{q_1, q'})$. Hence

$$w' \in f(w_1)f(w_2) \subseteq s((q, q_1)K_{q_1,q'}) \subseteq s(K_{q,q'})$$

So, for any word w in R, we can find a state q in F such that $w \in R_{q_0, q}$. Then, we have:

$$\forall w' \in f(w_0), w' \in s(K_{q_0, q}) \subseteq s(K)$$

Hence, we have $f(R) \subseteq s(K)$.

□

As a matter of fact, Theorem 12.7.12 allows us to state that the image of a rational language by a semi-commutation function is always in Ocl. So we state:

Theorem 12.7.13 *Let f be a semi-commutation function defined on an alphabet Σ. The following assertions are equivalent:*

1. *f is algebraic rational*

2. *The semi-commutation graph of f does not contain any subgraph of the kind*
   •→•—•←•→•   *or*   •—•—•←•

3. *For each rational language R, $f(R) \in$ Ocl.*

4. *For each rational bounded language R , $f(R) \in$ Alg*

Proof:
  1 $\Longleftrightarrow$ 2 from Theorem 12.7.12.
  2 $\Longrightarrow$ 3 because constructions which give us the image by f of a rational language use $D_1'^*$ and D_1^* which are in Ocl and operations under which Ocl is closed.
  3 $\Longrightarrow$ 4 is obvious.
  4 $\Longrightarrow$ 1 when looking at the proof of Theorem 12.7.12.

□

In the particular case of partial commutation , Theorem 12.7.12 becomes:

Theorem 12.7.14 *A partial commutation function is algebraic rational if and only if its commutation graph does not contain a path whose length is 3*

12.8   Applications of Semi-Commutations

In the well known works of A.Mazurkiewicz, traces have been applied to describe and study behaviours of concurrent systems and of Petri nets.

Within this framework, E. Ochmański in [208], [209], [210] defined concurrent systems and processes as some subsets of a semi-trace monoid and investigates there properties. We present only some of the results obtained by E. Ochmański, among others the Diamond Property.

From an other point of view it seems quite natural to invoke semi-commutations to describe concurrent behaviours of Petri nets: an action b (or transition) depends on an other a if at some moment of an execution, ab is enabled but not ba. This condition can be explicit with static properties of Petri nets. So we identify concurrent behaviours of Petri nets with semi-traces. This approach was simultaneously done in [208] and in [142]. In the third part of this section, we describe only some connections between semi-commutations and Petri nets.

12.8.1   More Properties of Derivations

Definition 12.8.1 *Let $u, w \in \Sigma^*$ be such that $\forall x \in \Sigma, |u|_x \leq |w|_x$. We denote by* left$(w, u)$ *the leftmost subword of w in which each letter of u appears with the same number of occurrences, and only letters of u appear and by* right(w, u) *the rightmost subword of w in which each letter of u appears with the same numbers of occurrences, and only letters of u appear.*

If num *is a enumeration on Σ^*,*

$$\text{left}(w, u) = \text{denum}(\Pi_{\text{num}(u)}(\text{num}(w)))$$

$$\text{right}(w, u) = \widetilde{v} \ with v = \text{denum}(\Pi_{\text{num}(\widetilde{u})}(\text{num}(\widetilde{w})))$$

where $\widetilde{u}$ is the reverse of u.

Lemma 12.8.2 *Let $u, v, w \in \Sigma^*$.*

If $w \xrightarrow[\theta]{*} uv$ then $w \xrightarrow[\theta]{*}$ left(w, u)right(w, v), left$(w, u) \xrightarrow[\theta]{*} u$ and right$(w, v) \xrightarrow[\theta]{*} v$.

Proof: Let num be a enumeration of Σ^* as defined in Section 12.3. Then $w \xrightarrow[\theta]{*} uv$ if and only if num$(w) \xrightarrow[\theta]{*}$ num(uv). If we set $u'v' = $ num(uv) with $u' = $ num(u), we have $\text{num}(w) \xrightarrow[\theta]{*} u'v'$. Then

$$
\begin{aligned}
\text{left}(\text{num}(w), u') &= \Pi_{u'}(\text{num}(w)) \\
\text{denum}(\text{left}(\text{num}(w), u')) &= \text{left}(w, u) \\
\text{left}(\text{num}(w), v') &= \Pi_{v'}(\text{num}(w)) \\
\text{denum}(\text{left}(\text{num}(w), v')) &= \text{left}(w, v)
\end{aligned}
$$

Set $w' = \text{left}(\text{num}(w), u')\text{right}(\text{num}(w), v')$.

Then $E(\text{num}(w)) \setminus E(w') \subseteq E(\text{num}(w)) \setminus E(u'v')$: if $(a, b) \in E(\text{num}(w)) \setminus E(w')$, then $a \in \text{alph}(v')$, $b \in \text{alph}(u')$ and $(a, b) \in E(\text{num}(w)) \setminus E(u'v')$. So $E(\text{num}(w)) \setminus E(w') \subseteq \theta_{num}$ and $\text{num}(w) \xrightarrow[\theta]{*} w'$ (Permutation Lemma). And we conclude with the Enumeration Lemma that $w \xrightarrow[\theta]{*} \text{left}(w, u)\text{right}(w, v)$.

Moreover it is clear that $\Pi_{u'}\text{num}(w) = \text{left}(\text{num}(w), u') \xrightarrow[\theta]{*} \Pi_{u'}(u'v') = u'$ as well as $\text{right}(\text{num}(w), v') \xrightarrow[\theta]{*} v'$ and if we remove numbers, we obtain $\text{left}(w, u) \xrightarrow[\theta]{*} u$ and $\text{right}(w, v) \xrightarrow[\theta]{*} v$.

$\square$

Lemma 12.8.3 *Let θ be a semi-commutation relation defined over Σ.*

If $w \xrightarrow[\theta]{*} xau$, $w \xrightarrow[\theta]{*} xbv$ for some words $w, x, u, v \in \Sigma^*$ and $a \neq b \in \Sigma$, then $(a, b) \in \theta$ or $(b, a) \in \theta$ and there exist $z \in \Sigma^*$ such that $w \xrightarrow[\theta]{*} xabz$ and $w \xrightarrow[\theta]{*} xbaz$.

Proof: Let us set $w' = \text{left}(w, x)$ and $w'' = \text{right}(w, au) = \text{right}(w, bv)$. By Lemma 12.8.2, we have $w \xrightarrow[\theta]{*} w'w''$, $w' \xrightarrow[\theta]{*} x$, $w'' \xrightarrow[\theta]{*} au$ and $w'' \xrightarrow[\theta]{*} bv$. If $w'' = z_1 a z_2 b z_3$ with $|z_1|_a = 0$ and $|z_1 a z_2|_b = 0$, we get from the Projection Lemma that $a \times \text{alph}(z_1) \subseteq \theta$ and $b \times \text{alph}(z_1 a z_2) \subseteq \theta$. So $(b, a) \in \theta$ and $w'' \xrightarrow[\theta]{*} baz_1 z_2 z_3$.

Thus $w \xrightarrow[\theta]{*} w'w'' \xrightarrow[\theta]{*} xw'' \xrightarrow[\theta]{*} xbaz_1 z_2 z_3 \xrightarrow[\theta]{*} xabz_1 z_2 z_3$ and we get the result with $z = z_1 z_2 z_3$. The case when $w'' = z_1 b z_2 a z_3$ is solved in the same way. $\square$

12.8.2 Semi-Commutation and Concurrent Systems

Let $M = \mathbb{M}(\Sigma, \theta)$ be a semi-trace monoid. Recall that elements of M are of the kind $f_\theta(u)$ where $u \in \Sigma^*$.

We define the order $\leq$ on $\mathbb{M}(\Sigma, \theta)$ by

$$
\forall t_1, t_2 \in \mathbb{M}(\Sigma, \theta), \ t_1 \leq t_2 \iff \exists s \in \mathbb{M}(\Sigma, \theta), t_1 s \subseteq t_2
$$

Definition 12.8.4 *A subset P of $(M, \leq)$ is a* system *in M if and only if it is backward closed, that is $\{t \in M \mid \exists s \in P, \ t \leq s\} \subseteq P$.*

Elements of a system are named states.

A subset P of $(M, \leq)$ is directed if and only if $\forall t_1, t_2 \in P, \exists t \in P, t_1 \leq t, t_2 \leq t$.

Any maximal (with respect to the set inclusion) directed subset of a system is called a process.

A system S is deterministic *if and only if it is directed, that is if and only if the only process included in it is itself.*

The maximal concurrent process *of a process P is the set*

$$MC(P) = \{t \in P \mid \forall s \in P, t \subseteq s \Rightarrow t = s\}$$

Definition 12.8.5 *For a given process P, if $t \in P$, we define the set of generators of t: gen(t) by*

$$gen(t) = \{u \in \Sigma^* \mid t = f_\theta(u)\}$$

It is clear that $gen(t)$ is closed under the commutation relation $\theta \cap \theta^{-1}$.

Lemma 12.8.6 *Let P be a process of $(M, \leq)$. For any state t of P, there exists a unique maximally concurrent state of P including t: we denote it by $MC_P(t)$ or $MC(t)$ if there is no ambiguity on P.*

Proof: Since semi-traces are finite sets, the existence is obvious.

Let $s, r \in MC(P)$ such that $t \subseteq s$ and $t \subseteq r$. Since P is directed, there exist $q \in P$ such that $s \leq q$ and $r \leq q$, that is $s\alpha \subseteq q$ and $r\beta \subseteq q$ for some $\alpha, \beta \in M$. If we choose one generator:g_p for each semi-trace p, we have $g_s \xrightarrow[\theta]{*} g_t$, $g_r \xrightarrow[\theta]{*} g_t, g_q \xrightarrow[\theta]{*} g_s g_\alpha$ and $g_q \xrightarrow[\theta]{*} g_r g_\beta$. If we set $w_1 = \text{left}(g_q, g_s) = \text{left}(g_q, g_t)$ and $w_2 = \text{right}(g_q, g_\alpha) = \text{right}(g_q, g_\beta)$, we get by Lemma 12.8.2: $g_q \xrightarrow[\theta]{*} w_1 w_2$ and $w_1 \xrightarrow[\theta]{*} g_s, w_1 \xrightarrow[\theta]{*} g_r$. Therefore on one side $f_\theta(w_1) \leq q$ and thus $f_\theta(w_1) \in P$ since $q \in P$ and P is backward closed and on the other side $f_\theta(w_1) = s = t$ since $s, t \in MC(P)$. So the uniqueness is proved.   □

Lemma 12.8.7 *Let P be a process and $t, s \in P$.*

$$t \leq s \Rightarrow MC(t) \leq MC(s)$$

Proof: Let us set $t = f_\theta(u)$, $s = f_\theta(v)$ and let $u_g \in Gen(MC(t))$ and $v_g \in Gen(MC(s))$. We have $u_g \xrightarrow[\theta]{*} u$ and $\exists x \in \Sigma^*, v_g \xrightarrow[\theta]{*} v \xrightarrow[\theta]{*} ux$.

Since P is directed, we can find words w, α, β of Σ^* such that $f_\theta(w) \in P$, $MC(s) \leq f_\theta(w)$ and $MC(t) \leq f_\theta(w)$ that is $w \xrightarrow[\theta]{*} u_g \alpha$ and $w \xrightarrow[\theta]{*} v_g \beta$. From Lemma 12.8.2, there exist words $u_0 = \text{left}(w, u_g), u_1, v_0 = \text{left}(w, v_g), v_1$ such that $w \xrightarrow[\theta]{*} u_0 u_1, u_0 \xrightarrow[\theta]{*} u_g, w \xrightarrow[\theta]{*} v_0 v_1, v_0 \xrightarrow[\theta]{*} v_g$. As u_g and v_g are generators, $f_\theta(u_0) = f_\theta(u_g)$ and $f_\theta(v_0) = f_\theta(v_g)$. Moreover, since $f_\theta(u) \leq f_\theta(v)$, each letter of $\text{alph}(u) = \text{alph}(u_g)$ appears in v and so in v_g with a greater number of occurrences.

Hence $u_0 = \text{left}(w, u_g) = \text{left}(v_0, u)$ and since $v_0 \xleftrightarrow[\theta]{*} v_g \xrightarrow[\theta]{*} ux$ we get $v_0 \xrightarrow[\theta]{*}$
$\text{left}(v_0, u)\text{right}(v_0, x) = u_0\text{right}(v_0, x)$. We conclude that

$$v_g \xleftrightarrow[\theta]{*} v_0 \xrightarrow[\theta]{*} u_0\text{right}(v_0, x) \xleftrightarrow[\theta]{*} u_g\text{right}(v_0, x)$$

and $MC(t) = f_\theta(u_g) \leq MC(s) = f_\theta(v_g)$. $\square$

The Diamond Property seems to be a very natural requirement for concurrent
processes: it is something like confluence of concurrent executions....

Definition 12.8.8 (Diamond Property) *Let $(M, \leq)$ a discrete poset.*
Let sNt if and only if $s \neq t$ and $\{z \in M | s \leq z \leq t\} = \{s, t\}$. We have $N^* = \leq$.
We say that (M, N) is
forward diamond *if and only if*

$$\forall s, t', t'' \in M, \, sNt', sNt'' \Rightarrow \exists! q \in M, t'Nq, t''Nq$$

backward diamond *if and only if*

$$\forall s, t', t'' \in M, \, t'Ns, t''Ns \Rightarrow \exists! q \in M, qNt', qNt''$$

diamond *if it is forward and backward diamond.*

There are however processes without the Diamond Property:

Example 12.8.9 Let $\Sigma = \{a, b, c\}$ and $\theta = \{(a, b), (b, a), (c, a), (c, b)\}$.
Here, the system S has two processes P_1 and P_2 as shown in Fig. 12.6. For
$t = f_\theta(abc)$, we have $MC_{P_1}(t) = f_\theta(acb) \neq f_\theta(bca) = MC_{P_2}(t)$.

In fact systems always satisfy a property which is a weaker Diamond Property:

Proposition 12.8.10 *Let P be a system of $(M, \leq)$. If $t \in M$, if a, b are two*
different letters of the alphabet of M such that $ta \in P$ and $tb \in P$ and if there exists
$s \in P$ such that $ta \leq s$ and $tb \leq s$ then either $(a, b) \in \theta$ and $t.f_\theta(ab)$ is the least
upper bound of ta and tb or $(b, a) \in \theta$ and $t.f_\theta(ba)$ is the least upper bound of ta
and tb.

Proof: Let $u \in Gen(t)$ and $w \in Gen(s)$. We have $w \xrightarrow[\theta]{*} ua\alpha$ and $w \xrightarrow[\theta]{*} ub\beta$
for some $\alpha, \beta \in \Sigma^*$. By Lemma 12.8.6, we conclude that (a, b) or $(b, a) \in \theta$ and
there exists $\gamma \in \Sigma^*$ such that $w \xrightarrow[\theta]{*} uab\gamma$ and $w \xrightarrow[\theta]{*} uba\gamma$. So $f_\theta(uab) \in P$ and
$f_\theta(uba) \in P$. If $(a, b) \in \theta$, then $f_\theta(uab)$ is an upper bound of ta and tb. And it is the
least upper bound since if $f_\theta(z)$ is an upper bound of ta and tb, we have $z \xrightarrow[\theta]{*} ua\mu$
and $z \xrightarrow[\theta]{*} ub\nu$ hence $z \xrightarrow[\theta]{*} uab\xi$ and $f_\theta(uab) \leq f_\theta(z)$. Symmetrically if $(b, a) \in \theta$,
$f_\theta(uba)$ is the least upper bound of ta and tb.

$\square$

Observe that in the above example, the maximally concurrent processes of P_1 and P_2 have the Diamond Property. We are going to see that in fact, $MC(P)$ is always diamond for any process P. For that, we introduce and give some properties of the restriction of the order to $MC(P)$.

Definition 12.8.11 *Let P be a process and $t, s \in MC(P)$.*
$t N_{MC} s$ if and only if $s \neq t$ and $\{q \in MC(P), t \leq q \leq s\} = \{t, s\}$

Lemma 12.8.12 *Let p be a process of $\mathbb{M}(\Sigma, \theta)$. Let $s, t \in MC(P)$. The three following assertions are equivalent:*

1. $t N_{MC} s$

2. $\exists a \in \Sigma$, $s = MC(ta)$

3. $s = t'at''$ with $t't'' = t$

Proof:
$1 \Rightarrow 2$
We have for some $u \in gen(t), v \in gen(s)$: $f_\theta(u) = t N_{MC} s = f_\theta(v)$. So for some word $z \in \Sigma^*$, $v \xrightarrow{*}_{\theta} uz$ and $z \neq \varepsilon$ (if not, $t = s$). Let us set $z = az'$ with $a \in \Sigma$. We get $f_\theta(u) \leq f_\theta(ua) \leq f_\theta(v)$ and with Lemma 12.8.7, $f_\theta(u) \leq MC(f_\theta(ua)) \leq f_\theta(v)$. By hypothesis, we get $MC(f_\theta(ua)) = f_\theta(v)$, $v \xrightarrow{*}_{\theta} ua$ and $z' = \varepsilon$. So $s = MC(f_\theta(ua)) = MC(ta)$.
$2 \Rightarrow 3$
If $u \in gen(t)$ and if $v \in gen(s)$, there is a derivation $v \xrightarrow{*}_{\theta} ua$. So we can write $v = u'au''$ with $|u''|_a = 0$. So with the Projection Lemma and Lemma 12.8.2, we get $a \times alph(u'') \subseteq \theta$ and $u'u'' \xrightarrow{*}_{\theta} u$. Since $f_\theta(u) = t$ is in $MC(P)$, $f_\theta(u) = f_\theta(u'u'') = f_\theta(u')f_\theta(u'')$. If we set $t' = f_\theta(u')$ and $t'' = f_\theta(u'')$ we get the result.
$3 \Rightarrow 1$
If $u' \in gen(t'), u'' \in gen(t''), u \in gen(t)$ and $v \in gen(s)$, we have $v \xleftrightarrow{*}_{\theta} u'au''$ and $u \xleftrightarrow{*}_{\theta} u'u''$. Let w be such that $f_\theta(w) \in MC(P)$ and $f_\theta(u) \leq f_\theta(w) \leq f_\theta(v)$. If $f_\theta(u) \neq f_\theta(w)$, then $|u| < |w|$. And $|w| \leq |v|$. So $|w| = |v| = |u| + 1$ and $v \xrightarrow{*}_{\theta} w$. Since $f_\theta(v) \in MC(P)$, we get $f_\theta(v) = f_\theta(w)$.   □

Proposition 12.8.13 *Let P be a process of $\mathbb{M}(\Sigma, \theta)$. The set $MC(P)$ of maximally concurrent states of P has the Diamond Property.*

Proof:

$MC(P)$ is forward diamond: let $t = f_\theta(u), s', s'' \in MC(P)$. If $tN_{MC}s', tN_{MC}s'$, then by Lemma 12.8.12, there exist $a, b \in \Sigma$ such that $s' = MC(ta)$ and $s'' = MC(tb)$. On the other hand, since P is directed, we can find $z = f_\theta(w) \in P$ such that $s' \leq z$ and $s'' \leq z$. So $w \xrightarrow{*}_{\theta} ua\alpha$ and $w \xrightarrow{*}_{\theta} ub\beta$ for some words $\alpha, \beta \in \Sigma^*$. By Lemma 12.8.6 we get $(a, b) \in \theta$ or $(b, a) \in \theta$ and there exist γ such that $w \xrightarrow{*}_{\theta} uab\gamma$ and $w \xrightarrow{*}_{\theta} uba\gamma$. Hence if $(a, b) \in \theta$, $f_\theta(uab)$ is the least upper bound of $f_\theta(ua)$ and $f_\theta(ub)$ (if $(b, a) \in \theta$, $f_\theta(uba)$ is the least upper bound of $f_\theta(ua)$ and $f_\theta(ub)$), and by Lemma 12.8.7, $MC(f_\theta(uab)) = MC(f_\theta(uba)) = MC(s'b) = MC(s''a)$ is a upper bound of $MC(f_\theta(ua)) = s'$ and $MC(f_\theta(ub)) = s''$. And we conclude with Lemma 12.8.12 that $s'N_{MC}MC(f_\theta(uab))$ and $s''N_{MC}MC(f_\theta(uba))$.

$MC(P)$ is forward diamond: Let $t, s', s'' \in MC(P)$ be such that $s'N_{MC}t$ and $s''N_{MC}t$. With Lemma 12.8.12, we have $t = MC(s'a) = MC(s''b)$ where a, b are two different letters (if $a = b$, then $s' = s''$). So if $u \in Gen(t), v' \in gen(s')$ and $v'' \in gen(s'')$, $u \xrightarrow{*}_{\theta} v'a$, $u \xrightarrow{*}_{\theta} v''b$ and there is a factorization $u = u_1au_2bu_3$ with $|u_3|_b = 0$ and $|u_2bu_3|_a = 0$ (or $u = u_1bu_2au_3$ with $|u_3|_a = 0$ and $|u_2au_3|_b = 0$). From Lemma 12.8.2, we can write

$$u \xrightarrow{*}_{\theta} u_1u_2bu_3a, u_1u_2bu_3 \xrightarrow{*}_{\theta} v'$$

$$u \xrightarrow{*}_{\theta} u_1au_2u_3b, u_1au_2u_3 \xrightarrow{*}_{\theta} v''$$

and since v' and v'' are generators, $f_\theta(u_1au_2u_3) = s''$ and $f_\theta(u_1u_2bu_3) = s'$. Hence there is a derivation $u \xrightarrow{*}_{\theta} u_1u_2u_3ab$ and $(a, b) \in \theta$. Thus $f_\theta(u_1u_2u_3) \leq f_\theta(u_1u_2u_3a) \leq f_\theta(u_1au_2u_3) = s''$ and symmetrically $f_\theta(u_1u_2u_3) \leq f_\theta(u_1u_2u_3b) \leq f_\theta(u_1u_2bu_3) = s'$. Clearly if we set $q = MC(f_\theta(u_1u_2u_3))$, we get $s' = MC(qa)$ and $s'' = MC(qb)$ and with Lemma 12.8.12, $qN_{MC}s'$ and $qN_{MC}s''$. To prove that q is unique, let us consider $q' \in MC(P)$ such that $q'N_{MC}s'$ and $q'N_{MC}s''$. By Lemma 12.8.12, there exist $c, d \in \Sigma$ such that $s' = MC(q'c)$ and $s'' = MC(q'd)$. Then $t = MC(q'ca) = MC(q'db)$ so $c = b, d = a$ and $q = q'$. □

12.8.3 Application to Petri-Net

Definition 12.8.14 *A Petri net $N = (P, T, In, Out)$ is defined by a finite set of places: P, a finite set of transitions: T, and by two applications from T to 2^P: the forward incidence In and the backward incidence Out.*

A marking of a Petri net is an application from P to $\mathbb{N}$.

A place-transition system is a couple $S = (N, m_0)$ where N is a Petri net and m_0 is a marking called the initial marking.

A transition $t \in T$ is enabled from the marking m if for each place p of $In(t)$, $m(p) \geq 1$. We denote the fact that t is enabled under the marking m by $m[t > m'$

where m', the follower marking, is defined for each place p of P by

$$
\begin{aligned}
m'(p) &= m(p) \text{ if } p \in P \setminus (In(t) \cup Out(t)) \\
&= m(p) + 1 \text{ if } p \in Out(t) \setminus In(t) \\
&= m(p) - 1 \text{ if } p \in In(t) \setminus Out(t) \\
&= m(p) \text{ if } p \in In(t) \cap Out(t)
\end{aligned}
$$

If $w = t_1 \ldots t_n \in T^*$, we write $m[w >$ if there exist $m_1, \ldots m_{n-1}, m_n$ such that $m[t_1 > m_1[t_2 > m_2 \ldots m_{n-1}[t_n > m_n$. We also write $m[w > m_n$.

The set of behaviours associated to a system S is defined by

$$
L(S) = \{ w \in T^* \mid m_0[w >\}
$$

For a given Petri net $N = (P, T, In, Out)$, it seems quite natural to define the following semi-dependence relation: The transition b depends on the transition a if and only if there is a marking m of N such that ab is enabled but ba is not enabled.

In fact we can decide if a transition depends on an other only with the configuration of the net:

Property 12.8.15 *Let $N = (P, T, In, Out)$ be a Petri net and $a, b \in T$. Transition b depends on transition a if and only if there exists a place $p \in P$ such that $p \in Out(a) \cap In(b) \setminus In(a) \cap Out(b)$.*

Proof: For the sufficient condition, let p be a place in $Out(a) \cap In(b)$. We have two cases:

1. If $p \notin In(a)$, consider a marking m such that $\forall q \in In(a), m(q) = 1$ and $\forall q \in In(b) \setminus p, m(q) = 1$. Then it is clear that ab is enabled from m but not ba (b is not enabled).

2. If $p \in In(a)$, then $p \notin Out(b)$. Let m be a marking which satisfies $\forall q \in In(a), m(q) = 1$ and $\forall q \in In(b), m(q) = 1$. Then ab and b are enabled from m but not ba.

We prove now the necessary condition: since ab is enabled from a marking m, we have $m[a > m'$ and $\forall p \in In(a), m(p) \geq 1, \forall p \in In(b), m'(p) \geq 1$. We now distinguish two cases:

1. If b is not enabled from m, then there exists $q \in In(b)$ such that $m(q) = 0$. But $m'(q) \geq 1$, so $q \in Out(a)$. Moreover as $m(q) = 0$ and a is enabled from m, $q \notin In(a)$.

2. If b is enabled but not ba, then we have $m[b > m''$ and $\forall p \in In(b), m(p) \geq 1$. But there exists $q \in In(a)$ such that $m''(q) = 0$. Since $m(q) \leq 1$ (a is enabled), $q \in In(b), m(q) = 1$ and $q \notin Out(b)$. Moreover ab is enabled and $q \in In(a) \cap In(b)$ hence $m'(q) = 1$ and $q \in Out(a)$.

$\square$

Observe that the semi-dependence relation is defined for arbitrary nets. For pure nets (without elementary loops), the definition we give is the same as this proposed by E. Ochmański in [209].

So if $N = (P, T, In, Out)$ is a Petri net, let θ be the semi commutation relation defined in the following way:

$$(a, b) \in \theta \Leftrightarrow a \neq b \text{ and } Out(a) \cap In(b) \setminus In(a) \cap Out(b) = \emptyset$$

It is easy to see that if $S = (N, m_0)$ is a place/transition system and if $L(S)$ is the set of behaviours of S,

$$L(S) = f_\theta(L(S))$$

and

$$L(S) \text{ is backward closed. } (uv \in L(S) \Rightarrow u \in L(S))$$

So the set of concurrent behaviours of S defined by $CB(S) = \{f_\theta(u) \mid u \in L(S)\}$ with the order $\leq$ defined previously on semi-traces is a system in the way defined in the previous section.

It is also interesting to characterize sets of behaviours of place/transition systems in term of other languages families and classical operators on them

It is easy to see that such sets are not always recognizable:

Example 12.8.16

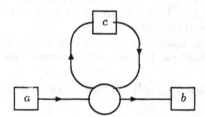

The set of behaviours of this place/transition system S_0 is equal to the left factors of the language $L(S_0) = f_\theta((ac^*b)^*(ac^*a^* + \varepsilon))$ where $\theta = \{(b, a), (c, a), (b, c)\}$.

In the case when there is an initial marking in the place of this system: k marks for instance,

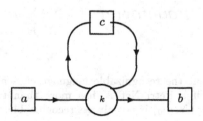

we get

$$
\begin{aligned}
L(S) &= f_\theta(b^{k-1}c^*b(ac^*b)^*(ac^*a^* + \varepsilon)) + \sum_{j=1}^{k-2} f_\theta(b^j c^*(ac^*a^* + \varepsilon)) \\
&= f_\theta(b^{k-1}c^*b(ac^*b)^*(ac^*a^* + \varepsilon) + \sum_{j=1}^{k-2} b^j c^*(ac^*a^* + \varepsilon))
\end{aligned}
$$

These languages can be defined as the closure of a recognizable language under the semi-commutation relation associated to the Petri net. It is not always the case, but in fact a Petri net can be decomposed into simple nets with only one place and each transition linked to this place: thus the set of behaviours of a place/transition system can be expressed by the synchronized product of languages like this above, or in an other way, we are going to prove that each set of behaviours of a place/transition system is the image by an inverse homomorphism of the closure of a recognizable language under a semi commutation function.

Lemma 12.8.17 *If $S = (N, m_0)$ is a place/transition system where N defines the semi commutation relation θ, then $L(S) = f_\theta(R)$ for some recognizable language R.*

Proof: If $N = (\{p\}, T, In, Out)$, we can build a partition of T in the following way: $T = P \cup C \cup I$ with $P = \{t \in T \mid p \in Out(t) \setminus In(t)\}$, $C = \{t \in T \mid p \in In(t) \setminus Out(t)\}$ and $I = \{t \in T \mid p \in In(t) \cap Out(t)\}$.

In each of these sets, transitions have exactly the same action on the place p. So the Petri net N defined the following semi-commutation θ:

$$
\theta = \{(c, p) \mid c \in C,\ p \in P\} \cup \{(c, i) \mid c \in C,\ i \in I\} \cup \{(i, p) \mid i \in I,\ p \in P\}
$$

and if $m_0(p) = k$, we get as in the previous example

$$
\begin{aligned}
L(S) &= f_\theta(C^{k-1}I^*C(PI^*C)^*(PI^*P^* + \varepsilon)) + \sum_{j=1}^{k-2} f_\theta(C^j I^*(PI^*P^* + \varepsilon)) \\
&= f_\theta(C^{k-1}I^*C(PI^*C)^*(PI^*P^* + \varepsilon) + \sum_{j=1}^{k-2} C^j I^*(PI^*P^* + \varepsilon))
\end{aligned}
$$

$\square$

We can remark that the recognizable language chosen in this proof is in fact $MAX\theta(L(S))$. But if a Petri Net N has more than two places the language $MAX\theta(L(S))$ for $S = (N, m_0)$ is not always recognizable:

Example 12.8.18

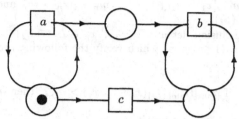

The semi-commutation relation which is defined by this place/transition system S is $\theta = \{(b,a),(c,a),(b,c)\}$. But, clearly, in $L(S)$ it is not possible to use any of the corresponding rules: $ba \longrightarrow ab, ca \longrightarrow ac$ or $bc \longrightarrow cb$ because transition b can not occur before transition a nor transition c and transition c can not occur before transition a. Then the only language which satisfies that its θ-closure is equal to $L(S)$ is $L(S)$ itself, and it is easy to see that $L(S)$ is equal to the left factors of the language $\{a^n c b^p \mid n \geq p\}$ which is not regular.

But we have always the following result:

Proposition 12.8.19 *For each place/transition system S we can find a recognizable language R, a semi commutation relation θ and an homomorphism h such that $L(S) = h^{-1}(f_\theta(R))$.*

Proof: Let us set $S = (N, m_0)$ with $N = (P, T, In, Out)$, and $P = \{1, 2, \ldots p\}$. We define p place/transition systems $S_i = (\{N_i\}, m_{0,i})$ where $N_i = (\{i\}, T_i, In_i, Out_i)$, $T_i = \{t \in T \mid i \in In(t) \cup Out(t)\}$ and In_i, Out_i are defined on T_i by $In_i(t) = In(t) \cap \{i\}$ and $Out_i(t) = Out(t) \cap \{i\}$. $m_{0,i}$ is the restriction of m_0 to the place i.
Let $L_i = L(S_i)$.
We prove that L is the synchronized product of L_i's:

$$L = L_1 \sqcap L_2 \sqcap \ldots \sqcap L_p = \{w \in T^* \mid \forall i \in P, \Pi_{\mathrm{alph}(L_i)}(w) \in L_i\}$$

To prove that $L \subseteq L_1 \sqcap L_2 \sqcap \ldots \sqcap L_p$, let w be a word of L. If we set for each $i \in P$ $X_i = \mathrm{alph}(L_i) = In^{-1}(i) \cup Out^{-1}(i)$ and $w_i = \Pi_{X_i}(w) = x_1 x_2 \ldots x_n$, we can write

$$w = \alpha_0 x_1 \alpha_1 x_2 \ldots \alpha_{n-1} x_n \alpha_n$$

and there exist markings

$$m_0[\alpha_0 > m_0'[x_1 > m_1[\alpha_1 > m_1'[x_2 > m_2 \ldots m_n[\alpha_n > m_n'$$

with $\forall k \geq 0$, $m_k(i) = m_k'(i)$ since only letters of X_i may modify the numbers of marks in the place i. And when we restrict our observation to the place i, it is clear that for $j \geq 1$, if $i \in Out(x_j) \setminus In(x_j)$, $m_j(i) = m_{j-1}'(i) + 1$ and if $i \in In(x_j)$, then $m_{j-1}'(i) \geq 1$ and $m_j(i) = m_{j-1}'(i) - 1$ if $x_j \notin Out(i)$, $m_j(i) = m_{j-1}'(i)$ if $x_j \in Out(i)$.

So in S_i we get $m_{0,i}[x_1 > m_{1,i}[x_2 > \ldots m_{n-1,i}[x_n > m_n$ and we conclude that $w_i = x_1 x_2 \ldots x_n \in L(S_i)$.

For the reverse inclusion, let $w = x_1 x_2 \ldots x_n \in L_1 \sqcap L_2 \sqcap \ldots \sqcap L_p$. We may define n markings m_j $(1 \leq j \leq n)$ which verify the following property:

$$\forall j \geq 1, \ \forall i \in P, \text{ if } m_{0,i}[\Pi_{\text{alph}(L_i)}(x_i x_2 \ldots x_j) > m_{j,i}, \text{ then } m_j(i) = m_{j,i}(i)$$

Since for every place i and for each $j \geq 1$, $\Pi_{\text{alph}(L_i)}(x_i x_2 \ldots x_j) \in L_i$, it is easy to see that

$$
\begin{aligned}
m_{j+1}(i) &= m_j(i) \text{ if } i \notin In(x_j) \cup Out(x_j) \\
&= m_j(i) + 1 \text{ if } i \in Out(x_j) \setminus In(x_j) \\
&= m_j(i) - 1 \text{ if } i \in In(x_j) \setminus Out(x_j) \\
&= m_j(i) \text{ if } i \in In(x_j) \cap Out(x_j)
\end{aligned}
$$

Hence $m_0[x_1 > m_1[x_2 > \ldots m_{n-1}[x_n > m_n$.

On the other hand, the synchronized product of languages can be obtained in the following way:

We know from the previous lemma that for each place i, $L_i = f_{\theta_i}(R_i)$

For each place $i \in P$, let h_i be the morphism defined on $T_i = \text{alph}(L_i)$ by:

$$\forall x \in \text{alph}(L_i), \ h_i(x) = (x, i)$$

and θ_i' the semi commutation relation defined by

$$\theta_i' = \{((x, i), (y, i)) \mid (x, y) \in \theta_i$$

Then $\forall i \in P$, $L_i = h_i^{-1}(f_{\theta_i}(h(R_i)))$.

Let h be the morphism defined on T by

$$\text{if } \{i_1, i_2, \ldots i_{p_i}\} = In(t) \cup Out(t), \ h(t) = (t, i_1)(t, i_2) \ldots (t, i_{p_i})$$

and let

$$\theta = \bigcup_{i=1}^{i=n} \theta_i \ \cup \{((x, i), (y, j)) \mid i \neq j\}$$

It is easy to see that

$$L(S) = h^{-1}(f_\theta(h_1(R_1) h_2(R_2) \ldots h_p(R_p)))$$

□

12.9 Conclusion

General semi-commutations or partial commutations are, in some sense, too powerful. Indeed, each recursively enumerable language can be expressed as $g \circ h^{-1} \circ f_\theta(R)$ where h and g are morphisms, θ is a partial commutation, and R a regular language (see [40]). This implies that many problems concerning semi-commutations are undecidable (K. Reinhardt [234], personal communication 1992). Thus it may be interesting to study restricted semi-commutations in order to get better decision properties. Such a family was defined in [126].

Definition 12.9.1 *A counter semi-commutation θ over the alphabet Σ is a semi-commutation such that for every (b,a) in θ either $\{b\} \times (\Sigma \setminus \{b\}) \subseteq \theta$ or $(\Sigma \setminus \{a\}) \times \{a\} \subseteq \theta$.*

It turns out that counter semi-commutations are exactly those preserving the family MC of multi-counter languages (see [126]), that is the smallest family closed under intersection and rational transduction which contains $D_1'^*$.

Theorem 12.9.2 *A semi-commutation θ over the alphabet Σ is a counter semi-commutation if and only if for every multi-counter language $L \subseteq \Sigma^*$, $f_\theta(L)$ is a multi-counter language.*

Due to the decidability of the reachability problem for vector addition systems, the emptiness problem is decidable in MC. This implies some decidability results on counter semi-commutations (see [126]). An other interesting property of this family of semi-commutations is obtained by using the composition criterion.

Definition 12.9.3 *A semi-commutation family T over Σ is said to be closed under composition if: $\forall \theta, \theta' \in T, f_{\theta'} \circ f_\theta = f_{\theta \cup \theta'}$ with $\theta \cup \theta' \in T$.*

Theorem 12.9.4 *The family of counter semi-commutations over Σ is closed under composition.*

Then it is natural to wonder whether there exist other semi-commutation families closed under composition. As a matter of fact, it turns out that the family of counter semi-commutations is the largest family closed under composition. But, firstly, we have to define precisely what is a semi-commutation family.

Definition 12.9.5 *Two semi-commutations θ and θ' over Σ are shape-equivalent if there exists a permutation σ over Σ such that $(b,a) \in \theta$ if and only if $(\sigma(b), \sigma(a)) \in \theta'$.*

Clearly, θ and θ' are shape-equivalent if and only if their commutation graphs are equal up to the labels of the vertices.

Definition 12.9.6 *A semi-commutation family over an alphabet Σ is a set of semi-commutations over Σ which is saturated by the shape-equivalence.*

Theorem 12.9.7 *Each semi-commutation family over Σ closed under composition is included in the family of counter semi-commutations over Σ.*

In section 12.7, algebraic-rational semi-commutations have been defined, that is, semi-commutations θ such that $R \in \text{Reg} \Longrightarrow f_\theta(R) \in \text{Alg}$. Except for the empty semi-commutation, there is no semi-commutation μ such that $R \in \text{Rec} \Longrightarrow f_\mu(R) \in$ Rec. However, if we take R in $\text{Reg}_\theta(\Sigma^*)$ for some semi-commutation θ, the problem becomes not trivial at all. For instance, if $\Sigma = \{a, b\}, \theta = \{(b, a)\}$ and $\mu = \theta \cup \theta^{-1}$, then $R \in \text{Reg}_\theta(\Sigma^*)$ implies $f_\mu(R) \in \text{Reg}_\mu(\Sigma^*)$. Thus it is worth to define the notion of compatibility between semi-commutations:

Definition 12.9.8 *Let θ and θ' be semi-commutations over the alphabet Σ. Then θ' is compatible with θ if for every $R \in \text{Reg}_\theta(\Sigma^*)$, $f_{\theta'}(R) \in \text{Reg}_{\theta'}(\Sigma^*)$.*

If θ is a partial commutation, it is clear that θ' is compatible with θ if and only if $\theta' \subseteq \theta$. In the general case, E. Ochmański and P. A. Wacrenier get a nice characterization ([211]):

Theorem 12.9.9 *Let θ and θ' be semi-commutations over the alphabet Σ. Then θ' is compatible with θ if and only if for every $A, B \subseteq \Sigma$ such that $(A \cup B, \bar{\theta} \cup \bar{\theta}'^{-1})$ is strongly connected, $B \times A \subseteq \theta'$ implies $B \times A \subseteq \theta$.*

This powerful result has several interesting direct implications:

Corollary 12.9.10 *Let θ and θ' be semi-commutations over the alphabet Σ with $\theta' \subseteq \theta^{-1}$. Then θ' is compatible with θ.*

Corollary 12.9.11 *Let θ and θ' be semi-commutations over the alphabet Σ with $\theta \subseteq \theta'$. Then θ' is compatible with θ if and only if $f_{\theta'} = f_{\theta' \cap \theta^{-1}} \circ f_\theta$.*

Corollary 12.9.12 *Let θ and θ' be semi-commutations over the alphabet Σ with $\theta' = \theta \cup \theta^{-1}$. Then θ' is compatible with θ if and only if θ is a confluent semi-commutation.*

These last very recent results on semi-commutations presented in this section are particularly useful: for instance Theorem 12.9.9 may be used for the study of morphisms of semi-trace monoids. Nevertheless, some notions are still missing inside the theory of semi-commutations.

Among the most important ones, we have seen in section 12.6 that Ochmański's theorem (Theorem 12.6.15) on partial commutations cannot be extended to semi-commutations in order to give a rational construction for the set of regular θ-closed languages: the notion of a *good* iteration on θ-closed languages has to be found.

Another important tool of recognizability, the notion of finite automaton for regular θ-closed languages, is still missing for semi-commutations. In Chapter 7 such automata are defined for partial commutations. These asynchronous automata work in such a way that regular languages which are recognized must be closed under the corresponding partial commutation. In the case of semi-commutations, we have to define for automata a behaviour which ensures that for any state q of the automaton, and for any pair of letters (a, b) in the corresponding semi-commutation relation, the state reached from q after reading ba is *better* (in the sense of Proposition 12.6.9) than the state reached from q after reading ab. As a matter of fact, this second problem is closely related to the first one since loops in such automata correspond with iterations in terms of rational expressions.

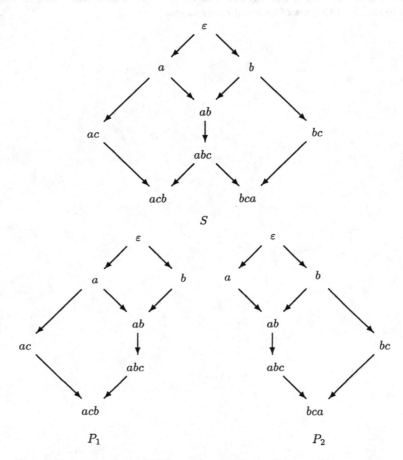

Figure 12.6: The system S does not satisfy the Diamond Property.

Bibliography

[1] IJ. Aalbersberg and G. Rozenberg, Theory of traces, *Theoretical Computer Science*, 60:1–82, 1988.

[2] IJ. Aalbersberg and E. Welzl, Trace languages defined by regular string languages, *R.A.I.R.O. — Informatique Théorique et Applications*, 20:103–119, 1986.

[3] IJ. J. Aalbersberg, *Studies in Trace Theory*, PhD thesis, Leiden University, 1987.

[4] IJ. J. Aalbersberg and H. J. Hoogeboom, Characterizations of the decidability of some problems for regular trace languages, *Mathematical Systems Theory*, 22:1–19, 1989.

[5] IJ. J. Aalbersberg and G. Rozenberg, Traces, dependency graphs and DNLC grammars, *Discrete Applied Mathematics*, 11:299–306, 1985.

[6] E. Abe, *Hopf algebras*, Cambridge University Press, 1977.

[7] A. V. Anisimov and D. E. Knuth, Inhomogeneous sorting, *International Journal of Computer and Information Sciences*, 8:255–260, 1979.

[8] A. Arnold, A syntactic congruence for rational ω-languages, *Theoretical Computer Science*, 39:333–335, 1985.

[9] M. Bednarczyk, *Categories of Asynchronous Transition Systems*, PhD thesis, University of Sussex, 1987, Available as Report 1/88, School of Cognitive and Computing Sciences, University of Sussex.

[10] A. J. Bernstein, Analysis of programs for parallel processing, *IEEE Trans. Comp.*, EC-15(5):757–762, 1966.

[11] J. Berstel, *Transductions and context-free languages*, Teubner Studienbücher, Stuttgart, 1979.

[12] J. Berstel, D. Perrin, J. F. Perrot, and A. Restivo, Sur le théorème du défaut, *Journal of Algebra*, 60:179–189, 1979.

[13] J. Berstel and C. Reutenauer, *Rational series and their languages*, Number 12 in EATCS Monographs on Theoretical Computer Science, Springer, Berlin-Heidelberg-New York, 1988.

[14] A. Bertoni, A. Brambilla, G. Mauri, and N. Sabadini, An application of the theory of free partially commutative monoids: asymptotic densities of trace languages, In J. Gruska et al., editors, *Proceedings of the 10th Symposium on Mathematical Foundations of Computer Science (MFCS'81)*, Strbske' Pleso

(CSFR) 1981, number 118 in Lecture Notes in Computer Science, pages 205–215, Berlin-Heidelberg-New York, 1981, Springer.

[15] A. Bertoni and M. Goldwurm, On the prefixes of a random trace and the membership problem for context-free trace languages, In L. Huguet and A. Poli, editors, *Applied Algebra, Algebraic Algorithms and Error-Correcting Codes (Proceedings AAECC 5), Menorca (Spain), June 15-19, 1987*, number 356 in Lecture Notes in Computer Science, pages 35–59, Berlin-Heidelberg-New York, 1989, Springer.

[16] A. Bertoni, M. Goldwurm, and N. Sabadini, Analysis of a class of algorithms for problems on trace languages, In T. Beth and M. Clausen, editors, *Applicable Algebra, Error-Correcting Codes, Combinatorics and Computer Algebra (Proceedings AAECC 4), Karlsruhe (FRG) September 23-26,1986*, number 307 in Lecture Notes in Computer Science, pages 202–214, Berlin-Heidelberg-New York, 1988, Springer.

[17] A. Bertoni, P. Massazza, and N. Sabadini, Holonomic generating functions and context-free languages, *International Journal of Foundations of Computer Science*, 3(2):181–191, 1992.

[18] A. Bertoni, G. Mauri, and N. Sabadini, Context-free trace languages, In *Proceedings of the 7th Coll. on Trees in Algebra and Programming (CAAP'82), Lille (France)*, pages 32–42, 1982.

[19] A. Bertoni, G. Mauri, and N. Sabadini, Equivalence and membership problems for regular trace languages, In *Proceedings of the 9th International Colloquium on Automata, Languages and Programming (ICALP'82)*, number 140 in Lecture Notes in Computer Science, pages 61–71, Berlin-Heidelberg-New York, 1982, Springer.

[20] A. Bertoni, G. Mauri, and N. Sabadini, A hierarchy of regular trace languages and some combinatorial applications, In A. Ballester, D. Cardus, and E. Trillas, editors, *Proceedings of the 2nd World Conf. on Mathematics at the service of man, Las Palmas (Canary Island) Spain*, pages 146–153, Universidad Politecnica de Las Palmas, 1982.

[21] A. Bertoni, G. Mauri, and N. Sabadini, Concurrency and commutativity, Technical report, Instituto di Cibernetica, Università di Milano, 1983, Presented at the Workshop on Petri nets, Varenna (Italy), 1982.

[22] A. Bertoni, G. Mauri, and N. Sabadini, Unambiguous regular trace languages, In G. Demetrovics, J. Katona and A. Salomaa, editors, *Proceedings of the Coll. on Algebra, Combinatorics and Logic in Computer Science*, volume 42 of *Colloquia Mathematica Soc. J. Bolyai*, pages 113–123, North Holland, Amsterdam, 1985.

[23] A. Bertoni, G. Mauri, and N. Sabadini, Membership problems for regular and context free trace languages, *Information and Computation*, 82:135–150, 1989.

[24] A. Bertoni and N. Sabadini, Generating functions of trace languages, *Bulletin of the European Association for Theoretical Computer Science (EATCS)*, 35:106–112, June 1988.

[25] E. Best and R. Devillers, Sequential and concurrent behaviour in Petri net theory, *Theoretical Computer Science*, 55:87–136, 1987.

[26] E. Best and C. Fernandez, *Non-sequential Processes, A Petri Net View*, Number 13 in EATCS Monographs on Theoretical Computer Science, Springer, Berlin-Heidelberg-New York, 1988.

[27] P. Bonizzoni, G. Mauri, and G. Pighizzini, About infinite traces, In V. Diekert, editor, *Proceedings of the ASMICS workshop Free Partially Commutative Monoids, Kochel am See, Oktober 1989*, Report TUM-I9002, Technical University of Munich, pages 1–10, 1990.

[28] N. Bourbaki, *Algèbres et groupes de Lie*, volume 2, 3, CCLS, 1972.

[29] C. Brown and D. Gurr, Temporal logic and categories of Petri nets, In A. Lingas, R. Karlsson, and S. Carlsson, editors, *Proceedings of the 20th International Colloquium on Automata, Languages and Programming (ICALP'93), Lund (Sweden) 1993*, number 700 in Lecture Notes in Computer Science, pages 570–581, Berlin-Heidelberg-New York, 1993, Springer.

[30] M. C. Browne, E. M. Clarke, and O. Grümberg, Characterizing finite Kripke structures in propositional temporal logic, *Theoretical Computer Science*, 59:115–131, 1988.

[31] D. Bruschi, G. Pighizzini, and N. Sabadini, On the existence of the minimum asynchronous automaton and on decision problems for unambiguous regular trace languages, *Information and Computation*, 108(2):262–285, 1994.

[32] V. Bruyère, C. De Felice, and G. Guaiana, Coding with traces, In P. Enjalbert, E. Mayr, and K. W. Wagner, editors, *Proceedings of the 11th Annual Symposium on Theoretical Aspects of Computer Science (STACS'94), 1994*, number 775 in Lecture Notes in Computer Science, pages 353–364, Berlin-Heidelberg-New York, 1994, Springer.

[33] J. Büchi, On a decision method in restricted second order arithmetic, In E. Nagel et al., editors, *Proc. Internat. Congress on Logic, Methodology and Philosophy of Science*, pages 1–11, Stanford Univ. Press, Stanford, CA, 1960.

[34] P. Cartier and D. Foata, *Problèmes combinatoires de commutation et réarrangements*, Number 85 in Lecture Notes in Mathematics, Springer, Berlin-Heidelberg-New York, 1969.

[35] K. T. Chen, R. H. Fox, and R. C. Lyndon, Free differential calculus, IV, *Ann. of Maths.*, 68(1):81–95, 1958.

[36] C. Choffrut, Free partially commutative monoids, Technical Report 86/20, LITP, Université Paris 7 (France), 1986.

[37] N. Chomsky and M. P. Schützenberger, The algebraic theory of context-free languages, In *Comp. Prog. and Formal Systems*, pages 118–161, Amsterdam, 1963, North-Holland.

[38] M. Chrobak and W. Rytter, Unique decipherability for partially commutative alphabets, *Fundamenta Informaticae*, X:323–336, 1987.

[39] E. M. Clarke, E. A. Emerson, and A. P. Sistla, Automatic verification of finite state concurrent systems using temporal logic specifications: A practical approach, *ACM Transactions on Programming Languages and Systems*, 8(2):244–263, 1986.

[40] M. Clerbout, *Commutations Partielles et Familles de Langages*, Thèse, Université des Sciences et Technologies de Lille (France), 1984.

[41] M. Clerbout and M. Latteux, Partial commutations and faithful rational transductions, *Theoretical Computer Science*, 35:241–254, 1985.

[42] M. Clerbout and M. Latteux, Semi-Commutations, *Information and Computation*, 73:59–74, 1987.

[43] M. Clerbout, M. Latteux, and Y. Roos, Decomposition of partial commutations, In M. S. Paterson, editor, *Proceedings of the 17th International Colloquium on Automata, Languages and Programming (ICALP'90), Warwick (England) 1990*, number 443 in Lecture Notes in Computer Science, pages 501–511, Berlin-Heidelberg-New York, 1990, Springer.

[44] S. A. Cook, A taxonomy of problems with fast parallel algorithms, *Information and Control*, 64:2–22, 1985.

[45] R. Cori and Y. Métivier, Approximation of a trace, asynchronous automata and the ordering of events in a distributed system, In *Proceedings of the 15th International Colloquium on Automata, Languages and Programming (ICALP'88)*, number 317 in LNCS, pages 147–161, Springer, 1988.

[46] R. Cori, Y. Métivier, and W. Zielonka, Asynchronous mappings and asynchronous cellular automata, *Information and Computation*, 106:159–202, 1993.

[47] R. Cori and D. Perrin, Automates et commutations partielles, *R.A.I.R.O. — Informatique Théorique et Applications*, 19:21–32, 1985.

[48] R. Cori, E. Sopena, M. Latteux, and Y. Roos, 2-asynchronous automata, *Theoretical Computer Science*, 61:93–102, 1988.

[49] J. W. de Bakker, W.-P. de Roever, and G. Rozenberg, editors, *Stepwise Refinement of Distributed Systems, Proc. of REX Workshop*, number 430 in Lecture Notes in Computer Science, Berlin-Heidelberg-New York, 1989, Springer.

[50] M. P. Delest and G. Viennot, Algebraic languages and polyominoes enumeration, *Theoretical Computer Science*, 34:169–206, 1984.

[51] W. Dicks, An exact sequence for rings of polynomials in partly commuting indeterminates, *Journal of Pure and Applied Algebra*, 22:215–228, 1980.

[52] V. Diekert, Transitive orientations, Möbius functions and complete semi-Thue systems for free partially commutative monoids, In T. Lepistö et al., editors, *Proceedings of the 15th International Colloquium on Automata, Languages and Programming (ICALP'88), Tampere (Finland) 1988*, number 317 in Lecture Notes in Computer Science, pages 176–187, Berlin-Heidelberg-New York, 1988, Springer.

[53] V. Diekert, *Combinatorics on Traces*, Number 454 in Lecture Notes in Computer Science, Springer, Berlin-Heidelberg-New York, 1990.

[54] V. Diekert, On the concatenation of infinite traces, In C. Choffrut et al., editors, *Proceedings of the 8th Annual Symposium on Theoretical Aspects of Computer Science (STACS'91), Hamburg 1991*, number 480 in Lecture Notes in Computer Science, pages 105–117, Berlin-Heidelberg-New York, 1991, Springer, Appeared also in Theoretical Computer Science [57].

[55] V. Diekert, Mathematical aspects of trace theory, *Mitt. Math. Ges. Hamburg*, 12:1171–1181, 1992, Special issue of the tricentenary.

[56] V. Diekert, Möbius functions and confluent semi-commutations, *Theoretical Computer Science*, 108:25–43, 1993.

[57] V. Diekert, On the concatenation of infinite traces, *Theoretical Computer Science*, 113:35–54, 1993, Special issue STACS 91.

[58] V. Diekert, A partial trace semantics for Petri nets, *Theoretical Computer Science*, 134:87–105, 1994, Special issue of ICWLC 92, Kyoto (Japan).

[59] V. Diekert, P. Gastin, and A. Petit, Rational and recognizable complex trace languages, *Information and Computation*, to appear.

[60] V. Diekert, P. Gastin, and A. Petit, Recognizable complex trace languages, In A. Tarlecki, editor, *Proceedings of the 16th Symposium on Mathematical Foundations of Computer Science (MFCS'91), Kazimierz Dolny (Poland) 1991*, number 520 in Lecture Notes in Computer Science, pages 131–140, Berlin-Heidelberg-New York, 1991, Springer.

[61] V. Diekert and A. Muscholl, Deterministic asynchronous automata for infinite
      traces, In P. Enjalbert, A. Finkel, and K. W. Wagner, editors, *Proceedings
      of the 10th Annual Symposium on Theoretical Aspects of Computer Science
      (STACS'93), Würzburg 1993*, number 665 in Lecture Notes in Computer Sci-
      ence, pages 617–628, Berlin-Heidelberg-New York, 1993, Springer, Extended
      version in [62].

[62] V. Diekert and A. Muscholl, Deterministic asynchronous automata for infinite
      traces, *Acta Informatica*, 31:379–397, 1994.

[63] V. Diekert and A. Muscholl, A note on Métivier's construction of asyn-
      chronous automata for triangulated graphs, *Fundamenta Informaticae*, to
      appear 1995, Special issue on Formal Language Theory.

[64] V. Diekert, E. Ochmański, and K. Reinhardt, On confluent semi-commutation
      systems – decidability and complexity results, *Information and Computation*,
      110:164–182, 1994, A preliminary version was presented at ICALP'91, Lecture
      Notes in Computer Science 510 (1991).

[65] E. W. Dijkstra, Self-stabilizing systems in spite of distributed control, *Com-
      munications of ACM*, 17(11):643–644, 1974.

[66] R. P. Dilworth, A decomposition theorem for partially ordered sets, *Annals
      of Mathematics*, 51:161–166, 1950.

[67] G. A. Dirac, On rigid circuit graphs, Abh. Math. Sem. 25, Univ. Hamburg,
      1961.

[68] D. Z. Dorovic, A generalization of Witt's formulae, *Journal of Algebra*,
      11:262–278, 1987.

[69] C. Droms, Graph groups, coherence and three-manifolds, *Journal of Algebra*,
      106(2):484–489, 1985.

[70] C. Droms, Isomorphisms of graph groups, *Proceedings of the American Math-
      ematical Society*, 100:407–408, 1987.

[71] C. Droms, Subgroup of graph groups, *Journal of Algebra*, 110:519–522, 1987.

[72] C. Droms, Residual nilpotence of graph groups, manuscript, 1992.

[73] M. Droste, Concurrency, automata and domains, In M. S. Paterson, editor,
      *Proceedings of the 17th International Colloquium on Automata, Languages
      and Programming (ICALP'90), Warwick (England) 1990*, number 443 in Lec-
      ture Notes in Computer Science, pages 195–208, Berlin-Heidelberg-New York,
      1990, Springer.

[74] C. Duboc, Commutations dans les monoïdes libres: un cadre théorique pour
      l'étude du parallelisme, Thèse, Faculté des Sciences de l'Université de Rouen,
      1986.

[75] C. Duboc, Mixed product and asynchronous automata, *Theoretical Computer Science*, 48:183–199, 1986.

[76] C. Duboc, On some equations in free partially commutative monoids, *Theoretical Computer Science*, 46:159–174, 1986.

[77] G. Duchamp, *Algorithmes sur les polynômes en variables non commutatives*, Thèse de doctorat, Université Paris 7, 1987.

[78] G. Duchamp, On the free partially commutative Lie algebra, Technical report 89-74, LITP – Université Paris 7, 1989.

[79] G. Duchamp and D. Krob, The lower central series of the free partially commutative group, Technical Report 90.64, LITP, Paris, 1990.

[80] G. Duchamp and D. Krob, Partially commutative formal power series, In I. Guessarian, editor, *Semantics of Systems of Concurrent Processes*, number 469 in Lecture Notes in Computer Science, pages 256–276, Berlin-Heidelberg-New York, 1990, Springer.

[81] G. Duchamp and D. Krob, Computing with P.B.W. in enveloping algebras, In G. Jacob and F. Lamnabhi-Lagarrigue, editors, *Algebraic Computing in Control*, volume 165 of *Lecture notes in control and information sciences*, pages 223–240, Berlin-Heidelberg-New York, 1991, Springer.

[82] G. Duchamp and D. Krob, Factorisations dans le monoïde partiellement commutatif libre, *C.R.A.S. Paris, Série I*, 312(1):189–192, 1991.

[83] G. Duchamp and D. Krob, Lazard's factorizations of free partially commutative monoids, In J. Leach-Albert, B. Monien, and M. Rodriguez Artalejo, editors, *Proceedings of the 18th International Colloquium on Automata, Languages and Programming (ICALP'91), Madrid (Spain) 1991*, number 510 in Lecture Notes in Computer Science, pages 242–253, Berlin-Heidelberg-New York, 1991, Springer.

[84] G. Duchamp and D. Krob, The central lower series of the free partially commutative group, *Semigroup Forum*, 45:385–394, 1992.

[85] G. Duchamp and D. Krob, The free partially commutative Lie algebra: bases and ranks, *Advances in Maths.*, 95(1):92–126, 1992.

[86] G. Duchamp and D. Krob, On the partially commutative shuffle product, *Theoretical Computer Science*, 96:405–410, 1992.

[87] G. Duchamp and D. Krob, Free partially commutative structures, *Journal of Algebra*, 156(2):318–361, 1993.

[88] G. Duchamp and D. Krob, Partially commutative Magnus transformations, *International Journal of Algebra and Computation*, 3(1):15–41, 1993.

[89] G. Duchamp and J. Y. Thibon, Simple orderings for free partially commutative groups, *International Journal of Algebra and Computation*, 2(3):351–355, 1992.

[90] W. Ebinger, *Charakterisierung von Sprachklassen unendlicher Spuren durch Logiken*, Dissertation, Institut für Informatik, Universität Stuttgart, 1994.

[91] W. Ebinger and A. Muscholl, Logical definability on infinite traces, *Theoretical Computer Science*, to appear. A preliminary version appeared in Proceedings of the 20th International Colloquium on Automata, Languages and Programming (ICALP'93), Lund (Sweden) 1993, Lecture Notes in Computer Science 700, 1993.

[92] A. Ehrenfeucht, H. J. Hoogeboom, and G. Rozenberg, Combinatorial properties of dependence graphs, *Information and Computation*, 114(2):315–328, 1994.

[93] A. Ehrenfeucht and G. Rozenberg, On the structure of dependence graphs, In K. Voss, H. J. Genrich, and G. Rozenberg, editors, *Concurrency and Nets*, pages 141–170, Berlin-Heidelberg-New York, 1987, Springer.

[94] S. Eilenberg, *Automata, Languages and Machines*, volume A, Academic Press, New York and London, 1974.

[95] S. Eilenberg and M. P. Schützenberger, Rational sets in commutative monoids, *Journal of Algebra*, 13:173–191, 1969.

[96] C. C. Elgot and J. E. Mezei, On relations defined by generalized finite automata, *IBM J. Research and Development*, 9:47–68, 1965.

[97] E. A. Emerson, Temporal and modal logic, In J. van Leeuwen, editor, *Handbook of Theoretical Computer Science*, volume B, chapter 16, pages 995–1072, Elsevier Science Publisher B. V., 1990.

[98] E. A. Emerson and J. Y. Halpern, Decision procedures and expressiveness in the temporal logic of branching time, *Journal of Computer and System Sciences*, 30:1–24, 1985.

[99] E. A. Emerson and J. Srinivasan, Branching time temporal logic, In J. W. de Bakker, W.-P. de Roever, and G. Rozenberg, editors, *Linear Time, Branching Time and Partial Order in Logics and Models for Concurrency*, number 354 in Lecture Notes in Computer Science, pages 123–172, Berlin-Heidelberg-New York, 1988, Springer.

[100] H. Fauconnier, Sémantique asynchrone et comportements infinis en CSP, *Theoretical Computer Science*, 54:277–298, 1987.

[101] P. C. Fischer and A. L. Rosenberg, Multitape non writing automata, *Journal of Computer and System Sciences*, 2:88–101, 1968.

[102] L. Fix and O. Grumberg, Verification of temporal properties, Technical Report TR 93-1368, CS Cornell Univ., Ithaca NY, Aug. 1993.

[103] P. Flajolet, Analytic models and ambiguity of context-free languages, *Theoretical Computer Science*, 49:283–309, 1987.

[104] M. P. Flé and G. Roucairol, On serializability of iterated transactions, In *Proceedings of the 15th ACM SIGACT-SIGOPS Symp. on Princ. of Distrib. Comp., Ottawa (1982)*, pages 194 – 200, 1982.

[105] M. P. Flé and G. Roucairol, Maximal serializability of iterated transactions, *Theoretical Computer Science*, 38:1–16, 1985.

[106] M. Fliess, *Sur certaines familles de séries formelles*, Thèse d'état, Université Paris 7, 1972.

[107] M. Fliess, Matrices de Hankel, *J. Math. Pures et Appl.*, 53:197–224, 1974.

[108] P. Gastin, *Un modèle distribué*, Thèse, LITP, Université Paris 7 (France), 1987.

[109] P. Gastin, Infinite traces, In I. Guessarian, editor, *Proceedings of the Spring School of Theoretical Computer Science on Semantics of Systems of Concurrent Processes*, number 469 in Lecture Notes in Computer Science, pages 277–308, Berlin-Heidelberg-New York, 1990, Springer.

[110] P. Gastin, Un modèle asynchrone pour les systèmes distribués, *Theoretical Computer Science*, 74:121–162, 1990.

[111] P. Gastin, Recognizable and rational trace languages of finite and infinite traces, In C. Choffrut et al., editors, *Proceedings of the 8th Annual Symposium on Theoretical Aspects of Computer Science (STACS'91), Hamburg 1991*, number 480 in Lecture Notes in Computer Science, pages 89–104, Berlin-Heidelberg-New York, 1991, Springer.

[112] P. Gastin, E. Ochmański, A. Petit, and B. Rozoy, Decidability of the Star problem in $A^* \times \{b\}^*$, *Information Processing Letters*, 44:65–71, 1992.

[113] P. Gastin and A. Petit, Asynchronous automata for infinite traces, In W. Kuich, editor, *Proceedings of the 19th International Colloquium on Automata, Languages and Programming (ICALP'92), Vienna (Austria) 1992*, number 623 in Lecture Notes in Computer Science, pages 583–594, Berlin-Heidelberg-New York, 1992, Springer.

[114] P. Gastin and A. Petit, Poset properties of complex traces, In I. M. Havel and V. Koubek, editors, *Proceedings of the 17th Symposium on Mathematical Foundations of Computer Science (MFCS'92), Prague, (Czechoslovakia), 1992*, number 629 in Lecture Notes in Computer Science, pages 255–263, Berlin-Heidelberg-New York, 1992, Springer.

[115] P. Gastin, A. Petit, and W. Zielonka, A Kleene theorem for infinite trace
      languages, In J. Leach-Albert, B. Monien, and M. Rodriguez Artalejo, ed-
      itors, *Proceedings of the 18th International Colloquium on Automata, Lan-
      guages and Programming (ICALP'91), Madrid (Spain) 1991*, number 510 in
      Lecture Notes in Computer Science, pages 254–266, Berlin-Heidelberg-New
      York, 1991, Springer.

[116] P. Gastin, A. Petit, and W. Zielonka, An extension of Kleene's and
      Ochmański's theorems to infinite traces, *Theoretical Computer Science*,
      125:167–204, 1994.

[117] P. Gastin and B. Rozoy, The poset of infinitary traces, *Theoretical Computer
      Science*, 120:101–121, 1993.

[118] R. Gerth, R. Kuiper, D. Peled, and W. Penczek, A partial order approach to
      branching time logic model checking, In *Proceedings of the Third Israel Sym-
      posium on Theory of Computing and Systems (ISTCS'95), Tel Aviv, Israel,
      January 4-6, 1995*, 1995.

[119] P. Godefroid, Using partial orders to improve automatic verification methods,
      In E. M. Clarke, editor, *Proceedings of the 2nd International Conference on
      Computer-Aided Verification (CAV '90), Rutgers, New Jersey, 1990*, number
      531 in Lecture Notes in Computer Science, pages 176–185, Berlin-Heidelberg-
      New York, 1991, Springer.

[120] P. Godefroid and P. Wolper, A partial approach to model checking, In
      Proceedings of the 6th IEEE Symposium on Logic in Computer Science, pages
      406–415, 1991.

[121] M. Goldwurm, Evaluations of the number of prefixes of traces: an application
      to algorithm analysis, In V. Diekert, editor, *Proceedings of the ASMICS
      workshop Free Partially Commutative Monoids, Kochel am See, Oktober 1989*,
      Report TUM-I9002, Technical University of Munich, pages 68– 80, 1990.

[122] M. Goldwurm, Some limit distributions in analysis of algorithms for prob-
      lems on trace languages, *International Journal of Foundations of Computer
      Science*, 1(3):265–276, 1990, Also appeared in Proc. 3rd Italian Conference
      of Theoretical Computer Science, World Scientific 1989, 285-298.

[123] M. Goldwurm, Probabilistic estimation of the number of prefixes of a trace,
      Theoretical Computer Science, 92:249–268, 1992.

[124] U. Goltz, R. Kuiper, and W. Penczek, Propositional temporal logics and
      equivalences, In W. R. Claveland, editor, *Proceedings of the Third Inter-
      national Conference on Concurrency Theory CONCUR'92*, number 630 in
      Lecture Notes in Computer Science, pages 222–235, Berlin-Heidelberg-New
      York, 1992, Springer.

[125] M. C. Golumbic, *Algorithmic Graph Theory and Perfect Graphs*, Academic Press, New York, 1980.

[126] D. Gonzalez, *Décomposition de semi-commutations*, Thèse, Université des Sciences et Technologies de Lille (France), 1993.

[127] J. Grabowsky, On partial languages, *Ann. Soc. Math. Pol.*, 4(2):428–498, 1981.

[128] R. L. Graham, B. L. Rothschild, and J. H. Spencer, *Ramsey Theory*, John Wiley & Sons, New York, 1980.

[129] G. Guaiana, A. Restivo, and S. Salemi, Star-free trace languages, *Theoretical Computer Science*, 97:301–311, 1992.

[130] M. Hall, A basis for free Lie rings and higher commutators in free groups, *Proceedings of the American Mathematical Society*, 1:575–581, 1950.

[131] D. Harel, Recurring dominoes: Making the highly undecidable highly understandable, *Annals of Discrete Mathematics*, 24:51–72, 1985.

[132] T. Harju and J. Karhumäki, Decidability of the multiplicity equivalence of multitape finite automata, *Theoretical Computer Science*, 78:347–355, 1991.

[133] K. Hashiguchi, A decision procedure for the order of regular events, *Theoretical Computer Science*, 8:69–72, 1979.

[134] K. Hashiguchi, Recognizable closures and submonoids of free partially commutative monoids, *Theoretical Computer Science*, 86:233–241, 1991.

[135] K. Hashiguchi and K. Yamada, String matching problems over free partially commutative monoids, *Information and Computation*, 101:131–149, 1992.

[136] P. Henrici, *Applied and computational complex analysis*, volume vol. 2, J. Wiley & Sons, New Jork, 1977.

[137] J. I. Hmelevskii, *Equations in Free Semigroups*, Number 107, 1976.

[138] C. A. R. Hoare, Communicating sequential processes, *Communications of the Association of Computing Machinery*, 8(21), 1978.

[139] C. A. R. Hoare, *Communicating Sequential Processes*, Prentice-Hall International, London, 1985.

[140] P. W. Hoogers, H. C. M. Kleijn, and P. S. Thiagarajan, A trace semantics for Petri nets, In W. Kuich, editor, *Proceedings of the 19th International Colloquium on Automata, Languages and Programming (ICALP'92), Vienna (Austria) 1992*, number 623 in Lecture Notes in Computer Science, pages 595–604, Berlin-Heidelberg-New York, 1992, Springer.

[141] G. Hotz and V. Claus, *Automatentheorie und Formale Sprachen, Band III*, Bibliographisches Institut, Mannheim, 1972.

[142] D. V. Hung and E. Knuth, Semi-commutations and Petri nets, *Theoretical Computer Science*, 64:67–81, 1989.

[143] O. H. Ibarra, Reversal-bounded multicounter machines and their decision problems, *Journal of the Association of Computing Machinery*, 25:116–133, 1978.

[144] D. Janssens and G. Rozenberg, A characterization of context-free string languages by directed node-label controlled graph grammars, *Acta Informatica*, 16:63–85, 1981.

[145] S. Jesi, G. Pighizzini, and N. Sabadini, Probabilistic asynchronous automata, In V. Diekert, editor, *Proceedings of a workshop of the ESPRIT Basic Research Action No 3166: Algebraic and Syntactic Methods in Computer Science (ASMICS), Kochel am See, Bavaria, FRG (1989)*, Report TUM-I9002, Technical University of Munich, pages 99–114, 1990, To appear in Mathematical Systems Theory.

[146] M. Karonski, A review of random graphs, *Journal of Graph Theory*, 6:349–389, 1982.

[147] M. Katsura and Y. Kobayashi, Lyndon traces and shuffle algebras, manuscript, 1992.

[148] M. Katsura and Y. Kobayashi, The shuffle algebra and its derivations, *Theoretical Computer Science*, 115:359–369, 1993.

[149] S. Katz and D. Peled, Defining conditional independence using collapses, In M. Z. Kwiatkowska, M. W. Shields, and R. M. Thomas, editors, *Semantics for Concurrency*, Workshops in Computing, pages 262–280, Berlin-Heidelberg-New York, 1990, Springer.

[150] S. Katz and D. Peled, Interleaving set temporal logic, *Theoretical Computer Science*, 75(3):21–43, 1991.

[151] S. Katz and D. Peled, Verification of distributed programs using representative interleaving sequences, *Distributed Computing*, 6:107–120, 1992.

[152] K. H. Kim, L. Makar-Limanov, J. Neggers, and F. W. Roush, Graph algebras, *Journal of Algebra*, 64:46–51, 1980.

[153] K. H. Kim and F. W. Roush, Homology of certain algebras defined by graphs, *Journal of Pure and Applied algebra*, 17:179–186, 1980.

[154] N. Klarlund, M. Mukund, and M. Sohoni, Determinizing asynchronous automata, In S. Abiteboul and E. Shamir, editors, *Proceedings of the 21st International Colloquium on Automata, Languages and Programming (ICALP'94), Jerusalem (Israel) 1994*, number 820 in Lecture Notes in Computer Science, pages 130–141, 1994.

[155] S. C. Kleene, Representation of events in nerve nets and finite automata, In M. Shannon, editor, *Automata Studies*, pages 3–40, 1956.

[156] D. E. Knuth, J. Morris, and V. Pratt, Fast pattern matching in strings, *SIAM Journal of Computing*, 6:323–350, 1977.

[157] Y. Kobayashi, Partial commutation, homology and the Möbius inversion formula, In M. Ito, editor, *Words, Languages and Combinatorics (Kyoto, Japan 1990)*, pages 288–298, World Scientific, Singapore, 1992.

[158] Y. Kobayashi, Partially commutative shuffling, manuscript, 1992.

[159] R. König, Graphs and free partially commutative monoids, *Theoretical Computer Science*, 78:319–346, 1991.

[160] D. Krob and P. Lalonde, Partially commutative Lyndon words, In P. Enjalbert, A. Finkel, and K. W. Wagner, editors, *Proceedings of the 10th Annual Symposium on Theoretical Aspects of Computer Science (STACS'93), Würzburg 1993*, number 665 in Lecture Notes in Computer Science, pages 237–246, Berlin-Heidelberg-New York, 1993, Springer.

[161] M. Kwiatkowska, *Fairness for non-interleaving concurrency*, PhD Thesis, University of Leicester (UK), 1989.

[162] M. Kwiatkowska, On infinitary trace languages, Technical Report 31, University of Leicester (UK), 1989.

[163] M. Kwiatkowska, A metric for traces, *Information Processing Letters*, 35:129–135, 1990.

[164] M. Kwiatkowska, On the domain of traces and sequential composition, In S. Abramsky and T. S. E. Maibaum, editors, *Proceedings of the 16th Coll. on Trees in Algebra and Programming (CAAP'91), Brighton (UK)*, number 493 in Lecture Notes in Computer Science, pages 42–56, Berlin-Heidelberg-New York, 1991, Springer.

[165] M. Kwiatkowska and M. Stannett, On transfinite traces, In V. Diekert and W. Ebinger, editors, *Proceedings ASMICS Workshop Infinite Traces, Tübingen*, Bericht 4/92, pages 123–157, Universität Stuttgart, Fakultät Informatik, 1992.

[166] R. E. Ladner, Application of model-theoretic games to discrete linear orders and finite automata, *Information and Computation*, 33:281–303, 1977.

[167] G. Lallement, *Semigroups and Combinatorial Applications*, John Wiley & Sons, New York, 1979.

[168] P. Lalonde, *Contribution à la théorie des empilements*, volume 4 of *Publications du LACIM*, Université du Québec à Montréal, 1990.

[169] P. Lalonde, Empilements de Lyndon et bases d'algèbres de Lie, In M. Delest, G. Jacob, and P. Leroux, editors, *Actes du colloque "Séries formelles et combinatoire algébrique"*, pages 275–286, 1991.

[170] P. Lalonde, Lyndon heaps: an analogue of Lyndon words in partially commutative monoids, manuscript, 1992.

[171] A. Lascoux and M. P. Schützenberger, Le monoïde plaxique, In *Quaderni de "La ricerca scientifica"*, volume 109, 1981.

[172] M. Latteux, Cônes rationnels commutatifs, *Journal of Computer and System Sciences*, 18:307–333, 1979.

[173] J. D. Lawson, The versatile continuous order, In M. Main, A. Melton, M. Mislove, and D. Schmidt, editors, *Proceedings of the Workshop on Mathematical Foundations of Programming Language Semantics*, number 298 in Lecture Notes in Computer Science, pages 134–160, Berlin-Heidelberg-New York, 1988, Springer.

[174] M. Lazard, Sur les groupes nilpotents et les anneaux de Lie, *Ann. Sci. ENS*, 3(71):101–190, 1954.

[175] M. Lazard, Groupes, anneaux de Lie et problème de Burnside, Technical report, Inst. Mat. dell. Universita Roma, 1960.

[176] A. Lentin and M.-P. Schützenberger, Combinatorial problem in the theory of free monoids, In Box et al., editors, *Proceedings of the conference held at the University of North Carolina at Chapel Hill*, pages 128–144, North Carolina Press, 1967.

[177] F. W. Levi, On semigroups, *Bull. Calcutta Math. Soc.*, 36:141–146, 1944.

[178] M. Li and P. Vitanyi, How to share concurrent asynchronous wait-free variables, In *Proceedings of the 16th International Colloquium on Automata, Languages and Programming (ICALP'89), Stresa (Italy) 1989*, number 372 in Lecture Notes in Computer Science, pages 488–505, Berlin-Heidelberg-New York, 1989, Springer.

[179] O. Lichtenstein and A. Pnueli, Checking that finite state concurrent programs satisfy their linear specification, In *Proceedings of the 12th ACM Symposium on Principles of Programming Languages*, pages 97–107, 1985.

[180] H.-N. Liu, C. Wrathall, and K. Zeger, Efficient solution of some problems in free partially commutative monoids, *Information and Computation*, 89:180–198, 1990.

[181] K. Lodaya, R. Parikh, R. Ramanujam, and P. S. Thiagarajan, A logical study of distributed transition systems, *Information and Computation*, 1994, to appear.

[182] M. Lothaire, *Combinatorics on Words*, Addison-Wesley, Reading, M.A., 1983.

[183] R. E. Lyndon and P. E. Schupp, *Combinatorial group theory*, Springer, Berlin-Heidelberg-New York, 1977.

[184] S. MacLane, *Categories. For the Working Mathematician*, Number 5 in Graduate Texts in Mathematics, Springer, Berlin-Heidelberg-New York, 1970.

[185] W. Magnus, Beziehungen zwischen Gruppen und Idealen in einem speziellen Ring, *Math. Ann.*, CXI:259–280, 1935.

[186] W. Magnus, A. Kharass, and D. Solitar, *Combinatorial group theory*, Dover, 1976.

[187] G. S. Makanin, The problem of solvability of equations in free semigroups, *Math. USSR Izvestiya*, 21:483–546, 1983.

[188] Z. Manna and A. Pnueli, *The Temporal Logic of Reactive and Concurrent Systems, Specification*, Springer, 1991.

[189] A. Mazurkiewicz, Concurrent program schemes and their interpretations, DAIMI Rep. PB 78, Aarhus University, Aarhus, 1977.

[190] A. Mazurkiewicz, Trace theory, In W. Brauer et al., editors, *Petri Nets, Applications and Relationship to other Models of Concurrency*, number 255 in Lecture Notes in Computer Science, pages 279–324, Berlin-Heidelberg-New York, 1987, Springer.

[191] A. Mazurkiewicz, Solvability of the asynchronous ranking problem, *Information Processing Letters*, 28:221–224, 1988.

[192] A. Mazurkiewicz, E. Ochmański, and W. Penczek, Concurrent systems and inevitability, *Theoretical Computer Science*, 64:281–304, 1989.

[193] J. D. Mc Knight, Kleene quotient theorem, *Pacific Journal of Mathematics*, pages 1343–1352, 1964.

[194] Y. Métivier, On recognizable subsets of free partially commutative monoids, In L. Kott, editor, *Proceedings of the 13th International Colloquium on Automata, Languages and Programming (ICALP'86), Rennes (France) 1986*, number 226 in Lecture Notes in Computer Science, pages 254–264, Berlin-Heidelberg-New York, 1986, Springer.

[195] Y. Métivier, Une condition suffisante de reconnaissabilité dans un monoïde partiellement commutatif, *R.A.I.R.O. — Informatique Théorique et Applications*, 20:121–127, 1986.

[196] Y. Métivier, An algorithm for computing asynchronous automata in the case of acyclic non-commutation graph, In T. Ottmann, editor, *Proceedings of the 14th International Colloquium on Automata, Languages and Programming (ICALP'87), Karlsruhe (FRG) 1987*, number 267 in Lecture Notes in Computer Science, pages 226–236, Berlin-Heidelberg-New York, 1987, Springer.

[197] Y. Métivier and G. Richomme, On the star operation and the finite power property in free partially commutative monoid, In P. Enjalbert, E. Mayr, and K. W. Wagner, editors, *Proceedings of the 11th Annual Symposium on Theoretical Aspects of Computer Science (STACS'94), 1994*, number 775 in Lecture Notes in Computer Science, pages 341–352, Berlin-Heidelberg-New York, 1994, Springer.

[198] A. Muscholl, On the complementation of Büchi asynchronous cellular automata, In S. Abiteboul and E. Shamir, editors, *Proceedings of the 21st International Colloquium on Automata, Languages and Programming (ICALP'94), Jerusalem (Israel) 1994*, number 820 in Lecture Notes in Computer Science, pages 142–153, Springer, 1994.

[199] M. Nielsen, G. Plotkin, and G. Winskel, Petri nets, event structures and domains, part 1, *Theoretical Computer Science*, 13:85–108, 1981.

[200] M. Nielsen, G. Rozenberg, and P. S. Thiagarajan, Behavioural notions for elementary net systems, *Distributed Computing*, 4:45–59, 1990.

[201] M. Nielsen, G. Rozenberg, and P. S. Thiagarajan, Transition systems, event structures and unfoldings, Submitted for publication, 1993.

[202] E. Ochmański, Petri nets and concurrent grammars (in Polish), Technical Report 233/CYF/79, 1979.

[203] E. Ochmański, Automatic construction of concurrent programs (in Polish), Technical Report 130/CYF/81, 1981.

[204] E. Ochmański, *Regular trace languages (in Polish)*, PhD thesis, Warszawa, 1984.

[205] E. Ochmański, Regular behaviour of concurrent systems, *Bulletin of the European Association for Theoretical Computer Science (EATCS)*, 27:56–67, Oct 1985.

[206] E. Ochmański, Occurrence traces – processes of elementary net systems, In *Advances in Petri Nets 88*, number 340 in Lecture Notes in Computer Science, pages 331–342, Berlin-Heidelberg-New York, 1988, Springer.

[207] E. Ochmański, On morphisms of trace monoids, In R. Cori and M. Wirsing, editors, *Proceedings of the 5th Annual Symposium on Theoretical Aspects of Computer Science (STACS'88)*, number 294 in Lecture Notes in Computer Science, pages 346–355, Berlin-Heidelberg-New York, 1988, Springer.

[208] E. Ochmański, Semi-commutationes for Place/Transition Systems, *Bulletin of the European Association for Theoretical Computer Science (EATCS)*, 38:191–198, 1989.

[209] E. Ochmański, Semi-Commutation and Petri Nets, In V. Diekert, editor, *Proceedings of the ASMICS workshop Free Partially Commutative Monoids, Kochel am See 1989*, Report TUM-I9002, Technical University of Munich, pages 151–166, 1990.

[210] E. Ochmański, Modelling concurrency with semi-commutations, In I. M. Havel and V. Koubek, editors, *Proceedings of the 17th Symposium on Mathematical Foundations of Computer Science (MFCS'92), Prague, (Czechoslovakia), 1992*, number 629 in Lecture Notes in Computer Science, pages 412–420, Berlin-Heidelberg-New York, 1992, Springer.

[211] E. Ochmański and P. A. Wacrenier, On regular compatibility of semi-commutations, In A. Lingas, R. Karlsson, and S. Carlsson, editors, *Proceedings of the 20th International Colloquium on Automata, Languages and Programming (ICALP'93), Lund (Sweden) 1993*, number 700 in Lecture Notes in Computer Science, pages 445–456, Berlin-Heidelberg-New York, 1993, Springer.

[212] F. Otto and C. Wrathall, Overlaps in free partially commutative monoids, *Journal of Computer and System Sciences*, 42:186–198, 1991.

[213] J. P. Pécuchet, Sur la détermination du rang d'une équation dans le monoïde libre, *Theoretical Computer Science*, 16:337–340, 1981.

[214] D. Peled, Interleaving set temporal logic, Master thesis, Technion, Israel, 1987.

[215] D. Peled, All from one, one from all: on model checking using representatives, In *Proceedings of the 5th International Conference on Computer Aided Verification, Greece*, number 697 in Lecture Notes in Computer Science, pages 409–423, Berlin-Heidelberg-New York, 1993, Springer.

[216] D. Peled, Combining partial order reductions with on-the-fly model checking, In *Proceedings of 6th International Conference on Computer Aided Verification, Stanford, California*, number 818 in Lecture Notes in Computer Science, pages 377–390, Berlin-Heidelberg-New York, June 1994, Springer.

[217] D. Peled, S. Katz, and A. Pnueli, Specifying and proving serializability in temporal logic, In *Proceedings of the Sixth Annual IEEE Symposium on Logic in Computer Science (LICS '91)*, 1991.

[218] D. Peled and A. Pnueli, Proving partial order properties, *Theoretical Computer Science*, 126:143–182, 1994, A preliminary version appeared in the proceedings of ICALP'90, Lecture Notes in Computer Science 443, Springer.

[219] W. Penczek, A concurrent branching time temporal logic, In E. Börger, H. Kleine Büning, and M. M. Richter, editors, *Proceedings of the 3rd Workshop on Computer Science Logic*, number 440 in Lecture Notes in Computer Science, pages 337–354, Berlin-Heidelberg-New York, 1990, Springer.

[220] W. Penczek, On temporal logics for trace systems, In V. Diekert and W. Ebinger, editors, *Proceedings ASMICS Workshop Infinite Traces, Tübingen*, Bericht 4/92, pages 158–204, Universität Stuttgart, Fakultät Informatik, 1992.

[221] W. Penczek, Axiomatizations of temporal logics on trace systems, In P. Enjalbert, A. Finkel, and K. W. Wagner, editors, *Proceedings of the 10th Annual Symposium on Theoretical Aspects of Computer Science (STACS'93), Würzburg 1993*, number 665 in Lecture Notes in Computer Science, pages 452–462, Berlin-Heidelberg-New York, 1993, Springer, the full version to appear in Fundamenta Informaticae.

[222] W. Penczek, Temporal logics for trace systems: On automated verification, *International Journal of Foundations of Computer Science*, 4:31–67, 1993.

[223] D. Perrin, Partial commutations, In *Proceedings of the 16th International Colloquium on Automata, Languages and Programming (ICALP'89), Stresa (Italy) 1989*, number 372 in Lecture Notes in Computer Science, pages 637–651, Berlin-Heidelberg-New York, 1989, Springer.

[224] D. Perrin and J.-E. Pin, First-order logic and star-free sets, *Journal of Computer and System Sciences*, 32:393–406, 1986.

[225] D. Perrin and J. E. Pin, Mots Infinis, Tech. Rep. LITP 93.40, Université Paris 7 (France), 1993, Book to appear.

[226] C. A. Petri, Fundamentals of a theory of asynchronous information flow, In *Proc. of IFIP Congress'62, North Holland, Amsterdam (1962)*, pages 386 – 390, 1962.

[227] G. Pighizzini, *Recognizable trace languages and asynchronous automata*, PhD thesis, Università di Milano, February 1993.

[228] G. Pighizzini, Synthesis of nondeterministic asynchronous automata, In M. Droste and Y. Gurevich, editors, *Semantics of programming languages and model theory*, number 5 in Algebra, Logic and Applications, pages 109–126, Gordon and Breach Science Publ., 1993.

[229] G. Pighizzini, Asynchronous automata versus asynchronous cellular automata, *Theoretical Computer Science*, 132:179–207, 1994.

[230] V. R. Pratt, Modelling concurrency with partial orders, *International Journal of Parallel Programming*, 15(1):33–71, 1986.

[231] M. O. Rabin and D. Scott, Finite automata and their decision problems, In E. F. Moore, editor, *Sequential Machines: Selected Papers*, Addison-Wesley, 1964.

[232] H. Rasiowa and R. Sikorski, *The Mathematics of Metamathematics*, PWN, Warszawa, 1970.

[233] R. Ree, Lie elements and an algebra associated with shuffles, *Ann. of Maths.*, 68:210–220, 1958.

[234] K. Reinhardt, *Prioritätszählerautomaten und die Synchronisation von Halbspursprachen*, Dissertation, Institut für Informatik, Universität Stuttgart, 1994.

[235] W. Reisig, *Petri Nets (an Introduction)*, Number 4 in EATCS Monographs on Theoretical Computer Science, Springer, Berlin-Heidelberg-New York, 1985.

[236] G. Richomme, Some trace monoids where both the Star Problem and the Finite Power Property Problem are decidable, In I. Privara et al., editors, *Proceedings of the 19th Symposium on Mathematical Foundations of Computer Science (MFCS'94), Kosice (Slovakia) 1994*, number 841 in Lecture Notes in Computer Science, pages 577–586, Berlin-Heidelberg-New York, 1994, Springer.

[237] J. G. Rosenstein, *Linear orderings*, Academic Press, New York, 1982.

[238] G. Rozenberg, Behaviour of elementary net systems, In W. Brauer, editor, *Petri nets: central models and their properties; advances in Petri nets; proceedings of an advanced course, Bad Honnef, 8.-19. Sept. 1986, Vol. 1*, number 254 in Lecture Notes in Computer Science, pages 60–94, Berlin-Heidelberg-New York, 1986, Springer.

[239] B. Rozoy and P. S. Thiagarajan, Event structures and trace monoids, *Theoretical Computer Science*, 91(2):285–313, 1991.

[240] W. Rytter, Some properties of trace languages, *Fundamenta Informaticae*, VII:117–127, 1984.

[241] J. Sakarovitch, On regular trace languages, *Theoretical Computer Science*, 52:59–75, 1987.

[242] J. Sakarovitch, The "last" decision problem for rational trace languages, In I. Simon, editor, *Proceedings of the 1st Latin American Symposium on Theoretical Informatics (LATIN'92)*, number 583 in Lecture Notes in Computer Science, pages 460–473, Berlin-Heidelberg-New York, 1992, Springer.

[243] A. Salomaa, *Formal Laguages*, Academic Press, 1973.

[244] A. Salomaa and M. Soittola, *Automata theoretic aspects of formal power series*, Springer, 1978.

[245] V. Sassone, M. Nielsen, and G. Winskel, Deterministic behavioural models for concurrency, In A. Borzyszkowski et al., editors, *Proceedings of the 18th Mathematical Foundations of Computer Science (MFCS'93), Gdansk (Polen) 1993*, number 711 in Lecture Notes in Computer Science, pages 682–692, Berlin-Heidelberg-New York, 1993, Springer.

[246] W. Schmitt, Hopf algebras and identities in free partially commutative monoids, *Theoretical Computer Science*, 73:335–340, 1990.

[247] M. P. Schützenberger, Sur une propriété combinatoire des algèbres de Lie libres pouvant être utilisée dans un problème de mathématiques appliquées, In *Séminaire Dubreuil-Pisot, Année 1958-59*, 1958.

[248] M. P. Schützenberger, On a factorization of free monoids, *Proceedings of the American Mathematical Society*, 16:21–24, 1965.

[249] M. P. Schützenberger, On finite monoids having only trivial subgroups, *Information and Control*, 8:190–194, 1965.

[250] H. Servatius, Automorphisms of graph groups, *Journal of Algebra*, 126(1):34–60, 1989.

[251] H. Servatius, C. Droms, and B. Servatius, Surface subgroups of graph groups, *Proceedings of the American Mathematical Society*, 106(3):573–578, 1989.

[252] H. Servatius, C. Droms, and B. Servatius, The finite basis extension property and graph groups, In P. Latiolais, editor, *Topology and combinatorial group theory*, volume 1440 of *Lecture Notes in Mathematics*, Springer, 1990.

[253] M. W. Shields, Adequate path expressions, In G. Kahn, editor, *Proceedings of the international symposium on Semantics of Concurrent Computation, Evian (France) 1979*, number 70 in Lecture Notes in Computer Science, pages 249–265, Berlin-Heidelberg-New York, 1979, Springer.

[254] M. W. Shields, Non-sequential behaviour, part 1, Int. Report CSR-120-82, Dept. of Computer Science, University of Edinburgh, 1982.

[255] M. W. Shields, Concurrent machines, *Computer Journal*, 28:449–465, 1985.

[256] I. Simon, Limited subsets of a free monoid, In *Proceedings of the 19th IEEE Annual Symposium on Foundations of Computer Science*, pages 143–150, North Carolina Press, 1967.

[257] E. W. Stark, Concurrent transition systems, *Theoretical Computer Science*, 64:221–269, 1989.

[258] P. S. Thiagarajan, Elementary net systems, In W. Brauer, editor, *Petri nets: central models and their properties; advances in Petri nets; proceedings of an advanced course, Bad Honnef, 8.-19. Sept. 1986, Vol. 1*, number 254 in Lecture Notes in Computer Science, pages 26–59, Berlin-Heidelberg-New York, 1986, Springer.

[259] P. S. Thiagarajan, A trace based extension of linear time temporal logic, In *Proceedings of the 9th Annual IEEE Symposium on Logic in Computer Science (LICS'94)*, Lecture Notes in Computer Science, pages 438–447, 1994.

[260] J. Y. Thibon, Intégrité des algèbres de séries formelles sur un alphabet partiellement commutatif libre, *Theoretical Computer Science*, 41, 1985.

[261] W. Thomas, Classifying regular events in symbolic logic, *Journal of Computer and System Sciences*, 25:360–376, 1982.

[262] W. Thomas, Automata on infinite objects, In J. v. Leeuwen, editor, *Handbook of Theoretical Computer Science*, chapter 4, pages 133–191, Elsevier Science Publishers B. V., 1990.

[263] W. Thomas, On logical definability of trace languages, In V. Diekert, editor, *Proceedings of a workshop of the ESPRIT Basic Research Action No 3166: Algebraic and Syntactic Methods in Computer Science (ASMICS), Kochel am See, Bavaria, FRG (1989)*, Report TUM-I9002, Technical University of Munich, pages 172–182, 1990.

[264] A. Valmari, Stubborn sets for reduced state space generation, In *Proceedings of 10th International Conference on Application and Theory of Petri Nets*, volume 2, pages 1–22, 1989.

[265] M. Y. Vardi and P. Wolper, An automata-theoretic approach to automatic program verification, In D. Kozen, editor, *Proceedings of the First Annual IEEE Symposium on Logic in Computer Science (LICS'86)*, pages 322–331, 1986.

[266] S. Varricchio, On the decidability of the equivalence problem for partially commutative rational power series, *Theoretical Computer Science*, 99(2):291–299, 1992.

[267] G. Viennot, *Algèbres de Lie libres et monoïdes libres*, Thèse d'état, Université Paris 7, 1974.

[268] G. Viennot, *Algèbres de Lie libres et monoïdes libres*, volume 691 of *Lecture Notes in Mathematics*, Springer, 1978.

[269] X. G. Viennot, Heaps of pieces I: Basic definitions and combinatorial lemmas, In G. Labelle et al., editors, *Proceedings Combinatoire énumerative, Montréal, Québec (Canada) 1985*, number 1234 in Lecture Notes in Mathematics, pages 321–350, Berlin-Heidelberg-New York, 1986, Springer.

[270] P. A. Wacrenier, *Semi-commutations et reconnaissabilité*, Thèse, Université des Sciences et Technologies de Lille (France), 1993.

[271] G. Winskel, Categories of models for concurrency, In S. D. Brookes, editor, *Seminar on concurrency: Carnegie-Mellon University, Pittsburgh, PA, July 9-11, 1984*, number 197 in Lecture Notes in Computer Science, Berlin-Heidelberg-New York, 1984, Springer.

[272] G. Winskel, An introduction to event structures, In J. W. de Bakker, W.-P. de Roever, and G. Rozenberg, editors, *Linear Time, Branching Time and Partial Order in Logics and Models for Concurrency*, number 354 in Lecture Notes in Computer Science, pages 123–172, Berlin-Heidelberg-New York, 1988, Springer.

[273] G. Winskel and M. Nielsen, Models for concurrency, To appear in Handbook of Logic in Computer Science, Oxford University Press.

[274] P. Wolper, On the relation of programs and computations to models of temporal logic, In *Proceedings of the Colloquium on Temporal Logic in Specification, Altrincham, UK, 1987*, number 398 in Lecture Notes in Computer Science, pages 75–123, Berlin-Heidelberg-New York, 1989, Springer.

[275] C. Wrathall, The word problem for free partially commutative groups, *Journal of Symbolic Computation*, 6:99–104, 1988.

[276] C. Wrathall, Free partially commutative groups, In D. Du and G. Hu, editors, *Combinatorics, Computing and Complexity (Proceedings of the Intern. Symp on Combinatorial Optimization, Tianjin 1988)*, Mathematics and Its Applications: Chinese series, pages 195–216, Science Press, Beijing and Kluwer Academic Publishers, Dordrecht/Boston/London, 1989.

[277] W. Zielonka, Notes on finite asynchronous automata, *R.A.I.R.O. — Informatique Théorique et Applications*, 21:99–135, 1987.

[278] W. Zielonka, Safe executions of recognizable trace languages by asynchronous automata, In A. R. Mayer et al., editors, *Proceedings of the Symposium on Logical Foundations of Computer Science, Logic at Botik '89, Pereslavl-Zalessky (USSR) 1989*, number 363 in Lecture Notes in Computer Science, pages 278–289, Berlin-Heidelberg-New York, 1989, Springer.

About the Editors

Volker Diekert graduated in mathematics in 1980 from the University of Hamburg, Germany. He spent the academic year 1977-78 at the Université des Sciences et Techniques du Languedoc in Montpellier, France where he studied with Prof. Alexander Grothendieck and obtained a Diplôme des Études Superieures. In 1983 he earned his Ph. D. in mathematics at the University of Regensburg, Germany under the direction of Prof. Jürgen Neukirch. In 1984 he moved to computer science. He was research assistent first at the University of Hamburg, and then at the Technical University of Munich where he received his Habilitation in 1989. In 1991 he became a full professor at the Departement of Computer Science of the University of Stuttgart, where he currently holds the chair for Theoretical Computer Science. He was visiting professor at the University of Hamburg (1987) and at the Université de Paris, Orsay (1991).

Professor Diekert has published about 40 journal and conference papers and a monograph. He has been a member of the program committee or invited speaker at major conferences on theoretical computer science. He is involved in European Basic Research Actions. In 1989 and 1991 he organized international workshops on trace theory. His current research interests include: (1) the theory of concurrent systems, in particular the theory of traces and the theory of infinite behavior, (2) formal languages, (3) complexity theory, (4) algebraic methods in computer science.

Grzegorz Rozenberg received his Master and Engineer degree in computer science in 1965 from the Technical University of Warsaw, Poland. In 1968 he obtained his Ph. D. in mathematics at the Polish Academy of Sciences, Warsaw. Since then he has held full time positions at the Polish Academy of Science (assistant professor), Utrecht University, The Netherlands (assistant professor), State University of New York at Buffalo, U.S.A. (associate professor), and University of Antwerp, Belgium (professor). Since 1979 he has been a professor at the Department of Computer Science at Leiden University and an adjoint professor at the University of Colorado at Boulder, U.S.A.

Professor Rozenberg was the President of the European Association for Theoretical Computer Science (EATCS), 1985-1994, and he is currently the chairman of the Steering Committee for International Conferences on Theory and Applications of Petri Nets. He has published more than 250 papers, is a (co-)editor of about 20 books and co-authored 3 books. He is the editor of the Bulletin of the EATCS, the editor of the series Advances in Petri Nets (Springer-Verlag), and a co-editor of the Monographs in Theoretical Computer Science (Springer-Verlag). He has been a member of the program committees for practically all major conferences on theoretical computer science in Europe.

Professor Rozenberg is involved in a number of externally funded research projects on both national and international levels. His current research interests are: (1) the theory of concurrent systems, in particular the theory of Petri nets, the theory of transition systems, and the theory of traces, (2) the theory of graph transformations, (3) formal language and automata theory, (4) mathematical structures useful in computer science - in particular the theory of 2-structures.

He is a Foreign Member of the Finnish Academy of Sciences and Letters, a member of Academia Europaea, and a doctor honoris causa of the University of Turku, Finland.

THE
BOOK
OF
TRACES